T0189287

Lecture Notes in Computer Science   12572

More information about this subseries at http://www.springer.com/series/7409

Jakub Lokoč · Tomáš Skopal ·
Klaus Schoeffmann · Vasileios Mezaris ·
Xirong Li · Stefanos Vrochidis ·
Ioannis Patras (Eds.)

MultiMedia Modeling

27th International Conference, MMM 2021
Prague, Czech Republic, June 22–24, 2021
Proceedings, Part I

 Springer

Editors
Jakub Lokoč 🆔
Charles University
Prague, Czech Republic

Tomáš Skopal 🆔
Charles University
Prague, Czech Republic

Klaus Schoeffmann 🆔
Klagenfurt University
Klagenfurt, Austria

Vasileios Mezaris 🆔
CERTH-ITI
Thessaloniki, Greece

Xirong Li 🆔
Renmin University of China
Beijing, China

Stefanos Vrochidis 🆔
CERTH-ITI
Thessaloniki, Greece

Ioannis Patras 🆔
Queen Mary University of London
London, UK

ISSN 0302-9743   ISSN 1611-3349 (electronic)
Lecture Notes in Computer Science
ISBN 978-3-030-67831-9   ISBN 978-3-030-67832-6 (eBook)
https://doi.org/10.1007/978-3-030-67832-6

LNCS Sublibrary: SL3 – Information Systems and Applications, incl. Internet/Web, and HCI

This Springer imprint is published by the registered company Springer Nature Switzerland AG
The registered company address is: Gewerbestrasse 11, 6330 Cham, Switzerland

Preface

These two-volume proceedings contain the papers accepted at MMM 2021, the 27th International Conference on MultiMedia Modeling.

Organized for more than 25 years, MMM has become a respected and well-established international conference bringing together excellent researchers from academic and industrial areas. During the conference, novel research works from MMM-related areas (especially multimedia content analysis; multimedia signal processing and communications; and multimedia applications and services) are shared along with practical experiences, results, and exciting demonstrations. The 27th instance of the conference was organized in Prague, Czech Republic on June 22–24, 2021. Due to the COVID-19 pandemic, the conference date was shifted by five months, however the Proceedings were published in January in accordance with the original plan. Despite the pandemic, MMM 2021 received a large number of submissions organized in different tracks.

Specifically, 211 papers were submitted to seven MMM 2021 tracks. Each paper was reviewed by at least two reviewers (but mostly three) from the Program Committee, while the TPC chairs and special event organizers acted as meta-reviewers. Out of 166 regular papers, 73 were accepted for the proceedings. In particular, 40 papers were accepted for oral presentation and 33 papers for poster presentation. Regarding the remaining tracks, 16 special session papers were accepted as well as 2 papers for a demo presentation and 17 papers for participation at the Video Browser Showdown 2021. Overall, the MMM 2021 program comprised 108 papers from the seven tracks with the following acceptance rates:

Tracks	#Papers	ACCEPTANCE rates
Full papers (oral)	40	24%
Full papers (oral + poster)	73	44%
Demos	2	67%
SS1: MAPTA	4	50%
SS2: MDRE	5	71%
SS3: MMARSat	3	100%
SS4: MULTIMED	4	67%
Video Browser Showdown	17	94%

The special sessions are traditionally organized to extend the program with novel challenging problems and directions. The MMM 2021 program included four special sessions:

- SS1: Multimedia Analytics: Perspectives, Tools, and Applications (MAPTA)
- SS2: Multimedia Datasets for Repeatable Experimentation (MDRE)
- SS3: Multimodal Analysis and Retrieval of Satellite Images (MMARSat)
- SS4: Multimedia and Multimodal Analytics in the Medical Domain and Pervasive Environments (MULTIMED)

Besides the four special sessions, the anniversary 10th Video Browser Showdown represented an important highlight of MMM 2021 with a record number of 17 participating systems in this exciting (and challenging!) competition. In addition, two highly respected speakers were invited to MMM 2021 to present their impressive talks and results in multimedia-related topics. Specifically, we would like to thank Cees Snoek from the University of Amsterdam, and Pavel Zezula from Masaryk University.

Last but not least, we would like to thank all members of the MMM community who contributed to the MMM 2021 event. We also thank all authors of submitted papers, all reviewers, and all members of the MMM 2021 organization team for their great work and support. They all helped MMM 2021 to be an exciting and inspiring international event for all participants!

January 2021

Jakub Lokoč
Tomáš Skopal
Klaus Schoeffmann
Vasileios Mezaris
Xirong Li
Stefanos Vrochidis
Ioannis Patras

Organization

Organizing Committee

General Chairs

Jakub Lokoč	Charles University, Prague
Tomáš Skopal	Charles University, Prague

Program Chairs

Klaus Schoeffmann	Klagenfurt University
Vasileios Mezaris	CERTH-ITI, Thessaloniki
Xirong Li	Renmin University of China

Special Session and Tutorial Chairs

Werner Bailer	Joanneum Research
Marta Mrak	BBC Research & Development

Panel Chairs

Giuseppe Amato	ISTI-CNR, Pisa
Fabrizio Falchi	ISTI-CNR, Pisa

Demo Chairs

Cathal Gurrin	Dublin City University
Jan Zahálka	Czech Technical University in Prague

Video Browser Showdown Chairs

Klaus Schoeffmann	Klagenfurt University
Werner Bailer	Joanneum Research
Jakub Lokoč	Charles University, Prague
Cathal Gurrin	Dublin City University

Publicity Chairs

Phoebe Chen	La Trobe University
Chong-Wah Ngo	City University of Hong Kong
Bing-Kun Bao	Nanjing University of Posts and Telecommunications

Publication Chairs

Stefanos Vrochidis	CERTH-ITI, Thessaloniki
Ioannis Patras	Queen Mary University of London

Steering Committee

Phoebe Chen	La Trobe University
Tat-Seng Chua	National University of Singapore
Kiyoharu Aizawa	University of Tokyo
Cathal Gurrin	Dublin City University
Benoit Huet	Eurecom
Klaus Schoeffmann	Klagenfurt University
Richang Hong	Hefei University of Technology
Björn Þór Jónsson	IT University of Copenhagen
Guo-Jun Qi	University of Central Florida
Wen-Huang Cheng	National Chiao Tung University
Peng Cui	Tsinghua University

Web Chair

František Mejzlík   Charles University, Prague

Organizing Agency

Conforg, s.r.o.

Special Session Organizers

Multimedia Datasets for Repeatable Experimentation (MDRE)

Cathal Gurrin	Dublin City University, Ireland
Duc-Tien Dang-Nguyen	University of Bergen, Norway
Björn Þór Jónsson	IT University of Copenhagen, Denmark
Klaus Schoeffmann	Klagenfurt University, Austria

Multimedia Analytics: Perspectives, Tools and Applications (MAPTA)

Björn Þór Jónsson	IT University of Copenhagen, Denmark
Stevan Rudinac	University of Amsterdam, The Netherlands
Xirong Li	Renmin University of China, China
Cathal Gurrin	Dublin City University, Ireland
Laurent Amsaleg	CNRS-IRISA, France

Multimodal Analysis and Retrieval of Satellite Images

Ilias Gialampoukidis	Centre for Research and Technology Hellas, Information Technologies Institute, Greece
Stefanos Vrochidis	Centre for Research and Technology Hellas, Information Technologies Institute, Greece
Ioannis Papoutsis	National Observatory of Athens, Greece

Guido Vingione   Serco Italy, Italy
Ioannis Kompatsiaris   Centre for Research and Technology Hellas,
                                Information Technologies Institute, Greece

MULTIMED: Multimedia and Multimodal Analytics in the Medical Domain and Pervasive Environments

Georgios Meditskos   Centre for Research and Technology Hellas,
                               Information Technologies Institute, Greece
Klaus Schoeffmann   Klagenfurt University, Austria
Leo Wanner   ICREA – Universitat Pompeu Fabra, Spain
Stefanos Vrochidis   Centre for Research and Technology Hellas,
                               Information Technologies Institute, Greece
Athanasios Tzioufas   Medical School of the National and Kapodistrian
                               University of Athens, Greece

MMM 2021 Program Committees and Reviewers Regular and Special Sessions
Program Committee

Olfa Ben Ahmed   EURECOM
Laurent Amsaleg   CNRS-IRISA
Evlampios Apostolidis   CERTH ITI
Ognjen Arandjelović   University of St Andrews
Devanshu Arya   University of Amsterdam
Nathalie Aussenac   IRIT CNRS
Esra Açar   Middle East Technical University
Werner Bailer   JOANNEUM RESEARCH
Bing-Kun Bao   Nanjing University of Posts and Telecommunications
Ilaria Bartolini   University of Bologna
Christian Beecks   University of Munster
Jenny Benois-Pineau   LaBRI, UMR CNRS 5800 CNRS,
                               University of Bordeaux
Roberto Di Bernardo   Engineering Ingegneria Informatica S.p.A.
Antonis Bikakis   University College London
Josep Blat   Universitat Pompeu Fabra
Richard Burns   West Chester University
Benjamin Bustos   University of Chile
K. Selçuk Candan   Arizona State University
Ying Cao   City University of Hong Kong
Annalina Caputo   University College Dublin
Savvas Chatzichristofis   Neapolis University Pafos
Angelos Chatzimichail   Centre for Research and Technology Hellas
Edgar Chavez   CICESE
Mulin Chen   Northwestern Polytechnical University
Zhineng Chen   Institute of Automation, Chinese Academy of Sciences
Zhiyong Cheng   Qilu University of Technology
Wei-Ta Chu   National Cheng Kung University

Andrea Ciapetti	Innovation Engineering
Kathy Clawson	University of Sunderland
Claudiu Cobarzan	Klagenfurt University
Rossana Damiano	Università di Torino
Mariana Damova	Mozaika
Minh-Son Dao	National Institute of Information and Communications Technology
Petros Daras	Information Technologies Institute
Mihai Datcu	DLR
Mathieu Delalandre	Université de Tours
Begum Demir	Technische Universität Berlin
Francois Destelle	Dublin City University
Cem Direkoğlu	Middle East Technical University – Northern Cyprus Campus
Jianfeng Dong	Zhejiang Gongshang University
Shaoyi Du	Xi'an Jiaotong University
Athanasios Efthymiou	University of Amsterdam
Lianli Gao	University of Science and Technology of China
Dimos Georgiou	Catalink EU
Negin Ghamsarian	Klagenfurt University
Ilias Gialampoukidis	CERTH ITI
Nikolaos Gkalelis	CERTH ITI
Nuno Grosso	
Ziyu Guan	Northwest University of China
Gylfi Gudmundsson	Reykjavik University
Silvio Guimaraes	Pontifícia Universidade Católica de Minas Gerais
Cathal Gurrin	Dublin City University
Pål Halvorsen	SimulaMet
Graham Healy	Dublin City University
Shintami Chusnul Hidayati	Institute of Technology Sepuluh Nopember
Dennis Hoppe	High Performance Computing Center Stuttgart
Jun-Wei Hsieh	National Taiwan Ocean University
Min-Chun Hu	National Tsing Hua University
Zhenzhen Hu	Nanyang Technological University
Jen-Wei Huang	National Cheng Kung University
Lei Huang	Ocean University of China
Ichiro Ide	Nagoya University
Konstantinos Ioannidis	CERTH ITI
Bogdan Ionescu	University Politehnica of Bucharest
Adam Jatowt	Kyoto University
Peiguang Jing	Tianjin University
Hyun Woo Jo	Korea University
Björn Þór Jónsson	IT-University of Copenhagen
Yong Ju Jung	Gachon University
Anastasios Karakostas	Aristotle University of Thessaloniki
Ari Karppinen	Finnish Meteorological Institute

Jiro Katto	Waseda University
Junmo Kim	Korea Advanced Institute of Science and Technology
Sabrina Kletz	Klagenfurt University
Ioannis Kompatsiaris	CERTH ITI
Haris Kontoes	National Observatory of Athens
Efstratios Kontopoulos	Elsevier Technology
Markus Koskela	CSC – IT Center for Science Ltd.
Yu-Kun Lai	Cardiff University
Woo Kyun Lee	Korea University
Jochen Laubrock	University of Potsdam
Khiem Tu Le	Dublin City University
Andreas Leibetseder	Klagenfurt University
Teng Li	Anhui University
Xirong Li	Renmin University of China
Yingbo Li	Eurecom
Wu Liu	JD AI Research of JD.com
Xueting Liu	The Chinese University of Hong Kong
Jakub Lokoč	Charles University
José Lorenzo	Atos
Mathias Lux	Klagenfurt University
Ioannis Manakos	CERTH ITI
José M. Martinez	Universidad Autònoma de Madrid
Stephane Marchand-Maillet	Viper Group – University of Geneva
Ernesto La Mattina	Engineering Ingegneria Informatica S.p.A.
Thanassis Mavropoulos	CERTH ITI
Kevin McGuinness	Dublin City University
Georgios Meditskos	CERTH ITI
Robert Mertens	HSW University of Applied Sciences
Vasileios Mezaris	CERTH ITI
Weiqing Min	ICT
Wolfgang Minker	University of Ulm
Marta Mrak	BBC
Phivos Mylonas	National Technical University of Athens
Henning Muller	HES-SO
Duc Tien Dang Nguyen	University of Bergen
Liqiang Nie	Shandong University
Tu Van Ninh	Dublin City University
Naoko Nitta	Osaka University
Noel E. O'Connor	Dublin City University
Neil O'Hare	Yahoo Research
Jean-Marc Ogier	University of La Rochelle
Vincent Oria	NJIT
Tse-Yu Pan	National Cheng Kung University
Ioannis Papoutsis	National Observatory of Athens
Cecilia Pasquini	Universität Innsbruck
Ladislav Peška	Charles University

Yannick Prie	LINA – University of Nantes
Manfred Jürgen Primus	Klagenfurt University
Athanasios Psaltis	Centre for Research and Technology Hellas, Thessaloniki
Georges Quénot	Laboratoire d'Informatique de Grenoble, CNRS
Miloš Radovanović	University of Novi Sad
Amon Rapp	University of Torino
Stevan Rudinac	University of Amsterdam
Borja Sanz	University of Deusto
Shin'ichi Satoh	National Institute of Informatics
Gabriella Scarpino	Serco Italia S.p.A.
Simon Scerri	Fraunhofer IAIS, University of Bonn
Klaus Schoeffmann	Klagenfurt University
Matthias Schramm	TU Wien
John See	Multimedia University
Jie Shao	University of Science and Technology of China
Wen-Ze Shao	Nanjing University of Posts and Telecommunications
Xi Shao	Nanjing University of Posts and Telecommunications
Ujjwal Sharma	University of Amsterdam
Dongyu She	Nankai University
Xiangjun Shen	Jiangsu University
Koichi Shinoda	Tokyo Institute of Technology
Hong-Han Shuai	National Chiao Tung University
Mei-Ling Shyu	University of Miami
Vasileios Sitokonstantinou	National Observatory of Athens
Tomáš Skopal	Charles University
Alan Smeaton	Dublin City University
Natalia Sokolova	Klagenfurt University
Gjorgji Strezoski	University of Amsterdam
Li Su	UCAS
Lifeng Sun	Tsinghua University
Machi Symeonidou	DRAXIS Environmental SA
Daniel Stanley Tan	De La Salle University
Mario Taschwer	Klagenfurt University
Georg Thallinger	JOANNEUM RESEARCH
Christian Timmerer	Klagenfurt University
Athina Tsanousa	CERTH ITI
Athanasios Tzioufas	NKUA
Shingo Uchihashi	Fuji Xerox Co., Ltd.
Tiberio Uricchio	University of Florence
Guido Vingione	Serco
Stefanos Vrochidis	CERTH ITI
Qiao Wang	Southeast University
Qifei Wang	Google
Xiang Wang	National University of Singapore
Xu Wang	Shenzhen University

Zheng Wang	National Institute of Informatics
Leo Wanner	ICREA/UPF
Wolfgang Weiss	JOANNEUM RESEARCH
Lai-Kuan Wong	Multimedia University
Tien-Tsin Wong	The Chinese University of Hong Kong
Marcel Worring	University of Amsterdam
Xiao Wu	Southwest Jiaotong University
Sen Xiang	Wuhan University of Science and Technology
Ying-Qing Xu	Tsinghua University
Toshihiko Yamasaki	The University of Tokyo
Keiji Yanai	The University of Electro-Communications
Gang Yang	Renmin University of China
Yang Yang	University of Science and Technology of China
You Yang	Huazhong University of Science and Technology
Zhaoquan Yuan	Southwest Jiaotong University
Jan Zahálka	Czech Technical University in Prague
Hanwang Zhang	Nanyang Technological University
Sicheng Zhao	University of California, Berkeley
Lei Zhu	Huazhong University of Science and Technology

Additional Reviewers

Hadi Amirpour	Hanyuan Liu
Eric Arazo	Katrinna Macfarlane
Gibran Benitez-Garcia	Danila Mamontov
Adam Blažek	Thanassis Mavropoulos
Manliang Cao	Anastasia Moumtzidou
Ekrem Çetinkaya	Vangelis Oikonomou
Long Chen	Jesus Perez-Martin
Přemysl Čech	Zhaobo Qi
Julia Dietlmeier	Tomas Soucek
Denis Dresvyanskiy	Vajira Thambawita
Negin Ghamsarian	Athina Tsanousa
Panagiotis Giannakeris	Chenglei Wu
Socratis Gkelios	Menghan Xia
Tomáš Grošup	Minshan Xie
Steven Hicks	Cai Xu
Milan Hladik	Gang Yang
Wenbo Hu	Yaming Yang
Debesh Jha	Jiang Zhou
Omar Shahbaz Khan	Haichao Zhu
Chengze Li	Zirui Zhu

Contents – Part I

Contents – Part II

Crossed-Time Delay Neural Network for Speaker Recognition

Liang Chen[1], Yanchun Liang[2], Xiaohu Shi[1], You Zhou[1], and Chunguo Wu[1,2]([✉])

[1] Key Laboratory of Symbolic Computation and Knowledge Engineering of Ministry of Education, College of Computer Science and Technology, Jilin University, Changchun 130012, People's Republic of China
wucg@jlu.edu.cn

[2] Zhuhai Laboratory of Key Laboratory of Symbol Computation and Knowledge Engineering of Ministry of Education, School of Computer, Zhuhai College of Jilin University, Zhuhai 519041, People's Republic of China

Abstract. Time Delay Neural Network (TDNN) is a well-performing structure for deep neural network-based speaker recognition systems. In this paper we introduce a novel structure, named Crossed-Time Delay Neural Network (CTDNN) to enhance the performance of current TDNN for speaker recognition. Inspired by the multi-filters setting of convolution layers from convolution neural networks, we set multiple time delay units with different context size at the bottom layer and construct a multilayer parallel network. The proposed CTDNN gives significant improvements over original TDNN on both speaker verification and identification tasks. It outperforms in VoxCeleb1 dataset in verification experiment with a 2.6% absolute Equal Error Rate improvement. In few shots condition, CTDNN reaches 90.4% identification accuracy, which doubles the identification accuracy of original TDNN. We also compare the proposed CTDNN with another new variant of TDNN, Factorized-TDNN, which shows that our model has a 36% absolute identification accuracy improvement under few shots condition. Moreover, the proposed CTDNN can handle training with a larger batch more efficiently and hence, utilize calculation resources economically.

Keywords: Speaker recognition · Time delay neural network · Feature embedding · Acoustic modeling

1 Introduction

The Speaker recognition system verifies or identifies a speaker's identity based on speaker's voice. It can be divided into speaker verification and speaker identification, where speaker verification aims to verify whether an utterance corresponds to a given identity and speaker identification aims to identify a speech from all enrolled speakers.

The original version of this chapter was revised: A typo in the third author's name has been corrected. The correction to this chapter is available at
https://doi.org/10.1007/978-3-030-67832-6_59

© Springer Nature Switzerland AG 2021, corrected publication 2021
J. Lokoč et al. (Eds.): MMM 2021, LNCS 12572, pp. 1–10, 2021.
https://doi.org/10.1007/978-3-030-67832-6_1

According to the different testing scenario, speaker recognition can also be categorized into closed-set or open-set settings. For closed-set scenario, all testing identities are enrolled in the training set, therefore it can be regarded as a classification problem. For open-set scenario, the testing identities are not previously seen in the training set, which is closer to real world application since new identities will be added to the system continually. To address that problem, each utterance must be mapped into an embedding space where cosine similarity is used to evaluate whether two utterances correspond to one same identity. The current studies mainly focus on the open-set speaker recognition problem.

Recently, deep neural network has been widely applied to learning speakers' embedding through the learning process of classification such as x-vectors and have shown great priority in performance [1] than traditional statistical models such as HMM-GMM [2] and i-vectors. Time delay layer is an important component among DNN-based models due to its ability to capture feature from sequent audio data.

Time Delay Neural Network was regarded as the ancestor of convolution neural network [1]. It is effective in capturing features from long range temporal contexts and is widely used in speech related field such as speaker recognition system automatic speech recognition and speech synthesis [3]. The TDNN architecture, shown in Fig. 1, uses a modular and incremental method to create larger networks from sub-components [4]. The time delay architecture can be regarded as a convolution on sequence data where a 1-dimension filter scans through the input sequence and generate an output at each step with the strategy of weight-sharing. Many related works have focused on TDNN, such as TDNN-LSTM [5], TDNN-BLSTM [6], CNN-LSTM-TDNN [7] and FTDNN [8]. References [5–7] focus on combining TDNN with different components to construct better model and reference [8] proposed a variant of TDNN through low-rank matrix factorization and skip connection to overcome gradient explosion problem for TDNN-based network structures.

We propose the crossed-time delay neural network as a variant of TDNN, named CTDNN. The multiple-filters mechanism of a convolution layer from CNN inspires us to set different time delay units at the bottom layer of the network. In CNN, each filter with different parameters in the same convolution layer captures different characteristics of the input by generating different feature maps, which ultimately helps to classify the input image. In the original TDNN, there is only one filter per layer, which restricts the model's feature extraction and generalization ability according to our analysis and experiments. The proposed structure has three main advantages:

- The time delay units with different context size in the same layer help to extract more heterogeneous features.
- The structure is wider, but not deeper, which avoids gradient explosion and vanishing problem arising occasionally in the training process and guarantees the generalization ability.
- Our model works well with large batch, compared to FTDNN, which enables it to utilize calculation resources in a more efficient way without alternating the batches frequently.

2   Baseline Models

The network architecture of our speaker recognition baseline systems is the same as the original x-vector system in [1] and the improved architecture FTDNN in [8].

The TDNN architecture shown in Fig. 1 is applied in x-vector system. Initial transforms are learnt on narrow contexts and the deeper layers process the hidden activations from a wider temporal context. Hence the higher layers have the ability to learn wider temporal relationships [1]. The time delay architecture can be regarded as a one-dimension convolution on sequence data where a 1-d filter scans through the input sequence by the strategy of weight-sharing. The time delay layers is followed by the statistical pooling(SP) layer which computes the statistical feature by computing the mean and variance. Fully connected layers and SoftMax are posed after the SP layer to project the sequence into speaker's identity. During back-propagation, the lower time delay layers are updated by a gradient accumulated over all the time steps of the input sequence. Thus, the lower layers of the network are forced to learn translation invariant feature transforms [1].

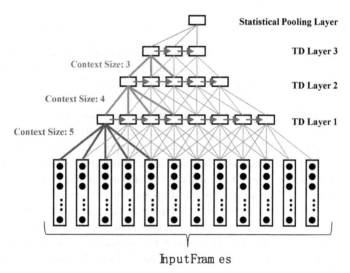

Fig. 1. An example for the original TDNN. Time delay (TD) layer 1, 2 and 3 each has a context size of 5, 4 and 3

The FTDNN is a factored form of TDNN which is structurally similar to TDNN, whose layers have been compressed via singular value decomposition to reduce the number of parameters, and uses shortcut connection [9] and highway connections in order to avoid gradient diffusion problems in deeper neural network.

3   Crossed-Time Delay Neural Network

The proposed CTDNN is shown in Fig. 2, which is a wide and shallow structure rather than a narrow and deep structure. It combines the Crossed-Time delay layers and the statistical pooling layers.

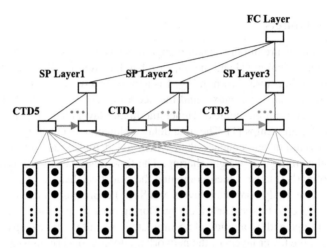

Fig. 2. The structure of CTDNN. Three parallel time delay units as CTD 5, 4 and 3 are marked.

3.1 Crossed-Time Delay Layer

We set different time delay units in the bottom layer to directly extract features from the input sequence. Each unit has a different context frame size, which means they take a different number of frames of MFCC feature as input. In Fig. 2, the context frame sizes are 5, 4 and 3 marked as Crossed-Time Delay (CTD) unit 5, CTD unit 4 and CTD unit 3. Each unit scans the input sequence separately and output a fixed size vector at each step till the end of the sequence. In other words, we can regard the different time delay units as different filters and each of them take the sequence as input and outputs different feature maps. The CTDNN layers can also be stacked vertically to form a deeper hierarchy structure, in this case, each feature map should be allocated a new time delay unit.

It seems against the consensus that the deep and narrow network is better than the wide and shallow one as discussed in [10]. However, the extension of the layer width is not to simply add more neurons and connections, but to extract features at different frequencies or paces. We exploit the strength of the structure from two perspectives including the heterogeneous feature extraction and the more feasible training process.

Heterogeneous Feature Extraction
Using crossed-time delay units can extract more heterogeneous feature than that of a TDNN. Since the raw audio is viewed as short-time stationary signal, it has to be framed to short-time pieces at a fixed frequency to further analyze the audio and extract other features like MFCC. In original TDNN models, the time delay units are stacked vertically, and each unit has fixed reception field and parameters within connections. This single-line structure has the bottom layer to domain the feature extraction capacity, which limits the generalization ability of the model.

Take the model shown in Fig. 1 as an example. The bottom layer has a context size of 5, so it takes in 5 frames of MFCC feature at a time. The second layer has an input size of 4, and it takes in four features from the bottom layer as input, which enlarges its context size to 8 dues to the tree-like vertical structure. However, the second layer does not actually take input from a context size of 8 but the linear combination of 4 short sequences at the size of 5. So does the deeper layers. So, the key of the model is up to the bottom layer. With a fixed set of parameters and context size, the feature it gets is homogeneous since there are features that range more or less than 5 frames because of the short-time stationary property of audio signal and those features cannot be captured by one fixed-context-size time delay unit.

As shown in Fig. 2, we set 3 time-delay units each with a different context size at the bottom layer. During back-propagation, due to the different context size, the lower layers of the network are updated by a gradient accumulated over different time steps of the input temporal context. Hence, the lower layers of the network are forced to learn different feature transforms, which enlarges the feature extraction capacity of the model.

Training Convenience

Shallow networks are more feasible to train and converge, especially on small datasets. Training might suffer from gradients vanishing or exploding problems during the process of back-propagation in deep neural network. The literature [10] found that relatively small network sizes have obvious computational advantages when training on small dataset. We leverage the depth and width of CTDNN in our experiments and find that building two CTDNN layers can outperform 5 normal TDNN layers in both common and few-shots learning tasks.

3.2 Statistical Concatenation

Since the context size of time delay unit differs in the bottom layer, the output of the units will have different length. Instead of doing statistical pooling on all the output in one time, we compute the mean and standard deviation for each time delay unit's output and concatenate the results parallel before the fully connected layer.

4 Experiments

We conducted our experiments on the open VoxCeleb1 [12] dataset and VCC2016 [13] dataset to test the models' performance under large and few samples condition. To be more specific, an open-set text-independent verification experiment was performed with VoxCeleb1 dataset and a close-set text-independent classification experiment was done with VCC2016 dataset since it has limited number of speakers (Table 1).

4.1 Preprocessing

For VoxCeleb1 the acoustic features were 30-dimensional MFCC features extracted every 10 ms and the frame size for short-time Fourier transform (STFT) was 25 ms. And for VCC2016 the acoustic features were 13-dimensional MFCC features and others are the same with VoxCeleb1. In order to obtain the same length inputs, we duplicate the short-length input and cut off the extra length to make all the input at the same length (1000 frames for Voxceleb1 and 300 for VCC2016). No more enhancing or aligning methods were implemented. Our model was implemented with PyTorch.

Table 1. Dataset details. Average length is the average number of frames after preprocessing in each dataset.

Dataset name	Num speakers	Total utterances	Average length
VoxCeleb1	1251	14425	791
VCC2016	10	1134	270
VCC2016 (Mini)	10	162	255

4.2 Model Configuration

Table 2. Model settings

	TDNN	FTDNN	CTDNN
1	TD [−2,2]	TD [−2,2]	CTD [−4,4]; CTD [−2,2]; CTD [−1,1]
2	TD [−1,2]	FTD Layer	CTD [−1,1] * 3
3	TD [−3,3]	FTD Layer	SC
4	TD [2, 7]	FTD Layer	FC
5	SP	FTD Layer	FC
6	FC	FTD Layer	SoftMax
7	FC	FTD Layer	
8	SoftMax	FTD Layer	
9		FTD Layer	
10		FC	
11		SP	
12		FC	
13		FC	
14		SoftMax	

In Table 2, FC stands for the Fully Connected layer, SP for Statistical Pooling Layer and SC stands for Statistical Concatenation. We construct the TDNN and FTDNN structure the same as [1] and [8]. TDNN structure combines of 4 TDNN layers. FTDNN has up to 14 layers, i.e., the deepest structure in our experiments. All the Time Delay layers in the three models have batch normalized input and are activated by ReLU. Dropout and skip-connection policies are only involved in FTDNN not in TDNN and CTDNN. To be recognized, the proposed CTDNN has a wider and shallower structure. We set 3 time-delay units in the first and second layer.

4.3 Training Parameters Settings

We used cross entropy as the loss function. Adam optimizer was used and the training batch size was 128 in VCC2016 and 50 in VoxCeleb1. The learning rate was fixed to 0.0001 for CTDNN and TDNN and 0.001 for FTDNN. Early Stopping was used to prevent overfitting.

4.4 Embedding Extraction and Verification

Embeddings were extracted after SP layer for TDNN and after SC Layer for CTDNN. Linear Discriminative Analysis was applied to reduce the embeddings' dimensions as well as alleviate the influence due to channel differences. We reduced the dimensions to 400 for CTDNN and 250 for TDNN since the CTDNN embedding's size is larger. We train the LDA model on the training data and apply it to the testing data to evaluate the performance of the systems. Cosine similarity was applied to all test cases in the testing part of VoxCeleb1 dataset to compute the similarity between two utterance and get the EER of the system.

5 Results

5.1 VoxCeleb1

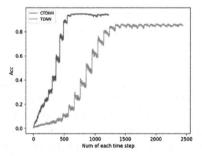

Fig. 3. Learning curve of VoxCeleb1 experiment. Each time step equals to 10 batches. The accuracy was tested on training data.

Figure 3 shows the update of accuracy on training data during the classification training process. The CTDNN structure converged sooner than the original TDNN and reach a higher training accuracy. Table 3 shows the result of TDNN's and CTDNN's identification performance on VoxCeleb1 dataset. CTDNN outperformed the TDNN structure by 30% improvement on EER.

Table 3. EER and converging epochs on VoxCeleb1 dataset

Structure	EER	Epochs
TDNN	0.054	31
CTDNN	**0.0382**	**12**

5.2 Vcc2016

Table 4 shows the results on two experiments. In both experiments, our CTDNN outperforms the other structures, especially in few samples learning in which the accuracy is more than 2 times of the original TDNN. Moreover, the experiments show that the performance of FTDNN gets worse when batch size grows and can't converge with the batch size of 128. We then tune the batch size and find 32 is the most proper setting for the first experiment. However, FTDNN can't work well with any batch size compared to CTDNN in few samples condition.

Table 4. Best Top1 test accuracy

Structure	VCC2016	VCC2016(Mini)
TDNN	0.778	0.448
CTDNN	**0.992**	**0.904**
FTDNN 32	0.965	0.662
FTDNN 128	0.608	0.681

The reason for FTDNN can't do well with large batch size is actually a general problem as discussed in [11]. There is still no consensus on how to tune batch size for different models. Different models might have different best batch size on different tasks. A large batch can significantly speed up the training while might suffer from loss in accuracy compared with small batch. From that perspective, the fact that CTDNN can achieve higher accuracy with large batch size also suggests that it can take full advantage of the GPU resources and speed up the training process.

Figure 4 and 5 shows the curves of test accuracy during training. It can be seen that CTDNN comes to convergence with higher accuracy than other models in both experiments.

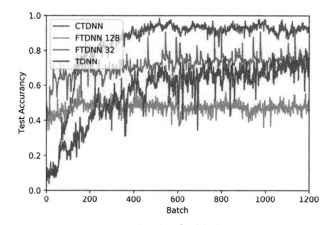

Fig. 4. Learning curve of VCC2016 experiment

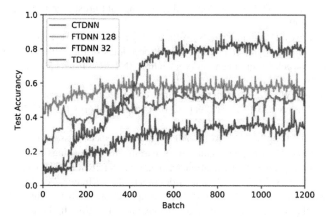

Fig. 5. Learning curve of VCC2016 (minus) experiment

6 Conclusion

In this work, we analyzed and examined the performance the new structure CTDNN on both speaker identification and verification tasks. Our analysis suggests that the crossed-time delay units can extract heterogeneous features therefore achieve better feature extraction ability. And our two experiments proved our analysis and showed the of large batch capacity of CTDNN.

TDNN was once the precursor of convolution neural network, now we apply the characteristics from CNN to improve TDNN and gain improvements. In the future we will explore more application of CTDNN such as using it to improve different TDNN based model and combine it with embedding extraction system like x-vector to find out its effect on speaker embeddings. Furthermore, there are still to explore about the relation between CTD units' parameters and feature capturing ability such as the number and the size of each CTD unit.

Acknowledgements. This work is supported by the National Natural Science Foundation of China (61772227, 61876069, 61876207 and 61972174), the Key Development Project of Jilin Province (20180201045GX and 20180201067GX), the Jilin Natural Science Foundation (20200201163JC), the Guangdong Key-Project for Applied Fundamental Research (2018KZDXM076), and the Guangdong International Cooperation of Science and Technology (2020A0505100018).

References

1. Snyder, D., Garcia-Romero, D., Sell, G., Povey, D., Khudanpur, S.: X-vectors : robust dnn embeddings for speaker recognition. In: Center for Language and Speech Processing & Human Language Technology, Center of Excellence the Johns Hopkins Un, Icassp 2018, pp. 5329–5333 (2018)
2. Jin, M., Yoo, C.D.: Speaker verification and identification. Behav. Biometrics Hum. Identif. Intell. Appl., 264–289 (2009). https://doi.org/10.4018/978-1-60566-725-6.ch013
3. Karaali, O., Corrigan, G., Gerson, I., Massey, N.: Text-to-speech conversion with neural networks: a recurrent TDNN approach. In: Proceedings of Eurospeech 1997, Rhodes, Greece, pp. 561–564 (1997)
4. Peddinti, V., Povey, D., Khudanpur, S.: A time delay neural network architecture for efficient modeling of long temporal contexts.pdf. In: Proceedings of the Annual Conference of the International Speech Communication Association, INTERSPEECH 2015, vol. 2015-Janua, pp. 2–6 (2015)
5. Liu, B., Zhang, W., Xu, X., Chen, D.: Time delay recurrent neural network for speech recognition. J. Phys. Conf. Ser. **1229**(1) (2019). https://doi.org/10.1088/1742-6596/1229/1/012078
6. Qin, Y., Lee, T., Feng, S., Hin Kong, A.P.: Automatic speech assessment for people with aphasia using TDNN-BLSTM with multi-task learning. In: Proceedings of Annual Conference of International Speech Communication Association, INTERSPEECH, vol. 2018-Septe, no. September, pp. 3418–3422 (2018). https://doi.org/10.21437/Interspeech.2018-1630
7. Miao, X., McLoughlin, I., Yan, Y.: A new time-frequency attention mechanism for TDNN and CNN-LSTM-TDNN, with application to language identification. In: Proceedings of Annual Conference International Speech Communication Association, INTERSPEECH, vol. 2019-Septe, pp. 4080–4084 (2019). https://doi.org/10.21437/Interspeech.2019-1256
8. Povey, D., et al.: Semi-orthogonal low-rank matrix factorization for deep neural networks. In: Proceedings of Annual Conference International Speech Communication Association, INTERSPEECH, vol. 2018-Septe, no. 2, pp. 3743–3747 (2018). https://doi.org/10.21437/Interspeech.2018-1417
9. He, K., Zhang, X., Ren, S., Sun, J.: Deep residual learning for image recognition. In: Proceedings of IEEE Computer Society Conference Computer Vision Pattern Recognition, vol. 2016-December, pp. 770–778 (2016). https://doi.org/10.1109/CVPR.2016.90.
10. Mhaskar, H.N., Poggio, T.: Deep vs. shallow networks: an approximation theory perspective. Anal. Appl. **14**(6), 829–848 (2016). https://doi.org/10.1142/S0219530516400042
11. He, F., Liu, T., Tao, D.: control batch size and learning rate to generalize well: theoretical and empirical evidence. In: Nips, no. NeurIPS, p. 10 (2019)
12. Nagrani, A., Chung, J.S., Zisserman, A.: VoxCeleb: a large-scale speaker identification dataset. In: Interspeech 2017, pp. 2616–2620 (2017). https://doi.org/10.21437/Interspeech.2017-950.
13. Toda, T., et al.: The Voice Conversion Challenge 2016, pp. 1632–1636 (2016). https://doi.org/10.21437/Interspeech.2016-1066.

An Asymmetric Two-Sided Penalty Term for CT-GAN

Huan Zhao[⊠], Yu Wang, Tingting Li, and Yuqing Zhao

College of Computer Science and Electronic Engineering, Hunan University,
Changsha, China
hzhao@hnu.edu.cn

Abstract. Generative Adversarial Networks (GAN) is undoubtedly one of the most outstanding deep generation models in the tasks such as image-to-image translation and image generation. In recent years, many improved algorithms have been proposed for GAN, and Wasserstein GAN with a consistency term (CT-GAN) has been noticed because of excellent stability. However, we find that its penalty term is not only too restrictive, but also ignores the boundary region of model distribution. This makes it challenging to enforce 1-Lipschitz constraint required by CT-GAN. In this paper, we propose a more efficient and less restrictive penalty term, named asymmetric two-sided penalty, to enforce the 1-Lipischtz constraint. As a application, we introduce Wasserstein GAN with Asymmetric Two-sided Penalty (WGAN-AP). In addition, we use Spectral Normalization enforcing generator to enhance the stability of our model. Through experiments on image generation task, our WGAN-AP shows stability and superiority compared to the state-of-the-art methods in terms of Inception Score and Fréchet Inception Distance. In particular, The Inception Score of our WGAN-AP achieves 9.14 and 8.41 separately on CIFAR-10 dataset in supervised and unsupervised tasks, which exceeds that of state-of-the-art models.

Keywords: CT-GAN · 1-Lipschitz constraint · Penalty term

1 Introduction

In recent years, deep learning has developed rapidly and made outstanding achievements in computer vision [23,35], speech [4] and natural language processing [7,10]. However, the training of deep learning models requires a large number of samples, which are often very costly to obtain. So, there spring up a lot of researches on deep generation model which can generate new samples by learning the internal probability distribution of data [18,22].

Since it has trouble in approximating many intractable probabilistic computations, initial deep generation model has not been widely used until the birth of Generative Adversarial Nets (GAN) [12], which simultaneously trains two deep neural networks: a generator and a discriminator. The generator keep approximating the data distribution to generate more realistic samples. And the

© Springer Nature Switzerland AG 2021
J. Lokoč et al. (Eds.): MMM 2021, LNCS 12572, pp. 11–23, 2021.
https://doi.org/10.1007/978-3-030-67832-6_2

discriminator is trained to distinguish generated samples from real data. This game allows GAN to continuously generate samples and modify them towards higher quality. With no doubt, GAN has become one of the most outstanding deep generation models, and its variants have achieved great success in various tasks [6,8,11,16,21,28]. However, with the development of research, the Jensen-Shannon Divergence (JSD) used by GAN has been proved to cause some training problems such as gradient vanishing and mode collapse [3].

Wasserstein GAN (WGAN) [3] was proposed as a solution to these issues. WGAN uses Kantorovich-Rubinstein duality [32] and 1-Lipschitz theory to implement Earth-Mover (EM) distance. Meanwhile, how to enforce 1-Lipschitz constraint was introduced as a new challenge.

In original WGAN, weight clipping was used to enforce 1-Lipschitz constraint, which has been proven to cause the discriminator to tend to learn oversimplified functions [13]. Meanwhile, [13] proposed a better way to enforce 1-Lipschitz, via a Gradient Penalty (WGAN-GP). Since then, a variety of regularization methods have emerged prominently.

Based on WGAN-GP, [34] introduced a additive consistency term to avoid the discriminator violating the 1-Lipschitz constraint freely in the surrounding region of the data distribution. Other recent work proposed innovative penalty term to replace gradient penalty. For example, [9] proposed a exponential gradient penalty term without adding any computation burden to enforce 1-Lipschitz constraint; WGAN-LP argued that gradient penalty is overly restrictive and proposed the Lipschitz penalty, which applied one-sided penalty [27].

Apart from traditional gradient penalty, [24] provided a new direction and proposed spectral normalization. In addition, several alternative model architecture and objective functions have been proposed to enforce 1-Lipschitz constraints (e.g., [1,2]). Although these methods demonstrate advanced robustness, the complete implementation of 1-Lipschitz constraint remains challenging.

In this paper, we propose an alternative asymmetric two-sided penalty term for CT-GAN to enforce the 1-Lipschitz constraint, so as to enhance the stability and performance. Our contributions are as follow:

1. Firstly, we review the regularization technique of CT-GAN. we find its penalty term not only too restrictive but also ignore the boundary region of model distribution, which leads the implementation of the 1-Lipschitz constraint to become difficult.
2. Secondly, we propose an asymmetric two-sided penalty to enforce 1-Lipschitz constraint. As an application, we introduce WGAN with Asymmetric Two-sided Penalty (WGAN-AP). It boosts the performance of CT-GAN and reduces computational effort.
3. Finally, on CIFAR-10, MNIST and toy datasets, we demonstrate the stability and superiority of our model in terms of Inception Score and Fréchet Inception Distance. Particularly, the Inception Score of our WGAN-AP achieves 9.14 and 8.41 respectively on CIFAR-10 dataset in supervised and unsupervised tasks, which boosts that of state-of-the-art models.

The remainder of the paper is organized as follows: In Sect. 2, we provide a review of existing methods (e.g. WGAN, WGAN-GP and CT-GAN) for better understanding. In Sect. 3, we present the motivation and implementation of our asymmetric two-sided penalty. Besides, we introduce our WGAN-AP. Section 4 uses experimental studies demonstrating the stability and superiority of our proposed method. Finally, Sect. 5 shows the conclusion of this paper.

2 Background

2.1 WGAN

Due to the use of JSD in the original GAN, if the discriminator reaches the optimal state $D_G^*(x) = P_{data}(x)/(P_{data}(x) + P_g(x))$(let P_{data} be a real data distribution and P_g be a model distribution on $\mathbb{R}^n$), the loss function will fall to a constant in general. [3] proves that this is the main reason for the instability of GAN. As an alternative, it propose to minimize the Earth-Mover (EM) distance.

$$W(P_{data}, P_g) = \inf_{\gamma \in \prod(P_{data}, P_g)} \mathbb{E}_{(x,y) \sim \gamma}[||x - y||], \tag{1}$$

But computing the infimum in Eq. (1) is difficult. In order to avoid the disadvantages, [3] using Kantorovich-Rubinstein duality[32] and 1-Lipschitz theory simplifying Eq. (1) as:

$$W(P_{data}, P_g) = \max_{D \in Lip_1} \mathbb{E}_{x \sim P_{data}}[D(x)] - \mathbb{E}_{z \sim P_z}[D(G(z))]. \tag{2}$$

Then, the Wasserstein Generative Adversarial Nets (WGAN) is proposed, the objective is defined as:

$$\min_G \max_{D \in Lip_1} L(D, G) = \mathbb{E}_{x \sim P_{data}}[D(x)] - \mathbb{E}_{z \sim P_z}[D(G(z))]. \tag{3}$$

Thus, how to enforce the 1-Lipschitz constraint during the training is crucial. WGAN uses weight clipping as a solution. Specifically, the weight ω is clipped to lie within a compact space $[-c, c]$ after each iteration. However, the discriminator tends to learn oversimplified functions due to weight clipping [13].

2.2 WGAN-GP

To solve the problem caused by weight clipping, [13] introduces a gradient penalty to WGAN (WGAN-GP). By noting that a differentiable function is 1-Lipschitz if and only if it has gradients with norm at most 1 everywhere, the gradient penalty limits the norm of the gradient between P_{data} and P_g:

$$GP|_{\dot{x}} = \mathbb{E}_{\dot{x} \sim P_{\dot{x}}}[(||\nabla_{\dot{x}} D(\dot{x})||_2 - 1)^2], \tag{4}$$

where $\dot{x}$ is equal to $\delta x + (1 - \delta)G(z), \delta \sim U[0, 1]$. The training objective of the discriminator is to minimize Eq. (5).

$$L = \mathbb{E}_{z \sim P_z}[D(G(z))] - \mathbb{E}_{x \sim P_{data}}[D(x)] + \lambda GP|_{\dot{x}}. \tag{5}$$

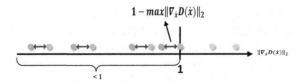

Fig. 1. A simplified two-dimensional schematic of our main idea about asymmetric two-sided penalty. We focus on the left region. The green dots demonstrate the real norm of data points, and the orange ones show the norm that we expect these to achieve after our punishment. The red two-way arrows have the same length, representing the fixed increment we set. (Color figure online)

2.3   CT-GAN

Although WGAN-GP achieves a great improvement in performance, it still does not fully enforce 1-Lipschitz constraints. [34] argue that the discriminator can violate the 1-Lipschitz constraint freely in the surrounding region of P_{data}. Based on this, it introduces an additive consistency term to WGAN-GP (CT-GAN), which realizes the continuity of the region around P_{data} by constraining the perturbed data points:

$$CT|_{x',x''} = \mathbb{E}_{x \sim P_{data}}[max(0, d(D(x'), D(x''))) + 0.1 * d(D_-(x'), D_-(x'') - M')], \tag{6}$$

where x', x'' are two perturbed points of real data, M' is a constant and $D_-(\cdot)$ represents the second-to-last layer of the discriminator. Therefore, the final objective is described as:

$$L = \mathbb{E}_{z \sim P_z}[D(G(z))] - \mathbb{E}_{x \sim P_{data}}[D(x)] + \lambda_1 GP|_{\dot{x}} + \lambda_2 CT|_{x',x''}. \tag{7}$$

3   Our Approach

3.1   Asymmetric Two-Sided Penalty

Main Idea. In WGAN and its variants, to enforce the 1-Lipschitz constraint, the discriminator function $D(x)$ has to implement

$$|D(x) - D(y)| \leq ||x - y||_2, \tag{8}$$

that is

$$||\nabla_{\dot{x}} D(\dot{x})||_2 \leq 1, \tag{9}$$

where $\dot{x}$ is equal to $\delta x + (1-\delta)G(z), \delta \sim U[0,1]$. Thus, when $||\nabla_{\dot{x}} D(\dot{x})||_2 > 1$, we need to constrain the norm of the gradient so that it can learn to approximate the required interval.

Definition 1. *Given a coupling $C(x,y)$, where $x \sim P_{data}, y \sim P_g$, when the discriminator is optimal, we can obtain an optimal coupling $C^*(x,y)$.*

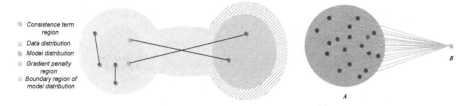

Fig. 2. Illustration of the constrained region of CT-GAN. These dots represent the sampling points. The yellow and green region represent P_{data} and P_g respectively. The purple and blue parts represent the constraint region of gradient penalty and consistence term respectively. And the red region is a sign for the boundary of P_g. (Color figure online)

Fig. 3. An example showing that the constraint power distribution between region A and dot B. The higher the line density, the stronger the constraint power.

WGAN-GP proves that if $D(x)$ is differentiable and the coupling $(x, y) \sim C^*(x, y)$, then $||\nabla_{\dot{x}} D(\dot{x})||_2 = 1$. Therefore, CT-GAN retains the two-sided penalty $\mathbb{E}_{\dot{x} \sim P_{\dot{x}}}(||\nabla_{\dot{x}} D(\dot{x})||_2 - 1)^2$ for limiting the norm of the gradient to approach 1 everywhere, even when $||\nabla_{\dot{x}} D(\dot{x})||_2 < 1$. However, in the actual training process, we sample independently from the marginal distributions P_{data} and P_g. This means that the collected coupling (x, y) probably lies outside the support of $C^*(x, y)$ and $||\nabla_{\dot{x}} D(\dot{x})||_2$ approach to one is unnecessarily when $||\nabla_{\dot{x}} D(\dot{x})||_2 < 1$.

In order to solve the computational burden and the damage to discriminator caused by the two-sided penalty, we propose an asymmetric two-sided penalty. When the norm of the gradient is greater than 1, we reserve the gradient penalty of CT-GAN, encouraging the norm of the gradient to go towards 1 everywhere. And when the norm of the gradient is less than 1, the most direct solution is to remove constraints such as WGAN-LP [27]. But increasing the gradient of lines connecting an arbitrary coupling $C(x, y)$, to some extent, is beneficial for discriminator to distinguish real and generated samples, so as to better guide generator. Thus, when $||\nabla_{\dot{x}} D(\dot{x})||_2 < 1$, as shown in Fig. 1, we propose to constrain all gradients with a fixed increment so that each gradient approaches a target slightly greater than itself. To avoid violating the 1-Lipschitz constraint, we set this increment to $1 - max||\nabla_{\dot{x}} D(\dot{x})||_2$. For each coupling $C(x, y)$, our penalty term of this part is constructed as

$$\{||\nabla_{\dot{x}} D(\dot{x})||_2 - [||\nabla_{\dot{x}} D(\dot{x})||_2 + (1 - max||\nabla_{\dot{x}} D(\dot{x})||_2)]\}^2, \tag{10}$$

that is

$$min(||\nabla_{\dot{x}} D(\dot{x})||_2 - 1)^2. \tag{11}$$

Therefore, our asymmetric two-sided penalty is constructed as

$$AP|_{\dot{x}} = \begin{cases} \mathbb{E}_{\dot{x} \sim P_{\dot{x}}}[(||\nabla_{\dot{x}} D(\dot{x})||_2 - 1)^2] & ||\nabla_{\dot{x}} D(\dot{x})||_2 > 1; \\ min[(||\nabla_{\dot{x}} D(\dot{x})||_2 - 1)^2] & ||\nabla_{\dot{x}} D(\dot{x})||_2 \leqslant 1. \end{cases} \tag{12}$$

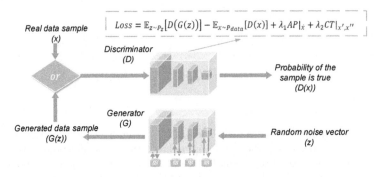

Fig. 4. Illustration of the structure of our WGAN-AP. The generator G receives a random noise vector $z \sim P_z$ as input, generate a sample $G(z)$. The discriminator D receives a sample and outputs the probability $D(x)$ that the sample is true.

Sampling Method. In practice, we can only achieve a finite sampling, considering an example in Fig. 3. Suppose we need to enforce a constraint between region A and dot B, the closer the region in A is to dot B, the denser the line. It means that the more marginal the region, the less constrained it will be. Therefore, the discriminator function has the highest probability of violating the 1-Lipschitz constraint in the boundary region of P_{data} and P_g. Although the consistence term of CT-GAN constrains the boundary region of P_{data}, but as shown in Fig. 2, the probability of the discriminator function to violating 1-Lipschitz in the boundary region of P_g remains high.

Therefore, for some tasks with large samples, we add noise to each generated data point, defining the perturbed model distribution P'_g. Then, we sampling uniformly along straight lines between pairs of samples to define $P_{\dot{x}}$, which are sampled from P_{data} and P'_g respectively. To some extent, this method expands the sampling range of the model distribution, and better constrains the boundary region of P_g by sampling beyond the required range.

3.2 WGAN with Asymmetric Two-Sided Penalty

We use our asymmetric two-sided penalty instead of two-sided penalty in CT-GAN. Figure 4 shows the framework of our WGAN-AP. Different from the previous training framework for GAN, we implement spectral normalization for the weight matrix in each layer of the generator network. And we advance an innovative loss function based on our AP, which is defined as bellow:

$$L = \mathbb{E}_{z \sim P_z}[D(G(z))] - \mathbb{E}_{x \sim P_{data}}[D(x)] + \lambda_1 AP|_{\dot{x}} + \lambda_2 CT|_{x',x''}, \qquad (13)$$

where $\dot{x}$ is equal to $\delta x + (1 - \delta)y, \delta \sim U[0, 1]$. x is sampled from P_{data} and y is sampled from the perturbed model distribution P'_g.

Algorithm 1. The algorithm for training WGAN-AP.

Require: the batch size $B = 64$, Adam hyperparameters $\alpha = 0.0003, \beta_1 = 0, \beta_2 = 0.99$, the weight coefficients $\lambda_1 = 10, \lambda_2 = 2$, number of iterations $iter = 10^6, N = 5$.

1: **for** $iter$ of training iterations **do**
2:     **for** $1, \cdots, N$ **do**
3:         **for** $i = 1, \cdots, B$ **do**
4:             Sample real data $x = \{x_1, \cdots, x_B\} \sim P_{data}$, perturbed generated data $y = \{y_1, \cdots, y_B\} \sim P_g'$, random vector $z \sim P_z$ and a number $\delta \sim U[0, 1]$.
5:             $\dot{x} \leftarrow \delta x + (1 - \delta)y$
6:             $L^{(i)} \leftarrow D(G(z)) - D(x) + \lambda_1 AP|_{\dot{x}} + \lambda_2 CT|_{x', x''}$
7:         **end for**
8:         $\theta_d \leftarrow Adam(\nabla_{\theta_d} \frac{1}{B} \sum_{i=1}^{B} L^{(i)}, \theta_d, \alpha, \beta_1, \beta_2)$
9:     **end for**
10:     Sample B random vectors $z^{(i)}$ and weight matrixes $\omega^{(i)}$.
11:     $\omega \leftarrow \frac{\omega^{(i)}}{\sigma(\omega^{(i)})}$
12:     $\theta_g \leftarrow Adam(\nabla_{\theta_g} \frac{1}{B} \sum_{i=1}^{B} -D(G(z^{(i)})), \theta_g, \alpha, \beta_1, \beta_2, \omega^{(i)})$
13: **end for**

Generator Constraint. Based on recent evidence that the performance of the generator is also closely related to the stability of GAN [25]. To further improve the stability of the model, before updating the generator, we apply the spectral normalization used for discriminator in SNGAN [24] to the generator. We divide the weight matrix of each layer in the generator network by its maximum singular value to enhance the stability.

Training Algorithm. The complete procedure for training WGAN-AP in this paper is outlined in Algorithm 1.

4   Experiments

In this section, we use Inception score (IS) [30], Fréchet inception distance (FID) [15] evaluating the stability and performance of WGAN-AP on toy datasets, prevalent MNIST [20] and CIFAR-10 [19] datasets. All experiments execute on tensorflow-gpu 1.12.0, CUDA 10.0 and python 3.6.5.

4.1   Datasets and Evaluation

MNIST is a handwritten digital dataset.It provides 60000 training samples and 10000 test samples. **CIFAR-10** is an RGB image dataset containing 10 types of ordinary objects.It provides 50000 training samples and 10000 test samples of size $32 * 32$. And we also use several **toy** datasets, including 8 Gaussians, 25 Gaussians and Swiss roll.

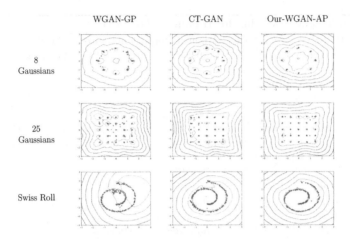

Fig. 5. Value surfaces of the discriminator on 8 Gaussians, 25 Gaussians and Swiss roll. The orange and green dots describes real data samples and generated data samples respectively. The curves represent the value surfaces of discriminator. (Color figure online)

Table 1. Inception score of the state-of-the-art GANs on CIFAR-10

Method	Supervised IS	Unsupervised IS
SteinGANs [33]	6.35	–
DCGANs [29]	6.58	6.16 ± 0.07
Improved GANs [30]	8.09 ± 0.07	–
AC-GANs [26]	8.25 ± 0.07	–
WGAN-GP [13]	8.42 ± 0.10	7.86 ± 0.07
SGANs [17]	8.59 ± 0.12	–
BEGAN [5]	–	5.62
CT-GAN [34]	8.81 ± 0.13	8.12 ± 0.12
SN-GAN [24]	–	8.22 ± 0.05
BWGAN [1]	–	8.31 ± 0.07
Our WGAN-AP	$\mathbf{9.14 \pm 0.13}$	$\mathbf{8.41 \pm 0.08}$

In the mainstream GAN experiments, **IS** is an important evaluation indicator. It evaluates both the quality and diversity of generated images. The higher its value, the better the model performs. But recent work pointed out that IS can't measure how well the generator approximates the real distribution [31]. So, we introduced **FID** to evaluate the fidelity of the generated images. And the lower its value, the better the model performs.

4.2   Results

Performance Evaluation

Toy First of all, we use several toy datasets for preliminary evaluation as depicted in Fig. 5. Due to the small sample size, we didn't disturb the generated samples. Then, we compare our WGAN-AP with WGAN-GP and CT-GAN after 100000 iterations. The best case is that the generated samples (green dots) overlap with the real samples (orange dots). So, it's not hard to see that the data distribution generated by our WGAN-AP is closer to the real data distribution.

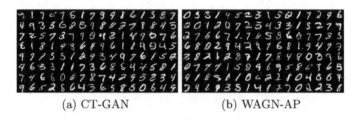

(a) CT-GAN   (b) WAGN-AP

Fig. 6. Generated images of CT-GA N (a) and Our WGAN-AP (b) on MNIST.

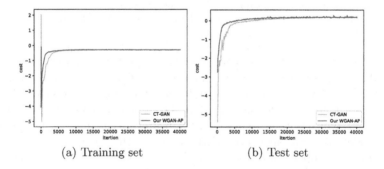

(a) Training set   (b) Test set

Fig. 7. Convergence curves of the discriminator cost on training set (a) and test set (b) of MNIST. The orange curve shows the cost of CT-GAN. The green curve shows the cost of Our WGAN-AP. (Color figure online)

CIFAR-10 We use ResNet comparing our WGAN-AP with the state-of-the-art GANs on CIFAR-10 datasets for both supervised and unsupervised task. Following the experiment setup of [34], firstly, we use 50000 training samples to calculate IS, and then we select the best model to report the IS on the test samples. We set the training steps to 100000. As shown in Table 1, compared to the state-of-the-art GANs, our WGAN-AP achieves the highest scores of 9.14

Table 2. FID scores of various WGANs on CIFAR-10

Table 2: FID scores of various WGANs on CIFAR-10

Method	WGAN-GP	CT-GAN	Our WGAN-AP
Generated samples			
FID	17.57	12.88	**11.77**

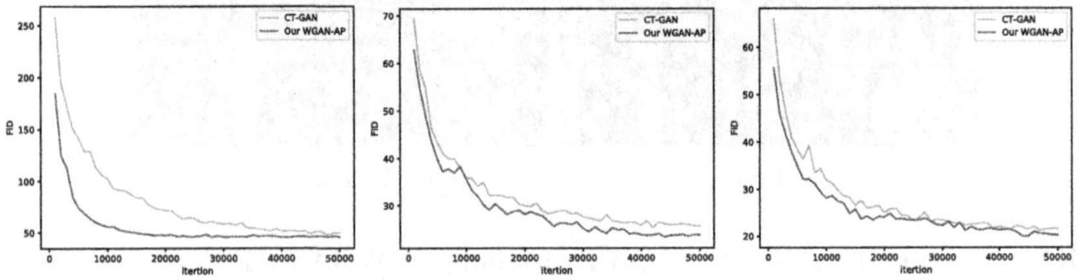

(a) ConvNet   (b) ResNet with LN   (c) ResNet

Fig. 8. Trend curves of FID scores. FID scores of CT-GAN and Our WGAN-AP during training are described by the orange and green curve respectively. They are trained in ConNet (a), ResNet with layernorm (b) and ResNet (c). (Color figure online)

and 8.41 in supervised and unsupervised tasks respectively. In order to evaluate the validity of the generated image, we also use FID to evaluate the trained model. Table 2 shows the FID scores and generated images of WGAN-GP, CT-GAN and our trained model on CIFAR-10 datasets. Our WGAN-AP achieves a score of 11.77, which is lower than CT-GAN. It proves that the samples generated by our model are more authentic. Further to say, these generated images also demonstrate the superiority of our model. You can see that the images of our WGAN-AP have a better topology, especially the image in row 4, column 7 is almost indistinguishable from the real car.

Stability Evaluation

MNIST To make a fair comparison, we follow [34] and use 1000 samples of MNIST to generate handwritten digital images. We set the training steps to 50000, and because of the sample size is small, we did not disturb the generated samples in the sampling stage. Figure 6 shows the generated samples with CT-GAN and our WGAN-AP respectively. We can see that our WGAN-AP generates more realistic and clearer handwritten digital images. Then, Fig. 7 shows the convergence curves of the discriminator cost by CT-GAN and WGAN-AP.

To highlight the convergence rate, we only show the results of the first 4000 iterations. It is clear that WGAN-AP converges to a stationary state faster on both the training and test sets.

CIFAR-10 For evaluating the stability of our model, we choose three different architectures, which are ConvNet[29], ResNet[14] and ResNet with layernorm (LN). The first two are frequently used in GAN. And, considering normalization technology for the discriminator has an effect on stability, we add the last one. After 50000 training steps, we compare our model with CT-GAN in these different architectures as shown in Fig. 8, and all experiments are conducted on CIFAR-10 with FID. Compared to CT-GAN, our WGAN-AP maintains a lower FID throughout the training process, regardless of the architecture. Finally, our WGAN-AP obtains FID of 45.54, 23.37 and 19.94 in three architectures respectively. It exceeds CT-GAN, which obtains 47.66, 25.64, 21.24. In conclusion, our model is less susceptible to architecture changes.

5   Conclusion

In this paper, we propose an asymmetric two-sided penalty to enforce the 1-Lipschitz constraint, which exceeds the performance of CT-GAN and reduces computational effort. Besides, for enhancing the stablility of Wasserstein GANs, we apply the spectral normalization to generator. We demonstrate the stability and performance of WGAN-AP over the state-of-the-art GANs across a variety of datasets.

Acknowledgments. This work was supported by National Key R&D Program of China (2018YFC0831800).

References

1. Adler, J., Lunz, S.: Banach Wasserstein GAN. In: NIPS, Montréal, pp. 6754–6763 (2018)
2. Anil, C., Lucas, J., Grosse, R.B.: Sorting out Lipschitz function approximation. In: ICML, Long Beach, pp. 291–301 (2019)
3. Arjovsky, M., Chintala, S., Bottou, L.: Wasserstein GAN. arXiv preprint arXiv:1701.07875 (2017)
4. Bao, F.: Improving speech emotion recognition via generative adversarial networks. Master's thesis (2019)
5. Berthelot, D., Schumm, T., Metz, L.: Began: Boundary equilibrium generative adversarial networks. arXiv preprint arXiv:1703.10717 (2017)
6. Bousmalis, K., Silberman, N., Dohan, D., Erhan, D., Krishnan, D.: Unsupervised pixel-level domain adaptation with generative adversarial networks. In: CVPR, Venice, pp. 3722–3731 (2017)
7. Chen, Q., Zhuo, Z., Wang, W.: Bert for joint intent classification and slot filling. arXiv preprint arXiv:1902.10909 (2019)

8. Chen, X., Duan, Y., Houthooft, R., Schulman, J., Sutskever, I., Abbeel, P.: Infogan: interpretable representation learning by information maximizing generative adversarial nets. In: NIPS, Barcelona, pp. 2172–2180 (2016)
9. Cui, S., Jiang, Y.: Effective Lipschitz constraint enforcement for Wasserstein GAN training. In: ICCIA, Beijing, pp. 74–78 (2017)
10. Dauphin, Y.N., Fan, A., Auli, M., Grangier, D.: Language modeling with gated convolutional networks. In: ICML, Sydney, pp. 933–941 (2017)
11. Dong, H., Liang, X., Shen, X., Wu, B., Chen, B.C., Yin, J.: FW-GAN: flow-navigated warping GAN for video virtual try-on. In: ICCV, Seoul, pp. 1161–1170 (2019)
12. Goodfellow, I., et al.: Generative adversarial nets. In: NIPS, Montreal, pp. 2672–2680 (2014)
13. Gulrajani, I., Ahmed, F., Arjovsky, M., Dumoulin, V., Courville, A.C.: Improved training of Wasserstein GANs. In: NIPS, Long Beach, pp. 5767–5777 (2017)
14. He, K., Zhang, X., Ren, S., Sun, J.: Deep residual learning for image recognition. In: CVPR, Las Vegas, pp. 770–778 (2016)
15. Heusel, M., Ramsauer, H., Unterthiner, T., Nessler, B., Hochreiter, S.: GANs trained by a two time-scale update rule converge to a local nash equilibrium. In: NIPS, Long Beach, pp. 6626–6637 (2017)
16. Huang, R., Zhang, S., Li, T., He, R.: Beyond face rotation: global and local perception GAN for photorealistic and identity preserving frontal view synthesis. In: CVPR, Venice, pp. 2439–2448 (2017)
17. Huang, X., Li, Y., Poursaeed, O., Hopcroft, J., Belongie, S.: Stacked generative adversarial networks. In: CVPR, Honolulu, pp. 5077–5086 (2017)
18. Kingma, D.P., Welling, M.: Auto-encoding variational bayes. In: ICLR, Banff (2014)
19. Krizhevsky, A., Hinton, G.: Learning multiple layers of features from tiny images. Computer Science Department, University of Toronto, Technical Report 1 (2009)
20. LeCun, Y., Bottou, L., Bengio, Y., Haffner, P.: Gradient-based learning applied to document recognition. Proc. IEEE **86**(11), 2278–2324 (1998)
21. Ledig, C., et al.: Photo-realistic single image super-resolution using a generative adversarial network. In: CVPR, Venice, pp. 4681–4690 (2017)
22. Li, Y., Swersky, K., Zemel, R.: Generative moment matching networks. In: ICML, Lille, pp. 1718–1727 (2015)
23. Li, Z., Zha, Z., Cao, Y.: Deep palette-based color decomposition for image recoloring with aesthetic suggestion. In: MMM, Daejeon, pp. 127–138 (2020)
24. Miyato, T., Kataoka, T., Koyama, M., Yoshida, Y.: Spectral normalization for generative adversarial networks. In: ICLR, Vancouver (2018)
25. Odena, A., et al.: Is generator conditioning causally related to GAN performance? In: ICML, Stockholm, pp. 3846–3855 (2018)
26. Odena, A., Olah, C., Shlens, J.: Conditional image synthesis with auxiliary classifier gans. In: ICML, Sydney, pp. 2642–2651 (2017)
27. Petzka, H., Fischer, A., Lukovnikov, D.: On the regularization of Wasserstein GANs. In: ICLR, Vancouver (2018)
28. Qiao, T., Zhang, J., Xu, D., Tao, D.: Mirrorgan: learning text-to-image generation by redescription. In: CVPR, Long Beach, pp. 1505–1514 (2019)
29. Radford, A., Metz, L., Chintala, S.: Unsupervised representation learning with deep convolutional generative adversarial networks. In: ICLR, San Juan (2016)
30. Salimans, T., Goodfellow, I., Zaremba, W., Cheung, V., Radford, A., Chen, X.: Improved techniques for training GANs. In: NIPS, Barcelona, pp. 2234–2242 (2016)

31. Shmelkov, K., Schmid, C., Alahari, K.: How good is my GAN? In: ECCV, Munich, pp. 218–234 (2018)
32. Villani, C.: Optimal Transport: Old and New. Springer, Heidelberg (2008). https://doi.org/10.1007/978-3-540-71050-9
33. Wang, D., Liu, Q.: Learning to draw samples: With application to amortized MLE for generative adversarial learning. arXiv preprint arXiv:1611.01722 (2016)
34. Wei, X., Gong, B., Liu, Z., Lu, W., Wang, L.: Improving the improved training of wasserstein GANs: a consistency term and its dual effect. In: ICLR, Vancouver (2018)
35. Zhou, J., Chen, J., Liang, C., Chen, J.: One-shot face recognition with feature rectification via adversarial learning. In: MMM, Daejeon, pp. 290–302 (2020)

Fast Discrete Matrix Factorization Hashing for Large-Scale Cross-Modal Retrieval

Huan Zhao$^{(\boxtimes)}$, Xiaolin She, Song Wang, and Kaili Ma

Hunan University, Changsha, China
{hzhao,shexiaolin,swang17,makaili}@hnu.edu.cn

Abstract. Hashing-based cross-modal retrieval methods have obtained considerable attention due to their efficient retrieval performance and low storage cost. Recently, supervised methods have demonstrated their excellent retrieval accuracy. However, many methods construct a massive similarity matrix by labels and disregard the discrete constraints imposed on the hash codes, which makes it unscalable and results in undesired performance. To overcome these shortcomings, we propose a novel supervised hashing method, named Fast Discrete Matrix Factorization Hashing (FDMFH), which focuses on correlations preservation and the hash codes learning with the discrete constraints. Specifically, FDMFH utilizes matrix factorization to learn a latent semantic space in which relevant data share the same semantic representation. Then, the discriminative hash codes generated by rotating quantization and linear regression preserve the original locality structure of training data. Moreover, an efficient discrete optimization method is used to learn the unified hash codes with a single step. Extensive experiments on two benchmark datasets, MIRFlickr and NUS-WIDE, verify that FDMFH outperforms several state-of-the-art methods.

Keywords: Cross-modal retrieval · Hashing · Discrete optimization · Supervised

1 Introduction

With the rapid development of information technology and the popularization of smart devices, multimedia data has shown an explosive growth trend, which attracts much attention in performing precise and efficient multimedia retrieval [1]. In recent years, hashing-based cross-modal retrieval methods have been widely studied due to their remarkable retrieval and storage efficiency [2]. These methods embed heterogeneous data from their respective original feature space into a Hamming space composed of compact hash codes. Therefore, the Hamming distance calculated by bit-wise XOR operations can be used to measure the similarities between queries and the retrieval set. For instance, if two data points are similar, their hamming distance will be as small as possible, and vice versa.

© Springer Nature Switzerland AG 2021
J. Lokoč et al. (Eds.): MMM 2021, LNCS 12572, pp. 24–36, 2021.
https://doi.org/10.1007/978-3-030-67832-6_3

According to whether label information is available, cross-modal hashing methods can be organized into two categories: unsupervised methods [3–6] and supervised methods [7–13]. Unsupervised methods generally concentrate on mapping multi-modal features into hash codes while maximizing the correlations of heterogeneous data. For example, Collective Matrix Factorization Hashing (CMFH) [3] firstly applies the collective matrix factorization technology to learn the unified hash codes with latent factor model from heterogeneous data. Latent Semantic Sparse Hashing (LSSH) [4] generates the unified hash codes by employing sparse coding and matrix factorization for images and texts respectively.

In many real scenarios, the supervised information such as semantic labels is available for multi-modal data. Thus, many supervised methods, which attempt to preserve semantic information obtained from labels, almost achieve higher accuracy than unsupervised methods. Representatively, Semantic Correlation Maximization (SCM) [7] attempts to leverage the to-be-learned binary code inner products to approximate the pairwise similarities constructed by given label vector. As a supervised extension of CMFH, Supervised Matrix Factorization Hashing (SMFH) [9] learns the hash codes with a latent semantic space by incorporating a Laplacian matrix, which makes it unscalable for large-scale datasets. Liu *et al.* [10] proposed another method termed Supervised Matrix Factorization Hashing (SMFH) to define a sampling matrix by randomly sampling parts of the similarity matrix, which effectively avoids huge storage requirements. Label Consistent Matrix Factorization Hashing (LCMFH) [11] transforms multi-modal data into the latent semantic space where the unified representations are the linear combinations of semantic features with labels as coefficients.

Furthermore, some discrete methods have been proposed to further obtain satisfactory retrieval accuracy. Semantics-Preserving Hashing (SePH) [14] learns the hash codes via minimizing the KL-divergence of the derived probability distribution in Hamming space and the probability distribution transformed by the semantic affinities. Composite Correlation Quantization (CCQ) [5] jointly rotates the original features into a correlation-maximal isomorphic space, and learns composite quantizers that transform the isomorphic features into compact binary codes in a bit-by-bit way. Discrete Cross-modal Hashing (DCH) [15] uses the discrete cyclic coordinate descent (DCC) [16] iteratively to solve each bit of the hash codes.

Although the proposed supervised methods have demonstrated their excellent retrieval accuracy, there are still the following problems to be solved. First, many methods construct a similarity matrix to guide the coding process, which requires massive calculation and storage, making them unscalable to large-scale scenarios. Second, the relaxation-based methods ignore the discrete constraints imposed on the hash codes, resulting in large quantization error and undesired performance. Third, numerous discrete methods learn the hash codes bit by bit, which is relatively more time-consuming.

To address the above issues, we propose a novel supervised cross-modal hashing method termed Fast Discrete Matrix Factorization Hashing (FDMFH). As illustrated in Fig. 1, the proposed FDMFH that consists of three parts generates

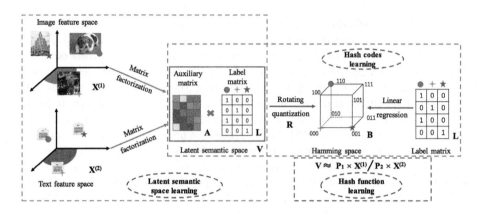

Fig. 1. Framework of the proposed FDMFH, illustrated with toy data.

the unified hash codes for heterogeneous data. It first utilizes collective matrix factorization to learn a latent semantic space, where different data points with the same category share the same representation. Then a rotation is found so as to minimize the quantization error between the Hamming space and the latent semantic space, and a regression of labels of data to the corresponding hash code further ensures the discrimination of the hash codes. Finally, it learns the linear projection as the modality-specific hash function to generate the hash codes for out-of-sample data in the retrieval phase. The main contributions of our proposed FDMFH can be summarized as follows:

- We propose a novel supervised cross-modal hashing method to learn discriminative hash codes while maximizing the correlations between multimodal data. Moreover, it reduces the quantization error and preserves the discrimination of labels into the hash codes.
- An efficient discrete optimization method is used to learn the hash codes directly without continues relaxation. It has a closed-form solution for the hash codes learning with a single step, which is suitable for large-scale scenarios.
- Our extensive experiments on two real-world datasets demonstrate the advantages of FDMFH under various cross-modal scenarios and show that FDMFH outperforms several state-of-the-art methods.

The remainder of this paper is organized as follows. Section 2 presents the details of our proposed method. The experimental results and analysis are provided in Sect. 3. Finally, Sect. 4 presents the conclusions of this work.

2   Proposed Method

In this section, we present the details of the proposed FDMFH. Without loss of generality, we choose bi-modal data for introduction, *e.g.* images and texts, which can be easily extended to the scenarios with multi-modality.

2.1   Problem Formulation

Suppose that we have a set of n training instances that consist of image-text pairs, $\mathbf{X}^{(1)} \in \mathbb{R}^{d_1 \times n}$ for images and $\mathbf{X}^{(2)} \in \mathbb{R}^{d_2 \times n}$ for texts. In general, the dimension d_1 of image feature is not equal to the dimension d_2 of text feature. Without loss of generality, we consider that both image features and text features are zero-centered, i.e., $\sum_{i=1}^{n} \mathbf{x}_i^{(1)} = 0$ and $\sum_{i=1}^{n} \mathbf{x}_i^{(2)} = 0$. Besides, the class labels $\mathbf{L} \in \{0,1\}^{c \times n}$ are provided, where c denotes the total number of categories. If the i-th entity belongs to the j-th category, $\mathbf{L}_{ji} = 1$, otherwise $\mathbf{L}_{ji} = 0$.

Based on such data given above, FDMFH aims to learn the unified hash codes matrix $\mathbf{B} = \{\mathbf{b}_i\}_{i=1}^{n} \in \{-1,1\}^{r \times n}$ for all training instances, where r means the length of the to-be-learnt hash codes. Moreover, in this paper, $\|\cdot\|_F$ denotes the Frobenius norm of a matrix. The $\text{sgn}(\cdot)$ is an element-wise sign function outputs -1 for negative numbers and $+1$ otherwise.

2.2   Fast Discrete Matrix Factorization Hashing

Latent Semantic Space Learning. Various modalities of a multimedia entity have different feature representations, which makes it difficult to realize the comprehensive utilization between them. Fortunately, matrix decomposition has been proved to be an effective way to transform original multimodal data into a common latent semantic space $\mathbf{V} \in \mathbb{R}^{r \times n}$, which consists of the unified representation and preserves the correlations of heterogeneous data. Furthermore, following previous work in [11], we leverage an auxiliary matrix $\mathbf{A} \in \mathbb{R}^{r \times c}$ to merge label information into the latent semantic space as $\mathbf{V} = \mathbf{AL}$, which guarantees that the unified representations are consistent with the corresponding semantic labels. To achieve this, the latent semantic space learning of bi-modal data can be formulated as:

$$\min_{\mathbf{U_m},\mathbf{A}} \sum_{m=1}^{2} \alpha_m \left\| \mathbf{X}^{(\mathbf{m})} - \mathbf{U_m AL} \right\| + \lambda Re \left(\mathbf{U_m}, \mathbf{AL} \right), \tag{1}$$

where α_m is the balance parameter and $\sum_{m=1}^{2} \alpha_m = 1$, λ is the tradeoff parameter, $\mathbf{U_m} \in \mathbb{R}^{d_m \times r}$ captures the higher-level features of data, the regularization term $Re(\cdot)$ is denoted as $Re(\cdot) = \|\cdot\|_F^2$ to avoid overfitting.

Hash Function Learning. The learned latent semantic space $\mathbf{V}$ are only applicable to training data. For out-of-sample instances, they need to be retrained to learn the unified semantic representations, which will take a lot of time. Hence, we learn two modality-specific linear projection matrices for mapping newcome instances into the latent semantic space for latent semantic representations by

$$\min_{\mathbf{P_m}} \sum_{m=1}^{2} \left\| \mathbf{V} - \mathbf{P_m X}^{(\mathbf{m})} \right\|_F^2 + \lambda Re \left(\mathbf{P_m} \right), \tag{2}$$

where $\mathbf{P_1} \in \mathbb{R}^{r \times d_1}$ and $\mathbf{P_2} \in \mathbb{R}^{r \times d_2}$ are the projection matrices for images and texts, respectively.

Learning Discriminative Hash Codes. After learning the latent semantic space $\mathbf{V}$, we can further quantify the latent semantic representation to generate the unified hash codes. However, many existing methods use the threshold function to embed data points in the latent semantic space into the Hamming space, which will undoubtedly cause large quantization error and reduce the discriminability of hash codes. To overcome this drawback, we firstly rotate the latent semantic space and then transform it into the Hamming space to ensure the maximum correlation between the latent semantic space and the Hamming space. We further define the following formulation:

$$\min_{\mathbf{B},\mathbf{R}} \|\mathbf{B} - \mathbf{RV}\|_F^2 \quad s.t. \ \mathbf{B} \in \{-1,1\}^{r \times n}, \mathbf{R}^T\mathbf{R} = \mathbf{I}, \tag{3}$$

where $\mathbf{R} \in \mathbb{R}^{r \times r}$ is an orthogonal rotation matrix. Thus, the locality structure of the original feature space will be preserved in the Hamming space as much as possible [17].

For the purpose of generating more discriminative hash codes for original multi-modal data, we can assume that its corresponding label can be predicted by the hash code, so as to ensure that the generated hash codes preserve semantic information as much as possible. According to [18], regressing $\mathbf{L}$ to $\mathbf{B}$ which will accelerate the algorithm is the same as regressing $\mathbf{B}$ to $\mathbf{L}$. So we can minimize the error of regression procedure by the following formulation:

$$\min_{\mathbf{B},\mathbf{W}} \gamma \left\| \mathbf{B} - \mathbf{W}^T\mathbf{L} \right\|_F^2 + \lambda Re\left(\mathbf{W}\right), \tag{4}$$

where $\mathbf{W} \in \mathbb{R}^{c \times r}$ is a linear classifier and γ is a weighted parameter. The term we used includes the inter- and intra-class properties in the learned hash code while the similarity matrix of size $n \times n$ is not constructed. Furthermore, it stabilizes the hashing coding algorithm [19,20]. To summarize, the hash codes learning procedure can be formulated as followed:

$$\min_{\mathbf{B},\mathbf{R},\mathbf{W}} \|\mathbf{B} - \mathbf{RV}\|_F^2 + \gamma \left\| \mathbf{B} - \mathbf{W}^T\mathbf{L} \right\|_F^2 + \lambda Re\left(\mathbf{W}\right)$$
$$s.t. \ \mathbf{B} \in \{-1,1\}^{r \times n}, \mathbf{R}^T\mathbf{R} = \mathbf{I}. \tag{5}$$

2.3 Optimization Algorithm

The optimization problem of FDMFH is non-convex with respect to all matrix variables jointly. Fortunately, the subproblems are convex with respect to each matrix variable while fixing the rests. Therefore, We introduce an alternating optimization method shown below.

Update $\mathbf{U_m}$: Fixing other matrix variables and letting the derivative of Eq. (1) with respect to $\mathbf{U_m}$ equal 0, we can obtain the closed form solution of $\mathbf{U_m}$:

$$\mathbf{U_m} = \mathbf{X}^{(m)} \mathbf{L}^T \mathbf{A}^T \left(\mathbf{ALL}^T \mathbf{A}^T + \frac{\lambda}{\alpha_m} \mathbf{I} \right)^{-1}. \tag{6}$$

Update $\mathbf{A}$: Fixing other matrix variables and letting the derivative of Eq. (1) with respect to $\mathbf{A}$ equal 0, we can obtain the closed form solution of $\mathbf{A}$:

$$\begin{aligned}
\mathbf{A} = &\left[\alpha_1 \mathbf{U_1}^T \mathbf{U_1} + \alpha_2 \mathbf{U_2}^T \mathbf{U_2} + 2\lambda \mathbf{I} \right]^{-1} \\
&\times \left[\alpha_1 \mathbf{U_1}^T \mathbf{X}^{(1)} \mathbf{L}^T + \alpha_2 \mathbf{U_2}^T \mathbf{X}^{(2)} \mathbf{L}^T \right] \\
&\times \left(\mathbf{LL}^T \right)^{-1}.
\end{aligned} \tag{7}$$

Update $\mathbf{P_m}$: Fixing other matrix variables and letting the derivative of Eq. (2) with respect to $\mathbf{P_m}$ equal 0, we can obtain the closed form solution of $\mathbf{P_m}$:

$$\mathbf{P_m} = \mathbf{VX}^{(m)T} \left(\mathbf{X}^{(m)} \mathbf{X}^{(m)T} + \lambda \mathbf{I} \right)^{-1}. \tag{8}$$

Update $\mathbf{R}$: Learning $\mathbf{R}$ by fixing other matrix variables, Eq. (5) can be rewritten as:

$$\min_{\mathbf{R}} \| \mathbf{B} - \mathbf{RV} \|_F^2 \quad s.t. \ \mathbf{R}^T \mathbf{R} = \mathbf{I}. \tag{9}$$

Obviously, this subproblem is an Orthogonal Procrustes problem and can be solved exactly by leveraging Singular Value Decomposition(SVD). More specifically, we can obtain $\mathbf{BV}^T = \mathbf{ESF}^T$ by taking SVD operation, and then the orthogonal rotation matrix $\mathbf{R}$ can be updated by $\mathbf{R} = \mathbf{EF}^T$.

Update $\mathbf{W}$: Fixing other matrix variables and letting the derivative of Eq. (5) with respect to $\mathbf{W}$ equal 0, we can obtain the closed form solution of $\mathbf{W}$:

$$\mathbf{W} = \left(\mathbf{LL}^T + \frac{\lambda}{\gamma} \mathbf{I} \right)^{-1} \mathbf{LB}^T. \tag{10}$$

Update $\mathbf{B}$: Learning $\mathbf{B}$ by fixing other matrix variables, Eq. (5) can be reformulated as:

$$\begin{aligned}
\min_{\mathbf{B}} \ &\left(\| \mathbf{B} \|_F^2 - 2tr \left(\mathbf{B}^T (\mathbf{RV}) \right) + \| \mathbf{RV} \|_F^2 \right) \\
&+ \gamma \left(\| \mathbf{B} \|_F^2 - 2tr \left(\mathbf{B}^T \left(\mathbf{W}^T L \right) \right) + \left\| \mathbf{W}^T \mathbf{L} \right\|_F^2 \right) \\
&s.t. \ \mathbf{B} \in \{-1, 1\}^{r \times n}.
\end{aligned} \tag{11}$$

$\| \mathbf{B} \|_F^2$ is a constant since $\mathbf{B}$ consists of -1 and 1, Eq. (11) is equivalent to

$$\min_{\mathbf{B}} - 2tr \left(\mathbf{B}^T \left(\mathbf{RV} + \gamma \mathbf{W}^T \mathbf{L} \right) \right) \quad s.t. \ \mathbf{B} \in \{-1, 1\}^{r \times n}. \tag{12}$$

Thus, we can obtain the closed form solution of $\mathbf{B}$ as below:

$$\mathbf{B} = \mathrm{sgn}(\mathbf{RV} + \gamma \mathbf{W}^T \mathbf{L}). \tag{13}$$

Obviously, $\mathbf{B}$ can be solved with a single step rather than bit-by-bit iteratively, which accelerates the training process and is suitable for large-scale scenarios. The training procedure of our FDMFH is summarized in Algorithm 1.

Algorithm 1. Fast Discrete Matrix Factorization Hashing

Input:
  Matrices $\mathbf{X}^{(1)}$, $\mathbf{X}^{(2)}$, $\mathbf{L}$; the length of code r, model parameters α_1, γ and λ.
1: Center $\mathbf{X}^{(1)}$ and $\mathbf{X}^{(2)}$ by means. Initialize $\mathbf{U}_1$, $\mathbf{U}_2$, $\mathbf{A}$, $\mathbf{R}$ and $\mathbf{W}$ as zero-centered random matrices respectively, and $\mathbf{B}$ as a binary matrix randomly.
2: **repeat**
3:    Update $\mathbf{U}_1$ and $\mathbf{U}_2$ by Eq. (6);
4:    Update $\mathbf{A}$ by Eq. (7);
5: **until** convergence or maximum number of iterations.
6: Calculate $\mathbf{V} = \mathbf{AL}$.
7: Calculate $\mathbf{P}_1$ and $\mathbf{P}_2$ by Eq. (8).
8: **repeat**
9:    Update $\mathbf{R}$ via SVD;
10:   Update $\mathbf{W}$ by Eq. (10);
11:   Update $\mathbf{B}$ by Eq. (13);
12: **until** convergence or maximum number of iterations.
Output:
  Unified hash codes $\mathbf{B}$, matrices $\mathbf{P}_1$, $\mathbf{P}_2$ and $\mathbf{R}$.

2.4   Out-of-Sample Extension

For a new query instance $\tilde{\mathbf{x}}^{(m)} \notin \mathbf{X}^{(m)}$, $m = 1, 2$, its corresponding unified hash code $\tilde{\mathbf{b}}$ can be generated via the trained modality-specific projection matrix $\mathbf{P}_m$ and the orthogonal rotation matrix $\mathbf{R}$. We can obtain the hash function for out-of-sample extension: $\tilde{\mathbf{b}} = h\left(\tilde{\mathbf{x}}^{(m)}\right) = \mathrm{sgn}\left(\mathbf{R}\mathbf{P}_m \tilde{\mathbf{x}}^{(m)}\right).$

Table 1. The statistics of two benchmark datasets.

Database	Total	Training size	Query size	Categories	Image feature	Text feature
MIRFlickr	16738	15902	836	24	150-d	500-d
NUS-WIDE	184711	10000	1866	10	500-d	1000-d

3   Experiment

In this section, we perform the comparisons between FDMFH and the baseline methods on two benchmark datasets to verify the superior retrieval performance of FDMFH. Furthermore, the parameter sensitivity and the training time cost of FDMFH will be demonstrated.

3.1   Experiment Settings

In the experiments, two benchmark datasets, MIRFlickr [21] and NUS-WIDE [22], are selected to evaluate the effectiveness of FDMFH. The statistics of two database are depicted in Table 1. We choose several state-of-art cross-modal hashing methods to compare with our proposed FDMFH, including unsupervised methods CMFH [3], LSSH [4], and supervised methods SCM [7], SePH [14], SMFH [10], DCH [15], LCMFH [11]. Because CMFH, LSSH and SePH require large computational cost, we randomly select 10,000 instances to train all models on NUS-WIDE. For our proposed FDMFH, we set the parameters as: $\alpha_1 = 0.5$, $\gamma = 2$, $\lambda = 0.0001$ for MIRFlickr, and $\lambda = 0.001$ for NUS-WIDE. The convergence threshold, maximum number of iterations for the latent semantic space learning and the hash codes learning are set to 0.01, 10 and 20, respectively. Following [4], mAP@50, precision-recall curve and topN-precision curve [23] are utilized to measure the retrieval performance on both the Image-query-Text tasks and the Text-query-Image tasks.

Table 2. mean Average Precision (mAP) comparison on two standard datasets.

Task	Method	MIRFlickr				NUS-WIDE			
		16 bits	32 bits	64 bits	128 bits	16 bits	32 bits	64 bits	128 bits
Image query Text	CMFH	0.6558	0.6470	0.6551	0.6438	0.4757	0.5015	0.4960	0.4934
	LSSH	0.6549	0.6618	0.6631	0.6806	0.4960	0.5105	0.5172	0.5249
	SMFH	0.6053	0.6385	0.6764	0.6873	0.5684	0.5972	0.6119	0.6004
	SCM	0.6952	0.7061	0.7068	0.7208	0.5857	0.6225	0.6220	0.6113
	SePH	0.6888	0.7020	0.7119	0.7141	0.5864	0.5892	0.5975	0.5993
	DCH	0.7784	0.7866	0.8230	0.8320	0.6423	0.6587	0.6682	0.6799
	LCMFH	0.7970	0.8292	0.8475	0.8521	0.6879	0.7160	0.7706	0.7867
	FDMFH	**0.8112**	**0.8444**	**0.8587**	**0.8654**	**0.7120**	**0.7528**	**0.7844**	**0.7878**
Text query Image	CMFH	0.7305	0.7357	0.7654	0.7819	0.4802	0.5115	0.5143	0.5245
	LSSH	0.7125	0.7475	0.7696	0.7717	0.6117	0.6266	0.6529	0.6664
	SMFH	0.6030	0.6571	0.7167	0.7422	0.5975	0.6719	0.6580	0.6617
	SCM	0.7050	0.7160	0.7217	0.7395	0.6089	0.6443	0.6734	0.6507
	SePH	0.7826	0.8057	0.8188	0.8300	0.7368	0.7479	0.7607	0.7646
	DCH	0.8946	0.9075	0.9120	0.9172	0.8053	0.8242	0.8244	0.8420
	LCMFH	0.9158	0.9294	0.9298	0.9388	0.8165	0.8473	0.8655	0.8729
	FDMFH	**0.9298**	**0.9355**	**0.9444**	**0.9459**	**0.8616**	**0.8723**	**0.8880**	**0.8890**

3.2   Experimental Results

Results on MIRFlickr. The mAP scores of all methods on MIRFlickr are shown in Table 2. From Table 2, we have the following observations. First, FDMFH shows best performance than baseline methods on both tasks with various code length, confirming that FDMFH is suitable for large-scale scenarios. Second, the mAP scores of all methods increase with the code length, because the longer codes can encode more semantic information for instances. Third, the mAP scores of the Text-query-Image tasks are generally higher than these of the Image-query-Text tasks, which means that the texts can better describe the semantic of the image-text pairs compared to the images.

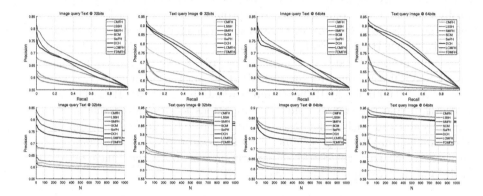

Fig. 2. Precision-recall curves (top) and topN-precision curves (buttom) on MIRFlickr varying code length.

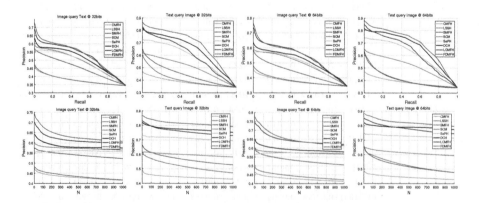

Fig. 3. Precision-recall curves (top) and topN-precision curves (buttom) on NUS-WIDE varying code length.

The precision-recall curves and the topN-precision curves are plotted in Fig. 2. As we can see, FDMFH also achieves the best performance among all methods. Besides, the performance of SMFH is worse than unsupervised CMFH, which shows that SMFH is sensitive to input data and cannot achieve satisfactory performance on all datasets.

Results on NUS-WIDE. Table 2 also reports the mAP scores of all methods on NUS-WIDE, and the precision-recall curves and the topN-precision curves are demonstrated in Fig. 3. Similar to the results obtained on MIRFlickr, FDMFH still achieves the best performance compared with baseline methods, and as the length of the codes increases, the results are also better. In addition, we can observe that the supervised methods achieve better performance than the unsupervised methods, which also verifies that the label information can further improve the retrieval accuracy.

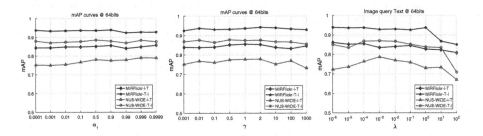

Fig. 4. Parameter sensitivity analysis.

Table 3. Comparison of training time (second) on NUS-WIDE under varying the size of training set.

Method/Training size	2000	5000	10000	50000	100000
CMFH	3.482	13.67	32.29	421.7	1412
LSSH	53.64	131.2	244.8	1260	–
SMFH	1.655	2.294	6.817	43.65	81.47
SCM	18.31	17.51	18.98	18.98	20.65
SePH	817.6	1792	3110	–	–
DCH	2.402	5.241	8.822	33.14	66.12
LCMFH	1.059	2.055	3.808	17.28	33.85
FDMFH	0.344	0.596	1.026	5.227	9.580

3.3 Parameter Sensitivity Analysis

In the previous experiments, we simply initialize the parameters on two datasets. In this section, we will perform sensitivity analysis on all parameters by fixing the values of other parameters and varying the value of one parameter. This series of experiments are performed with the code length of 64 bits.

α_1 balances the importance of both modal. The larger α_1 is, the greater the influence of the images on the performance. In particular, when α_1 is equal to 0.5, the influence of the images is equal to the texts. Combining the two retrieval tasks, we can observe from Fig. 4 that FDMFH shows superior and stable performance when $\alpha_1 \in [0.5, 0.9]$.

γ controls the influences of the rotating quantization term and the linear regression term in the hash codes learning part. When γ is too large, our modal just focuses on linear regression while ignoring rotating quantization. When γ is too small, rotating quantization will become more important. As shown in Fig. 4, we can find that FDMFH is not sensitive to γ when $\gamma \in [0.01, 100]$.

λ controls the weight of the regularization term. When λ is too small, the constraints of the regularization term will be reduced, the model is prone to overfitting, otherwise the model will be underfitting. As can be seen from Fig. 4, when the λ is larger than 1, the mAP scores decreases significantly. Therefore, λ can be easily chosen from the range between $[10^{-4}, 1]$.

3.4 Time Cost Analysis

To verify the efficiency of FDMFH, we sample different numbers of data points in NUS-WIDE to construct training set and record the training time of different methods with the fixed code length of 64 bits. The training time for each method are shown in Tabel 3, and all results are retained with four significant digits. Among them, "–" means that the training time cost is too high, and we do not report in this experiment. We can observe that CMFH, LSSH and SePH take higher time cost than other methods. The reason is that CMFH is subject to the strict convergence condition, LSSH has to extract the sparse representation of images, and SePH needs to construct the semantic affinities matrix and train kernel features. Furthermore, FDMFH demonstrates its efficiency and proves that it can be adapted to large-scale dataset scenarios.

4 Conclusion

In this paper, we propose a novel supervised hashing method, named Fast Discrete Matrix Factorization Hashing (FDMFH), for large-scale cross-modal retrieval. FDMFH utilizes the semantic labels as supervision during the latent semantic space learning process and the hash codes learning process without similarity matrix. Based on the rotating quantization term, FDMFH avoids the large quantization error while hash codes preserve the original locality structure of training data. In addition, an efficient discrete optimization method is used to learn the hash codes with a single step. Extensive experiments on two real-world datasets verify the stable and superior performance of FDMFH. In future work, we plan to extend FDMFH into a non-linear model such as a deep neural network to capture the underlying nonlinear structure, which further preserves the semantic correlations from the multimodal data.

Acknowledgments. This work was supported by National Key R&D Program of China (2018YFC0831800).

References

1. Wang, J., Liu, W., Kumar, S., Chang, S.: Learning to hash for indexing big data–a survey. Proc. IEEE **104**(1), 34–57 (2016)
2. Peng, Y., Huang, X., Zhao, Y.: An overview of cross-media retrieval: concepts, methodologies, benchmarks, and challenges. IEEE Trans. Circuits Syst. Video Technol. **28**(9), 2372–2385 (2018)
3. Ding, G., Guo, Y., Zhou, J.: Collective matrix factorization hashing for multimodal data. In: CVPR, pp. 2075–2082 (2014)
4. Zhou, J., Ding, G., Guo, Y.: Latent semantic sparse hashing for cross-modal similarity search. In: SIGIR, pp. 415–424 (2014)
5. Long, M., Cao, Y., Wang, J., Yu, P.S.: Composite correlation quantization for efficient multimodal retrieval. In: SIGIR, pp. 579–588 (2016)
6. Su, S., Zhong, Z., Zhang, C.: Deep joint-semantics reconstructing hashing for large-scale unsupervised cross-modal retrieval. In: ICCV, pp. 3027–3035 (2019)
7. Zhang, D., Li, W.J.: Large-scale supervised multimodal hashing with semantic correlation maximization. In: AAAI, pp. 2177–2183 (2014)
8. Cao, Y., Liu, B., Long, M., Wang, J.: Cross-modal hamming hashing. In: Ferrari, V., Hebert, M., Sminchisescu, C., Weiss, Y. (eds.) ECCV 2018. LNCS, vol. 11205, pp. 207–223. Springer, Cham (2018). https://doi.org/10.1007/978-3-030-01246-5_13
9. Tang, J., Wang, K., Shao, L.: Supervised matrix factorization hashing for cross-modal retrieval. IEEE Trans. Image Process. **25**(7), 3157–3166 (2016)
10. Liu, H., Ji, R., Wu, Y., Hua, G.: Supervised matrix factorization for cross-modality hashing. In: IJCAI, pp. 1767–1773 (2016)
11. Wang, D., Gao, X.B., Wang, X., He, L.: Label consistent matrix factorization hashing for large-scale cross-modal similarity search. IEEE Trans. Pattern Anal. Mach. Intell. **41**(10), 2466–2479 (2019)
12. Zhao, H., Wang, S., She, X., Su, C.: Supervised matrix factorization hashing with quantitative loss for image-text search. IEEE Access **8**, 102051–102064 (2020)
13. Zhang, X., Lai, H., Feng, J.: Attention-aware deep adversarial hashing for cross-modal retrieval. In: Ferrari, V., Hebert, M., Sminchisescu, C., Weiss, Y. (eds.) ECCV 2018. LNCS, vol. 11219, pp. 614–629. Springer, Cham (2018). https://doi.org/10.1007/978-3-030-01267-0_36
14. Lin, Z., Ding, G., Hu, M., Wang, J.: Semantics-preserving hashing for cross-view retrieval. In: CVPR, pp. 3864–3872 (2015)
15. Xu, X., Shen, F., Yang, Y., Shen, H.T., Li, X.: Learning discriminative binary codes for large-scale cross-modal retrieval. IEEE Trans. Image Process. **26**(5), 2494–2507 (2017)

16. Shen, F., Shen, C., Liu, W., Shen, H.T.: Supervised discrete hashing. In: CVPR, pp. 37–45 (2015)
17. Gong, Y., Lazebnik, S., Gordo, A., Perronnin, F.: Iterative quantization: a procrustean approach to learning binary codes for large-scale image retrieval. IEEE Trans. Pattern Anal. Mach. Intell. **35**(12), 2916–2929 (2013)
18. Gui, J., Liu, T., Sun, Z., Tao, D., Tan, T.: Fast supervised discrete hashing. IEEE Trans. Pattern Anal. Mach. Intell. **40**(2), 490–496 (2017)
19. Watson, G.A.: Characterization of the subdifferential of some matrix norms. Linear Alg. Appl. **170**, 33–45 (1992)
20. Hoerl, A.E., Kennard, R.W.: Ridge regression: applications to nonorthogonal problems. Technometrics **12**(1), 69–82 (1970)
21. Huiskes, M.J., Lew, M.S.: The MIR flickr retrieval evaluation. In: ICMR, pp. 39–43 (2008)
22. Chua, T.S., Tang, J., Hong, R., Li, H., Luo, Z., Zheng, Y.: NUS-WIDE: a real-world web image database from national university of Singapore. In: CIVR, pp. 48–56 (2009)
23. Baeza-Yates, R., Ribeiro-Neto, B.: Modern Information Retrieval, vol. 463. ACM Press, New York (1999)

Fast Optimal Transport Artistic Style Transfer

Ting Qiu[1,2], Bingbing Ni[1,2]($\boxtimes$), Ziang Liu[1], and Xuanhong Chen[1,2]

[1] Shanghai Jiao Tong University, Shanghai 200240, China
{776398420,nibingbing,acemenethil,chen19910528}@sjtu.edu.cn
[2] Hisilicon, Shenzhen, China

Abstract. Artistic style transfer plays an important role in the culture and entertainment industry. However, contemporary stylization approaches are suffering from two obstacles: 1) the low temporal efficiency and 2) the improper stylization metrics. To address these issues, we present a real-time style transfer framework optimized by the optimal transport theory. On the one hand, we design our learning scheme as a feed-forward network which can translate high-resolution images at the real-time speed; On the other hand, instead of learning the style manipulation unconstrained in the tensor space, we introduce the optimal transport optimization tool to ensure the stylization to be conducted along the style-manifold. Extensive experiments on Place365 and Wiki-art well demonstrate the excellent temporal efficiency as well as the convincing stylization effect of the proposed framework.

Keywords: Style transfer · Image translation · Optimal transport

1 Introduction

Artistic style transfer is a vital non-real rendering technology in computer graphics, which possesses the ability to re-create a photograph in the artistic creation way. Recently, style transfer [2,3,5,8,11–13,16,27] based on Convolution Neural Network [14] makes great progress in generating pleasing results. However, there are two core issues never be addressed at the same time: the appropriate stylization metric and the fast online inference speed. In this work, we aim to design a real-time artistic style transfer scheme which learns the artistic style via the optimal transport theory [17,19].

Great majority of style transfer approaches [2,5,8,11,26] employs the Gram Matrix [5] as their stylization metric. Although these schemes have demonstrated limited success in generating beautiful results, their stylization results are more like the tone adjustment and texture mapping of the original image, rather than the artistic reconstruction according to the content. The reason is that their stylization metric, Gram Matrix, plays a defective role for evaluating the style characteristic differences, leading to the texture-level alpha-blending results (Fig. 1).

© Springer Nature Switzerland AG 2021
J. Lokoč et al. (Eds.): MMM 2021, LNCS 12572, pp. 37–49, 2021.
https://doi.org/10.1007/978-3-030-67832-6_4

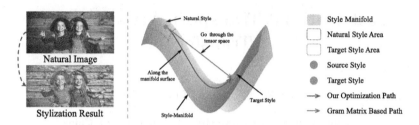

Fig. 1. Our method treats the style transfer as an optimal transport problem. In this way, our framework will manipulate the style distribution along the style-manifold leading to the excellent stylization effect.

Exhaustively, the style is the textural and structural description for an image [23]. It actually distributes along the **style-manifold surface**. Consequently, manipulating the style should considerate the geometry characteristics of the style-manifold rather than directly going through the tensor space. Inspired by this idea, the optimal transport schemes are introduced into the style transfer field. Kolkin N. *et al.* [13] (STROTSS) propose an optimization-based style transfer algorithm which replaces the Gram Matrix with a relaxed earth moving distance [15]. In this way, STROTSS achieves a significantly improvement in the stylization effect. However, STROTSS suffers from the heavy computational burden, leading to infeasible deployment in the real-time application scenes.

In order to tackle the mentioned difficulties (*i.e.*, the low temporal efficiency and the improper stylization metrics) in the style transfer, we propose a real-time feed-forward framework (called *fast optimal transport artistic style transfer, FOTAST*) to learn to manipulate the image style along the style-manifold surface following intrinsic geometry properties of the style distribution. In detail, for the temporal efficiency, we design our framework as a simple but powerful autoencoder-like network. To chase the idea of residual learning [9], we introduce some res-blocks to further increase the capacity of our framework, which largely strengthens the generalization-ability of our model. For the improper stylization metrics, we re-design the common used style loss (*i.e.*, Gram Matrix based euclidean distance of the pre-trained VGG [22] features) to considerate the manifold inherent nature of image styles. Actually, Gram Matrix is just an eccentric covariance matrix for an image/a feature, which acts as the texture-pattern descriptor in the style transfer. However, directly optimizing the euclidean distance of two Gram Matrices is equal to manipulate the style along a line in the tensor space. Such an optimization way ignores the geometry properties of style-manifold, leading to texture-level alpha-blending effect. Inspired by [13,15], we replace the Gram Matrix with the well-designed relaxed earth moving distance, videlicet, we translate the style transfer problem of our framework into an optimal transport problem. Under this idea, our model will learn to explore the style along the style-manifold, which encourages our framework to produce more convincing and artistically reconstructed results.

Extensive experimental results well demonstrate the effectiveness and high visual quality achieved by our framework.

2   Related Work

Style Transfer. Traditionally style transfer creates mathematical or statistical models for each style to render content images [4,10]. Since the convolutional neural network is used in this task, style transfer steps into a new level. The first neural style transfer algorithm based on the deep neural network is proposed by Gatys et al. [5], which re-renders the stylization image via the iterative gradient-based optimization approaches. Sequentially, Gatys et al. [6] keep improving the visual effect of style transfer. The feed-forward-based methods [12,24] use an auto-encoder for faster inference speed, and [12] also proposes perceptual loss for better semantic transferring. [11] proposes adaptive instance normalization by learning mean values and variance of channel-wise features. Recently [27] evaluates the effectiveness of self-attention mechanism in style transfer, and[13] uses local self-similarity as style loss. Most of these approaches employ the Gram Matrix as the quantitative metric for style transfer.

Optimal Transport. Optimal transport constructs distance between distributions. Our method uses a classical distance in optimal transport, named Earth Mover's Distance(EMD) [17,19]. EMD has been widely used in the computer vision [18,19], image retrieval [21] and natural language processing [15]. And recently [1] employs EMD distance in generative adversarial networks.

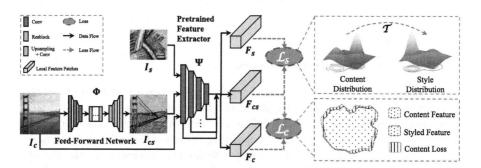

Fig. 2. This figure presents our optimization framework. Our method employs a feed-forward network to directly transfer images. During the training process, the pre-trained feature extractor obtains multi-layer features from the content, style and styled images(I_c, I_s and I_{cs}), and then generates a series of candidate feature patches F_c, F_s and F_{cs}. Our loss consists of content loss $\mathcal{L}_c$ and style loss $\mathcal{L}_s$, where $\mathcal{L}_c$ measures the similarity of F_c and F_{cs}, $\mathcal{L}_s$ uses optimal transport to optimize the distance between F_s and F_{cs}.

3   Methodology

The essential idea behind the style transfer is to align the style distribution between the content and style images. Unfortunately, **Gram Matrix based** approaches present limited capability to handle such a complicated alignment problem. To tackle the distribution alignment difficulty, we propose the *fast optimal transport artistic style transfer (FOTAST)*. In detail, our *FOTAST* treats the style transfer as an **optimal transport problem** instead of a Gram Matrix based optimization. In this way, our framework manipulates the style distribution along the **style-manifold** resulting in the excellent stylization effect. Furthermore, *FOTAST* is designed as a feed-forward pipeline rather than an optimization process [13], which endows the ability to perform real-time.

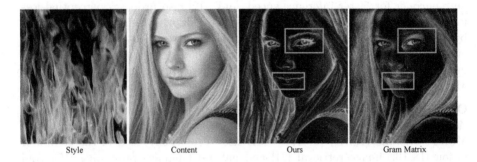

Style   Content   Ours   Gram Matrix

Fig. 3. The figure shows the different visual effect of our method and Gram Matrix as style loss, training and testing in the same condition. (Color figure online)

3.1   Fast Style Transfer Framework

Contemporary optimization-based stylization approaches are suffering from the low temporal efficiency, which largely limits the application scenes. To design a real-time stylization scheme, we follow the network structure guidelines set forth by [3]. As shown in Fig. 2, our learning framework consists of two main parts: 1) the feed-forward transfer network Φ for fast inference; 2) the feature extractor Ψ for calculating losses. Instead of per-pixel optimization, our feed-forward network fits the optimization process by learning massive samples. After the training process, our framework can directly perform stylization without the online optimization. Therefore, our network significantly reduces temporal and spatial complexity, making the application of style transfer a reality.

In detail, the feed-forward part of our pipeline is a simple but powerful autoencoder-like fully convolutional network. It makes our network able to process images of any spatial size. Our network contains an encoder with 3 CNN layers, and a decoder with 3 upsampling CNN layers, as shown in Fig. 2. Considering that pooling will degrade the performance of the generative model, we employ the strided convolutions for downsampling. Additionally, we use the upsampling + convolution way for features upsampling to avoid the checkerboard artifacts. To chase the idea of residual learning [9], we introduce some res-blocks to further increase the capacity of our framework. These res-blocks largely strengthens the stability and generalization-ability of our model, as in Fig. 5.

3.2 Learn to Style Transfer via Optimal Transport

The improper stylization metric is a notorious difficulty in style transfer. Although mainstream works [2,5,8,11,26] use Gram Matrix based euclidean distance in style tensor space, their training networks are easy to stuck in local optimal solution. As shown in Fig. 3, with same training conditions, the Gram Matrix method generates dissimilar color and texture from the style image. It also causes artifacts in local details (*e.g.*, white noise in flat areas). The reason is that all textural and structural representations of styles are actually distributes along the style-manifold surface. However, Gram Matrix based euclidean distance, essentially an eccentric covariance matrix, shifts directly in the tensor space, instead of moving along the geometry characteristic of the style-manifold. Therefore, it ignores the geometry property of style-manifold and leads to the texture-level alpha-blending results.

To pursue the minimal geometry distance between content and style representations, we translate the style transfer problem of our framework into a optimal transport problem. Inspired by [13,15], we replace the Gram Matrix with the well-designed Earth Mover's Distance (EMD) [19], which carries out the content distributions along the style-manifold surface. We propose the style loss as follows.

Style Loss. Note that $\mathcal{T}$ is the transport matrix and $c(i,j)$ is the cost matrix, x and y are the transported mass. EMD is defined as follows:

$$\mathcal{E} = \min_{\mathcal{T} \geq 0} \sum_{i=1}^{m} \sum_{j=1}^{n} \mathcal{T}_{ij} c(i,j),$$

$$s.t. \quad \sum_{j=1}^{n} \mathcal{T}_{ij} = x_i, \quad \sum_{i=1}^{m} \mathcal{T}_{ij} = y_j, \quad \forall i \in \{1,\ldots,m\}, \quad \forall j \in \{1,\ldots,n\}, \quad (1)$$

where $c(i,j)$ can be different metrics. We explore several measurement methods, and choose cosine distance as $c(i,j)$, because cosine distance can accurately measure the similarity of features with faster computation.

Unfortunately, normal optimal transport methods for style transfer imposes extremely high requirements on the solution, because of the large amount of style and content representations. For faster distance computation, we employ Relaxed Earth Mover's Distance (REMD) inspired by [15]. All features are considered to own equal mass, which means $x_i = 1/m$, $y_j = 1/n$. And we remove one constraint, obtaining tighter bounds, to relax the EMD optimization problem:

$$\mathcal{E}_x = \frac{1}{m} \sum_{j=1}^{n} \min_{i} c(i,j), \quad \mathcal{E}_y = \frac{1}{n} \sum_{i=1}^{m} \min_{j} c(i,j). \quad (2)$$

And the style loss is defined as:

$$\mathcal{L}_{style} = \max(\mathcal{E}_x, \mathcal{E}_y). \tag{3}$$

Fig. 4. This is an example of high-resolution style transferring. Then content image has 3440×1476 pixels. When zooming in, our method still retains a significant perceptual performance in details.

3.3 Optimization Objectives

During the training process, the pre-trained feature extractor obtains multi-layer features from the content, style and styled images, and then generates a series of candidate feature patches. The loss function in our method consists of content and style components, which is defined as follows:

$$\mathcal{L}_{total} = \mathcal{L}_{content} + \alpha \mathcal{L}_{style}, \tag{4}$$

where α is to balance the magnitude of style loss, here we set α as 6.

Content Loss. Our content loss is a selective object. Note that I_c, I_s and I_{cs} to be content, style and styled images. Let F_c and F_{cs} present feature vectors extracted from I_c and I_{cs}, the content loss can be presented as:

$$\mathcal{L}_{content} = \ell(F_c, F_{cs}) = \begin{cases} \ell_{perceptual}(F_c, F_{cs}) \\ \ell_{self-similarity}(F_c, F_{cs}) \end{cases}, \tag{5}$$

where in different conditions, we decide to choose perceptual loss [12] or self-similarity descriptors [20] as ℓ. Let M, N and H denote the width, length and channels of F_c and F_{cs}, l present a convolutional layer, perceptual loss can be calculated as:

$$\ell^l_{perceptual}(F_c, F_{cs}) = \frac{1}{M_l N_l H_l} \, \|F_c^l - F_{cs}^l\|_2^2. \tag{6}$$

Let $\mathcal{C}_{ij}^{I_c}$ and $\mathcal{C}_{ij}^{I_{cs}}$ be the pairwise cosine distance matrix of F_c and F_{cs}, where $i, j = \{1, \ldots N\}$, the self-similarity can be measured as follows:

$$\ell_{self-similarity}(F_c, F_{cs}) = \frac{1}{N^2} \sum_{i,j} \left| \frac{\mathcal{C}_{ij}^{I_{cs}}}{\sum_i \mathcal{C}_{ij}^{I_{cs}}} - \frac{\mathcal{C}_{ij}^{I_c}}{\sum_i \mathcal{C}_{ij}^{I_c}} \right|. \tag{7}$$

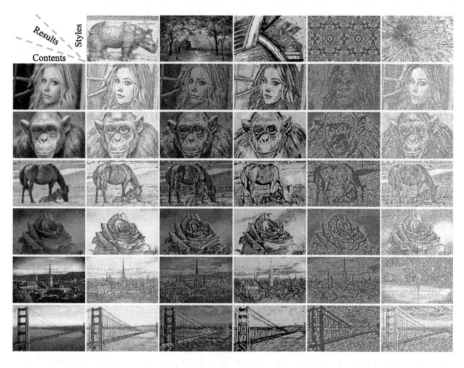

Fig. 5. In order to fully reflect the generalization-ability of our method, we show the visual effect of different content images transferred by different styles.

4 Experiments

4.1 Implementation Details

The structure of our feed-forwardnetwork is as shown in Fig. 2. It contains 3 CNN layers, 5 residual blocks [9] and 3 upsampling CNN layers. All residual blocks use Instance Normalization, followed by a SeLU non-linear activation layer. As discussed in [12], our pre-trained feature extractor uses layers $relu1\_2$, $relu2\_2$, $relu3\_3$ and $relu4\_4$ of VGG-19 [22] network, which is pre-trained by ImageNet [7] dataset. Our feed-forwardnetwork is trained on Wiki-art [11] and Place365 [25] dataset, respectively as our style and content images.

Baseline. We choose 7 representative mainstream models as our baseline: AAMS [27], WCT [16], AdaIN [11], Swap [3], NST [5], FNST [12], STROTSS [13]. We follow their official codes and training scheme for fair comparison.

4.2 Qualitative Analysis

As in Fig. 5, we show the visual effect of different content images transferred by different styles, including painting styles and pure texture maps. In each style, the content images have been fully reconstructed by style information (*e.g.*, line strokes are learned in third column), rather than element stitching. It also better reserves the elements of the style images (*e.g.*, column 5). This figure reflects that our *FOTAST* has strong stability and generalization-ability.

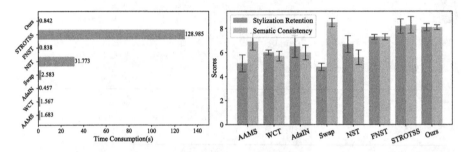

Fig. 6. The left figure presents the average time-consumption of inference in different methods. The right figure shows the scores of the user study, including stylization retention and semantic consistency.

Comparison. We compare our *FOTAST* with 7 state-of-art methods. Our experiments choose the most representative style images from galleries, photographs and other art works. As shown in Fig. 8, on the one hand, the visual effect of our method is close to STROTSS (*e.g.*, column 1 and 6) and even better (*e.g.*, column 2 and 4), while we greatly improve the speed (**100× faster** as shown in Fig. 6) with higher stability. On the other hand, we have a significant advantage over other methods. Our content semantics are accurately maintained, simultaneously it also preserves the characteristics of target style images (*e.g.*, the textures of the marble is well maintained in column 4). FNST and NST are more like pasting the texture to the surface of the content image, and it can't express style characteristics in some local details (*e.g.*, column 4 and 6). Even though Swap owns better details of content images, it's missing much style information. As for AdaIN, WCT and AAMS, their methods cause severe distortion in local structures and have low generalization-ability. Therefore, *FOTAST* maintains better perceptual performance in both content and style information, as well as high feed-forward speed.

Ultra High Resolution. We evaluate our method on 4k images, and the experiment proves that our method owns significant results in high-resolution images.

As shown in Fig. 4, we employ 6 different styles on a 3440×1476 image. When zooming in the figure, the transferred image has clear style textures while maintaining an accurate content structure.

4.3   Quantitative Analysis

In the quantitative analysis, we adopted time-consumption measurement and user study of stylization effects.

Time-Consumption. We randomly selected 1000 images (resized as 512×512) from Place365 dataset, scattered in 10 different styles in Wiki-art dataset, for testing their inference time-consumption on NVIDIA 1080Ti GPU. With the results in Fig. 6, feed-forward-based methods (*i.e.*, AAMS, WCT, Swap, FNST and Ours) are on average 2 orders of magnitude faster than optimization-based methods (*i.e.*, NST and STROTSS) except for AdaIN. Even in these feed-forward-based methods, the inference speed of ours is still among the best.

User Study. We carefully pick 50 groups of images, each contains one content image, one style image and 8 styled images (involving results from AAMS [27], WCT [16], AdaIN [11], Swap [3], NST [5], FNST [12], STROTSS [13] and ours). Then we ask 70 participants to attend our study. Each participant watches all styled images in one group in random order, and has limited time for to score from 0 to 10 (10 points is Best, 0 point is the worst). We use stylization retention to present the degree of stylization, and semantic consistency to denote the retention of semantic information (*e.g.*, contours and micro-structures). The mean scores of all methods attended are calculated and shown in Fig. 6. The study presents that our *FOTAST* performs close to STROTSS in stylization retention and semantic consistency, higher than FNST and other approaches. And Our method has stronger stability (less variance) and generalization-ability than STROTSS.

Fig. 7. We show the different effects of self-similarity and perceptual loss as content loss, training and testing in the same condition.

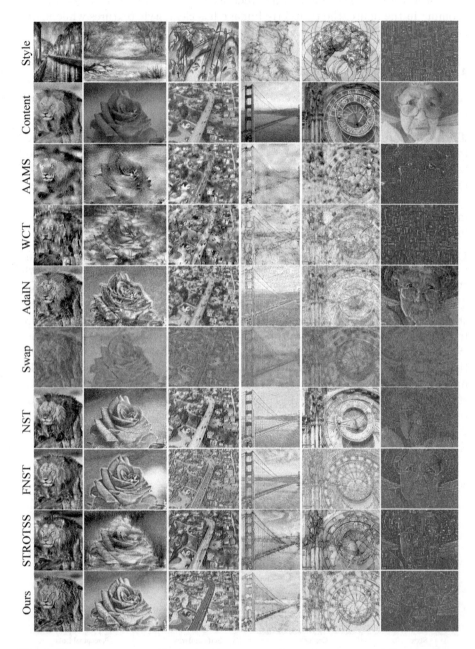

Fig. 8. We compare our method with 7 representative mainstream models as our baseline: AAMS [27], WCT [16], AdaIN [11], Swap [3], NST [5], FNST [12], STROTSS [13], where we train and test these methods in the same condition.

4.4   Ablation Study

Two important components of our method are content loss and style loss. We study the effectiveness of these two losses by replacing one of them individually.

Content Loss. We treat self-similarity and perceptual loss as content loss respectively, and the model is trained with the same strategy in implementation details. With the results in Fig. 7, we observe that self-similarity performs more semantic-like rather than structure-like. The results of self-similarity retains similarities of content and style information, expressing the texture of the style more accurately while maintaining the outline of the content. On the contrary, perceptual loss performs more structure-like, and the style textures feels to be post on content images.

Style Loss. To evaluate the visual effect of style loss, we replace REMD by normal Gram Matrix. As in Fig. 3, our method has a significant advantage over Gram Matrix. Our content semantics (*e.g.*, the girl's eyes) are accurately maintained, while it also preserves the features of target style images. However, Gram Matrix is more like pasting the texture to the surface of the content image, and it can't express style characteristics in some local details at all (*e.g.*, the girl's eyes and mouth are still the original appearances).

5   Conclusion

In this paper, we propose a fast artistic style transfer framework based on optimal transport, aiming at better stylization performance and lower time-consumption. Our experiments of qualitative and quantitative analysis present the advantages over other state-of-art methods, and the ablation studies evaluate the effectiveness of our method.

Acknowledgement. This work was supported by National Science Foundation of China (U20B200011, 61976137) and Shanghai Jiao Tong University, Shanghai 200240, China. This work was partially supported by Hisilicon.

References

1. Arjovsky, M., Chintala, S., Bottou, L.: Wasserstein GAN. arXiv preprint arXiv:1701.07875 (2017)
2. Babaeizadeh, M., Ghiasi, G.: Adjustable real-time style transfer (2020)
3. Chen, T.Q., Schmidt, M.: Fast patch-based style transfer of arbitrary style. arXiv: Computer Vision and Pattern Recognition (2016)
4. Efros, A.A., Freeman, W.T.: Image quilting for texture synthesis and transfer. In: Proceedings of the 28th Annual Conference on Computer Graphics and Interactive Techniques, pp. 341–346 (2001)
5. Gatys, L.A., Ecker, A.S., Bethge, M.: A neural algorithm of artistic style. arXiv: Computer Vision and Pattern Recognition (2015)

6. Gatys, L.A., Ecker, A.S., Bethge, M.: Image style transfer using convolutional neural networks. In: Proceedings of the IEEE Conference on Computer Vision and Pattern Recognition, pp. 2414–2423 (2016)
7. Geirhos, R., Rubisch, P., Michaelis, C., Bethge, M., Wichmann, F.A., Brendel, W.: Imagenet-trained CNNs are biased towards texture; increasing shape bias improves accuracy and robustness. arXiv preprint arXiv:1811.12231 (2018)
8. Ghiasi, G., Lee, H., Kudlur, M., Dumoulin, V., Shlens, J.: Exploring the structure of a real-time, arbitrary neural artistic stylization network. arXiv: Computer Vision and Pattern Recognition (2017)
9. He, K., Zhang, X., Ren, S., Sun, J.: Deep residual learning for image recognition, pp. 770–778 (2016)
10. Hertzmann, A.: Painterly rendering with curved brush strokes of multiple sizes. In: Proceedings of the 25th Annual Conference on Computer Graphics and Interactive Techniques, pp. 453–460 (1998)
11. Huang, X., Belongie, S.: Arbitrary style transfer in real-time with adaptive instance normalization. In: Proceedings of the IEEE International Conference on Computer Vision, pp. 1501–1510 (2017)
12. Johnson, J., Alahi, A., Fei-Fei, L.: Perceptual losses for real-time style transfer and super-resolution. In: Leibe, B., Matas, J., Sebe, N., Welling, M. (eds.) ECCV 2016. LNCS, vol. 9906, pp. 694–711. Springer, Cham (2016). https://doi.org/10.1007/978-3-319-46475-6_43
13. Kolkin, N., Salavon, J., Shakhnarovich, G.: Style transfer by relaxed optimal transport and self-similarity. In: Proceedings of the IEEE Conference on Computer Vision and Pattern Recognition, pp. 10051–10060 (2019)
14. Krizhevsky, A., Sutskever, I., Hinton, G.E.: Imagenet classification with deep convolutional neural networks, pp. 1097–1105 (2012)
15. Kusner, M., Sun, Y., Kolkin, N., Weinberger, K.: From word embeddings to document distances. In: International Conference on Machine Learning, pp. 957–966 (2015)
16. Li, Y., Fang, C., Yang, J., Wang, Z., Lu, X., Yang, M.: Universal style transfer via feature transforms, pp. 386–396 (2017)
17. Monge, G.: Mémoire sur la théorie des déblais et des remblais. De l'Imprimerie Royale (1781)
18. Ren, Z., Yuan, J., Zhang, Z.: Robust hand gesture recognition based on finger-earth mover's distance with a commodity depth camera. In: Proceedings of the 19th ACM International Conference on Multimedia, pp. 1093–1096 (2011)
19. Rubner, Y., Tomasi, C., Guibas, L.J.: A metric for distributions with applications to image databases. In: Sixth International Conference on Computer Vision (IEEE Cat. No. 98CH36271), pp. 59–66. IEEE (1998)
20. Shechtman, E., Irani, M.: Matching local self-similarities across images and videos. In: IEEE Conference on Computer Vision and Pattern Recognition, pp. 1–8. IEEE (2007)
21. Shirdhonkar, S., Jacobs, D.W.: Approximate earth mover's distance in linear time. In: IEEE Conference on Computer Vision and Pattern Recognition, pp. 1–8. IEEE (2008)
22. Simonyan, K., Zisserman, A.: Very deep convolutional networks for large-scale image recognition (2014)
23. Ulyanov, D., Vedaldi, A., Lempitsky, V.: Instance normalization: the missing ingredient for fast stylization. arXiv: Computer Vision and Pattern Recognition (2016)

24. Ulyanov, D., Vedaldi, A., Lempitsky, V.: Improved texture networks: maximizing quality and diversity in feed-forward stylization and texture synthesis. In: Proceedings of the IEEE Conference on Computer Vision and Pattern Recognition, pp. 6924–6932 (2017)

25. Wu, Z., Song, C., Zhou, Y., Gong, M., Huang, H.: Pair-wise exchangeable feature extraction for arbitrary style transfer. arXiv preprint arXiv:1811.10352 (2018)

26. Yang, S., Wang, Z., Wang, Z., Xu, N., Liu, J., Guo, Z.: Controllable artistic text style transfer via shape-matching GAN, pp. 4442–4451 (2019)

27. Yao, Y., Ren, J., Xie, X., Liu, W., Liu, Y.J., Wang, J.: Attention-aware multi-stroke style transfer. In: Proceedings of the IEEE Conference on Computer Vision and Pattern Recognition, pp. 1467–1475 (2019)

Stacked Sparse Autoencoder for Audio Object Coding

Yulin Wu[1], Ruimin Hu[1,2(✉)], Xiaochen Wang[1,3], Chenhao Hu[1], and Gang Li[1]

[1] National Engineering Research Center for Multimedia Software,
School of Computer Science, Wuhan University, Wuhan, China
{wuyulin,hrm,clowang,huchenhao,ligang10}@whu.edu.cn
[2] Hubei Key Laboratory of Multimedia and Network Communication Engineering,
Wuhan University, Wuhan, China
[3] Collaborative Innovation Center of Geospatial Technology, Wuhan, China

Abstract. Compared with channel-based audio coding, the object-based audio coding has a definite advantage in meeting the user's demands of personalized control. However, in the conventional Spatial Audio Object Coding (SAOC), each frame is divided into 28 sub-bands. All frequency points in one sub-band share the common parameter. Under the SAOC framework, the bitrate can be saved, but aliasing distortion is prone to occur, which will influence the listening experience of audiences. In order to obtain higher perceptual quality, we propose a Stacked Sparse Autoencoder (SSAE) pipeline as overlapped modules. Each module extracted the efficient feature of side information from its preceding module. Then we can reduce the dimensionality of side information parameters for saving bitrate, and well reconstruct audio objects, thereby providing favorable auditory perception. Compared with conventional SAOC, TS-SAOC, and SVD-SAOC, both objective and subjective results show that the proposed method can achieve the best sound quality of the output signal at the same bitrate.

Keywords: SAOC · Stacked sparse autoencoder · Dimensionality reduction

1 Introduction

Three-dimensional (3D) audio denotes an audio object with 3 degrees of freedom, such as azimuth, elevation, and distance. It can form a sound image at any position in 3D space. With the development of 3D audio and video, the demand for interactive and personalized listening experience is growing rapidly. Conventional channel-based audio coding technology is limited by the number of channels, and it can't meet the user's needs of personalized reconstruction, especially in immersive scenes, such as digital interactive theater and virtual reality games. Thus object-based coding method represented by immersive audio combines intuitive content creation and optimal reproduction in a wide range

© Springer Nature Switzerland AG 2021
J. Lokoč et al. (Eds.): MMM 2021, LNCS 12572, pp. 50–61, 2021.
https://doi.org/10.1007/978-3-030-67832-6_5

of playback configurations, which use a suitable rendering system. The object-based coding framework has been used successfully in commercial cases. Dolby Atmos [1] is popular in home theaters and enables a highly accurate immersive listening experience, with birds or helicopters flying overhead, rain falling from above, and thunder from any direction.

The typical representative of object-based coding is Spatial Audio Object Coding (SAOC) [2–4], which is originated from Spatial Audio Coding (SAC) [5]. The core idea of SAOC is to transmit multiple object signals with only a downmix and side information parameters, which can encode various audio objects at a low bitrate simultaneously. On the basis of the framework, many research institutions and scholars are focusing on improving the sound quality of audio objects, but the recovered object in the previous works contains other objects' components. This phenomenon is called aliasing distortion.

In order to reduce aliasing distortion and further improve the coding performance, we introduce an efficient compression method Stacked Sparse Autoencoder (SSAE) owing to reduce the dimensionality of side information. An autoencoder is a type of neural network that is efficient in dimensionality reduction. The basic idea of auto encoder is trying to compress data from input into a low-dimensional code and try to decompress that code as well as reconstruct an output that as similar to the original data as possible. This process forces the autoencoder to engage in capturing inherent features of the input in its hidden representation. SSAE is a type of autoencoder with efficient data compression. So we put forward a side information representation modeling based on SSAE.

The rest of this paper is organized as follows. We first review the related work about SAOC in Sect. 2 and then illustrate relevant techniques that SSAE is based upon in Sect. 3. In Sect. 4, we evaluate the proposed method under different audio objects in terms of subjective and objective measures. Lastly, we conclude in Sect. 5.

2 Related Work

The general structure of the state-of-art methods is depicted in Fig. 1. At the encoder, the inputs are J monophonic audio objects denoted by S_j. Firstly the side information matrix θ of each object is calculated, then the θ is quantized to yield $\bar{\theta}$, which is transmitted with downmix $\sum_j S_j$ of all the objects to the decoder. At the decoder, all the objects are reconstructed by using the estimation of side information $\hat{\theta}$ and the downmix $\sum_j S_j$.

SAOC downmixes multiple audio objects and transmits the side information extracted by each object to compress signals. Compared with transmitting all objects separately, the bitrate of the SAOC structure is much cheaper. However, when the number of audio objects increases and the code bitrate is limited, the reconstructed audio objects of SAOC will bring spectral aliasing. It won't be audience-friendly.

It is well known that the design of audio codes is to address the trade-off among low bitrate, high perceptual quality, low complexity, and delay. Many

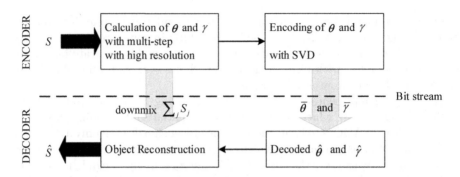

Fig. 1. The general structure of the state-of-art methods. The black parts represent conventional SAOC [2], black parts plus purple parts represent multi-step SAOC [6,13], and black parts plus red parts represent SVD-SAOC [11]. (Color figure online)

of the previous methods have worked towards the goal. Two-step SAOC (TS-SAOC) was proposed in [6], it classifies all the object signals into an audio target object (usually referring to the vocal object) and normal audio objects, the framework encodes the residual γ of the target object, quantized value $\bar{\gamma}$ of the residual work as supplementary information, which can help decode the target signal. So perfect gain of the target object can be obtained. However, it may not be only one target object in practical application. Moreover, the bitrate overhead of residual coding is large, and distortion among normal audio objects is still obvious.

By exploiting the inter-object sparsity of audio objects in the perceptual time-frequency domain, the compression framework of psychoacoustic-based analysis-by-synthesis (PABS) has been proposed in [7]. It compresses the side information of multiple audio objects into two audio mixture with retaining the most critical object signals at a time-frequency bin. However, the sparsity between objects will gradually decrease as the number of audio objects increases.

Intra-Object Sparsity Object Coding (IOSOC) [8] compresses multiple simultaneously occurring audio objects into only a mono downmix signal with side information based on the intra-object sparsity. The extracted frequency positions need to be recorded working as supplementary information. It can improve perceptual quality. However, the total number of preserved time-frequency instants among simultaneously occurring audio objects in one frame is limited to 1024. Perceptual performance varies greatly between different audio objects.

Dimensionality Reduction for ISS (DRISS) method was proposed in [9], which introduces random tensor compression. The method uses higher-order singular value decompositions (HOSVD) to reduce computational complexity and transmits less quantized parameters to the decoder with the help of the inference algorithm. Although the method allows significant bitrate savings as low as 0.1 kbps, the reconstructed audio quality is still very poor.

Recent research [10,11] makes a lot of contributions in reducing the degree of spectrum aliasing. In [10], the non-negative matrix factorization (NMF) method is applied to object parameter coding to reduce the high bitrate caused by more sub-bands in a frame. Especially SVD-SAOC [11] not only determines the optimal number of sub-band according to signal distortion but also uses the singular value decomposition (SVD) to reduce the dimensionality of transmitting parameters under finely divided sub-bands, and it can reduce aliasing distortion.

Zhang S et al. utilizes the sparsity of objects in the sparse domain [12] and uses the binary mask as side information, finally combines with the downmix signals to reconstruct audio objects from the downmix signals based on the sparsity of each audio object.

Multi-step SAOC coding structure [13] extracts residual and spatial information of all objects by cyclic chosen module and uses SVD to compress the residual information. So it can save bitrate with an optimized frequency energy sorting strategy, but it inevitably brings about the problem of error propagation.

Existing methods can be divided into three categories, and one compensates the missing part of audio objects with multi-step residual coding [6,13], another utilizes the sparsity of audio objects to compress signals [7,8,12], the other uses dimensionality reduction algorithms to compress parameters [9–11]. However, residual coding will bring about the problem of error propagation. The sparsity of objects will change with the categories and the number of audio objects in practical application. The dimensionality reduction algorithms are to transform the input linearly, and the reconstruction error is significant.

As we know, there are many dimensionality reduction methods. The Principal Component Analysis (PCA) module [14] is the classical one, but it can't well estimate the final number of dimensionality reduction. The SVD module is to transform the input linearly, and SSAE is nonlinear. In theory, the reconstruct error of SSAE will be lower than that of PCA and SVD. Because of its nonlinearity, there will be less information loss. In recent years, SSAE has been proven to be effective in extracting features in image processing tasks [15]. However, there was no report about representing side information with the SSAE model in object-based coding. For these reasons, we choose this module. The input of the audio encoder (AE) module in [12] is the downmix signal, while the input of the SSAE module in our method is the side information. That is the core difference.

We try to solve the problems that remained in the previous work and improve coding performance, and we put forward the SSAE-SAOC method to investigate the perceptual quality of the reconstructed objects.

3   Proposed Approach

3.1   Structure of SSAE-SAOC

The structure of the proposed method SSAE-SAOC is displayed in Fig. 2. The input mono audio objects $(S_1, S_2, ..., S_J)$ are transformed into time-frequency domain by a Modified Discrete Cosine Transform (MDCT), denoted by $O_1, O_2, ..., O_J$, where $j \in \{1, 2, ..., J\}$ represent the index of the object, $G_1, G_2, ..., G_J$ represent the side information matrices, $\hat{G}_1, \hat{G}_2, ..., \hat{G}_J$ are the

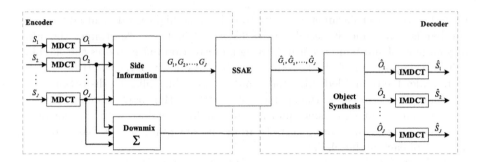

Fig. 2. The overall structure of the proposed method SSAE-SAOC.

reconstructed matrices derived by SSAE for all audio objects, the output mono audio objects $(\hat{S}_1, \hat{S}_2, ..., \hat{S}_J)$ are transferred by an Inverse Modified Discrete Cosine Transform (IMDCT).

The side information matrixes are also called Object Level Differences (OLD), which is defined by:

$$G_j(i,b) = \frac{P_j(i,b)}{P_{max}(i,b)} \begin{cases} 1 \leq i \leq I \\ 1 \leq j \leq J \\ 1 \leq b \leq B \end{cases} \tag{1}$$

Table 1. Partition boundaries for bandwidths of 2 ERB, MDCT size of 2048, and sampling rate of 44.1 kHz.

A_0	A_1	A_2	A_3	A_4	A_5	A_6	A_7	A_8	A_9
0	3	7	11	15	19	23	27	31	39
A_{10}	A_{11}	A_{12}	A_{13}	A_{14}	A_{15}	A_{16}	A_{17}	A_{18}	A_{19}
47	55	63	79	95	111	127	159	191	223
A_{20}	A_{21}	A_{22}	A_{23}	A_{24}	A_{25}	A_{26}	A_{27}	A_{28}	–
255	287	319	367	415	479	559	655	1025	–

Where $P_j(i,b) = \sum\limits_{k=A_{b-1}}^{A_b-1} [S_j(i,k)]^2$ is the estimated power of the j_{th} audio object, A_{b-1} and $A_b - 1$ are the beginning and end points of b_{th} sub-band. $P_{max}(i,b)$ is the maximum power of the input audio objects at the b_{th} sub-band in the i_{th} frame, respectively. I, J, and B are the number of frames, audio objects, and sub-bands, respectively. Sub-band division of SAOC is according to near twice width of the equivalent rectangle bandwidth (ERB) [16], as shown in Table 1. There are 28 sub-bands in a frame. All frequency points involved in one sub-band of an object share the same side information parameter. Such as in the second sub-band, the side information parameter of frequency points 3–6 is the same, which means frequency points 3–6 are treated equally. But in fact, the energy of frequency points 3–6 are not equal. That is why the decoded objects of SAOC have serious aliasing distortion.

3.2   Architecture of Stacked Sparse Autoencoder

AE is an unsupervised neural network with three layers [17], including an input layer, a hidden layer, and an output layer. The input layer denotes original inputs, the hidden layer represents learned features, and the output layer represents reconstruction, which has the same size as the input layer. An AE is also composed of the encoder and the decoder. The encoder consists of an input layer and a hidden layer, and it works as transforming the original inputs into hidden representation codes. The decoder consists of a hidden layer and an output layer, and it works as reconstructing the original inputs with the learned hidden representation codes. The structure of AE is shown in Fig. 3.

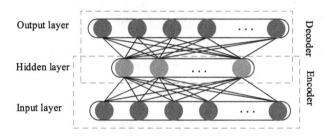

Fig. 3. The structure of AE.

The encoder maps the input vector x to the hidden layer with a non-linear function:

$$y = \mathcal{F}(\mathbb{W}x + b) \tag{2}$$

Where $x \in \mathbb{R}^{N \times 1}$ represents the input vector. N denotes the number of signals. $\mathcal{F}$ is the activation function, which commonly used Log-sigmoid function (Logsig), $\mathbb{W}$ is the weight matrix of the encoder, and b is the bias vector of the encoder.

The decoder process is defined as follows:

$$\hat{x} = \mathcal{F}'(\mathbb{W}'y + b') \tag{3}$$

Where $\mathcal{F}'$ is the transfer function of the decoder, which can be linear (Purelin). $\mathbb{W}'$ and b' are the weights and biases of the decoder.

The definition of the cost function $\mathcal{J}_{cost}$ is:

$$\mathcal{J}_{cost} = [\frac{1}{N}\sum_{i=1}^{N}(\frac{1}{2}\|\hat{x}_i - x_i\|^2)] + \frac{\lambda}{2}\sum_{l=1}^{n_l-1}\sum_{i=1}^{s_l}\sum_{j=1}^{s_{l+1}}(\mathbb{W}_{ji}^{(l)})^2 + \beta\sum_{j=1}^{s_l}KL(\rho\|\hat{\rho}_j) \tag{4}$$

Cost function $\mathcal{J}_{cost}$ includes three terms, the first is an average sum-of-squares error term, and the second is a regularization term, λ denotes the weight decay parameter, n_l represents the number of layers, s_l is the number of neurons in the l_{th} layer (not counting the bias unit), the last is the Kullback-Leibler (KL) divergence between a Bernoulli random variable with mean ρ and $\hat{\rho}_j$. β controls the weight of sparsity penalty term.

A stacked sparse autoencoder can be viewed as a stack of multiple autoencoders (AEs). It is a type of deep neural network consisting of one input layer, multiple hidden layers, and a softmax layer. The activated hidden layer is fed into the next AE. SSAE extracts the features layer by layer, and the resulting features are more representative and have a small dimensionality.

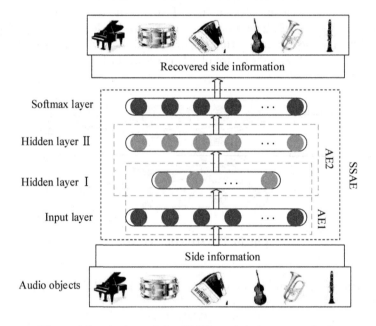

Fig. 4. The pipeline of the SSAE module in our method.

As shown in Fig. 4, two AEs are used to extract features for the training phase. In our network, all the normalized side information of audio objects is input to the SSAE module, and AE1 compress the parameters to get the representation of the features in hidden layer I. AE2 continues to extract efficient features based on the output of AE1, and the last layer is a Softmax classifier. In the output, a linear transformation of the network is applied to the Softmax, and it should be noted that the size of Softmax is the same as the input layer.

4   Experimental Evaluation

4.1   Experiments Conditions

To assess the performance of our proposed SSAE-SAOC, we report a series of experiments on the DSD100 dataset [18]. It composes of 100 different songs. Each song contains $J = 4$ objects sampled at 44.1 kHz with 16 bits resolution: bass, drums, accompaniment, and vocals. The track lengths vary from 2:20 to 4:50 min.

Objective evaluation metrics in tests are signal-to-distortion ratio (SDR, in dB) and signal-to-interferences ratio (SIR, in dB), which are calculated by the BSS_EVAL toolbox [19,20]. We use the SDR metric when analyzing the reconstruction error between the decoded audio objects and the original audio objects. The SIR metric can reflect the degree of frequency aliasing distortion.

The time-frequency transformation method is MDCT with the size of 2048 points and 50% overlapping. Downmix signals are compressed by MPEG AAC codes at 128 kbps. We compare the proposed method with the baseline methods at a fixed bitrate of 5 kbps per object. SAOC, TS-SAOC, and SVD-SAOC are the baseline methods. Because SVD-SAOC [11] finely divides a frame into 112 sub-bands, so we also follow the sub-band dividing technique.

4.2   SSAE Model Training

In the training phase, we use the loss function defined in Eq. (4). Training is to maximize the chances of reconstruction of the side information. Firstly, calculated side information parameters are fed into the SSAE model. Then the loss between the input (original side information parameters) and the output (recovered side information parameters) will be computed.

The complete DSD100 training set with 50 songs is used. The duration of training audio is about 14 h. The test material for the experimental evaluation is shown in Table 2. It consists of 6 actual songs from the DSD100 dataset represented by recording id A–F. Each recording has four active audio objects and lasts no more than 20 s.

Table 2. Description of test material.

ID	Names	List of audio objects	Style
A	One minute smile	Bass, drums, accompaniment, vocals	Power Pop
B	Stitch up	Bass, drums, accompaniment, vocals	Indie Pop/Rock
C	Sea of leaves	Bass, drums, accompaniment, vocals	Uptempo Indie Roc
D	Ghost	Bass, drums, accompaniment, vocals	Leftfield Pop/Electronica
E	The wind	Bass, drums, accompaniment, vocals	Melodic Indie Rock
F	We feel alright	Bass, drums, accompaniment, vocals	Gothic Electro

The detailed initialization parameters used in training work are listed in Table 3.

Table 3. Parameters of the proposed SSAE model.

Parameters	AE1	AE2	Softmax layer
Max epochs	400	400	400
L2Weight regularization λ	0.004	0.002	–
Sparsity regularization β	4	4	–
Sparsity proportion ρ	0.15	0.1	–

4.3   Test Results and Data Analysis

As shown, Fig. 5(a) and 5(b) are the average SDR and SIR of all audio objects in the same recording. And all audio objects are encoded respectively by SAOC, TS-SAOC, SVD-SAOC, and SSAE-SAOC. Compared with conventional SAOC and TS-SAOC, all the results of our proposed method SSAE-SAOC are apparently much better, which verifies the effectiveness of the proposed method to improve the perceptual quality with the same bitrate. Moreover, all the SDRs of SSAE-SAOC have an absolute advantage over SVD-SAOC. It is because that SSAE has a non-linear structure and extracts efficient features of side information while reducing the dimensionality. Thus, the proposed SSAE-SAOC can better rebuild the audio objects. The SIR of SSAE-SAOC is also better than SVD-SAOC, which can also prove that our method can reduce aliasing distortion to a certain extent.

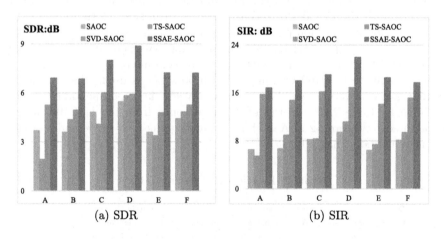

(a) SDR   (b) SIR

Fig. 5. Objective test results.

The average objective results of all test materials are shown in Table 4. Our method has the highest SDR and SIR than the other methods. The largest SDR means the reconstructed objects by our method have the least distortion to original objects. Meanwhile, the largest SIR indicates each reconstructed object by our method suffers the least interference from other objects. Compared with

SAOC and TS-SAOC, our method can averagely improve the SDR and SIR by about 3.34 dB and 10.67 dB, respectively.

Table 4. The average objective results of all test materials.

	SAOC	TS-SAOC	SVD-SAOC	SSAE-SAOC
SDR	4.26	4.06	5.36	**7.50**
SIR	7.57	8.46	15.48	**18.69**

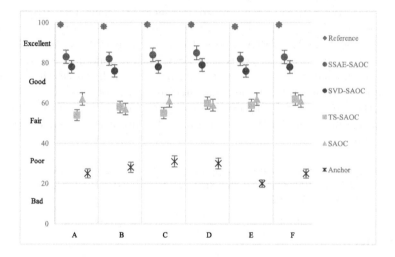

Fig. 6. The MUSHRA scores of six recordings.

We choose 13 listeners aged 20 to 35 to evaluate the quality of decoded audio objects. The MUSHRA method is performed in the subjective test [21]. The subjective test results for different methods with 95% confidence intervals are shown in Fig. 6. The MUSHRA score of each recording file is derived by averaging scores obtained for all objects in the recording. A MUSHRA test is performed to measure the subjective perceptual quality with six conditions: anchor, SAOC, TS-SAOC, SVD-SAOC, SSAE-SAOC, and hidden reference. The hidden reference is the original audio objects. The anchor is obtained by filtering the original object with the 3.5 kHz low-pass filter.

It can be observed that SSAE-SAOC has the highest MUSHRA scores for all the test files and is stable in the excellent range. SSAE-SAOC outperforms SAOC and TS-SAOC at the same bitrate, and it raises the perceived sound quality by about 20 MUSHRA points. Moreover, the scores of SSAE-SAOC are slightly higher than SVD-SAOC. It shows that our method can extract better features of parameters to achieve dimensionality reduction. So, SSAE-SAOC can improve not only perceptual quality but also be competitive in suppressing other objects.

The MUSHRA scores are consistent with objective test results, so the effectiveness of our method can be further demonstrated.

5   Conclusions

In this paper, we proposed a new object-based audio coding method SSAE-SAOC, and our approach can provide high coding quality. The test results demonstrate that our method reaches a higher coding level than the state of art methods. Compared with SAOC and TS-SAOC at the same bitrate, the value of SDR and SIR can be improved averagely by about 3.34 dB and 10.67 dB, respectively. The proposed method can also improve the perceived sound quality by about 20 MUSHRA points. Compared with SVD-SAOC, the proposed method's main advantage is that SSAE has a non-linear structure and captures the efficient feature of the side information, which enables the recovered object to be more accurate. As demonstrated in a series of thorough experimental tests, the objective and subjective results both confirm that our method gets the best performance under the circumstance of multiple active audio objects in the meantime.

Acknowledgment. This work was supported by the National Key R&D Program of China (No. 2017YFB1002803) and the National Nature Science Foundation of China (No. 61701194, No. U1736206).

References

1. Dolby Laboratories: Dolby ATMOS cinema specifications (2014). http://www.dolby.com/us/en/technologies/dolby-atmos/dolby-atmos-specifications.pdf
2. Herre, J., Purnhagen, H., Koppens, J., Hellmuth, O., Engdegrd, J., Hilper, J.: Valero ML (2012) MPEG spatial audio object coding - the ISO/MPEG standard for efficient coding of interactive audio scenes. J. Audio Eng. Soc. **60**(9), 655–673 (2012)
3. Herre, J., Hilpert, J., Kuntz, A., Plogsties, J.: MPEG-H 3D audio-the new standard for coding of immersive spatial audio. IEEE J. Sel. Top. Signal Process. **9**(5), 770–779 (2015)
4. Herre, J., Disch, S.: New concepts in parametric coding of spatial audio: from SAC to SAOC. In: IEEE International Conference on Multimedia and Expo (ICME), pp. 1894–1897. IEEE (2007)
5. Herre, J., et al.: Spatial audio coding: next-generation efficient and compatible coding of multichannel audio. In: Audio Engineering Society Convention, vol. 117 (2004)
6. Kim, K., Seo, J., Beack, S., Kang, K., Hahn, M.: Spatial audio object coding with two-step coding structure for interactive audio service. IEEE Trans. Multimedia **13**(6), 1208–1216 (2011)

7. Zheng, X., Ritz, C., Xi, J.: A psychoacoustic-based analysis-by-synthesis scheme for jointly encoding multiple audio objects into independent mixtures. In: IEEE International Conference on Acoustics, Speech and Signal Processing, pp. 281–285. IEEE (2013)

8. Jia, M., Yang, Z., Bao, C., Zheng, X., Ritz, C.: Encoding multiple audio objects using intra-object sparsity. IEEE/ACM Trans. Audio Speech Lang. Process. **23**(6), 1082–1095 (2015)

9. Rohlfing, C., Cohen, J. E., Liutkus, A.: Very low bitrate spatial audio coding with dimensionality reduction. In: IEEE International Conference on Acoustics, Speech and Signal Processing (ICASSP), New Orleans, LA, pp. 741–745 (2017)

10. Wu, T., Hu, R., Wang, X., Ke, S., Wang, J.: High quality audio object coding framework based on non-negative matrix factorization. China Commun. **14**(9), 32–41 (2017)

11. Wu, T., Hu, R., Wang, X., Ke, S.: Audio object coding based on optimal parameter frequency resolution. Multimedia Tools Appl. **78**(15), 20723–20738 (2019)

12. Zhang, S., Wu, X., Qu, T.: Sparse autoencoder based multiple audio objects coding method. In: Audio Engineering Society Convention, vol. 146. Audio Engineering Society (2019)

13. Hu, C., Hu, R., Wang, X., Wu, T., Li, D.: Multi-step coding structure of spatial audio object coding. In: Ro, Y.M., et al. (eds.) MMM 2020. LNCS, vol. 11961, pp. 666–678. Springer, Cham (2020). https://doi.org/10.1007/978-3-030-37731-1_54

14. Ilin, A., Raiko, T.: Practical approaches to principal component analysis in the presence of missing values. J. Mach. Learn. Res. **11**(1), 1957–2000 (2010)

15. Mariem, G., Ammar, L., Ridha, E., Mourad, Z.: Stacked sparse autoencoder and history of binary motion image for human activity recognition. Multimedia Tools Appl. **78**, 2157–2179 (2019)

16. Faller, C., Baumgarte, F.: Binaural cue coding-part II: schemes and applications. IEEE Trans. Speech Audio Process. **11**(6), 520–531 (2003)

17. Wang, Y., Yao, H., Zhao, S.: Auto-encoder based dimensionality reduction. Neurocomputing **184**(5), 232–242 (2016)

18. Liutkus, A., Fabian-Robert, S., Rafii, Z., Kitamura, D., Rivet, B.: The 2016 Signal Separation Evaluation Campaign (2017). https://sigsep.github.io/datasets/dsd100.html

19. Fevotte, C., Gribonval R., Vincent, E.: BSS_EVAL Toolbox User Guide. IRISA, Technical report 1706 (2005). http://www.irisa.fr/metiss/bss_eval/user_guide.pdf

20. Vincent, E., Gribonval, R., Fevotte, C.: Performance measurement in blind audio source separation. IEEE Trans. Audio Speech Lang. Process. **14**(4), 1462–1469 (2006)

21. ITU Radiocommunication Bureau: "BS.1534-3: Method for the subjective assessment of intermediate quality level of coding systems," Recommendation ITUR BS. 1534 (2015)

A Collaborative Multi-modal Fusion Method Based on Random Variational Information Bottleneck for Gesture Recognition

Yang Gu[1,2,3(✉)] , Yajie Li[1,2,4] , Yiqiang Chen[1,2,3,4], Jiwei Wang[1,2], and Jianfei Shen[1,2]

[1] Institute of Computing Technology, Chinese Academy of Sciences, Beijing 100190, China
guyang@ict.ac.cn
[2] Beijing Key Laboratory of Mobile Computing and Pervasive Device, Beijing 100190, China
[3] Peng Cheng Laboratary, Shenzhen 518000, China
[4] Xiangtan University, Xiangtan 411105, China

Abstract. Gesture is a typical human-machine interaction manner, accurate and robust gesture recognition can assist to achieve more natural interaction and understanding. Multi-modal gesture recognition can improve the recognition performance with the help of complex multi-modal relationship. However, it still faces the challenge of how to effectively balance the correlation and redundancy among different modalities, so as to guarantee the accuracy and robustness of the recognition. Hence, in this paper, a collaborative multi-modal learning method based on Random Variational Information Bottleneck (RVIB) is proposed. With random local information selection strategy, some information is compressed by information bottleneck, and the rest is retained directly, so as to make full use of effective redundant information while eliminating invalid redundant information. Experiments on open dataset show that the proposed method can achieve 95.77% recognition accuracy for 21 dynamic gestures, and can guarantee the recognition accuracy when some modality is missing.

Keywords: Multi-modal fusion · Information bottleneck · Random regularization · Gesture recognition

1 Introduction

Nowadays, data acquisition becomes even more convenient, which provides a solid foundation for Multi-Modal Learning (MML). Compared with the uni-modal learning, MML can accomplish the task better with the help of complex relationship among different modalities [1,2], and has been successfully applied

© Springer Nature Switzerland AG 2021
J. Lokoč et al. (Eds.): MMM 2021, LNCS 12572, pp. 62–74, 2021.
https://doi.org/10.1007/978-3-030-67832-6_6

to lots of fields, such as speech recognition [3], information retrieval [4], human-computer interaction [5], et al.

Gesture is a typical human-computer interaction manner, gesture recognition with high accuracy and robustness can assist to achieve more natural interaction and understanding. MML especially Multi-modal Fusion (MF) is an effective way to achieve better recognition performance. However, it still faces the challenge of how to effectively fuse the complex multi-modal relationship, especially the correlation and redundancy. Correlation mainly refers to the relevance for the same gesture, such as the strong relevance between video information and skeleton information, which can deal with the problem of missing modalities or the unrobustness of the model when data quality is poor [1]. Information Bottleneck (IB) [6] with a rigid theoretical framework, is an efficient representation for input variables, which compresses the noisy data as much as possible while retaining the information most relevant to the output variables. Therefore, information bottleneck and multi-modal learning have been naturally coupled: through information bottleneck, we can learn the strongly correlated fusion representation of the output. The useless redundancy mainly includes the complex and unpredictable environment noise of some modality collected in real scenario, which can cause information conflict, and improper learning of useless redundancy will deteriorate the model performance [7]. While maintaining some appropriate redundancy can improve the generalization ability and robustness of model.

Hence, aiming at the problem of how to effectively balance useful correlation and redundancy for multi-modal gesture recognition, we propose a multi-modal fusion method based on Random Variational Information Bottleneck (RVIB). By innovatively introducing random information selection strategy and IB, the model can improve its recognition ability and robustness, and experimental results on open dataset show that the proposed RVIB can achieve the recognition accuracy of 95.77% for 21 dynamic gestures, and can also guarantee the recognition accuracy when some modality is missing.

2 Related Work

For multi-modal gesture recognition, researchers have conducted massive studies from different perspectives. Convolutional Neural Network (CNN) based features and Long Short-Term Memory (LSTM) based deep sequence models were quite popular recently. Tur et al. [8] provided a framework composed of three modules: two CNN modules for feature extraction and dimension reduction, one HMM module for sequence classifier to solve isolated gesture recognition problem, results showed HMMs can achieve 90.15% accuracy in Montalbano dataset [9] using RGB and Skeletal data. Xiao et al. [10] proposed a new multi-modal learning framework for sign language recognition, which used LSTM and Couple Hidden Markov Model (CHMM) to fuse hand and skeleton information, so as to solve the side-effect caused by complex background, different illumination, etc.

Multi-modal fusion can be implemented at different stage/level. Neverova et al.[11] carried out the multi-modal gesture recognition work, Moddrop, from the feature level, which first conducted unimode learning, then fused RGB video and depth video modalities, further fused skeleton and audio modalities, finally implemented multi-modal fusion through two fully connected layers. Joze et al. [12] proposed an intermediate fusion framework with Multimodal Transfer Module (MMTM), which can be embedded at different levels, enabling the multi-modal learning ability by recalibrating the channel-wise features in each CNN stream. And the follow-up work [13] from the same team as in [11] further optimized the fusion order of modality automatically by neural network, so as to dig out the effective redundancy and complementary information between different modalities as much as possible. Abavisani et al. [2] proposed a decision level fusion framework, which leveraged the knowledge from multiple modalities in training uni-modal network for hand gesture recognition.

The effectiveness of multi-modal fusion mainly reflected in the proper usage of the relationships between different modalities. Ben et al. [14] put forward a fusion framework BLOCK for multi-modal representation based on the block-term tensor decomposition, which optimized the trade-off between the expressiveness and complexity of the fusion model, and experimental results indicated that BLOCK was able to represent subtle combinations between modalities while maintaining powerful uni-modal representations. To get the effective representation of information, Information Bottleneck [6] has been regarded as a theoretical framework that can provide boundary of information relevance. Ma et al. [15] put forward a multi-modal learning method based on information bottleneck to solve the skip-modal generation problem, which can learn the correspondence between modalities from unpaired data, and results showed the approach can improve the performance on traditional cross-modal generation. Even though information bottleneck and multi-modal learning have been naturally coupled, the work was still not fully developed. And in this paper, an innovative multi-modal fusion method based on Random Variational Information Bottleneck for gesture recognition was proposed to balance the relevance and redundancy among different modalities so as to ensure the accuracy and robustness of recognition model.

3   Methodology

In this section, we first introduced the principle of information bottleneck and variational information bottleneck, then explained the principle of proposed RVIB, finally introduced the network structure of RVIB used in this work.

3.1   Variational Information Bottleneck

Information bottleneck was proposed in 2000 [6] to explain and enhance the generalization ability of neural network. The main idea is: for input data X, the corresponding output (label) is Y, the representation for neural network is Z, then the goal of information bottleneck is to maximize the mutual information $I(Z, Y)$ between Y and Z, and minimize the mutual information $I(Z, X)$ between X and Z, so as to reserve the most useful data and discard other information.

The optimization of information bottleneck has two parts of mutual information, as shown in Eq. (1). Where β is used to control the hyper-parameter, and $\boldsymbol{\theta}$ is the parameter needed to be learned. The optimization goal is to maximize:

$$R_{IB}(\boldsymbol{\theta}) = I(Z, Y; \boldsymbol{\theta}) - \beta I(Z, X; \boldsymbol{\theta}) \tag{1}$$

Here, mutual information is represented by Kullback-Leibler (KL) divergence. If Eq. (1) is directly considered as the objective function, it is difficult to calculate, and also difficult to update the network parameters by backpropagation. Therefore, Alemi et al. [16] proposed to construct a lower boundary of Eq. (1) by means of variational inference, and used the reparameterization trick to update the parameters with gradient back-propagation. Through variational approximation and considering the non-negative property of KL divergence, we have:

$$
\begin{aligned}
I(Z, Y) = D_{KL}\left(p(y, z) \| p(y)p(z)\right) &= \int dy dz p(y, z) \log \frac{p(y, z)}{p(y)p(z)} \\
&= \int dy dz p(y, z) \log \frac{p(y|z)}{p(y)} \geq \int dy dz p(y, z) \log \frac{q(y|z)}{p(y)} \\
&= \int dy dz p(y, z) \log q(y|z) - \int dy p(y) \log p(y) \\
&= \int dy dz p(y, z) \log q(y|z) + H(Y)
\end{aligned}
\tag{2}
$$

In Eq. (2), $q(y|z)$ is the variational approximation of $p(y|z)$, $H(Y)$ is the entropy of ground-truth label which is not related to the optimization function, hence it can be neglected. For the second term in Eq. (1), the marginal distribution of hidden variable z is difficult to calculate directly, and similarly $p(z)$ is also replaced by its variational approximation $r(z)$, combined with the non-negative characteristics of KL divergence, it becomes:

$$D_{KL}(p(Z), r(Z)) \geq 0 \Rightarrow \int dz p(z) \log p(z) \geq \int dz p(z) \log r(z) \tag{3}$$

Hence, we can get the upper boundary as follows:

$$I(Z, X) = \int dz dx p(x, z) \log \frac{p(z|x)}{p(z)} \leq \int dx dz p(x) p(z|x) \log \frac{p(z|x)}{r(z)} \tag{4}$$

Combining Eq. (2) and Eq. (4) together, we can have the lower boundry of the optimization function, which is :

$$
\begin{aligned}
I(Z, Y) - \beta I(Z, X) &\geq \int dx dy dz p(x) p(y|x) p(z|x) \log q(y|z) \\
&- \beta \int dx dz p(x) p(z|x) \log \frac{p(z|x)}{r(z)} = L
\end{aligned}
\tag{5}
$$

For neural network, to optimize Eq. (5), the training dataset can be seen as the approximation of joint distribution $p(x, y)$, then Eq. (5) becomes:

$$L \approx \frac{1}{N} \sum_{n=1}^{N} \left[\int dz p\left(z|x_n\right) \log q\left(y_n|z\right) - \beta p\left(z|x_n\right) \log \frac{p\left(z|x_n\right)}{r(z)} \right] \tag{6}$$

If neural network is considered as encoder-decoder structure, then the encoder can be seen as the multi-dimensional joint Gaussian distribution $p(z|x) = \mathcal{N}\left(z|f_e^\mu(x), f_e^\Sigma(x)\right)$, where f represents the network learning parameter μ and Σ. When reparametrization trick is used, $p(z|x)dz$ becomes $p(\epsilon)d\epsilon$, which makes the sampling of z independent of the network parameters and can be updated with gradient back propagation. Hereby, the objective function of IB becomes:

$$J_{IB} = \frac{1}{N} \sum_{n=1}^{N} \mathbb{E}_{\epsilon \sim p(\epsilon)} \left[-\log q\left(y_n | f\left(x_n, \epsilon\right)\right)\right] + \beta D_{KL}\left(p\left(Z|x_n\right), r(Z)\right) \quad (7)$$

As shown in Eq. (7), the first term ϵ can be calculated by expectation. For the second term, normal distribution $\mathcal{N}(0, I)$ is used as the prior distribution of z. When variational IB is applied to multi-modal classification task, the first term in Eq. (7) can be replaced by classic cross entropy. If we want to compress the information by IB, then we can directly add the second term in Eq. (7) with a constraint coefficient β.

3.2   Random Variational Information Bottleneck

Information bottleneck is mainly used to compress information, however for multi-modal learning process, retaining some redundancy can improve the accuracy and robustness of the model. Therefore, randomness is introduced in our work to preserve redundancy. Regularization based on randomness has been widely used in deep learning due to its simplicity and effectiveness. And the well-known Dropout [17] improves the robustness (generalization ability) of the network by randomly inactivating nodes. Therefore, we propose RVIB, balancing information compression and information redundancy to ensure the recognition accuracy and robustness.

Specifically, when IB is applied to multi-modal fusion layer for information compression, not all of the information is used, only partial information is selected by a certain probability from input layer, while the rest is directly put into a fully connected layer with the width equal to the width of IB (which is the number of independent Gaussian distribution components for hidden variables z), which is combined with the output of IB as the input for the next layer. The reason for superposing the output in proportion is to make the weight consistency between compression and non-compression information.

The sampling strategy for IB has randomness, which may lead to the output of the network unstable. Hence, we refer to the work in [16], in the prediction/testing stage, the sampling strategy for vector z (the sampling for the vector in Eq. (7)) is to average the result of multiple times sampling.

The output of the neural network with the structure illustrated in Fig.1 can be expressed as:

$$y_{rvib} = p_{comp} * y + (1 - p_{comp}) * y_{fc} \quad (8)$$

Where y is the output of IB, and the input of IB is randomly selected from the input vector by compression ratio p_{comp}; y_{fc} is the output of fully connected layer, and the input of the fully connected layer are the retained information after random selection. We adopt this random information selection strategy in training stage to guarantee the recognition accuracy and robustness.

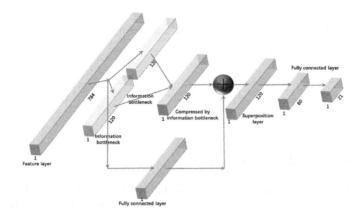

Fig. 1. Multi-modal fusion network with RVIB

4   Experiment

To verify the effectiveness of the proposed RVIB, experiments were carried out on public multi-modal gesture recognition dataset Montalbano [9] from different aspects. The configuration for the experiment was: Ubuntu OS, two Intel Xeon CPUs (2.40 GHz, 14-core, 28-thread), and a Titan XP GPU with 12G memory.

4.1   Data Processing

Montalbano [9] contained four modalities: RGB video, depth video, skeleton data, and audio data for 21 gesture categories (including 20 labeled gestures and 1 non-gesture). Together there were 13,858 gesture instances and the data was preprocessed according to [11]: continuous frame flow was sampled with different step, analyzed with different time scale. New instances can be formed by inconsecutive frames. In our experiment, in order to decrease calculation cost, we used the same step (step = 4), and each instance contained 5 frames. By this way, the new instance corresponded to the original 17 frames' time span, which was roughly equivalent to the period of one hand gesture. Finally we got 107,061 instances. Existing work [11] showed the effectiveness of early stage fusion strategy. Hence, we first utilized CNN to extract the feature for different modality, then used classifier to fine-tune and fuse the different modalities. What is more, as RGB video and depth video were strongly correlated, we fused these two modalities first, then combined them with skeleton data and audio data. The hyper-parameters for the neural network processing each modality were given in Table 1, where FC represented Fully Connected layer. The two/three dimension convolutional layer parameters were denoted as Conv2D/3D-(number of channels * receptive field size). The max pooling layer was represented as Mp-(receptive field size).

Table 1. Neural network structure for data processing

Parameter configuration										
Skeleton	Input-(183*5)	FC1-(700)	FC2-(400)	FC3-350)	Output-(21)	–	–	–	–	–
Video	Input-(36*36*5)	Conv3D-(25*5*5*3)	Mp-(2*2*3)	Conv2D-(25*5*5)	Mp-(1*1)	FC1-(900)	FC2-(450)	Output-(21)	VideoFusion-(84)	FusionOutput-(21)
Audio	Input-(40*9)	Conv2D-(25*5*5)	Mp-(1*1)	FC1-(700)	FC2-(350)	Output-(21)	–	–	–	–

4.2 Experimental Analysis

For experiment validation, we adopted the model used in [11] with three modalities (video, skeleton and audio) as basic model, where RGB video and depth had already been fused on the preprocessing stage. The feature dimension for the corresponding modality was: 84, 350, 350. 10-fold cross validation was used to verify the recognition accuracy, and for each fold there were 96,355 training instances and 10,706 testing instances. The experiments were conducted from three aspects: 1) exploring the optimal sampling and superposition strategies; 2) exploring the effects of different hyper-parameters, and 3) performance comparison for different multi-modal fusion methods. And the network structure for RVIB was already illustrated in Fig. 1.

4.2.1 Exploring the Optimal Sampling and Superposition Strategies

As sampling strategy for hidden variable and superposition strategy for fully connected layer directly affected the network structure and performance, we first explored the effect for the above two strategies.

(1) Different sampling strategies

Sampling strategies for hidden variable had two situations: training period sampling strategy and testing period sampling strategy. Here, three sampling strategies were validated: 1) "training 1 testing 1"; 2) "training 12 testing 12"; and 3) "training 1 testing 12". Where "training 1 testing 1" meant hidden variable was sampled once for training, once for testing, and other strategies can be inferred in the same way. For this experiment, the constraint coefficient was fixed as $\beta = 1e-4$, the width of IB was 120, and the superposition strategy was superposed by compression ratio. The results for different sampling strategies were illustrated in Table 2.

From the above result, the optimal sampling strategies were: "training 1 testing 12", which was reasonable. As sampling once on training stage can enlarge parameters' searching range so as to jump out of local optimum; while sampling 12 times and averaging them on predication stage can ensure the output as stable as possible. The above strategies took the stability of the model in to account, and also guaranteed the optimum searching space during the training stage.

(2) Different superposition strategies

To explore the effect of different superposition strategies, according to the superposition between IB and fully connected layer, we designed 2 schemes: 1) superposition by equal proportion; 2) superposition by compression ratio p_{comp}. For this experiment, the width of IB was 120, the constraint coefficient $\beta = 1e-4$, the sampling strategy for hidden variable was "training 1 testing 12", and the result for different superposition strategies ware given in Table 3.

Table 2. Performance for different sampling strategies

Recognition accuracy(%)		Compression ratio				
		0.2	0.4	0.6	0.8	1
Sampling strategy	Training 1, testing 1	95.22	94.22	92.68	91.76	87.50
	Training 12, testing 12	95.34	94.34	91.02	88.42	91.85
	Training 1, testing 12	**95.57**	94.85	94.25	91.59	94.28

Table 3. Performance for different superposition strategies

Recognition accuracy(%)		Compression ratio				
		0.2	0.4	0.6	0.8	1
Superposition strategy	By equal proportion	95.42	94.82	94.14	89.25	10.41
	By compression ratio	**95.57**	94.85	94.25	91.59	94.28

From the result in Table 3, it was obvious that with the increase of compression ratio, the recognition performance for equal proportion superposition strategy declined sharply, only 10.41% when $p_{comp} = 1$. The reason for this phenomenon was that during the training process when $p_{comp} = 1$, all the data had been selected into IB layer, none for the fully connected layer, the result of superposition layer only came from the output of IB. Therefore the parameter for fully connected layer cannot be updated with back propagation, which were all random values. During testing process data went through both IB layer and fully connected layer, when superposing them by equal proportion, the random values generated by fully connected layer played a vital role in fusion layer, which destroyed the effective information learned by IB and made the output of the network chaotic. While for superposition strategy by compression ratio, the output of superposition layer when $p_{comp} = 1$ was also come from the IB layer, therefore, the result could maintain to a similar level, which verified that the superposition strategy by compression ratio was reasonable.

4.2.2   Exploring the Effects of Different Hyper-parameters

In this part, the effects of different hyper-parameters were discussed, including constraint coefficient β, compression ratio p_{comp} and width of IB, to get the optimal hyper-parameter combination.

(1) Exploring optimal combination of constraint coefficient and compression ratio

For this experiment, the width for IB was 120, sampling strategy and superposition strategy were the optimal ones according the previous experiment. The result for different combinations of constraint coefficient and compression ratio was given in Table 4. In Table 4, when either the compression ratio p_{comp} or constraint coefficient value β was too large, which was similar to the situation when the width of IB was too small, information was compressed too much, leading to the decrease of learning ability and low recognition accuracy. When either the compression ratio p_{comp} or the constraint coefficient value β was too small, which equaled to IB under-fitting, leading to low recognition performance. When p_{comp} and β had proper value, IB can both compress invalid information and retain some useful redundancy to improve the accuracy and stability of the model. Specifically, compared with the basic network, when $\beta = 1e-4$, $p_{comp} = 0.1$, the recognition accuracy was improved.

We further analyzed the reason why compressing 10% information was the most effective. As the proposed method in this paper was feature-level fusion, most of the invalid information had already been filtered during feature extraction period for the single modality. Considering the left invalid redundancy, IB worked well when $p_{comp} = 0.1$.

Table 4. Performance for different constraint coefficient and compression ratio

Recognition accuracy (%)		Compression ration										
		1	0.9	0.8	0.7	0.6	0.5	0.4	0.3	0.2	0.1	0
Constraint coefficient	1	55.56	55.56	55.56	55.56	55.56	55.56	55.96	55.56	55.82	55.56	95.05
	0.5	55.56	55.56	55.56	55.56	57.91	55.99	55.59	59.94	55.56	55.56	95.05
	10^-1	55.56	55.56	55.56	56.36	56.36	55.56	56.71	93.14	94.91	94.91	95.0
	10^-2	55.56	56.85	91.71	92.88	93.59	94.22	94.88	95.02	95.2	95.28	94.91
	10^-3	89.48	84.3	89.28	93.54	93.19	93.37	94.65	95.25	95.6	95.51	95.2
	10^-4	94.28	89.48	91.59	92.65	94.25	94.17	94.85	95.28	95.57	**95.77**	94.97
	10^-5	94.65	94.2	92.97	93.51	93.82	93.99	94.88	95.17	95.37	95.48	95.05
	10^-6	94.2	93.91	94.14	94.37	93.82	94.05	95.0	95.6	95.62	95.48	94.8
	10^-7	94.82	94.97	94.11	94.02	93.42	94.37	94.54	95.28	95.71	95.48	95.31
	0	94.42	94.8	94.37	93.97	94.05	94.68	94.8	95.25	95.65	95.2	95.0

(2) Exploring the optimal width of IB

For this experiment, the sampling strategy and superposition strategy were the optimal ones as previous, the constraint coefficient $\beta = 1e-4$, and the compression ration changed in the range [0,1] with step 0.1. Result for different combination of IB's width and compression ratio was given in Table 5.

From Table 5, when the compression ratio $p_{comp} = 0.1$, the width for IB was 120, and when $p_{comp} = 0.2$, the width for IB was 300, the model achieved the best performance. However, the larger the width was, the more computation cost it would be. Hence, in order to save the resource, the optimal value for IB's width was set to be 120.

Besides, when there was no IB, the proposed method degenerated to Moddrop [11] (the basic model), which recognition accuracy was 95.17%. From the result we can find out that there were many combinations of compression ratio p_{comp} and IB's width that made the proposed method outperform Moddrop, which verified the effectiveness of RVIB for gesture recognition.

Summarizing the experiments above, the optimal network configuration for the proposed method was: constraint coefficient $\beta = 1e-4$, compression ration $p_{comp} = 0.1$, the width for IB was 120, the sampling strategy and superposition strategy was "training 1 testing 12" and "superposition by compression ratio". With the above configuration the network achieved its optimal recognition accuracy 95.77%.

Table 5. Performance for different compression ratio and IB's width

Recognition accuracy(%)		Compression ratio										
		0	0.1	0.2	0.3	0.4	0.5	0.6	0.7	0.8	0.9	1.0
Width for IB	80	94.62	95.6	95.51	95.62	95.17	94.37	93.85	92.99	92.28	85.22	94.11
	96	94.88	95.54	95.31	95.54	94.94	93.77	94.05	92.74	91.76	93.31	93.71
	120	94.97	**95.77**	95.57	95.28	94.85	94.17	94.25	92.65	91.59	89.48	94.28
	256	95.17	95.14	95.57	95.14	94.71	94.62	93.25	92.57	91.42	92.57	93.08
	300	95.0	95.31	**95.77**	95.11	94.6	93.68	93.65	92.57	92.57	88.02	94.14

4.2.3 Performance Comparison for Different Fusion Methods

In this section, we mainly compared the performance of proposed RVIB method with other multi-modal fusion methods.

(1) Performance when no modalities missing

We compared the recognition performance of the proposed RVIB with other commonly used multi-modal fusion method: variational IB [16], Moddrop [11], Modout [13] and BLOCK [14]. The reasons for comparing with these methods were: variational IB was the work which the proposed method derived from; Moddrop and Modout ware representative works for multi-modality gesture recognition in the recent years; and BLOCK was the recently effective works to get the better representation and subtle combination of multi-modalities through their complex relationships. Comparison results were shown in Table 6.

From Table 6, the proposed RVIB had 95.77% recognition accuracy, which was 1.35% higher than variational IB, 0.60% higher than ModDrop, 0.86% higher than Modout, 1.32% higher than BLOCK. This verified the effectiveness of the proposed method, which can utilize the complex relationship between multi-modalities to improve the recognition accuracy.

Table 6. Performance for different multi-modal fusion methods

Methods	Recognition accuracy(%)		
	Full modalities	Audio missing	Skeleton missing
IB [16]	94.42	93.17	90.94
ModDrop [11]	95.17	94.17	91.65
Modout [13]	94.91	93.79	91.62
BLOCK [14]	94.45	94.20	**93.48**
RVIB	**95.77**	**94.54**	92.45

(2) **Performance when modality missing**

Except for improving the recognition accuracy, the proposed method has the ability of high robustness/stableness. Hence, we further conducted the experiments when some modality was missing. Table 6 showed the results when audio modality or skeleton modality was missing.

From Table 6, when audio modality was missing, the recognition performance decreased, however the proposed RVIB still outperformed other methods. As audio information was not as dominant as video and skeleton for gesture recognition, the performance decrease was mild. When skeleton modality was missing, the recognition performance decreased sharply for all the methods except BLOCK. The accuracy improvement of the proposed RVIB over IB, ModDrop, and Modout was 1.51%, 0.8%, and 0.83% respectively, the improvement became bigger than that with no modality missing, which proved the better stability of the proposed method than the others'. The result of BLOCK when skeleton modality missing was higher than proposed method might because that Block had the ability of representing the fine interactions between modalities while maintaining powerful uni-modal representations with block-superdiagonal tensor decomposition. However, considering the overall performance for the three situation in Table 6, the proposed RVIB was still competitive.

5   Conclusion

To solve the problem of how to balance the relationship between correlation and redundancy for multi-modal gesture recognition, a collaborative multi-modal fusion method based on random variational information bottleneck was proposed in this paper. Based on information bottleneck, RVIB innovatively brought in the random information selection strategy, which compressed part of the information by information bottleneck, while retaining part of the original information, so as to balance the elimination of invalid redundant information and the utilization of effective redundant information. Experimental results on the open dataset proved the effectiveness and robustness of the proposed method.

At this stage, the work was mainly conducted at the feature level, and in the future we would explore the automatically fusion strategy and representation strategy at different levels to further improve the recognition performance.

Acknowledgments. This work was supported by National Key Research and Development Plan of China (No. 2017YFB1002802), Natural Science Foundation of China (No. 61902377), and Beijing Natural Science Foundation (No. 4194091).

References

1. Baltrušaitis, T., Ahuja, C., Morency, L.-P.: Multimodal machine learning: a survey and taxonomy. IEEE Trans. Pattern Anal. Mach. Intell. **41**(2), 423–443 (2018)
2. Abavisani, M., Joze, H.R.V., Patel, V.M.: Improving the performance of unimodal dynamic hand-gesture recognition with multimodal training. In: Proceedings of the IEEE Conference on Computer Vision and Pattern Recognition, pp. 1165–1174 (2019)
3. Caglayan, O., Sanabria, R., Palaskar, S., Barraul, L., Metze, F.: Multimodal grounding for sequence-to-sequence speech recognition. In: IEEE International Conference on Acoustics, Speech and Signal Processing (ICASSP), ICASSP 2019, pp. 8648–8652. IEEE (2019)
4. Hu, P., Zhen, L., Peng, D., Liu, P.: Scalable deep multimodal learning for cross-modal retrieval. In: Proceedings of the 42nd International ACM SIGIR Conference on Research and Development in Information Retrieval, pp. 635–644 (2019)
5. Zhang, J., Wang, B., Zhang, C., Xiao, Y., Wang, M.Y.: An EEG/EMG/EOG-based multimodal human-machine interface to real-time control of a soft robot hand. Front. Neurorobot. **13**, 7 (2019)
6. Tishby, N., Pereira, F.C., Bialek, W.: The information bottleneck method. arXiv preprint physics/0004057 (2000)
7. Karpathy, A., Toderici, G., Shetty, S., Leung, T., Sukthankar, R., Fei-Fei, L.: Large-scale video classification with convolutional neural networks. In: Proceedings of the IEEE conference on Computer Vision and Pattern Recognition, pp. 1725–1732 (2014)
8. Tur, A.O., Keles, H.Y.: Evaluation of hidden Markov models using deep CNN features in isolated sign recognition. arXiv preprint arXiv:2006.11183 (2020)
9. Escalera, S., et al.: ChaLearn looking at people challenge 2014: dataset and results. In: Agapito, L., Bronstein, M.M., Rother, C. (eds.) ECCV 2014. LNCS, vol. 8925, pp. 459–473. Springer, Cham (2015). https://doi.org/10.1007/978-3-319-16178-5_32
10. Xiao, Q., Qin, M., Guo, P., Zhao, Y.: Multimodal fusion based on LSTM and a couple conditional hidden Markov model for Chinese sign language recognition. IEEE Access **7**, 112258–112268 (2019)
11. Neverova, N., Wolf, C., Taylor, G., Nebout, F.: ModDrop: adaptive multi-modal gesture recognition. IEEE Trans. Pattern Anal. Mach. Intell. **38**(8), 1692–1706 (2015)
12. Joze, H.R.V., Shaban, A., Iuzzolino, M.L., Koishida, K.: MMTM: multimodal transfer module for CNN fusion. In: Proceedings of the IEEE/CVF Conference on Computer Vision and Pattern Recognition (CVPR), June 2020
13. Li, F., Neverova, N., Wolf, C., Taylor, G.: Modout: learning multi-modal architectures by stochastic regularization. In: 12th IEEE International Conference on Automatic Face & Gesture Recognition (FG 2017), pp. 422–429. IEEE (2017)
14. Ben-Younes, H., Cadene, R., Thome, N., Cord, M.: Block: bilinear superdiagonal fusion for visual question answering and visual relationship detection. In: Proceedings of the AAAI Conference on Artificial Intelligence vol. 33, pp. 8102–8109 (2019)

15. Ma, S., McDuff, D., Song, Y.: Unpaired image-to-speech synthesis with multimodal information bottleneck. In: Proceedings of the IEEE International Conference on Computer Vision, pp. 7598–7607 (2019)
16. Alemi, A.A., Fischer, I., Dillon, J.V., Murphy, K.: Deep variational information bottleneck. arXiv preprint arXiv:1612.00410 (2016)
17. Srivastava, N., Hinton, G., Krizhevsky, A., Sutskever, I., Salakhutdinov, R.: Dropout: a simple way to prevent neural networks from overfitting. J. Mach. Learn. Res. **15**(1), 1929–1958 (2014)

Frame Aggregation and Multi-modal Fusion Framework for Video-Based Person Recognition

Fangtao Li, Wenzhe Wang, Zihe Liu, Haoran Wang, Chenghao Yan, and Bin Wu$^{(\boxtimes)}$

Beijing University of Posts and Telecommucations, Beijing, China
{lift,wangwenzhe,ziheliu,wanghaoran,chenghao_yan,wubin}@bupt.edu.cn

Abstract. Video-based person recognition is challenging due to persons being blocked and blurred, and the variation of shooting angle. Previous research always focused on person recognition on still images, ignoring similarity and continuity between video frames. To tackle the challenges above, we propose a novel Frame Aggregation and Multi-Modal Fusion (FAMF) framework for video-based person recognition, which aggregates face features and incorporates them with multi-modal information to identify persons in videos. For frame aggregation, we propose a novel trainable layer based on NetVLAD (named AttentionVLAD), which takes arbitrary number of features as input and computes a fixed-length aggregated feature based on the feature quality. We show that introducing an attention mechanism into NetVLAD effectively decreases the impact of low-quality frames. For the multi-model information of videos, we propose a Multi-Layer Multi-Modal Attention (MLMA) module to learn the correlation of multi-modality by adaptively updating correlation Gram matrix. Experimental results on iQIYI-VID-2019 dataset show that our framework outperforms other state-of-the-art methods.

Keywords: Person recognition · Video understanding · VLAD · Multi-modal

1 Introduction

Person recognition in videos is a basic task for video understanding. Different from person recognition in images, video-based person recognition has the following difficulties and challenges: (1) The expressions, angles, and clarity of the

This work is supported by the National Key Research and Development Program of China (2018YFC0831500), the National Natural Science Foundation of China under Grant No. 61972047, the NSFC-General Technology Basic Research Joint Funds under Grant U1936220 and the Fundamental Research Funds for the Central Universities (2019XD-D01).

© Springer Nature Switzerland AG 2021
J. Lokoč et al. (Eds.): MMM 2021, LNCS 12572, pp. 75–86, 2021.
https://doi.org/10.1007/978-3-030-67832-6_7

person may vary in videos. (2) Videos are more informative than images, which means the model that can use information effectively tends to be more complicated. Most of the current research is still stuck in recognition based on frames. In general, when extended to video-based person recognition, the essence of the study is to use frames as units of recognition, but with the addition of pooling or voting to aggregate the results. However, this aggregation method neglects the quality of frames, which may lead to misidentification.

To tackle this problem, a natural idea is to remove low-quality frames during data preprocessing. However this method places high requirements on how to measure the quality of frames. It will also reduce the generalization of the model. Another widely used method is to equip models with the ability to learn frame quality. To this end, NeXtVLAD [8] apply a non-linear activation function as a simple attention mechanism, and GhostVLAD [21] implicitly achieves this goal by "Ghost" clusters, which can help the network ignore low-resolution or low-quality frames. However, these heuristic rules are incapable of the complex cases in the real world.

In some extreme cases, the resolution of the face in the video is so low that the clear face cannot be recognized, so we can only rely on other information such as audio, text, *etc.*, to help identify of the person. However, most methods integrate multi-modal information through pooling, concatenation, or heuristic rules, which is over-simplified in complex real-world scenarios.

In this work, we propose a Frame Aggregation and Multi-Modal Fusion (FAMF) framework for video-based person recognition. To measure the quality of different frames, we propose a Vector of Locally Aggregated Descriptors with cluster attention (AttentionVLAD) algorithm. In order to enhance the robustness of the model and better handle the extreme case where the face is completely obscured, we introduce a Multi-Layer Multi-Modal Attention (MLMA) module to use multi-modal information for joint projections. Finally, we evaluate the performance of our framework through experiments on the iQIYI-VID-2019 dataset [10]. The experimental results show the effectiveness of our framework.

In short, our contribution is as follows:

1. We propose a FAMF framework to recognize persons in videos, which considers both frame quality and multi-modal information for end-to-end recognition.
2. For frame aggregation, we propose a new trainable feature aggregation module named AttentionVLAD, which uses attention mechanism to adjust the weight of aggregated output. For multi-modal fusion embedding, we propose a MLMA module inspired by attention mechanism, which uses continuous convolutional layers to obtain the multimodal attention weights.
3. We verify the effectiveness of the proposed framework on the iQIYI-VID-2019 dataset. Our approach outperforms other state-of-the-art methods without any model begging or data augmentation.

2 Related Work

Person Recognition. Person recognition has been widely studied in different research areas. In general, face recognition is the most important sub-task for person recognition, while person re-identification (person Re-ID), speaker identification, *etc.*, can also be regarded as part of person recognition.

As one of the most studied sub-questions of person recognition, face recognition has achieved great success along with the arising of deep learning. For face recognition on still images, many algorithms perform quite well. ArcFace [3] reached a precision of 99.83% on LFW [6] dataset, which outperforms the human performance. Person re-identification aims to identify the pedestrian in case the face is blurred or invisible. Many algorithms [13,20] performs well on this task. However, most of these algorithms use the body as a crucial feature for identification, and they have not addressed the problem of changing clothes yet. For speaker recognition, i-vector [2] is a widely used algorithm for a long time. More recently, d-vector based on deep learning [7] became increasingly popular and performs well. However, the large amount of noise in the real scene along with the misalignment of the speakers and the characters in the video is the restricted factors that affect the further application of this technology.

Multi-modal Fusion. For multi-modal fusion, early works concatenate embeddings to learn a larger multi-modal embedding. However this may lead to a potential loss of information between different modalities. Recent studies on learning multi-modal fusion embeddings apply neural network to incorporate modalities. Tensor Fusion Network (TFN) [18] calculates the outer-product of video, audio and text features to represent comprehensive features. Liu *et al.* [11] developed a low rank method for building tensor networks to reduce computational complexity caused by outer-product. Adversarial representation learning and graph fusion network [12] are also applied for multi-modal fusion. In recent years, some researchers apply attention mechanism on multi-modal fusion. Liu *et al.* [9] proposed a Multi-Modal Attention (MMA) module, which reweight modalities through a Gram Metrix of self-attention. Tsai *et al.* [15] built a multi-modal transformer to learn interactions between modalities. Xuan *et al.* [17] proposed a cross-modal attention network, which concentrates on specific locations, time segments and media adaptively.

Feature Aggregation. In the early stages of the development of image recognition, many encoding methods were proposed to aggregate image descriptors into a template representation. Along with the era of deep learning, some researchers integrate these algorithms into neural networks, such as NetFV [14] and NetVLAD [1]. Recently, Lin *et al.* [8] proposed a NeXtVLAD model for video classification, which decreases the number of parameters by group convolution. Zhong *et al.* [21] introduced a feature aggregation module named GhostVLAD for set-based face recognition, which dramatically downweights blurry and low-resolution images by ghost clusters, and GhostVLAD surpassed the state-of-the-art methods on IJB-B [16] dataset.

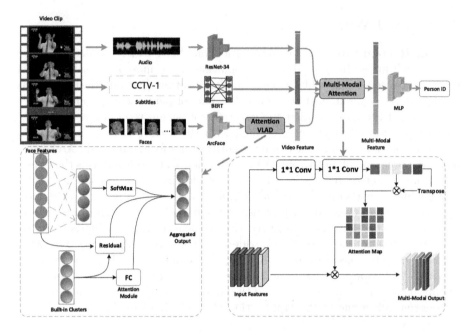

Fig. 1. An overview of the process of identifying the person in a given video clip. The FAMF framework consists of a feature extractor, a frame feature aggregation module, a multi-modal fusion module and a classifier. Face embeddings are aggregated by AttentionVLAD and fused with other modal embeddings by MLMA.

3   Our Framework

3.1   Overview

In this paper, we regard person recognition as a classification task, which means given a piece of video, we expect our model can determine the label of the main characters in the video. As shown in Fig. 1, our framework consists of four modules:

Feature Extractor. In this stage, we mainly perform video pre-processing and feature extraction. Multi-modal information such as face, audio, body, text, *etc.*, will be extracted from the input video. Then we use pre-trained models to extract embedding respectively.

Frame Aggregation Module. A video is composed of continuously changing frames, which means if a face is detected in a certain frame, it is likely that its adjacent frames also contain the face with the same label, despite their angle, expression or clarity may be varied. To measure the quality of faces and eliminate the complexity caused by the different number of faces in different clips, we propose a frame feature aggregation module based on NetVLAD. Taking any number of features as input, this module can generate a fixed-length embedding as a video-level face feature. More details can be found in Sect. 3.2.

Multi-modal Fusion Module. Multi-modal features of a video clip are likely to be complementary and redundant. In this stage, we apply a multi-modal attention module to learn the weight of corresponding multi-modal features and readjust the multi-modal features according to the weight. This module will be introduced in detail in Sect. 3.3.

Classifier. Based on the premise that we focus on supervised person recognition in video, we use a Multi-Layer Perceptron (MLP) as a classifier to predict the identity of the person.

3.2   AttentionVLAD for Frame Aggregation

One key problem of video-based person recognition is that people do not appear in all frames of the video, the clarity and the quality of each frame is also varied. If all detected face features are concatenated as input, although all the information of visual cues are retained, the model will be memory-cost, which has a great negative impact on model training and storage. In previous research, NetVLAD is a widely used layer to aggregate low-level features. In this section, we propose an improved frame features aggregation layer, AttentionVLAD, to improve the impact of low-quality frames.

NetVLAD. Given N D-dimensional features $X \in \mathbb{R}^{N*D}$ extracted from the input video clip, which are likely to be extracted in an arbitrary manner using an arbitrary pre-trained model, such as N frame features extracted by ResNet [5], or N face features extracted by ArcFace [3], all these N features are aggregated into feature $V \in \mathbb{R}^{D*K}$ where K is a hyper-parameter indicating the number of trainable clusters. The formula is shown as below:

$$V(j, k) = \sum_{i=1}^{N} \alpha_k(x_i)(x_i(j) - c_k(j)), \tag{1}$$

$$\alpha_k(x_i) = \frac{e^{a_k^T x_i + b_k}}{\sum_{k'=1}^{K} e^{a_k^T x_i + b_k}}, \tag{2}$$

where $\{x_i \in \mathbb{R}^D, i = 1...N\}$ is the input features, $\{c_k \in \mathbb{R}^D, i = 1...K\}$ is the N-dimensional centre of cluster k, $\{a_k\}$, $\{b_k\}$ and $\{c_k\}$ are trainable parameters. $\alpha_k(x_i)$ is the soft-assignment weight of input feature x_i for cluster c_k.

AttentionVLAD. Based on NetVLAD, we proposed a novel feature aggregation module with cluster attention named AttentionVLAD, which is applied to
adjust the weight of low-quality feature in the aggregation stage. In our experiment, AttentionVLAD is deployed on face modal, since face is the crucial modal
for person recognition. Given the number of trainable clusters K and N D-
dimensional features $X \in \mathbb{R}^{N*D}$, which are the output of the feature extractor,
where N refers to the number of faces, respectively. The aggregated output feature $V \in \mathbb{R}^{D*K}$ can be generated as below:

$$V(j, k) = \sum_{i=1}^{N} \phi(c_k)\alpha_k(x_i)(x_i(j) - c_k(j)), \tag{3}$$

$$\alpha_k(x_i) = \frac{e^{a_k^\top x_i + b_k}}{\sum_{k'=1}^{K} e^{a_k^\top x_i + b_k}}, \tag{4}$$

where x_i refers to the i-th feature, c_k is the N-dimensional anchor point of
cluster k, $\{a_k\}$, $\{b_k\}$ and $\{c_k\}$ are trainable parameters. α is the soft-assignment
weight of input feature for cluster c. $\phi(c_k)$ is an attention weight for cluster k
implemented by a full-connected layer. $\alpha_k(x_i)$ is the soft-assignment weight of
input feature x_i for cluster c_k, as in NetVLAD [1]. Note that we calculate the
similarity by the cluster center, and adjust the weight of aggregated feature,
which is different with self-attention.

The improvement of AttentionVLAD lies in the cluster attention function,
which can learn the feature quality implicitly. To learn the impact of face quality
on prediction result, an easy way is to measure the weight at the instance level,
e.g. adding a non-linear activation for each feature. However, due to the complexity of the feature, the activation function may not learn the weight as expected.
Another way is to use trainable clusters to adjust weights implicitly. This idea
first appeared in GhostVLAD [21], which uses G ghost clusters to collect features
of low-quality and drop them in the output. In fact, GhostVLAD [21] can be
regarded as a specialization of AttentionVLAD when K of the cluster attention
weight $\phi(c_k)$ in proposed AttentionVLAD are 1 and G of them are 0. In other
words, compared to the binary cluster weight of 0 or 1 in GhostVLAD [21], AttentionVLAD can achieve better results with adaptive stepwise cluster weights.

Another explanation of AttentionVLAD is that it introduces the information
of trainable clusters themselves into the output. A key point of NetVLAD [1]
is that it uses residuals of the input and the trainable clusters to represent the
aggregation template. Although residuals can retain the input information well,
the distribution and scale of input is completely ignored. Which infer the quality
of features. In order to rehabilitate this information in aggregation output, we
use cluster weight as a scalar to fuse the residuals between inputs and clusters,
which is calculated by the attention mechanism.

3.3   MLMA for Multi-modal Fusion

Given a video clip with a main character appearing, in the ideal case, we can only
rely on the detected face to determine the identity of the character. However, the

face of person will inevitably be blurred or blocked, or we can not even detect a clear face in the entire video. In this situation, we can use other information about the video to predict the identity. To eliminate the redundancy of multi-modal information and use complementary information as much as possible, we devise a Multi-Layer Multi-Modal Attention (MLMA) module to fuse the multi-modal features according to the weights.

Given features $X \in \mathbb{R}^{(K_1+K_2)*D}$, where K_1 refers to the number of the clusters in AttentionVLAD, and K_2 refers to the number of the other multi-modal feature of the source video, such as audio, body, text, textitetc., and D is the dimension of features. The weight of each modal can be yielded through the continuous convolution layer and a soft-max activation:

$$Y_i = \sum_{j}^{K_1+K_2} X_j \frac{e^{Z_{j,i}}}{\sum_i e^{Z_{j,i}}}, \tag{5}$$

$$Z = (W_{F_1} W_{F_2} X)^\top (W_{F_1} W_{F_2} X), \tag{6}$$

where Z is the Gram matrix of multi-modal attention weight, W are trainable parameters. Y_i represents the summation of products between cross-correlation weights and feature X_j.

The MLMA is inspired by SAGAN [19] and MMA [9]. For multi-modal feature in videos, MLMA can efficiently capture the inter-modal correlation. From the perspective of enhancing correlation and reducing redundancy, a modal of feature that is inconsistent with other modal of feature will be amplified after fusion by MLMA, implying that they are weakly correlated. In another point of view, if a certain modal is missing, MLMA will try to replace it by another strongly related and similarly distributed feature, which is important to compensate the loss when some features are missing.

Our motivation is to improve the matrix acquisition method of Gram matrix of multi-modal features. MMA [9] has shown that using Gram matrix can better incorporate multi-modal features, since it is simpler and more effective in capturing the feature correlation. However, it simply uses a convolution layer to reduce the number of feature channels at one-time, and then multiply with the transpose of embedding to get Gram matrix. Residual connection and L2-regularization are also applied. We have found in experiments that if features are processed by two consecutive convolutional layers, better results can be achieved, and the effect of residual connection and L2-regularization term is not obvious. Therefore, we did not use these tricks.

4   Experiments

4.1   Dataset

The iQIYI-VID-2019 dataset [10] is a large-scale benchmark for multi-modal person identification. It contains more than 200K videos of 10,034 celebrities. To the best of our knowledge, it is the largest video dataset for person recognition

Fig. 2. Some challenging cases of iQIYI-VID-2019 dataset. From left to right: occlusion, weak light, invisible face, small face, and blur.

Table 1. Comparison with state-of-the-art methods on iQIYI-VID-2019 dataset. A higher mAP value is better.

Method	Frame Aggregation	Multi-Modal Fusion	mAP
Liu *et al.* [9]	NetVLAD	MMA	0.8246
GhostVLAD [21]	GhostVLAD	Concat	0.8109
NeXtVLAD [8]	NeXtVLAD	Concat	0.8283
FAMF-mf	NetVLAD	MLMA	0.8295
FAMF-fa	AttentionVLAD	MMA	0.8610
FAMF(Ours)	AttentionVLAD	MLMA	**0.8824**

so far. In 2019, the whole dataset including test set was released in ACM MM workshop. The dataset contains both video clips and the official features of face, head, body and audio. We removed the noise data from the training set in the preprocessing stage, and do not apply any data augmentation in experiment. All models are trained on the training set and evaluated on the validation set. Some challenging cases are shown in Fig. 2.

4.2   Results

We use Mean Average Precision (mAP) to evaluate the performance of models, mAP can be calculated as:

$$mAP(Q) = \frac{1}{|Q|} \sum_{i=1}^{|Q|} \frac{1}{m_i} \sum_{j=1}^{n_i} Precision(R_{i,j}), \qquad (7)$$

where Q is the set of person ID to retrieve, m_i is the number of positive examples for the i-th ID, n_i is the number of positive examples within the top k retrieval results for the i-th ID, and $R_{i,j}$ is the set of ranked retrieval results from the top until getting j positive examples. In our implementation, only the top 100 retrievals are kept for each person ID.

Table 1 shows the performance comparison of our model with the baseline models on iQIYI-VID-2019 dataset [10]. We mainly compared with some state-of-the-art person recognition methods. NetVLAD+MMA means we use NetVLAD [1] for temporal aggregation and Multi-Modal Attention [9] for multi-modal feature fusion. This is also the official baseline model of iQIYI-VID-2019 [10]. GhostVLAD and NeXtVLAD are implemented with reference to [21]

[8], respectively. FAMF-mf means we only apply AttentionVLAD for frame aggregation, while FAMF-fa means we replace MMA [9] with MLMA. For a complete version, the result is shown as in *row* 6, which adopts AttentionVLAD for frame aggregation and MLMA for multi-modal fusion.

Fig. 3. The weight of different faces in a same video is shown on the above of faces. The contribution of blurred or blocked faces is significantly reduced, and the weight of clear, unobstructed faces is still close to 1.

We select some video clips randomly in the test set, and print the weight of different keyframes, as shown in Fig. 3. *row* 1 shows two videos in which faces that are obscured or blurred (*column* 1, 2, 5, 6) have significantly lower weights compared to clear and unobscured faces. Two videos in *row* 2 show that the frames of low resolution have significant low weight (*column* 1 *to* 4). These examples indicating the cluster attention mechanism has the ability to learn image quality.

4.3   Implementation Details

Preprocessing. During data preprocessing, for visual features of each video, such as face, body, *etc.*, if the number of features is greater than the frame number N (we set $N = 24$), then we sampled N features for each video randomly without repeating, otherwise we sampled repeatedly until the number of features is equal to N. Note that the number N can be different during training and testing stage. For audio information, we use the official audio embedding directly. For text or subtitle of a certain video clip, we choose one frame and use the return value of Baidu OCR API as the text, then take the output of pre-trained BERT [4] as text feature. If a certain modal is missing, we use a zero vector as the corresponding embedding.

Model Settings. The classifier consists of 3 fully-connected(FC) layers, of which the first two layers are used as input and hidden layers, and the output of the last layer is mapped to the labels. Between two adjacent FC layers, we add a Batch-Normalization layer. Dropout is not applied. The dimension of all hidden layers is set to 4096, while the output dimension of the last FC layer is 10,034.

Table 2. Experimental results for using different modality information.

Cues	mAP
Face	0.8656
Face + Body	0.8776
Face + Audio	0.8688
Face + Text	0.8685
Face + Audio + Text	0.8385
Face + Audio + Body	**0.8824**
Face + Body + Text	0.8669
Face + Audio + Body + Text	0.8761

The hyper-parameter K of AttentionVLAD is 8, and in MLMA, the dimension of two hidden layers are 128 and 32, respectively.

Training Strategy. All of the models are optimized by Adam Optimizer, and the loss function is Cross-Entropy Loss. The learning rate of AttentionVLAD and the other parameters are initialized as 0.04 and 0.004, respectively. After training for 50 epochs, the learning rates are divided by 10 for every 10 epochs. At training stage, the size of mini-batch is 4,096.

4.4   Ablation Study

AttentionVLAD. Firstly we analyze the performance of different aggregation methods. From Table 1, we can find that AttentionVLAD outperforms the other aggregation modules such as NetVLAD [1] (*row 4 vs. row 5*). As mentioned in Sect. 3.2, AttentionVLAD can drop low-quality features in steps. Under the premise of using only face features, the cluster attention mechanism can improve the representation.

MLMA. For multi-modal information fusion, we mainly compared results with MMA [9]. The improvement of the effect can be considered as being affected by the two-layer convolutional layer. It can extract more information than the one-layer convolution in the original method. In the case that the increased memory overhead can be ignored, it can improve the mAP by 0.02 to 0.8824 (*row 4 vs. row 6*).

Multi-modal Information. The effect of multi-modal information is shown in Table 2. We assume that face feature is of most importance in person identification, while other features are relatively auxiliary. Taking face feature as a baseline, adding audio feature can raise the performance significantly. We presume it is because audio feature is not strongly correlated with the face feature, which adds less redundant information to enhance the robustness of the model. The attention weight is shown as Fig. 4, where the *row 1* to *row 8* refer to the

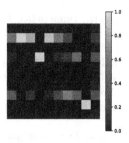

Fig. 4. Attention weight of multi-modal features. The first eight columns, the ninth column, and the tenth column of the matrix show the cross-correlation weights of face, audio, body, respectively.

8 features from AttentionVLAD, the last row refers to the audio feature, and the last row refers to body feature, respectively. The result shows that body feature tends to be replaced by face feature, while the audio feature has a high probability to be independent to concatenate with other features.

Hyper Parameters. Finally, we discuss the impact of the number of clusters K on the performance. We compare the results for $K = 2, 4, 8, 16$, respectively. Results show that when K is 2 or 4, the model performs not well ($mAP = 0.7952$ *vs.* 0.8824), proving that the aggregate feature does not effectively filter out the information in each frame feature. The model achieves the best performance when $K = 8$. In theory, further increasing K can still improve the effect. However, it may cause the problem of out of memory. When $K = 16$ ($mAP = 0.8323$), in order to train the model, we have to reduce the batch size.

5 Conclusion

In this paper, we first propose a novel FAMF framework for video-based person recognition. A new feature aggregation module named AttentionVLAD, and a multi-modal feature fusion module MLMA are then proposed. Given a video clip, we first extract multi-modal feature by pre-train model, then for face feature, AttentionVLAD is applied to generate a fix-length template. The Attention-VLAD uses cluster attention mechanism to learn face quality. Then a MLMA module is applied to fuse multi-modal features, which reweights multi-modal features by two convolution layers. The experiment results on iQIYI-VID-2019 dataset show that our model outperforms other person recognition methods.

References

1. Arandjelovic, R., Gronat, P., Torii, A., Pajdla, T., Sivic, J.: NetVLAD: CNN architecture for weakly supervised place recognition. In: CVPR, pp. 5297–5307 (2016)

2. Dehak, N., Kenny, P.J., Dehak, R., Dumouchel, P., Ouellet, P.: Front-end factor analysis for speaker verification. IEEE Trans. Audio Speech Lang. Process. **19**(4), 788–798 (2010)

3. Deng, J., Guo, J., Xue, N., Zafeiriou, S.: ArcFace: additive angular margin loss for deep face recognition. In: CVPR, pp. 4690–4699 (2019)

4. Devlin, J., Chang, M.W., Lee, K., Toutanova, K.: BERT: pre-training of deep bidirectional transformers for language understanding. arXiv preprint arXiv:1810.04805 (2018)

5. He, K., Zhang, X., Ren, S., Sun, J.: Deep residual learning for image recognition. In: CVPR, pp. 770–778 (2016)

6. Huang, G.B., Mattar, M., Berg, T., Learned-Miller, E.: Labeled faces in the wild: a database forstudying face recognition in unconstrained environments (2008)

7. Li, C., et al.: Deep speaker: an end-to-end neural speaker embedding system. arXiv preprint arXiv:1705.02304 650 (2017)

8. Lin, R., Xiao, J., Fan, J.: NeXtVLAD: an efficient neural network to aggregate frame-level features for large-scale video classification. In: ECCV, p. 0 (2018)

9. Liu, Y., et al.: iQIYI-VID: a large dataset for multi-modal person identification. arXiv preprint arXiv:1811.07548 (2018)

10. Liu, Y., et al.: iQIYI celebrity video identification challenge. In: ACM MM, pp. 2516–2520 (2019)

11. Liu, Z., Shen, Y., Lakshminarasimhan, V.B., Liang, P.P., Zadeh, A.B., Morency, L.P.: Efficient low-rank multimodal fusion with modality-specific factors. In: ACL, pp. 2247–2256 (2018)

12. Mai, S., Hu, H., Xing, S.: Modality to modality translation: an adversarial representation learning and graph fusion network for multimodal fusion. In: AAAI, pp. 164–172. AAAI Press (2020)

13. Song, G., Leng, B., Liu, Y., Hetang, C., Cai, S.: Region-based quality estimation network for large-scale person re-identification. In: AAAI (2018)

14. Tang, P., Wang, X., Shi, B., Bai, X., Liu, W., Tu, Z.: Deep FisherNet for object classification. arXiv preprint arXiv:1608.00182 (2016)

15. Tsai, Y.H.H., Bai, S., Liang, P.P., Kolter, J.Z., Morency, L.P., Salakhutdinov, R.: Multimodal transformer for unaligned multimodal language sequences. In: ACL, pp. 6558–6569 (2019)

16. Whitelam, C., et al.: IARPA Janus benchmark-B face dataset. In: CVPR, pp. 90–98 (2017)

17. Xuan, H., Zhang, Z., Chen, S., Yang, J., Yan, Y.: Cross-modal attention network for temporal inconsistent audio-visual event localization. In: AAAI, pp. 279–286. AAAI Press (2020)

18. Zadeh, A., Chen, M., Poria, S., Cambria, E., Morency, L.P.: Tensor fusion network for multimodal sentiment analysis. arXiv preprint arXiv:1707.07250 (2017)

19. Zhang, H., Goodfellow, I., Metaxas, D., Odena, A.: Self-attention generative adversarial networks. In: ICML, pp. 7354–7363 (2019)

20. Zheng, Z., Yang, X., Yu, Z., Zheng, L., Yang, Y., Kautz, J.: Joint discriminative and generative learning for person re-identification. In: CVPR, pp. 2138–2147 (2019)

21. Zhong, Y., Arandjelović, R., Zisserman, A.: GhostVLAD for set-based face recognition. In: Jawahar, C.V., Li, H., Mori, G., Schindler, K. (eds.) ACCV 2018. LNCS, vol. 11362, pp. 35–50. Springer, Cham (2019). https://doi.org/10.1007/978-3-030-20890-5_3

An Adaptive Face-Iris Multimodal Identification System Based on Quality Assessment Network

Zhengding Luo, Qinghua Gu, Guoxiong Su, Yuesheng Zhu[✉],
and Zhiqiang Bai

School of Electronic and Computer Engineering, Peking University, Beijing, China
{luozd,guqh,suguoxiong,zhuys,baizq}@pku.edu.cn

Abstract. In practical applications, face-iris multimodal recognition systems may suffer from performance degradation when image acquisition is not constrained strictly. One way to diminish the negative effect of poor-quality samples is to incorporate quality assessment (QA) into face-iris fusion schemes. However, existing face and iris QA approaches are limited by specific types of distortions or requiring particular reference images. To tackle this problem, an adaptive face-iris multimodal identification system based on quality assessment network is proposed. In the system, the face-iris quality assessment network (FaceIrisQANet) can measure face-iris relative quality scores given their image features, achieving distortion-generic and referenceless QA. Different from most deep neural networks, the FaceIrisQANet employs biologically inspired generalized divisive normalization (GDN) instead of rectified linear unit (ReLU) as activation function. Additionally, face and iris are assigned adaptive weights according to their relative quality scores at the score level fusion scheme. Experimental results on three face-iris multimodal datasets show that our system not only provides a good recognition performance but also exhibits superior generalization capability.

Keywords: Face-iris multimodal biometric recognition · Face-iris relative image quality assessment · Adaptive score level fusion

1 Introduction

Traditional identification techniques include password-based schemes and token-based schemes. Biometric recognition refers to automatic identification using certain physiological or behavioral biometric traits, which have an edge over traditional recognition approaches because they cannot be stolen or shared [12]. Face recognition is known as the most popular and iris recognition as one of the most accurate recognition technologies [14,30]. However, unimodal face and iris recognition are limited by some inherent drawbacks including sensitivity to noisy data, vulnerability to spoofing and unacceptable error rates, etc. It is studied that face-iris multimodal recognition combining face and iris information

© Springer Nature Switzerland AG 2021
J. Lokoč et al. (Eds.): MMM 2021, LNCS 12572, pp. 87–98, 2021.
https://doi.org/10.1007/978-3-030-67832-6_8

can effectively overcome the limitations of individual modalities [4, 27]. Though face-iris multimodal identification systems have been deployed for various applications from border control, citizen authentication to forensic, how to deal with face-iris samples of poor quality is still an ongoing research topic [25].

Matching score level fusion is the most popular fusion scheme due to ease in assessing and combining different matchers [21]. Conventional score level fusion rules include weighted sum rule, sum rule, min rule and max rule [11]. Biometric image quality is highly related to the recognition accuracy, which plays an important role in optimizing overall recognition performance [8, 22]. There have been some face and iris quality assessment (QA) approaches studied in the literature. Several relevant QA works for face and iris are summarized in Table 1. As shown in the Table 1, most of the existing face and iris QA approaches are limited by specific types of distortions such as contrast, occlusion and brightness [1–3, 7], these approaches suffer from lack of generality in the presence of unknown distortions.

Table 1. Summary of some image quality measure works for face and iris

Modality	Type of quality factors	Quality metric method
Face [3]	Facial expressions	Classifier based on eigenface
Face [2]	Contrast, brightness, focus etc.	Integrating all quality factors
Face [9]	Distortion-generic	A neural network named FaceQnet
Iris [1]	Gray level, contrast, smoothness, etc.	Classifier based on all quality factors
Iris [7]	Feature correlation, occlusion etc.	Combining all quality factors
Iris [13]	Distortion-generic	Differential sign-magnitude statistics

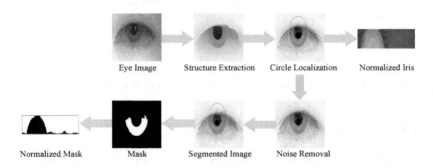

Fig. 1. Illustration of the key steps of iris segmentation and normalization.

In order to achieve distortion-generic QA, Jenadeleh et al. [13] utilized statistical features of the local difference sign-magnitude transform to measure iris quality. The distortion-generic face QA network proposed in [9] needed a third party software to select high-quality gallery image for each subject, which may bring about additional bias and complexity. Besides, blind (i.e. no-reference) QA technology for face and iris is also important, since reference information is not always available or reliable in real-world scenarios [20]. Additionally, Johnson et al. [15] compared using the individual QA and relative QA used in the face-iris fusion scheme and found that relative QA presents better performance.

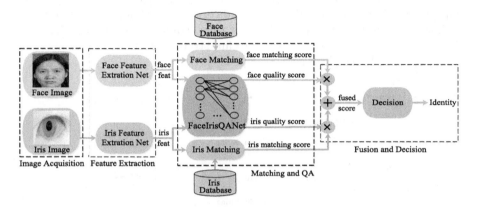

Fig. 2. Overall system architecture. Image Acquisition: A preprocessed face-iris pair as the input. Feature Extraction: Using pretrained networks to extract features. Matching: Matching the extracted feature with other features stored in the database. QA: FaceIrisQANet measures face-iris relative quality scores based on their features. Fusion and Decision: A quality controlled weighted sum rule and the identity is decided.

From the analysis above, development of a distortion-generic blind face-iris relative QA approach is highly desirable. Our work aims to enhance face-iris multimodal recognition performance by incorporating a face-iris quality assessment network (FaceIrisQANet). The main contributions are summarized as follows: (1) Joint face-iris identification contributes to improving the limited recognition ability of unimodal biometrics. (2) The FaceIrisQANet can achieve distortion-generic and no-reference QA, measuring face-iris relative quality scores based on their image features. Besides, GDN instead of ReLU function is used as activation layer in the FaceIrisQANet. (3) Face and iris are assigned adaptive weights depended on their relative quality scores when they are combined at the score level. (4) Experiments on three face-iris multimodal datasets demonstrate that the proposed system consistently outperforms unimodal recognition systems, multimodal recognition systems without QA and multimodal recognition systems with other QA approaches.

The remainder of this paper is organized as follows: Sect. 2 presents the composition of the adaptive face-iris multimodal identification system and especially describes the FaceIrisQANet. Section 3 includes the datasets and experiments performed. Finally, Sect. 4 gives the conclusions of this paper.

2 Proposed System

2.1 Preprocessing

Prior to recognition, the acquired face and iris images need to be preprocessed respectively to obtain suitable inputs of the system. For face preprocessing, the MTCNN face detector [29] is utilized to conduct face detection and alignment. For iris segmentation and normalization, the approach as shown in Fig. 1 is employed to get normalized iris images and corresponding noise masks from the eye image. Accurate iris segmentation is of great significance to the overall recognition performance, therefore, a coarse-to-fine strategy is adopted to segment iris region from the background and noisy pixels [31].

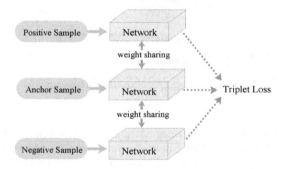

Fig. 3. Triplet training architecture for feature extraction network. The distance of genuine pair (positive-anchor) is reduced and meanwhile the distance of imposter pair (anchor-negative) is enlarged during training.

2.2 Feature Extraction

The overall diagram of the proposed system consisting of five modules is presented in Fig. 2. After preprocessing, the network [24] and network [32] are used to extract features for face and iris respectively, which have been proven to be effective feature extraction models. Since the global and structural information is the optimal for face representation, the face feature extraction network has a quite deep architecture. But different from face, the iris feature extraction network [32] does not use very deep architecture for the reason that the discriminative iris information mainly comes from small and local patterns.

Besides, both the feature extraction networks for face and iris are trained with a triplet architecture illustrated in Fig. 3. The weights of three identical networks trained in parallel are shared during training. The anchor-positive pair belongs to the same person while the anchor-negative pair comes from different persons. The triplet loss function [24] is defined as:

$$L = \frac{1}{N} \sum_{i=1}^{N} \left[\left\| \boldsymbol{f}_i^A - \boldsymbol{f}_i^P \right\|^2 - \left\| \boldsymbol{f}_i^A - \boldsymbol{f}_i^N \right\|^2 + \alpha \right]_+ , \tag{1}$$

where N is the number of triplet samples in a mini-batch, $\boldsymbol{f}_i^A$, $\boldsymbol{f}_i^P$, $\boldsymbol{f}_i^N$ represent the feature maps of anchor, positive, negative images in the i-th triplet respectively. α is a preset margin to control the desired distance between anchor-positive and anchor-negative. The symbol $[\bullet]_+$ corresponds to $\max(\bullet, 0)$. During training, anchor-positive distance is reduced and anchor-negative distance is enlarged through optimization of the triplet loss.

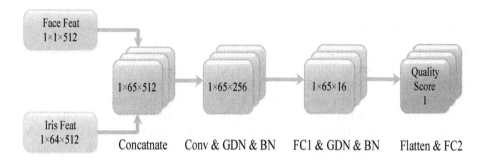

Fig. 4. Architecture of FaceIrisQANet. Output size: channel × height × width.

2.3 Matching

The matching module represents comparison of the obtained feature with all other features stored in the database. Generally, the matching score refers to either the similarity or distance between the compared features. For face matching, Euclidean Distance (ED) used to measure the difference between two face features is defined as follows:

$$ED\left(f^1, f^2\right) = \sqrt{\sum\nolimits_{(x,y)\in(M,N)} \left(f_{x,y}^1 - f_{x,y}^2\right)^2}, \tag{2}$$

where f^1, f^2 represent the compared face features, x,y are the spatial coordinates of face features and M, N means the row and column dimension of the face features. The smaller value of ED represents that the more likely f^1 and f^2 belong to the same subject.

Unlike face features, binary features are generally used in iris recognition works, since they are more resistant to various noise and consume smaller storage. Accordingly, Hamming Distance (HD) is employed to compute the matching score between two binarized iris features [19], which is calculated as:

$$HD = \frac{\sum_{j=1}^{N} X_j(XOR)Y_j(AND)Xn_j(AND)Yn_j}{N - \sum_{k=1}^{N} Xn_k(OR)Yn_k}, \tag{3}$$

where X_j and Y_j are the two compared bit-wise iris templates, Xn_j and Yn_j are their corresponding noise masks. N is the total number of bits of each iris template. Only those bits of iris features corresponding to '0' bits in both iris masks could be used to compute HD.

Additionally, in order to account for rotational inconsistencies, one template is successively shifted so that a number of HD values are calculated between two bit-wise iris features. This method is suggested by Daugman [14], which aims to correct for misalignment in normalised iris patterns. Finally, from the calculated HD values, the lowest one is taken as the matching score.

2.4   FaceIrisQANet

Network Architecture. Quality estimation is actually a regression problem and neural network has proven to be useful in regression prediction of image quality [18]. The proposed FaceIrisQANet showed in Fig. 4 mainly includes a convolutional layer with kernel size of 3×3 (stride of 1×2 and padding of 1) and two fully connected (FC) layers. At first, the iris feature of size $1 \times 64 \times 512$ is concatenated with the face feature of size $1 \times 1 \times 512$ in the second dimension, so that the fused feature of size $1 \times 65 \times 512$ is obtained. Then both the convolutional layer and FC1 layer are followed by generalized divisive normalization (GDN) activation layer and batch normalization (BN) layer. After that, the feature is flattened prior to the FC2 layer. As a result, the face-iris relative quality score is the value outputted by the FC2 layer.

GDN Activation Function. ReLU and its variants have become the dominant activation functions in deep neural networks. However, they generally require a substantially large number of model parameters to achieve good performance. In the FaceIrisQANet, we adopt a GDN transform as the activation function that is biologically inspired and has proven effective in assessing image quality. It is demonstrated that GDN has the capability of reducing model parameters and meanwhile maintaining similar quality prediction performance [17]. Given an S-dimensional linear convolutional activation $\mathbf{x}(m, n) = [x_1(m, n), \cdots, x_S(m, n)]^T$ at spatial location (m, n), the GDN transform is defined as:

$$y_i(m, n) = \frac{x_i(m, n)}{\left(\beta_i + \sum_{j=1}^{S} \gamma_{ij} x_j(m, n)^2\right)^{\frac{1}{2}}}, \qquad (4)$$

where $\mathbf{y}(m, n) = [y_1(m, n), \cdots, y_S(m, n)]^T$ is the normalized activation vector at spatial location (m, n). The weight matrix γ and the bias vector β are parameters in GDN to be optimized. Both of them are confined to $[0, +\infty)$ so as to ensure the legitimacy of the square root operation in the denominator and are shared across spatial locations.

Generation of the Groundtruth. The total error rate named as TER here is the sum of false accept rate (FAR) and false reject rate (FRR). For the i-th face-iris pair, the iris matching score vector and face matching score vector are denoted as S_i^{iris} and S_i^{face}, which are computed based on two different matching systems. Therefore, min-max normalization is performed prior to generation of the groundtruth. Let W_i^{iris} and W_i^{face} be the weights assigned to iris and face, face-iris groundtruth relative quality scores $(GQ_i^{iris}, GQ_i^{face})$ are generated as:

(1) At first, the min-max normalization technique is employed to normalize the matching score vectors S_i^{iris} and S_i^{face}:

$$S_i^{iris} = \frac{S_i^{iris} - \min}{\max - \min}, \; S_i^{face} = \frac{S_i^{face} - \min}{\max - \min}.$$

(2) The weights W_i^{iris} is varied over the range $[0, 1]$ in steps of 0.001 and $W_i^{face} = 1 - W_i^{iris}$ is satisfied.

(3) The weighted sum of scores S_i is computed as:

$$S_i = W_i^{iris} S_i^{iris} + (1 - W_i^{iris}) S_i^{face}.$$

(4) GQ_i^{iris} is the weight of iris achieving minimum TER of S_i computed as:

$$GQ_i^{iris} = \operatorname{argmin} TER(S_i; W_i^{iris}), \; GQ_i^{face} = 1 - GQ_i^{iris}.$$

Then face and iris features and the generated GQ_i^{iris} or GQ_i^{face} are used to train FaceIrisQANet in training dataset. ℓ_1 -norm is employed as the loss function. Once trained, the FaceIrisQANet can be seen as a "black box" that receives face and iris features and outputs face-iris relative quality scores $(Q_i^{iris}, Q_i^{face} = 1 - Q_i^{iris})$, which achieves distortion-generic and referenceless QA.

Table 2. Summary of some conventional score level fusion rules.

Score level fusion rule	Formula
Weighted sum rule	$S_i = W^{iris} S_i^{iris} + W^{face} S_i^{face}$
Sum rule	$S_i = S_i^{iris} + S_i^{face}$
Min rule	$S_i = min(S_i^{iris}, S_i^{face})$
Max rule	$S_i = max(S_i^{iris}, S_i^{face})$

2.5 Fusion and Decision

Some conventional score level fusion rules are summarized in Table 2, it is shown that the quality information is not incorporated in these rules. However, in the proposed system, face matching score vector S_i^{face} and iris matching score vector S_i^{iris} are merged by a quality-controlled weighted sum rule as follows:

$$S_i = Q_i^{iris} S_i^{iris} + Q_i^{face} S_i^{face}. \tag{5}$$

The adaptive weights of face matching score vector and iris matching score vector are assigned given Q_i^{iris} and Q_i^{face} for every face-iris pair. Finally, the fused score S_i is compared with a predefined threshold to decide the identity of the user.

3   Experiments and Results

In order to comprehensively evaluate the performance of the proposed system, receiver operating characteristic (ROC) curve, total error rate (FAR+FRR) and equal error rate (EER) are used to present the overall recognition performance. The decision thresholds for the employed three datasets are 0.70, 0.63 and 0.69 respectively, since the lowest total error rate of training set is obtained when using these thresholds.

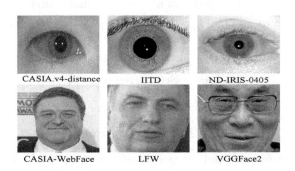

Fig. 5. Sample images from employed face and iris datasets.

3.1   Face-Iris Multimodal Datasets

A main problem for multimodal biometrics research is the lack of available real-user datasets (i.e. multiple modalities come from the same person). To solve the problem, many related experiments in multi-biometrics are performed on created chimeric datasets (i.e. multiple modalities come from different users) [6]. Therefore, three face datasets and iris datasets shown in Fig. 5 are combined to generates three face-iris multimodal datasets:

(1) CASIA-WEB multimodal dataset is the combination of CASIA.v4-distance iris database[1] and CASIA-WebFace face database [28]. The dataset contains 976 face-iris samples from 122 subjects.
(2) IITD-LFW multimodal dataset is made up of IITD iris database [16] and Labeled faces in the wild face database [10], which includes 1065 face-iris pairs from 213 subjects.
(3) ND-VGG multimodal dataset consists of ND-IRIS-0405 iris dataset [23] and VGGFace2 face dataset [5]. There are 3040 face-iris samples from 304 subjects in the dataset. The ratio of training samples to test samples is 1:1 for CASIA-WEB multimodal dataset and ND-VGG multimodal dataset, and the ratio is 3:2 for IITD-LFW multimodal dataset.

---

[1] http://biometrics.idealtest.org.

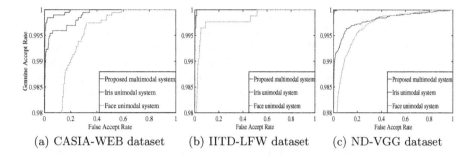

(a) CASIA-WEB dataset   (b) IITD-LFW dataset   (c) ND-VGG dataset

Fig. 6. Comparison with unimodal recognition systems on three face-iris datasets.

Table 3. Performance comparison with non quality-based score fusion rules

Score level fusion rule	CASIA-WEB		IITD-LFW		ND-VGG	
	FAR+FRR	EER	FAR+FRR	EER	FAR+FRR	EER
Quality controlled fusion	0.0095	0.0046	0.0019	0.0012	0.0026	0.0014
Weighted sum rule	0.0111	0.0061	0.0052	0.0023	0.0118	0.0062
Sum rule	0.6301	0.1547	0.1185	0.0070	0.4376	0.0384
Min rule	0.0338	0.0067	0.0127	0.0023	0.0172	0.0021
Max rule	0.1134	0.0154	0.0411	0.0035	0.0469	0.0111

Red represents the best value and blue takes the second place.

3.2   Comparison with Unimodal Biometrics

In order to explore the influence of multimodal biometrics, our system is compared with the face and iris unimodal recognition systems [24,32]. The comparison ROC curves can be found in Fig. 6, which shows that our system consistently outperforms face and iris unimodal recognition systems on three datasets.

Specifically, our system have a significant improvement over face and iris unimodal recognition systems on CASIA-WEB and ND-VGG datasets. For the comparison on IITD-LFW dataset, we obtain similar performance with iris unimodal recognition system due to the high-quality of IITD iris dataset. Apart from this, it is noticeable that the worse recognition performance is always obtained by face unimodal recognition system, because the three face datasets captured in unconstrained environments are of quite poor quality. However, the performance of our system are little affected by the poor quality of face samples, which denotes that our system can effectively diminish the negative effect brought by poor-quality samples.

3.3   Comparison with Non Quality-Based Fusion Rules

Four commonly used score fusion rules illustrated in Table 2 are used as our baseline fusion rules, and there is no quality information in these rules. For the weighted sum rule, all users are assigned the same face weight W^{face} and iris weight W^{iris}, which are computed given the EER of face and iris in training set [26]. Comparison results of different score fusion rules can be found in Table 3.

As shown in Table 3, the best performance is always achieved by our fusion rule on three multimodal datasets. The weighted sum rule and min rule take the second place in the terms of total error rate and EER. On average, our quality-controlled fusion rule outperforms 51.95% and 35.25% by the second place in terms of total error rate and EER respectively. Therefore, using the quality-controlled fusion rule can reduce the recognition error rate effectively compared with non quality-based fusion rules.

Table 4. Comparison of other quality measure approaches for iris and face

Iris and face QA methods	CASIA-WEB		IITD-LFW		ND-VGG	
	FAR+FRR	EER	FAR+FRR	EER	FAR+FRR	EER
Ours (FaceIrisQANet)	0.0095	0.0046	0.0019	0.0012	0.0026	0.0014
Baseline1 [9,13]	0.0146	0.0075	0.0032	0.0020	0.0052	0.0029
Baseline2 [2,13]	0.0133	0.0072	0.0038	0.0023	0.0084	0.0049
Baseline3 [7,9]	0.0145	0.0083	0.0046	0.0021	0.0050	0.0026
Baseline4 [2,7]	0.0145	0.0084	0.0054	0.0029	0.0077	0.0047
Baseline5 [20]	0.0146	0.0081	0.0035	0.0021	0.0061	0.0030

Red represents the best value and blue takes the second place.

3.4 Comparison with Other QA Approaches

Different combinations of the iris QA methods [7,13] and face QA methods [2,9] are taken as baselines to compare with the proposed FaceIrisQANet. As summarized in Table 1, these QA approaches include both distortion-specific QA [2,7] and distortion-generic QA [9,13]. Besides, the blind/referenceless image spatial quality evaluator (BRISQUE) [20] is seen as another benchmark to assess iris and face image quality. The comparison results of different QA approaches for iris and face on three datasets can be found in Table 4.

According to Table 4, using the FaceIrisQANet consistently obtains the best recognition performance. Besides, as mentioned in Sect. 2, our FaceIrisQANet can achieve distortion-generic blind QA for face and iris only based on their features. Though the baseline1 are also distortion-generic QA approaches for face and iris, which has not obtained satisfactory performance compared with the FaceIrisQANet. Additionally, our method surpasses 36.11% and 46.15% in terms of EER over baseline2 and baseline3 respectively, which delivers the second best performance on CASIA-WEB dataset and ND-VGG dataset.

4 Conclusion

An adaptive face-iris multimodal identification system based on quality assessment network is developed in this paper. As discussed in the experiments section, the proposed system offers a superior recognition performance and generalizes well on different face-iris multimodal datasets, which arises from the benefits of multimodal biometrics, the FaceIrisQANet and quality-controlled fusion scheme. It is demonstrated that incorporating the FaceIrisQANet into the score level fusion scheme can deliver a lower recognition error rate. Additionally, the

FaceIrisQANet differs from previous QA approaches for face and iris in that it is distortion-generic and no-reference, which benefits from better generality and practicality capability. As future work we will explore more quality dependent multimodal recognition approaches.

Acknowledgment. This work was supported in part by NSFC-Shenzhen Robot Jointed Founding under Grant U1613215, in part by the Shenzhen Municipal Development and Reform Commission (Disciplinary Development Program for Data Science and Intelligent Computing), and in part by the Key-Area Research and Development Program of Guangdong Province under Grant 2019B010137001.

References

1. Abate, A.F., Barra, S., Casanova, A., Fenu, G., Marras, M.: Iris quality assessment: a statistical approach for biometric security applications. In: Castiglione, A., Pop, F., Ficco, M., Palmieri, F. (eds.) CSS 2018. LNCS, vol. 11161, pp. 270–278. Springer, Cham (2018). https://doi.org/10.1007/978-3-030-01689-0_21
2. Abaza, A., Harrison, M.A., Bourlai, T.: Quality metrics for practical face recognition. In: Proceedings of the 21st International Conference on Pattern Recognition, pp. 3103–3107. IEEE (2012)
3. Abdel-Mottaleb, M., Mahoor, M.H.: Application notes-algorithms for assessing the quality of facial images. IEEE Comput. Intell. Mag. **2**(2), 10–17 (2007)
4. Ammour, B., Bouden, T., Boubchir, L.: Face-iris multimodal biometric system based on hybrid level fusion. In: 41st International Conference on Telecommunications and Signal Processing, pp. 1–5. IEEE (2018)
5. Cao, Q., Shen, L., Xie, W., Parkhi, O.M., Zisserman, A.: VGGFace2: a dataset for recognising faces across pose and age. In: 13th IEEE International Conference on Automatic Face and Gesture Recognition, pp. 67–74. IEEE (2018)
6. Dorizzi, B., Garcia-Salicetti, S., Allano, L.: Multimodality in biosecure: Evaluation on real vs. virtual subjects. In: IEEE International Conference on Acoustics Speech and Signal Processing Proceedings, vol. 5, p. V. IEEE (2006)
7. Du, Y., Belcher, C., Zhou, Z., Ives, R.: Feature correlation evaluation approach for iris feature quality measure. Signal Process. **90**(4), 1176–1187 (2010)
8. Grother, P., Tabassi, E.: Performance of biometric quality measures. IEEE Trans. Pattern Anal. Mach. Intell. **29**(4), 531–543 (2007)
9. Hernandez-Ortega, J., Galbally, J., Fierrez, J., Haraksim, R., Beslay, L.: FaceQnet: quality assessment for face recognition based on deep learning. In: 12th IAPR International Conference On Biometrics, pp. 1–8 (2019)
10. Huang, G.B., Ramesh, M., Berg, T., Learned-Miller, E.: Labeled faces in the wild: a database for studying face recognition in unconstrained environments. Technical report 07–49, University of Massachusetts, Amherst, October 2007
11. Jain, A., Nandakumar, K., Ross, A.: Score normalization in multimodal biometric systems. Pattern Recognit. **38**(12), 2270–2285 (2005)
12. Jain, A.K.: Technology: biometric recognition. Nature **449**(7158), 38 (2007)
13. Jenadeleh, M., Pedersen, M., Saupe, D.: Realtime quality assessment of iris biometrics under visible light. In: Proceedings of the IEEE Conference on Computer Vision and Pattern Recognition Workshops, pp. 443–452 (2018)
14. John, D.: How iris recognition works. IEEE Trans. Circ. Syst. Video Technol. **14**(1), 21–30 (2004)

15. Johnson, P.A., Hua, F., Schuckers, S.: Comparison of quality-based fusion of face and iris biometrics. In: 2011 International Joint Conference on Biometrics, pp. 1–5. IEEE (2011)

16. Kumar, A., Passi, A.: Comparison and combination of iris matchers for reliable personal authentication. Pattern Recognit. **43**(3), 1016–1026 (2010)

17. Li, Q., Wang, Z.: Reduced-reference image quality assessment using divisive normalization-based image representation. IEEE J. Sel. Topics Sig. Process. **3**(2), 202–211 (2009)

18. Ma, K., Liu, W., Zhang, K., Duanmu, Z., Wang, Z., Zuo, W.: End-to-end blind image quality assessment using deep neural networks. IEEE Trans. Image Process. **27**(3), 1202–1213 (2017)

19. Masek, L.: Recognition of human iris patterns for biometric identification. Ph.D. thesis, Master's thesis, University of Western Australia (2003)

20. Mittal, A., Moorthy, A.K., Bovik, A.C.: No-reference image quality assessment in the spatial domain. IEEE Trans. Image Process. **21**(12), 4695–4708 (2012)

21. Morizet, N., Gilles, J.: A new adaptive combination approach to score level fusion for face and iris biometrics combining wavelets and statistical moments. In: Bebis, G., et al. (eds.) ISVC 2008. LNCS, vol. 5359, pp. 661–671. Springer, Heidelberg (2008). https://doi.org/10.1007/978-3-540-89646-3_65

22. Nandakumar, K., Chen, Y., Jain, A.K., Dass, S.C.: Quality-based score level fusion in multibiometric systems. In: 18th International Conference on Pattern Recognition, vol. 4, pp. 473–476. IEEE (2006)

23. Phillips, P.J., et al.: FRVT 2006 and ice 2006 large-scale experimental results. IEEE Trans. Pattern Anal. Mach. Intell. **32**(5), 831–846 (2009)

24. Schroff, F., Kalenichenko, D., Philbin, J.: FaceNet: a unified embedding for face recognition and clustering. In: Proceedings of the IEEE Conference on Computer Vision and Pattern Recognition, pp. 815–823 (2015)

25. Sim, H.M., Asmuni, H., Hassan, R., Othman, R.M.: Multimodal biometrics: weighted score level fusion based on non-ideal iris and face images. Expert Syst. Appl. **41**(11), 5390–5404 (2014)

26. Snelick, R., Uludag, U., Mink, A., Indovina, M., Jain, A.: Large-scale evaluation of multimodal biometric authentication using state-of-the-art systems. IEEE Trans. Pattern Anal. Mach. Intell. **27**(3), 450–455 (2005)

27. Soleymani, S., Dabouei, A., Kazemi, H., Dawson, J., Nasrabadi, N.M.: Multi-level feature abstraction from convolutional neural networks for multimodal biometric identification. In: 24th International Conference on Pattern Recognition, pp. 3469–3476. IEEE (2018)

28. Yi, D., Lei, Z., Liao, S., Li, S.Z.: Learning face representation from scratch. Computer Science (2014)

29. Zhang, K., Zhang, Z., Li, Z., Qiao, Y.: Joint face detection and alignment using multitask cascaded convolutional networks. IEEE Sig. Process. Lett. **23**(10), 1499–1503 (2016)

30. Zhao, W., Chellappa, R., Phillips, P.J., Rosenfeld, A.: Face recognition: a literature survey. ACM Comput. Surv. (CSUR) **35**(4), 399–458 (2003)

31. Zhao, Z., Ajay, K.: An accurate iris segmentation framework under relaxed imaging constraints using total variation model. In: Proceedings of the IEEE International Conference on Computer Vision, pp. 3828–3836 (2015)

32. Zhao, Z., Kumar, A.: Towards more accurate iris recognition using deeply learned spatially corresponding features. In: Proceedings of the IEEE International Conference on Computer Vision, pp. 3809–3818 (2017)

Thermal Face Recognition Based on Multi-scale Image Synthesis

Wei-Ta Chu[1(✉)] and Ping-Shen Huang[2]

[1] National Cheng Kung University, Tainan, Taiwan
`wtchu@gs.ncku.edu.tw`
[2] National Chung Cheng University, Chiayi, Taiwan
`kevin971227@gmail.com`

Abstract. We present a transformation-based method to achieve thermal face recognition. Given a thermal face, the proposed model transforms the input to a synthesized visible face, which is then used as a probe to compare with visible faces in the database. This transformation model is built on the basis of a generative adversarial network, mainly with the ideas of multi-scale discrimination and various loss functions like feature embedding, identity preservation, and facial landmark-guided texture synthesis. The evaluation results show that the proposed method outperforms the state of the art.

Keywords: Thermal face recognition · Image synthesis · Multi-scale

1 Introduction

With the rage of COVID-19 in the world, infrared images have attracted more and more attention because they are formed based on heat signals from the skin tissues. In addition, they are also widely used in many domains like night-time surveillance and access control. Compared with images in the visible spectrum, infrared images are less affected by visual appearance changes caused by lighting/illumination variations.

Infrared images can be categorized into four groups according to the wavelengths sensed, including near infrared (NIR, 0.75 μm–1.4 μm), short-wave infrared (SWIR, 1.4 μm–3.0 μm), mid-wave infrared (MWIR, 3.0 μm–8.0 μm), and long-wave infrared (LWIR, 8.0 μm–15.0 μm). NIR and SWIR imaging are reflection-based and their visual appearance is similar to visible images. They are called "reflected infrared". MWIR and LWIR images measure material emissivity and temperature, and they are called "thermal infrared".

Thermal face recognition aims to identify a person captured in the thermal spectrum by matching the most similar image captured in the visible spectrum. It is thus a cross-spectrum matching task. For this purpose, we need a non-linear mapping from the thermal spectrum to the visible spectrum while preserving the identity information. In this work, we present a model based on the generative

© Springer Nature Switzerland AG 2021
J. Lokoč et al. (Eds.): MMM 2021, LNCS 12572, pp. 99–110, 2021.
https://doi.org/10.1007/978-3-030-67832-6_9

adversarial networks (GANs) [9] to synthesize visible faces from given thermal faces, and the generated faces will be matched against a gallery of visible faces.

Recent advances in GANs has witnessed success in various applications, including style transfer [1], image super resolution [2] and face completion [3]. GANs are composed of a generator and a discriminator. The former learns how to synthesize image, and the latter learns to discriminate between real images and synthesized image. In order to synthesize visible faces of better quality, we consider facial landmark information and identity information in the proposed network. Besides, at the stage of extracting features in the generator, we attempt to force the model to better extract features for image synthesis. For the discriminator, we develop multiple discriminators at different image scales in order to synthesize finer details of faces.

Contributions of this work are summarized as follows.

- We present a GAN-based thermal to visible face synthesis system with the ideas of integrating facial landmark information and identity information.
- We demonstrate the importance of image resolution for face synthesis from the thermal spectrum to the visible spectrum.

The rest of this paper is organized as follows. Sect. 2 provides the literature survey on thermal face recognition. Sect. 3 provides details of the proposed method. The evaluation protocols and performance are described in Sect. 4, followed by the conclusion in Sect. 5.

2   Related Works

Existing thermal to visible face recognition works can be roughly grouped into two categories: (1) mapping thermal faces and visible faces into the common feature space and then achieving recognition; (2) transforming thermal faces into the visible spectrum, and then conducting recognition.

2.1   Feature Embedding

One of the seminal works of this category is deep perceptual mapping (DPM) [7]. Sarfraz and Stiefelhagen extracted dense SIFT features from patches of thermal face images, and then used an auto-encoder to map features into a common space which is shared with the features extracted from visible face images. Given a thermal face image, they extracted features and found the visible face with the most similar features to determine identity. Saxena et al. [8] used a shared weight convolutional neural network to extract features from face images of different spectrums, and proposed a metric learning method to distinguish whether the input paired face images come from the same person.

2.2   Image Transformation

GANs are widely used in the image synthesis task. Song et al. [10] developed GANs to transform NIR faces into visible faces. They proposed a two-path model to jointly consider global information representing texture of the entire image, and local information representing texture around the eyes. Zang et al. [11] proposed a thermal-to-visible GAN (TV-GAN) that transforms thermal faces into visible faces while retaining identity information. They used an architecture based on Pix2Pix [1], with the discriminator added an additional function to discriminate identity. Recently, Mallat et al. [12] used Cascaded Refinement Networks (CRN) [13] to consider information of thermal faces at multiple scales and targeted at synthesizing finer texture.

Inspired by the two categories of studies, we propose a GAN-based model to do image transformation as well as integrate the concept of feature embedding. In addition, the generator additionally considers facial landmark information and identity information to make synthesized face more realistic.

3   Thermal Face Recognition

The thermal face recognition problem can be divided into two parts: (1) image transformation and (2) face matching. Given a thermal face image T, we would like to find a function f that synthesizes the corresponding visible face, i.e., $f(T) = Q$. In this work, we learn the function f based on a GAN. Assuming that we have a set of visible faces as the gallery set $\mathcal{G}$, and the synthesized face image is the probe Q, thermal face recognition is done by matching the probe with images in $\mathcal{G}$. The probe is recognized as the individual who is in $\mathcal{G}$ and is the most similar face to Q.

3.1   Baseline Model

Framework. We first describe a baseline model to do image transformation. It consists of a generator G and a discriminator D. The goal of G is to synthesize visible faces from thermal faces, while the discriminator D aims to distinguish real images from the synthesized ones. The generator is built on the architecture proposed by Johnson et al. [14], which consists of a convolutional layer, a series of residual blocks and a transposed convolutional layer. A thermal face of 512×512 pixels is passed through these components and a synthesized visible face of resolution 512×512 pixel is output.

We adopt multi-scale discriminators proposed by Wang et al. [4] as the discriminators. Two discriminators D_1 and D_2 that have identical architecture are developed to deal with different scales of image. Specifically, we downsample the synthesized image and the corresponding visible image from 512×512 to 256×256. The 512×512 synthesized image and visible image are fed to D_1, while the 256×256 versions are fed to D_2. Two different discriminators handle different scales of discrimination. Results of discrimination at different scales encourage the generator to synthesize not only the global look but also finer details of face images. Figure 1 shows architecture of the baseline model.

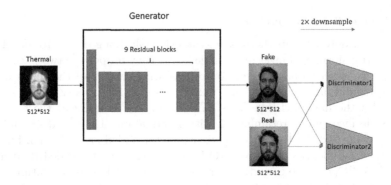

Fig. 1. Network architecture of the baseline model.

Loss Functions of Baseline Model. The baseline model consists of an adversarial loss [9], a feature matching loss [4], and a perceptual loss [14]. The training dataset consists of thermal-visible face pairs $\{(t_i, x_i)\}$, where t_i is a thermal face image and x_i is a corresponding visible face image. For a conventional GAN, the objective of the generator G is to maximize the probability of the discriminator D making a mistake (mis-discriminate the synthesized image and real image), while the objective of D is to maximize the probability of making a correct decision (correctly discriminate the synthesized image and real image). With multi-scale discriminators D_1 and D_2, the adversarial loss $\mathcal{L}_{GAN}$ is defined as

$$
\begin{aligned}
\mathcal{L}_{GAN}(G, D_1, D_2) = {} & \mathbb{E}_{(t,x)}[\log D_1(t, x) + \log D_2(t, x)] \\
& + \mathbb{E}_{t,x}[\log(1 - D_1(t, G(x)) + \log(1 - D_2(t, G(x))].
\end{aligned}
\tag{1}
$$

Feature matching loss [4] is further designed to guide network learning. Features are extracted from multiple layers of the discriminator. These intermediate representations are used to learn the matching between the real and the synthesized image. The feature matching loss $\mathcal{L}_{FM}$ is calculated as:

$$
\mathcal{L}_{FM}(G, D_k) = \mathbb{E}_{(t,x)} \sum_{i=1}^{M} \frac{1}{N_i}[\| D_k^{(i)}(t, x) - D_k^{(i)}(t, G(t)) \|_1],
\tag{2}
$$

where $D_k^{(i)}$ represents the output feature maps of the ith layer of D_k, and M is the total number of layers. The notation $\|\cdot\|_1$ denotes the L_1 norm, and the value N_i denotes the number of elements in a layer.

The perceptual loss $\mathcal{L}_P$ [14] is designed to measure the semantic difference between the synthesized image and the real image. It is defined as:

$$
\mathcal{L}_P(G) = \mathbb{E}_{(t,x)} \| \Phi_P(G(t)) - \Phi_P(x) \|_1,
\tag{3}
$$

where Φ_P denotes the features extractor based on the VGG-19 network [15] pretrained on the ImageNet dataset [16]. The features are extracted at multiple layers, and are then concatenated to be image representations. The loss is the L_1 norm between representations of synthesized images and real images.

Finally, the overall loss function used in the baseline model is $\mathcal{L}(G, D_1, D_2) = \mathcal{L}_{GAN} + \lambda_{FM}\mathcal{L}_{FM} + \lambda_P\mathcal{L}_P$, and the baseline model is trained by solving the minimax game: $\min_G \max_{D_1, D_2} \mathcal{L}(G, D_1, D_2)$.

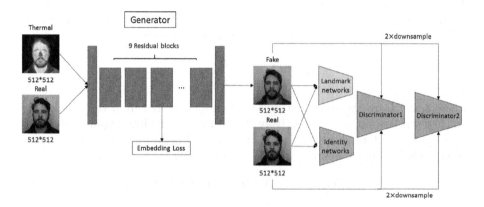

Fig. 2. Architecture of proposed method.

3.2   Proposed Model

In order to further improve quality of synthesized images, we propose three major designs to improve the baseline model. Figure 2 illustrates the complete architecture of the proposed method.

Feature Embedding. As mentioned in Sect. 2, studies of thermal face recognition can be categorized into the ones with image transformation and the ones with feature embedding. The baseline model mentioned in Sect. 3.1 is based on image transformation. However, we would like to further take the concept of feature embedding in constructing the generator. We hope that in the generation process, features extracted from the thermal face can be embedded into the ones similar to the features extracted from the corresponding visible face. To achieve this, we feed the paired thermal face and visible face to the generator, and calculate the distance between features extracted from an intermediate layer of the generator. The embedding loss function $\mathcal{L}_E$ is defined as:

$$\mathcal{L}_E(G) = \mathbb{E}_{(t,x)}\|\Phi_E(t) - \Phi_E(x)\|_1, \tag{4}$$

where $\Phi_E(t)$ and $\Phi_E(x)$ denote the feature maps output by the third residual block of the generator by giving the thermal image t and the corresponding visible face x, respectively.

Facial Landmarks. The resolution of thermal faces is usually low, and less texture information can be utilized to achieve good image synthesis. To improve synthesized details on eyes, nose, and mouth, and their relative positions, we further consider positions of facial landmarks. The idea is: if the synthesized image is good, the facial landmarks detected from it would be closer to that detected from the corresponding visible face. We use a facial landmarks detector Φ_L proposed by Bulat et al. [17] to detect 68 facial landmarks, and then calculate the normalized mean error (NME) between the positions of landmarks detected from the synthesized face and the corresponding visible face.

$$NME = \sum \frac{\|l - \tilde{l}\|_2}{Kd} \times 100\%, \tag{5}$$

where l and $\tilde{l}$ are the coordinates of landmarks detected from the visible face and the synthesized face, respectively. The value d is the interpupillary distance between the centers of two eyes, and the value K is the number of facial landmarks. The landmark loss function $\mathcal{L}_L$ is defined as:

$$\mathcal{L}_L(G) = \mathbb{E}_{(t,x)} NME(\Phi_L(G(t)), \Phi_L(x)), \tag{6}$$

where Φ_L conceptually denotes the landmark detection module that outputs coordinates of landmarks l and $\tilde{l}$.

Identity. The final target of image synthesis is to achieve accurate face recognition. Therefore, preserving identity information is certainly needed. To do this, we extract high-level identity-specific features by an architecture IR-50 with Arc-Face Φ_I (an improved version of the vanilla ResNet-50 [18]) [19] pre-trained on the MS-Celeb-1M dataset [20], and then calculate the cosine similarity between the synthesized face and the corresponding visible face. The identity loss function $\mathcal{L}_I$ is designed as:

$$\mathcal{L}_I(G) = \mathbb{E}_{(t,x)}(1 - \cos(\Phi_I(G(t), \Phi_I(x))). \tag{7}$$

Combining the aforementioned loss functions with that in the baseline model, the overall loss function of our proposed model is finally formulated as:

$$\mathcal{L} = \mathcal{L}_{GAN} + \lambda_{FM}\mathcal{L}_{FM} + \lambda_P\mathcal{L}_P + \lambda_E\mathcal{L}_E + \lambda_L\mathcal{L}_L + \lambda_I\mathcal{L}_I. \tag{8}$$

4   Evaluation

4.1   Dataset

We evaluate the proposed approach based on the Eurecom VIS-TH database provided in [5]. The data were collected from 50 subjects of different ages, gender, and ethnicities. The resolution of visible face images are 1920×1080 pixels, and the resolution of thermal face images are 160×120 pixels with a wavelength range of $7.5\,\mu m$–$13.5\,\mu m$. Visible faces and thermal faces were captured in pairs for each subject. There are 21 different capture settings, and thus this dataset contains $50 \times 2 \times 21 = 2100$ images in total. The 21 settings can be divided into five groups:

- **Neutral**: 1 pair captured with standard illumination, frontal view, neutral expression.
- **Expression**: 6 pairs captured with different expressions: happy, angry, sad, surprised, blinking, and yawning.
- **Head pose**: 4 pairs captured with different head poses: up, down, right at 45° and left at 45°.
- **Occlusion**: 5 pairs captured with varying occlusions: eyeglasses, sunglasses, cap, mouth occluded by hand, and eye occluded by hand.
- **Illumination**: 5 pairs captured with different illuminations: ambient light, rim light, key light, fill light, all lights on, and all lights off.

4.2   Evaluation Protocol

To fairly compare with [12], we follow their evaluation protocol. Both visible faces and thermal faces are resized into 128×128 pixels. However, in face synthesis, higher resolution images are required to retain the details of the facial features. Therefore, we upsample visible faces from 128×128 pixels to 512×512 pixels, and take them as the ground truth. To avoid blur effects caused by simple upsampling, we adopt a super-resolution model proposed by Wang et al. [2], and get a result like Fig. 3(b). We can see that this super-resolution face is clearer than the face obtained by a simple upsampling method shown in Fig. 3(a). We will show that this difference causes performance gap in the following. Please notice that this upsampling process still make us fairly compare with [12], because both methods start from 128×128 thermal faces and visible faces. We don't get extra information in addition to the thermal-visible pairs.

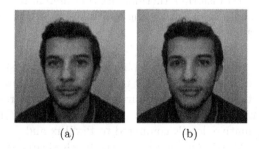

(a)   (b)

Fig. 3. Examples showing face obtained by direct upsampling (left) and by the super resolution (right) method provided in [2].

To recognize the synthesized face, we follow the settings in [12], and use the LightCNN [6] to extract facial features. The extracted features of the probe image are compared with features of gallery images. A test image is recognized according to the nearest neighbor measured by cosine similarity. In the evaluation, the ten-fold cross validation scheme is used. For each fold, paired faces of 45 subjects are used to train the model, except for the ones acquired in total darkness. The thermal faces of the remaining 5 subjects are tested by feeding to the proposed model. The average test accuracy in ten folds will be reported.

4.3 Performance of Thermal Face Recognition

Baselines. To evaluate the performance of thermal face recognition, we need to do face matching between the probe set and the gallery set. Following [12], the synthesized visible faces from the thermal spectrum are the probe set, and all the neutral images of 50 subjects are the gallery set. Please notice again that only the 50 neutral faces are used as the gallery set. Based on this protocol, we compare the proposed model with several baselines:

- **Visible**: All the original visible face images are taken as the probes. This setting can be seen as the upper bound of LightCNN-based recognition, because it is simply a simple visible face recognition task.
- **Thermal**: All thermal face images are directly taken as the probes. This setting can be seen as the lower bound of LightCNN-based recognition, because no transformation is done for recognition. It shows how the modality gap influences recognition performance.
- **Pix2Pix** [1]: We can adopt the typical image-to-image translation work proposed in [1] to translate a thermal face into a visible face. Then the transformed face is used to recognize based on LightCNN.
- **TV-GAN** [11]: Zhang et al. used an architecture based on Pix2Pix to transform thermal face images into visible face images, added with a discriminator to consider identity of the generated face image. This approach is also used in performance comparison.
- **CRN** [12]: This is the state of the art. Mallat et al. used a cascaded refined network (CRN) to transform a thermal faces of different resolutions into a visible face. The main idea is considering multiple scales of images to synthesize more texture details.

Transformation Results. Figure 4 shows sample transformation results obtained by different methods. The first column shows the source thermal faces, and the results in the second to the fourth columns are the results of Pix2Pix, TV-GAN, CRN, and ours, respectively. As can be seen, the CRN method synthesizes more informative details compared to Pix2Pix and TV-GAN, but some facial parts remain blurry. Our method gives much clearer synthesized results on important facial parts like eyes, nose, and mouth.

Figure 5 shows sample results obtained by the baseline model mentioned in Sect. 3.1 and our complete model. Comparing them with the ground truth side-by-side, we see the complete model relatively yields more texture details, especially when the face is non-frontal. These results visually show effectiveness of the complete model with the loss functions mentioned in Sect. 3.2.

Recognition Accuracy. Table 1 shows recognition accuracies of various methods. The numbers shown in the parentheses of the leading column is the number of faces for each corresponding individual. For Pix2Pix and TV-GAN, we directly quote the values provided in [12]. Reasonably all methods work better than directly using thermal images as the probe. This shows that the image transformation methods to synthesize visible-like images are required to reduce the modality gap. TV-GAN works better than Pix2Pix because the discriminator takes into account more identity information during synthesis. Unlike Pix2Pix and TV-GAN, which are based on L1 Loss function making them sensitive to image misalignment, CRN uses the contextual loss to process images that are not fully aligned. The recognition accuracy of CRN is increased to 57.61%. The baseline model mentioned in Sect. 3.1 already achieves accuracy greater than Pix2Pix and TV-GAN. With the helps of the designed feature embedding loss, landmark loss and identity loss, the complete model improves to 58.27% accuracy, which outperforms the state-of-the-art CRN on the Eurecom dataset.

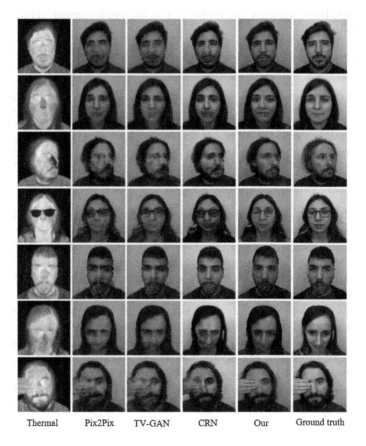

Thermal   Pix2Pix   TV-GAN   CRN   Our   Ground truth

Fig. 4. Sample transformation results obtained by different methods.

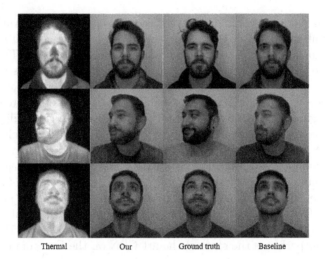

Thermal   Our   Ground truth   Baseline

Fig. 5. Sample transformation results obtained by the baseline model and the proposed complete model.

Table 1. Comparison of face recognition accuracy for various methods.

	Visible	Thermal	Pix2Pix [1]	TV-GAN [11]	CRN [12]	Baseline	Our
Neutral (1)	100.00	32.00	48.00	54.00	82.00	82.00	**90.00**
Expression (6)	99.66	23.00	37.33	38.33	**67.66**	57.00	63.33
Head pose (4)	80.50	12.50	14.50	15.50	**30.00**	23.00	28.00
Occlusion (5)	98.80	14.40	16.40	25.00	**44.80**	31.60	39.20
Illumination (5)	87.20	15.60	29.60	35.20	63.60	58.00	**70.80**
Average	95.23	19.50	29.17	33.61	57.61	50.32	**58.27**

Ablation Studies. To demonstrate the effectiveness of different loss functions, we evaluate our model trained based on several combinations. Table 2 shows recognition accuracies obtained based on different combinations. Without considering the designed losses, the first row corresponds to the baseline method. By considering more loss functions, the recognition accuracy is gradually improved, while the complete model yields the best performance.

We further explore the influence of image resolutions on performance. Several settings are designed during training: (1) input image size is 128×128; (2) input image size is 512×512 pixels (direct upsampling without super resolution); (3) input image size is 512×512 pixels (upsampling by super resolution). Table 3 shows performance variations. As can be seen, even without taking extra information, image upsampling benefits image synthesis. If the upsampling is done by the super resolution technique [2], further performance gain can be obtained.

Table 2. Recognition accuracies obtained based on different loss functions.

Feature embedding	Landmark	Identity	Accuracy
			50.32
		✓	53.57
	✓		51.17
✓			51.21
	✓	✓	56.10
✓	✓	✓	**58.27**

Table 3. Performance variations when images of different resolutions are used as the input.

Settings	Accuracy
128 * 128	38.97
512 * 512 (w/o SR)	54.59
512 * 512 (w. SR)	**58.27**

5 Conclusion

We have presented a GAN-based model to transform thermal face images into visible-like face images. In the proposed network, loss functions based on feature embedding, landmark detection, and identity are jointly added to a GAN considering multi-scale discrimination. Experimental results show that our model is better than the state of the art in terms of quantitative measure (recognition performance) and qualitative measure (visual synthesized results). We also demonstrate the importance of image resolution for face synthesis.

On the other hand, our synthesis results for side-view faces are still not good enough. In the future, we hope to improve recognition performance, and develop a real-time thermal face recognition system by integrating thermal face detection, tracking, and recognition.

Acknowledgment. This work was partially supported by Qualcomm Technologies, Inc. under the grant number B109-K027D, and by the Ministry of Science and Technology, Taiwan, under the grant 108-2221-E-006-227-MY3, 107-2923-E-194-003-MY3, and 109-2218-E-002-015.

References

1. Isola, P., Zhu, J., Zhou, T., Efros, A.A.: Image-to-image translation with conditional adversarial networks. In: Proceedings of CVPR, pp. 5967–5976 (2017)
2. Wang, X., et al.: ESRGAN: enhanced super-resolution generative adversarial networks. In: Proceedings of ECCV Workshops (2018)

3. Li, Y., Liu, S., Yang, J., Yang, M.: Generative face completion. In: Proceedings of CVPR, pp. 5892–5900 (2017)
4. Wang, T., Liu, M., Zhu, J., Tao, A., Kautz, J., Catanzaro, B.: High-resolution image synthesis and semantic manipulation with conditional GANs. In: Proceedings of CVPR, pp. 8798–8807 (2018)
5. Mallat, K., Dugelay, J.: A benchmark database of visible and thermal paired face images across multiple variations. In: Proceedings of International Conference of the Biometrics Special Interest Group, pp. 1–5 (2018)
6. Wu, X., He, R., Sun, Z., Tan, T.: A light CNN for deep face representation with noisy labels. IEEE TIFS **13**, 2884–2896 (2018)
7. Sarfraz, M.S., Stiefelhagen, R.: Deep perceptual mapping for thermal to visible face recognition. In: Proceedings of BMVC (2015)
8. Saxena, S., Verbeek, J.: Heterogeneous face recognition with CNNs. In: Hua, G., Jégou, H. (eds.) ECCV 2016. LNCS, vol. 9915, pp. 483–491. Springer, Cham (2016). https://doi.org/10.1007/978-3-319-49409-8_40
9. Goodfellow, I.J., et al.: Generative adversarial nets. In: Proceedings of NIPS, pp. 2672–2680 (2014)
10. Song, L., Zhang, M., Wu, X., He, R.: Adversarial discriminative heterogeneous face recognition. In: Proceedings of AAAI (2018)
11. Zhang, T., Wiliem, A., Yang, S., Lovell, B.C.: TV-GAN: generative adversarial network based thermal to visible face recognition. In: Proceedings of ICB (2018)
12. Mallat, K., Damer, N., Boutros, F., Kuijper, A., Dugelay, J.: Cross-spectrum thermal to visible face recognition based on cascaded image synthesis. In: Proceedings of ICB (2019)
13. Chen, Q., Koltun, V.: Photographic image synthesis with cascaded refinement networks. In: Proceedings of ICCV, pp. 1511–1520 (2017)
14. Johnson, J., Alahi, A., Fei-Fei, L.: Perceptual losses for real-time style transfer and super-resolution. In: Leibe, B., Matas, J., Sebe, N., Welling, M. (eds.) ECCV 2016. LNCS, vol. 9906, pp. 694–711. Springer, Cham (2016). https://doi.org/10.1007/978-3-319-46475-6_43
15. Simonyan, K., Zisserman, A.: Very deep convolutional networks for large-scale image recognition. In: Proceedings of ICLR (2015)
16. Russakovsky, O., et al.: ImageNet large scale visual recognition challenge. Int. J. Comput. Vis. **115**(3), 211–252 (2015). https://doi.org/10.1007/s11263-015-0816-y
17. Bulat, A., Tzimiropoulos, G.: How far are we from solving the 2D & 3D face alignment problem? In: Proceedings of ICCV, pp. 1021–1030 (2017)
18. He, K., Zhang, X., Ren, S., Sun, J.: Deep residual learning for image recognition. In: Proceedings of CVPR, pp. 770–778 (2016)
19. Deng, J., Guo, J., Xue, N., Zafeiriou, S.: Arcface: additive angular margin loss for deep face recognition. In: Proceedings of CVPR, pp. 4690–4699 (2019)
20. Guo, Y., Zhang, L., Hu, Y., He, X., Gao, J.: MS-Celeb-1M: a dataset and benchmark for large-scale face recognition. In: Leibe, B., Matas, J., Sebe, N., Welling, M. (eds.) ECCV 2016. LNCS, vol. 9907, pp. 87–102. Springer, Cham (2016). https://doi.org/10.1007/978-3-319-46487-9_6

Contrastive Learning in Frequency Domain for Non-I.I.D. Image Classification

Huan Shao, Zhaoquan Yuan[✉], Xiao Peng, and Xiao Wu

School of Information Science and Technology,
Southwest Jiaotong University, Chengdu 610031, China
{bk2015112265,pengx}@my.swjtu.edu.cn, zqyuan@swjtu.edu.cn,
wuxiaohk@home.swjtu.edu.cn

Abstract. Non-I.I.D. image classification is an important research topic for both academic and industrial communities. However, it is a very challenging task, as it violates the famous hypothesis of independent and identically distributed (I.I.D.) in conventional machine learning, and the classifier minimizing empirical errors on training images does not perform well on testing images. In this work, we propose a novel model called Contrastive Learning in Frequency Domain (CLFD) to learn invariant representations for Non-I.I.D. image classification. In CLFD, model learning includes two steps: contrastive learning in the frequency domain for pre-training, and image classification with fine-tuning. In the first pre-training step, anchor, positive and negative images are transformed by Discrete Cosine Transform (DCT) and then projected into vector space. This step is to obtain stable invariant features by minimizing the contrastive loss. In the step of image classification with fine-tuning, the features from ResNet are mapped into the label space by a simple fully connected layer, and the classification loss is utilized to fine-tune the parameters in the ResNet. Extensive experiments conducted on public NICO dataset demonstrate the effectiveness of the proposed CLFD, which outperforms the state-of-the-art methods.

Keywords: Non-I.I.D. image classification · Contrastive learning · Frequency domain learning

1 Introduction

With the recent development of deep learning, the task of image classification has been rapidly advanced [9,11]. CNN-based models show marvellous performance for this task, which learn a function on the labelled image training dataset and predict on the unseen test images. The effectiveness of this kind of approaches benefits from the famous hypothesis that the training data and testing data are independent and identically distributed (I.I.D.). However, this hypothesis is easily broken and the distribution shift is common in many practical applications [10].

© Springer Nature Switzerland AG 2021
J. Lokoč et al. (Eds.): MMM 2021, LNCS 12572, pp. 111–122, 2021.
https://doi.org/10.1007/978-3-030-67832-6_10

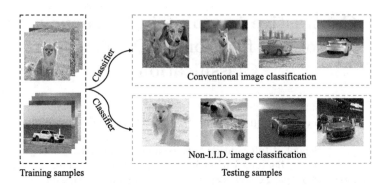

Fig. 1. Difference between conventional image classification and Non-I.I.D. image classification.

Therefore, research towards Non-I.I.D. image classification plays an important role in both academic and industrial communities.

In this paper, we focus on the task of Non-I.I.D. (Non-Independent and Identically Distributed) image classification, where we aim to learn a predictive model under the distribution shift between the training data and testing data. Specifically, our work is established upon the recently proposed NICO (Non-I.I.D. Image dataset with Contexts) dataset which is delicately designed for Non-I.I.D. image classification [10]. The difference between Non-I.I.D. image classification and conventional image classification is illustrated in Fig. 1. In the configuration of conventional image classification, training and testing images are with identical contexts for each class (e.g., dog in the context of grassland, car in the context of beach). In the task of our Non-I.I.D. image classification, the classifier is trained in some contexts, while tested in other unseen contexts.

Non-I.I.D. image classification is a very challenging and largely understudied problem. There is no unified effective framework for Non-I.I.D. classification in the statistical machine learning community and the classifier minimizing empirical errors on training images is not necessarily with minimal test error on testing images. Recently, some efforts are made to advance this topic. Typically, they try to discover the contribution degree of each image feature for the label to find the stable feature representations. Causality is integrated into the classifier to estimate the effect of every dimensional feature for the label by treating features as intervention variables and labels as outcome variables [15,16]. However, these methods require learning a set of sample weights for every batch of samples during training, which makes it time-consuming and takes up a lot of computing resources.

In this paper, we try to handle the Non-I.I.D. image classification from another aspect of invariant feature learning. Despite the distribution shift in our task, there exist some invariant features belonging to the objects of the class in both training and testing data. For example, for dogs, the invariant features include the eyes, tails, and hairs, etc. No matter what context dogs in, they should consist of these features. Contrastive Learning has been considered as an effective way to learn useful representations of images, showing the potential to learn the invariant features under different distributions [2,8]. Meanwhile, it has been proven that learning in the frequency domain can help to avoid information loss and occupier of excessive computing resources [6,20].

Based on the above ideas, in this paper, we propose a novel method, called Contrastive Learning in Frequency Domain (CLFD), for Non-I.I.D. image classification. We integrate the frequency domain learning into the framework of contrastive learning to learn invariant representations for images. Specifically, the whole learning process includes two steps: contrastive learning in the frequency domain for pre-training, and image classification with fine-tuning. In the first pre-training step, anchor, positive and negative images generated from data augmentations are transformed into the frequency domain by Discrete Cosine Transform (DCT), and then the feature maps are projected into vector space through ResNet and Multi-layer Perceptron (MLP) respectively. In the vector space, a contrastive loss is computed to train the parameters of ResNet and MLP. In the step of fine-tuning, the features from ResNet are mapped into label space by a simple fully connected (FC) layer, and the classification loss is used to fine-tune the parameters in ResNet.

The contribution of this paper can be summarized as follows:

- We propose a novel model Contrastive Learning in Frequency Domain (CLFD) combining the contrastive learning and frequency domain learning for Non-I.I.D. image classification.
- We conduct comprehensive experiments on the public NICO [10] dataset under different Non-I.I.D. settings to validate the effectiveness of our CLFD over existing state-of-the-art methods.
- We also prove that transforming images to the frequency domain can benefit the training of contrastive learning, and CLFD may be a potentially useful method for a wide range of applications, other than image classification.

2   Related Work

2.1   Non-I.I.D. Image Classification

Non-I.I.D. image classification is not widely studied although it is important for computer vision and multimedia. The main reason may be lacking a well-designed public dataset. To support related research, NICO is constructed and released [10]. Existing methods for Non-I.I.D. image classification are mainly based on causal inference motivated by the idea that the variables with causal effect on output should be stable under different distributions. Typically, a causally regularized learning algorithm is proposed to learn a set of sample weights which aims to de-correlate each dimension of the image feature, considering every dimension of the feature as a treated variable [15]. Furtherly, A ConvNet with batch balancing method is developed to exploit the CNN model for general Non-I.I.D. image classification [10]. However, the decomposition of image features into a single dimension may not be conducive to the model's

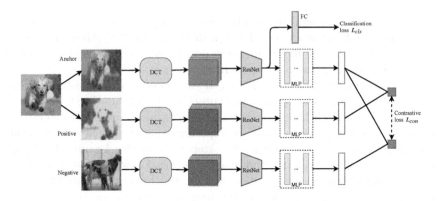

Fig. 2. The architecture of our proposed CLFD.

understanding of the image. Some features may need to be related in multiple dimensions. What's more, these methods treat each dimension of the feature equally. However, the importance is different from each other among different dimensional features to the classification task. Our method firstly prunes unnecessary features for image classification and learns stable features under different distributions through contrastive learning.

Intuitively, Non-I.I.D. image classification can be solved by transfer learning. However, we argue that the task of Non-I.I.D. image classification is slightly different from the tasks of both domain adaptation and domain generalization. In domain adaptation, the testing data need to be fed into training models to learn the invariant representations between training data and testing data [4,13], while the testing images are unseen during training in our Non-I.I.D. image classification task. Domain generalization is a field closely related to domain adaptation, which works for scenarios where the distribution of the target domain is unknown [5,12]. However, these models require the training data to be defined into multiple domains explicitly and we know which domain each sample belongs to, and this kind of configuration is not needed in our task.

2.2 Contrastive Learning

Contrastive learning, which is an unsupervised representation learning method, has obtained many breakthrough results in learning invariant representations. The basic idea is to maximize the mutual information between different views of the same sample by minimizing a contrastive loss, which was first proposed in [7]. A research hotspot in contrastive learning is the way to construct positive and negative samples [14,19]. Inspired by previous work, [2] explores the benefits of larger batch size and a nonlinear head in the network. Following the contrastive learning framework presented in [2], we extend the contrastive learning into the frequency domain.

2.3   Learning in the Frequency Domain

Recently, some methods to learn in the frequency domain for images are presented. [1,3,17] propose to do inference directly on compressed image representations such as Discrete Cosine Transform (DCT) [1,18]. [20] proposes a frequency-domain learning approach without much modification to the CNN network structure, achieving improvement in both performance and training efficiency. Based on the frequency-domain model, a learning-based channel selection method was also proposed to prune some unnecessary frequency components for inference, which significantly reduce computing consumption.

3   Proposed Method

In this section, we introduce our proposed Contrastive Learning in Frequency Domain (CLFD) model for Non-I.I.D. image classification. The architecture of our CLFD is illustrated in Fig. 2. The model learning includes contrastive learning in the frequency domain for pre-training and image classification with fine-tuning two steps. In the first pre-training step, anchor, positive and negative images are transformed by Discrete Cosine Transform (DCT) and then are projected into vector space through ResNet and Multi-layer Perceptron (MLP) respectively. This step is to train the ResNet (and MLP) and obtain the stable invariant features by maximizing the similarity between the anchor and positive sample while minimizing the similarity between the anchor and negative samples. In the step of image classification with fine-tuning, the features from ResNet are mapped into label space by a simple fully connected layer, and the classification loss is utilized to fine-tune the parameters in ResNet and FC.

3.1   Contrastive Learning in Frequency Domain for Pre-training

Data Pre-processing. Inspired by [2], each image is augmented randomly twice to obtain two augmented examples, which are considered as the anchor and positive samples respectively (they constitute a positive pair), and the augmented samples from other images in the same batch are regarded as negative samples (the anchor and negative samples constitute negative pairs). As a result, for a batch of size N, there are N positive pairs and $2N(N - 1)$ negative pairs. The data augmentation operations in our paper include ResizedCrop, HorizontalFlip, GaussianBlur, ColorJitter and Grayscale, with a probability of $0.5, 0.5, 0.8, 0.8, 0.2$ to be executed respectively.

Frequency Transformation. Following [20], the augmented data are transformed into the frequency domain to further improve the performance of the model. We firstly transfer the image from the RGB colour space into the YCbCr colour space. The data of Cb and Cr channels are compressed, for they are colour-related and less important than brightness information represented by the Y component. As a result, the training process is accelerated and can occupy less computing resources. Then each of the three Y, Cb, and Cr channel undergoes a DCT to obtain multiple sets of coefficients in the frequency domain, which is divided into 8×8 blocks. The blocks with the same frequency are grouped into one group to preserve the spatial relationship information, resulting in 192 channels. After these transforms, the image size becomes $64C \times H/8 \times W/8$ from $C \times H \times W$ ($C = 3, H = 112, W = 112$ in our experiments). However, not all of these channels are indispensable for our task, which means that we can prune the unnecessary ones to reduce computational complexity. Similar to [20], 24 channels are reserved for further training, while other channels are omitted without a negative impact on model performance. Finally, we obtain the feature maps with a size of $24 \times 14 \times 14$.

Contrastive Learning. Our model is built based on the classic resnet50 [9] without complicated modify. The first four layers are removed and the input size of the conv layer is changed to fit the input size of frequency-domain feature maps $\mathbf{x} \in \mathcal{R}^{24 \times 14 \times 14}$. After the projection of ResNet, A 2048-dimensional representation is obtained and then fed into an MLP layer, resulting in a 128-dimensional vector $\mathbf{z}$. Note that the parameters of both the ResNet and MLP for three branches of anchor, positive and negative samples are shared. The similarity of two samples is measured by the cosine similarity, which is defined as

$$sim(\mathbf{z}_i, \mathbf{z}_j) = \frac{\mathbf{z}_i \cdot \mathbf{z}_j}{max(||\mathbf{z}_i||_2 \cdot ||\mathbf{z}_j||_2, \epsilon)}, \tag{1}$$

where the ϵ is a real number with small values to avoid division by zero. Based on the cross-entropy loss, the contrastive loss of a sample pair $\mathbf{z}_i, \mathbf{z}_j$ is defined as:

$$\mathcal{L}_{con}(i, j) = -\log \frac{\exp(sim(\mathbf{z}_i, \mathbf{z}_j)/\tau)}{\sum_{k=1}^{2N}\{\exp(sim(\mathbf{z}_i, \mathbf{z}_k)/\tau)|k \neq i\}}, \tag{2}$$

where τ is the temperature parameter and set to 0.5 in our experiment. During contrastive training, each of the $2N$ samples will be regarded as an anchor to calculate the loss in Eq. 2 with all other $2N - 1$ samples. The model is optimized to minimize the pre-training loss:

$$\mathcal{L}_{pret} = \sum_{k=1}^{N} \mathcal{L}_{con}(2k - 1, 2k) + \mathcal{L}_{con}(2k, 2k - 1). \tag{3}$$

We argue that the stable invariant representations can be learned by the contrastive learning in the frequency domain in the pre-training step. The similarity of positive pairs is maximized while that of negative pairs decreases during the contrastive training. A positive pair (anchor and the positive sample) are generated from the same image by the data augmentation, and they can be considered as different views for the same image. Therefore, when the learned representations of the two views are similar, it means that the learned features are invariant with respect to the transformations in data augmentation. Also, DCT transforms the spatial domain into the orthogonal frequency domain, which is helpful for feature selection and invariant feature learning.

Algorithm 1: Contrastive Learning in Frequency Domain

Input: Training data $D_{train} = \{(\mathbf{x}_i, \mathbf{y}_i | i = 1, 2, \cdots, N)\}$.
Output: Parameters θ of ResNet and FC.

1 **for** *each batch* **do**
2   **for** *each image* **do**
3   Draw two random compositions of augmentations t, t';
4        $\tilde{\mathbf{x}}_{2k-1} = DCT(t(\mathbf{x}_k)), \tilde{\mathbf{x}}_{2k} = DCT(t'(\mathbf{x}_k))$;
5   **end**
6   Project feature maps into the vector space by ResNet and MLP;
7   Optimize the parameters of ResNet and MLP by minimizing $\mathcal{L}_{pret}$ acorrding Eq.3;
8 **end**
9 **for** *each batch* **do**
10    $\tilde{\mathbf{x}} = DCT(t(\mathbf{x}))$;
11   Project feature maps into the label space by ResNet and FC to get $\widehat{\mathbf{y}}$;
12   Optimize the parameters of ResNet and FC by minimizing $\mathcal{L}_{cls}$ acorrding Eq.4;
13 **end**
14 Output parameters of the ResNet and FC.

3.2 Image Classification with Fine-Tuning

In the fine-tuning step, the features extracted from ResNet are fed into an FC (fully connected) layer and softmax layer to compute the probabilities of each class. The cross-entropy loss is used to fine-tune the parameters of ResNet and FC:

$$\mathcal{L}_{cls} = -\sum_{n=1}^{N} \sum_{k=1}^{K} \mathbf{y}_{nk} \log \widehat{\mathbf{y}}_{nk}, \tag{4}$$

where $\widehat{\mathbf{y}}$ and $\mathbf{y}$ are the predicted probabilities and the ground truth label respectively. N denotes the batch size, and K is the number of classes.

The learning process of the proposed Contrastive Learning in Frequency Domain (CLFD) is summarized in Algorithm 1.

4 Experiment

In order to evaluate the efficiency of the proposed model, extensive experiments are conducted on the public NICO dataset [10], by comparing our proposed CLFD with existing state-of-the-art methods.

4.1 Datasets Description

The NICO dataset [10] is a public benchmark especially designed for Non-I.I.D. image classification task. It consists of two superclasses, namely *Animal* and *Vehicle*, and there are 10 classes in *Animal* and 9 classes in *Vehicle* respectively.

Table 1. The accuracy on testing datasets of two superclasses in the proportional bias setting, with fixing the dominant ratio of training data to 5:1.

Superclass	Animal					Vehicle				
Dominant ratio	1:5	1:1	2:1	3:1	4:1	1:5	1:1	2:1	3:1	4:1
CNN	36.42	37.85	39.38	39.63	40.41	50.13	52.19	51.73	51.66	49.22
CNBB [10]	39.86	41.41	43.75	43.53	46.42	57.64	53.82	54.07	54.78	58.09
Our full model	**48.07**	**49.08**	**49.60**	**50.07**	**51.74**	**63.53**	**61.64**	**61.84**	**61.70**	**63.46**
w/o CLR	43.27	44.43	46.00	47.34	48.82	59.47	59.09	58.55	58.44	59.60
w/o DCT	43.57	45.54	46.43	46.86	48.65	58.47	56.54	56.27	56.66	59.17

Table 2. The accuracy on testing datasets of two superclasses in the combined bias setting, with fixing the dominant ratio of testing data to 1:1.

Superclass	Animal					Vehicle				
Dominant ratio	1:1	2:1	3:1	4:1	5:1	1:1	2:1	3:1	4:1	5:1
CNN	37.74	35.44	35.34	35.24	35.94	52.16	51.12	51.33	55.89	56.37
CNBB [10]	38.46	40.20	34.82	33.73	32.67	58.01	58.40	57.69	57.23	55.77
Our full model	**41.24**	**41.42**	**40.55**	**38.50**	**37.58**	**62.53**	**59.32**	**60.04**	**60.75**	61.81
w/o CLR	40.88	40.86	39.48	38.12	37.03	57.74	57.10	57.29	59.39	**62.34**
w/o DCT	39.27	38.51	37.46	35.51	35.73	56.06	58.24	59.93	59.81	58.38

Different from the conventional datasets for image classification, NICO labels images with both the main concept and contexts, which enables it to provide various Non-I.I.D. settings. By adjusting the number of images of different contexts in the training and test set, different degrees of distribution shift can be flexibly controlled. The number of pictures contained in each context ranges from tens to hundreds, and there are 188 contexts and nearly 25,000 images in total.

4.2 Experimental Setup

Non-I.I.D. Settings. In this paper, we conduct the experiments on two super-classes of the NICO dataset with two Non-I.I.D. settings, namely *Proportional bias* and *Combined bias* respectively. **(1) *Proportional bias* setting.** In the setting of *Proportional bias*, all the contexts appear in both training and testing data, but with different proportion. One context is selected as the dominant context for each class, which means that the number of images with this context has the largest proportion. A dominant ratio η is defined as $\eta = \frac{N_{dominant}}{N_{minor}}$, where $N_{dominant}$ and N_{minor} denote the number of images with the dominant context and the average number of pictures with other contexts, respectively. As with the work [10], we fix the dominant ratio of training data to 5:1, and vary the dominant ratio of testing data from 1:5 to 4:1. **(2) *Combined bias* setting.** In the setting of *Combined bias*, the proportional bias and the compositional bias [10] are combined, where some contexts appearing in the testing data are new to training data. Again, as with the work [10], we randomly choose 7 contexts for training and the other 3 contexts for testing. In this setting, the η of testing data is fixed to 1:1, and the η of training data is adjusted from 1:1 to 5:1.

Baselines. In order to verify the effectiveness of contrastive pre-training and frequency domain transformation, we choose two kinds of models as baselines. **(1) CNN.** The ResNet with batch normalization is taken as the basic model, and images in the spatial domain are fed into the model. Only classification loss is computed to training the parameters in the network. **(2) CNBB** [10]. It treats each dimension of the feature in the image as a treated variable, while other dimensions as confounding factors. The basic idea is to learn a set of sample weights to make each dimension of the image feature decorrelated and evaluate the causal effect of each dimension of features on the output. For each batch of data, it first optimizes the sample weights by minimizing the confounder balancing loss and then calculate the weighted to optimize the model parameters. CNBB is also built based on the ResNet, which is the same as our models.

Ablation Study. We further provide the ablation study of CLFD to analyze the importance of the two proposed components: **(1) CLFD w/o CLR.** Based on CNN, this model is trained with data transformed into the frequency domain, but without contrastive learning for representations. **(2) CLFD w/o DCT.** The discrete cosine transform is removed from our full model, and the images are in the spatial domain. The model is pre-trained by contrastive learning before fine-tuning for the classification task.

Technical Details. For a fair comparison, all parameters and hardware for the four models are the same during the training. All the methods are implemented using Pytorch. The batch size during contrastive learning is 256, and the training loss is optimized using Adam optimizer with learning rate $lr = 1e{-}4$ in contrastive pre-training and $3e{-}4$ in classification fine-tuning respectively. We report the classification accuracy on the testing data for all methods, which is shown in Sect. 4.3.

4.3   Experimental Results

The experimental results in Table 1 are obtained in the *Proportional bias* setting. We can see that our proposed method achieves state-of-the-art performance in all configurations, which illustrates the effectiveness of our CLFD model. It is also shown that both the methods of CLFD w/o CLR and w/o DCT outperform the CNN and CNBB models, while worse than our full model, which illustrates that both frequency transform and contrastive learning are helpful for our Non-I.I.D. image classification.

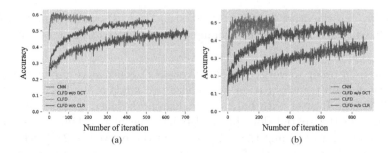

Fig. 3. Classification accuracy curves on (a) animal validation set under proportional bias setting and (b) vehicle validation set under combined bias setting.

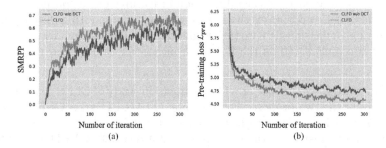

Fig. 4. The curves of (a) accuracy and (b) contrastive loss during the pre-training. SMRPP is short for Similarity Maximization Ratio of the Positive Pair, which is defined as the proportion of positive sample pairs that have the greatest similarity.

Table 2 reports the testing accuracy under the *Combined bias* setting. Our CLFD outperforms the other methods in almost all the settings. We can see that the results in the *Combined bias* setting are lower than that of the *proportional bias* setting, which indicates that the distribution shift of combined bias is harsher.

To illustrate the learning process, we plot the accuracy curve with the number of iterations on the validation dataset whose distribution is similar to testing data to avoid overfitting. we plot the accuracy on the validation set after every iteration on the training set during training. Figure 3 shows the curves of accuracy under two bias settings, which shows the effectiveness of the DCT and contrastive learning. We can see that both contrastive learning and DCT help to improve accuracy. What's more, the speed of training is significantly faster with contrastive pre-training, which makes the model learn a better representation of data.

To get insight into the CLFD for pre-training and the effect of the DCT, we also analyze related metrics during the pre-training progress. As the final image classification is not the optimization objective of contrastive learning during the pre-training, we need some metrics to measure the effectiveness of contrastive training. In this paper, we define a new metric named Similarity Maximization

Ratio of the Positive Pair (SMRPP) as the proportion of positive sample pairs that have the greatest similarity. Models with higher SMRPP can learn better representations to distinguish from different samples. Therefore, it is reasonable to take SMRPP as an indicator to measure the effectiveness of contrastive training. The pre-training loss $\mathcal{L}_{pret}$ obviously is another metric for pre-training. Also, to understand the contribution of DCT in the pre-training step, we plot the curves of SMRPP and $\mathcal{L}_{pret}$ against the number of iterations for our proposed models trained in the frequency (CLFD) and spatial domain (CLFD w/o DCT) respectively, which is shown in Fig. 4. It is obvious that the SMRPP and loss in the frequency domain are better than that in the spatial domain. We can conclude that transforming images to the frequency domain can benefit the training of contrastive learning, and CLFD may be a potentially useful method for a wide range of applications, other than image classification.

5 Conclusion

In this paper, we propose a novel Contrastive Learning in Frequency Domain (CLFD) model for the task of Non-I.I.D. image classification by integrating the contrastive learning and frequency domain learning to learn invariant representations. Extensive experiments show that our method helps to improve the performance of the Non-IID image classification. Our future works will explore disentangled representation learning with the framework of contrastive learning. Also, we will apply our method to some other related datasets to test its performance.

Acknowledgment. This work was supported in part by the National Natural Science Foundation of China under Grants 61802053 and 61772436, the Sichuan Science and Technology Program under Grant 2020YJ0037 and 2020YJ0207, the Foundation for Department of Transportation of Henan Province under Grant 2019J-2-2, and the Fundamental Research Funds for the Central Universities under Grant 2682019CX62.

References

1. Ahmed, N., Natarajan, T., Rao, K.R.: Discrete cosine transform. IEEE Trans. Comput. **C-23**(1), 90–93 (1974)
2. Chen, T., Kornblith, S., Norouzi, M., Hinton, G.: A simple framework for contrastive learning of visual representations. arXiv preprint arXiv:2002.05709 (2020)
3. Ehrlich, M., Davis, L.S.: Deep residual learning in the jpeg transform domain. In: Proceedings of the IEEE/CVF International Conference on Computer Vision (ICCV), October 2019
4. Ganin, Y., Lempitsky, V.: Unsupervised domain adaptation by backpropagation. In: Bach, F., Blei, D. (eds.) Proceedings of the 32nd International Conference on Machine Learning. Proceedings of Machine Learning Research, vol. 37, pp. 1180–1189. PMLR, Lille, France, 07–09 Jul 2015
5. Ghifary, M., Kleijn, W.B., Zhang, M., Balduzzi, D.: Domain generalization for object recognition with multi-task autoencoders. In: Proceedings of the IEEE International Conference on Computer Vision (ICCV), December 2015

6. Gueguen, L., Sergeev, A., Kadlec, B., Liu, R., Yosinski, J.: Faster neural networks straight from JPEG. In: Bengio, S., Wallach, H., Larochelle, H., Grauman, K., Cesa-Bianchi, N., Garnett, R. (eds.) Advances in Neural Information Processing Systems, vol. 31, pp. 3933–3944. Curran Associates, Inc. (2018)

7. Hadsell, R., Chopra, S., LeCun, Y.: Dimensionality reduction by learning an invariant mapping. In: 2006 IEEE Computer Society Conference on Computer Vision and Pattern Recognition (CVPR 2006), vol. 2, pp. 1735–1742 (2006)

8. He, K., Fan, H., Wu, Y., Xie, S., Girshick, R.: Momentum contrast for unsupervised visual representation learning. In: Proceedings of the IEEE/CVF Conference on Computer Vision and Pattern Recognition (CVPR), June 2020

9. He, K., Zhang, X., Ren, S., Sun, J.: Deep residual learning for image recognition. In: Proceedings of the IEEE Conference on Computer Vision and Pattern Recognition (CVPR), June 2016

10. He, Y., Shen, Z., Cui, P.: Towards non-I.I.D. image classification: a dataset and baselines. Pattern Recogn. **110**, 07383 (2020)

11. Krizhevsky, A., Sutskever, I., Hinton, G.E.: ImageNet classification with deep convolutional neural networks. In: Pereira, F., Burges, C.J.C., Bottou, L., Weinberger, K.Q. (eds.) Advances in Neural Information Processing Systems, vol. 25, pp. 1097–1105. Curran Associates, Inc. (2012)

12. Li, D., Yang, Y., Song, Y.Z., Hospedales, T.M.: Deeper, broader and artier domain generalization. In: Proceedings of the IEEE International Conference on Computer Vision (ICCV), October 2017

13. Long, M., Zhu, H., Wang, J., Jordan, M.I.: Deep transfer learning with joint adaptation networks. In: International conference on machine learning, pp. 2208–2217 (2017)

14. van den Oord, A., Li, Y., Vinyals, O.: Representation learning with contrastive predictive coding. arXiv, arXiv-1807 (2018)

15. Shen, Z., Cui, P., Kuang, K., Li, B., Chen, P.: Causally regularized learning with agnostic data selection bias. In: Proceedings of the 26th ACM International Conference on Multimedia, pp. 411–419, MM 2018. Association for Computing Machinery, New York (2018)

16. Shen, Z., Cui, P., Zhang, T., Kuang, K.: Stable learning via sample reweighting. In: AAAI, pp. 5692–5699 (2020)

17. Torfason, R., Mentzer, F., Ágústsson, E., Tschannen, M., Timofte, R., Gool, L.V.: Towards image understanding from deep compression without decoding. In: International Conference on Learning Representations (2018)

18. Watson, A.B.: Image compression using the discrete cosine transform. Math. J. **4**(1), 81 (1994)

19. Wu, Z., Xiong, Y., Yu, S.X., Lin, D.: Unsupervised feature learning via non-parametric instance discrimination. In: Proceedings of the IEEE Conference on Computer Vision and Pattern Recognition (CVPR), June 2018

20. Xu, K., Qin, M., Sun, F., Wang, Y., Chen, Y.K., Ren, F.: Learning in the frequency domain. In: Proceedings of the IEEE/CVF Conference on Computer Vision and Pattern Recognition (CVPR), June 2020

Group Activity Recognition by Exploiting Position Distribution and Appearance Relation

Duoxuan Pei, Annan Li$^{(\boxtimes)}$, and Yunhong Wang

The State Key Laboratory of Virtual Reality Technology and Systems,
Beihang University, Beijing 100191, China
{peidx,liannan,yhwang}@buaa.edu.cn

Abstract. Group activity recognition in multi-person scene videos is a challenging task. Most previous approaches fail to provide a practical solution to describe the person relations and distribution within the scene, which is important for understanding group activities. To this end, we propose a two-stream relation network to simultaneously deal with both position distribution information and appearance relation information. For the former, we build Position Distribution Network (PDN) to obtain the spatial position distribution. For the latter, we propose Appearance Relation Network (ARN) to explore the appearance relation of the individuals in scene. We fuse the two clues, i.e. position distribution and appearance relation, to form the global representation for group activity recognition. Extensive experiments on two widely-used group activity datasets demonstrate the effectiveness and superiority of the proposed framework.

Keywords: Group activity recognition · Position information · Graph Convolutional Network

1 Introduction

Group activity recognition has attracted increasing attention both in academia and industry over the past decades. It is widely applied in many sophisticated tasks, *i.e.* video surveillance, sports analysis, and event detection.

Previous approaches attempt to tackle down this problem by constructing hand-craft descriptors to model spatial-temporal information. Choi *et al.* [2] extract contextual description from the local area around the individuals to recognize group activities. This paradigm is further enhanced by introducing the local structural learning [3]. Lan *et al.* [12] propose a graphical model by considering interactions on the social role level, aggregating more details to model the scene-level features.

Recently, benefit from the strong discriminative capabilities of the CNN/RNN models, deep learning methods [4,6,9,17,19,21] have made great progress in group activity recognition task. Earlier approaches [6,9] are inclined

© Springer Nature Switzerland AG 2021
J. Lokoč et al. (Eds.): MMM 2021, LNCS 12572, pp. 123–135, 2021.
https://doi.org/10.1007/978-3-030-67832-6_11

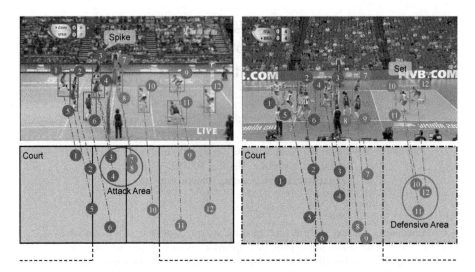

Fig. 1. Illustration of position distribution in the Volleyball dataset (upper row lists the original frames and the bottom row shows the corresponding players position in the court). Players are densely distributed in areas where the activities occur, and sparsely distributed in other areas.

to aggregate the individual-level features to scene-level ones by employing the basic pooling strategies, without considering the relations among the individuals. Later, some methods [17,22] alleviate this problem by excavating the relations among persons to better model the activities, suggesting a promising alternative and the advanced relation modeling techniques, such as Graph Convolutional Network (GCN). Despite the progresses of existing deep models, however, we found that most of them solely take the appearance information into consideration, and simply arrange the individual-level features in the aggregation stage. Such measures neglect an important clue, *i.e.* the position distribution of persons, which provides discriminative information for group activity understanding. As shown in Fig. 1, there exists specific relative position patterns among the typical group activities in volleyball games. For example, players are densely distributed in areas where attack or defensive activities occur, while players in other areas are sparsely distributed. Spike generally appears near the net while pass and digging activities often occur near the end line of the competition terrain. Based on the considerations above, it is desirable to model the position distribution and simultaneously comprise the appearance clue.

To this end, we propose a two-stream relation network which leverages both appearance and relative position information for group activity recognition. To be specific, we design the Position Distribution Network (PDN) to model the position distribution of the individuals within scene and design the Appearance Relation Network (ARN) to model the appearance relation of individuals. In PDN and ARN, we construct graphs for position and appearance nodes to represent the topological structures. Graph convolutions are then applied on the two types of graphs to abstract the position distribution and appearance information. These clues are combined to depict both the global perspective and the local details, thus reach a more discriminative representation of group activities.

Our contributions can be summarized as follows:

- We propose the Position Distribution Network (PDN) to model the position distribution of the individuals.
- We propose a two-stream relation network, which consists of PDN and ARN, capable of both modeling the distribution and appearance clues for group activity.
- Extensive experiments are carried out on two benchmarks, *i.e.,* Volleyball [9] and Collective Activity [2] dataset, on which our approach outperforms state-of-the-art and demonstrate the effectiveness.

2 Related Work

Current methods on action recognition can be roughly divided into traditional feature based ones and deep feature based ones.

Generally, traditional methods design hand-crafted features for modeling contextual information in group activities. Choi *et al.* [2,3] create a context descriptor from a person and his/her neighbors and extend the model with structure learning method. Lan *et al.* [12,13] propose an adaptive latent structure learning that represents hierarchical relationships ranging from lower person-level information. However, the above models are based on the traditional hand-crafted features, which suffer from representative limitations.

Then many deep learning based methods [1,5,8,9,19,21] have achieved significant results on group activity recognition. Ibrahim *et al.* [9] design a two-stage deep temporal model, establishes an LSTM model to represent the dynamic appearance of individuals and an LSTM model to aggregate human level information. Bagautdinov *et al.* [1] build a framework for joint detection and activity recognition of multiple people. Wang *et al.* [21] propose a recurrent context modeling scheme based on LSTM network to fuse person-level, group-level, and scene-level contexts for group activity recognition.

More recently, many works tend to modeling the relations of players, report new state-of-the-art performance. Qi *et al.* [17] propose a semantic graph to describe the spatial context of the whole scene and integrates temporal factors into the structural-RNN for temporal modeling. Ibrahim *et al.* [8] design a hierarchical network to extract and build connections between individuals. Kong *et al.* [11] propose a model to simultaneously deal with two issues, *i.e.* attending to key persons and modeling the context, via a hierarchical attention and context modeling framework and obtain promising performance. Wu *et al.* [22] create an actor relation graph convolutional network to capture the appearance and position relation between actors, showing the effectiveness of Graph Convolutional Network (GCN) [10,16].

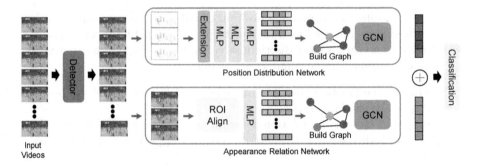

Fig. 2. Overview of our framework. Given a sequence of sampled video frames, we first generate bounding boxes for players via a pre-trained detector. The Position Distribution Network takes the boxes as input and explores the spatial position distribution of players. Based on the player image regions, the Appearance Relation Network is responsible for capturing their appearance relations within the scene. We both build graphs using position/appearance features, and employ graph convolution to abstract the two kinds of clues. The outputs of the networks are then fused to produce the group-level features for the final group activity classification, where $\oplus$ indicates the concatenation operation.

3   Method

This paper aims at recognizing group activities by exploiting the position and appearance clues. For this purpose, we build Position Distribution Network (PDN) and Appearance Relation Network (ARN) to explore the spatial position distribution and appearance relation of players within the scene. In the following, we first present an overview of our framework and then introduce the PDN, ARN respectively.

3.1   Framework

Figure 2 shows the overview of our framework. Given a sampled video sequence, we first generate bounding boxes for players via a pre-trained Faster-RCNN detector [18]. Afterwards, our approach takes two key phrases for modeling the position distribution and appearance relation.

- **Position Distribution Modeling.** We create the PDN to model the spatial position distribution of players. As the bounding boxes of the individuals only contain low-level relations (only 4-dimensional), we design an extension block that contains several Multi-Layer Perceptron (MLP) to excavate richer position features. In PDN, multiple graphs are built to represent the player position topological structure. We then use the Graph Convolutional Networks (GCN) to investigate the position distribution.
- **Appearance Relation Modeling.** We build the ARN to explore the appearance relations information. RoIAlign [7] is adopted to extract the

player appearance features, which are used to construct graphs to capture relation information among players. Then GCN is applied on the graphs to generate appearance relation features.

The output of PDN and ARN, *i.e.* position distribution and appearance relation, are fused to form the group-level feature. We use the softmax classification layer to make the final group activity classification.

3.2   Position Distribution Network

Position Feature Extension. As mentioned above, it is an intuitive way to directly take 4-dimensional bounding boxes for the relative position modeling. But such low-level clues can not be adopted for the position modeling directly since they have a certain gap from the real world information. Instead, we employ a position extension block which contains a multi-layer perceptron for mapping these low-level clues to high-level representations. Benefit from its powerfully mapping ability, we are able to mine more effective position information.

In a sporting scene, the scale of a player implies the depth clue. As Fig. 3 shows, when a player locates closer from the camera, the scale is larger, and vice versa. As we know, it is not straightforward to map the image coordinates to real world based on single frame, and such a prior knowledge could bring better performance. We then exploit the scales to alleviate the gap between two coordinates. Moreover, in the match, players usually perform different actions, incurring frequent shape variation. Apart from that the image region sequence could represent the actions, modeling the ratio slope variation is lightweight and also discriminative. For example, as shown in Fig. 3, a *blocking* sample with ratio slope of bounding box is 3.7 and a *digging* sample with ratio slope of bounding box is 0.7 in Volleyball dataset. Based on the aforementioned considerations, we design extension layer that extend the original bounding box from four-dimensional to nine-dimensional, as Eq. (1) shows, including the coordinates of center point, the length, width and aspect ratio and the slope of bounding box.

$$\mathbf{F_{ex}} = \{(b_i, \frac{x_{i1} + x_{i2}}{2}, \frac{y_{i1} + y_{i2}}{2}, |x_{i1} - x_{i2}|, |y_{i1} - y_{i2}|, |\frac{y_{i1} - y_{i2}}{x_{i1} - x_{i2}}|) \\ |i = 1, 2, \cdots, N\} \quad (1)$$

where $b_i = (x_{i1}, y_{i1}, x_{i2}, y_{i2})$ refers to the bounding box, N is the bounding box number in one frame.

To improve the representation ability, after the position extension, we also use function $f_{em}(\cdot)$ to transform extended features $\mathbf{F_{ex}}$ to an embedded space $\mathbf{F_{em}}$. As shown in Fig. 2, the function $f_{em}(\cdot)$ consists of several multilayer perceptrons (MLPs), responsible for better approximating to the real positions in the court.

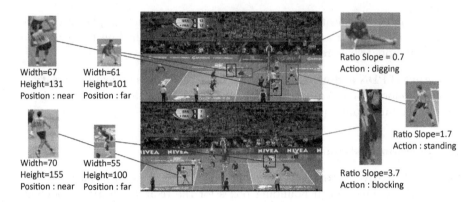

Fig. 3. Illustration of scale and shape changes of players in the scene.

Building Position Graph. In PDN, we build graphs based on position features to explicitly model spatial position distribution relations. The graph consists of nodes and edges, while the former can be regarded as input and the latter can be represented by a matrix. Here, the nodes are embedding position features $\mathbf{F_{em}} = \{a_i | i = 1, \cdots, N\}$, where N is number of bounding boxes in one frame and a_i denotes the i-th player position feature. We construct the matrix $\mathbf{G} \in \mathbb{R}^{N \times N}$ to represent the graph topology, where the value $\mathbf{G}_{i,j}$ indicates the distribution relation of node j and i. In our work, we employ the following function to compute relation value

$$\mathbf{G}_{i,j} = \frac{f_{dp}(a_i, a_j)}{\sum_{j=1}^{N} f_{dp}(a_i, a_j)}, \tag{2}$$

where $f_{dp}(a_i, a_j)$ denotes the position relation of i-th and j-th feature a_i and a_j, which denotes the features b_i and b_j after extension and embedding. We then discuss different forms of relation computing.

Dot-Product: The dot-product operation is an effective way to estimate the relation between two features. Intuitively, players who are close to each other have higher similarity in position, and it is significant for capturing the spatial player distribution when improving the relation extent of local scope. The similarity is computed as

$$f_{dp}(a_i, a_j) = \frac{(a_i)^{\mathbf{T}} a_j}{\sqrt{d}}, \tag{3}$$

where $\sqrt{d}$ is the dimension of embedding features, and a_i denotes the features b_i after extension and embedding.

Distance Encoding: Compared to dot-product, the distance is a more intuitive way to represent the relation of two positions. Here we consider two distance metrics, depicted as

$$f_{dp}(a_i, a_j) = \frac{1}{\mathbf{W} f_{dis}(a_i, a_j) + \mathbf{bias}}, \tag{4}$$

where $f_{dis}(\cdot)$ is a distance function *i.e. Euclidean* and cosine distance. We then transform the result to a scalar with weight $\mathbf{W}$ and bias $\mathbf{bias}$, followed by a reciprocal function.

Graph Convolution on Graphs. Based on the graphs, we can perform position distribution information modeling. Inspired by [10,15], we use Graph Convolutional Network (GCN), which takes graphs as input, recursively update the inner parameters, and output the high level position distribution features for group activity recognition. The output $\mathbf{F_{out}}$ of PDN can be calculated as follows:

$$\mathbf{F_{out}} = \mathbf{G} f_{em}(\mathbf{F_{ex}}) \mathbf{W_{graph}}, \tag{5}$$

where $\mathbf{G} \in \mathbb{R}^{N \times N}$ denotes the matrix representation of the graph, $\mathbf{F_{ex}} \in \mathbb{R}^{N \times d}$ is the extended bounding box feature, $\mathbf{W_{graph}} \in \mathbb{R}^{d_e \times d_o}$ is a learnable weight matrix in GCN.

3.3   Appearance Relation Network

As depicted in Sect. 1, many studies emphasis the importance of appearance relation modeling. In our work, we also design a relation network, namely ARN, that make use of appearance information and provide complementarity to PDN.

We first extract appearance feature for each player, which serve as the input of ARN. Specifically, we adopts Inception-v3 [20] to extract a multi-scale feature map for each frame. Then we apply RoIAlign [7] to extract the features for each individual bounding box from the frame feature map. After that, a linear layer transform the aligned features to embedding space.

Upon these appearance features, we build appearance relation graphs, where each node denotes appearance features for each player. We use the same relation computing methods in PDN to construct the edges. Finally, we apply the GCN to conduct appearance features reasoning based on the graphs. The output of ARN carries the high level appearance relation features for group activity recognition.

The output of PDN and ARN, *i.e.* the position distribution and the appearance relation features are combined to form the group-level representation. We use the softmax classification layer to make the final group activity classification. The whole framework can be trained in an end-to-end manner with back propagation and standard cross entropy loss.

4   Experiments

In order to validate the two-stream relation network, we conduct extensive experiments on the Volleyball [9] and the Collective Activity datasets. The datasets, settings and results are described in the subsequent.

4.1 Datasets and Settings

Datasets: The Volleyball dataset [9] is composed of 4,830 clips gathered from 55 volleyball games, with 3,493 training clips and 1,337 for testing. Each clip is labeled with one of 8 group activity annotations (*right set, right spike, right pass, right win point, left set, left spike, left pass* and *left win point*). Only the middle frame of each clip is annotated with the bounding boxes as well as the individual actions from nine personal action annotations (*waiting, setting, digging, failing, spiking, blocking, jumping, moving* and *standing*). Following [17], we used frames from 2/3 of the video sequences for training, and the remaining for testing.

The Collective Activity dataset [2] contains 44 short video sequences from five group activities (*crossing, waiting, queueing, walking* and *talking*) and six individual actions (*N.A., crossing, waiting, queueing, walking* and *talking*). The group activity annotation for each frame is defined as the activity in which most people participate. We adopt the same experimental setting as [11].

Settings: We employ Faster R-CNN as the detector for the our two-stream relation network. The positions of player will be further encoded to a D_V-dim vector for Volleyball dataset and embedding feature D_A-dim vector for Group Activity dataset by a multi layer sub-network. Because the position information of Group Activity dataset is more complex, we set D_V to 64 and D_A to 128 which are obtained by experiment. The graph is then built based on the position vectors. The Inception-v3 [20] is utilized as the backbone of the proposed framework. Following previous literature like [22], we take three frames for training and nine for test in each clip. The implementation is based on PyTorch.

For the Volleyball dataset, we train the network for 300 epochs with the bach size at 40 and the learning rate annealing from 0.001 to 0.00001. For the Collective Activity dataset, the model is trained for 150 epochs and the batch size is set at 16. The learning rate of is annealing from 0.001 to 0.00001.

Table 1. Quantitative performance on Volleyball dataset.

Methods	Backbone	Accuracy
HDTM [9]	AlexNet	81.9%
CERN [19]	VGG16	83.3%
stagNet [17]	VGG16	87.6%
HRN [8]	VGG19	89.5%
SSU [1]	Inception v3	86.2%
ARG [22]	Inception v3	91.5%
Ours	Inception v3	**92.2%**

4.2   Comparison to the State-of-the-Art

We compare the proposed two-stream relation network with the state-of-the-art on both two benchmarks. HDTM [9], CERN [19], stagNet [17], HRN [8], SSU [1] and ARG [22] are taken as the counterparts.

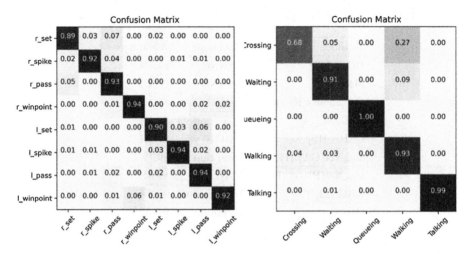

Fig. 4. Volleyball dataset confusion matrix (left) and Collective dataset confusion matrix (right) for group activity recognition.

The accuracies of different methods on Volleyball dataset are summarized in Table 1. It can be observed that the proposed method achieves the best score, and is superior to HDTM, CERN, stagNet and HRN with the smaller backbone. (*i.e.* Inception v3 vs. VGG-16). When using the same backbone, our approach still performs better than the other attempts. The performance of ARG [22] is similar to ours when employing the same backbone. Benefiting from the proposed combination of position distribution and appearance relation information, our approach achieves better description of the spatial information, the performance is then significantly boosted from 91.5% to 92.2%.

Table 2 shows the comparisons on Collective Activity dataset, we can see that our method still reaches the best scores among the counterparts, demonstrating the strong generalization ability of the proposed framework. The improvements to ARG is relatively smaller on Collective Activity dataset since there are uncertain number of people in each group activity on the Collective Activity dataset. Both the results on these benchmarks prove that the effectiveness of our method in modeling the persons' relations and distributions. In addition, we draw the confusion matrices based on our approach in Fig. 4, where promising recognition accuracies (≥90%) are obtained in terms of the majority of group activities in Volleyball and nearly 100% recognized for the queue, talking in Collective Activity dataset.

4.3 Ablation Studies

In this subsection, we show extensive ablation studies on the Volleyball dataset to investigate the impact of numbers of the graphs N_g, dimensions of the embedding feature D_V and various edges definitions E.

Table 2. Quantitative performance on Collective Activity dataset.

Methods	Backbone	Accuracy
HDTM [9]	AlexNet	81.5%
SIM [4]	AlexNet	81.2%
Cardinality Kernel [6]	None	83.4%
SBGAR [14]	Inception-v3	86.1%
CERN [19]	VGG16 v3	87.2%
stagNet(GT) [17]	Inception v3	89.1%
stagNet(PRO) [17]	VGG16	87.9%
ARG [22]	Inception v3	90.2%
Ours	Inception v3	**90.33%**

Multiple Graphs: We carefully tune the number of the relative position graphs N_g used in both two steams on Volleyball dataset. The results are illustrated in Table 3. As shown in Table 3, the accuracy will be slightly boosted when N_g increases, indicating more graphs will improve the discriminative ability of the model. But when N_g is set larger than 16, the performance drops from 92.22% to 92%, it may caused by the over-fitting. We set N_g at 16 for the PDN in our experiments.

Table 3. Comparison of different number of graphs on Volleyball dataset.

Number	1	4	8	16	32
Accuracy	91.85%	92.07%	92.00%	**92.22%**	92.00%

Embedding Feature Dimension: We tune the value of the dimension of the embedded feature D_V experimentally in Table 4. We can find that when D_V is set at 64, the model reaches the best score. It incurs the increase in error rate. We set D_V at 64 in our model. According to these results, we set D_V at 64 in our models.

Table 4. Comparison of different dimension of embedding feature on Volleyball dataset.

Dimension	9	16	32	64	128	256
Accuracy	91.55%	92.07%	92.15%	**92.22%**	91.55%	91.92%

Comparison of Various Edges: There are various types of the distance metric in the computation of GCN, (*i.e.* Euclidean Distance, Cosine Distance and Dot Product). The results are stated in Table 5.

Table 5. Comparison of different edges on Volleyball dataset.

Edges	Accuracy
Euclidean Distance	91.32%
Cosin Distance	91.25%
Dot-Product	**92.22%**

From Table 5, we can find that our model reaches the best performance when the metric is set as dot product, almost 1% higher than the other ones. It may indicate that the dot-product can better encoding the spatial information in these videos.

5   Conclusion

This paper present a two-stream relation network for modeling persons' relation and position distribution information in group activities. To take advantages of two clues, we build PDN and ARN respectively. By combining them, our framework can better explore the global and local details in the group. The extensive experiment results on Volleyball and Collective Activity dataset prove the effectiveness and generalization ability.

Acknowledgments. This work was supported by the Foundation for Innovative Research Groups through the National Natural Science Foundation of China (Grant No. 61421003) and CCF-Tencent Rhino-Bird Research Fund.

References

1. Bagautdinov, T., Alahi, A., Fleuret, F., Fua, P., Savarese, S.: Social scene understanding: end-to-end multi-person action localization and collective activity recognition. In: Proceedings of the IEEE conference on computer vision and pattern recognition, pp. 4315–4324 (2017)

2. Choi, W., Shahid, K., Savarese, S.: What are they doing?: Collective activity classification using spatio-temporal relationship among people. In: 2009 IEEE 12th International Conference on Computer Vision Workshops, ICCV Workshops, pp. 1282–1289. IEEE (2009)
3. Choi, W., Shahid, K., Savarese, S.: Learning context for collective activity recognition. In: IEEE Conference on Computer Vision and Pattern Recognition, pp. 3273–3280 (2011)
4. Deng, Z., Vahdat, A., Hu, H., Mori, G.: Structure inference machines: recurrent neural networks for analyzing relations in group activity recognition. In: Proceedings of the IEEE Conference on Computer Vision and Pattern Recognition, pp. 4772–4781 (2016)
5. Direkoğlu, C., O'Connor, N.E.: Temporal segmentation and recognition of team activities in sports. Mach. Vis. Appl. **29**(5), 891–913 (2018). https://doi.org/10.1007/s00138-018-0944-9
6. Hajimirsadeghi, H., Yan, W., Vahdat, A., Mori, G.: Visual recognition by counting instances: a multi-instance cardinality potential kernel. In: Proceedings of the IEEE Conference on Computer Vision and Pattern Recognition, pp. 2596–2605 (2015)
7. He, K., Gkioxari, G., Dollár, P., Girshick, R.B.: Mask R-CNN. In: IEEE International Conference on Computer Vision, pp. 2980–2988 (2017)
8. Ibrahim, M.S., Mori, G.: Hierarchical relational networks for group activity recognition and retrieval. In: European Conference on Computer Vision, pp. 742–758 (2018)
9. Ibrahim, M.S., Muralidharan, S., Deng, Z., Vahdat, A., Mori, G.: A hierarchical deep temporal model for group activity recognition. In: Proceedings of the IEEE Conference on Computer Vision and Pattern Recognition, pp. 1971–1980 (2016)
10. Kipf, T.N., Welling, M.: Semi-supervised classification with graph convolutional networks. In: International Conference on Learning Representations (2017)
11. Kong, L., Qin, J., Huang, D., Wang, Y., Gool, L.V.: Hierarchical attention and context modeling for group activity recognition. In: IEEE International Conference on Acoustics, Speech and Signal Processing, pp. 1328–1332 (2018)
12. Lan, T., Sigal, L., Mori, G.: Social roles in hierarchical models for human activity recognition. In: IEEE Conference on Computer Vision and Pattern Recognition, pp. 1354–1361 (2012)
13. Lan, T., Wang, Y., Yang, W., Robinovitch, S.N., Mori, G.: Discriminative latent models for recognizing contextual group activities. IEEE Trans. Pattern Anal. Mach. Intell. **34**(8), 1549–1562 (2012)
14. Li, X., Choo Chuah, M.: SBGAR: semantics based group activity recognition. In: Proceedings of the IEEE International Conference on Computer Vision, pp. 2876–2885 (2017)
15. Liu, L., Zhou, T., Long, G., Jiang, J., Yao, L., Zhang, C.: Prototype propagation networks (PPN) for weakly-supervised few-shot learning on category graph. In: International Joint Conferences on Artificial Intelligence (IJCAI) (2019)
16. Liu, L., Zhou, T., Long, G., Jiang, J., Zhang, C.: Learning to propagate for graph meta-learning. In: Neural Information Processing Systems (NeurIPS) (2019)
17. Qi, M., Qin, J., Li, A., Wang, Y., Luo, J., Van Gool, L.: stagNet: an attentive semantic RNN for group activity recognition. In: Proceedings of the European Conference on Computer Vision (ECCV), pp. 101–117 (2018)
18. Ren, S., He, K., Girshick, R., Sun, J.: Faster R-CNN: towards real-time object detection with region proposal networks. In: Advances in Neural Information Processing Systems, pp. 91–99 (2015)

19. Shu, T., Todorovic, S., Zhu, S.: CERN: confidence-energy recurrent network for group activity recognition. In: IEEE Conference on Computer Vision and Pattern Recognition, pp. 4255–4263 (2017)
20. Szegedy, C., Vanhoucke, V., Ioffe, S., Shlens, J., Wojna, Z.: Rethinking the inception architecture for computer vision. In: IEEE Conference on Computer Vision and Pattern Recognition, pp. 2818–2826 (2016)
21. Wang, M., Ni, B., Yang, X.: Recurrent modeling of interaction context for collective activity recognition. In: IEEE Conference on Computer Vision and Pattern Recognition, pp. 7408–7416 (2017)
22. Wu, J., Wang, L., Wang, L., Guo, J., Wu, G.: Learning actor relation graphs for group activity recognition. In: IEEE Conference on Computer Vision and Pattern Recognition, pp. 9964–9974 (2019)

Multi-branch and Multi-scale Attention Learning for Fine-Grained Visual Categorization

Fan Zhang$^{(\boxtimes)}$ 🆔, Meng Li 🆔, Guisheng Zhai 🆔, and Yizhao Liu 🆔

School of MEIE, China University of Mining and Technology (Beijing), Beijing, China
leozhang1995@foxmail.com

Abstract. ImageNet Large Scale Visual Recognition Challenge (ILSVRC) is one of the most authoritative academic competitions in the field of Computer Vision (CV) in recent years. But applying ILSVRC's annual champion directly to fine-grained visual categorization (FGVC) tasks does not achieve good performance. To FGVC tasks, the small inter-class variations and the large intra-class variations make it a challenging problem. Our attention object location module (AOLM) can predict the position of the object and attention part proposal module (APPM) can propose informative part regions without the need of bounding-box or part annotations. The obtained object images not only contain almost the entire structure of the object, but also contains more details, part images have many different scales and more fine-grained features, and the raw images contain the complete object. The three kinds of training images are supervised by our multi-branch network. Therefore, our multi-branch and multi-scale learning network(MMAL-Net) has good classification ability and robustness for images of different scales. Our approach can be trained end-to-end, while provides short inference time. Through the comprehensive experiments demonstrate that our approach can achieves state-of-the-art results on CUB-200-2011, FGVC-Aircraft and Stanford Cars datasets. Our code will be available at https://github.com/ZF1044404254/MMAL-Net.

Keywords: FGVC · Classification · Attention · Location · Scale

1 Introduction

How to tell a dog's breed? This is a frequently asked question because dogs have similar characteristics. The FGVC direction of CV research focuses on such issues, and it is also called sub-category recognition. In recent years, it is a very popular research topic in CV, pattern recognition and other fields. It's purpose is to make a more detailed sub-class division for coarse-grained large categories (e.g. classifying bird species [1], aircraft models [2], car models [3], etc.).

Many papers [4–7] have shown that the key to fine-grained visual categorization tasks lies in developing effective methods to accurately identify informative

J. Lokoč et al. (Eds.): MMM 2021, LNCS 12572, pp. 136–147, 2021.
https://doi.org/10.1007/978-3-030-67832-6_12

regions in an image. They leverage the extra annotations of bounding box and part annotations to localize significant regions. However, obtaining such dense annotations of bounding box and part annotations is labor-intensive, which limits both scalability and practicality of real-world fine-grained applications. Other methods [8–11] use an unsupervised learning scheme to localize informative regions. They eliminate the need for the expensive annotations, but how to focus on the right areas and use them is still worth investigating.

An overview of our MMAL-Net is shown in Fig. 1. Our method has three branches in training phase, whose raw branch mainly studies the overall characteristics of the object, and AOLM needs to obtain the object's bounding box information with the help of the feature maps of the raw image from this branch. As the input of object branch, the finer scale of object image is very helpful for classification, because it contains the structural features of the target as well as the fine-grained features. Then, APPM proposes several part regions with the most discrimency and less redundancy according to the feature maps of object image. The part branch sends the part image clipped from the object image to the network for training. It enables the network to learn fine-grained features of different parts in different scales. Unlike RA-CNN [12], the parameters of CNN and FC in our three branches are shared. Therefore, through the common learning process of the three branches, the trained model has a good classification ability for different scales and parts of object. In the testing phase, RA-CNN [12] and NTS-Net [10] need to calculate the feature vectors of the multiple part region images and then concat these vectors for classification. But the best classification performance is simply obtained by the result of object branch in our approach. So our approach can reduce some calculations and inference time while achieving high accuracy.

Our main contributions can be summarized as follows:

- Our multi-branch network can be trained end-to-end and learn object's discriminative regions for recognition effectively.
- The AOLM does not increase the number of parameters, so we do not need to train a proposal network like RA-CNN [12]. The accuracy of object localization is achieved by only using category labels.
- We present an attention part proposal method(APPM) without the need of part annotations. It can select multiple ordered discriminative part images, so that the model can effectively learn different scales parts's fine-grained features.
- State-of-the-art performances are reported on three standard benchmark datasets, where our method stable outperforms the state-of-the-art methods and baselines.

2 Related Works

In the past few years, the accuracy of benchmark on open datasets has been improved based on deep learning and fine-grained classification methods. They can be classified as follows: 1) By end-to-end feature encoding; 2) By localization-classification subnetworks.

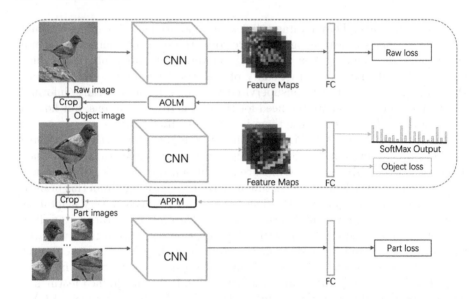

Fig. 1. The overview of our proposed MMAL-Net in the training phase, The red branch is raw branch, the orange branch is object branch, and the blue branch is part branch. In the dotted green box is the network structure for the test phase. The CNN (Convolutional Neural Networks) and FC (Fully Connection) layer of the same color represent parameter sharing. Our multi-branch all use cross entropy loss as the classification loss.

2.1 By End-to-End Feature Encoding

This kind of method directly learns a more discriminative feature representation by developing powerful deep models for fine-grained recognition. The most representative method among them is Bilinear-CNN [4], which represents an image as a pooled outer product of features derived from two bilinear models, and thus encodes higher order statistics of convolutional activations to enhance the mid-level learning capability. Thanks to its high model capacity, it achieves clear performance improvement on a wide range of visual tasks. However, the high dimensionality of bilinear features still limits its further generalization. In order to solve this problem, [13,14] try to aggregate low-dimensional embeddings by applying tensor sketching. They can reduce the dimensionality of bilinear features and achieve comparable or higher classification accuracy.

2.2 By Localization-Classification Subnetworks

This kind of method trains a localization subnetwork with supervised or weakly supervised to locate key part regions. Then the classification subnetwork uses the information of fine-grained regions captured by the localization subnetwork to further enhance its classification capability. Earlier works [5–7] belong to full supervision method depend on more than image-level annotations to locate semantic key parts. [7] trained a region proposal network to generate proposals of informative image parts and concatenate multiple part-level features as a whole image representation toward final fine-grained recognition. However, maintaining such dense part annotations increases additional location labeling cost. Therefore, [8–11] take advantage of attention mechanisms to avoid this problem. There is no need of bounding box annotations and part annotations except image-level annotation.

3 Method

3.1 Attention Object Location Module (AOLM)

This method was inspired by SCDA [15]. SCDA uses a pre-trained model to extract image features for fine-grained image retrieval tasks. We improve it's positioning performance as much as possible through some measures. At the first, we describe the process of generating object location coordinates by processing the CNNs feature map as the Fig. 2 illustrated.

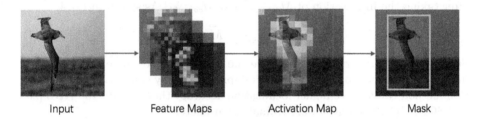

| Input | Feature Maps | Activation Map | Mask |

Fig. 2. The pipeline of the AOLM, we first get an activation map by aggregating the feature maps in the channel dimension, then obtain a bounding box according to activation map.

We use $F \in R^{C \times H \times W}$ to represent feature maps with C channels and spatial size $H \times W$ output from the last convolutional layer of an input image X and f_i is the i-th feature map of the corresponding channel. As shown in Eq. 1,

$$A = \sum_{i=0}^{C-1} f_i \tag{1}$$

activation map A can be obtained by aggregating the feature maps F. We can visualize where the deep neural networks focus on for recognition simply and locate the object regions accurately from A. As shown in Eq. 2, $\bar{a}$ is the mean value of A.

$$\bar{a} = \frac{\sum_{x=0}^{W-1} \sum_{y=0}^{H-1} A(x,y)}{H \times W} \tag{2}$$

$\bar{a}$ is used as the threshold to determine whether the element at that position in A is a part of object, and (x, y) is a particular position in a $H \times W$ activation map. Then we initially obtained a coarse mask map $\widetilde{M}_{conv\_5c}$ from the last convolutional layer $Conv\_5c$ of ResNet-50 [16] according to Eq. 3.

$$\widetilde{M}_{(x,y)} = \begin{cases} 1 & \text{if } A_{(x,y)} > \bar{a} \\ 0 & \text{otherwise} \end{cases} \tag{3}$$

On the basis of the experimental results, we find that the object is often in the largest connected component of $\widetilde{M}_{conv\_5c}$, so the smallest bounding box containing the largest connected area is used as the result of our object location. SCDA [15] uses a VGG16 [17] pre-trained on ImageNet as backbone network can achieve better position accuracy, but ResNet-50 [16] pre-trained on ImageNet does not reach a similar accuracy rate and dropped significantly in our experiments. So we use the training set to continue train ResNet-50 for improving object location accuracy and experiments in Subsect. 4.5 verify the effectiveness of this approach. Then, inspired by [15] and [18] the performance of their methods all benefit from the ensemble of Multiple layers. So we get the activation map of the output of $Conv\_5b$ according to Eq. 1, which is one block in front of $Conv\_5c$. Then we can get $\widetilde{M}_{conv\_5b}$ according to Eq. 3, and finally we can get a more accurate mask M after taking the intersection of $\widetilde{M}_{conv\_5c}$ and $\widetilde{M}_{conv\_5b}$. As shown in Eq. 4.

$$M = \widetilde{M}_{conv\_5c} \cap \widetilde{M}_{conv\_5b} \tag{4}$$

Subsequent experimental results prove the effectiveness of these approaches to improve object location accuracy. This improved weakly supervised object location method can achieve higher localization accuracy than ACOL [19], ADL [20] and SCDA [15], without adding trainable parameters.

3.2   Attention Part Proposal Module(APPM)

Although AOLM can achieve higher localization accuracy, but there are some positioning results are part of the object. We improve the robustness of the model to this situation through APPM and part branch. It will be demonstrated in the next section. By observing the activation map A, we find that the area with high activation value of the activation map are often the area where the key part are located, such as the head area in the example. Using the idea of sliding window in object detection to find the windows with information as part images. Moreover, we implemented the traditional sliding window approach with full convolutional network to reduce the amount of calculation, just like Overfeat [21] gets the feature map of different windows from the feature map output from the previous branch. Then we aggregate each window's activation map A_w in the channel dimension and get its activation mean value $\bar{a}_w$ according to Eq. 5,

$$\bar{a}_w = \frac{\sum_{x=0}^{W_w-1} \sum_{y=0}^{H_w-1} A_w(x,y)}{H_w \times W_w} \tag{5}$$

H_w, W_w are the height and width of a window's feature map. We sort by the $\bar{a}_w$ value of all windows. The larger the $\bar{a}_w$ is, the larger the informativeness of this part region is, as shown in Fig. 3. However, we cannot directly select the first few windows, because they are often adjacent to the largest $\bar{a}_w$ windows and contain approximate the same part, but we hope to select as many different parts as possible. In order to reduce region redundancy, we adopt non-maximum suppression (NMS) to select a fixed number of windows as part images with different scales. By visualizing the output of this module in Fig. 4, it can be seen that this method proposed some ordered, different importance degree part regions.

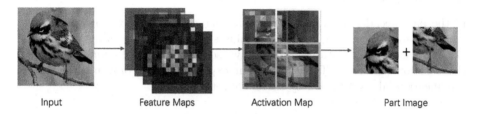

Input   Feature Maps   Activation Map   Part Image

Fig. 3. The simple pipeline of the APPM. We use red, orange, yellow, green colors to indicate the order of windows' $\bar{a}_w$. (Color figure online)

3.3 Architecture of MMAL-Net

In order to make the model fully and effectively learn the images obtained through AOLM and APPM. During the training phase, we construct a three branches network structure consisting of raw branch, object branch, and part branch, as shown in Fig. 1. The three branches share a CNN for feature extraction and a FC layer for classification. Our three branches all use cross entropy loss as the classification loss. As shown in Eq. 6, 7, and 8, respectively.

$$L_{raw} = -\log(P_r(c)) \tag{6}$$

$$L_{object} = -\log(P_o(c)) \tag{7}$$

$$L_{parts} = -\sum_{n=0}^{N-1} \log(P_{p(n)}(c)) \tag{8}$$

where c is the ground truth label of the input image, P_r, P_o are the category probabilities of the last softmax layer output of the raw branch and object branch, respectively, $P_{p(n)}$ is the output of the softmax layer of the part branch corresponding to the nth part image, N is the number of part images. The total loss is defined as:

$$L_{total} = L_{raw} + L_{object} + L_{parts} \tag{9}$$

The total loss is the sum of the losses of the three branches, which work together to optimize the performance of the model during backpropagation. It enables the final convergent model to make classification predictions based on the overall structural characteristics of the object or the fine-grained characteristics of a part. The model has good object scale adaptability, which improves the robustness in the case of inaccurate AOLM localization. During the testing phase, we removed the part branch so as to reduce a large amount of calculations, so our method will not take too long to predict in practical applications. MMAL-Net achieves the state-of-the-art performance because of a reasonable and effective framework.

4   Experiments

4.1   Datasets

In the past decade, the vision community has released many benchmark fine-grained datasets covering diverse domains such as birds [1], aircraft [2], cars [3], etc. These three datasets are widely used as benchmarks for fine-grained classification (shown in Table 1). In our experiments, we only use the image classification labels provided by these datasets.

Table 1. Introduction of the three datasets used in this paper.

Datasets	Object	Class	Train	Test
CUB-200-2011 (CUB) [1]	Bird	200	5994	5794
FGVC-Aircraft (AIR) [2]	Aircraft	100	6667	3333
Stanford Cars (CAR) [3]	Car	196	8144	8041

4.2   Implementation Details

In all our experiments, we first preprocess images to size 448×448 to get input image for raw branch and object branch. The object image is also scaled into 448×448, but all part images are resized to 224×224 for part branch. We construct windows with three broad categories of scales: $\{[4 \times 4, 3 \times 5], [6 \times 6, 5 \times 7], [8 \times 8, 6 \times 10, 7 \times 9, 7 \times 10]\}$ for activation map of 14×14 size, and the number of a raw image's part images is $N = 7$, among them $N_1 = 2, N_2 = 3, N_3 = 2$. N_1, N_2 and N_3 are the number of three broad categories of scales windows mentioned above. ResNet-50 [16] pre-trained on ImageNet is used as the backbone of our network structure. During training and testing, we do not use any other annotations other than image-level labels. Our optimizer is SGD with the momentum of 0.9 and the weight decay of 0.0001, and a mini-batch size of 6 on a Tesla P100 GPU. The initial learning rate is 0.001 and multiplied by 0.1 after 60 epoch. We use Pytorch as our code-base.

4.3   Performance Comparison

We compared the baseline methods mentioned above on three commonly used fine-grained classification datasets. The experimental results are shown in the Table 2. By comparison, we can see that our method achieves the best accuracy currently available on these three datasets.

Table 2. Comparison results on three common datasets. Train Anno. represents using bounding box or part annotations in training.

Methods	Train Anno.	CUB	AIR	CAR
ResNet-50 [16]		84.5	90.3	92.7
Bilinear-CNN [4]		84.1	84.1	91.3
SPDA-CNN [5]	✓	85.1	–	–
KP [14]		86.2	86.9	92.4
RA-CNN [12]		85.3	–	92.5
MA-CNN [9]		86.5	89.9	92.8
OSME+MAMC [22]		86.5	–	93.0
PC [23]		86.9	89.2	92.9
HBP [24]		87.1	90.3	93.7
Mask-CNN [6]	✓	87.3	–	–
DFL-CNN [25]		87.4	92.0	93.8
HSnet [7]	✓	87.5	–	–
NTS-Net [10]		87.5	91.4	93.9
MetaFGNet [26]		87.6	–	–
DCL [27]		87.8	**92.2**	**94.5**
TASN [11]		**87.9**	–	93.8
Ours		**89.6**	**94.7**	**95.0**

4.4   Ablation Studies

The ablation study is performed on the CUB dataset. Without adding any of our proposed methods, the ResNet-50 [16] obtained an accuracy of 84.5% under the condition that the input image resolution is 448×448. In order to verify the rationality of the training structure of our three branches, we remove the object branch and part branch respectively. After removing the object branch, the best accuracy is 85.0% from the raw branch, a drop of 4.6%. This proves the great contribution of AOLM and object branch to improve the classification accuracy. After removing the part branch, the best accuracy is 87.3% from the object branch, down 2.3%. The results of the experiment show that part branch and APPM can improve the robustness of the model when facing AOLM unstable positioning results. The above experiment has shown that the three branches of our method all have a significant contribution to the final accuracy in the training phase.

4.5   Object Localization Performance

Percentage of Correctly Localized Parts (PCP) metric is the percentage of predicted boxes that are correctly localized with more than 50% IOU with the ground-truth bounding boxes. The following experiments were carried out with

ResNet-50 [16] as the backbone network. On the CUB dataset, the best result of AOLM in terms of the PCP metric for object localization is 85.1%. AOLM clearly exceeds SCDA's [15] 76.8% and the recent weakly supervised object location methods ACOL's [19] 46.0% and ADL's [20] 62.3%. As shown in Table 3, the ensemble of multiple layers significantly improves object location accuracy. Through the experiment, we find that the object location accuracy using the pre-trained model directly is 65.0%. However, it rise to 85.1% after one iteration of training. And as the training progressed, CNN paid more and more attention to the most discerning region to improve classification accuracy which leads to localization accuracy drops to 71.1%. The object images predicted when the localization Accuracy is 85.1% and 71.1% are used for testing, and the classification accuracy is quite due to part branch make model has good adaptability to object's scale. For convenience, we use a convergent model for object localization and classification, instead of using the model of the first iteration for object localization for higher localization accuracy.

Table 3. Object localization accuracy on CUB-200-2011.

Methods	Localization accuracy
ACOL [19]	46.0%
ADL [20]	62.3%
SCDA [15]	**76.8%**
AOLM(conv_5c)	82.2%
AOLM(conv_5b & conv_5c)	**85.1%**

4.6   Model and Inference Time Complexity

Unlike RA-CNN [12] and NTS-Net [10], the former has three branches with independent parameters and needs to train a subnetwork to propose finer scale images and the latter needs to train a navigator network to propose regions with large amount of information (such as different body parts of birds). Our MMAL-Net has some advantages in terms of parameter volume over them. First, the three branches parameters are shared, and secondly the AOLM and APPM modules do not require training, do not add additional parameter amounts. Thirdly their calculation amount is relatively smaller. Finally, better classification performance is achieved by MMAL-Net. Compared with the ResNet-50 baseline, our method yields a significantly better result (+4.1%) with the same parameter volume. As for inference time, RA-CNN needs to calculate the output of three branches and fuse them; NTS-Net needs to extract and fuse the 4 proposal local image features of the input image. Above reasons make their inference time relatively longer and our method has a shorter inference time. It only needs to calculate the output of the first two branches and does not need to fuse them, because the classification results are based on the output of the second branch (object branch). For more accurate comparison, we conducted an inference time test on Tesla P100 and the input image size is 448×448. The inference time of MMAL-Net and NTS-Net are summarized as follows: the running time on an image of NTS-Net is about 5.61 ms, and ours method's running time on an image is about 1.80 ms. Based on the above analysis, lower model and inference time complexity both add extra practical value to our proposed method.

4.7   Visualization of Object and Part Regions

In order to visually analyze the areas of concern for our AOLM and APPM, we draw the object's bounding boxes and part regions proposed by AOLM and APPM in Fig. 4. In the first column, we use red and green rectangles to denote the ground truth and predicted bounding box in raw image. It is very helpful for classification that the positioned areas of objects often cover an almost complete object. In columns two through four, we use red, orange, yellow, and green rectangles to represent the regions with the highest average activation values in different scales proposed by APPM, with red rectangle denoting the highest one. Figure 4 conveys that the proposed area does contain more fine-grained information and the order is more reasonable on the same scale, which are very helpful for model's robustness to scale. We can find that the most discriminative regions of birds are head firstly, then is body, which is similar to human cognition.

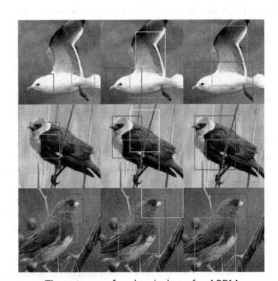

AOLM results   Three types of scale windows for APPM

Fig. 4. Visualization of object and part regions. (Color figure online)

5   Conclusion

In this paper, we propose an effective method for fine-grained classification without bounding box or part annotations. The multi-branch structure can make full use of the images obtained by AOLM and APPM to achieve excellent performance. Our algorithm is end-to-end trainable and achieves state-of-the-art results in CUB-200-2001 [1], FGVC Aircraft [2] and Stanford Cars [3] datasets. The future work is how to set the number and size of windows adaptively to further improve the classification accuracy.

References

1. Wah, C., Branson, S., Welinder, P., Perona, P., Belongie, S.: The Caltech-UCSD Birds-200-2011 Dataset. Technical report CNS-TR-2011-001, California Institute of Technology (2011)
2. Maji, S., Rahtu, E., Kannala, J., Blaschko, M., Vedaldi, A.: Fine-grained visual classification of aircraft. arXiv preprint arXiv:1306.5151 (2013)
3. Krause, J., Stark, M., Deng, J., Fei-Fei, L.: 3D object representations for fine-grained categorization. In: 4th International IEEE Workshop on 3D Representation and Recognition (3dRR-13), Sydney, Australia (2013)
4. Lin, T.Y., RoyChowdhury, A., Maji, S.: Bilinear CNN models for fine-grained visual recognition. In: CVPR, pp. 1449–1457 (2015)
5. Zhang, H., et al.: SPDA-CNN: unifying semantic part detection and abstraction for fine-grained recognition. In: Proceedings of the IEEE Conference on Computer Vision and Pattern Recognition, pp. 1143–1152 (2016)
6. Wei, X.S., Xie, C.W., Wu, J.: Mask-CNN: localizing parts and selecting descriptors for fine-grained image recognition. arXiv preprint arXiv:1605.06878 (2016)
7. Lam, M., Mahasseni, B., Todorovic, S.: Fine-grained recognition as HSnet search for informative image parts. In: CVPR, pp. 2520–2529 (2017)
8. Zhao, B., Wu, X., Feng, J., Peng, Q., Yan, S.: Diversified visual attention networks for fine-grained object classification. IEEE Trans. Multimedia **19**(6), 1245–1256 (2017)
9. Zheng, H., Fu, J., Mei, T., Luo, J.: Learning multi-attention convolutional neural network for fine-grained image recognition. In: ICCV, pp. 5209–5217 (2017)
10. Yang, Z., Luo, T., Wang, D., Hu, Z., Gao, J., Wang, L.: Learning to navigate for fine-grained classification. In: ECCV, pp. 420–435 (2018)
11. Zheng, H., Fu, J., Zha, Z.J., Luo, J.: Looking for the devil in the details: learning trilinear attention sampling network for fine-grained image recognition. In: CVPR, pp. 5012–5021 (2019)
12. Fu, J., Zheng, H., Mei, T.: Look closer to see better: recurrent attention convolutional neural network for fine-grained image recognition. In: CVPR, pp. 4438–4446 (2017)
13. Gao, Y., Beijbom, O., Zhang, N., Darrell, T.: Compact bilinear pooling. In: CVPR, pp. 317–326 (2016)
14. Cui, Y., Zhou, F., Wang, J., Liu, X., Lin, Y., Belongie, S.: Kernel pooling for convolutional neural networks. In: CVPR, pp. 2921–2930 (2017)

15. Wei, X.S., Luo, J.H., Wu, J., Zhou, Z.H.: Selective convolutional descriptor aggregation for fine-grained image retrieval. IEEE Trans. Image Process. **26**(6), 2868–2881 (2017)
16. He, K., Zhang, X., Ren, S., Sun, J.: Deep residual learning for image recognition. In: CVPR, pp. 770–778 (2016)
17. Simonyan, K., Zisserman, A.: Very deep convolutional networks for large-scale image recognition. arXiv preprint arXiv:1409.1556 (2014)
18. Long, J., Shelhamer, E., Darrell, T.: Fully convolutional networks for semantic segmentation. In: CVPR, pp. 3431–3440 (2015)
19. Zhang, X., Wei, Y., Feng, J., Yang, Y., Huang, T.S.: Adversarial complementary learning for weakly supervised object localization. In: CVPR, pp. 1325–1334 (2018)
20. Choe, J., Shim, H.: Attention-based dropout layer for weakly supervised object localization. In: CVPR, pp. 2219–2228 (2019)
21. Sermanet, P., Eigen, D., Zhang, X., Mathieu, M., Fergus, R., LeCun, Y.: OverFeat: integrated recognition, localization and detection using convolutional networks. arXiv preprint arXiv:1312.6229 (2013)
22. Sun, M., Yuan, Y., Zhou, F., Ding, E.: Multi-attention multi-class constraint for fine-grained image recognition. In: ECCV, pp. 805–821 (2018)
23. Dubey, A., Gupta, O., Guo, P., Raskar, R., Farrell, R., Naik, N.: Pairwise confusion for fine-grained visual classification. In: ECCV, pp. 70–86 (2018)
24. Yu, C., Zhao, X., Zheng, Q., Zhang, P., You, X.: Hierarchical bilinear pooling for fine-grained visual recognition. In: Proceedings of the European Conference on Computer Vision (ECCV), pp. 574–589 (2018)
25. Wang, Y., Morariu, V.I., Davis, L.S.: Learning a discriminative filter bank within a CNN for fine-grained recognition. In: CVPR, pp. 4148–4157 (2018)
26. Zhang, Y., Tang, H., Jia, K.: Fine-grained visual categorization using meta-learning optimization with sample selection of auxiliary data. In: Proceedings of the European Conference on Computer Vision (ECCV), pp. 233–248 (2018)
27. Chen, S., Bai, Y., Zhang, W., Mei, T.: Destruction and construction learning for fine-grained image recognition. In: CVPR, pp. 5157–5166 (2019)

Dense Attention-Guided Network for Boundary-Aware Salient Object Detection

Zhe Zhang[1,2], Junhui Ma[1,2], Panpan Xu[1,2], and Wencheng Wang[1,2(✉)]

[1] State Key Laboratory of Computer Science, Institute of Software,
Chinese Academy of Sciences, Beijing, China
whn@ios.ac.cn
[2] University of Chinese Academy of Sciences, Beijing, China

Abstract. Recently, salient object detection methods have achieved significant performance with the development of deep supervised learning. However, most existing methods just simply combine low-level and high-level features, which do not consider that the features of each level should contribute to the features of other levels during learning. To overcome the situation, this paper presents a Dense Attention-guided Network (DANet), which builds dense attention-guided information flows to integrate multi-level features. Specifically, we propose a Residual Attention Module (RAM) to highlight important features and suppress unimportant ones or background noises. In the network, the attention-guided features are transferred to other levels through dense connections, and a Feature Aggregation Module (FAM) is employed to adaptively fuse the multi-level feature maps. For accurate boundary estimation, we further design a novel boundary loss function to preserve the edges of salient regions. The experiments show that the proposed DANet achieves state-of-the-art performance on six widely used salient object detection benchmarks under different evaluation metrics. Besides, Our method runs at a speed of 26 fps on a single GPU and does not need any pre-processing and post-processing.

Keywords: Salient object detection · Computer vision · Image processing · Deep learning

1 Introduction

Salient object detection aims to locate the most visually attractive regions in an image, which has been applied in many applications, such as image segmentation [2], visual tracking [4] and so on. Although lots of approaches have been investigated, salient object detection is still a big challenge in computer vision. Traditional salient object detection approaches [27,32] mainly depend on handcraft features to capture the salient objects, which is often failed in complex scenes. Benefited from the development of the convolutional neural network and

© Springer Nature Switzerland AG 2021
J. Lokoč et al. (Eds.): MMM 2021, LNCS 12572, pp. 148–161, 2021.
https://doi.org/10.1007/978-3-030-67832-6_13

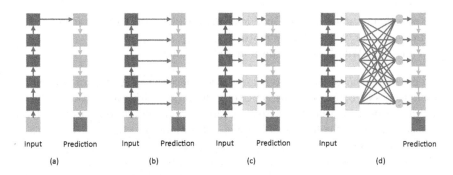

Fig. 1. Comparison with different network architectures. (a) FCN. (b) U-net. (c) Attention-based network. (d) Our dense attention-guided network.

large-scale datasets [21,27], the recent deep learning-based methods [5,15,23] have achieved great success.

Nowadays, most deep learning-based salient object detection approaches [5,8] are based on fully convolutional network (FCN) [12], which is composed of multiple convolutional and pooling layers, as shown in Fig. 1(a). Although FCN can progressively expand the receptive field and produce high-level semantic information, it reduces the size of feature maps and loses some structural details. In order to make better use of the low-level characteristics in salient object detection, several approaches [10,11,13,15] are presented based U-net architecture [16]. These methods combine the low-level and high-level features to generate more accurate saliency maps, as shown in Fig. 1(b). With the development of the attention mechanism [19], attention-based network [23,31] are proposed to highlight the important features while filtering noises, as shown in Fig. 1(c). However, the features of each level should contribute to the features of other levels during the learning, existing methods cannot make full use of multi-level features, which may generate inaccurate saliency maps.

To deal with the challenge mentioned above, we propose a dense attention-guided network (DANet) to capture the correlation between multi-level feature maps and suppress the negative effect, as shown in Fig. 1(d). Similar to most deep learning-based methods [1,5,15], we accept the encoder-decoder structure as our base architecture. The feature map from each encoder block will be fed into our residual attention module (RAM), compared with the simple stacked attention mechanisms, our RAM use the residual structure which can improve the representational capability and highlight the important features as well as suppressing the unimportant ones. Then we transfer each attention-guided feature map to other levels through dense connections. Next, we design a feature aggregation module (FAM) that adaptively combines the multi-level feature maps. Besides, a novel boundary loss function is presented to preserve the edge of salient objects, we convert the traditional dilated operation in morphology to convolutional layer to produce the boundary maps of both ground truth and predicted saliency map, where Euclidean distance is used to measure the similarity between the two boundary maps.

Our main contributions are summarized as follows:

- We propose a novel dense attention-guided network (DANet) for accurately predicting saliency maps. Our DANet combines multi-level feature maps to simultaneously incorporate coarse semantics and fine details through dense connections. Specifically, the RAM can obtain more discriminative and effective features, and the FAM is able to adaptively fuse multi-level feature maps.
- We present a new boundary loss function to guide the network to learn the accurate contours of salient objects, which is also helpful to locate the salient regions.
- Our method can run at a real-time speed of 26 FPS in a single GPU. The experimental results demonstrate the superiority and effectiveness of the proposed model compared with other 15 state-of-the-art methods on six widely used benchmarks.

2   Related Work

Traditional Methods: Early salient object detection methods [27,32] usually have some prior assumptions, such as color contrast, background prior and center prior. Since these methods mainly rely on hand-crafted features, they often produce coarse saliency maps in complex scenes.

FCN Methods: Recently, the deep learning-based methods have performed great development. Many methods [5,8,29] use the fully convolutional neural network (FCN) [12] to extract high-level semantic features. Li et al. [8] introduce an end-to-end deep contrast network including a pixel level fully convolutional stream and a segment-level spatial pooling stream for salient object detection. Zhang et al. [29] integrate multi-level features by concatenating feature maps from both high-level and low-level.

U-Net Models: Salient object detection methods [10,11,13,15] based on U-Net [16] achieve gratifying performance because U-Net structure can capture more spatial information and further multi-scale feature fusion. Zhang et al. [29] offer a generic aggregating multi-level convolutional feature framework for salient object detection. Qin et al. [15] present the residual refinement module and hybrid loss function to produce saliency objects with clear boundaries. However, these methods just simply combine the low-level and high-level features without distinction, which yield inaccurate saliency maps.

Attention-Based Approaches: With the development of attention mechanisms, several attention-based methods are employed. Wang et al. [23] present a pyramid attention model, which the former extends the regular attention mechanisms with multi-scale information to improve saliency representation.

Zhao et al. [31] propose a context-aware pyramid feature extraction module and a context-aware attention module for capturing multi-scale features. However, as discussed in [20], simple stacking of attention mechanisms may degrade the model, therefore we use the residual attention mechanism to improve the representational capability of the model in salient object detection.

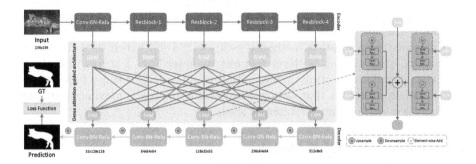

Fig. 2. The pipeline of our proposed dense attention-guided network: DANet.

3   Proposed DANet

The pipeline of our DANet is shown in Fig. 2. In this section, we first describe our dense attention-guided architecture in Sect. 3.1. The residual attention module is presented in Sect. 3.2. Section 3.3 illustrates the feature aggregation module. Our loss function is introduced in Sect. 3.4.

3.1   Dense Attention-Guided Architecture

Similar to most deep learning-based salient object detection methods [15,31], our encoder network can use VGG [17], ResNet [3], etc. To avoid overfitting and reducing computation, we use Resnet-34 [3] as our encoder network. For an input image I, we first resize I to 256×256, then our encoder network can generate feature maps from the first convolutional layer and 4 residual blocks. We denote the 5 feature maps as F^i ($i = 1, 2, 3, 4, 5$). Each feature map F^i is firstly sent to the residual attention-guided module (RAM) to be optimized since RAM can highlight the crucial features and filter out the background noises, we denote the output feature maps from RAM as F_{RAM}^i. Then the F_{RAM}^i is transferred to other feature blocks through dense connections. Next, the feature aggregation module (FAM) is able to adaptively combine the multi-level feature maps, we denote the output feature maps from FAM as F_{FAM}^i. Finally, each F_{FAM}^i is sent to the decoder network to generate the saliency map. The output feature maps of our dense attention-guided architecture can be defined as:

$$F_{output}^i = FAM^i(RAM^n(F_{input}^n), RAM^{n-1}(F_{input}^{n-1}), ..., RAM^1(F_{input}^1)) \quad (1)$$

where F_{input}^i represents the feature maps after the encoder network. F_{output}^n means the output feature maps from dense attention-guided architecture. Here, $n = 5$ because we have 5 feature maps as mentioned above. RAM can highlight the important features and filter noises, which is described in Sect. 3.2. FAM can adaptively integrate multi-level feature maps, which is illustrated in Sect. 3.3. In this way, each integrated feature map will simultaneously incorporate coarse semantics and fine details.

Compared with existing methods, such as DSS [5], which uses short connections to pass the higher-level features to lower-level features, our dense attention-guided architecture enables optimized multi-level features to be guided to each other, it ensures that the hierarchical information is maximized utilization between feature maps of different levels.

3.2   Residual Attention Module

It is obvious that different features have different effects on salient object detection. However, most existing methods just combine low-level and high-level features without distinction. Low-level features usually have structural details but also contain noises, high-level features often carry rich semantic information but also include the unimportant ones. These noises or unimportant features will influence the generation of precise saliency maps. Hence, we propose a residual attention module (RAM) to highlight the crucial features and suppress unnecessary ones.

As discussed in [20], simply stacking the attention mechanisms will lead to an obvious performance drop. Therefore, we use the residual structure to obtain more accurate and distinctive features. Our residual attention module can be defined as follows:

$$F_{RAM}^i = F_{input}^i \oplus (F_{input}^i \otimes W^i) \quad (2)$$

where F_{RAM}^i is the output of the RAM, F_{input}^i is the feature map from the encoder network. $\oplus$ is the element-wise addition and $\otimes$ is the element-wise multiplication. W^i is the residual attention weight, which ranges from [0,1] through *Sigmoid* function. The detailed computation of W^i is shown in Fig. 3. It can be seen that we use the convolution-relu layer and channel concatenation to capture the crucial features. Note that the final 1×1 convolution is used to reduce the channel number to equal the input.

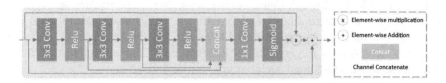

Fig. 3. Our residual attention module.

3.3   Feature Aggregation Module

Considering the inconsistent resolution of multi-level feature maps, if we just simply upsample or downsample the feature maps of other levels, the features may lose important information or even produce noise to mislead feature learning, since upsampling will bring redundant noise while downsampling will lose several feature information.

In order to make full use of the features of different levels and suppress the redundant noises, we design the feature aggregation module (FAM) to adaptively fuse the hierarchical features and keep the effectiveness of features, the visualization of FAM is shown in Fig. 2. Our FAM can be defined as follows:

$$F_{FAM}^i = \sum_{j=1}^{5}(Conv - Relu(Conv - Relu(\varphi(F_{RAM}^j)))) \tag{3}$$

F_{FAM}^i is the output feature that will be fed into the decoder network. $\sum$ is the element-wise addition for the feature maps of all levels. $Conv - Relu$ is the 3×3 convolutional layer followed by a $relu$ activate layer, which is applied to correct the negative effect of upsampling/downsampling. φ is the upsampling/downsampling layer that adjusts features of different levels to the same resolution.

3.4   Loss Function

For predicting more accurate boundary-aware saliency maps, we use multiple loss functions to train our model. The loss function is defined as follows:

$$L = (1 - \alpha)(l_{ce} + l_{ssim}) + \alpha l_b \tag{4}$$

where l_{ce} is the cross-entropy loss, l_{ssim} is the ssim loss [15], l_b is the proposed boundary loss. The α is weight parameter to balance the salient objects and salient edges, in our experiment, we found that $\alpha = 0.15$ is suitable.

Most deep learning-based methods [5,31] use cross-entropy loss function to represent the cost of wrong prediction. It can be defined as:

$$l_{ce} = - \sum_{i=0}^{size(Y)} (Y_i \log(P_i) + (1 - Y_i \log(1 - P_i))) \tag{5}$$

where Y_i is value of ground truth of pixel i, P_i is value of predicted saliency map of pixel i.

SSIM can capture the structural information in an image. Hence, we adopt the SSIM loss function used in [15], it can be defined as

$$l_{ssim} = 1 - \frac{(2\mu_x\mu_y + C_1)(2\sigma_{xy} + C_2)}{(\mu_x^2 + \mu_y^2 + C_1)(\sigma_x^2 + \sigma_y^2 + C_2)} \qquad (6)$$

where x and y are two corresponding patches cropped from the predicted map P and the ground truth Y. μ_x, μ_y and σ_x, σ_y are the mean and standard deviations of x and y respectively, σ_{xy} is their covariance, $C_1 = 0.01^2$ and $C_2 = 0.03^2$ are used to avoid dividing by zero.

In addition, we propose a new boundary loss function to preserve the boundary of salient objects and locate the salient regions. We convert the dilated operation in morphology to convolutional layers, then the boundary loss function can be defined as:

$$l_b = Euc(conv_d(P) - P, conv_d(Y) - Y) \qquad (7)$$

where $Euc(m, n)$ is the Euclidean distance between m and n, $conv_d$ represents the convolutional layer with the kernel size 3×3 and the weights are equal to 1. The predict saliency map or ground truth will be dilated through $conv_d$, so the boundary map can be obtained by the subtraction between the dilated map and the original map. The visualization of our predicted boundary map is shown in Fig. 4.

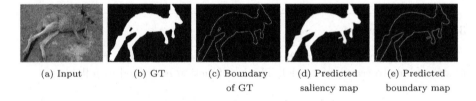

| (a) Input | (b) GT | (c) Boundary of GT | (d) Predicted saliency map | (e) Predicted boundary map |

Fig. 4. Comparison of our predicted map with GT.

4   Experiments

4.1   Datasets and Evaluation Metrics

Datasets. The performance evaluation is utilized on six standard benchmark datasets: ECSSD [26], HKU-IS [7], PASCAL-S [9], DUT-OMRON [27] DUTS-test [21] and SOD [14].

Evaluation Metrics. Same as [15,28], we employ maximum F-measure, S-measure, MAE scores, PR curve and F-measure curve as evaluation measures to quantitatively evaluate our improvements.

Table 1. The F_β^{max}, S_m and MAE of different salient object detection approaches on all test datasets. The best two results are shown in red and blue. "+" means the results are generated with post-processing by CRF. Note that RBD [32] and DRFI [6] are traditional methods without backbone. BANet [18] does not provide the predicted saliency maps on SOD dataset.

	Backbone	SOD			ECSSD			HKU-IS			PASCALS			DUT-test			DUT-OMRON		
		F_β^{max}	S_m	MAE	F_β^{max}	S_m	MAE	F_β^{max}	S_m	MAE	F_β^{max}	S_m	MAE	F_β^{max}	S_m	MAE	F_β^{max}	S_m	MAE
RBD [32]	-	0.648	0.586	0.228	0.712	0.683	0.172	0.720	0.699	0.142	0.654	0.675	0.193	0.583	0.631	0.152	0.628	0.679	0.142
DRFI [6]	-	0.701	0.625	0.223	0.782	0.732	0.170	0.777	0.740	0.144	0.691	0.686	0.196	0.649	0.669	0.154	0.664	0.696	0.150
UCF [30]	VGG-16	0.807	0.763	0.148	0.903	0.884	0.069	0.888	0.875	0.062	0.819	0.793	0.111	0.772	0.777	0.111	0.729	0.760	0.120
Amulet [29]	VGG-16	0.796	0.755	0.144	0.915	0.894	0.059	0.897	0.886	0.051	0.834	0.807	0.099	0.777	0.796	0.084	0.743	0.780	0.098
DSS+ [5]	VGG-16	0.845	0.746	0.122	0.921	0.882	0.052	0.866	0.815	0.059	0.836	0.807	0.102	0.778	0.749	0.069	0.745	0.733	0.075
NLDF+ [13]	VGG-16	0.840	0.759	0.123	0.905	0.875	0.063	0.858	0.838	0.060	0.827	0.806	0.101	0.758	0.758	0.077	0.679	0.681	0.107
R^3Net+ [1]	ResNeXt	0.848	0.762	0.124	0.934	0.910	0.040	0.921	0.900	0.034	0.844	0.811	0.100	0.835	0.823	0.057	0.804	0.816	0.063
DRGL [22]	ResNet-50	0.845	0.774	0.103	0.922	0.903	0.041	0.910	0.895	0.036	0.857	0.834	0.081	0.828	0.831	0.049	0.774	0.805	0.062
PiCANetR [11]	ResNet-50	0.867	0.780	0.104	0.935	0.917	0.047	0.919	0.905	0.043	0.874	0.840	0.073	0.862	0.859	0.049	0.819	0.831	0.065
MLMS [24]	VGG-16	0.862	0.789	0.106	0.930	0.911	0.044	0.922	0.906	0.039	0.864	0.837	0.079	0.852	0.851	0.046	0.791	0.805	0.068
BMPM [28]	VGG-16	0.863	0.782	0.105	0.927	0.908	0.041	0.921	0.903	0.040	0.863	0.835	0.078	0.854	0.848	0.048	0.792	0.809	0.064
PAGE+ [23]	VGG-16	0.842	0.765	0.108	0.934	0.910	0.037	0.921	0.902	0.031	0.853	0.823	0.083	0.841	0.834	0.047	0.794	0.818	0.059
BASNet [15]	ResNet-34	0.851	0.772	0.112	0.942	0.916	0.037	0.929	0.909	0.032	0.861	0.831	0.084	0.860	0.853	0.047	0.811	0.836	0.056
CPD [25]	ResNet-50	0.859	0.771	0.110	0.939	0.918	0.037	0.925	0.906	0.034	0.865	0.843	0.078	0.865	0.858	0.042	0.797	0.824	0.056
BANet [18]	ResNet-50	-	-	-	0.941	0.923	0.035	0.931	0.913	0.032	0.871	0.838	0.077	0.872	0.866	0.039	0.802	0.832	0.059
Ours	ResNet-34	0.870	0.784	0.103	0.942	0.918	0.036	0.934	0.916	0.030	0.881	0.851	0.072	0.884	0.867	0.038	0.824	0.833	0.054

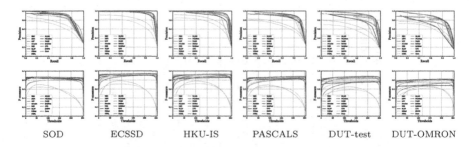

SOD   ECSSD   HKU-IS   PASCALS   DUT-test   DUT-OMRON

Fig. 5. Illustration of PR curves (the first row) and F-measure curves (the second row) on the six widely tested datasets.

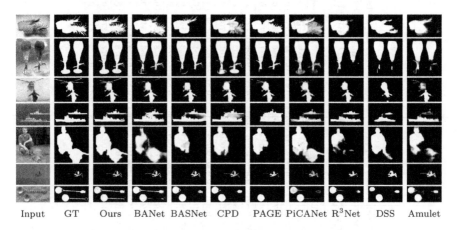

Input   GT   Ours   BANet   BASNet   CPD   PAGE   PiCANet   R³Net   DSS   Amulet

Fig. 6. Visual comparison with state-of-the-arts.

4.2 Implementation Details

We adopt ResNet-34 [3] which is pre-trained on Imagenet as our backbone. The DUTS-train dataset [21] is used to train our model. As suggested in [10], we do not use the validation set and train the model until training loss converges. In order to make the model robust, we use some data augmentation techniques: random brightness and contrast changing, and random horizontal flipping. In training period, similar to [15], we use the Adam optimizer to train the model with the learning rate $lr = 1e-3$, betas $= (0.9, 0.999)$, eps $= 1e-8$, weight decay $= 0$. Our model is trained on a single 1080Ti GPU with a mini-batch size of 16, and it takes about 12 h to train the whole model. The inference for a 400×300 image only takes 0.038 s (26 fps).

4.3 Comparison with State-of-the-Arts

We compare our method with other 15 state-of-the-art approaches on six widely used datasets, including BANet [18], CPD [25], BASNet [15], PAGE [23],

BMPM [28], MLMS [24], PiCANet [11], DGRL [22], R³Net [1], NLDF [13], DSS [5], Amulet [29], UCF [30], DRFI [6] and RBD [32]. For fair comparisons, we use saliency maps provided by the authors or their released codes with default settings.

Quantitative Evaluation. In Table 1, we show our quantitative comparison results. We evaluate and compare our proposed method with other salient object detection methods from F-measure, MAE, and S-measure. As we can see, our method performs favorably against the state-of-the-arts in terms of both regional and boundary measures. Particularly, our method achieves the best performance on all datasets in F_β^{max}.

Besides the numerical comparisons, we plot the precision-recall curves and F-measure curves of all compared methods over all six datasets. As shown in Fig. 5, the solid red line which denotes the proposed method outperforms all other methods at most thresholds. Particularly, we achieve the best performance on all datasets in F-measure curves.

Qualitative Evaluation. In Fig. 6, It shows the qualitative comparison of the results with eight state-of-the-art methods. It turns out that our model can handle various challenging scenarios, including images with low contrast (row 2, 6), complex object boundaries (row 1,4,7), varying object scale (row 3) and object touching image boundary (row 5). It is worth mentioning that due to the RAM and the boundary loss function, our results can not only highlight the salient object but also maintain coherent edges of salient regions. For example, other methods can not accurately locate and detect salient objects in 3rd image due to complex scenes and varying object scale. However, our approach has better performance because of complementary multi-level features and boundary preservation.

Table 2. Ablation study on different architectures and loss functions. B: baseline model. DAA: dense attention-guided architecture. RAM: residual attention module. FAM: feature aggregation module. l_{ce}: cross-entropy loss. l_s: ssim loss. l_b: boundary loss.

Architecture and loss function	F_β^{max}	MAE
B + l_{ce}	0.928	0.048
B + DAA + l_{ce}	0.931	0.046
B + DAA + FAM + l_{ce}	0.934	0.044
B + DAA + FAM + RAM + l_{ce}	0.938	0.041
B + DAA + FAM + RAM + l_{ce} + l_s	0.940	0.039
B + DAA + FAM + RAM + l_{ce} + l_b	0.940	0.038
B + DAA + FAM + RAM + l_{ce} + l_s + l_b	0.942	0.036

Table 3. Ablation study on SSAM and our RAM.

Architecture	F_β^{max}	MAE
SSAM	0.937	0.042
RAM	0.942	0.036

4.4 Ablation Study

In order to investigate the importance of different modules in our method, we conduct the ablation study on the ECSSD dataset, as shown in Table 2, where a higher F_β^{max}, and lower MAE correspond to better results. The proposed model contains all components (i.e. baseline model only includes encoder and decoder, dense attention-guided architecture, residual attention module, feature aggregation module, and three loss functions) that achieve the best performance. Specifically, DAA can merge features of different levels, RAM is able to effectively improve the extraction of important features, FAM overcomes the wrong prediction generated by upsampling and downsampling in feature aggregation, and the loss function can improve the overall structural and edge quality of predicted saliency map. It turns out that all components are necessary for the proposed method to yield the best salient object detection result.

As discussed in Sect. 3.2, simply stacking the attention mechanisms will lead to an obvious performance drop. Here, we also make the ablation study on the ECSSD dataset to verify the effectiveness of our RAM, as shown in Table 3. SSAM means simply stacking the attention mechanisms instead of our RAM. Compared with SSAM, our RAM can effectively improve the quality of the saliency map.

5 Conclusion

In this paper, a novel salient object detection model named Dense Attention-guided Network (DANet) is proposed. We build a dense attention-guided architecture to transfer the hierarchical information, which can maximize the usage of the information flow between multi-level features. In addition, we design the residual attention module (RAM) and feature aggregation module (FAM) in the architecture to make full use of the features. RAM can focus on the crucial features as well as suppress the noises, and FAM can adaptively integrate the multi-level features. Besides, we present a new boundary loss function to preserve the edges of salient objects. The proposed method can achieve superior performance and produce visually favorable results. Experimental results on six widely used datasets verified that our proposed method outperforms 15 state-of-the-art methods under different evaluation metrics. Furthermore, our model has efficient inference speed and runs on GPUs in real-time.

Acknowledgement. This paper is partially supported by the National Natural Science Foundation of China under Grant No. 62072446. Many thanks to the anonymous reviewers for their valuable suggestions.

References

1. Deng, Z., et al.: R3Net: recurrent residual refinement network for saliency detection. In: Proceedings of the 27th International Joint Conference on Artificial Intelligence, pp. 684–690. AAAI Press (2018)
2. Donoser, M., Urschler, M., Hirzer, M., Bischof, H.: Saliency driven total variation segmentation. In: 2009 IEEE 12th International Conference on Computer Vision, pp. 817–824 (2009)
3. He, K., Zhang, X., Ren, S., Sun, J.: Deep residual learning for image recognition. In: Proceedings of the IEEE Conference on Computer Vision and Pattern Recognition, pp. 770–778 (2016)
4. Hong, S., You, T., Kwak, S., Han, B.: Online tracking by learning discriminative saliency map with convolutional neural network. In: International Conference on Machine Learning, pp. 597–606 (2015)
5. Hou, Q., Cheng, M.M., Hu, X., Borji, A., Tu, Z., Torr, P.H.: Deeply supervised salient object detection with short connections. In: Proceedings of the IEEE Conference on Computer Vision and Pattern Recognition, pp. 3203–3212 (2017)
6. Jiang, H., Wang, J., Yuan, Z., Wu, Y., Zheng, N., Li, S.: Salient object detection: a discriminative regional feature integration approach. In: Proceedings of the IEEE Conference on Computer Vision and Pattern Recognition, pp. 2083–2090 (2013)
7. Li, G., Yu, Y.: Visual saliency based on multiscale deep features. In: Proceedings of the IEEE Conference on Computer Vision and Pattern Recognition, pp. 5455–5463 (2015)
8. Li, G., Yu, Y.: Deep contrast learning for salient object detection. In: Proceedings of the IEEE Conference on Computer Vision and Pattern Recognition, pp. 478–487 (2016)
9. Li, Y., Hou, X., Koch, C., Rehg, J.M., Yuille, A.L.: The secrets of salient object segmentation. In: Proceedings of the IEEE Conference on Computer Vision and Pattern Recognition, pp. 280–287 (2014)
10. Liu, N., Han, J.: DHSNet: deep hierarchical saliency network for salient object detection. In: Proceedings of the IEEE Conference on Computer Vision and Pattern Recognition, pp. 678–686 (2016)
11. Liu, N., Han, J., Yang, M.H.: PiCANet: learning pixel-wise contextual attention for saliency detection. In: Proceedings of the IEEE Conference on Computer Vision and Pattern Recognition, pp. 3089–3098 (2018)
12. Long, J., Shelhamer, E., Darrell, T.: Fully convolutional networks for semantic segmentation. In: Proceedings of the IEEE conference on computer vision and pattern recognition, pp. 3431–3440 (2015)
13. Luo, Z., Mishra, A., Achkar, A., Eichel, J., Li, S., Jodoin, P.M.: Non-local deep features for salient object detection. In: Proceedings of the IEEE Conference on Computer Vision and Pattern Recognition, pp. 6609–6617 (2017)
14. Movahedi, V., Elder, J.H.: Design and perceptual validation of performance measures for salient object segmentation. In: 2010 IEEE Computer Society Conference on Computer Vision and Pattern Recognition-Workshops, pp. 49–56. IEEE (2010)

15. Qin, X., Zhang, Z., Huang, C., Gao, C., Dehghan, M., Jagersand, M.: BASNet: boundary-aware salient object detection. In: Proceedings of the IEEE Conference on Computer Vision and Pattern Recognition, pp. 7479–7489 (2019)
16. Ronneberger, O., Fischer, P., Brox, T.: U-Net: convolutional networks for biomedical image segmentation. In: Navab, N., Hornegger, J., Wells, W.M., Frangi, A.F. (eds.) MICCAI 2015. LNCS, vol. 9351, pp. 234–241. Springer, Cham (2015). https://doi.org/10.1007/978-3-319-24574-4_28
17. Simonyan, K., Zisserman, A.: Very deep convolutional networks for large-scale image recognition. arXiv preprint arXiv:1409.1556 (2014)
18. Su, J., Li, J., Zhang, Y., Xia, C., Tian, Y.: Selectivity or invariance: boundary-aware salient object detection. In: Proceedings of the IEEE International Conference on Computer Vision, pp. 3799–3808 (2019)
19. Vaswani, A., et al.: Attention is all you need. In: Advances in Neural Information Processing Systems, pp. 5998–6008 (2017)
20. Wang, F., et al.: Residual attention network for image classification. In: Proceedings of the IEEE Conference on Computer Vision and Pattern Recognition, pp. 6450–6458 (2017)
21. Wang, L., et al.: Learning to detect salient objects with image-level supervision. In: Proceedings of the IEEE Conference on Computer Vision and Pattern Recognition, pp. 136–145 (2017)
22. Wang, T., et al.: Detect globally, refine locally: a novel approach to saliency detection. In: Proceedings of the IEEE Conference on Computer Vision and Pattern Recognition, pp. 3127–3135 (2018)
23. Wang, W., Zhao, S., Shen, J., Hoi, S.C., Borji, A.: Salient object detection with pyramid attention and salient edges. In: Proceedings of the IEEE Conference on Computer Vision and Pattern Recognition, pp. 1448–1457 (2019)
24. Wu, R., Feng, M., Guan, W., Wang, D., Lu, H., Ding, E.: A mutual learning method for salient object detection with intertwined multi-supervision. In: Proceedings of the IEEE Conference on Computer Vision and Pattern Recognition, pp. 8150–8159 (2019)
25. Wu, Z., Su, L., Huang, Q.: Cascaded partial decoder for fast and accurate salient object detection. In: Proceedings of the IEEE Conference on Computer Vision and Pattern Recognition, pp. 3907–3916 (2019)
26. Yan, Q., Xu, L., Shi, J., Jia, J.: Hierarchical saliency detection. In: Proceedings of the IEEE Conference on Computer Vision and Pattern Recognition, pp. 1155–1162 (2013)
27. Yang, C., Zhang, L., Lu, H., Ruan, X., Yang, M.H.: Saliency detection via graph-based manifold ranking. In: Proceedings of the IEEE Conference on Computer Vision and Pattern Recognition, pp. 3166–3173 (2013)
28. Zhang, L., Dai, J., Lu, H., He, Y., Wang, G.: A bi-directional message passing model for salient object detection. In: Proceedings of the IEEE Conference on Computer Vision and Pattern Recognition, pp. 1741–1750 (2018)
29. Zhang, P., Wang, D., Lu, H., Wang, H., Ruan, X.: Amulet: aggregating multi-level convolutional features for salient object detection. In: Proceedings of the IEEE International Conference on Computer Vision, pp. 202–211 (2017)
30. Zhang, P., Wang, D., Lu, H., Wang, H., Yin, B.: Learning uncertain convolutional features for accurate saliency detection. In: Proceedings of the IEEE International Conference on Computer Vision, pp. 212–221 (2017)

31. Zhao, T., Wu, X.: Pyramid feature attention network for saliency detection. In: Proceedings of the IEEE Conference on Computer Vision and Pattern Recognition, pp. 3085–3094 (2019)
32. Zhu, W., Liang, S., Wei, Y., Sun, J.: Saliency optimization from robust background detection. In: Proceedings of the IEEE Conference on Computer Vision and Pattern Recognition, pp. 2814–2821 (2014)

Generative Image Inpainting by Hybrid Contextual Attention Network

Zhijiao Xiao$^{(\boxtimes)}$ and Donglun Li

College of Computer Science and Software Engineering,
Shenzhen University, Shenzhen 510680, China
`cindyxzj@szu.edu.cn, lidonglun@email.szu.edu.cn`

Abstract. Image inpainting is a challenging task due to the loss of the image information. Recently, GAN-based approaches have shown promising performance
in the field of image inpainting. For this task, a superior similarity measurement of extracted patches from known and missing regions is important. Existing
approaches usually adopt cosine distance to measure this similarity for missing
region reconstruction. However, from the semantic-level perspective, these methods often generate content with inconsistent color and disorder structure due to
the ignorance of the magnitude distance of the attended patches. To resolve this
problem, we propose a Hybrid Contextual Attention Network (HCA-Net) with
a novel attention module called hybrid contextual attention module (HCAM).
HCAM takes account of both cosine distance and Euclidean distance as the measurement of the extracted patches and gives a better prediction of missing features. Besides, a Spectral-Normalization patch discriminator and the cosine loss
are added into the model for patch-level and pixel-level consistency enhancement. Extensive results on three public datasets (Paris Street View, Celeba-HQ,
and Places2), have both validated that our approach significantly outperforms the
state-of-the-art approaches.

Keywords: Image inpainting · HCA-Net · HCAM

1 Introduction

Image inpainting is a traditional technique that originated from the European cultural
renaissance. This technique aims to synthesize plausible and realistic content in the
missing region. It can also be extended to remove unsatisfactory parts (i.e. objects,
scratches, watermarks) in photos. Current inpainting methods are usually divided into
two categories, traditional methods and GAN-based methods. Traditional methods can
be divided into two classes: Diffusion-based methods [2] and Exemplar-based methods
[1, 12]. Diffusion-based methods model the entire inpainting process as a partial differential equation (PDE) and reconstruct the image by iterative updating the corresponding
equation until convergence. Exemplar methods, like PatchMatch [1], try to search the
most relevant patch from the complete part based on the similarity between the known
and unknown patches, and then fill the content for the hole in the image with it. These
methods often perform well when the hole is thin or the texture is regular. However,

© Springer Nature Switzerland AG 2021
J. Lokoč et al. (Eds.): MMM 2021, LNCS 12572, pp. 162–173, 2021.
https://doi.org/10.1007/978-3-030-67832-6_14

because of their weakness in capturing the high-level semantic structure of the image, they will usually produce blur and inconsistent results especially when the hole is huge or the texture is complicated and non-repetitive.

In recent years, deep convolution neural network (CNN) has shown a strong ability in capturing semantic structure information and helped overcome the shortcomings of traditional image inpainting methods. Thanks to that, recent researches on image inpainting cast their sight on using generative adversarial network (GAN) to accomplish the image inpainting task. GAN-based inpainting methods first encode the mask image into potential feature spaces and decode them to generate image similar to ground-truth image. However, this kind of methods such as context-encoder (CE) [10] and global-local network (GL) [4], tend to produce blur results and distort structures due to their low efficiency in utilizing the distant spatial location information for missing features reconstruction. Therefore, some methods [15, 16] attempt to learn and utilize the relation between missing and known region patches to encourage the generate image consistency. These methods such as contextual attention estimates the weight of each attended high-level feature map patches for missing feature reconstruction. These methods usually adopt the cosine distance as the measurement of the weight of each attended patches and performs well. However, only applying the cosine distance to estimate the similarity is not enough. It ignores the magnitude of the extracted patches.

Thus, in this paper, we proposed a network Hybrid Contextual Attention Network (HCA-Net) with a novel attention module, Hybrid Contextual Attention Module (HCAM) to resolve this issue. HCAM adopts a new similarity measurement that combines the original cosine distance with Euclidean distance on the magnitude of the extract patches, and achieves a better performance. Besides, for the purpose of training a model to process irregular mask or random location mask, the conventional global and local discriminator is replaced with a spectral-normalization [9] based patch discriminator. Furthermore, an additive cosine loss is introduced into the training process to help promote the color and structure consistency of the generated content. Extensive experiment on public image datasets, such as faces dataset Celeba-HQ (Face), scenery datasets Paris Street View and Places2, has demonstrated that the proposed method generates better results compared to the state-of-the-art methods. In summary, the main contributions of HCA-Net are summarized as follow:

- We unify the coarse-to-refine network with an attention module, **H**ybrid **C**ontextual **A**ttention **M**odule (HCAM) and a Spectral-Normalization Patch(SN-Patch) discriminator. HCAM adopts a novel measurement of the relation between extract patches from foreground and background to improve the inpainting performance and SN-Patch discriminator helps deal with random damaged images.
- We design a new joint loss function which first considers cosine loss in the inpainting task to provide better color and structure consistency generated results
- Experiment has shown that the proposed attention module performs better than the previous attention module and the proposed model obtains a better results compared to the existing models.

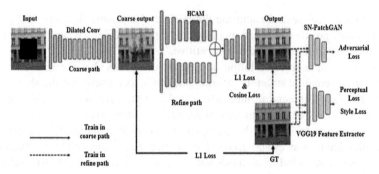

Fig. 1. The architecture of HCA-Net (It contains three parts: a coarse-to-refine network, a SN-Patch discriminator and a pre-trained VGG19 features extractor)

2 Related Work

In this part, we will describe relevant previous works on image inpainting in two categories: Generative model based inpainting and Attention based inpainting.

Generative Model Based Inpainting. With rapid improvement of deep learning in recent years, GAN becomes a common and effective method in the generation task. For the inpainting task, Pathak et al. [10] first introduced a context-encoder (CE) which borrows the idea of GAN. CE uses an additive adversarial loss to alleviate the blurriness caused by only minimizing l1 or l2 difference between the reference and inpainted image. However, it has a limitation that it only processes an image with center square mask and ignores the consistency inside the hole. To alleviate this problem, Iizuka et al. [4] designed a global and local discriminator that classify both missing region and entire image as true or fake to enforce the consistency inside the missing region, but the result lacks detail information and suffers boundary artifacts.

Attention Based Inpainting. Attention mechanism has made a great breakthrough in the field of computer vision [13, 18]. In the area of image processing, the attention mechanism aims to locate the most important part in an image and helps model the relevant information patch at the distant location. In the inpainting task, Yu et al. [15] proposed a contextual attention module (CAM) to fill the missing patches with similar patches from known region at the high-level feature maps. The CAM utilizes cosine distance to estimate the weight score, and generate semantic consistent results. However, it remains a challenge to generate more realistic results. Inspired by traditional methods [12, 14], only consider the cosine distance as the measurement of similarity ignores the Euclidean distances of attended pixel values. To address this problem, we design a novel model Hybrid Contextual Attention Module (HCAM), which considers both cosine distance and Euclidean distances of attended pixel values to provide a more efficient model of similarity for missing features reconstruction, so as to improve the visual and semantic consistency of inpainting result (Fig. 2).

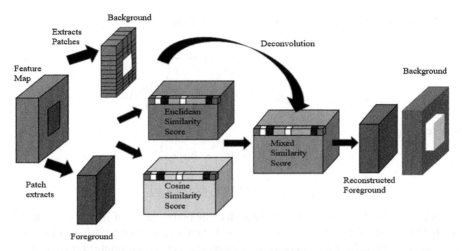

Fig. 2. The design of hybrid contextual attention module HCAM)

3   Hybrid Contextual Attention Network (HCA-Net)

3.1   Architecture of HCA-Net

As shown in Fig. 1, the proposed HCA-Net consists of three parts: a coarse-to-refine generator, a SN-Patch discriminator, and a pre-trained VGG19 features extractor. The generator works as the repair habit of painters. The coarse network generates an intermediate rough result for refinement. The refine network contains two parallel branches: coarse branch and refine branch. The coarse branch provides a larger receptive field by a consecutive dilation layer, and the refine branch reconstructs the feature maps by a module called HCAM which will be detailed introduced in the next section. For the sake of the random appearance of damage in an image, the previous global and local discriminator is replaced with a spectral-normalization Patch discriminator for patch-level consistency enhancement.

3.2   Hybrid Contextual Attention Module

Conventional CAM applies the cosine distance to calculate the similarity for patches extracted from the foreground and background of feature maps. However, the feature representation will be distorted after convolution and normalizing. To alleviate this problem, we propose a new attention module called hybrid contextual attention module (HCAM). Different from CAM, HCAM takes account for both cosine distance and Euclidean distance of the magnitude of the vector form of extracted 3×3 patches to compute the similarity $s_{x,y,x',y'}$.

In HCAM, we first extract 3×3 patches $\{f_{x,y}\}$, $\{b_{x',y'}\}$ from the foreground and background feature maps, respectively. Then for each $b_{x',y'}$, we match it with $\{f_{x,y}\}$ and calculate two kinds of similarity between them. The cosine similarity $c_{(x,y),(x',y')}$ and the

Euclidean similarity $d'_{(x,y),(x',y')}$ are computed as follows:

$$c_{(x,y),(x',y')} = < \frac{f_{x,y}}{|f_{x,y}|}, \frac{b_{x',y'}}{|b_{x',y'}|} > \tag{1}$$

$$d'_{(x,y),(x',y')} = \tanh(-(\frac{d_{(x,y),(x',y')} - mean(d_{*,(x',y')})}{std(d_{*,(x',y')})}) \tag{2}$$

where

$$d_{(x,y),(x',y')} = ||f_{x,y} - b_{x',y'}||^2 \tag{3}$$

$$s^*_{x,y,x',y'} = softmax_{x'y'}(\lambda s_{x,y,x',y'}) \tag{4}$$

Since the Euclidean distance similarity has the output range of $[0, \infty)$, it is hard to apply the softmax function. Therefore, we use formula (2) to limit its value within $[-1, 1]$ in each channel. Then, we apply a scaled softmax function as formula (4) to map these two similarities $c_{x,y,x',y'}$ and $d'_{x,y,x',y'}$ into the value range of $[0, 1)$ in each channel to gain the attention score $c^*_{x,y,x',y'}$ and $d^*_{x,y,x',y'}$. To combine $c^*_{x,y,x',y'}$ and $d^*_{x,y,x',y'}$, a parameter α is utilized to balance them as formula (5):

$$s_{x,y,x',y'} = \alpha c^*_{x,y,x',y'} + (1-\alpha)d^*_{x,y,x',y'} \tag{5}$$

Based on the characteristic of the softmax function, the parameter α, which ranges from $[0, 1]$, is used to balance the attention score gained by calculating the cosine distance and Euclidean distance. In this way, it is ensured that the score $s_{x,y,x',y'}$ will be summed up to 1 in each channel. Finally, similar to CAM, the extracted 3x3 background patches $\{b_{x',y'}\}$ are set as deconvolution filters and deconvoluted with the ultimate attention score $s_{x,y,x',y'}$ for features of foreground refinement.

3.3 Loss Function

In the training progress of HCA-Net, the coarse and refine stage is optimized simultaneously. For the coarse path, the original reconstruction loss is adopted to guide for an intermediate coarse result generation. While, for the refine stage, several losses are introduced for better reconstruction and described as follows:

Pixel Reconstruct Loss. The pixel reconstruct loss minimize the l1-norm distance between the output image $I_{out} = f(I_{in})$ and the ground-truth image I_{gt}.

$$L_{rec} = ||I_{out} - I_{gt}|| \tag{6}$$

Adversarial Loss. Based on previous work [10], integrating adversarial loss to train the model would alleviate the blurriness caused by minimizing l1 loss but the gradient of the generator can easily disappear. To solve this problem, motivated by [6], hinge loss is used to substitute the original adversarial loss in training, which is defined as:

$$L_{G_{adv}} = -E_{x \sim P_{sample}}[D(x)] \tag{7}$$

$$L_{D_{adv}} = E_{x \sim P_{data}}[\min(0, -1 + D(x))] - E_{x \sim P_{sample}}[\min(0, -1 - D(x))] \tag{8}$$

Perceptual Loss. Since only using element-wise loss would lack enough high-level semantics information, we introduce perceptual loss [5] to help capture more high level structure,

$$L_{per} = \frac{1}{C_j H_j w_j} ||\phi_j(I_{out}) - \phi_j(I_{gt})||_2^2 \tag{9}$$

where φ is the pre-trained VGG19 network feature extractor [11], and $\varphi(\cdot)$ is the corresponding feature maps of the j-th layer. We select relu1_2, relu2_2, and relu3_2 layer to compute the perceptual loss.

Style Loss. To preserve the style consistency, the style loss is taken into consideration. With the help of the style loss, our model could learn the style information from background

$$L_{sty} = \frac{1}{C_j H_j w_j} ||G(\phi_j(I_{out})) - G(\phi_j(I_{gt}))||_2^2 \tag{10}$$

where φ is the pre-trained VGG19 network feature extractor, G denotes the Gram matrix, j denotes the layer of the feature map. Similar to the calculation of perceptual loss, the feature maps of layers elu1_2, relu2_2, and relu3_2 are selected to compute this loss.

Cosine Loss. Inspired by ExpandNet [8], a LDR-to-HDR translation work that requires consistent HDR output images, the cosine loss is taken into consideration for pixel-level consistency. It performs better in maintaining color consistency and reducing color shift and is defined as:

$$L_{cos} = 1 - \frac{1}{K} \sum_{j=i}^{K} \frac{I_{out}^j \cdot I_{gt}^j}{||I_{out}^j||_2 ||I_{gt}^j||_2} \tag{11}$$

where I^j is the j-th RGB pixel vector of image I, while K is the total number of pixels of the image.

Overall Loss. In summary, the overall object function for our model lies as follows:

$$L_{total} = \lambda_{sty} L_{sty} + \lambda_{per} L_{per} + \lambda_{rec} L_{rec} + \lambda_{adv} L_{adv} + \lambda_{cos} L_{cos} \tag{12}$$

where $\lambda_{sty}, \lambda_{per}, \lambda_{rec}, \lambda_{adv}, \lambda_{cos}$ are the tradeoff parameters for the style, perceptual, reconstruction, adversarial, and cosine losses, respectively.

4   Experiments

4.1   Datasets

Experiments are conducted on three public image datasets, including a face dataset Celeba-HQ, and two scenery datasets, Paris Street View and Places2.

– Celeba-HQ [7]: Celeba-HQ is a high-quality version of Celeba dataset. It has 30,000 images, and we randomly select 28,000 images of the dataset for training and 2,000 for testing.
– Paris Street View [10]: Paris dataset has 14,900 training images and 100 test images, which are collected from the street views of Paris. Each image contains the information of buildings in Paris and the structure of buildings such as windows and doors.
– Places2 [19]: Places2 is a challenging dataset that contains more than 1 million training images from 365 categories of scenes. Since the amount of Places2 test dataset is too large, we take the validation set of Places2 instead, as our test set for comparison.
– Mask Datasets: We use two kinds of mask datasets: center mask and irregular mask dataset. The center mask dataset covers 25% area of the image in random places as a square form. The irregular mask dataset is generated by the irregular mask generation method proposed by [16], and each generated irregular mask covers 10%–50% of the image randomly.

4.2   Training Details

In the preprocessing stage, the training images are resized to 256×256. In particular, for Paris Street View, the images are cropped into three parts: left, center and right. Each part is 537×537 and will be resized to 256×256 for training. During training, the commonly-used mask generation algorithm proposed by [16] is applied for irregular mask generation. Based on the basis of experimental observations, the hyperparameters are set as $\lambda_{sty} = 100$, $\lambda_{per} = 0.1$, $\lambda_{rec} = 1$, $\lambda_{adv} = 0.1$ and $\lambda_{cos} = 5$. For all the datasets, the batch size is set as 8. A special learning rule TTUR [3] that set the learning rate as $lr_g = 0.0001$ and $lr_d = 0.0004$ for generator and discriminator respectively, is adopted in training progress. We adopt the Adam Optimizer where β_1 is 0.5, and β_2 is 0.999 to optimize our model. All the experiments are implemented in PyTorch and conducted on an Ubuntu 16.08 System with 11G NVIDIA 1080Ti GPU.

4.3   Performance Evaluation

We conduct both qualitative and quantitative comparison experiments on the test set of the three public datasets with using the proposed method HCA-Net and the following three state-of-the-art GAN-based inpainting methods:

– CA [15]: A two-stage based network with a contextual attention module for finer refinement
– GATE [16]: An inpainting network which take gate convolution instead of conventional convolution
– PEN [17]: A pyramid-fill encoder-decoder network for image inpainting which is based on U-Net structure

Quantitative Comparisons. The comparison is conducted under two conditions, center mask and irregular mask. For the center mask condition, the test images are masked with a 128×128 center square mask. While, for irregular mask, a irregular mask generation approach from [16] is used to generate a 10,000 irregular mask dataset. Then we shuffle them and apply the same mask for the same test image. As CA and PEN-Net do not provide pre-trained model based on the irregular mask, we only compare the results produced by HCA-Net and Gate. We use mean Absolute Error (MAE), Peak Signal-to-Noise Ratio (PSNR), Structural Similarity (SSIM), and Fréchet Inception Distance (FID) as evaluation metrics. As shown in Table 1, our approach obtains a superior performance both on Celeba-HQ and Places2 in PSNR, SSIM, and MAE, and gains a second better fid score. Since our fid score is close to that of Gate, we deprecated the gate convolution for faster inpainting in our work.

Table 1. Comparison results on public datasets with PSNR, SSIM, MAE and FID under two condition (center mask and 10%–50% irregular mask). ↑ higher is better, ↓ lower is better (The best result is in bold form)

Datasets		Celeba-HQ		Places2	
Mask type		Center mask	Irregular mask	Center mask	Irregular mask
PSNR↑	CA	19.810	–	24.132	–
	PEN	20.579	–	25.485	–
	GATE	20.404	26.101	25.580	29.641
	Our method	**21.668**	**28.489**	**26.172**	**30.851**
SSIM↑	CA	0.742	–	0.864	–
	PEN	0.731	–	0.894	–
	GATE	0.736	0.922	0.900	0.963
	Our method	**0.778**	**0.940**	**0.910**	**0.968**
MAE↓	CA	5.31%	–	3.32%	–
	PEN	5.15%	–	2.83%	–
	GATE	5.55%	2.65%	2.58%	1.68%
	Our method	**4.20%**	**1.82%**	**2.38%**	**1.20%**
FID↓	CA	7.169	–	9.543	–
	PEN	16.759	–	9.920	–
	GATE	6.683	**1.12**	**7.048**	**2.752**
	Our method	**6.066**	1.29	7.887	2.805

Visual Results. Figure 3 shows the visual results of our method and those of the three state-of-the-art approaches on Celeba-HQ. CA is effective in finer details repair, but the results tend to be color inconsistent. Gated treats the missing region and the known region respectively, but performs poor in generating plausible content. PEN-Net reconstructs the content from multi-level features but the content between the missing region and the known region tends to be discontinuous. In comparison to these methods, the purposed HCA-Net tends to generate more visual-pleasing and natural results. In addition, as shown in Fig. 4, our method also produces a more consistent result in the condition of irregular masks.

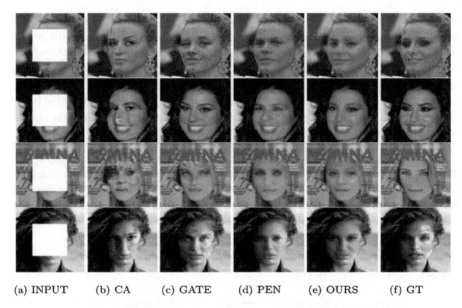

(a) INPUT   (b) CA   (c) GATE   (d) PEN   (e) OURS   (f) GT

Fig. 3. The visual results of different methods on Celeba-HQ

4.4 Ablation Study

Parameter Selection and Evaluation of HCAM. To evaluate the performance of HCAM and select an appropriate value of α for further experiment, we train our model on dataset Celeba-HQ, where we let the values of α ranged from 0 to 1. Since the result generated by GAN may be stochastic, we take the mean PSNR of the last 5 epochs test results for comparison. Then this result is taken as a guide to select a suitable value of α for further experiment.

(a) INPUT   (b) GATE   (c) OURS   (d) GT

Fig. 4. The inpaint result based on irregular mask by our method ((a) input, (b) gate, (c) ours, and (d) ground-truth)

As the guidance of Table 2, we set α = 0.5 for other datasets. Then, we compare the results produced by HCAM with results generated by using cosine distance or Euclidean distance to demonstrate the efficiency of HCAM. As shown in Table 3, the HCAM performs better than the other two methods both in PSNR and SSIM.

Table 2. Comparison of the mean psnr of test results produced by the last 5 epochs model trained with different α

α	0.1	0.2	0.3	0.4	0.5	0.6	0.7	0.8	0.9
PSNR	26.120	26.131	26.153	26.157	26.172	26.146	26.150	26.139	26.122

Table 3. Comparisons of the performance obtained by our method with that obtained by cosine distance and Euclidean distance

Measurements	Cosine	Euclidean	Ours
PSNR	26.1089	26.1434	**26.1719**
SSIM	0.9062	0.9077	**0.9096**

Evaluation of Loss Function. We set the values of hyperparameters $(\lambda_{sty}, \lambda_{per}, \lambda_{cos})$ as zero to evaluate the role of perceptual loss, style loss, and cosine loss. The visual results are shown in Fig. 5, and we can find that the generation result of the default setting is more natural. Without cosine loss, the pixel is inconsistent when zooming in the image. While, without the perceptual and style loss, the inpaint result lacks enough structure information. Moreover, as shown in Table 4, the model which is trained by overall loss performs better than those trained by other settings.

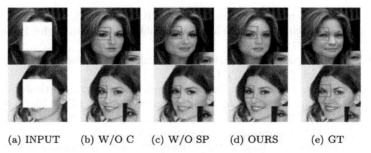

(a) INPUT   (b) W/O C   (c) W/O SP   (d) OURS   (e) GT

Fig. 5. Visual comparisons of different loss setting: (a) input, (b) result without cosine loss (c) result without perceptual and style loss (d) original (e) gt (Best view in zoom-in)

Table 4. Comparisons of the performance of different loss setting

Methods	PSNR	SSIM
w/o cosine loss	25.63	0.901
w/o perceptual loss and style loss	26.08	0.906
Default Setting	26.17	0.910

5   Conclusion and Future Work

In this paper, we propose a coarse-to-refine based network (HCA-Net) to address the image inpainting problem. We designed a new contextual attention module HCAM that better models the relation between extracted image patches. Besides, we introduced the cosine loss to enforce the consistency of generative image. Extensive experiments on public datasets have shown that our proposed method outperforms the previous inpainting methods. However, our work shows poor performance when the information is not enough. In our future work, we will analyze and overcome this problem and simplify our model for fast image inpainting.

Acknowledgement. This work was supported in part by the National Natural Science Foundation of China (Grant 62002230).

References

1. Barnes, C., Shechtman, E., Finkelstein, A., Goldman, D.B.: PatchMatch: a randomized correspondence algorithm for structural image editing. ACM Trans. Graph. (Proc. SIGGRAPH) **28**(3), 1–11 (2009)
2. Bertalmio, M., Sapiro, G., Caselles, V., Ballester, C.: Image inpainting. In: Proceedings of the 27th Annual Conference on Computer Graphics and Interactive Techniques, pp. 417–424 (2000)
3. Heusel, M., Ramsauer, H., Unterthiner, T., Nessler, B., Hochreiter, S.: Gans trained by a two time-scale update rule converge to a local nash equilibrium. Adv. Neural. Inf. Process. Syst. **30**, 6626–6637 (2017)
4. Iizuka, S., Simo-Serra, E., Ishikawa, H.: Globally and locally consistent image com-pletion. ACM Trans. Graph. (ToG) **36**(4), 1–14 (2017)
5. Johnson, J., Alahi, A., Fei-Fei, L.: Perceptual losses for real-time style transfer and super-resolution. In: Leibe, B., Matas, J., Sebe, N., Welling, M. (eds.) ECCV 2016. LNCS, vol. 9906, pp. 694–711. Springer, Cham (2016). https://doi.org/10.1007/978-3-319-46475-6_43
6. Lim, J.H., Ye, J.C.: Geometric gan. arXiv preprint arXiv:1705.02894 (2017)
7. Liu, Z., Luo, P., Wang, X., Tang, X.: Deep learning face attributes in the wild. In: Proceedings of International Conference on Computer Vision (ICCV) (2015)
8. Marnerides, D., Bashford-Rogers, T., Hatchett, J., Debattista, K.: Expandnet: a deep convolutional neural network for high dynamic range expansion from low dynamic range content. In: Computer Graphics Forum, vol. 37, pp. 37–49. Wiley Online Library (2018)
9. Miyato, T., Kataoka, T., Koyama, M., Yoshida, Y.: Spectral normalization for generative adversarial networks. arXiv preprint arXiv:1802.05957 (2018)

10. Pathak, D., Krahenbuhl, P., Donahue, J., Darrell, T., Efros, A.A.: Context en- coders: feature learning by inpainting. In: Proceedings of the IEEE Conference on Computer Vision and Pattern Recognition, pp. 2536–2544 (2016)
11. Simonyan, K., Zisserman, A.: Very deep convolutional networks for large-scale image recognition. arXiv preprint arXiv:1409.1556 (2014)
12. Ting, H., Chen, S., Liu, J., Tang, X.: Image inpainting by global structure and texture propagation. In: Proceedings of the 15th ACM international conference on Multimedia, pp. 517–520 (2007)
13. Wang, X., Girshick, R., Gupta, A., He, K.: Non-local neural networks. In: Proceedings of the IEEE Conference on Computer Vision and Pattern Recognition, pp. 7794–7803 (2018)
14. Xu, Z., Sun, J.: Image inpainting by patch propagation using patch sparsity. IEEE Trans. Image Process. **19**(5), 1153–1165 (2010)
15. Yu, J., Lin, Z., Yang, J., Shen, X., Lu, X., Huang, T.S.: Generative image inpainting with contextual attention. In: Proceedings of the IEEE Conference on Computer Vision and Pattern Recognition, pp. 5505–5514 (2018)
16. Yu, J., Lin, Z., Yang, J., Shen, X., Lu, X., Huang, T.S.: Free-form image inpainting with gated convolution. In: Proceedings of the IEEE International Conference on Computer Vision, pp. 4471–4480 (2019)
17. Zeng, Y., Fu, J., Chao, H., Guo, B.: Learning pyramid-context encoder network for high-quality image inpainting. In: Proceedings of the IEEE Conference on Computer Vision and Pattern Recognition, pp. 1486–1494 (2019)
18. Zhong, S.h., Liu, Y., Zhang, Y., Chung, F.l.: Attention modeling for face recognition via deep learning. In: Proceedings of the Annual Meeting of the Cognitive Science Society, vol. 34 (2012)
19. Zhou, B., Khosla, A., Lapedriza, A., Torralba, A., Oliva, A.: Places2: a large-scale database for scene understanding. Arxiv preprint (2015)

Atypical Lyrics Completion Considering Musical Audio Signals

Kento Watanabe[✉][iD] and Masataka Goto[✉][iD]

National Institute of Advanced Industrial Science and Technology (AIST),
Central 2, 1-1-1 Umezono, Tsukuba, Ibaraki, Japan
{kento.watanabe,m.goto}@aist.go.jp

Abstract. This paper addresses the novel task of lyrics completion for creative support. Our proposed task aims to suggest words that are (1) atypical but (2) suitable for musical audio signals. Previous approaches focused on fully automatic lyrics generation tasks using language models that tend to generate frequent phrases (e.g., "I love you"), despite the importance of atypicality for creative support. In this study, we propose a novel vector space model with negative sampling strategy and hypothesize that embedding multimodal aspects (words, draft sentences, and musical audio signals) in a unified vector space contributes to capturing (1) the atypicality of words and (2) the relationships between words and the moods of music audio. To test our hypothesis, we used a large-scale dataset to investigate whether the proposed multimodal vector space model suggests atypical words. Several findings were obtained from experiment results. One is that the negative sampling strategy contributes to suggesting atypical words. Another is that embedding audio signals contributes to suggesting words suitable for the mood of the provided music audio.

Keywords: Lyrics completion · Natural language processing · Multi-modal embedding

1 Introduction

Lyrics are important in conveying emotions and messages in popular music, and the recently increasing popularity of user-generated content on video sharing services makes writing lyrics popular even for novice writers. Lyrics writers, however, unlike the writers of prose text, need to create attractive phrases suitable for the given music. Thus, writing lyrics is not an easy job.

This difficulty has motivated a range of studies for computer-assisted lyrics writing [9,10,13]. For example, Watanabe et al. (2018) train a Recurrent Neural Network Language Model (RNN-LM) that generates fluent lyrics while maintaining compatibility between the boundaries of lyrics and melody structures. Those studies, however, aim to generate lyrics fully automatically. Even if language models generate perfect lyrics, a fully automatic generation system cannot support writers because it ignores their intentions.

© Springer Nature Switzerland AG 2021
J. Lokoč et al. (Eds.): MMM 2021, LNCS 12572, pp. 174–186, 2021.
https://doi.org/10.1007/978-3-030-67832-6_15

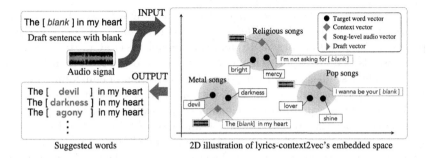

Fig. 1. Overview of lyrics completion task. Our model predicts words similar to the input draft sentences and musical audio signals.

In this study, for creative support instead of lyrics generation, we design a lyrics completion task to recommend candidate words for the blank in a given sentence (Fig. 1). Specifically, we focus on the following two properties of lyrics. (1) Lyrics sometimes depend on the *moods* of music audio (e.g., 'love" is often used in ballad songs, "kill" is often used in metal songs). However, no text completion system suggests words that are appropriate for the mood of music audio. Thus, we propose a task in which a system recommends words suitable for the mood of a given song excerpt represented as an audio signal. (2) *Atypicality* is important in writing lyrics; to make lyrics attractive, writers consider both typical and atypical phrases. However, previous research on automatic lyrics generation has used language models that predict highly frequent (i.e., *typical*) words. Creative support systems need also to recommend unusual and rare (i.e., *atypical*) words while maintaining the fluency of the sentence.

We therefore propose a multimodal vector space model (VSM), *lyrics-context2vec*, that, given a draft sentence with a blank, suggests atypical words while maintaining the relationship with the mood of music audio. With lyrics-context2vec, input vectors (i.e., combinations of music audios and draft sentences) and output vectors (i.e., atypical words) are located near each other in a unified high-dimensional vector space (Fig. 1). This model suggests atypical words because we use typical words as negative examples in its training.

The contributions of this study are summarized as follows: (1) We propose, for creative support, a novel multimodal vector space model that captures the relationship between atypical words and the mood of music audio. (2) We demonstrate that our model suggests words suitable for the mood of the input musical audio signal. (3) We demonstrate that our model suggests words more atypical than those suggested by RNN-LMs.

2   Related Work

We first discuss the related work on vector space models focusing on music. Weston et al. (2011) proposed a model for embedding acoustic signals, artist tags, and social tags in a unified vector space [15]. They designed several relationships based on assumptions such as *"the songs created by an artist are correlated"*. Lopopolo and van Miltenburg (2015) and Karamanolakis et al. (2016) used a bag-of-audio-words (BoAW) approach and vectorized audio words by utilizing social tags [3,6]. Their studies shared with ours the motivation of embedding multiple aspects in vector spaces but dealt only with audio and metadata without lyrics even though lyrics are an important element that conveys messages and emotions of music. Yu et al. (2019) and Watanabe and Goto (2019) embedded different aspects (i.e., lyric word and song sound) into a unified vector space [12,16]. To the best of our knowledge, there has been no study modeling the relationship between a draft sentence of lyrics (a sentence with a blank) and music audio simultaneously.

We then discuss the related work on automatic lyrics generation. Barbieri et al. (2012), Potash et al. (2015), and Watanabe et al. (2018) proposed models that generate lyrics under a range of constraints provided in terms of topic, rhyme, rhythm, part-of-speech, and so on [1,10,14]. Oliveira et al. (2007) and Watanabe et al. (2018) proposed language models that generate singable lyrics based on melody segment positions [9,13]. However, they used language models that tend to generate typical words and did not focus on the atypicality of lyrics.

This paper thus can be considered the first work that tackles the novel lyrics completion task by dealing with both of those relationship and atypicality.

3   Lyrics-Audio Data

To model the relationship between lyrics and moods of music audio, we obtained 458,572 songs, each consisting of a pair comprising a text file of English lyrics and an audio file of a music excerpt[1]. Here each text file contains all sentences of the lyrics of a song, and each audio file is a short popular-music excerpt (30 s, 44.1 kHz) that was collected from the Internet and originally provided for trial listening. In this study, we embedded the moods of audio signals as well as the words of lyrics directly into a unified vector space without using metadata such as genre tags because those tags are too coarse. The total duration of all the excerpted audio files was more than 159 days.

3.1   Bag-of-Audio-Words

To represent the mood feature of a short music excerpt, we use a discrete symbol called an *audio-word (aw)* [5]. The bag-of-audio-words (BoAW) creation procedure is as follows. (1) Each music excerpt is downsampled to 22,050 Hz. (2) *LibROSA*, a python package for music and audio analysis, is used to extract 20-dimensional mel-frequency cepstral coefficients (MFCCs) with the FFT size of 2048 samples and the hop size of 512 samples. This result is represented as an

---

[1] In our experiments, English lyrics text were provided by a lyrics distribution company.

MFCC matrix (20×1280). (3) The MFCC matrix is divided into 128 submatrices (20×10) without overlap. (4) To create a vocabulary of k audio-words, we apply the $k\text{-}means\text{++}$ algorithm to all the divided MFCCs of all the songs. In other words, each k-th cluster corresponds to an audio-word (aw). In this study we made 3000 audio-words.

4   Atypical Word Completion Model Considering Audio

In this section we propose a multimodal vector space model *lyrics-context2vec* that, given a music audio signal and a draft sentence with a blank, suggests atypical words while maintaining the relationship with the mood of the music audio. Specifically, lyrics-context2vec suggests N-best atypical words $w^1, ..., w^N$ that could fit with the context. Here we assume three types of contexts: (1) the words on the left side of the blank, (2) the words on the right side of the blank, and (3) the BoAW converted from the audio signal.

This model is useful for creative support because it helps a user (lyrics writer) come up with new ideas for a song by looking at atypical words suitable for it. There are two technical problems in recommending atypical words suitable for the music audio. First, since most statistical models (e.g., RNN-LM) learn to predict highly frequent words, it is hard to suggest atypical words that are important for creative support. Second, how to model the relationship between words and musical audio signals is not obvious.

To address the first problem, we focus on the negative sampling strategy in word2vec [8]. This strategy was proposed for the purpose of approximation because computation of loss function is time-consuming. We, however, use negative sampling for the purpose of suppression of typical word recommendation because we want to suggest *atypical* words for creative support. Since negative examples are drawn from the distribution of highly frequent words, it is expected that input vectors of contexts are located far from vectors of typical words. It is not obvious that the negative sampling contributes to suggesting atypical words.

To address the second problem, we utilize the mechanism of *lyrics2vec* proposed by [12]. In lyrics2vec, co-occurring audio-words and lyric words are located near each other under the assumption that *some words of lyrics are written depending on the musical audio signal* (e.g., words about love tend to be used in ballad songs).

4.1   Model Construction

Lyrics-context2vec is based on lyrics2vec and context2vec [7]. Formally, context2vec is a vector space model that encodes left draft words $w_1, ..., w_{t-1}$ and right draft words $w_{t+1}, ..., w_T$ into latent vectors z_1 and z_2, respectively, using two Recurrent Neural Networks (RNNs). Then the target word vector $v(w_t)$ and a vector that is nonlinearly transformed from the latent vectors are mapped closely into a unified vector space. The loss function of context2vec E_{c2v} is

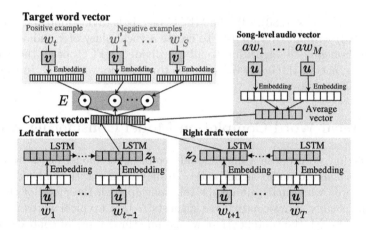

Fig. 2. Overview of the proposed lyrics-context2vec model.

defined so that the inner product of the target word vector $\boldsymbol{v}(w_t)$ and the non-linearly transformed vector is maximized:

$$E_{c2v} = -\log\sigma\Big(\boldsymbol{v}(w_t)^{\mathsf{T}} \cdot \mathrm{MLP}([\boldsymbol{z}_1, \boldsymbol{z}_2])\Big) - \sum_{s=1}^{S} \log\sigma\Big(-\boldsymbol{v}(w_s')^{\mathsf{T}} \cdot \mathrm{MLP}([\boldsymbol{z}_1, \boldsymbol{z}_2])\Big), \quad (1)$$

where $\sigma(\cdot)$ is a sigmoid function. To obtain an x-dimensional word vector representation, we define an embedding function $\boldsymbol{v}(\cdot)$ that maps the target word to an x-dimensional vector. S is the number of negative examples w_s'. $[\boldsymbol{z}_1, \boldsymbol{z}_2]$ denotes a concatenation of latent vectors $\boldsymbol{z}_1$ and $\boldsymbol{z}_2$. $\mathrm{MLP}(\cdot)$ stands for multilayer perceptron (MLP). In this loss function, negative examples w_s' are sampled from the distribution $P(w_s') = D(w_s')^{0.75} / \sum_{w' \in V} (D(w')^{0.75})$ where V is the vocabulary and $D(w')$ is the document frequency of a word w'. In other words, since frequent words tend to be sampled as negative examples, we expect that a draft sentence vector and the vector of highly frequent typical words are located far away from each other. When computing word completion, our system displays target words with high cosine similarity to the input context vector $\mathrm{MLP}([\boldsymbol{z}_1, \boldsymbol{z}_2])$.

Then we extend context2vec to suggest atypical words suitable for both the music audio and the draft sentence by embedding three aspects (i.e., target words, draft sentences, and song-level audio). The structure of this extended model is illustrated in Fig. 2. We concatenate song-level audio and draft vectors and define the loss function E so that the concatenated vector $[\boldsymbol{z}_1, \boldsymbol{z}_2, \frac{1}{M}\sum_{m=1}^{M} \boldsymbol{u}(aw_m)]$ is located close to the target word vector $\boldsymbol{v}(w)$:

$$E = -\log\sigma\Big(\boldsymbol{v}(w_t)^{\mathsf{T}} \cdot [\boldsymbol{z}_1, \boldsymbol{z}_2, \frac{1}{M}\sum_{m=1}^{M} \boldsymbol{u}(aw_m)]\Big)$$

$$- \sum_{s=1}^{S} \log\sigma\Big(-\boldsymbol{v}(w_s')^{\mathsf{T}} \cdot [\boldsymbol{z}_1, \boldsymbol{z}_2, \frac{1}{M}\sum_{m=1}^{M} \boldsymbol{u}(aw_m)]\Big), \quad (2)$$

where we define the dimension of draft vectors z_1, z_2 as d and define an embedding function $u(\cdot)$ that maps the context word/audio-word to a d-dimensional vector. Thus the dimension of target word vectors $v(\cdot)$ is $x = 3d$. M is the number of audio-words in the song. We define the average of audio-word vectors as a song-level audio vector.

In the original context2vec the concatenated vector connects to an MLP, but lyrics-context2vec uses the concatenated vector directly without an MLP. This is because it is useful for lyrics writers to be able to flexibly change the contexts (draft sentence and music audio) to obtain the suggested words. For example, even if a user provides only the left draft vector z_1, the lyrics-context2vec can suggest appropriate words by computing the cosine similarity between the word vector $v(w_t)$ and the concatenated vector $[z_1, \mathbf{0}, \mathbf{0}]$[2]. Models with an MLP cannot provide this flexibility since all the three vectors are always required to compute an MLP. We therefore do not use an MLP in the proposed model.

5   Experiments

In order to evaluate whether lyrics-context2vec can suggest (1) atypical words and (2) words suitable for music audio, we designed word completion tasks. The input of these tasks is $T-1$ draft words $w_1, ..., w_{t-1}, w_{t+1}, ..., w_T$ of each sentence in a test song. Therefore the model needs to fill in the t-th blank with a word. We used the following *Score* to evaluate the performance of models in the lyrics completion task:

$$Score@N = \frac{\sum_{r \in R} \mathbb{1}(r \in \{h^1, ..., h^N\})}{|R|}, \tag{3}$$

where r denotes the correct word and $|R|$ is the number of blanks in the test data. $h^1, ..., h^N$ are the top N words suggested by the model. $\mathbb{1}(\cdot)$ is the indicator function. In this study we calculated $Score@N$, with N ranging from 1 to 20 under the assumption that our support system suggests 20 words to users.

Here it is important to define which word in each sentence is the correct word r. We designed four types of correct answers:

Typicality. We defined a randomly chosen word in each sentence of the test song as the correct word r. In this metric, high-frequency words tend to be chosen as the correct answer. In other words, this metric is a measure of typical word completion.

Atypicality. We first calculated the document frequency of words of the test song and then defined the minimum-document-frequency word in each sentence as the correct word. This metric is a measure of atypical word completion.

Music+Typicality. In each sentence of the test song, we extracted the word most similar to the music audio of the song by using the pre-trained lyrics2vec that

---
[2] $\mathbf{0}$ is the zero vector that has all components equal to zero.

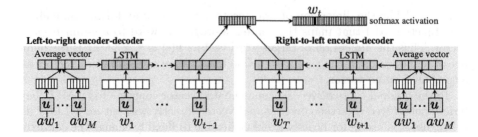

Fig. 3. Overview of Encoder-Decoder model.

was proposed by Watanabe and Goto [12]. If the document frequency of the extracted word was more than 1,000, we defined this word as the correct word for the sentence and did not use the other words. This metric is a measure of prediction of *typical* words suitable for the music audio of the song.

Music+Atypicality. We extracted the word most similar to the music audio of the song as with Music+Typicality. If the document frequency of the extracted word was less than or equal to 1,000, we defined this word as the correct word for the sentence and did not use the other words. This metric is a measure of prediction of *atypical* words suitable for the music audio of the song.

5.1 Comparison Methods

To investigate the effect of our lyrics-context2vec, we compared the following four models. (1) *Bi-RNN-LM*, a standard bidirectional RNN-LM trained with lyrics without audio information. (2) *Encoder-Decoder*, a Bi-RNN-LM in which the song-level audio vector $\frac{1}{M}\sum_{m=1}^{M} \boldsymbol{u}(aw_m)$ is input to the initial RNN state (Fig. 3). (3) *Context2vec*, a context2vec [7] without a multilayer perceptron (MLP). (4) *Lyrics-context2vec*, the proposed model.

The RNN-LM type models (Bi-RNN-LM and Encoder-Decoder) predict words with high predictive probability in the blank, and the VSM-type models (context2vec and lyrics-context2vec) predict the most similar words in the blank.

5.2 Settings

Dataset. We randomly split our dataset into 80-10-10% divisions to construct the training, validation, and test data. From those, we used the words whose frequency was more than 20 and converted the others to a special symbol ⟨unk⟩.

Parameters. In all models, we utilized Long Short-Term Memory (LSTM) [2] as the RNN layer. We chose $d = 300$ for the dimension of the audio-word vector $\boldsymbol{u}(\cdot)$ and the dimension of the LSTM hidden state $\boldsymbol{z}$. We chose $x = 900$ for the dimension of the target word vector $\boldsymbol{v}(\cdot)$. We used negative sampling with $S = 20$ negative examples. We used a categorical cross-entropy loss for outputs of RNN-LM type models. We used Adam [4] with an initial learning rate of 0.001 for parameter optimization and used a mini-batch size of 100. Training was run for 10 epochs, and the model used for testing was the one that achieved the best Music+Atypicality score on the validation set. In this study, we utilized the pre-trained lyrics2vec [12] for Music+Typicality and Music+Atypicality; this lyrics2vec was trained with the same parameters as lyrics-context2vec.

5.3   Results

Figure 4(a) shows the result of the typical word completion task (Typicality). As shown in this figure, RNN-LM type models achieved higher scores than VSM type models. This is because the RNN-LM type models are trained to maximize the probability of generating highly frequent phrases. Interestingly, we can see that there is no difference between the scores of Bi-RNN-LM and Encoder-Decoder. This indicates that audio information does not contribute to predicting typical words. We speculated that typical words are strongly correlated with draft sentences rather than audio.

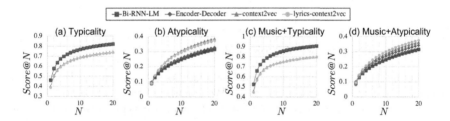

Fig. 4. Results of the lyrics completion tasks.

Regarding the task of predicting the typical words suitable for music audio (Fig. 4(c)), we can observe results similar to those for the task Typicality. This reinforces the fact that typical words can be predicted from only the draft sentence, without using audio information.

Regarding the atypical word completion (Fig. 4(b)), VSM type models achieved higher scores than RNN-LM type models. This indicates that negative sampling contributes to suppression of typical word completion. Overall, for atypical word completion tasks it is desirable to use a VSM with negative sampling rather than a language model aimed at generating highly frequent phrases.

Regarding the main task Music+Atypicality (Fig. 4(d)), lyrics-context2vec predicted atypical words suitable for music audio better than all other models. This means that our model captures both the atypicality and the relationship between a music audio and words simultaneously. Moreover, we can see that lyrics-context2vec performs better than context2vec, and Encoder-Decoder performs better than Bi-RNN-LM. This indicates that using audio information contributes to suggesting atypical words suitable for the music audio.

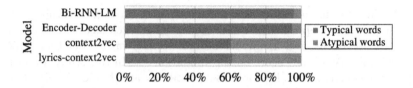

Fig. 5. Ratio of the suggested typical/atypical words.

Table 1. Effect of multilayer perceptron (MLP).

Score@20	The proposed lyrics-context2vec w/o MLP	lyrics-context2vec with MLP
Typicality	0.738	**0.742**
Atypicality	**0.372**	0.351
Music+Typicality	0.799	**0.807**
Music+Atypicality	**0.376**	0.351

5.4   Ratio of Suggested Atypical Words

In all completion tasks, we calculated how many of the top 20 words suggested by each model were typical or atypical. We calculated the document frequency of words and assumed that the top 10% of them are typical words (i.e., the remaining 90% are atypical words).

Figure 5 shows the ratio of typical/atypical words suggested by each model. As we can see in this figure, VSM type models suggested many more atypical words than RNN-LM type models did. This result confirms our intuition that negative sampling contributes to suppression of typical word completion while RNN-LM type models maximize the probability of predicting typical words.

6   Discussions

6.1   Effect of Multilayer Perceptron (MLP)

For the purpose of developing a support system that allows the user to flexibly change the contexts (draft sentence and music audio), we omitted the MLP from our lyrics-context2vec even though an MLP is used in the original context2vec. Here we investigate whether excluding the MLP has a negative impact on word completion tasks. To check the effect of an MLP, we compared the performance of lyrics-context2vec with that of the model with an MLP.

Table 1 summarizes the results. Regarding typical word completion tasks Typicality and Music+Typicality, the model without an MLP achieved almost the same performance as the model with an MLP. Interestingly, the model without an MLP improved the performance of atypical word completion tasks Atypicality and Music+Atypicality. We thus confirmed that excluding the MLP does not have a negative impact for our purposes.

Table 2. The suggested words for draft sentences and songs. We highlight atypical words in bold. Here we calculated the document frequency of words and assumed that the top 10% of them are typical words and the remaining 90% are atypical words. Words are shown in descending order of similarity or prediction probability.

Draft	Music audio	Model	Suggested words
I [ ] you	No audio	Bi-RNN-LM	love, need, know, want, remember, thought, miss, promise, understand, believe, see, like, think, tell, told, **appreciate**, worship, wanted, loved, hate
		context2vec	love, **appreciate**, adore, **implore**, **guarantee**, promise, followed, miss, want, worship, **trusted**, thank, **approached**, believed, need, remember, watched, **entertain**, **assure**, recognize
	Killing Time (Metal)	Encoder-Decoder	**despise**, know, want, thought, remember, followed, wish, **await**, believe, need, love, **summon**, watched, promise, understand, will, **suffocate**, **defy**, **implore**, **destroyed**
		lyrics-context2vec (the proposed model)	**despise**, **await**, **trusted**, **appreciate**, remember, followed, worship, **implore**, believed, thank, hate, **reject**, **assure**, adore, promised, **consume**, **warned**, **possess**, **beckon**, **destroyed**
	Amazing Grace (Pop)	Encoder-Decoder	love, want, need, adore, know, remember, thought, believe, hear, miss, promise, found, will, worship, thank, followed, understand, have, loved, believed
		lyrics-context2vec (the proposed model)	adore, **appreciate**, love, **overheard**, promise, remember, **enfold**, **await**, **forsake**, promised, **hypnotize**, recognize, need, followed, missed, **surround**, thank, follow, deliver, thought
The [ ] in my heart	No audio	Bi-RNN-LM	pain, deep, place, thunder, fire, devil, beating, voices, hole, poison, wind, sun, darkness, burning, love, feeling, song, world, beat, light
		context2vec	**tremors**, pain, devil, **sparkles**, **pounding**, **dagger**, deep, echo, magic, poison, **conflicts**, echoes, diamonds, **toxins**, hunger, hole, **bloodlust**, burning, demon, **blackness**
	Killing Time (Metal)	Encoder-Decoder	pain, deep, burning, fire, hole, world, dead, darkness, feeling, beauty, devil, silence, drowning, shadows, words, dream, demons, power, wind, thunder
		lyrics-context2vec (the proposed model)	hole, devil, burning, emptiness, **blackness**, pain, darkness, demons, **dagger**, hatred, **tremors**, void, fire, **agony**, holes, **essence**, **coldness**, **plague**, **needles**, deep
	Amazing Grace (Pop)	Encoder-Decoder	deep, pain, dream, wind, song, thunder, fire, tears, music, feeling, stars, burning, sunshine, silence, hole, darkness, love, answer, beauty, words
		lyrics-context2vec (the proposed model)	**pains**, ringing, **brightness**, deep, **cuckoo**, angels, **teardrops**, **ache**, roses, **falcon**, music, wind, **waltzes**, troubles, pain, **lump**, **birdie**, melody, **elements**, devil

6.2   Examples of Suggested Words

In the results of lyrics completion tasks, we observed that our lyrics-context2vec suggests an atypical word suitable for the provided music audio. In order to interpret this observation intuitively, we investigated words suggested when draft sentences were fixed and the input music audio was changed. Table 2 shows the top 20 words suggested by each model. In this table, atypical words whose document frequency is among the lowest 90% are shown in bold. We can see that the bolded rare words (e.g., "guarantee" and "entertain") appear more often in word sets suggested by VSM type models than in word sets suggested by RNN-LM type models. This observation supports our claim that negative sampling suppresses typical word completion.

Regarding the calm song *Amazing Grace*, lyrics-context2vec and Encoder-Decoder tended to suggest emotional and positive words (e.g., "missed" and "brightness"). On the other hand, regarding the metal song *Killing Time*, lyrics-context2vec and Encoder-Decoder tended to suggest explicit and negative expressions (e.g., "destroyed" and "darkness"). This indicates that both RNN-LM and VSM type models with song-level audio vectors successfully suggest words suitable for the mood of the provided music audio. These results are consistent with the result of the lyrics completion tasks in Sect. 5. The audio and words used in this table are available at an anonymized web page (https://kentow.github.io/mmm2021/index.html).

7   Conclusion and Future Work

This paper addresses the novel task of lyrics completion for creative support. Our proposed task aims to suggest words that are (1) atypical and (2) suitable for the musical audio signal. Previous work focused on fully automatic lyrics generation using language models that tend to predict highly frequent phrases (e.g., "I love you"), despite the importance of atypicality in creative support.

In this study, we proposed lyrics-context2vec, a multimodal vector space model that suggests atypical but appropriate words for the given music audio and draft sentence. In the vector space of lyrics-context2vec, a vector corresponding to an atypical word in a song and a song-level audio vector corresponding to an audio excerpt of the song are located near each other. Moreover, we trained the models to suggest atypical words by embedding the highly frequent word vector away from the song-level audio vector. No previous study has ever conducted such an analysis of the word completion task focusing on atypicality and relationship with music audio.

In lyrics completion tasks we used a large-scale dataset to investigate whether the proposed multi-aspect vector model suggests atypical but appropriate lyrics. Several findings were obtained from experiment results. One is that the negative sampling strategy contributes to suggesting atypical words. Another is that embedding audio signals contributes to suggesting words suitable for the mood of the provided music audio. We conclude that embedding multiple aspects into a vector space contributes to capturing atypicality and relationship with audio.

We plan to incorporate the proposed lyrics-context2vec model into a writing support system and conduct a user study evaluating that system. We also plan to investigate the behavior of our method when using powerful language models such as Transformers [11] instead of LSTMs. Future work will also include application of this model to different types of texts in which atypical words are effective, such as poetry and advertising slogans.

Acknowledgements. The authors appreciate SyncPower Corporation for providing lyrics data. This work was supported in part by JST ACCEL Grant Number JPM-JAC1602, and JSPS KAKENHI Grant Number 20K19878 Japan.

References

1. Barbieri, G., Pachet, F., Roy, P., Esposti, M.D.: Markov constraints for generating lyrics with style. In: Proceedings of the 20th European Conference on Artificial Intelligence, pp. 115–120 (2012)
2. Hochreiter, S., Schmidhuber, J.: Long short-term memory. Neural Comput. **9**(8), 1735–1780 (1997)
3. Karamanolakis, G., Iosif, E., Zlatintsi, A., Pikrakis, A., Potamianos, A.: Audio-based distributional representations of meaning using a fusion of feature encodings. In: INTERSPEECH, pp. 3658–3662 (2016)
4. Kingma, D.P., Ba, J.: Adam: a method for stochastic optimization. In: Proceedings of the 3rd International Conference on Learning Representations (ICLR 2015) (2015)
5. Liu, Y., Zhao, W.L., Ngo, C.W., Xu, C.S., Lu, H.Q.: Coherent bag-of audio words model for efficient large-scale video copy detection. In: Proceedings of the ACM International Conference on Image and Video Retrieval, pp. 89–96 (2010)
6. Lopopolo, A., van Miltenburg, E.: Sound-based distributional models. In: Proceedings of the 11th International Conference on Computational Semantics, pp. 70–75 (2015)
7. Melamud, O., Goldberger, J., Dagan, I.: context2vec: Learning generic context embedding with bidirectional LSTM. In: Proceedings of the 20th SIGNLL Conference on Computational Natural Language Learning, pp. 51–61 (2016)
8. Mikolov, T., Sutskever, I., Chen, K., Corrado, G., Dean, J.: Distributed representations of words and phrases and their compositionality. In: Proceedings of the 26th Annual Conference on Neural Information Processing Systems, pp. 3111–3119 (2013)
9. Oliveira, H.R.G., Cardoso, F.A., Pereira, F.C.: Tra-la-lyrics: an approach to generate text based on rhythm. In: Proceedings of the 4th International Joint Workshop on Computational Creativity, pp. 47–55 (2007)
10. Potash, P., Romanov, A., Rumshisky, A.: GhostWriter: using an LSTM for automatic Rap lyric generation. In: Proceedings of the 2015 Conference on Empirical Methods in Natural Language Processing, pp. 1919–1924 (2015)
11. Vaswani, A., et al.: Attention is all you need. In: Advances in Neural Information Processing Systems 30: Annual Conference on Neural Information Processing Systems 2017, pp. 5998–6008 (2017)
12. Watanabe, K., Goto, M.: Query-by-Blending: a music exploration system blending latent vector representations of lyric word, song audio, and artist. In: Proceedings of the 20th Annual Conference of the International Society for Music Information Retrieval, pp. 144–151 (2019)
13. Watanabe, K., Matsubayashi, Y., Fukayama, S., Goto, M., Inui, K., Nakano, T.: A melody-conditioned lyrics language model. In: Proceedings of the 16th Annual Conference of the North American Chapter of the Association for Computational Linguistics: Human Language Technologies, pp. 163–172 (2018)

14. Watanabe, K., Matsubayashi, Y., Inui, K., Nakano, T., Fukayama, S., Goto, M.: LyriSys: an interactive support system for writing lyrics based on topic transition. In: Proceedings of the 22nd Annual Meeting of the Intelligent User Interfaces Community, pp. 559–563 (2017)
15. Weston, J., Bengio, S., Hamel, P.: Multi-tasking with joint semantic spaces for large-scale music annotation and retrieval. J. New Music Res. **40**(4), 337–348 (2011)
16. Yu, Y., Tang, S., Raposo, F., Chen, L.: Deep cross-modal correlation learning for audio and lyrics in music retrieval. ACM Trans. Multimed. Comput. Commun. Appl. **15**(1), 1–16 (2019)

Improving Supervised Cross-modal Retrieval with Semantic Graph Embedding

Changting Feng[1], Dagang Li[1,2]($\boxtimes$), and Jingwei Zheng[1]

[1] School of ECE, Peking University Shenzhen Graduate School, Shenzhen, China
fengct@pku.edu.cn
[2] International Institute of Next-Generation Internet, Macau University of Science and Technology, Taipa, Macao, Special Administrative Region of China
dagang.li@ieee.org

Abstract. This paper focuses on the use of embedding with global semantic relations to improve the cross modal retrieval. Our method smoothly bridges the heterogeneity gap by graph embedding and then obtains discriminative representation by supervised learning. First, we construct a semantic correlation graph based on the intra-modal similarity and the semantic propagation of pairwise information. Then, embeddings are learnt from the graph semantic structure which enables all the cross-modal data to be mapped into the same space. Second, based on the previous embeddings, we adopt a simple one-branch neural network to enhance the discrimination of the representation by minimizing the discrimination loss and reconstruction loss. Experimental results on three widely-used benchmark datasets clearly demonstrate the improvement of the proposed approach over the state-of-the-art cross-modal retrieval methods.

Keywords: Cross-modal retrieval · Graph embedding · Neural network

1 Introduction

With the rapid growth of multimedia data such as texts, images and videos on the Internet, we are exposed to increasingly different types of data every day. It is common for us to associate different types of data that complement each other to describe the same events or topics. As a result, cross-modal retrieval is becoming increasingly important, through which users can get the results with various media types by taking one of the media type as a query.

However, it is well known that inconsistent distributions and representations of different modalities, such as image and text, cause the heterogeneity gap, which makes it very difficult to measure the cross-modal similarity [15]. To bridge the heterogeneity gap, a large number of cross-modal retrieval methods have been proposed [24]. Most of the existing methods follow the idea of learning a

© Springer Nature Switzerland AG 2021
J. Lokoč et al. (Eds.): MMM 2021, LNCS 12572, pp. 187–199, 2021.
https://doi.org/10.1007/978-3-030-67832-6_16

common space, in which the similarity of different modalities can be computed directly by using the same distance metrics.

The traditional method using statistical correlation analysis is the basic paradigm of common space learning. As one of the most representative works in traditional methods, Canonical Correlation Analysis (CCA) [6] learns a linear projection to a common space by making cross-modal data pairs maximally correlated. However, the real world cross-modal data contains rich correlation that is too complex for the linear projection to model. To address this issue, some kernel-based methods have been proposed, but their performance heavily relies on the choice of kernel function, while it is still an open issue to select the kernel function for particular cross-modal retrieval application [13].

Inspired by the progress of deep neural network (DNN), a large number of DNN-based methods have been proposed to learn the complex nonlinear correlation of cross-modal data in an unsupervised [1,3] or supervised [22,25,30] manner. Conventional DNN-based methods typically focus on how to find a better way to project different modal data into a common space base on the correlation limited to data pair or within the mini-batch. As a result, only partial semantic similarity information of the whole data corpus has been considered. Zhang et al. [29] preserve the similarity information by using a multimodal graph built upon pairwise constraints and K-nearest neighbors. Then the embedding learnt from the graph was used as the cross-modal representation. Although this method can utilize both the labeled and unlabeled data, the pairwise constraints cannot properly explore the inter-modal correlation. To fully explore the semantic similarities, Wu et al. [26] construct a semantic graph for multi-label cross-modal dataset, and learn a full semantic structure-preserved embedding by preserving the local and global semantic structure consistencies as well as local geometric structure consistency. However, using label to construct the graph, result in the fully connection within category, which leads to high time and space complexity, and cannot deal with the unlabeled data.

Accordingly, we present a novel cross-modal learning architecture which preserve various correlations of cross-modal data and learn discriminative representation between semantic categories. The intra-modal and inter-modal similarity is described by our semantic correlation graph built upon K-nearest-neighbors and semantic propagation of pairwise information. In the semantic correlation graph, each data sample from cross-modal dataset is viewed as a semantic vertex, and the various semantic correlation can be captured by the graph embedding learned from the graph context. Moreover, we adopt a one-branch supervised learner to reinforce the label information, by minimizing the discrimination loss in common space and label reconstruction loss in label space.

The main contributions of our work are as follows:

- We propose a novel cross-modal learning architecture, which smoothly bridge the heterogeneity gap between different modalities and use a one-branch supervised learner to explore the semantic discrimination both in the common space and the label space.

- A semantic propagation of inter-modal correlation is developed to construct a semantic balance graph, which has good consistency in semantic and good efficiency in construction.
- Benefit from the semantic correlation graph embedding, we adopt a one-branch neural network to nonlinearly project the embedding into the common space, which contains much less parameters than the widely used two-branch approach.
- Experimental results on widely-used benchmark datasets show the effectiveness of the proposed method comparing to the state-of-the-art methods for cross-modal retrieval.

2   Related Work

In this section, we briefly reviewed the existing cross-modal retrieval methods. The methods can be roughly divided into two categories: binary representation learning [7] and real-valued representation learning [22,25]. The binary representation approaches were also called as cross-modal hashing, and they aim to map the heterogeneous data into a common Hamming space, in which the cross-modal retrieval task can be processed more efficiently. But the representations are encoded to binary, which may result in the loss of information [14].

The proposed method in this paper belongs to the category of real-valued representation methods. A variety of approaches have been proposed to learn the real-valued common representation subsapce [24]. Traditional methods usually learn a latent common space by maximizing the correlation between different modalities, such as CCA [6], Partial Least Squares (PLS) [19], and Multi-set CCA (MCCA) [18]. However these traditional unsupervised approaches ignore some useful semantic information, which is import to discriminate the multi-model data. To exploit the label information, many semi-supervised and supervised approaches were proposed [4].

Moreover, some cross-modal learning methods employed graph for better exploring the semantic relevance of multi-modal data. Zhai et al. [28], proposed Joint Representation Learning (JRL) which incorporate graph regularization into the cross-modal retrieval. With graph regularization, JRL explore jointly the correlation and semantic information in the dataset, regardless of whether the sample is labeled or not. Wang et al. [23] further propose a unified multimodal graph for all media type to better select coupled feature and preserves the inter-modality and intra-modality similarity relationships.

Since deep neural network (DNN) provide better non-linear representation which traditional methods does not have, DNN have recently been employed in many cross-modal methods. Some works extended traditional models into deep methods, such as deep canonical correlation analysis (DCCA) [1], which uses two subnetworks to learn nonlinear transformations into a latent common subspace, where the resulting representations are highly linearly correlated. Inspired by metric learning, Wang et al. [25] proposed a two-branch neural network training by the objective function which combines the cross-view ranking constraints with the within-view structure preservation constraints.

Moreover, graph methods were also consider by some DNN-based methods to model various semantic correlation of cross-modal data. Zhang et al. [29] introduced graph embedding layer which is learned based on the label information and the structure of graph built upon pairwise constraints and KNN. Wu et al. [26] proposed a semantic structure-preserved embedding which is learned toward local and global semantic structure consistencies as well as local geometric structure consistency. The recently proposed methods: ACMR [22] and DSCMR [30], learned discriminative representation and modality-invariant representation simultaneously. ACMR learn invariant feature by employing the adversarial learning and DSCMR use the weight sharing strategy as well as the modality invariant loss. They both exploited semantic label information for discriminative feature and achieved promising performance on cross-modal retrieval tasks.

Although many cross-modal deep methods have been proposed, there is a need to exploit the various relevance of multi-modal data in a global view and capture the nonlinear relation of label information. To achieve this goal, our methods use semantic correlation graph to obtain embedding with rich information and use a nonlinear supervised learner to learn discrimination of them.

3   Proposed Method

3.1   Problem Formulation

Without loss of generality, we focus on cross-modal retrieval for bi-modal data, such as images and text. Assume we have n_v images $\mathcal{V} = \{v_1, \cdots, v_{n_v}\}$ and n_t texts $\mathcal{T} = \{t_1, \cdots, t_{n_t}\}$. Each image is represented as a data point $v_i \in \mathbf{R}^{d_v}$, each text is represented as a data point $t_i \in \mathbf{R}^{d_t}$ and n_i is use to denote an image or a text. In addition, we have the pairwise information which is denoted as image-text pairs: $\Psi = \{(\mathbf{v}_i, \mathbf{t}_i)\}_{i=1}^n$, where v_i and t_i represent the ith instance of image and text. Each image-text pairs is along with a semantic label vector $y_i = [y_{1i}, y_{2i}, \ldots, y_{ai}] \in \mathbf{R}^a$, where a is the categories number. Label vector y_i indicates what labels the image and text has, and $y_{ij} = 1$ if the ith instance belongs to the j category, otherwise $y_{ij} = 0$.

Since the original feature of images and text lie in the different representation space with inconsistent distribution, their similarity cannot be directly measure. Our goal is to project the original feature into a common hidden space that can well preserve the intra-modal similarity and capture the pairwise label information and semantic classification information.

3.2   Framework of the Proposed Method

This paper mainly focuses on leveraging the various correlation of the cross-modal dataset to bridge the heterogeneity gap smoothly and leveraging the label information to learn discrimination of representation in the common space. The general framework of the proposed method is shown in Fig. 1, from which we can see that it consist of three feature spaces: the embedding space, the common hidden space and the label space. And the last two of them are learned together as a supervised learner.

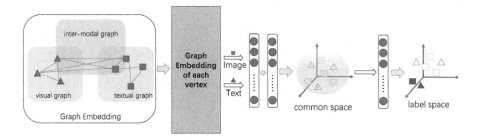

Fig. 1. The general framework of our method.

Graph Embedding. In the embedding space, the similar same modal data should be close and the different modal data with similar meaning should be close as well. Therefore, we build a graph to incorporate the correlation of the intra-modal similarity, the pairwise information and the inter-modal similarity. In this graph, every images and texts is regard as a semantic data point.

Firstly, we preserve the intra-modal similarity of the original feature space by connecting the similar data point from the same modal. Take v_i and v_j as an example, they are connected if one of them is among the other's k-nearest neighbor and weight of edge (v_i, v_j) is defined as follow:

$$w_{ij} = \begin{cases} s\left(v_i, v_j\right), v_i \in N_k\left(v_j\right) \\ 0, v_i \notin N_k\left(v_j\right) \end{cases}$$

The similarity function is $s\left(v_i, v_j\right) = \frac{1}{2}cos(v_i, v_j)$, and the $N_k\left(v_j\right)$ denotes the k-nearest neighbor of v_j.

Secondly, the one-to-one pairwise information are applied as the bridge to connect the different modalities. For example, if v_i and t_i are in pairs, they are connected and the weight of the edge is set to 1, because the pairwise information indicates that these different modal data represent the same underlying content.

However, only use the one-to-one pairwise information to connect the cross-modal data may lead to semantic bias illustrating in Fig. 2a, which would make the data point biased towards intra-modal data and neglect some inter-modal correlation. To address this problem, we propose a semantic propagation method to built up a balance inter-modal correlation. As show in Fig. 2b, image v_i not only connect to its pair text t_i, but also connect to the neighbor of t_i and the weight of edge (v_i, t_j) is defined as follow:

$$\hat{w}_{ij} = \begin{cases} s\left(t_i, t_j\right), t_j \in N_k\left(t_i\right) \\ 0, t_j \notin N_k\left(t_i\right) \end{cases}$$

By using the semantic propagation to construct the semantic graph, we connect all the data into a unified graph with rich semantic structure and enforce vertex with similar semantic information closely connected with each other. Next, we need to learn a embedding that can well preserve the graph context of each vertex.

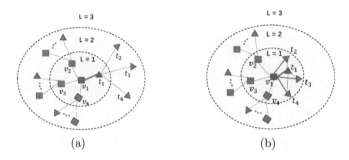

Fig. 2. Illustration showing the important role of semantic propagation. (a) show the graph only with KNN connection and one-to-one pairwise connection. For image v_1, its **first-order** neighbour only contain its KNN $\{v_2, v_3, v_4\}$ and $\{t_1\}$. As v_1 and t_1 represent the same underlying content, these connection lead to a semantic bias of the intra-modal KNN $\{v_2, v_3, v_4\}$ and inter-modal KNN $\{t_2, t_3, t_4\}$. (b) show the graph after semantic propagation of v_1, where both the intra-modal and inter-modal KNN are the same order neighbour of v_1

Motivated by node2vec [5], which learn latent representation of each vertex in a graph. We use skip-gram model [11] to learn the semantic graph embedding to the data points. Let $g(\cdot)$ be the mapping function projecting vertex to graph embedding. With the assumption of vertex independence, we have the probability of observing the neighborhood $N(n_i)$ for each vertex n_i as follow:

$$p\left(N\left(n_i\right) \mid n_i\right) = \Pi_{n_j \in N(n_i)} \frac{\exp\left(g\left(n_i\right)^T g\left(n_j\right)\right)}{\sum_{n_k \in V} \exp\left(g\left(n_i\right)^T g\left(n_k\right)\right)}$$

However, the denominator of the above softmax function requires a huge amount of computation. So we use negative sampling to approximate it. The basic idea of negative sampling is to use logistic regression to distinguish the target vertex from the noise distribution vertex. Taking vertex n_i as an example, we randomly select k_1 nodes that are not connected to the target node as negative samples, and the negative sample set is expressed as $N\prime(n_i)$. We select k_2 nodes from all connected nodes as the set of neighbor nodes and it is expressed as $N(n_i)$, and the objective function of vertex n_i in the graph becomes the minimize loss function as follow: 098

$$l_G\left(n_i\right) = -\sum_{n_j \in N(n_i)} \log \sigma\left(g\left(n_i\right)^T g\left(n_j\right)\right) - \sum_{n_k \in N'(n_i)} \log \sigma\left(-g\left(n_i\right)^T g\left(n_k\right)\right)$$

$$(1)$$

In this way, we bridge the heterogeneity gap between modes and uniformly represent all the cross-modal data by project them into the embedding space. After learning the graph embedding, there still a need to improve the discrimination of the representation for better performance in cross-modal retrieval tasks.

Supervised Learning. Different from other supervised DNN-based cross-modal methods, we use a simple one branch deep neural network to learn a common hidden space, which is inspired by the Siamese network [27]. For the discrimination of the representation, we need to enforce different-category samples to be far apart while the same-category samples lie as close as possible. We achieve this goal by maximizing the likelihood function defined as follow:

$$p\left(I_{ij}|c_i,c_j\right) = \begin{cases} \sigma\left(s(c_i,c_j)\right), & if\ I_{ij}=1 \\ 1-\sigma\left(s(c_i,c_j)\right), & otherwise \end{cases}$$

where $c_i = f_1(g(n_i))$, and c_i denotes the feature in the common space, f_1 denotes the mapping function from graph embedding space to common embedding space, and $\sigma\left(x\right) = \frac{1}{1+e^{-x}}$ is the sigmoid function. As we can see, the larger $p(1|c_i,c_j)$ wants, the bigger the similarity $s(c_i,c_j)$ needs to be and the larger $p(0|c_i,c_j)$ wants, the smaller $s(c_i,c_j)$ needs to be. Therefore, maximizing this likelihood function is a suitable way for learning discrimination representation. Moreover, maximizing the likelihood is equivalent to minimizing the negative log likelihood function. Therefore, to make the learning process more effective, we adopt the negative log likelihood as objective function:

$$l_C = \frac{1}{n^2}\sum_{i,j=1}^{n}\left(\log\left(1+e^{s(c_i,c_j)}\right)-I_{ij}s(c_i,c_j)\right) \tag{2}$$

Furthermore, we reinforce the discrimination of the representation by reconstructing label information, which is inspired by the Autoencoder [21] that use the reconstruction ability to learn latent representation. We use a linear classifier to project the common space representation into the label space, and the reconstruction loss is defined as:

$$l_L\left(n_i\right) = \left\|f_2(c_i)-y_i\right\|_F^2 \tag{3}$$

where f_2 is the linear classifier, and $\left\|\cdot\right\|_F$ denotes the Frobenius-norm.

Combining the discrimination loss Eq. (2) in common space and the reconstruction loss Eq. (3) in label space, we obtain the objective function for the supervised learner as follow:

$$l = l_C + l_L \tag{4}$$

3.3   Implementation Details

The proposed method can be divided into two part. For the semantic correlation graph, it is implemented by a single embedding layer which hidden dimension size is 300 and follow an operation of computing the objective function. For the one-branch supervised learner, we use two fully-connected layers with Rectified Linear Unit (ReLU) [12] activation function to project embedding into common space, and a fully-connected layers is follow as a linear classifier for the label space. The hidden units for the first two layers are 512 and 1024, and the last layer is determined by the categories number of the dataset.

We use the cosine similarity function to select 8 nearest neighbors on original feature space for each data point to build the graph. When sampling on graph, the random walk length is set to 10, and the window size is set to 3. The sampling is performed 5 times to get the final training data.

Our model are trained by back-propagation and mini-batch stochastic gradient descent based technique. Adam [9] optimiser is employed and its learning rate is given by 10^{-5} and the batch size is 50. The entire network is trained on a Nvidia GTX 2080 Ti GPU in PyTorch with the maximal number of epochs as 500.

4   Experiment

4.1   Datasets and Feature

As shown in Table 1, we follow the dataset partition scheme and feature exaction strategies from [15,30] making these a fair comparison. For images, each of them is represented by a 4096-dimensional feature extracted from the fc7 layer of VGGNet [20], which has been pre-trained on ImageNet and fine-tune on image classification task of each dataset. For text, we extract a 300-dimensional feature for each text by the sentence CNN [8] that has been pre-trained on each dataset. It is notable that all the compared methods adopt the same features as our method.

Table 1. The statistics of the three datasets used in the experiments, where "/" in columns "Instance" stands for the number of train/test/validation pairs.

Dataset	Label	Instance	Image feature	Text feature
Wikipedia [17]	10	2173/231/462	4096D VGG	300D TextCNN
Pascal Sentence [16]	20	800/100/100	4096D VGG	300D TextCNN
NUS-WIDE-10k [2]	10	8000/1000/1000	4096D VGG	300D TextCNN

4.2   Evaluation Metric

To evaluate the performance of our methods, we perform cross-modal retrieval tasks as retrieving one modality by another modality query, i.e., text retrieval using an image query (image-to-text) and image retrieval using a text query (text-to-image). We adopt mean average precision (mAP) [17] which is widely used in retrieval task to evaluate the search quality. Give a query and a set of retrieved samples, and the sample is relevant when it share a same label with the query, the average precision (AP) is defined as: $AP = \frac{1}{R_N} \sum_{j=1}^{N}(\frac{R_j}{j} \times I(j))$, where $I(j) = 1$ if the j-th retrieved sample is relevant with the query and $I(j) = 0$ otherwise, and R_j is define as: $R_j \sum_{i=1}^{j} I(i)$. Then, the average of the AP on all the queries is the final evaluation result of mAP.

4.3   Comparison Results

To evaluate the effectiveness of our method, we compare the proposed method with six state-of-the-art methods in the experiments, including three traditional methods, namely CCA [6], MCCA [18], JRL [28], as well as three DNN-based methods, namely SSPE [26], ACMR [22], DSCMR [30]. The mAP scores of our method and the compared methods on all the three wide-used datasets are shown in Tables 2, 3, 4. From the table, we can see that our methods out performs other methods. Compared with the best competitor our method achieves the improvements of 2.3%, 3.2% and 2.6% in term of the average mAP scores on Pascal Sentences [16], Wikipedia [17], and NUS-WIDE-10k [2] datasets.

Table 2. Experiments on Pascal Sentence dataset

Method	CCA	MCCA	JRL	SSPE	ACMR	DSCMR	Ours
Image2Text	0.225	0.664	0.527	0.669	0.671	0.711	**0.737**
Text2Image	0.227	0.689	0.534	0.625	0.676	0.717	**0.724**
Average	0.226	0.677	0.531	0.647	0.674	0.714	**0.731**

Table 3. Experiments on Wikipedia dataset

Method	CCA	MCCA	JRL	SSPE	ACMR	DSCMR	Ours
Image2Text	0.134	0.341	0.449	0.512	0.477	0.521	**0.534**
Text2Image	0.133	0.307	0.418	0.463	0.434	0.478	**0.491**
Average	0.134	0.324	0.434	0.488	0.456	0.500	**0.513**

4.4   Model Analysis

Figure 3a shows the experiment results of the validate mAP as function of training epoch on Wikipedia dataset. It can be clearly seen from Fig. 3a that the score increase fast at first and stay stable after 100 epoch, which indicates that our model converges monotonously and fast. We also test our model with various

Table 4. Experiments on NUS-WIDE-10k dataset

Method	CCA	MCCA	JRL	SSPE	ACMR	DSCMR	Ours
Image2Text	0.378	0.448	0.586	0.585	0.588	0.611	**0.617**
Text2Image	0.394	0.462	0.598	0.591	0.599	0.615	**0.634**
Average	0.386	0.455	0.592	0.588	0.594	0.613	**0.626**

k-nearest neighbour to construct the semantic graph for embedding. As shown in Fig. 3b, with the increasing number of neighbour vertex been chosen, the mAP score first increases and then slightly decreases. Because small number of K can not preserve enough correlation information, while large number of K increase the dissimilar semantic connection. For efficiency we choose 8 as the value of K.

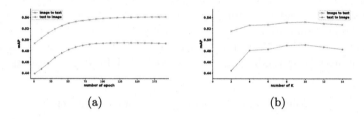

(a)   (b)

Fig. 3. Modal analysis on Wikipedia. (a) Validation performance with different numbers of epochs. (b) Impact of the numbers of k-nearest neighbour

4.5   Impact of Different Components

In order to visually demonstrate the effect of our method, we adopt t-SNE [10] to project the feature into a two dimensional visualization plan which shows the distribution of data intuitively. Figure 4 shows the distribution of features in different spaces during the learning process of Wikipedia dataset. The original space feature visualize are displayed in Fig. 4a, 4b. We can see that the original space of each mode is very different, and there is a semantic gap between modes, which can not be compared.

Figure 4c, 4d show the image and text representation in the graph embedding space. In this space, the feature have not been well discriminated yet, but they retain the clustering characteristics which represent the intra-modal information of the original space. More importantly, we can see from Fig. 4e that image and text features of the same category are well mixed together which means the inter-modal information is well used to cross the modality gap.

The result of the common space features are displayed in Fig. 4f, 4g, 4e. We can see that the discrimination loss of the common space and the reconstruction of the label space are powerful to enhance the semantic information. In the common space, the features of the muti-modal dataset are effectively separates into several semantic clusters which are much more discriminative than those in the graph embedding space.

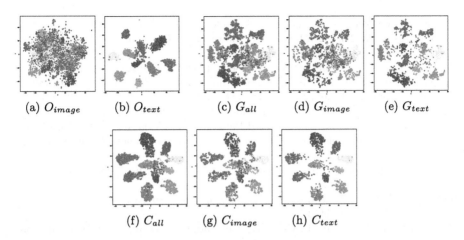

(a) O_{image} (b) O_{text} (c) G_{all} (d) G_{image} (e) G_{text}

(f) C_{all} (g) C_{image} (h) C_{text}

Fig. 4. Visualization of features in different spaces, where O, G, C represents the Original space, Graph embedding space, Common space

5   Conclusion

In this paper, we proposed a novel approach to fully exploit the intra-modal similarity, pairwise information, inter-modal correlation and label information of the cross-modal data. We built a semantic balance graph by the semantic propagation of pairwise information, so that we can bridge the heterogeneity gap smoothly. And nonlinear neural network is applied to enrich the label information. Comprehensive experiments conducted on three benchmark datasets showed that our proposed model achieves superior performance compared to state-of-the-art methods.

Acknowledgments. This work was supported by National Key R&D Program of China (2019YFB1804400).

References

1. Andrew, G., Arora, R., Bilmes, J., Livescu, K.: Deep canonical correlation analysis. In: International Conference on Machine Learning, pp. 1247–1255 (2013)
2. Chua, T.S., Tang, J., Hong, R., Li, H., Luo, Z., Zheng, Y.: NUS-WIDE: a real-world web image database from National University of Singapore. In: Proceedings of the ACM International Conference on Image and Video Retrieval, pp. 1–9 (2009)
3. Feng, F., Wang, X., Li, R.: Cross-modal retrieval with correspondence autoencoder. In: Proceedings of the 22nd ACM International Conference on Multimedia, pp. 7–16 (2014)
4. Gong, Y., Ke, Q., Isard, M., Lazebnik, S.: A multi-view embedding space for modeling internet images, tags, and their semantics. Int. J. Comput. Vision **106**(2), 210–233 (2013). https://doi.org/10.1007/s11263-013-0658-4

5. Grover, A., Leskovec, J.: node2vec: Scalable feature learning for networks. In: Proceedings of the 22nd ACM SIGKDD International Conference on Knowledge Discovery and Data Mining, pp. 855–864 (2016)
6. Hotelling, H.: Relations between two sets of variates. In: Kotz, S., Johnson, N.L. (eds.) Breakthroughs in Statistics. SSS, pp. 162–190. Springer, New York (1992). https://doi.org/10.1007/978-1-4612-4380-9_14
7. Jiang, Q.Y., Li, W.J.: Deep cross-modal hashing. In: Proceedings of the IEEE Conference on Computer Vision and Pattern Recognition, pp. 3232–3240 (2017)
8. Kim, Y.: Convolutional neural networks for sentence classification. arXiv preprint arXiv:1408.5882 (2014)
9. Kingma, D.P., Ba, J.: Adam: a method for stochastic optimization. arXiv preprint arXiv:1412.6980 (2014)
10. van der Maaten, L., Hinton, G.: Visualizing data using t-SNE. J. Mach. Learn. Res. **9**, 2579–2605 (2008)
11. Mikolov, T., Sutskever, I., Chen, K., Corrado, G.S., Dean, J.: Distributed representations of words and phrases and their compositionality. In: Advances in Neural Information Processing Systems, pp. 3111–3119 (2013)
12. Nair, V., Hinton, G.E.: Rectified linear units improve restricted Boltzmann machines. In: ICML (2010)
13. Peng, X., Xiao, S., Feng, J., Yau, W.Y., Yi, Z.: Deep subspace clustering with sparsity prior. In: IJCAI, pp. 1925–1931 (2016)
14. Peng, Y., Huang, X., Zhao, Y.: An overview of cross-media retrieval: concepts, methodologies, benchmarks, and challenges. IEEE Trans. Circuits Syst. Video Technol. **28**(9), 2372–2385 (2017)
15. Peng, Y., Qi, J.: CM-GANs: cross-modal generative adversarial networks for common representation learning. ACM Trans. Multimed. Comput. Commun. Appl. (TOMM) **15**(1), 1–24 (2019)
16. Rashtchian, C., Young, P., Hodosh, M., Hockenmaier, J.: Collecting image annotations using Amazon's Mechanical Turk. In: Proceedings of the NAACL HLT 2010 Workshop on Creating Speech and Language Data with Amazon's Mechanical Turk, pp. 139–147 (2010)
17. Rasiwasia, N., et al.: A new approach to cross-modal multimedia retrieval. In: ACM International Conference on Multimedia, pp. 251–260 (2010)
18. Rupnik, J., Shawe-Taylor, J.: Multi-view canonical correlation analysis. In: Conference on Data Mining and Data Warehouses (SiKDD 2010), pp. 1–4 (2010)
19. Sharma, A., Jacobs, D.W.: Bypassing synthesis: PLS for face recognition with pose, low-resolution and sketch. In: CVPR 2011, pp. 593–600. IEEE (2011)
20. Simonyan, K., Zisserman, A.: Very deep convolutional networks for large-scale image recognition. arXiv preprint arXiv:1409.1556 (2014)
21. Vincent, P., Larochelle, H., Bengio, Y., Manzagol, P.A.: Extracting and composing robust features with denoising autoencoders. In: Proceedings of the 25th International Conference on Machine Learning, pp. 1096–1103 (2008)
22. Wang, B., Yang, Y., Xu, X., Hanjalic, A., Shen, H.T.: Adversarial cross-modal retrieval. In: Proceedings of the 25th ACM International Conference on Multimedia, pp. 154–162 (2017)
23. Wang, K., He, R., Wang, L., Wang, W., Tan, T.: Joint feature selection and subspace learning for cross-modal retrieval. IEEE Trans. Pattern Anal. Mach. Intell. **38**(10), 2010–2023 (2015)
24. Wang, K., Yin, Q., Wang, W., Wu, S., Wang, L.: A comprehensive survey on cross-modal retrieval. arXiv preprint arXiv:1607.06215 (2016)

25. Wang, L., Li, Y., Lazebnik, S.: Learning deep structure-preserving image-text embeddings. In: Proceedings of the IEEE Conference on Computer Vision and Pattern Recognition, pp. 5005–5013 (2016)

26. Wu, Y., Wang, S., Huang, Q.: Learning semantic structure-preserved embeddings for cross-modal retrieval. In: Proceedings of the 26th ACM International Conference on Multimedia, pp. 825–833 (2018)

27. Zagoruyko, S., Komodakis, N.: Learning to compare image patches via convolutional neural networks. In: Proceedings of the IEEE Conference on Computer Vision and Pattern Recognition, pp. 4353–4361 (2015)

28. Zhai, X., Peng, Y., Xiao, J.: Learning cross-media joint representation with sparse and semisupervised regularization. IEEE Trans. Circuits Syst. Video Technol. **24**(6), 965–978 (2014)

29. Zhang, Y., Cao, J., Gu, X.: Learning cross-modal aligned representation with graph embedding. IEEE Access **6**, 77321–77333 (2018)

30. Zhen, L., Hu, P., Wang, X., Peng, D.: Deep supervised cross-modal retrieval. In: Proceedings of the IEEE Conference on Computer Vision and Pattern Recognition, pp. 10394–10403 (2019)

Confidence-Based Global Attention Guided Network for Image Inpainting

Zhilin Huang, Chujun Qin, Lei Li, Ruixin Liu, and Yuesheng Zhu[✉]

School of Electronic and Computer Engineering, Peking University, Shenzhen, China
{zerinhwang03,chujun.qin,csleili,anne_xin,zhuys}@pku.edu.cn

Abstract. Most of recent generative image inpainting methods have shown promising performance by adopting attention mechanisms to fill hole regions with known-region features. However, these methods tend to neglect the impact of reliable hole-region information, which leads to discontinuities in structure and texture of final results. Besides, they always fail to predict plausible contents with realistic details in hole regions due to the ineffectiveness of vanilla decoder in capturing long-range information at each level. To handle these problems, we propose a confidence-based global attention guided network (CGAG-Net) consisting of coarse and fine steps, where each step is built upon the encoder-decoder architecture. CGAG-Net utilizes reliable global information to missing contents through an attention mechanism, and uses attention scores learned from high-level features to guide the reconstruction of low-level features. Specifically, we propose a confidence-based global attention layer (CGA) embedded in the encoder to fill hole regions with reliable global features weighted by learned attention scores, where reliability of features is measured by automatically generated confidence values. Meanwhile, the attention scores learned by CGA are repeatedly used to guide the feature prediction at each level of the attention guided decoder (AG Decoder) we proposed. Thus, AG Decoder can obtain semantically-coherent and texture-coherent features from global regions to predict missing contents. Extensive experiments on Paris StreetView and CelebA datasets validate the superiority of our proposed approach through quantitative and qualitative comparisons with existing methods.

Keywords: Image inpainting · Encoder-decoder · Attention mechanism

1 Introduction

Image inpainting is a task of restoring the missing or damaged parts of images in computer vision. In practice, many image inpainting approaches have been proposed in wide application ranges, such as photo editing, image-based rendering, etc. The main challenge of image inpainting is to generate semantically plausible and visually realistic results for missing regions [27].

© Springer Nature Switzerland AG 2021
J. Lokoč et al. (Eds.): MMM 2021, LNCS 12572, pp. 200–212, 2021.
https://doi.org/10.1007/978-3-030-67832-6_17

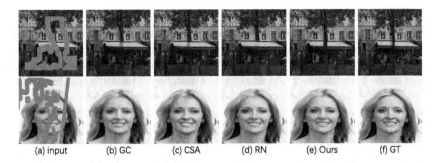

|(a) input|(b) GC|(c) CSA|(d) RN|(e) Ours|(f) GT|

Fig. 1. Qualitative comparisons of inpainting results by Gated Conv (GC) [28], Coherent Semantic Attention (CSA) [13], Region Normalization (RN) [29], our model and ground truth (GT). [Best viewed with zoom-in.]

Traditionally, this task is settled with diffusion-based or patch-based approaches [1,4,17,30]. These methods only work well for stationary textural regions, and they fail to generate semantic information on non-stationary images. To make up for it, early learning-based methods [8,18,26] are proposed to formulate inpainting as a conditional image generation problem by using convolutional encoder-decoder network, where the encoder learns a latent feature representation of the image and the decoder reasons about the missing contents [18]. Unfortunately, these methods often create boundary artifacts and blurry results inconsistent with known regions. Recently, some approaches [21,27,28] adopt spatial attention mechanisms in encoder to effectively encode the latent representation by fully utilizing long-range contextual information. Firstly, they extract patches in known regions and hole regions of the high-level feature map, and then take known-region patches as references to calculate attention scores with hole-region patches. Finally, they fill the hole regions with known-region patches weighted by the attention scores.

However, most existing attention-based image inpainting methods [20,21,27] tend to completely ignore the impact of holes features which may be not well-inferred, or just model the correlation between adjacent hole-region features in a certain direction [13], which leads to discontinuous structures and textures in final results, as shown in the first row of Fig. 1. Moreover, due to limited size of the vanilla convolutional kernel and receptive field, they cannot effectively utilize distant information at each level of the vanilla decoder. Thus, they always fail to reason about realistic details in hole regions, as shown in the second row of the Fig. 1.

To handle these problems, we propose a confidence-based global attention guided network (CGAG-Net) which divides the inpainting task into coarse and fine steps as shown in Fig. 2(a). In the coarse step, a simple dilated convolutional network [27] generates preliminary results for the next step. And in the fine step, a confidence-based global attention layer (CGA) we proposed is applied to the high-level features of the encoder to reconstruct semantic continuous features in the hole regions by taking feature patches from both holes and known regions as references. Considering the fact that indiscriminately model the correlation within the hole regions to reconstruct missing contents will introduce unreliable (i.e., poorly-inferred) information and results in blurriness, CGA automatically generates confidence values to measure the reliability of information for each channel at each spatial location of reference patches. The confidence values are able to highlight reliable information and suppress unreliable one.

In addition, we propose an attention guided decoder (AG Decoder) to fill hole regions from high-level to low-level by repeatedly applying a guided attention module (GA) we proposed to the decoder. Since the attention scores learned from high-level features reflect the correlation of spatial location between semantically-coherent features, they can be taken as the guidance of the attention mechanism to fill hole regions of low-level features with semantically-coherent and texture-coherent patches. By using the attention scores learned from high-level feature map to guide GA at shallow layers of the AG Decoder, our model can generate both semantically and visually plausible results. Furthermore, we propose a multi-scale gated block (MSGB) embedded in the encoder to capture valid information at various scales by adopting multiple gated convolutions [28] with different kernel sizes and connecting them in a hierarchical style. Extensive experiments on standard datasets Paris StreetView [3] and CelebA [15] demonstrate that the proposed approach can generate higher-quality inpainting results in irregular holes than existing methods.

The main contributions of this paper are summarized as follows:

• We propose a confidence-based global attention layer (CGA) to consider the impact of reliable global features on the reconstruction of missing contents, according to the automatically generated confidence values which can highlight reliable information of features and suppress unreliable one.

• An attention guided decoder (AG Decoder) is proposed to fill hole regions at each level with semantically-coherent and texture-coherent features under the guidance of attention scores from CGA.

• MSGB is designed to capture information at various scales by adopting multiple gated convolutions with different kernel sizes and connecting them in a hierarchical style.

2   Related Work

2.1   Learning-Based Image Inpainting

Learning-based methods for image inpainting [2, 7, 11, 14, 16, 22, 24] always use deep learning and adversarial training strategy [6] to predict the missing contents in hole regions. One of the early learning-based methods, Context Encoder [18] takes adversarial training into a encoder-decoder architecture to fill the holes in feature-level. On the basis of Context Encoder, Iizuka et al. [8] propose global and local discriminators to generate better results with regard to overall consistency as well as more detail. Yang et al. [26] propose a multi-scale neural patch synthesis approach to generate high-frequency details. Liu et al. [12] propose an automatic mask generation and update mechanism to focus on valid pixels in the feature map for better results. Inspired by [12], Yu et al. [28] propose a gated convolution and SN-PatchGAN to better deal with irregular masks.

2.2 Attention-Based Image Inpainting

Recently, spatial attention mechanism is introduced in image inpainting task to model long-range dependencies within features [19,23]. Yan et al. [25] introduce a shift operation and a guidance loss to restore features in the decoder by utilizing the information in corresponding encoder layers. Yu et al. [27] propose a novel contextual attention layer to explicitly utilize the feature in known-regions as references to make better predictions. Liu et al. [13] propose a coherent semantic attention layer to model the correlation between adjacency features in hole regions for continuity results.

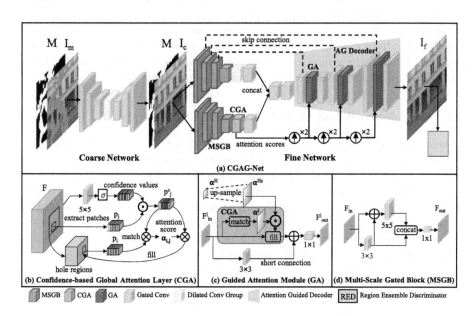

Fig. 2. The architecture of our proposed confidence-based global attention guided network (CGAG-Net).

3 Approach

3.1 Overview

Our model confidence-based global attention guided network (CGAG-Net) divides image inpainting task into coarse and fine steps, where each step is built upon the encoder-decoder architecture, as shown in Fig. 2(a). In the coarse step, we adopt the same structure of the coarse network in [27]. The coarse network takes the concatenation of the masked image I_m and the binary mask M as input to generate the coarse prediction I_c. In the fine step, we take the concatenation of I_c and M as input of the fine network to obtain the finer result I_f. The fine network consists of two parallel encoders and an attention guided decoder (AG Decoder). The multi-scale gated block (MSGB) is embedded in each layer of two encoders to capture the information at different scales. The top encoder focuses on hallucinating contents with a dilated convolution group (i.e., stacked dilated convolutions). And the confidence-based global attention layer (CGA) is embedded in the deepest layer of the bottom encoder, which enables the encoder to reconstruct the semantically continuous contents with reliable patches from the global. Then, the output from two encoders are fused together and fed into the attention guided decoder (AG Decoder). The AG Decoder repeatedly uses a guided attention module (GA) to reconstruct hole-region features from high-level to low-level. Meanwhile, the attention scores learned in CGA is up-sampled to the corresponding resolution to guide the filling process of GA at each level of the AG Decoder. In addition, skip connections [13] are introduced to concatenate features from each layer of the top encoder and corresponding layers of AG Decoder. Finally, the region ensemble discriminator (RED) proposed in [19] is introduced to act as global and local discriminator simultaneously.

3.2   Confidence-Based Global Attention Layer

In order to model the correlation between hole-region features and avoid introducing unreliable information into hole regions, we propose a confidence-based global attention layer (CGA), as shown in Fig. 2(b).

CGA first takes the feature map F as input of a gated convolution [28] with an activation function, and then sigmoid function is applied on the output of the gated convolution to get confidence values in a confidence map C for each channel at each spatial location of F. The confidence values in C are between 0 and 1 (0 represents completely unreliable, and vice versa). The next, F^c is obtained by computing element-wise multiplication between C and F:

$$C_{x,y} = \sigma(\phi(W_c(F))) \tag{1}$$

$$F^c_{x,y} = C_{x,y} \odot F_{x,y} \tag{2}$$

where W_c denotes the convolutional filters, σ denotes the sigmoid function, $\odot$ denotes the element-wise multiplication and ϕ can be any activation functions. After extracting patches p and p^c from hole regions of F and the global (both hole regions and known regions) of F^c respectively, CGA takes patches p^c as references to calculate the cosine similarity with p:

$$s_{i,j} = <\frac{p_i}{||p_i||_2}, \frac{p^c_j}{||p^c_j||_2}> \tag{3}$$

where p_i and p_j^c are the i-th patch and the j-th patch of p and p^c respectively. Finally, the softmax is applied on the channel of similarities to obtain attention scores α and then CGA fills hole regions with patches p^c weighted by α:

$$\alpha_{i,j} = softmax(\frac{exp(s_{i,j})}{\sum_{i=1}^{N} exp(s_{i,j})}) \tag{4}$$

$$p_i = \sum_{i}^{N} \alpha_{i,j} \cdot p_j^c \tag{5}$$

Compared with existing attention mechanisms for image inpainting [21,25, 27,28], our CGA additionally considers the impact of reliable information in whole hole regions to generate continuous results. The confidence values generated by CGA in an adaptive manner are able to highlight the reliable information for each channel at each spatial location of the feature map and suppress unreliable one. It is worth noting that confidence values are only applied on reference patches. In this way, our CGA can avoid the situation that a hole-region patch always have a large attention score with itself when CAG additionally takes hole-region patches as references. And the generalization ability of learned attention scores is enhanced simultaneously. The contextual attention layer proposed in [27] can be regarded as a special case of our CGA, where confidence values for each channel of features are 0 in hole regions and 1 in known regions.

3.3 Attention Guided Decoder

In order to generate semantically and texture plausible results, we propose an attention guided decoder (AG Decoder). Under the guidance of the attention scores learned from high-level features, a guided attention module (GA) is repeatedly applied on features at each level of AG Decoder to reconstruct the missing contents with semantically-coherent and texture-coherent information. The GA consists of CGA and a short connection which can ease the flow of information and stabilize the training process, as shown in Fig. 2(c).

In the l-th layer of AG Decoder, GA first obtains the attention score $\alpha_{i,j}^l$ between the patch pair, p_i^l and p_j^{cl}, by taking the same strategy as mentioned in Sect. 3.2, where p_i^l is the i-th hole-region patch and p_j^{cl} is the j-th reference patch. Furthermore, in order to maintain the semantic coherency between generated textures and surroundings, we use the attention map α^H learned from high-level features by CGA to guide the hole filling process of GA at each level of the AG Decoder, where α^H reflects the correlation of spatial location between semantically-coherent features. Thus, α^H is up-sampled to the corresponding resolution with scale factor s to obtain the up-sampled attention score map α^{Hs}. After that, softmax is applied on the result of the element-wise multiplication between α^{Hs} and α^l to get the guided attention score map α^{Gl}. In this way, only elements with high values in both α^{Hs} and α^l will have high values in α^{Gl}. That is to say, only if two patches in a patch pair have both high semantic and textural coherency, can they obtain a high attention score in α^{Gl}. Finally, we reconstruct hole regions with p^{cl} weighted by α^{Gl}. The process can be formulated as follows:

$$\alpha^{Gl} = softmax(\alpha^{Hs} \odot \alpha^l) \tag{6}$$

$$p_i^l = \sum_{i=1}^{N} \alpha_{i,j}^{Gl} \cdot p_j^{cl} \tag{7}$$

3.4   Multi-scale Gated Block

Extracting features at different scales is essential for CNN models to capture important contextual information. Inspired by Res2Net [5] and Gated Conv [28], we propose multi-scale gated block (MSGB), as shown in Fig. 2(d), to extract valid features at various scales by adopting multiple gated convolutions with different kernel sizes and connecting them in a hierarchical style. The gated convolution proposed in [28] can distinguish valid pixels/features from invalid ones, thereby preventing predicted results from being affected by harmful information.

Let F_{in} and F_{out} be the input and the output feature map of MSGB, $GC_{i \times i}(\cdot)$ be the gated convolution [28] with kernel size i. MSGB first extracts features with a 3×3 gated convolution in the input feature map F_{in} to get the output $F_{3 \times 3}$. Instead of simply fusing features at different scales, MSGB uses element-wise sum operation between $F_{3 \times 3}$ and F_{in} before feeding F_{in} into a 5×5 gated convolution. After using a 1×1 gated convolution to reduce channels of the concatenation of $F_{3 \times 3}$ and $F_{5 \times 5}$, MSGB fuses information at different scales to obtain the output F_{out}. The process can be formulated as follows:

$$F_{3 \times 3} = \phi(GC_{3 \times 3}(F_{in})) \tag{8}$$

$$F_{5 \times 5} = \phi(GC_{5 \times 5}(F_{3 \times 3} + F_{in})) \tag{9}$$

$$F_{out} = \phi(GC_{1 \times 1}(concat([F_{3 \times 3}, F_{5 \times 5})))) \tag{10}$$

where $\phi(\cdot)$ denotes the activation function. We select LeakyReLU as activation function in our experiments.

Compared with simply fusing multi-scale information in a parallel style, our MSGB can obtain larger receptive fields without using extra parameters. Specifically, when we take $F_{3 \times 3}$ as the input of a 5×5 gated convolution, the output will have a larger receptive field than the output obtained by taking F_{in} as the input of the 5×5 gated convolution due to the connection explosion effect [5].

3.5   Loss Function

To make constrains that the output of the coarse network and the fine network should approximate the ground-truth image, following [27], we use L1 distance as our reconstruction loss L_{rec}. Besides, We adopt region ensemble discriminator (RED) [19] as global and local discriminator to calculate the adversarial loss L_{adv} in each pixel individually, which drives our model to handle various holes with arbitrary shapes and generate visually pleasing results. To address the gradient vanishing problem in generator, we employ the hinge version of the adversarial loss [13]. Moreover, we use the perceptual loss [9] L_{per} to generate plausible contents by measuring the similarity between high-level structure.

In summary, the overall loss function of the proposed CGAG-Net is as follows:

$$L_{total} = \lambda_{rec} \cdot L_{rec} + \lambda_{adv} \cdot L_{adv} + \lambda_{per} \cdot L_{per} \tag{11}$$

where λ_{rec}, λ_{adv}, λ_{per} are hyper-parameters for the reconstruction, adversarial and perceptual losses.

4   Experiments

4.1   Experiment Settings

We evaluate our model on two datasets: Paris StreetView [3] and CelebA [15]. For these two datasets, we use the original train, validation and test splits. And we obtain irregular masks which are classified based on different hole-to-image area ratios from Partial Conv [12]. The training and testing process are conducted on masks with 20%–40% hole-to-image area ratio. Besides, we follow [28] to adopt the same data augmentation such as flipping during training process. Our model is optimized by Adam algorithm [10] with learning rate of 1×10^{-4} and $\beta 1 = 0.5$. The hyper-parameters are set as $\lambda_{rec} = 1.0$, $\lambda_{per} = 1.0$, $\lambda_{adv} = 0.01$. And we train on an Nvidia Titan X Pascal GPU with a batch size of 1. All masks and images for training and testing are with the size of 256×256.

We compare our method with five methods: Partial Conv (PC) [12], Contextual Attention (CA) [27], Gated Conv (GC) [28], Coherent Semantic Attention (CSA) [13] and Region Normalization (RN) [29].

4.2   Qualitative Comparisons

Figure 3 present inpainting results of different methods on testing images from Paris StreetView and CelebA datasets. For all methods, no post-processing step is performed to ensure fairness. As shown in Fig. 3, PC, CA and RN are effective in generate semantically plausible results, but the results present distorted structures and lack realistic details. Compared with previous methods, GC and CSA can generate richer details, but the results still have discontinuous textures and boundary artifacts. This is mainly because they neglect the impact of hole-region features and the ineffectiveness of vanilla decoder in capturing distant information of low-level features. Compared with these methods, our model is able to generate semantically and visually plausible results with clear boundaries and continuous textures in hole regions.

208   Z. Huang et al.

Fig. 3. Example cases of qualitative comparison on the Paris StreetView and CelebA datasets. [Best viewed with zoom-in.]

Table 1. Quantitative comparison results over Paris StreetView [3] and CelebA [15] datasets with irregular masks between PC [12], CA [27], GC [28], CSA [13], RN [29] and Ours. $^-$ Lower is better. $^+$ Higher is better.

Datasets	Paris StreetView						CelebA					
Methods	PC	CA	GC	CSA	RN	Ours	PC	CA	GC	CSA	RN	Ours
MAE$^-$	3.884	3.386	3.283	3.245	3.491	**3.143**	3.307	3.144	2.887	3.060	2.849	**2.709**
SSIM$^+$	0.879	0.901	0.903	0.904	0.892	**0.906**	0.909	0.917	0.921	0.925	**0.927**	**0.927**
PSNR$^+$	27.981	28.810	29.082	29.112	28.691	**29.309**	28.131	28.470	29.057	29.427	29.448	**29.603**

4.3 Quantitative Comparisons

We use images from the testing set of Paris StreetView and CelebA datasets with irregular masks to make comparisons. We take MAE, PSNR, SSIM as evaluation metrics to quantify the performance of models. Table 1 lists the comparison results which present our method outperforms all other methods in these measurements on both Paris StreetView and CelebA datasets.

Table 2. Quantitative comparisons over Paris StreetView between CA [27] and CGA. $^-$ Lower is better. $^+$ Higher is better.

	MAE$^-$	SSIM$^+$	PSNR$^+$
With CA	3.283	0.903	29.082
With CGA (all 1)	3.345	0.903	29.077
With CGA	**3.271**	**0.904**	**29.154**

4.4   Ablation Study

Effect of CGA. In order to demonstrate the effect of our CGA, we adopt the architecture of Gated Conv [28] and replace the contextual attention layer (CA) [27] with CGA to make both qualitative and quantitative comparisons on the Paris StreetView testing set. Also, to validate the effect of confidence values, we set all confidence values in CGA as 1 to make a comparison. As present in Tab 2, by adopting CGA we proposed, the mode can achieve the best performance in all metrics. As shown in the areas marked with red bounding boxes in Fig. 4, CA fails to generate continuous structures and textures in hole regions. And directly modeling the correlation (all confidence values are set to 1) between hole-region features in CGA will cause blurriness. By adopting our CGA with automatically generated confidence values which can highlight reliable information of hole-region features and suppress unreliable one, the model is able to generate continuous structures and textures in hole regions.

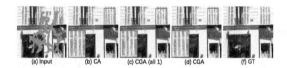

Fig. 4. The effect of CGA. [Best viewed with zoom-in.]

Effect of AG Decoder. We make a comparison on the Paris StreetView testing set to demonstrate the effect of our AG Decoder. Figure 5 presents that the model can generate semantically plausible results but contain blurriness, when we replace the AG Decoder in our model with vanilla decoder (without using attention mechanisms). Without the guidance of attention scores learned from high-level features, AG Decoder fails to generate textures consistent with surroundings. When we adopt AG Decoder under the guidance of attention scores learned from high-level features, our model can generate semantically and visually plausible results.

(a) Input   (b) vanilla decoder   (c) AG Decoder   (d) AG Decoder   (f) GT
                              (without guidance)

Fig. 5. The effect of AG Decoder. [Best viewed with zoom-in.]

Effect of MSGB. To verify the effect of MSGB, we replace the gated convolutions in the encoder of GC [28] with two types of MSGB which connects multiple gated convolutions in different styles (hierarchical and parallel) to make a comparison. For fair comparison, we keep the number of model parameters the same. As shown in Table 3, when adopting MSGB with gated convolutions connected in a hierarchical style, the model can obtain the best performance in all metrics.

Table 3. Quantitative comparisons between Gated Conv [28] and MSGB on CelebA dataset. $^-$ Lower is better. $^+$ Higher is better.

	MAE$^-$	SSIM$^+$	PSNR$^+$
With Gated Conv	2.887	0.921	29.057
With MSGB (parallel)	2.868	**0.924**	29.251
With MSGB (hierarchical)	**2.858**	**0.924**	**29.334**

5   Conclusion

In this paper, we propose a confidence-based global attention guided network (CGAG-Net) with two key components, a confidence-based global attention layer in the encoder and an attention guided decoder to synthesize missing contents in masked images. By measuring reliability of global features and predicting missing contents at each level of the attention guided decoder with semantically-coherent and texture-coherent features, our CGAG-Net can generate semantically and visually plausible results with continuous structures and textures. Extensive experiments on different datasets demonstrate that our methods can significantly outperforms other state-of-the-art approaches in image inpainting.

Acknowledgement. This work was supported in part by the Shenzhen Municipal Development and Reform Commission (Disciplinary Development Program for Data Science and Intelligent Computing), and in part by the Key-Area Research and Development Program of Guangdong Province (2019B010137001).

References

1. Barnes, C., Shechtman, E., Finkelstein, A., Goldman, D.B.: PatchMatch: a randomized correspondence algorithm for structural image editing. ACM Trans. Graph. **28**(3), 24 (2009)
2. Demir, U., Ünal, G.B.: Patch-based image inpainting with generative adversarial networks. CoRR abs/1803.07422 (2018)
3. Doersch, C., Singh, S., Gupta, A., Sivic, J., Efros, A.A.: What makes Paris look like Paris? Commun. ACM **58**(12), 103–110 (2015)
4. Efros, A.A., Leung, T.K.: Texture synthesis by non-parametric sampling. In: ICCV, pp. 1033–1038. IEEE Computer Society (1999)
5. Gao, S., Cheng, M., Zhao, K., Zhang, X., Yang, M., Torr, P.H.S.: Res2Net: a new multi-scale backbone architecture. CoRR abs/1904.01169 (2019)
6. Goodfellow, I.J., et al.: Generative adversarial nets. In: NIPS, pp. 2672–2680 (2014)
7. Han, X., Wu, Z., Huang, W., Scott, M.R., Davis, L.: FiNet: compatible and diverse fashion image inpainting. In: ICCV, pp. 4480–4490. IEEE (2019)
8. Iizuka, S., Simo-Serra, E., Ishikawa, H.: Globally and locally consistent image completion. ACM Trans. Graph. **36**(4), 107:1–107:14 (2017)
9. Johnson, J., Alahi, A., Fei-Fei, L.: Perceptual losses for real-time style transfer and super-resolution. In: Leibe, B., Matas, J., Sebe, N., Welling, M. (eds.) ECCV 2016. LNCS, vol. 9906, pp. 694–711. Springer, Cham (2016). https://doi.org/10.1007/978-3-319-46475-6_43
10. Kingma, D.P., Ba, J.: Adam: a method for stochastic optimization. In: ICLR (Poster) (2015)
11. Liao, L., Hu, R., Xiao, J., Wang, Z.: Edge-aware context encoder for image inpainting. In: ICASSP, pp. 3156–3160. IEEE (2018)
12. Liu, G., Reda, F.A., Shih, K.J., Wang, T.-C., Tao, A., Catanzaro, B.: Image inpainting for irregular holes using partial convolutions. In: Ferrari, V., Hebert, M., Sminchisescu, C., Weiss, Y. (eds.) ECCV 2018. LNCS, vol. 11215, pp. 89–105. Springer, Cham (2018). https://doi.org/10.1007/978-3-030-01252-6_6
13. Liu, H., Jiang, B., Xiao, Y., Yang, C.: Coherent semantic attention for image inpainting. In: ICCV, pp. 4169–4178. IEEE (2019)
14. Liu, S., Guo, Z., Chen, J., Yu, T., Chen, Z.: Interleaved zooming network for image inpainting. In: ICME Workshops, pp. 673–678. IEEE (2019)
15. Liu, Z., Luo, P., Wang, X., Tang, X.: Deep learning face attributes in the wild. In: ICCV, pp. 3730–3738. IEEE Computer Society (2015)
16. Ma, Y., Liu, X., Bai, S., Wang, L., He, D., Liu, A.: Coarse-to-fine image inpainting via region-wise convolutions and non-local correlation. In: IJCAI, pp. 3123–3129 (2019). ijcai.org
17. Newson, A., Almansa, A., Gousseau, Y., Pérez, P.: Non-local patch-based image inpainting. Image Process. Line **7**, 373–385 (2017)
18. Pathak, D., Krähenbühl, P., Donahue, J., Darrell, T., Efros, A.A.: Context encoders: feature learning by inpainting. In: CVPR, pp. 2536–2544. IEEE Computer Society (2016)
19. Shin, Y., Sagong, M., Yeo, Y., Kim, S., Ko, S.: PEPSI++: fast and lightweight network for image inpainting. CoRR abs/1905.09010 (2019)
20. Song, Y., et al.: Contextual-based image inpainting: infer, match, and translate. In: Ferrari, V., Hebert, M., Sminchisescu, C., Weiss, Y. (eds.) ECCV 2018. LNCS, vol. 11206, pp. 3–18. Springer, Cham (2018). https://doi.org/10.1007/978-3-030-01216-8_1

21. Wang, N., Li, J., Zhang, L., Du, B.: MUSICAL: multi-scale image contextual attention learning for inpainting. In: IJCAI, pp. 3748–3754 (2019). ijcai.org
22. Wang, Y., Tao, X., Qi, X., Shen, X., Jia, J.: Image inpainting via generative multi-column convolutional neural networks. In: NeurIPS, pp. 329–338 (2018)
23. Xie, C., et al.: Image inpainting with learnable bidirectional attention maps. In: ICCV, pp. 8857–8866. IEEE (2019)
24. Xiong, W., et al.: Foreground-aware image inpainting. In: CVPR, pp. 5840–5848. Computer Vision Foundation/IEEE (2019)
25. Yan, Z., Li, X., Li, M., Zuo, W., Shan, S.: Shift-Net: image inpainting via deep feature rearrangement. In: Ferrari, V., Hebert, M., Sminchisescu, C., Weiss, Y. (eds.) Computer Vision – ECCV 2018. LNCS, vol. 11218, pp. 3–19. Springer, Cham (2018). https://doi.org/10.1007/978-3-030-01264-9_1
26. Yang, C., Lu, X., Lin, Z., Shechtman, E., Wang, O., Li, H.: High-resolution image inpainting using multi-scale neural patch synthesis. In: CVPR, pp. 4076–4084. IEEE Computer Society (2017)
27. Yu, J., Lin, Z., Yang, J., Shen, X., Lu, X., Huang, T.S.: Generative image inpainting with contextual attention. In: CVPR, pp. 5505–5514. IEEE Computer Society (2018)
28. Yu, J., Lin, Z., Yang, J., Shen, X., Lu, X., Huang, T.S.: Free-form image inpainting with gated convolution. In: ICCV, pp. 4470–4479. IEEE (2019)
29. Yu, T., et al.: Region normalization for image inpainting. In: AAAI, pp. 12733–12740. AAAI Press (2020)
30. Zhang, Q., Lin, J.: Exemplar-based image inpainting using color distribution analysis. J. Inf. Sci. Eng. **28**(4), 641–654 (2012)

Multi-task Deep Learning for No-Reference Screen Content Image Quality Assessment

Rui Gao, Ziqing Huang, and Shiguang Liu[✉]

College of Intelligence and Computing, Tianjin University, Tianjin 300350, China
lsg@tju.edu.cn

Abstract. The past decades have witnessed growing development of image quality assessment (IQA) for natural images (NIs). However, since screen content images (SCIs) exhibit different visual characteristics from the NIs, few of NIs-oriented IQA methods can be directly applied on SCIs. In this paper, we present a quality prediction approach specially designed for SCIs, which is based on multi-task deep learning. First, we split a SCI into 32×32 patches and design a novel convolutional neural network (CNN) to predict the quality score of each SCI patch. Then, we propose an effective adaptive weighting algorithm for patch-level quality score aggregation. The proposed CNN is built on an end-to-end multi-task learning framework, which integrates the histogram of oriented gradient (HOG) features prediction task to the SCI quality prediction task for learning a better mapping between input SCI patch and its quality score. The proposed adaptive weighting algorithm for patch-level quality score aggregation further improves the representation ability of each SCI patch. Experimental results on two-largest SCI-oriented databases demonstrate that our proposed method is superior to the state-of-the-art no-reference IQA methods and most of the full-reference IQA methods.

Keywords: No-reference image quality assessment · Screen content images · Multi-task learning · Histogram of oriented gradient

1 Introduction

With the rapid development of various multimedia applications and social communication systems over the internet, screen content images (SCIs) have been widely introduced in people's daily life, such as online education, online browsen, remote screen sharing, etc. Undoubtedly, the visual quality of SCIs has a significant influence on viewing experience of the client side. Hence, it's highly desired to devise an effective image quality assessment (IQA) method aiming to automatically predict the objective quality of SCIs. However, as composite images, SCIs have significantly different properties compared to natural images (NIs).

Supported by the Natural Science Foundation of China under grant no. 61672375.

J. Lokoč et al. (Eds.): MMM 2021, LNCS 12572, pp. 213–226, 2021.
https://doi.org/10.1007/978-3-030-67832-6_18

Thus the IQA models devised for NIs can not be directly employed in quality prediction of SCIs. Specifically, NIs containing natural scenes usually hold relatively smooth edges, complicated shapes and rich color with slow color change, while SCIs involve a mixture of sources which come down to natural content and computer-generated content (texts, charts, maps, graphics, symbols, etc.), especially contain plenty of text content, which results in SCIs have multiple sharp edges, high contrast, relatively uncomplicated shapes and little color variance. Consequently, there is a strong need to design a SCIs-oriented IQA method. At present, the objective IQA methods for SCIs can be classified into three categories depending on the accessibility of reference images: full reference (FR), reduced reference (RR) and no reference (NR). The NR-IQA model is more practicable due to its fewer restrictions and broader application prospects, of which one is based on the hand-crafted features and regression model that is also referred to as a two-step framework, and the other is based on the CNN model, also called as end-to-end framework.

For the end-to-end framework, Zuo et al. [19] devised a novel classification network to train the distorted image patches for predicting the quality scores, and weights determined by gradient entropy were applied to fuse the quality scores of textual and pictorial images patches. In [3], a well designed CNN architecture was presented to evaluate the quality scores of small patches, and representative patches were selected according to the saliency map to accelerate the quality score aggregation for the SCIs. Chen et al. [2] proposed a naturalization module to transform IQA of NIs into IQA of SCIs. It's not hard to conclude that most of CNNs-based NR-IQA methods for SCIs split SCIs into patches aiming to acquire enough training data and simply assign the subjective quality score of an image to all the local patches as their local quality label. This is problematic because local perceptual quality is not well-defined and not always consistent with the image quality score. To partially represent the region-wise perceptual quality variation for SCIs, an adaptive weighting method is proposed to fuse the local quality for the quality of distorted image. However, most of existing methods focus on edge or gradient information as the important factor, even ignore the whole content information of SCI. Therefore, there is a strong desire for effective network structure designed for accurate quality prediction results and effective strategy of fusing local quality, which motivate us to propose an effective NR-IQA approach tailored for SCIs.

In this work, we suggest a novel CNN-based multi-task learning model specifically designed for SCIs. Now that the contents of SCIs are rich in texture, gradient and contrast information, considering that the human visual system (HVS) is highly sensitive to edge and texture information often encountered in SCIs, we design a histogram of oriented gradient (HOG) aided convolutional neural network to evaluate quality scores of SCI patches by exploring HOG features of SCIs as predictive information source, which is shortened as HOGAMTL. The main contributions lie in three aspects:

(1) A valid multi-task learning network is developed by taking the advantages of HOG features, which induces the CNN feature extractor to extract more

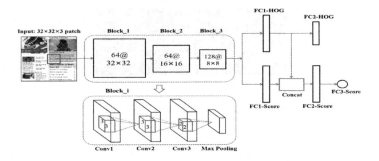

Fig. 1. An illustration of the architecture of our multi-task learning CNN model.

texture features inherited from SCIs' contents. It achieves promising performance on benchmark databases and surpasses the compared methods.

(2) Considering influence of the different image patches' contents on the quality of the image, VLSD and local entropy are involved in acquiring the local weight of each patch. That ensures our model follows the characteristic of HVS.

(3) Unlike other adaptive weighting methods which simply regard the local weight as the patch's weight for quality aggregation, our method embeds global weight in the estimation of each patch's weight, which further enhances the representation ability of each SCI patch.

2   The Proposed SCI-IQA Method

Figure 1 illustrates the devised multi-task learning CNN architecture, which consists of two learning tasks, namely HOG features prediction task and quality score prediction task. The former assists the latter in training and learning a better map between the input image patch and its quality score. The overall pipeline of our approach is depicted into two parts. First, we detail our proposed CNN model, then we present a quality aggregation algorithm to fuse the local quality scores for obtaining a quality score of the image.

2.1   Patch-Level IQA Score Prediction

Image Preprocessing. Regarding that CNN is sensitive to the mean value of the input data, the proposed CNN model for patch-level quality score prediction takes locally normalized SCI patches as input, which is defined as:

$$\hat{I}(i,j,d) = \frac{I(i,j,d) - \mu(i,j,d)}{\sigma(i,j,d) + C} \tag{1}$$

$$\mu(i,j,d) = \sum_{k=-K}^{K} \sum_{l=-L}^{L} \omega_{k,l} I_{k,l}(i,j,d) \tag{2}$$

(a)   (b)   (c)   (d)

Fig. 2. Examples of patch selection.

$$\sigma(i,j,d) = \sqrt{\sum_{k=-K}^{K} \sum_{l=-L}^{L} \omega_{k,l}(I_{k,l}(i,j,d) - \mu(i,j,d))^2} \qquad (3)$$

where $\omega = \{\omega_{k,l}|k = -K,\ldots,K, l = -L,\ldots,L\}$ is a 2D circularly-symmetric Gaussian weighting function sampled out to three standard deviations and rescaled to a unit volume. $I(i,j,d)$ denotes the pixel value. $K=L=3$ mean the normalization window sizes, and $C=1$ is a constant that prevents division by zero.

Network Training. The architecture of our proposed CNN model for SCI patch quality score prediction is shown in Fig. 1. Corresponding to two prediction tasks, there are two outputs in this multi-learning network, which are 36 dimensions output of HOG features (denoted by FC$_2$-HOG) and one dimension output of SCI patch quality score (denoted by FC$_3$-Score). For the auxiliary HOG prediction task, considering the characteristic that SCIs contain more edge and texture information, we believe that HOG can always represent distortion situation of SCIs adequately and induce the CNN feature extractor to extract more texture features. The details about HOG extraction could refer to [4].

As a NR-IQA model, quality score prediction is the main task of our proposed HOGAMTL. It shares the CNN feature extractor with HOG features prediction task and concatenates feature vectors of two tasks to get a new feature vector for quality prediction task. Then the quality score of a patch is obtained by this new feature vector. The framework of our CNN model is demonstrated in Fig. 1. The max pooling layer is introduced to decrease the training parameter size, which also tends to preserve more image texture information. That is consistent with the characteristics of SCIs. Taking distorted SCI patches preprocessed, we feed them into our proposed network to learn their HOG features and quality scores. The specific training objective function is defined as

$$O = \frac{1}{N} \sum_{n=1}^{N} (|H_p^n - H_g^n|_1 + |S_p^n - S_g^n|_1) \qquad (4)$$

where H_p^n represents the predicted HOG features of the n-th image patch in a batch with N patches, H_g^n denotes HOG label, S_p^n is the predicted score via concatenating the feature vectors from HOG prediction task, and S_g^n is the ground truth value. The parameters can be learnt in an end-to-end manner by minimizing the sum of the two L_1-norm loss functions, which comes from the HOG prediction task and quality score prediction task individually.

2.2   Image-Level IQA Score Generation

SCI Patch Selection. With the trained multi-task learning CNN model, each input $32 \times 32 \times 3$ SCI patch is predicted for getting a quality score scalar. However, there are a few pure-color patches without containing any contents, whose quality has little impact on the image quality evaluation, even might generate undesired noise for the final quality estimation. Therefore, we need to get rid of these pure-color patches and select SCI patches containing content information as candidates to obtain the image visual quality score. We mainly refer to [14] to select candidate patches. The result is provided in Fig. 2(d), in which the gray patches belong to the pure-color parts appeared in the original image. Finally, we remove these unimportant patches and reserve these patches that make a difference in terms of the image quality evaluation.

Patch-Level Weight Evaluation. After selecting suitable candidate SCI patches, there is a need for weighting each patch on account of their different characteristics. As there are two main types of regions in SCI, i.e., textual region and pictorial region. Since HVS is sensitive to texture information, the textual region would always draw more attention than the pictorial region. Correspondingly, textual image patch's quality always supplies a larger impact on the image quality estimation than pictorial patch's quality. Additionally, in some cases, the pictorial region occupies a large proportion in the image, which determines the pictorial patches also have high weights, even higher than those of the textual patches for IQA. Consequently, a comprehensive weight index is needed by taking into account both textual and pictorial weights, and adaptively determining which patch owns higher quality weight for its source image quality evaluation. Based on this observation, we assume that the quality of a SCI is jointly affected by tow factors: the importance of textual and pictorial regions, and the areas of the two regions, which is detailed as follows.

(a) Local weight based on VLSD and ALE: The local weight of each patch is responsible for its own local properties. Concerning that LSD mainly emphasizes textual region and local entropy feature prefers to highlight pictorial region, which was stated earlier, we compute the variance of LSD (VLSD) and the average value of local entropy (ALE) of each patch to reflect their characteristics. Accordingly, the two features of VLSD and the ALE tend to highlight textual and pictorial patches, which is illustrated in Figs. 3(a) and 3(b). The highlighted regions are marked with red boxes to emphasize the difference between the VLSD map and the ALE map. It can be observed that patches with greater value supply more information to image perception. Therefore, these patches deserve to be assigned higher weights for IQA. Correspondingly, the great VLSD value and ALE value can exactly depict and measure local weight of these patches. The two feature values of VLSD and ALE are calculated as

$$VLSD = \frac{1}{N} \sum_{n=1}^{N} (\sigma(i,j) - \bar{\sigma})^2 \tag{5}$$

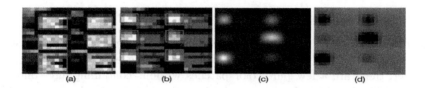

Fig. 3. Examples of local weight and global weight indicators.

$$ALE = \frac{1}{N} \sum_{n=1}^{N} E(i,j) \tag{6}$$

$$W_l = VLSD^{\rho_1} \times ALE^{\rho_2} \tag{7}$$

where $N=1024$, which is the number of pixels in the 32×32 image patch, $\sigma(i,j)$ is computed with Eq. (3) for getting LSD map of the patch, and $\bar{\sigma}$ is the mean value of the LSD map, thus the result of $VLSD$ represents the variance of LSD map of this patch. By the same token, $E(i,j)$ is calculated from the local entropy map of the patch, and then Eq. (6) is applied to compute the average value of the local entropy map. At this point, two weight indicators are obtained for each patch and they need to be combined to form the local weight of this image patch via Eq. (7). The given exponent ρ_1 and ρ_2 are two positive integers that are utilized to adjust the relative importance of $VLSD$ and ALE. In our study, the values of ρ_1 and ρ_2 are variable to adapt to different image databases. We provisionally set these two parameters as 2.0 and 6.0, respectively.

(b) Global weight based on region area: The global weight of each patch aims at the property of the image. According to the type of SCI contents, there are two types of regions: textual region and pictorial region. Facing the fact that humans always pay more attention to the type of the contents covering larger region area instead of the type of contents only occupying a small region area of the image, even if this kind of contents are rich in texture information. For that reason, the content information distribution of the image need to be considered as computing its patches' weights. We call the weight depending on the content region area as global weight, which can be determined through the saliency map. Besides, we observe that the fast saliency map (SM) calculation is a positive way to distinguish the textual regions from the pictorial regions of SCIs, as demonstrated in Fig. 3(c). It's obvious that the saliency map will mostly assign large salient values to pictorial regions instead of textual regions. To put it another way, small salient pixel values in a region suggest that this part is likely to be a textual region. Consequently, we count the number of textual patches and pictorial patches of each SCI respectively, according to the saliency map of SCI. Specifically, we transform the pixel-level salient value to patch-level salient value by computing the maximum value only in each patch for the saliency map. The result is presented in Fig. 3(d) and the calculation is described as

$$S = max\left\{s(i,j)\right\}, i \in [1, N'], j \in [1, N'] \tag{8}$$

where N' is set as the patch size, $s(i,j)$ is saved as pixel-level salient value, and S is saved as patch-level salient value. Then, for each SCI, we count the S values ranging from 0 to 0.03 in order to obtain the number of patches whose contents are inclined to be textual information. Therefore, the remaining patches belong to pictorial patches. Notably, the value of 0.03 is small enough to contain all of textual patches of SCI as much as possible, which is concluded through experiment. Eventually, we obtain the individual amount of pictorial patches and textual patches in one image and they can represent the global weight of each patch, and we also classify these patches into two categories: textual patches and pictorial patches through judging the S value of each patch. If this patch belongs to a textual patch, the patch's global weight equals to the amount of all textual patches of its source image. Similarly, if this patch is regarded as a pictorial patch, its global weight equals to the amount of all pictorial patches.

Quality Aggregation. Given a test distorted screen content image, based on the above analysis, we obtain the quality score of each patch predicted by the multi-task learning network and the corresponding local weight and global weight. A weighted summation method is employed to fuse quality scores of these patches which is calculated as

$$Q = \frac{\sum_{i=1}^{M} Q_i \times (W_{l_i} + W_{g_i})}{\sum_{i=1}^{M} (W_{l_i} + W_{g_i})} \tag{9}$$

where Q_i is the score of the $i-th$ patch and its local weight W_{l_i} is calculated by Eq. (7). Besides, through assessing the type of this patch and count the amount of all patches of its corresponding type in this given image, the global weight W_{g_i} is assigned. M is the number of the patches except pure-color patches of the test image, and Q is the final quality score of the test image.

3   Experimental Results

3.1   Databases and Evaluation Methodology

We employed two widely used SCI databases, i.e., the screen content image quality assessment database (SIQAD) and the screen content image database (SCID), which contain 980 and 1800 high-quality annotated SCIs, respectively. Four measures were leveraged to evaluate the performance of IQA for SCIs: Pearson Linear Correlation Coefficient (PLCC), Spearman Rank Order Correlation Coefficient (SROCC), Kendall rank-order correlation coefficient (KROCC), and Root Mean Square Error (RMSE).

3.2   Performance Comparison

Ablation Studies. We conducted ablation experiment on network architecture to examine whether the performance of the proposed multi-task learning model is superior. The baseline model is the quality prediction task without concat layer. Then we added the HOG feature prediction task and concat layer, respectively. The evaluation is illustrated in Fig. 4. The result of the single-task learning model containing quality score prediction task simply is marked in green, named as STL. The multi-task learning model without concat layer is marked in blue, in which the HOG prediction task fails to aid the quality prediction task and only the CNN extractor is shared between the two tasks, named as HOG-MTL, and the multi-task learning model with concat layer is marked in orange, in which the HOG prediction task successfully aids the quality prediction task, shortly named as HOGAMTL. As presented in Fig. 4, the performance is improved when HOG features are introduced and the accuracy will further increase as the HOG prediction task aids the quality prediction task by the concat layer, which confirms HOG prediction task is effective for visual quality prediction of SCIs.

In order to show the advantage of our proposed quality aggregation algorithm, we conducted another ablation study on weighting strategy. Specifically, each SCI patch is assigned with the same weight (i.e., average weighting strategy), the local weight computed with Eq. (7), the global weight obtained through Eq. (8) and the combination weight via fusing local weight with global weight in Eq. (8), respectively. Table 1 lists the performance evaluation results of different weighting strategies for IQA of SCIs. In this table, the first-ranked, the second-ranked and the third-ranked performance value of each evaluation criteria are boldfaced in red, blue and black, separately. It can be clearly observed from this table, as we assign the combination weight consisting of local weight and global weight to the image patch, the performance will be superior. In contrast, if we get rid of either kind of the two weights, the performance would decrease.

Besides, there is an interesting phenomenon that the local weighting achieves significant improvement comparing with average and global weighting on SIQAD. This could be explained by considering that more massive texts exist in SIQAD than in SCID. If we only adopt global weighting strategy, maybe it will fail to notice the presence of pictorial regions, which leads to the unfairness. By the same logic, if we only adopt average weighting strategy, it will fail to notice the peculiarity of a large number of texts. Consequently, local weighting strategy considering both characteristics of textual and pictorial regions is better.

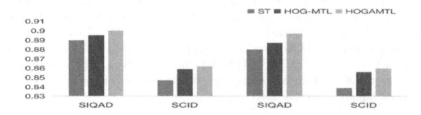

Fig. 4. PLCC and SROCC based on different network models on SIQAD and SCID database. The left two groups denote the PLCC values and the right two groups represent the SROCC values.

Table 1. Evaluation results based on different weighting strategy

Criteria	SIQAD				SCID			
	SROCC	PLCC	KROCC	RMSE	SROCC	PLCC	KROCC	RMSE
Average	**0.8580**	**0.8648**	**0.6677**	**7.2667**	0.8398	0.8454	0.6444	7.1468
Global	0.8398	0.8499	0.6478	7.6269	**0.8526**	**0.8592**	**0.6602**	**6.8463**
Local	**0.8960**	**0.8984**	**0.7262**	**6.3558**	0.8542	0.8598	0.6651	6.8332
Local+Global	0.8962	0.9000	0.7265	6.3535	0.8569	0.8613	0.6679	6.7991

Overall and Individual Performance Comparison. In order to verify the overall capability, our proposed NR-IQA model HOGAMTL was compared with multiple FR and NR-SCIQA models, including SIQM [10], ESIM, SVQI [8], SFUW [6], GFM [16], MDQGS [7], SQMS [9], BQMS [11], SIQE [12], OSM [15], NRLT [5], IGM [18], PICNN [2], TFSR [17], QOD [13], and CBIQA [1]. In contrast with the NR-IQA of SCIs models, the first three performance figures of each measurement criterion (i.e., PLCC, SROCC and RMSE) in each row are indicated in bold, and from the first to the third are individually marked red, blue and black. It can be obviously observed that the proposed HOGAMTL yields the best overall performance on the SCID database, compared with other state-of-the-art NR-SCIQA methods. On the SIQAD database, our method achieves the third-place overall performance but almost comparable to the top two models. Certainly, HOGAMTL even surpasses various FR-IQA of SCIs models. Specifically, the performance of HOGAMTL is higher than all advanced FR-IQA of SCIs model listed in Table 2 on the SIQAD database in three metrics, and it also beats nearly all FR-IQA of SCIs models on the SCID database except ESIM, SFUW and GFM highlighted in green. For the sake of comprehensive performance comparisons over multiple databases, Table 2 exhibits the average performances of different IQA methods on these two databases. It can be obviously observed that the proposed HOGAMTL almost yields the highest PLCC and SROCC in both Direct Average and Weighted Average performance comparisons apart from PLCC value of Direct Average, yet the metric value (0.8807) is intensely approximate to the top value (0.882). Consequently, it's obvious that HOGAMTL offers comprehensive performance over multiple databases.

To more comprehensively evaluate each IQA model's ability on assessing image quality's degradations caused by each distortion type, Table 3 reports the results of comparison experiment conducted on the SIQAD database. HOGAMTL surpasses most of FR-SCIQA models excluding CC distortion type. Among these NR-SCIQA models, HOGAMTL yields the most top-three performances (18 times) same as model CBIQA. Yet HOGAMTL is among the first-place models 12 times beyond CBIQA (9 times) with 3 times, which is presented in the last row of Table 3. That proves the superiority capability of our proposed method. Table 4 exhibits the results conducted on the SCID database. Differently from before, this time the top three models are evaluated under the participation of FR-IQA of SCIs models. As shown in Table 4, the proposed

Table 2. Comparisons among the proposed and other FR and NR models

	Criteria	SIQM	ESIM	SVQI	SFUW	GFM	MDQGS	SQMS	BQMS	SIQE	OSM	NRLT	IGM	PICNN	TFSR	QOD	CBIQA	Our
		FR	FR	FR	FR	FR	FR	FR	NR	NR	NR	NR	NR	NR	NR	NR	NR	
SIQAD	PLCC	0.8520	0.8788	0.8911	0.8910	0.8828	0.8839	0.8870	0.7549	0.7904	0.8306	0.8442	0.8834	0.896	0.8618	0.9008	0.9109	0.9000
	SROCC	0.8450	0.8632	0.8836	0.8800	0.8735	0.8822	0.8803	0.7223	0.7593	0.8007	0.8202	0.8634	0.897	0.8354	0.8888	0.8976	0.8962
	RMSE	7.4936	6.8310	6.4965	6.4990	6.7234	6.6951	6.6110	9.3042	8.7899	7.9331	7.5957	–	6.790	7.4951	6.2258	5.8930	6.3535
SCID	PLCC	0.8303	0.8630	0.8604	0.8590	0.8760	–	0.8557	0.6487	0.6371	–	0.6625	–	–	0.8017	–	0.8531	0.8613
	SROCC	0.8086	0.8478	0.8386	0.8950	0.8759	–	0.8320	0.6138	0.6034	–	0.6454	–	–	0.7840	–	0.8377	0.8569
	RMSE	7.8920	7.1552	7.2178	7.3100	6.8310	–	7.3276	10.7787	10.9202	–	10.6452	–	–	8.8041	–	7.3930	6.7991
Direct Average	PLCC	0.8412	0.8709	0.8758	0.875	0.8794	–	0.8714	0.7018	0.7138	–	0.7534	–	–	0.8318	–	0.882	0.8807
	SROCC	0.8268	0.8555	0.8611	0.8875	0.8747	–	0.8562	0.6681	0.6814	–	0.7328	–	–	0.8097	–	0.8677	0.8766
Weighted Average	PLCC	0.8379	0.8686	0.8712	0.8703	0.8783	–	0.8667	0.6861	0.6911	–	0.7266	–	–	0.8229	–	0.8735	0.875
	SROCC	0.8214	0.8532	0.8545	0.8897	0.8751	–	0.849	0.652	0.6584	–	0.707	–	–	0.8021	–	0.8588	0.8708

Table 3. Performance comparisons on seven distortion types on SIQAD

	Distortions	SIQM FR	ESIM FR	SVQI FR	SFUW FR	GFM FR	MDQGS FR	SQMS FR	BQMS NR	SIQE NR	NRLT NR	TFSR NR	QOD NR	CBIQA NR	Our
PLCC	GN	0.8921	0.8891	0.9031	0.8870	0.8990	0.8982	0.900	0.8372	0.0883	0.9131	**0.9291**	0.913	**0.9317**	**0.9177**
	GB	0.9124	0.9234	0.9132	0.9230	0.9143	0.9195	0.912	0.7558	0.8033	0.8949	**0.9367**	**0.925**	0.9148	0.9535
	MB	0.8565	0.8886	0.8722	0.8780	0.8662	0.8421	0.867	0.7237	0.7810	**0.8993**	**0.9243**	0.889	0.8846	0.9282
	CC	0.7902	0.7641	0.8087	0.8290	0.8107	0.8011	0.803	0.7209	0.6030	**0.8131**	0.6563	**0.837**	0.9229	0.7049
	JC	0.7717	0.7999	0.7953	0.7570	0.8398	0.7885	0.786	0.7653	**0.8339**	0.7932	0.8334	0.830	**0.9036**	0.9138
	J2C	0.7940	0.7888	0.8342	0.8150	0.8486	0.8606	0.826	0.7909	**0.8535**	0.6848	0.8347	0.818	**0.9143**	0.9368
	LSC	0.7204	0.7915	0.8283	0.7590	0.8288	0.8316	0.813	0.8427	**0.8921**	0.7228	0.8069	**0.867**	0.9294	0.8128
	ALL	0.8520	0.8788	0.8911	0.8910	0.8828	0.8839	0.8870	0.7549	0.7904	0.8842	0.8616	**0.9008**	0.9109	**0.9000**
SROCC	GN	0.8711	0.8757	0.8909	0.8690	0.8795	0.8882	0.886	0.8346	0.8280	0.8966	0.9144	0.905	**0.9143**	0.8692
	GB	0.9102	0.9239	0.9129	0.9170	0.9132	0.9192	0.915	0.7627	0.7942	0.8812	**0.9311**	**0.916**	0.8971	0.9365
	MB	0.8401	0.8938	0.8753	0.8740	0.8699	0.8345	0.869	0.7176	0.7748	**0.8919**	**0.9148**	0.871	0.8708	0.9184
	CC	0.7055	0.6108	0.7131	0.7220	0.7038	0.6644	0.695	**0.7260**	0.8199	0.7072	0.6498	0.700	0.9075	0.5835
	JC	0.7754	0.7989	0.7925	0.7500	0.8434	0.7856	0.789	0.7661	**0.8388**	0.7698	0.8377	0.815	**0.8848**	0.8922
	J2C	0.7771	0.7827	0.8282	0.8120	0.8444	0.8622	0.819	0.7919	**0.8493**	0.6761	0.8354	0.795	**0.8911**	0.9562
	LSC	0.7255	0.7958	0.8412	0.7540	0.8445	0.8513	0.829	0.8267	**0.8843**	0.6978	0.7948	**0.882**	0.9046	0.7898
	ALL	0.8450	0.8632	0.8836	0.8800	0.8735	0.8822	0.8803	0.7223	0.7593	0.8202	0.8354	**0.8888**	0.8976	**0.8962**
RMSE	GN	7.0165	6.8272	6.4044	8.8760	6.6835	6.5576	6.921	8.1615	19.0113	-	5.3105	6.150	**5.3292**	**5.9159**
	GB	5.8367	5.8270	6.1550	5.5920	6.1459	5.9639	6.611	8.8390	8.2689	-	**5.2141**	5.772	**5.3767**	4.4336
	MB	6.0869	5.9639	6.3604	6.2360	6.5184	7.0121	7.204	9.2398	8.6522	-	**5.5266**	**5.762**	6.0794	4.6997
	CC	8.1079	8.1141	7.3996	7.0480	7.3638	7.5284	7.743	9.2114	12.4155	-	10.5005	**6.939**	5.0375	9.351
	JC	5.6548	5.6401	5.6969	6.1430	5.1009	5.7787	5.983	8.5874	7.3633	-	**5.2541**	5.460	5.5912	3.7027
	J2C	6.0820	6.3877	5.7309	6.0230	5.4985	5.2930	6.050	8.4164	7.1150	-	**5.6377**	6.000	**5.4480**	3.1189
	LSC	5.3576	5.2150	4.7751	5.5550	4.7736	4.7382	5.104	7.8336	6.5744	-	5.6217	4.338	**5.2539**	**5.3892**
	ALL	7.4936	6.8310	6.4965	6.4990	7.2234	6.6951	6.6110	9.3042	8.7899	0.8202	7.4951	**6.2258**	5.8930	**6.3535**
	Number	-	-	-	-	-	-	-	0	0	0	2	1	9	12

Table 4. Performance comparisons on nine distortion types on SCID

	Distortions	SIQM (FR)	ESIM (FR)	SVQI (FR)	GFM (FR)	SQMS (FR)	CBIQA (NR)	Our (NR)
PLCC	GN	0.9269	**0.9563**	0.9362	**0.9497**	0.9298	0.9182	0.9722
	GB	**0.9266**	0.8700	0.9130	**0.9156**	0.9081	0.9296	0.8579
	MB	0.9152	0.8824	0.8997	**0.9023**	0.8968	**0.903**	0.8983
	CC	0.7821	0.7908	0.8266	**0.8787**	**0.8441**	0.9067	0.7584
	JC	0.9226	**0.9421**	0.9356	**0.9392**	0.9302	0.8992	0.9558
	J2C	0.9076	**0.9457**	0.9513	0.9226	**0.9468**	0.9028	0.9410
	CSC	0.0683	0.0694	0.0919	0.8728	0.0628	**0.8527**	**0.6167**
	CQD	0.8385	**0.9005**	0.9047	0.8928	0.8986	**0.9042**	0.7842
	HEVC	0.8316	0.9108	0.8496	**0.8740**	**0.8515**	0.8363	0.8379
	ALL	0.8303	**0.8630**	0.8604	0.8760	0.8557	0.8531	**0.8613**
SROCC	GN	0.9133	**0.9460**	0.9191	**0.9370**	0.9155	0.8962	0.9641
	GB	0.9232	0.8699	0.9079	**0.9081**	**0.9079**	0.9063	0.8401
	MB	**0.9006**	0.8608	**0.8842**	0.8892	0.8814	0.8725	0.9107
	CC	0.7435	0.6182	0.7705	**0.8225**	**0.8027**	0.8797	0.5300
	JC	0.9158	**0.9455**	**0.9287**	0.9281	0.9236	0.8959	0.9558
	J2C	0.8935	**0.9359**	0.9367	0.9085	**0.9320**	0.8923	0.9006
	CSC	0.0617	0.1037	0.0790	0.8736	0.0814	**0.8396**	**0.5350**
	CQD	0.8301	0.8868	0.8957	0.8907	**0.8913**	**0.8955**	0.7505
	HEVC	0.8517	0.9036	0.8665	**0.8712**	**0.8667**	0.8261	0.8569
	ALL	0.8086	**0.8478**	0.8386	0.8759	0.8320	0.8377	**0.8569**
RMSE	GN	4.8222	**3.6760**	4.4179	**3.9378**	4.6250	4.9014	2.7681
	GB	4.0989	5.2213	4.3194	**4.2566**	4.4336	**4.3107**	5.3026
	MB	**4.7388**	5.1431	4.7709	4.6121	4.8352	5.1268	**4.6197**
	CC	6.1281	5.4790	**5.0374**	4.2732	**4.7995**	5.0742	5.3783
	JC	6.7341	**5.0373**	5.3055	5.2011	5.5181	**4.5375**	4.4987
	J2C	7.2951	5.1695	**4.9058**	6.1385	5.1191	**4.2713**	**4.8037**
	CSC	9.8394	9.8156	9.7977	4.8031	9.8199	**5.1742**	7.1440
	CQD	7.1976	**5.5607**	**5.4481**	5.7592	5.6110	4.9035	8.7329
	HEVC	8.197	**5.7446**	7.3381	6.7590	7.2938	5.3346	**6.2844**
	ALL	7.8920	**7.1552**	7.2178	**6.8310**	7.3276	7.3930	6.7991
	Number	3	2	4	7	0	6	8

Table 5. Performance in cross database validation

	Training (SIQAD)	
Testing (SCID)	PLCC	SROCC
GN	0.8434	0.8084
GB	0.7637	0.7342
MB	0.8865	0.8745
CC	0.7517	0.6627
JC	0.8494	0.8258
J2C	0.8621	0.8445
ALL	0.8267	0.8186

model delivers excellent performance with 8 times among the first-place models and renders more promising performance on SCID database compared with results with method CBIQA on SIQAD, which further verifies the robustness of HOGAMTL. We also trained the model on the whole SIQAD database and tested on SCID database. As shown in Table 5, there is a acceptable performance decline compared to training on SCID database, which represents a strong generalization performance of our model.

4   Conclusion

In this paper, a multi-task deep learning model had been proposed for NR-SCIQA. We first introduced the HOG prediction task to our multi-task learning model and let this task to aid the quality prediction task, then we designed a quality aggregation algorithm to obtain the final quality score of screen content image. The comparison experiments verified the superior performance and generalization of our method. For the future work, we will continue to explore better texture features to aid the deep learning more precisely.

References

1. Bai, Y., Yu, M.: Jiang: learning content-specific codebooks for blind quality assessment of screen content images. Sig. Process. **161**(20), 248–258 (2019)
2. Chen, J., Shen, L., Zheng, L., Jiang, X.: Naturalization module in neural networks for screen content image quality assessment. IEEE Sig. Process. Lett. **25**(11), 1685–1689 (2018)
3. Cheng, Z., Takeuchi, M.: A fast no-reference screen content image quality prediction using convolutional neural networks. In: Proceedings of the IEEE International Conference on Multimedia & Expo Workshops, pp. 1–6 (2018)
4. Dalal, N., Triggs, B.: Histograms of oriented gradients for human detection. In: Proceedings of the IEEE Computer Society Conference on Computer Vision and Pattern Recognition, pp. 886–893 (2005)

5. Fang, Y., Yan, J., Li, L., Wu, J., Lin, W.: No reference quality assessment for screen content images with both local and global feature representation. IEEE Trans. Image Process. **27**(4), 1600–1610 (2017)

6. Fang, Y., Yan, J., Liu, J., Wang, S., Li, Q., Guo, Z.: Objective quality assessment of screen content images by uncertainty weighting. IEEE Trans. Image Process. **26**(4), 2016–2027 (2017)

7. Fu, Y., Zeng, H., Ma, L., Ni, Z., Zhu, J., Ma, K.K.: Screen content image quality assessment using multi-scale difference of gaussian. IEEE Trans. Circ. Syst. Video Technol. **28**(9), 2428–2432 (2018)

8. Gu, K., Qiao, J., Min, X., Yue, G., Lin, W., Thalmann, D.: Evaluating quality of screen content images via structural variation analysis. IEEE Trans. Vis. Comput. Graph. **24**(10), 2689–2701 (2017)

9. Gu, K., et al.: Saliency-guided quality assessment of screen content images. IEEE Trans. Multimedia **18**(6), 1098–1110 (2016)

10. Gu, K., Wang, S., Zhai, G., Ma, S., Lin, W.: Screen image quality assessment incorporating structural degradation measurement. In: Proceedings of the IEEE International Symposium on Circuits and Systems (ISCAS), pp. 125–128 (2015)

11. Gu, K., Zhai, G., Lin, W., Yang, X., Zhang, W.: Learning a blind quality evaluation engine of screen content images. Neurocomputing **196**, 140–149 (2016)

12. Gu, K., Zhou, J., Qiao, J.F., Zhai, G., Lin, W., Bovik, A.C.: No-reference quality assessment of screen content pictures. IEEE Trans. Image Process. **26**(8), 4005–4018 (2017)

13. Jiang, X., Shen, L., Feng, G., Yu, L., An, P.: Deep optimization model for screen content image quality assessment using neural networks. arXiv preprint arXiv:1903.00705 (2019)

14. Kim, J., Lee, S.: Deep learning of human visual sensitivity in image quality assessment framework. In: Proceedings of the IEEE Conference on Computer Vision and Pattern Recognition, pp. 1676–1684 (2017)

15. Lu, N., Li, G.: Blind quality assessment for screen content images by orientation selectivity mechanism. Sig. Process. **145**, 225–232 (2018)

16. Ni, Z., Zeng, H., Ma, L., Hou, J., Chen, J., Ma, K.K.: A gabor feature-based quality assessment model for the screen content images. IEEE Trans. Image Process. **27**(9), 4516–4528 (2018)

17. Yang, J., Liu, J., Jiang, B., Lu, W.: No reference quality evaluation for screen content images considering texture feature based on sparse representation. Sig. Process. **153**(89), 336–347 (2018)

18. Yue, G., Hou, C., Yan, W., Choi, L.K., Zhou, T., Hou, Y.: Blind quality assessment for screen content images via convolutional neural network. Digit. Sig. Process. **91**, 21–30 (2019)

19. Zuo, L., Wang, H., Fu, J.: Screen content image quality assessment via convolutional neural network. In: Proceedings of the IEEE International Conference on Image Processing, pp. 2082–2086 (2016)

Language Person Search with Pair-Based Weighting Loss

Peng Zhang[1,2], Deqiang Ouyang[2,3], Chunlin Jiang[3], and Jie Shao[2,3(✉)]

[1] Guizhou Provincial Key Laboratory of Public Big Data, Guizhou University,
Guiyang 550025, China
[2] Center for Future Media, School of Computer Science and Engineering, University
of Electronic Science and Technology of China, Chengdu 611731, China
{pengzhang,ouyangdeqiang}@std.uestc.edu.cn, shaojie@uestc.edu.cn
[3] Sichuan Artificial Intelligence Research Institute, Yibin 644000, China
jclxhu552@163.com

Abstract. Language person search, which means retrieving specific person images with natural language description, is becoming a research hotspot in the area of person re-identification. Compared with person re-identification which belongs to image retrieval task, language person search poses challenges due to heterogeneous semantic gap between different modal data of image and text. To solve this problem, most existing methods employ softmax-based classification loss in order to embed the visual and textual features into a common latent space. However, pair-based loss, as a successful approach of metric learning, is hardly mentioned in this task. Recently, pair-based weighting loss for deep metric learning has shown great potential in improving the performance of many retrieval-related tasks. In this paper, to better correlate person image with given language description, we introduce pair-based weighting loss which encourages model to assign appropriate weights to different image-text pairs. We have conducted extensive experiments on the dataset CUHK-PEDES and the experimental results validated the effectiveness of our proposed method.

Keywords: Language person search · Deep metric learning · Pair weighting

1 Introduction

Recently, language person search, as illustrated in Fig. 1, has drawn dramatic attention from academic research especially after the introduction of CUHK-PEDES dataset [14]. As an extension task of person re-identification [4,16,21] that is essentially an image retrieval task, language person search is believed to get closer to real scenarios. For example, in a scene of crime, it is always hard for police to get explicit and accurate information like a picture of the criminal. However, we can sometimes get oral descriptions about the criminal's appearance from a witness. Thus, research on this topic is of great practical

© Springer Nature Switzerland AG 2021
J. Lokoč et al. (Eds.): MMM 2021, LNCS 12572, pp. 227–239, 2021.
https://doi.org/10.1007/978-3-030-67832-6_19

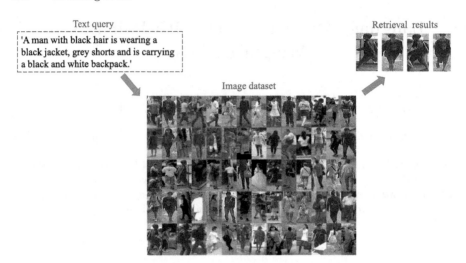

Fig. 1. Given a textual description, language person search aims at retrieving the most relevant person images from an image dataset.

value. Despite sharing a lot in common with person re-identification, language person search is basically a different task and can be classified into a cross-modal retrieval problem. Given a natural language description that is considered to be a modality of text, language person search requires retrieving another modality information of person images that match the descriptions. Compared with the task of person re-identification, language person search concerns information of different modalities, i.e., text and image. Data of different modalities has an inconsistent distribution which means a heterogeneous semantic gap. Although describing a same person, features from language and image have huge differences which makes it nearly impossible for us to directly retrieve images according to the text description. How to minimize the distances between features regardless of modality under the same identity and maximize the distances between those of different identities is no doubt playing a decisive role in the model performance.

In general, existing works either construct a similarity score learning model or try to learn a joint embedding space for image and text. In [14], as a pioneer, Li *et al.* adopted a visual attention mechanism to weight the contributions of different visual units for each word and developed a recurrent neural network with gated neural attention (GNA-RNN) to estimate the similarity between image and language description. In [13], Li *et al.* exploited identity-level information and proposed a novel cross-modal cross-entropy (CMCE) loss to correlate the features of text and image of the same identity. In addition, they presented an effective co-attention mechanism where spatial attention relates words to specific image regions and latent semantic attention helps extract a more consistent textual feature against the variation of sentence structure. In [3,11], Chen *et al.* and Ji *et al.* proposed other similarity score learning algorithms.

While these methods have achieved significant performance, they either pay a high price to design a well-crafted and complicated model which focuses on part-based features of person images or extract more discriminative textual feature using more advanced language model such as BERT [6] which has high requirements for computing resources. We observe that many existing works [18,30,32,33] have applied softmax-based classification loss in order to classify feature vectors into the correct category and meanwhile increase the similarity of the matched feature pair of image and text. However, as another popular loss function of metric learning, pair-based losses [29] have been hardly adopted in the task of language person search. Pair-based loss, which is expressed in terms of pairwise cosine similarity, aims to minimize the distance of positive pairs while maximizing the discrepancy of negative pairs and it has demonstrated an impressive capability of improving model performance in the task of face recognition [22] and person re-identification [9]. However, as pairs are constructed randomly from training samples, pair-based loss encounters a key problem that redundant and less informative pairs overwhelm the training process giving rise to slow convergence and model degeneration. To solve this problem, recent works have been dedicated to improving pair sampling schemes. In [29], Wang *et al.* cast the pair sampling problem into a general pair weighting formulation.

Language person search is essentially a cross-modality retrieval problem which is obviously different from single-modality retrieval tasks such as face recognition and person re-identification. In this task, pair sample is randomly constructed from person image and language description creating matched or unmatched image-text pair. To exploit the informative pair as well as to be more resistant to redundant and less informative pair, we introduce pair-based weighting loss for the first time in this task.

Briefly, the contributions of this paper can be summarized into two folds:

- To better exploit the information of the matched and unmatched image-text pairs in the task of language person search, we introduce a pair-based weighting loss that will encourage the model to focus more on the informative pairs.
- We have conducted extensive experiments to prove the effectiveness of our framework and experimental results have demonstrated the superiority of our proposed method on the CUHK-PEDES dataset.

2 Related Work

2.1 Language Person Search

Language person search develops from person re-identification. Compared with attribute-based person re-identification [25,26,28] which retrieves person images corresponding to a pre-defined set of attributes, language person search has complete freedom form in describing person's appearance. In summary, there are roughly two research directions in this task. One is joint embedding learning and the other is pairwise similarity learning [32]. Joint embedding learning tries to project features from different modalities onto a common latent space where the similarity between image and text features can be directly compared.

Pairwise similarity learning emphasizes learning to predict a matching score by a dedicated network that fuses image and text features. In [14], Li et al. proposed a framework to measure the correlation degree of each word with different visual feature units and to get a similarity score between sentence and image. In [13], Li et al. developed an identity-aware two-stage deep learning framework with a CMCE loss to fully take advantage of identity information. In [33], Zheng et al. first adopted a convolution neural network to process textual information while most studies use RNN. In [32], Zhang and Lu presented an effective cross-modal projection matching (CMPM) and a cross-modal projection classification (CMPC) loss function to learn discriminative embedding features. In all the above mentioned methods, few of them have taken pair-based loss into consideration, let al.one how to weight different pairs appropriately. In this paper, to exploit the informative pairs as fully as possible we adopt pair-based weighting loss.

2.2 Deep Metric Learning

Measuring the distances and preserving an appropriate distance relationship between pair of samples play an essential role in many applications, such as person re-identification, face recognition and image retrieval. A variety of loss functions related to deep metric learning have been applied and achieved good performance in many deep learning frameworks. Generally, the metric loss function can be classified into two categories, softmax-based losses and pair-based metric losses [17]. The softmax-based loss has been well developed and exerted great influence in face recognition. Some well-known face recognition losses including L-Softmax loss [20], A-Softmax loss [19], AM-Softmax loss [27] and Arcface loss [5] all belong to softmax-based loss. Pair-based metric loss is designed for the purpose of preserving an appropriate distance structure for pair samples including positive and negative pairs. Some of the most representative pair-based metric loss include Contrastive loss [7], Triplet loss [22] and Triplet-Center loss [8]. As for pair weighting, lifted structure loss [24], N-pair loss [23] and Multi-Similarity (MS) loss [29] introduce effective weighting schemes to assign a larger weight to a more informative pair. In this paper, we concentrate on pair-based weighting loss. Compared with traditional pair-based losses such as contrastive loss and triplet loss, pair-based weighting loss distinguishes itself by introducing the concept of pair weighting which can be regarded as a scheme of allocating different attentions for pair samples. In [31], Wei et al. proposed a universal weighting framework to treat pair samples with different weight values for cross-modal tasks.

3   The Proposed Approach

In this section, we describe the details of our model as shown in Fig. 2. We first formulate the task of language person search and introduce our baseline framework. Then, we explain the pair-based weighting loss and how to apply it to our task. Finally, we present the objective function of our model.

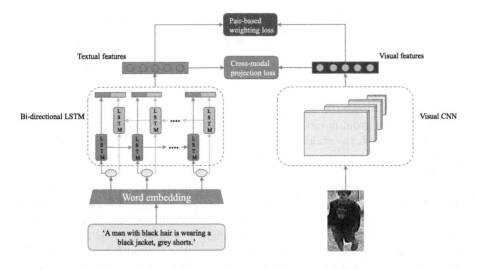

Fig. 2. Architecture of our proposed model.

3.1 Baseline Framework

Person image and its corresponding text description will be input into feature extractors which include image feature extractor and text feature extractor to process image and text information, respectively. As for text description, sentences are preprocessed into 512D word vectors through word embedding layers. To further extract text features, Bi-LSTM network [34] is adopted to get the initial text features.

With regard to image features, pre-trained MobileNet [10] is used as our backbone model. We adjust the input image size to 224×224 and obtain features from the last pooling layer of the backbone model. Subsequently, a fully convolutional layer is added to get the output as the final image features.

Let us assume there are n person images and corresponding descriptions in a mini-batch. The image-text pairs are denoted as $\{(\boldsymbol{x}_i, \boldsymbol{z}_j), y_{i,j}\}_{j=1}^{n}$, where $y_{i,j} = 1$ indicates the image-text pair is a matched pair, while $y_{i,j} = 0$ means the unmatched ones. The probability of matching $\boldsymbol{x}_i$ to $\boldsymbol{z}_i$ is formulated as:

$$p_{i,j} = \frac{\exp\left(\boldsymbol{x}_i^\top \overline{\boldsymbol{z}}_j\right)}{\sum_{k=1}^{n} \exp\left(\boldsymbol{x}_i^\top \overline{\boldsymbol{z}}_k\right)} \quad \text{s.t. } \overline{\boldsymbol{z}}_j = \frac{\boldsymbol{z}_j}{\|\boldsymbol{z}_j\|}. \tag{1}$$

In a mini-batch, the true matching probability of $(\boldsymbol{x}_i, \boldsymbol{z}_j)$ is calculated as:

$$q_{i,j} = \frac{y_{i,j}}{\sum_{k=1}^{n} y_{i,k}}. \tag{2}$$

Then, the matching loss from image to text is calculated as:

$$\mathcal{L}_i = \sum_{j=1}^{n} p_{i,j} \log \frac{p_{i,j}}{q_{i,j} + \epsilon}, \tag{3}$$

$$\mathcal{L}_{i2t} = \frac{1}{n} \sum_{i=1}^{n} \mathcal{L}_i, \tag{4}$$

Finally, the cross-modal projection matching (CMPM) loss is defined as:

$$\mathcal{L}_{\text{cmpm}} = \mathcal{L}_{i2t} + \mathcal{L}_{t2i}, \tag{5}$$

where ϵ is set to avoid numerical problems. $\mathcal{L}_{t2i}$ indicates the matching loss from text to image with the similar derivation procedure to $\mathcal{L}_{i2t}$. The CMPM loss is essentially a relative entropy which encourages p_i to have the same probability distribution as q_i.

Compared with the CMPM loss, the cross-modal projection classification (CMPC) loss is a softmax-based loss that classifies the projection of text features onto image features rather than classifies the original features. The advantage of CPMC loss lies in its integration of similarity of matched pair and softmax-based classification loss. We denote image features extracted from MobileNet by $\mathcal{X} = \{x_i\}_{i=1}^{N}$, text features from Bi-LSTM by $\mathcal{Z} = \{z_i\}_{i=1}^{N}$ and the label set $\mathcal{Y} = \{y_i\}_{i=1}^{N}$ from M classes. M indicates the number of identities. The CMPC loss is written as follows.

$$\mathcal{L}_{ipt} = \frac{1}{N} \sum_{i} - \log \left(\frac{\exp\left(W_{v_i}^{\top} \hat{x}_i\right)}{\sum_j \exp\left(W_j^{\top} \hat{x}_i\right)} \right) \quad \text{s.t. } \|W_j\| = 1, \hat{x}_i = x_i^{\top} z_i \cdot z_i, \tag{6}$$

$$\mathcal{L}_{tpi} = \frac{1}{N} \sum_{i} - \log \left(\frac{\exp\left(W_{y_i}^{\top} \hat{z}_i\right)}{\sum_j \exp\left(W_j^{\top} \hat{z}_i\right)} \right) \quad \text{s.t. } \|W_j\| = 1, \hat{z}_i = z_i^{\top} \bar{x}_i \cdot \bar{x}_i, \tag{7}$$

where W_{v_i} and W_j denote the y_i-th and j-th columns of weight matrix W. The final CMPC loss is calculated by

$$\mathcal{L}_{cmpc} = \mathcal{L}_{ipt} + \mathcal{L}_{tpi}. \tag{8}$$

The cross-modal projection loss can be eventually written as

$$\mathcal{L}_{cmp} = \mathcal{L}_{cmpm} + \mathcal{L}_{cmpc}. \tag{9}$$

3.2   Pair-Based Weighting Loss

It is important to notice that in the language person search task, there is only several matched image-text pairs for each identity compared with a large number of unmatched pairs. However, in the CMPM and CMPC loss, we only take advantage of the unweighted matched pairs but ignore the informative unmatched pairs which leads to slow convergence and poor performance. In many metric learning literatures, effective hard sample mining and pair weighting strategies have been proposed for models to deal with the enormous amount of pairs. Specifically in our task, the number of positive pairs and negative ones is imbalanced with negative pairs overwhelming positive ones. Under these circumstances, a suitable pair weighting mechanism is indispensable.

According to the focal loss [15] and the MS loss [29], it is believed that the weight of positive pair is inversely proportional to its similarity value while the weight of negative pair is in proportion to its similarity value. In this paper, we define weight of a pair sample as the derivative of pair-based loss with respect to the pair similarity in accordance with the weight definition in [29]. For simplicity and convenience, we especially adopt a binomial pair-based weighting loss for our task. After giving the formulation, we will further give a mathematical proof of the validity of our proposed loss.

In this loss, we refer to (x_i, z_i) as a positive pair and $(x_i, z_{j,i \neq j})$ as a negative pair. S_{ij} indicates the similarity score of (x_i, z_j). We denote $N_{x_i} = \{S_{ij,i \neq j}\}$ as a set of similarity scores for all negative pairs of sample x_i, and $N_{t_j} = \{S_{iz,z \neq i}\}$ as the set of similarity scores for all negative pairs of sample z_j. Our pair-based weighting loss can be finally written as:

$$
\mathcal{L}_{pwl} = \frac{1}{N} \sum_{i=1}^{i=N} \left[\sum_{p=0}^{2} a_p S_{ii}^p + \sum_{q=0}^{2} b_q Max \{N_{x_i}\}^q \right]
$$
$$
+ \frac{1}{N} \sum_{j=1}^{j=N} \left[\sum_{p=0}^{2} a_p S_{jj}^p + \sum_{q=0}^{2} b_q Max \{N_{z_j}\}^q \right]
$$
(10)

where $Max \{N_{x_i}\}$ and $Max \{N_{z_i}\}$ represent the hardest negative pair of image feature x_i and text feature z_i, respectively, $\{a_p\}_{p=0}^{p=2}$ and $\{b_q\}_{q=0}^{q=2}$ are hyper-parameters. Specifically, we denote the weight of a negative pair $(x_i, z_{j,i \neq j})$ as

$$
w_{ij} = \frac{\partial \mathcal{L}_{pwl}}{\partial S_{ij}},
$$
(11)

which equals the derivative of pair-based weighting loss with respect to the pair similarity.

To make our explanations more concise and clear, we ignore the similarity of positive pair and depict the relation between the similarity value of negative pair and the pair-based weighting loss value in Fig. 3. We can observe that as the similarity of negative pair increases, the loss value increases. Moreover, the pair weight w_{ij}, i.e, derivative of the loss value with respect to negative pair similarity also increases as the similarity value increases. In other words, through the binomial pair-based weighting loss, we implement the principle that the weight of negative pair should be in proportion to its similarity value.

3.3   Objective Function

For convenience, we refer to the baseline loss as:

$$
\mathcal{L}_{baseline} = \mathcal{L}_{cmp} = \mathcal{L}_{cmpm} + \mathcal{L}_{cmpc},
$$
(12)

and the overall objective function is written as:

$$\mathcal{L} = \mathcal{L}_{baseline} + \mathcal{L}_{pwl}. \tag{13}$$

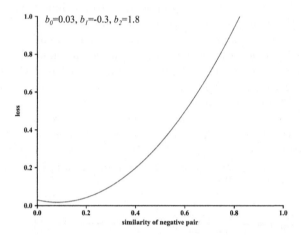

Fig. 3. As similarity of negative pair increases, both its related pair-based weighting loss and the pair weight w_{ij} increase.

4   Experiment

4.1   Dataset and Implementation Details

So far, the CUHK-PEDES dataset is the only public dataset for the task of person search with natural language description. In CUHK-PEDES, there are a total of 40,206 pedestrian images of 13,003 identities. It contains 80,440 natural language descriptions with each image accompanied by about two sentence descriptions. We follow the protocol in [14] and split the dataset into three subsets for training, validation, and test. The training set contains 11,003 identities with 34,054 images and 68,108 sentence descriptions. The validation set and test set both have 1,000 identities and 3,074 images with 6,158 and 6,156 textual descriptions respectively.

We use Adam optimizer with a learning rate being 0.0002 to train our model. The batch size is 16. As for the binomial pair-based weighting loss, we set $\{a_0 = 0.5, a_1 = -0.7, a_2 = 0.2, b_0 = 0.03, b_1 = -0.3, b_2 = 1.8\}$.

To test the model performance, we first extract image features from MobileNet and textual features from Bi-LSTM, respectively. Then, we calculate the cosine distance between image and text feature vectors after normalization. We adopt Recall@K(K = 1,10) accuracy as our evaluation criterion. The code to reproduce the results of our work is available at https://github.com/pengzhanguestc/pair_weighting_loss.

4.2   Performance Comparison

In this section, we make a comparison in terms of performance evaluation between our proposed method and some existing algorithms on the CUHK-PEDES dataset. These methods include LSTM Q+norm [1], GNA-RNN [14], Latent Co-attention [13], GLA [2], Dual Path [33], CAN [12], MCCL [30] and A-GANet [18]. Compared with all these above dedicated and sophisticated methods, our proposed method is obviously more efficient by employing the pair-wised weighting loss. We can see the considerable performance improvement from Table 1.

Table 1. Comparison of person search results (R@K (%)) on CUHK-PEDES dataset.

Method	R@ 1	R@ 10
Deeper LSTM Q+norm [1]	17.19	57.82
GNA-RNN [14]	19.05	53.64
Latent Co-attention [13]	25.94	60.48
GLA [2]	43.58	76.26
Dual Path [33]	44.40	75.07
CAN [12]	45.52	76.98
MCCL [30]	50.58	79.06
A-GANet [18]	**53.14**	81.95
Baseline	49.37	79.27
Baseline+PWL	52.76	**82.36**

4.3   Visualization of Retrieval Results

We conduct qualitative comparisons on our proposed method. In Fig. 4, we present the top-5 retrieval results for each given text description on CUHK-PEDES dataset. Figure 4(b) shows the results of the baseline model while Fig. 4(c) shows the results of baseline model enhanced with pair-based weighting loss. We can see that the latter one performs obviously better than the former one. It can be inferred that pair-based weighting loss exerts a positive influence on the retrieval performance.

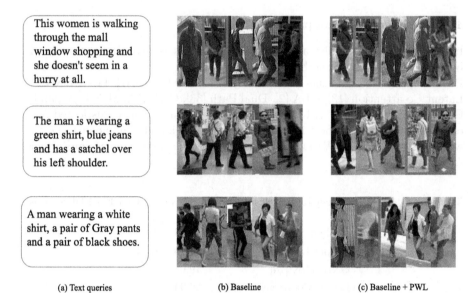

This women is walking through the mall window shopping and she doesn't seem in a hurry at all.

The man is wearing a green shirt, blue jeans and has a satchel over his left shoulder.

A man wearing a white shirt, a pair of Gray pants and a pair of black shoes.

(a) Text queries   (b) Baseline   (c) Baseline + PWL

Fig. 4. Examples of top-5 language person search results by different algorithms, including (b) Baseline, (c) Baseline+PWL. Corresponding images are marked by green bounding boxes. (Color figure online)

5   Conclusion

Language person search can be regarded as a cross-modal retrieval task whose performance has a close relation with full exploitation of informative pair samples, mainly negative ones. In this paper, we propose to combine our task with pair-based weighting loss, which has obtained extraordinary achievement in deep metric learning. Experimental results convincingly prove that pair-based weighting loss makes a considerable improvement in the task of language person search. Limited by the lack of dataset resources in text-based person search, our experiments are conducted only on the CUHK-PEDES dataset. In the future, we would like to collect dataset from the existing person description resources and validate our methods on the new dataset. In addition, we plan to design a weighting function which is more advanced and more adapted to this task.

Acknowledgments. This work was supported by Major Scientific and Technological Special Project of Guizhou Province (No. 20183002) and Sichuan Science and Technology Program (No. 2019YFG0535).

References

1. Antol, S., et al.: VQA: visual question answering. In: 2015 IEEE International Conference on Computer Vision, ICCV 2015, Santiago, Chile, 7–13 December 2015, pp. 2425–2433 (2015)

2. Chen, D., et al.: Improving deep visual representation for person re-identification by global and local image-language association. In: Ferrari, V., Hebert, M., Sminchisescu, C., Weiss, Y. (eds.) ECCV 2018, Part XVI. LNCS, vol. 11220, pp. 56–73. Springer, Cham (2018). https://doi.org/10.1007/978-3-030-01270-0_4

3. Chen, T., Xu, C., Luo, J.: Improving text-based person search by spatial matching and adaptive threshold. In: 2018 IEEE Winter Conference on Applications of Computer Vision, WACV 2018, Lake Tahoe, NV, USA, 12–15 March 2018, pp. 1879–1887 (2018)

4. Dai, J., Zhang, P., Wang, D., Lu, H., Wang, H.: Video person re-identification by temporal residual learning. IEEE Trans. Image Process. **28**(3), 1366–1377 (2019)

5. Deng, J., Guo, J., Xue, N., Zafeiriou, S.: Arcface: additive angular margin loss for deep face recognition. In: IEEE Conference on Computer Vision and Pattern Recognition, CVPR 2019, Long Beach, CA, USA, 16–20 June 2019, pp. 4690–4699 (2019)

6. Devlin, J., Chang, M., Lee, K., Toutanova, K.: BERT: pre-training of deep bidirectional transformers for language understanding. In: Proceedings of the 2019 Conference of the North American Chapter of the Association for Computational Linguistics: Human Language Technologies, NAACL-HLT 2019, Minneapolis, MN, USA, 2–7 June 2019, volume 1 (Long and Short Papers), pp. 4171–4186 (2019)

7. Hadsell, R., Chopra, S., LeCun, Y.: Dimensionality reduction by learning an invariant mapping. In: 2006 IEEE Computer Society Conference on Computer Vision and Pattern Recognition (CVPR 2006), 17–22 June 2006, New York, NY, USA, pp. 1735–1742 (2006)

8. He, X., Zhou, Y., Zhou, Z., Bai, S., Bai, X.: Triplet-center loss for multi-view 3D object retrieval. In: 2018 IEEE Conference on Computer Vision and Pattern Recognition, CVPR 2018, Salt Lake City, UT, USA, 18–22 June 2018, pp. 1945–1954 (2018)

9. Hermans, A., Beyer, L., Leibe, B.: In defense of the triplet loss for person re-identification. CoRR abs/1703.07737 (2017)

10. Howard, A.G., et al.: Mobilenets: efficient convolutional neural networks for mobile vision applications. CoRR abs/1704.04861 (2017)

11. Ji, Z., Li, S., Pang, Y.: Fusion-attention network for person search with free-form natural language. Pattern Recogn. Lett. **116**, 205–211 (2018)

12. Jing, Y., Si, C., Wang, J., Wang, W., Wang, L., Tan, T.: Cascade attention network for person search: Both image and text-image similarity selection. CoRR abs/1809.08440 (2018)

13. Li, S., Xiao, T., Li, H., Yang, W., Wang, X.: Identity-aware textual-visual matching with latent co-attention. In: IEEE International Conference on Computer Vision, ICCV 2017, Venice, Italy, 22–29 October 2017, pp. 1908–1917 (2017)

14. Li, S., Xiao, T., Li, H., Zhou, B., Yue, D., Wang, X.: Person search with natural language description. In: 2017 IEEE Conference on Computer Vision and Pattern Recognition, CVPR 2017, Honolulu, HI, USA, 21–26 July 2017, pp. 5187–5196 (2017)

15. Lin, T., Goyal, P., Girshick, R.B., He, K., Dollár, P.: Focal loss for dense object detection. In: IEEE International Conference on Computer Vision, ICCV 2017, Venice, Italy, 22–29 October 2017, pp. 2999–3007 (2017)

16. Lin, Y., et al.: Improving person re-identification by attribute and identity learning. Pattern Recogn. **95**, 151–161 (2019)

17. Liu, H., Cheng, J., Wang, W., Su, Y.: The general pair-based weighting loss for deep metric learning. CoRR abs/1905.12837 (2019)

18. Liu, J., Zha, Z., Hong, R., Wang, M., Zhang, Y.: Deep adversarial graph attention convolution network for text-based person search. In: Proceedings of the 27th ACM International Conference on Multimedia, MM 2019, Nice, France, 21–25 October 2019, pp. 665–673 (2019)

19. Liu, W., Wen, Y., Yu, Z., Li, M., Raj, B., Song, L.: Sphereface: deep hypersphere embedding for face recognition. In: 2017 IEEE Conference on Computer Vision and Pattern Recognition, CVPR 2017, Honolulu, HI, USA, 21–26 July 2017, pp. 6738–6746 (2017)

20. Liu, W., Wen, Y., Yu, Z., Yang, M.: Large-margin softmax loss for convolutional neural networks. In: Proceedings of the 33nd International Conference on Machine Learning, ICML 2016, New York City, NY, USA, 19–24 June 2016, pp. 507–516 (2016)

21. Liu, Z., Wang, D., Lu, H.: Stepwise metric promotion for unsupervised video person re-identification. In: IEEE International Conference on Computer Vision, ICCV 2017, Venice, Italy, 22–29 October 2017, pp. 2448–2457 (2017)

22. Schroff, F., Kalenichenko, D., Philbin, J.: Facenet: a unified embedding for face recognition and clustering. In: IEEE Conference on Computer Vision and Pattern Recognition, CVPR 2015, Boston, MA, USA, 7–12 June 2015, pp. 815–823 (2015)

23. Sohn, K.: Improved deep metric learning with multi-class n-pair loss objective. In: Lee, D.D., Sugiyama, M., von Luxburg, U., Guyon, I., Garnett, R. (eds.) Advances in Neural Information Processing Systems 29: Annual Conference on Neural Information Processing Systems NIPS 2016, 5–10 December 2016, Barcelona, Spain, pp. 1849–1857 (2016)

24. Song, H.O., Xiang, Y., Jegelka, S., Savarese, S.: Deep metric learning via lifted structured feature embedding. In: 2016 IEEE Conference on Computer Vision and Pattern Recognition, CVPR 2016, Las Vegas, NV, USA, 27–30 June 2016, pp. 4004–4012 (2016)

25. Su, C., Zhang, S., Xing, J., Gao, W., Tian, Q.: Deep attributes driven multi-camera person re-identification. In: Leibe, B., Matas, J., Sebe, N., Welling, M. (eds.) ECCV 2016, Part II. LNCS, vol. 9906, pp. 475–491. Springer, Cham (2016). https://doi.org/10.1007/978-3-319-46475-6_30

26. Vaquero, D.A., Feris, R.S., Tran, D., Brown, L.M., Hampapur, A., Turk, M.A.: Attribute-based people search in surveillance environments. In: IEEE Workshop on Applications of Computer Vision (WACV 2009), 7–8 December, 2009, Snowbird, UT, USA, pp. 1–8 (2009)

27. Wang, F., Cheng, J., Liu, W., Liu, H.: Additive margin softmax for face verification. IEEE Signal Process. Lett. **25**(7), 926–930 (2018)

28. Wang, J., Zhu, X., Gong, S., Li, W.: Transferable joint attribute-identity deep learning for unsupervised person re-identification. In: 2018 IEEE Conference on Computer Vision and Pattern Recognition, CVPR 2018, Salt Lake City, UT, USA, 18–22 June 2018, pp. 2275–2284 (2018)

29. Wang, X., Han, X., Huang, W., Dong, D., Scott, M.R.: Multi-similarity loss with general pair weighting for deep metric learning. In: IEEE Conference on Computer Vision and Pattern Recognition, CVPR 2019, Long Beach, CA, USA, 16–20 June 2019, pp. 5022–5030 (2019)

30. Wang, Y., Bo, C., Wang, D., Wang, S., Qi, Y., Lu, H.: Language person search with mutually connected classification loss. In: IEEE International Conference on Acoustics, Speech and Signal Processing, ICASSP 2019, Brighton, United Kingdom, 12–17 May 2019, pp. 2057–2061 (2019)

31. Wei, J., Xu, X., Yang, Y., Ji, Y., Wang, Z., Shen, H.T.: Universal weighting metric learning for cross-modal matching. In: IEEE Conference on Computer Vision and Pattern Recognition, CVPR 2020, Seattle, WA, USA, 16–20 June 2020, pp. 13005–13014 (2020)
32. Zhang, Y., Lu, H.: Deep cross-modal projection learning for image-text matching. In: Ferrari, V., Hebert, M., Sminchisescu, C., Weiss, Y. (eds.) ECCV 2018, Part I. LNCS, vol. 11205, pp. 707–723. Springer, Cham (2018). https://doi.org/10.1007/978-3-030-01246-5_42
33. Zheng, Z., Zheng, L., Garrett, M., Yang, Y., Xu, M., Shen, Y.: Dual-path convolutional image-text embeddings with instance loss. ACM Trans. Multimed. Comput. Commun. Appl. **16**(2), 511–5123 (2020)
34. Zhou, P., et al.: Attention-based bidirectional long short-term memory networks for relation classification. In: Proceedings of the 54th Annual Meeting of the Association for Computational Linguistics, ACL 2016, 7–12 August 2016, Berlin, Germany, Volume 2: Short Papers (2016)

DeepFusion: Deep Ensembles for Domain Independent System Fusion

Mihai Gabriel Constantin$^{(\boxtimes)}$, Liviu-Daniel Ştefan, and Bogdan Ionescu

University "Politehnica" of Bucharest, Bucharest, Romania
`mihai.constantin84@upb.ro`

Abstract. While ensemble systems and late fusion mechanisms have proven their effectiveness by achieving state-of-the-art results in various computer vision tasks, current approaches are not exploiting the power of deep neural networks as their primary ensembling algorithm, but only as inducers, i.e., systems that are used as inputs for the primary ensembling algorithm. In this paper, we propose several deep neural network architectures as ensembling algorithms with various network configurations that use dense and attention layers, an input pre-processing algorithm, and a new type of deep neural network layer denoted the Cross-Space-Fusion layer, that further improves the overall results. Experimental validation is carried out on several data sets from various domains (emotional content classification, medical data captioning) and under various evaluation conditions (two-class regression, binary classification, and multi-label classification), proving the efficiency of DeepFusion.

Keywords: Ensemble learning · Deep neural networks · Deep ensembles

1 Introduction

Ensemble systems have demonstrated to be effective models for solving a large variety of problems in several domains, including image [14] and video [28] classification, speech recognition [6], and broader data stream processing [11] to name but a few. *Ensemble learning* is a universal term for methods that employ a pool of *inducers* to generate predictions, typically in supervised machine learning tasks. Despite the current advances in knowledge discovery, single learners did not obtain satisfactory performances when dealing with complex data, such as class imbalance, high-dimensionality, concept drift, noisy data, etc. In this context, ensemble learning tries to fill this gap by obtaining a strong learner based on the experience of the myriad of classifiers it incorporates. Selecting an appropriate set of inducers according to the classification problem for obtaining an accurate ensemble is still an open research problem [11,24]. As ensemble accuracy is governed by the law of large numbers, one must consider the relationships between *accuracy* and *diversity* of the inducers within an ensemble. Here, diversity refers to the capability of the inducers of responding differently

© Springer Nature Switzerland AG 2021
J. Lokoč et al. (Eds.): MMM 2021, LNCS 12572, pp. 240–252, 2021.
https://doi.org/10.1007/978-3-030-67832-6_20

to the same input. This paradigm is supported by the no-free-lunch theorem formulated by Wolpert [26]. Concretely, given a learning task, where N inducers are independently trained on a specific data set, it is improbable that the errors from these N individual learners are completely uncorrelated. However, it is more probable that the ensemble accuracy can surpass the average accuracy of its members if they promote high diversity in predictions. Finding the optimal accuracy-diversity trade-off has been actively studied [19], showing that ensemble error decreases as base model error decreases and diversity increases. Nevertheless, the pioneering work in [17] shows that the relationships between accuracy and diversity of the members in an ensemble are more complex, and it is not guaranteed that enhancing ensemble diversity improves the predictive results. This raises an essential technical research question: *How to create high accuracy ensembles to account for all the aforementioned factors?* To answer this question, we aim to model the bias learned by each classifier in the ensemble setting and the correlations between the biases via a consensus learning method, to perform retrieval robustly, and improve the performance of the inducers.

Several methods have been used in the literature, starting from AdaBoost [8] with it's variants, e.g., soft margin AdaBoost [22] and Gradient boosting machines [10] with improved iterations as XGBoost [4], to Bagging [2] and Random Forests [3]. Despite the success of DNNs in recent years, there is currently little literature on the integration of ensemble learning in deep neural networks. Recent works use ensembles to boost over features [7], where deep neural networks are trained, in an entangled setting, stacking diverse data representations. To the extent of our knowledge, DNNs have not been explored as *ensembling learners*, where the input is represented by the prediction of a plethora of classifiers. One of the reasons is that the popular CNN layers are designed to learn patterns based on how the data is organized in space, whereas in ensembles the pixels are substituted with predictions of different classifiers that are not correlated.

In this context, the contribution of this work is 5-fold: (i) we introduce a set of novel ensembling techniques that use deep neural networks; (ii) we further enhance the performance of our deep ensembling methods by adding attention layers to the networks, with the particular role of filtering the input created by the inducer systems; (iii) we introduce a novel input pre-processing method, that groups the data according to the overall correlation between inducers, allowing for a better analysis of the input and for the introduction of more complex processing layers; (iv) we introduce a novel deep learning layer, called Cross-Space-Fusion layer that optimally utilizes the new pre-processed data and further enhances the results of the deep ensembling methods; (v) the proposed approaches are not dependent on a particular category of learning tasks or data. Evaluation is carried out on a set of diverse tasks, targeting several types of machine learning problems: two-class regression, binary classification, and multi-label classification. We achieve state-of-the-art performance compared to other traditional ensembling techniques and best performers from the literature. To allow reproducibility, we publish the code on GitHub[1]. The code is developed in Python 3 and is tested on the Keras 2.2.4 and Tensorflow 1.12 libraries.

2   Proposed Method

For a standard ensembling system, given a set S of M samples and a set F of N classifier or regression inducer algorithms, each algorithm will produce an output for every given sample $y_{i,j}, i \in [1, N], j \in [1, M]$, as follows:

$$
\begin{cases} S = \begin{bmatrix} s_1 \ s_2 \ ... \ s_M \end{bmatrix} \\ F = \begin{bmatrix} f_1 \ f_2 \ ... \ f_N \end{bmatrix} \end{cases} \Rightarrow Y = \begin{bmatrix} y_{1,1} & \cdots & y_{1,M} \\ \cdot & \cdot & \cdot \\ \cdot & \cdot & \cdot \\ y_{N,1} & \cdots & y_{N,M} \end{bmatrix} \tag{1}
$$

Ensembling systems involve the creation of a new aggregation algorithm E, that can detect and learn patterns in a training set composed of image or video samples, inducers, and their outputs, and apply those patterns on a validation set to produce a new output for every sample, e_i, that is a better prediction of the ground truth values of the validation set. Furthermore, a generalized ensembling system must take into account the type of output required by the studied problem. Therefore, while in binary classification tasks, the output values are $e_i \in \{0, 1\}$ and in regression tasks the values are $e_i \in [0, 1]$ or $[-1, 1]$, for multi-label prediction, e_i is actually represented by a vector of values for each of the L labels assigned to the dataset. With this in mind, we propose the DeepFusion approach – to deploy several DNN architectures that take as input a set of inducer predictions and produce new outputs e for the given samples. Our assumption is that deep architectures will be able to learn the biases of different inducers, no matter how high or low their performance is. We therefore propose three different types of network architectures: dense networks (Sect. 2.1), attention augmented dense architectures (Sect. 2.2) and finally, dense architectures augmented with a novel type of layer, called Cross-Space-Fusion layer (Sect. 2.3).

2.1   Dense Networks

Given their ability to classify input data into output labels correctly, dense layers have represented an integral part of deep neural networks in many domains. In our particular case, we use a set of dense layers for combining the inputs of all inducers and, in the training phase, learn the biases of the inducer systems and adapt the internal parameters of the dense layers in a manner that will allow the prediction of validation data. Considering that dense layers need no special assumption with regards to the nature of the input, we believe using them is also useful for creating a domain-independent ensembling system. Figure 1 presents the diagram of the dense network approach.

To optimize the results of our dense networks, we start by building a system that searches for the best parameters of these networks. We accomplish this

---

[1]   https://github.com/cmihaigabriel/DeepFusionSystem_v2.

by varying several parameters of the dense network: (i) the optimum width by testing the following number of neurons per layer: $\{25, 50, 500, 1000, 2000, 5000\}$; (ii) the depth of the network by changing the number of dense layers, testing the following values: $\{5, 10, 15, 20, 25\}$; (iii) adding or removing batch normalization layers between the dense layers. We validate these architectures in our experiments and change these parameters until the best architecture with regards to prediction capabilities is detected.

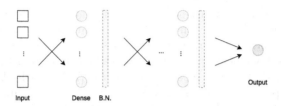

Fig. 1. DeepFusion dense network architecture (DF-Dense): variable number of layers, number of neurons per layer and the presence or absence of BN layers.

2.2 Dense Networks with Attention Layers

While in the previous step we try to discover the best dense network, in this section we focus on boosting the predictive power of our approach by inserting soft-attention estimators after the last dense layer in the structure. Our intuition is that such mechanisms will learn to attend to specific informative features, by unveiling the relationships between individual classifiers. We denote the input vector as x_i, the soft attention vector as a_i with $a \in [0, 1]$, the learned attention mask $\hat{a}_i$ is then computed by element-wise multiplication of input vector and the attention mask: $\hat{a}_i = a_i \odot x_i$. Finally, the attention mask is learned in a supervised fashion with back-propagation. The pipeline of our proposed approach called DF-Attn is depicted in Fig. 2.

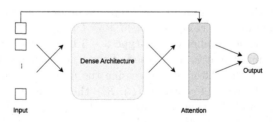

Fig. 2. DF-Attn architecture: attention masks automatically discover mutually complementary individual classifiers and disable the counterproductive ones.

2.3   Dense Networks with Cross-Space-Fusion Layers

The final architecture augmentation is represented by a novel type of layer, the Cross-Space-Fusion (*CSF*) layer, that can exploit spatial correlations, and several input pre-processing (*decoration*) techniques that allow the implementation of the CSF layer. While the introduction of convolutional layers has greatly improved the performance of deep neural networks [16] by allowing the spatial processing of data, several aspects hinder the use of such layers. First of all, given the input matrix Y, with the shape presented in Eq. 1, there is no intrinsic spatial information associated with such an input; therefore, some input decoration techniques should be used to generate these spatial correlations.

To generate spatial information, we choose to pre-process the input data and decorate each element with output scores and data from the most similar inducers. Given an image or video sample $s_i, i \in [1, M]$, each of the N inducer algorithms will produce a set of scores, $Y_i = \begin{bmatrix} y_{1,i} & y_{2,i} & \dots & y_{N,i} \end{bmatrix}$, and, as mentioned before, this kind of input has no intrinsic spatial correlation associated with it. In the first step of the input decoration technique, we analyze the correlation between the individual inducers $f_i, i \in [1, N]$. This correlation can be determined by any standard method, such as Pearson's correlation score, but, to ensure an optimized learning process we will use the same metric as the task we are processing. Given any $f_i, i \in [1, N]$ inducer system, that produces the vector $\bar{f}_i = \begin{bmatrix} \bar{f}_1 & \bar{f}_2 & \dots & \bar{f}_M \end{bmatrix}$ of outputs across the entire set of samples, and a vector of correlation scores $cr_i = \begin{bmatrix} cr_{1,i} & cr_{2,i} & \dots & cr_{N-1,i} \end{bmatrix}$ between this inducer and all the other inducers can be generated. We then create the following structures:

$$C_{i,j} = \begin{bmatrix} c_{1,i,j} & c_{2,i,j} & c_{3,i,j} \\ c_{8,i,j} & s_{i,j} & c_{4,i,j} \\ c_{7,i,j} & c_{6,i,j} & c_{5,i,j} \end{bmatrix}, R_{i,j} = \begin{bmatrix} r_{1,i,j} & r_{2,i,j} & r_{3,i,j} \\ r_{8,i,j} & 1 & r_{4,i,j} \\ r_{7,i,j} & r_{6,i,j} & r_{5,i,j} \end{bmatrix} \quad (2)$$

In this example, each element $s_{i,j}$, representing the prediction produced by inducer i for sample j, is decorated with scores from the similar systems, $c_{1,i,j}$ representing the most similar system, $c_{2,i,j}$ representing the second most similar system and so on. For the second dimension of our new matrix we input the correlation scores for the most similar system ($r_{1,i,j}$), the second most similar ($r_{2,i,j}$) and so on, with the value 1 as centroid, corresponding to the initial $s_{i,j}$ element. Finally, the new input of our deep ensembling models is represented by a 3-dimensional matrix, composed of $M \times N$ $C_{i,j}$-type 3×3 bi-dimensional elements and the same number of $R_{i,j}$-type 3×3 bi-dimensional elements. We denote the entire input matrix, composed of these structures with I_{proc} and its size is $(3 \times N, 3 \times M, 2)$. After pre-processing the input I_{proc}, it is fed into the CSF layer. For each group of centroids (C_i, R_i), the neural network learns a set of parameters $\alpha_{k,i}$ and $\beta_{k,i}$ that will process each sample as following, therefore combining the elements in each centroid:

$$\begin{bmatrix} \frac{\alpha_{1,i}*s_i+\beta_{1,i}*c_{1,i}*r_{1,i}}{2} & \frac{\alpha_{2,i}*s_i+\beta_{2,i}*c_{2,i}*r_{2,i}}{2} & \frac{\alpha_{3,i}*s_i+\beta_{3,i}*c_{3,i}*r_{3,i}}{2} \\ \frac{\alpha_{8,i}*s_i+\beta_{8,i}*c_{8,i}*r_{8,i}}{2} & s_i & \frac{\alpha_{4,i}*s_i+\beta_{4,i}*c_{4,i}*r_{4,i}}{2} \\ \frac{\alpha_{7,i}*s_i+\beta_{7,i}*c_{7,i}*r_{7,i}}{2} & \frac{\alpha_{6,i}*s_i+\beta_{6,i}*c_{6,i}*r_{6,i}}{2} & \frac{\alpha_{5,i}*s_i+\beta_{5,i}*c_{7,i}*r_{5,i}}{2} \end{bmatrix} \quad (3)$$

The number of parameters used by the CSF layer per centroid pair is 16, thus generating $16 \times M$ parameters that are trained, where M is the total number of inducers. The output of the CSF layer is finally processed by Average Pooling layers, thus generating a single value for each (C_i, R_i) centroid group and, thus, outputting the same sized matrix as the input before the pre-processing step. We test two setups with regard to data processing. In the first setup, denoted *8S*, all the 8-most similar inducer values are populated in I_{proc}, while in the second setup, denoted *4S*, only the 4-most similar ones are populated. A diagram of the Cross-Space-Fusion architecture is presented in Fig. 3.

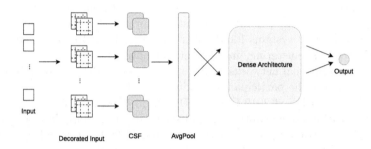

Fig. 3. Cross-Space-Fusion augmented architecture: initial pre-processing steps and the architecture of the entire network (DF-CSF).

3   Experimental Setup

3.1   Training Protocol

To perform the ensembling of the systems we search for the best performing dense architecture by using the setup presented in Sect. 2.1. Results are tested against the validation set, and the best performing dense architecture is then augmented with attention layers in the third step and with Cross-Space-Fusion layers in the fourth step. The input is modified for the use of the CSF layers, as described in Sect. 2.3. As presented in Sect. 2.3, the CSF layers are applied directly to the dense architecture, and not to its attention augmented variant. For each network, training is performed for 50 epochs, with a batch size of 64, and mean squared error loss for the regression experiments and binary crossentropy for the classification and labeling experiments. We use an Adam optimizer [12], with an initial learning rate of 0.01.

3.2   Data Sets

We empirically verify the performance of our approaches, by conducting the experiments on two data sets, namely: the Emotional Impact of Movies [5], and the ImageCLEFmed Concept Detection [20]. These data were validated during the yearly MediaEval[2] and ImageCLEF[3] benchmark initiatives, for multimedia evaluation, and cross-language annotation and retrieval of images, respectively.

The MediaEval 2018 Emotional Impact of Movies [5] is a data set for automatic recognition of emotion in videos, in terms of valence, arousal, and fear. Out this regard, the data set offers annotations for two tasks, namely (i) valence and arousal prediction (denoted *Arousal-Valence*), a two-class regression task, consisting of 54 training/validation movies with a total duration of approx. 27 h, and 12 testing movies with a total duration of approx. 9 h, and (ii) fear detection (denoted *Fear*), a binary classification task, consisting of 44 training/validation movies, with a total duration of more than 15 h, and 12 testing movies with a total duration of approx. 9 h. We considered all the systems participating in the benchmarking campaign, namely 30 systems for the valence and arousal prediction task, and 18 systems for the fear detection task. Inducers ranged from linear SVR/SVM, clustering, multi-layer perceptron, to bidirectional LSTMs, temporal convolutional networks, and ensembles. For a detailed description, the reader may access the participants working notes here[4].

The ImageCLEFmed 2019 Concept Detection (denoted *Caption*) is a multi-label classification image captioning and scene understanding data set [20] consisting of 56,629 training, 14,157 validation, and 10,000 test radiology examples with multiple classes (medical concepts) associated with each image, extracted from the PMC Open Access [23] and Radiology Objects in COntext [21]. In total, there are 5,528 unique concepts, whereas the distribution limits per images in the training, validation, and test sets is between 1–72, 1–77, and 1–34 concepts, respectively. We have considered all the systems participating in the benchmarking campaign, namely 58 systems with inducers ranging from clustering, logistic regression, to ResNet-101, LSTM, CheXNet and ensembles. For a detailed description, the reader may access the participants working notes here[5].

3.3   Evaluation

Ensemble accuracy is governed by the law of large numbers, typically requiring tens of systems to provide learning guarantees and significantly boost the performance. However, they are not used in practice, as it is impossible to implement or retrieve so many systems from the authors, or even to re-run them in identical conditions. In addition, there is no general criterion or best practices in this respect in the literature. In this context, current approaches use a limited number of inducers, e.g., less than 10 [18], which most likely are not representative for a full-scale experiment. To overcome this issue, we have incorporated all the systems developed and submitted in the respective benchmarking competitions and performed all the experiments solely on the test data, as provided by the task organizers, in a repeated k-fold cross validation manner. In this regard,

---

[2]   http://www.multimediaeval.org/.

[3]   https://www.imageclef.org/.

[4]   http://ceur-ws.org/Vol-2283/.

[5]   http://ceur-ws.org/Vol-2380/.

the split samples are randomized, and 100 partitions are generated to assure a thorough coverage of the data, using two protocols: (i) 75% training and 25% testing (KF75), and (ii) 50% training and 50% testing (KF50).

Performance evaluation is carried out via the official metrics released by the authors of the data, namely: (i) for the MediaEval 2018 Emotional Impact of Movies data set, we use the Mean Square Error (MSE) and the Pearson's Correlation Coefficient (PCC) for the valence and arousal prediction task, with MSE being the primary metric, and Intersection over Union (IoU) of time intervals, for the fear detection task, and (ii) for the ImageCLEFmed 2019 Concept Detection, the F1-scores computed per image and averaged across all test images. The metrics are computed as average values over all the partitions.

4   Results and Discussion

This section presents and analyzes the results of the proposed DeepFusion methods (Sect. 2) with regards to the three tasks described in Sect. 3.2. We use the best-performing systems submitted at their respective benchmarking competitions as baselines for comparing our methods, and these methods also represent the best performing inducer systems for our DeepFusion approach.

For the Arousal-Valence data, the best performing method is developed by Sun et al. [25], using a traditional late fusion approach, with results of MSE = 0.1334 and PCC = 0.3358 for arousal and MSE = 0.0837 and PCC = 0.3047 for valence. For the Fear data, the best performing system is developed by Yi et al. [27], using a series of convolutional networks, and achieving a IoU result of 0.1575. Finally, for the Caption data, the best results are achieved by Kougia et al. [15], with a deep learning system that achieves an F1 score of 0.2823.

Another group of baseline methods is represented by classical ensembling approaches. We test several traditional late fusion strategies such as: weighted fusion (denoted LFweight), based on the ranking of individual inducers, taking the maximum inducer score value (LFmax) and taking the average and median values of inducer scores (LFavg, LFmed) for the regression tasks, and max voting (LFvote) for the classification tasks [13]. Furthermore, we also add two boosting mechanisms: AdaBoost [9] (BoostAda) and Gradient Boosting [10] (BoostGrad). For these traditional late fusion approaches we choose inducer combinations that maximize their performance.

4.1   Ablation Studies

Network size heavily influences the performance of the network. In cases when the network is too large, due to a lack of sufficient training samples or due to low dimensionality of the inputs, the network can encounter problems such as the exploding gradient problem [1]. Figure 4 presents such a case, studied on the Arousal-Valence data. The arousal and valence graphs represent a network setup of 5 dense layers and a variation of network width. It is interesting to observe that, for numbers of neurons that surpass 1,000, the network is not able to learn the inducer biases, and the MSE results are lower than the state-of-the-art (SOA) results. Furthermore, in those particular cases, the value of the PCC metric approaches 0, denoting that perhaps the network outputs values close to neutral for the validation samples [5]. Also, the addition of BN layers contributed to the performance of the arousal detection network, allowing for a transition to a larger network, from 50 neurons/layer, to 500.

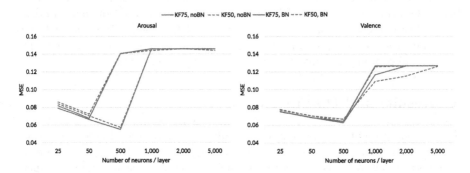

Fig. 4. Ablation study with regards to the influence of network depth and batch normalization layers, on the Arousal-Valence data.

Finally, it is worth noting that, for the DF-CSF architecture, there are differences with regards to the optimal input decoration mechanism. While for the regression data, Arousal-Valence, the best performing decoration scheme uses only 4 similar systems for decorating each input sample (4S), for the classification and multi-labeling data, Fear and Caption, the best performances for the DF-CSF architectures uses all the 8 most similar systems in decorating the input samples (8S). The difference in results is most evident for the Fear data, where the DF-CSF-8S architecture has an IoU result of 0.2242, while the DF-CSF-4S architecture has a result of 0.2173. The difference between the optimal approach with regards to the decoration mechanism proves that for different approaches and tasks, different decoration mechanisms must be employed and that newer variations of our mechanism may provide even better results.

4.2 Results

The results of our proposed DeepFusion architectures are presented in Table 1. As expected, training on a KF75 split produces better results than KF50, but in both scenarios the results clearly surpass the state-of-the-art and the traditional late fusion approaches. It is important to note that the results for the traditional late fusion approaches did not improve state-of-the-art results by a large margin, and in some cases, performed worse than the SOA systems. Overall the best performing architecture is represented by the CSF layer augmented networks.

For the Arousal-Valence data, the best performing DF-Dense architecture is composed, for both arousal and valence, of a 5 layer network, with each layer having 500 neurons and uses batch normalization layers between the dense layers.

Table 1. Results for the three datasets: Arousal-Valence, with MSE and PCC metrics, Fear, with IoU metric and Caption, with F1-score metric. For reference, we present the best performing state-of-the-art systems [15,25,27] (SOA) and the traditional late fusion mechanisms. We present the best performing dense (DF-Dense), attention (DF-Attn) and Cross-Space-Fusion (DF-CSF) architectures. The best results for each type of data split are presented (KF75 and KF50), including the original (orig.) split for the SOA systems and the best performing overall architectures for each split are presented in bold.

System	Split	Arousal (MSE)	Arousal (PCC)	Valence (MSE)	Valence (PCC)	Fear (IoU)	Caption (F1)
SOA	orig	0.1334	0.3358	0.0837	0.3047	0.1575	0.2823
LFweight	orig	0.1297	0.2819	0.0831	0.3011	–	–
LFmax	orig	0.1374	0.3135	0.0851	0.2563	–	–
LFavg	orig	0.1316	0.3347	0.0821	0.2916	–	–
LFmed	orig	0.1310	0.3340	0.0820	0.2902	–	–
LFvote	orig	–	–	–	–	0.1381	0.2511
BoostAda	KF75	0.1253	0.3828	0.0783	0.4174	0.1733	0.2846
BoostGrad	KF75	0.1282	0.3911	0.0769	0.3972	0.1621	0.2834
DF-Dense	KF75	0.0549	0.8315	0.0626	0.8101	0.2129	0.3740
	KF50	0.0571	0.8018	0.0640	0.7876	0.1938	0.3462
DF-Attn	KF75	0.0548	0.8339	0.0626	0.8107	0.2140	0.3659
	KF50	**0.0568**	0.8036	0.0640	0.7888	0.1913	0.3522
DF-CSF	KF75	**0.0543**	**0.8422**	**0.0625**	**0.8123**	**0.2242**	**0.3912**
	KF50	**0.0568**	**0.8073**	**0.0637**	**0.7903**	**0.2091**	**0.3610**

Even though the state-of-the-art results were high with regards to MSE [25], 0.1334 for arousal and 0.0837 for valence, our DF-Dense systems managed to improve those results, reaching to 0.0549 and 0.0626. Both the DF-Attn and DF-CSF networks further improved these results, with the CSF network being the best overall performer; however, the difference in results to DF-Dense was not very substantial. Another interesting analysis can be performed on the PCC results. Here, our proposed networks significantly improve the results, indicating a better understanding of borderline cases, as theorized in the competition overview paper [5]. The state-of-the-art results are improved to a maximum of 0.8422 for arousal and 0.8123 for valence by the DF-CSF network. Regarding the DF-CSF network, the architecture performed best with the 4S setup.

For the Fear data, the optimal DF-Dense configuration is composed of a 10 layer network, with each layer having 500 neurons, and no batch normalization layers. This configuration achieves a final score of 0.2129, increasing the state-of-the-art result by 35.17%. Furthermore, both the DF-Attn and the DF-CSF configurations increase this score, with a maximum IoU of 0.2242, representing a 42.35% increase over the original performance, for an 8S setup of DF-CSF.

Finally, for the Caption data, the best performing DF-Dense configuration is represented by a 5 layer network, with 500 neurons per layer and no batch normalization. This configuration achieves an F1-score of 0.3740, increasing the state-of-the-art results by 32.48%. Interestingly, for the KF75 split, the DF-Attn network does not perform better than the DF-Dense network. However, similar to the other datasets, the best performing system is the DF-CSF, with an F1-score of 0.3912, under the 8S setup.

5   Conclusions and Future Work

In this paper, we present a set of novel ensembling techniques, that use DNN architectures as the primary ensembling learner. Our architectures integrate dense and attention layers, but also a novel input decoration technique, that creates spatial information out of inducer outputs and a novel deep neural network layer, the Cross-Space-Fusion layer, that is able to manipulate the newly created spatial information. We evaluate our approaches on three tasks from diverse domains (emotional content processing and medical image captioning) and with diverse problem formulations (two-class regression, binary classification, and multi-label classification). We validate our results by comparing them with the current state of the art on the three tasks and with traditional ensembling approaches. Results show significant improvements, by a margin of at least 38.58%, therefore validating our DeepFusion methods and techniques.

Given the encouraging results presented in this paper, future developments of our methods may prove useful for solving even more tasks under different problem formulations. Considering the usefulness of our input decoration method, some further work towards improving the results may include incorporating a larger set of decoration methods, or adding both similar and dissimilar inducers in the decoration scheme. We also believe that further work on the Cross-Space-Fusion layer may provide even better results.

Acknowledgements. This work was funded under project SMARTRetail, agreement 8PTE/2020, grant PN-III-P2-2.1-PTE-2019-0055, Ministry of Innovation and Research, UEFISCDI and AI4Media "A European Excellence Centre for Media, Society and Democracy", grant #951911, H2020 ICT-48-2020.

References

1. Bengio, Y., Simard, P., Frasconi, P.: Learning long-term dependencies with gradient descent is difficult. IEEE Trans. Neural Netw. **5**(2), 157–166 (1994)
2. Breiman, L.: Bagging predictors. Mach. Learn. **24**(2), 123–140 (1996). https://doi.org/10.1007/BF00058655
3. Breiman, L.: Random forests. Mach. Learn. **45**(1), 5–32 (2001)
4. Chen, T., Guestrin, C.: Xgboost: a scalable tree boosting system. In: Proceedings of the 22nd ACM SIGKDD International Conference on Knowledge Discovery and Data Mining, pp. 785–794. ACM (2016)

5. Dellandréa, E., Huigsloot, M., Chen, L., Baveye, Y., Xiao, Z., Sjöberg, M.: The mediaeval 2018 emotional impact of movies task. In: MediaEval (2018)
6. Deng, L., Platt, J.C.: Ensemble deep learning for speech recognition. In: Fifteenth Annual Conference of the International Speech Communication Association (2014)
7. Feichtenhofer, C., Pinz, A., Zisserman, A.: Convolutional two-stream network fusion for video action recognition. In: Proceedings of the IEEE Conference on Computer Vision and Pattern Recognition, pp. 1933–1941 (2016)
8. Freund, Y., Schapire, R., Abe, N.: A short introduction to boosting. J. Jpn. Soc. Artif. Intell. **14**(771–780), 1612 (1999)
9. Freund, Y., Schapire, R.E.: A desicion-theoretic generalization of on-line learning and an application to boosting. In: Vitányi, P. (ed.) EuroCOLT 1995. LNCS, vol. 904, pp. 23–37. Springer, Heidelberg (1995). https://doi.org/10.1007/3-540-59119-2_166
10. Friedman, J.H.: Greedy function approximation: a gradient boosting machine. Ann. Stat. **29**, 1189–1232 (2001)
11. Gomes, H.M., Barddal, J.P., Enembreck, F., Bifet, A.: A survey on ensemble learning for data stream classification. ACM Comput. Surv. **50**(2), 1–36 (2017)
12. Kingma, D.P., Ba, J.: Adam: a method for stochastic optimization. arXiv preprint arXiv:1412.6980 (2014)
13. Kittler, J., Hatef, M., Duin, R.P., Matas, J.: On combining classifiers. IEEE Trans. Pattern Anal. Mach. Intell. **20**(3), 226–239 (1998)
14. Kontschieder, P., Fiterau, M., Criminisi, A., Rota Bulo, S.: Deep neural decision forests. In: Proceedings of the IEEE International Conference on Computer Vision, pp. 1467–1475 (2015)
15. Kougia, V., Pavlopoulos, J., Androutsopoulos, I.: AUEB NLP group at image-clefmed caption 2019. In: CEUR Workshop Proceedings, CLEF2019, pp. 09–12 (2019)
16. Krizhevsky, A., Sutskever, I., Hinton, G.E.: Imagenet classification with deep convolutional neural networks. In: Advances in Neural Information Processing Systems, pp. 1097–1105 (2012)
17. Kuncheva, L.I., Whitaker, C.J.: Measures of diversity in classifier ensembles and their relationship with the ensemble accuracy. Mach. Learn. **51**(2), 181–207 (2003)
18. Li, X., Huo, Y., Jin, Q., Xu, J.: Detecting violence in video using subclasses. In: 2016 ACM Conference on Multimedia Conference, pp. 586–590 (2016)
19. Liu, L., et al.: Deep neural network ensembles against deception: Ensemble diversity, accuracy and robustness. arXiv preprint arXiv:1908.11091 (2019)
20. Pelka, O., Friedrich, C.M., García Seco de Herrera, A., Müller, H.: Overview of the imageclefmed 2019 concept detection task. CLEF working notes, CEUR (2019)
21. Pelka, O., Koitka, S., Rückert, J., Nensa, F., Friedrich, C.M.: Radiology Objects in COntext (ROCO): a multimodal image dataset. In: Stoyanov, D., et al. (eds.) LABELS/CVII/STENT -2018. LNCS, vol. 11043, pp. 180–189. Springer, Cham (2018). https://doi.org/10.1007/978-3-030-01364-6_20
22. Rätsch, G., Onoda, T., Müller, K.R.: Soft margins for AdaBoost. Mach. Learn. **42**(3), 287–320 (2001). https://doi.org/10.1023/A:1007618119488
23. Roberts, R.J.: Pubmed central: The genbank of the published literature (2001)
24. Sagi, O., Rokach, L.: Ensemble learning: a survey. Wiley Interdisc. Rev. Data Min Kowl. Discov. **8**(4), e1249 (2018)
25. Sun, J.J., Liu, T., Prasad, G.: GLA in mediaeval 2018 emotional impact of movies task. In: Proceedings of the MediaEval 2018 Workshop (2018)

26. Wolpert, D.H.: The supervised learning no-free-lunch theorems. In: Roy, R.K., Köppen, M., Ovaska, S., Furuhashi, T. (eds.) Soft Computing and Industry, pp. 25–42. Springer, London (2002). https://doi.org/10.1007/978-1-4471-0123-9_3
27. Yi, Y., Wang, H., Li, Q.: CNN features for emotional impact of movies task. In: Proceedings of MediaEval 2018 Workshop (2018)
28. Zhou, Z.H., Feng, J.: Deep forest: towards an alternative to deep neural networks. In: Proceedings of the Twenty-Sixth International Joint Conference on Artificial Intelligence, IJCAI-17, pp. 3553–3559 (2017)

Illuminate Low-Light Image via Coarse-to-fine Multi-level Network

Yansheng Qiu[1,2(✉)], Jun Chen[1,2(✉)], Xiao Wang[1,2], and Kui Jang[1,2]

[1] National Engineering Research Center for Multimedia Software, School of
Computer Science, Wuhan University, Wuhan 430072, China
{2019202110004,chenj}@whu.edu.cn
[2] Hubei Key Laboratory of Multimedia and Network Communication Engineering,
Wuhan University, Wuhan 430072, China

Abstract. Images under low light or against light are of low readability and visibility which in turn cause performance degradation of many computer vision tasks. As the crucial research objects for low-brightness image enhancement, reflectance as an invariant has color information, and illuminance as a variable has brightness information. Existing technologies prefer to represent the reflectance and illumination in the same network depth directly, which ignores the internal discrepancy and correlation of these two components, further causing the details vanished and artifacts noises. Consequently, we propose coarse-to-fine multi-level decouple and fusion network (CMDFN) to decompose the restoration tasks into two sub-tasks, and use decouple network (CMDN) to learn the joint features of reflectance and illumination at different network depths. To refine the joint representation and revise color information, fusion network (CMFN) is applied to promote the illuminations map by extracting the complementary and redundant information from the reflectance map. Finally, we integrate the refined illumination and reflectance to reproduce the predicted image. Especially, in CMFN, we introduce a process based on discriminate attention mechanism to balance the noise. Experimental results have demonstrated that our proposed network is superior other state of the art methods, both visually and quantitatively.

Keywords: Low light enhancement · Retinex · Reflectance · Illumination

1 Introduction

Underexposure causes significant effects on image quality, and thus greatly reduces the precision of vision-oriented tasks, such as [7,17,18,20]. Therefore, there is a pressing need to develop effective technologies to improve the exposure conditions to promote the readability. Recent years have witnessed the development of the enhancement approaches to light up low exposure images. The early traditional attempts can be roughly divided into two categories, including histogram equalization (HE) [12] and Retinex theory [10]. HE mainly redistribute

© Springer Nature Switzerland AG 2021
J. Lokoč et al. (Eds.): MMM 2021, LNCS 12572, pp. 253–264, 2021.
https://doi.org/10.1007/978-3-030-67832-6_21

the light intensity on the histogram of the output image to meet certain constraints to increase the contrast of the image. However, they barely consider real illumination factors, usually making enhanced results visually vulnerable and inconsistent with real scenes. Based on Retinex theory, researchers propose single-scale Retinex (SSR) [9] and multi-scale Retinex (MSR) [8]. SSR restricts the smoothness of the illumination map through gaussian filtering. MSR extends SSR with multiscale gaussian filters and color restoration. However, their performance often depends on elaborate parameter tuning so that they are not robust enough to complex real-world scenarios (Fig. 1).

Fig. 1. From left to right: low exposure images, illumination, reflectance, enhanced images. Obviously, reflectance has more information than illumination, especially between the color reflections of objects.

With the development of deep learning, researchers gradually realized internal discrepancy and correlation of illumination and reflectance.Yang et al. [19] propose a pipeline to employ imge from LDR into HDR in order to obtain details which is not easily explore in LDR. Chen et al. [14] propose to enhance images in RAW format, but show unsatisfactory performance in JPEG format, thus limiting the practical applications. Cai et al. [1] apply the convolution network to strengthen reflectance and illumination respectively. However, the performance is limited by the separation accuracy of these two components. Wei et al. [2] propose RetinexNet to separate reflectance and illumination from low-brightness and high-brightness image pairs. Although RetinexNet exhibits better effect than that of the traditional methods, it still ignores the discrepancy between reflectance and illumination. As shown in Fig. 2, RetinexNet has excellent brightness while causing noise-contaminated results. Based on RetinexNet, Zhang et al. [23] introduce the Retinex manner, and consequently decouple the observed low-light image into two smaller subspaces, expecting to be better and easier optimized. However, the discrepancy between the reflectance and the illumination in the enhanced subnetwork is still ignored, which may cause the daub phenomenon, especially in the intersection of light and dark. As shown in Fig. 2, KinD blurs the skylight structure and sky, reducing the brightness of the chandelier to make it partially invisible.

To tackle these limitations above, we propose a decouple network (CMDN) to decompose the learning process of mapping the low-light input to the high-quality result based on Retinex theory, and construct a fusion network (CMFN) for low-light image enhancement. As shown in Fig. 3, coarse-to-fine multi-level

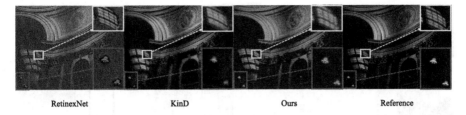

RetinexNet   KinD   Ours   Reference

Fig. 2. Restoration examples by RetinexNet [2], KinD [23] and ours. Both RetinexNet and KinD have difficulty handling where light meets shade. RetinexNet produced virtual shadows on the treatment of the chandelier, and KinD reduced the brightness so that one of the lights was not fully displayed. In the skylight treatment, although RetinexNet retained the structure, it generated a lot of noise, and KinD blurred the structure. Our method not only displays the brightness of the chandelier normally but also retains a clear structure.

decouple and fusion network(CMDFN) is a two-level network. In the first stage, we divide the decomposition of low-brightness images into two parallel subtasks, which learn to optimize the reflectance and illumination information respectively, thereby reducing the difficulty of learning. In the second stage, the reflectance is deeply represented, and at the same time, the correlation with the illumination is learned to assist in updating the illumination information and achieve the refinement representation of the brightness characteristics. Finally, the two are merged to achieve low-light image. According to the difference between the two features, features are extracted from different levels of the network to achieve coarse representation. The whole network is trained end-to-end to avoid noise amplification and error accumulation.

2   Method

In order to simulate the human retinal system, Land et al. propose the Retinex theory [10], which assumes that the observed image consists of two components: reflectance and illumination. The theory can be defined as:

$$S = R \odot I \tag{1}$$

where S represents the observed image, R represents the reflectance which is constant and I represents the illumination which is alterable. The relationship between R and I is defined as $\odot$, which is element-wise multiplication. Based on Retinex theory, we propose a new structure to lighten the image. As schematically illustrated in Fig. 3, our network framework consists of two sub-networks: CMDN and CMFN network. In CMDN, we encode the joint representation of reflectance and illumination from the input image at different network depths. Then the coarse representation of these two components go into CMFN for a refinement. Specifically, we apply a unet to extract the deep features of the

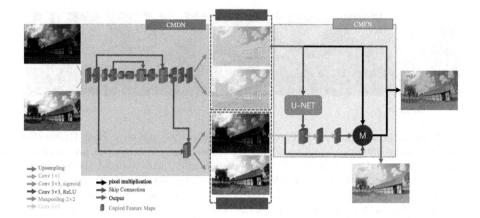

Fig. 3. The architecture of coarse-to-fine multi-level decouple and fusion network (CMDFN). Two branches correspond to the reflectance and illumination, respectively. From the perspective of functionality, it also can be divided into two steps, including CMDN and CMFN. Module M stands for processing based on discriminate attention mechanism. The top-to-bottom portion of the reflectance part from the low-exposure image and the normal image respectively, as well as the illumination part.

reflectance, and revise the illumination map by learning the correlated coefficient between the joint features. Finally, we combine the adjusted illumination and reflectance to produce the enhanced result.

2.1 Coarse-to-fine Multi-level Decouple Network

Since Eq. (1) is ill-posed, it is difficult to design a constraint function adaptive to various scenarios. Therefore, we try to address this problem in a data-driven way. The previous deep learning approach generate the optimal approximation by minimizing the distance between the predicted results and ground truth. Unfortunately, there is no ground-truth of reflectance and illumination. Motivated by RetinexNet [2], we learn the decomposition method from high/low exposure photo pairs. Different from RetinexNet, we obtain reflectance from deeper networks than illumination. To get the expectant result, we made the following constraint:

$$L_D = \beta_d L_{recon} + \gamma_d L_{decom_r} + \delta_d L_{decom_i} \tag{2}$$

where L_{recon}, L_{decom_r} and L_{decom_i} respectively represent the reconstruction loss, decomposed reflectance loss and decomposed illumination loss and β_d, γ_d and δ_d denote the coefficients to balance each loss function, which are all set to 1 when network is trained. In order to decompose the image with Retinex theory, we limit the direction of the network output by $L_{recon} = \sum_{i=low,high} \sum_{j=low,high} \|R_i \odot I_j - S_j\|_1$, where $\|\cdot\|_1$ is the ℓ^1 norm. $L_{decom_r} = 0.1 * \|R_{low} - R_{high}\|_2 - 0.01 * SSIM(R_{low}, R_{high})$ is used to ensure the consistency of reflectance in structure and color, where $\|\cdot\|_2$ means the ℓ^2 norm and

Fig. 4. From left to right: low exposure images, illumination, reflectance.

$SSIM(\cdot, \cdot)$ means the structural similarity measurement. Decomposed illumination requires excellent smoothness and structural consistency. Thus, we employ $L_{decom_i} = 0.08 * L_{ismooth} + 0.1 * L_{iconsist}$ to get the desired result. $L_{ismooth} = \left\| \frac{\nabla I_l}{max(|\nabla I_l|, \epsilon)} \right\|_1 + \left\| \frac{\nabla I_l}{max(|\nabla I_l|, \epsilon)} \right\|_1$ makes sure illumination is smooth, where ∇ denotes the gradient containing ∇x (horizontal) and ∇y (vertical) directions. And the ϵ is defined as a small positive constant (0.01 in this work) for avoiding zero denominator. $L_{iconsist} = \|S \odot exp(-5 * S)\|_1$ with $S = | \nabla I_{low} | + | \nabla I_{high} |$ is used to get the structural consistency of illumination (Fig. 4).

CMDN contains two branches corresponding to the reflectance and illumination, respectively. The reflectance branch first uses a convolutional layer to extract features from the input images, followed by a 5-layer network like the variation of U-net [13]. Finally, two convolutional (conv) layers with ReLU layer and a conv layer with Sigmoid layer are followed. While the illumination branch is composed of a conv+ReLU layer taking feature of image as the input and a conv layer on concatenated feature maps from the deep of reflectance branch (to learn the residual brightness from the reflectance), finally followed by a Sigmoid layer.

It should be specified that we adopt high/low exposure photo pairs to optimize CMDN, while only a low-brightness image is necessary for testing.

2.2   Discriminate Attention Mechanism

Fig. 5. From left to right: illumination, attention map, enhanced illumination.

As schematically illustrated in Fig. 3, we obtain illumination information from reflectance, which can not only supplement the details lost in CMDN, but also serve as a reference to adjust the illumination. However, it is difficult to design an appropriate weighting value for all scenarios, which will lead to overexposure when is large and will lead to insufficient brightness when is small. Therefore, we introduce discriminate attention mechanism to design a relationship between reflectance, illumination and enhanced illumination for competing for the weighting in the enhanced illumination. The relationship is as follow:

$$I_{delta} = I_{low} * M_A + R_{low} * (1 - M_A) \tag{3}$$

where I_{low} and R_{low} denote the decomposed illumination and reflectance, I_{delta} refers to the enhanced illumination and M_A is the discriminate attention map. As shown in Fig. 5, discriminate attention map can well extract the structure information and brightness information existing in reflectance, which is crucial for the further refinement of the illumination map. Experiments show that this indirect enhancing method is one percentage point higher than the direct one on the final PSNR (Peak Signal to Noise Ratio).

2.3   Coarse-to-fine Multi-level Fusion Network

To further refine the representation of the reflectance and illumination while preserving the image textures, we apply to learn the correlated feature of these two components for a revision. CMFN uses the deeper information of reflectance, and combine with illumination as the input.

The main purpose of CMFN is to brighten I_{low} which need to keep getting closer and closer to I_{high}. Thus we employ $L_{consit} = \|I_{delta} - I_{high}\|_2$ and $L_{grd} = \|\nabla I_{delta} - \nabla I_{high}\|_2$ to do that. In order to make the output of the whole structure reach the expectation, we also use $L_{relight} = \|R_{low} \odot I_{delta} - S_{high}\|_1$ to guide the direction of the network. Therefore, the loss function of CMFN is as follows:

$$L_E = \beta_e L_{consit} + \gamma_e L_{grd} + \delta_e L_{relight} \tag{4}$$

where β_e, γ_e and δ_e denote the coefficients to balance each loss function, which are all set to 1 when network is trained.

As illustrated in Fig. 3, CMFN contains two branches to deal with the reflectance and illumination. As for reflectance, a typical 5-layer U-net explores the deep brightness information of reflectance which CMDN may ignore, followed a conv layer with ReLU to integrate residual information. Afterwards, features of illumination is combined with deep reflectance, followed two conv layers. Afterwards, reflectance (convert to grayscale), combined map and illumination are input into discriminate attention mechanism to obtain the enhanced illumination. In the end, the lighted image is combined by enhanced illumination and reflectance in pixel multiplication way.

3   Experiment

3.1   Implementation Details

We use the LOL dataset [2] as the training dataset, which contains 500 low/normal-light image pairs. Different form other datasets like LIME [6] dataset and NPE [15] dataset which are retouched by post-production, most images are collected by changing exposure time and ISO. And it covers a broad range of lighting conditions, scenes, subjects, and styles.

For the CMDN, batch size is set to be 10 and patch-size to be 48×48. While for the CMFN, the batch size is set to be 4 and the patch-size to be 384×384. We train the both nets with 60 epochs. Each convolution stride is 1 and kernel size 3. Each down-sampling uses maxpooling with stride 2 and kernel size 2. Resize connection is a bilinear interpolation operation in CMDN, while it is nearest interpolation in CMFN. We use the stochastic gradient descent (SGD) technique for optimization.

3.2   Comparison

Quantitative Comparison. PSNR and SSIM are used for quantitative comparison. Although this is not an absolute indicator, overall, high PSNR and SSIM values correspond to fairly good results. the competitors are BIMEF [21], SRIE [5], CRM [22], Dong [3], LIME [6], MF [4], RRM [11], Retinex-Net [2],

Fig. 6. From left to right: low exposure images, reflectance, enhanced illumination, enhanced images.

GLAD [16], MSR [9], NPE [15] and KinD [23], which are state-of-the-art methods (Fig. 6).

The score of each competitor on the LOL dataset is shown in the Table 1. For each low-light image tested, there is a high light counterpart. Therefore, we can use PSNR and SSIM (structural similarity index) to evaluate the results of the network. From the scores, our result stands out from the rest.

Visual Comparison. We show visual comparison Retinex-net [2], KinD [23] and ours in Fig. 7. Comparing the results, we noticed two important improvements in our results. First of all, our method can restore more details and better contrast. It's not going to be partially blurred like KinD [23]. At the bottom of Fig. 7, the side walls of the cavern and the rocks of the creek, KinD has blurred their structure. Although Retinex-net [2] can restore rocks, it produces a lot of noise. However, we can clearly reproduce their structures, and even see the reflection of sunlight on the rocks. Second, it also displays more appropriate brightness to make the enhanced results look realistic. In the third row of Fig. 7, we show the light on a sunny day, while the brightness of KinD [23] is similar to that of a rainy day.

Table 1. Quantitative comparison on LOL dataset in terms of PSNR and SSIM. The best results are highlighted in bold.

Metrics	BIMEF	CRM	Dong	LIME	MF	RRM	SRIE
PSNR	13.8753	17.2033	16.7165	16.7586	18.7916	13.8765	11.8552
SSIM	0.5771	0.6442	0.5824	0.5644	0.6422	0.6577	0.4979

Metrics	Retinex-Net	MSR	NPE	GLAD	KinD	Ours	
PSNR	16.7740	13.1728	16.9697	19.7182	20.8665	**23.0421**	
SSIM	0.5594	0.4787	0.5894	0.7035	0.8022	**0.8377**	

Table 2. The **deep** represents to learn R and I from different depths, and the **normal** represents not to. $\sqrt{}$ represents to use discriminate attention mechanism, and $\times$ represents not to. Quantitative comparison on LOL dataset in terms of PSNR and SSIM. The best results are highlighted in bold.

CMDN	CMFN	Discriminate attention	PSNR	SSIM
Normal	Normal	$\times$	16.7740	0.5594
Deep	Normal	$\times$	20.8665	0.8022
Deep	Deep	$\times$	22.0780	0.8280
Deep	Deep	$\sqrt{}$	**23.0421**	**0.8377**

3.3 Ablation Study

Network Structure Ablation. Our method consists of two kinds of modules. CMDN is responsible for decomposing image into reflectance and illumination from different depths. CMFN is responsible for combining reflectance with deeper information and illumination. Especially, in CMFN, a strategy based on discriminate attention mechanism is introduced to learn the relationship between I, R and I_{delta}. Changing either of them increase the noise or lead to the distortion.

Here, we take the LOL dataset as an example to do the ablation study. Considering the network we built may not be able to achieve the effect of existing algorithms, we adopted KinD and Retinex-net respectively instead of ignoring

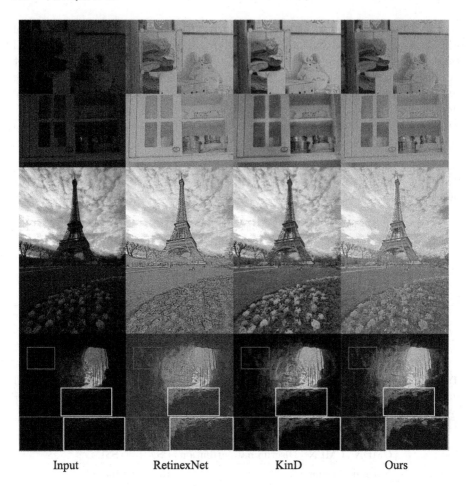

| Input | RetinexNet | KinD | Ours |

Fig. 7. Visual comparison with Retinex-Net and KinD.

depth in CMFN and ignoring depth in CMDN and CMFN. In addition, we verified the effect of discriminate attention mechanism on the final result. All results are shown in Table 2. We can conclude that the subnetworks which consider different depths of R and L will improve the final result. In the CMFN, the introduction of the discriminate attention mechanism has greatly improved the PSNR, and it has also been slightly improved on the SSIM.

Loss Function Ablation. In order to guide the brightness adjustment of the image, in CMDN, we use L_{recon} to limit the network to decompose the image in Retinex theory, use L_{decom_r} to ensure the consistency of structure and color reflectivity, and use L_{decom_i} to ensure smooth lighting and structural consistency. In CMFN, we use L_{consit} and L_{grd} to incrementally I_{low} which needs to keep getting closer and closer to I_{high}. In order to ensure that the reinforcement

Table 3. Quantitative comparison between different loss functions on LOL dataset in terms of PSNR and SSIM (w/o - without). The best results are highlighted in bold.

L_{recon}	$L_{relight}$	L_{decom_i}	L_{decom_r}	L_{grd}	L_{consit}	PSNR	SSIM
With	With	w/o	w/o	w/o	w/o	11.7133	0.5291
With	With	With	w/o	w/o	w/o	18.7291	0.6315
With	With	With	With	w/o	w/o	20.3350	0.7322
With	With	With	With	With	w/o	22.6062	0.7950
With	With	With	With	With	With	**23.0421**	**0.8377**

direction of the network remains the same we use $L_{relight}$ to restrict. Both L_{recon} and $L_{relight}$ urge the network to train in theory Retinex theory, so we do not add them to ablation experiment.

As shown in Table 3, the experimental results reveal that in our method the result has been progressively improved with increase of the loss component. They convincingly proved the effectiveness of each loss component.

4   Conclusion

In this paper, we have presented a novel end-to-end network for enhancing low-light photos. Depending on Retinex theory, we analyze that reflectance and illumination exist the internal discrepancy and correlations. Therefore, we mine reflectance and illumination in different network depths of the CMDN. Based on the characteristic of reflectance, we exploit the correlated information of reflectance in CMFN to refine the illumination map. Besides, CMFN adopts discriminate attention mechanism in the result processing. Experiments have demonstrated that our design is significantly better than the most state-of-the-art alternatives, both quantitatively and visually.

Acknowledgements. The research was supported by the National Nature Science Foundation of China under Grant U62071338, 1903214 and 62071339, by National Key R&D Program of China (No. 2017YFC0803700).

References

1. Cai, J., Gu, S., Zhang, L.: Learning a deep single image contrast enhancer from multi-exposure images. IEEE Trans. Image Process. **27**(4), 2049–2062 (2018)
2. Wei, C., Wang, W., Yang, W., Liu, J.: Deep retinex decomposition for low-light enhancement. In: BMVC (2018)
3. Dong, X., et al.: Fast efficient algorithm for enhancement of low lighting video. In: ICME, pp. 1–6 (2011)
4. Fu, X., Zeng, D., Huang, Y., Liao, Y., Ding, X., Paisley, J.: A fusion-based enhancing method for weakly illuminated images. Signal Process. **129**, 82–96 (2016)

5. Fu, X., Zeng, D., Huang, Y., Zhang, X.P., Ding, X.: A weighted variational model for simultaneous reflectance and illumination estimation. In: IEEE CVPR, pp. 2782–2790 (2016)
6. Guo, X., Li, Y., Ling, H.: Lime: low-light image enhancement via illumination map estimation. IEEE Trans. Image Process. **26**(2), 982–993 (2017)
7. Jiang, K., Wang, Z., Yi, P., Wang, G., Gu, K., Jiang, J.: ATMFN: adaptive-threshold-based multi-model fusion network for compressed face hallucination. IEEE Trans. Multim. **22**(10), 2734–2747 (2020)
8. Jobson, D.J., Rahman, Z.U., Woodell, G.A.: A multiscale retinex for bridging the gap between color images and the human observation of scenes. IEEE Trans. Image Process. **6**(7), 965–976 (1997)
9. Jobson, D.J., Rahman, Z.U., Woodell, G.A.: Properties and performance of a center/surround retinex. TIP **6**(3), 451–462 (1997)
10. Land, E.H.: The retinex theory of color vision. Sci. Am. **237**(6), 108–129 (1977)
11. Li, M., Liu, J., Yang, W., Sun, X., Guo, Z.: Structure-revealing low-light image enhancement via robust retinex model. IEEE Trans. Image Process. **27**(6), 2828–2841 (2018)
12. Pisano, E.D., et al.: Contrast limited adaptive histogram equalization image processing to improve the detection of simulated spiculations in dense mammograms. J. Digit. Imaging **11**(4), 193–200 (1998)
13. Ronneberger, O., Fischer, P., Brox, T.: U-Net: convolutional networks for biomedical image segmentation. In: Navab, N., Hornegger, J., Wells, W.M., Frangi, A.F. (eds.) MICCAI 2015. LNCS, vol. 9351, pp. 234–241. Springer, Cham (2015). https://doi.org/10.1007/978-3-319-24574-4_28
14. Wang, R., Zhang, Q., Fu, C.W., Shen, X., Zheng, W.S., Jia, J.: Underexposed photo enhancement using deep illumination estimation. In: IEEE CVPR, pp. 6849–6857 (2019)
15. Wang, S., Zheng, J., Hu, H.M., Li, B.: Naturalness preserved enhancement algorithm for non-uniform illumination images. IEEE Trans. Image Process. **22**(9), 3538–3548 (2013)
16. Wang, W., Wei, C., Yang, W., Liu, J.: Gladnet: low-light enhancement network with global awareness. In: IEEE FG, pp. 751–755 (2018)
17. Wang, X., et al.: When pedestrian detection meets nighttime surveillance: A new benchmark. In: Bessiere, C. (ed.) IJCAI, pp. 509–515 (2020)
18. Wang, X., et al.: S^{3}d: scalable pedestrian detection via score scale surface discrimination. IEEE Trans. Circuits Syst. Video Technol. **30**(10), 3332–3344 (2020)
19. Yang, X., Xu, K., Song, Y., Zhang, Q., Wei, X., Lau, R.W.: Image correction via deep reciprocating hdr transformation. In: IEEE CVPR, pp. 1798–1807 (2018)
20. Yi, P., Wang, Z., Jiang, K., Shao, Z., Ma, J.: Multi-temporal ultra dense memory network for video super-resolution. IEEE Trans. Circuits Syst. Video Technol. **30**(8), 2503–2516 (2020)
21. Ying, Z., Li, G., Gao, W.: A bio-inspired multi-exposure fusion framework for low-light image enhancement. CoRR abs/1711.00591 (2017)
22. Ying, Z., Li, G., Ren, Y., Wang, R., Wang, W.: A new low-light image enhancement algorithm using camera response model. In: IEEE ICCV, pp. 3015–3022 (2017)
23. Zhang, Y., Zhang, J., Guo, X.: Kindling the darkness: a practical low-light image enhancer. In: ACM MM, pp. 1632–1640 (2019)

MM-Net: Learning Adaptive Meta-metric for Few-Shot Biometric Recognition

Qinghua Gu[(⊠)], Zhengding Luo, Wanyu Zhao, and Yuesheng Zhu[(⊠)]

Communication and Information Security Lab,
School of Electronic and Computer Engineering, Peking University, Shenzhen, China
{guqh,luozd,wyzhao,zhuys}@pku.edu.cn

Abstract. Deep Convolutional Neural Network (DCNN) has pushed forward the development of deep biometric recognition. However, it is resource-consuming to train existing deep networks with plenty of labeled training data in actual scenarios. Therefore, in this paper, we exploit few-shot learning for biometric recognition, which can solve many actual problems with limited training samples, such as video surveillance and suspect detection. Specifically, we propose a novel adaptive meta-metric network (MM-Net) for few-shot biometric recognition. Instead of traditional task-invariant distance metrics, a novel meta-metric learner is proposed to measure the similarities between queries and class embeddings under different tasks adaptively. Moreover, we introduce focal loss to address the class imbalance problem in few-shot biometric recognition, and make the classifiers focus on hard-classified samples. Experimental results on three different biometric datasets demonstrate the superior performance of our MM-Net over other few-shot learning approaches.

Keywords: Few-shot learning · Biometric recognition · Meta-metric · Focal loss

1 Introduction

The great progress of biometric recognition [12,15] in recent years has made large-scale biometric identification possible for many practical applications. However, these approaches usually require a large amount of labeled data and Deep Convolutional Neural Network (DCNN) embedding models [11,13,19], which is time-consuming and resource-consuming. Moreover, due to the limitation of training samples in many scenarios, it is essential to study the few-shot problem for real-world scenarios [5,23], such as gate ID identification, passport identification, and law enforcement.

Standard few-shot learning [24] can adapt to recognize new classes when only few labeled support samples are available. Figure 1 shows the example of few-shot face recognition in 5-way 1-shot setting. For each episode, there are 5 classes with 1 sample each class in support set and 2 samples for evaluation in query set. The classifiers for standard few-shot face recognition can identify new

© Springer Nature Switzerland AG 2021
J. Lokoč et al. (Eds.): MMM 2021, LNCS 12572, pp. 265–277, 2021.
https://doi.org/10.1007/978-3-030-67832-6_22

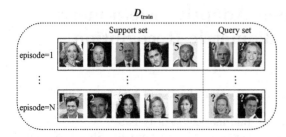 

Fig. 1. Example of few-shot face recognition in 5-way 1-shot setting. It aims to recognize the query images in query set based on few samples in support set. The D_{test} has a disjoint class label space with D_{train}.

classes in D_{test} through few support samples based on a simple and effective network architecture, which is very helpful in practical applications.

Most existing few-shot learning approaches focus on optimizing model parameters based on meta-learning [6,16], or utilize fixed metrics [20,24] to learn transferable distance distribution between images [18]. However, these approaches are not effective enough for few-shot biometric recognition, because biometric images are quite different from general images. In general, there are two main challenges in few-shot biometric tasks: (1) Firstly, a simple framework needs to be designed with strong generalization performance for recognizing new categories when lacking support samples. (2) Secondly, many biometric images have similar features [1] (e.g., palmprint images) and these categories are difficult to accurately identify, which is not so obvious in general images.

In this paper, we propose a novel focal loss based adaptive meta-metric network (MM-Net) for few-shot biometric recognition. Specifically, we consider designing a general few-shot recognition framework for different biometric datasets. It is crucial to ensure that the network maintains good generalization performance when dealing with different tasks. Meanwhile, we consider that there are much more similar contours and local features between biometric images than general images. For these reasons, the task-invariant fixed distance metrics [20,24] do not work well in few-shot biometric recognition tasks anymore. Therefore, we propose a novel adaptive meta-metric based on a ResNet Block [22], which combines meta-learning [17] and distance metric [7]. The meta-metric learns to measure the consistencies between queries and class embeddings in different tasks flexibly, rather than the invariable distance measurement between images. The learned class embeddings can distinguish biometric images efficiently by reducing intra-class variance.

Moreover, the widely used Cross-Entropy (CE) Loss has a tendency to be influenced heavily by trivial samples in case of data imbalance. In the biometric recognition tasks, there are no particularly distinctive features for a big proportion of the biometric images. Therefore, training under such an environment results in a CE loss based system focusing itself more towards samples with distinctive features, whereas it should be giving more priority towards the harder common classes. This problem will be more serious in few-shot learning because the number of support set is very small. To address this issue, we extend focal loss [14] to the multi-class few-shot biometric recognition cases. Focal loss, which addresses class imbalance by dynamically scaling the standard CE loss, focuses the training towards the various hard-classified samples while reducing the influence of easy-classified samples on the system.

In short, our main contributions are in three-fold.

- We develop a benchmark task framework for standard few-shot biometric recognition and a novel adaptive meta-metric learner is proposed to measure the nonlinear similarities between images and categories.
- To the best of our knowledge, this is the first time that focal loss has been used in few-shot learning to focus on hard-classified samples.
- We conduct experiments on three different biometric datasets, including face and palmprint datasets. Experimental results show the competitive improvements continuously compared to other few-shot learning baselines.

2 Related Work

In this part, we briefly review the related works about biometric recognition, few-shot learning, and loss function.

Biometric Recognition. Most achievements of deep biometric recognition have relied on a large amount of labeled biometric data for the training process of the model. In recent years, some models [4,9] are trained with the specific training set, which contains some classes with a large amount of labeled data, and some classes with only one labeled samples. Although these approaches can identify categories that have appeared once in the training set, they are not effective to recognize new classes that have never been seen.

Our topic is quite different from theirs since that our model can recognize new classes by relying on few labeled supporting samples effectively. Moreover, Our MM-Net is a general framework for different biometric few-shot recognition rather than specific biological features, because the adopted episodic training mechanism can guarantee a strong generalization performance in different tasks.

Few-Shot Learning. In recent years, a large number of studies on few-shot learning have been proposed, most of them can be divided into meta-learning based and metric-learning based. For the former, a meta-learner that learns to optimize model parameters extracts some transferable knowledge between tasks to leverage in the context of few-shot learning [6,16]. The metric-learning based approaches [20,21,24] mainly focus on learning transferable embeddings and the distance distribution between images.

However, most of these approaches tend to focus on few-shot classification of general images (e.g., ImageNet). In our work, a novel MM-Net is proposed for few-shot learning tasks in biometric recognition, which combines the advantages of two types of above approaches. On the one hand, our MM-Net learns class

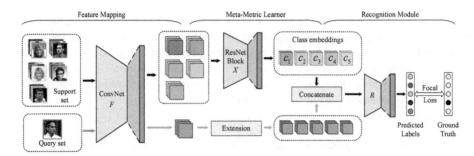

Fig. 2. The architecture of our MM-Net for a few-shot face recognition task in 5-way K-shot setting. The meta-metric learner performs deep nonlinear measurement between the query images and the class embeddings of each support category $c_i (i = 1, 2, 3, 4, 5)$. Then, the focal loss is calculated between the predicted labels and the ground truth to further optimize the network parameters.

embeddings based on the support samples adaptively. On the other hand, the nonlinear deep image-to-class measurement we adopted is more effective than the previous task-invariant image-to-image measurement.

Loss Functions. For most few-shot classification tasks, most of them use CE loss to train the model [6,8,16,24], they ignore that the problem of class imbalance will be more obvious when the samples are less than the general classification task. For biometric images, some of them have obvious characteristics, but there are still many pictures existing only slight differences. In this case, the imbalance of categories cannot be ignored for few-shot biometric recognition. Lin et al. [14] proposed a new loss called focal loss, which addresses class imbalance by dynamically scaling the standard CE loss such that the loss associated with easily classifiable examples are down-weighted. In this paper, we adapt the focal loss into few-shot biometric recognition to address the issue of class imbalance.

3   Proposed Approach

3.1   Task Formulation

Take few-shot face recognition as an example, it can be formulated as training a classifier to recognize the remaining face images when given few support face images in each class. More specifically, suppose we have a (small) support set S which consists of C different classes and K face image samples each class, few-shot face recognition aims to classify the query face images in query set Q which consists of the face images selected in the remaining images in the above C classes. This setting is called the C-way K-shot [24] in few-shot face recognition. The support set S and query set Q can be described as:

$$S = \left\{ x_1^1, \ldots, x_K^1, \ldots, x_1^C, \ldots, x_K^C \right\} \tag{1}$$

$$Q = \left\{ x_{K+1}^1, \ldots, x_{K+N}^1, \ldots, x_{K+1}^C, \ldots, x_{K+N}^C \right\} \tag{2}$$

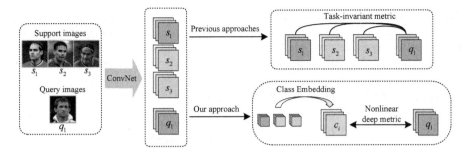

Fig. 3. A comparison of our meta-metric learner with other previous approaches. Instead of image-to-image measurements, our meta-metric learner measures the similarities between the queries and class embeddings.

Where N is the number of query samples for each class.

However, the model will suffer from overfitting if we directly train the classifier, because the training set D_{train} has a disjoint class label space with the test set D_{test} for few-shot face recognition. Therefore, we introduce a novel meta-metric learner to learn the similarities between query face images and support categories adaptively, and train the model upon episodic training mechanism.

3.2   Model Description

Figure 2 shows the illustration of the proposed focal loss based adaptive meta-metric network (MM-Net) for a few-shot face recognition task in 5-way K-shot setting. Both support samples and queries learn feature maps based on the ConvNet F, any suitable CNNs can be used here. The ConvNet here does not contain the fully connected layers, as it is only used to learn feature maps of images.

Meta-Metric Learner. In most previous approaches, task-invariant image-to-image distance metrics (e.g., Cosine Similarity [24] and Euclidean Distance [20]) are usually used to measure the distance between images. Figure 3 shows the comparison of our meta-metric learner with other previous approaches. There are two key differences between our approach and others: (1) the objects of measurement; (2) the choices of metrics.

First, we consider that the measurement between images is not efficient enough to accurately identify biometric images due to lacking support face samples. Therefore, we perform residual embedding X for the feature maps of support category c_i based on a ResNet Block, and measure the similarities between the query images and support categories directly. Second, we combine meta-learning with distance metric, the Recognition Module R can adaptively measure the deep nonlinear similarities between the query images and support categories in different tasks. For a query sample x, its predicting probability distribution P over C support classes can be formulated as:

$$P = \{p_1, \ldots, p_i, \ldots, p_C\} = R(X(F(c_i)), F(x)) \tag{3}$$

Focal Loss. Inspired by CE loss, focal loss is proposed to address the extreme class imbalance between foreground and background classes during training. In this paper, we consider that the biometric category imbalance is more significant in few-shot learning due to lacking support samples. In this case, we introduce focal loss to address this issue.

The CE loss for binary classification can be described as:

$$\mathrm{CE}(p, y) = \begin{cases} -\log(p) & \text{if } y = 1 \\ -\log(1 - p) & \text{otherwise} \end{cases} \tag{4}$$

In the above $y \in \{\pm 1\}$ specifies the ground-truth class and $p \in [0, 1]$ is the model's estimated probability for the class with label $y = 1$. For notational convenience, we define p_t:

$$p_t = \begin{cases} p & \text{if } y = 1 \\ 1 - p & \text{otherwise} \end{cases} \tag{5}$$

and rewrite $\mathrm{CE}(p, y) = \mathrm{CE}(p_t) = -\log(p_t)$.

For differentiating between easy/hard examples, the focal loss reshapes the loss function to down-weight easy examples and thus focus training on hard negatives. In this paper, we extend the FL to the multi-class few-shot biometric recognition cases. For a query biometric sample (x, Y), the one-hot vector $Y = \{y_1, \dots, y_i, \dots, y_C\}$ represents its true labels, which has the dimension of $1 \times C$. We assume that the probability of the query x being predicted as the ith label is p_i. Then, a modulating factor $(1 - p_i)^\lambda$ is added to the CE loss, with tunable focusing parameter $\lambda \geq 0$. The FL can be defined as:

$$\mathrm{FL}(P, Y) = -\sum_{i=1}^{C} (1 - p_i)^\lambda y_i \log p_i \tag{6}$$

From the Eq. 6, we can find that when a query is misclassified (i.e., $y_i = 1$ and p_i is small), the modulating factor $(1 - p_i)^\lambda$ is close to 1, and the loss is not greatly affected. As $p_i \to 1$, the factor is close to 0, and the loss for these well-classified queries is down-weighted. When $\lambda = 0$, FL is equivalent to CE, and as λ is increased the effect of the modulating factor is likewise increased. Comparing to CE loss, FL can be adjusted according to the degree of class imbalance in different datasets to achieve the best performance. More details will be shown in Sect. 4.3 and 4.4.

3.3   Network Architecture

In our work, we define a 64-Conv block, and each block consists of a convolutional layer which including 64 filters of size 3×3, a batch normalization layer, and a ReLU nonlinear activation layer. Besides, we define a 64-Conv-MP block, which contains a 64-Conv block and a 2×2 max-pooling layer. The network architecture of our MM-Net is shown in Fig. 4. For the ConvNet, we choose two

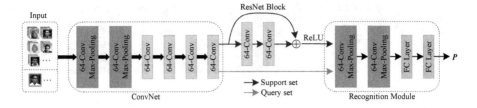

Fig. 4. The network architecture of our MM-Net.

64-Conv-MP blocks and four 64-Conv blocks, and both support set and query set share the same network parameters. As for the class embedding part, we define a Residual Block, which contains two 64-Conv blocks including one linear identity mapping. Meanwhile, two 64-Conv-MP blocks and two fully-connected layers are used to classify the learned deep feature representations in Recognition Module R.

3.4 Training Strategy

The training strategy in Matching Networks [24] called episodic training mechanism has achieved good performance in few-shot learning, and it will be adopted in our work. More specifically, in each training episode of C-way K-shot setting, we randomly sample C classes and K samples each class from training set D_{train} to compose a training support set S_{train} (e.g., $C=5$, $K=5$, the S_{train} will has 25 samples). At the same time, we randomly select some samples of the remaining parts of the above C classes to compose a training query set Q_{train}.

Next, the MM-Net is trained to minimize the error predicting the class labels of images in the Q_{train} conditioned on the S_{train}. After thousands of training episodes, the trained model can adaptively perform C-way K-shot recognition when encountering new classes in D_{test}, because the classifier has learned how to evaluate intrinsic connections between queries and support classes.

4 Experiments

4.1 Dataset

As shown in Fig. 5, two face datasets and one palmprint dataset are used to evaluate the performance of our MM-Net. In order to make the datasets suitable for our few-shot learning tasks, two few-shot face recognition datasets are devised based on MS-Celeb-1M [10] and VGG-Face2 [2] respectively.

***mini*MS-Celeb-1M.** It contains 200 classes selected randomly from MS-Celeb-1M, with an average of 75 face samples per class. We split the whole dataset into 130, 30, and 40 classes for training, validation, and testing.

***mini*VGG-Face2.** It consists of approximately 42000 face images with 140 classes, each having 250–350 examples. In particular, the images here are closer

(a). miniMS-Celeb-1M   (b). miniVGG-Face2   (c). PolyU-NIR

Fig. 5. Three different biometric datasets used in our experiments.

Table 1. The comparative results of few-shot biometric recognition in the 5-way 5-shot setting.

Model	Dataset		
	$mini$MS-Celeb-1M	$mini$VGG-Face2	PolyU-NIR
Meta-Learning LSTM [16]	88.63 ± 0.46%	73.60 ± 0.62%	92.37 ± 0.13%
MAML [6]	94.86 ± 0.23%	76.24 ± 0.74%	97.70 ± 0.09%
Matching Net [24]	89.30 ± 0.31%	69.53 ± 0.35%	89.85 ± 0.24%
GNN [8]	93.62 ± 0.27%	78.19 ± 0.58%	94.20 ± 0.11%
Prototypical Nets [20]	92.47 ± 0.34%	79.45 ± 0.51%	93.56 ± 0.19%
MM-Net(CE Loss)	**95.87 ± 0.24%**	**82.31 ± 0.57%**	**98.39 ± 0.08%**
MM-Net(Focal Loss)	**97.78 ± 0.18%**	**83.95 ± 0.54%**	**99.86 ± 0.06%**

to real scenes, and many faces have occlusion or interference, which is more challenging for few-shot face recognition. We split the dataset into 90, 20, and 30 classes for training, validation, and testing.

PolyU-NIR. As for the PolyU-NIR palmprint dataset, 6000 grayscale images from 500 different palms of 250 people are collected, including 195 males and 55 females. For each palm, 12 images are collected in two sessions. We split the dataset into 325, 75, and 100 classes for training, validation, and testing.

4.2   Experimental Settings

For few-shot face recognition, we execute six settings (i.e., 5/10-way 1/5/10-shot with 15/10/5 queries each class for 1/5/10-shot respectively). In spite of lacking samples for each palm, we execute 5/10/15-way 1/3/5-shot with 10/8/6 queries each class for 1/3/5-shot for few-shot palmprint recognition. We construct 300000 training episodes and 6000 test episodes in all the few-shot biometric recognition tasks, the 95% confidence interval of accuracies is also recorded.

In particular, the hyperparameter λ can adjust the rate at which easy samples are down-weighted when the classes are imbalanced. After comparative testing, we choose $\lambda = 1.0$ on $mini$MS-Celeb-1M and PolyU-NIR, $\lambda = 3.5$ on $mini$VGG-Face2. The experiments prove that focal loss performs better than CE Loss ($\lambda = 0$) on both two datasets.

Table 2. Few-shot face recognition results of MM-Net.

Setting	Dataset		
		*mini*MS-Celeb-1M	*mini*VGG-Face2
5-way	1-shot	92.28 ± 0.48%	69.98 ± 0.88%
	5-shot	97.78 ± 0.18%	83.95 ± 0.54%
	10-shot	98.15 ± 0.15%	86.61 ± 0.47%
10-way	1-shot	86.52 ± 0.45%	54.07 ± 0.67%
	5-shot	96.45 ± 0.15%	74.61 ± 0.46%
	10-shot	97.11 ± 0.13%	78.83 ± 0.39%

Table 3. Few-shot palmprint recognition results of MM-Net.

Shot	Way		
	5-way	10-way	15-way
1-shot	99.54 ± 0.11%	99.13 ± 0.12%	99.10 ± 0.09%
3-shot	99.84 ± 0.05%	99.80 ± 0.05%	99.65 ± 0.06%
5-shot	99.86 ± 0.06%	99.83 ± 0.05%	99.81 ± 0.04%

4.3 Experimental Results

Few-Shot Face Recognition. Table 1 shows the experimental results of our MM-Net and other competitive few-shot learning approaches in 5-way 5-shot setting, including Meat-Learning LSTM [16], MAML [6], Matching Net [24], GNN [8] and Prototypical Nets [20]. In Meat-Learning LSTM and MAML, they learn the network optimization process and transfer knowledge to few-shot face recognition tasks. As for Prototypical Nets, it calculates a mixed loss by fusing CE Loss and the mean distance of queries to prototypes. Compared with these approaches, our MM-Net leads to some persistent improvements on two datasets, which is benefit from adopted focal loss and proposed adaptive meta-metric. More specifically, we gain the largest improvement over the second result by 2.92% and 4.50% on *mini*MS-Celeb-1M and *mini*VGG-Face2.

In order to fully demonstrate the performance of our model in different settings, we performed various experiments on the two datasets, and the results are recorded in Table 2. It is reasonable that in the case of the same number of classes, the more support samples are better for improving face recognition. Another observation is that the performance on *mini*MS-Celeb-1M is better than *mini*VGG-Face2, because the face images on *mini*VGG-Face2 contain more complicated scenes and noises.

Few-Shot Palmprint Recognition. Table 3 shows the experimental results on PolyU-NIR, the MM-Net behaves continuously effectively in few-shot palmprint recognition tasks of all the settings. More specifically, the accuracies have

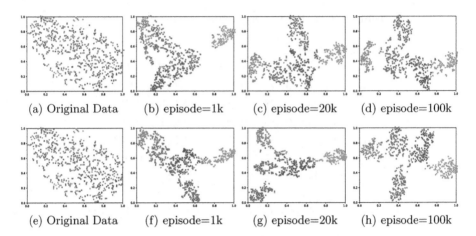

(a) Original Data   (b) episode=1k   (c) episode=20k   (d) episode=100k

(e) Original Data   (f) episode=1k   (g) episode=20k   (h) episode=100k

Fig. 6. The 2-D distributions of learned features under the supervision of (a)–(d): Cross-Entropy Loss and (e)–(h): Focal Loss ($\lambda = 3.5$) in 5-way 5-shot setting on $mini$VGG-Face2. Different training episodes lead to different deep feature distributions. The points with different colors denote features from 5 different classes, and 120 query faces each class are chosen randomly to demonstrate.

exceeded 99% in all the experiments. The experimental results show that the MM-Net can identify palmprint images adaptively and accurately with only few support samples in different tasks.

For comparison, we present the results of some baselines in the 5-way 5-shot palmprint recognition in Table 1. Our MM-Net achieves a competitive result compared to popular few-shot recognition approaches. Experiments on three datasets show that the proposed approach can maintain excellent generalization performance in different few-shot recognition tasks.

4.4 Discussion

Visualization. In order to show the training process intuitively, we visualize the deep feature distributions of the query images using t-SNE [3] visualization tool in 5-way 5-shot setting on $mini$VGG-Face2. As shown in Fig. 6 (e)–(h), we separately map the deeply learned features of query images to a 2-dimensional space after different training episodes. With the number of training episodes increases, the samples belonging to the same class become more and more compact, which is very advantageous for few-shot face recognition.

Moreover, Fig. 6 (a)–(d) shows the 2-D distributions of learned features under the supervision of CE loss with the same distance metric. We can observe that: under the supervision of CE loss, although the deeply learned features are separable, they are not discriminative enough, since many hard-classified faces interfere with each other. In contrast, the discriminative power of feature maps can be significantly enhanced with focal loss because inter-class variations are increased and intra-class variations are reduced.

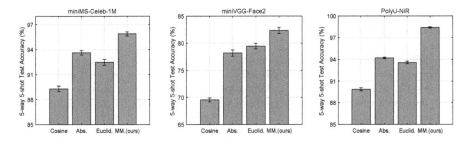

Fig. 7. The 5-way 5-shot face recognition accuracies with different metrics.

Effect of Metrics. In Sect. 3.2 and previous experiments, we have proved that focal loss is much more effective than CE loss in few-shot face recognition tasks. In this part, we investigate the effect of different metrics on the performance of few-shot face recognition when using the same CE loss. The experimental results on two datasets are shown in Fig. 7. We can find that our adaptive Meta-Metric (MM.) indeed performs better than other task-invariant metrics, including Cosine Similarity, Absolute Difference and Euclidean Distance.

5   Conclusion

In this paper, we propose a novel focal loss based adaptive meta-metric network (MM-Net) for few-shot biometric recognition. Our framework utilizes the focal loss that dynamically scales the cross-entropy loss, enabling the classifiers to focus on hard-classified samples. Moreover, the proposed adaptive meta-metric contributes to classify queries effectively in different tasks. In the future, we will explore the few-shot learning and biometric recognition in our future work.

Acknowledgement. This work was supported in part by the Shenzhen Municipal Development and Reform Commission (Disciplinary Development Program for Data Science and Intelligent Computing), and in part by the Key-Area Research and Development Program of Guangdong Province (2019B010137001).

References

1. Bhatt, H.S., Singh, R., Vatsa, M., Ratha, N.K.: Improving cross-resolution face matching using ensemble-based co-transfer learning. IEEE Trans. Image Process. **23**(12), 5654–5669 (2014)
2. Cao, Q., Shen, L., Xie, W., Parkhi, O.M., Zisserman, A.: VGGFace2: a dataset for recognising faces across pose and age. In: Proceedings of the 13th IEEE International Conference on Automatic Face Gesture Recognition, pp. 67–74, May 2018
3. Dimitriadis, G., Neto, J.P., Kampff, A.R.: T-SNE visualization of large-scale neural recordings. Neural Comput. **30**(7), 1750–1774 (2018)

4. Ding, Z., Guo, Y., Zhang, L., Fu, Y.: One-shot face recognition via generative learning. In: Proceedings of the 13th IEEE International Conference on Automatic Face Gesture Recognition, pp. 1–7, May 2018
5. Fei-Fei, L., Fergus, R., Perona, P.: One-shot learning of object categories. IEEE Trans. Pattern Anal. Mach. Intell. **28**(4), 594–611 (2006)
6. Finn, C., Abbeel, P., Levine, S.: Model-agnostic meta-learning for fast adaptation of deep networks. In: Proceedings of the 34th International Conference on Machine Learning, vol. 70, pp. 1126–1135, March 2017
7. Fouad, S., Tino, P., Raychaudhury, S., Schneider, P.: Incorporating privileged information through metric learning. IEEE Trans. Neural Netw. Learn. Syst. **24**(7), 1086–1098 (2013)
8. Garcia, V., Bruna, J.: Few-shot learning with graph neural networks. arXiv preprint arXiv:1711.04043, November 2017
9. Guo, Y., Zhang, L.: One-shot face recognition by promoting underrepresented classes. arXiv preprint arXiv:1707.05574, July 2017
10. Guo, Y., Zhang, L., Hu, Y., He, X., Gao, J.: MS-Celeb-1M: a dataset and benchmark for large-scale face recognition. In: Leibe, B., Matas, J., Sebe, N., Welling, M. (eds.) ECCV 2016. LNCS, vol. 9907, pp. 87–102. Springer, Cham (2016). https://doi.org/10.1007/978-3-319-46487-9_6
11. He, K., Zhang, X., Ren, S., Sun, J.: Deep residual learning for image recognition. In: Proceedings of the IEEE Conference on Computer Vision and Pattern Recognition, pp. 770–778, June 2016
12. He, R., Wu, X., Sun, Z., Tan, T.: Wasserstein CNN: learning invariant features for NIR-VIS face recognition. IEEE Trans. Pattern Anal. Mach. Intell. **41**(7), 1761–1773 (2019)
13. Krizhevsky, A., Sutskever, I., Hinton, G.E.: ImageNet classification with deep convolutional neural networks. In: Proceedings of the Advances in Neural Information Processing System, pp. 1097–1105, December 2012
14. Lin, T.Y., Goyal, P., Girshick, R., He, K., Dollár, P.: Focal loss for dense object detection. In: Proceedings of the IEEE International Conference on Computer Vision, pp. 2980–2988, October 2017
15. Mantecón, T., del-Blanco, C.R., Jaureguizar, F., García, N.: Visual face recognition using bag of dense derivative depth patterns. IEEE Signal Process. Lett. **23**(6), 771–775 (2016)
16. Ravi, S., Larochelle, H.: Optimization as a model for few-shot learning (2016)
17. Santoro, A., Bartunov, S., Botvinick, M., Wierstra, D., Lillicrap, T.: Meta-learning with memory-augmented neural networks. In: Proceedings of the 33rd International Conference on Machine Learning, pp. 1842–1850, June 2016
18. Shao, L., Zhu, F., Li, X.: Transfer learning for visual categorization: a survey. IEEE Trans. Neural Netw. Learn. Syst. **26**(5), 1019–1034 (2015)
19. Simonyan, K., Zisserman, A.: Very deep convolutional networks for large-scale image recognition. arXiv preprint arXiv:1409.1556, September 2014
20. Snell, J., Swersky, K., Zemel, R.: Prototypical networks for few-shot learning. In: Advances in Neural Information Processing Systems, vol. 30, pp. 4077–4087 (2017)
21. Sung, F., Yang, Y., Zhang, L., Xiang, T., Torr, P.H.S., Hospedales, T.M.: Learning to compare: relation network for few-shot learning. In: Proceedings of the IEEE Conference on Computer Vision and Pattern Recognition, pp. 1199–1208, June 2018

22. Szegedy, C., Ioffe, S., Vanhoucke, V., Alemi, A.A.: Inception-v4, inception-ResNet and the impact of residual connections on learning. In: Proceedings of the 31st AAAI Conference on Artificial Intelligence, pp. 4278–4284, February 2017
23. Tan, X., Chen, S., Zhou, Z.H., Zhang, F.: Face recognition from a single image per person: a survey. Pattern Recogn. **39**(9), 1725–1745 (2006)
24. Vinyals, O., Blundell, C., Lillicrap, T., Wierstra, D., et al.: Matching networks for one shot learning. In: Proceedings of the Advances in Neural Information Processing Systems, vol. 29, pp. 3630–3638 (2016)

A Sentiment Similarity-Oriented Attention Model with Multi-task Learning for Text-Based Emotion Recognition

Yahui Fu[1], Lili Guo[1], Longbiao Wang[1(✉)], Zhilei Liu[1], Jiaxing Liu[1], and Jianwu Dang[1,2]

[1] Tianjin Key Laboratory of Cognitive Computing and Application, College of Intelligence and Computing, Tianjin University, Tianjin, China
{fuyahui,liliguo,longbiao_wang,zhileiliu,jiaxingliu}@tju.edu.cn
[2] Japan Advanced Institute of Science and Technology, Ishikawa, Japan
jdang@jaist.ac.jp

Abstract. Emotion recognition based on text modality has been one of the major topics in the field of emotion recognition in conversation. How to extract efficient emotional features is still a challenge. Previous studies utilize contextual semantics and emotion lexicon for affect modeling. However, they ignore information that may be conveyed by the emotion labels themselves. To address this problem, we propose the sentiment similarity-oriented attention (SSOA) mechanism, which uses the semantics of emotion labels to guide the model's attention when encoding the input conversations. Thus to extract emotion-related information from sentences. Then we use the convolutional neural network (CNN) to extract complex informative features. In addition, as discrete emotions are highly related with the Valence, Arousal, and Dominance (VAD) in psychophysiology, we train the VAD regression and emotion classification tasks together by using multi-task learning to extract more robust features. The proposed method outperforms the benchmarks by an absolute increase of over 3.65% in terms of the average F1 for the emotion classification task, and also outperforms previous strategies for the VAD regression task on the IEMOCAP database.

Keywords: Sentiment similarity-oriented attention · Text emotion recognition · VAD regression · Multi-task learning · Convolutional neural network

1 Introduction

Text emotion recognition has emerged as a prevalent research topic that can make some valuable contributions, not only in social media applications like

Y. Fu and L. Guo—Contributed equally to this work.

© Springer Nature Switzerland AG 2021
J. Lokoč et al. (Eds.): MMM 2021, LNCS 12572, pp. 278–289, 2021.
https://doi.org/10.1007/978-3-030-67832-6_23

Facebook, Twitter and Youtube, but also in more innovative area such as human-computer interaction. It is significant to extract effective textual features for emotion recognition but still a challenging task.

In the traditional studies, distributed representations or pre-trained embeddings are playing important roles in state-of-the-art sentiment analysis systems. For example, predictive methods Word2Vec [1] and Glove [2], which can capture multi-dimensional word semantics. Beyond word-semantics, there has been a big efforts toward End-to-End neural network models [3] and achieved better performance by fine-tuning the well pre-trained models such as ELMO [4] and BERT [5]. However, these representations are based on syntactic and semantic information, which do not enclose specific affective information.

To conduct affective information into training, [6–9] introduced lexical resources to enrich previous word distributions with sentiment-informative features, as lexical values are intuitively associated with the word's sentiment polarity and strength. Especially, [8] proposed a lexicon-based supervised attention model to extract sentiment-enriched features for document-level emotion classification. Similarly, [7] introduced a kind of affect-enriched word distribution, which was trained with lexical resources on the Valence-Arousal-Dominance dimensions. These studies demonstrate the effectiveness of sentiment lexicons in emotion recognition. However, it's limited in lexicon vocabulary coverage, and the valence of one sentence is not simply the sum of the lexical polarities of its constituent words [10]. Emojis are also thought high correlated to affect, therefore, [11] proposed a model named Deepmoji that adopted a bidirectional long short-term memory (BLSTM) with an attention mechanism. The Deepmoji predicted emojis from text on a 1246 million tweet corpus and achieved a good results. Nevertheless, it needs huge effort to collect tweets. In addition, none of these researches consider the semantics of the emotion labels themselves.

To address the above problems, we propose a sentiment similarity-oriented attention (SSOA) mechanism, which uses the label embeddings to guide the network to extract emotion-related information from input sentences. First of all, we compute the sentiment similarity between input sentences and emotion labels. Then we apply the valence value that selected from an affective lexicon as the sentiment polarity. After training the model, we can obtain SSOA, the value of which represents the weight of each emotion contributes to the final representations. Finally, we use CNN to capture complex linguistic features as it has been wildly used for text emotion recognition and shown promising performances such as [12,13]. Furthermore, [14] indicated that emotion state can be considered as a point in a continuous space, which is described by the dimensions of valence (V, the pleasantness of the stimulus), arousal (A, the intensity of emotion produced) and dominance (D, the degree of power/control exerted by a stimulus), meanwhile, discrete emotions are highly correlated with VAD in psychophysiology. Therefore, in this work, we adopt a multi-task model for both discrete emotion classification and dimensional VAD regression to enrich robustness.

To summarize, our main contributions are as follows: 1) we propose a sentiment similarity-oriented attention mechanism to encode sentiment-informative representations by incorporating label semantics. 2) we propose to leverage the inter-dependence of two related tasks (i.e. discrete emotion recognition and dimensional VAD recognition) in improving each other's performance. The rest of this paper is organized as follows. Section 2 introduces the proposed method, sentiment similarity-oriented attention mechanism with multi-task learning. We then conduct a series of comparative experiments and validation studies in Sect. 3. Section 4 gives the conclusions.

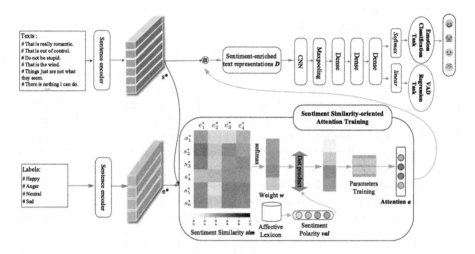

Fig. 1. This is the overall framework: sentiment similarity-oriented attention model with multi-task learning for text-based emotion recognition. We introduce sentiment similarity and sentiment polarity to compute affective attention. Then, we use this attention to construct sentiment-enriched text representations for both emotion classification and VAD regression task with multi-task learning.

2   Sentiment Similarity-Oriented Attention Model with Multi-task Learning

Figure 1 gives the overall framework. First, the sentence encoder approach is used to generate representations for all the input texts and emotional labels. Then we adopt the proposed sentiment similarity-oriented attention mechanism to obtain the sentiment-enriched text representations, followed by a CNN to extract deep informative features. In addition, we introduce multi-task learning for both emotion classification and VAD regression to extract more robust representations.

2.1   Sentence Encoder

[15] has published two kinds of universal sentence encoder for sentence embedding, one is trained with Transformer encoder [16], while the other is based on deep averaging network (DAN) architecture [17], and all of them can be obtained from the TF Hub website. We use the first one (USE_T) for our sentence encoder part to encode texts and emotion labels into sentence embeddings. Rather than learning label embeddings from radome, we also explore using contextual embeddings from transformer-based models. This allow us to use richer semantics derived from pre-training. The reason that we use sentence embeddings not conventional pre-trained word embeddings as when computing emotion of one sentence based on word level may cause sentiment inconsistency. For example, in a sentence sample *'You are not stupid.'* word *not* and *stupid* are both represent negative emotion, if just concatenate them to represent the emotion of this sentence, it is negative, which should be positive.

2.2   Sentiment Similarity-Oriented Attention

In this section, we introduce our proposed SSOA mechanism more explicitly. The main idea behind the SSOA mechanism is to compute affective attention scores between the labels and the representations of the input sentences that is to be classified. Formally, let $S = \{s_1...s_i...s_N\}$ be the set of the sentences in the database, where N is the total number of training data set. $E = \{e_1, e_2, e_3, e_4\}$ be the set of four emotion labels (Happy, Angry, Neutral, Sad) same as in [18], $Val = \{val_1, val_2, val_3, val_4\}$ be the set of valence scores of the emotions, which selected from ANEW lexicon [19]. We define val_i as the sentiment polarity of each emotion e_j, which is a real number and indicates the strength of each emotion.

For each s_i in S, $1 \leq i \leq l$, where l is batch size. And each e_j in E, $1 \leq j \leq 4$, we directly assess their sentence embedding s_i^* and e_j^* respectively, produced by the sentence encoder. For the pairwise sentiment similarity $sim\left(s_i^*, e_j^*\right)$, we compute it based on the method proposed in [15], that first compute the cosine similarity of the sentence embedding and emotion embedding, then use arccos to convert the cosine similarity into an angular distance, which had experimented to have better performance on sentiment similarity computing, that is,

$$sim\left(s_i^*, e_j^*\right) = \left(1 - \arccos\left(\frac{s_i^{*\top} e_j^*}{\| s_i^* \| \| e_j^* \|}/\pi\right)\right) \tag{1}$$

where $s_i^{*\top}$ represents the transpose of s_i^*. For each $sim\left(s_i^*, e_j^*\right)$, we use the softmax function to compute the weight probability $w_{i,j}$ as:

$$w_{i,j} = \frac{\exp\left(sim\left(s_i^*, e_j^*\right)\right)}{\sum_{j=1}^4 \exp\left(sim\left(s_i^*, e_j^*\right)\right)} \tag{2}$$

Then the affective attention $a_{i,j}$ that sentence s_i oriented on each emotion is computed as below:

$$a_{i,j} = \alpha * (val_j w_{i,j}) \tag{3}$$

We add a scaling hyper-parameter α to increase the range of possible probability values for each conditional probability term. The sentiment-enriched text representations D can be induced as follows:

$$D = \sum_{i=1}^{l} \sum_{j=1}^{4} W_s s_i^* a_{i,j} \tag{4}$$

where W_s denotes sentence-level weight matrices, $D \in \mathbb{R}^{l \times 4d^s}$, and d^s is the size of sentence embedding.

2.3   Multi-task Learning

In this subsection, we introduce multi-task learning for both emotion classification and VAD regression task, as the knowledge learned in one task can usually improve the performance of another related task and enrich robustness of different type tasks [20,21]. Each sentence s_i in the training corpus has the following feature and label set $[s_i^*, (y_{emo,i}, y_{val,i}, y_{aro,i}, y_{dom,i})]$, where s_i^* represents the sentence embedding of s_i, and $(y_{emo,i}, y_{val,i}, y_{aro,i}, y_{dom,i})$ represent the associated categorical emotion, dimensional valence, arousal and dominance label separately. We apply CNN and three dense layers as informative feature extractor, then H^* is the final document vector. The probability of emotion classification task is computed by a *softmax* function:

$$P(y_{emo}) = softmax(W_e H^* + b_e) \tag{5}$$

where W_e and b_e are the parameters of the *softmax* layer. We use categorical cross entropy loss function for the first task, the objective function of this system is as follows:

$$J_e = -\frac{1}{l} \sum_{i=1}^{l} log P(y_{emo,i}) [y_{emo,i}] \tag{6}$$

where $y_{emo,i}$ is the expected class label of sentence s_i and $P(y_{emo,i})$ is the probability distribution of emotion labels for s_i. However, for the continuous labels, the *softmax* layer is not applicable, we use the *linear* function to predict the values for the VAD regression task. Then the predict value $y_{val|aro|dom,i}^p$ for sentence s_i is calculated using the following formula:

$$y_{val|aro|dom,i}^p = linear(W_s h_i^* + b_s) \tag{7}$$

where h_i^* represents the final vector of sentence s_i, W_e and b_e represent weights and bias respectively. Given l training sentences, we use the mean squared error loss function for VAD analysis, the loss between predicted dimensional values $y_{val|aro|dom,i}^p$ and original continuous labels $y_{val|aro|dom,i}^o$ is calculated as below:

$$L_{s,val|aro|dom} = \frac{1}{3l} \sum_{i=1}^{l} \left(y_{val|aro|dom,i}^p - y_{val|aro|dom,i}^o \right)^2 \tag{8}$$

Then the objective function for the whole system is:

$$J = J_e + \beta * (L_{s,act} + L_{s,aro} + L_{s,dom}) \qquad (9)$$

where β is the hyper-parameter to control the influence of the loss of the regression function to balance the preference between classification and regression disagreements.

3   Experiments and Analysis

3.1   Database and Lexicon

The IEMOCAP Emotion Database. The Interactive Emotional Dyadic Motion Capture (IEMOCAP) database [22] contains videos of ten unique speakers acting in two different scenarios: scripted and improvised dialog with dyadic interactions. We only use the transcript data. To compared with state-of-the-art approaches, we use four emotion categories and three sentiment dimensions with 5531 utterances in this study. The four-class emotion distribution is: 29.6% happy, 30.9% neutral, 19.9% anger and 19.6% sad. Note that happy and excited category in the original annotation are included into happy class to balance data distribution between classes. For valence, arousal and dominance labels, self-assessment are used for annotation, in which the scale is from 1 to 5. In this paper, we focus on speaker-independent emotion recognition. We use the first eight speakers from session one to four as the training set, and session five as the test set.

The ANEW Affective Lexicon. The emotional values of the English words in Affective Norms for English Words (ANEW) [19] were calculated by means of measuring the psychological reaction of a person to the specific word. It contains real-valued scores for valence, arousal and dominance (VAD) on a scale of 1–9 each, corresponding to the degree from low to high for each dimension respectively. We select the *Valence* rating as the sentiment polarity which can distinguish different emotions of distinct words with the scale ranging from unpleasant to pleasant.

3.2   Experimental Setup

Following [15], we set the dimension of the sentence embedding to 512. We use a convolutional layer with 16 filters each for kernel size of (4,4) and a max-pooling layer with the size of (2,2). As for dense layers, we use three hidden dense layers with 1024, 512 and 256 units and ReLU activation [23] separately. For regularization, we employ Dropout operation [24] with dropout rate of 0.5 for each layer. We set the mini-batch size as 50 and epoch number as 120, Adam [25] optimizer with a learning rate 0.0002, clipnorm as 5. And we set the parameter β to 1.0 to control the strength of the cost function for the VAD regression task.

We evaluate the experimental results of both single-task learning (STL) and multi-task learning (MTL) architecture. In the single-task architecture, we build separate systems for emotion classification and VAD regression, whereas in multi-task architecture a join-model is learned for both of these problems.

3.3   Experimental Results and Analysis

Comparison to State-of-the-art Approaches: To quantitatively evaluate the performance of the proposed model, we compare our method with currently advanced approaches. The following are the commonly used benchmarks:

Tf-idf+Lexicon+DNN [9]: Introducing affective *ANEW* [19] lexicon and the term frequency-inverse document frequency (*tf-idf*) to construct the text features with DNN for emotion classification on IEMOCAP.

CNN [26]: A efficient architecture which achieves excellent results on multiple benchmarks including sentiment analysis.

LSTMs [27]: Two conventional stacked LSTM layers for emotion detection using the text transcripts of IEMOCAP.

Deepmoji [11]: Using the millions of texts on social media with emojis to pre-train the model to learn representations of emotional contents.

BiGRU+ATT [28]: A BiGRU network with the classical attention (ATT) mechanism.

BiLSTM+CNN [29]: Incorporating convolution with BiLSTM layer to sample more meaningful information.

BERT$_{BASE}$ [5]: Bidirectional encoder with 12-layer Transformer blocks, which obtains new state-of-the-art results on sentence-level sentiment analysis.

Table 1. F1, Accuracy for the comparative experiments in emotion classification framework. Acc. = Accuracy(%), Average(w) = Weighted average(%). The best results are in bold.

ID	Model	IEMOCAP									
		Happy		Anger		Neutral		Sad		Average(W)	
		Acc.	F1	Acc.	F1	Acc.	F1	Acc.	F1	Acc.	F1
1	Tf-idf+Lexicon+DNN [9]	63.80	69.29	68.24	67.64	60.68	58.84	62.86	57.69	63.89	63.39
2	CNN [26]	64.71	69.00	72.35	64.23	60.16	59.08	62.45	62.70	64.92	63.75
3	LSTMs [27]	60.41	69.08	71.18	66.30	61.72	59.18	68.98	62.25	65.57	64.20
4	Deepmoji [11]	58.37	66.15	61.18	63.03	72.14	61.56	63.67	66.10	63.84	64.21
5	BiGRU+ATT [28]	60.18	68.73	76.47	67.01	59.64	58.79	71.02	64.33	66.83	64.72
6	BiLSTM+CNN [29]	63.57	70.60	71.76	67.59	63.80	61.17	66.53	62.21	66.42	65.40
7	BERT$_{BASE}$ [5]	59.05	69.23	72.35	65.78	67.19	63.70	73.88	66.54	68.12	66.31
Proposed	USE_T+SSOA+CNN	**69.91**	**72.88**	71.18	**70.14**	**67.71**	**65.74**	72.24	**71.08**	**70.26**	**69.96**

In order to evaluate the performance, we present accuracy and F1-score for emotion classification task. As for VAD regression work, we use the mean squared

Table 2. MSE and r for the comparative experiments in VAD regression framework

ID	Model	IEMOCAP					
		Valence		Arousal		Dominance	
		MSE	r	MSE	r	MSE	r
1	Tf-idf+Lexicon+DNN [9]	0.755	0.435	0.536	0.277	0.638	0.318
2	CNN [26]	0.731	0.471	0.544	0.345	0.619	0.359
3	LSTMs [27]	0.626	0.575	0.413	0.425	0.536	0.447
4	Deepmoji [11]	0.655	0.499	0.417	0.421	0.514	0.458
5	BiGRU+ATT [28]	0.674	0.478	0.439	0.378	0.561	0.416
6	BiLSTM+CNN [29]	0.685	0.466	0.433	0.400	0.531	0.442
7	BERT$_{BASE}$ [5]	0.566	0.587	0.416	0.464	0.564	0.460
Proposed	USE_T+SSOA+CNN	**0.523**	**0.603**	**0.402**	0.446	**0.511**	**0.486**

error (MSE) and pearson correlation coefficient (r) to evaluation the performance, in which the lower MSE value and higher r correlation, the better performance. Experimental results of different methods in single task framework are shown in Table 1 and Table 2.

As shown in Table 1, our proposed model outperforms the state-of-the-art approaches with the absolute increase of more than 3.65%, 2.14% on average weighted F1, accuracy in the emotion classification task. As for VAD regression task, we can see from Table 2 that the proposed model *USE_T+SSOA+CNN* has better performance of consistently lower MAE and higher r. The results of the comparative experiments demonstrate the effectiveness of our proposed model. In order to illustrate the performance of our proposed SSOA mechanism and multi-task training, we do further researches in the following part.

Validation Studies of Proposed Model: We apply Universal Sentence Encoder which is trained with Transformer [15] (USE_T) to encode input texts into sentence embeddings and use CNN as the feature extractor. Therefore **USE_T+CNN** is the basic architecture and we control it as invarient.

USE_T+ATT+CNN: In order to validate our proposed SSOA mechanism, we also consider the most useful self-attention mechanism [16], which decide the importance of features for the prediction task by weighing them when constructing the representation of text.

USE_T+SSOA+CNN (STL): It is our work in single task framework, which uses SSOA mechanism to compute attention scores between the label and the representations of the sentences in the input that is to be classified. This can then be used to appropriately weight the contributions of each sentence to the final representations.

USE_T+SSOA+CNN (MTL): To demonstrates the effectiveness of incorporating VAD regression with emotion classification, we experiment this model

Table 3. Results (%) of Validation studies on emotion classification task

Model	IEMOCAP									
	Happy		Anger		Neutral		Sad		Average(W)	
	Acc	F1	Acc	F1	Acc	F1	Acc	F1	Acc	F1
USE_T+CNN	60.63	69.61	70.59	67.61	73.44	66.04	69.80	67.99	68.61	67.81
USE_T+ATT+CNN	69.00	70.77	68.82	68.82	69.01	65.11	66.12	69.53	68.24	68.56
USE_T+SSOA+CNN (STL)	66.97	73.27	70.00	71.47	71.61	64.94	69.80	68.95	69.60	69.66
USE_T+SSOA+CNN (SML)	**69.91**	72.88	**71.18**	70.14	67.71	**65.74**	**72.24**	71.08	**70.26**	**69.96**

Table 4. Results of validation studies on VAD regression task

Model	IEMOCAP					
	Valence		Arousal		Dominance	
	MSE	r	MSE	r	MSE	r
USE_T+CNN	0.595	0.570	0.431	0.418	0.563	0.464
USE_T+ATT+CNN	0.571	0.582	0.463	0.415	0.554	0.459
USE_T+SSOA+CNN(STL)	0.546	0.591	0.405	0.441	0.526	0.470
USE_T+SSOA+CNN(MTL)	**0.523**	**0.603**	**0.402**	**0.446**	**0.511**	**0.486**

in the multi-task framework which trained with both categorical emotion labels and dimensional valence, arousal, dominance labels.

From Table 3 and Table 4, some conclusions can be drawn as following: (1) Both *USE_T+ATT+CNN* with self-attention and *USE_T+SSOA+CNN* with our SSOA have a better performance than with no attention mechanism as expected. (2) Compared with *USE_T+ATT+CNN*, our *USE_T+SSOA+CNN* model achieves a relatively better result, especially achieves improvement about 2.5% in Happy, 2.65% in Anger on F1-score, and have accuracy improvement about 2.6% in Neutral, 3.68% in Sad separately. The results demonstrate that semantics of emotion labels can guide a model's attention when representing the input conversation and our proposed SSOA mechanism is able to capture sentiment-aware features, meanwhile, self-attention mechanism usually weights

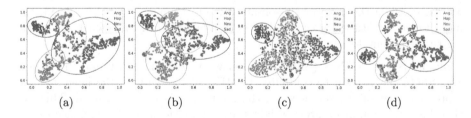

(a)   (b)   (c)   (d)

Fig. 2. t-SNE visualization of validation studies on emotion classification. (a):USE_T+CNN,   (b):USE_T+ATT+CNN,   (c):USE_T+SSOA+CNN(STL)   (d):USE_T+SSOA+CNN(MTL)

features based on semantic and context information which is not effective enough for emotion recognition. (3) Comparatively, as is shown in the last row, when both the problems are learned and evaluated in a multi-task learning framework, we observe performance enhancement for both tasks as well, which illustrates the effectiveness of multitask framework. And as we assume there are two reasons that VAD regression and emotion classification can assist each other task. On the one hand, emotions are high correlated with valence-arousal-dominance space. On the other hand, we take emotion labels into attention computing, which can help to capture more valence and arousal features.

Furthermore, in order to validate the effectiveness of our proposed method on different emotions, we introduce the t-Distributed Stochastic Neighbor Embedding (t-SNE) [30] for visualizing the deep representations as shown in Fig. 2. We can see that compared with Fig. 2 (a), the points which represent Anger in Fig. 2 (b) can be distinguished more easily. The points which represent Happy and Sad have similar performance. Compared with Fig. 2 (b), all the four emotion points have better discrimination in Fig. 2(c) which means the deep representations extracted by our model are more sentiment-aware. However, we can observe from Fig. 2(c) that most confusions are concentrated between Anger, Sad with Neutral. We assume the reason is that Anger and Sad hold the lowest percentage in IEMOCAP, which would not trained enough in our SSOA training process. Besides, the dataset we use is multimodal, a few utterances such as *"Yeah"*, *"I know"* carrying non-neutral emotions were misclassified as we do not utilize audio and visual modality in our experiments. In Fig. 2(d), Sad can be distinguished better, we assume it's because Sad is one kind of negative valence and arousal values emotion according to Valence-Arousal representation [18], whose prediction would be more easy with the help of VAD.

Overall, the proposed *USE_T+SSOA+CNN* with multi-task learning model outperforms the other comparative and ablation studies. It is reasonable to assume that the proposed model is good at capturing both semantic and emotion features not only in emotion classification but also the VAD regression task.

4   Conclusion

In this paper, we proposed a sentiment similarity-oriented attention mechanism, which can be used to guide the network to extract emotion-related information from input sentences to improve classification and regression accuracy. In addition, to extract more robust features, we jointed dimensional emotion recognition using multi-task learning. The effectiveness of our proposed method has been verified under a series of comparative experiments and validation studies on IEMOCAP. The results show that the proposed method outperforms previous text-based emotion recognition by 6.57% from 63.39% to 69.96%, and show better robustness. In the future work, we will make improvements of the proposed model by introducing speech information into SSOA computation.

Acknowledgements. This work was supported in part by the National Key R&D Program of China under Grant 2018YFB1305200, the National Natural Science Foundation of China under Grant 61771333 and the Tianjin Municipal Science and Technology Project under Grant 18ZXZNGX00330.

References

1. Mikolov, T., Chen, K., Corrado, G., Dean, J.: Efficient estimation of word representations in vector space. arXiv preprint arXiv:1301.3781 (2013)
2. Pennington, J., Socher, R., Manning, C.D.: Glove: global vectors for word representation. In: Proceedings of the 2014 Conference on Empirical Methods in Natural Language Processing (EMNLP), pp. 1532–1543 (2014)
3. Winata, G.I., et al.: CAiRE_HKUST at SemEval-2019 task 3: hierarchical attention for dialogue emotion classification. arXiv preprint arXiv:1906.04041 (2019)
4. Peters, M.E., et al.: Deep contextualized word representations. arXiv preprint arXiv:1802.05365 (2018)
5. Devlin, J., Chang, M.-W., Lee, K., Toutanova, K.: BERT: pre-training of deep bidirectional transformers for language understanding. arXiv preprint arXiv:1810.04805 (2018)
6. Araque, O., Zhu, G., Iglesias, C.A.: A semantic similarity-based perspective of affect lexicons for sentiment analysis. Knowl.-Based Syst. **165**, 346–359 (2019)
7. Khosla, S., Chhaya, N., Chawla, K.: Aff2Vec: affect-enriched distributional word representations. arXiv preprint arXiv:1805.07966 (2018)
8. Zou, Y., Gui, T., Zhang, Q., Huang, X.-J.: A lexicon-based supervised attention model for neural sentiment analysis. In: Proceedings of the 27th International Conference on Computational Linguistics, pp. 868–877 (2018)
9. Kim, E., Shin, J.W.: DNN-based emotion recognition based on bottleneck acoustic features and lexical features. In: ICASSP 2019–2019 IEEE International Conference on Acoustics, Speech and Signal Processing (ICASSP), pp. 6720–6724. IEEE (2019)
10. Mohammad, S.M.: Sentiment analysis: detecting valence, emotions, and other affectual states from text. In: Emotion Measurement, pp. 201–237. Elsevier (2016)
11. Felbo, B., Mislove, A., Søgaard, A., Rahwan, I., Lehmann, S.: Using millions of emoji occurrences to learn any-domain representations for detecting sentiment, emotion and sarcasm. arXiv preprint arXiv:1708.00524 (2017)
12. Du, J., Gui, L., He, Y., Xu, R.: A convolutional attentional neural network for sentiment classification. In: 2017 International Conference on Security, Pattern Analysis, and Cybernetics (SPAC), pp. 445–450. IEEE (2017)
13. Yang, X., Macdonald, C., Ounis, I.: Using word embeddings in Twitter election classification. Inf. Retrieval J. **21**(2–3), 183–207 (2018). https://doi.org/10.1007/s10791-017-9319-5
14. Marsella, S., Gratch, J.: Computationally modeling human emotion. Commun. ACM **57**(12), 56–67 (2014)
15. Cer, D., et al.: Universal sentence encoder for English. In: Proceedings of the 2018 Conference on Empirical Methods in Natural Language Processing: System Demonstrations, pp. 169–174 (2018)
16. Vaswani, A., et al.: Attention is all you need. In: Advances in Neural Information Processing Systems, pp. 5998–6008 (2017)
17. Iyyer, M., Manjunatha, V., Boyd-Graber, J., Daumé III, H.: Deep unordered composition rivals syntactic methods for text classification. In: Proceedings of the 53rd Annual Meeting of the Association for Computational Linguistics and the 7th International Joint Conference on Natural Language Processing (Volume 1: Long Papers), pp. 1681–1691 (2015)

18. Giannakopoulos, T., Pikrakis, A., Theodoridis, S.: A dimensional approach to emotion recognition of speech from movies. In: 2009 IEEE International Conference on Acoustics, Speech and Signal Processing, pp. 65–68. IEEE (2009)

19. Warriner, A.B., Kuperman, V., Brysbaert, M.: Norms of valence, arousal, and dominance for 13,915 English lemmas. Behav. Res. Methods **45**(4), 1191–1207 (2013). https://doi.org/10.3758/s13428-012-0314-x

20. Tafreshi, S., Diab, M.: Emotion detection and classification in a multigenre corpus with joint multi-task deep learning. In: Proceedings of the 27th International Conference on Computational Linguistics, pp. 2905–2913 (2018)

21. Akhtar, Md.S., Chauhan, D.S., Ghosal, D., Poria, S., Ekbal, A., Bhattacharyya, P.: Multi-task learning for multi-modal emotion recognition and sentiment analysis. arXiv preprint arXiv:1905.05812 (2019)

22. Busso, C., et al.: IEMOCAP: interactive emotional dyadic motion capture database. Lang. Resour. Eval. **42**(4), 335–359 (2008). https://doi.org/10.1007/s10579-008-9076-6

23. Nair, V., Hinton, G.E.: Rectified linear units improve restricted Boltzmann machines. In: Proceedings of the 27th International Conference on Machine Learning (ICML-10), pp. 807–814 (2010)

24. Hinton, G.E., Srivastava, N., Krizhevsky, A., Sutskever, I., Salakhutdinov, R.R.: Improving neural networks by preventing co-adaptation of feature detectors. arXiv preprint arXiv:1207.0580 (2012)

25. Kingma, D.P., Ba, J.: Adam: a method for stochastic optimization. arXiv preprint arXiv:1412.6980 (2014)

26. Kim, Y.: Convolutional neural networks for sentence classification. arXiv preprint arXiv:1408.5882 (2014)

27. Tripathi, S., Beigi, H.: Multi-modal emotion recognition on IEMOCAP dataset using deep learning. arXiv preprint arXiv:1804.05788 (2018)

28. Yang, Z., Yang, D., Dyer, C., He, X., Smola, A., Hovy, E.: Hierarchical attention networks for document classification. In: Proceedings of the 2016 Conference of the North American Chapter of the Association for Computational Linguistics: Human Language Technologies, pp. 1480–1489 (2016)

29. Zhou, P., Qi, Z., Zheng, S., Xu, J., Bao, H., Xu, B.: Text classification improved by integrating bidirectional LSTM with two-dimensional max pooling. arXiv preprint arXiv:1611.06639 (2016)

30. Van Der Maaten, L.: Accelerating t-SNE using tree-based algorithms. J. Mach. Learn. Res. **15**(1), 3221–3245 (2014)

Locating Visual Explanations for Video Question Answering

Xuanwei Chen, Rui Liu, Xiaomeng Song, and Yahong Han[✉]

College of Intelligence and Computing, Tianjin University, Tianjin, China
yahong@tju.edu.cn

Abstract. Although promising performance has been reported for Video Question Answering (VideoQA) in recent years, there is still a large gap for human to truly understand the model decisions. Besides, beyond a short answer, complementary visual information is desirable to enhance and elucidate the content of QA pairs. To this end, we introduce a new task called Video Question Answering with Visual Explanations (VQA-VE), which requires to generate answers and provide visual explanations (i.e., locating relevant moments within the whole video) simultaneously. This task bridges video question answering and temporal localization. They are two separate and typical visual tasks and come with our challenge. For training and evaluation, we build a new dataset on top of ActivityNet Captions by annotating QA pairs with temporal ground-truth. We also adopt a large-scale benchmark TVQA. Towards VQA-VE, we develop a new model that is able to generate complete natural language sentences as answers while locating relevant moments with various time spans in a multi-task framework. We also introduce two metrics to fairly measure the performance on VQA-VE. Experimental results not only show the effectiveness of our model, but also demonstrate that additional supervision from visual explanations can improve the performance of models on traditional VideoQA task.

Keywords: Visual explanations · Video question answering · Open-ended dataset

1 Introduction

Video question answering (VideoQA) has recently attracted researchers from multimedia, computer vision and artificial intelligence. As a multi-modal task, the goal of it is to jointly understand visual contents and natural languages. There are a range of datasets [13, 21, 22] and models [5, 25] proposed to boost the research. Although promising performance has been reported, recent efforts [1, 16] have pointed out that models can show good performance only by exploiting strong language prior without truly understanding the visual contents, since answers in some datasets present imbalanced length distributions. Under these circumstances, it is desirable to let models provide explanations with predicted answers for human to prove their rationalities.

© Springer Nature Switzerland AG 2021
J. Lokoč et al. (Eds.): MMM 2021, LNCS 12572, pp. 290–302, 2021.
https://doi.org/10.1007/978-3-030-67832-6_24

In this paper, we introduce a new task called Video Question Answering with Visual Explanations (VQA-VE). To solve VQA-VE, models are not only required to generate answers given questions and videos, but also expected to provide visual explanations (i.e., locate relevant moments within the whole video) for predicted answers. As shown in Fig. 1, a visual explanation can be taken as an evidence to justify if predicted answers are convincible and traceable [15], or as a supplementary to provide relevant information on the context of QA pairs, or even as a specification to indicate vague expressions or abstract concepts in QA pairs vividly. Therefore, visual explanations for answers play an important role in the interaction of question-answering. As mentioned in [20], open-ended QA form enables much wider applications than multiple choice since candidate choices are not easy to obtain in practical setting. Therefore, in order to further evaluate the task of VQA-VE, we construct a new dataset called Activity-QA on top of the ActivityNet Captions dataset [9].

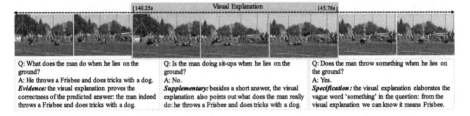

Fig. 1. VQA-VE requires to provide visual explanations for predicted answers. There are advantages for visual explanations: (Left) visual explanation can serve as an evidence to justify the correctness of answers; (Middle) visual explanation can provide supplementary information for the content of QA pairs; (Right) visual explanation can give clear indication to elaborate the vague expressions in QA pairs.

VQA-VE bridges video question answering and temporal localization of typical visual tasks. Visual explanations can range across multiple time scales, thus models need to deal with short as well as long sequences of video frames. These challenges motivate us to develop a new model of multi-task framework to generate answers and provide visual explanations simultaneously. Specifically, we design an answer prediction module to generate natural language sentences as answers based on fully fused cross-modal features, as well as a localization module to locate relevant moments with various time spans using semantic information as guidance. We design two metrics by a well-devised merge scheme with two widely used metrics in temporal localization and video question answering. From experiment results we can find that additional supervision from visual explanations can help models achieve better performance on traditional VideoQA task.

2   Related Work

Explanations for Video Question Answering: Most previous works [11,15] focused on explanations for ImageQA. Our work owns key differences with them:

we focus on visual explanations for VideoQA, and argue that the visual explanations generated by highlighting relevant spatial regions is insufficient for videos. For VideoQA, a popular way to visually explain predicted answers is using temporal attention to indicate 'where to look'. However, it lacks a well-defined task and appropriate dataset with labeled ground-truth time stamps to explicitly explore and measure the visual explanations directly. We notice Lei *et al.* [10] also constructed a dataset with temporally annotated QA pairs. However, they still worked on traditional VideoQA task that treated temporal annotation as an additional resource to generate answers. To fill this gap, we propose a new task which requires generating answers and locating visual explanations simultaneously. We also construct a new dataset and two metrics to facilitate its research.

Temporal Localization: Many attempts [6,12,24] of temporal localization aim to detect temporal boundaries of actions or events in untrimmed videos. Although VQA-VE also requires models to temporally localize relevant moments within the video, it goes beyond the case of using natural languages to retrieve the visual contents. Instead, visual explanations and QA pairs are complementary with each other and both serve as guides to enhance the generation of one another.

3   A New Dataset: Activity-QA

3.1   Dataset Collection

VQA-VE consists of two coupled sub-tasks: answers generation and visual explanations. It needs corresponding datasets which have temporally annotated QA pairs. Unfortunately, most existing datasets fail to meet such requirement. Therefore, we build a new dataset called Activity-QA on top of ActivityNet Captions [9].

First we remove videos which only contain static images or blurred scenes. Then we instruct human annotators to give 'valid' QA pairs with the start time and end time to mark the relevant moment, according to video contents and temporally annotated sentence descriptions in ActivityNet Captions. 'valid' means each QA pair is only related to one part in the whole video. In order to construct a video-specific dataset that is different from the image case, we impose constraint according to the temporal and dynamic characteristics of videos: QA pairs we construct are guaranteed to focus on the evolving of events or actions. To ensure the quality of our dataset, we double check the QA pairs. Since video contents in original dataset are diverse, QA pairs that strictly satisfy our demands are hard to construct. In total we collect 12059 QA pairs for 7034 long untrimmed videos. We split them into training and test set for experiment.

We notice a dataset TVQA [10] which also provides temporally annotated QA pairs. Compared with it, ours has two advantages: (1) Our QA form is open-ended. As mentioned in [20], it is a more general and challenging task than the multiple choice form in TVQA. (2) Our QA pairs feature action-centric and time-centric while some QA pairs in TVQA are only about static objects. It allows to find answers by observing single frame with no consideration of temporal dependency of videos, which reduces the native challenges of videos. In order to fully evaluate our task and model, however, we also conduct experiments on TVQA.

3.2   Dataset Analysis

Open-ended: Activity-QA is an open-ended dataset that natural language sentences are expected to be produced word by word as answers. Besides enabling much wider applications, open-ended puts forward higher requirements for models to deal with natural languages, because answers are expected to be complete and fluent sentences instead of one option. Also, without candidates, models can hardly utilize prior information related to answers in the test process. These all bring up more challenges. The length distribution of our questions and answers are shown in Fig. 2. Compared with other open-ended VideoQA datasets [20], our QA pairs are longer. In addition, since our videos are about real-world scenes and collected from Youtube, QA pairs share rich vocabulary diversity. The total number of words appearing in our QA pairs is 4992.

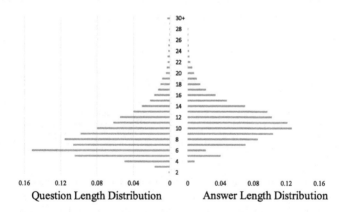

Fig. 2. Length distributions of questions and answers.

Action-Centric and Time-Centric: Corresponding to the dynamic and temporal characteristics of videos, our QA pairs feature action-centric and time-centric. Specifically, questions in Activity-QA are all about the evolving of events or actions. Therefore, to get correct answers, reasoning about temporal clues of videos needs to be well addressed. Besides, most of our questions contain temporal adverbial such as 'after', 'at first', 'the second time' *etc*, which serves as the key to answer questions and locate relevant moments accurately.

Double-Check: After constructing temporally annotated QA pairs, we double check each one manually for ensuring their reasonability and validity. During the double-check process, although the inter-human awareness on the start/end of an event is different, we ensure each QA pair only matches one exact part in the whole video for eliminating the ambiguity when models provide visual explanations. We also believe that these deviations can be ignored after downsampling the video frames. Under those strict standards, we collect 12059 temporally annotated QA pairs for 7034 videos in total.

4   The Proposed Model

4.1   Problem Formulation

The overview of our model is shown in Fig. 3. We denote a long untrimmed video as $V = \{v_t\}_{t=1}^T$, where T is the total frame number of the video. Each video is associated with a set of temporally annotated QA pairs: $Q = (q_i, s_i, t_i^{qs}, t_i^{qe})_{i=1}^M$, where M is the total QA pair number of the video. q_i and s_i denote question and answer which contain various length sequences of words $(w_1, w_2, \ldots, w_n) \in W$. Each q_i and s_i is coupled with a time stamp (t_i^{qs}, t_i^{qe}) as the start and end time of the relevant moment, i.e., the visual explanation in the whole video. Given a video V and a question q_i, the task is to generate an answer s_i' and a time stamp of visual explanation $\left(t_i^{qs'}, t_i^{qe'}\right)$ for the predicted answer.

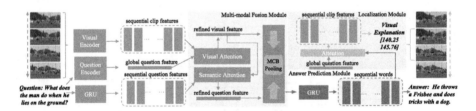

Fig. 3. An overview of our model. The visual encoder, question encoder, and GRU extract clip features and question features. Then multi-modal fusion module refines cross-modal features by visual attention, semantic attention and MCB Pooling to fully fuse refined features. Finally, answer prediction module and localization module are used to generate answers and provide visual explanations.

4.2   Visual Encoder

First, in order to deal with visual explanations which can range across short as well as long sequences of video frames, we use sliding window method to generate a set of candidate clips for each video. Specifically, clips of one video can be represented as $C = (c_i, t_i^{cs}, t_i^{ce})_{i=1}^M$, where M is the total clip number of the video, (t_i^{cs}, t_i^{ce}) denote the start time and end time of the clip c_i. To construct visual feature, we first linearly transform ResNet-200 features from ActivityNet [8] pretrained model into 500 dimension as same as the FC7 layer of C3D features [17], then concatenate them. Features of all clips from one video form sequential clip features $(f_{v1}, f_{v2}, \ldots, f_{vM})$.

4.3   Question Encoder

We extract word feature f_{lqi} by a single-layer GRU [2] for representing each word w_i in the question, then assemble them into sequential question features $(f_{lq1}, f_{lq2}, \ldots, f_{lqn})$ for capturing order and contextual information of the question. Besides, we extract global question feature f_{gq} for representing the semantic information of the whole question. We embed each word as a 300 dimensional vector through an random initialized embedding matrix. Then we feed them into a 512 dimensional single-layer GRU and pick the final hidden state as global question feature.

4.4   Multi-modal Fusion Module

Multi-modal fusion module aims to fully fuse the feature from visual contents and natural languages. We employ visual attention and semantic attention, and use rich ways to combine the generated features. The sequential clip features $(f_{v1}, f_{v2}, \ldots, f_{vM})$ from visual encoder, the sequential question features $(f_{lq1}, f_{lq2}, \ldots, f_{lqn})$ from GRU, and the global question feature f_{gq} from question encoder are input to this module.

First, we employ visual attention that uses global question feature to calculate attention weights for sequential clip features. This mechanism targets to help model selectively focus on semantic-related clips and filter out irrelevant visual information with questions as guidance to get refined visual feature f_V. We then employ semantic attention that uses refined visual feature to calculate attention weights for sequential question features. This mechanism helps model pay different levels of attention to words so as to interpret the whole question based on visual contents then get refined question feature f_Q. Finally, we adopt Multimodal Compact Bilinear pooling [4] to get a joint representation which is an effective multi-modal features fusion method.

4.5   Prediction Module

Our prediction module is used to solve compositional task: generate natural language sentences as answers and locate visual explanations. It consists of two sub-modules: answer prediction module and localization module.

Answer Prediction Module: In answer prediction module, we employ a single-layer GRU to generate each word of answers step by step. The multi-modal representation from multi-modal fusion module serves as an initial state to GRU for guiding the answer generation. The final hidden state of GRU is the input to localization module.

Localization Module: We concatenate the final hidden state of GRU in answer prediction module with global question feature to form semantic guidance for locating visual explanations. Specifically, we use it to calculate attention weights for sequential clip features and assign weights to them to get weighted clip features. Then we feed all weighted clip features into two FC layers to generate localization predicted results: the last FC layer outputs one relevant score and two location regression offsets for each clip. The relevant score denotes the relevant degree between the clip and the QA pair. The location regression offsets denote the differences between ground-truth offsets and predicted offsets. The ground-truth offsets are calculated as:

$$
\begin{aligned}
t_{i,j}^{gs} &= t_i^{qs} - t_j^{cs} \\
t_{i,j}^{ge} &= t_i^{qe} - t_j^{ce}
\end{aligned}
\tag{1}
$$

where $t_{i,j}^{gs}$ and $t_{i,j}^{ge}$ denote the start time offset and end time offset between clip j and QA pair i. t_i^{qs} and t_i^{qe} are the start time and end time of QA pair i, t_j^{cs} and t_j^{ce} are the start time and end time of clip j. The location regression offsets help model adjust the temporal boundaries of the input clip so as to locate relevant moments more accurately.

4.6   Multi-task Loss

The total loss L consists of two parts: L_{ans} for answer loss and L_{loc} for localization loss, and L is formulated as:

$$
L = L_{ans} + \omega L_{loc}
\tag{2}
$$

where ω is a hyper-parameter to balance two loss. For L_{ans} we calculate cross entropy loss, and for L_{loc} we motivated by [6] and calculate as:

$$
L_{loc} = L_{score} + \mu L_{offset}
\tag{3}
$$

where L_{score} is loss for relevant score, and L_{offset} is loss for location regression offsets, μ is a hyper-parameter to balance two loss. Specifically, L_{score} is calculated as:

$$
L_{score} = \frac{1}{N} \sum_{i=1}^{N} \sum_{j=1}^{M} [\lambda log(1 + exp(-z_{i,j=gt})) \\
+ log(1 + exp(z_{i,j \neq gt}))]
\tag{4}
$$

where N is the batch size, M is the total number of clips, $z_{i,j}$ is the relevant score between clip j and QA pair i, $j = gt$ means clip j is the matched clip. λ is a hyper-parameter to balance the number of matched clips and mismatched clips. This loss encourages matched clip has positive score while mismatched one has negative score. And L_{offset} is calculated as:

$$L_{offset} = \frac{1}{N} \sum_{i=1}^{N} \sum_{j=1}^{M} [R(t_{i,j}^{gs} - t_{i,j}^{ps}) + R(t_{i,j}^{ge} - t_{i,j}^{pe})] \tag{5}$$

where $t_{i,j}^{gs}$ and $t_{i,j}^{ge}$ are ground-truth offsets between clip j and QA pair i, $t_{i,j}^{ps}$ and $t_{i,j}^{pe}$ are predicted offsets output by model. $R(\cdot)$ denotes L1 distance function (we also experiment with Smooth-L1 distance function and L2 distance function and find L1 distance function is better). This loss encourages the smallest differences between predicted and ground-truth offsets so as to adjust the clip boundaries, making them closer to the ground-truth boundaries.

5 Experiment

5.1 Training Sample

To deal with visual explanations with various time spans, we use multi-scale temporal sliding windows to collect clips according to the frame number of videos in two datasets. At training time, we use (32, 64, 128, 256, 512) for Activity-QA and (9, 15, 21, 33, 45) for TVQA, with 80% overlap between adjacent clips for dense sampling. At test time, we use coarse sampling for speeding up, with (256, 512) for Activity-QA and (15, 45) for TVQA. For each temporally annotated QA pair $(q_i, s_i, t_i^{qs}, t_i^{qe})$, we assign a sliding window clip $(c_j, t_j^{cs}, t_j^{ce})$ as a matched one if it has the largest IoU with the ground-truth time stamp (t_i^{qs}, t_i^{qe}). We also stipulate that non Intersection over Length (nIoL) [6] between the matched clip and the ground-truth time stamp is smaller than 0.15, because we want most part of the matched clip overlap with the ground-truth. Under these constraints, each QA pair is aligned with only one matched clip. To avoid redundant mismatched samples, we also filter out clips whose IoU smaller than 0.1 with the ground-truth when training (at test time we feed all clips into the model).

5.2 Evaluation Metric

VQA-VE is a compositional task that requires to generate answers and locate relevant moments simultaneously. We consider both and design two new metrics which can fairly measure the performance on VQA-VE. First, we calculate answer quality and localization quality separately by two widely used metrics. For localization quality, we calculate the IoU of localization predicted result $(t_j^{cs} + t_{i,j}^{ps}, t_j^{ce} + t_{i,j}^{pe})$ and ground-truth (t_i^{qs}, t_i^{qe}). For answer quality, we use WUPS and set threshold as 0.0 and 0.9 following the previous works [14, 20]. Then we combine them to measure the whole task quality. When calculated IoU is higher than the given threshold, we set it to 1.0, otherwise 0.0, and multiply with the WUPS score as the whole task quality. In this case, we consider the predicted answer is valid only if models can provide a convincing and accurate visual explanation (IoU with ground-truth is higher than the given threshold) for it. Specifically, we compute 'WUPS=n, IoU=m' which means we set threshold n for WUPS and m for IoU, and '$R@t$' means the top-t results we pick to calculate the IoU.

5.3 Baseline Methods

VQA-VE requires generating natural language sentences as answers and locating relevant moments simultaneously. Therefore, we use methods proposed in the previous work [20,23] for open-ended VideoQA as answer prediction module and combine with our localization module to construct some baseline methods. Specifically, **E-SS** [23] extends Sequence-to-Sequence model [18], **E-VQA** [23] uses two GRU to encode videos and questions, and **E-SA** [20] applies soft attention [19] on sequential video features. Besides, we use **CTRL** [6] proposed for language based temporal localization as localization module and combine with our answer prediction module as another baseline method. We also experiment with different variants of our model: **QA-VE** is our proposed model, **V-mean** and **S-mean** use temporal mean pooling instead of visual attention or semantic attention, **AM-C** uses element-wise addition, element-wise multiplication and concatenation [6] instead of MCB Pooling to fuse cross-modal features, and **R-loss** uses the loss only for the relevant clips instead of L_{offset}. The relevant clips are based on the relevant score $z_{i,j}$.

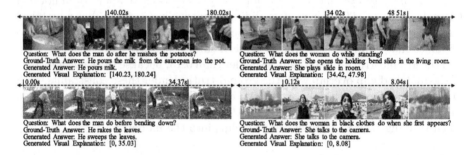

Fig. 4. Qualitative results generated by our proposed model on Activity-QA. Time stamps above the dashed line denote ground-truth time stamps of visual explanations, and words in red are generated results by our proposed model.

5.4 Experiments on Activity-QA

We report the results on Activity-QA in Table 1. From the result we can see that our model achieves the best performance over other methods on all three metrics, demonstrating its effectiveness. Besides, we notice performances of all methods on 'WUPS = 0.9' are more lower than 'WUPS = 0.0', suggesting that generating complete and long sentences as answers that as similar as (threshold higher than 0.9) the ground-truth is challenging.

Table 1. Performances on Activity-QA evaluated by metric (R@5).

Method	WUPS = 0.0			WUPS = 0.9		
	IoU = 0.1	IoU = 0.3	IoU = 0.5	IoU = 0.1	IoU = 0.3	IoU = 0.5
E-VQA	22.94	17.75	10.19	2.86	2.12	1.26
E-SS	25.14	19.36	11.13	4.14	3.18	1.71
E-SA	25.88	18.82	10.17	3.64	2.55	1.22
CTRL	23.62	17.52	10.26	4.54	3.47	2.18
Q-mean	33.70	23.64	12.36	6.75	6.76	2.17
S-mean	33.63	23.78	12.41	8.14	5.68	2.82
AM-C	38.88	29.11	16.44	10.69	7.79	4.39
R-loss	47.72	35.69	19.73	5.30	3.99	2.15
QA-VE	**55.33**	**41.66**	**23.60**	**10.89**	**7.83**	**4.54**

The reason for inferior performances of VideoQA based methods might be that they don't fully fuse cross-modal features. Besides, we notice CTRL based model performs better to some extend compared with other baseline methods on 'IoU = 0.5'. The reason we suggest is that the former additionally concatenates features of QA pairs for localization, demonstrating visual explanations are related to both questions and answers.

For variants of our model, the inferior performances of V-mean and S-mean indicate the order information is crucial for understanding the contents. Besides, temporal mean pooling may destroy the sequential structure of videos and questions. For videos, capturing the temporal correlations of frames or clips can learn the time order and development of events or actions. For questions, temporally accumulating the understanding of words and their context is beneficial to comprehend the meaning of the whole sentence. In addition, the performance of QA-VE suggests that MCB Pooling performs better than simple operations and concatenation when fusing cross-modal features. We also find that the loss only for the relevant clips is not sufficient by the experiments on R-loss. This result shows that reducing location regression offsets can improve global performances. There is an obvious relation between locating explanations and answering process. We also show some qualitative results generated by our model in Fig. 4.

Table 2. Performance on TVQA evaluated by metric (R@5).

Method	WUPS = 0.0			WUPS = 0.9		
	IoU = 0.1	IoU = 0.3	IoU = 0.5	IoU = 0.1	IoU = 0.3	IoU = 0.5
E-VQA	16.30	12.40	2.80	3.36	2.52	0.70
E-SS	11.60	9.17	2.85	2.97	2.31	0.75
E-SA	19.54	9.75	1.47	5.13	2.64	0.39
CTRL	13.96	8.79	1.50	3.64	2.33	0.36
Q-mean	17.69	12.15	2.73	4.56	2.99	0.71
S-mean	10.57	7.88	2.12	2.77	2.01	0.63
AM-C	20.62	14.22	2.90	5.17	3.61	0.82
R-loss	25.92	18.32	4.70	4.15	3.17	0.73
QA-VE	**26.71**	**19.20**	**5.20**	**5.43**	**3.99**	**1.01**

Table 3. Performance on traditional VideoQA task.

Method	Activity-QA			TVQA		
	W0	W9	METEOR	W0	W9	METEOR
Q-A	39.12	11.21	12.61	21.73	4.34	8.45
AM-C	46.38	12.11	13.77	24.97	5.27	9.79
QA-VE	**64.74**	**13.31**	**14.05**	**31.70**	**6.49**	**11.32**

5.5   Experiments on TVQA

TVQA 152.5K temporally annotated QA pairs 21.8K videos. We report the results in Table 2. Since TVQA only provides ResNet-101 [7] features, we use it as sequential clip features. We extend TVQA into open-ended by using the correct candidate as the answer. The results are consistent with Activity-QA. However, we notice the overall performance on TVQA compared with Activity-QA are lower. We suggest the reasons are three-folds: (1) Features from ResNet101 may leads to inferior performance. (2) The average length of QA pairs in TVQA is 76.2, such longer dependency may not be well captured by GRU. (3) Some QA pairs in TVQA are only about static objects, it may hard to locate accurate evidences for them from temporal dimension.

5.6   Experiments on Traditional VideoQA Task

We do further experiments that only measure the answer quality by WUPS and METEOR [3] to evaluate the impact of visual explanations on traditional open-ended Video-QA task. METEOR is a popular metrics for video caption and used to score answers by aligning them to ground truths. Here we adopt it as a reference and 'Wn' means we set threshold n for WUPS. We use our proposed model as **QA-VE** and the model that only contains answer prediction module as **Q-A**.

In other words, we train **QA-VE** with the multi-task loss and train **Q-A** only with the answer loss. From Table 3 we can see that **QA-VE** performs better. It suggests that with the sub-task of providing visual explanations, models can achieve better performance on traditional VideoQA task. We believe the reason might be that locating the correct moment means models can filter out redundant visual contents to catch the semantic-related visual clues in relative range compared with the whole long video. The results support the complementary nature between visual explanations and QA in that the supervision of visual explanations help models predict more accurate answers.

6   Conclusion

In this paper, we propose a new task called VQA-VE, which requires to generate answers and provide visual explanations for predicted answers simultaneously. To facilitate its research, we construct a new dataset called Activity-QA and adopt TVQA. We also develop a new model of multi-task framework to address it and design two metrics to fairly measure the performance on VQA-VE. Experimental results not only show the effectiveness of our model, but also suggest that additional supervision of visual explanations can help models better solve traditional VideoQA task.

Acknowledgement. This work is supported by the NSFC (under Grant 61876130, 61932009).

References

1. Antol, S., et al.: VQA: visual question answering. In: ICCV (2015)
2. Cho, K., et al.: Learning phrase representations using RNN encoder-decoder for statistical machine translation. In: EMNLP (2014)
3. Denkowski, M., Lavie, A.: Meteor universal: Language specific translation evaluation for any target language. In: Proceedings of the Ninth Workshop on Statistical Machine Translation, pp. 376–380 (2014)
4. Fukui, A., Park, D.H., Yang, D., Rohrbach, A., Darrell, T., Rohrbach, M.: Multimodal compact bilinear pooling for visual question answering and visual grounding. arXiv preprint arXiv:1606.01847 (2016)
5. Gao, J., Ge, R., Chen, K., Nevatia, R.: Motion-appearance co-memory networks for video question answering. In: CVPR (2018)
6. Gao, J., Sun, C., Yang, Z., Nevatia, R.: Tall: temporal activity localization via language query. In: ICCV (2017)
7. He, K., Zhang, X., Ren, S., Sun, J.: Deep residual learning for image recognition. In: CVPR (2016)
8. Heilbron, F.C., Escorcia, V., Ghanem, B., Niebles, J.C.: ActivityNet: a large-scale video benchmark for human activity understanding. In: CVPR (2015)
9. Krishna, R., Hata, K., Ren, F., Fei-Fei, L., Niebles, J.C.: Dense-captioning events in videos. In: ICCV (2017)
10. Lei, J., Yu, L., Bansal, M., Berg, T.L.: TVQA: localized, compositional video question answering. In: EMNLP (2018)

11. Liang, J., Jiang, L., Cao, L., Kalantidis, Y., Li, L.J., Hauptmann, A.G.: Focal visual-text attention for memex question answering. IEEE Trans. Pattern Anal. Mach. Intell. **41**(8), 1893–1908 (2019)

12. Lin, T., Zhao, X., Su, H., Wang, C., Yang, M.: BSN: boundary sensitive network for temporal action proposal generation. In: Ferrari, V., Hebert, M., Sminchisescu, C., Weiss, Y. (eds.) ECCV 2018. LNCS, vol. 11208, pp. 3–21. Springer, Cham (2018). https://doi.org/10.1007/978-3-030-01225-0_1

13. Maharaj, T., Ballas, N., Rohrbach, A., Courville, A., Pal, C.: A dataset and exploration of models for understanding video data through fill-in-the-blank question-answering. In: CVPR, pp. 7359–7368 (2017)

14. Malinowski, M., Fritz, M.: A multi-world approach to question answering about real-world scenes based on uncertain input. In: NIPS, pp. 1682–1690 (2014)

15. Park, D.H., et al.: Multimodal explanations: justifying decisions and pointing to the evidence. In: CVPR (2018)

16. Song, X., Shi, Y., Chen, X., Han, Y.: Explore multi-step reasoning for video question answering. In: ACM MM (2018)

17. Tran, D., Bourdev, L., Fergus, R., Torresani, L., Paluri, M.: Learning spatiotemporal features with 3D convolutional networks. In: ICCV (2015)

18. Venugopalan, S., Rohrbach, M., Donahue, J., Mooney, R., Darrell, T., Saenko, K.: Sequence to sequence - video to text. In: ICCV (2015)

19. Xu, K., et al.: Show, attend and tell: neural image caption generation with visual attention. In: ICML (2015)

20. Xue, H., Zhao, Z., Cai, D.: Unifying the video and question attentions for open-ended video question answering. IEEE TIP **26**, 5656–5666 (2017)

21. Yu, Y., Ko, H., Choi, J., Kim, G.: End-to-end concept word detection for video captioning, retrieval, and question answering. In: CVPR (2017)

22. Yu, Z., et al..: ActivityNet-QA: a dataset for understanding complex web videos via question answering. arXiv preprint arXiv:1906.02467 (2019)

23. Zeng, K., Chen, T., Chuang, C., Liao, Y., Niebles, J.C., Sun, M.: Leveraging video descriptions to learn video question answering. In: AAAI (2017)

24. Zhao, Y., Xiong, Y., Wang, L., Wu, Z., Tang, X., Lin, D.: Temporal action detection with structured segment networks. In: ICCV (2017)

25. Zhao, Z., et al.: Open-ended long-form video question answering via adaptive hierarchical reinforced networks. In: IJCAI, pp. 3683–3689 (2018)

Global Cognition and Local Perception Network for Blind Image Deblurring

Chuanfa Zhang, Wei Zhang, Feiyu Chen, Yiting Cheng, Shuyong Gao, and Wenqiang Zhang$^{(\boxtimes)}$

Shanghai Key Laboratory of Intelligent Information Processing,
School of Computer Science, Fudan University, Shanghai, China
wqzhang@fudan.edu.cn

Abstract. Nowadays, people are more and more used to taking pictures with handheld devices. However, the photos taken by handheld devices are easy to blur. Recent state-of-the-art methods for image deblurring often restore image through multiple stages, which leads to excessive network parameters and slow running speed, and makes it difficult to apply to mobile devices. While one-stage image deblurring methods have fewer parameters and faster running speed, the performance of their models is not so satisfactory. To solve these problems, we propose a lightweight one-stage image deblurring network called Global Cognition and Local Perception Network (GCLPN) in this paper. We design the Global Cognition Module (GCM) to obtain global feature descriptors and present the Local Perception Module (LPM) to help image reconstruction in local regions. Furthermore, we introduce a gradient loss that focuses on subtle image texture information during network training. Experimental results illustrate that our GCLPN surpasses the state-of-the-art methods in standard metrics of PSNR and SSIM with the least number of parameters (about 1.7M) and real-time running speed (about 0.37 s per 720×1280 image).

Keywords: Blind image deblurring · Deep learning · Lightweight neural network · Global and local cognition · Gradient loss

1 Introduction

Blind image deblurring aims to restore the blurred image into the corresponding sharp image. It is also used as a pre-processing step of other computer vision tasks (e.g. image classification, object detection, etc.). A blurred image can be modeled as,

$$B = K \otimes I + N, \tag{1}$$

where B, K, I, N, and $\otimes$ denote the blurred images, blur kernel, original sharp images, additive noise, and convolution operation, respectively. And this is a

This work was supported by Fudan University-CIOMP Joint Fund (FC2019-005), National Key R&D Program of China (2019YFC1711800).

© Springer Nature Switzerland AG 2021
J. Lokoč et al. (Eds.): MMM 2021, LNCS 12572, pp. 303–314, 2021.
https://doi.org/10.1007/978-3-030-67832-6_25

highly ill-posed problem, because for a give input B, its solution K and I are not unique.

In recent years, Convolutional Neural Network (CNN) has achieved excellent performance in a variety of computer vision tasks, including image deblurring [2,5]. The state-of-the-art CNN based methods usually employ the multi-stage scheme to get sharp image output progressively. As shown in Fig. 1(a), following a multi-scale manner [4,11,14], the image is restored from lower resolution to higher resolution. And a multi-patch manner [18] is illustrated in Fig. 1(b). This manner first restores small patches then gradually expands to the whole image. Although multi-stage methods have achieved good performance, the cumbersome parameters and long running time make these methods can not satisfy the requirements of the practical application on robots or mobile devices.

The one-stage CNN based methods [1,9,10] try to restore image directly from the original resolution input. The one-stage methods have fewer parameters and faster running speed than multi-stage methods but have worse performance than multi-stage methods due to the lack of the global view of image understanding.

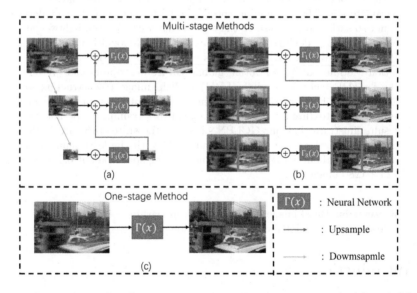

Fig. 1. The pipelines of multi-stage networks and one-stage network. (a) and (b) are multi-stage methods, and (c) is the pipeline of the one-stage method.

In this paper, we design a Global Cognition and Local Perception Network (GCLPN) for blind image deblurring. Considering the practical value of GCLPN, we employ a one-stage framework instead of the multi-stage framework due to the heavy parameters and slow running speed multi-stage framework has. And to make up for the defect that the one-stage model is difficult to gain the overall image features, we propose a Global Cognition Module (GCM) to extract the global information of the input image, which is effective in promoting performance with no extra parameters introduced. Furthermore, we design a Local Perception Module (LPM) for the dynamic combination of the local and the global features. As for loss function, to tackle the problem that traditional Mean Square Error (MSE) loss usually leads to smooth output and ignores the heterogeneousness of texture, we introduce a gradient loss function to help restore image texture. Further experiments show the superiority of our GCLPN.

Our contributions are summarized as follows:

- We propose a one-stage blind image deblurring network called Global Cognition and Local Perception Network (GCLPN). Our GCLPN contains GCM and LPM, GCM is used to extract the global feature, LPM is used to combine the local feature and the global feature dynamically. Experimental results show that GCM and LPM can improve network performance with a small number of parameters introduced.
- We introduce a gradient loss function based on the gradient changes on the x-axis and y-axis. Due to the gradient variety usually occur on object texture, our gradient loss can correct the smooth texture caused by MSE loss.
- Our GCLPN not only achieves the state-of-the-art performance of PSNR and SSIM but also has fewer parameters and faster running speed compared to other image deblurring methods.

2   Related Work

2.1   Image Deblurring

Multi-stage Deblurring. The pipeline of Multi-stage deblurring methods is shown in Fig. 1 (a) and (b). Fig. 1 (a) follows a coarse-to-fine protocol, restores the image from the lower-resolution to the higher-resolution gradually [4,11,14]. And Fig. 1 (b) follows a patch-to-whole protocol, restores the image from several patches to the whole image [17]. However, the huge amount of parameters and slow running speed make it difficult to put multi-stage methods into the use of mobile phones, robots, and other embedded devices. Different from these works, our GCLPN has a higher practical application value with less memory cost and faster running speed.

One-Stage Deblurring. Based on Generative Adversarial Networks (GAN), Kupyn et al. [9,10] proposed 2 one-stage image deblurring networks, called DeblurGAN and DeblurGANv2. DeblurGAN [9] simply stacked 9 ResBlocks as the generator and DeblurGANv2 [10] follow the FPN framework to explore the trade-off between performance and efficiency of different backbones. Although DeblurGAN and DeblurGANv2 have less parameter and shorter running time than multi-stage methods, the performance of DeblurGAN and DeblurGANv2 is barely satisfactory especially when processing large image blur due to the small size of the receptive field. Aljadaany et al. [1] designed a one-stage image deblurring network based on Douglas-Rachford iterations, but a large number of parameters limit the running speed. While our GCLPN, with the cooperation of the GCM and LPM, achieves better performance than multi-stage methods.

2.2   Attention Mechanism

The attention mechanism aims to help the network focus on the important information on the feature map. It can be explained using human biological systems. For example, the human visual processing system tends to focus selectively on parts of the image while ignoring other irrelevant information. And the attention mechanism has been used in many natural language processing tasks and computer vision tasks. The Transformer [15] proposes the self-attention mechanism to draw global dependencies of inputs and applies it in machine translation. The NL [16] explores the effectiveness of the non-local operation in the spatial dimension for videos and images. The SE-Net [6] gets the channel relationship of the feature map through a "Squeeze-and-Excitation" manner. In this paper, to get the long-range information, we add a self-attention at the beginning of GCM, and to obtain the importance of each pixel, we propose a point-wise attention module called LPM.

3   Proposed Method

In this section, we give the details about our Global Cognition and Local Perception Network (GCLPN). First, we show the overall architecture of GCLPN in Sect. 3.1. Second, we introduce our Global Cognition Module (GCM) to capture the global image features in Sect. 3.2. GCM helps restore the large image blur but performs badly when blur limit in a small region. And to enable the network to recognize the local blur and global blur adaptively, we design the Local Perception Module (LPM) in Sect. 3.3. Finally, as the MSE loss tends to produce smooth output, we propose the gradient loss to force the network to understand the importance of sharpness in Sect. 3.4.

3.1   Network Architecture

Our GCLPN is built on an encoder-decoder framework. And the downsample and upsample are performed by a convolution and a deconvolution of two-stride, respectively. Our encoder consists of three levels, the first level and the second level have the same architecture of seven convolutional layers, three residual links, and four Leaky Rectified Linear Units (Leaky ReLu). And we stack two GCMs in the third level. Our decoder also has three levels with the same architecture of one convolutional layer and two deformable blocks. The pipeline of our GCLPN demonstrates in Fig. 2.

Note that, the deformable convolution [3,19] is used for image reconstruction in our GCLPN. The intuition is that traditional convolutional layers perform convolution operators within a grid, while deformable convolutional layers learn an offset so the convolution operators are more flexible. And deformable convolution is robust when dealing with the image that contains blurred region and sharp region simultaneously.

Moreover, we add an LPM between the encoder and the decoder because either the direct sum or concatenate can not exchange the information from

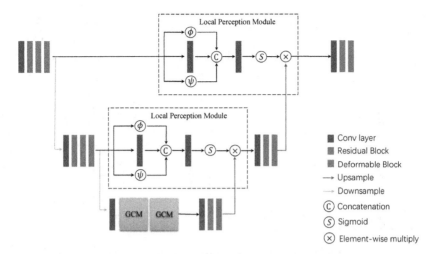

Fig. 2. The pipeline of our proposed network. We use residual blocks for the feature extraction and use deformable blocks for image reconstruction. ϕ and ψ indicate the mean value and the max value along the channel dimension, respectively.

the encoder to decoder sufficiently. Our LPM first extracts the local position descriptors then combines the local position descriptors and the global features in a dynamic way. The experiment shows LPM outperforms the sum or concatenate. More details of LPM is shown in Sect. 3.3.

3.2 Global Cognition Module

The predicted image of One-stage image deblurring methods usually contains many artifacts [9,10] due to the lack of global cognition of the input image, especially when the whole input image is blurred. To tackle this problem, we design the Global Cognition Module (GCM) to produce the global cognition information of the input image.

As demonstrated in Fig. 3, our GCM first consists of a self-attention layer, which can be defined as:

$$Attention_{i,j} = \sum_{k,l \in \mathcal{N}} \sigma(A_{i,j}^T B_{k,l}) X_{k,l}, \tag{2}$$

where $\mathcal{N}$ is the whole location lattice, σ is a sigmoid function, A is the query, B is the key, and $X \in \mathbb{R}^{h \times w \times d_{in}}$ is the input. Then we split the output into groups, each group passes a convolutional layer with the output of the former group together. This procedure can be modeled as:

$$y_i = \omega_i(p_i + y_{i-1}), \tag{3}$$

$$out = \delta(\mathcal{C}(y_i))(i = 0, 1, 2, 3), \tag{4}$$

where $p_i \in \mathbb{R}^{\frac{d_{in}}{4} \times h \times w}(i = 0, 1, 2, 3)$ is equally divided from input $x \in \mathbb{R}^{d_{in} \times h \times w}$ along channels, ω represents a convolution layer, $\mathcal{C}$ denotes concatenation through the channel dimension and δ is a Leaky Relu non-linear layer.

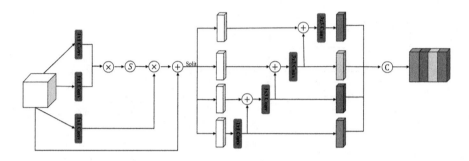

Fig. 3. Our Global Cognition Module (GCM).

3.3   Local Perception Module

As mentioned above, GCM tends to extract a global feature descriptor, which is beneficial for removing large blur kernels. Nevertheless, the global feature is dominated by sharp information when blur happens in a small region, and in this case, the global feature has less ability for blur region restoration. To enhance the perception for local region blur we design a Local Perception Module (LPM).

As the feature map after GCM has a global receptive field and our LPM aims to get a local perception of the image. Thus, we choose the feature map before GCM as the input of LPM. Specifically, for each level l, we use E_{out}^l, D_{in}^l and D_{out}^l denote the output of the encoder, the input of decoder and the output of the decoder. The local perception is gained by:

$$lp_1 = \omega_1(E_{out}^l), \tag{5}$$

$$lp_2 = \phi(E_{out}^l), \tag{6}$$

$$lp_3 = \psi(E_{out}^l), \tag{7}$$

$$LP = \mathcal{C}(lp_i)(i = 1, 2, 3), \tag{8}$$

where $\omega_1 \in \mathcal{R}^{1 \times d_{in} \times 1 \times 1}$ is a point-wise convolutional layer, $\phi(x) \in \mathcal{R}^{n \times 1 \times h \times w}$ and $\psi(x) \in \mathcal{R}^{n \times 1 \times h \times w}$ are the mean value and the max value of an input $x \in \mathbb{R}^{n \times d \times h \times w}$ along channel dimension. Note that, all the operations are performed in the channel dimension because the input E_{out}^l already has a local receptive filed and we want to compress the local information into more representative information in this step.

Considering that our network should dynamically choose the importance of local features and global features under different inputs, we utilize LP to form a score map and use the score map combine with D_{out}^l. This procedure is modeled as:

$$Score = \sigma(\omega_2(LP))(i = 1, 2, 3), \tag{9}$$

$$D^l_{in} = Score \otimes D^{l-1}_{out}, \tag{10}$$

where $\omega_2 \in \mathcal{R}^{1 \times 3 \times 1 \times 1}$ is a convolutional layer, σ is a sigmoid function, and $\otimes$ is element-wise multiply operation.

3.4 Loss

Our GCLPN leverages three losses. The first loss is Mean Square Error (MSE) loss, which is widely used in image deblurring [4,11,14,17,18].

$$\mathcal{L}_{MSE} = \frac{1}{N} \sum_{i=1}^{h} \sum_{j=1}^{w} ||I_{i,j} - I^*_{i,j}||^2_2, \tag{11}$$

where $N = h * w$ is the number of total pixel of the input image, and $I_{i,j}$, $I^*_{i,j}$ are the predicted output and the ground truth at pixel (i, j), respectively.

$\mathcal{L}_{MSE}$ pays more attention to reducing the difference in image contents and has less ability when handling subtle texture features. As image deblurring task needs to restore sharp object boundary, we use a gradient loss during training that can be expressed as:

$$\mathcal{L}_{gradient} = ||(\nabla x(I) - \nabla x(I^*))||_2 + ||(\nabla y(I) - \nabla y(I^*))||_2, \tag{12}$$

where ∇x and ∇y represent the spatial derivative along with the horizontal and vertical directions, respectively. As shown in Fig. 4, MSE loss is calculated in terms of Fig. 4 (a) and Fig. 4 (c). So MSE cares more about image color and content, the blurring of the boundary does not have a significant effect on the value of MSE. MSE tends to minimize the average difference, and the averaged boundary that MSE produced can be seen as another form of image blur. But our gradient loss is calculated in terms of Fig. 4 (b) and Fig. 4 (d). The gradient loss has eliminated the interfere of image color and content and focuses on the difference of image texture. Adversarial loss and perceptual loss [7] are two ways to optimize the metric of SSIM, but both of those losses need an extra network, which means extra forward and backward process, and slow training speed. So we directly optimize the SSIM in the following means:

$$\mathcal{L}_s = 1 - SSIM(I, I^*). \tag{13}$$

Our total loss is defined as:

$$\mathcal{L}_{overall} = \alpha \mathcal{L}_{MSE} + \beta \mathcal{L}_{gradient} + \gamma \mathcal{L}_s, \tag{14}$$

where α, β and γ are hyper-parameters.

| (a) | (b) | (c) | (d) |

Fig. 4. The difference between images and corresponding gradient maps. (a) and (c) represent blurry image and original sharp image, respectively. (b) is the gradient map of (a) and (d) is the gradient map of (c).

4   Experiments

4.1   Details

We evaluate our GCLPN on a single NVIDIA Titan Xp GPU and implement the network using PyTorch. GCLPN is trained on GOPRO dataset [11], which contains 3214 image pairs. Following the same protocol in [11], 2103 image pairs are used for training and the remaining 1111 pairs for evaluation. We adopt Adam with $\beta_1 = 0.9$, $\beta_2 = 0.999$ and $\epsilon = 10^{-8}$ to optimize our model. The initial learning rate is set to 0.0001 and decay to 0. The hyper-parameters α, β and γ are set to 1, 0.1, 0.1, respectively. The network is trained for 5000 epochs with the batch size of 8.

Table 1. Quantitative results on GOPRO dataset.

Method	[8]	[13]	[5]	[12]	[11]	[9]	[14]	[10]	[17]	[1]	[4]	**GCLPN**
PSNR	23.64	24.64	27.19	28.94	29.08	28.70	30.26	28.17	30.21	30.35	30.92	**31.24**
SSIM	0.824	0.843	0.908	0.922	0.914	0.958	0.934	0.925	0.934	**0.961**	0.942	**0.946**
Parm(M)	–	–	–	–	21	–	6.4	3.3	5.4	6.7	2.8	**1.7**
Time	1 h	20 m	–	–	3.09 s	0.85 s	1.87 s	0.04 s	0.02 s	1.2 s	1.6 s	**0.37 s**

4.2   Metric

The standard metrics of image deblurring are Peak Signal-Noise Ratio (PSNR) and Structural Similarity (SSIM). PSNR measures image similarity from the difference between pixels, and SSIM measures image similarity from brightness, contrast, and structure.

$$PSNR = 10 log_{10}(\frac{MAX}{\mathcal{L}_{MSE}}),$$

$$SSIM = \frac{(2\mu_I\mu_{I^*} + c_1)(2\sigma_{II^*} + c_2)}{(\mu_I^2 + \mu_{I^*}^2 + c_1)(\sigma_I^2 + \sigma_{I^*}^2 + c_2)},$$

where MAX is the max pixel value of the image (usually 255 or 1), μ_I, μ_{I^*}, σ_I, σ_{I^*} and σ_{II^*} are the mean value, variance, and covariance of image I and I^*, respectively. And $c1 = 0.01L$, $c2 = 0.03L$ are constants, where L is the range of pixel values. With the PSNR and SSIM measure the quantity of the network output, we also evaluate the efficiency of our GCLPN by network parameters and running time.

4.3 Evaluation

To verify the effectiveness of our GCLPN, we compare it with existing state-of-the-art image deblurring approaches a thorough quantitative and qualitative experiment.

We evaluate the predicted image with the standard metrics of Peak Signal-Noise Ratio (PSNR) and Structural Similarity (SSIM) on the GOPRO testing set. The quantitative results of our GCLPN and other state-of-the-art methods are shown in Table 1. Our GCLPN produces superior results (31.24dB in PSNR and 0.946 in SSIM) comparing to the recent state-of-the-art multi-stage method [4]. And compared with [4], GCLPN also reduces the network parameter by 60% and increases the running time by 432%.

As demonstrated in Fig. 5, we also select some representative methods (one-stage methods DeblurGANv2 [10] and multi-stage methods SRN [14] and PSS-SRN [4]) for qualitative evaluation. The doorframe in the first row and the legs of pedestrians in the last row show that our network is better than SRN and PSS-SRN at restoring the local regions and preserving details of the image. And DeblurrGANv2 contains many artifacts when the entire input image is blurred (e.g. the second and last row in Fig. 5), but our GCLPN produces more reasonable results due to the global cognition provided by GCM.

Table 2. Ablation study of our method. DB and GL represent the DeformableBlocks and Gradient Loss. Rwrs, rwc and rws are abbreviations for "replaced with resblocks", "replaced with concatenation" and "replaced with summation", respectively.

Model	GCLPN1	GCLPN2	GCLPN3	GCLPN4	GCLPN5	GCLPN6	GCLPN (final)
DB	Rwrs	✓	✓	✓	✓	✓	✓
GCM	Rwrs	Rwrs	✓	✓	✓	✓	✓
LPM	Rwc	Rwc	Rwc	Rwc	Rws	✓	✓
GL				✓	✓		✓
PSNR	29.81	30.12	30.29	30.63	30.52	31.02	31.24
SSIM	0.928	0.934	0.940	0.943	0.942	0.944	0.946

4.4 Ablation Study

To evaluate the effectiveness of the functional component proposed by our network, we design several baseline networks and show the ablation study result in Table 2. From GCLPN1, GCLPN2, GCLPN3, GCLPN6 to GCLPN(final),

| DeblurGANv2[8] | SRN[2] | PSS-SRN[5] | GCLPN |

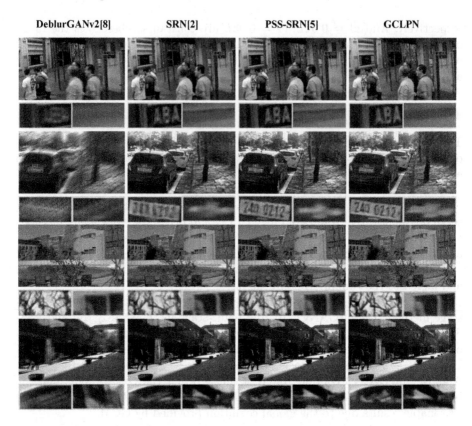

Fig. 5. Qualitative evaluation. From left to right are the predicted sharp image and two zoom-in detail picture use [4, 10, 14] and our GCLPN, respectively.

we gradually add our proposed modules until getting the final network, and the metrics of PSNR and SSIM indicate that every component is effective in promoting the network performance. Furthermore, our LPM achieves much better performance than feature map concatenation or summation due to the local perception mechanism and the dynamic combination with the global feature, compared GCLPN4 and GCLPN5 with GCLPN (final).

5 Conclusion

In this paper, we propose a one-stage network with fewer parameters and higher running speed. Our network has fewer artifacts than previous one-stage networks and outperforms recent state-of-the-art multi-stage networks. Our GCLPN first uses GCM to get a global view of the input image and then uses LPM to help local region reconstruction. Moreover, as MSE loss leads the output object boundary to be somewhat smooth, the gradient loss is proposed to preserve more texture information. The ablation evaluations and experimental comparisons demonstrate that the proposed GCLPN outperforms state-of-the-art methods under standard metrics of PSNR and SSIM while reducing 60% parameters and increasing 432% running speed compared with multi-stage methods.

References

1. Aljadaany, R., Pal, D.K., Savvides, M.: Douglas-Rachford networks: learning both the image prior and data fidelity terms for blind image deconvolution. In: IEEE Conference on Computer Vision and Pattern Recognition. CVPR 2019, Long Beach, CA, USA, 16–20 June 2019 (2019). https://doi.org/10.1109/CVPR.2019.01048
2. Chakrabarti, A.: A neural approach to blind motion deblurring. In: Leibe, B., Matas, J., Sebe, N., Welling, M. (eds.) ECCV 2016. LNCS, vol. 9907, pp. 221–235. Springer, Cham (2016). https://doi.org/10.1007/978-3-319-46487-9_14
3. Dai, J., et al.: Deformable convolutional networks. In: IEEE International Conference on Computer Vision. ICCV 2017, Venice, Italy, 22–29 October 2017 (2017). https://doi.org/10.1109/ICCV.2017.89
4. Gao, H., Tao, X., Shen, X., Jia, J.: Dynamic scene deblurring with parameter selective sharing and nested skip connections. In: IEEE Conference on Computer Vision and Pattern Recognition. CVPR 2019, Long Beach, CA, USA, 16–20 June 2019 (2019). https://doi.org/10.1109/CVPR.2019.00397
5. Gong, D., et al.: From motion blur to motion flow: a deep learning solution for removing heterogeneous motion blur. In: 2017 IEEE Conference on Computer Vision and Pattern Recognition. CVPR 2017, Honolulu, HI, USA, 21–26 July 2017 (2017). https://doi.org/10.1109/CVPR.2017.405
6. Hu, J., Shen, L., Sun, G.: Squeeze-and-excitation networks. In: 2018 IEEE Conference on Computer Vision and Pattern Recognition. CVPR 2018, Salt Lake City, UT, USA, 18–22 June 2018 (2018). https://doi.org/10.1109/CVPR.2018.00745
7. Johnson, J., Alahi, A., Fei-Fei, L.: Perceptual losses for real-time style transfer and super-resolution. In: Leibe, B., Matas, J., Sebe, N., Welling, M. (eds.) ECCV 2016. LNCS, vol. 9906, pp. 694–711. Springer, Cham (2016). https://doi.org/10.1007/978-3-319-46475-6_43
8. Kim, T.H., Lee, K.M.: Segmentation-free dynamic scene deblurring. In: 2014 IEEE Conference on Computer Vision and Pattern Recognition. CVPR 2014, Columbus, OH, USA, 23–28 June 2014 (2014). https://doi.org/10.1109/CVPR.2014.348
9. Kupyn, O., Budzan, V., Mykhailych, M., Mishkin, D., Matas, J.: DeblurGAN: blind motion deblurring using conditional adversarial networks. In: 2018 IEEE Conference on Computer Vision and Pattern Recognition. CVPR 2018, Salt Lake City, UT, USA, 18–22 June 2018 (2018). https://doi.org/10.1109/CVPR.2018.00854
10. Kupyn, O., Martyniuk, T., Wu, J., Wang, Z.: DeblurGAN-v2: deblurring (orders-of-magnitude) faster and better. In: 2019 IEEE/CVF International Conference on Computer Vision. ICCV 2019, Seoul, Korea (South), 27 October–2 November 2019 (2019). https://doi.org/10.1109/ICCV.2019.00897
11. Nah, S., Kim, T.H., Lee, K.M.: Deep multi-scale convolutional neural network for dynamic scene deblurring. In: 2017 IEEE Conference on Computer Vision and Pattern Recognition. CVPR 2017, Honolulu, HI, USA, 21–26 July 2017 (2017). https://doi.org/10.1109/CVPR.2017.35

12. Ramakrishnan, S., Pachori, S., Gangopadhyay, A., Raman, S.: Deep generative filter for motion deblurring. In: 2017 IEEE International Conference on Computer Vision Workshops. ICCV Workshops 2017, Venice, Italy, 22–29 October 2017 (2017). https://doi.org/10.1109/ICCVW.2017.353

13. Sun, J., Cao, W., Xu, Z., Ponce, J.: Learning a convolutional neural network for non-uniform motion blur removal. In: IEEE Conference on Computer Vision and Pattern Recognition. CVPR 2015, Boston, MA, USA, 7–12 June 2015 (2015). https://doi.org/10.1109/CVPR.2015.7298677

14. Tao, X., Gao, H., Shen, X., Wang, J., Jia, J.: Scale-recurrent network for deep image deblurring. In: 2018 IEEE Conference on Computer Vision and Pattern Recognition. CVPR 2018, Salt Lake City, UT, USA, 18–22 June 2018 (2018). https://doi.org/10.1109/CVPR.2018.00853

15. Vaswani, A., et al.: Attention is all you need. In: Advances in Neural Information Processing Systems 30: Annual Conference on Neural Information Processing Systems 2017, Long Beach, CA, USA, 4–9 December 2017 (2017)

16. Wang, X., Girshick, R.B., Gupta, A., He, K.: Non-local neural networks. In: 2018 IEEE Conference on Computer Vision and Pattern Recognition. CVPR 2018, Salt Lake City, UT, USA, 18–22 June 2018 (2018). https://doi.org/10.1109/CVPR.2018.00813

17. Zhang, H., Dai, Y., Li, H., Koniusz, P.: Deep stacked hierarchical multi-patch network for image deblurring. In: IEEE Conference on Computer Vision and Pattern Recognition. CVPR 2019, Long Beach, CA, USA, 16–20 June 2019 (2019). https://doi.org/10.1109/CVPR.2019.00613

18. Zhang, J., et al.: Dynamic scene deblurring using spatially variant recurrent neural networks. In: 2018 IEEE Conference on Computer Vision and Pattern Recognition. CVPR 2018, Salt Lake City, UT, USA, 18–22 June 2018 (2018). https://doi.org/10.1109/CVPR.2018.00267

19. Zhu, X., Hu, H., Lin, S., Dai, J.: Deformable convnets V2: more deformable, better results. In: IEEE Conference on Computer Vision and Pattern Recognition. CVPR 2019, Long Beach, CA, USA, 16–20 June 2019 (2019). https://doi.org/10.1109/CVPR.2019.00953

Multi-grained Fusion for Conditional Image Retrieval

Yating Liu[1] and Yan Lu[2(✉)]

[1] School of Software, University of Science and Technology of China, Hefei, China
liuyat@mail.ustc.edu.cn
[2] School of Information Science and Technology, University of Science
and Technology of China, Hefei, China
luyan17@mail.ustc.edu.cn

Abstract. We tackle a new task *conditional image retrieval*, where the query includes an image and a corresponding additional text, with the aim to search the most similar target images in the whole gallery database. The additional text describes the additional conditions for the query image. Previous methods always represent the query pairs by fusing features at the deeper layer, which neglects the fine-grained relationships between the image and the different stages of the sentence. In this paper, we propose a Multi-Grained Fusion (MGF) module to mine the multi-grained relationships in the query pairs to fuse features more effectively. To further improve the performance, we propose an unsupervised Online Groups Matching (OGM) loss to make the feature include more identity information. Extensive experiments show that our method outperforms other state-of-the-art approaches.

Keywords: Image retrieval · Multi-grained · Unsupervised learning

1 Introduction

The image retrieval system aims to search the target images when the user gives a query. Traditional methods always treat this topic by learning discriminative features [1] or designing better distance metrics [2,3]. In standard image retrieval, queries and galleries are all in image form. This paradigm is simple, which can not meet diverse needs. The *conditional image retrieval* [4] is a new challenging topic that can compensate for more flexible demands. In this task setting, each query is represented as the paired form including an image and an additional text. The text gives additional conditions which describe the semantic modification from the query image to the target gallery images, like Fig. 1 shows. The retrieval system will return the target gallery images which are relative to the query pair. This new image retrieval topic allows the user to give more related query information by the natural language, which widely broadens the application range of the image retrieval. But this form also introduces several new challenges.

In the conditional image retrieval, the query is represented by the paired form which includes two modality data. So the retrieval algorithm needs to generate

© Springer Nature Switzerland AG 2021
J. Lokoč et al. (Eds.): MMM 2021, LNCS 12572, pp. 315–327, 2021.
https://doi.org/10.1007/978-3-030-67832-6_26

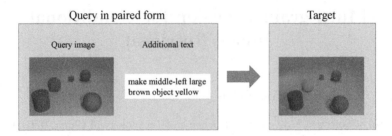

Fig. 1. Illustration of the conditional image retrieval: each query is represented as the paired form including an image and an additional text. The text represents additional conditions for the query image. The goal is to search the relative targets in whole gallery database.

the features which include both image and text information for each query pair. This leads to the first problem: How to fuse information effectively from two modalities in each query pair. Text Image Residual Gating (TIRG) [4] tries to solve this problem by directly fusing deeper features of the query image and the corresponding text together. This method only fuses deep global features from two modalities. It focuses on the coarse-grained relationships which represent the correspondence between the image and the overall sentence. But it neglects the fine-grained relationships between the image and different stages in the language descriptor, such as correspondences between the image and each word or component in the sentence, which brings lower performances. To solve this problem, in this paper, we propose a Multi-Grained Fusion (MGF) module to fuse features in both fine-grained and coarse-grained levels. This fusion method constructs a novel multi-level conditioned attention module to mine multi-grained relationships between the image and each component in the language descriptor, which is more flexible than single coarse-grained fusion methods.

To train the model for the conditional image retrieval well, existing methods only use the embedding loss (the triplet loss) but without utilizing the identity classification loss. Because in the training stage, the training data are as the form of groups. Each group consists of a query pair (an image and a text) and a target gallery image. It's easy to train with the triplet loss in a mini-batch but hard to use the classification loss because we don't have a distinct identity definition. According to our knowledge, the existing state-of-the-art methods in related image retrieval tasks, such as person re-identification [5], often use both the embedding loss and the classification loss together to make the features carry richer identity (ID) information. Only training with the embedding loss results in unsatisfied performances. The core obstacle of utilizing classification loss is the definition of identity. In standard retrieval, each sample belongs to a clearly defined ID and each ID has a certain amount of data. But in the conditional image retrieval, it's not. So in this paper, we propose an Online Groups Matching (OGM) loss which is motivated by unsupervised feature learning. The proposed loss doesn't need the clear ID definition but can guide features to include more identity information, which is complementary with the embedding loss.

The contributions of this paper are two-fold. First, we propose a Multi-Grained Fusion (MGF) module to fuse information in query pairs effectively. The method can mine multi-grained relationships between different modality data, which can generate better fusion features. Second, we provide the Online Groups Matching (OGM) loss which leads the idea of unsupervised learning into this task to carry richer ID information. In extensive experiments, the proposed method outperforms other state-of-the-art approaches.

2   Related Work

Image Retrieval. The image retrieval system aims to search the target images when the user gives a query. In standard image retrieval, queries and galleries are all in image form. Many traditional approaches extract local invariant features [6] from images. Then they aggregate these local invariant features into a single representation for the entire image. e.g., bag-of-words [7], VLAD [8,9] and fish vector [10]. In the last few years, extracting image representations based on a convolutional neural network (CNN) [1,5] has attracted people's interest. So many methods based on neural networks have emerged [11–13]. With the development of GPU parallel computing, neural network methods have drawn more attention.

Unsupervised Learning. Unsupervised learning has received increasing attention in recent years because most data in nature is unlabeled. And sometimes, it's time- and resource-consuming to label data precisely. Wu et al. [14] treated each sample as a separate category to build an instance-based classifier. He et al. [15] proposed MoCo which built a dynamic dictionary with a queue and a moving-averaged encoder to facilitate contrastive unsupervised learning. In this paper, we focus on treating the feature learning task which is difficult to define the identity for each data. It's an intuitive way to utilize the unsupervised learning method to tackle this topic and we propose our Online Groups Matching (OGM) loss.

Conditional Image Retrieval. Conditional image retrieval is a new challenging topic, where each query is represented as the paired form includes an image and an additional text. Han et al. [16] proposed an automatic spatially-aware concept discovery approach which combined attribute spatial representations and attribute semantic representations to get more discriminative representations. TIRG [4] solved this problem by directly adding deeper features of the image and the corresponding text together. Vo et al. [17] learned a shared embedding space for both the source domain and the target domain. Yu et al. [18] proposed the Curling Network which could measure the semantic differential relationships between images with respect to a query text. Previous

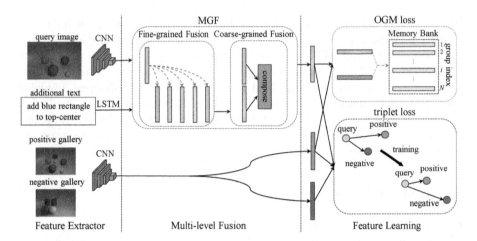

Fig. 2. The architecture of our method. There are three stages: first, in the feature extracting stage, each image is passed through a convolutional neural network and each text is sent to long short-term memory. Second, these features are sent to our MGF including fine-grained fusion and coarse-grained fusion. Third, we use the embedding loss and our proposed OGM loss to learn features better.

methods always represented the query pairs by fusing features at the deeper layer, which neglected the fine-grained relationships between the image and the different stages of the sentence. In this paper, we propose a Multi-Grained Fusion (MGF) module to mine multi-grained relationships between query images and corresponding texts. Except that, we design the OGM loss to further train our model more effectively.

3   Proposed Method

The architecture of our method is shown in Fig. 2. In the feature extracting stage, every image is passed through a convolutional neural network (CNN) and each sentence is sent to a long short-term memory (LSTM). Different with other methods, we utilize all hidden state vectors $\{h_0, h_1, \ldots, h_{L-1}\}$ as our text features instead of the commonly used final one, where L is the length of the text. This allows us to mine the fine-grained relationships between the image and the text descriptor. And then the query image features and text features are feed into the proposed Multi-Grained Fusion (MGF) module. The MGF mines the multi-grained relationships to generate fusion features for each query pair. After getting query representations and gallery representations, we train features by our proposed Online Groups Matching (OGM) loss and the embedding loss (the triplet loss) together.

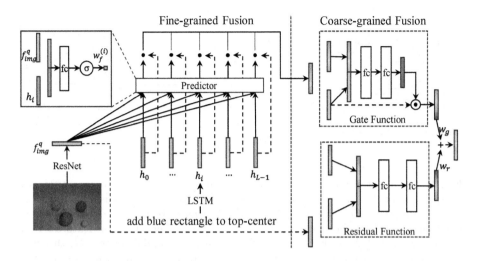

Fig. 3. The details of our Multi-Grained Fusion module.

3.1 Multi-grained Fusion Module

The input of our MGF are the query image features f_{img}^q and text features $f_{text}^q = [h_0, h_1, \ldots, h_{L-1}]$, where $h_i \in \mathbb{R}^d$. The MGF module fuses these features in both fine-grained and coarse-grained level. The details of our MGF are shown in Fig. 3. We first concatenate f_{img}^q and each text component h_i ($i \in [0, 1, \ldots, L-1]$) together. Then we send them into a predictor to compute the weighted values $W_f = [w_f^{(0)}, w_f^{(1)}, \ldots, w_f^{(L-1)}]$:

$$w_f^{(i)} = \sigma(W_{fc}\left[f_{img}^q, h_i\right] + b_{fc}) \tag{1}$$

where $[\cdot, \cdot]$ means the concatenation operation. W_{fc} and b_{fc} are learnable weights in the predictor. σ is the activation function and we use sigmoid here. W_f represents the fine-grained relationships between the query image and each component in the additional query text. So we use these fine-grained relation values to weight the corresponding output of the LSTM. And compose them together as the fine-grained fusion result:

$$\phi_f = \frac{1}{L} \cdot W_f (f_{text}^q)^T = \frac{1}{L} \sum_{i=0}^{L-1} w_f^{(i)} \cdot h_i \tag{2}$$

where $\cdot^T$ means transpose. ϕ_f means the fine-grained fusion output. Fine-grained features contain the relationships between images and each component of the sentences, but these features lack of direct correlation between images and the entire sentence. So we utilize feature-fused method [4] to mine the coarse-grained relationships:

$$q = w_g \cdot Gate(f_{img}^q, \phi_f^T) + w_r \cdot Res(f_{img}^q, \phi_f^T) \tag{3}$$

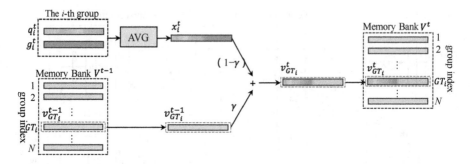

Fig. 4. The updated process of our memory bank, after getting features of the i-th group, we send them into an element-wise average module to get a new feature x_i^t at the t-th iteration. We take the GT_i-th row of memory bank $v_{GT_i}^{t-1}$ at the $(t-1)$-th iteration, and GT_i is the ground-truth group number of the i-th input features. Then compose x_i^t and $v_{GT_i}^{t-1}$ by element-wise addition to get an update of the GT_i-th row of memory bank $v_{GT_i}^t$. Finally, we put back this new update $v_{GT_i}^t$ to our memory bank at the t-th iteration.

where q represents the query image features. w_g and w_r are learnable weights to balance the gate function and the residual function. These two fuctions are written as:

$$Gate(f_{img}^q, \phi_f^T) = \sigma(W_{g2} \cdot \text{RELU}(W_{g1} \cdot [f_{img}^q, \phi_f^T] + b_{g1}) + b_{g2}) \odot f_{img}^q$$
$$Res(f_{img}^q, \phi_f^T) = W_{r2} \cdot \text{RELU}(W_{r1} \cdot [f_{img}^q, \phi_f^T] + b_{r1}) + b_{r2} \tag{4}$$

where $W_{g1}, W_{g2}, b_{g1}, b_{g2}$ and $W_{r1}, W_{r2}, b_{r1}, b_{r2}$ are learnable weights for the gate function and the residual function respectively. $\odot$ means element-wise product. The coarse-grained module directly connects the features of images and texts, which is complementary to the fine-grained module. So using these two modules can achieve better results.

3.2   Online Groups Matching Loss

In this section, we focus on how to train features better. We don't have a clear definition of the identity (ID). Only using the embedding loss does not contain ID information, which results in unsatisfied performance. So we propose the OGM loss, which is motivated by the unsupervised feature learning, to make features carry more ID information.

We first count the number of groups in the overall training dataset and give each group a unique ID. The query pair and the gallery target image in each group are assigned the same ID[1]. The total number of groups is N. Then we follow the Non-parametric Softmax Classifier [19] to use the memory bank to train features. The implementation of the memory bank is a $N \times d$ matrix V,

---

[1] In a few cases, one gallery sample may be the targets of different groups simultaneously. We define that these groups belong to a same identity.

where d is the dimension of the feature vectors. The GT_i-th row of V stores the memory features of the i-th group, and GT_i is the ground-truth group number of the i-th input features. The memory bank is updated by the following equation:

$$v^t_{GT_i} = \gamma v^{t-1}_{GT_i} + (1 - \gamma)x^t_i \tag{5}$$

where $\gamma \in [0, 1]$ is the memory coefficient, which is used to balance the last time bank features with the current input one. The superscript t represents the current time which is equal to the last iteration. The $v^t_{GT_i}$ is the memory feature of the i-th group data at the t-th iteration in the memory bank. x^t_i is the i-th group feature obtained by the t iteration model. The x^t_i is computed by averaging the query and gallery features (q^t_i and g^t_i) in the i-th group at the t-th iteration:

$$x^t_i = 0.5(q^t_i + g^t_i) \tag{6}$$

where g is the gallery image features. We use the CNN that extracted the query image features to extract the gallery features. In other words, whatever for the query or gallery images, we use the same image feature extractor. The overall update strategy is shown in Fig. 4. As the training progresses, the memory bank is equivalent to taking the moving average on the model output features at different times. Based on that, our OGM loss computes the cosine similarities between the memory bank features with the current time features. And then the overall loss value for the current iteration is computed as follow:

$$L_{OGM} = -\frac{1}{2B} \sum_{i=1}^{B} \{ log\{ \underbrace{\frac{exp\{cos(v^t_{GT_i}, q^t_i)/\tau\}}{\sum_{j=1}^{N} exp\{cos(v^t_j, q^t_i)/\tau\}}}_{\text{query term}} \} + log\{ \underbrace{\frac{exp\{cos(v^t_{GT_i}, g^t_i)/\tau\}}{\sum_{j=1}^{N} exp\{cos(v^t_j, g^t_i)/\tau\}}}_{\text{gallery term}} \}\}$$

$$\tag{7}$$

where B is the batch size. τ is the temperature parameter. The query term constrains that the query features should be close to its corresponding memory feature v_{GT_i} and far away from other memory features v_j ($j \neq GT_i$), which makes query features more discriminative. The gallery item plays the same role. The update of the memory bank and the calculation of the loss function are alternated in each iteration. Whether for query or gallery, we use the same memory bank. So the memory bank can further break the gap between the query domain and the gallery domain, which leads to better results.

Except that, we follow TIRG [4] to use the soft triplet loss as the embedding loss which can be written as:

$$L_{triplet} = \frac{1}{MB} \sum_{i=1}^{B} \sum_{m=1}^{M} log\{1 + exp\{||q_i, g^+_i|| - ||q_i, g^-_{i,m}||\}\} \tag{8}$$

where q_i, g^+_i and $g^-_{i,m}$ are the query feature (anchor), the target feature (positive) and the negative feature (negative) respectively. $||\cdot, \cdot||$ means the Euclidean distance metric. Subscript m means the negative index of the i-th group. M is

Table 1. Comparison with other state-of-the-art approaches. The best result is in bold and the second best is underlined. We use Recall@1 as our evaluation indicator on CSS dataset.

Methods	Datasets						
	Fashion 200k		MIT States		CSS		
	Recall@1	Recall@10	Recall@1	Recall@10	3d→3d	2d→3d	2d→2d
Image only [4]	3.5	22.7	$3.3^{\pm 0.1}$	$20.9^{\pm 0.1}$	6.3	6.3	–
Text only [4]	1.0	12.3	$7.4^{\pm 0.4}$	$32.7^{\pm 0.8}$	0.1	0.1	–
Han et al. [16]	6.3	19.9	–	–	–	–	–
Concat [4]	$11.9^{\pm 1.0}$	$39.7^{\pm 1.0}$	$11.8^{\pm 0.2}$	$42.1^{\pm 0.3}$	$60.6^{\pm 0.8}$	27.3	–
Show & Tell [25]	$12.3^{\pm 1.1}$	$40.2^{\pm 1.7}$	$11.9^{\pm 0.1}$	$42.0^{\pm 0.8}$	$33.0^{\pm 3.2}$	6.0	–
Para–Hashing [27]	$12.2^{\pm 1.1}$	$40.0^{\pm 1.1}$	–	–	$60.5^{\pm 1.9}$	31.4	–
Attribute Op. [26]	–	–	$8.8^{\pm 0.1}$	$39.1^{\pm 0.3}$	–	–	–
Relationship [28]	$13.0^{\pm 0.6}$	$40.5^{\pm 0.7}$	$\underline{12.3}^{\pm 0.5}$	$42.9^{\pm 0.9}$	$62.1^{\pm 1.2}$	30.6	–
FiLM [29]	$12.9^{\pm 0.7}$	$39.5^{\pm 2.1}$	$10.1^{\pm 0.3}$	$38.3^{\pm 0.7}$	$65.6^{\pm 0.5}$	43.7	–
TIRG [4]	$\underline{14.1}^{\pm 0.6}$	$\underline{42.5}^{\pm 0.7}$	$12.2^{\pm 0.4}$	$\underline{43.1}^{\pm 0.3}$	$\underline{73.7}^{\pm 1.0}$	46.6	–
TIRG[1] [4]	$12.2^{\pm 2.5}$	$39.0^{\pm 3.5}$	$12.2^{\pm 0.9}$	$42.4^{\pm 0.5}$	$69.9^{\pm 1.1}$	$\underline{52.5}$	72.3
Vo et al. [17]	–	–	–	–	72.0	43.0	$\underline{73.0}$
Ours	$\mathbf{16.0}^{\pm 0.7}$	$\mathbf{44.6}^{\pm 0.7}$	$\mathbf{13.1}^{\pm 0.5}$	$\mathbf{43.6}^{\pm 0.5}$	$\mathbf{74.2}^{\pm 0.5}$	**62.8**	**79.6**

the number of negative cases for q_i in one batch. In other words, we mine M hard negative samples in one batch for each query.

We combine these two losses with a hyper-parameter λ which can be formulated as below: $L_{total} = L_{triplet} + \lambda L_{OGM}$ where λ is a hyper-parameter used to balance the triplet loss and OGM loss. Features which contain identity information improve our method performance.

4   Experiments

In this section, we briefly introduce experimental settings in experiments and then compare the performance of our method with other state-of-the-art approaches.

4.1   Experimental Settings

Datasets. Fashion 200k [16] is a commercial dataset which consists of more than 200,000 images in five categories (dress, top, pants, skirt and jacket). Each image has an associated product description such as "blue destroyed boyfriend jeans" or "leather jackets". There are about 172k and 31k of queries for training and testing. MIT States [20] has about 60k images in objects, scenes, and materials. Each image is labeled by the form of adjective + noun such as "young tiger" or "dry river". There are 245 nouns and 115 adjectives in the whole dataset. CSS dataset [4] is a generating synthesized object dataset which consists of 19k

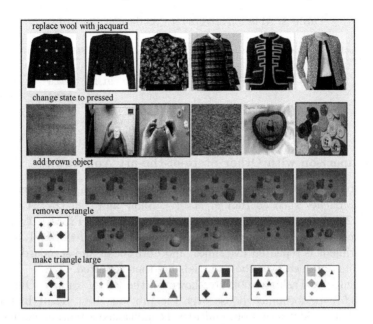

Fig. 5. Examples of our method. The 1st row, the 2nd row and the 3rd to 5th row show the result of Fashion 200k, MIT States and CSS dataset respectively. The correct results are framed by blue. (Color figure online)

training images and 19k testing images. Each image can be viewed as a 9 (3×3) grid scene, so each image contains 9 positions such as top left, bottom right. The additional text describes the conditions. e.g., "add gray circle to top-left" and "make bottom-right purple triangle gray". Each image can be rendered in 2d version and 3d version[2].

Implementation Details. We implement our method based on the Pytorch. We use ResNet18 [21] pretrained on ImageNet [22] and LSTM [23] with random initial to get image features (output size = 512) and text features (hidden size = 512) respectively. The memory bank is initialized by zero. The batch size is 32. We train model in 160k iterations with a momentum optimizer whose learning rate and weight decay parameters are 1e-2 and 1e-6 respectively. Following TIRG [4], we use the instance classification loss instead of the soft triplet loss on Fashion 200K. For the hyper-parameters, we choose $\lambda = 1/3$, $\tau = 1/10$ and $\gamma = 1/2$. We build our experiment environments on the TIRG [4] open-source codes. So we also compare our methods with the re-implemented TIRG[1] [4].

---

[2] The re-implemented TIRG based on the release codes [24].

Table 2. Ablation studies on CSS dataset (2d→2d).

Coarse grained	Fine grained	Triplet Loss	OGM Loss	Recall@1	Recall@5	Recall@10	Recall@50
✓		✓		72.3	91.3	94.6	98.4
✓	✓	✓		75.9	91.4	94.6	98.5
✓		✓	✓	74.3	92.6	94.8	98.5
✓	✓	✓	✓	79.6	93.9	96.6	99.0

4.2 Comparison with Other State-of-the-art Approaches

We evaluate the performance of our method and compare with other state-of-the-art approaches such as Han *et al.* [16], Show and Tell [25], Attribute as Operator [26], Parameter hashing [27], Relationship [28], FiLM [29], TIRG [4] and Vo *et al.* [17]. We evaluate the performance with *Recall@k* (k = 1, 5, 10, 50). Each experiment is repeated five times, and both mean and standard deviation of the results obtained over the five trials are then reported.

The results on Fashion 200k are shown on the left of Table 1. Our method gains a 13.5% performance boost over the previous best result in terms of Recall@1. This validates that our multi-level conditioned attention module mines the multi-grained relationships in the query pairs, whose relationships are more flexible than single coarse-grained fusion methods. This shows that our method has better application values for the commercial.

The results on MIT States are shown on the middle of Table 1. Our method gains a 6.5% performance boost over the state-of-the-art approaches in terms of Recall@1. It shows that our method can achieve satisfying performances for the retrieval of objects, scenes and materials, which demonstrate the wide application value of our method.

The results on CSS dataset are shown on the right of Table 1. There are three settings on this dataset. Specifically, from 3d to 3d (3d→3d), from 2d to 3d (2d→3d) and from 2d to 2d (2d→2d). We only use Recall@1 as our evaluation indicator. Our approach outperforms other approaches with a 0.7% and 9% performance improvement on the setting of 3d→3d and 2d→2d respectively. Especially, when facing setting 2d→3d, our method outperforms the state-of-the-art methods with a large improvement (19.6%). This represents that the features extracted by our method are more discriminative, which can provide higher recall than other methods. Except the numerical experiments, we also give an example of the retrieval results of our methods. The results are shown in Fig. 5, which provides the satisfying results.

4.3 Ablation Study

In this section, we explore the effectiveness of each component of the proposed methods. We conduct our study on the commonly used CSS dataset (2d→2d). The baseline method is the TIRG (coarse-grained fusion + triplet loss).

Effect of MGF: We evaluate how much improvement can be made by MGF (coarse-grained fusion + fine-grained fusion). We test the results whatever the loss functions are. For the triplet loss, comparing the 1st row and the 2nd row of Table 2, the MGF brings about a 5% performance boost over the baseline method in terms of Recall@1. For our proposed OGM loss, the results are shown in 3rd and 4th rows. The fine-grained fusion brings 7.1% performance boost because our module mines multi-grained relationships in query pairs and provides better fusion results.

Effect of Unsupervised Learning: We aim to quantify the contribution of unsupervised learning. The results are shown in the 2nd and 4th row of Table 2. Our OGM loss can always achieve gains with different models which demonstrates that our loss functions can be widely used.

The last row of Table 2 shows that our multi-grained module and OGM loss jointly contributed to the final result which achieve 79.6 in Recall@1 which brings about a 10.1% performance boost.

5 Conclusion

In this paper, we propose a multi-level fusion method of conditional image retrieval. Our method constructs a novel multi-level conditioned attention module to mine multi-grained relationships in query pairs, so it can provide better fusion results. Besides, we apply unsupervised learning to our method and propose an Online Groups Matching loss to improve final performance. Extensive experiments validate the superior performance of our method, as well as the effectiveness of each component.

References

1. Chen, B., Deng, W.: Hybrid-attention based decoupled metric learning for zero-shot image retrieval. In: Computer Vision and Pattern Recognition (2019)
2. Bai, S., Tang, P., Torr, P.H., Latecki, L.J.: Re-Ranking via metric fusion for object retrieval and person re-identification. In: Computer Vision and Pattern Recognition (2019)
3. Chen, B., Deng, W.: Energy confused adversarial metric learning for zero-shot image retrieval and clustering. In: Proceedings of the AAAI Conference on Artificial Intelligence (2019)
4. Vo, N., et al.: Composing text and image for image retrieval - an empirical odyssey. In: Computer Vision and Pattern Recognition (2019)
5. Lu, Y., et al.: Cross-modality Person re-identification with shared-specific feature transfer. In: Computer Vision and Pattern Recognition, pp. 13379–13389. IEEE Computer Society (2020)
6. Lowe, D.G.: Distinctive image features from scale-invariant keypoints. Int. J. Comput. Vis. **60**(2), 91–110 (2004). https://doi.org/10.1023/B:VISI.0000029664.99615.94

7. Sivic, J., Zisserman, A.: Video google: a text retrieval approach to object matching in videos. In: Proceedings Ninth IEEE International Conference on Computer Vision (2003)
8. Jégou, H., Douze, M., Schmid, C., Pérez, P.: Aggregating local descriptors into a compact image representation. In: Computer Vision and Pattern Recognition, pp. 3304–3311. IEEE Computer Society (2010)
9. Arandjelovic, R., Gronat, P., Torii, A., Pajdla, T., Sivic, J.: NetVLAD: CNN architecture for weakly supervised place recognition. In: Computer Vision and Pattern Recognition, pp. 5297–5307. IEEE Computer Society (2016)
10. Perronnin, F., Liu, Y., Sánchez, J., Poirier, H.: Large-scale image retrieval with compressed fisher vectors. In: Computer Vision and Pattern Recognition, pp. 3384–3391. IEEE Computer Society (2010)
11. Wu, D., Dai, Q., Liu, J., Li, B., Wang, W.: Deep incremental hashing network for efficient image retrieval. In: Computer Vision and Pattern Recognition (2019)
12. Yuan, L., et al.: Central similarity quantization for efficient image and video retrieval. In: Computer Vision and Pattern Recognition (2020)
13. Klein, B., Wolf, L.: End-To-end supervised product quantization for image search and retrieval. In: Computer Vision and Pattern Recognition (2019)
14. Wu, Z., Xiong, Y., Yu, S. X., Lin, D.: Unsupervised feature learning via non-parametric instance discrimination. In: Computer Vision and Pattern Recognition, pp. 3733–3742. IEEE Computer Society (2018)
15. He, K., Fan, H., Wu, Y., Xie, S., Girshick, R.: Momentum contrast for unsupervised visual representation learning. In: Computer Vision and Pattern Recognition, pp. 9729–9738. IEEE Computer Society (2020)
16. Han, X., et al.: Automatic spatially-aware fashion concept discovery. In: The IEEE International Conference on Computer Vision (2017)
17. Vo, N., Jiang, L., Hays, J.: Let's Transfer Transformations of Shared Semantic Representations. arXiv preprint arXiv:1903.00793 (2019)
18. Yu, Y., Lee, S., Choi, Y., Kim, G.: CurlingNet: Compositional Learning between Images and Text for Fashion IQ Data. arXiv preprint arXiv:2003.12299 (2020)
19. Xiao, T., Li, S., Wang, B., Lin, L., Wang, X.: Joint detection and identification feature learning for person search. In: Computer Vision and Pattern Recognition, pp. 3415–3424. IEEE Computer Society (2017)
20. Isola, P., Lim, J.J., Adelson, E.H.: Discovering states and transformations in image collections. In: Computer Vision and Pattern Recognition, pp. 1383–1391. IEEE Computer Society (2015)
21. He, K., Zhang, X., Ren, S., Sun, J.: Deep residual learning for image recognition. In: Computer Vision and Pattern Recognition, pp. 770–778. IEEE Computer Society (2016)
22. Deng, J., Dong, W., Socher, R., Li, L.J., Li, K., Fei-Fei, L.: Imagenet: a large-scale hierarchical image database. In: Computer Vision and Pattern Recognition, pp. 248–255. IEEE Computer Society (2009)
23. Hochreiter, S., Schmidhuber, J.: Long short-term memory. Neural Comput. 9(8), 1735–1780 (1997)
24. Vo, N., et al.: https://github.com/google/tirg
25. Kato, K., Li, Y., Gupta, A.: Compositional learning for human object interaction. In: Proceedings of the European Conference on Computer Vision (ECCV), pp. 234–251 (2018)
26. Nagarajan, T., Grauman, K.: Attributes as operators: factorizing unseen attribute-object compositions. In: Proceedings of the European Conference on Computer Vision (ECCV), pp. 169–185 (2018)

27. Noh, H., Seo, P.H., Han, B.: Image question answering using convolutional neural network with dynamic parameter prediction. In: Computer Vision and Pattern Recognition, pp. 30–38. IEEE Computer Society (2016)
28. Santoro, A., et al.: A simple neural network module for relational reasoning. In: Advances in Neural Information Processing Systems, pp. 4967–4976 (2017)
29. Perez, E., Strub, F., De Vries, H., Dumoulin, V., Courville, A.: Film: visual reasoning with a general conditioning layer. In: Thirty-Second AAAI Conference on Artificial Intelligence (2018)

A Hybrid Music Recommendation Algorithm Based on Attention Mechanism

Weite Feng, Tong Li$^{(\boxtimes)}$, Haiyang Yu, and Zhen Yang

Faculty of Information Technology, Beijing University of Technology,
Engineering Research Center of Intelligent Perception and Autonomous Control,
Ministry of Education, Beijing, China
fengwt@emails.bjut.edu.cn, {litong,yuhaiyang,yangzhen}@bjut.edu.cn

Abstract. Music recommendation systems based on deep learning have been actively explored using hybrid approaches. However, most of the models proposed by previous studies adopt coarse-grained embedding approaches (e.g., CNNs) to characterize audio features. Users' fine-grained preferences for music content have not been effectively explored yet. In this work, we propose a hybrid music recommendation model based on attention mechanism, which integrates user's historical behaviour records and audio content and can capture the user's fine-grained preferences for music content due to the introduction of attention mechanism. We experimented with a subset of the last.fm-1b dataset (30,753 users, 10,000 songs, 1533,245 interactions). The experimental results show that our method outperforms baselines approaches.

Keywords: Music recommendation · Attention mechanism · User behavior · Audio content

1 Introduction

In recent years, with the development of the Internet, it has become more and more convenient for people to get music from music streaming media services. Provide users with personalized music recommendations has become an essential requirement for those companies. Thus, the music recommendation algorithm has been widely used in the industry and attracted the attention of many scholars in academia. However, due to the semantic gap (the relationship between music features and user preferences is hard to describe) between user context and music content [14], mining the relationship between user preferences and audio content remains a challenge.

Current approaches to solving the problems of music recommendation can be broadly divided into Collaborative Filtering (CF) and Content-Based Filtering (CBF) [18]. The CF approach, because of its good extensibility, has been widely used in the recommendation system. This method uses the user's historical behaviour record to infer the user's preference for a song, which is a practical

© Springer Nature Switzerland AG 2021
J. Lokoč et al. (Eds.): MMM 2021, LNCS 12572, pp. 328–339, 2021.
https://doi.org/10.1007/978-3-030-67832-6_27

approach. However, it suffers from the cold-start problem. The CBF approach, which uses the song's label or audio content to calculate the similarity of the song and then generate recommendations, can solve the cold start problem of the item. However, it is not easy to extract user preferences from the user's historical behaviour record.

To better explore the relationship between users' listening records and audio contents, attempts have been made to fill the semantic gap using hybrid methods (combining listening records with audio content). A prominent approach is the deep content-based music recommendation model proposed by Oord et al. This method maps the audio content into the item latent factor obtained from the CF method by training a neural network [14]. Inspired by Neural Collaborative Filtering (NCF) [9], Lee et al. propose a deep content-user embedding model, that combines the user-item interaction and music audio content in an end-to-end fashion [12]. However, those approaches still have drawbacks. We argue that music content contains a wealth of information. Intuitively, users have different preferences for different parts of the music content, demanding fine-grained preferences. However, existing approaches, which use Convolutional Neural Networks (CNN) or Recurrent Neural Networks (RNN) to embed audio content into vectors, can only deal with coarse-grained preferences and thus limit their recommendation performance.

To solve this problem, we get inspiration from the recent use of Attention mechanisms, which have recently been used as an effective means to capture user preferences. Chen et al. used the attention mechanism in the Attentive Collaborative Filtering (ACF) model to capture users' preferences for different parts of the multimedia content [2]. In the task of automatic music annotation, Yu et al. introduced the attention mechanism when modelling the audio content, which significantly improved the accuracy of annotation [20]. As such, we argue that appropriate deployment of the attention mechanism can effectively mine users' fine-grained preferences of music content.

In this paper, we propose a hybrid music recommendation algorithm based on attention mechanism, which combines user-item interaction with music audio and captures users' fine-grained preferences for audio content using an attention mechanism. Specifically, we use an architecture based on NCF to extract user preferences from the user's historical behaviour record. On top of that, we add an audio attention layer to calculates user preferences for each part of the audio content. The input of the model is the one-hot vector of a particular user and a specific song, as well as the corresponding audio signal, and the output of the model is the probability that the user likes the song. We experimented with a subset of the last.fm-1b dataset (30,753 users, 10,000 songs, 1533,245 interactions). The experimental results show that our method outperforms baselines.

2   Related Works

Our work is related to two main research areas, that is, content-based and hybrid music recommendation and attention-based recommendation system.

2.1   Content-Based and Hybrid Music Recommendation

Research on music recommendation using deep learning techniques usually uses Deep Neural Networks (DNNs) to obtain the vector representation of songs from audio content or text metadata. And these vector representations are either used directly for content-based recommendation systems, integrated into matrix factorization approaches, or used to build hybrid recommendation systems [17].

The work of Oord et al. is the first to introduce deep learning technology into the music recommendation system [14]. They trained Convolutional Neural Network (CNN) to study the relationship between music content and the latent factor representations of music items. This allows a new music item to get a vector representation via CNN, alleviating the problem of cold starts on the item side. Besides audio content, attempts have been made to add more ancillary information. Oramas et al. propose an approach to creating separate representations of music artists and music tracks, and integrate both into a hybrid music recommendation system [15].

Since the separation of the audio feature learning phase from the collaborative filtering phase may produce suboptimal solutions, people began to try to build hybrid recommendation models in an end-to-end manner [12]. Using a new model based on a deep belief network and a probabilistic graph model, Wang et al. unified the two-stage tasks in music recommendation (audio feature extraction and recommendation generation) into an automatic process [19]. Liang et al. propose a hybrid music recommendation system that integrates content features learned via an MLP as prior to probabilistic matrix factorization [13]. Lee et al. propose deep content-user embedding model, which uses the MLP to learn the embedding of user and item, and meanwhile obtains the embedding of audio content through a CNN. They finally combine the user-item interaction and music audio content in an end-to-end fashion [12].

To sum up, much work has been done to integrate audio content into the collaborative filtering recommendation systems. However, these methods do not investigate users' historical behaviour records in depth, and cannot mine users' fine-grained preferences of audio content. The development of neural network technology and the application of attention mechanism in the recommendation system makes it possible to solve this problem. We will introduce the use of attention mechanism in the recommendation system in the next subsection.

2.2   Attention-Based Recommendation System

The attention mechanism is activated by visual attention. For example, people only need to focus on specific parts of visual input to understand or recognize them. Applying an attention mechanism to a recommendation system, we can filter out non-informational content, select the most representative items [2], and simultaneously provide good interpretability [22].

Chen et al. proposed an Attentive Collaborative Filtering model (ACF), which introduced a two-layer attention mechanism on top of the latent factor model [2]. In the ACF model, an item-level attention mechanism is used to select the item that best represents the user, and a component-level attention mechanism is used to select the most representative content in the multimedia items. The introduction of attention mechanism improves the performance of CF method.

In the study of social media, Zhang et al. proposed a co-attention based hashtag recommendation model that integrates both visual and textual information [21]. They first used the attention mechanism to select the critical content from the picture with the help of the tweet information, chosen then the essential parts from the tweet with the extracted image content, and finally generated the recommendation of the hashtag. In the domain of the heterogeneous information network, Shi et al. use an attention mechanism to select important meta-paths for users to generate high-quality recommendations [10]. The introduction of attention mechanism not only improves the performance of the recommendation system, but also brings better interpretability.

In general, the attention mechanism is widely used in recommendation systems and has achieved good results. This makes it possible to use it to explore users' fine-grained preferences for music.

3   Method

In this section, we will introduce our proposed Hybrid Music Recommendation Algorithm (HMRA). The architecture of the model is shown in Fig. 1.

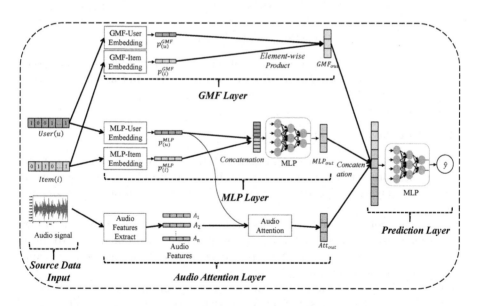

Fig. 1. The overall framework of our proposed model.

In general, the inputs of the model are one-hot vectors of users and items, as well as audio files of the music associated with them. The output of the model is the probability that the user like the song. To better excavate the user's personality preference from the user's historical behaviour record, we used a Generalized Matrix Factorization (GMF) layer and a Multi-Layer Perceptron (MLP) layer to model the complex interactions between users and items. These two layers can effectively learn the linear and non-linear relationships between users and items, respectively [9]. In addition, an audio attention layer is used to capture the user's preferences for the audio content. After fusing the information from the user's historical behaviour record and the audio content, we designed another MLP layer (we call it the prediction layer) to model the complex relationship between them and generate predictive ratings. We will introduce each layer in detail in the following subsections, respectively.

3.1   Generalized Matrix Factorization Layer

As matrix factorization is the most popular model for recommendation and has been investigated extensively, being able to recover it allows a recommendation model to mimic a large family of factorization models [9].

For this reason, we uses a GMF layer to implement matrix factorization, the input of this layer is the one-hot vector of user and item, which will be mapped into low-dimensional vectors after an embedding layer respectively. The low-dimensional user and item vectors obtained can be regarded as the implicit vector representation of user and item. Let the user one-hot vector be V_u^U and item one-hot vector be V_i^I, the function of the GMF layer is as follow:

$$\text{GMF}_{out} = P_G^T V_u^U \odot Q_G^T V_i^I \tag{1}$$

Where P_G and Q_G are parameters that map V_u^U and V_i^I to a low-dimensional space, and $\odot$ denotes the element-wise product of vectors. In this way, our model can mimic matrix factorization to some extent.

3.2   Multi-layer Perceptron Layer

According to the study of He et al. [9], a GMF layer is not enough to capture the complex interaction between users and items, so we refer to their design and use an MLP layer to capture the more complex relationship between users and items.

In our model, the one-hot vectors of users and items are mapped into low-dimensional vectors by embedding layer, respectively. A common way to incorporate features from users and items is to concatenate them together. This approach is prevalent in multimodal tasks [21].

However, vector concatenation does not account for any interactions between user and item, which is insufficient for modeling the collaborative filtering [9]. Therefore, We adopts an MLP layer to learn the complex interaction between users and items, which endowing the model with operability and non-linear capability. MLP is a commonly used neural network structure and a general function approximation method that can fit complex functions [5]. MLP can be viewed as a layer upon layer of neural networks, map a set of input vectors to a set of output vectors. In our model, the input of MLP is the one-hot vector of user and item. Let the user one-hot vector be V_u^U and item one-hot vector be V_i^I. When MLP has only one layer, the function of the MLP layer is as follow:

$$MLP_{out} = a\left(W^T \begin{bmatrix} P_M^T V_u^U \\ Q_M^T V_i^I \end{bmatrix} + b\right) \tag{2}$$

Where P_M and Q_M are parameters that map V_u^U and V_i^I to a low-dimensional space. W and b are parameters of MLP layer. a denotes the Relu activation function.

As the number of MLP layers increases, the fitting ability of MLP will also become stronger. An L-layers MLP can be expressed as a composite form of the above formula, which can be expressed as follows:

$$MLP_{out} = a_L\left(W_L^T\left(a_{L-1}\left(\ldots a_2\left(W_2^T \begin{bmatrix} P_M^T V_u^U \\ Q_M^T V_i^I \end{bmatrix} + b_2\right)\ldots\right)\right) + b_L\right) \tag{3}$$

Where P_M and Q_M are parameters that map V_u^U and V_i^I to a low-dimensional space. W_L and b_L are parameters of the L-th layer of MLP. a denotes the Relu activation function.

As for the structural design of neural networks, a common strategy is tower mode, in which each layer of the network uses fewer neurons than the previous layer. The premise is that by using fewer neurons in higher-level networks, they can learn more abstractive information from the data [7]. So we empirically set the number of neurons in the neural network to be half as many at each layer as at the previous layer.

So far, the GMF layer and MLP layer are used to deal with users' historical behavior records. The GMF layer uses a linear kernel to model the implicit relationships between users and items. The MLP layer uses a non-linear kernel to fit the interaction function between users and items. The combination of the two layers contributes to mining user preferences from the user's historical behavior records.

3.3 Audio Attention Layer

Music content contains a wealth of information, and users should intuitively have different preferences for different parts of a song. Therefore, being able to mine users' fine-grained preferences for a particular piece of music will help us to make recommendations. Thus, we designed an audio attention layer that calculates the user's preferences for different parts of the audio content. The input of this layer is the user's embedding and audio features. This layer can calculate the user's preference for each part of the audio (attention weight) through the attention mechanism. Finally, we embedded the audio content via the weighted sum of the audio features and the attention weights. In this way, we can excavate the user's fine-grained preferences for audio content.

The audio attention layer first receives the audio signal and then performs audio feature extraction. Because the Mel-Frequency Cepstral Coefficient (MFCC) can represent the timbre and chromagram can give pitch information [3], in this work, we take these two audio features as two-dimensional representations of music. Besides these two-dimensional audio features, some one-dimensional audio features can also help us describe music better. The zero-crossing rate represents the rhythm of the music, and the spectral centroid of the spectrum represents the brightness of the sound [6], so we also use those two audio features to describe music. In our dataset, each song is sampled for $40\,s$, and the sampling rate is 22050 Hz. MFCC and chromagram is performed with a frame size of 8192 and 50% overlaps between adjacent frames so that we get audio features with the size of $216 * 34$.

The calculated audio features can be represented by a matrix A, and A_i represents the i-th vector in the audio features matrix. Combining with user vector p_u, we use a two-layer neural network to calculate the attention weight a_i of each audio feature vector. The formula is as follows:

$$a_i = \mathrm{h}^{\mathrm{T}} a \left(\mathrm{W}^T \begin{bmatrix} \mathrm{p_u} \\ \mathrm{A_i} \end{bmatrix} + \mathrm{b} \right) \tag{4}$$

Where h, W and b are parameters in the neural network, and a is the Relu activation function. In particular, to improve the flexibility of the model, the GMF layer and the MLP layer will embed the user's one-hot vector, respectively. Therefore, there will be two latent vectors p_u of one user in the model. By using p_u from different layers, we will get two different ways to calculate the weight of attention. We will discuss these two ways in Sect. 4.4.

The final attention weights are obtained by normalizing the above attentive scores over all the audio features using the softmax function:

$$\beta_{\mathrm{i}} = \frac{\exp\left(\mathrm{a_i}\right)}{\sum_{\mathrm{j}=1}^{|\mathrm{A}|} \exp\left(\mathrm{a_j}\right)} \tag{5}$$

After we get the final attention weight, by the weighted sum of the audio content and its attention weight, we can get the embedding of the audio content. let Att_{out} be the final embedding of audio, it can be calculate as follows:

$$Att_{\mathrm{out}} = \sum_{i=1}^{|A|} \beta_i \cdot A_i \tag{6}$$

3.4 Prediction Layer

Due to the addition of music content, the relationship between users and items will become more complex, so we need the model to have a more potent learning ability to learn the complicated relationship between users' historical behavior records and music content. Therefore, after combining the output of the GMF layer GMF_{out} and the production of the MLP layer MLP_{out} as well as the music content Att_{out}, we used a multi-layer neural network to generate the final prediction score. The formula is as follows:

$$\hat{y}_{ui} = a_L \left(h^T \left(a_{L-1} \left(\ldots a_2 \left(W_2^T \begin{bmatrix} \text{MLP}_{out} \\ \text{GMF}_{out} \\ \text{Att}_{out} \end{bmatrix} + b_2 \right) \ldots \right) \right) + b_L \right) \quad (7)$$

Where h, W and b_i are parameters in the neural network, and a is the Relu activation function. By default, to prevent overfitting, the layer number of the network is set to 3. We also use the same tower structure as MLP layer to design the neural network.

So far, we have mined users' personality preferences from the user's historical behavior records through the GMF and MLP layers. We then used an audio attention layer to mine users' fine-grained preferences for audio content and obtained audio embedding. Finally, we output a user's predicted score of a song through the combination of three layers.

4 Experiments

In this section, we will conduct experiments to answer the following research questions:

- RQ1 Whether the proposed method can effectively improve the performance of traditional methods?
- RQ2 Whether the attention mechanism is effective?

4.1 Dataset Descriptions

To explore the influence of attention mechanism on the recommendation. We need to provide the model audios that are complete. As far as we know, none of the existing public datasets meet our requirements. Therefore, we extracted a subset from the last.fm-1b dataset that is widely used in the field of music recommendation [16], and download corresponding audio files from the music streaming media to construct the dataset used in our experiment.

Dataset Constructions. Because of the massive size of the last.fm-1b dataset, it will take a lot of time to do experiments on the whole dataset. So we deleted the listening records before 2014 from the complete set, then extracted the top 10,000 songs we could download from the song set (some songs could not be downloaded due to copyright restrictions or other reasons). Based on this song set, the listening records irrelevant to the song set are deleted. In the listening record, repeated listening records generated by users listening to the same song at different times will be saved only once. To ensure the quality of the dataset, we deleted the user whose interaction records were less than 10. In the end, our dataset contains 30,753 users, 10,000 songs, and 1,533,245 interactive records, with data sparsity of 99.50%.

4.2   Experimental Settings

Parameter Settings. To determine the hyperparameters of our model, the batch size will be tested according to the ascending gradient [128,256,512,1024]. The learning rate will be tested according to the ascending gradient [0.0001, 0.0005, 0.001, 0.005]. The output size of MLP and GMF will be tested according to the rising gradient [8,16,32,64].

Evaluation Protocols. To evaluate the effectiveness of our model, we use a leave-one-out evaluation method, which is widely used in other works [1]. For each user, we treat the latest song the user listens to as a test set and the rest as a training set. Since sorting all the songs in the dataset would take a lot of time, we adopted a common strategy [4], for each user, 99 items that have not been interacted with are randomly sampled and add to the test set, and only those 100 items are sorted for each user to form recommendations. The following two indicators measure the quality of sorting: *Hit Ratio* (HR) and *Normalized Discounted Cumulative Gain* (NDCG) [8]. HR intuitively measures whether the test item appears in the top-n list, while NDCG accounts for the position of the hits by assigning a higher score to the top-ranked hits. We calculated two metrics for each test user and calculated their average as the result of each round of testing.

Baselines. We will choose the following methods to compare with our proposed method:

- **ItemPop**: Items are ranked according to their popularity and number of interactions.
- **WMF** [11]: Uses a weighted matrix factorization algorithm to obtain implicit representations of users and items, and generates recommendation through inner vector products. It is a classical matrix factorization algorithm.
- **NeuMF** [9]: This is the state of the art neural network-based recommendation method.

4.3   Performance Comparison (RQ1)

Figure 2 shows the performance of $HR@10$ and $NDCG@10$ of each algorithm under different predictive factors. For MF methods WMF, the number of predictive factors is equal to the number of latent factors. For NeuMF, the number of predictive factors represents the dimensions of the output of the MLP layer and the GMF layer. Since ItemPop's performance is poor and its methods do not involve the number of predictors, it will not be listed separately here.

As can be seen from Fig. 2, the method we proposed is better than each baseline except when the number of predictive factors is equal to 8. When the number of predictors is set to 8, NeuMF performs slightly better than our method. We think that when the predictor is equal to 8, the information from collaborative

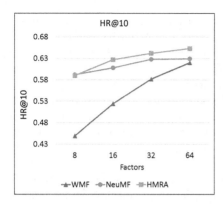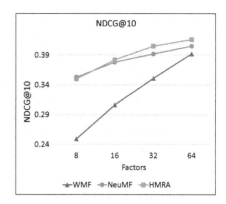

Fig. 2. Performance of HR@10 and NDCG@10 w.r.t. the number of predictive factors.

filtering cannot be fully expressed in the input of the model prediction layer (At that time, the dimensions of the audio embedding are 32, while the sum of the dimensions of the output of the MLP layer and the GMF layer is only 16). This finding indicates that it is crucial to model the user's historical behaviour when building the hybrid recommendation algorithm. Excessive introduction of content information may bring more noise to the model and reduce the recommendation performance.

A clear trend can be observed in Fig. 2 as well. As the predictive factors increase, our model gets increasingly better than the baseline. According to our analysis, content information from audio has a complex nature, which means that we need complex functions to model its relationship with user interests. As the dimension of the predictive factors increases, the width of the prediction layer model also increases, which enables our model to better model the content information of audio. This phenomenon shows once again that because deep learning can learn complex features, the application of deep learning method in content-based recommendation system can significantly improve the performance of the recommendation system.

4.4 Whether the Attention Mechanism is Effective (RQ2)

Table 1. Performance of HR@10 and NDCG@10 w.r.t. different kinds of attention

	Attention-with-MLP		Attention-with-GMF		w/o Attention	
Factors	HR	NDCG	HR	NDCG	HR	NDCG
8	**0.590**	**0.350**	0.567	0.348	0.383	0.201
16	**0.627**	0.382	0.623	**0.384**	0.488	0.275
32	**0.642**	**0.405**	0.640	0.403	0.523	0.293
64	0.653	**0.416**	**0.655**	0.414	0.607	0.361

To verify the effectiveness of the attention mechanism, we compare different implementations of it (Attention-with-MLP and Attention-with-GMF) and without them (w/o Attention). As shown in Table 1, we can see that the attention mechanism has a significant impact on the experimental results. With the attention mechanism, both of the two implementations we gave (Attention-with-MLP and Attention-with-GMF) have achieved good results. Mostly, Attention-with-MLP is going to be slightly better than Attention-with-GMF. This phenomenon indicates that the GMF layer and the MLP layer have learned the same information about the user. Without the attention mechanism (all the attention weights are set to 1), the experimental results would be inferior. This phenomenon shows that the ability to distinguish important parts of the audio content and effectively remove the noise data will have a significant effect on the music recommendation system.t effect on the music recommendation system.

5   Conclusions and Future Work

In this paper, we present the hybrid music recommendation algorithm based on the attention mechanism. Based on NCF, an attention layer is introduced to fully explore the relationship between the user's behaviour records and the user's fine-grained preference for music content in an end-to-end way. Experiments show that our method is better than the traditional method.

In future work, we will consider introducing more side information, such as lyrics or knowledge graphs. This allows us to embed songs better. At the same time, we will consider how to integrate more information about the user, which is not currently considered in this model.

Acknowledgement. This work is partially supported by the National Natural Science of Foundation of China (No.61902010, 61671030), Beijing Excellent Talent Funding-Youth Project (No.2018000020124G039).

References

1. Bayer, I., He, X., Kanagal, B., Rendle, S.: A generic coordinate descent framework for learning from implicit feedback. In: Proceedings of the 26th International Conference on World Wide Web, pp. 1341–1350 (2017)
2. Chen, J., Zhang, H., He, X., Nie, L., Liu, W., Chua, T.: Attentive collaborative filtering: Multimedia recommendation with item- and component-level attention. In: Proceedings of the 40th International ACM SIGIR Conference on Research and Development in Information Retrieval, pp. 335–344 (2017)
3. Choi, K., Fazekas, G., Cho, K., Sandler, M.: A tutorial on deep learning for music information retrieval. arXiv: Computer Vision and Pattern Recognition (2017)
4. Elkahky, A., Song, Y., He, X.: A multi-view deep learning approach for cross domain user modeling in recommendation systems. In: Proceedings of the 24th International Conference on World Wide Web, pp. 278–288 (2015)
5. Goodfellow, I., Bengio, Y., Courville, A.: Deep Learning. The MIT Press, Cambridge (2016)

6. Grey, J.M., Gordon, J.W.: Perceptual effects of spectral modifications on musical timbres. J. Acoust. Soc. Am. **63**(5), 1493–1500 (1978)
7. He, K., Zhang, X., Ren, S., Sun, J.: Deep residual learning for image recognition. In: Proceedings of the IEEE Conference on Computer Vision and Pattern Recognition, pp. 770–778 (2016)
8. He, X., Chen, T., Kan, M., Chen, X.: TriRank: review-aware explainable recommendation by modeling aspects. In: Proceedings of the 24th ACM International on Conference on Information and Knowledge Management, pp. 1661–1670 (2015)
9. He, X., Liao, L., Zhang, H., Nie, L., Hu, X., Chua, T.: Neural collaborative filtering. In: Proceedings of the 26th International Conference on World Wide Web, pp. 173–182 (2017)
10. Hu, B., Shi, C., Zhao, W.X., Yu, P.S.: Leveraging meta-path based context for top- n recommendation with a neural co-attention model. In: Proceedings of the 24th ACM SIGKDD International Conference on Knowledge Discovery and Data Mining, pp. 1531–1540 (2018)
11. Hu, Y., Koren, Y., Volinsky, C.: Collaborative filtering for implicit feedback datasets. In: Eighth IEEE International Conference on Data Mining, pp. 263–272 (2009)
12. Lee, J., Lee, K., Park, J., Park, J., Nam, J.: Deep content-user embedding model for music recommendation. arXiv: Information Retrieval (2018)
13. Liang, D., Zhan, M., Ellis, D.P.: Content-aware collaborative music recommendation using pre-trained neural networks. In: Proceedings of the 16th International Society for Music Information Retrieval Conference, ISMIR 2015. International Society for Music Information Retrieval, pp. 295–301 (2015)
14. Van den Oord, A., Dieleman, S., Schrauwen, B.: Deep content-based music recommendation. In: Advances in Neural Information Processing Systems, pp. 2643–2651 (2013)
15. Oramas, S., Nieto, O., Sordo, M., Serra, X.: A deep multimodal approach for cold-start music recommendation. In: Proceedings of the 2nd Workshop on Deep Learning for Recommender Systems, pp. 32–37 (2017)
16. Schedl, M.: The LFM-1b dataset for music retrieval and recommendation. In: Proceedings of the 2016 ACM on International Conference on Multimedia Retrieval, pp. 103–110 (2016)
17. Schedl, M.: Deep learning in music recommendation systems. Front. Appl. Math. Stat. **5**, 44 (2019)
18. Schedl, M., Zamani, H., Chen, C.-W., Deldjoo, Y., Elahi, M.: Current challenges and visions in music recommender systems research. Int. J. Multimed. Inf. Retrieval **7**(2), 95–116 (2018). https://doi.org/10.1007/s13735-018-0154-2
19. Wang, X., Wang, Y.: Improving content-based and hybrid music recommendation using deep learning. In: Proceedings of the 22nd ACM International Conference on Multimedia, pp. 627–636 (2014)
20. Yu, Y., Luo, S., Liu, S., Qiao, H., Liu, Y., Feng, L.: Deep attention based music genre classification. Neurocomputing **372**, 84–91 (2020)
21. Zhang, Q., Wang, J., Huang, H., Huang, X., Gong, Y.: Hashtag recommendation for multimodal microblog using co-attention network. In: Proceedings of the Twenty-Sixth International Joint Conference on Artificial Intelligence, IJCAI-17, pp. 3420–3426 (2017)
22. Zhang, S., Yao, L., Sun, A., Tay, Y.: Deep learning based recommender system: a survey and new perspectives. ACM Comput. Surv. **52**(1), 5 (2019)

Few-Shot Learning with Unlabeled Outlier Exposure

Haojie Wang, Jieya Lian, and Shengwu Xiong$^{(\boxtimes)}$

School of Computer Science and Technology, Wuhan University of Technology,
Wuhan, China
{wanghj18,jylian,xiongsw}@whut.edu.cn

Abstract. Few-shot learning aims to train a classifier which can recognize a new class from a few examples like a human. Recently, some works have leveraged auxiliary information in few-shot learning, such as textual data, unlabeled visual data. But these data are positive data, they are close related to the training data. Different from such experimental settings, people can also get knowledge from negative data to better recognize a new class. Inspired by this, we exposure a few unlabeled outliers in each few-shot learning tasks to assist the learning of the classifier. To the best of our knowledge, we are the first ones who propose to utilize outliers to improve few-shot learning. We propose a novel method based on meta-learning paradigms to utilize unlabeled outliers. We not only utilize unlabeled outliers to optimize the meta-embedding network but also adaptively leverage them to enhance the class prototypes. Experiments show that our outlier exposure network can improve few-shot learning performance with a few unlabeled outliers exposure.

Keywords: Few-shot learning · Outlier exposure · Meta-learning

1 Introduction

Deep learning has achieved fantastic performance in areas such as speech, vision, and language [6]. However, training a deep network usually requires a lot of labeled data. They will be overfitting in low data regimes while manually annotating data is time-consuming, laborious, and expensive. In contrast, a human can recognize a new class from only a few examples. Recently, few-shot learning has attracted considerable attention, as it aims to produce models that can generalize from a small number of labeled data.

In the few-shot learning domain, most approaches are based on meta-learning (learn to learn) paradigms. They construct a lot of few-shot learning tasks. Each task contains the support set (a few labeled training examples from every class) and the query set (the testing data). For each task, given the support set, we need to predict the labels of the query data. These tasks are split into

---

H. Wang and J. Lian–Equal contribution.

© Springer Nature Switzerland AG 2021
J. Lokoč et al. (Eds.): MMM 2021, LNCS 12572, pp. 340–351, 2021.
https://doi.org/10.1007/978-3-030-67832-6_28

training tasks and testing tasks. The model is trained on the training tasks to extract information across tasks (meta-training) and tested on the testing tasks to measure its performance (meta-testing).

These methods can be mainly divided into two types, metric-based [8,13, 14,16,17,19] and optimization-based [1,7,9,12]. Metric-based approaches aim to learn proper representations, which minimize intra-class distances and maximize inter-class distances. The most representative method is Prototypical networks [14], it aims to learn a metric space in which classification can be performed by computing Euclidean distances to every class prototypes, which is computed as the mean of embedded support examples for each class. Optimization-based approaches aim to find a set of model parameters that can be adapted with a few steps of gradient descent to new individual tasks. Most optimization-based approaches are built on the basis of model-agnostic meta-learning (MAML) [1], which aims to train a model's parameters such that a small number of gradient updates will lead to fast learning on a new task.

Recently, some works have leveraged auxiliary information in few-shot learning. Xing et al. [18] introduced textual data in few-shot learning. They add the word embedding of classes to each tasks' support set. Besides, they propose AM3, which adaptively combines information from two modalities, outperforms by a considerable margin to the single-modality few-shot learning. Ren et al. [10] construct a semi-supervised few-shot scenario where unlabeled examples are also available within each task. They consider two situations: one where all unlabeled examples belong to the same set of classes as the support set of the task, as well as the more challenging situation where examples from other distractor classes are also provided. When the unlabeled images contain irrelevant classes (distractors), they try to identify distractors and reduce the impact of them as much as possible. They predict the labels of unlabeled examples then leverage these data to enhance class prototypes, improving their predictions of testing data. Zhang et al. [20] leverage fake data generated by a non-perfect generator in MetaGAN to learn sharper decision boundaries. People can not only get knowledge from positive unlabeled data but also can get knowledge from pure negative unlabeled examples to better recognize a new class. In anomaly detection, Hendrycks et al. [3] propose leveraging diverse, realistic outlier datasets to enable the detection of novel forms of anomalies. Inspired by this, we consider a scenario where the new classes are learned in the presence of additional unlabeled outlier data.

In this work, we introduce unlabeled outliers in few-shot learning. We propose a novel method that utilizes outliers in both training and testing phases based on meta-learning paradigms, instead of only using outliers to optimize the embedding network in the training phase. We adaptively leverage outliers to enhance the class prototypes. To the best of our knowledge, we are the first ones who utilize outlier data to improve few-shot learning. Experiments show that our outlier exposure network can improve the few-shot learning performance with a few unlabeled outliers exposure.

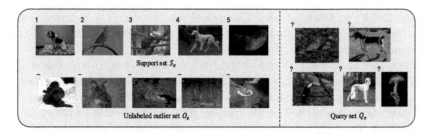

Fig. 1. Example of an episode (few-shot classification task) in our outlier exposure setup. Each episode includes support data, query data and unlabeled outlier data. The left side of the dashed line illustrates the training data including support set S_e (at the top row) and unlabeled outlier set O_e (at the bottom row). The right side of the dashed line illustrates the query set Q_e. The support set and query set share the same label space, and the unlabeled outlier set's label space is disjoint with their label space.

2 Background

We start with defining precisely the current paradigm for few-shot learning and the prototypical networks approach to this problem followed by a brief explanation of learning vector quantization.

2.1 Problem Definition

Few-shot learning models are trained on D_{train} and tested on D_{test}. D_{train} has its own label space C_{train} that is disjoint with D_{test}. D_{test} only has a few labeled samples with each class in C_{test}.

In order to perform meta-learning and extract transferrable knowledge that allows us to generalize better classifiers from a small amount of labeled data, most approaches follow the episodic training paradigm. They build K-shot, N-way episodes to match inference that will be encountered at test time. Each episode e is formed by randomly selecting N classes from C_{train} and then sampling two sets of images from these classes: K labeled samples from each of the N classes to act as the support set $S_e = (\boldsymbol{x}_i, y_i)_{i=1}^{N \times K}$, a fraction of the remainder of those N classes' samples to serve as the query set $Q_e = (\boldsymbol{q}_i, y_i)_{i=1}^{Q}$.

Training on these episodes is done by feeding support set to the model and updating its parameters by minimizing the loss of the predictions on samples in the query set.

$$L(\theta) = \underset{(S_e, Q_e)}{\mathbb{E}} - \sum_{t=1}^{Q} log p_\theta(y_t | \boldsymbol{q}_t, S_e) \tag{1}$$

The model must take in a small number of labeled examples and produce a classifier that can be applied to new classes. So episodic training encourages the model to have good generalization on the new episodes. Due to this analogy, training under episodic training is referred to as learning to learn or meta-learning.

2.2 Prototypical Networks

Prototypical networks [14] have attracted significant attention because of its simplicity and effectiveness in few-shot learning. It aims to learn prototypes for each class and predict the labels of query data by computing Euclidean distances to the prototype of each class. More precisely, prototypical networks learn an embedding function f, which maps examples into space where examples from the same class are close and those from different classes are far. A further reason for the success of prototypical networks is they use a non-parametric nearest classifier with all parameters lie in the embedding function, which alleviates the overfitting problem.

Prototypical networks compute prototype $\boldsymbol{p}_c$ (of class c) by averaging the embeddings of all support samples of class c.

$$\boldsymbol{p}_c = \frac{1}{|S_e^c|} \sum_{(\boldsymbol{s}_i, y_i) \in S_e^c} f(\boldsymbol{s}_i) \tag{2}$$

where S_e^c is the subset of support which belongs to class c. This model assigns a probability over any class c based on a softmax over negative distances between $\boldsymbol{q}_t$ and each prototype:

$$p(y = c | \boldsymbol{q}_t, P) = \frac{exp(-d(f(\boldsymbol{q}_t), \boldsymbol{p}_c))}{\sum_{k=1}^N exp(-d(f(\boldsymbol{q}_t), \boldsymbol{p}_k))} \tag{3}$$

where $P = \{\boldsymbol{p}_1, ... \boldsymbol{p}_N\}$ denotes the set of class prototypes. The model is trained by minimizing Eq. 1, iterating over training episodes and performing stochastic gradient descent update for each episode.

2.3 Learning Vector Quantization

We further utilize outliers to optimize class prototypes through Learning Vector Quantization(LVQ).

Kohonen's Learning Vector Quantization is a nonparametric classification scheme that classifies query data by comparing them to k prototypes called Voronoi Vectors [5]. The locations of these vectors are determined from training data through a learning algorithm as follows.

Let $\{(\boldsymbol{x}_i, y_{\boldsymbol{x}_i})\}_{i=1}^N$ be the training data, $y_{\boldsymbol{x}_i}$ is the label of $\boldsymbol{x}_i$. $V = \{\boldsymbol{v}_1, ..., \boldsymbol{v}_k\}$ is Voronoi vectors. Once the Voronoi vectors are initialized, training proceeds by taking a sample $(\boldsymbol{x}_j, y_{\boldsymbol{x}_j})$ from the training set, finding the closest Voronoi vector and adjusting its value according to Eqs. 4, 5 where $\eta \in (0, 1)$. After several passes through the data, the Voronoi vectors converge and training is complete.

Suppose $\boldsymbol{v}_c$ is the closest Vector and it is adjusted as follows:

if $y_{\boldsymbol{v}_c} = y_{\boldsymbol{x}_j}$

$$\boldsymbol{v}_c' = \boldsymbol{v}_c + \eta(\boldsymbol{x}_j - \boldsymbol{v}_c) \tag{4}$$

if $y_{\boldsymbol{v}_c} \neq y_{\boldsymbol{x}_j}$

$$\boldsymbol{v}_c' = \boldsymbol{v}_c - \eta(\boldsymbol{x}_j - \boldsymbol{v}_c) \tag{5}$$

The other Voronoi vectors are not modified.

This update affects that if x_j and v_c have the same labels then v_c is moved closer to x_j, however, if they have different labels then v_c is moved away from x_j.

3 Few-Shot Learning with Unlabeled Outlier Exposure

We now define the unlabeled outlier setting considered in this work.

Different from classic few-shot learning, we introduce an additional unlabeled outlier dataset D_{out} which has its own label space that is disjoint with D_{train} and D_{test}. For each episode e, we add an unlabeled outlier set $O_e = \{\tilde{x}_1, ..., \tilde{x}_M\}$ which is sampled from D_{out} into the classification task. Figure 1 shows the composition of an episode in our experimental setup.

We add an outlier exposure loss to optimize the network. Besides, we search the nearest outliers then adaptively update prototypes by LVQ mechanism. Details can be found in Algorithm 1.

Algorithm 1. Training strategy of few-shot learning with unlabeled outlier exposure.

Input: An Episode e including S_e, Q_e, O_e
Output: Episodic loss $\mathcal{L}(\theta)$ for sampled episode e.
Compute $P = \{p_1, ... p_N\}$ with Eq 2.
Compute outlier exposure loss $\mathcal{L}_{OE}(\theta)$ with Eq 6.
{update prototypes by adaptive LVQ}
for c in N **do**
    $\tilde{x}_{t*} \leftarrow FindNearest(O_e, p_c)$
    $\eta_c = h(p_c, f(\tilde{x}_{t*}))$
    $p'_c = (1 + \eta_c)p_c - \eta_c f(\tilde{x}_{t*})$
end for
Compute Cross-Entropy loss $\mathcal{L}_{CE}(\theta)$ with updated prototypes $P' = \{p'_1, ... p'_N\}$ via Eq 3.
$\mathcal{L}(\theta) \leftarrow \mathcal{L}_{CE}(\theta) + \gamma \mathcal{L}_{OE}(\theta)$

3.1 Outlier Exposure Loss

We add a constraint to optimize the embedding network by computing the cross-entropy between outlier samples and uniform distribution over N classes.

$$L_{OE}(\theta) = \mathbb{E}_{O_e} - \sum_{t=1}^{M} \sum_{c=1}^{N} \frac{1}{N} log p_\theta(c|\tilde{x}_t, P) \tag{6}$$

In Sect. 3.1, we describe the N-way K-shot classification problem. As we mentioned before, D_{out} has its own label space that is disjoint with D_{train} and

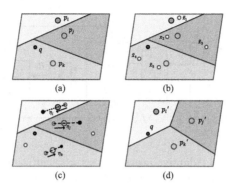

Fig. 2. Qualitative example of how our model works. Now we have a few-shot classification task. (a) Assume query sample q has category i. The closest prototype to the query sample q is p_k. (b) We add some outliers in this task. (c) The adaptive LVQ mechanism modify the position of prototypes, given the nearest outliers. (d) After using adaptive LVQ mechanism to update the prototypes, the prototypes' position are modified. And the closest prototype to the query is now the one of the category i, correcting the classification

D_{test}. Outliers do not belong to any class of the N classes. So the outlier should equally far away from N prototypes. In other words, the classification result vector of outlier should satisfy the uniform distribution. By adding such constraint, i.e. outlier exposure loss, we aim to make prototypes far away from these outliers in embedding space.

3.2 Adaptive LVQ Mechanism

To further utilize outlier samples in both the training tasks and testing tasks, we adaptively utilize outliers to enhance class prototypes. We use Fig. 2 to illustrate the Adaptive LVQ mechanism. Figure 3 describes the framework of the proposed model.

We utilize LVQ to enhance class prototypes by the following equation:

$$\boldsymbol{p}'_c = (1 + \eta_c)\boldsymbol{p}_c - \eta_c f(\tilde{\boldsymbol{x}}_{t*}) \tag{7}$$

in which $\tilde{\boldsymbol{x}}_{t*}$ is the nearest outlier to prototype $\boldsymbol{p}_c$. We use Euclidean distance as the distance function. The coefficient η_c is conditioned on prototypes and outliers calculated as

$$\eta_c = h(\boldsymbol{p}_c, f(\tilde{\boldsymbol{x}}_{t*})) \tag{8}$$

where η_c is the adaptive coefficient and h denotes an adaptive coefficient producing network with parameters θ_h.

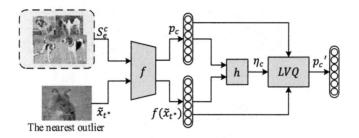

Fig. 3. The framework of Adaptive Learning Vector Quantization (LVQ) mechanism. The final prototype is modified by adaptive LVQ mechanism. f is the embedding function. The coefficient η_c is conditioned on the representation of prototype and its nearest outlier. h is an adaptive coefficient producing network

3.3   Total Loss

Combining Eq. 1 and 6 gives us final loss

$$L(\theta) = \mathop{\mathbb{E}}_{(S_e, Q_e)} - \sum_{t=1}^{Q_e} log p_\theta(y_t | \boldsymbol{q}_t, P') + \gamma L_{OE} \tag{9}$$

where $\theta = \{\theta_f, \theta_h\}$ is the set of parameters, γ is the weighting factor of outlier exposure, $P' = \{\boldsymbol{p}'_1, ...\boldsymbol{p}'_N\}$ is the updated prototypes.

4   Experiments

We conduct our experiments with widely used few-shot learning dataset: mini-ImageNet [17].

4.1   Datasets

The miniImageNet dataset is a modified version of the ILSVRC-12 dataset[11] that includes 60, 000 color images of size 84×84 with 100 classes, each having 600 examples. We follow on the split provided by [9], using 64 classes for training, 16 for validation, and 20 for testing.

The outlier dataset is also a subset of the ILSVRC-12 dataset [11]. We randomly sample 50 classes from ILSVRC-12 dataset which are disjoint with mini-ImageNet dataset. Each class has around 1,300 images. Note that we don't use the labels of the outlier dataset in both training and testing.

4.2   Implementation Details

We build our model on top of prototypical network [14] and FEAT [19]. But the proposed method can potentially be applied to any metric-based approaches.

Table 1. Few-shot classification accuracy on test split of the miniImageNet. In each Semi-k methods, 100 unlabeled data without distractors are provided for each task.

Model	Test accuracy	
	5-way 1-shot	5-way 5-shot
MatchNet [17]	$43.40 \pm 0.78\%$	$51.09 \pm 0.71\%$
ProtoNets [14]	$49.42 \pm 0.78\%$	$68.20 \pm 0.66\%$
MAML [1]	$48.70 \pm 1.84\%$	$63.11 \pm 0.92\%$
RelationNet [16]	$51.38 \pm 0.82\%$	$67.07 \pm 0.69\%$
MetaGan [20]	$52.71 \pm 0.64\%$	$68.63 \pm 0.67\%$
Semi-k-Means [10]	$50.09 \pm 0.45\%$	$64.59 \pm 0.28\%$
Semi-k+Cluster [10]	$49.03 \pm 0.24\%$	$63.08 \pm 0.18\%$
Semi-k+Masked [10]	$50.41 \pm 0.31\%$	$64.39 \pm 0.24\%$
DSN [13]	$51.78 \pm 0.96\%$	$68.96 \pm 0.69\%$
FEAT [19]	$55.15 \pm 0.20\%$	$71.61 \pm 0.16\%$
Our (ProtoNet)	$53.36 \pm 0.20\%$	$71.12 \pm 0.16\%$
Our (FEAT)	$\mathbf{55.43} \pm 0.20\%$	$\mathbf{71.74} \pm 0.16\%$

We consider a four-layer convolution network (ConvNet) which has the same architecture used in several recent works [10,13,14,16,17,19,20] as embedding function. It contains 4 repeated convolutional blocks. In each block, there are a 64-filter 3×3 convolution, a batch normalization layer, a ReLU, and a max-pooling with size 2. The input images are resized to $84 \times 84 \times 3$. Our adaptive coefficient producing network contains one hidden layer with 300 units and outputs a single scalar for η_c. The representation of one prototype and its nearest outlier are concatenated as the input of our adaptive network. We use ReLU non-linearity [2] and dropout [15]. The coefficient of dropout is set to 0.6.

We also use an additional pre-training strategy, which is suggested by [8,12]. At first, the backbone network is followed by a fully-connected layer with softmax. It is trained to classify all classes in the meta-training set. The trained weights are then used to initialize the embedding function.

We use Euclidean distance as the distance function in the nearest neighbor algorithm. Inspired by Oreshkin et al. [8], we set the metric scale coefficient to 32.

During the training, stochastic gradient descent (SGD) with Adam [4] optimizer is employed, with the initial learning rate set to be 1e-4. Models are trained for 200 iterations and the learning rate is reduced by a factor of ten every 50 iterations. Each iteration contains 100 episodes.

The weight γ in Eq. 9 is set to 0.2 in 5-way 1-shot setting and 0.5 in 5-way 5-shot setting.

During the testing, we batch 15 query images per class in each episode for evaluation. We update class prototypes by adaptive LVQ mechanism with their nearest outliers, then classify query data by computing Euclidean distance

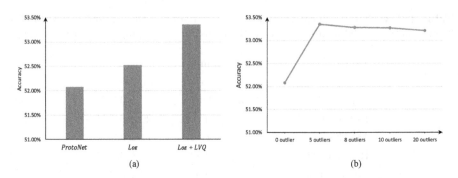

Fig. 4. Ablation study. (a) Comparison of stripped-down version model in 5-way 1-shot regime. (b) Comparison of our model for different number of outliers per-task.

between the updated prototypes and query data. The classification accuracies are computed by averaging over 10,000 randomly generated episodes from the meta-testing set.

4.3   Results

Experimental results on MiniImagenet are shown in Table 1. The compared methods are all use ConvNet as backbone. We can see that our method outperforms many methods, such as ProtoNets, RelationNet and Semi-k-Means with the same backbone network. We build our model on top of prototypical network [14] and FEAT [19]. But the proposed method can potentially be applied to any metric-based approaches.

Table 2. Classification accuracy comparison of our method and re-implemented Semi-k-Means on MiniImageNet. Semi-k-Means method is re-implement with pretraining. We provide 25 unlabeled data without distractors for each task.

Model	Test accuracy	
	5-way 1-shot	5-way 5-shot
Semi-k-Means [10]	$52.70 \pm 0.23\%$	$69.33 \pm 0.17\%$
Our (ProtoNet)	$53.36 \pm 0.20\%$	$71.12 \pm 0.16\%$

To make fair comparisons, we reimplement semi-supervised few-shot learning [10] with pre-training, and the re-implementation method achieves better results than previously reported ones.

We only reimplement the *Semi-k-Means* method cause the *Semi-k+Cluster* method and *Semi-k+Masked* method are designed for the situation where there are some distractors in unlabeled data. In no-distractor semi-supervised settings, *Semi-k-Means* method has the best performance. In the case of the same amount of unlabeled data, no-distractor setting has better performance than distractor setting under all methods of Semi-few [10]. We provide 5 unlabeled data without distractors for each class, i.e. 25 unlabeled data for each class. The experiment results are shown in Table 2.

We can see that the re-implementation method achieves better results. We only exposure 5 unlabeled outliers for each task, but our method still outperforms *Semi-k-means* method. It is clear that our method is more effective than *Semi-k-means* method and its variant.

We also compare our full model with a stripped-down version (without the L_{OE} or adaptive LVQ mechanism) in one-shot regime to further analyze the effectiveness of our model. Figure 4(a) can show that outlier exposure loss and adaptive LVQ mechanism are both effect.

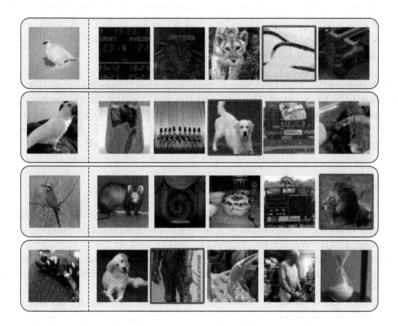

Fig. 5. Tasks which contains outliers that are visually similar to support samples. The left images are outlier data. We circle the similar support samples with red boxes. (Color figure online)

Besides, we evaluate the effection of the number of outliers. From Fig. 4(b), we can hardly observe the improvements in test accuracy when the number of outliers per task grows from 5 to 20. So it is enough to use only 5 outliers under our model. As future work, we may focus on how to better learn statistical information from a larger outlier dataset.

We randomly sample some tasks to analyze in which situation our method works better. We evaluate two trained models on these sampled tasks. The first one is our full model (built on ProtoNet). The second one is its baseline ProtoNet with pre-training. We found that when there are some outliers which are visually similar to the support samples (Note that outliers belong to different classes with support samples), our method works better. In the tasks shown in Fig. 5, our average accuracy is 15% higher than its baseline ProtoNet. We think such phenomenon is due to similar but different outliers can help the model learn sharper decision boundary.

5   Conclusion

In this work, we propose a novel semi-supervised few-shot learning paradigm, where unlabeled data are pure outliers. To utilize these unlabeled data, we propose outlier exposure loss to optimize the embedding network and adaptive LVQ mechanism to enhance class prototypes conditioned on class prototypes and their nearest outliers. Our proposed method shows consistent improvements compared to our baselines. As future work, we are working on how to better learn statistical information of a larger outlier dataset.

Acknowledgments. This work was in part supported by the National Key Research and Development Program of China (Grant No. 2017YFB1402203), the National Natural Science Foundation of China (Grant No. 61702386). the Defense Industrial Technology Development Program (Grant No. JCKY2018110C165), Major Technological Innovation Projects in Hubei Province (Grant No. 2019AAA024).

References

1. Finn, C., Abbeel, P., Levine, S.: Model-agnostic meta-learning for fast adaptation of deep networks. In: Proceedings of the 34th International Conference on Machine Learning, ICML, vol. 70, pp. 1126–1135 (2017)
2. Glorot, X., Bordes, A., Bengio, Y.: Deep sparse rectifier neural networks. In: Proceedings of the Fourteenth International Conference on Artificial Intelligence and Statistics, AISTATS, vol. 15, pp. 315–323 (2011)
3. Hendrycks, D., Mazeika, M., Dietterich, T.G.: Deep anomaly detection with outlier exposure. In: 7th International Conference on Learning Representations, ICLR (2019)
4. Kingma, D.P., Ba, J.: Adam: a method for stochastic optimization. In: 3rd International Conference on Learning Representations, ICLR (2015)
5. Kohonen, T.: Learning vector quantization. In: Self-Organizing Maps, pp. 175–189 (1995)
6. LeCun, Y., Bengio, Y., Hinton, G.: Deep learning. Nature **521**(7553), 436–444 (2015)
7. Li, Z., Zhou, F., Chen, F., Li, H.: Meta-SGD: learning to learn quickly for few-shot learning. arXiv preprint arXiv:1707.09835 (2017)
8. Oreshkin, B., López, P.R., Lacoste, A.: TADAM: task dependent adaptive metric for improved few-shot learning. In: Advances in Neural Information Processing Systems, NeurIPS, pp. 721–731 (2018)
9. Ravi, S., Larochelle, H.: Optimization as a model for few-shot learning. In: 5th International Conference on Learning Representations, ICLR (2017)

10. Ren, M., et al.: Meta-learning for semi-supervised few-shot classification. In: 6th International Conference on Learning Representations, ICLR (2018)
11. Russakovsky, O., et al.: ImageNet large scale visual recognition challenge. Int. J. Comput. Vis. **115**(3), 211–252 (2015)
12. Rusu, A.A., et al: Meta-learning with latent embedding optimization. In: 7th International Conference on Learning Representations, ICLR (2019)
13. Simon, C., Koniusz, P., Nock, R., Harandi, M.: Adaptive subspaces for few-shot learning. In: Proceedings of the IEEE/CVF Conference on Computer Vision and Pattern Recognition, CVPR, pp. 4136–4145 (2020)
14. Snell, J., Swersky, K., Zemel, R.: Prototypical networks for few-shot learning. In: Advances in Neural Information Processing Systems, NeurIPS, pp. 4077–4087 (2017)
15. Srivastava, N., Hinton, G.E., Krizhevsky, A., Sutskever, I., Salakhutdinov, R.: Dropout: a simple way to prevent neural networks from overfitting. J. Mach. Learn. Res. **15**(1), 1929–1958 (2014)
16. Sung, F., Yang, Y., Zhang, L., Xiang, T., Torr, P.H., Hospedales, T.M.: Learning to compare: relation network for few-shot learning. In: Proceedings of the IEEE/CVF Conference on Computer Vision and Pattern Recognition, CVPR, pp. 1199–1208 (2018)
17. Vinyals, O., Blundell, C., Lillicrap, T., Wierstra, D.: Matching networks for one shot learning. In: Advances in Neural Information Processing Systems, pp. 3630–3638 (2016)
18. Xing, C., Rostamzadeh, N., Oreshkin, B.N., Pinheiro, P.O.: Adaptive cross-modal few-shot learning. In: Advances in Neural Information Processing Systems, NeurIPS, pp. 4848–4858. Curran Associates, Inc. (2019)
19. Ye, H.J., Hu, H., Zhan, D.C., Sha, F.: Few-shot learning via embedding adaptation with set-to-set functions. In: Proceedings of the IEEE/CVF Conference on Computer Vision and Pattern Recognition, CVPR, pp. 8808–8817 (2020)
20. Zhang, R., Che, T., Ghahramani, Z., Bengio, Y., Song, Y.: MetaGAN: an adversarial approach to few-shot learning. In: Advances in Neural Information Processing Systems, NeurIPS, pp. 2371–2380 (2018)

Fine-Grained Video Deblurring
with Event Camera

Limeng Zhang, Hongguang Zhang, Chenyang Zhu, Shasha Guo, Jihua Chen,
and Lei Wang[✉]

College of Computer Science and Technology,
National University of Defense Technology, Changsha, China
{zhanglimeng,leiwang}@nudt.edu.cn

Abstract. Despite CNN-based deblurring models have shown their superiority on solving motion blurs, how to restore photorealistic images from severe motion blurs remains an ill-posed problem due to the loss of temporal information and textures. Video deblurring methods try to extract meaningful temporal information in multiple consecutive blurry frames during a long period of time. However, the information obtained in such a coarse period is overcomplicated, and all frames may suffer from severe motion blurs. Event cameras such as Dynamic and Active Pixel Vision Sensor (DAVIS) can simultaneously produce gray-scale Active Pixel Sensor (APS) frames and events, which capture motions as the events at very high temporal resolution, *i.e.*, $1\,\mu s$, and provide useful information for blurry APS frames. In this paper, we propose a deep fine-grained video deblurring pipeline consisting of a deblurring module and a recurrent module to address severe motion blurs. Concatenating the blurry image with event representations at a fine-grained temporal period, our proposed model achieves state-of-the-art performance on both popular GoPro and real blurry datasets captured by DAVIS, and is capable of generating high frame-rate video by applying a tiny shift to event representations in the recurrent module.

Keywords: Video deblurring · Video reconstruction · High
frame-rate · Event camera

1 Introduction

Conventional cameras require long exposure time to accumulate light from scenes, therefore object movements and camera shakes during the exposure time may lead to complex blurs in captured frames. The motion deblurring task aims at calculating and removing blurs from captured blurry images, and restoring sharp and clean images. However, the restoration of a single image is a highly ill-posed deconvolutional task.

CNN-based deblurring methods have shown their superiority in non-uniform motion deblurring tasks. Early methods follow the idea of setting a variety of priors or regularization, or substitute some operators with learned models [12,

© Springer Nature Switzerland AG 2021
J. Lokoč et al. (Eds.): MMM 2021, LNCS 12572, pp. 352–364, 2021.
https://doi.org/10.1007/978-3-030-67832-6_29

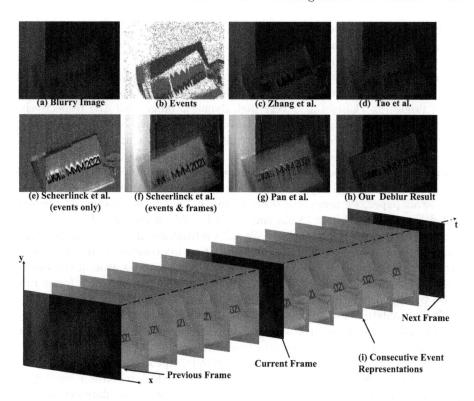

Fig. 1. The motivation of our model. A severe motion-blurred image (a) can hardly be restored by state-of-the-art deep learning model [20,24] (c) (d) with a blurry image. [16] proposes a complementary filter which can use only events (e) or events combined with the blurry image (f). [13] (g) formulates the relationship between events and blurry images via an EDI model. (h) refers to our proposed fine-grained video deblurring model (FGVD), which learns to concatenate consecutive recurrent event representations (i) in a fine-grained manner with a blurry image to restore a photorealistic image.

17,19,22]. Recent methods design end-to-end networks to learn the connections between blurry images and the corresponding sharp images without estimating the blur kernels [11,20,24,25].

Despite previous methods have achieved significant improvements, they fail in challenging cases due to image degradations, *e.g.*, severe motion blurs and high dynamic range.

To address this ill-posed problem, previous works [7,18] propose to leverage multiple consecutive blurry frames as inputs, which contain richer temporal information and textures. However, the benefits from such a design are marginal as all these intensity frames suffer from severe motion blurs. Instead of merely relying on the blurry images, we propose to leverage the motion information recorded by an event camera to address the motion deblurring problem.

Event-based cameras [3] are bio-inspired vision sensors that work differently from traditional cameras. Instead of accumulating light intensity during the fixed exposure time, the event camera records the changes of intensity asynchronously in microseconds. The output of the event camera is a stream of events shaped in a four-dimensional array (x, y, t, p) that encodes time, location, and polarity of brightness changes at a very high dynamic range (140 dB) respectively. Though the image shown in Fig. 1(a) is severely blurry, the corresponding event information Fig. 1(b) is abundant. Figure 1(i) are consecutive recurrent event representations in fine-grained around the latent sharp image. Those event representations contain clear outlines and dense information, which provides the possibility to restore blurry images under severe motion blurs.

In this paper, we propose a deep deblurring and reconstructing framework called Fine-grained Video Deblurring (FGVD), which consists of a deblurring network and a recurrent module. We take advantage of event camera's high temporal resolution that records the full motion information, and concatenate blurry image with several consecutive event representations around the blurry image to restore the latent sharp image. Then we reconstruct a high frame rate video by applying a tiny shift to event representations in the recurrent model.

We formulate the deblurring task as the residual learning between blurry images and latent sharp images. Inspired by [24], we use an efficient multi-patch hierarchical encoder-decoder architecture. By dividing the inputs into multiple localized patches, the model can more effectively capture the non-uniform blur kernels via residual learning among different levels, which requires a small filter size and leads to a fast inference runtime. We generate the simulated event data with ESIM [14], and evaluate the performance of our model on GoPro dataset [11]. Both qualitative and quantitative results show state-of-the-art performance $w.r.t.$ Peak Signal to Noise Ratio (PSNR) as depicted in Fig. 2. As [6] has no experimental data yet, we refer to the performance mentioned in their paper as shown by the purple dotted line. We further evaluate our model on a real event camera dataset [13] captured by DAVIS240C [3] and our event blurry datasets captured by DAVIS346. Our qualitative results show that our deblurring model can effectively restore photorealistic sharp images and reconstruct high frame rate videos in challenging scenarios.

Our contributions in this paper are listed as follows.

- We propose a novel and effective pipeline, namely FGVD, consisting of a deblurring network and a recurrent module to address motion deblurring and video reconstruction.
- We investigate the complementary relationship between the blurry frame and consecutive recurrent event representations, which provide fine-grained motion information for deblurring.
- Our evaluations on both synthesis and real datasets show that our proposed pipeline achieves state-of-the-art results on both qualitative and quantitative evaluations.

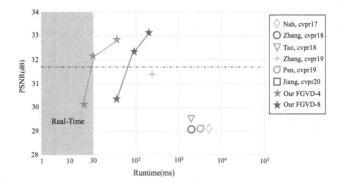

Fig. 2. The PSNR vs. runtime of state-of-the-art motion deblurring models on the GoPro dataset [11]. The blue region indicates real-time inference runtime. FGVD-4 and 8 represent the number of layers of our deblurring model (detailed in Sect. 3.4). The three stars in each line indicate the performance of models without events, with a single event representation, and with continuous event representations respectively. Our model achieves the highest PSNR of 33.02 dB for 1280×720 images. (Color figure online)

2   Related Work

Image Deblurring and Video Deblurring . [19] proposes a convolution neural network to estimate locally blur kernel, then uses the conventional energy-based optimization to estimate the latent sharp image. [5] uses a fully convolutional neural network to estimate optical flow from a single blurry image, then restore the blurry image from the estimated optical flow. [11] proposes a multi-scale CNN to restore sharp images in an end-to-end manner without estimating blur kernel. [20] proposes a coarse-to-fine SRN-Deblurnet to restore the blurry image on different levels. [7] proposes to take consecutive multiple frames as input, restoring the middle sharp image. [24] proposes a deep hierarchical multi-patch network via fine-to-coarse hierarchical representations, exploiting the deblurring cues at different scales. It is the first real-time deep motion deblurring model for 720p images at 30 fps. Recently, [13] formulates a deblurring task to an optimization problem by solving a single variable non-convex problem called the Event-based Double Integral (EDI) model.

Event Based Intensity Image Reconstruction. Event cameras such as DAVIS [3] and DVS [9] record intensity changes at a microsecond level do not suffer from motion blur. [1] proposes to estimate optical flow and intensity images simultaneously by minimizing energy. [2] learns a sparse patch-based dictionary to match event patches to gradient patch, then reconstruct intensity via Poisson integration. [10] restores intensity images through manifold regularization. DAVIS camera uses a share camera sensor that can simultaneously output events and intensity images (APS). Due to the noise and loss of details reconstructed with only events, [16] proposes an asynchronous event-driven complementary filter to combine the APS frame with events. [15] proposes a full convolutional recurrent UNet-like architecture to reconstruct intensity images from events only.

3 Method

3.1 Formulation

Intensity frames captured by the traditional camera may suffer from motion blur due to their long exposure time. Non-uniform motion deblurring remains a highly ill-posed problem due to the loss of important information e.g.. time information and image textures are destroyed.

Existing video deblurring methods reduce motion blurs using multiple frames to exploit the temporal information. Different from those coarser temporal information extracted from a long period, we propose to investigate the complete temporal information in the event steam in single exposure time. This allows more details to be restored, and it is easy to generate high frame rate videos. If we want to use fine-grained event representations to help deblurring task, we should first investigate the relationship between blurry frame and event representations.

We denote the blurry image input as B, a set of events as $E(t)$. Our objective is to restore sharp images and videos from blurry images and corresponding events. To this end, we should build a relationship between them. Inspired by [13], we have:

$$L(t) = L(t - T) + cE(t) \tag{1}$$

Equation 1 shows that the adjacent images can be related by integrating the events between the exposure time, where t refers to the current timestamp and T refers to the exposure time and $L(t)$ refers to the latent sharp image of the current timestamp. Because the previous latent image is impossible to get, we decide to exploit the complete information of the event, with a recurrent representation of the event, we can approximately get the similarly sharp image as $L(t - T)$.

We then further investigate the history information hidden in the event representations sequence, similar to the traditional video deblurring method. Define a finer time duration t_0, we can create any number of n event representations around the latent image $E(t) = \{e_1, e_2, e_3, ..., e_n\}$, $e_n = e(t - T + n * t_0)$, restore $L(t)$ more detailed and generate high frame rate video as,

$$\begin{cases} L(t) = & L(t - T) + c\{e_1, e_2, ..., e_{n-1}, e_n\} \\ L(t + t_0) = & L(t - T + t_0) + c\{e_2, e_3, ..., e_n, e_{n+1}\} \\ ..., \end{cases}$$

In general, we formulate the deblurring and video reconstruction tasks as residual learning ones and exploit the complete information encoded in the event representations in a fine-grained temporal step t_0. After we get a restored frame, we concatenate it with corresponding consecutive event representations with a tiny t_0 shift to get the next estimated frame $L(t + t_0)$. We then repeat this process to reconstruct a high frame rate video.

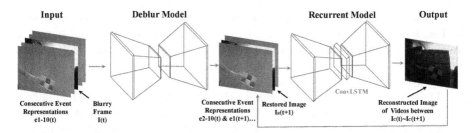

Fig. 3. Overview of our proposed Fine-Grained Video Deblur model (FGVD). The input of the deblur model is the concatenation of a blurry image $I(t)$ and consecutive event representations $e_{1-10}(t)$ around it, we use 10 as an example here. The deblurred image $I_R(t)$ is then stacked with shift representations group as input for the recurrent model to generate high frame rate video.

3.2   Overall Architecture

The overall of our framework is depicted in Fig. 3. By simultaneously inputting blurry images with corresponding events, our network can output a sequence of deblurred images to reconstruct a high frame rate video. We will introduce the consecutive event representations in Sect. 3.3. We use a deep multi-patch network as our deblur model (refer to Sect. 3.4 for details).

The architecture of the Recurrent Model is a popular encoder-decoder network with a convlstm model [23]. We first use the deblur model to restore a sharp image, then concatenate the sharp image with corresponding consecutive event representations for the next finer timestamp. The output of the Recurrent Model will continue to take as input to generate the next frame.

3.3   Event Representations

In order to be able to process the event stream, we need to convert the event stream into an image-like channel representation. A natural choice is to directly integrate the event on a $2D$ plane. [27] proposed to encode the events in a spatial-temporal voxel grad.

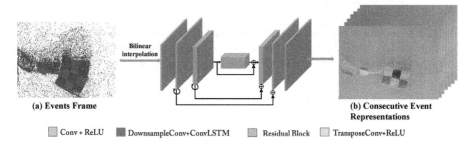

Fig. 4. The demonstration of the recurrent model generating consecutive event representations. (a) Directly integrate events frame. (b) consecutive event representations.

We use the architecture in Fig. 4 to generate our consecutive event representations inspired by [15]. The direct integration Fig. 4(a) or the spatial-temporal voxel or others frame like representation [4,21,26] may suffer from noise or lack details because of sparsity with little events. We need a representation that is similar to the latent sharp image with rich information as (b).

The event frame in Fig. 4(a) implies that the intensity image (APS) suffers from severe motion blurs during the exposure time. Because the model can generate event representations at a very high frame rate, the reconstructed event representations in Fig. 4(b) is clear. We apply a tiny time shift t_0 recurrent module to generate a large number of dense event representations around the blurry image, which supplement richer information about motion blurs.

3.4   Deblurring Model

[24] proposes a hierarchical multi-patch network inspired by Spatial Pyramid Matching [8]. The model as shown in Fig. 5 makes the lower level focus on local information to produce residual information for the coarser level, and achieves state-of-the-art performance with a fast inference runtime. B_i is the i_{th} level input which is the sum of the original blurred image and the output of the previous layer S_{i+1}.

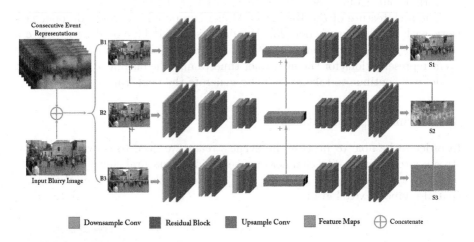

Fig. 5. The architecture of our used deblur model. The figure is a simple (1-2-4) model. The notation (1-2-4) indicates the numbers of image patches from the coarsest to the finniest level. *i.e.*, a vertical split at the second level, $2 \times 2 = 4$ splits at the third level.

4   Experiments

4.1   Implementation

Synthetic Dataset. In order to quantitatively compare our experiment results, we use the popular GoPro blurry dataset [11], which consists of 3214 pairs of blurred and sharp images captured at 720×1280 resolution. To get the simulated event data, we employ the ground-truth images to generate simulated event data based on ESIM [14].

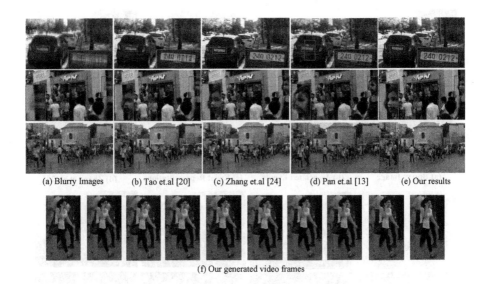

(a) Blurry Images   (b) Tao et.al [20]   (c) Zhang et.al [24]   (d) Pan et.al [13]   (e) Our results

(f) Our generated video frames

Fig. 6. Visual comparisons on GoPro dataset. Zoom in for the best view.

Real Dataset. We evaluate our method on the real blurry event dataset [13], captured by DAVIS-240C [3] under different conditions, such as indoor, outdoor, low lighting conditions, and different motion patterns such as camera shake, object motion. Besides, we also recorded a real event datasets with DAVIS-346 for testing.

Our experiments are implemented in Pytorch and evaluated on a single NVIDIA Tesla P100 GPU. The framework is trained in two consecutive steps. During the training of the deblur model, we randomly crop 256×256 patches from original blurry images, and forward these patches as inputs of each level. We normalize blurry and sharp images to $[0, 1]$ and subtract 0.5. The training batch size is set to 6. We employ Adam solver for training, where the learning rate is set to 0.0001, which is decayed by 0.1 per 500 epoch. The models are totally trained for 2000 epochs. During the training of the recurrent module, we fix the parameters of the deblurring model. The Adam optimizer of 0.0001 learning rate is used to train the recurrent module.

4.2   Experimental Results

We compare our proposed pipeline with previous deblurring works including conventional deblurring methods [13], learning-based deblurring methods [7,11, 20,24] and event-based image reconstruction methods [16].

Evaluation on Synthetic GoPro Dataset. The images shown in Fig. 6 demonstrate that our deblurred images achieve the best view quality, which

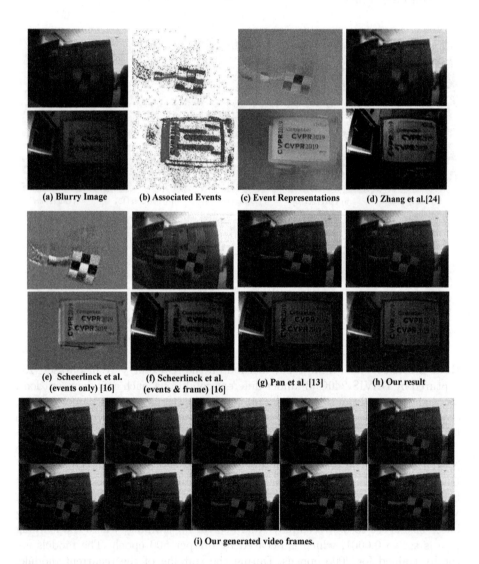

(a) Blurry Image   (b) Associated Events   (c) Event Representations   (d) Zhang et al.[24]

(e) Scheerlinck et al.   (f) Scheerlinck et al.   (g) Pan et al. [13]   (h) Our result
(events only) [16]   (events & frame) [16]

(i) Our generated video frames.

Fig. 7. Visual comparisons on real blurry event dataset [13] in low lighting and complex dynamic conditions.

is sharp and photorealistic. The qualitative comparisons in Table 1 show that our proposed model achieves a significant improvement in terms of PSNR.

Evaluation on the Real Dataset. As shown in Fig. 7, previous learning-based model (d) fails to restore the sharp images due to the lack of temporal information associated with motions. (e) The reconstruction with only events (due to the intense image blurry) loses backgrounds and has artifacts. A clear image is restored by EDI (g), but it suffers from noises and is non-photorealistic. Our method leverages the consecutive recurrent representations as supplementary information and successfully restores a sharp image (h). Following we generate a high frame-rate video using the recurrent module (i).

Table 1. Quantitative comparisons on the GoPro dataset 720p [11]. PSNR in dB, Runtime in ms, Model Size in MB. All models are tested under the same blurry condition and we use the pre-training models provided by these methods to conducting extensive testing. We train our model three times to get the average performance.

Models	PSNR	SSIM	Runtime	Model size
Sun et al. [19]	25.30	0.8511	12000	54.1
Gong et al. [5]	26.05	0.8632	9600	39.2
Jin et al. [7]	26.98	0.8922	1100	57.3
Tao et al. [20]	30.26	0.9342	1600	33.6
Nah et al. [11]	29.08	0.9135	4300	303.6
Pan et al. [13]	29.06	0.9430	3220	**0.51**
Zhang (1-2-4) [24]	30.21	0.9023	**17**	21.7
Stack2-VMPHN [24]	31.50	**0.9483**	552	86.8
Baseline-A	32.25	0.9285	31	57.8
Baseline-B	32.44	0.9301	97	64.7
FGVD-4 (Our)	32.82	0.9348	61	57.8
FGVD-8 (Our)	**33.02**	0.9362	121	64.7

Ablation Study. Here we perform ablation studies to demonstrate the efficiency of the consecutive event representations. Baseline-A in Table 1 is our FGVD-4 model using only a single event representation, and Baseline-B refers to FGVD-8. We test these models on both synthesis and real datasets. The results shown in Fig. 8 demonstrates that using the consecutive event representations in deblurring network can significantly improve the quality of deblurred images.

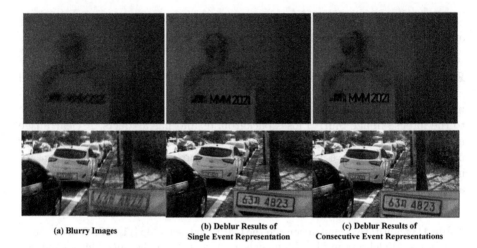

(a) Blurry Images   (b) Deblur Results of Single Event Representation   (c) Deblur Results of Consecutive Event Representations

Fig. 8. Ablation study. (a) The Blurry Images. (b) Deblur results of Baseline-B. (c) Deblur results of our FGVD-8.

5   Conclusion

In this paper, we propose a fine-grained video deblur and reconstruct model, namely FGVD, to restore and reconstruct high frame-rate sharp videos. We formulate the deblurring task as a residual learning process between blurry images and the latent sharp images in FGVD. Our experimental results demonstrate that the dense consecutive event representations can provide fine-grained motion information which is beneficial to restore sharp images. We achieve significant improvements in deblurring performance on both synthetic and real datasets, and successfully reconstructed high frame-rate sharp videos. Due to the low resolution of current event cameras, we want to build up a camera system, which employs an event camera to assist the high-resolution RGB camera, to address non-uniform motion deblurring problem in future works.

Acknowledge. This work is funded by the National Key R&D Program of China (2018YFB2202603), HGJ of China (2017ZX01028-103-002), and in part by the National Natural Science Foundation of China (61802427 & 61832018).

References

1. Bardow, P., Davison, A.J., Leutenegger, S.: Simultaneous optical flow and intensity estimation from an event camera. In: Proceedings of the IEEE Conference on Computer Vision and Pattern Recognition, pp. 884–892 (2016)
2. Barua, S., Miyatani, Y., Veeraraghavan, A.: Direct face detection and video reconstruction from event cameras. In: 2016 IEEE Winter Conference on Applications of Computer Vision (WACV), pp. 1–9. IEEE (2016)

3. Brandli, C., Berner, R., Yang, M., Liu, S.C., Delbruck, T.: A 240× 180 130 db 3 μs latency global shutter spatiotemporal vision sensor. IEEE J. Solid-State Circ. **49**(10), 2333–2341 (2014)
4. Chen, Y., Chen, W., Cao, X., Hua, Q.: Intensity-image reconstruction for event cameras using convolutional neural network. In: ICASSP 2020–2020 IEEE International Conference on Acoustics, Speech and Signal Processing (ICASSP), pp. 1973–1977. IEEE (2020)
5. Gong, D., et al.: From motion blur to motion flow: a deep learning solution for removing heterogeneous motion blur. In: The IEEE Conference on Computer Vision and Pattern Recognition (CVPR), July 2017
6. Jiang, Z., Zhang, Y., Zou, D., Ren, J., Lv, J., Liu, Y.: Learning event-based motion deblurring. In: Proceedings of the IEEE/CVF Conference on Computer Vision and Pattern Recognition, pp. 3320–3329 (2020)
7. Jin, M., Meishvili, G., Favaro, P.: Learning to extract a video sequence from a single motion-blurred image. In: Proceedings of the IEEE Conference on Computer Vision and Pattern Recognition, pp. 6334–6342 (2018)
8. Lazebnik, S., Schmid, C., Ponce, J.: Beyond bags of features: spatial pyramid matching for recognizing natural scene categories. In: 2006 IEEE Computer Society Conference on Computer Vision and Pattern Recognition (CVPR 2006), vol. 2, pp. 2169–2178. IEEE (2006)
9. Lichtsteiner, P., Posch, C., Delbruck, T.: A 128 backslashtimes 128 120 db 15 backslashmu s latency asynchronous temporal contrast vision sensor. IEEE J. Solid-State Circ. **43**(2), 566–576 (2008)
10. Munda, G., Reinbacher, C., Pock, T.: Real-time intensity-image reconstruction for event cameras using manifold regularisation. Int. J. Comput. Vis. **126**(12), 1381–1393 (2018)
11. Nah, S., Hyun Kim, T., Mu Lee, K.: Deep multi-scale convolutional neural network for dynamic scene deblurring. In: Proceedings of the IEEE Conference on Computer Vision and Pattern Recognition, pp. 3883–3891 (2017)
12. Pan, L., Hartley, R., Liu, M., Dai, Y.: Phase-only image based kernel estimation for single image blind deblurring. In: Proceedings of the IEEE Conference on Computer Vision and Pattern Recognition, pp. 6034–6043 (2019)
13. Pan, L., Scheerlinck, C., Yu, X., Hartley, R., Liu, M., Dai, Y.: Bringing a blurry frame alive at high frame-rate with an event camera. In: Proceedings of the IEEE Conference on Computer Vision and Pattern Recognition, pp. 6820–6829 (2019)
14. Rebecq, H., Gehrig, D., Scaramuzza, D.: ESIM: an open event camera simulator. In: Conference on Robot Learning, pp. 969–982 (2018)
15. Rebecq, H., Ranftl, R., Koltun, V., Scaramuzza, D.: Events-to-video: bringing modern computer vision to event cameras. In: Proceedings of the IEEE Conference on Computer Vision and Pattern Recognition, pp. 3857–3866 (2019)
16. Scheerlinck, C., Barnes, N., Mahony, R.: Continuous-time intensity estimation using event cameras. In: Jawahar, C.V., Li, H., Mori, G., Schindler, K. (eds.) ACCV 2018. LNCS, vol. 11365, pp. 308–324. Springer, Cham (2019). https://doi.org/10.1007/978-3-030-20873-8_20
17. Schuler, C.J., Hirsch, M., Harmeling, S., Schölkopf, B.: Learning to deblur. IEEE Trans. Pattern Anal. Mach. Intell. **38**(7), 1439–1451 (2015)
18. Su, S., Delbracio, M., Wang, J., Sapiro, G., Heidrich, W., Wang, O.: Deep video deblurring for hand-held cameras. In: Proceedings of the IEEE Conference on Computer Vision and Pattern Recognition, pp. 1279–1288 (2017)

19. Sun, J., Cao, W., Xu, Z., Ponce, J.: Learning a convolutional neural network for non-uniform motion blur removal. In: Proceedings of the IEEE Conference on Computer Vision and Pattern Recognition, pp. 769–777 (2015)
20. Tao, X., Gao, H., Shen, X., Wang, J., Jia, J.: Scale-recurrent network for deep image deblurring. In: Proceedings of the IEEE Conference on Computer Vision and Pattern Recognition, pp. 8174–8182 (2018)
21. Wang, L., Ho, Y.S., Yoon, K.J., et al.: Event-based high dynamic range image and very high frame rate video generation using conditional generative adversarial networks. In: Proceedings of the IEEE Conference on Computer Vision and Pattern Recognition, pp. 10081–10090 (2019)
22. Xiao, L., Wang, J., Heidrich, W., Hirsch, M.: Learning high-order filters for efficient blind deconvolution of document photographs. In: Leibe, B., Matas, J., Sebe, N., Welling, M. (eds.) ECCV 2016. LNCS, vol. 9907, pp. 734–749. Springer, Cham (2016). https://doi.org/10.1007/978-3-319-46487-9_45
23. Xingjian, S., Chen, Z., Wang, H., Yeung, D.Y., Wong, W.K., Woo, W.C.: Convolutional LSTM network: a machine learning approach for precipitation nowcasting. In: Advances in Neural Information Processing Systems, pp. 802–810 (2015)
24. Zhang, H., Dai, Y., Li, H., Koniusz, P.: Deep stacked hierarchical multi-patch network for image deblurring. In: Proceedings of the IEEE Conference on Computer Vision and Pattern Recognition, pp. 5978–5986 (2019)
25. Zhang, J., et al.: Dynamic scene deblurring using spatially variant recurrent neural networks. In: Proceedings of the IEEE Conference on Computer Vision and Pattern Recognition, pp. 2521–2529 (2018)
26. Zhu, A.Z., Yuan, L., Chaney, K., Daniilidis, K.: Unsupervised event-based learning of optical flow, depth, and egomotion. In: Proceedings of the IEEE Conference on Computer Vision and Pattern Recognition, pp. 989–997 (2019)
27. Zhu, A.Z., Yuan, L., Chaney, K., Daniilidis, K.: Unsupervised event-based optical flow using motion compensation. In: Proceedings of the European Conference on Computer Vision (ECCV), pp. 711–714 (2018)

Discriminative and Selective Pseudo-Labeling for Domain Adaptation

Fei Wang, Youdong Ding$^{(\boxtimes)}$, Huan Liang, and Jing Wen

Department of Film and Television Engineering, Shanghai Engineering Research
Center of Motion Picture Special Effects, Shanghai University,
Shanghai 200072, People's Republic of China
{s852989587,ydding,Lianghuan,winjing}@shu.edu.cn

Abstract. Unsupervised domain adaptation aims to transfer the knowledge of source domain to a related but not labeled target domain. Due to the lack of label information of target domain, most existing methods train a weak classifier and directly apply to pseudo-labeling which may downgrade adaptation performance. To address this problem, in this paper, we propose a novel discriminative and selective pseudo-labeling (DSPL) method for domain adaptation. Specifically, we first match the marginal distributions of two domains and increase inter-class distance simultaneously. Then a feature transformation method is proposed to learn a low-dimensional transfer subspace which is discriminative enough. Finally, after data has formed good clusters, we introduce a structured prediction based selective pseudo-labeling strategy which is able to sufficiently exploit target data structure. We conduct extensive experiments on three popular visual datasets, demonstrating the good domian adaptation performance of our method.

Keywords: Unsupervised domain adaptation · Pseudo-labeling · Discriminative learned subspace

1 Introduction

In a large number of machine learning methods, models trained with labeled training data may lead to large errors when directly apply to testing data. This is mainly because two kinds of data are sampled from different distributions and there are large domain discrepancy between two domains. For example, images can be very different with different shooting angles, backgrounds or lighting conditions. Moreover, although we can acquire generous images from the Internet, labeling them is a time-consuming and expensive work. Unsupervised domain adaptation (UDA) aims to reduce these domain discrepancy and leverage the knowledge from labeled source domain to unlabeled target domain [1].

Most UDA approaches aim to learn a domain-invariant projection and project source domain and target domain into a subspace where the data distributions can be aligned adequately. Transfer component analysis (TCA) [2] only matched

© Springer Nature Switzerland AG 2021
J. Lokoč et al. (Eds.): MMM 2021, LNCS 12572, pp. 365–377, 2021.
https://doi.org/10.1007/978-3-030-67832-6_30

the marginal distributions, joint distribution adaptation (JDA) [3] improved it by matching conditional distributions concurrently. Based on JDA, many UDA methods [4–8] have been proposed. In order to match the conditional distributions, these UDA approaches need to get labels of target domain (which utilize the class information of source domain). These methods all trained a weak classifier like 1-NN or SVM to get pseudo labels while ignored the uncertainty of labels' accuracy which may cause catastrophic errors in the learning process. In other words, the errors of last iteration may deliver to the next iteration and degrade the adaptation performance.

On the other hand, it is not enough to only minimize the domain discrepancy because Ben-David et al. [9] have illustrated that the generalization error of target domain trained from source domain is identified by the both domain divergence and classifier performance in source domain. As for the classification problems, the basic idea is that instances of the same class should be clustered together, while different class should be separated sufficiently far. In this way, the discriminative power of source domain can pass to the target domain naturally. Inspired by this idea, visual domain adaptation was proposed to [10] improve JDA [3] by forming compact clusters which can preserve more separability. Domain-irrelevant class clustering (DICE) [6] utilized clustering theory to increase the intra-class compactness in both domains. Selective Pseudo-Labeling (SPL) [11] was based on locality preserving projections (LPP) [12] and proposed a new pseudo-labeling strategy. However, they both overlooked the inter-class distance, which is beneficial for adaptation performance. Note that, a discriminative subspace is imperative for pseudo-labeling, because if data tend to form discrete clusters, then instances in the same cluster are more likely to share a label (In other words, if two classes are too close, instances can be easily classified into wrong classes).

In this paper, we propose a discriminative and selective pseudo-labeling (DSPL) method to tackle these two issues. DSPL aims to learn a discriminative feature-invariant subspace where source domain and target domain can be aligned well to reduce domain discrepancy. Specifically, we first match the marginal distributions and increase inter-class distance simultaneously. Then, we propose a discriminative subspace learning method which is beneficial for pseudo-labeling. Finally, we introduce a selective pseudo-labeling strategy which sufficiently consider structural information of target domain.

Our contributions can be summarized as:

- We propose a novel discriminative pseudo-labeling method for domain adaptation, DSPL is able to align the distributions well and perform selective pseudo-labeling which keep the consecutiveness of labels' accuracy.
- We propose a discriminative subspace learning method which fully exploit the class information of both domains to preserve compactness within-class and separability between-class.
- We conduct extensive experiments on three widely-used domain adaptation datasets and compare with seven relevant state-of-the-art baseline methods, demonstrating the good performance of our proposed approach.

2   Related Work

In this section, we briefly review some UDA methods. Because DSPL is a kind of feature based method. We will introduce related work in three aspects, including: distribution alignment, subspace learning and deep learning methods. In distribution alignment, many effective methods have been proposed [2–5]. TCA [2] firstly performed the marginal distribution alignment by a MMD [17] function. JDA [3] enhanced TCA by exploiting the same class information and jointly matched the both marginal and conditional distribution. Balanced distribution adaptation [4] added a balanced factor to manually weight the two kinds of distributions. Joint geometrical and statistical alignment (JGSA) [5] are proposed to learn map the source domain and the target domain into two coupled subspaces and then reduced the geometrical shift and distribution shift simultaneously. Besides, JGSA also considered the source-domain discriminative information. However, these works all trained a base classifier (1-NN or SVM) to predict pseudo labels of target domain, which may downgrade the adaptation performance.

Apart from the distribution alignment methods, the goals of subspace learning methods are using the learning subspaces of two domains to represent the original space which are invariant across domains. The work of [13] aimed to represent the original feature by the subspaces which are described by the base vectors. Correlation alignment [14] adapted second-order statistics of source domain and target domain to minimize the domain discrepancy. Geodesic flow kernel [15] are proposed to learn a geodesic flow kernel on a manifold between domains. Manifold embedded distribution alignment (MEDA) [8] extended the idea of samples in manifold and learned a domain-invariant classifier in the Grassmann manifold.

Domain Adaptation have achieved remarkable performance with the rapid development of deep learning. Deep domain confusion [16] is the first domain adaptation work with linear MMD loss in a single layer network. Deep adaptation networks [18] added multiple-kernel MMD to adapt the discrepancy on several fully connected layers. Joint adaptation networks [19] enhanced it by using a joint MMD loss to align joint discrepancy in multiple task-specific layers. Contrastive Adaptation Network [20] optimizes the intra-class and inter-class domain discrepancy through an alternating update strategy. Inspired by the idea of generative adversarial networks, adversarial learning has become a mainstream approach which can help learn more discriminative representations. The work of [21] aligned feature distributions in a network by inverse backpropagation. Unlike most adversarial learning based methods, Incremental Collaborative and Adversarial Network [22] additionally learned informative domain representations and iteratively performed a sample selection.

In short, our method combined the advantages of distribution alignment and subspace learning. However, our method differs from existing works mainly in two aspects. Firstly, we propose a discriminative subspace learning method which explicitly model both intra-class and inter-class information. Secondly, instead of using a weak classifier to predict labels, we conduct a selective pseudo-labeling strategy which exploit the cluster structure of target data.

3 Proposed Method

3.1 Notations and Problem Definition

Suppose that $D_s = \{(x_s^i, y_s^i)\}_{i=1}^{n_s}$ denotes n_s instances and corresponding labels of the source domain and $D_t = \{(x_t^i)\}_{i=1}^{n_t}$ denotes n_t unlabeled data in the target domain. In UDA, source domain matrix $X_s \in \mathbb{R}^{d \times n_s}$ and target domain matrix $X_t \in \mathbb{R}^{d \times n_t}$ share the same dimensionality d. Similarly, $Y_s \in \mathbb{R}^{n_s \times 1}$ and $Y_t \in \mathbb{R}^{n_t \times 1}$ denote the label matrices of the source domain and target domain, respectively. Because the source domain D_s and the target domain D_t are sampled from different distributions, there will be large discrepancy between two domains. The goal of UDA is to learn a feature projection $\varphi(\bullet)$ by using the labeled domain D_s which can sufficiently align the both marginal and conditional distributions like $P_s(\varphi(X_s)) = P_t(\varphi(X_t))$ and $P_s(Y_s|\varphi(X_t)) = P_t(Y_s|\varphi(X_t))$. Then a classifier is learned to predict the labels $y_t \in Y_t$ for D_t.

3.2 Marginal Distributions Alignment

Different from [11] using PCA to reduce the data dimensionality. We follow TCA [2] to match the marginal distributions and reduce the high dimensional deep features simultaneously. The objective function of TCA is defined as:

$$\min \|\frac{1}{n_s} \sum_{i=1}^{n_s} A^T x_i - \frac{1}{n_t} \sum_{j=1}^{n_t} A^T x_j\|^2 = \min \operatorname{tr}\left(A^T X M_0 X^T A\right) \tag{1}$$

where M_0 is the MMD matrix and is computed as follows:

$$(M_0)_{ij} = \begin{cases} 1/n_s^2, & x_i, x_j \in D_s \\ 1/n_t^2, & x_i, x_j \in D_t \\ -1/n_s n_t, & \text{otherwise} \end{cases} \tag{2}$$

Although the deep features can be clustered well, which means the same-class samples of source domain are 'close' enough, we still need to ensure that different-class samples should be as 'far' as possible. Therefore, we follow [23] to introduce a repulsive force distance, it is computed as:

$$\max \sum_{c=1}^{C} \left\| \frac{1}{n_s^{(c)}} \sum_{x_i \in D_s^{(c)}} A^T x_i - \frac{1}{\sum_{r \in G_s} n_s^{(r)}} \sum_{x_j \in D_s^{(r)}} A^T x_j \right\|^2 = \max \sum_{c=1}^{C} \operatorname{tr}\left(A^T X M_S X^T A\right) \tag{3}$$

where $G_s = \{\{1 \ldots C\} - \{c\}\}$, c is the cth class of source domain and M_S is computed as follows:

$$(M_S)_{ij} = \begin{cases} 1/n_s^{(c)2}, & x_i, x_j \in D_s^{(c)} \\ 1/n_s^{(r)^2}, & x_i, x_j \in D_s^{(r)} \\ -1/n_s^{(c)}n_s^{(r)}, & \begin{cases} x_i \in D_s^{(c)}, x_j \in D_s^{(r)} \\ x_i \in D_s^{(r)}, x_j \in D_s^{(c)} \end{cases} \\ 0, & \text{otherwise.} \end{cases} \tag{4}$$

Equation (3) means that the inter-class distance of source domain should be 'far' away. Combine (1) (3) and we can get the following eigenvalue problem:

$$(X(M_0 - \mu \sum_{c=1}^{C} M_S)X^T + \lambda I)A = XHX^T A\Phi \tag{5}$$

where μ and λ are two trade-off parameters. $H = I - \frac{1}{n_s+n_t}\mathbf{1}\mathbf{1}^{\mathbf{T}}$ is the centering matrix. Note that XHX^T aims to avoid the trivial solution and it is equivalent to PCA. By solving this eigenvalue problem, we can get the d_1 corresponding eigenvectors of the d_1 smallest eigenvalues $A = [a_1, \ldots, a_{d_1}] \in \mathbb{R}^{d \times d_1}$ and the new data feature representation: $X_s' = A^T X_s$ and $X_t' = A^T X_t$.

3.3 Discriminative Subspace Learning

It is not enough to match only marginal distributions because the class information between domains has not be sufficiently utilized. LPP [12] aims to preserve data structure after subspace learning. The objective function of LPP is:

$$\min_P \sum_{i,j} \left\| P^T x_i' - P^T x_j' \right\|_2^2 Q_{ij} \tag{6}$$

where $P \in \mathbb{R}^{d_1 \times d_2}$ is the learned feature projection, x_i' and x_j' are source domain and target domain data after marginal distributions alignment, respectively. The similarity matrix Q is defined as:

$$Q_{ij} = \begin{cases} 1, y_i = y_j \\ 0, \text{ otherwise} \end{cases} \tag{7}$$

which means if two samples share the same class no matter which domain they are, they should be as 'close' as possible after projection. Although we have ensured that source domain is discriminative enough in last section which implies that different class of target domain would be 'far' away, we can not guarantee that after subspace learning, the discriminant information is still preserved. Hence, we use discriminant locality preserving projections (DLPP) [24] to learn a discriminative feature projection P which can significantly reduce domain shift. The objective function of DLPP can be defined as:

$$\max_P \frac{\text{tr}\left(P^T(X'DX'^T + FNF^T)P\right)}{\text{tr}\left(P^T\left(X'LX'^T + I\right)P\right)} \tag{8}$$

where $L = D - Q$ is the laplacian matrix, D is computed as: $D_{ii} = \sum_j Q_{ij}$. The L2 regularization $\text{tr}\left(P^T P\right)$ is added to avoid numerical instability issues. $F = [f_1, f_2, \ldots, f_c] \in \mathbb{R}^{c \times d_1}$ is the mean of different classes in source domain. Because the uncertainty of target domain, we only maximize the inter-class distance of source domain. $N = E - B$, B is the weight matrix between two classes' mean, it is defined as: $B_{ij} = \exp\left(- \|f_i - f_j\|^2 / t\right)$, where t can be determined empirically; $E_{ii} = \sum_j B_{ij}$. Maximizing the numerator tends to separate f_i and f_j as 'far' as possible, while minimizing the denominator tends to ensure x_i and x_j 'close' enough.

Equation (8) is equivalent to the following eigenvalue problem:

$$(X' DX'^T + FNF^T)P = \left(X' LX'^T + I\right) P\Psi \tag{9}$$

By solving this eigenvalue problem, we can get the d_2 corresponding eigenvectors of the d_2 largest eigenvalues $P = [p_1, \ldots, p_{d_2}] \in \mathbb{R}^{d_1 \times d_2}$. The projected data can be computed as: $Z_s = P^T X'_s$ and $Z_t = P^T X'_t$

Because there are no labels in target domain, in next section, we will describe how to get the pseudo labels of target domain.

3.4   Pseudo Labels Prediction

The aforementioned discriminative subspace has fully paved the way for obtaining pseudo labels. Instead of using a standard classifier, we follow [11] to introduce a structured prediction based selective pseudo-labeling method. After marginal and conditional distributions using Eq. (5) and Eq. (9), the learned subspace has been discriminative enough. In this way, one way to predict the target labels is that if one sample is closer to one certain class, it is more likely to belong to this class. Then the target labels can be defined as following equation:

$$p_1\left(y|x^t\right) = \frac{\exp\left(- \left\|z^t - \overline{z}^s_y\right\|\right)}{\sum_{y=1}^{|\mathcal{Y}|} \exp\left(-\|z^t - \overline{z}^s_y\|\right)} \tag{10}$$

where z^t and $\overline{z}^s_i$ are the target data and the mean of source class i after projection, respectively. On the other hand, if the target domain forms nice clusters, the structural information of target domain can be used to improve classification performance [25]. Specifically, we use K-means to form y clusters which are initialised with the class means of source domain, then the target labels can be calculated as:

$$p_2\left(y|x^t\right) = \frac{\exp\left(- \left\|z^t - \overline{z}^t_y\right\|\right)}{\sum_{y=1}^{|\mathcal{Y}|} \exp\left(-\|z^t - \overline{z}^t_y\|\right)} \tag{11}$$

where $\overline{z}^t_i$ denotes the i-th cluster center of target domain. It is better to take advantage of both of them, then the label of a given x^t can be calculated as:

$$\hat{y}^t = \arg\max_{y \in \mathcal{Y}} \{p_1\left(y|\boldsymbol{x}^t\right), p_2\left(y|\boldsymbol{x}^t\right)\} \tag{12}$$

Instead of using all target samples in subspace learning, it is better to progressively select samples because incorrect samples may cause wrong error accumulation during learning. In this case, we select kn_t/T samples in k-th iterations where T is the number of iterations. For each class c, top kn_t^c/T high-probability samples is selected. The pseudo code is shown in Algorithm 1.

Algorithm 1. Discriminative selective pseudo-labeling for unsupervised domain adaptaion

---

Require: Source data and labels:X_s, Y_s, target data: X_t, parameters: $T, d_1, d_2, \mu, \lambda$;
Ensure: Target labels y_t;
1: Marginal distributions alignment using Eq.(5) ;
2: Solve Eq.(9) to get the initialized project matrix P_0 with only source data;
3: Predict the target labels using Eq.(12);
4: **while** $k < T$ **do**
5:    $k \leftarrow k + 1$;
6:    Select kn_t/T target samples;
7:    Update project matrix P using Eq.(9) with all source data and selective target data;
8:    Update labels of target domain using Eq.(12).
9: **end while**

---

4   Experiments

4.1   Datasets

Office-31 is the most popular image benchmark dataset for domain adaptation. It contains 4,652 real-world objects images with 31 categories from three different domains:Amazon (A), Webcam (W), DSLR (D). We constructed 6 transfer tasks: $A \to W$, $D \to W$, $W \to D$, $A \to D$, $D \to A$, $W \to A$.

Office-Caltech is based on **Office-31** and introduce a new domain Caltech-256 (C) for studying larger discrepancy. It contains 30,607 images with 256 categories. Ten overlapping classes are selected to the dataset. We constructed 12 transfer tasks: $C \to A$, ... , $D \to W$.

Office-Home is a challenging dataset which contains 65 kinds of object images crawled from ofiice and home settings. There are 15,588 images from four kinds of domains: Art (Ar), Clipart (Cl), Product (Pr) and Real-world (Rw). We constructed 12 transfer tasks: $Ar \to Cl$, ... , $Rw \to Pr$.

Figure 1 highlights the differences among different domains with example images from the category of MONITOR and TV on Office-Caltech and Office-Home.

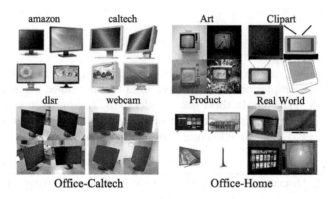

Fig. 1. Example images from the MONITOR category in amazon, caltech, dlsr and webcam on Office-Caltech and example images from the TV category in Art, Clipart, Product and Real World on Office-Home

4.2 Experimental Setting

For fair comparison, we adopt Decaf6 [26] features for **Office-Caltech** and ResNet50 features for **Office-31** and **Office-Home**. The ResNet50 features are described in [11]. For different datasets, we set different parameters, $T = 10, \lambda = 0.1$ for all three datasets, **Office-31**($d_1 = 800, d_2 = 200, \mu = 0.5$), **Office-Caltech**($d_1 = 100, d_2 = 80, \mu = 0.1$), **Office-Home**($d_1 = 1300, d_2 = 100, \mu = 0.2$). The parameters are set according to the original papers to obtain the optimal results for all compared methods. In the training process, all labeled source domain samples and all unlabeled target domain samples are adopted.

4.3 Experimental Results and Analysis

We compare our method with 7 state-of-the-arts, including TCA [2], JDA [3], JGSA [5], DICE [6], MEDA [8], CAPLS [27] and SPL [11]. The classification accuracy of unlabeled target domain on three datasets are shown in the Table 1, Table 2 and Table 3 respectively. We can observe from the tables that DSPL outperformed in 19 tasks of all 30 tasks and performed best in average on all three datasets. The results clearly indicated the outstanding adaptation performance of DSPL. The existing methods all have limitations which can not handle domain adaptation in some tasks. For example, TCA, JDA, JGSA and DICE all trained a weak classifier to predict target labels which may lead to misclassification. CAPLS and SPL did not learn a discriminative enough subspace to adapt two domains where there still exists large domain discrepancy. Since these datasets are selected from numerous domains, including real-world, art, product and clipart images, DSPL is able to tackle domain adaptation issues well.

There are mainly three components in DSPL: marginal distributions alignment (MDA), discriminative subspace learning (DSL) and selective pseudo labeling (SPL). We conducted an ablation study to evaluate the importance of each

Table 1. Accuracy (%) on Office-31 datasets

Task	TCA	JDA	JGSA	DICE	MEDA	CDPLS	SPL	DSPL
$A \rightarrow W$	72.6	76.1	85.2	78.5	86.2	90.6	**92.7**	91.7
$D \rightarrow W$	96.9	97.1	97.9	98.7	97.2	98.6	98.2	**99.1**
$W \rightarrow D$	98.2	97.2	**100.0**	99.6	99.4	99.6	99.8	99.8
$A \rightarrow D$	72.5	76.3	86.8	80.9	85.3	88.6	93.0	**93.8**
$D \rightarrow A$	65.0	69.4	71.2	68.5	72.4	75.4	76.4	**79.2**
$W \rightarrow A$	62.0	68.2	71.0	67.6	74.0	76.3	76.8	**79.2**
Average	77.9	80.7	85.4	82.3	85.7	88.2	89.6	**90.5**

Table 2. Accuracy (%) on Office-Caltech datasets

Task	TCA	JDA	JGSA	DICE	MEDA	CDPLS	SPL	DSPL
$C \rightarrow A$	89.0	91.0	91.4	92.3	**93.4**	90.8	92.7	**93.4**
$C \rightarrow W$	75.6	82.4	86.8	93.6	**95.6**	85.4	93.2	91.2
$C \rightarrow D$	84.7	87.9	93.6	93.6	91.1	95.5	**98.7**	97.5
$A \rightarrow C$	83.1	85.0	84.9	85.9	87.4	86.1	87.4	**88.7**
$A \rightarrow W$	76.3	83.1	81.0	86.4	88.1	87.1	95.3	**96.3**
$A \rightarrow D$	84.7	86.6	88.5	89.8	88.1	**94.9**	89.2	90.4
$W \rightarrow C$	79.0	85.3	85.0	85.3	**93.2**	88.2	87.0	87.9
$W \rightarrow A$	81.3	91.1	90.7	90.7	**99.4**	92.3	92.0	93.6
$W \rightarrow D$	**100.0**	**100.0**	**100.0**	**100.0**	99.4	**100.0**	**100.0**	99.4
$D \rightarrow C$	81.7	85.1	86.2	87.4	87.5	88.8	88.6	**90.3**
$D \rightarrow A$	89.0	91.0	92.0	92.5	93.2	93.0	92.9	**93.3**
$D \rightarrow W$	98.6	99.7	99.7	99.0	97.6	**100.0**	98.6	**100.0**
Average	85.3	86.2	90.0	91.4	92.8	91.8	93.0	**93.5**

component. For MDA and DSL, we adopt a standard classifier (1-NN) to predict the pseudo labels as previous works do [3,5,6]. The ablation study is shown in Fig. 2. The figure indicates that each component is crucial for improving accuracy. Among them, discriminative subspace learning is the most important because there is large domain shift and it is also critical for the final pseudo-labeling.

4.4 Parameter Sensitivity and Visualization Analysis

In this section, we first analyze the parameter sensitivity of DSPL. There are five parameters in DSPL: $T, \lambda, d_1, d_2, \mu$. To ensure the optimal performance of the our method, we empirically set $T = 10, \lambda = 0.1$ for all three datasets. Classification accuracy w.r.t. d_1, d_1 and μ for three datasets are shown in Fig. 3. As we can see, when the value of d_1, d_2 are too small, it will degrade classification performance.

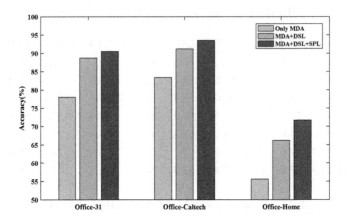

Fig. 2. Ablation study on three datasets.

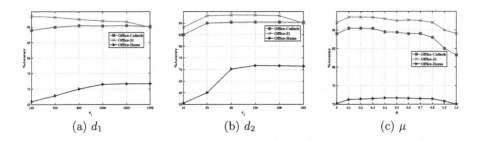

(a) d_1 (b) d_2 (c) μ

Fig. 3. (a)~(c): Classification accuracy w.r.t. d_1, d_1 and μ.

Table 3. Accuracy (%) on Office-Home datasets

Task	TCA	JDA	JGSA	DICE	MEDA	CDPLS	SPL	DSPL
$Ar \rightarrow Cl$	41.2	43.3	44.7	50.7	51.1	**56.2**	54.5	54.2
$Ar \rightarrow Pr$	60.4	62.4	65.2	72.6	74.6	78.3	77.8	**78.4**
$Ar \rightarrow Rw$	65.3	66.2	69.3	77.2	76.4	80.2	**81.9**	81.8
$Cl \rightarrow Ar$	48.4	48.0	51.9	59.7	62.3	66.0	65.1	**67.1**
$Cl \rightarrow Pr$	58.4	59.1	66.1	73.4	77.7	75.4	78.0	**78.4**
$Cl \rightarrow Rw$	60.4	60.3	65.0	73.5	75.7	78.4	81.1	**81.3**
$Pr \rightarrow Ar$	50.5	50.8	57.6	62.0	63.8	66.4	66.0	**66.6**
$Pr \rightarrow Cl$	43.3	45.5	46.6	50.4	51.9	53.2	53.1	**53.8**
$Pr \rightarrow Rw$	69.1	71.5	73.2	79.4	79.9	81.1	82.8	**83.2**
$Rw \rightarrow Ar$	60.5	60.1	62.5	67.3	68.1	**71.6**	69.9	71.5
$Rw \rightarrow Cl$	46.6	48.5	49.8	55.3	54.2	56.1	55.3	**57.4**
$Rw \rightarrow Pr$	74.1	75.0	76.5	81.3	82.3	84.3	86.0	**86.1**
Average	56.5	57.6	60.7	66.9	68.2	70.6	71.0	**71.7**

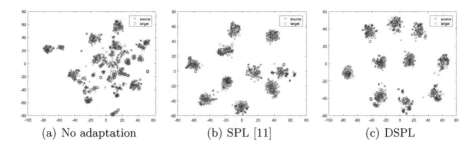

(a) No adaptation   (b) SPL [11]   (c) DSPL

Fig. 4. (a)∼(c): The t-SNE visualizations on $A \rightarrow W$ task.

The reason lies on that if d_1, d_2 are too small, the learning subspace may lose much feature information. When d_1, d_2 are big enough, they has little influence on DSPL. There is a large range of μ ($\mu \in [0.1, 0.5]$) can be selected to obtain optimal methods. However, if μ is too large, it may remove some useful features. To summarize, our proposed method is insensitive to parameters, showing the robustness of DSPL.

Figure 4 shows the t-SNE visualizations on $A \rightarrow W$ task. The blue points represent the instances of source domain, while the red points represent target domain. We can observe from the figure that if there is no adaptation, it is hardly to directly apply source domain to target domain for the large domain discrepancy. Compared to SPL , DSPL outperforms on separating different class away which is crucial for pseudo labeling. Besides, the target domain and source domain are highly overlapped which is easily for classification.

5   Conclusion

We propose a novel domain adaptation method discriminative selective pseudo-labeling (DSPL). Compared to the existing approaches, instead of using a standard classifier, we introduce a selective pseudo-labeling strategy which can significantly boost domain adaptation performance. Moreover, we propose a discriminative subspace learning method which is crucial for predicting labels. We conduct experiments on three well-known datasets with seven state-of-the-art methods. The experimental results and ablation study validate the excellent classification accuracy and effectiveness of DSPL.

Acknowledgment. This work was funded by the National Natural Science Foundation of China (Grant No. 61303093, 61402278).

References

1. Wang, Q., Breckon, T.P.: A survey on transfer learning. IEEE Trans. Knowl. Data Eng. **22**(10), 1345–1359 (2010)

2. Pan, S.J., Tsang, I.W., Kwok, J.T., Yang, Q.: Domain adaptation via transfer component analysis. IEEE Trans. Neural Netw. **22**(2), 199–210 (2011)
3. Long, M., Wang, J., Ding, G., Sun, J., Yu, P.S.: Transfer feature learning with joint distribution adaptation. In: ICCV, pp. 2200–2207 (2013)
4. Wang, J., Chen, Y., Hao, S., Feng, W., Shen, Z.: Balanced distribution adaptation for transfer learning. In: ICDM, pp. 1129–1134 (2017)
5. Zhang, J., Li, W., Ogunbona, P.: Joint geometrical and statistical alignment for visual domain adaptation. In: CVPR, pp. 5150–5158 (2017)
6. Liang, J., He, R., Sun, Z., Tan, T.: Aggregating randomized clustering-promoting invariant projections for domain adaptation. IEEE Trans. Pattern Anal. Mach. Intell. **41**(5), 1027–1042 (2019)
7. Li, S., Song, S., Huang, G., Ding, Z., Wu, C.: Domain invariant and class discriminative feature learning for visual domain adaptation. IEEE Trans. Image Process. **27**(9), 4260–4273 (2018)
8. Wang, J., Feng, W., Chen, Y., Yu, H., Huang, M., Yu, P.S.: Visual domain adaptation with manifold embedded distribution alignment. In: ACM MM, pp. 402–410 (2018)
9. David, S.B., Blitzer, J., Crammer, K., Pereira, F.: Analysis of representations for domain adaptation. In: NIPS, pp. 137–144 (2006)
10. Tahmoresnezhad, Jafar, Hashemi, Sattar: Visual domain adaptation via transfer feature learning. Knowl. Inf. Syst. **50**(2), 585–605 (2016). https://doi.org/10.1007/s10115-016-0944-x
11. Wang, Q., Breckon, T.P.: Unsupervised domain adaptation via structured prediction based selective Pseudo-Labeling. In: AAAI, pp. 6243–6250 (2020)
12. He, X., Niyogi, P.: Locality preserving projections. In: NIPS, pp. 153–160 (2003)
13. Fernando, B., Habrard, A., Sebban, M., Tuytelaars, T.: Unsupervised visual domain adaptation using subspace alignment. In: ICCV, pp. 2960–2967 (2013)
14. Sun, B., Feng, J., Saenko, K.: Return of frustratingly easy domain adaptation. In: AAAI, pp. 2058–2065 (2016)
15. Gong, B., Shi, Y., Sha, F., Grauman, K.: Geodesic flow kernel for unsupervised domain adaptation. In: CVPR, pp. 2066–2073 (2012)
16. Tzeng, E., Hoffman, J., Zhang, N., Saenko, K.: Darrell, T.: Deep domain confusion: maximizing for domain invariance. arXiv preprint arXiv:1412.3474abs/1412.3474 (2014)
17. Gretton, A., Borgwardt, K.M., Rasch, M.J., Schölkopf, B., Smola, A.J.: A Kernel two-sample test. J. Mach. Learn. Res. **13**, 723–773 (2012)
18. Long, M., Cao, Y., Wang, J., Jordan, M.I.: Learning transferable features with deep adaptation networks. In: ICML, pp. 97–105 (2015)
19. Long, M., Zhu, H., Wang, J., Jordan, M.I.: Deep transfer learning with joint adaptation networks. In: ICML, pp. 2208–2217 (2017)
20. Kang, G., Jiang, L., Yang, Y., Hauptmann, A.G.: Unsupervised domain adaptation with similarity learning. In: CVPR, pp. 4893–4902 (2018)
21. Ganin, Y., Lempitsky, V.S.: Unsupervised domain adaptation by backpropagation. In: ICML, pp. 1180–1189 (2015)
22. Zhang, W., Ouyang, W., Li, W., Xu, D.: Collaborative and adversarial network for unsupervised domain adaptation. In: CVPR, pp. 3801–3809 (2018)
23. Luo, L., Chen, L., Lu, Y., Hu, S.: Discriminative label consistent domain adaptation. arXiv preprint arXiv:1802.08077 (2018)
24. Yu, W., Teng, X., Liu, C.: Face recognition using discriminant locality preserving projections. Image Vis. Comput. **24**(3), 239–248 (2006)

25. Zhang, Z., Saligrama, V.: Zero-shot recognition via structured prediction. In: ECCV, pp. 533–548 (2016)
26. Donahue, J., Jia, Y., Vinyals, O., Hoffman, J., Zhang, N., Tzeng, E.: DeCAF: a deep convolutional activation feature for generic visual recognition. In: ICML, pp. 647–655 (2014)
27. Wang, Q., Bu, P., Breckon, T.P.: Unifying unsupervised domain adaptation and zero-shot visual recognition. In: IJCNN, pp. 1–8 (2019)

Multi-level Gate Feature Aggregation with Spatially Adaptive Batch-Instance Normalization for Semantic Image Synthesis

Jia Long[1] and Hongtao Lu[1,2(✉)]

[1] Key Lab of Shanghai Education Commission for Intelligent Interaction
and Cognitive Engineering, Department of Computer Science and Engineering,
Shanghai Jiao Tong University, Shanghai, China
{longjia,htlu}@sjtu.edu.cn
[2] MoE Key Lab of Artificial Intelligence, AI Institute,
Shanghai Jiao Tong University, Shanghai, China

Abstract. In this paper, we focus on the task of generating realistic images given an input semantic layout, which is also called semantic image synthesis. Most of previous methods are based on conditional generative adversarial networks mechanism, which is stacks of convolution, normalization, and non-linearity layers. However, these methods easily generate blurred regions and distorted structures. There are two limits existing: their normalization layers are unable to make a good balance between keeping semantic layout information and geometric changes; and cannot effectively aggregated multi-level feature. To address the above problems, we propose a novel method which incorporates multi-level gate feature aggregation mechanism (GFA) and spatially adaptive batch-instance normalization (SPAda-BIN) for semantic image synthesis. Experiments on several challenging datasets demonstrate the advantage of the proposed method over existing approaches, in terms of both visual fidelity and quantitative metrics.

Keywords: Image-to-image translation · Normalization · Multi-level feature fusion · Semantic image synthesis

1 Introduction

When we see a semantic layout, we will naturally imagine the real image corresponding to it. Skilled painter can even create close to real photos based on semantic layout. From this we will consider a question, can we train such a model that is transformed into a real scene based on a novel semantic layout?

Existing semantic image synthesis methods, such as pix2pix [12], cascaded refinement Networks (CRN) [3], semi-parametric image synthesis (SIMS) [18], are mainly built by stacking convolutional, normalization, and non-linearity layers, although they can generate relatively reasonable real images based on the

© Springer Nature Switzerland AG 2021
J. Lokoč et al. (Eds.): MMM 2021, LNCS 12572, pp. 378–390, 2021.
https://doi.org/10.1007/978-3-030-67832-6_31

semantic segmentation mask, these methods still have many problems. As shown in Fig. 4 and Fig. 5, we can see that some blurred areas appear in the scene generated according to the semantic segmentation mask and some structures are is distorted. There are two main reasons for these failures. First, the normalization used in existing methods are incapable of making a trade-off between keeping semantic layout information and geometric changes. Secondly, previous methods are unable to design a reasonable method to effectively aggregate high-level features and low-level features simultaneously. An obvious disadvantage is that a massive useful information and useless information are mixed together.

To solve the first issue, we proposed spatially-adaptive batch-instance normalization which can adaptively select a proper ratio between batch normalization and instance normalization. It can also keep the semantic layout information consistent with the change of picture style. In contrast to BIN [17], our scaling λ and shifting β are tensors, not vectors. For the second issue, we introduce a multi-level gate feature aggregation mechanism to effectively combine richer semantic information of high-level features and detailed information of low-level features. In order to better measure the usefulness of each feature vector and control the information spread, we use the gating mechanism [4,9].

In our paper, we explore the task of realistic picture generation from semantic segmentation mask. We conduct experiments on several challenging datasets including the Cityscapes [5], the ADE20K [23], and the COCO-Stuff [2].

In summary, the contributions of this paper are follows:

- We introduce a multi-level gate feature aggregation mechanism to aggregate features of different levels. Unlike previous methods, we use the gating mechanism to measure the usefulness of each feature vector, and control information propagation.
- We proposed a spatially adaptive batch-instance normalization for our task. This new normalization could make a suitable trade-off between batch normalization and instance normalization in spatial domain.
- We show the effectiveness of the proposed method by extensive qualitative, quantitative and human preference experiments on the COCO-Stuff [2], Cityscapes [5] and ADE20K [23] datasets.

2 Related Work

2.1 Normalization

Recent related work have shown that CNN feature statistics (*e.g.*, mean and variance [10], Gram matrix [8]) can be used to directly describe the image style. Specifically, Instance normalization (IN) [10] eliminates the effect of style variation by directly normalizing the feature statistics of the image and is used more often than Layer Normalization (LN) [1] or Batch Normalization (BN) [11] in style transfer. We propose an spatially adaptive batch-instance normalization (SPAda-BIN) to adaptively select a proper ratio between BN and IN in three dimensions. Through the SPAda-BIN, our model could keep semantic layout information consistent and geometric changes naturally.

2.2   Multi-level Feature Fusion

In deep convolutional neural networks, the top layers often lack of fine detailed information of the input images. The U-Net [19] adds skip connections between the encoder and decoder to reuse different level features. In context contrasted local (CCL) model [15], it locally aggregates every two adjacent feature maps of the pyramid into a feature map until the last one is left.

2.3   Gating Mechanism

In deep neural networks, gates are commonly utilized to control information propagation. The highway network [20] uses gates to make training deep network feasible. The work in [7] used gates for information control between adjacent layers. The difference from them is that the multi-level feature maps of our method are fused through the gating mechanism. Through this mechanism the useful information in the multi-level features can be adjusted to the correct position and the useless information can also be effectively suppressed.

3   The Proposed Method

In this section, we introduce our method based on multi-level gate feature aggregation with spatially adaptive batch-instance normalization for translating semantic mask to realistic photos. The architecture of our image generator is shown in Fig. 1. The generator is based on an U-Net encoder-decoder architecture with spatially adaptive batch-instance normalization (SPAda-BIN) residual blocks. The skip connections is replaced by multi-level gate feature aggregation (GFA), shown in Fig. 2 which is applied between corresponding layers in the encoder and decoder.

We adopt multi-scale discriminators which consist of three discriminators that discriminate different resolution versions of the generated images. They can guide the generator to generate globally consistent images; and the discriminator at the finest scale encourages the generator to produce image with better details.

3.1   Multi-level Gate Feature Aggregation

Given L feature maps $\{\mathbf{X}^i \in \mathbb{R}^{C^i \times H^i \times W^i}\}_{i=1}^{L}$ extracted from networks, they are sorted by their depth in the network, the semantics increase as the network depth increases, but the details decrease. C^i, H^i, W^i are the number of channels, height and width of the i-th feature map respectively. Due to the downsampling operation, higher-level feature maps have lower resolution, $H_{i+1} < H_i, W_{i+1} < W_i$. In semantic map feature, the top high-level feature map X_L contains rich semantic informations, but the major limitation of X_L is its low spatial resolution without detailed information. In contrast, feature maps of low level from shallow layers are with high resolution, but with few semantic informations. Therefore, combining the complementary advantages of multi-level feature maps will achieve

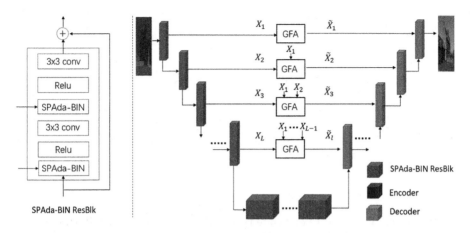

Fig. 1. The architecture of our generator, we combine SPAda-BIN residual blocks and Gate Feature Aggregation model to U-Net encoder-decoder architecture

the purpose of high resolution and rich semantics, and this operation can be abstracted as an aggregation process.

$$\{X_1, X_2, ..., X_L\} \rightarrow \{\tilde{X}_1, \tilde{X}_2, ..., \tilde{X}_L\} \tag{1}$$

where $\tilde{X}_l$ is the fused feature map for the l-th level. Addition is a straightforward operation to combine feature maps by adding features at each position, but it mixes useful information with a lot of trivial features together.

The most fundamental purpose of multi-level feature fusion is to gather useful information under the interference of a large amount of useless information. In order to measure the importance of each feature vector in the feature map and aggregate the information accordingly, we use the gating mechanism. In our method, multi-level gate feature aggregation is designed to achieve additive aggregation by controlling the information flow with the gates. Each level l is associated with a gate map $G_l \in [0, 1]^{H_l \times W_l}$. With these gate maps, our additive aggregation is formally defined as

$$\tilde{X}_l = X_l \cdot (1 + G_l) + \sum_{i=1}^{l-1} G_i \cdot X_i \cdot (1 - G_l) \tag{2}$$

where $\cdot$ denotes element-wise multiplication broadcasting in the channel dimension, each gate map $G_l = sigmoid(w_i * X_i)$ is estimated by a convolutional layer parameterized with $w_i \in \mathbb{R}^{C_i \times 1 \times 1}$. The detailed operation can be seen in Fig. 2.

Our multi-level gate feature aggregation method is mainly inspired by the gated fully fusion (GFF) [14]. The difference between our method and the GFF is that when the number of network layers deepens, all different level features before this level will be aggregated with the current level features through the gate mechanism, instead of directly combining the current features with the

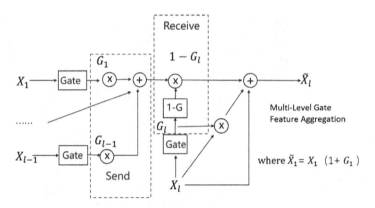

Fig. 2. The proposed Multi-Level Gate Feature Aggregation module (GFA), where G_l is the gate map generated from X_l. $\tilde{X}_l$ is the aggregated feature map.

features of all other levels. The reason is that high-level features are rich in semantic information but lack of details. As shown in Fig. 2, in addition to the aggregated feature $\tilde{X}_l$, there is a feature map through encoding and SPAda-BIN resnet block inputting to decoding. We consider that features in decoding contains certain semantic information, so the lower the level of features is, the fewer features it aggregates. An extreme example is $\tilde{X}_1 = X_1 \cdot (1 + G_1)$.

3.2   Spatially-Adaptive Batch-Instance Normalization

Let $\mathbf{f}^t \in \mathbb{R}^{N \times C^t \times H^i \times W^t}$ denote the activations of the t-th layer of a deep convolutional network for a batch of N samples, C^t is the number of channels in the layer, H^t and W^t be the height and width of the activation map in the layer. In our model, we proposed a new normalization method called the spatially adaptive batch-instance normalization as shown in Eqs. (3)–(5), where $f^t_{n,c,x,y}$ is the activation at the site before normalization and $\mu_c^{t(B)}$ and $\sigma_c^{t(B)}$ are the bath mean and standard deviation of the activations in channel c. The batch-normalized response in the t-th activation map is:

$$\hat{x}_B^t = \frac{f^t_{n,c,x,y} - \mu_c^{t(B)}}{\sigma_c^{t(B)}}, \tag{3}$$

$$\mu_c^{t(B)} = \frac{1}{NH^tW^t} \sum_{n,x,y} f^t_{n,c,x,y}, \tag{4}$$

$$\sigma_c^{t(B)} = \sqrt{\frac{1}{NH^tW^t} \sum_{n,x,y} ((f^t_{n,c,x,y})^2 - (\mu_c^{t(B)})^2)} \tag{5}$$

On the other hand, instance-normalization normalizes each example in the mini-batch independently using per-instance feature statistics, we denote the mean $\mu_c^{t(I)}$ and variance $\sigma_c^{t(I)}$. The instance-normalized response in the t-th activation is defined as

$$\hat{x}_I^t = \frac{f_{n,c,x,y}^t - \mu_c^{t(I)}}{\sigma_c^{t(I)}}, \tag{6}$$

$$\mu_c^{t(I)} = \frac{1}{NH^tW^t} \sum_{n,x,y} f_{n,c,x,y}^t, \tag{7}$$

$$\sigma_c^{t(I)} = \sqrt{\frac{1}{NH^tW^t} \sum_{n,x,y} ((f_{n,c,x,y}^t)^2 - (\mu_c^{t(I)})^2)} \tag{8}$$

We aim to find the balance between keeping semantic layout information and geometric changes, so we proposed spatially-adaptive batch-instance Normalization (SPAda-BIN). Figure 3 illustrates the SPAda-BIN design.

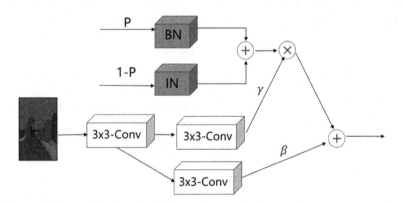

Fig. 3. In our SPAda-BIN, we first project the semantic mask onto the embedding space, and then perform convolution to generate modulation parameters λ and β. In contrast to other normalization method, λ and β are not vectors, but tensors with spatial dimensions.

What we have in common with Batch-Instance Normalization is that the activation is normalized in the channel-wise manner and then modulated with learned scale and bias. In contrast to the Batch-Instance Normalization, we use the symbol $\lambda_{c,h,w}^t$ and $\beta_{c,h,w}^t$ to denote the functions that convert semantic segmentation mask to the scaling and bias values at the site (c, y, x) in the t-th activation map. We implement the functions $\lambda_{c,h,w}^t$ and $\beta_{c,h,w}^t$ using a simple convolutional network.

The input feature map through our normalization will output an activation value at site $(n \in N, c \in C^t, x \in H^t, y \in W^t)$:

$$\lambda_{c,h,w}^t (p.\hat{x}_B^t + (1-p)\hat{x}_I^t) + \beta_{c,h,w}^t, \qquad (9)$$

$$p \leftarrow clip_{[0,1]}(p - \tau \triangle p), \qquad (10)$$

Where $\lambda_{c,h,w}^t, \beta_{c,h,w}^t$ are the learned modulation parameters of the normalization layer. τ is the learning rate and $\triangle p$ indicates the parameter update vector. We can limit the value of p within the range of [0, 1] simply by applying a limit in the parameter update step. In tasks where instance normalization is important, the generator will adjust the value of p close to 1, while the value of p is close to 0 in the task where the batch normalization is important.

3.3   Loss Function

The full loss function includes the following losses:

L_1 loss: Similar to most image-to-image translation model, we also adopt an L_1 loss to encourage the generated image $G(x)$ from a semantic mask x to be close to its ground truth image y. The L_1 loss is given by

$$\mathcal{L}_{L_1}(G) = \mathbf{E}_{(x,y)}\big[||y - G(x)||_1\big] \qquad (11)$$

Adversarial loss: The purpose of using adversarial loss is to match the distribution of the translated image with the distribution of the target image. D_k denote the discriminators of different scales, and adversarial loss is given by

$$\mathcal{L}_{adv}(G; D) = \sum_{i=0}^{3} \big[\mathbf{E}_{(x,y)}\big[log D_k(x, y)\big] \qquad (12)$$

$$+ \ \mathbf{E}_x\big[log(1 - log D_k(x, G(X)))\big]\big] \qquad (13)$$

Feature matching loss: specifically, we extract features from multiple layers of the discriminator and learn to match these intermediate representations from the real and the generated image. We denote the i-th layer feature extractor of discriminator D_k as $D_k^{(i)}$ (from input to the i-th layer of D_k). The feature matching loss is given by

$$\mathcal{L}_{FM}(G) = \mathbf{E}_{(x,y)} \sum_{i=1}^{T} \frac{1}{N_i} ||D_k^{(i)}(x, y) - D_k^{(i)}(x, G(x))||_1]$$

Where T is the total number of layers and N_i denotes the number of elements in each layer.

Full Objective: By combining the above loss functions, the full objective function of our model is

$$\min_G \max_D \mathcal{L}_{adv}(G; D) + \lambda \mathcal{L}_{L_1}(G) + \mu \mathcal{L}_{FM}(G) \qquad (14)$$

where λ, μ are the weights that balance the importance of each item.

4 Experiment

We use the U-Net architecture as the base architecture of our generator model, and use multi-scale discriminator for the discriminator [22]. The optimization algorithm is Adam [13] optimizer with momentum parameters with $\beta_1 = 0.45$ and $\beta_2 = 0.999$. All the images are resized to 256×256 in our experiments.

4.1 Datasets

We conduct experiments on tree benchmark datasets.

ADE20K dataset [23] consists of 20,210 training and 2,000 validation images. The dataset contains challenging scenes with 150 semantic classes.

COCO-Stuff [2] is derived from the COCO dataset [16]. It has 118,000 training images and 5,000 validation images captured from diverse scenes. It has 182 semantic classes.

Cityscapes dataset [6] contains street scene images captured in German cities. The training and validation set sizes are 3,000 and 500 respectively.

We train the competing semantic image synthesis methods [3,12,18] on the same training set and report their results on the same validation set for each dataset.

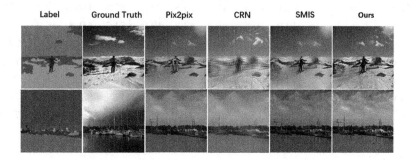

Fig. 4. Visual comparison of semantic image synthesis results on the COCO-Stuff dataset

4.2 Evaluation Metrics

For our real scene generation from semantic layout task, in addition to evaluate the quality of the generated images, we must also consider the semantic information contained in the image. Specifically, We run a semantic segmentation model on the generated image and compare the degree of matching between the predicted segmentation mask and the ground truth input. We use both the mean Intersection over Union (mIoU) and the pixel accuracy (accu) for measuring the

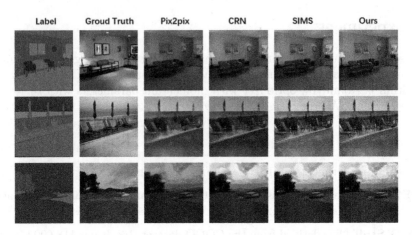

Fig. 5. Visual comparison of semantic image synthesis results on the ADE20K dataset

Table 1. Quantitative comparison. For the mIoU and accu, higher is better. For the FID, lower is better. Experiment on COCO-Stuff, AED20K and Cityscapes dataset

Method	COCO-Stuff			AED20K			Cityscapes		
	FID	mIoU	accu	FID	mIoU	accu	FID	mIoU	accu
pix2pix	127.2	12.9	41.6	90.7	18.3	65.2	116.3	49.4	75.0
CRN	72.1	23.4	40.1	75.8	22.3	67.6	103.5	52.1	76.8
SIMS	40.2	10.5	46.3	42.3	19.2	71.5	**50.3**	46.9	74.1
Ours w/o SPAda-BIN	68.7	21.3	43.7	70.5	21.2	68.4	87.4	51.1	73.0
Ours w/o GFA	81.2	14.5	37.9	82.4	18.8	66.5	93.8	47.5	75.2
Ours w/D_p	52.6	26.1	46.8	54.3	26.1	70.8	79.2	55.8	78.5
Ours w/BIN	42.3	29.7	54.1	48.2	28.5	71,1	83.4	57.3	76.8
Ours	**28.9**	**34.6**	**62.7**	**37.3**	**35.4**	**73.1**	75.6	**60.1**	**79.6**

semantic information contained in the generated picture. In order to measure the quality of the generated image, we employ Fréchet Inception Distance (FID).

MIoU: Mean Intersection over Union calculates the ratio of the intersection and union of two sets. In the problem of semantic segmentation, these two sets are ground truth and predicted segmentation.

Accu: Pixel accuracy is a simple measurement method, it is the proportion of correctly marked pixels to total pixels.

FID: Fréchet Inception Distance employs an Inception network [21] to extract features and calculates the Wasserstein-2 distance between features of generated images and real images. The lower the FID value is, the distance more closer between the distribution of synthesized results and the distribution of real images.

4.3   Baselines

We compare our method with three state-of-the-art semantic image synthesis models: the pix2pix model [12], the cascaded refinement network (CRN) [3], and the semi-parametric image synthesis method (SIMS) [18]. Our experiments use the author's original implementation and recommended hyperparameters.

Pix2Pix [12] model is a significant GAN-based image-to-image translation framework. This method is the first to use conditional generative adversarial networks to solve image-to-image translation problems and lay the foundation for following related work.

CRN [3] model uses multiple cascaded resolution multiplying feed-forward network modules, the resolution is gradually doubled, eventually achieve high image resolution. Each resolution multiplying modules works at their respective resolutions.

SIMS [18] uses a semi-parametric approach that combines the advantages of parametric model and non-parametric model to synthesize real segments from the training set and refine the boundaries between segments.

4.4   Quantitative Comparisons

As show in Table 1. We perform experiments on three different data sets and compare with the state-of-the-art methods. For the COCO-Stuff, our full model achieves an FID score of 29.4, which is about 1.4 times better than the previous leading method; the mIoU/accu score is 34.6/62.7, which is 1.48/1.35 times better than the state-of-the-art method. For the ADE20K, our full models achieves an FID/accu score of 37.3, which is beyond previous leading method 4.8/1.6 in score; the mIoU score is 35.4, which is 1.6 times better than the previous leading method. For the Cityscapes dataset, we observed that the SIMS model produces a better FID score than our methods but has poor performance on semantic segmentation evaluation.

Table 2. User preference study. The numbers indicate the percentage of users who favor the results of the proposed method over those of the competing method

Dataset	Ours vs pix2pix	Ours vs CRN	Ours vs SIMS
COCO-Stuff	91.36	77.47	73.47
ADE20K	87.18	73.65	85.21
Cityscapes	58.39	61.57	49.89

4.5   Qualitative Results

In Fig. 4 and Fig. 5, we provide qualitative visual comparisons of the competing methods. We found that the images generated by our method with much better details and visual quality. Especially for diverse scenes in the COCO-Stuff and ADE20K dataset.

4.6   Human Evaluation

We conducted an user preference study that to evaluate the perceptual quality of generated images, 20 users participated in these experiments. The users are given unlimited time to make the selection for pick up the more realistic images. For each comparison, we randomly choose 500 generated images for each dataset.

Table 2 shows the results of experiment. Obviously, we find that users prefer our results on other datasets, especially on the COCO-Stuff and ADE20K datasets. For the Cityscapes, even pictures generated by those methods have high fidelity, our method is still the best in comprehensive comparison.

4.7   Ablation Study

We performed ablation study to evaluate the importance of each component of our proposed model. We used FID/mIoU/accu to evaluate on three different datasets. As show in last five row in Table 1. The experiments were performed by removing each specific moudle from our complete model and then training the rest of model without the absent part. When we remove the SPAda-BIN/GFA, its performance drops drastically compared to the full model. Multi-scale discriminator also helps to improve the performance of our model. We also use BIN to replace SPAda-BIN, and compare the results with our method.

5   Conclusion

In this paper, we have proposed multi-level gate feature aggregation with spatially-adaptive batch-Instance normalization generate visually reasonable real scene from semantic layout. The multi-level gate feature aggregation uses gating mechanism to measure the usefulness of each feature vector and effectively aggregate multi-level feature. Our spatially adaptive batch-Instance normalization could adaptively makes a suitable trade-off between batch normalization and instance normalization in space. Extensive experiments show the effectiveness of our proposed method, including four evaluation metric and visual observation.

Acknowledgment. This paper is supported by NSFC (Nos. 61772330, 61533012, 61876109), China Next Generation Internet IPv6 project (Grant No. NGII20170609) and Shanghai authentication key Lab. (2017XCWZK01).

References

1. Ba, J.L., Kiros, J.R., Hinton, G.E.: Layer normalization (2016)
2. Caesar, H., Uijlings, J., Ferrari, V.: COCO-stuff: thing and stuff classes in context (2016)
3. Chen, Q., Koltun, V.: Photographic image synthesis with cascaded refinement networks (2017)
4. Cho, K., et al.: Learning phrase representations using RNN encoder-decoder for statistical machine translation. Comput. Sci. (2014)
5. Cordts, M., et al.: The cityscapes dataset for semantic urban scene understanding. In: The IEEE Conference on Computer Vision and Pattern Recognition (CVPR), June 2016
6. Cordts, M., et al: The cityscapes dataset for semantic urban scene understanding (2016)
7. Ding, H., Jiang, X., Shuai, B., Qun Liu, A., Wang, G.: Context contrasted feature and gated multi-scale aggregation for scene segmentation. In: The IEEE Conference on Computer Vision and Pattern Recognition (CVPR), June 2018
8. Gatys, L.A., Ecker, A.S., Bethge, M.: Image style transfer using convolutional neural networks. In: 2016 IEEE Conference on Computer Vision and Pattern Recognition (CVPR) (2016)
9. Hochreiter, S., Schmidhuber, J.: Long short-term memory. Neural Comput. **9**(8), 1735–1780 (1997)
10. Huang, X., Belongie, S.: Arbitrary style transfer in real-time with adaptive instance normalization (2017)
11. Ioffe, S., Szegedy, C.: Batch normalization: accelerating deep network training by reducing internal covariate shift (2015)
12. Isola, P., Zhu, J.Y., Zhou, T., Efros, A.A.: Image-to-image translation with conditional adversarial networks (2016)
13. Kingma, D., Ba, J.: Adam: a method for stochastic optimization. Comput. Sci. (2014)
14. Li, X., Zhao, H., Han, L., Tong, Y., Yang, K.: GFF: gated fully fusion for semantic segmentation (2019)
15. Lin, D., Ji, Y., Lischinski, D., Cohen-Or, D., Huang, H.: Multi-scale context intertwining for semantic segmentation. In: Ferrari, V., Hebert, M., Sminchisescu, C., Weiss, Y. (eds.) ECCV 2018. LNCS, vol. 11207, pp. 622–638. Springer, Cham (2018). https://doi.org/10.1007/978-3-030-01219-9_37
16. Lin, T.Y., et al.: Microsoft COCO: common objects in context (2014)
17. Nam, H., Kim, H.E.: Batch-instance normalization for adaptively style-invariant neural networks. In: Bengio, S., Wallach, H., Larochelle, H., Grauman, K., Cesa-Bianchi, N., Garnett, R. (eds.) Advances in Neural Information Processing Systems 31, pp. 2558–2567. Curran Associates, Inc. (2018). http://papers.nips.cc/paper/7522-batch-instance-normalization-for-adaptively-style-invariant-neural-networks.pdf
18. Qi, X., Chen, Q., Jia, J., Koltun, V.: Semi-parametric image synthesis. In: The IEEE Conference on Computer Vision and Pattern Recognition (CVPR), June 2018
19. Ronneberger, O., Fischer, P., Brox, T.: U-Net: convolutional networks for biomedical image segmentation (2015)
20. Srivastava, R.K., Greff, K., Schmidhuber, J.: Training very deep networks. Comput. Sci. (2015)

21. Szegedy, C., et al.: Going deeper with convolutions (2014)
22. Wang, T.C., Liu, M.Y., Zhu, J.Y., Tao, A., Kautz, J., Catanzaro, B.: High-resolution image synthesis and semantic manipulation with conditional GANs (2017)
23. Zhou, B., Hang, Z., Puig, X., Fidler, S., Barriuso, A., Torralba, A.: Scene parsing through ade20k dataset. In: IEEE Conference on Computer Vision & Pattern Recognition (2017)

Robust Multispectral Pedestrian Detection via Uncertainty-Aware Cross-Modal Learning

Sungjune Park[1], Jung Uk Kim[1], Yeon Gyun Kim[2], Sang-Keun Moon[3], and Yong Man Ro[1(✉)]

[1] Image and Video Systems Laboratory, School of Electrical Engineering, KAIST, Daejeon, Republic of Korea
{sungjune-p,jukim0701,ymro}@kaist.ac.kr
[2] Agency for Defense Development, Daejeon, Republic of Korea
yg_kim@add.re.kr
[3] Korea Electric Power Corporation (KEPCO) Research Institute, Daejeon, Republic of Korea
sk.moon@kepco.co.kr

Abstract. With the development of deep neural networks, multispectral pedestrian detection has been received a great attention by exploiting complementary properties of multiple modalities (*e.g.,* color-visible and thermal modalities). Previous works usually rely on network prediction scores in combining complementary modal information. However, it is widely known that deep neural networks often show the overconfident problem which results in limited performance. In this paper, we propose a novel uncertainty-aware cross-modal learning to alleviate the aforementioned problem in multispectral pedestrian detection. First, we extract object region uncertainty which represents the reliability of object region features in multiple modalities. Then, we combine each modal object region feature considering object region uncertainty. Second, we guide the classifier of detection framework with soft target labels to be aware of the level of object region uncertainty in multiple modalities. To verify the effectiveness of the proposed methods, we conduct extensive experiments with various detection frameworks on two public datasets (*i.e.,* KAIST Multispectral Pedestrian Dataset and CVC-14).

Keywords: Multispectral pedestrian detection · Cross-modal learning · Object region uncertainty

1 Introduction

Object detection has shown remarkable developments with the advent of the deep neural networks (DNNs), and it has been applied into many real-world applications such as autonomous driving and artificial surveillance systems [6, 32,34]. Recently, multispectral data (*e.g.,* color-visible and thermal data) have been adopted to utilize complementary information of two modalities [1,10,31].

© Springer Nature Switzerland AG 2021
J. Lokoč et al. (Eds.): MMM 2021, LNCS 12572, pp. 391–402, 2021.
https://doi.org/10.1007/978-3-030-67832-6_32

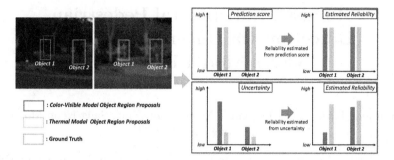

Fig. 1. In the color-visible modality (*left*), the bounding box is not estimated well. Therefore, the quality of object region feature would be poor, and the reliability of the modal feature should reflect it. However, prediction scores tend to be overconfident, thus, object region uncertainty is required to represent the reliability properly.

Since the complementary property of multispectral data is known to achieve additional performance gain, several works have studied on multispectral pedestrian detection [22,23,27,36]. The key idea of the multispectral pedestrian detection is how to combine two modalities in an effective way. In [23], two features corresponding to the object region of interests (RoIs) (we call it object region feature), are combined by using the illumination score from an additional module. The illumination score, which predicts whether the image is captured at day or night, acts as an importance weight for each modal object region feature. Also, [36] combines object region features of two modalities by weighting each prediction score to indicate the reliability of object region features.

However, these methods have limitations on representing the reliability of object region feature. The illumination score of [23] mainly focused on the whole scene rather than estimating the reliability of each object region feature. That is, [23] overlooked that object region features could have different degrees of the reliability due to shade, occlusion, and so on, even though objects belong to the same modality. Also, [36] used the prediction score to deal with each object region feature, but it could bring another problem. For example, as shown in Fig. 1, when the estimated object region is misaligned (*i.e.*, the leftmost red bounding box), which means it cannot contain the object properly, the reliability of object region feature should be low. However, the prediction score could be large even in the misaligned case, because deep neural networks (DNNs) usually accompany the overconfidence problem [5,15]. Therefore, the prediction score is insufficient to represent the reliability of object region features as well.

To alleviate these limitations, in this paper, we present a novel cross-modal learning approach by measuring the uncertainty of object region feature. The uncertainty of object region feature could display the extent of bounding box deviation from the desirable object region, so that, it can represent the quality of object region feature. We call this uncertainty *object region uncertainty*. To estimate object region uncertainty for each object region feature, we adopt two-stage region-based detectors (*e.g.,* Faster R-CNN and FPN) which extract RoI features for object samples. The proposed learning approach can be divided into two folds. First, we estimate object region uncertainty to measure the reliability for each object region feature. Based on object region uncertainty, we acquire uncertainty-aware cross-modal fusion (UCF) weights. UCF weights represent the relative reliability of each modal object region feature, and we can combine two modal features minimizing the effect of less reliable modal object feature. Second, we propose an uncertainty-aware feature learning (UFL). Usually, classification loss is trained with hard target labels (*i.e.*, 1 for the correct class). However, in UFL, we adjust hard labels to soft labels according to the level of object region uncertainty. Therefore, the detection framework can be trained with soft target labels on uncertain object region features. Consequently, we achieve performance improvements on two public datasets (*i.e.*, KAIST Multispectral Pedestrian Dataset [14] and CVC-14 [8]) with various detection frameworks.

The main contributions of this paper are as follows: (1) In multispectral pedestrian detection, this paper is the first work that employs uncertainty-aware cross-modal fusion (UCF) for effective modal object region feature fusion. (2) Also, uncertainty-aware feature learning (UFL) is proposed to train network elastically being aware of how uncertain object region feature is. With the above contributions, we achieve performance improvements which result in comparable pedestrian detection performances with the other state-of-the-art methods.

2   Related Work

2.1   Multispectral Pedestrian Detection

Multispectral pedestrian detection has been studied for various real-world applications, such as, autonomous driving and intelligent surveillance systems [6,32,34]. Several works usually make use of complementary information in color-visible and thermal modalities [22,23,27,36]. [27] constructed three pathways (*i.e., color, thermal and fusion pathways*), and treated them as independent modalities assigning a weight for each path using an additional channel weight fusion layer. [22] simply incorporated the segmentation task with a pixel-level loss to improve performances. In [23], an additional illumination module was attached to give weights for modal feature fusion. Also, [36] combined both modal features with attention weights using their prediction scores. In this paper, we generate uncertainty-aware cross-modal fusion (UCF) weights to combine modal object region features effectively, and present an uncertainty-aware feature learning (UFL) method by using object region uncertainty.

2.2   Aleatoric Uncertainty

Aleatoric uncertainty represent a noise which is inherent in input observation as described in [15]. Aleatoric uncertainty can be divided into two types: *homoscedastic* and *heteroscedastic* uncertainty. While the first one remains constant independent of input, the second uncertainty varies with input, and have

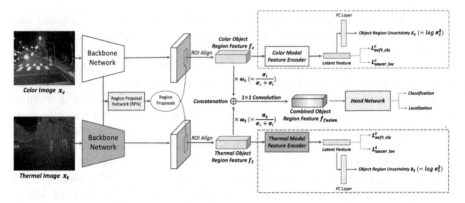

Fig. 2. The overall architecture of the proposed framework. The orange and blue dotted boxes represent the modal feature encoder paths to extract object region uncertainty and to learn modal object features for each modality. (Color figure online)

large uncertainty values according to the level of input noise [21,26]. So that, heteroscedastic uncertainty can be more meaningful in computer vision area.

By adopting aforementioned concept, [12] tried to enhance a bounding box regression for more accurate object detection. [12] extracted the uncertainty using the transformed regression (described in Sect. 3.1). Then, the uncertainty is used to select probable bounding boxes and to acquire more accurate localization results, during non-maximum suppression (NMS) process. We also utilize the transformed regression to acquire the object region uncertainty regarding location predictions. Then, we estimate the reliability of object region features acquiring UCF weights from object region uncertainty. Also, we propose a UFL approach to train the detection framework depending on the degree of the object region uncertainty.

3   Proposed Method

The overall architecture of the proposed methods is shown in Fig. 2. Each modal feature is passed through their own feature encoder. The transformed localization L_{uncer_loc} is to predict bounding boxes and to learn extracting object region uncertainty, σ. Then, σ is used to measure the reliability of color-visible and thermal object region features, f_c and f_t, acquiring uncertainty-aware cross-modal fusion (UCF) weights, ω_c and ω_t. Also, the transformed classification L_{soft_cls} is conducted to guide the detection framework with soft target labels based on σ, that is, uncertainty-aware feature learning (UFL). The combined object region feature, f_{fusion}, then, makes a final prediction with the traditional classification and localization training losses. More details are described in the subsections below.

3.1 Preliminaries

Most of object detection frameworks usually take bounding box regression for object localization [16–19, 24, 29]. During localization, the level of misalignment can be estimated by modifying the traditional bounding box regression [12]. The transformed regression loss for object localization is as follows,

$$L_{loc} = \frac{(x_g - x_e)^2}{2\sigma^2} + \frac{\log \sigma^2}{2}, \tag{1}$$

where x_g and x_e are ground-truth and estimated bounding box coordinates, respectively, and σ represents uncertainty estimation that comes from additional fully connected layer in the form of log scale s as shown in Fig. 2. During training phase, when the object region is uncertain where bounding box is easy to be misaligned from the desirable object region, σ is trained to be large to minimize the loss, Eq. (1). In other case, when bounding box is estimated well $(x_g \approx x_e)$, σ would be relatively small. Therefore, it could display the level of object region uncertainty, and it can be used to measure the reliability of object region features.

In practice, we train the detection framework to predict $s = \log \sigma^2$, therefore,

$$L_{loc} = \frac{(x_g - x_e)^2}{2}e^{-s} + \frac{1}{2}s. \tag{2}$$

By combining the above equation and traditional smooth L1 regression [7], the final transformed localization becomes as follows,

$$L_{uncer\_loc} = \begin{cases} \frac{(x_g - x_e)^2}{2}e^{-s} + \frac{1}{2}(x_g - x_e)^2 + \frac{1}{2}s & \text{if } |x_g - x_e| \leq 1, \\ (|x_g - x_e| - \frac{1}{2})e^{-s} + |x_g - x_e| + \frac{s-1}{2} & \text{otherwise.} \end{cases} \tag{3}$$

3.2 Uncertainty-Aware Cross-Modal Fusion (UCF)

Since a naive feature fusion cannot guide which modal feature is more reliable (or useful) to the detection framework, the framework has no choice but to simply combine different modal features. Therefore, to determine the reliability of each modal object region feature, we utilize object region uncertainty, σ_c and σ_t. If one modal object region feature is less reliable, it would be better to refer to the other modal feature for effective fusion. To this end, we generate uncertainty-aware cross-modal fusion (UCF) weights for both modal features as follows,

$$\omega_c = \frac{\sigma_t}{\sigma_c + \sigma_t}, \qquad \omega_t = \frac{\sigma_c}{\sigma_c + \sigma_t}, \tag{4}$$

$$f_{fusion} = \omega_c f_c \oplus \omega_t f_t, \tag{5}$$

where $\sigma_t = e^{\frac{1}{2}s_t}$ and $\sigma_c = e^{\frac{1}{2}s_c}$. ω_c and ω_t represent the relative level of reliability for f_c and f_t, respectively, which are UCF weights. Here, $\oplus$ denotes concatenation. Due to UCF, for example, if σ_t is larger than σ_c, ω_t becomes smaller than ω_c, minimizing the effect of f_t. After that, the combined feature, f_{fusion}, is acquired to make a final prediction.

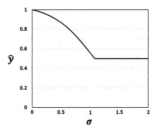

Fig. 3. $\hat{y}$ function of object region uncertainty σ.

3.3   Uncertainty-Aware Feature Learning (UFL)

In general object detection, cross-entropy is widely adopted with hard target labels (*i.e.,* 1 for the correct class) for the classification task. We adjust hard labels by using object region uncertainty σ. The motivation is, it is widely known that hard target labels often make deep neural networks overfitted in uncertain samples [2]. When training neural networks, it is necessary to consider reducing the effect of uncertain object region features. Therefore, we generate soft target labels for the correct class according to object region uncertainty σ. For example, we guide the detection framework that the object feature is uncertain by giving a soft label (*e.g.,* $\hat{y} = 0.6$). For that, we make an uncertainty-aware label generation function to acquire soft labels for the correct class as follows,

$$g(\sigma) = \frac{-1}{1 + e^{-3(\sigma-1)}} + \frac{2 + e^3}{1 + e^3}, \tag{6}$$

$$\hat{y} = max(g(\sigma), 0.5), \tag{7}$$

where $\sigma \in \{\sigma_c, \sigma_t\}$, and it is shown in Fig. 3. We set the least value of the soft label as 0.5 for the highly uncertain object region features to have the same probability whether it is foreground or background. Thus, we can apply uncertainty-aware soft target labels into cross-entropy classification loss as follows,

$$L_{soft} = -\frac{1}{N} \sum_{i=1}^{N} \hat{y}_i log f(x_i; \theta). \tag{8}$$

N is the number of samples, $\hat{y}_i$ is the acquired soft target label, $f(x_i; \theta)$ is the network output of input image x_i given network parameters θ.

To leave the detection framework to be guided with hard labels, we integrate L_{soft} with the traditional classification loss which uses hard target labels by employing a balancing hyperparameter α as [13,33],

$$L_{soft\_cls} = \alpha L_{hard\_cls} + (1 - \alpha)L_{soft}. \tag{9}$$

Finally, the total loss function becomes as follows,

$$L_{total} = L_{OD} + \underbrace{L^c_{soft\_cls} + L^c_{uncer\_loc}}_{\text{color-visible}} + \underbrace{L^t_{soft\_cls} + L^t_{uncer\_loc}}_{\text{thermal}}, \tag{10}$$

Table 1. Pedestrian detection performances (Miss Rate) on KAIST dataset.

Method	Backbone	Proposed Method	All	Day	Night
CWF + APF [27]	VGG16	–	31.36	31.79	20.82
Halfway Fusion [25]	VGG16	–	25.75	24.88	26.59
Fusion RPN [20]	VGG16	–	20.67	19.55	22.12
IAF-RCNN [23]	VGG16	–	15.73	15.36	14.99
IATDNN + IAMSS [9]	VGG16	–	14.95	14.55	18.26
CIAN [35]	VGG16	–	14.12	14.67	15.72
MSDS-RCNN [22]	VGG16	–	11.63	10.60	11.13
AR-CNN [36]	VGG16	–	9.34	9.94	8.38
Faster R-CNN [29]	VGG16	–	15.21	17.80	10.28
		✓	**11.22**	**13.31**	**7.70**
FPN [24]	ResNet-50	–	11.85	13.90	8.14
		✓	**9.26**	**10.95**	**5.78**
	ResNet-101	–	11.01	12.49	8.49
		✓	**7.80**	**9.10**	**4.96**

Table 2. Pedestrian detection performances (Miss Rate) on CVC-14 dataset.

Method	Backbone	Proposed Method	All	Day	Night
DPM (visible) [8]	VGG16	–	–	25.20	76.40
MACF [27]	VGG16	–	73.58	66.30	78.16
ACF [27]	VGG16	–	60.10	61.30	48.20
Halfway Fusion [27]	VGG16	–	31.99	36.29	26.29
Choi et al. [3]	VGG16	–	47.30	49.30	43.80
Park et al. [27]	VGG16	–	37.00	38.10	34.40
CWF + APF [27]	VGG16	–	26.29	28.67	23.48
AR-CNN [36]	VGG16	–	22.10	24.70	18.10
Faster R-CNN [29]	VGG16	–	27.62	34.93	19.01
		✓	**23.88**	**32.86**	**13.30**
FPN [24]	ResNet-50	–	20.05	30.34	9.30
		✓	**16.71**	**24.52**	**8.10**
	ResNet-101	–	16.55	25.35	7.38
		✓	**15.11**	**22.21**	**7.27**

where L_{OD} represents the traditional classification and localization losses for object detection [24,29].

4 Experiments

4.1 Experimental Setup

Datasets and Evaluation Metrics. We conducted experiments on two public multispectral pedestrian detection datasets: KAIST Multispectral Pedestrian Dataset (we refer it as KAIST dataset) [14] and CVC-14 [8]. KAIST dataset is composed of 95,328 color (RGB) and thermal image pairs, and 2,252 image pairs are used for test evaluation. Each image resolution is 512×640. CVC-14 dataset consists of 7,085 training and 1,433 test image pairs with resolution of 471×640. Each dataset is divided into three categories: All, Day, and Night. Day and Night indicate the images which are captured in the day and night time, respectively. All set denotes a combination of Day and Night sets.

In both datasets, we used a log miss rate (MR) for an evaluation metric. MR is calculated by averaging over false positive per image (FPPI) with the range of $[10^{-2}, 10^{0}]$ following [4]. In this metric, the lower MR score means the better detection performance.

Implementation Details. To verify the effectiveness of our methods, we used two widely-used detection frameworks, Faster R-CNN and FPN [24,29], with three backbone networks (*i.e.,* ResNet-50, ResNet-101, and VGG16 [11,30]) using Pytorch [28]. For Faster R-CNN, we adopted VGG16 for fair comparison with other existing methods, and we employed ResNet-50 and ResNet-101 for FPN. We trained all the frameworks using stochastic gradient descent (SGD)

Table 3. The effectiveness comparison between prediction scores and uncertainty-aware cross-modal fusion (UCF) weights for modal feature fusion.

Fusion Weights		Miss Rate (%)
Color-visible(w_c)	Thermal(w_t)	
Baseline (no fusion weights)		11.01
P_{fg}^c	P_{fg}^t	10.5
$\lvert P_{fg}^c - P_{bg}^c \rvert$	$\lvert P_{fg}^t - P_{bg}^t \rvert$	9.87
$\dfrac{\sigma_t}{\sigma_c+\sigma_t}$	$\dfrac{\sigma_c}{\sigma_c+\sigma_t}$	**9.16**

with 4 TITAN XP GPUs having 1 image batch per each GPU. We trained the detection frameworks for the first 2 epochs with 0.008 initial learning rate, and another epoch with the learning rate decayed by a factor of 0.1. The number of region of interests (RoI) are set to 256, and we used $\alpha = 0.8$ for Eq. (9).

4.2   Performance Comparison

We investigated the effectiveness of the proposed methods. As shown in Table 1, on KAIST dataset, the proposed methods achieved performance improvements on all the three detection frameworks by showing MR improvement margin of 2 to 4.5. Especially, in the case of Faster R-CNN, the detection performances were improved by 3.99, 4.49, and 2.58 MR in All, Day and Night set, respectively. Furthermore, on CVC-14 dataset, similar tendency is shown in Table 2. More specifically, for Faster R-CNN, performance showed 3.74, 2.07, and 5.71 MR improvement margins in the three sets. Interestingly, when the backbone network was ResNet-101, we achieved the state-of-the-art performance. These experiments verified that the proposed methods (*i.e.*, UCF and UFL), which consider object region uncertainty, brings detection performance improvements in the general frameworks.

4.3   Effectiveness Comparison Between Prediction Score and Object Region Uncertainty

In this section, we compared the detection performance on KAIST dataset by changing the fusion weights for each object region feature. FPN framework is adopted for the backbone network with ResNet-101. Note that, to investigate the effect of fusion weights, we did not utilize UFL. In Table 3, P_{fg}^c and P_{fg}^t represent prediction scores of foreground (*i.e.*, pedestrian), while P_{bg}^c and P_{bg}^t mean probabilities of backgrounds in both modalities (*i.e.*, $P_{fg}^c + P_{bg}^c = 1$). In the first row, the baseline represents the detection framework that conducts a simple feature fusion using concatenation. In the second row, classification score of two modalities, P_{fg}^c and P_{fg}^t, were weighted to each object region feature. In the third row, following [36], considering both foreground and background together, we used $\lvert P_{fg}^c - P_{bg}^c \rvert$ and $\lvert P_{fg}^t - P_{bg}^t \rvert$ to represent the reliability of both

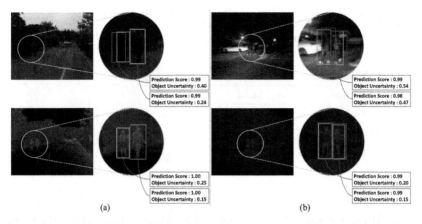

Fig. 4. The visualization results for two image pairs, (a) and (b), show that prediction scores tend to be overconfident regardless of whether bounding box is estimated well or not. Green and red boxes represent ground-truth and estimated bounding boxes, respectively. Object region uncertainty represents the degree of deviation in estimated bounding box properly rather than prediction score.

modal object region features. The last row is for UCF weights which employ object region uncertainty to represent the reliability of each modal object region feature. Considering the object region uncertainty showed superior performances than other methods. It demonstrated that UCF weights are more effective than prediction score for representing the reliability of modal object region features.

Furthermore, we analyzed it with visualization results. Intuitively, when the bounding box is not well-estimated (misaligned from the desirable object region), the effect of corresponding object region feature should be minimized. However, as shown in Fig. 4, although some of the estimated bounding boxes (*red box*) in color-visible modality were misaligned and could not contain the corresponding object suitably, the prediction scores tended to be overconfident showing high scores. Therefore, it had a limitation to represent the reliability of each modal object region feature properly. On the other hand, our object region uncertainty showed an appropriate tendency even in the misaligned case showing high uncertainty. Note that, high uncertainty value means low reliability, while high prediction score means high reliability. As shown in the figure, the uncertainty values were large when color-visible modal bounding boxes were not estimated well, while showing low values for well-estimated thermal case. From this analysis, we verified that the proposed UCF could be a more considerate fusion guidance.

4.4   Ablation Studies

Impact of the UCF and UFL. To verify the effectiveness of the proposed UCF and UFL, we conducted ablation studies on KAIST dataset. As shown in Table. 4, when we applied UCF weights only for effective feature fusion, the detection performance was enhanced by 1.85 MR. Also, when we applied UFL

Table 4. The ablation studies to show the effectiveness of each proposed method.

Model	Miss Rate (%)
Baseline	11.01
With UCF	9.16
With UFL	8.96
With UCF and UFL	**7.80**

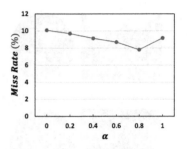

Fig. 5. Impact of α varying from 0 to 1 with an interval of 0.2.

only, 2.05 MR was improved when compared with the performance of the baseline (*i.e.*, simple fusion framework with FPN ResNet-101). Finally, we achieved 3.21 MR improvement by applying UCF and UFL at the same time. From the ablation studies, we showed that each proposed method is effective to combine and learn two modal object region features properly in multispectral pedestrian detection.

Variations on hyperparameter α. As shown in Eq. (9), we used a balancing hyperparameter, $\alpha = 0.8$, between classification losses which use hard and soft target labels. To investigate the impact of α, we conducted experiments with varying α from 0 to 1 with an interval of 0.2 on KAIST dataset. FPN framework is adopted for the backbone network with ResNet-101. As shown in Fig. 5, although it showed performances of small variations with varying α, it displayed better detection performances consistently when compared with the baseline performance (*i.e.*, 11.01 %). Note that, $\alpha = 1$ means the traditional classification loss with hard target labels solely, and $\alpha = 0$ is the case that used the classification loss with soft target labels only. While it is beneficial to train the framework with hard target labels and soft target labels together [13], we verified that soft target labels are required to guide the detection framework for uncertain object region features showing superior performance to baseline.

5 Conclusion

In this paper, we introduced an uncertainty-aware cross-modal learning approach to employ complementary characteristics of two modal data. First, we presented an uncertainty-aware cross-modal fusion (UCF) weights to give reliability weights to both modal object region features. By using UCF weights, we could combine each complementary object region feature effectively. Second, we proposed an uncertainty-aware feature learning (UFL) to train the detection framework with soft target labels according to the level of object region uncertainty. Therefore, we could inform the detection framework whether object region feature is uncertain or not, so that the effect of uncertain object region features could decrease. Finally, through comprehensive experiments, we verified the effectiveness of the proposed framework with various detection baselines.

References

1. Cao, Y., Guan, D., Wu, Y., Yang, J., Cao, Y., Yang, M.Y.: Box-level segmentation supervised deep neural networks for accurate and real-time multispectral pedestrian detection. ISPRS J. Photogramm. Remote Sens. **150**, 70–79 (2019)
2. Chang, J., Lan, Z., Cheng, C., Wei, Y.: Data uncertainty learning in face recognition. In: Proceedings of the IEEE/CVF Conference on Computer Vision and Pattern Recognition, pp. 5710–5719 (2020)
3. Choi, H., Kim, S., Park, K., Sohn, K.: Multi-spectral pedestrian detection based on accumulated object proposal with fully convolutional networks. In: 2016 23rd International Conference on Pattern Recognition (ICPR), pp. 621–626. IEEE (2016)
4. Dollár, P., Wojek, C., Schiele, B., Perona, P.: Pedestrian detection: a benchmark. In: 2009 IEEE Conference on Computer Vision and Pattern Recognition, pp. 304–311. IEEE (2009)
5. Gal, Y., Ghahramani, Z.: Dropout as a Bayesian approximation: representing model uncertainty in deep learning. In: International Conference on Machine Learning, pp. 1050–1059 (2016)
6. Geiger, A., Lenz, P., Urtasun, R.: Are we ready for autonomous driving? The KITTI vision benchmark suite. In: 2012 IEEE Conference on Computer Vision and Pattern Recognition, pp. 3354–3361. IEEE (2012)
7. Girshick, R., Donahue, J., Darrell, T., Malik, J.: Rich feature hierarchies for accurate object detection and semantic segmentation. In: Proceedings of the IEEE Conference on Computer Vision and Pattern Recognition, pp. 580–587 (2014)
8. González, A., et al.: Pedestrian detection at day/night time with visible and fir cameras: a comparison. Sensors **16**(6), 820 (2016)
9. Guan, D., Cao, Y., Yang, J., Cao, Y., Yang, M.Y.: Fusion of multispectral data through illumination-aware deep neural networks for pedestrian detection. Inf. Fusion **50**, 148–157 (2019)
10. Gupta, S., Girshick, R., Arbeláez, P., Malik, J.: Learning rich features from RGB-D images for object detection and segmentation. In: Fleet, D., Pajdla, T., Schiele, B., Tuytelaars, T. (eds.) ECCV 2014. LNCS, vol. 8695, pp. 345–360. Springer, Cham (2014). https://doi.org/10.1007/978-3-319-10584-0_23
11. He, K., Zhang, X., Ren, S., Sun, J.: Deep residual learning for image recognition. In: Proceedings of the IEEE Conference on Computer Vision and Pattern Recognition, pp. 770–778 (2016)
12. He, Y., Zhu, C., Wang, J., Savvides, M., Zhang, X.: Bounding box regression with uncertainty for accurate object detection. In: Proceedings of the IEEE Conference on Computer Vision and Pattern Recognition, pp. 2888–2897 (2019)
13. Hinton, G., Vinyals, O., Dean, J.: Distilling the knowledge in a neural network. arXiv preprint arXiv:1503.02531 (2015)
14. Hwang, S., Park, J., Kim, N., Choi, Y., So Kweon, I.: Multispectral pedestrian detection: benchmark dataset and baseline. In: Proceedings of the IEEE Conference on Computer Vision and Pattern Recognition, pp. 1037–1045 (2015)
15. Kendall, A., Gal, Y.: What uncertainties do we need in Bayesian deep learning for computer vision? In: Advances in Neural Information Processing Systems, pp. 5574–5584 (2017)
16. Kim, J.U., Kwon, J., Kim, H.G., Lee, H., Ro, Y.M.: Object bounding box-critic networks for occlusion-robust object detection in road scene. In: 2018 25th IEEE International Conference on Image Processing (ICIP), pp. 1313–1317. IEEE (2018)

17. Kim, J.U., Kwon, J., Kim, H.G., Ro, Y.M.: BBC net: bounding-box critic network for occlusion-robust object detection. IEEE Trans. Circuits Syst. Video Technol. **30**(4), 1037–1050 (2019)
18. Kim, J.U., Park, S., Ro, Y.M.: Towards human-like interpretable object detection via spatial relation encoding. In: 2020 IEEE International Conference on Image Processing (ICIP), pp. 3284–3288. IEEE (2020)
19. Kim, J.U., Ro, Y.M.: Attentive layer separation for object classification and object localization in object detection. In: 2019 IEEE International Conference on Image Processing (ICIP), pp. 3995–3999. IEEE (2019)
20. Konig, D., Adam, M., Jarvers, C., Layher, G., Neumann, H., Teutsch, M.: Fully convolutional region proposal networks for multispectral person detection. In: Proceedings of the IEEE Conference on Computer Vision and Pattern Recognition Workshops, pp. 49–56 (2017)
21. Le, Q.V., Smola, A.J., Canu, S.: Heteroscedastic Gaussian process regression. In: Proceedings of the 22nd International Conference on Machine Learning, pp. 489–496 (2005)
22. Li, C., Song, D., Tong, R., Tang, M.: Multispectral pedestrian detection via simultaneous detection and segmentation. arXiv preprint arXiv:1808.04818 (2018)
23. Li, C., Song, D., Tong, R., Tang, M.: Illumination-aware faster R-CNN for robust multispectral pedestrian detection. Pattern Recognit. **85**, 161–171 (2019)
24. Lin, T.Y., Dollár, P., Girshick, R., He, K., Hariharan, B., Belongie, S.: Feature pyramid networks for object detection. In: Proceedings of the IEEE Conference on Computer Vision and Pattern Recognition, pp. 2117–2125 (2017)
25. Liu, J., Zhang, S., Wang, S., Metaxas, D.N.: Multispectral deep neural networks for pedestrian detection. arXiv preprint arXiv:1611.02644 (2016)
26. Nix, D.A., Weigend, A.S.: Estimating the mean and variance of the target probability distribution. In: Proceedings of 1994 IEEE International Conference on Neural Networks (ICNN 1994), vol. 1, pp. 55–60. IEEE (1994)
27. Park, K., Kim, S., Sohn, K.: Unified multi-spectral pedestrian detection based on probabilistic fusion networks. Pattern Recognit. **80**, 143–155 (2018)
28. Paszke, A., et al.: Automatic differentiation in pytorch (2017)
29. Ren, S., He, K., Girshick, R., Sun, J.: Faster R-CNN: towards real-time object detection with region proposal networks. In: Advances in Neural Information Processing Systems, pp. 91–99 (2015)
30. Simonyan, K., Zisserman, A.: Very deep convolutional networks for large-scale image recognition. arXiv preprint arXiv:1409.1556 (2014)
31. Song, S., Xiao, J.: Deep sliding shapes for amodal 3D object detection in RGB-D images. In: Proceedings of the IEEE Conference on Computer Vision and Pattern Recognition, pp. 808–816 (2016)
32. Torabi, A., Massé, G., Bilodeau, G.A.: An iterative integrated framework for thermal-visible image registration, sensor fusion, and people tracking for video surveillance applications. Comput. Vis. Image Underst. **116**(2), 210–221 (2012)
33. Tung, F., Mori, G.: Similarity-preserving knowledge distillation. In: Proceedings of the IEEE International Conference on Computer Vision, pp. 1365–1374 (2019)
34. Wang, X., Wang, M., Li, W.: Scene-specific pedestrian detection for static video surveillance. IEEE Trans. Pattern Anal. Mach. Intell. **36**(2), 361–374 (2013)
35. Zhang, L., et al.: Cross-modality interactive attention network for multispectral pedestrian detection. Inf. Fusion **50**, 20–29 (2019)
36. Zhang, L., Zhu, X., Chen, X., Yang, X., Lei, Z., Liu, Z.: Weakly aligned cross-modal learning for multispectral pedestrian detection. In: Proceedings of the IEEE International Conference on Computer Vision, pp. 5127–5137 (2019)

Time-Dependent Body Gesture Representation for Video Emotion Recognition

Jie Wei, Xinyu Yang$^{(\boxtimes)}$, and Yizhuo Dong

Xi'an Jiaotong University, Xi'an, China
yxyphd@mail.xjtu.edu.cn

Abstract. Video emotion recognition has recently become a research hotspot in the field of affective computing. Although large parts of studies focus on facial cues, body gestures are the only available cues in some scenes such as video monitoring systems. In this paper, we propose a body gesture representation method based on body joint movements. To reduce the model complexity and promote the understanding of video emotion, this method uses body joint information to represent body gestures and captures time-dependent relationship of body joints. Furthermore, we propose an attention-based channelwise convolutional neural network (ACCNN) to retain the independent characteristics of each body joint and learn key body gesture features. Experimental results on the multimodal database of Emotional Speech, Video and Gestures (ESVG) demonstrate the effectiveness of the proposed method, and the accuracy of body gesture features is comparable with that of facial features.

Keywords: Video emotion recognition · Body joints · Gesture representation · Channelwise convolution

1 Introduction

Emotion is the origin of human psychological activities and behaviors. Understanding the emotion of the other side and giving the reasonable emotional responses could facilitate the communication between people. Also, understanding user emotional state could optimize the machine service manners [9]. For example, vehicles with emotion recognition systems can detect the driver's emotion in real-time, so as to avoid traffic accidents caused by the upset and subdued states [16]. Video monitoring devices equipped with emotion recognition systems can track the emotion changes of anyone who is suspicious, and then can predict possible behaviors and improve the emergency response capacity. As emotion plays an increasingly important role in human-human and human-computer interactions [13], the research of automatic emotion recognition has attracted more attention in academic community.

© Springer Nature Switzerland AG 2021
J. Lokoč et al. (Eds.): MMM 2021, LNCS 12572, pp. 403–416, 2021.
https://doi.org/10.1007/978-3-030-67832-6_33

At present, 95% of research on video emotion recognition focus on facial expressions, and the rest focus on speech information [4]. However, it is difficult to capture vocal and facial expressions clearly in some reconnaissance and surveillance videos, and body gestures are the only available evidences in this case [1]. Nonverbal behavior and psychological research have found that body gesture can also convey emotional information [15]. Ekman et al. [8] pointed out that compared with facial expressions which are self-controlled intentionally, body gestures are usually more difficult to be controlled, thus can get more accurate emotional information.

However, most of the research for body gesture analysis focuses on pose estimation, action recognition, and so on [6,24], with insufficient attention given to emotion recognition [5,20]. Despite the fact, from limited empirical research, we can find out they focus on designing the handcrafted body movement features. The extraction process of these handcrafted features is complicated, and there are no clear protocols to distinguish different emotional labels. Recently, with the development of deep learning in the field of computer vision, deep models have been extended to gesture emotion recognition [2,23]. These studies explored the emotional cues of body gestures and built various deep networks to learn spatial-temporal information directly from videos. However, it requires extensive time and resources to process original videos using deep models. Treating all pixels with equal weights can not highlight the body gesture movements which are crucial to the emotional understanding.

With this insight, we propose a novel video emotion recognition method based on body gesture movements. First, 25 body joints are selected to present body gestures and the positions of these key joints are detected to record the change information. This step can reduce the time of subsequent processing and retain important body gesture information. Second, the changes of these key joints are temporally aggregated to obtain the time-dependent relationship of consecutive frames. Finally, we propose an attention-based channelwise convolutional neural network (ACCNN) to recognize the emotion. This network can retain the independent characteristics of each key joint by using channelwise convolutional layers and maximize the advantages of key body gesture features by using attention mechanism.

The contributions of our work are as follows:

1) We propose a body gesture representation method. This method aggregate body joints information temporally to capture the changes of body gesture in consecutive frames, which contains rich temporal information and greatly reduces the amount of calculation.

2) We propose an ACCNN model to recognize the emotional states. The model can retain the independent characteristics of each key joint and maximize the weight of important features, and further improve the accuracy of emotion recognition.

2   Related Work

Recognizing emotional state with body gestures is an important research aspect of human social psychology [17]. Wallbott et al. [22] pointed out that the body language recognition may benefit from various psychological protocols. Therefore, early research usually defined general body movement protocols for emotions [10,11]. For example, anger is encoded by shoulders moved upwards, arms stretched forwards or sideways; fear is encoded by hands or arms clenched, elbows dragged inward to show a conservative gesture; surprise is encoded by opening arms, hands burying the face or mouth.

With the development of machine learning, the research of body gesture emotion recognition has shifted to the feature selection of movements. Camurri et al. [5] proposed a set of body movement features includes low-level physical measurements (e.g., position, speed, and acceleration of body parts), overall motion description features (e.g., motion fluency, impulsiveness, and directness), and so on, and traditional models, such as SVM, are used to recognize emotional states. Saha et al. [20] considered extracting movement features by computing the distance, acceleration, and angle between 11 joints of the upper body, and then, different machine learning algorithms are used to recognize basic human emotions. Piana et al. [18] extracted more global expressive features of body gesture (e.g., contraction index, impulsiveness, and fluidity) from three-dimensional data of 15 joints while explored various intermediate and advanced features to recognize emotions. Psaltis et al. [19] extracted six types of human movement features from body joints, including velocity, acceleration, distances between hands, forward and backward leaning of the torso. Each type of features was trained separately, and then, output probabilities of these features were fused to predict the emotional states. The above methods design a large number of movement features from body joints information, but the extraction process of handcrafted features is relatively complex and time-consuming.

In recent years, the development of deep learning in the field of image processing has promoted the research of gesture emotion recognition. Sun et al. [23] proposed extracting deep spatial features by using CNN model and extracting temporal features by using BLSTM model, then hierarchical fusion strategy was considered to improve emotion recognition performance. Barros et al. [2] proposed a multichannel convolutional neural network with each of channels contained a two-layer convolutional structure. The training processes of each channel was shared to realize emotion classification. Deng et al. [7] proposed an attention-based BLSTM to represent the correlations between human movements and emotions. The advantage of this model is that it can better represent various emotions by exploiting the movement data. Barros et al. [3] proposed a cross-channel convolutional neural network that incorporates attention mechanism to learn the location of rich emotional expressions, which is conductive to improve the accuracy of emotion recognition. The above methods get effective emotion recognition performance using an end-to-end form, but the process of learning features from the original video directly may contain too many noises.

Meanwhile, deep models with high complexity and large number of parameters require more computing resources.

Based on this situation, we propose a body gesture representation method. This method retains the temporal information of videos and reduces the time for training by aggregating joints information in the time order. Also, we propose an ACCNN model which adds attention mechanism to maximize the weight of important features. With these steps, the accuracy of emotion recognition can be significantly improved.

3   Proposed Method

In this section, the proposed body gesture movements-based method for emotion recognition is introduced. There are three steps. First, position of the 25 body joints of each video frame is marked. Second, the changes of these key joints are reprented. Finally, the ACCNN model is trained for emotion recognition.

3.1   Body Joints Marked

The position information of key joints (e.g., head, hands, and torso) is sufficient to construct body gestures in images or videos without the need for overall visual information [14]. With this phenomenon, this paper considers using the position information of key joints in videos, which can reduce computing resources. In addition, all pixels of body joints are of the same importance, which can avoid the effect of pixel differences.

For videos, we use the OpenPose method [6] proposed by Carnegie Mellon University to obtain the position information of key joints. OpenPose is the first realtime multi-person 2D pose estimation method based on deep learning, which has excellent robustness to occlusion and truncation.

25 body joints are selected as key joints: 5 for the body trunks, 12 for the arms and 8 for the legs. The marking process is shown in Fig. 1. The information of each joint is represented as a sparse matrix I_t^i. (x_t^i, y_t^i) is denoted as the position coordinates for joint i in frame t, and the value of it is set to 1 (red point) while the remaining positions set to 0 (black point). Because the resolutions of different video are inconsistent, we rescale the matrix I_t^i to make the x and y coordinates less than 64. Therefore, in this work, for each video clip, we can get T description images $I_t = (I_t^1, I_t^2, ..., I_t^{25})$ of 25 channels with a 64×64 resolution.

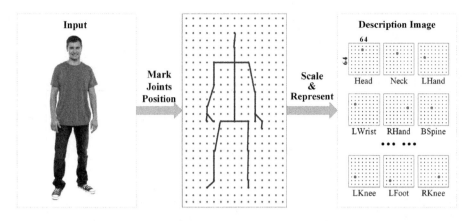

Fig. 1. An example of marking the position of body joints.

3.2 Body Gestures Representation

In Sect. 3.1, we obtain the description images of each joint at each frame according to the coordinates of the body joints. Next, we consider the continuous changes of body gestures and propose two body gesture representation methods.

3.2.1 Representation Method Without Timeline

The changes of body gesture are essentially the stacking of body gestures of continuous frames in the time order. The easiest way to realize the change presentation of body gestures is to encode the temporal relationship. We establish a relationship $W(t)$, which can be regarded as assigning the same weight to the description images in the same time and different weights in different time. And then, the description images of all moments are aggregated to obtain change representation of body gestures.

For different situations, we propose two ways to establish the relationship that are linear relationship $W(t) = \frac{T}{T-1}(t-1)$ and non-linear relationship $W(t) = \frac{1}{T-1}(t^2 - t)$. The core idea of this representation method is to assign the minimum weight to the first frame and the maximum weight to the last frame, while the middle frames are assigned to corresponding weights based on temporal relationships.

Taking the linear relationship as an example, the process is shown in Fig. 2. First, the description images of different times are assigned to different weights $W(t)$, so the description image at time t is represented as $G_t = I_t \cdot W(t)$. Then, the representation results of different times are aggregated. Based on this, the change representation of body gestures is obtained $G = \sum G_t$, in which $G_t = (G_t^1, G_t^2, ..., G_t^{25})$.

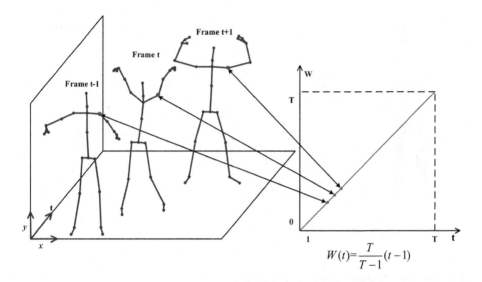

$$W(t) = \frac{T}{T-1}(t-1)$$

Fig. 2. Time-dependent body gesture representation without timeline.

3.2.2   Representation Method with Timeline

For some change situations of body gesture in videos, there exists a slight problem with the above representation. For example, for the repetitive back and forth movements with opposite starting direction, the change representation of body gestures may be identical because of the final aggregate operation. Although the representation of the non-linear relationship can solve this problem to some extent, it is still impossible to completely avoid the same representation for different changes of gesture. Therefore, in this section, to make up for the deficiency of the above representation method, we propose to use the trajectory of body joints to represent the changes.

If each body joint is tracked over time, the trajectory that describe how the corresponding body joint moves can be built. We propose to establish the coordinate systems between the time-axis and the X-axis, the time-axis and the Y-axis, respectively. There will form two trajectories in different directions based on above coordinate systems, so as to achieve a complete change representation of body gestures. Specifically, the joint coordinate (x_i^t, y_i^t) of each frame t is split, then two trajectories of different directions $R_x^i = (x_i^1, x_i^2, ..., x_i^T)$ and $R_y^i = (y_i^1, y_i^2, ..., y_i^T)$ are established according to the time order. Finally, the trajectories of different joints are aggregated, and the change representation of body gestures are obtained $R = (R_x^1, R_y^1, R_x^2, R_y^2, ..., R_x^{25}, R_y^{25})$. An example of the visualization results of the 25 joints trajectories is shown in Fig. 3. Figure 3(a) shows the trajectories of neutral, with little fluctuation over time. Figure 3(b) shows the trajectories of happiness, which fluctuates greatly over time.

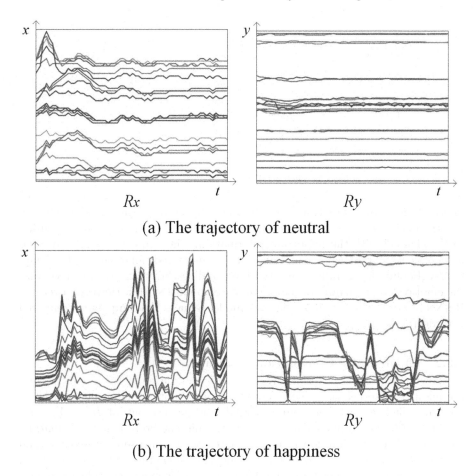

(a) The trajectory of neutral

(b) The trajectory of happiness

Fig. 3. Time-dependent body gesture representation with timeline.

3.3   ACCNN Model

3.3.1   Model Structure

The overall structure of the ACCNN model is shown in Fig. 4. The output is the emotion category, and the input is the change representation of body gestures obtained in Sect. 3.2. For the first representation method, the number of input channels is 25, and for the second is 25×2. The representation of body gestures has more simplified information compare with the original image, so the proposed model architecture just needs a shallow network and does not require any pretraining.

Specifically, the proposed ACCNN model includes two streams. The one consists of two blocks, and each block contains the conventional convolution layer, BN layer, and RELU layer. The other consists of two blocks, channelwise convolutional layer and attention layer. Each input channel represents different joint

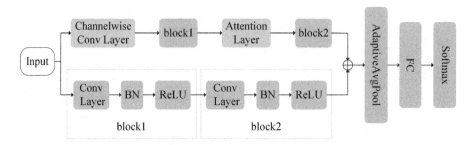

Fig. 4. The structure of ACCNN model.

information, channelwise convolutional layer can retain the independent characteristics of each joint, and attention layer enable the model to pay more attention
to the channel with the important information. The two streams are executed
independently, and then the information is aggregated, followed by the Adap-
tiveAvgPooling layer, fully-connected layer and the Softmax layer, to recognize
the emotions. The amount of parameters are about 5×10^2k. However, even the
ResNet18 are about 3×10^4k, thus our model reduces the complexity compared
with deep models.

3.3.2   Channelwise Convolutional Layer

As shown in Fig. 5(a), the input is $H_1 \times W_1 \times C_1$ and the kernel is $h_1 \times w_1 \times C_1$, and
the number of kernels is c_1. For conventional convolution, all elements of input
are multiplied by each kernel and merged, and get the output $H_2 \times W_2 \times c_1$.
In this work, each input channel represents different body joints information,
and channelwise convolution layer is adopted to perform separate convolution
operation for each channel to retain the independent characteristics of each joint.

The channelwise convolution layer performs independent convolution operation on each channel, and each channel data has the corresponding convolution
kernel. As shown in Fig. 5(b), the input is $H_1 \times W_1 \times C_1$ and the kernel is
$h_1 \times w_1 \times C_1$, and channelwise convolution requires that the number of kernel is
equal to the number of input channels C_1. The $H_1 \times W_1$ of channel C_i performs

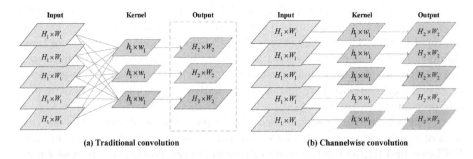

Fig. 5. The comparison of traditional and channelwise convolution.

convolution operation with the $h_1 \times w_1$ of corresponding channel, and get the final output $H_2 \times W_2 \times C_1$.

3.3.3 Attention Layer

Since the contribution of each joint for different emotions are not exactly consistent, the attention layer is added to pay more attention to the joints with the more relatively information. Each input channel represents information of different joints, and thus the Squeeze-and-Excitation structure [12] is used to achieve attention mechanism on the channel dimension. It enables the model to pay more attention to the channel with important information, while suppress the unimportant channel information.

The specific structure of Squeeze-and-Excitation is shown in Fig. 6. First, the AdaptiveAvgPool layer performs Squeeze operations to obtain the global features of channel level. Second, two fully-connected layers perform the Excitation operation to learn the relationship between each channel and get the weight of different channels. Finally, the original input is multiplied by the corresponding weights to get the output.

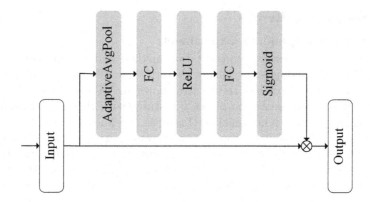

Fig. 6. The structure of Squeeze-and-Excitation.

4 Experimental Results

4.1 Dataset

The performance of the proposed method is evaluated on publicly available multimodal database of Emotional Speech, Video and Gestures (ESVG) [21]. A total of 16 professional actors were recorded for seven emotions: neutral state, sadness, surprise, fear, disgust, anger, happiness, and they were presented with a short scenario describing the emotion they had to present before recording. Each person was recorded separately, and all emotions were acted out 5 times. The public part of the database includes 13 actors - 7 female and 6 male, and the total number of videos amounted to 455.

4.2 Experimental Setup

We used two experimental schemes during the experiments, subject-dependent and subject-independent. In the first scheme, we use 5-fold cross-validation, in which all videos were split uniformly into 5 folds, so the subjects that appeared in the training set appear in the test set. In the second scheme, we use leave-one-subject-out cross-validation, in which all actors were split into 13 folds, so the subjects that appeared in the training set did not appear in the test set.

The model is built on PyTorch framework with Adam optimizer. The initial learning rate is set to 0.001 and reduce it by 0.5 times for every 50 epochs, and a total of 200 epochs are executed in the training stage.

In order to further present the effectiveness of the proposed method, we also considered two baseline experiments. 1) The pretrained network extracts deep features of the facial expression, and SVM are used to identify emotion. 2) The pretrained network extracts deep features of the facial expression, and LSTM are used to identify emotion. In addition, the score fusion that sum score vectors of different methods is used to show the performance improvement after fusing different methods.

4.3 Experimental Results

4.3.1 Subject-Dependent Experiment

From the aspects of gesture representation method and recognition model, we conducted corresponding experiments to verify the effectiveness of proposed. The performance comparison results are shown in Table 1. First, the performance of change representation of body gestures with timeline (trajectory) is better compared to without timeline (linear & non-linear). Second, the recognition accuracy of fusing the proposed two representation methods is improved compared to single. It illustrates that there exists the complementarity between the two methods. Finally, the proposed emotion recognition model ACCNN have improved the recognition performance compared to traditional convolutional networks, which shows that channelwise convolution and attention mechanisms are more superior in the change representation of body gestures.

Table 1. Performance comparison of different representation methods and recognition models.

	Traditional convolution (%)	ACCNN model (%)
Without timeline (Linear)	59.46	62.56
Without timeline (Non-Linear)	55.01	59.41
With timeline (Trajectory)	83.58	86.24
Fusion (Linear + Trajectory)	85.05	**88.35**

In order to comprehend the recognition performance more intuitively, the recognition accuracy for each emotion is further analyzed. The experimental comparison results are shown in Fig. 7. First, the recognition accuracy of each emotion has been improved after fusing the proposed two representation methods, which further verifies the complementarity of the two methods. Second, "Neutral" has the best recognition performance compared with the others, and the recognition is 100% correct after fusion. Finally, compared with the representation method of removing timeline, establishing timeline improves recognition accuracy for all emotional categories.

To further demonstrate the effectiveness of the proposed method, we compare the recognition performance with baseline and the facial expression-based methods. The experimental comparation results are shown in Table 2. First, the proposed method has greatly improved the recognition accuracy compared with the gesture-based baseline, which shows the superiority of our method in gesture emotion recognition. Second, the proposed method provides comparable results to facial expression-based baseline and other methods. In addition, our proposed method and facial expression-based method are fused to further improve the recognition accuracy to 92.53%, indicating the advantages of fusing the gestures and facial expressions information.

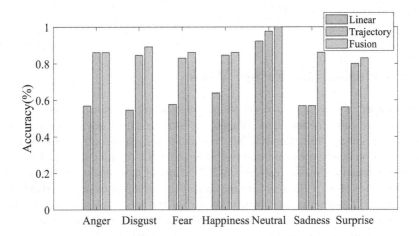

Fig. 7. Recognition accuracy for each emotion category.

Table 2. Emotion recognition performance comparison with other methods.

Method		Accuracy(%)
Baseline(gesture-based) [21]		62.83
Baseline(facial expression-based) [21]		**94.67**
SVM	Resnet101 feature	78.90
	VGGFACE feature	87.69
LSTM	Resnet101 feature	67.85
	VGGFACE feature	77.69
Our proposed		88.35
Fusion(SVM_VGGFACE + Trajectory)		**92.53**

4.3.2 Subject-Independent Experiment

This section compares the recognition performance of subject-independent experiments with facial expression-based methods. The experimental results are shown in Table 3. First, compared with subject-dependent experiments, the recognition accuracy is greatly reduced, which shows that the individual difference of emotion expression has a great impact on the recognition performance. Second, the recognition accuracy of facial expression-based method decreases less compared to gesture-based method, indicating that facial expression features are less affected by individual differences. Finally, the fusion of the proposed method and facial expression-based method also improve the recognition accuracy to 61.1%.

Table 3. Emotion recognition performance comparison with other methods.

Method		Accuracy (%)
SVM	Resnet101 feature	48.57
	VGGFACE feature	58.24
LSTM	Resnet101 feature	51.65
	VGGFACE feature	56.48
Our proposed		54.29
Fusion (SVM_VGGFACE + Trajectory)		**61.10**

5   Conclusion and Future Work

In this paper, we propose a novel video emotion recognition method based on body gesture movements. The changes of body gestures are represented with joints information, and the ACCNN model is used to recognize emotion. The representation method can reduce the complexity for training and capture time-dependent relationship of gestures. ACCNN model can retain the independent characteristics of each channel and maximize the advantages of important channel features. The experimental results show that the proposed method is effective. In addition, the fusion of proposed method and facial expression-based method effectively improves the accuracy of emotion recognition.

In the future work, we will continue research on gesture emotion recognition, and further consider multimodal-based emotion recognition methods to obtain better recognition performance.

References

1. Aviezer, H., Trope, Y., Todorov, A.: Body cues, not facial expressions, discriminate between intense positive and negative emotions. Science **338**(6111), 1225–1229 (2012). https://doi.org/10.1126/science.1224313
2. Barros, P., Jirak, D., Weber, C., Wermter, S.: Multimodal emotional state recognition using sequence-dependent deep hierarchical features. Neural Netw. **72**, 140–151 (2015). https://doi.org/10.1016/j.neunet.2015.09.009

3. Barros, P., Parisi, G., Weber, C., Wermter, S.: Emotion-modulated attention improves expression recognition: a deep learning model. Neurocomputing **253**, 104–114 (2017). https://doi.org/10.1016/j.neucom.2017.01.096
4. Beatrice, D.G.: Why bodies? Twelve reasons for including bodily expressions in affective neuroscience. Philos. Trans. R. Soc. Lond. Ser. B Biol. Sci. **364**(1535), 3475–3484 (2009). https://doi.org/10.1098/rstb.2009.0190
5. Camurri, A., Lagerlöf, I., Volpe, G.: Recognizing emotion from dance movement: comparison of spectator recognition and automated techniques. Int. J. Hum. Comput. Stud. **59**(1–2), 213–225 (2003). https://doi.org/10.1016/S1071-5819(03)00050-8
6. Cao, Z., Simon, T., Wei, S.E., Sheikh, Y.: Realtime multi-person 2D pose estimation using part affinity fields. In: Proceedings of the IEEE Conference on Computer Vision and Pattern Recognition, pp. 1302–1310, July 2017. https://doi.org/10.1109/CVPR.2017.143
7. Deng, J.J., Leung, C.H.C., Mengoni, P., Li, Y.: Emotion recognition from human behaviors using attention model. In: 2018 IEEE First International Conference on Artificial Intelligence and Knowledge Engineering (AIKE), pp. 249–253, September 2018. https://doi.org/10.1109/AIKE.2018.00056
8. Ekman, P.: Mistakes when deceiving. Ann. N. Y. Acad. Sci. **364**(1), 269–278 (1981). https://doi.org/10.1111/j.1749-6632.1981.tb34479.x
9. Filntisis, P.P., Efthymiou, N., Koutras, P., Potamianos, G., Maragos, P.: Fusing body posture with facial expressions for joint recognition of affect in child-robot interaction. IEEE Robot. Autom. Lett. **4**(4), 4011–4018 (2019). https://doi.org/10.1109/LRA.2019.2930434
10. Gunes, H., Piccardi, M.: A bimodal face and body gesture database for automatic analysis of human nonverbal affective behavior. In: 18th International Conference on Pattern Recognition (ICPR 2006), pp. 1148–1153, August 2006. https://doi.org/10.1109/ICPR.2006.39
11. Gunes, H., Piccardi, M.: Fusing face and body gesture for machine recognition of emotions. In: ROMAN 2005. IEEE International Workshop on Robot and Human Interactive Communication, 2005, pp. 306–311, October 2005. https://doi.org/10.1109/ROMAN.2005.1513796
12. Hu, J., Shen, L., Sun, G.: Squeeze-and-excitation networks. In: Proceedings of the IEEE Conference on Computer Vision and Pattern Recognition, pp. 7132–7141, June 2018. https://doi.org/10.1109/CVPR.2018.00745
13. Izard, C.E., Ackerman, B.P., Schoff, K.M., Fine, S.E.: Self-Organization of Discrete Emotions, Emotion Patterns, and Emotion-Cognition Relations, pp. 15–36. Cambridge Studies in Social and Emotional Development, Cambridge University Press (2000). https://doi.org/10.1017/CBO9780511527883.003
14. Li, J., Wang, C., Zhu, H., Mao, Y., Fang, H.S., Lu, C.: CrowdPose: efficient crowded scenes pose estimation and a new benchmark. In: 2019 IEEE/CVF Conference on Computer Vision and Pattern Recognition (CVPR), pp. 10855–10864, June 2019. https://doi.org/10.1109/CVPR.2019.01112
15. Matsumoto, D., Frank, M., Hwang, H.: Nonverbal Communication: Science and Applications. Sage Publications (2012). https://doi.org/10.4135/9781452244037
16. Nass, C., Jonsson, I.M., Harris, H., Reaves, B., Endo, J., Brave, S., Takayama, L.: Improving automotive safety by pairing driver emotion and car voice emotion. In: CHI '05 Extended Abstracts on Human Factors in Computing Systems, CHI EA 2005, New York, NY, USA, pp. 1973–1976. Association for Computing Machinery (2005). https://doi.org/10.1145/1056808.1057070

17. Pease, B., Pease, A.: The Definitive Book of Body Language: The Hidden Meaning Behind People's Gestures and Expressions. Bantam (2008)
18. Piana, S., Staglianò, A., Odone, F., Camurri, A.: Adaptive body gesture representation for automatic emotion recognition. ACM Trans. Interact. Intell. Syst. **6**(1), 1–31 (2016). https://doi.org/10.1145/2818740
19. Psaltis, A., Kaza, K., Stefanidis, K., Thermos, S., Apostolakis, K.C.: Multimodal affective state recognition in serious games applications. In: IEEE International Conference on Imaging Systems and Techniques, pp. 435–439, October 2016. https://doi.org/10.1109/IST.2016.7738265
20. Saha, S., Datta, S., Konar, A., Janarthanan, R.: A study on emotion recognition from body gestures using kinect sensor. In: 2014 International Conference on Communication and Signal Processing, pp. 056–060, April 2014. https://doi.org/10.1109/ICCSP.2014.6949798
21. Sapiński, T., Kamińska, D., Pelikant, A., Ozcinar, C., Avots, E., Anbarjafari, G.: Multimodal database of emotional speech, video and gestures. In: International Conference on Pattern Recognition, pp. 153–163, August 2018
22. Siegman, A.W., Feldstein, S.: Nonverbal Behavior and Communication. Psychology Press (2014)
23. Sun, B., Cao, S., He, J., Yu, L.: Affect recognition from facial movements and body gestures by hierarchical deep spatio-temporal features and fusion strategy. Neural Netw. **105**, 36–51 (2017). https://doi.org/10.1016/j.neunet.2017.11.021
24. Weng, J., Liu, M., Jiang, X., Yuan, J.: Deformable pose traversal convolution for 3D action and gesture recognition. In: Ferrari, V., Hebert, M., Sminchisescu, C., Weiss, Y. (eds.) ECCV 2018. LNCS, vol. 11211, pp. 142–157. Springer, Cham (2018). https://doi.org/10.1007/978-3-030-01234-2_9

MusiCoder: A Universal Music-Acoustic Encoder Based on Transformer

Yilun Zhao[1,2(✉)] and Jia Guo[2]

[1] Zhejiang University/University of Illinois at Urbana-Champaign Institute,
Zhejiang University, Haining, China
`zhaoyilun@zju.edu.cn`
[2] YouKu Cognitive and Intelligent Lab, Alibaba Group, Hangzhou, China
`{yilun.zyl,gj243069}@alibaba-inc.com`

Abstract. Music annotation has always been one of the critical topics in the field of Music Information Retrieval (MIR). Traditional models use supervised learning for music annotation tasks. However, as supervised machine learning approaches increase in complexity, the increasing need for more annotated training data can often not be matched with available data. In this paper, a new self-supervised music acoustic representation learning approach named MusiCoder is proposed. Inspired by the success of BERT, MusiCoder builds upon the architecture of self-attention bidirectional transformers. Two pre-training objectives, including Contiguous Frames Masking (CFM) and Contiguous Channels Masking (CCM), are designed to adapt BERT-like masked reconstruction pre-training to continuous acoustic frame domain. The performance of MusiCoder is evaluated in two downstream music annotation tasks. The results show that MusiCoder outperforms the state-of-the-art models in both music genre classification and auto-tagging tasks. The effectiveness of Musi-Coder indicates a great potential of a new self-supervised learning approach to understand music: first apply masked reconstruction tasks to pre-train a transformer-based model with massive unlabeled music acoustic data, and then finetune the model on specific downstream tasks with labeled data.

Keywords: Music information retrieval · Self-supervised representation learning · Masked reconstruction · Transformer

1 Introduction

The amount of music has been growing rapidly over the past decades. As an effective measure for utilizing massive music data, automatically assigning one music clip a set of relevant tags, providing high-level descriptions about the music clip such as genre, emotion, theme, are of great significance in MIR community [5,39].

Supported by Alibaba Group, and Key Laboratory of Design Intelligence and Digital Creativity of Zhejiang Province, Zhejiang University.

ⓒ Springer Nature Switzerland AG 2021
J. Lokoč et al. (Eds.): MMM 2021, LNCS 12572, pp. 417–429, 2021.
https://doi.org/10.1007/978-3-030-67832-6_34

Some researchers have applied several supervised learning models [14,20,22,28], which are trained on human-annotated music data. However, the performance of supervised learning method are likely to be limited by the size of labeled dataset, which is expensive and time consuming to collect.

Recently, self-supervised pre-training models [23,24,31,37], especially BERT, dominate Natural Language Processing (NLP) community. BERT proposes a Masked Language Model (MLM) pre-training objective, which can learn a powerful language representation by reconstructing the masked input sequences in pre-training stage. The intuition behind this design is that a model available to recover the missing content should have learned a good contextual representation. In particular, BERT and its variants [25,38,40] have reached significant improvements on various NLP benchmark tasks [36]. Compared with the text domain whose inputs are discrete word tokens, in acoustics domain, the inputs are usually multi-dimensional feature vectors (e.g., energy in multiple frequency bands) of each frame, which are continuous and smoothly changed over time. Therefore, some particular designs need to be introduced to bridge the gaps between discrete text and contiguous acoustic frames. We are the first to apply the idea of masked reconstruction pre-training to the continuous music acoustic domain. In this paper, a new self-supervised pre-training scheme called Musi-Coder is proposed, which can learn a powerful acoustic music representations through reconstructing masked acoustic frame sequence in pre-training stage.

Our contributions can be summarized as:

1. We present a new self-supervised pre-training model named MusiCoder. Musi-Coder builds upon the structure of multi-layer bidirectional self-attention transformers. Rather than relying on massive human-labeled data, MusiCoder can learn a powerful music representation from unlabeled music acoustic data, which is much easier to collect.
2. The reconstruction procedure of BERT-like model is adapted from classification task to regression task. In other word, MusiCoder can reconstruct continuous acoustic frames directly, which avoids an extra transformation from continuous frames to discrete word tokens before pre-training.
3. Two pre-training objectives, including Contiguous Frames Masking (CFM) and Contiguous Channels Masking (CCM), are proposed to pre-train Musi-Coder. The ablation study shows that both CFM and CCM objectives can effectively improve the performance of MusiCoder pre-training.
4. The MusiCoder is evaluated on two downstream tasks: GTZAN music genre classification and MTG-Jamendo music auto-tagging. And MusiCoder outperforms the SOTA model in both tasks. The success of MusiCoder indicates a great potential of applying transformer-based masked reconstruction pre-training in Music Information Retrieval (MIR) field.

2   Related Work

In the past few years, pre-training models and self-supervised representation learning have achieved great success in NLP community. Huge amount of self-

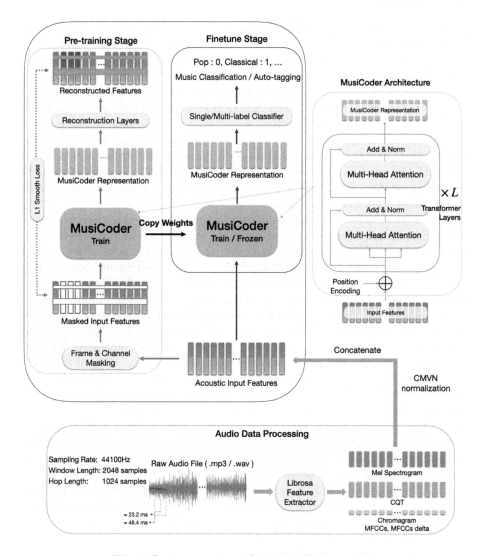

Fig. 1. System overview of the MusiCoder model

supervised pre-training models based on multi-layer self-attention transformers [34], such as BERT [12], GPT [30], XLNet [38], Electra [9] are proposed. Among them, BERT is perhaps the most classic and popular one due to its simplicity and outstanding performance. Specifically, BERT is designed to reconstruct the masked input sequences in pre-training stage. Through reconstructing the missing content from a given masked sequence, the model can learn a powerful contextual representation.

More recently, the success of BERT in NLP community draws the attention of researchers in acoustic signal processing field. Some pioneering works

[2,23,24,31,37] have shown the effectiveness of adapting BERT to Automatic Speech Recognition (ASR) research. Specifically, they design some specific pre-training objectives to bridge the gaps between discrete text and contiguous acoustic frames. In vq-wav2vec [2], input speech audio is first discretized to a K-way quantized embedding space by learning discrete representation from audio samples. However, the quantization process requires massive computing resources and is against the continuous nature of acoustic frames. Some works [7,23,24,31,37] design a modified version of BERT to directly utilize continuous speech. In [7,23,24], continuous frame-level masked reconstruction is adapted in BERT-like pre-training stage. In [37], SpecAugment [27] is applied to mask input frames. And [31] learns by reconstructing from shuffled acoustic frame orders rather than masked frames.

As for MIR community, representation learning has been popular for many years. Several convolutional neural networks (CNNs) based supervised methods [8,14,20,22,28] are proposed in music understanding tasks. They usually employ variant depth of convolutional layers on Mel-spectrogram based representations or raw waveform signals of the music to learn effective music representation, and append fully connected layers to predict relevant annotation like music genres, tags. However, training such CNN-based models usually requires massive human-annotated data. And in [6,17], researchers show that compared with supervised learning methods, using self-supervision on unlabeled data can significantly improve the robustness of the model. Recently, the self-attention transformer has shown promising results in symbolic music generation area. For example, Music Transformer [18] and Pop Music Transformer [19] employ relative attention to capture long-term structure from music MIDI data, which can be used as discrete word tokens directly. However, compared with raw music audio, the size of existing MIDI dataset is limited. Moreover, transcription from raw audio to MIDI files is time-consuming and not accurate. In this paper, we proposed MusiCoder, a universal music-acoustic encoder based on transformers. Specifically, MusiCoder is first pre-trained on massive unlabeled music acoustic data, and then finetuned on specific downstream music annotation tasks using labeled data.

3 MusiCoder Model

A universal transformer-based encoder named MusiCoder is presented for music acoustic representation learning. The system overview of proposed MusiCoder is shown in Fig. 1.

3.1 Input Representation

For each input frame t_i, its vector representation x_i is obtained by first projecting t_i linearly to hidden dimension H_{dim}, and then added with sinusoidal positional encoding [34] defined as following:

$$PE_{(pos,2i)} = sin(pos/10000^{2i/H_{dim}})$$
$$PE_{(pos,2i+1)} = cos(pos/10000^{2i/H_{dim}})$$

(1)

The positional encoding is used to inject information about the relative position of acoustic frames. The design of positional encoding makes the transformer encoder aware of the music sequence order.

3.2 Transformer Encoder

A multi-layer bidirectional self-attention transformer encoder [34] is used to encode the input music acoustic frames. Specifically, a L-layer transformer is used to encode the input vectors $X = \{x_i\}_{i=1}^N$ as:

$$H^l = Transformer_l(H^{l-1})$$

(2)

where $l \in [1, L]$, $H^0 = X$ and $H^L = [h_1^L, ..., h_N^L]$. We use the hidden vector h_i^L as the contextualized representation of the input token t_i. The architecture of transformer encoder is shown in Fig. 1.

3.3 Pre-training Objectives

The main idea of masked reconstruction pre-training is to perturb the inputs by randomly masking tokens with some probability, and reconstruct the masked tokens at the output. In the pre-training process, a reconstruction module, which consists of two layers of feed-forward network with GeLU activation [16] and layer-normalization [1], is appended to predict the masked inputs. The module uses the output of the last MusiCoder encoder layer as its input. Moreover, two new pre-training objectives are presented to help MusiCoder learn acoustic music representation.

Objective 1: Contiguous Frames Masking (CFM). To avoid the model exploiting local smoothness of acoustic frames, rather than only mask one span with fixed number of consecutive frames [24], we mask several spans of consecutive frames dynamically. Given a sequence of input frames $X = (x_1, x_2, ..., x_n)$, we select a subset $Y \subset X$ by iteratively sampling contiguous input frames (spans) until the masking budget (e.g., 15% of X) has been spent. At each iteration, the span length is first sampled from a geometric distribution $\ell \sim Geo(p)$. Then the starting point of the masked span is randomly selected. We set $p = 0.2$, $\ell_{min} = 2$ and $\ell_{max} = 7$. The corresponding mean length of span is around 3.87 frames (≈ 179.6 ms). In each masked span, the frames are masked according to the following policy: 1) replace all frames with zero in 70% of the case. Since each dimension of input frames are normalized to have zero mean value, setting the masked value to zero is equivalent to setting it to the mean value. 2) replace all frames with a random masking frame in 20% of the case. 3) keep the original frames unchanged in the rest 10% of the case. Since MusiCoder will only receive acoustic frames without masking during inference time, policy 3) allows the model to receive real inputs during pre-training, and resolves the pretrain-fintune inconsistency problem [12].

Objective 2: Contiguous Channels Masking (CCM). The intuition of channel masking is that a model available to predict the partial loss of channel information should have learned a high-level understanding along the channel axis. For log-mel spectrum and log-CQT features, a block of consecutive channels is randomly masked to zero for all time steps across the input sequence of frames. Specifically, the number of masked blocks, n, is first sampled from $\{0, 1, \ldots, H\}$ uniformly. Then a starting channel index is sampled from $\{0, 1, \ldots, H - n\}$, where H is the number of total channels.

Pre-training Objective Function.

$$Loss(x) = \begin{cases} 0.5 \cdot x^2 & if \ |x| < 1 \\ |x| - 0.5 & otherwise \end{cases} \qquad (3)$$

The Huber Loss [15] is used to minimize reconstruction error between masked input features and corresponding encoder output. Huber Loss is a robust L1 loss that is less sensitive to outliers. And in our preliminary experiments, we found that compared with L1 loss used in [24], using Huber loss will make the training process easier to converge.

3.4   MusiCoder Model Setting

We primarily report experimental results on two models: MusiCoderBase and MusiCoderLarge. The model settings are listed in Table 1. The number of Transformer block layers, the size of hidden vectors, the number of self-attention heads are represented as L_{num}, H_{dim}, A_{num}, respectively.

Table 1. The proposed model settings

	L_{num}	H_{dim}	A_{num}	#parameters
MusiCoderBase	4	768	12	29.3M
MusiCoderLarge	8	1024	16	93.1M

4   Experiment Setup

4.1   Dataset Collection and Preprocess

Table 2. Statistics on the datasets used for pre-training and downstream tasks

Task	Datasets	#clips	Duration (hours)	Description
Pre-training	Music4all	109.2K	908.7	–
	FMA-large	106.3K	886.4	–
	MTG-Jamendo[a]	37.3K	1346.9	–
Classification	GTZAN	1000	8.3	100 clips for each genre
Auto-tagging	MTG-Jamendo[b]	18.4K	157.1	56 mood/theme tags

[a,b] For MTG-Jamendo dataset, we removed music clips used in Auto-tagging task when pre-training.

As shown in Table 2, the pre-training data were aggregated from three datasets: Music4all [13], FMA-Large [11] and MTG-Jamendo [4]. Both Music4all and FMA-Large datasets provide 30-s audio clips in .mp3 format for each song. And MTG-Jamendo dataset contains 55.7K music tracks, each with a duration of more than 30 s. Since the maximum time stamps of MusiCoder is set to 1600, those music tracks exceeding 35 s would be cropped into several music clips, the duration of which was randomly picked from 10 s to 35 s.

GTZAN music genre classification [32] and MTG-Jamendo music auto-tagging tasks [4] were used to evaluate the performance of finetuned MusiCoder. GTZAN consists of 1000 music clips divided into ten different genres (blues, classical, country, disco, hip-hop, jazz, metal, pop, reggae & rock). Each genre consists of 100 music clips in .wav format with a duration of 30 s. To avoid seeing any test data in downstream tasks, for pre-training data, we filtered out those music clips appearing in downstream tasks.

Audio Preprocess. The acoustic music analysis library, Librosa [26], provides flexible ways to extract features related to timbre, harmony, and rhythm aspect of music. In our work, Librosa was used to extract the following features from a given music clip: Mel-scaled Spectrogram, Constant-Q Transform (CQT), Mel-frequency cepstral coefficients (MFCCs), MFCCs delta and Chromagram, as detailed in Table 4. Each kind of features was extracted at the sampling rate of 44,100 Hz, with a Hamming window size of 2048 samples ($\approx$46 ms) and a hop size of 1024 samples ($\approx$23 ms). The Mel Spectrogram and CQT features were transformed to log amplitude with $S' = ln(10 \cdot S + \epsilon)$, where S, ϵ represents the feature and an extremely small number, respectively. Then Cepstral Mean and Variance Normalization (CMVN) [29,35] were applied to the extracted features for minimizing distortion caused by noise contamination. Finally these normalized features were concatenated to a 324-dim feature, which was later used as the input of MusiCoder (Table 3).

Table 3. Acoustic features of music extracted by Librosa

Feature	Characteristic	Dimension
Chromagram	Melody, Harmony	12
MFCCs	Pitch	20
MFCCs delta	Pitch	20
Mel-scaled Spectrogram	Raw Waveform	128
Constant-Q Transform	Raw Waveform	144

4.2   Training Setup

All our experiments were conducted on 5 GTX 2080Ti and can be reproduced on any machine with GPU memory more than 48 GBs. In pre-training stage, MusiCoderBase and MusiCoderLarge were trained with a batch size of 64 for 200k and 500k steps, respectively. We applied the Adam optimizer [21] with $\beta_1 = 0.9$, $\beta_2 = 0.999$ and $\epsilon = 10^{-6}$. And the learning rate were varied with warmup schedule [34] according to the formula:

$$lrate = H_{dim}^{-0.5} \cdot min(step\_num^{-0.5}, step\_num \cdot warmup\_steps^{-1.5}) \quad (4)$$

where *warmup_steps* was set as 8000. Moreover, library Apex was used to accelerate the training process and save GPU memory.

For downstream tasks, we performed an exhaustive search on the following sets of parameters. The model that performed the best on the validation set was selected. All the other training parameters remained the same as those in pre-training stage:

Table 4. Parameter settings for downstream tasks

Parameter	Candidate value
Batch size	16, 24, 32
Learning rate	2e−5, 3e−5, 5e−5
Epoch	2, 3, 4
Dropout rate	0.05, 0.1

5 Results

5.1 Music Genre Classification

Table 5. Results of GTZAN music classification task

Models	Accuracy
Hand-crafted features + SVM [3]	87.9%
CNN + SVM [8]	89.8%
CNN+MLP based ensemble [14]	94.2%
MusiCoderBase	**94.2%**
MusiCoderLarge	**94.3%**
Theoretical maximum score [32]	94.5%

Since GTZAN dataset only contains 1000 music clips, the experiments were conducted in a ten-fold cross-validation setup. For each fold, 80, 20 songs of each genre were randomly selected and placed into the training and validation split, respectively. The ten-fold average accuracy score is shown in Table 5. In prevoious work, [3] applied low-level music features and rich statistics to predict music genres. In [8], researchers first used a CNN based model, which was trained on music auto-tagging tasks, to extract features. These extracted features were then applied on SVM [33] for genre classification. In [14], the authors trained two models: a CNN based model trained on a variety of spectral and rhythmic features, and an MLP network trained on features, which were extracted from a model for music auto-tagging task. Then these two models were combined in a majority voting ensemble setup. The authors reported the accuracy score as 94.2%. Although some other works reported their accuracy score higher than 94.5%, we set 94.5% as the state-of-the-art accuracy according to the analysis in [32], which demonstrates that the inherent noise (e.g., repetitions, mis-labelings, distortions of the songs) in GTZAN dataset prevents the perfect accuracy score from surpassing 94.5%. In the experiment, MusiCoderBase and MusiCoderLarge achieve accuracy of 94.2% and 94.3%, respectively. The proposed models outperform the state-of-the-art models and achieve accuracy score close to the ideal value.

5.2 Music Auto-tagging

For the music auto-tagging task, two sets of performance measurements, ROC-AUC macro and PR-AUC macro, were applied. ROC-AUC can lead to over-optimistic scores when data are unbalanced [10]. Since the music tags given in the MTG-Jamendo dataset are highly unbalanced [4], the PR-AUC metric was also introduced for evaluation. The MusiCoder model was compared with other

Table 6. Results of MTG-Jamendo music auto-tagging task

	Models	ROC-AUC macro	PR-AUC macro
	VQ-VAE+CNN [20]	72.07%	10.76%
	VGGish [4]	72.58%	10.77%
	CRNN [22]	73.80%	11.71%
	FA-ResNet [22]	75.75%	14.63%
	SampleCNN (reproduced) [28]	76.93%	14.92%
	Shake-FA-ResNet [22]	77.17%	14.80%
Ours	MusiCoderBase w/o pre-training	77.03%	15.02%
	MusiCoderBase with CCM	81.93%	19.49%
	MusiCoderBase with CFM	81.38%	19.51%
	MusiCoderBase with CFM+CCM	**82.57%**	**20.87%**
	MusiCoderLarge with CFM+CCM	**83.82%**	**22.01%**

state-of-the-art models competing in the challenge of MediaEval 2019: Emotion and Theme Recognition in Music Using Jamendo [4]. We used the same train-valid-test data splits as the challenge. The results are shown in Table 6. For VQ-VAE+CNN [20], VGGish [4], CRNN [22], FA-ResNet [22], Shake-FA-ResNet [22] models, we directly used the evaluation results posted in the competition leaderboard[1]. For SampleCNN [28], we reproduced the work according to the official implementation[2]. As the results suggest, the proposed MusiCoder model achieves new state-of-the-art results in music auto-tagging task.

Ablation Study. Ablation study were conducted to better understand the performance of MusiCoder. The results are also shown in Table 6. According to the experiemnt, even without pre-training, MusiCoderBase can still outperform most SOTA models, which indicates the effectiveness of transformer-based architecture. When MusiCoderBase is pre-trained with objective CCM or CFM only, a significant improvement over MusiCoderBase without pre-training is observed. And MusiCoderBase with CCM and CFM pre-training objectives combined achieves better results. The improvement indicates the effectiveness of pre-training stage. And it shows that the designed pre-training objectives CCM and CFM are both the key elements that drives pre-trained MusiCoder to learn a powerful music acoustic representation. We also explore the effect of model size on downstream task accuracy. In the experiment, MusiCoderLarge outperforms MusiCoderBase, which reflects that increasing the model size of MusiCoder will lead to continual improvements.

---

[1] https://multimediaeval.github.io/2019-Emotion-and-Theme-Recognition-in-Music-Task/results.

[2] https://github.com/tae-jun/sample-cnn.

6 Conclusion

In this paper, we propose MusiCoder, a universal music-acoustic encoder based on transformers. Rather than relying on massive human labeled data which is expensive and time consuming to collect, MusiCoder can learn a strong music representation from unlabeled music acoustic data. Two new pre-training objectives Contiguous Frames Masking (CFM) and Contiguous Channel Masking (CCM) are designed to improve the pre-training stage in continuous acoustic frame domain. The effectiveness of proposed objectives is evaluated through extensive ablation studies. Moreover, MusiCoder outperforms the state-of-the-art model in music genre classification on GTZAN dataset and music auto-tagging on MTG-Jamendo dataset. Our work shows a great potential of adapting transformer-based masked reconstruction pre-training scheme to MIR community. Beyond improving the model, we plan to extend MusiCoder to other music understanding tasks (e.g., music emotion recognition, chord estimation, music segmentation). We believe the future prospects for large scale representation learning from music acoustic data look quite promising.

References

1. Ba, J.L., Kiros, J.R., Hinton, G.E.: Layer normalization. arXiv preprint arXiv:1607.06450 (2016)
2. Baevski, A., Schneider, S., Auli, M.: vq-wav2vec: Self-supervised learning of discrete speech representations. arXiv preprint arXiv:1910.05453 (2019)
3. Baniya, B.K., Lee, J., Li, Z.N.: Audio feature reduction and analysis for automatic music genre classification. In: 2014 IEEE International Conference on Systems, Man, and Cybernetics (SMC), pp. 457–462. IEEE (2014)
4. Bogdanov, D., Won, M., Tovstogan, P., Porter, A., Serra, X.: The mtg-jamendo dataset for automatic music tagging. In: Machine Learning for Music Discovery Workshop, International Conference on Machine Learning (ICML 2019), Long Beach, CA, United States (2019). http://hdl.handle.net/10230/42015
5. Bu, J., Tan, S., Chen, C., Wang, C., Wu, H., Zhang, L., He, X.: Music recommendation by unified hypergraph: combining social media information and music content. In: Proceedings of the 18th ACM international conference on Multimedia, pp. 391–400 (2010)
6. Carmon, Y., Raghunathan, A., Schmidt, L., Duchi, J.C., Liang, P.S.: Unlabeled data improves adversarial robustness. In: Advances in Neural Information Processing Systems, pp. 11192–11203 (2019)
7. Chi, P.H., Chung, P.H., Wu, T.H., Hsieh, C.C., Li, S.W., Lee, H.y.: Audio albert: a lite bert for self-supervised learning of audio representation. arXiv preprint arXiv:2005.08575 (2020)
8. Choi, K., Fazekas, G., Sandler, M., Cho, K.: Transfer learning for music classification and regression tasks. arXiv preprint arXiv:1703.09179 (2017)
9. Clark, K., Luong, M.T., Le, Q.V., Manning, C.D.: Electra: Pre-training text encoders as discriminators rather than generators. arXiv preprint arXiv:2003.10555 (2020)
10. Davis, J., Goadrich, M.: The relationship between precision-recall and roc curves. In: Proceedings of the 23rd International Conference on Machine Learning, pp. 233–240 (2006)

11. Defferrard, M., Benzi, K., Vandergheynst, P., Bresson, X.: FMA: a dataset for music analysis. arXiv preprint arXiv:1612.01840 (2016)
12. Devlin, J., Chang, M.W., Lee, K., Toutanova, K.: BERT: pre-training of deep bidirectional transformers for language understanding. arXiv preprint arXiv:1810.04805 (2018)
13. Domingues, M., et al.: Music4all: a new music database and its applications, July 2020. https://doi.org/10.1109/IWSSIP48289.2020.9145170
14. Ghosal, D., Kolekar, M.H.: Music genre recognition using deep neural networks and transfer learning. In: Interspeech, pp. 2087–2091 (2018)
15. Girshick, R.: Fast r-cnn. In: Proceedings of the IEEE International Conference on Computer Vision, pp. 1440–1448 (2015)
16. Hendrycks, D., Gimpel, K.: Gaussian error linear units (gelus). arXiv preprint arXiv:1606.08415 (2016)
17. Hendrycks, D., Mazeika, M., Kadavath, S., Song, D.: Using self-supervised learning can improve model robustness and uncertainty. In: Advances in Neural Information Processing Systems, pp. 15663–15674 (2019)
18. Huang, C.Z.A., et al.: Music transformer: generating music with long-term structure. In: International Conference on Learning Representations (2018)
19. Huang, Y.S., Yang, Y.H.: Pop music transformer: generating music with rhythm and harmony. arXiv preprint arXiv:2002.00212 (2020)
20. Hung, H.T., Chen, Y.H., Mayerl, M., Zangerle, M.V.E., Yang, Y.H.: Mediaeval 2019 emotion and theme recognition task: a vq-vae based approach
21. Kingma, D.P., Ba, J.: Adam: A method for stochastic optimization. arXiv preprint arXiv:1412.6980 (2014)
22. Koutini, K., Chowdhury, S., Haunschmid, V., Eghbal-zadeh, H., Widmer, G.: Emotion and theme recognition in music with frequency-aware RF-regularized cnns. arXiv preprint arXiv:1911.05833 (2019)
23. Ling, S., Liu, Y., Salazar, J., Kirchhoff, K.: Deep contextualized acoustic representations for semi-supervised speech recognition. In: ICASSP 2020–2020 IEEE International Conference on Acoustics, Speech and Signal Processing (ICASSP), pp. 6429–6433. IEEE (2020)
24. Liu, A.T., Yang, S.W., Chi, P.H., Hsu, P.C., Lee, H.Y.: Mockingjay: unsupervised speech representation learning with deep bidirectional transformer encoders. In: ICASSP 2020–2020 IEEE International Conference on Acoustics, Speech and Signal Processing (ICASSP), pp. 6419–6423. IEEE (2020)
25. Liu, Y., et al.: Roberta: a robustly optimized bert pretraining approach. arXiv preprint arXiv:1907.11692 (2019)
26. McFee, B., et al.: librosa: audio and music signal analysis in python. In: Proceedings of the 14th Python in Science Conference, vol. 8, pp. 18–25 (2015)
27. Park, D.S., et al.: Specaugment: a simple data augmentation method for automatic speech recognition. arXiv preprint arXiv:1904.08779 (2019)
28. Pons, J., Nieto, O., Prockup, M., Schmidt, E., Ehmann, A., Serra, X.: End-to-end learning for music audio tagging at scale. arXiv preprint arXiv:1711.02520 (2017)
29. Pujol, P., Macho, D., Nadeu, C.: On real-time mean-and-variance normalization of speech recognition features. In: 2006 IEEE International Conference on Acoustics Speech and Signal Processing Proceedings, vol. 1, pp. I-I. IEEE (2006)
30. Radford, A., Narasimhan, K., Salimans, T., Sutskever, I.: Improving language understanding by generative pre-training (2018). http://s3-us-west-2.amazonaws.com/openai-assets/researchcovers/languageunsupervised/languageunderstandingpaper.pdf

31. Song, X., et al.: Speech-xlnet: unsupervised acoustic model pretraining for self-attention networks. arXiv preprint arXiv:1910.10387 (2019)
32. Sturm, B.L.: The gtzan dataset: Its contents, its faults, their effects on evaluation, and its future use. arXiv preprint arXiv:1306.1461 (2013)
33. Suykens, J.A., Vandewalle, J.: Least squares support vector machine classifiers. Neural Process. Lett. **9**(3), 293–300 (1999)
34. Vaswani, A., et al.: Attention is all you need. In: Advances in Neural Information Processing Systems, pp. 5998–6008 (2017)
35. Viikki, O., Laurila, K.: Cepstral domain segmental feature vector normalization for noise robust speech recognition. Speech Commun. **25**(1–3), 133–147 (1998)
36. Wang, A., Singh, A., Michael, J., Hill, F., Levy, O., Bowman, S.R.: Glue: a multitask benchmark and analysis platform for natural language understanding. arXiv preprint arXiv:1804.07461 (2018)
37. Wang, W., Tang, Q., Livescu, K.: Unsupervised pre-training of bidirectional speech encoders via masked reconstruction. In: ICASSP 2020–2020 IEEE International Conference on Acoustics, Speech and Signal Processing (ICASSP) pp. 6889–6893. IEEE (2020)
38. Yang, Z., Dai, Z., Yang, Y., Carbonell, J., Salakhutdinov, R.R., Le, Q.V.: Xlnet: generalized autoregressive pretraining for language understanding. In: Advances in Neural Information Processing Systems, pp. 5753–5763 (2019)
39. Zhang, K., Zhang, H., Li, S., Yang, C., Sun, L.: The pmemo dataset for music emotion recognition. In: Proceedings of the 2018 ACM on International Conference on Multimedia Retrieval, pp. 135–142 (2018)
40. Zhang, Z., Han, X., Liu, Z., Jiang, X., Sun, M., Liu, Q.: Ernie: enhanced language representation with informative entities. arXiv preprint arXiv:1905.07129 (2019)

DANet: Deformable Alignment Network for Video Inpainting

Xutong Lu[✉] and Jianfu Zhang

Department of Computer Science, Shanghai Jiao Tong University,
Shanghai 200240, China
{luxutong,c.sis}@sjtu.edu.cn

Abstract. The goal of video inpainting is to fill the missing holes in a given video sequence. Due to the additional dimension, the video inpainting task is considerably more challenging to generate a plausible result than the image inpainting task. In this paper, we propose a novel video inpainting network based on deformable alignment, named **D**eformable **A**lignment **Net**work (DANet). Given several consecutive images, DANet can align the image features from the global-level to pixel-level in a coarse-to-fine fashion. After alignment, DANet applies a fusion block to fuse the aligned features with neighboring frames and generates an inpainted frame. The coarse-to-fine alignment architecture ensures a better fusion result, which leads to temporal and spatial consistency combined with the fusion block. Experiment results demonstrate that DANet is more semantically correct and temporally coherent, and is comparable with state-of-the-art video inpainting methods.

Keywords: Video inpainting · Alignment Network · Computer vision

1 Introduction

Video inpainting algorithms aim to fill the missing regions in a given video sequence while maintaining temporal and spatial consistency and coherency. With the rapid growth in internet media, inpainting has become more impactful in the computer vision field. Video inpainting algorithms can be used for video editing and restoration tasks such as object removal or old video restoration. However, the video inpainting methods are still immature for practical application. Although image inpainting algorithms have made significant progress in recent years, video inpainting is still challenging due to the additional time dimension. It is non-trivial to apply image inpainting methods directly to video tasks because of the high requirement for both spatial and temporal consistency and coherency.

Traditional video inpainting methods [5–7,14] may suffer in heavy computation costs introduced by the cumbersome optimization process. Deep Learning video inpainting methods [3,12,22] are more efficient than traditional methods.

© Springer Nature Switzerland AG 2021
J. Lokoč et al. (Eds.): MMM 2021, LNCS 12572, pp. 430–442, 2021.
https://doi.org/10.1007/978-3-030-67832-6_35

Lee *et al.* [12] designed a deep neural network for alignment and a copy-and-paste module for feature level inpainting. However, their method can only align the images coarsely, causing failures when the foreground is moving. The method proposed in [22] achieved pixel-level alignment by propagating the pixels according to the flow map. Nevertheless, it is not an end-to-end system, and the flow map generation network may cause some significant inconsistency caused by the domain shift brought by external data. Existing deep video inpainting methods are still not effective enough for real-world applications, and the research field of deep video inpainting is worthy of more attention to exploring.

In this paper, we propose a novel deep video inpainting network based on deformable alignment, named **D**eformable **A**lignment **Net**work (DANet). Our idea is inspired by traditional video inpainting methods based on frame alignment [5,6]. Our DANet is a new architecture for video inpainting. To better use the redundant information in the image sequence, DANet fuses the feature after alignment rather than using them directly. The main components of our proposed DANet are the coarse-to-fine alignment module and the feature fusion block. The coarse alignment module extends the idea proposed by the STN network [8] to the video inpainting task. It estimates the affine matrix by embedded input of a reference feature map and a target feature map, then aligns the two features in the global-level by the affine matrix as a coarse alignment procedure. To further enhance the alignment accuracy, we introduce the deformable convolutional network to video inpainting to accomplish pixel-level alignment in features. To avoid the impact of missing regions caused by small kernel windows inside the missing regions, the global convolution scheme [17] is applied to estimate the offsets in missing regions efficiently with a larger kernel size. After the coarse-to-fine alignment procedure, the fusion block fuses the feature map with aligned reference feature maps to enhance the consistency and coherency of synthesized frames. The fusion block calculates the feature similarity map of the target frame and the reference frames and then fuses these frames by the dot product. Experimental results show that DANet is faster than the traditional methods and overcomes the problems we mentioned in [12,22]. Our results are comparable to the state-of-the-art method, and many experiments are carried out in the DAVIS dataset.

In summary, the major contribution of our paper is as follows:

- We propose a coarse-to-fine alignment network architecture for video inpainting that can conduct feature level alignment between images that contain large holes, and avoid the problem that optical flow may fail when the large movement occurs.
- To the best of our knowledge, DANet is the first video inpainting method based on deformable alignment. We apply a global convolution scheme to extend the deformable convolution to the video inpainting task and achieved a reliable result.
- We propose a novel feature fusion method to combine reference frame features based on similarity map between frames to enhance consistency and coherency of the generated frames.

- We conduct experiments on the DAVIS dataset. It achieves reasonable performance and plausible results in video inpainting task, and is compatible with state-of-the-art video inpainting methods.

The rest of this paper is organized as follows. Section 2 introduces the related work of image inpainting and video inpainting. Section 3 describes our DANet architecture in detail. Section 4 presents our experimental setting, results of performance comparisons. Section 5 is the conclusion and future works.

2 Related Work

2.1 Image Inpainting

Image inpainting algorithms aim to fill the missing regions of an image. When the missing region is relatively small or simple, good results can be obtained by traditional image inpainting algorithms. The traditional methods are mainly based on the patch match rule [1,2,4]. Take [4] as an example: this kind of method divides the missing regions into small patches and determines their priority. For each missing patch in order of priority, it then searches for the best-match patch from the known region and updates the missing patch.

Learning-based methods use deep neural networks to learn and predict the possible distribution of the missing regions. Many deep generative models have been proposed since the context-encoder method was introduced in [16]. Vanilla convolutional neural networks for image inpainting cause mistakes due to the convolutions on the missing region. Liu *et al.* applied the partial convolutional layer to solve this problem in [13]. They also solved the blurred results problem through the perceptual and the style loss without the adversarial loss. Yu *et al.* proposed a contextual attention module and gated convolutional layer in [24]. The contextual attention module can measure the similarity between the known region patches and the completed region patches. Gated convolution is similar to partial convolution for handling the convolution in the missing region.

2.2 Video Inpainting

Compared to image inpainting, the video inpainting task is more challenging because of the high requirement of spatial and temporal consistency. Meanwhile, video sequences also have some redundant information. A good video inpainting algorithm which can achieve high temporal and spatial consistency at the same time should utilize the redundant information properly. Some traditional methods [5,6] exploit redundant information by aligning frames of the video sequence. Granados *et al.* [6] proposed an alignment method based on homographies, and the optical flow method was applied to maintain temporal consistency. Ebdelli *et al.* [5] introduced an improved alignment method and applied sliding windows to reduce time complexity. Some other papers extend traditional image inpainting methods to video inpainting. Newson *et al.* proposed a 3D patch match method in [14]. They also exploited texture features and applied the multi-resolution scheme to maintain temporal consistency. Huang *et al.* [7] proposed an optical flow method to optimize the 3D patch-match procedure while maintaining temporal consistency. This method suffers from heavy computation costs introduced by the cumbersome optimization process as all the other traditional methods.

With the progress made in deep image inpainting, learning-based video inpainting methods were proposed. Kim *et al.* [10] proposed a network with a 3D encoder and 2D decoder to complete the missing region with higher efficiency. They designed a feedback architecture and applied warping loss to maintain temporal consistency. Liu *et al.* [3] extended gated convolution and partial convolution proposed in [13,24] to 3D and applied them in video inpainting. A 3D patch-GAN was designed by them to acquire higher temporal consistency. Similar to 3D convolution methods, optical flow can also extract temporal information. Xu *et al.* [22] designed a deep flow completion network to fill the missing region in the optical-flow map. Then they propagate the pixels according to the completed flow map. For the unpainted region, the deep image inpainting method proposed in [24] was applied. Kim *et al.* [11] utilized the optical flow at the feature level. A recurrent feedback module and a memory layer were designed to maintain temporal consistency. Copy-and-Paste Networks (CPNet) [12] utilized an alignment network to align the image sequence. Then the copy-and-paste network is applied to extract and fuse the aligned features. Onion-Peel Networks (OPNet) [15] proposed a contextual attention module for better temporal consistency. To exploit richer contextual information, it progressively filled the hole from the hole boundary.

3 Proposed Method

3.1 Deformable Alignment Network Architecture

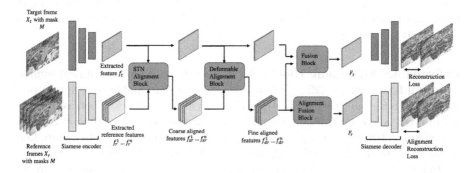

Fig. 1. The architecture of DANet. It mainly consists of 2 parts. The first part is the coarse-to-fine alignment network, while the second part is the feature fusion network.

We introduce a novel Deformable Alignment Network (DANet), which is depicted in Fig. 1, to accomplish the video inpainting task with higher consistency. The goal of our DANet is to generate inpainted frames $\{\hat{Y}\}$ from the input frames $\{X\}$ with missing holes $\{M\}$. Our DANet takes several consecutive images in a video as the input. One of them is treated as the target frame X_t while the others are reference frames X_r. The output of DANet is the completed target frame $\hat{Y}_t$. DANet mainly contains two steps. The first step is to align the related features from coarse to fine by our STN alignment block and deformable alignment block. The second step is to fuse the aligned features according to the similarity map between reference frames and the target frame to get the completed result $\hat{Y}_t$.

Alignment based methods can only align the images coarsely, causing failures when the foreground is moving. The flow map generation network in optical-flow-based methods may cause some significant inconsistency due to the domain shift brought by external data. Our novel coarse-to-fine deformable alignment module is proposed to solve these problems. The coarse alignment module extends the STN network to the video inpainting task. The built-in deformable alignment block is proposed to enhance the alignment accuracy further.

STN Alignment Block. The DANet firstly extracts features of all input frames $\{X\}$ by an encoder network similar with [24] and take one of them as the target frame's feature f_t and the others reference features f_r. Then f_t and each reference feature f_r^i are passed to STN Alignment block, which is depicted in Fig. 2. f_t and f_r^i are embedded together and passed to affine matrix generator. The output of the affine matrix generator is a 2×3 affine matrix A_θ. This affine matrix can transform the reference feature f_r^i to f_{sr}^i which is coarsely aligned to f_t. The affine transformation procedure can be formalized as:

$$\begin{pmatrix} x_k^{i,sr} \\ y_k^{i,sr} \end{pmatrix} = T_\theta(G_k) = A_\theta \begin{pmatrix} x_k^{i,r} \\ y_k^{i,r} \\ 1 \end{pmatrix} = \begin{bmatrix} \theta_{11} & \theta_{12} & \theta_{13} \\ \theta_{21} & \theta_{22} & \theta_{23} \end{bmatrix} \begin{pmatrix} x_k^{i,r} \\ y_k^{i,r} \\ 1 \end{pmatrix}. \tag{1}$$

The affine matrix generator network is differentiable [8]. Thus the STN Alignment block can be trained jointly and it can align the reference feature and target feature coarsely.

Deformable Alignment Block. To achieve feature-level alignment similar to optical flow methods [22], we take advantage of deformable convolution proposed by Tian et al. [19]. We firstly estimate feature-level offset between target feature and reference feature. Then deformable convolution is applied to align the reference feature to target feature with the guidance of the offset map. Our architecture of the deformable alignment block is shown in Fig. 2.

Deformable alignment block concatenates the input target frame feature f_t, and one of the reference features f_{sr}^i similarly with STN alignment block. The embedded feature is passed to a global convolution block to generate the offset map. If the kernel size is small, the convolution occurs in the missing region

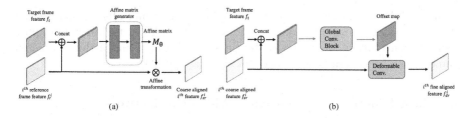

(a)   (b)

Fig. 2. (a): Detailed illustration of the STN alignment block. It aligns the features coarsely at the feature map level. (b): Detailed illustration of the deformable alignment block. It aligns the features finely at the feature pixel level.

will not produce meaningful results. Global convolution [17] is designed to solve the locality problem in convolutional networks. In our DANet, it is applied to estimate the offsets in missing regions with a larger kernel size to avoid such situations. We enlarge the receptive field to make the offset estimation meaningful by combining $1 \times k + k \times 1$ and $k \times 1 + 1 \times k$ ($k = 5, 7, 12$ in our implementation) convolution layers. For each feature-level pixel, the global convolution block generates an offset $(\delta x_i, \delta y_i)$. Then the coarsely aligned feature f_{sr}^i is transformed to finely aligned feature f_{dr}^i with the guidance of offset map through deformable convolution [20].

Fusion Block. After the coarse-to-fine alignment procedure, the DANet obtains all aligned reference features f_{dr}. DANet can generate a proper result if the aligned and target features are correctly fused. We propose a novel but simple method to fuse the features of target and reference frames. It is depicted in Fig. 3.

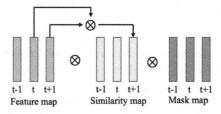

Fig. 3. Detailed illustration of the feature fusion block.

Firstly, the target feature f_t and reference features f_{dr} are passed to a simple two-layer convolutional neural network to extract low-level features further. Then we calculate the similarity map by applying dot product between target feature f_t' and all features $\{f'\}$. After that, DANet multiples the similarity maps, original feature maps, and masks together to produce the fused features $\{F\}$. The masks here are resized and aligned together with images in the coarse-to-fine alignment block, and they use the same affine matrix and offset generated by the embedded features. We concatenate the fused features together and apply a simple convolution to get the finally fused feature F_t. Finally, the completed frame $\hat{Y}_t$ can be generated by a decoder similar with [24].

3.2   Loss Functions of Deformable Alignment Network

Our DANet is an end-to-end network, and it is trained jointly. The reconstruction loss between the completed target frame and the ground truth is calculated, and the losses for the missing region and the non-missing region should be calculated separately:

$$\mathcal{L}_{\text{hole}} = \sum_t^N \left\| M_t \odot (\hat{Y}_t - Y_t) \right\|_1, \tag{2}$$

$$\mathcal{L}_{\text{non-hole}} = \sum_t^N \left\| (1 - M_t) \odot (\hat{Y}_t - Y_t) \right\|_1, \tag{3}$$

where t is the target frame index of the image sequence, and M_t is the mask of target frame. Perceptual, style, and total variation loss are also calculated in order to improve visual quality:

$$\mathcal{L}_{\text{perceptual}} = \frac{1}{P} \cdot \sum_p^P \left\| f_p \left(\hat{Y}_{\text{comp}} \right) - f_p(Y) \right\|_1, \tag{4}$$

$$\mathcal{L}_{\text{style}} = \frac{1}{P} \cdot \sum_p^P \left\| G_p^f \left(\hat{Y}_{\text{comp}} \right) - G_p^f(Y) \right\|_1, \tag{5}$$

where $\hat{Y}_{comp}$ is the combination of $\hat{Y}_t$ in the missing region and X_t in the other regions, f is the output of the pooling layer of VGG-16 in our implementation, p is the pooling index, G is the gram matrix multiplication [9]. Each frame's TV loss is calculated and added together to ensure spatial smoothness.

To get a better inpainting result, we have designed another referential feature fusion block to fuse only the aligned reference features, depicted in Fig. 1. The fusion procedure is relatively simple: all aligned reference features are concatenated together and passed to a simple neural network. The output is delivered to the same decoder to decode the referential result $\hat{Y}_{r^t}$. r^t stands for the fusion result of referential frames except for the target frame t.

The referential result does not have any information about X_t except the alignment information. We additionally calculate the reconstruction loss between $\hat{Y}_{r^t}$ and Y_t, which can help the coarse-to-fine alignment module converge better and faster:

$$\mathcal{L}_{\text{hole(referential)}} = \sum_t^N \left\| M_t \odot (\hat{Y}_{r^t} - Y_t) \right\|_1, \tag{6}$$

$$\mathcal{L}_{\text{non-hole(referential)}} = \sum_t^N \left\| (1 - M_t) \odot (\hat{Y}_{r^t} - Y_t) \right\|_1.$$ (7)

The total-loss function is:

$$\begin{aligned}
\mathcal{L} = {} & 3 \cdot \mathcal{L}_{\text{hole(referential)}} + 2 \cdot \mathcal{L}_{\text{non-hole(referential)}} + 10 \cdot \mathcal{L}_{\text{hole}} \\
& + 6 \cdot \mathcal{L}_{\text{non-hole}} + 0.01 \cdot \mathcal{L}_{\text{perceptual}} + 24 \cdot \mathcal{L}_{\text{style}} + 0.1 \cdot \mathcal{L}_{\text{tv}}.
\end{aligned}$$ (8)

The weight for each loss is empirically determined.

4 Experiments

4.1 Datasets Synthesis and Training Details

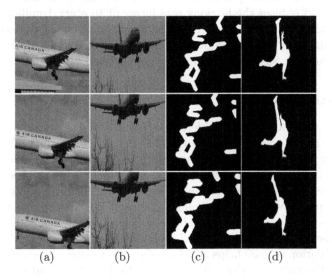

(a)   (b)   (c)   (d)

Fig. 4. Dataset composition. (a) are generated from the Place2 Dataset [25] by successive random transformations. (b) are the video frames from the Youtube-VOS dataset [21]. (c) are the randomly generated masks with successive random transformations. (d) are the masks from the Youtube-VOS dataset and the DAVIS dataset [18]. The training image sequences are generated by randomly choosing from (a) and (b), while the mask sequences are generated by randomly choosing from (c) and (d)

Video inpainting aims to fill the spatial and temporal holes. The inputs of video inpainting algorithms are image sequences with holes and masks indicating the missing regions. There is no video inpainting dataset till now. We synthesized a dataset for video inpainting using image sequences in Places2 Dataset [25] and Youtube-VOS Dataset [21], masks in the Youtube-VOS Dataset and the

DAVIS2017 Dataset [18]. An example of our composited dataset is shown in Fig. 4.

Some of the image sequences are randomly sampled from the Youtube-VOS dataset, and the others are generated by successive random transformations utilizing the Places2 image dataset. We applied random crops and random affine operations like shear, scale, and rotation on the single image in the Places2 dataset. The image sequences are selected from the combined dataset, and we can control each part's ratio to handle the training process. Some of the mask sequences are sampled from the Youtube-VOS dataset and DAVIS dataset, and the others are generated by successive random transformations using randomly generated masks. The mask sequences can be selected from the combined mask dataset, and the ratio of each kind of mask can also be handled. Finally, a training sample is composited by combining an image sequence and a mask sequence.

The DANet model is trained on hardware with two NVIDIA Telsa V100 GPUs. We resize five frames of one composited video to 256×256 as the input of the DANet. Our training batch size is 24, while Adam optimizer's learning rate is 5×10^{-5} and reduces the learning rate factor of 10 every 1 million iterations. In the first training step, we set the ratio of generated image sequence 80% for better training the STN subnetwork. Then we set the ratio of Youtube-VOS image sequences to 80% to finetune the whole network.

4.2   Ablation Study

In Table 1, we evaluate how different structures of DANet affect inpainting results. For a fair comparison, we remove one part each time of our DANet without any other modifications. As shown in Table 1, every removal of the module will decrease PSNR and SSIM. The Alignment Fusion Blocks is vital for the coarse-to-fine alignment module to learn better from the input sequences. Thus the removal will cause a significant impact on the training process and make the result worse. The deformable alignment block will enhance the alignment accuracy by accomplishing pixel-level alignment in features. Moreover, the global convolution scheme helps avoid missing offset caused by small kernel windows inside the missing regions. The result in Table 1 shows that the deformable alignment block and the global convolution block can help the DANet achieve better inpainting results.

Table 1. Experiment results about the structure design for the fixed region inpainting on the DAVIS2017 dataset

Method	PSNR	SSIM
DANet w/o. Deformable Alignment Block	27.24	0.44
DANet w/o. Global Convolution Block	27.83	0.45
DANet w/o. Alignment Fusion Block	26.92	0.44
DANet	**27.96**	**0.46**

4.3 Experiments on DAVIS Dataset

We carry out the foreground object removal experiment and fixed region inpainting experiment on the DAVIS dataset to analyze the performance of our DANet. The model we used to conduct the experiments is not trained with the DAVIS image dataset. Both quantitative and qualitative analyses are provided.

Table 2. Quantitative results for the fixed region inpainting on the DAVIS2017 dataset

Method	PSNR	SSIM
Deepfill [23]	16.47	0.14
Newson *et al.* [14]	24.72	0.43
Huang *et al.* [7]	27.39	0.44
CPNet [12]	27.68	**0.46**
Ours	**27.96**	0.46

The quantitative result of fixed region inpainting is depicted in Table 2. In this experiment, each frame of the generated video is masked by a fixed square region at the center of the frame. The target is to fill the fixed holes. We calculate the PSNR and SSIM in the same way as [13,22]. As shown in Table 2, directly apply image inpainting algorithm [23] to video results in bad performance. Compared to traditional video inpainting methods [7,14], deep methods have better performance because they can handle complex motions to some extends. Moreover, our approach achieves the best performance on the

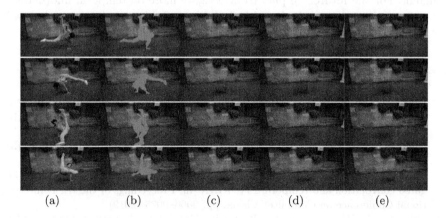

(a)   (b)   (c)   (d)   (e)

Fig. 5. Qualitative comparison of object removal results for the scenes breakdance-flare from DAVIS2017 dataset. (a) are the original frames. (b) are the input frames with masks. (c) are the results of Deep flow-guided video inpainting [22]. (d) are the results of Copy-and-paste networks [12]. (e) are the results of our method.

PSNR and the same performance as CPNet [12] on the SSIM due to the ability of deformable alignment and novel fusion architecture.

In addition to the quantitative evaluation, we also carried out experiments for video object removal on the DAVIS dataset. In this task, the input of DANet is DAVIS video frames with its segmentation masks. The object removal task has broader application prospects, and our DANet shows a better performance. The qualitative comparison result is depicted in Fig. 5. Figure 5(a) are the original image sequence in the DAVIS dataset, and the name of this video clip is breakdance-flare. Figure 5(b) are images with missing regions. Figure 5(c) are the outputs of the deep flow-guided model [22]. It is easy to see that the completed missing region is shaking between frames. The main reason for this phenomenon is the network estimating optical flow may output wrong estimations when the foreground is moving fast or under some other conditions. The deep flow-guided model may accumulate small errors and sometimes produce bad results. Figure 5(d) are the outputs of CPNet [12] and Fig. 5(e) are the results of our DANet. These two results are more temporal consistent, while our DANet is more precise in details than CPNet's results. The PSNR and SSIM results in Table 2 also indicate the same conclusion.

5 Conclusions and Future Work

In this paper, we propose a Deformable Alignment Network (DANet) to solve the video inpainting problem. We design the STN alignment block and the deformable alignment block to accomplish the coarse-to-fine alignment procedure. A novel fusion block is proposed to fuse the aligned features. Experiments are conducted on the DAVIS dataset, and the results demonstrate that our DANet has better performance and is more semantically correct and temporally coherent. For the future, we plan to investigate more on temporal information. The temporal consistency is the critical problem of video inpainting, and we will try to construct more temporal constraints to optimize our method.

References

1. Bertalmio, M., Sapiro, G., Caselles, V., Ballester, C.: Image inpainting. In: Proceedings of the 27th Annual Conference on Computer Graphics and Interactive Techniques, pp. 417–424 (2000)
2. Chan, T.: Local inpainting models and TV inpainting. SIAM J. Appl. Math. **62**(3), 1019–1043 (2001)
3. Chang, Y.L., Liu, Z.Y., Lee, K.Y., Hsu, W.: Free-form video inpainting with 3D gated convolution and temporal PatchGAN. In: Proceedings of the IEEE International Conference on Computer Vision, pp. 9066–9075 (2019)
4. Criminisi, A., Pérez, P., Toyama, K.: Region filling and object removal by exemplar-based image inpainting. IEEE Trans. Image Process. **13**(9), 1200–1212 (2004)
5. Ebdelli, M., Le Meur, O., Guillemot, C.: Video inpainting with short-term windows: application to object removal and error concealment. IEEE Trans. Image Process. **24**(10), 3034–3047 (2015)

6. Granados, M., Kim, K.I., Tompkin, J., Kautz, J., Theobalt, C.: Background inpainting for videos with dynamic objects and a free-moving camera. In: Fitzgibbon, A., Lazebnik, S., Perona, P., Sato, Y., Schmid, C. (eds.) ECCV 2012. LNCS, vol. 7572, pp. 682–695. Springer, Heidelberg (2012). https://doi.org/10.1007/978-3-642-33718-5_49

7. Huang, J.B., Kang, S.B., Ahuja, N., Kopf, J.: Temporally coherent completion of dynamic video. ACM Trans. Graph. (TOG) **35**(6), 1–11 (2016)

8. Jaderberg, M., Simonyan, K., Zisserman, A.: Spatial transformer networks. In: Advances in Neural Information Processing Systems, pp. 2017–2025 (2015)

9. Johnson, J., Alahi, A., Fei-Fei, L.: Perceptual losses for real-time style transfer and super-resolution. In: Leibe, B., Matas, J., Sebe, N., Welling, M. (eds.) ECCV 2016. LNCS, vol. 9906, pp. 694–711. Springer, Cham (2016). https://doi.org/10.1007/978-3-319-46475-6_43

10. Kim, D., Woo, S., Lee, J.Y., Kweon, I.S.: Deep blind video decaptioning by temporal aggregation and recurrence. In: Proceedings of the IEEE Conference on Computer Vision and Pattern Recognition, pp. 4263–4272 (2019)

11. Kim, D., Woo, S., Lee, J.Y., Kweon, I.S.: Deep video inpainting. In: Proceedings of the IEEE Conference on Computer Vision and Pattern Recognition, pp. 5792–5801 (2019)

12. Lee, S., Oh, S.W., Won, D., Kim, S.J.: Copy-and-paste networks for deep video inpainting. In: Proceedings of the IEEE International Conference on Computer Vision, pp. 4413–4421 (2019)

13. Liu, G., Reda, F.A., Shih, K.J., Wang, T.-C., Tao, A., Catanzaro, B.: Image inpainting for irregular holes using partial convolutions. In: Ferrari, V., Hebert, M., Sminchisescu, C., Weiss, Y. (eds.) ECCV 2018. LNCS, vol. 11215, pp. 89–105. Springer, Cham (2018). https://doi.org/10.1007/978-3-030-01252-6_6

14. Newson, A., Almansa, A., Fradet, M., Gousseau, Y., Pérez, P.: Video inpainting of complex scenes. SIAM J. Imaging Sci. **7**(4), 1993–2019 (2014)

15. Oh, S.W., Lee, S., Lee, J.Y., Kim, S.J.: Onion-peel networks for deep video completion. In: Proceedings of the IEEE International Conference on Computer Vision, pp. 4403–4412 (2019)

16. Pathak, D., Krahenbuhl, P., Donahue, J., Darrell, T., Efros, A.A.: Context encoders: feature learning by inpainting. In: Proceedings of the IEEE Conference on Computer Vision and Pattern Recognition, pp. 2536–2544 (2016)

17. Peng, C., Zhang, X., Yu, G., Luo, G., Sun, J.: Large kernel matters-improve semantic segmentation by global convolutional network. In: Proceedings of the IEEE Conference on Computer Vision and Pattern Recognition, pp. 4353–4361 (2017)

18. Pont-Tuset, J., Perazzi, F., Caelles, S., Arbeláez, P., Sorkine-Hornung, A., Van Gool, L.: The 2017 davis challenge on video object segmentation. arXiv preprint arXiv:1704.00675 (2017)

19. Tian, Y., Zhang, Y., Fu, Y., Xu, C.: TDAN: temporally-deformable alignment network for video super-resolution. In: Proceedings of the IEEE/CVF Conference on Computer Vision and Pattern Recognition, pp. 3360–3369 (2020)

20. Wang, X., Chan, K.C., Yu, K., Dong, C., Change Loy, C.: EDVR: video restoration with enhanced deformable convolutional networks. In: Proceedings of the IEEE Conference on Computer Vision and Pattern Recognition Workshops (2019)

21. Xu, N., et al.: YouTube-VOS: a large-scale video object segmentation benchmark. arXiv preprint arXiv:1809.03327 (2018)

22. Xu, R., Li, X., Zhou, B., Loy, C.C.: Deep flow-guided video inpainting. In: Proceedings of the IEEE Conference on Computer Vision and Pattern Recognition, pp. 3723–3732 (2019)

23. Yu, J., Lin, Z., Yang, J., Shen, X., Lu, X., Huang, T.S.: Generative image inpainting with contextual attention. In: Proceedings of the IEEE Conference on Computer Vision and Pattern Recognition, pp. 5505–5514 (2018)
24. Yu, J., Lin, Z., Yang, J., Shen, X., Lu, X., Huang, T.S.: Free-form image inpainting with gated convolution. In: Proceedings of the IEEE International Conference on Computer Vision, pp. 4471–4480 (2019)
25. Zhou, B., Lapedriza, A., Khosla, A., Oliva, A., Torralba, A.: Places: a 10 million image database for scene recognition. IEEE Trans. Pattern Anal. Mach. Intell. **40**(6), 1452–1464 (2017)

Deep Centralized Cross-modal Retrieval

Zhenyu Wen[(✉)] and Aimin Feng

Nanjing University of Aeronautics and Astronautics, Nanjing 211106, China
wzydyx2@163.com

Abstract. The mainstream of cross-modal retrieval approaches generally focus on measure the similarity between different types of data in a common subspace. Most of these methods are based on pairs or triplets of instances, which has the following disadvantages: 1) due to the high discrepancy of pairs and triplets, there might be a large number of zero-losses, and the model cannot be updated under these circumstances. 2) global information in the common subspace cannot be fully exploited to deliver cross-modal retrieval tasks. To solve the above problems, we present a novel cross-modal retrieval method, called Deep Centralized Cross-modal Retrieval (DCCMR). Specifically, we first learn a center for embeddings of each class in the common space, then a double-quadruplet-center-loss function is proposed to force the distance between samples and centers from different classes to be larger than distance from the same class. To the best of our knowledge, the proposed DCCMR could be one of the first works to utilize the combination of quadruplet loss and center loss, leading to more stable results. Comprehensive experimental results on three widely-used benchmark datasets verify that our method achieves comparable performance compared with the state-of-the-art cross-modal retrieval methods as well as the usefulness and effectiveness of our DCCMR.

Keywords: Cross-modal retrieval · Representation learning · Quadruplet loss · Center loss

1 Introduction

Cross-modal retrieval [1] provides a paradigm to take one type of data as the query and retrieve relevant data of another type (e.g., image and text), which has attracted considerable attention from many researchers. The key problem of cross-modal retrieval is how to measure the content similarity between different types of data, which is known as heterogeneity gap [2]. Many existing methods follow the idea of representation learning to bridge the heterogeneity gap, projecting data samples from different modalities into a common subspace where the similarity can be measured directly by common distance metrics.

It is notable that many cross-modal methods were proposed on the basis of pairs or triplets of data samples. Specifically, the learning process of these methods rely on the selection of instances, e.g., triplet-based methods can be regarded as an extended form of pair-based methods, three samples are considered at one time, two of which belong

© Springer Nature Switzerland AG 2021
J. Lokoč et al. (Eds.): MMM 2021, LNCS 12572, pp. 443–455, 2021.
https://doi.org/10.1007/978-3-030-67832-6_36

to the same class and the third one belongs to a different class. By imposing larger distance between negative pair than positive pair, the intra-class compactness and inter-class discrepancy are enforced. This learning paradigm leads to three disadvantages: 1) Due to the high discrepancy of pairs or triplets, it is easily to yield cases when loss equals zero, under which the model cannot be updated. 2) The normal triplet or pair loss fail to fully exploit global information in the common space, e.g., the compactness characteristic from the same semantic class. 3) Single triplet loss only considers the relationship between positive pair and negative pair, but ignores the relationship among negative pairs.

In this paper, we propose a novel cross-modal retrieval method, called Deep Centralized Cross-modal Retrieval (DCCMR), which solves the above three problems. The framework of DCCMR is shown in Fig. 1. Specifically, based on the concept of quadruplet loss and center loss, we propose an objective function that simultaneously enhances the discriminative power of embedding and learns discriminative features with deep metric learning. During learning process, the model utilizes samples and centers of sample embeddings to form a quadruplet-center-loss. Under this formulation, different identities with same semantic label are projected into adjacent regions. Meanwhile, the objective function imposes margin between negative centers. The main contributions and novelty of this work can be summarized as follows:

- We use a double-quadruplet schema to bridge the heterogeneity gap in cross-modal retrieval tasks. To the best of our knowledge, this could be one of the first works to do so.
- A joint objective function utilizing centers of class-based embedding is formulated to structure the latent space. Unlike most of existing methods, our proposed method is based on centers of embeddings instead of single embedding, thus taking global information into consideration. Through our method, both the fine-grained and the high-level semantic information could be exploited in an end-to-end manner to learn the common representations for heterogeneous data.
- We introduce an adaptive learning schema to tune the gradient update in the gradient descent and back-propagation algorithms used for training our model.

2 Related Work

Cross-modal retrieval aims at retrieving relevant items that are of different nature with respect to the query format, e.g., querying an image dataset with text description(text-to-image). The main challenge is to measure the similarity between different modalities of data, which is known as heterogeneity gap. In the Information Retrieval (IR) Community, early works have circumvented this issue by learning a common representation space, where the similarity between samples from different modalities can be measured directly. These methods are briefly reviewed from the following two aspects: traditional methods and deep-based methods.

Traditional cross-modal retrieval methods mainly learn a linear mapping matrix by optimizing statistical values. Canonical Correlation Analysis (CCA) [3] is one of the most representative work. Data is divided into different cross modal pairs (e.g., image

/ text pairs), and CCA learns a subspace that maximizes the relationship between pairs of data. Some works based on CCA have also been applied in cross-modal retrieval tasks. To employ semantic labels as discriminative information, [4] uses CCA to get the common space of image and text, and then a log probability is used to get the semantics. A supervised form of CCA is used in [5] to improve the accuracy of retrieval. Joint representation learning (JRL) in [6] jointly explore the correlation and semantic information in a unified optimization framework. To extend traditional linear paradigm to nonlinear models, some works such as Kernel CCA (KCCA) [7] apply kernel trick, although the learned representation is limited due to the predetermined kernel.

Deep neural network (DNN) has achieved great success in many applications such as image classification and object detection [8, 9]. DNN has shown better performance on learning nonlinear relation compared with kernel trick, and is widely used to project multi-modal data in a high-level common subspace [10]. [11] applies an extended form of restricted Boltzmann machine to common space learning, and proposes a double-modal deep self-encoder. On the basis of traditional methods, Deep Canonical Correlation Analysis (DCCA, [12, 13]) can be regarded as a nonlinear extended form of CCA, which can be used to learn the complex nonlinear relationship between cross-modal data. Recently, some works focus on utilizing the inter-(e.g., image and text) and intra-modality (e.g., only image) correlation to improve the common representation learning ability, such as Cross-Media Multiple Deep Network (CMDN) [14] and Cross-modal Correlation Learning (CCL) [10].

Many existing studies on cross-modal retrieval focus on utilizing pairwise or triplet-wise representation learning. Therefore, these methods fail to fully explore the relation between samples and their centers in common subspace, as well as relation between different centers. On the contrary, our proposed method can learn the common discriminative representations using both global information (e.g., relation between two centers with different semantic label) and fine-grained information (e.g., relation between a sample and its corresponding semantic center).

3 Our Approach

In the following paragraphs, we first introduce the formulation of the cross-modal retrieval problem. Then our Deep Centralized Cross-modal Retrieval (DCCMR) method to learn the common subspace of data from different modalities is presented, including the framework of DCCMR, the objective function and the adaptive learning schema. At last, we provide more details of the proposed method.

3.1 Problem Formulation

Consider the cross-modal retrieval task for bimodal data, e.g., image and text. Assume that there is a collection of n instances in the form of image-text pair, denoted as $\Psi = \left\{ \chi_i^1, \chi_i^2 \right\}_{i=1}^n$, where χ_i^1 is an instance from image modality and χ_i^2 is an instance from text modality. $\gamma_i = \left[y_{i1}, y_{i2}, \ldots, y_{ic} \right] \in \{0, 1\}^c$ is allocated to each image-text pair as a semantic label, where c is the number of semantic categories. If the ith belongs to the kth semantic category, then $y_{ik} = 1$, otherwise $y_{ik} = 0$.

Since data from different modalities cannot be directly used to measure their similarity, the cross-modal learning aims to solve the heterogeneity gap by learning two functions for both modality: $u_i = f_1(\chi_i^1; \Theta_1)\mathbb{R}^d$ and $v_i = f_2(\chi_i^2; \Theta_2)\mathbb{R}^d$, where d is the dimensionality of representation of heterogeneous data in the common subspace, Θ_1 and Θ_2 are the parameters of the two functions f_1 and f_2. In the common space, the similarity between embeddings can be measured directly. Specifically, cross-modal learning enforce similarity between pairs with the same semantic label to be larger than those with different semantic labels. The relevant samples of different modalities can be returned given one query of certain modality.

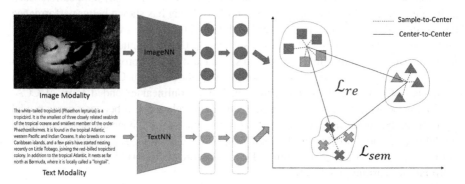

Fig. 1. Overview of our DCCMR. Different shapes (e.g., triangle, square, cross) indicate different categories, data from image are colored in blue and data from text are in red. Data are first inputed to respective network, followed by several fully connected layers to map them into common subspace. (Color figure online)

3.2   Network Architecture

Many existing cross-media retrieval methods are based on pairwise relation, enforcing the similarity of samples from the same category to be larger than the similarity of samples from different categories, which might cause some issues: (1) Failing to fully exploit global information – Constraints only consider samples instead of their centers. (2) Training difficulty – Since some labels would be easier to infer than others, and there exists high discrepancy among different pairs, there would be lots of cases when loss equals zero during training process, and the model cannot be updated under these circumstances. (3) Limits of learning discriminative features – Most of existing works focus on similar and dissimilar pairs, but ignore the relation among those embeddings with different labels. In fact, the similarity of samples from the same category should not only be larger than the similarity of samples from different categories, but also be larger than the similarity between two different negative categories. Through this we enforce between-class distance to be larger than in-class distance.

The general framework of the proposed method is shown in Fig. 1, from which we can see that it includes two sub-networks, one for image modality and another for text modality, and they are both trained in an end-to-end manner. They aim to learn the transform functions that can project data of image and text into a common subspace, in which the between-class variation is maximized while the within-class variation is minimized. Inputs are first embedded through respective network, then as input of several fully connected layers that map features into the latent space.

3.3 Objective Function

We design a new loss function to drive the learning of our DCCMR-Net, which jointly considers retrieval loss and semantic loss. Furthermore, we adopt a double-quadruplet schema to ensure the compactness characteristic of features from the same category and the sparsity characteristic of features from different categories. The new designed loss function is defined as follows:

$$\mathcal{L} = \mathcal{L}_{re} + \lambda \mathcal{L}_{sem} \tag{1}$$

where $\mathcal{L}_{re}$ is the loss associated with the retrieval task and $\mathcal{L}_{sem}$ is the loss coming with the semantic information.

Retrieval Loss. The objective of the retrieval loss $\mathcal{L}_{re}$ is to learn cross-modal embeddings by gathering matching items together and discriminating irrelevant ones. We propose to use a loss function ℓ_{re} based on a particular quadruplet $\left(x_q, c_{pos}, c_{neg}^i, c_{neg}^j\right)$, consisting of a query x_q, the center of its matching counterparts c_{pos} and two different centers of dissimilar items c_{neg}^i and c_{neg}^j in the other modality. The center is calculated by mean value of each dimension from samples with same label in common space. The retrieval loss function $\mathcal{L}_{re}$ is the aggregation of the individual loss ℓ_{re} over all quadruplets.

$$\ell_{re}\left(x_q, c_{pos}, c_{neg}^i, c_{neg}^j\right) = \left[d\left(x_q, c_{pos}\right) - d\left(x_q, c_{neg}\right) + \alpha_1\right]_+ \\ + \sum_{i,j}\left[d\left(x_q, c_{pos}\right) - d\left(c_{neg}^i, c_{neg}^j\right) + \alpha_2\right]_+ \tag{2}$$

In Eq. (2), we apply the quadruplet loss function [15] to minimize the intra-class variance and maximize the inter-class variance, where $d(x, y)$ expresses the L2 distance. By adopting quadruplet loss, our DCCMR enforce the feature outputs of different categories to be more dissimilar than those of same category. This objective function also ensures that distances between samples and corresponding centers are smaller than distances between different centers. α_1 and α_2 are the normally used margin in metric learning. Through imposing margin in both Eq. (2) and Eq. (3), we ensure the distance between dissimilar objects to be larger enough than distance between similar objects.

Semantic Loss. $\mathcal{L}_{sem}$ acts as a regularization capable of taking advantage of semantic information in the multi-modal alignment. For a given query x_q' and its corresponding label, we want to make sure that related items from the same modality are closer to each other than to non-related ones. To achieve this, we propose the individual quadruplet loss ℓ_{sem}:

$$\ell_{sem}\left(x_q', c_{pos}', c_{neg}^{i'}, c_{neg}^{j'}\right) = \left[d\left(x_q', c_{pos}'\right) - d\left(x_q', c_{neg}'\right) + \alpha_1\right]_+ \\ + \sum_{i,j}\left[d\left(x_q', c_{pos}'\right) - d\left(c_{neg}^{i'}, c_{neg}^{j'}\right) + \alpha_2\right]_+ \tag{3}$$

Different from Eq. (2), all items in $\mathcal{L}_{sem}$ come from the same modality, by which we encourage instances of the same class from the same modality to stay closer to each other.

3.4 Adaptive Learning Schema

As commonly used in deep learning, we adopt the Adam algorithm [16] which approximates the true gradient over mini-batches to update the model. The update term is generally computed by aggregation of the gradient using the average over all quadruplets in the mini-batch. However, our double-quadruplet learning framework is a difficult learning problem, since the updating process needs to concern both the high-level and fine-grained information, i.e., centers for different classes and embedding from a specific sample. This strategy tends to cost lots of resources as the model updating and embeddings changing, especially when the size of the training set grows. To tackle this issue, we propose an adaptive strategy considers an update term δ_{adp}, which takes into account informative quadruplets only. More formally, given a mini-batch $\mathcal{B}$, the matching center c_{pos}^i and unmatched center c_{neg}^j with respect to a query x_i, and $\mathbb{N}_i$ the set of centers with different categories from x_i, the loss is defined as:

$$
\begin{aligned}
\mathcal{L} &= \sum_{i \in \mathcal{B}} \Big\{ \sum_{j \in \mathbb{N}_i} \Big\{ \Big[d\Big(x_i, c_{pos}^i\Big) - d\Big(x_i, c_{neg}^j\Big) + \alpha_1 \Big]_+ \\
&+ \sum_{k,l \in \mathbb{N}_i} \Big[d\Big(x_i, c_{pos}^i\Big) - d\Big(c_{neg}^k, c_{neg}^l\Big) + \alpha_2 \Big]_+ \Big\} \Big\} \\
&= \sum_{i,j,k,l} \Big\{ \Big[d\Big(x_i, c_{pos}^i\Big) - d\Big(x_i, c_{neg}^j\Big) + \alpha_1 \Big]_+ \\
&+ \Big[d\Big(x_i, c_{pos}^i\Big) - d\Big(c_{neg}^k, c_{neg}^l\Big) + \alpha_2 \Big]_+ \Big\}
\end{aligned}
\tag{4}
$$

With the loss formed as a quadruplet considering only four indices, the adaptive learning strategy avoids wasting much resource on storing temporary variables, and can adaptively learn centers for embeddings, thus the update term δ_{adp} is defined by:

$$
\delta_{adp} = \sum_{i \in \mathcal{B}} \left(\sum_{j,k,l \in \mathbb{N}_i} \frac{\nabla \mathcal{L}_{ins}(i,j,k,l,\Theta)}{|\mathcal{B}|} \right)
\tag{5}
$$

where Θ is the trainable parameters, $|\mathcal{B}|$ is the number of quadruplets contributing to the cost, and $\nabla \mathcal{L}_{ins}$ is the normally used back-propagation derivative term in deep learning.

3.5 Implementation Details

Our implementation use two sub-networks for image and text modality. The sub-network for image has the same configuration with 19-layer VGGNet, and the sub-network for text uses the Word2Vec model. Three fully connected layers are followed to learn the common representation with Rectified Linear Unit (ReLU) [17] as the active function. Specifically, data from image modality is extracted from the fc7 layer in VGGNet as a 4096-dimensional feature vector, while text is represented as 300-dimensional feature vector after the Word2Vec.

For training, we use the ADAM optimizer with a learning rate of 5×10^{-3} and an epoch number of 20. The balance factor λ in Eq. (1) is set as 0.5 to control the contribution of semantic loss, the two margins α_1 and α_2 we impose in Eq. (2) and Eq. (3) are set as 1 and 0.5 following [15].

4   Experiment

To demonstrate the effectiveness of the proposed method, we conduct experiments on three widely-used benchmark datasets: the Wikipedia dataset [18], the NUS-WIDE-10k dataset [19] and PKU XMedia dataset [20, 21] and compare with state-of-the-art methods.

4.1   Datasets and Features

The Wikipedia dataset is the most widely-used dataset for cross-modal retrieval. It consists of 2,866 pairs of image and text, with a label from 10 semantic classes (i.e., art, biology, history, etc.). The NUS-WIDE-10k dataset is classified into 10 categories, with a total of 10,000 images and corresponding tags. The PKU XMedia dataset has up to five modalities such as images, texts, videos, audio clips and 3D models, we simply take data from image and text as usage. Note that features of PKU XMedia has been provided by their authors as shown in Table 1, and has a total of 5000 pairs and 20 categories.

Table 1. Statistical results of the three benchmark datasets

Dataset	Modality	Train	Validate	Test	Label	Feature
Wikipedia	Image	2173	231	462	10	4096D VGG
	Text	2173	231	462	10	300D W2V
NUS-WIDE-10k	Image	8000	1000	1000	10	4096D VGG
	Text	8000	1000	1000	10	300D W2V
XMedia	Image	4000	500	500	20	4096D VGG
	Text	4000	500	500	20	3000D BoW

4.2   Evaluation Metric

Following [2], we adopt the mean average precision (mAP) as the evaluation to judge the cross-modal retrieval performance for compared methods. Both ranking information and precision can be simultaneously considered with mAP metric. The final result consists of two cross-modal tasks: 1) using image as query and retrieval text samples (Image2Text). 2) using text as query and retrieval image samples (Text2Image).

4.3   Comparison with State-of-the-Art Methods

We verify the effectiveness of the proposed method by comparing with eight state-of-the-art methods, including four traditional methods, which are CCA [3], MCCA [22], JRL [6] and MvDA [23], as well as four DNN-based methods, namely DCCA [13], CMDN [14], CCL [10]and DSCMR [24]. The result of the proposed DCCMR and the compared methods are shown on Tables 2, 3 and 4 with the best result shown in boldface. Five of these compared methods are pair-based, namely CCA, MCCA, JRL, DCCA, DSCMR, while CCL is triplet-based. MvDA and CMDN is neither pair-based nor triplet-based. Our DCCMR is quadruplet-based.

Table 2. Performance comparison in terms of mAP scores on the Wikipedia dataset.

Method	Image2Text	Text2Image	Average	Tuples
CCA	0.249	0.196	0.223	4,719,756
MCCA	0.271	0.209	0.240	4,719,756
JRL	0.339	0.250	0.295	4,719,756
MvDA	0.288	0.259	0.274	N/A
DCCA	0.301	0.286	0.294	4,719,756
CMDN	0.441	0.477	0.459	N/A
CCL	0.481	0.442	0.462	3,415,530,092
DSCMR	**0.521**	**0.478**	**0.499**	**4,719,756**
Our DCCMR	0.478	0.482	0.479	3,168,234

Table 2 gives the experiment result on Wikipedia dataset, which has 2173 image/text pairs and 10 labels in training set. During training process, pair-based methods use pairs to construct the common subspace, thus the number of pairs for training would be $2 \times C(2173, 2)$, which is 4,719,756. The number of triplets for triplet-based methods would be $2 \times C(2173, 3)$, which is 3,415,530,092. According to Eq. (4), our DCCMR use quadruplets of samples and centers, hence the number of quadruplets would be $2 \times 2173 \times 9 \times 9 \times 9$, which is 3,168,234. It can be seen that even DCCMR use less tuples to construct the common subspace, it reaches the second best average mAP with only 0.02 behind.

Table 3 gives the experiment result on NUS-WIDE-10k dataset, which has 8000 image/text pairs and 10 labels in training set. Similar to the computing process on Wikipedia, the number of tuples for pair-based and triplet-based methods would be 63,992,000 and 170,602,672,000, respectively. Tuples for DCCMR would be 11,664,000. Our method achieves the best average mAP with the least tuples usage. Because of the larger scale of NUS-WIDE-10k, the global information in the common subspace contributes more compared with Wikipedia, leading to better performance and less tuples usage.

Table 3. Performance comparison in terms of mAP scores on the NUS-WIDE-10k dataset.

Method	Image2Text	Text2Image	Average	Tuples
CCA	0.263	0.250	0.257	63,992,000
MCCA	0.358	0.345	0.352	63,992,000
JRL	0.544	0.510	0.527	63,992,000
MvDA	0.563	0.544	0.554	N/A
DCCA	0.571	0.559	0.565	63,992,000
CMDN	0.512	0.495	0.504	N/A
CCL	0.568	0.569	0.569	170,602,672,000
DSCMR	0.604	0.599	0.603	63,992,000
Our DCCMR	**0.629**	**0.616**	**0.622**	**11,664,000**

Table 4. Performance comparison in terms of mAP scores on the PKU XMedia dataset.

Method	Image2Text	Text2Image	Average	Tuples
CCA	0.119	0.114	0.117	15,996,000
MCCA	0.149	0.137	0.143	15,996,000
JRL	0.195	0.213	0.204	15,996,000
MvDA	0.599	0.601	0.600	N/A
DCCA	0.550	0.528	0.539	15,996,000
CMDN	0.662	0.624	0.643	N/A
CCL	0.712	0.685	0.699	21,317,336,000
DSCMR	0.793	0.779	0.796	15,996,000
Our DCCMR	**0.848**	**0.855**	**0.852**	**54,872,000**

Table 4 gives the experiment result on XMedia dataset. DCCMR also achieves the best average mAP as 0.852, with an improvment of 0.056 from the second competitor. Our method use quadruplets formed by samples and centers to structure the common subspace. In XMedia, the number of samples and semantic centers in training set is 4000 and 20, respectively. In that case, the number of tuples from pair-based methods would be $2 \times C(4000, 2)$, which is 15,996,000, while our quadruplet-based method use $2 \times 4000 \times 19 \times 19 \times 19$, leading to more tuples compared with pair-based methods. Cause XMedia use articles crawled from Internet as texts, while NUS-WIDE-10k use tags corresponding to images as texts, the cross-modal information in XMedia would be more, leading to better performance.

The experiment result on three datasets show that DCCMR achieves comparable performance compared with other SOTA methods. Besides, the number of tuples used by our method can be greatly reduced compared with triplet-based methods. Due to the utilization of global information, the discrimination can be well preserved in common subspace, leading to high performance on both two cross-modal retrieval tasks.

4.4 Visualization of the Learned Representation

We adopt the t-SNE approach [25] to embed the learned representations into a 2-dimensional visualization panel. For comparison, we show the original t-SNE embeddings for images and texts in PKU XMedia dataset on Fig. 2(d) and Fig. 2(e), respectively. From the observation, the distribution in image and text modalities are largely different.

Figure 2(a) and Fig. 2(b) show the 2-dimensional distribution of the representations of images and texts in the common subspace, they are mixed in Fig. 2(c). It can be seen that through our DCCMR, the discrimination of samples from different semantic categories are well preserved in common space, and effectively separates the distribution into different semantic clusters.

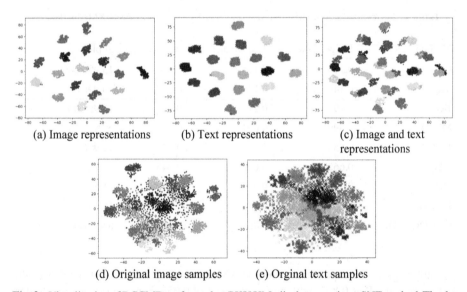

(a) Image representations   (b) Text representations   (c) Image and text representations

(d) Original image samples   (e) Orginal text samples

Fig. 2. Visualization of DCCMR performed on PKU XMedia dataset using t-SNE method. The dot denotes samples from image modality while cross denotes samples from text modality. Different color indicates different semantic categories. (Color figure online)

4.5 Ablation Study

We evaluate the effectiveness of our model DCCMR, which includes both retrieval loss and semantic loss, in different setups, and having the following objectives.

Evaluating the impact of the retrieval loss: we use **DCCMR_re** which refers to our model with only the retrieval loss term $\mathcal{L}_{re}$ in Eq. (1).

Evaluating the impact of the semantic loss: we use **DCCMR_sem** which refers to our model with only the semantic loss term $\mathcal{L}_{sem}$ in Eq. (1).

Evaluating the impact of λ which controls the balance of retrieval loss and semantic loss: we use **DCCMR_re + sem**, which we treat both loss terms equally and λ in Eq. (1) is set as 1 in this situation.

Table 5. Impact of different part of our DCCMR.

Method	Image2Text	Text2Image	Average
DCCMR_re	0.672	0.656	0.664
DCCMR_sem	0.516	0.503	0.510
DCCMR_re + sem	0.733	0.748	0.741
Full DCCMR	**0.852**	**0.855**	**0.854**

Table 5 show the performance comparisons of our DCCMR and its three variations in terms of mAP on XMedia Dataset. From the result we can see that the full DCCMR performs best compared with other variations, indicating the contribution of the retrieval loss, the semantic loss and the balance control between them. Furthermore, **DCCMR_re** highly outperforms **DCCMR_sem**, this is because retrieval is the main focus of the schema, and semantic loss acts as a regularization, therefore cannot replace $\mathcal{L}_{re}$, although the improvement on **DCCMR_re + sem** shows its contribution compared with single **DCCMR_re**. These results also prove the effectiveness of introducing both inter-modality and intra-modality information for multimodal learning.

5 Conclusion

In this paper, we propose a novel approach DCCMR for learning cross-modal embedding (image to text, and vice versa). Our main contribution relies on a joint retrieval and classification learning framework, in which centers of class-based embeddings are utilized, and a double-quadruplet schema is used in the model to output with a larger inter-class variation and a smaller intra-class variation compared with general triplet or pairwise methods. For learning the double-quadruplet learning schema, we propose an adaptive strategy for informative quadruplet mining. Comprehensive experimental results on three widely-used multimodal datasets have demonstrated the effectiveness of our proposed DCCMR.

References

1. Peng, Y., Huang, X., Zhao, Y.: An overview of cross-media retrieval: concepts, methodologies, benchmarks, and challenges. IEEE Trans. Circuits Syst. Video Technol. **28**(9), 2372–2385 (2017)
2. Wang, K., Yin, Q., Wang, W., et al.: A comprehensive survey on cross-modal retrieval. arXiv preprint arXiv:1607.06215 (2016)

3. Hotelling, H.: Relations between two sets of variates. In: Kotz S., Johnson N.L. (eds.) Breakthroughs in Statistics, pp. 162–190. Springer, New York (1992). https://doi.org/10.1007/978-1-4612-4380-9_14

4. Rasiwasia, N., Costa Pereira, J., Coviello, E., et al.: A new approach to cross-modal multimedia retrieval. In: Proceedings of the 18th ACM International Conference on Multimedia, pp. 251–260 (2010)

5. Sharma, A., Kumar, A., Daume, H., et al.: Generalized multiview analysis: a discriminative latent space. In: 2012 IEEE Conference on Computer Vision and Pattern Recognition, pp. 2160–2167. IEEE (2012)

6. Zhai, X., Peng, Y., Xiao, J.: Learning cross-media joint representation with sparse and semisupervised regularization. IEEE Trans. Circ. Syst. Video Technol. 24(6), 965–978 (2013)

7. Akaho, S.: A kernel method for canonical correlation analysis (2006). arXiv preprint cs/0609071

8. Peng, X., Feng, J., Xiao, S., et al.: Structured autoencoders for subspace clustering. IEEE Trans. Image Process. 27(10), 5076–5086 (2018)

9. Zhou, J.T., Zhao, H., Peng, X., et al.: Transfer hashing: from shallow to deep. IEEE Trans. Neural Netw. Learn. Syst. 29(12), 6191–6201 (2018)

10. Peng, Y., Qi, J., Huang, X., et al.: CCL: cross-modal correlation learning with multigrained fusion by hierarchical network. IEEE Trans. Multimedia 20(2), 405–420 (2017)

11. Ngiam, J., Khosla, A., Kim, M., et al.: Multimodal deep learning. In: Proceedings of the 28th International Conference on Machine Learning (ICML-2011), pp. 689–696 (2011)

12. Yan, F., Mikolajczyk, K.: Deep correlation for matching images and text. In: Proceedings of the IEEE Conference on Computer Vision and Pattern Recognition, pp. 3441–3450 (2015)

13. Andrew, G., Arora, R., Bilmes, J., et al.: Deep canonical correlation analysis. In: International Conference on Machine Learning, pp. 1247–1255 (2013)

14. Peng, Y., Huang, X., Qi, J.: Cross-media shared representation by hierarchical learning with multiple deep networks. In: IJCAI, pp. 3846–3853 (2016)

15. Chen, W., Chen, X., Zhang, J., et al.: Beyond triplet loss: a deep quadruplet network for person re-identification. In: Proceedings of the IEEE Conference on Computer Vision and Pattern Recognition, pp. 403–412 (2017)

16. Kingma, D.P., Ba, J.: Adam: a method for stochastic optimization. arXiv preprint arXiv:1412.6980 (2014)

17. Nair, V., Hinton, G.E.: Rectified linear units improve restricted boltzmann machines. In: Proceedings of the 27th International Conference on Machine Learning (ICML-2010), pp. 807–814 (2010)

18. Pereira, J.C., Coviello, E., Doyle, G., et al.: On the role of correlation and abstraction in cross-modal multimedia retrieval. IEEE Trans. Pattern Anal. Mach. Intell. 36(3), 521–535 (2013)

19. Chua, T.-S., Tang, J., Hong, R. , Li, H., Luo, Z., Zheng, Y.: NUS-WIDE: a real-world web image database from national university of Singapore. In: ACM International Conference on Image and Video Retrieval (CIVR), pp. 1–9 (2009)

20. Peng, Y., Zhai, X., Zhao, Y., Huang, X.: Semi-supervised crossmedia feature learning with unified patch graph regularization. IEEE Trans. Circ. Syst. Video Technol. (TCSVT) 26(3), 583–596 (2016)

21. Zhai, X., Peng, Y., Xiao, J.: Learning cross-media joint representation with sparse and semi-supervised regularization. IEEE Trans. Circ. Syst. Video Technol. (TCSVT) 24(6), 965–978 (2014)

22. Rupnik, J., Shawe-Taylor, J.: Multi-view canonical correlation analysis. In: Conference on Data Mining and Data Warehouses (SiKDD 2010), pp. 1–4 (2010)

23. Kan, M., Shan, S., Zhang, H., et al.: Multi-view discriminant analysis. IEEE Trans. Pattern Anal. Mach. Intell. 38(1), 188–194 (2015)

24. Zhen, L., Hu, P., Wang, X., et al.: Deep supervised cross-modal retrieval. In: Proceedings of the IEEE Conference on Computer Vision and Pattern Recognition, pp. 10394–10403 (2019)
25. Maaten, L., Hinton, G.: Visualizing data using t-SNE. J. Mach. Learn. Res. **9**(Nov), 2579–2605 (2008)

Shot Boundary Detection Through Multi-stage Deep Convolution Neural Network

Tingting Wang[1], Na Feng[1], Junqing Yu[1(✉)], Yunfeng He[1], Yangliu Hu[1],
and Yi-Ping Phoebe Chen[2]

[1] School of Computer Science and Technology, Huazhong University of Science
and Technology, Wuhan, China
{fengna,yjqing}@hust.edu.cn
[2] Department of Computer Science and Information Technology,
La Trobe University, Melbourne, VIC 3086, Australia
phoebe.chen@latrobe.edu.au

Abstract. Fast and accurate shot segmentation is very important for content-based video analysis. However, existing solutions have not yet achieved the ideal balance of speed and accuracy. In this paper, we propose a multi-stage shot boundary detection framework based on deep CNN for shot segmentation tasks. The process is composed of three stages, which are respectively for candidate boundary detection, abrupt detection and gradual transition detection. At each stage, deep CNN is used to extract image features, which overcomes the disadvantages of hand-craft feature-based methods such as poor scalability and complex calculation. Besides, we also set a variety of constraints to filter as many non-boundaries as possible to improve the processing speed of the model. In gradual transition detection, we introduce a scheme that can infer the gradual position by computing the probability signals of the start, mid and end of the gradual transition. We conduct experiments on ClipShots and the experimental results show that the proposed model achieves better performance on abrupt and gradual transition detection.

Keywords: Shot boundary detection · Convolution neural network · Abrupt transition · Gradual transition

1 Introduction

The research of shot boundary detection has been carried on for many years. However, due to the diversity of the gradual transition and the interference in the video, such as sudden light changes, rapid movement of objects or cameras, etc., the problem of shot boundary detection is still not well solved. Most methods use the shallow visual features designed by prior knowledge and lack the ability to describe high-level semantic information. Fast detection methods usually analyze spatial information and adopt simple identification mechanisms, and the results

© Springer Nature Switzerland AG 2021
J. Lokoč et al. (Eds.): MMM 2021, LNCS 12572, pp. 456–468, 2021.
https://doi.org/10.1007/978-3-030-67832-6_37

are not as good as expected. To improve the accuracy, some methods adopt more complex feature combination and identification mechanism, resulting in high computational cost and slower speed. Since shot segmentation is used as a preprocessing step for video content analysis, it is important to simultaneously improve the accuracy and speed of shot boundary detection.

In recent years, thanks to the development of Graphics Processing Unit (GPU) and large-scale datasets, deep learning has achieved major breakthroughs in speed and efficiency on image and video analysis issues. Compared with manually designed features, its ability to automatically learn and extract high-level semantic feature expression can better reflect the diversity of data. However, there are few studies on applying CNN to shot segmentation.

In this paper, we propose a CNN-based multi-stage shot boundary detection framework (SSBD). It is divided into three stages. The first stage is to generate candidate boundaries where the shot transition may occur. CNN is used as the feature extractor of the frame and then the most non-boundaries are quickly excluded by calculating the difference between adjacent frames. In the second stage, 3D CNN is used to further identify the abrupts, gradual transitions and non-boundaries. Threshold mechanism is adopted to obtain candidate gradual frames from the latter two. The third stage is to detect gradual transitions. We still adopt 3D CNN to predict the probability that each candidate frame belongs to the start, mid and end of the transition, and then the position can be determined by strong peaks of these three probability signals.

The contributions of our work can be summarized as follows:

- We propose a shot boundary detection framework and conduct experiments on ClipShots. The results show that the proposed model performs better than others.
- We put forward a variety of constraints in the process of shot boundary detection, which can quickly and accurately filter out non-shot boundaries to improve the processing speed and reduce calculations.
- We introduce a scheme in the gradual transition detection, which calculates the probability signals of the start, mid and end of the transition, and then the position can be determined according to the strong peaks of these signals.

2   Related Works

Traditionally, most shot boundary detection methods mainly rely on well-designed hand-crafted features. The basic idea is to achieve shot segmentation by finding the changing rule of the difference between frames at the shot boundary. These methods usually includes three steps: visual content representation (feature extraction), construction of continuous signals (similarity measure), and the shot boundary classification of the continuous signals (shot boundary identification). The features used by these methods include color histograms [1,2], edges [3], mutual information and entropy [4], wavelet representation [5], speeded up robust features (SURF) [6], motion information [5,7,8] and many other manual features [9–11]. The threshold mechanism [4,12–14] has been widely used in the decision-making stage, but recently most researchers employ statistical learning algorithms to identify shot boundaries.

In order to eliminate the interference caused by illumination and camera or object movement, some methods tend to make use of complex features and continuous calculations but cannot achieve real-time analysis. As the basis of high-level video content analysis, efficient detection of shot boundaries is also important. [2] proposes a method for fast detection based on singular value decomposition and pattern matching. [6] employs SURF descriptors and HSV histogram to describe the visual feature of the image, and detect abrupt and gradual transitions by calculating the similarity between adjacent frames. In addition, the paper also proposes a GPU-based computing framework to achieve real-time analysis. [15] proposes a multi-modal visual features-based framework, which uses the discontinuity signal calculated based on SURF and RGB histogram. The above methods only use the spatial features of the image, and the processing speed is very fast but at the cost of the accuracy.

Encouraged by the successful application of deep learning on visual tasks, researchers have begun to use deep learning to achieve shot boundary detection in the past two years, but there are still few related works. [16] proposes a method based on interpretable labels learned by CNN. It uses a similar mechanism as in [2] to eliminate non-boundary frames, and then adopt the pixel-wise difference and the adaptive threshold-based method to detect abrupt. For gradual transition, it uses CNN to get labels of the previous and next frames of one candidate segment and analyze the relationships between those labels to judge if the segment has gradual transition in it. [17] and [18] apply 3D CNN to identify abrupt and gradual transitions. [19] introduces a cascade framework that can achieve rapid and accurate shot segmentation. It first extracts CNN features of the image to filter non-boundaries and then uses 2D CNN and 3D CNN to identify the abrupt and gradual transitions. Although these methods have made improvements on shot boundary detection, there are still some problems, such as the inability to accurately localize the boundaries, the lack of tolerance for variable shot lengths, etc.

3   Methodology

This part describes the proposed method in detail. Firstly, we use CNN to extract the spatial feature of each frame in the video and then detect possible shot boundaries by calculating the difference between adjacent frames. Secondly, 3D CNN is used to extract the spatio-temporal features of the candidate boundary frames and their neighbors to identify the abrupt transitions. At the same time, the probability threshold is used to generate candidate gradual frames. Finally, predicting the probability that each candidate gradual frame belongs to the start, mid and end of the transition, and the position can be derived from strong peaks of these three probability signals. The pipeline is illustrated in Fig. 1.

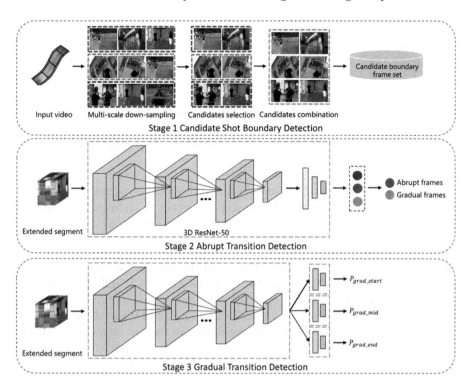

Fig. 1. The pipeline of SSBD. It consists of three stages. In the first stage, multiple scales are used to sample the video and then pick out potential shot boundary frames by calculating the difference between frames. In the second stage, the candidate frames are expanded into segments and 3D ResNet-50 is used to predict abrupts and candidate gradual frames. In the third stage, we use 3D CNN to predict the probability that each candidate frame belongs to the start, mid, and end of the gradual transition, and then construct the probability signal function to infer the position of the transition.

3.1 Candidate Shot Boundary Detection

Shot is a group of images continuously captured by the same camera. The visual content of the image in the same shot is continuous in time and space but inconsistent in different shots. We adopt the visual difference between two consecutive frames as the measure of visual continuity, it can be seen that the difference maintains a stable change rate within the same shot, but changes significantly when the shot transition occurs. Therefore, we compare the difference with the predefined threshold to preserve the shot boundaries. If the difference between two consecutive frames is greater than the threshold, it can be considered that a shot transition occurs. The specific steps are as follows:

1. Use CNN to extract the spatial feature of each frame in the video sequence and denote it by F_i.

2. Calculate the difference d_i between the i-th and the i+1-th frames by the following equation

$$d_i = 1 - \frac{<F_i, F_{i+1}>}{\|F_i\| \|F_{i+1}\|} \tag{1}$$

where $<F_i, F_{i+1}>$ represents the dot product of F_i and F_{i+1}, $\|F_i\|$ represents the L2 norm of F_i.
3. Calculate the mean value μ_G of the difference of all frames in the video sequence.
4. For the i-th frame, if it satisfies $(d_i > \lambda d_{i-1} \cup d_i > \lambda d_{i+1}) \cap d_i > \gamma \mu_G$, it is regarded as a candidate boundary frame. λ specifies the minimum change rate of visual content when shot transition occurs, γ and μ_G constitute the global static threshold of the difference between frames.

Since the length of the gradual transition varies greatly, we use multiple temporal scales to downsample the video and then merge the candidate frames obtained at different scales. When two candidate frames at different scales are very close (within five frames), only the candidate frame at the lower scale is retained. In the experiment, we use scales of 1, 2, 4, 8, 16, and 32. In addition, we consider VGG-16, ResNet-50 and SqueezeNet as feature extraction networks and use the output of high layers as feature representations. Specifically, the fc6 of VGG16, the pool5 of ResNet-50 and the pool10 of SqueezeNet.

3.2   Abrupt Detection

The input of the abrupt detection model is a set of continuous frames centered on the candidate frame. For the candidate frame x, it is expanded 7 and 8 frames forward and backward respectively to form a segment with a length of 16. When x is the first or last frame of the video, that is, $x - 7$ is less than 0 or $x + 8$ is greater than the total number of video frames, it needs to be looped multiple times to form a 16-frame segment. After that, we choose 3D ResNet-50 as the classification network and output the probability that the frame is abrupt, gradual and non-boundary. To prevent some negative samples from being predicted as abrupts, simple post-processing is performed on all abrupt frames:

1. For abrupt frame x and its neighbor $x + 1$, calculate the HSV histograms H_x and H_{x+1}, where H is set to 18, S is set to 16 and V is set to 16.
2. Calculate the Bhattacharyya distance d between H_x and H_{x+1} by the following equation

$$d(H_x, H_{x+1}) = \sqrt{1 - \frac{1}{\sqrt{\bar{H}_x \bar{H}_{x+1} N^2}} \sum_I \sqrt{H_x(I) \cdot H_{x+1}(I)}} \tag{2}$$

3. Compare d with the threshold T. If $d < T$, it is considered that there is no abrupt at x. Experiments show that the best result is obtained when T is set to 0.36.

Although the abrupt detection network also outputs predictions of gradual transitions and non-shot boundaries, the lack of gradual transition training samples may lead to inaccurate recognition. Therefore, in addition to those boundaries predicted to be gradual transitions, the non-boundaries whose gradual transition probability is greater than or equal to the threshold p are also retained as the potential gradual transitions. They are all the inputs for the next stage. In the experiment, p is set to 0.1.

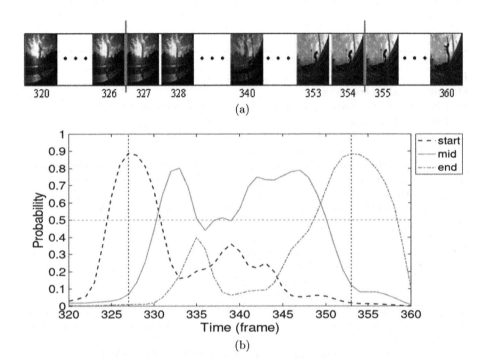

Fig. 2. Example of gradual transition prediction. (a) displays a gradual transition in [327,353], (b) shows three state probability signals of the gradual transition.

3.3   Gradual Transition Detection

This stage aims to locate the gradual transitions in the video. Inspired by [20], the model we build identifies three gradual transition states: start (the first frame of the transition), end (the last frame of the transition), and mid (any frame between the first and last of the transition). After obtaining all candidate gradual frames, we first expand them into candidate segments and then use 3D CNN to compute the probability that each frame in the segments belongs to the above three states. Finally, gradual transitions can be determined based on these three signals.

For a given candidate gradual frame x, it is expanded n frames forward and backward respectively to form a candidate segment with a length of $2n+1$.

Since the segment cannot overlap the abrupt, it should not span the abrupt closest to x. Let N_{total} be the total number of video frames. $C_{left}(x)$ represents the abrupt frame closest to the left of x, if the value is -1, there is no abrupt. $C_{right}(x)$ represents the abrupt frame closest to the right of x, if the value is $N_{total} - 1$, there is no abrupt. L_{min} represents the minimum length of the shot. In this paper, we use the last frame of the previous shot to represent the abrupt. Thus, the candidate interval of x is $(\max(C_{left}(x)+1+L_{min}, x-n+1), \min(x + n - 1, C_{right}(x) - L_{min}))$. In the experiment, n takes 25 and L_{min} is set to 1.

Algorithm 1. Process of gradual transition detection

Input: Smooth probability signal $g_{start}(t)$, $g_{mid}(t)$ and $g_{end}(t)$;
Output: Gradual transitions;
1: Find all the maximum points in $g_{mid}(t)$, each is denoted by m_i;
2: **for** $i = 1,2,3,...$ **do**
3:     **if** $g_{mid}(m_i) \geq Th_{mid}$ **then**
4:         **for** $j = m_i$ to $m_i - separation$ **do**
5:             find the strong peaks of $g_{start}(t)$ (the probability is not less than $Th_{s,e}$)
6:             **if** there is a strong peak of $g_{end}(t)$ between two consecutive strong peaks **then**
7:                 end the scan and keep the strong peak points on the right
8:             **end if**
9:         **end for**
10:        **if** $g_{start}(t)$ has one or more strong peak points **then**
11:            choose the point that maximizes the value of $g_{start}(t)$ as the start of the gradual transition denoted by s_i
12:            **for** $k = m_i$ to $m_i + separation$ **do**
13:                find the strong peaks of $g_{end}(t)$ (the probability is not less than $Th_{s,e}$)
14:                **if** there is a strong peak of $g_{start}(t)$ between two consecutive strong peaks **then**
15:                    end the scan and keep the strong peak points on the left
16:                **end if**
17:            **end for**
18:            **if** $g_{end}(t)$ has one or more strong peak points **then**
19:                choose the point that maximizes the value of $g_{end}(t)$ as the end of the gradual transition denoted by e_i. The gradual transition interval is $(s_i, e_i, g_{mid}(m_i))$
20:            **end if**
21:        **end if**
22:    **end if**
23: **end for**
24: Perform NMS on all gradual transitions. When multiple gradual transitions overlap, only the transition with the largest $g_{mid}(m_i)$ is retained.

Three state probabilities need to be calculated for each frame in the candidate segment. Given a frame in the segment, we extend it forward and backward by

8 frames respectively to form a segment with a length of 17 as the input of the gradual transition detection network. When it is the first or last frame of the video, it needs to be looped multiple times. After obtaining three probability values of each frame, the probability signal $f_M(t)$ is defined according to the following equation, where $M \in$(start, mid, end) and s_t represents the segment centered on frame t.

$$f_M(t) = Pr(M \mid s_t) \tag{3}$$

Figure 2 gives an example. Although the original probability signal can indicate the occurrence of the gradual transition, it is not very smooth. We perform window function on $f_M(t)$ to obtain the smooth signal $g_M(t)$. In the next processing, we first determine the transition center by the peak value in $g_{mid}(t)$. Then, a scan is performed within a limited range along the time axis to determine if there are strong peaks in $g_{start}(t)$ and $g_{end}(t)$. If so, the gradual transition boundary can be localized based on these strong peaks. The process of gradual transition detection is described in Algorithm 1.

In the experiment, Th_{mid} is set to 0.5, *separation* is set to 40, $Th_{s,e}$ is set to 0.5. For gradual transitions with a length of 1 or 2 frames, there may not be a maximum point in $g_{mid}(t)$ that meets the requirements in Algorithm 1. Thus, we add steps to detect such transition. Traverse $g_{start}(t)$, if there is a strong peak point s_i that is not included in the found gradual transition, and a strong peak point e_i of $g_{end}(t)$ is found in $[s_i, s_i + 1]$, the interval $[s_i, e_i]$ is considered as the gradual transition.

4 Experiments

In this part, we will illustrate the experiments on candidate shot boundary detection, abrupt detection and gradual transition detection. All experiments are performed on the ClipShots dataset.

4.1 Evaluation of Candidate Shot Boundary Detection

Evaluation of Different Parameter Values. The parameters λ and γ specify change rate of the difference value between frames and threshold respectively, which control the strictness of the decision-making conditions in step four in Sect. 3.1. We compare the performance of the algorithm with different parameter values, and the results are shown in Table 1. We calculate the ratios of the candidate boundary frames (CBF) to the total frames (TF), the retained abrupts (RA) to the total abrupts (TA), the retained gradual transitions (RG) to the total gradual transitions (TG). It can be seen that as the parameter value increases, more non-boundary frames will be filtered, and more real shot transitions will be lost at the same time. The loss rate of the gradual transition is higher than that of the abrupt, which is in line with the rule that the visual content changes less during the gradual transition.

Evaluation of Different Features. The output of pool10 of SqueezeNet, fc6 of VGG-16 and pool5 of ResNet-50 trained on ImageNet are directly used as the feature representation. Table 2 lists the performance of these models. In addition to the three indicators in Table 1, we also calculate the speed. We adjust the values of λ and γ to make the total number of candidate boundaries obtained on different features close. It can be seen that these three models can achieve better results on shot boundary detection, especially abrupt. SqueezeNet with the fewest parameters is the fastest.

Table 1. Performance of candidate shot boundary detection with different parameter values

Parameter values	CBF/TF (%)	RA/TA (%)	RG/TG (%)
$\lambda = 2$, $\gamma = 0.7$	16.56	99.23	97.91
$\lambda = 2.5$, $\gamma = 0.9$	10.65	98.92	96.6
$\lambda = 3$, $\gamma = 1$	8	98.63	94.77
$\lambda = 3.5$, $\gamma = 1.2$	5.93	98.28	92.29

Table 2. Performance of candidate shot boundary detection with different features

Feature	CBF/TF (%)	RA/TA (%)	RG/TG (%)	Speed (Frames Per Second)
SqueezeNet	16.23	99.23	97.91	1000
VGG-16	16.1	99.16	97.81	129.9
ResNet-50	16.26	99.05	97.70	250

4.2 Evaluation of Abrupt Detection

Training Set. We rebuilt the training set. First, the candidate boundary detection is performed on all videos in the ClipShots training set to obtain a set of video frames. Then, some sampling operations are executed on the video frame set: (1) Sample all video frames whose ground truth is abrupt. (2) Sample all video frames whose ground truth is gradual transition. (3) Randomly sample the video frames whose ground truth is non-boundary, and the number of frames is equal to the sum of the abrupt and gradual frames. In the end, we obtain 116017 abrupt frames, 58623 gradual frames and 174640 non-boundary frames.

Implementation Detail. The size of the input image is 112×112. We use the 3D ResNet-50 pre-trained on the Kinetics dataset published in [21] to initialize the network. SGD is adopted to update the parameters and the momentum is set to 0.9. The batch size is 64 and the initial learning rate is set to 0.001.

Performance. Table 3 shows the results of abrupt detection. We first perform the candidate shot boundary detection on all videos in the ClipShots test set and then perform abrupt detection on the previous output. For comparison, we also add the experimental results of [17–19], which are derived from [19].

Table 3. Performance of abrupt detection on ClipShots

Method	Precision (%)	Recall (%)	F1-measure (%)
DeepSBD [17]	73.1	92.1	81.5
FCN [18]	41.0	9.3	15.1
DSM [19]	77.6	93.4	84.8
Ours (without post-processing)	87.1	90.9	89.0
Ours (with post-processing)	90.8	89.7	90.3

It can be seen that the precision and F1-measure of the proposed model are the highest, improving by at least 10% and 4%, but the recall is lower than DeepSBD and DSM. Compared with DeepSBD and FCN which adopt 8 and 4 convolutional layers, we employ a deeper network with 50 layers to extract features, so the learning and representation capabilities of video content are stronger. Compared with DSM, we adopt the 3D CNN which performs spatio-temporal convolution in all convolutional layers, while in DSM, the input multi-frame is simply regarded as a multi-channel image, which is equivalent to only fusing the temporal information of the video in the first convolutional layer. This is not enough for the spatiotemporal analysis of the input segment. In addition, with post-processing, the precision is increased by 3.7%, but the recall is reduced by 1.2%, and F1-measure is only increased by 1.3%. This shows that post-processing has limited improvement on abrupt detection.

4.3 Evaluation of Gradual Transition Detection

Original Label Translation. Training gradual transition detection network requires three labels: y_{start}, y_{mid} and y_{end}. Due to the extreme imbalance of positive and negative samples (especially y_{start} and y_{end}), and the high similarity of frames near the long-span gradual transition but with different labels, simple 0, 1 labels makes CNN learning unstable. Inspired by [22], we translate y_{start} and y_{end} to force the label of the frames near the gradual transition to be greater than 0. As a result, we can minimize the difference between positive and negative samples while increasing the tolerance for similar training data.

Training Set. The training set is constructed from ClipShots and only_gradual [19]. Sampling four frames from each gradual transition, of which three frames must be the start, mid and end frames, and the last frame is randomly selected. One frame is randomly sampled in the range of 21 frames before and after the gradual transition, and five frames are randomly sampled from the non-gradual frames. In the end, the training set contains 208296 samples, and the ratios of positive and negative for start, mid and end are 1:4.55, 1:2.85, and 1:4.54.

Implementation Detail. We use the 3D ResNet-50 pre-trained on the Kinetics dataset to initialize the body part of the network, and use SGD with momentum of 0.9 to update the parameters. The batch size is 50 and the initial learning rate is set to 0.001.

Performance. Table 4 lists the performance of the gradual transition detection on ClipShots. We perform a complete shot boundary detection process on all videos in the ClipShots test set and the comparison results come from [19].

Table 4. Performance of gradual transition detection on ClipShots

Method	Precision (%)	Recall (%)	F1-measure (%)
DeepSBD [17]	83.7	38.6	52.8
FCN [18]	39.3	5.3	9.3
DSM [19]	84.0	90.4	87.0
Ours	88.1	81.3	84.6

It can be seen that the proposed model performs better than DeepSBD and FCN due to the deeper network. However, even though the network in DSM has only 18 layers, the F1-measure of ours is 2.4% lower than it. The reasons are as follows: (1) The input of the gradual transition detection model is the output of the previous stage where 7.2% of the ground truth has been lost. This directly leads to a low recall. (2) The input length of the model is 17 frames and down-sampling is performed on multiple convolutional layers, while the input length of DSM is 64 frames without any down-sampling operation, making full use of temporal information.

5   Conclusion

In this paper, we propose a shot boundary detection framework based on deep CNN. Three stages are designed to achieve fast and accurate performance, namely candidate shot boundary detection, abrupt detection and gradual transition detection. We introduce a scheme in gradual transition detection, which is to determine the position of the gradual transition by calculating the probability signals of the start, mid and end of the transition. Our method achieves better results on ClipShots dataset. One existing drawback of the proposed method is that there is still a large number of repeated calculations in gradual transition detection. In addition, the mining of difficult negative samples is insufficient. In future work, we will try to improve the network structure and add more negative samples in training to improve the robustness of the model to sudden light change, fast motion and occlusion.

References

1. Zhang, C., Wang, W.: A robust and efficient shot boundary detection approach based on fished criterion. In: 20th ACM International Conference on Multimedia, pp. 701–704 (2012)
2. Lu, Z.-M., Shi, Y.: Fast video shot boundary detection based on SVD and pattern matching. IEEE Trans. Image Process. **22**(12), 5136–5145 (2013)
3. Adjeroh, D.-A., Lee, M.-C., Banda, N., Kandaswamy, U.: Adaptive edge-oriented shot boundary detection. J. Image Video Proc. **2009**, 859371 (2009)
4. Cernekova, Z., Pitas, I., Nikou, C.: Information theory-based shot cut/fade detection and video summarization. IEEE Trans. Circ. Syst. Video Technol. **16**(1), 82–91 (2006)
5. Priya, L., Domnic, S.: Walsh-hadamard transform kernel-based feature vector for shot boundary detection. IEEE Trans. Image Process. **23**(12), 5187–5197 (2014)
6. Apostolidis, E., Mezaris, V.: Fast shot segmentation combining global and local visual descriptors. 2014 IEEE International Conference on Acoustics, Speech and Signal Processing (ICASSP), pp. 6583–6587. IEEE (2014)
7. Mohanta, P.-P., Saha, S.-K., Chanda, B.: A model-based shot boundary detection technique using frame transition parameters. IEEE Trans. Multimedia **14**(1), 223–233 (2012)
8. Lian, S.: Automatic video temporal segmentation based on multiple features. Soft Comput. **15**(3), 469–482 (2011)
9. Baraldi, L., Grana, C., Cucchiara, R.: Shot and scene detection via hierarchical clustering for re-using broadcast video. In: Azzopardi, G., Petkov, N. (eds.) CAIP 2015. LNCS, vol. 9256, pp. 801–811. Springer, Cham (2015). https://doi.org/10.1007/978-3-319-23192-1_67
10. Lankinen, J., Kamarainen, J.-K.: Video shot boundary detection using visual bag-of-words. In: International Conference on Computer Vision Theory and Applications, pp. 788–791 (2013)
11. Thounaojam, D.-M., Thonga, M.K., Singh, K.-M., Roy, S.: A genetic algorithm and fuzzy logic approach for video shot boundary detection. Comput. Intell. Neurosci. **2016**, 1–11 (2016)
12. Yusoff, Y., Christmas, W.-J., Kittler, J.: Video shot cut detection using adaptive thresholding. In: Proceedings of the British Machine Conference, pp. 1–10. BMVA Press (2000)
13. Wu, X., Yuan, P.-C., Liu, C., Huang, J.: Shot boundary detection: an information saliency approach. In: 2008 Congress on Image and Signal Processing, pp. 808–812. IEEE (2010)
14. Xia, D., Deng, X., Zeng, Q.: Shot boundary detection based on difference sequences of mutual information. In: 4th International Conference on Image and Graphics (ICIG 2007), pp. 389–394. IEEE (2007)
15. Tippaya, S., Sitjongsataporn, S., Tan, T., Khan, M.-M., Chamnongthai, K.: Multi-modal visual features-based video shot boundary detection. IEEE Access **5**, 12563–12575 (2017)

16. Tong, W., Song, L., Yang, X., Qu, H., Xie, R.: CNN-based shot boundary detection and video annotation. In: 2015 IEEE International Symposium on Broadband Multimedia Systems and Broadcasting, pp. 1–5. IEEE (2015)
17. Hassanien, A., Elgharib, M.-A., Selim, A., Hefeeda, M., Matusik, W.: Large-scale, fast and accurate shot boundary detection through spatio-temporal convolutional neural networks. arXiv preprint arXiv: 1705.03281 (2017)
18. Gygli, M.: Ridiculously fast shot boundary detection with fully convolutional neural networks. In: 2018 International Conference on Content-Based Multimedia Indexing, pp. 1–4. IEEE (2018)
19. Tang, S., Feng, L., Kuang, Z., Chen, Y., Zhang, W.: Fast video shot transition localization with deep structured models. In: Jawahar, C.V., Li, H., Mori, G., Schindler, K. (eds.) ACCV 2018. LNCS, vol. 11361, pp. 577–592. Springer, Cham (2019). https://doi.org/10.1007/978-3-030-20887-5_36
20. Nibali, A., He, Z., Morgan, S., Greenwood, G.: Extraction and classification of diving clips from continuous video footage. In: 2017 IEEE Conference on Computer Vision and Pattern Recognition Workshops (CVPRW), pp. 94–104. IEEE (2017)
21. Hara, K., Kataoka, H., Satoh, Y.: Can spatiotemporal 3D CNNs retrace the history of 2D CNNs and imagenet?. In: 2018 IEEE/CVF Conference on Computer Vision and Pattern Recognition, pp. 6546–6555. IEEE (2018)
22. Victor, B., He, Z., Morgan, S., Miniutti, D.: Continuous video to simple signals for swimming stroke detection with convolutional neural networks. In: 2017 IEEE Conference on Computer Vision and Pattern Recognition Workshops (CVPRW), pp. 122–131. IEEE (2017)

Towards Optimal Multirate Encoding for HTTP Adaptive Streaming

Hadi Amirpour[1]([✉]), Ekrem Çetinkaya[1], Christian Timmerer[1,2], and Mohammad Ghanbari[1,3]

[1] University of Klagenfurt, Klagenfurt, Austria
hadi@itec.aau.at
[2] Bitmovin, Klagenfurt, Austria
[3] University of Essex, Colchester, UK

Abstract. *HTTP Adaptive Streaming* (HAS) enables high quality streaming of video contents. In HAS, videos are divided into short intervals called segments, and each segment is encoded at various quality/bitrates to adapt to the available channel rate. Multiple encoding of the same content imposes high cost for video content providers. To reduce the time-complexity of encoding multiple representations, state-of-the-art methods typically encode the highest quality representation first and reuse the information gathered during its encoding to accelerate the encoding of the remaining representations. As encoding the highest quality representation requires the highest time-complexity compared to the lower quality representations, it would be a bottleneck in parallel encoding scenarios and the overall time-complexity will be limited to the time-complexity of the highest quality representation. In this paper and to address this problem, we consider all representations from the highest to the lowest quality representation as a potential, single reference to accelerate the encoding of the other, dependent representations. We formulate a set of encoding modes and assess their performance in terms of BD-Rate and time-complexity, using both VMAF and PSNR as objective metrics. Experimental results show that encoding a middle quality representation as a reference, can significantly reduce the maximum encoding complexity and hence it is an efficient way of encoding multiple representations in parallel. Based on this fact, a fast multirate encoding method is proposed which utilizes depth and prediction mode of a middle quality representation to accelerate the encoding of the dependent representations.

Keywords: HEVC · Video encoding · Multirate encoding · DASH

1 Introduction

According to the Cisco's Visual Networking Index (VNI), 82% of the Internet traffic will consist of video by 2022 [6]. This increase in video traffic along with improvements in video characteristics such as resolution, frame rate, and bit

© Springer Nature Switzerland AG 2021
J. Lokoč et al. (Eds.): MMM 2021, LNCS 12572, pp. 469–480, 2021.
https://doi.org/10.1007/978-3-030-67832-6_38

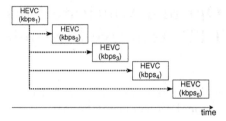

Fig. 1. The framework for the conventional, fast multirate encoding methods. A representation with $kbps_n$ has higher quality than a representation with $kbps_{n+1}$.

depth raises the need of developing a highly efficient video encoding environment. To meet the high demand for streaming high quality video over the Internet and to overcome the associated challenges, the Moving Picture Experts Group (MPEG) has developed a standard called *Dynamic Adaptive Streaming over HTTP* (MPEG-DASH) [15].

DASH is the standardized solution for *HTTP Adaptive Streaming* (HAS). The main idea behind HAS is to divide the video content into segments and encode each segment at various bitrates and resolutions, called *representations*, which are stored in plain HTTP servers. These representations are stored in order to continuously adapt the video delivery to the network conditions and device capabilities of the client.

High Efficiency Video Coding (HEVC) [16] is one of the latest standard video codecs that significantly improves encoding efficiency over its predecessor *Advanced Video Coding* (AVC) [17]. This encoding efficiency is achieved at the cost of an increased encoding time-complexity [11], which is a challenge for content providers. This is more crucial for DASH servers as they have to encode multiple representations of the same video segment [3].

On the other hand, as various representations are the same content encoded at different qualities or resolutions, their encoding information can be shared to accelerate the encoding of the other representations. This information includes, but is not limited to, CTU depth values, prediction modes, motion vectors, and reference frames. Several state-of-the-art approaches first encode *a single representation*, called a *reference representation* and then utilize its information to speed up the encoding process of the remaining representations, called *dependent representations*. Numerous approaches are proposed for fast multirate encoding ranging from limiting CU depth search levels [1,5,13,14,19] to reusing additional available information to help with other encoding decisions [7,10,12,18].

As shown in Fig. 1, conventional, fast multirate encoding approaches usually first encode the *highest quality* as the reference representation and reuse its information to reduce the time-complexity of the dependent representations and, thus, the overall time-complexity. For example, Fig. 2 shows the normalized time-complexity of encoding the *Kimono*1 sequence [4] at five bitrates (*i.e.*, different QPs indicated on the horizontal axis) using the unmodified HEVC Test

Model (HM). As shown in the figure the time-complexity increases with increasing bitrate/quality. In parallel encoding, all the representations are encoded simultaneously on different cores or machines. As encoding the highest quality representation has the highest time-complexity among other representations, the parallel encoding of multiple representations is limited to the encoding time-complexity of the highest quality representation.

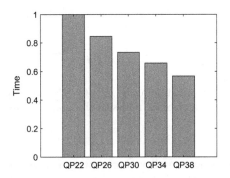

Fig. 2. The normalized time-complexity of encoding *Kimono*1 sequence at five bitrates.

The main contribution of this paper is to optimize the HAS encoding for efficient parallel multirate encoding. The remainder of the paper is organized as follows. In Sect. 2, we briefly cover related works. Section 3 describes the single reference multirate encoding and the corresponding experimental results. Our methodology is described in Sect. 4 including its comparison with the other modes. Finally, Sect. 5 concludes the paper.

2   Related Works

HEVC can gain about 50% bitrate reduction compared to AVC [16]. This improvement is achieved by using sophisticated encoding tools and the highest gain is achieved by introducing Coding Tree Units (CTUs) [11]. In HEVC, frames are first divided into slices and then they are further divided into square regions called CTUs. These CTUs are the main building blocks of HEVC and each CTU can be recursively divided into smaller square regions called Coding Units (CUs). Depth values from 0 to 3 are assigned to CU sizes from 64×64 to 8×8 pixels. An example of CTU partitioning is shown in Fig. 3. Fast CTU depth decision methods typically exploit the correlation between the depth value of spatially and/or temporally neighboring CTUs to avoid the search process for unnecessary CUs. Similarly, fast multirate encoding approaches use correlation between co-located CTUs in the reference and dependent representations to eliminate unnecessary CU searches.

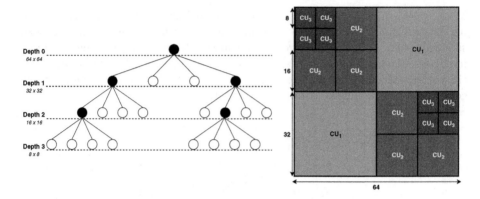

Fig. 3. An example CTU partitioning in HEVC. CUs are ordered from top-left to bottom-right in the graph and black nodes in the graph mean split decision is given for the current CU.

In [14], first the highest quality representation is encoded with unmodified HEVC. Its depth information is then used to encode the dependent representations. Based on the observation that CUs generally tend to have higher depth values in higher quality, when encoding dependent representations, only CUs for which their depth levels are smaller or equal to that of the co-located CU in the reference representation are searched. In this way, larger depths are skipped in the search and considerable time is saved.

Following this idea, a similar approach is used for representations with different resolutions [13]. Since the corresponding CTUs in different resolutions cover different areas, they do not match with each other. Therefore, a novel matching algorithm is proposed to obtain block structure information from the high resolution representation with an arbitrary downsampling ratio. This information is then used to skip unnecessary depth searches at lower resolutions.

The two above-mentioned methods are then combined to introduce an efficient multirate encoding method [12]. In addition to CTU depth values, additional information from the reference representation namely *prediction mode, intra mode, and motion vectors* [2] are used to accelerate encoding of lower quality and lower resolution representations.

A double bound approach for limiting possible CU depth values is proposed in [1]. Information from both the highest and the lowest quality representations is used to reduce encoding time-complexity. First, the highest quality representation is encoded with unmodified HEVC, then the information obtained from this encoding is used to encode the lowest quality representation similar to [14]. The remaining intermediate quality representations are encoded with a double bound approach for CU depth search and reference frame selection. In CU depth search, the possible depth level search window is limited by the highest depth value in the lowest quality representation and the lowest depth value in the highest quality representation. In addition, other reference frame searches are skipped if both the highest and the lowest quality representations have the same reference frame. The encoding order of this method is shown in Fig. 4.

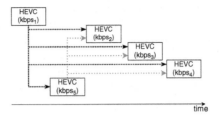

Fig. 4. The framework for the double bound multirate encoding method [1]

In [8], macro-block mode decision and intra/inter prediction information of the highest quality representation are shared with loweer quality representations using VP8.

An approach based on machine learning is proposed in [7]. The highest quality representation is encoded and then a random forest is used to determine which CU structure will be used in encoding lower quality representations. The CTU depth structure in the highest quality representation is used in [5] to limit the maximum depth search level in lower quality representations. If more time-complexity reduction is required, the search at the same CU depth in the corresponding CTU in the reference representation is skipped and searches are only performed at the lower CU depths.

Another approach proposes to first encode the lowest quality representation as the reference representation and then uses its information to limit the search processes while encoding the higher quality representations [9]. During encoding of the reference representation, a per-CTU analysis metadata file is created in addition to the HEVC bitstream itself. The higher quality representations can use this information in the rate-distortion optimization process. This metadata file includes information of CTU quad-tree structure, PU predictions, coding modes, and motion vectors. A similar framework is used in [10] for multiple resolution encoding using AOMedia's AV1. First the lowest resolution is encoded and its information is used to accelerate the higher resolution representations. Block structure similarity between different resolutions is used to determine early rate distortion optimization search termination.

In this paper, the performance of choosing various quality encodings as a reference representation is compared to find the optimal reference representation for parallel encoding.

3   Single Reference Multirate Encoding

3.1   Different Single Reference Multirate Encoding Modes

Several methods in the literature use the depth values of the highest quality encoding as an upper bound to limit the depth values in dependent representations to reduce time-complexity [5,13]. In parallel encoding, the amount of time-complexity reduction in all these approaches is limited by the encoding time of the highest quality representation.

Figure 5 shows the average encoding time-complexity of three different methods, namely *(i)* unmodified HEVC reference software (HM 16.20), *(ii)* single upper depth bound [14] and *(iii)* double bound approach [1] for encoding the video sequences used in this paper. We can see that despite the reduction in the time-complexity of dependent encodings, none of these approaches achieves a reduction in time-complexity of encoding the highest quality representation.

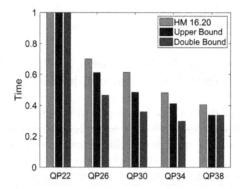

Fig. 5. Time reduction of different methods. Results are normalized average time-complexities for the dataset and resolutions used in this paper.

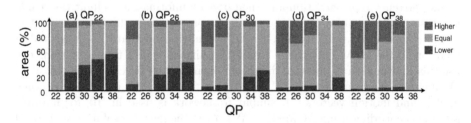

Fig. 6. Percentage of the area with CU depth greater, identical or lower than the reference encoding QPi ((a) QP_{22} (b) QP_{26} (c) QP_{30} (d) QP_{34} (e) QP_{38}).

Finding the relationship between the CU depth levels of different quality encodings can be helpful in understanding the effect of choosing different quality encodings as reference representations. Thus, the 1080p representation of the video sequences used in this paper (cf. Subsect. 3.2) are encoded with the HEVC reference software (HM 16.20). Figure 6 indicates the percentages of the areas with CU depth values smaller, identical, or greater than the corresponding reference representation. With growing QP, dependent representations tend to take larger CUs than co-located CUs in the reference encoding. Consequently, the

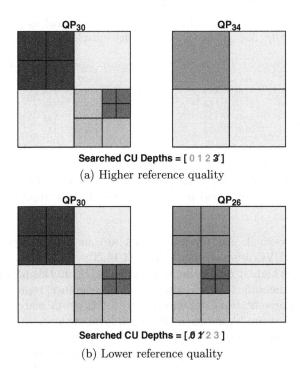

Searched CU Depths = [0 1 2 3̶]

(a) Higher reference quality

Searched CU Depths = [0̶ 1̶ 2 3]

(b) Lower reference quality

Fig. 7. CTU depth elimination example. QP_{30} is the reference representation.

Algorithm 1: CU depth search elimination algorithm.

Input: $QP_{current}$, $QP_{reference}$, CU_{xy}
Output: $Depths$
$Depth_{co} = Depths_{reference}[CU_{xy}]$
if $QP_{current} < QP_{reference}$ **then**
  $\lfloor$ $Depths = [Depth_{co} : 3]$
else if $QP_{current} > QP_{reference}$ **then**
  $\lfloor$ $Depths = [0 : Depth_{co}]$
Return: $Depths$

---

depth values smaller than that of the co-located CU in reference representation can be skipped from the search process. Inversely, for the dependent representations with lower QP than the reference representation, the depth values larger than that of the co-located CU in the reference representation can be skipped from the search process.

Therefore, CU depth search elimination in our experiments is done using the approach as shown in Algorithm 1. CU_{xy} is the location of current CU and $Depth_{co}$ is the depth value of the co-located CU in the reference representation. The elimination process is illustrated in Fig. 7 with an example.

Table 1. BDRate/ΔT for different encoding modes compared to *Mode 0* using the total time-complexity ΔT_t and the maximum time-complexity ΔT_m.

Mode	$BDRate_V$	$BDRate_P$	ΔT_t	$BDRate_V/\Delta T_t$	$BDRate_P/\Delta T_t$	ΔT_m	$BDRate_V/\Delta T_m$	$BDRate_P/\Delta T_m$
Mode 1	0.403	0.427	34.65 %	1.16	1.21	0.00 %	–	–
Mode 2	0.432	0.393	31.97 %	1.35	1.27	16.62 %	2.59	2.36
Mode 3	0.464	0.459	24.17 %	1.68	1.96	18.73 %	2.47	2.45
Mode 4	0.468	0.513	10.71 %	4.36	7.03	13.98 %	3.34	3.66
Mode 5	0.500	0.571	10.08 %	8.33	8.27	12.99 %	3.84	4.39

To find the optimal reference representation, N different encoding modes are selected which may correspond to the number of quality representations (*e.g.*, QPs):

- **Mode 0** (baseline): All representations are encoded independently with unmodified HEVC reference encoder (HM 16.20).
- **Mode 1**: The highest quality representation (QP_{22} in this paper) is encoded first using unmodified HEVC and used as reference representation. The dependent representations are encoded with CU depth search upper bound, *i.e.*, depths that are higher than the depth level of the co-located CU in the reference representation are skipped.
- **Mode 2, 3, ..., $(N-1)$**: One respective intermediate quality representation is encoded first using unmodified HEVC and used as reference representation. The dependent representations are encoded with CU depth search lower or upper bound depending on the quality level: *(i)* for representations with higher QP values than the reference representation, depth levels that are higher than the co-located CU in the reference representation are skipped; *(ii)* for the representations with QPs lower than the reference representation, depth levels that are lower than the co-located CU in the reference representation are skipped.
- **Mode N**: The lowest quality representation (QP_{38} in this paper) is encoded first using unmodified HEVC and used as reference representation. The dependent representations are encoded with CU depth search lower bound.

3.2   Experimental Evaluation

All experiments were conducted in the Google Cloud Compute Engine environment with *n1-highcpu-16* as machine type[1] which runs Ubuntu 18.04 operating system and is equipped with Intel Xeon Skylake vCPU with 16 cores and 14.4GB of memory. We used the following eight video sequences at three different resolutions (*1080p, 720p,* and *360p*) for our experiments: *Basketball Drive (50 fps), Kimono (24 fps), Park Joy, River Run, Blue Sky, River Bed, Rush Hour,* and *Sunflower (25 fps)*. These sequences are representative for a broad range of video

---

[1] https://cloud.google.com/compute/docs/machine-types#n1_machine_types.

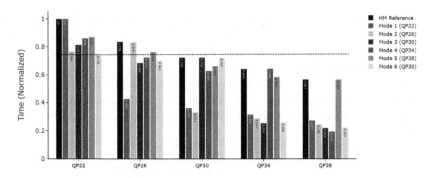

Fig. 8. Normalized average encoding time of different modes. Dotted line indicates the highest time-complexity of *mode 6*. It can be seen that there is at least one representation for each mode that has higher time-complexity compared to *mode 6*.

Table 2. Time reduction of different methods for the highest complexity encoding with BD-VMAF rate.

Mode	$BDRate_V$	$BDRate_P$	ΔT_m	$BDRate_V/\Delta T_m$	$BDRate_P/\Delta T_m$
Mode 3	0.464	0.459	18.73 %	2.47	2.45
Mode 6	0.539	0.504	25.66 %	2.10	1.96

characteristics. The actual encoding parameters are based on the *random access, main* configuration of the HEVC Common Test Conditions (CTC) [4].

The following metrics have been used: *(i)* Bjontegaard delta rate using PSNR (BDR_P), and *(ii)* Bjontegaard delta rate using VMAF (BDR_V). Five QP values are chosen for encoding of the video sequences to obtain multirate representations (*i.e.*, $N = 5$ in this paper): $\{QP_{22}, QP_{26}, QP_{30}, QP_{34}, QP_{38}\}$.

For all experiments, average metrics are obtained by encoding the eight above mentioned video sequences at three different resolutions (*i.e.*, 24 sequences per QP level in total). Each mode is encoded with five different QP values and, thus, the reported average results are averaged over 120 encodings per mode in total.

Table 1 shows the *(i)* BDR_P,*(ii)* BDR_V,*(iii)*reduction in encoding time ΔT, and *(iv)* BDRate/ΔT for different encoding modes compared to *Mode 0*. ΔT indicates the average time difference between encoding the sequences with the HEVC reference software and the corresponding encoding modes. It is calculated as shown in Eq. 1

$$\Delta T_t(mode_x) = \frac{1}{N} \sum_{i=1}^{N=5} 1 - \frac{T_{Mode_x}(QP_i)}{T_{Mode_0}(QP_i)} \qquad (1)$$

where $T_{Mode_x}(QP_i)$ denotes the encoding time-complexity of $Mode_x$ at QP_i. BD-Rate/ΔT is given to demonstrate the effectiveness of the approaches in both time-complexity reduction and bitrate increase. Lower BD-Rate/ΔT means better performance in complexity reduction. From these results, we can see that choosing the reference representation closer to the highest quality increases the total time saving and reduces rate disruption. On the other hand, choosing the reference representation closer to the lowest quality, reduces the average time saving and increases the rate disruption.

To better understand how these methods affect the performance of parallel encoding, the time-complexity reduction for each mode is calculated as Eq. 2 using the maximum time-complexity of each mode instead of its total time-complexity.

$$\Delta T_m(mode_x) = 1 - \frac{\max\limits_{1 \leq i \leq N}(T_{Mode_x}(QP_i))}{\max\limits_{1 \leq i \leq N}(T_{Mode_0}(QP_i))} \tag{2}$$

The simulation results for parallel encoding are given in Table 1 using VMAF and PSNR as objective metrics. This table is reported since the overall time-complexity reduction of the parallel encoding scenario is bounded by the highest time-complexity encoding which causes the bottleneck in the framework. It can be seen that choosing QP_{30} as the reference representation gives the most time-complexity reduction (18.73 %) and lowest BD-Rate/ΔT (2.47) using VMAF as the objective metric in terms of parallel encoding with a slight overall bitrate increase.

4   Improved Encoding Mode

Based on the results provided above, we propose to first encode the *middle quality representation* using the unmodified HEVC reference software and then encode dependent representations using the information obtained during this encoding.

Since the reference representation does not have the highest time-complexity, further information can be used in addition to limiting the depth values to accelerate encoding the highest time-complexity representation. Thus, we propose to use intra/inter prediction mode. Therefore, the proposed intra/inter prediction mode is applied only to encode QP_{22} as applying this to other dependent representations results in quality degradation while having no impact on the highest time-complexity. In order to reduce time-complexity of the QP_{22} even more, the *intra* mode is skipped for a CU when its co-located CU in the reference representation has been *inter* coded.

The percentage of inter coded CUs in QP_{22} when their co-located CU in QP_{30} have been encoded in inter mode is 94.3%. It is clear that the majority of the CUs are *inter* coded if their co-located CU has been *inter* encoded in the reference representation. Therefore, the *intra* coding can be skipped for the CUs when their co-located CU in the reference representation has been *inter* encoded without causing noticeable degradation. Our improved encoding method is defined as follows:

– **Mode M** (*i.e.*, $N+1$ and *Mode 6* for the actual implementation used in this paper): The middle quality representation $M/2$ (*i.e.*, QP_{30}) is encoded first using unmodified HEVC and used as reference representation. The dependent representations are encoded with CU depth search lower or upper bound depending on the quality level. Moreover, if *inter* coding mode is used in middle quality representation (QP_{30}), *intra* search is skipped while encoding the highest quality representation (QP_{22}).

Figure 8 shows the encoding times for the different encoding modes in order to better illustrate the parallel encoding performance of choosing different reference representations. The results have been summarized in Table 2. We can observe that using the improved Mode N (*Mode 6*), decreases BD-Rate/ΔT metric significantly. Thus, the improved mode can be efficiently used to encode all representations in parallel.

It can be seen in Fig. 8 that *Mode 2* achieves the most reduction in the time-complexity of QP_{22}. However, encoding QP_{26} (*i.e.*, the reference representation) takes more time, thus QP_{22} is not the most time-complex encoding in that scenario. Therefore, using *Mode 3* with QP_{30} as reference representation results in the most reduction in the highest time-complexity encoding (*i.e.*, QP_{22}).

5   Conclusion

In this paper, we investigated different approaches for efficient multirate encoding with respect to parallel encoding performance. Therefore, different quality encodings are chosen as reference representation and possible CU depth searches are eliminated while encoding remaining, dependent representations. Several experiments are conducted to measure the effect of choosing different quality levels as the reference representation. Based on these results we proposed an improved method by using the middle quality representation as the reference representation, which achieves the best overall results in terms of encoding time-complexity including significant improvements while encoding the highest quality representation (25.66% compared to unmodified HEVC reference software).

Acknowledgment. This research has been supported in part by the *Christian Doppler Laboratory ATHENA* (https://athena.itec.aau.at/).

References

1. Amirpour, H., Çetinkaya, E., Timmerer, C., Ghanbari, M.: Fast multi-rate encoding for adaptive http streaming. In: 2020 Data Compression Conference (DCC), pp. 358–358 (2020)
2. Amirpour, H., Ghanbari, M., Pinheiro, A., Pereira, M.: Motion estimation with chessboard pattern prediction strategy. Multimed. Tools Appli. **78**(15), 21785–21804 (2019)
3. Bentaleb, A., Taani, B., Begen, A.C., Timmerer, C., Zimmermann, R.: A survey on bitrate adaptation schemes for streaming media over http. IEEE Commun. Surv. Tutorials **21**(1), 562–585 (2019)
4. Bossen, F., et al.: Common test conditions and software reference configurations. JCTVC-L1100 12, 7 (2013)

5. Bubolz, T.L.A., Conceição, R.A., Grellert, M., Agostini, L., Zatt, B., Correa, G.: Quality and energy-aware HEVC transrating based on machine learning. IEEE Trans. Circuits Syst. I Regul. Pap. **66**(6), 2124–2136 (2019). https://doi.org/10.1109/TCSI.2019.2903978
6. Cisco: cisco visual networking index: forecast and methodology, 2017–2022 (White Paper) (2019)
7. De Praeter, J., et al.: Fast simultaneous video encoder for adaptive streaming. In: 2015 IEEE 17th International Workshop on Multimedia Signal Processing (MMSP), pp. 1–6, October 2015. https://doi.org/10.1109/MMSP.2015.7340802
8. Finstad, D.H., Stensland, H.K., Espeland, H., Halvorsen, P.: Improved multi-rate video encoding. In: 2011 IEEE International Symposium on Multimedia, pp. 293–300, December 2011. https://doi.org/10.1109/ISM.2011.53
9. Goswami, K., et al.: Adaptive multi-resolution encoding for ABR streaming. In: 2018 25th IEEE International Conference on Image Processing (ICIP), pp. 1008–1012, October 2018. https://doi.org/10.1109/ICIP.2018.8451485
10. Guo, B., Han, Y., Wen, J.: Fast block structure determination in Av1-based multiple resolutions video encoding. In: 2018 IEEE International Conference on Multimedia and Expo (ICME), pp. 1–6, July 2018. https://doi.org/10.1109/ICME.2018.8486492
11. Kim, I., Min, J., Lee, T., Han, W., Park, J.: Block partitioning structure in the HEVC standard. IEEE Trans. Circuits Syst. Video Technol. **22**(12), 1697–1706 (2012)
12. Schroeder, D., Ilangovan, A., Reisslein, M., Steinbach, E.: Efficient multi-rate video encoding for HEVC-based adaptive HTTP streaming. IEEE Trans. Circuits Syst. Video Technol. **28**(1), 143–157 (2018). https://doi.org/10.1109/TCSVT.2016.2599028
13. Schroeder, D., Ilangovan, A., Steinbach, E.: Multi-rate encoding for HEVC-based adaptive http streaming with multiple resolutions. In: 2015 IEEE 17th International Workshop on Multimedia Signal Processing (MMSP), pp. 1–6, October 2015. https://doi.org/10.1109/MMSP.2015.7340822
14. Schroeder, D., Rehm, P., Steinbach, E.: Block structure reuse for multi-rate high efficiency video coding. In: 2015 IEEE International Conference on Image Processing (ICIP), pp. 3972–3976, September 2015. https://doi.org/10.1109/ICIP.2015.7351551
15. Sodagar, I.: The MPEG-DASH standard for multimedia streaming over the internet. IEEE Multimed. **18**(4), 62–67 (2011). https://doi.org/10.1109/MMUL.2011.71
16. Sullivan, G.J., Ohm, J.R., Han, W.J., Wiegand, T.: Overview of the high efficiency video coding (HEVC) standard. IEEE Trans. Circuits Syst. Video Technol. **22**(12), 1649–1668 (2012)
17. Wiegand, T., Sullivan, G.J., Bjontegaard, G., Luthra, A.: Overview of the h.264/AVC video coding standard. IEEE Trans. Circuits Syst. Video Technol. **13**(7), 560–576 (2003)
18. Zaccarin, A., Boon-lock yeo: multi-rate encoding of a video sequence in the DCT domain. In: 2002 IEEE International Symposium on Circuits and Systems. Proceedings (Cat. No.02CH37353), vol. 2, pp. II-II, May 2002. https://doi.org/10.1109/ISCAS.2002.1011444
19. Çetinkaya, E., Amirpour, H., Timmerer, C., Ghanbari, M.: FaME-ML: fast multirate encoding for HTTP adaptive streaming using machine learning. In: 2020 IEEE International Conference on Visual Communications and Image Processing (VCIP) (2020)

Fast Mode Decision Algorithm for Intra Encoding of the 3rd Generation Audio Video Coding Standard

Shengyuan Wu[1,2], Zhenyu Wang[1,2], Yangang Cai[1,2], and Ronggang Wang[1,2(✉)]

[1] Peking University Shenzhen Graduate School, Shenzhen, China
{wsyuan,caiyangang}@pku.edu.cn, {wangzhenyu,rgwang}@pkusz.edu.cn
[2] Pengcheng Laboratory, Shenzhen, China

Abstract. The baseline profile of the third-generation Audio Video coding Standard (AVS3) was issued in March 2019, and achieves 23.52% BD-rate saving at the cost of doubled encoding time compared with AVS2, saves approximately 22% bitrate with over 7 times complexity compared with HEVC. uAVS3e works as the open source encoder for AVS3 baseline profile and has achieved almost 50 times encoding speed-up with 1.81% BD-rate loss when compared with the reference software of AVS3 (HPM4.0). In order to further reduce the complexity of AVS3 intra encoder, this paper proposed three speed-up strategies, including progressive rough mode search, sharing candidates among different prediction units (PU) and constraints on modes number of rate distortion optimization (RDO) based on statistics. The experimental results show that, the fast algorithms bring about 2 times encoding speed with 0.96% BD-rate loss under All Intra configuration.

Keywords: Intra prediction · Fast algorithm · AVS3 · uAVS3e

1 Introduction

AVS3 is the third-generation audio and video coding standard formulated by the AVS working group of China, and the baseline profile was completed on March 9, 2019, which achieves 23.52% BD-rate savings with doubled encoding time compared with AVS2 and approximately 22% BD-rate saving with over 7 times [1] complexity compared with HEVC [2].

AVS3 intra encoder can be divided into two major parts: rough mode decision (RMD) and rate distortion optimization (RDO) selection. In the RMD stage, it is necessary to calculate 33 intra modes, including performing a relatively simple Hadamard transform and then obtaining the value of SATD cost to approximate the rate distortion of the mode in the real RDO process. Five or four (mainly decided by aspect ratio) intra modes with the smallest SATD cost would be selected after RMD, which is used as the candidate modes for RDO to calculate, and a series of decision-making processes such as complex DCT transform

© Springer Nature Switzerland AG 2021
J. Lokoč et al. (Eds.): MMM 2021, LNCS 12572, pp. 481–492, 2021.
https://doi.org/10.1007/978-3-030-67832-6_39

and quantization are performed in RDO. Figure 1 provides a simple illustration to show the time-consuming distribution of Intra encoding as a reference. The testing video sequence is BQMall with the QP 35 under all-intra constraint.

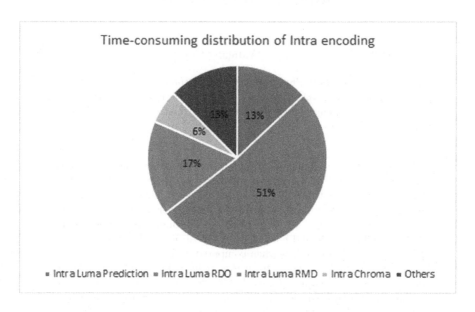

Fig. 1. Time-consuming distribution of Intra encoding.

According to statistics, the most time-consuming module is the RDO selection process, which accounts for more than 50% of the encoding time, followed by the RMD, which accounts for nearly 20% of the encoding time. Our acceleration strategies mainly lie in the two parts.

From the point of encoding tools, there are two main intra tools in AVS3, one is Derived Tree named DT [3] and the other is Intra Prediction Filter called IPF [4]. DT is a type of PU partition inherited from AVS2. Specifically, a CU in intra analysis used to be a whole PU (SIZE_2N×2N), which is taken as the basic unit of prediction. DT adds several PU types for CU to choose from. To be exact, it includes 2 symmetrical types: SIZE_2N×hN (2N × 0.5N), SIZE_hN×2N (0.5N × 2N) and 4 asymmetrical types: SIZE_2N×nU (2N × (N/2) + 2N × (3N/2)), SIZE_2N×nD (2N × (3N/2) + 2N × (N/2)), SIZE_nL×2N ((N/2) × 2N + (3N/2) × 2N) and SIZE_nR×2N ((3N/2) × 2N + (N/2) × 2N) (illustrated in Fig. 2). These new partitioning types of PU provide more flexible blocks for intra prediction, and shorten the prediction distance, bringing in BD-rate gain. The tool-off test for DT under All Intra (AI) configuration tells that the BD-rate would ascend by 0.69% with about 34% time going down. In the following paragraphs, we use DT-PU to represent all DT types of PU.

The intra prediction filter is designed to filter the boundary of the intra prediction block, so as to mitigate the distortion of the prediction block.

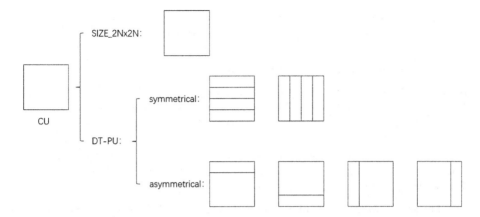

Fig. 2. The PU type of SIZE_2N×2N and derived tree.

The main idea is to further utilize the potential relationship between the reference pixels and the predicted pixels by filtering the predicted pixels according to the reference pixels. Fast algorithms should take the actual implementation method into account. Because the time complexity brought by the DT-PU is too large, IPF would not be operated on the DT-PU. When IPF is allowed in the current CU, only the SIZE_2N×2N block will perform complete calculations in both cases of no filtering and filtering, decide the optimal mode respectively, and finally compare the costs to determine whether current PU take the advantage of IPF or not. The tool-off test for IPF under AI configuration demonstrates it would save time by 26% while the BD-rate would go up by 1.16%.

G. Chen et al. [5] achieved predominant direction by calculating gradient histogram of current PU, in this way, prediction modes could be reduced. H. Zhang et al. [6] designed the progressive Rough Mode Search method which checks mode step by step with different search range, thereby reducing the count of modes checked by rough mode decision. Minghai Wang et al. [7] presented a method to improve candidate mode list based on the probability of the candidate modes to be selected as the best prediction mode. [8] propose fast intra prediction method based on characteristics to adaptively remove mode candidates. [9] decreases computational complexity based on texture complexity. [10] reduces modes calculation on the basis of texture direction. The information of adjacent PUs is made full use to cut-off mode decision complexity by [11].

This paper proposes acceleration strategies on AVS3 intra encoder and the remainder of this paper is organized as follows: Sect. 2 presents the speed-up methods. Experimental results, and analysis are shown in Sect. 3. Section 4 concludes this paper.

2   Acceleration Strategies

Based on the performance and complexity analysis on intra prediction in the previous section, RMD and RDO are the most time-consuming parts in intra encoding process. Therefore, the acceleration strategies of this article are mainly designed to reduce the complexity of RMD and RDO processes.

2.1 Progressive Rough Mode Search

In the rough mode selection process of intra prediction, the progressive Rough Mode Search (pRMS) method [6] was experimentally verified to be very efficient in [12] on AVS2, and this paper borrows the same idea of pRMS. Additionally, most probable modes (MPMs) are considered after the pRMS process. The core of pRMS is to first search intra modes coarsely in a wide range with a large step, and then shorten the search step and try to find the best mode progressively. The search process is described as followed:

(1) The search range of the first step: including DC, PLANAR, BILINEAR and 7 angular modes, 0,1,2,6,10,14,18,22,26,30, from which the strategy selects seven modes with the better SATD cost for the second step;
(2) The search range in the second step: according to the seven modes output in the first step, collect the angular modes with a distance of 2 among them. and select the 3 optimal SATD cost modes for the third step search;
(3) The search modes range of the third step: According to the three modes output in the second step, collect and calculate the angular modes with a distance of 1 among them.

Given that MPMs are very likely to be the best intra mode, it is necessary to check whether MPMs have been calculated during the pRMS search process. If not, the SATD cost of the MPMs are evaluated and may be included into RDO list according to SATD cost.

2.2 Shared Intra Mode RDO Candidates List

Based on the analysis in Sect. 1, Derived Tree (DT) and Intra Prediction Filter (IPF), have a great impact on the complexity of intra prediction. DT can achieve a BD-rate gain of 0.69% and a time increase of 34%, while IPF provides a BD-rate gain of 1.16% and a time cost of 26%.

In order to further exploiting the correlation between candidates list under different cases, this paper made some statistics. Figure 3 shows the correlation of candidate lists between different intra PUs.

The probability of IPF candidates coinciding with the non-IPF candidates of SIZE_2N×2N is 78% on average. This indicates a high similarity of intra mode candidates between IPF and non-IPF cases. Therefore, we can reuse the intra mode candidates of IPF-off case as the RDO candidates when IPF is on. In this case, the RMD process for IPF-on case can be skipped. On the other hand, from Fig. 3 it can be seen that only about 42% of the DT-PU candidates overlap with candidates of SIZE_2N×2N non-IPF cases (Although the probability of coincidence of the latter is not very high, we still conducted the following substitution experiments, the reasons would be given in Sect. 3.2).

Since MPMs have a quite high hitting rate in intra mode decision, MPMs will be used to replace some unlikely modes in the candidate list.

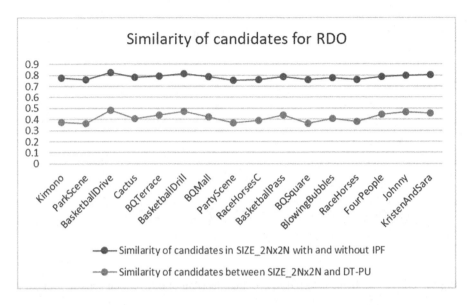

Fig. 3. Blue line presents the similarity of intra modes selected by RMD between two cases of SIZE_2N×2N in the same block CU, with and without IPF, orange line shows the similarity of intra prediction modes in the candidate lists selected by the DT-PU and the SIZE_2N×2N-type PU without IPF in the same CU. (Color figure online)

2.3 RDO Count Constraints

In addition to acceleration of the RMD process, the optimization of RDO is also investigated in this paper. The probability of blocks being selected with different size varies much in the final bitstream. Generally, if the texture of an area in the picture is particularly complex, then it is more likely to be divided into small blocks. For complex contents, we can reduce the number of candidate modes for RDO in the larger blocks, and provide more modes to RDO in the smaller ones. However, how to make precise constraints of the candidate number for RDO needs to be designed based on detailed statistical results.

Figure 4 shows the selection rate of different CU sizes in bitstreams of different QPs. The line chart also distinguishes DT-PU and SIZE_2N×2N PU. It can be seen the probability of DT-PU being selected in bitstream is relatively low when compared to SIZE_2N×2N. According to the line chart, a key point is first clarified that the RDO candidate count constraints here need to be designed corresponding to different QPs, because the selection rate of the same CU size in various QPs is rather different. For example, the same CU size of 4 × 4 here, the probability of being selected in bitstream is 5% when QP is 45, while the probability of being selected is 16% when QP is 27. Actually, it is also easy to understand, because the smaller the QP is, the richer the texture should be. And as a result, the CU partition would have a deeper depth, small CU would take a large proportion in the final bitstream.

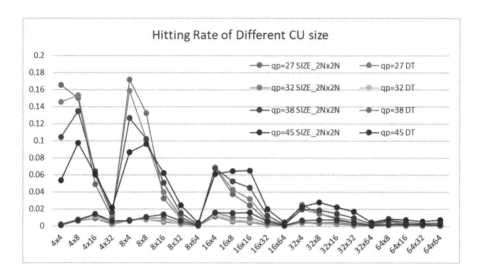

Fig. 4. The rate of being selected in the final decision of different cu sizes in four QPs.

In previous method, blocks of different sizes would be designed certain numbers for acceleration without taking QP into consideration. In this paper, different RDO candidate numbers are used for different CU sizes in different QPs. In order to enable the probability directly to guide the design of the candidate number of RDO, this strategy maps the probability to the corresponding counts interval. The original scheme on uAVS3e is to implement a simple limit on the number of RDO candidates. For CU with an aspect ratio equal to 1:4 or 1:8, only four candidates are supplied to RDO, and five for other CUs. This paper takes $(1, 5)$ as the mapping interval, assume the maximum probability of being selected is p, and the candidates count of CU size with the probability falling on $(1/2p, p)$ is set to 5, $(1/4p, 1/2p)$ is set to 4, $(1/8p, 1/4p)$ is set to 3, $(1/16p, 1/8p)$ is set to 2, and if the probability below $1/16p$, the count would be set to 1.

3   Experimental Results and Analysis

The experiments are all carried out on the open source platform, uAVS3e. uAVS3e [13] is the open source encoder for the baseline profile of AVS3. uAVS3e is designed to optimize the standard reference software High-Performance Model (HPM) [14,15], and maintained by the research team led by Professor Ronggang Wang. The main contributors include Peking University Shenzhen Graduate School, Peng Cheng Laboratory and Guangdong Bohua UHD Innovation Corporation. Currently, uAVS3e adopts wave-front parallel coding scheme (WPP), frame-level parallel algorithms, and assembly instruction optimization for key coding modules. By the end of June, 2020, uAVS3e has achieved nearly 50 times encoding speed compared with HPM4.0. In terms of compression efficiency, it brings 1.81% BD-rate loss for Y component, 16.03% BD-rate gain for U component and 19.51% gain for V component. In other words, if the YUV components are calculated in the ratio of 4:1:1, a comprehensive BD-rate gain of nearly 5% can be obtained.

The following experiments keep in accordance with the common test condition of AVS3. More specifically, 10s frames with a sampling ratio at 8 under All Intra configuration (AI) is used. All tests are conducted at the QPs of 27,32,38,45. The following subsections show the experimental results and analysis of the proposed fast algorithms under AI configuration. All the tables will provide the speed-up ratio directly, and time saving (TS) can be calculated as follows:

$$TS = \left(1 - \frac{1}{Speedupratio}\right) * 100\% \tag{1}$$

3.1 Progressive Rough Mode Search

Table 1 shows that pRMS with MPM checking can achieves 15% time saving with average 0.10% BD-rate loss. Based on the above description, the first search step requires a calculation of 10 modes.

Table 1. Time savings and BD-rate loss of pRMS with AI configuration.

Class	Sequence	BDrate (Y)	BDrate (U)	BDrate (V)	Speedup ratio
B	Kimono	0.05%	0.01%	−0.06%	1.22×
	ParkScene	0.05%	−0.11%	−0.06%	1.18×
	BasketballDrive	0.12%	0.08%	0.06%	1.21×
	Cactus	0.08%	0.17%	0.23%	1.18×
	BQTerrace	0.17%	0.26%	0.22%	1.16×
C	BasketballDrill	0.23%	0.21%	0.55%	1.17×
	BQMall	0.04%	0.05%	0.11%	1.17×
	PartyScene	0.07%	0.00%	0.11%	1.14×
	RaceHorsesC	0.06%	0.09%	−0.11%	1.16×
D	BasketballPass	0.17%	0.35%	0.33%	1.18×
	BQSquare	0.11%	0.16%	0.14%	1.13×
	BlowingBubbles	0.10%	0.01%	−0.19%	1.15×
	RaceHorses	0.06%	0.22%	−0.08%	1.15×
E	FourPeople	0.09%	−0.11%	0.09%	1.19×
	Johnny	0.10%	0.14%	0.31%	1.21×
	KristenAndSara	0.12%	0.03%	0.08%	1.20×
Average		0.10%	0.10%	0.11%	1.17×

The worst case is hit if the first step selects 7 angular modes. Because it means the largest search range for the second step. All the angular modes in step 1 have neighboring modes with distance of 2. When forming the searching mode list of step 2, some adjacent modes would overlap, for instance, the adjacent modes of mode 6 with a distance of 2 are mode 4 and mode 8, while mode 8 and mode 12 for mode 10, so in the worst case 8 modes need to be calculated in step 2. In the third step is that the 3 modes offered by step 2 is 3 non-adjacent angular modes, which means 6 modes need to be calculated. In the process of checking MPMs, the worst is that they are both not calculated before.

For the best case, the number of angular modes provided by step 1 is the least, so it's 4 angular modes except for 3 special modes (0,1,2), and step 2 would calculate 5 modes at least. In the process of checking MPMs, the best is that they both have been calculated.

In summary, 26 modes need to be calculated in the worst case, and 15 modes need to be calculated in the best case. As a result, RMD time can be greatly reduced.

3.2   Shared Intra Mode RDO Candidates List

Table 2 compares the performance and time complexity between the anchor and sharing candidates. In this method, we reuse the candidate list of SIZE_2N×2N PU selected by rough mode decision process when don't use IPF as the RDO candidate modes of SIZE_2N×2N PU with IPF on and different PU types in DT.

Table 2. Time savings and BD-rate loss of shared candidates list with AI configuration

Class	Sequence	BDrate (Y)	BDrate (U)	BDrate (V)	Speedup ratio
B	Kimono	−0.25%	0.17%	0.19%	1.42×
	ParkScene	−0.03%	0.82%	0.55%	1.41×
	BasketballDrive	−0.01%	0.46%	0.44%	1.43×
	Cactus	0.28%	0.77%	0.89%	1.45×
	BQTerrace	0.18%	0.62%	0.79%	1.42×
C	BasketballDrill	0.73%	0.92%	1.13%	1.44×
	BQMall	0.22%	0.83%	0.96%	1.39×
	PartyScene	0.23%	0.61%	0.65%	1.42×
	RaceHorsesC	0.20%	0.39%	0.60%	1.39×
D	BasketballPass	0.34%	1.12%	0.49%	1.42×
	BQSquare	0.53%	0.78%	0.90%	1.42×
	BlowingBubbles	0.41%	0.89%	0.67%	1.40×
	RaceHorses	0.35%	0.67%	0.40%	1.41×
E	FourPeople	0.35%	1.17%	1.44%	1.43×
	Johnny	0.30%	1.24%	1.11%	1.49×
	KristenAndSara	0.37%	0.85%	0.84%	1.45×
Average		0.26%	0.77%	0.75%	1.42×

The results show that when the candidate list selected by RMD of SIZE_2N×2N without IPF is shared between these different PUs, a large part of the rough selection time can be cut off. On this basis, in order to reduce the possibility of a more reliable mode being replaced, we check whether the MPMs exist in the candidate list before performing the real RDO process. The selection rate of MPMs is relatively high, so if MPM does not exist, this acceleration strategy will substitute MPM for one or two modes at the end of the candidate list, which is less likely to be selected by the RDO process. Through these ideas, this strategy of sharing the candidate list can save time by 29.6% and the BD-rate will increase by 0.26%.

According to the statistical results of Sect. 2.2, the candidates obtained by rough selection with DT-type PU do not match with the candidate lists obtained by SIZE_2N×2N well. However, in the method of sharing the candidate list, it still decides to share modes with the DT-PU. It can be easily observed that the proportion of DT-PU is very low in bitstream from the statistical results in Sect. 2.3. Consequently, the loss due to the low overlap rate of the candidate list has been alleviated.

3.3 RDO Count Constraints

Table 3 demonstrates the encoding time declines by 17% under the RDO count constraint strategy while the BD-rate escalates by 0.51%.

Table 3. Time savings and BD-rate loss of constraints on RDO mode counts with AI configuration

Class	Sequence	BDrate (Y)	BDrate (U)	BDrate (V)	Speedup ratio
B	Kimono	1.11%	1.02%	0.87%	1.13×
	ParkScene	0.52%	1.05%	0.56%	1.21×
	BasketballDrive	1.12%	1.13%	1.22%	1.19×
	Cactus	0.42%	0.60%	0.67%	1.21×
	BQTerrace	0.26%	0.64%	0.76%	1.23×
C	BasketballDrill	0.38%	0.38%	0.46%	1.19×
	BQMall	0.37%	0.44%	0.62%	1.22×
	PartyScene	0.19%	0.34%	0.27%	1.26×
	RaceHorsesC	0.23%	0.31%	0.35%	1.21×
D	BasketballPass	0.63%	0.34%	0.33%	1.21×
	BQSquare	0.23%	0.01%	0.15%	1.24×
	BlowingBubbles	0.43%	0.30%	0.22%	1.23×
	RaceHorses	0.31%	0.21%	−0.24%	1.22×
E	FourPeople	0.57%	0.83%	1.03%	1.19×
	Johnny	0.70%	0.77%	0.85%	1.18×
	KristenAndSara	0.59%	0.63%	0.78%	1.17×
Average		0.51%	0.56%	0.56%	1.21×

Constraints on the number of candidate modes for RDO is a very intuitive way to reduce the encoding time complexity, because RDO process is the most time-consuming module according to the analysis in Sect. 1.

However, the cost performance ratio is not particularly high by applying previous method to uAVS3e, which restricts fixed count of modes for RDO for every square CU block with size of 4 × 4, 8 × 8, 16 × 16, 32 × 32, 64 × 64. The phenomenon is mainly caused by two reasons. The first is the multiple tree partitioning structure adopted by AVS3, which not only includes square blocks under Quad-tree partitioning, but also rectangular blocks obtained by Binary-Tree and Extended Quad-Tree partitioning. The other is the influence brought about by QP.

As mentioned in Sect. 1, the number of intra modes used for RDO is 4 or 5 in the original setting. So it's natural to cut off the most unlikely modes according to the selecting rate of every position in candidates list, but the experiments results demonstrate the selecting rate is not enough to guide the constraints for RDO reduction. The key point is how to balance the loss and time-saving. The strategy of constraints on RDO modes count in this article mainly relies on the statistics of the decoder to acquire the probability of each block size being selected, and also take the influence of different QP into account. The impact of different QPs on the proportion of different block sizes in the bitstream is very large from the statistical result. Finally, fast trick based on the feature does work in intra encoding for time saving.

3.4   Overall Performance

Table 4 shows the experiment result of combining the above three acceleration strategies. The comprehensive acceleration strategy can bring 50% time saving and with a 0.96% BD-rate loss.

There is an inherent interaction between these three tools. On the one hand, pRMS weakens the accuracy of rough selection, which has an effect on the correctness of the shared candidate list, and further influences the RDO decision of PU that receive the shared candidate list. pRMS and the shared mode list together lower the accuracy of the rough selection stage, so the candidate modes sent to RDO may not be precise enough. Therefore, the accuracy of the final mode is further reduced after the number of RDO modes is limited. On the other hand, pRMS can speed up all PUs originally, but after sharing the candidate lists, most PUs no longer have the rough selection process, so pRMS only works with time saving for the rough mode decision process of SIZE_2N×2N without IPF. And the method to limit the count of RDO candidates directly reduces the count of RDO for all PUs, resulting in encoding time reduction.

In fact, uAVS3e is in development stage, and the code version is constantly updated. Its ultimate goal is to establish a complete set of compression speed levels control that can meet the needs of different application scenarios. At present, it mainly focuses on the low speed level with small BD-rate loss in exchange for more time saving. In the higher-speed version, DT-PU will be turned off. As a result, the time savings brought by the above three speed-up strategies will be greater.

Table 4. Overall performance with All Intra configuration

Class	Sequence	BDrate (Y)	BDrate (U)	BDrate (V)	Speedup ratio
B	Kimono	0.76%	1.86%	1.59%	1.97×
	ParkScene	0.35%	2.32%	1.58%	1.97×
	BasketballDrive	1.77%	2.92%	2.88%	2.08×
	Cactus	0.83%	1.88%	2.20%	1.99×
	BQTerrace	0.67%	1.91%	2.22%	1.97×
C	BasketballDrill	1.54%	2.58%	3.01%	2.07×
	BQMall	0.79%	1.85%	1.88%	1.99×
	PartyScene	0.41%	1.12%	1.05%	1.95×
	RaceHorsesC	0.51%	1.11%	1.26%	1.94×
D	BasketballPass	1.33%	2.30%	1.72%	2.03×
	BQSquare	0.84%	1.07%	1.28%	1.99×
	BlowingBubbles	0.85%	1.54%	1.55%	1.97×
	RaceHorses	0.80%	1.11%	0.76%	1.96×
E	FourPeople	1.08%	2.95%	3.22%	2.04×
	Johnny	1.52%	2.71%	3.05%	2.09×
	KristenAndSara	1.40%	2.34%	2.79%	2.04×
Average		0.96%	1.97%	2.00%	2.00×

4   Conclusion

This paper proposes several fast algorithms for AVS3 intra encoder, including fast mode decision, sharing candidate list, restricting RDO mode counts. The effectiveness of these algorithms is verified on uAVS3e, the open source encoder of baseline profile of AVS3. The experimental result show that the proposed algorithms can double encoding speed at the cost of 0.96% BD-rate loss under AI configuration.

Acknowledgements. Thanks to National Natural Science Foundation of China 61672063 and 61902008, Shenzhen Research Projects of JCYJ20180503182128089 and 201806080921419290.

References

1. Fan, K., et al.: Performance and computational complexity analysis of coding tools in AVS3. In: IEEE International Conference on Multimedia & Expo Workshops (ICMEW), pp. 1–6. IEEE (2020)
2. Sullivan, G.J., Ohm, J.R., Han, W.J., Wiegand, T.: Overview of the high efficiency video coding (HEVC) standard. IEEE Trans. Circ. Syst. Video Technol. **22**(12), 1649–1668 (2012)

3. Wang, L., Niu, B., Wei, Z., Xiao, H., He, Y.: CE1: Derived Mode. AVS workgroup Doc. M4540 (2018)
4. Fan, K., Wang, R., Li, G., Gao, W.: Efficient prediction methods with enhanced spatial-temporal correlation for HEVC. IEEE Trans. Circ. Syst. Video Technol. **29**(12), 3716–3728 (2018)
5. Chen, G., Liu, Z., Ikenaga, T., Wang, D.: Fast HEVC intra mode decision using matching edge detector and kernel density estimation alike histogram generation. In: IEEE International Symposium on Circuits and Systems (ISCAS), pp. 53–56. IEEE (2013)
6. Zhang, H., Ma, Z.: Fast intra mode decision for high efficiency video coding (HEVC). IEEE Trans. Circ. Syst. Video Technol. **24**(4), 660–668 (2013)
7. Wang, M., Wei, H., Fang, Y., Song, Y., Zhuang, Z.: Fast mode selection algorithm for HEVC intra encoder. In: IEEE International Conference on Automation, Electronics and Electrical Engineering (AUTEEE), pp. 169–172. IEEE (2018)
8. Zhang, M., Zhao, C., Xu, J.: An adaptive fast intra mode decision in HEVC. In: 19th IEEE International Conference on Image Processing, pp. 221–224. IEEE (2012)
9. Zhang, Q., Zhao, Y., Zhang, W., Sun, L., Su, R.: Efficient intra mode decision for low complexity HEVC screen content compression. PLOS One **14**(12), e0226900 (2019)
10. Zhang, Q., Wang, Y., Huang, L., Jiang, B.: Fast CU partition and intra mode decision method for H. 266/VVC. IEEE Access **8**, 117539–117550 (2020)
11. Shang, X., Wang, G., Fan, T., Li, Y.: Fast CU size decision and PU mode decision algorithm in HEVC intra coding. In: IEEE International Conference on Image Processing (ICIP), pp. 1593–1597. IEEE (2015)
12. Fan, K., Wang, R., Wang, Z., Li, G., Gao, W.: iAVS2: a fast intra-encoding platform for IEEE 1857.4. IEEE Trans. Circ. Syst. Video Technol. **27**(12), 2726–2738 (2016)
13. https://github.com/uavs3/uavs3e
14. https://gitlab.com/AVS3_Software/hpm
15. Fan, K., et al.: HPM: new reference software platform for AVS3. AVS workgroup Doc. M4510 (2018)

Graph Structure Reasoning Network for Face Alignment and Reconstruction

Xing Wang, Xinyu Li, and Suping Wu[✉]

School of Information Engineering, Ningxia University, Yinchuan 750021, China
wx_nxu@163.com, lxy_nxu@163.com, wspg123@163.com

Abstract. In the unconstrained scene, a large amount of self-occlusion and large poses occurs in the face. These occluded points lead to a huge challenge in face alignment and reconstruction. When performing 3DMM parameter regression, existing face alignment and reconstruction methods only consider reducing the error between the predicted point and the real point, which learn the relevant apparent information but ignore the face geometric contour structure information. Therefore, this paper proposes a graph structure reasoning network for face alignment and reconstruction. By constructing a contour map of the face structure with nose tip as the anchor, the errors between the predictably and actually established maps are optimized. When there is a large pose or occlusion, the neural network can infer the position of the invisible landmark through the contextual information of the visible landmark. Thus, the neural network effectively extracts the structural information of the human face and makes inference on the invisible points. Our GSRN has achieved significant results in both the face alignment and face reconstruction on the AFLW2000-3D and AFLW datasets.

Keywords: Face alignment · Face reconstruction · Graph structure reasoning network

1 Introduction

3D face reconstruction [1,2] and face alignment [3–5] are two basic and highly related topics in computer vision. In recent decades, research in these two fields has promoted each other. Blanz et al. [6] proposed a 3D deformable model (3DMM) of a 3D human face based on principal component analysis (PCA). 3DMM is a statistical parameter model which includes shape and texture parameters, and shape parameters include identity parameters and expression parameters. It approximates a three-dimensional human face as a linear combination of basic shapes and textures. It can handle 2D face images better with different poses and illumination. However, when the human face is under strong light or

This work was supported in part by the National Science Foundation of China under Grant 62062056, and in part by the Natural Science Foundation of China under Grant 61662059.

ⓒ Springer Nature Switzerland AG 2021
J. Lokoč et al. (Eds.): MMM 2021, LNCS 12572, pp. 493–505, 2021.
https://doi.org/10.1007/978-3-030-67832-6_40

has a large pose, there is a large amount of invisible apparent information, which causes a large error in the combined parameters of regression. Lei Jiang et al. [7] proposed a dual attention mechanism for moving dense networks for 3DMM parameter regression. DAMD-Net is a dual attention mechanism and an efficient end-to-end 3D face alignment framework. Through deep separable convolution, tightly connected convolution, and lightweight channel attention mechanism, a stable network model is established. Although this network improves the accuracy of 3DMM regression in the face landmark and reconstruction, this method only focuses on the learning of the apparent information of the face but ignores the geometric structure information of the face. In the case of extremely large poses, the effects of illumination and a large pose can degrade network performance. In order to solve the effects of illumination and large poses in extreme environments, Lee et al. [8], Qu et al. [9], and Liu et al. [10] proposed to discard landmarks that are self-occluded in large poses. It is processed as missing data to effectively extract the apparent information of the face model, thereby improving the accuracy of the regression. This method only enhances the apparent information of the face and does not consider the geometrical structure information of the face. Feng et al. [11] believed that the changes in the position of 3D face landmark are consistent with the changes in 3D face reconstruction shape, thus, they proposed the joint work of face landmark detection and 3D face reconstruction. During collaborative work, the information of the landmark position change of the face is used as the prior information for 3D face reconstruction to perform the face reconstruction regression. Although this method takes into account the face structure information, it is very time-consuming to perform regression by cascading regression.

To solve the problems of illumination and large poses in extreme environments and time consuming, we propose a graph structure reasoning network for face landmark detection and reconstruction (GSRN). When the face is occluded, the apparent information of the occluded part is missing, and the neural network cannot use the apparent information to align the face landmark. This brings great challenges to the prediction of neural networks. In order to better predict the occluded part, we could infer the invisible points by learning the apparent information of visible points and reasoning through the face structure. The position information of the points further improves the accuracy of the occluded part. In order to better predict the parameters of 3DMM, we also define parameter, reconstruction and 3D face landmark loss function to optimize the network. The network structure flowchart is shown in Fig. 1.

In summary, our contributions are as follows:

1) To address the problems of occlusion and a large pose in the unconstrained natural environment, we propose a graph structure reasoning network. Based on the apparent information of visible points, the graph structure is used to infer the invisible part points.
2) We introduce an advanced DAMD-Net network architecture as the basic network. DAMD-Net is a dual attention mechanism and an efficient end-to-end 3D face alignment framework. Through the channel and spatial attention

mechanism, the important apparent semantic information of the face will be extracted and the redundant information that is not important will be ignored, thereby improving the accuracy of the network regression parameters.

3) Comparisons with the state of the art methods, we experimentally demonstrate that our GSRN has significantly improved the 3D alignment and face reconstruction performance. The proposed face alignment and reconstruction method can deal with arbitrary poses and is more efficient.

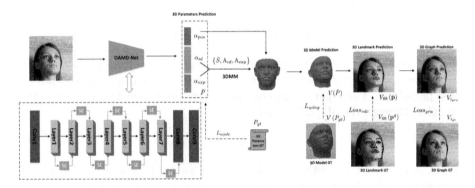

Fig. 1. The pipeline of our GSRN. It aims to train a DAMD-Net regressor model. The model takes the face image as input and outputs the coefficients α_{pos}, α_{id}, and α_{exp}. These coefficients are used to reconstruct a 3D face model through the 3DMM model. In the face model, 68 landmarks of the 3D face can be obtained through a fixed index. Finally, we build a graph structure model through 68 landmarks. In this process, the DAMD-Net regressor model is optimized by using parameter regression, face model, face landmarks and graph structure loss function.

2   Proposed Method

In this section, we introduce our proposed robust 3D face alignment and face reconstruction method, which fits a 3D morphable model by using a graph structure constrained reasoning learning network.

2.1   Graph Structure Reasoning Network

To better predict the occluded part, we propose a graph structure reasoning network for face landmark and reconstruction. We could infer the invisible points by learning the apparent information of visible points and reasoning through the face structure. The position information of the points further improves the accuracy of the occluded part. To better predict the parameters of 3DMM, we also define parameter, reconstruction and face landmark loss function to optimize the network.

Given a face image X, first the face image is sent to the convolutional layer of the convolutional neural network to extract the apparent and structural features of the human face. The extracted features can be expressed as:

$$F = W_c * X \tag{1}$$

where $*$ indicates a series of convolution, pooling, and activation operations, and W_c indicates all parameters. Feature F obtains identity, expression and pose parameters through full convolution:

$$\alpha_{id}, \quad \alpha_{\exp}, \quad \alpha_{pos} = f(F) \tag{2}$$

where f represents the full convolution structure, α_{id} represents the identity parameter, α_{exp} represents the expression parameter, and α_{pos} represents the pose parameter. These parameters can be used to obtain the face reconstruction model V through the 3DMM model:

$$V = \alpha_{id} * A_{id} + \alpha_{\exp} * A_{\exp} \tag{3}$$

where A_{id} stands for identity and A_{exp} stands for expression. By selecting corresponding points in the reconstructed face model according to a fixed index, 68 landmarks of human face V_{68} can be obtained:

$$V_{68} = V[ind, :, :] \tag{4}$$

Among them, ind represents the index of the landmark of the face in the face reconstruction model. The 68 landmarks are used to establish the graph structure to obtain $Loss_{gra}$ (For the specific establishment process, please refer to the next section).

2.2 Graph Represents Reasoning Loss Function

Existing regression methods only perform point-to-point regression without considering the relationship between points, so that convolutional neural networks only focus on the learning of the face apparent information, but lack the learning of the face spatial structure information. Therefore, we propose a graph representation loss function. This loss function restricts the overall and local aspects of the face structure, so that in the face alignment and reconstruction, the visible points are aligned by the apparent information. For invisible points, the position coordinates of invisible points are inferred by knowing the position coordinates of the visible points, so that it is very robust to occlusion and self-occlusion with large poses. This section will discuss the overall and local aspects of the graph to represent the inference loss function.

Overall Graph Structure Modeling. In an unconstrained scene, people will be affected by makeup, wearing jewelry, and their own hair, and there will also be large-scale occlusions. However, in the occlusion, the position of the nose tip is relatively unlikely to be blocked. Therefore, in this section, a map structure model is established with the nose tip as the center. As shown in Fig. 2.

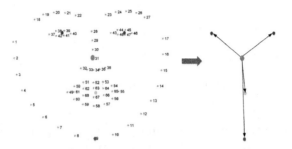

Fig. 2. Overall diagram of the global structure graph modeling. (Color figure online)

Set the map model with the nose tip as the center, that is, use the point (No.31) near it as the center point (red point). The cheek contour uses the No.9 point as the cheek restraint point. For the left eye, the landmark (No.37-No.42) of the left eye is used as the average to obtain the green point, and the right eye can be obtained by the same principle. The yellow area is obtained by averaging the key points from the No.49 landmark to the No.68 landmark in the mouth area. Therefore, the general calculation formula for the green and yellow points is as follows:

$$X_{avg} = \frac{1}{N}\sum_{i=1}^{N} X_i; \quad Y_{avg} = \frac{1}{N}\sum_{i=1}^{N} Y_i; \quad Z_{avg} = \frac{1}{N}\sum_{i=1}^{N} Z_i; \tag{5}$$

where X, Y, and Z represent the coordinate points. N represents the number of landmark in the eye or mouth area.

Take the red dot as the center to calculate the mean square error sum of the distance from the other four points to the red point and the real landmark from the red point to the other four landmarks. So the overall graph structure loss function is $Loss_{glo}$:

$$Loss_{glo} = \sum_{i=1}^{N} \left\| (V_{i_{pre}} - V_{red_{pre}}) - (V_{i_{gt}} - V_{red_{gt}}) \right\|^2 \tag{6}$$

V_i represents the X, Y, and Z coordinates of the two green, yellow, and purple dots, respectively. V_{red} represents the coordinates of the red dot.

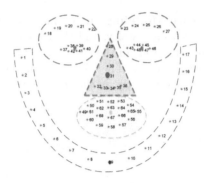

Fig. 3. Local structure partition. (Color figure online)

Partial Graph Structure Modeling. The local map structure divides the human face into five parts, which are the left eye area, right eye area, nose area, mouth area and cheek area. The specific situation is shown in Fig. 3.

In order to better perform the local landmark alignment and face reconstruction, we propose a local graph structure constraint loss function. In each region, we calculate the error between the distance from each point to the center point and the distance from each real point to the real center point in the region, and finally form the corresponding local loss function. For example, taking the left eye as an example, first calculate the distance between point No.18-No.22 and the green point, and then calculate the distance from point No.37-No.42 to the green point. Calculate the predicted and true errors and add them up to form the eye constraint map loss function $Loss_{eye}$. It is worth mentioning that when the posture is large, the landmark of the cheek area are easily occluded, so it is not enough to use the distance from the point on the cheek (No.0-No.17) to point No.9. Therefore, this method adds a constraint from each point on the human cheek to the point (No.31) on the nose tip so that the blocked cheek can be predicted well. So the local constraint $loss_{part}$:

$$Loss_{part} = Loss_{eye} + Loss_{nose} + Loss_{mou} + Loss_{yaw} \qquad (7)$$

Among them, $Loss_{eye}$, $Loss_{nose}$, $Loss_{mou}$, and $Loss_{yaw}$ represent the eye, nose, mouth and cheek area graph structure loss functions, respectively.

The overall loss function of graph learning is defined as:

$$Loss_{gra} = Loss_{glo} + Loss_{part} \qquad (8)$$

Other Loss Functions. To predict 3D parameters, we use the weighted parameter distance cost (WPDC) of Zhu [12] et al. Calculate the difference between the true 3D parameters and the predicted 3D parameters. The basic idea is to clearly model the importance of each parameter:

$$L_{wpdc} = \left(P_{gt} - \bar{P}\right)^T W \left(P_{gt} - \bar{P}\right) \qquad (9)$$

where $\bar{P}$ is the predicted value and P_{gt} is the true value. The diagonal matrix W contains weights. For each element of the shape parameter P, its weight is the inverse of the standard deviation obtained from the data used in the 3DMM training.

In order to accurately obtain the vertices of the human face. For 3D face vertices reconstructed using 3D parameters, using Wing Loss [13] is defined as:

$$L_{wing}(\Delta V(P)) = \begin{cases} \ln(1 + |\Delta V(P)|/\in) & if |\Delta V(P)| < \omega \\ |\Delta V(P)| - C & otherwise \end{cases} \quad (10)$$

where $\Delta V(P) = V(P_{gt}) - V(\bar{P})$, $V(P_{gt})$ and $V(\bar{P})$ are the ground truth of the 3D facial vertices and the 3D facial vertices reconstructed using the 3D parameters predicted by the network, respectively. ω and $\in$ are the log function parameters. $C = \omega - \omega \ln(1 + \omega/\epsilon)$ is a constant that smoothly links the piecewise-defined linear and nonlinear parts.

In order to accurately obtain the 68 landmarks of the human face. For 3D face landmark alignment, using VDC Loss [12] is defined as:

$$Loss_{vdc} = \|V_{68}(\bar{\mathbf{p}}) - V_{68}(\mathbf{p}^g)\|^2 \quad (11)$$

where $V_{68}(\cdot)$ is the face landmark.

3 Experiments

3.1 Data Augmentation and Implementation Details

The input of GSRN is a 2D image with the facial ROI localized by a face detector. In this paper, we use the Dlib SDK for face detection. We enlarge the detected face bounding box by a factor of 0.25 of its original size and crop a square image patch of the face ROI, which is scaled to 120×120. DAMD-Net outputs a 62-dimensional 3D parameter vector, including 40-dimensional identity parameter vector, 10-dimensional expression parameter vector and 12-dimensional pose vector. We use both real face images and generated face images to train our GSRN. Set the size of the hyperparameter batch size to 128. For the optimizer, the adaptive stochastic gradient descent method (Adam) is used. A total of 60 epochs of training, the learning rate of the first 15 epochs is 0.002, and the subsequent 15 epochs will decay to the original 0.2.

3.2 Comparative Evaluation

Comparison on AFLW. In the AFLW [14] dataset, 21,080 images are selected as test samples, and each sample has 21 landmark coordinates. During the test, the test set is divided into three subsets according to the absolute yaw angle of the test set: $[0°, 30°)$, $[30°, 60°)$, and $[60°, 90°]$, with 11596, 5457, and 4027 samples, respectively. Many classical methods have been tested on the AFLW dataset. Table 1 shows the results of the experimental normalized mean error. Figure 4 shows the corresponding CED curves.

Table 1. The NME(%) of face alignment results on AFLW and AFLW2000-3D

| Method | AFLW DataSet(21 pts) | | | | | AFLW2000-3D DataSet(68 pts) | | | | |
	[0°,30°)	[30°,60°)	[60°,90°]	Mean	Std	[0°,30°)	[30°,60°)	[60°,90°]	Mean	Std
CDM [15]	8.150	13.020	16.170	12.440	4.040	-	-	-	-	-
RCPR [16]	5.430	6.580	11.530	7.850	3.240	4.260	5.960	13.180	7.800	4.740
ESR [17]	5.660	7.120	11.940	8.240	3.290	4.600	6.700	12.670	7.990	4.190
SDM [18]	4.750	5.550	9.340	6.550	2.450	3.670	4.940	9.760	6.120	3.210
DeFA [19]	-	-	-	-	-	4.50	5.56	7.330	5.803	1.169
3DDFA(CVPR16) [12]	5.000	5.060	6.740	5.600	0.990	3.780	4.540	7.930	5.420	2.210
Nonlinear 3DMM [20]	-	-	-	-	-	-	-	4.700	-
DAMDNet(ICCVW19) [7]	4.359	5.209	6.028	5.199	0.682	2.907	3.830	4.953	3.897	0.837
GSRN(ours)	**4.253**	**5.144**	**5.816**	**5.073**	**0.638**	**2.842**	**3.789**	**4.804**	**3.812**	**0.801**

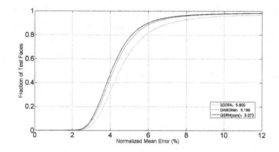

Fig. 4. The cumulative errors distribution (CED) curves on AFLW.

In order to prove the effectiveness of our GSRN for the alignment of face landmark in a large pose, we divide the AFLW [14] test data set into three subsets based on the absolute yaw angle: [0°,30°),[30°,60°) and [60°,90°]. The AFLW test data set is divided into 11596, 5457, and 4027 samples. Therefore, the CED curve of Fig. 5 is drawn. From left to right, the CED curves of small pose ([0°,30°)), medium pose ([30°,60°)), and large pose ([60°,90°]) are plotted.

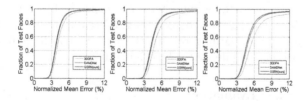

Fig. 5. The CED curves of the small, medium and large pose on AFLW.

From the above results, it can be seen that our method shows better results on the AFLW [14] dataset. Especially in the case of a large pose, the performance of our method is the best, which fully proves that the model has strong robustness under extreme large poses.

Comparison on AFLW2000-3D. In the AFLW2000-3D [12], it is divided into three subsets based on the absolute yaw angle: $[0°,30°),[30°,60°)$ and $[60°,90°]$ are 1312, 383, and 305 samples, respectively. Table 1 shows the experimental results. Figure 6 shows the corresponding CED curves. On AFLW2000-3D [12], the CED curve of the small, medium and large pose are also drawn, as shown in Fig. 7. Figure 8 shows a qualitative comparison of 3D face alignment. From the above results, we can see that our GSRN method is superior to other methods, especially in large poses, the model has strong robustness.

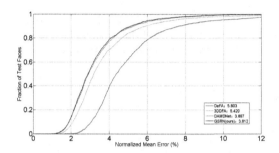

Fig. 6. The cumulative errors distribution (CED) curves on AFLW2000-3D.

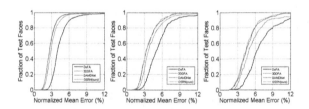

Fig. 7. The CED curve of the small, medium and large pose on AFLW2000-3D.

In order to prove the effectiveness of our model in 3D face reconstruction, we perform a comparison of a 3D normalized mean error on the AFLW2000-3D dataset, as shown in Table 2. The corresponding CED curve is plotted as shown in Fig. 9. In order to evaluate the quality of the reconstructed face, we add the texture of the face to the reconstructed face. If the face reconstruction is good, the relative position of the texture on the face is correct, otherwise, it is not good. Figure 10 shows a qualitative comparison of 3D face reconstruction. As can be seen from the figure, in 3DDFA, the position of the lips is not well-textured in the first and second pictures, and the texture of the human hand is not good in the third picture, and the background texture is pasted on the face in the fourth and fifth pictures, and texture of the mouth and nose is not good in the last picture. Therefore, our method has a good effect in face reconstruction. From the above results, we can see that our GSRN method is superior to other methods, especially under large poses, the model has strong robustness.

Fig. 8. Comparison of 3D face alignment. The first line is the original image, the second line is the alignment result of 3DDFA, and the third line is the alignment result of our GSRN. The blue circle shows that our GSRN is better than 3DDFA at face alignment.

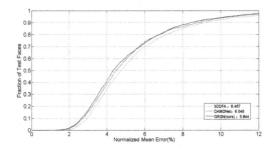

Fig. 9. The cumulative errors distribution (CED) curves on AFLW2000-3D.

Table 2. The NME(%) of face reconstruction results on AFLW2000-3D.

	3DDFA [12]	DAMDNet [7]	GSRN(Our)
[0°,30°)	4.877	4.672	4.543
[30°,60°)	6.086	5.619	5.368
[60°,90°]	8.437	7.855	7.620
Mean	6.467	6.049	5.844
Std	1.478	1.334	1.301

Runtime. GSRN has achieved good performance in 3D face alignment and reconstruction, and it is surprisingly lighter and faster. We compare the model parameters size and running time of PRN [21] and GSRN, as shown in Table 3.

The size of our GSRN model parameters is only 10.7M. The PRN [21] network structure uses an encoder and decoder structure. It is the network structure with the fewer model parameters in face alignment and reconstruction. However, this network structure requires 36M model parameters. The parameter size of our GSRN is less than PRN [21] by one third. From the data in Table 3, it can be seen that our GSRN is better than the PRN [21] network in terms of model

Table 3. Compare the model parameters size and running time of PRN and GSRN.

	PRN [21]	GSRN(ours)
Model parameter size	36M	10.7M
Each image runs in CPU time	0.23s	0.20s

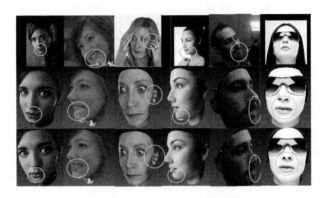

Fig. 10. Comparison of 3D face reconstruction. The first line is the original image, the second line is the result of 3DDFA reconstruction, and the third line is the result of our GSRN reconstruction. The blue circle shows that our GSRN is better than 3DDFA at face reconstruction.

parameter size and the running time of the test pictures in the model. The running time of our GSRN is defined from the input cropped facial image to the network output parameters. The hardware used for evaluation is Intel (R) Core (TM) i7-8750H CPU @ 2.20GHz.

4 Conclusion

In this paper, for the self-occlusion problem of a large pose, we propose a graph structure reasoning network, which well solves the problems of 3D face alignment and 3D face reconstruction simultaneously. We have designed the graph structure reasoning loss function. Based on the apparent information of visible points, the graph structure constraint reasoning learning is used to infer the invisible part points. The quantitative and qualitative results demonstrate our method is robust to a large pose. Experiments on two test datasets show that our method achieves significant improvements over others, and further show that our method runs faster than other methods and is suitable for real-time usage.

References

1. Yi, H., Li, C., Cao, Q., et al.: Mmface: a multi-metric regression network for unconstrained face reconstruction. In: Proceedings of the IEEE Conference on Computer Vision and Pattern Recognition (CVPR), pp. 7663–7672. IEEE (2019)

2. Tu, X., Zhao, J., Jiang, Z., et al.: Joint 3D face reconstruction and dense face alignment from a single image with 2D-assisted self-supervised learning. arXiv preprint arXiv:1903.09359 (2019)
3. Zhu, C., Liu, H., Yu, Z., et al.: Towards omni-supervised face alignment for large scale unlabeled videos. In: Association for the Advancement of Artificial Intelligence (AAAI), pp. 13090–13097(2020)
4. Zhu, C., Wu, S., Yu, Z., et al.: Multi-agent deep collaboration learning for face alignment under different perspectives. In: 2019 IEEE International Conference on Image Processing (ICIP), pp. 1785–1789. IEEE(2019)
5. Zhu, C., Li, X., Li, J., et al.: Spatial-temporal knowledge integration: robust self-supervised facial landmark tracking. In: Proceedings of the 28th ACM International Conference on Multimedia(MM), pp. 4135–4143 (2020)
6. Blanz, V., Vetter, T.: Face recognition based on fitting a 3d morphable model. IEEE Trans. Pattern Anal. Mach. Intell. **25**(9), 1063–1074 (2003)
7. Jiang, L., Wu, X.J., Kittler, J.: Dual attention mobDenseNet (DAMDNet) for robust 3D face alignment. In: Proceedings of the IEEE International Conference on Computer Vision Workshops (ICCVW2019) (2019)
8. Lee, Y.J., Lee, S.J., Park, K.R., Jo, J., Kim, J.: Single view-based 3D face reconstruction robust to self-occlusion. EURASIP J. Adv. Sig. Process. **2012**(1), 1–20 (2012)
9. Qu, C., Monari, E., Schuchert, T., Beyerer, J.: Fast, robust and automatic 3D face model reconstruction from videos. In: AVSS, pp. 113–118. IEEE (2014)
10. Liu, F., Zeng, D., Li, J., Zhao, Q.: Cascaded regressor based 3D face reconstruction from a single arbitrary view image. arXiv preprint arXiv:1509.06161 (2015)
11. Liu, F., Zeng, D., Zhao, Q., Liu, X.: Joint face alignment and 3D face reconstruction. In: Leibe, B., Matas, J., Sebe, N., Welling, M. (eds.) ECCV 2016. LNCS, vol. 9909, pp. 545–560. Springer, Cham (2016). https://doi.org/10.1007/978-3-319-46454-1_33
12. Zhu, X., Lei, Z., Liu, X., Shi, H., Li, S.Z.: Face alignment across large poses: a 3d solution. In: Proceedings of the IEEE Conference on Computer Vision and Pattern Recognition (2016), pp. 146–155 (2016)
13. Feng, Z.-H., Kittler, J., Awais, M., Huber, P., Wu, X.-J.: Wing loss for robust facial landmark localisation with convolutional neural networks. In: 2018 IEEE/CVF Conference on Computer Vision and Pattern Recognition (ICCV2018), pp. 2235–2245. IEEE (2018)
14. Koestinger, M., Wohlhart, P., Roth, P.M., Bischof, H.: Annotated facial landmarks in the wild: a large-scale, realworld database for facial landmark localization. In: Computer Vision Workshops (ICCV Workshops), pp. 2144–2151. IEEE (2011)
15. Yu, X., Huang, J., Zhang, S., Metaxas, D.N.: Face landmark fitting via optimized part mixtures and cascaded deformable model. Trans. Pattern Anal. Mach. Intell. **11**, 2212–2226 (2016)
16. Burgos-Artizzu, X.P., Perona, P., Dollar, P.: Robust face landmark estimation under occlusion. In: Proceedings of the IEEE International Conference on Computer Vision (ICCV2013), pp. 1513–1520 (2013)
17. Cao, X., Wei, Y., Wen, F., Sun, J.: Face alignment by explicit shape regression. Int. J. Comput. Vis. (IJCV2014) **107**(2), 177–190 (2014)
18. Yan, J., Lei, Z., Yi, D., Li, S.: Learn to combine multiple hypotheses for accurate face alignment. In: Proceedings of the IEEE International Conference on Computer Vision Workshops (ICCV Workshops), pp. 392–396 (2013)
19. Liu, Y., Jourabloo, A., Ren, W., Liu, X.: Dense face alignment. arXiv preprint arXiv:1709.01442 (2017)

20. Tran, L., Liu, X.: Nonlinear 3d face morphable model. In: Proceedings of the IEEE Conference on Computer Vision and Pattern Recognition (CVPR2018), pp. 7346–7355 (2018)
21. Feng, Y., Wu, F., Shao, X., et al.: Joint 3d face reconstruction and dense alignment with position map regression network. In: Proceedings of the European Conference on Computer Vision (ECCV2018), pp. 534–551 (2018)

Game Input with Delay – A Model of the Time Distribution for Selecting a Moving Target with a Mouse

Shengmei Liu$^{(\boxtimes)}$ and Mark Claypool

{sliu7,claypool}@wpi.edu

Worcester Polytechnic Institute, Worcester, MA 01609, USA

Abstract. Computer game player performance can degrade with delays from both the local system and network. Analytic models and simulations have the potential to enable exploration of player performance with delay as an alternative to time-intensive user studies. This paper presents an analytic model for the distributions of elapsed times for players doing a common game action – selecting a moving target with a mouse with delay – derived from results from prior user studies. We develop and validate our model, then demonstrate the use of our model via simulation, exploring player performance with different game configurations and delays.

Keywords: Moving target selection · Game player · Modeling · Fitts' law

1 Introduction

Computer games require timely responses to player actions in order to provide for an immersive, interactive experience. Unfortunately, computer input hardware and software always have some delay from when a player inputs a game command until the result is processed and rendered on the screen. Delays on most local computer system are at least 20 ms and can range much higher, up to about 250 ms for some platforms and game systems [11]. Games played over a network, such as multi-player game systems or cloud-based game streaming, have additional delays from the network and server processing as game data has to be transmitted to and from a server. Both local delays and network delays impact the player, degrading both player performance and player Quality of Experience (QoE) as total delay increases [3–5].

Research that studies delay and games typically conducts user studies with participants playing a game with controlled amounts of delay. While these studies can be effective for ascertaining player performance for specific games [1,2], and specific game actions [15], they are time-intensive, requiring months of time to design, setup, conduct and analyze. Moreover, user studies often can only gather data over the small range of game and system configurations tested because of the limited number of configuration parameters users can experience during a single test session. Moreover, some societal conditions (e.g., social distancing during a pandemic) can make organizing and executing traditional user studies impossible.

© Springer Nature Switzerland AG 2021
J. Lokoč et al. (Eds.): MMM 2021, LNCS 12572, pp. 506–518, 2021.
https://doi.org/10.1007/978-3-030-67832-6_41

As an alternative approach, analytic models of player performance and simulations of computer games can provide for a broad exploration of the impact of delay on game conditions without costly user studies. However, such an approach can only be effective if it accurately represents player performance. Data from studies that isolate "atoms" of game actions have the potential to provide the foundation for accurate analytic models of player performance, and resultant simulations that use them can help explain and predict the effects of delay for a wide range of games and delay conditions. This paper makes just such a contribution – an analytic model of a game action, based on user studies, validated and then demonstrated through simulation.

We use data gathered from two previous users studies with over 80 people that measured user performance for an atomic game action – selecting a moving target with a mouse. Users played a game that had them select targets that moved around the screen with different speeds and with different amounts of added delay. The studies recorded the elapsed time to select the target, coupled with a player-provided self-rating of skill.

We use the data from these studies in multivariate, multiple regression to derive models of: 1) the expected elapsed times for selecting a moving target with a mouse, and 2) the distribution of the elapsed times. Used together, these models provide an accurate representation of target selection times over a range of delays and target speeds and two levels of player skill and can be used both to predict performance directly from the model (using the expected value), but also put into discrete event simulations (using the distribution of values). We demonstrate the use of the models in analytic analysis and simulations of player performance for basic shooting games to predict the impact of delay for several game and system configurations.

The rest of this paper is organized as follows: Sect. 2 presents work related to this paper; Sect. 3 describes the user study datasets; Sect. 4 details the derivation and validation of our models; Sect. 5 evaluates game performance using analytic models and simulation; Sect. 6 describes some limitations of our work; and Sect. 7 summarizes our conclusions and possible future work.

2   Related Work

This section describes work related to the problem of modeling distributions for the time needed for users to select moving targets with delay.

2.1   Models of User Input

Fitts' law is a seminal work in human-computer interaction and ergonomics that describes the time to select a stationary target based on the target distance and target width [7]. Fitts' law has been shown to be applicable to a variety of conditions and input devices and has been extended to two dimensions [18], making it suitable for modeling target selection with a mouse [23]. However, Fitts' law by itself accounts for neither moving targets nor delay.

Jagacinski et al. [12], Hajri et al. [9], and Hoffmann [10] extended Fitts' law to moving targets, adding target speed to the model. Mackenzie and Ware [19] measured selection time and error rates when selecting stationary targets with delay, and Jota et al. [13] studied target selection and dragging with touch devices with delay. They found a pronounced multiplicative effect between delay and Fitts' Index of Difficulty (ID) [7], and proposed a modification to Fitts' law that incorporates delay by including an additional term. Teather et al. [24] measured selection time for stationary targets of different sizes and delays and jitter, and confirmed similar findings to MacKenzie and Ware [19] for Fitts' law's computations for ID. Friston et al. [8] confirmed earlier results of Fitts' law for low delay systems and compared their model to others.

The models proposed provide for expected elapsed times and, in some cases, errors, but do not model the distributions of the elapsed times. The latter is needed for simulations where player response times are selected from a range of possible values based on a model and then used in the simulation, as in the case of our work and needed by other simulators.

2.2   Game Actions

An overlapping research area studies the effects of delay on individual (aka *atomic*) game actions.

Raaen and Eg [22] conducted experiments with a simple button and dial interface, letting users adjust delay based on their perceptions. They found users are capable of perceiving even low amounts of delay (around 66 ms). Long and Gutwin [15] studied the effects of delay on intercepting a moving target. They found target speed directly affects the impact of delay, with fast targets affected by delays as low as 50 ms, but slower targets resilient to delays as high as 150 ms. Pavloyvych and Stuerzlinger [21] and Pavloyvych and Gutwin [20] studied target tracking for objects moving along Lissajous curves (smooth curves, with varying turns within the curve). They found tracking errors increase quickly for delays over 110 ms, but the effects of target velocity on errors is close to linear. Long and Gutwin [16] measured selection time for different sized moving targets. They found that the effects of delay are exacerbated by fast target speeds.

In general, while these approaches have helped understand delay and fundamental game actions, they generally have not applied a model to the data gathered, or if they have, the models are for average (expected) values and not the distributions of the values.

3   Datasets

We use two sets of data obtained from prior user studies [6]: *Set-A* and *Set-B*. Each data set was obtained from users playing a game with controlled amounts of delay where the game focused on a single player's action – selecting a moving target with a mouse. Selecting a moving target is an action common to many PC game genres, such as shooters (e.g., *Nuclear Throne*, Vlambeer, 2015 and *Call of Duty*, Activision, 2003).

3.1   Game

Both datasets are obtained from users playing a custom game called *Puck Hunt* that allows for the study of selecting a moving target with controlled amounts of delay.

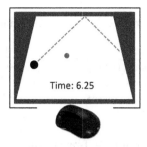

Fig. 1. *Puck Hunt.* Users click on a moving target (the puck) with the mouse cursor (a red ball). The game adds delay to the mouse input and varies the target speed between rounds.

In Puck Hunt, depicted in Fig. 1, the user proceeds through a series of short rounds, where each round has a large black ball, the puck/target, that moves with kinematics, bouncing off the edges of the screen. The user moves the mouse to control the small red ball (a.k.a., the cursor) and attempts to select the target by moving the ball over the target and clicking the mouse button. Once the user has successfully selected the target, the target disappears and a notification pops up telling the user to prepare for the next round. Thereupon pressing any key, a new round starts, with the target at a new starting location with a new orientation and speed. The user is scored via a timer that counts up from zero at the beginning of each round, stopping when the target is selected. The game settings and parameters were chosen based on pilot tests so as to provide for a range of difficulties – easy to hard. The size of the target is a constant 28 mm, not dissimilar to the size of a "duck" in the video game *Duck Hunt* (Nintendo, 1984).

In dataset Set-A, users select targets with three different speeds (150, 300 and 450 pixels/s) under 11 different delays (100 to 500 ms), with each combination of delay and speed encountered 5 times. In dataset Set-B, users select targets with three different speeds (550, 1100 and 1550 pixels/s) under 11 different delays (20 to 420 ms), with each combination of delay and speed encountered 5 times.

The game records objective measures of performance, including the elapsed time it took for the user to select the target.

3.2   Procedure

All user studies were conducted in dedicated computer labs with computer hardware more than adequate to support the games and LCD monitors.

For each study, participants first completed informed consent and demographic questionnaire forms before starting the game. The demographic questionnaire include the question "rate yourself as a computer gamer" with responses given on a 5 point scale (1 - low to 5 - high). The self-rating question was mandatory. The demographic question-tionnaire also included an optional gender question with choices for "male", "female", "other" and "prefer not to say" – only one user did not specify either male or female.

Table 1 summarizes the major dataset variables, with the bottom row, "Both", show-ing the users, gender, rounds and conditions for both datasets combined into one.

Table 1. Summary of dataset variables

Dataset	Usrs	Gender	Rounds	Conditions
Set-A	51	43 ♂, 8 ♀	167	3 speeds, 11 delays
Set-B	32	23 ♂, 8 ♀, 1?	167	3 speeds, 11 delays
Both	83	66 ♂, 16 ♀, 1?	334	6 speeds, 22 delays

Table 2. Self-rated skill

Dataset	1	2	3	4	5	$\bar{x}$	s
Set-A	1	3	5	24	18	4.1	0.9
Set-B	4	2	9	8	9	3.5	1.3
Both	5	5	14	32	27	3.9	1.1

Table 2 shows the breakdown of self-rated skills for each dataset, with the mean and standard deviation reported by $\bar{x}$ and s, respectively, in the last two columns. The bottom row shows the breakdown of both datasets combined into one. The datasets have a slight skew towards higher skills (mean skill slightly above 3 and mode 4 for each), but there are players of all skill levels in both sets.

4 Modeling Selection Time

This section describes our methods used to: a) process and analyze the user study data, and then, b) derive models for the distribution of elapsed times to select moving targets with delay.

4.1 Pre-processing

In Puck Hunt, if the user's time to select the target surpasses 30 s, the round ends, and the elapsed time for that round is recorded as a 30. These 30 s values are not the elapsed times that would have been recorded if the trial continued, and so artificially impact any model of selection time that includes them. Thus, we look to replace values of exactly 30 s with estimates of the larger values they likely would have had if the round had continued (and the user had kept trying) until the target was selected. In total, the game has 33 different combinations of speed and delay, called *difficulty levels*. For most difficulty levels, there are no elapsed times of 30 s. However, the higher difficulty levels (speeds above 500 px/s, and delays above 120 ms) have one or more 30 s values. We replace these 30 s values with randomly generated points above 30 s using previously derived models [6]. See our technical report for details [14].

Before modeling, we standardized the delay and target speed by subtracting the means and dividing by the standard deviations. The mean value for delay is 206 ms and the standard deviation is 122 ms. The mean value for target speed is 683 px/s and the standard deviation is 488 px/s.

The distribution of all elapsed times appears log-normal, which makes sense since human actions are impacted by many individual factors that, when put together, have an exponential distribution. We take the natural logarithm of the elapsed time to obtain a probability distribution that appears normal. The probability distribution of elapsed time at each difficulty level follows this pattern, too.

4.2   Modeling

We use multivariate, multiple regression to model the mean and standard deviation of the natural logarithm of the elapsed time. This will allow generation of distributions of elapsed times (using a normal distribution, then taking the exponent) for a given difficulty level, making it usable both for analytically modeling and for simulating game performance.

There are many possible models that fit the elapsed time data. We compare different regression models by using the coefficient of determination (the adjusted R^2) as a measurement of how well observed outcomes are replicated by the model. We fit a model with terms for delay, speed and a combined delay-speed term that is the most parsimonious in providing the desired prediction with as few terms as possible – for both mean and standard deviation. See our technical report for details on the models compared [14].

Our models for mean and standard deviation for the natural log of the elapsed time are:

$$mean(\,ln(T)\,) = k_1 + k_2 d + k_3 s + k_4 ds$$
$$stddev(\,ln(T)\,) = k_5 + k_6 d + k_7 s + k_8 ds$$

(1)

where the k parameters (e.g., k_1) are constants, d is the standardized delay ($d = \frac{D-206}{122}$) and s is the standardized speed ($s = \frac{S-683}{488}$).

Using Eq. 1 on our standardized user study data yields an adjusted R^2 for mean and standard deviation of 0.96 for both. The final model for the mean and standard deviation of the natural log of elapsed time is:

$$mean(\,ln(T)\,) = 0.685 + 0.506d + 0.605\,s + 0.196ds$$
$$stddev(\,ln(T)\,) = 0.567 + 0.126d + 0.225\,s + 0.029ds$$

(2)

With the models predicting mean and standard deviation for $ln(T)$, given speed and delay, the normal distribution with the predicted mean and standard deviation can be used to generate a distribution of logarithmic elapsed times and taking the exponent to get the elapsed times. Our model has excellent fit for the data with R^2 of 0.99 and root mean square error (RMSE) of 0.03.

4.3   Player Skills

Before modeling player skill, we assess if there is a difference in performance based on self-rated skills.

In the user studies, players rated their skills as computer gamers from 1 (low) to 5 (high). The mean self-rating is about 3.9, showing a slight skew towards having "high ability". Based on our user sample, we divided users into low skill (24 users with self-rating 1–3) and high skill (59 users with self-rating 4–5).

Since the games and test conditions are slightly different between the two user studies, we normalize the data based on the average performance of all users in the same dataset. For example, since the average elapsed time to select a target across all users and all trials for the Set-B dataset is 1.6 s, each individual user in the Set-B dataset has

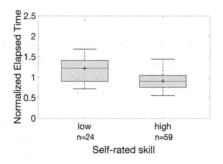

Fig. 2. Combined skill groups

their elapsed times divided by 1.6. Users with normalized values below 1 are better than average and values above 1 are worse than average – e.g., a normalized score of 0.9 is 10% better than the average while a 2.0 is twice as bad as the average.

Figure 2 shows boxplots of normalized elapsed time on the y-axis for users clustered by skill group on the x-axis. Each box depicts quartiles and median with the mean shown with a '+'. Points higher or lower than 1.4 × the inter-quartile range are outliers, depicted by the dots. The whiskers span from the minimum non-outlier to the maximum non-outlier. The x-axis "n=" labels indicate the number of participants in each skill group. From the figure, the mean and median of normalized elapsed times decrease (improve) with self-rated skill.

Since the elapsed time data is skewed right, comparisons of the two skill groups was done using a Mann-Whitney U test – a non-parametric test of the null hypothesis that it is equally likely that a randomly selected value from one group will be greater than or less than a randomly selected value from a second group. Effectively, this tests whether two independent self-rated skill group samples come from populations having the same distribution. The test results indicate that the elapsed time was larger for low skill players (*median* = 1.22) than for high skill players (*median* = 0.91), with $U = 321$, and $p < .001$.

Since self-rated skill appears to generally differentiate performance, we derive models for original elapsed time $ln(T)$ parameterized by skill as we did for all users before. The final models are shown in Table 3.

Table 3. Models of moving target selection time with delay

Skill	Model	Adjusted R^2
All	*mean*($ln(T)$) = $0.685 + 0.506d + 0.605s + 0.196ds$	0.96
	stddev($ln(T)$) = $0.567 + 0.126d + 0.225s + 0.029ds$	0.96
Low	*mean*($ln(T)$) = $0.850 + 0.560d + 0.672s + 0.212ds$	0.96
	stddev($ln(T)$) = $0.589 + 0.118d + 0.253s + 0.009ds$	0.88
High	*mean*($ln(T)$) = $0.605 + 0.468d + 0.625s + 0.208ds$	0.95
	stddev($ln(T)$) = $0.539 + 0.109d + 0.227s + 0.041ds$	0.96

4.4   Validation

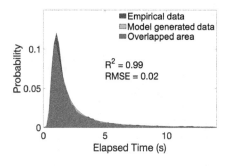
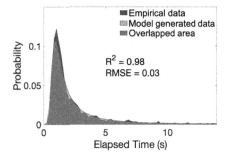

Fig. 3. Training   **Fig. 4.** Validation

To validate our model, we randomly select 20% of data from each difficulty level (combination of target speed and delay) for validation, and train a model on the remaining 80% of the data. Figure 3 depicts the resulting model fit to the training data, showing the elapsed time on the x-axis and the distribution of values on the y-axis. The data are shown with separate colors (blue and pink), with the purple color showing data overlap. The model fits the training data well with an R^2 of 0.99 and a RMSE of 0.03. Figure 4 depicts the trained model fit to the validation data. The model also fits the validation data well with R^2 at 0.98 and RMSE at 0.03. For the rest of this paper, we use the models trained on all of the data (Table 3) for our analysis and simulations.

5   Evaluation

As a demonstration of our model's use, we use the model to analytically model and simulate player performance for some game configurations. This allows us to explore the impact of game and system configuration on player performance over a range of delays not studied by the previous user studies.

5.1   Player Performance Versus Delay

We begin by comparing the impact of delay on performance for target selection compared to reaction time actions where a player responds immediately (e.g., by a key press or mouse click) to an event in the game. Using our model, selection time performance with delay is modeled analytically by $\frac{T(0)}{T(n)}$, where $T(n)$ is the mean elapsed time with delay at an average target speed at 450 px/s, calculated with our model. Reaction time actions are similarly modeled, but using the mathematical response time derivation by Ma et al. [17].

Figure 5 depicts the effects of delay on player performance for both actions. The x-axis is delay, in milliseconds, with a "0" representing the ideal case, and the y-axis the normalized performance with a "1" representing performance in the best case (0

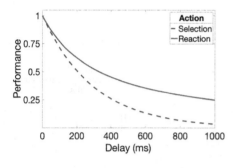
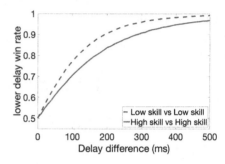

Fig. 5. Player performance versus delay (Color figure online)

Fig. 6. Win rate versus delay – Skill (Color figure online)

delay). The dashed blue line shows how player performance selecting a 450 px/s target decays with an increase in delay. The solid orange line shows how player reaction time performance decays with an increase in delay. From the figure, both actions have degraded by about 25% at a modest delay of 100 ms. However, the dashed blue line has a steeper decreasing trend than the solid orange line, indicating that delay has more impact on selection actions than on reaction actions.

5.2 Win Rate Versus Delay – Skill

We simulate a shooter game where two players try to select (shoot) a target before their opponent. Both players have an equal base delay, but one player has extra network delay to evaluate the effects of unequal amounts of delay on matches with players of equal skill. We simulate 100k iterations of the game for each combination of added delay and player skill. Figure 6 depicts the results. The x-axis is the delay difference for the two players, and the y-axis is the win rate of the player with lower delay. The dashed blue line is games with two low skill players, while the solid orange line is games with two high skill players. From the figure, even a modest delay difference of 100 ms makes it about 50% harder for the delayed player to win. The dashed blue line increases faster than the solid orange line, indicating delay impacts games with higher skill players less.

5.3 Win Rate Versus Delay – Target Speed

Figure 7 depicts how delay impacts win rate with different target speeds. This simulation is the same as before, but both players are of average skill and the target speed varies for each game. The x-axis is the delay difference for the two players, and the y-axis is the win rate of the player with lower delay. The dashed blue line is games with slow target speeds of 150 px/s, while the solid orange line is games with fast target speeds of 1150 px/s. The solid orange line increases faster than the dashed blue line, indicating delay impacts player performance more for higher target speeds (i.e., harder games).

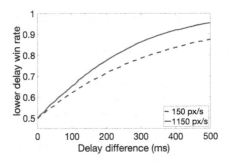

Fig. 7. Win rate versus delay for difference target speeds (Color figure online)

6 Limitations

The model is limited by the details recorded and varied by the underlying user studies. As such, the model is only accurate over the range of target speeds and delays tested. For example, this means the model may not be accurate in extrapolating results to very low delays, such as might be encountered in future high end gaming systems, nor may it well-represent extremely small or extremely fast targets.

While target selection is a common action in both 2D and 3D games, the user studies were for a 2D game only so the model may not be accurate in 3D where perspective (and, hence target sizes and on-screen speeds) may change with camera placement.

The self-rated skill is a coarse measure of player experience and a more detailed, multi-question self-assessment may provide for more accuracy in models of performance versus skill.

The studies including 66 males, but only 16 females and the vast majority are relatively young. Gamer demographics are much more evenly split across gender and more widely distributed by age.

7 Conclusion

With the growth in networking and cloud services, computer games are increasingly hosted on servers, adding significant delay between user input and rendered results. Understanding the impact of delay on game input can help build systems that better deal with the avoidable delays.

While user studies are effective for measuring the effects of delay on player performance, they are time intensive and, by necessity, typically have a limited range of game parameters they can test. Analytic models and simulations that mimic the behavior of players in games can complement user studies, providing for a broader range of evaluation. This approach is most effective if the game modeled and simulated incorporates observed user behavior.

This work leverages data gathered from two previous user studies [6] to build a model that can be used for just such approaches – analytic models and simulations. Eighty-three users playing 334 rounds of a game provided data on the time to select a moving target, the target moving with 6 different speeds and the mouse input subjected to 22 different amounts of delay.

We use multivariate, multiple regression to derive a model for the mean and standard deviation of the natural log of the elapsed time, with additive linear terms for delay and speed and a multiplicative interaction term. The same approach is used to model elapsed time distributions based on self-rated user skill – low (self-rated skill 1–3) and high (self-rated skill 4–5). Our derived models have an excellent fit (R^2 around 0.98 and low root mean square error) and can be used to generate a normal distribution of logarithmic elapsed times, then expanded to elapsed time by taking the exponential.

In addition to the main contribution of a model for the distribution of target selection times with delay, we demonstrate use of the model by analytically modeling and simulating player performance in a game that features target selection. The analytic modeling and simulation results show that for the evaluated game:

1 Even delay differences of only 100 ms make it about 50% harder to win.
2 High skill players are less affected by delay than low skill players.
3 Delay affects players more for faster targets.

There are several areas of potential future work.

While the models presented in this paper provide insights into a meaningful and fundamental measure of performance – the elapsed time to select – another measure of performance for selection is accuracy. Future work could model accuracy in a manner similar to the elapsed time models in this work, possibly being combined into a single model of performance.

The atomic action of moving target selection is only one of many fundamental game actions that are affected by delay. Future work could design and conduct user studies to gather data on the effects of delay on other atomic actions, for example, navigation. Such studies could provide data for additional models on these atomic game actions, allowing for richer simulations that can predict the effects of delay for a broader set of games.

References

1. Amin, R., Jackson, F., Gilbert, J.E., Martin, J., Shaw, T.: Assessing the impact of latency and jitter on the perceived quality of call of duty modern warfare 2. In: Kurosu, M. (ed.) HCI 2013. LNCS, vol. 8006, pp. 97–106. Springer, Heidelberg (2013). https://doi.org/10.1007/978-3-642-39265-8_11
2. Armitage, G.: An experimental estimation of latency sensitivity in multiplayer quake 3. In: Proceedings of the 11th IEEE International Conference on Networks (ICON), Sydney, Australia, September 2003
3. Chen, D.Y., Chen, K.-T., Yang, H.T.: Dude, the source of lags is on your computer. In: Proceedings of ACM Network and System Support for Games Workshop (NetGames), Denver, CO, USA, December 2013
4. Chen, K.T., Chang, Y.C., Hsu, H.J., Chen, D.Y., Huang, C.Y., Hsu, C.H.: On the quality of service of cloud gaming systems. IEEE Trans. Multimedia 16(2), 480–495 (2014)
5. Claypool, M., Claypool, K.: Latency and player actions in online games. Commun. ACM 49(11), 40–45 (2006)

6. Claypool, M., Eg, R., Raaen, K.: Modeling user performance for moving target selection with a delayed mouse. In: Proceedings of the 23rd International Conference on MultiMedia Modeling (MMM), Reykjavik, Iceland, January 2017

7. Fitts, P.M.: The information capacity of the human motor system in controlling the amplitude of movement. J. Exp. Psychol. **47**(6), 381–391 (1954)

8. Friston, S., Karlström, P., Steed, A.: The effects of low latency on pointing and steering tasks. IEEE Trans. Visual Comput. Graphics **22**(5), 1605–1615 (2016)

9. Hajri, A.A., Fels, S., Miller, G., Ilich, M.: Moving target selection in 2D graphical user interfaces. In: Campos, P., Graham, N., Jorge, J., Nunes, N., Palanque, P., Winckler, M. (eds.) INTERACT 2011. LNCS, vol. 6947, pp. 141–161. Springer, Heidelberg (2011). https://doi.org/10.1007/978-3-642-23771-3_12

10. Hoffmann, E.: Capture of moving targets: a modification of Fitts' law. Ergonomics **34**(2), 211–220 (1991)

11. Ivkovic, Z., Stavness, I., Gutwin, C., Sutcliffe, S.: Quantifying and mitigating the negative effects of local latencies on aiming in 3D shooter games. In: Proceedings of the ACM CHI Human Factors in Computing Systems, Seoul, Korea, pp. 135–144 (2015)

12. Jagacinski, R., Repperger, D., Ward, S., Moran, M.: A test of Fitts' law with moving targets. J. Hum. Factors Ergon. Soc. **22**(2), 225–233 (1980)

13. Jota, R., Ng, A., Dietz, P., Wigdor, D.: How fast is fast enough?: a study of the effects of latency in direct-touch pointing tasks. In: Proceedings of the ACM CHI Human Factors in Computing Systems, Paris, France (2013)

14. Liu, S., Claypool, M.: Game input with delay - a model for the time to select a moving target with a mouse. Technical report WPI-CS-TR-20-05, Computer Science Department at Worcester Polytechnic Institute, July 2020

15. Long, M., Gutwin, C.: Characterizing and modeling the effects of local latency on game performance and experience. In: Proceedings of the ACM Symposium on Computer-Human Interaction in Play (CHI Play), Melbourne, VC, Australia (2018)

16. Long, M., Gutwin, C.: Effects of local latency on game pointing devices and game pointing tasks. In: Proceedings of the ACM CHI Human Factors in Computing Systems, Glasgow, Scotland, UK, May 2019

17. Ma, T., Holden, J., Serota, R.A.: Distribution of human response times. Complexity **21**(6), 61–69 (2013)

18. MacKenzie, I.S., Buxton, W.: Extending Fitts' law to two-dimensional tasks. In: Proceedings of the ACM CHI Conference on Human Factors in Computing Systems, Monterey, CA, USA, pp. 219–226, May 1992

19. MacKenzie, I.S., Ware, C.: Lag as a determinant of human performance in interactive systems. In: Proceedings of ACM CHI Human Factors in Computing Systems (1993)

20. Pavlovych, A., Gutwin, C.: Assessing target acquisition and tracking performance for complex moving targets in the presence of latency and jitter. In: Proceedings of Graphics Interface, Toronto, ON, Canada, May 2012

21. Pavlovych, A., Stuerzlinger, W.: Target following performance in the presence of latency, jitter, and signal dropouts. In: Proceedings of Graphics Interface, St. John's, NL, Canada, pp. 33–40, May 2011

22. Raaen, K., Eg, R.: Instantaneous human-computer interactions: button causes and screen effects. In: Proceedings of the HCI International Conference, Los Angeles, CA, USA, August 2015

23. Soukoreff, R.W., MacKenzie, I.S.: Towards a standard for pointing device evaluation - perspectives on 27 years of Fitts' law research in HCI. Int. J. Hum.-Comput. Stud. **61**(6), 751–789 (2004)
24. Teather, R.J., Pavlovych, A., Stuerzlinger, W., MacKenzie, I.S.: Effects of tracking technology, latency, and spatial jitter on object movement. In: Proceedings of the IEEE Symposium on 3D User Interfaces, Lafayette, LA, USA, pp. 43–50 (2009)

Unsupervised Temporal Attention Summarization Model for User Created Videos

Min Hu[1], Ruimin Hu[1(✉)], Xiaocheng Wang[1,2], and Rui Sheng[1]

[1] National Engineering Research Center for Multimedia Software (NERCMS),
School of Computer Science, Wuhan University, Wuhan, China
2018202110006@whu.edu.cn, hurm1964@gmail.com, clowang@163.com,
shengrui20000130@gmail.com
[2] Shenzhen Institute of Wuhan University, Shenzhen, China

Abstract. Unlike surveillance videos, videos created by common users contain more frequent shot changes, more diversified backgrounds, and a wider variety of content. The existing methods have two critical issues for summarizing user-created videos: 1) information distortion 2) high redundancy among keyframes. Therefore, we propose a novel temporal attention model to evaluate the importance scores of each frame. Specifically, on the basis of the classical attention model, we combine the predictions of both encoder and decoder to ensure using integrate information to score frame-level importance. Further, in order to sift redundant frames out, we devise a feedforward reward function to quantify diversity, representativeness, and storyness properties of candidate keyframes in attention model. Last, the Deep Deterministic Policy Gradient algorithm is adopted to efficiently solve the proposed formulation. Extensive experiments on the public SumMe and TVSum datasets show that our method outperforms the state of the art by a large margin in terms of the F-score.

Keywords: Video summarization · Unsupervised learning · Attention mechanism

1 Introduction

With the development of self-media platforms, including YouTube, Instagram, and others, a tremendous amount of video data have been created and uploaded to the internet by ordinary users. In order to preview, storage, retrieval, and management easily, video summarization technique, aiming to represent an original video by means of a brief sketch, is studied widely at present. However, most contents in user-created videos, (e.g., videos from wearables), are captured randomly. Therefore, the scene changes frequently within a short time, drastically increasing the semantic information and causing disturbances from irrelevant data.

Supported by Basic Research Project of Science and Technology Plan of Shenzhen (JCYJ20170818143246278).

J. Lokoč et al. (Eds.): MMM 2021, LNCS 12572, pp. 519–530, 2021.
https://doi.org/10.1007/978-3-030-67832-6_42

For user-created videos, the existing approaches can be roughly classified into two categories: supervised and unsupervised learning techniques. Supervised learning needs the importance score label for each frame/shot. With the labels' monitoring, supervised methods show attractive performances. For instance, Zhang et al. [3] innovatively created a Long Short-Term Memory (LSTM [7])-based model to exploit inter-dependencies of frames into selecting keyframes and achieved significant improvements. Ji et al. [4] developed an attention-based video summarization model (M-AVS) which introduced the classical attention-based encoder-decoder structure (AM) [21] to further enhance the coding ability of single LSTM for a long input sequence. However, due to attention mechanism's operation that matches different position information to store feature-consistent data and neglect content's diversity. Thus, information distortion and redundancy occurred in the model. Additionally, the performance of supervised methods is related to the quality and quantity of the annotated data. Collecting a large amount of annotated video data as well as standard annotations are extremely labor-intensive.

Recently, unsupervised methods achieve promising performance and even match up with the accuracy of supervised learning methods. Mahasseni et al. [5] utilized a variational autoencoder (VAE) and generative adversarial networks (GANs) to learn keyframes without importance score labels. However, when dealing with long video sequence, the training of GAN-based model had difficulty in convergence. Zhou et al. [6] subsequently presented an end-to-end unsupervised model (DR-DSN) under reinforcement learning framework and adopted policy gradient to update the parameters in DR-DSN. Jing et al. [1] proposed to utilize the structure information between the sorce video and target summary video. In practice, DR-DSN shows slow learning ability because the cost computation lags behind model per step's selection.

In conclusion, it is fair to say that unsupervised methods are promising. But when handling a long sequence, the insufficient training leads to the difficulties in learning optimal selection policy. In contrary, although supervised methods, especially attention-based model, can deal with a long sequence well by means of selectively storing information, the high redundancy among keyframes as well as the limitation on supervised training are needed to be solved urgently.

In this work, a novel Temporal Attention Summarization model (TASM) is proposed and trained via an unsupervised fashion. Furthermore, in TASM, a combination mechanism of encoder and decoder is designed for obtaining as comprehensive as possible coded information. Second, we devise a feedforward properties reward, a comprehensive value of candidate keyframes' diversity, representativeness, and storyness scores, to enhance keyframes' variedness. Last, the Deep Deterministic Policy Gradient (DDPG) algorithm [20] is adopted to efficiently solve the proposed formulation, which alleviates the training problem in unsupervised methods.

1) To solve the issue of high redundant frames in summarizing user created video, we propose a comprehensive feedforward properties reward which combines the score of diversity, representativeness, and storyness property of candidate keyframes.
2) We propose to extend decoder's prediction to encoder's prediction, which can unitedly take advantages of data in both encoder and decoder rather than distorted information in decoder to decrease the negative affect from information distortion.

3) We first adopt DDPG to extend our model into unsupervised fashion under reinforcement learning framework. Comprehensive and detailed experiments, conducted on two general datasets, SumMe and TVSum, demonstrate that our method outperforms the state-of-the-art unsupervised method [6] by 18.4% and 2.1% F-score improvements, respectively.

2 Related Work

The area of supervised methods for video summarization is relatively mature. Gong et al. [8] treated video summarization as a "sequence-to-sequence" problem and designed a sequential determinantal point process algorithm (SeqDPP) to measure the diversity of the selected shots. Because LSTM can accurately capture the inter-dependencies in video frames, Zhang et al. [3] combined it with SeqDPP [8] to select keyframes that were semantically relevant and diverse. In addition, Ji [4] developed an LSTM-based encoder-decoder architecture that was trained using supervised method. Zhong et al. incorporate a self-attention mechanism into an encoder-decoder attention mechanism [2]. The performance of supervised methods of video summarization depends on the quality of the annotated dataset. However, it is extremely labor-intensive to generate high-quality annotated datasets. Compared with ground-truth labels, human-crafted criteria, including diversity and representativeness, have the same effect in training video summarization models. The disadvantage in unsupervised learning approaches, such as traditional clustering-based [9] and graph-based [10], is that they do not apply to general cases. Using the power of deep learning, methods based on GAN [5] and reinforcement learning [6] have been proposed for general applications. Even without the guidance of labels, methods, based on deep learning, can approach the performance of supervised learning methods.

3 Problem Formulation

Our baseline method is M-AVS [4] which formulates the video summarization problem as a sequence-to-sequence problem and adopts AM model, proposed by Dzmitry et al. [21], to model the selecting keyframes process.

Given a long video $X = \{x_t\}_{t=1}^T$, where $x_t \in \mathbb{R}^{w \times h \times c}$, w, h, c is per frame's width, height and channel, t is the number of the frames. The attention-based model outputs $Y = \{y_t\}_{t=1}^T, y_t \in [0, 1]$ is the t_{th} label which represents whether t_{th} frame is selected as key frame ("1" is true and "0" is false). The collection of the selected frames composes the final video summarization $X_{sub} = \{x_t | t \in E\}, E = \{t \in [1, T] | y_t = 1\}$.

The AM model consists of an encoder, an attention module, and a decoder. Generally, the encoder is a Bidirectional LSTM (Bi-LSTM [7]) to encode the input sequence into a context vector; the attention mechanism is designed for concentrating the relevant hidden states in encoder; the decoder is an LSTM for translating the context vector and outputting target prediction.

In the decoder, p_t is conditioned on a context vector c_t for each previous output p_{t-1} in Eq. (1) as:

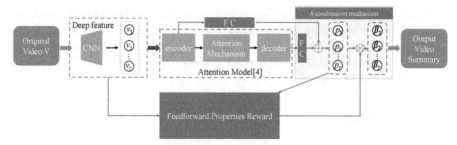

Fig. 1. The proposed model contains a feedforward reward and a combination mechanism for the attention model.

$$p_t = p\{p_t|p_1, p_2, ..., p_{t-1}, V\} = G(p_{t-1}, s_t, c_t), \tag{1}$$

where s_t is hidden state in LSTM for time t, computed by

$$s_t = F(p_{t-1}, s_{t-1}, c_t).$$

The context vector c_t is a weighted sum of the encoder's hidden states $(h_1, h_2, ..., h_T)$, computed by Eq. (4). Each hidden state h_t, $h_t = [h_t^f, h_t^b]$ in Bi-LSTM stores the backward and forward information (they are denoted as h_t^b and h_t^f, respectively) for t time, computed as Eq. (2)–Eq. (3):

$$h_t^f = f(W_1 v + \hat{W}_1 h_{t-1}^f + \hat{b}_1), \tag{2}$$

$$h_t^b = f(W_2 v + \hat{W}_2 h_{t+1}^b + \hat{b}_2), \tag{3}$$

$$c_t = \sum_{t'=1}^{T} (a_{t't} h_{t'}), \ t' \in [1, T], \tag{4}$$

where $f(\cdot)$ represents the nonlinear computation of LSTM, the $a_{t't}$ is an attention weight of encoder's hidden states, computed by Eq. (5):

$$a_{t't} = \frac{\exp(e_{t't})}{\sum_{k=1}^{T} \exp(e_{tk})}, \tag{5}$$

where $e_{t't} = \begin{cases} \text{score}(s_{t-1}, h_{t'}), \ t \in [2, T] \\ \text{score}(s_0, h_{t'}), \ t = 1 \end{cases}$ is an align model for scoring the matching level between t_{th}- and t'_{th}-information. The align model essentially measures the similarity of coded information in different position. Therefore, in [4], more similar data will be reserved in the context vector.

4 Main Components of Our Model

In this section, we will introduce the proposed model TASM. First, based on M-AVS [4], we design a feedforward properties reward, including diversity, representativeness, and storyness properties, to further sift unnecessary frames out. Furthermore, in order to ensure the accuracy of the importance score, a weighted sum of encoder's and decoder's predictions is utilized for determining the keyframes. The render pipeline is showed in Fig. 1.

4.1 Feedforward Properties Reward (FP-R)

Temporal importance score $B = \{\beta_t\}_{t=1}^T$ is obtained by weighting temporal probability $P = \{p_t\}_{t=1}^T$. Most notably, for t time, the β_t depends upon the output p_t of the proposed attention model (it will be described in part 4.2) and its corresponding feedforward reward k_t, computed as Eq. (6):

$$\beta_t = \frac{\exp(k_t \cdot p_t)}{\sum_{t'=1}^T \exp(k_{t'} \cdot p_{t'})}, \quad \sum_{t=1}^T p_t = 1, \tag{6}$$

Specifically, diversity, representativeness, and storyness are important properties for evaluating the quality of a video summarization. The k_t is a comprehensive score of candidate keyframes' diversity, representativeness, and storyness property. These properties functions have been applied to video summarization methods and achieved promising performance in [5, 6], computed by Eq. (7)–Eq. (9):

$$R_{diversity}(\tau) = \frac{1}{|E|(|E| - 1)} \sum_{t \in |E|} \sum_{t' \in |E|} \left(1 - \frac{\tau_t^T \tau_{t'}}{\|\tau_t\|_2 \|\tau_{t'}\|_2} \right), \tag{7}$$

$$R_{representative}(\tau) = \exp\left(-\frac{1}{|E|} \sum_{t=1}^{|E|} \min_{t' \in n} \|\tau_t - \tau_{t'}\|_2 \right), \tag{8}$$

$$R_{storyness}(E, T) = \exp\left\{ -\sum_j \left| (E_{j+1} - E_j) - \frac{|T|}{|E|} \right| \right\}, \tag{9}$$

where $|E|$ is the amount of candidate key frames, $|T|$ is the amount of video frames. Usually, K-mediods algorithm [12] determines clips' mediods $\tau_{t'}$ which has the minimal-distance summation with data points. The diversity function $R_{diversity}(\cdot)$ computes the cosine similarity between selected frames τ_t and the subset mediods $\tau_{t'}$; The representativeness function $R_{representative}(\cdot)$ is the exponential of squared errors between the selected frame τ_t and the nearest clips' mediods $\tau_{t'}$; The $R_{storyness}(\cdot)$ measures the level of uniform distribution of key frames by computing the distance between consecutive key frames' interval $E_{j+1} - E_j$ and mean interval $\frac{|T|}{|E|}$.

Referred the work of [23]. The weighted sum of three properties is denoted as Eq. (10),

$$k_t = \frac{1}{T}\left(0.2R_{diversity} + 0.23R_{representative} + 0.05R_{storyness}\right). \tag{10}$$

4.2 Bi-LSTM- and LSTM-Based Temporal Attention Model (Bi-LTAM)

On the baseline AM model, we make an improvement by expanding the prediction at decoder to encoder. The hidden states in decoder tend to store identical information because of the align mechanism in AM. However, encoder contains relatively original information. Therefore, we take advantage of data in both encoder and decoder for predicting the frames' importance scores, as Eq. (11) shows:

$$p_t = 0.5(de\_p_t + en\_p_t), \tag{11}$$

where the probability de_p_t for t time is predicted by LSTM as Eq. (1), en_p_t is predicted by encoder.

In Bi-LSTM, the forward- and backward-hidden states are denoted as h_t^f and h_t^b ($h_t^f \in \mathbb{R}^{256}$, $h_t^b \in \mathbb{R}^{256}$), The final output of encoder is $h_t = [h_t^b, h_t^f]$, $h_t \in \mathbb{R}^{512}$,which concatenates the h_t^f and h_t^b. The probability predicted by Bi-LSTM is computed as Eq. (12):

$$en\_p_t = \sigma(Wh_t), \tag{12}$$

where a FC layer that ends with a sigmoid function $\sigma(\cdot)$ predicts en_p_t for each frame.

4.3 Generating Video Summarization

The binary possibility set $Y = \{y_t\}_{t=1}^T$ indicates whether a frame is selected into the video summarization, which relies on the temporal importance score $B = \{\beta_t\}_{t=1}^T$ ($\beta_t \in [0, 1]$). The key frames are sampled according to the Bernoulli distribution [11], as shown in Eq. (13):

$$y_t = Bernoulli(\beta_t), \ y_t \in \{0, 1\}. \tag{13}$$

4.4 Training and Optimization

We adopt the DDPG algorithm to train TASM. The DDPG is a united algorithm of actor-critic and deterministic policy gradient algorithm [20], which contains two kinds of model, named actor and critic. Actor takes action according to the environment state; critic evaluates the actor's action and provides action-value. In this work, the proposed TASM is served as the actor and we develop a linear regression network to play as critic. The actor network aims to learn a policy μ_{θ^μ} by maximizing the expected actor-value as Eq. (14):

$$\max_{\theta^\mu} J(\mu) = E_{s: p^\beta}[Q^{\mu_{\theta^\mu}}(s, \mu_{\theta^\mu}(s))], \tag{14}$$

where θ^μ is parameter in the policy function, p^β is the state visitation distribution, s is hidden state in decoder, $Q^{\mu_{\theta^\mu}}(\cdot)$ is the actor-value function, modelled by the critic.

Following [20], we use deterministic policy gradient algorithm to take the derivative of $J(\mu)$.the parameters in critic is updated by minimizing SmoothL$_1$ Loss on the basis of the predicted action-value and the expected action-value.

5 Experiments

5.1 Implementation Details

Datasets. We verify the performance of our model on two public datasets: SumMe [13] and TVSum [14]. The SumMe dataset consists of 25 videos covering a wide range of topics, including sports and vacations. The video durations range from 1–6 min. More than 15 users generate human-created summaries and provide frame-level importance scores. TVSum contains 50 videos in 10 categories selected from YouTube. The videos are about 1–5 min in length, and the frame-level importance of each video is scored by 20 users. Two other datasets, YouTube [9] and the Open Video Project (OVP)[1], are used to augment the training data [5, 6]. The YouTube dataset contains 39 YouTube videos, and OVP contains 50 documentary videos.

Evaluation Metrics. For a fair comparison with the other methods, we adopt the commonly used evaluation metric the F-score [15]. Assuming that A is an algorithm-generated summary and B is a user-generated video summary, the precise P and the recall R are calculated using Eq. (15), and then the harmonic mean F-score is computed using Eq. (16) [2, 5, 6].

$$
\begin{aligned}
P &= \frac{overlapped\ duration\ of\ A\ and\ B}{duration\ of\ A}, \\
R &= \frac{overlapped\ duration\ of\ A\ and\ B}{duration\ of\ B}.
\end{aligned}
\tag{15}
$$

$$
F = (2 \times P \times R)/(P + R). \tag{16}
$$

Experimental Settings. Following the general down-sampling ratio [4, 6], we sample the video at 2 frames per second (fps) into a subset as an original input. The hidden-layer sizes of the attention modules based on the Bi-LSTM and LSTM are set to 256 and 512, respectively. The episode is N = 8, and the learning rate is 1e−4. The maximum epoch is 60, but the training process will be stopped early if the convergence occurs in 5 epochs in a row. We employ the standard 5-Fold Cross Validation (5FCV), which uses 80% of the videos for training and 20% for testing [5]. We run the TASM model five times and report the average performance.

---

[1] Open video project: https://open-video.org/.

5.2   Experiment Results

Comparison with Unsupervised Approaches. The previous unsupervised methods can be roughly classified into two categories: methods based on temporal structure (GANdpp [5] and DR-DSN [6]) and those not based on temporal structures (K-mediods, Vsumm [9], Web image [16], dictionary selection [17], online sparse coding [18], and co-archetypal [13]). It is obvious that on both datasets the methods based on temporal structures outperform those not based on temporal structures. Thus, we further devise a novel unsupervised temporal attention model TASM for video summarization.

Table 1. Comparison with unsupervised approaches.

Method	SumMe (F-score %)	TVSum (F-score %)
K-mediods	33.4	28.8
Vsumm [9]	33.7	–
Web image [16]	–	36
Dictionary selection [17]	37.8	42
Online sparse coding [18]	–	46
Co-archetypal [13]	–	50
GANdpp [5]	39.1	51.7
DR-DSN [6]	41.4	57.6
TASM	**49.0**	**58.8**

Compared to the previous methods, TASM improves the F-score by a large margin on both SumMe and TVSum datasets. As Table 1 shows, the F-scores of the proposed TASM are 18.4% and 2.1% higher than those of the state-of-the-art unsupervised method DR-DSN [6] on the SumMe and TVSum datasets, respectively.

Interestingly, compared to DR-DSN, the improvement of 18.4%, gained using the TASM on SumMe dataset, substantially exceeds the improvement on TVSum dataset. This is mainly because that the association within each shot of a video in the SumMe dataset is looser than that in TVSum. Thus it is more suitable to emphasis the diversity of keyframes in SumMe videos, which makes for a better performance on SumMe dataset.

Comparison with Supervised Approaches. Table 2 shows that the proposed unsupervised TASM outperforms than other supervised methods on SumMe dataset. Compared with the state-of-the-art supervised method M-AVS [4], the notable improvement by 10.3% on SumMe dataset can demonstrate the effectiveness of TASM on dealing with raw user-created videos. However, the results, gained using TASM, decreases by 3.7% on TVSum. Videos in TVSum dataset are edited by video producers and shots have compact association with each other. Therefore, diversity property is less important for videos in TVSum. Additionally, supervised methods theoretically can achieve better performance than unsupervised methods when there are adequate training samplings.

Table 2. Comparison with supervised approaches.

Method	SumMe (F-score %)	TVSum (F-score %)
Interestingness [13]	39.4	–
Submodularity [12]	39.7	–
Summary transfer [19]	40.9	–
Bi-LSTM [3]	37.6	54.2
Dpp-LSTM [3]	38.6	54.7
GANsup [5]	41.7	56.3
DR-DSNsup [6]	42.1	58.1
Li et al. [22]	43.9	52.7
M-AVS [4]	44.4	**61.0**
TASM	**49.0**	58.8

Although M-AVS and ours adopt same component-AM model, we make an improvement using a feedforward reward and a combination mechanism of encoder and decoder to solve the information redundancy and distortion problem in M-AVS. Thus, compared to Li et al. [22], it can be observed that M-AVS gains only 1 absolute points improvement on SumMe while the proposed STAM achieves 5 absolute points improvement.

Furthermore, we note the positive effects of the reinforcement-learning algorithm DDPG adopted in the TASM. Generally, supervised methods perform better than methods in unsupervised fashion. However, for the TASM, the unsupervised version achieves an F-score of 49.0% on the SumMe dataset and the supervised M-AVS achieves an F-score of 44.4%, as shown in Table 2. With the adoption of the DDPG algorithm, the unsupervised method achieves better performance than the supervised methods. Thus, we conclude that the reinforcement-learning algorithm is efficient within the framework of unsupervised training methods.

Comparison in Augmentation and Transfer Settings. We follow [5] and [6] for three settings: canonical, augmented, and transfer, which are denoted as C, A, and T, respectively, in Table 3. For setting A, we randomly pick 20% of the videos in a given dataset to test and combine the rest with the OVP and YouTube videos to use as a training dataset. For setting T, we use the entire given dataset for testing and the other three datasets for training. Setting C is the standard 5FCV.

Table 3. Comparison in augmentation and transfer settings (F-score %).

Method	SumMe			TVSum		
	C	A	T	C	A	T
Bi-LSTM [3]	37.6	41.6	40.7	54.2	57.9	56.9
Dpp-LSTM [3]	38.6	42.9	41.8	54.7	59.6	58.7
GANdpp [5]	39.1	43.4	–	51.7	59.5	–
DR-DSN [6]	41.4	42.8	42.4	57.6	58.4	57.8
M-AVS	44.4	46.1	–	61	61.8	–
TASM	**49.0**	**46.9**	**44.0**	**58.8**	59.4	58.2

On SumMe dataset, it can be seen that TASM achieves best performance in all three kinds of settings (C, A, T). For instant, in setting A, TASM outperforms M-AVS by 1.7% in terms of F-score.

Additionally, on TVSum dataset, TASM catches up with and even surpasses the existing unsupervised methods GANdpp and DR-DSN in setting C, A, and T. However, compared to supervised method, TASM shows slightly inferior performance. It mainly lies in the fact that videos in the OVP and YouTube datasets are user-edited as same as those in TVSum.

6 Conclusions

For summarizing user-created videos, the existing methods have two critical issues: 1) information distortion in model 2) high redundancy among keyframes. To address the critical issues, we design a novel attention model under the framework of attention-based encoder-decoder. To address the information distortion in decoder, we propose a combination mechanism which takes fully advantage of information in both encoder and decoder. For overcoming the redundancy problem in classical attention mechanism, a feedforward reward value, combing diversity, representativeness, and storyness, is adopted to modify the attention model's scoring directly. Last, the state-of-the-art reinforcement learning method, DDPG, is used solve the formulations to achieve speedy convergence. Extensive experiments on the public SumMe and TVSum datasets show that our proposed TASM model outperforms the state-of-the-art unsupervised methods. In the future, we would like to explore a higher efficient light weight spatio-temporal attention model for video summarization.

References

1. Zhang, J., et al.: A structure-transfer-driven temporal subspace clustering for video summarization. Multimedia Tools Appl. **78**(1), 24123–24145 (2019). https://doi.org/10.1007/s11042-018-6841-4
2. Ji, Z., et al.: Deep Attentive Video Summarization With Distribution Consistency Learning (2020)
3. Zhang, K., Chao, W.-L., Sha, F., Grauman, K.: Video summarization with long short-term memory. In: Leibe, B., Matas, J., Sebe, N., Welling, M. (eds.) ECCV 2016. LNCS, vol. 9911, pp. 766–782. Springer, Cham (2016). https://doi.org/10.1007/978-3-319-46478-7_47
4. Ji, Z., Xiong, K., Pang, Y., Li, X.: Video summarization with attention-based encoder-decoder networks. IEEE Trans. Circuits Syst. Video Technol **30** (6). Early Access (2020)
5. Mahasseni, B., Lam, M., Todorovic, S.: Unsupervised video summarization with adversarial LSTM networks. In: Proceedings of the IEEE Conference on Computer Vision and Pattern Recognition, pp. 202– 211 (2017)
6. Zhou, K., Qiao, Y., Xiang, T.: Deep reinforcement learning for unsupervised video summarization with diversity-representativeness reward. In: Thirty-Second AAAI Conference on Artificial Intelligence, pp. 7582–7589 (2018)
7. Lipton, Z.C., Berkowitz, J., Elkan, C.: A critical review of recurrent neural networks for sequence learning. arXiv preprint arXiv:1506.00019 (2015)
8. Gong, B., Chao, W.-L., Grauman, K., Sha, F.: Diverse sequential subset selection for supervised video summarization. In: Advances in Neural Information Processing Systems, pp. 2069–2077 (2014)
9. Avila, S.E.F.D., Lopes, A.P.B., da Luz Jr., A., de Albuquerque Arajo, A.: VSUMM: a mechanism designed to produce static video summaries and a novel evaluation method. Pattern Recogn. Lett. **32**(1), 56–68 (2011)
10. Lu, Z., Grauman, K.: Story-driven summarization for egocentric video. In: Proceedings of the IEEE Conference on Computer Vision and Pattern Recognition, pp. 2714–2721 (2013)
11. El-Ghoroury, H.N., Gupta, S.C.: Additive Bernoulli noise linear sequential circuits. IEEE Trans. Comput. **100**(10), 1119–1124 (1972)
12. Gygli, M., Grabner, H., Van Gool, L.: Video summarization by learning submodular mixtures of objectives. In: Proceedings of the IEEE Conference on Computer Vision and Pattern Recognition, pp. 3090–3098 (2015)
13. Gygli, M., Grabner, H., Riemenschneider, H., Van Gool, L.: Creating summaries from user videos. In: Fleet, D., Pajdla, T., Schiele, B., Tuytelaars, T. (eds.) ECCV 2014. LNCS, vol. 8695, pp. 505–520. Springer, Cham (2014). https://doi.org/10.1007/978-3-319-10584-0_33
14. Song, Y., Vallmitjana, J., Stent, A., Jaimes, A.: TVSum: summarizing web videos using titles. In: Proceedings of the IEEE Conference on Computer Vision and Pattern Recognition, pp. 5179–5187 (2015)
15. Lin, C.-Y.: Rouge: a package for automatic evaluation of summaries. In: Text Summarization Branches Out, pp. 74–81 (2004)
16. Khosla, A., Hamid, R., Lin, C.-J., Sundaresan, N.: Large-scale video summarization using web-image priors. In: Proceedings of the IEEE Conference on Computer Vision and Pattern Recognition, pp. 2698– 2705 (2013)
17. Elhamifar, E., Sapiro, G., Vidal, R.: Sparse modeling for finding representative objects. Preparation **4**(6), 8 (2012)
18. Zhao, B., Xing, E.P.: Quasi real-time summarization for consumer videos. In: Proceedings of the IEEE Conference on Computer Vision and Pattern Recognition, pp. 2513–2520 (2014)
19. Zhang, K., Chao, W.-L., Sha, F., Grauman, K.: Summary transfer: exemplar-based subset selection for video summarization. In: Proceedings of the IEEE Conference on Computer Vision and Pattern Recognition, pp. 1059–1067 (2016)

20. Lillicrap, T.P., et al.: Continuous control with deep reinforcement learning. Computer Science, vol. 23, no. 8, p. 187 (2015)
21. Dzmitry, B., Cho, K., Bengio, Y.: Neural machine translation by jointly learning to align and translate. Computer Science (2014)
22. Li, X., Zhao, B., Lu, X.: A general framework for edited video and raw video summarization. IEEE Trans. Image Process. **26**(8), 3652–3664 (2017)
23. Sreeja, M.U., Kovoor, B.C.: Towards genre-specific frameworks for video summarisation: a survey. J. Vis. Commun. Image Represent. **62**, 340–358 (2019)

Learning from the Negativity: Deep Negative Correlation Meta-Learning for Adversarial Image Classification

Wenbo Zheng[1,3], Lan Yan[3,4], Fei-Yue Wang[3,4], and Chao Gou[2(✉)]

[1] School of Software Engineering, Xi'an Jiaotong University, Xi'an, China
zwb2017@stu.xjtu.edu.cn
[2] School of Intelligent Systems Engineering, Sun Yat-sen University,
Guangzhou, China
gouchao@mail.sysu.edu.cn
[3] The State Key Laboratory for Management and Control of Complex Systems,
Institute of Automation, Chinese Academy of Sciences, Beijing, China
{Yanlan2017,feiyue.wang}@ia.ac.cn
[4] School of Artificial Intelligence, University of Chinese Academy of Sciences,
Beijing, China

Abstract. Adversarial images are commonly viewed negatively for neural network training. Here we present an opposite perspective: adversarial images can be used to investigate the problem of classifying adversarial images themselves. To this end, we propose a novel framework termed as **Deep Negative Correlation Meta-Learning**. In particular, we present a deep relation network to capture and memorize the relation among different samples. We further formulate a deep negative correlation learning, and design a novel meta-learning-based classifier to prevent overfitting and learn discriminative features. The final classification is derived from our relation network by learning to compare the features of samples. Experimental results demonstrate that our approach achieves significantly higher performance compared with other state-of-the-arts.

Keywords: Meta-Learning · Negative correlation · Adversarial images

1 Introduction

Deep neural networks (DNNs) are vulnerable to adversarial examples-maliciously crafted inputs that cause DNNs to make incorrect predictions. This phenomenon not only brings to light the limitations of neural networks, but also raises security risks to physical implementation of these models.

Over the years, many researchers have proposed ways to deal with adversarial image challenges. The modern deep neural networks can achieve high accuracy when the training distribution and test distribution are identically distributed [5]. Still, this assumption is frequently violated in practice. When the train and test distributions are mismatched, accuracy can plummet. All in all, many

© Springer Nature Switzerland AG 2021
J. Lokoč et al. (Eds.): MMM 2021, LNCS 12572, pp. 531–540, 2021.
https://doi.org/10.1007/978-3-030-67832-6_43

researchers propose two possible settlements recently: one is the data augmentation based approaches (for instance, Patch Uniform [3]); the other is "Divide-and-conquer" approaches, which means using two batch norm statistics, one for normal images and one auxiliary for adversarial images, for instance, Noisy Student [18]. However, improvements in these models are limited. Therefore, instead of focusing on defending against adversarial images, we concentrate on classifying the adversarial images themselves, where the only adversarial images are used to both train and test machine learning based models, not normal images used.

In this paper, we propose a novel meta-learning-based model for the adversarial image classification tasks, based on deep negative correlation learning strategy. We build a two-branch relation network via meta-learning. First, we use the embedding approach to do feature extraction of training images. In this process, we introduce deep negative correlation learning to our network. Then, to compare the features, we design a relation model that determines if they are from matching categories or not. We conduct experiments on DAmageNet [1] and Stylized-ImageNet [2] datasets. Experimental results show that our model performs better than similar works, and has strong robustness.

In summary, our main contributions are as follows:

☼ To the best of our knowledge, our work is the first to both define and show adversarial image classification on adversarial image datasets.

☼ We integrate deep negative correlation learning into the meta-based model, which can effectively prevent overfitting and learn the discriminative features on unseen class samples. To the best our knowledge, this is the first attempt to study the image classification approach based on deep negative correlation meta-learning.

☼ Our network is effective, and experimental results show that the proposed approach has strong robustness and outperforms existing methods.

2 Deep Negative Correlation Meta-Learning Based Approach

2.1 Problem Setup

Before elaborating on the proposed network, we briefly present the notations and prior knowledge.

There are three datasets [6,9,11,13,14,19–22]: a training set, a support set, and a test set. We can in principle train a classifier to assign a class label $\hat{y}$ to each sample $\hat{x}$ in the test set while we only use the support set. However, in most cases, the performance of such a classifier is usually not excellent because of the lack of the labeled samples in the support set. Therefore, we use the meta-learning on the training set to transfer the extracted knowledge to the support set. It aims to perform the few-shot learning on the support set better and classify the test set more successfully.

We propose novel matching networks [6,8,9,11,13–16,19–22] to solve the problem of adversarial image classification. Suppose there are m labeled samples for each of n unique classes in support set. We select randomly n classes from the training set with m labeled samples from each of the n classes to conduct the sample set $S = \{(x_i, y_i)\}^z_{i=1} (z = m \times n)$, and we select the remaining samples to conduct the query set $Q = \{(x_j, y_j)\}^v_{j=1}$. This sample/query set split is designed to simulate the support/test set that will be encountered at test time.

2.2   Network Formulation

When the traditional classifier (e.g., convolutional neural networks (CNNs)) are trained with adversarial images, most of which are noisy data, it can over-fit to such a dataset, resulting in poor classification performance. To address this issue, we suggest deep negative correlation meta-learning [10], the core of which is the generalization of negative correlation learning and meta-learning. Based on it, we propose a novel matching networks based on relational network [11] to solve the problem of adversarial image classification. First, we meta-learn a *negative correlation learning based feature extraction model*. The well-learned features of the query samples in the support set are then fed into relation networks to learn the similarity scores. Further, we conduct a few-shot classification based on these scores.

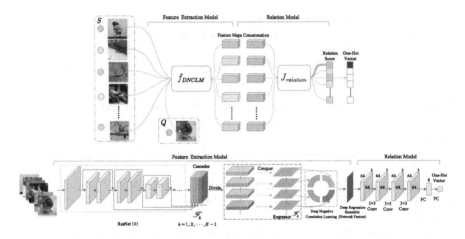

Fig. 1. The pipeline and network architecture of our model. Top: the pipeline of our model. Meta-classifier contains two modules: a feature extraction model and a relation model. The feature extraction model f_{DNCLM}, which means using deep negative correlation learning, produces feature maps to represent feature extraction function. The relation model $J_{relation}$ represents the similarity between the sample set S and query set Q; Bottom: the network architecture of our model. The classifier uses designed network based on ResNet-101 and deep negative correlation learning as feature extraction model, including the cascades of each Res-layer $\mathscr{F}_k, k = 1, 2, \cdots, K-1$ and a regressor $\mathscr{F}_K$. The output of this network can be regarded as network features, and then we apply the relation model.

Deep Negative Correlation Meta-Learning Based Classifier: As illustrated in Fig. 1, our matching network consists of two branches: a **feature extraction model** and a **relation model** during the training of our network.

Negative Correlation Learning Based Feature Extraction: Similar to Ref. [10], we design the network to learn a correlation regularized ensemble by aggregating each layer features. The network can be trained with the following objective:

$$\mathcal{L}_k = \frac{1}{2}(\mathscr{F}_k - Y)^2 - \lambda(\mathscr{F}_k - \widehat{\mathscr{F}})^2 \tag{1}$$

where $\mathscr{F}_k$ means the function of the k-th layer in network aiming to feature extraction, $\mathcal{L}_k$ means the loss function of k-th layer in the network, $\widehat{\mathscr{F}}$ means the function of averaging all layers in network, and Y means the ground-truth labels of samples.

We consider our task of adversarial image classification and further define the $\mathscr{F}_k$:

$$
\begin{aligned}
\mathscr{F}_k(x_i) &= \overbrace{\mathscr{F}_k}^{\text{Regressor}} \; \overbrace{(\mathscr{F}_{k-1} \cdots (\mathscr{F}_1(x_i) \cdots)}^{\text{Feature Extractors}}, \\
k &= 1, 2, \cdots, K \\
i &= 1, 2, 3 \cdots, m \times n
\end{aligned}
\tag{2}
$$

where k and i stands for the index for each layer and data samples. More specifically, each predictor in the ensemble consists of cascades of feature extractor $\mathscr{F}_k, k = 1, 2, \cdots, K - 1$ and a regressor $\mathscr{F}_K$. Motivated by the recent success of deep residual networks (ResNets) on image classification tasks, each feature extractor $\mathscr{F}_k$ is embodied by a typical layer of a ResNet.

Meta-Learning Based Relation Model: We further introduce a non-linear distance relation model to learn to compare the sample features in a few-shot classification.

Suppose sample x_j in the query set Q and sample x_i in the sample set S, we define the function f_{DNCLM} which represents feature extraction function using deep negative correlation learning based model (DNCLM) to produce feature maps $f_{DNCLM}(x_j)$ and $f_{DNCLM}(x_i)$. The feature maps are combined using the function C_{DNCLM}.

The combined feature map of the sample and query is used as the relation model $J_{relation}(\cdot)$ to get a scalar in range of 0 to 1 representing the similarity between x_i and x_j, which is called relation score. Suppose we have one labeled sample for each of n unique classes, our model can generate n relation scores $Judge_{i,j}$ for the relation between one query input x_j and training sample set examples x_i:

$$
\begin{aligned}
Judge_{i,j} &= J_{relation}(C_{DNCLM}(f_{DNCLM}(x_i), f_{DNCLM}(x_j))), \\
i &= 1, 2, \cdots, n
\end{aligned}
\tag{3}
$$

Furthermore, for m labeled samples for each of n unique classes, we use element-wise sum over our feature extraction model outputs of all samples from each training class to form this class's feature map. And this pooled class-level feature map is combined with the query image feature map as above.

We use mean square error (MSE) loss to train our model, regressing the relation score $Judge_{i,j}$ to the ground truth: matched pairs have similarity 1 and the mismatched pair have similarity 0.

$$Loss = \arg\min \sum_{i=1}^{n} \sum_{j=1}^{m} (Judge_{i,j} - (y_i == y_j))^2 \qquad (4)$$

2.3 Network Architecture

Our network architecture is shown in Fig. 1. Our network consists of two parts. The first part use ResNet-101 and fully convolutional layers for input images. In other words, we employ the ResNet-101 as $\mathscr{F}_k, k = 1, 2, \cdots, 101$, and one fully convolutional layer as a regressor $\mathscr{F}_{102}$; The second part, relation networks, learns to learn a deep distance metric to compare images, each of which is designed to simulate the few-shot setting. Once trained, relation networks are able to classify images of new classes by computing relaion scores between query images and the few examples of each new class without further updating the network.

Feature Extraction Model: We employ the ResNet-101 architecture [4] linked with one fully convolutional layer for learning the feature extraction model. When meta-learn the feature extraction, we used Adam optimizer [7] with a learning rate of 0.001 and a decay for every 50 epochs. We train 800 epochs when the loss starts to converge.

Relation Model: We use the 6-layer network architecture, which consists of four convolutional blocks and two fully-connected layers. Each of convolutional block is a 3×3 convolution with 64 filters followed by batch normalisation, ReLU non-linearity and 2×2 max-pooling. Finally, We use two fully-connected layers to have 8 and 1 outputs, respectively, followed by a sigmoid function to get the final similarity scores mentioned in Eq. (4). Other network settings are similar to our feature extraction model.

3 Experiments and Results

We evaluated the performance of our algorithm and compared approaches in terms of its accuracy.

3.1 Experimental Settings

The images of the two datasets are resized to $224 \times 224 \times 3$. On the DAmageNet dataset [1], we randomly choose a subset of 1000 classes with 20 samples of each class for training and testing. We choose only 15 face images of each class to construct a training set, and the remaining samples are test images; On the Stylized-ImageNet dataset [2], we use a similar experimental strategy to the DAmageNet dataset. In this paper, we use these settings to train and test our algorithm and comparison approaches for a fair comparison. We randomly choose 10 times as per the settings and take the average classification accuracy for comparison.

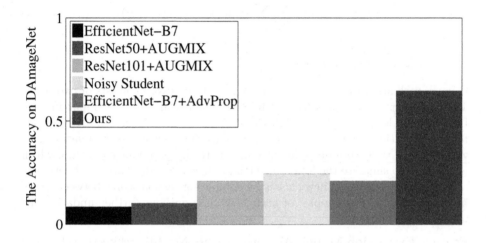

Fig. 2. Performance comparison on DAmageNet

3.2   Comparison Experiment

In this subsection, we compare the state-of-the-art baselines with our model on two datasets.

Baselines: We compare against various state-of-the-art baselines, including EfficientNet-B7 [12], ResNet50+AUGMIX [5], ResNet101+AUGMIX [5], Noisy Student [18], EfficientNet-B7+AdvProp [17].

Comparison with State-of-the-Art Methods. From Fig. 2, our model is better than others on two datasets. It can get the following two points:

Firstly, EfficientNet-B7 is deep-learning-based approach. Since this kind of approach cannot effectively handle noise datasets, the performances of this kind of approach is lower than ours.

Secondly, ResNet50+AUGMIX, ResNet101+AUGMIX, Noisy Student, and EfficientNet-B7+AdvProp are the "Divide-and-conquer" approaches. As this "Divide-and-conquer" approaches cannot deal with over-fitting and adversarial images' special distribution, the performance of these is lower than ours.

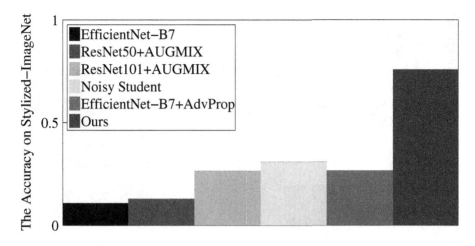

Fig. 3. Performance comparison on stylized-ImageNet

From the above two points, *it is clear that the design of deep negative corre-lation meta-learning is more effective than deep learning for adversarial image classification.* Moreover, by analyzing comparison results shown in Fig. 3, on the other dataset, we can get similar conclusions.

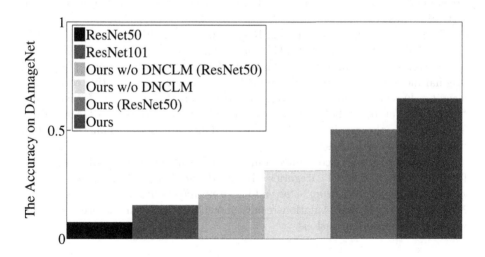

Fig. 4. The ablation results on DAmageNet

3.3   Ablation Experiment

In this subsection, in order to verify the reasonableness and effectiveness of *deep negative correlation learning based model*, we design the Ablation experiment.

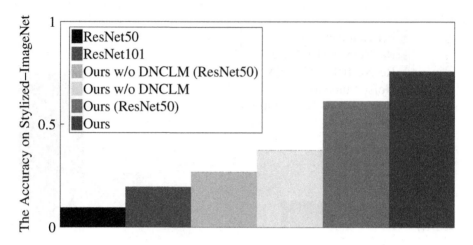

Fig. 5. The ablation results on stylized-ImageNet

In Fig. 4 and Fig. 5, "**Ours (ResNet50)**" means a variant of "Ours", which use ResNet50 instead of ResNet101; "**Ours w/o DNCLM**" means a variant of Ours, which removes deep negative correlation learning based model, and at this point, we use traditional meta-learning strategy; "**Ours w/o DNCLM (ResNet50)**" means a variant of "Ours w/o DNCLM", which use ResNet50 instead of ResNet101.

From Fig. 4, Ours is better than ResNet50, ResNet101, "Ours w/o DNCLM (ResNet50)", "Ours w/o DNCLM", and "Ours (ResNet50)", on DAmageNet, respectively. This means our model is more effective than all variants of Ours and original models (ResNet50 or ResNet101), due to our deep negative correlation learning. Further, from Fig. 4, Ours is better than ResNet101 on DAmageNet. "Ours (ResNet50)" is better "Ours w/o DNCLM (ResNet50)" on DAmageNet. This suggests the results of all variants of Ours are better than the original models (ResNet50 or ResNet101).

The above means, once trained, our network is able to extract discriminative features for unseen novel categories. *All in all, these suggest our design of deep negative correlation learning helps us to improve adversarial image classification.* Moreover, by analyzing Ablation results shown in Fig. 5, on the other dataset, we can get similar conclusions.

4   Conclusion

Adversarial samples are commonly considered an obstacle to training neural networks, and is generally only used as a test image to detect the performance of the trained neural network. Here we pose a different view: to use adversarial images for studying this kind of special samples themselves. In this paper, we propose a novel framework termed as deep negative correlation meta-learning to address this task. We build the two-branch relation network via meta-learning. First, we use the embedding approach to do feature extraction of training images. In this process, we introduce deep negative correlation learning to our network. Then, to compare the features, we design a relation model that determines if they are from matching categories or not. Experimental results demonstrate that our approach achieves significantly higher performance compared with state-of-the-arts.

Acknowledgment. This work is supported in part by the Key Research and Development Program of Guangzhou (202007050002), in part by the National Natural Science Foundation of China (61806198, 61533019, U1811463), and in part by the National Key Research and Development Program of China (No. 2018AAA0101502).

References

1. Chen, S., Huang, X., He, Z., Sun, C.: DAmageNet: a universal adversarial dataset. arXiv:1912.07160, December 2019
2. Geirhos, R., Rubisch, P., Michaelis, C., Bethge, M., Wichmann, F.A., Brendel, W.: Imagenet-trained CNNs are biased towards texture; increasing shape bias improves accuracy and robustness. In: ICLR (2019). https://openreview.net/forum?id=Bygh9j09KX
3. Gontijo Lopes, R., Yin, D., Poole, B., Gilmer, J., Cubuk, E.D.: Improving robustness without sacrificing accuracy with Patch Gaussian augmentation. arXiv:1906.02611, June 2019
4. He, K., Zhang, X., Ren, S., Sun, J.: Deep residual learning for image recognition. In: CVPR, June 2016
5. Hendrycks, D., Mu, N., Cubuk, E.D., Zoph, B., Gilmer, J., Lakshminarayanan, B.: AugMix: a simple data processing method to improve robustness and uncertainty. In: ICLR (2020)
6. Hsu, J., Chen, Y., Lee, H.: Meta learning for end-to-end low-resource speech recognition. In: ICASSP 2020–2020 IEEE International Conference on Acoustics, Speech and Signal Processing (ICASSP), pp. 7844–7848 (2020)
7. Kingma, D.P., Ba, J.: Adam: a method for stochastic optimization. arXiv:1412.6980, December 2014
8. Li, P., Wei, Y., Yang, Y.: Meta parsing networks: towards generalized few-shot scene parsing with adaptive metric learning. In: Proceedings of the 28th ACM International Conference on Multimedia, MM 2020, pp. 64–72. Association for Computing Machinery, New York (2020). https://doi.org/10.1145/3394171.3413944
9. Qiao, F., Zhao, L., Peng, X.: Learning to learn single domain generalization. In: The IEEE/CVF Conference on Computer Vision and Pattern Recognition (CVPR), June 2020
10. Shi, Z., Zhang, L., Liu, Y., Cao, X., Ye, Y., Cheng, M., Zheng, G.: Crowd counting with deep negative correlation learning. In: CVPR, pp. 5382–5390, June 2018. https://doi.org/10.1109/CVPR.2018.00564
11. Sung, F., Yang, Y., Zhang, L., Xiang, T., Torr, P.H., Hospedales, T.M.: Learning to compare: Relation network for few-shot learning. In: CVPR (2018)
12. Tan, M., Le, Q.: EfficientNet: rethinking model scaling for convolutional neural networks. In: ICML, pp. 6105–6114 (2019)

13. Verma, V.K., Brahma, D., Rai, P.: Meta-learning for generalized zero-shot learning (2019)
14. Vinyals, O., Blundell, C., Lillicrap, T., Kavukcuoglu, K., Wierstra, D.: Matching networks for one shot learning. In: NIPS (2016)
15. Wang, Q., Liu, X., Liu, W., Liu, A., Liu, W., Mei, T.: Metasearch: incremental product search via deep meta-learning. IEEE Trans. Image Process. **29**, 7549–7564 (2020). https://doi.org/10.1109/TIP.2020.3004249
16. Wang, Y., Yao, Q., Kwok, J.T., Ni, L.M.: Generalizing from a few examples: a survey on few-shot learning. ACM Comput. Surv. **53**(3) (2020). https://doi.org/10.1145/3386252
17. Xie, C., Tan, M., Gong, B., Wang, J., Yuille, A., Le, Q.V.: Adversarial examples improve image recognition. arXiv:1911.09665, November 2019
18. Xie, Q., Luong, M.T., Hovy, E., Le, Q.V.: Self-training with Noisy Student improves ImageNet classification. arXiv:1911.04252, November 2019
19. Yao, H., et al.: Automated relational meta-learning. In: International Conference on Learning Representations (2020). https://openreview.net/forum?id=rklp93EtwH
20. Zheng, W., Gou, C., Yan, L.: A relation hashing network embedded with prior features for skin lesion classification. In: Suk, H.-I., Liu, M., Yan, P., Lian, C. (eds.) MLMI 2019. LNCS, vol. 11861, pp. 115–123. Springer, Cham (2019). https://doi.org/10.1007/978-3-030-32692-0_14
21. Zheng, W., Gou, C., Yan, L., Mo, S.: Learning to classify: a flow-based relation network for encrypted traffic classification. In: Huang, Y., King, I., Liu, T., van Steen, M. (eds.) WWW 2020: The Web Conference 2020, Taipei, Taiwan, 20–24 April 2020, pp. 13–22. ACM/IW3C2 (2020). https://doi.org/10.1145/3366423.3380090
22. Zheng, W., Yan, L., Gou, C., Wang, F.: Federated meta-learning for fraudulent credit card detection. In: Bessiere, C. (ed.) Proceedings of the Twenty-Ninth International Joint Conference on Artificial Intelligence, IJCAI 2020, pp. 4654–4660 (2020). ijcai.org. https://doi.org/10.24963/ijcai.2020/642

Learning 3D-Craft Generation with Predictive Action Neural Network

Ze-yu Liu[1], Jian-wei Liu[1(✉)], Xin Zuo[1], and Weimin Li[2]

[1] Department of Automation, College of Information Science and Engineering, China University of Petroleum, Beijing Campus (CUP), Beijing 102249, China
`liujw@cup.edu.cn`
[2] School of Computer Engineering and Technology, Shanghai University, Shanghai, China

Abstract. We present a deep neural network to construct human-built *3D-Craft* houses in Minecraft environment. Instead of hard exploration on constrained game environment, we propose a method learning to imitate human building order with recorded action sequence. Previous methods consider the action sequence as stacked voxel representation. However, the stacked voxel representation suffers from unnecessary computation cost and limited sequence information. To address these problems, we consider the action sequence as ordered point sets in 3D space. Our network is based on encoder-decoder framework. The encoder jointly learns local geometry and global sequence order information. In order to generate 3D shapes in physical environment, the decoder makes two-stream predictions, including action position and constructing block type. We conduct quantitative and qualitative experiments on *3D-Craft* dataset, which demonstrates that the proposed method achieves the state-of-the-art performance in house building task.

Keywords: 3D house construction · Minecraft environment · Action sequence · Ordered point sets · Encoder-decoder framework

1 Introduction

Recently, generation modeling has received an extensive attention in a wide range of tasks, such as neural language generation [1], audio generation [6], and shape generation [14]. Numerous efforts have been devoted to these areas. In this paper, we present a generative model which aims to build 3D physical houses in Minecraft environment, which requires a sequence of carefully planned building actions. In order to know how human build numerous houses in 3D space, we train network to imitate human behavior with recorded sequence of actions. Our model is helpful to understand human planning process and can be extended to other generation tasks, such as 3D printing task because 3D printing also requires delicate construction order. Different from 2D environment, 3D environment is challenging and closer to real world. Planning to build physical houses in 3D

© Springer Nature Switzerland AG 2021
J. Lokoč et al. (Eds.): MMM 2021, LNCS 12572, pp. 541–553, 2021.
https://doi.org/10.1007/978-3-030-67832-6_44

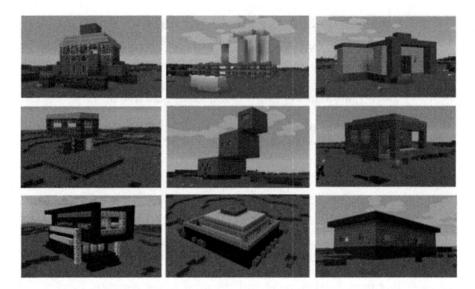

Fig. 1. Examples from the *3D-Craft* dataset [3]. Human build houses from scratch in the environment of Minecraft. The Cuberite server is used to collect crowd sourced annotation, which facilitates the model to imitate human behavior and generate realistic houses.

environment requires general knowledge of the environment, such as gravity. It is a hard problem due to potential complexity and large exploration space. Point cloud generation or reconstruction tasks [4,8,14,15] aim to generate target shape given single or multiple view image, while our task generates houses without given final constructed shape, and we target on learning natural human order by exploiting action sequences.

Previous works [3] model action sequences as stacked voxel, which is 4D sparse representation (0 or 1 to denote occupied or unoccupied). To express block type, [3] deploy additional type dimension, resulting in high dimensional sparse data. Normal voxel transformation such as 3D CNN adds large number of computation cost. Moreover, as the length of sequence grows, prior work uses fixed size of stacked frames which leads to limited sequence information. In order to overcome these problems, we first model action sequences as ordered point sets and propose a predictive neural network simultaneously modeling geometry and sequence information of the building process.

The house generation task can be divided into two stages, one involves understanding constructed blocks, and the other consists in making actions. With this in mind, we build our model based on encoder-decoder framework. The targets of encoder can be further decomposed into two parts, including geometric encoding and sequence modeling.

For encoder, we have two parts working together and combine the fine-gained features in the late fusion step. Furthermore, the model infers high-level constructing information, such as which position already constructed, which part of the house is building, and decides its current building phase. Analyzing the geometry structure of constructed blocks is related to 3D shape modeling [10,12,13,16]. The pioneering work of PointNet [13] represents detailed shape information of 3D object with coordinate format, which is storage efficient compared with sparse volumetric representation. It can be generalized to a wide range of tasks such as segmentation [13], recognition [11] and completion task [5]. However, PointNet considers shapes as unordered point sets, which lose detailed information of building process. Recently, [9] propose a network including multiple PointSIFT modules to process points. Each PointSIFT module uses ordered convolution operator to extract local feature. They believe deep learning benefit from ordered function, but they still solve problem on unordered point sets. In this paper, we deploy multi-layer perception (MLP) followed by asymmetric function to extract local geometry information. In order to capture intrinsic pattern between different actions in building process, we further extend geometry part with LSTM based attentive sequence modeling network.

For decoder, we deploy network to make two-stream predictions. One stream makes prediction of block type, while the other stream estimates the probabilities for each position. It is well demonstrated [2] that two stream network is beneficial for action recognition. As one stream contributes to spatial signal while the other stream exploits temporal cues. For 3D craft building task, we argue that two-stream predictions is helpful to retain individual properties for different prediction target. The intuition here is that the position stream extracts continuous geometry signal, while the block type stream exploits discrete category information. So we propose to decompose the encoder feature into two parts and conquer the task by two predictive streams.

The main contributions of our work are as follows:

- Different from previous works [3], we first consider action sequences as ordered point sets and apply multi-layer perception and asymmetric function to model geometry information.
- We extend encoder with LSTM to model order information of action sequence and propose two-stream decoder to predict building actions.
- To the best of our knowledge, our model is the first RNN-based model which jointly modeling order and geometry information for 3D craft building sequence.
- We propose a novel generative neural network for 3D house building task, which achieves the state-of-the-art performance on *3D-Craft* dataset with reasonable computational cost.

2   Predictive Action Neural Network

In this section, we first formulate the problem, and then elaborate the encoder and decoder framework in our model. Figure 2 depicts the overall architecture of the predictive action neural network. For simplicity, we denote the proposed network as PA-Net henceforth. Our network consists of an encoder and a two-stream decoder.

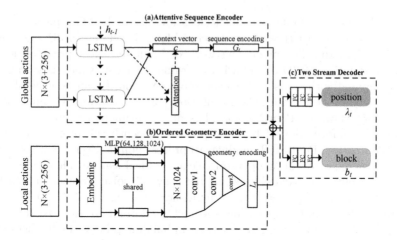

Fig. 2. The overview of proposed method, formed by (a) the attentive sequence encoder, (b) the ordered geometry encoder, (c) the two stream decoder.

2.1 Problem Definition

Suppose we have a 3D craft dataset $\mathcal{D}$ with N sequences of actions. Each action sequence is represented as an ordered set of actions $seq = \{A_1, \cdots, A_n\}$, where A_i is a vector representation of action. We denote each action as two parts, including continuous representation of coordinate (x, y, z) and discrete one-hot representation of block type $(c_1, \cdots, c_m)$, where $x, y, z \in \mathbb{R}$ and $c_i \in \{0, 1\}$.

For the house building task, given the previous constructed sequence $\{A_1, \cdots, A_{t-1}\}$, the goal is to predict next action A_t. In other words, the model defines a probability over the building sequence with joint probability

$$p(seq) = \prod_{t=1}^{T} p(A_t | A_1, \cdots, A_{t-1}) \tag{1}$$

With this in mind, we formulate each prediction as conditional probability,

$$p(A_t) = p(A_t | A_1, \cdots, A_{t-1}) \tag{2}$$

Since the choices of construction position and block type can be considered as two independent events, we further decompose the joint probability as the multiplication of $p(b_t | A_1, \cdots, A_{t-1})$ and $p(\lambda_t | A_1, \cdots, A_{t-1})$, where b_t and λ_t denote the prediction of block type and position respectively.

2.2   Ordered Geometry Encoder

Given the input sequence of length N, the goal of geometry encoder is to learn both geometric and structural information of constructed shapes. Moreover, we can understand which block is constructed, which is not, and potential relations between different parts of objects. Inspired by recent advances of point cloud technologies [10,12,13,16], we formulate the sequence of actions as ordered point sets. In our observation, human build numerous structures over large space of areas, but adjacent actions tend to be taken in the space with small radius. For example, in *3D-Craft train* set, the number of adjacent actions with distance of 7 and total number of actions are $1,023,717$ and $1,112,745$ respectively, which indicates at least 92% of adjacent actions occur in the nearby area. Therefore, to achieve an optimal trade-off, we follow previous work [3] and deploy local context with radius of D_l, which results in $(2D_l + 1) \times (2D_l + 1) \times (2D_l + 1)$ voxel space. To normalize data, we shift every coordinate relative to the last block since the next action is greatly influenced by local context centered around last position λ_{t-1}. We assume every position $p_{i,j,k}$ in voxel space is occupied by point $P_{i,j,k}$. For constructed position, we assign feature vector A to corresponding block, while for unreconstructed position, we assume the position is occupied by a special block "air". For seeking efficiency, we further reduce dimension by flattening the voxel data into ordered sequence of points $\{P_1, \cdots, P_n\}$, where n denotes the length of encoding space. To leverage powerful geometry representation, we deploy shape encoder which is based on PointNet [13]. Before feature extraction, we first compute a small transformation matrix to map the original coordinates into latent space. Then each point in ordered sequence is further encoded by shared MLP layers with hidden units of 64, 128 and 1024. In point cloud task, mainstream approaches [10,12,13,16] make unordered and transformation invariance assumptions. However, for house building task, the order matters significantly for the final decision. Because the same object with different construction order could lead to different actions. For example, a wall with the last action on left may lead to further construction on the left side, and vice versa. Furthermore, the scales and directions also contribute to the final target. We believe that ordered transformation such as convolution is beneficial for geometry encoder. With this in mind, we deploy order-aware encoding, which consists of multiple convolutional layers to aggregate point features. The final output of geometry encoder is denoted as L_t.

2.3   Attentive Sequence Encoder

It is popular [1,6,7] to model sequence conditional probability $p(A_t|A_1, \cdots, A_{t-1})$ with a RNN based neural network, where the context of sequence is modeled by a fixed size hidden variable h_t. Inspired by two stream network [2], geometry encoder captures spatial information, while sequence encoder exploits temporal cues in building process. We deploy LSTM to model order information between different actions. Since the next action is more related to nearby building blocks, we further filter actions based on a global encoding space with radius

D_g centered around the last block. Suppose the input of sequence encoder is $\{A_1, \cdots, A_n\}$. At every time step t, the LSTM hidden variable h_t is generated by

$$h_t = f(h_{t-1}, A_t) \tag{3}$$

where f is the LSTM updating function. After feeding the whole action sequence into recurrent model, we derive the hidden state h_t, which encapsulates the entire contextual information of the sequence. To enhance the recurrent model, we further incorporate the attention mechanism in the encoder. The intuition is that human tends to consider each action differently and focus on parts of the action sequence. In our approach, we generate a contextual vector c to highlight the importance of different actions in each time step

$$c = \sum_{t=1}^{T} \alpha(t)h_t \tag{4}$$

where $\alpha(t)$ is the importance vector, which is computed as follows

$$\alpha(i) = \frac{exp(score(h_i, h_t))}{\sum_{j=1}^{T} exp(score(h_j, h_t))} \tag{5}$$

Here the score function is denoted as

$$score(h_i, h_t) = h_i^T W_s h_t \tag{6}$$

which is a function to compute correlations between two vectors. With the help of Eq. (4), we can obtain the final sequence encoding by

$$G_t = W_g tanh(W_c[h_t; c]) \tag{7}$$

2.4   Late Feature Fusion

We then take advantage of a simple concatenation layer to combine the local geometry encoding L_t and global sequence encoding G_t and produce a feature vector C_t. The final encoding vector is able to capture both geometry and order information for building process. As depicted in Fig. 2, we adopt encoding C_t to predict the position λ_t and block type b_t at time step t.

2.5   Two Stream Predictor

The outputs of encoder rely on both local geometry and global sequence semantics. Previous work [3] on this task considers the prediction of block type depends on the position λ_t. In this work, we follow divide and conquer paradigm, and we find it better to model the prediction λ_t and b_t individually. Here we split the predictor into two streams, one stream is responsible for predicting the position, while the other stream contributes to the block type estimation. Based on the final encoding C_t, we apply multiple FC layers followed by a softmax layer to each stream. Since a local space with $D_l = 3$ already covers 90% situations, we follow [3] and limit position prediction within a local voxel space with radius $D_l = 3$ centered around the last block, which leads to 343 possible positions. For block type prediction, we deploy several linear layers to obtain a 256 dimension vector, which represents prediction scores for 256 possible building blocks.

2.6 Training by Effective Sampling

We train the entire network in an end-to-end fashion with stochastic gradient descent (SGD) algorithm. Each sequence with n observations $\{ob_1, \cdots, ob_n\}$ is randomly sampled during training. However, instead of taking all observations to perform sequential updates, we only consider the observation with next action in the nearby area as effective sample. Indeed, the numerous sequences are constructed by various annotators. We believe uncorrelated sampling is beneficial for full observation and can be generalized to various situations.

The training process is guided by the cross-entropy loss function, which consists of two parts, including position loss and block type loss. The losses define the distance between the predicted and the ground-truth action. Formally, given the observation $ob = \{A_1, \cdots, A_{t-1}\}$ and next action (λ_t, b_t), the position and block type losses are defined as follows:

$$\mathcal{L}_{position} = -\mathbb{E}_{(ob,\lambda_t)\sim\mathcal{D}} \log p(\lambda_t|A_1, \cdots, A_{t-1}) \tag{8}$$

$$\mathcal{L}_{block} = -\mathbb{E}_{(ob,b_t)\sim\mathcal{D}} \log p(b_t|A_1, \cdots, A_{t-1}) \tag{9}$$

The full training objective is to minimize the joint loss

$$\mathcal{L} = \mathcal{L}_{position} + \mathcal{L}_{block} \tag{10}$$

3 Experiments

In this section, we conduct several experiments for both order-aware generation and order recovery tasks. Extensive quantitative and qualitative results on *3D-Craft* dataset are reported to evaluate the effectiveness of our proposed method.

3.1 Dataset

We evaluate the performance of our proposed method on Facebook *3D-Craft* dataset [3]. The dataset is collected on the Minecraft game environment. Numerous human action sequences are recorded by Cuberite server. 3D house generation is a brand-new task, and provides a unique way to explore human actions. The *3D-Craft* dataset consists of more than 2,500 houses with 2.8 million building actions crowd sourced by more than 200 human players. The average steps to build a house is 635, and normally it takes 10.9 types of blocks to build a house. We follow [3] to process annotations and split the dataset into *train*, *val* and *test* sets. Here we choose the *train* set of 1750 houses with $1,074,647$ actions to train our network.

Table 1. Comparisons between our proposed method and other methods proposed by [3]. Our method ranks among the top of state-of-the-art models. For the MTC metric, lower value is better.

Methods	ACC@1 (%)	ACC@5 (%)	ACC@10 (%)	CCA	MTC	Normalized MTC (%)
LSTM	32.1	41.3	43.5	–	278.3	50.6
Naive inertia	38.7	47.0	48.3	1.8	287.7	52.5
Nearest neighbor	42.9	59.7	61.9	4.7	209.2	37.9
Naive VoxelCNN	–	–	–	2.2	430.5	–
Learned raster-scan	31.5	49.0	52.8	2.4	295.3	53.1
VoxelCNN	62.7	77.2	78.9	11.7	122.8	23.2
Ours	**67.3**	**79.8**	**82.4**	**13.8**	**108.2**	**20.0**

3.2   Implementation Details

All experiments are conducted with an NVIDIA Tesla V100 GPU using the PyTorch deep learning toolkit. The whole network is optimized with SGD algorithm with momentum of 0.9. The batch size is 64, and we train our network for 20 epochs. The initial learning rate is set to 0.1 for the first epoch and the learning rate decay is performed every 5 epoch. As an additional result, we also train our network with order reconstruction setting which gives the final shape before the generation starts. To make a fair comparison, we adopt the same data split setting and preprocessing steps in previous works [3]. For encoding space, we set parameters $D_l = 3$ and $D_g = 10$. The evaluation metric ACC@1 on *val* set is used to select the best model. Batch-normalization and ReLU activation are deployed after each fully connected layer. We follow [3] to evaluate the model performance. There are three types of metrics, including accuracy of next n step (ACC@N), number of consecutive correct actions (CCA) and number of mistakes to complete (MTC).

3.3   Order-Aware Generation Task

In this section, we conduct quantitative and qualitative experiments to analyze our proposed method and compare our results with other state-of-the-art methods on house building task.

Table 1 shows a comparison of various metrics between our methods and other methods on *3D-Craft* dataset. It can be seen our proposed method improves VoxelCNN by 4.6% in terms of ACC@1 and outperforms other methods, such as LSTM (by 35.2%), Naive Inertia (by 28.6%), Nearest Neighbor (by 24.4%) and Learned Raster-Scan (by 35.8%). Notably, our method achieves the top results on *3D-Craft* dataset with ACC@5 of 79.8%, ACC@10 of 82.4%, CCA of 13.8%, MTC of 108.2% and normalized MTC of 20.0%, which indicate the advantage of our proposed method. The LSTM method also utilizes recurrent module to leverage sequence information, but without explicitly modeling geometry structures of constructed blocks, the model fails in making accurate estimation. The Voxel-CNN [3] approach represents sequence as stacked voxel and exploits 3D convolution to model geometry and order information. The VoxelCNN model generates

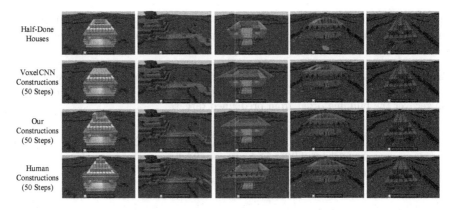

Fig. 3. Qualitative results generated by our model. *Top row*: given 50% constructed blocks; *Second row*: constructions from VoxelCNN [3] with 50 predicted blocks; *Third row*: constructions from our method with 50 predicted blocks; *Bottom row*: constructions from GT annotations with 50 predicted blocks.

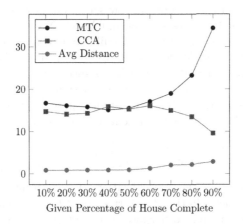

Fig. 4. Evaluation of MTC, CCA and Average Distance Between GT Actions given different construction progress. The model makes more mistakes when the house is almost finished.

houses decently well, but limited sequence information and high dimensional transformation hinder the real application of order-aware generative model. Our PA-Net not only avoids the high dimensional cost, but also boosts CCA metric to 13.8, which surpasses the original VoxelCNN model.

In additional analysis, we conduct experiments to learn how hard to predict the next action given different percentages of constructed blocks. Figure 4 shows the MTC, CCA and average distance between GT actions corresponding to different constructed percentages. This experiment shows that it is much harder to predict actions when the house is almost finished. This is likely because there are a lot of improvement works when the house is almost completed (larger than 70%). Improvement works bring higher uncertainty, which is challenging for our generative model.   We also present some qualitative results generated

Table 2. Qualitative results of order recovery from given target shape. We extend our network to take an additional input of the final shape, and test how well our model can recover the building order from predefined target.

Methods	ACC@1 (%)	ACC@10 (%)	MTC
Nearest neighbor	43.3	62.4	–
VoxelCNN	69.3	88.0	–
Ours	**70.7**	**89.5**	**101.5**

by our model. For each sample in the *test* set, given 50% constructed blocks, we let our model construct 50 steps. As shown in Fig. 3, our method is capable of imitating human behavior and generating reasonable houses. The first row presents half built houses, the bottom row shows the ground truths, other rows gives comparable results of our model and VoxelCNN [3]. It can be observed in the second column, our model try to build some complicated guard bars on both sides of the road, while the VoxelCNN model builds simplified blocks on one side of the road. Although our method is successful to imitate human build pattern, there is still a gap between predicted actions and GT annotations. This is likely because the high uncertainty in building process. Furthermore, the small mistakes may have large effects in subsequent predictions.

3.4   Order Recovery Task

It is of interest to study the generalization of our method in other task. In this section, we conduct additional experiments to transfer our method to order recovery task. Different from order-aware generation task, we provide the final shape before the construction starts. In this way, the generative model is guided by predefined target. The order recovery task is challenging since it is nontrivial to recover human order with final shapes. To this end, we extend our encoder with an additional module. For seeking efficiently and effectively, we deploy a module which is similar to the ordered geometry encoder. We report the performance of generalization experiment in Table 2. Our model is able to perform reasonable reconstruction which mimics human order. It can be observed in Table 2, our model achieves the top scores, which outperforms VoxelCNN in terms of ACC@1 (70.7% vs 69.3%) and ACC@5 (89.5% vs 88.0%).

3.5   Ablation Study

In this section, we analyze the effects of different modules in our network. For all experiments, we compare the ACC@1, ACC@10 and MTC metrics to analyze the contribution of different modules. As shown in Table 3, we construct three variants of our proposed method by removing specific module. For example, instead of two stream prediction, we follow [3] and build our decoder with factorized prediction, this result is denoted as "w/o two stream prediction". For encoder, both geometry and sequence encoder contribute to the final scores, as removing any of them degrades the performance. The possible reason is that geometry and sequence encoder provide complementary information. As for decoder, previous work [3] uses factorized prediction which predicts block type depends on position. As is revealed in Table 3, incorporating two stream prediction outperforms factorized prediction in terms of ACC@1 metric (67.3% vs 65.4%). This indicates that the semantic information required for determining position and block type is slightly different.

Table 3. Ablation study of ACC (%) and MTC performance on the *3D-Craft* dataset by performing the ablation tests with different modules.

Methods	ACC@1 (%)	ACC@10 (%)	MTC
Ours	67.3	82.4	108.2
w/o geometry information	60.3	77.3	132.3
w/o sequence information	64.6	81.2	114.0
w/o two stream prediction	65.4	81.7	110.5

4   Conclusions

In this paper, we present a novel generative model for 3D house building task. The proposed method decomposes the feature into geometry and sequence part. This decomposition is helpful for the network to exploit complementary information in parallel. To model geometry information, we first consider action sequence as ordered point sets and apply MLP to model spatial information. For sequence information, we leverage attentive sequence encoder to extract the most correlated temporal cues for action planing. With two kinds of information, we apply two stream prediction to determine block type and position of next action. The proposed contributions can effectively decrease the computation cost and were able to provide 4.6% ACC@1 and 2.1 CCA boosts over the VoxelCNN method on the brand-new *3D-Craft* benchmark. Our model can be generalized to order recover task, which is conditioned on predefined houses. Without losing generality, our model should be able to apply on similar generation tasks. Although our method achieves the best performance in house building task, it fails in understating house parts, such as door and wall. For future work, we plan to investigate this problem by assigning semantic labels and generate houses part by part.

Acknowledgement. This work was supported by the National Key R&D Program of China (No. 2017YFE0117500) and the Science Foundation of China University of Petroleum, Beijing (No. 2462020YXZZ023).

References

1. Bahdanau, D., Cho, K., Bengio, Y.: Neural machine translation by jointly learning to align and translate. In: Bengio, Y., LeCun, Y. (eds.) 3rd International Conference on Learning Representations, ICLR 2015, San Diego, CA, USA, 7–9 May 2015, Conference Track Proceedings (2015). http://arxiv.org/abs/1409.0473
2. Carreira, J., Zisserman, A.: Quo vadis, action recognition? A new model and the kinetics dataset. CoRR abs/1705.07750 (2017). http://arxiv.org/abs/1705.07750
3. Chen, Z., et al.: Order-aware generative modeling using the 3D-craft dataset. In: ICCV (2019)
4. Choy, C.B., Xu, D., Gwak, J., Chen, K., Savarese, S.: 3D-r2n2: a unified approach for single and multi-view 3D object reconstruction. CoRR abs/1604.00449 (2016). http://arxiv.org/abs/1604.00449
5. Deprelle, T., Groueix, T., Fisher, M., Kim, V., Russell, B., Aubry, M.: Learning elementary structures for 3D shape generation and matching. In: Wallach, H., Larochelle, H., Beygelzimer, A., d'Alché-Buc, F., Fox, E., Garnett, R. (eds.) Advances in Neural Information Processing Systems, vol. 32, pp. 7435–7445. Curran Associates, Inc. (2019). http://papers.nips.cc/paper/8962-learning-elementary-structures-for-3d-shape-generation-and-matching.pdf
6. Dhariwal, P., Jun, H., Payne, C., Kim, J.W., Radford, A., Sutskever, I.: Jukebox: a generative model for music. arXiv preprint arXiv:2005.00341 (2020)
7. Gregor, K., Danihelka, I., Graves, A., Wierstra, D.: DRAW: a recurrent neural network for image generation. CoRR abs/1502.04623 (2015). http://arxiv.org/abs/1502.04623
8. Henderson, P., Ferrari, V.: Learning single-image 3D reconstruction by generative modelling of shape, pose and shading. CoRR abs/1901.06447 (2019). http://arxiv.org/abs/1901.06447
9. Jiang, M., Wu, Y., Lu, C.: PointSIFT: a SIFT-like network module for 3D point cloud semantic segmentation. CoRR abs/1807.00652 (2018). http://arxiv.org/abs/1807.00652
10. Klokov, R., Lempitsky, V.S.: Escape from cells: deep Kd-networks for the recognition of 3D point cloud models. CoRR abs/1704.01222 (2017). http://arxiv.org/abs/1704.01222
11. Komori, J., Hotta, K.: AB-PointNet for 3D point cloud recognition. In: 2019 Digital Image Computing: Techniques and Applications (DICTA), pp. 1–6 (2019)
12. Qi, C.R., Yi, L., Su, H., Guibas, L.J.: PointNet++: deep hierarchical feature learning on point sets in a metric space. arXiv preprint arXiv:1706.02413 (2017)
13. Qi, C.R., Su, H., Mo, K., Guibas, L.J.: PointNet: deep learning on point sets for 3d classification and segmentation. CoRR abs/1612.00593 (2016). http://arxiv.org/abs/1612.00593

14. Sinha, A., Unmesh, A., Huang, Q., Ramani, K.: SurfNet: generating 3D shape surfaces using deep residual networks. CoRR abs/1703.04079 (2017). http://arxiv.org/abs/1703.04079
15. Xie, H., Yao, H., Zhang, S., Zhou, S., Sun, W.: Pix2vox++: multi-scale context-aware 3D object reconstruction from single and multiple images. Int. J. Comput. Vis. (IJCV) **128**, 2919–2935 (2020)
16. Zhou, Y., Tuzel, O.: Net: end-to-end learning for point cloud based 3D object detection. CoRR abs/1711.06396 (2017). http://arxiv.org/abs/1711.06396

Unsupervised Multi-shot Person Re-identification via Dynamic Bi-directional Normalized Sparse Representation

Xiaobao Li[1], Wen Wang[1], Qingyong Li[1(✉)], and Lijun Guo[2]

[1] Beijing Key Lab of Traffic Data Analysis and Mining, Beijing Jiaotong University, Beijing, China
{19112018,wangwen,liqy}@bjtu.edu.cn
[2] Faculty of Electrical Engineering and Computer Science, Ningbo University, Ningbo, Zhejiang, China
guolijun@nbu.edu.cn

Abstract. Due to the abundant priori information and the widespread applications, multi-shot based person re-identification has drawn increasing attention in recent years. In this paper, the high labeling cost and the huge unlabeled data motivate us to focus on the unsupervised scenario and a unified coarse-to-fine framework is proposed, named by Dynamic Bi-directional Normalized Sparse Representation (DBNSR). Specifically, the method designs an alternatively iterative mechanism to dynamically update the estimated cross-camera labels and progressively learn a discriminative metric. In each iteration, a Bi-directional Normalized Sparse Representation (BNSR) model is applied to estimate the label for each pair of cross-camera person sequences with bi-directional probabilities defined to encode their mutual correlation. With the estimated labels, we learn a keep-it-simple-and-straight-forward metric (KISSME) to further make BNSR model available in a more discriminative and lower-dimensional subspace. Extensive experiments on PRID 2011, iLIDS-VID and MARS three benchmarks show that our method performs favorably against state-of-the-arts.

Keywords: Person re-identification · Unsupervised · Sparse representation

1 Introduction

Person Re-identification (person reID), which aims to recognize a specific individual across non-overlapping camera views, is a crucial step of surveillance systems in modern society and has been widely researched in recent years [19]. In contrast with the single-shot scenario [13], multi-shot person re-ID [14,16] seeks to match two different sequences constituted by multiple person images of

© Springer Nature Switzerland AG 2021
J. Lokoč et al. (Eds.): MMM 2021, LNCS 12572, pp. 554–566, 2021.
https://doi.org/10.1007/978-3-030-67832-6_45

an identical subject. It is natural that richer spatial and temporal information is available in image sequences, which helps to enhance the robustness against the uncontrolled background noises. Though existing multi-shot based person reID methods have achieved superior performance, most of them consider the supervised learning context and rely on large volumes of labeled person images, which leads to high annotation cost and thus greatly limits the scalability for the real-world applications. To address such problem and further make sufficient use of the large amount of unlabeled data, unsupervised multi-shot person reID [4,9,11,16] has become a new focus in recent years.

Without the availability of labels, the majority of existing methods are less effective due to the drastic cross-view appearance variation. Therefore, it is usually accepted to be a key component in unsupervised person reID to estimate cross-camera pairwise labels as learning guidance. Currently, the label estimation technique has been explored in several existing unsupervised multi-shot person reID methods [4,9,15,16]. However, some of them [4,16] define the distance between two person image sequences by averaging all the distances between pairs of images belonging to either sequence respectively. Such a strategy ignores to mine the consistency between images within a sequence and fails to make use of the complementary information contained in each sequence. While others [9,15] merely consider unidirectional label estimation which neglects the mutual correlation of person sequences under different cameras and is thus liable to be affected by noises. As a result, the performance of these methods is still far behind the fully-supervised mode.

To overcome the above issues, this paper presents a unified coarse-to-fine framework to solve unsupervised multi-shot person reID problem, named by Dynamic Bi-directional Normalized Sparse Representation (DBNSR). We not only estimate the label for each pair of cross-camera person sequences efficiently, but also learn a discriminative metric simultaneously. In each iteration, a keep-it-simple-and-straight-forward metric (KISSME) metric is learned with the estimated labels, while in turn the labels are subsequently dynamically adjusted in an embedded subspace. For label estimation, we design a Normalized Sparse Representation (NSR) to indicate the similarity between cross-camera person images by creatively endow each sparse representation coefficient with a probability property. To further enhance robustness, we develop the Bi-directional Normalized Sparse Representation (BNSR). It filters the unreliable pairs by considering the bi-directional probabilities between two cameras, i.e., the probability from one camera to other one and that in reverse. Finally, having learned with the DBNSR framework, conventional discriminative methods can be conducted in the learned discriminative subspace based on the estimated pairwise labels, such as the Elasticnet sparse representation method [20]. Our contributions are summarized as follows:

(1) We present a natural yet non-trivial DBNSR method to solve the label estimation problem for unsupervised multi-shot person reID, which integrates label estimation and metric learning into a unified coarse-to-fine framework.

(2) We present a NSR method to calculate the similarity between person images by a global view, which effectively utilizes the complementary information within each person sequence and thus leads to more robust similarity measurement.

(3) We further propose a BNSR model by configuring NSR with Bi-directional strategy, which creatively encodes the mutual correlation of intraperson sequences under different cameras into the label estimation. It can effectively filter the unreliable pairwise labels and leads to more robust label estimation.

2   Proposed Method

In this work, we present a unified coarse-to-fine DBNSR framework for unsupervised multi-shot person reID. The overall schematic flowchart is shown in Fig. 1. The critical steps are elaborated in the following subsections.

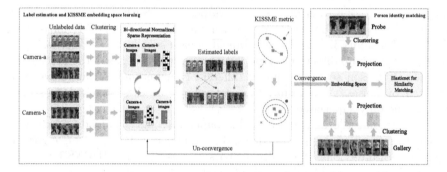

Fig. 1. Framework of the proposed DBNSR method. Given the person image sequences in Camera-a and Camera-b, we firstly exploit the k-means algorithm to represent each person sequence with the centroids of clusters. Then the BNSR model is constructed with the clustered person image sequences for label estimation of the cross camera. Meanwhile, an iterative mechanism is introduced. At each iteration, a KISSME metric is learned with the estimated pairwise labels and the BNSR model is updated. For testing, we generate the representations of each person image sequence in probe and gallery based on the k-means algorithm and project them into the learned KISSME embedding space. Finally, an Elasticnet sparse representation model is constructed to perform identity matching for persons.

2.1   Normalized Sparse Representation

A key component of person reID is to leverage the cross camera pairwise labels for metric model learning. However, such information is missing in unsupervised multi-shot person reID. To handle the issue, some works [11,16] attempt to treat the nearest samples as a positive pair with Euclidean distance as the similarity measurement. However, they usually compute the similarity between person image of the cross-camera one by one, which means that the correlations among person images in the same sequence are neglected. Unlike them, in this paper, we develop a Normalized Sparse Representation (NSR) model to measure the similarity among person images by a global perspective. In this manner, the relationships among person images are effectively involved in the process of the similarity computation.

Before introducing the NSR method, we first conduct clustering on each person image sequence for efficiently aggregating the information contained in each person sequence. In this manner, each of them is partitioned into several clusters by the k-means algorithm and thus can be represented by the set of clustering centroids.

Formally, suppose there are m clustered person image sequences $\{F^{(i)}\}_{i=1}^m$ from Camera-a and n clustered person image sequences $\{G^{(j)}\}_{j=1}^n$ from Camera-b. $F^{(i)} = [f_1^{(i)}, f_2^{(i)}, \cdots, f_k^{(i)}] \in \mathbb{R}^{d \times k}$ denotes the ith person image sequence in Camera-a, which contains d-dimensional feature representations of the k clustering centroids. Similarly, we also have $G^{(j)} = [g_1^{(j)}, g_2^{(j)}, \cdots, g_k^{(j)}]$.

Given a person image sequence $P \in \mathbb{R}^{d \times k}$ belonging to $\{F^{(i)}\}_{i=1}^m$, we aim to seek the most similar person image sequence from $\{G^{(j)}\}_{j=1}^n$ and treat them as a positive pair. To this end, we construct a sparse representation dictionary $D = [G^{(1)}, G^{(2)}, \cdots, G^{(n)}] \in \mathbb{R}^{d \times M}$ based on the n person image sequences in Camera-b. Each centroid feature vector in D is termed as an atom and $M = n \times k$ is the total number of atoms. Especially, let x_{lt} denotes the probability that the $t^{th}(t = 1, 2, \cdots, k)$ person image in P is represented by the $l^{th}(l = 1, 2, \cdots, M)$ person image from Camera-b. Furthermore, from the perspective of probability, we expect that the sum of the probabilities that the tth person image of P is represented by all person images from Camera-b is equal to 1, i.e., $\sum_{l=1}^M x_{lt} = 1$. Based on the above discussions, we develop a Normalized Sparse Presentation (NSR) model to formulate the similarity between person images,

$$\min_{X,E} \|X\|_1 + \frac{1}{2}\|E\|_F^2$$
$$s.t. DX + E = P, 0 \leq X \leq 1, 1_1^T X = 1_2^T \tag{1}$$

where $\|\cdot\|_1$ and $\|\cdot\|_F$ denote the l_1-norm and Frobenius norm respectively. $X \in \mathbb{R}^{M \times k}$ is a probability matrix with respect to P. $\|X\|_1$ enforces the sparsity of X. $E \in \mathbb{R}^{d \times k}$ is a residual matrix that is introduced to counter the negative impacts of image breakage and object occlusion on the model. The equality constraint $1_1^T X = 1_2^T$ together with nonnegative constraint $0 \leq X \leq 1$ guarantee the probability nature of x_{lt}. $1_1 \in \mathbb{R}^{M \times 1}$ and $1_2 \in \mathbb{R}^{k \times 1}$ are the vector of all ones.

Each element in X is used to measure the similarity between person images. The larger x_{lt} indicates that the tth person image of P and l^{th} person image in Camera-b are more likely treated as a positive pair. It can be rewritten as a convex problem easily and thus global optimal solution can be efficiently computed by the Alternating Direction Method of Multipliers (ADMM) algorithm [3].

For $F^{(i)}$, we have obtained a corresponding probability matrix $X^{(i)} = [x_1^{(i)}, x_2^{(i)}, \cdots, x_k^{(i)}] \in \mathbb{R}^{M \times k}$ by solving Eq. (1), where the column vector $x_t^{(i)}$ is a M-dimensional probability vector. Then we rewrite $x_t^{(i)}$ as n number of k-dimensional sub-vectors $\{x_{tj}^{(i)}\}_j^n$. Each sub-vector $x_{tj}^{(i)} = [x_{tj}^{(i)}[1], x_{tj}^{(i)}[2], \cdots , x_{tj}^{(i)}[k]]$ respectively contains the probabilities that $f_t^{(i)}$ in $F^{(i)}$ can be represented by the k number of images in $G^{(j)}$. Since the person images in a sequence have the same identity, we average all the probabilities in $\{x_{tj}^{(i)}\}_{t=1}^k$ to compute the probability of representing $F^{(i)}$ by $G^{(j)}, j = 1, 2, \cdots , n$, denoted as

$$p_{ij} = \frac{1}{k^2} \sum_{t=1}^k \sum_{c=1}^k x_{tj}^{(i)}[c] \tag{2}$$

therefore, by sorting $\{p_{ij} | j = 1, 2, \ldots , n\}$ in descending order, the pairwise label can be defined as follows.

$$y_{i\tau} = \begin{cases} 1, & \tau = \arg \max_j \{p_{ij} | j = 1, 2, \cdots , n\} \\ 0, & \text{otherwise} \end{cases} \tag{3}$$

where $y_{i\tau} = 1$ means that $F^{(i)}$ and $G^{(\tau)}$ are treated as a positive pair, otherwise $y_{i\tau} = 0$. Different from the existing SR based methods, which are mainly used for supervised person matching, our proposed NSR methd is designed to mine the associated probability between cross-camera sequences for unsupervised label estimation. Benefit from the advanced linear expression of sparse representation, our NSR method can calculate the similarity by a global view and can effectively use the intrinsic correlation among images within the same person image sequence. It is conducive to output more reliable pairwise labels.

2.2   Bi-directional NSR for Label Estimation

Inspired by the mutual correlation of person image sequences with same identity under different cameras, we further present a Bi-directional Normalized Sparse Representation (BNSR) model to filter the unreliable output of Eq. (3). The illustration of BNSR for pairwise label estimation is shown in Fig. 1. Specifically, given the unlabeled person image sequences in Camera-a and Camera-b respectively, two NSR models, forward and backward, are constructed. For the forward NSR, we construct the dictionary D in Eq. (1) based on $\{G^{(j)}\}_{j=1}^n$. In reverse, the dictionary D of the backward NSR is constructed based on $\{F^{(i)}\}_{i=1}^m$. With the estimated pairwise labels based on such two NSR models, we further refine the pairwise labels by

$$y_{i\tau} = \begin{cases} 1, & if \quad y_{i\tau}^{a \leftarrow b} = 1 \ \& \ y_{l\tau}^{b \leftarrow a} = 1 \ \& \ l == i \\ 0, & \text{otherwise} \end{cases} \tag{4}$$

where $y_{i\tau}^{a \leftarrow b}$ is the pairwise label output based on the forward NSR model and $y_{l\tau}^{b \leftarrow a}$ is outputted by the backward NSR model. we consider $F^{(i)}$ and $G^{(\tau)}$ as a positive pair only when there exists the maximum probability for them to represent each other, i.e., $l == i$.

2.3 Dynamic Bi-directional Normalized Spare Representation

To facilitate the performance of unsupervised multi-shot person reID, it is natural to learn a discriminative metric based on the pairwise labels outputted by BNSR. However, developing BNSR model in original feature space directly may result in unsatisfactory outputs due to the complex appearance variation. To tackle this issue, a Dynamic Bi-directional Normalized Sparse Representation (DBNSR) is proposed with an alternatively iterative strategy. It iteratively learns a discriminative KISSME metric [1] with the currently estimated labels and then in turn dynamically improves the BNSR model. Here we choose KISSME for its simple calculation to facilitate introducing our intrinsic novelty. In our DBNSR framework, it can be easily replaced by other advanced metric learning methods.

Formally, in each iteration, we have obtained pairs of training data $\{(f_t^{(i)}, g_l^{(\tau)}), y_{i\tau}\}$ according to the currently estimated pairwise labels. Similar with [1], by assuming a Gaussian structure of the difference space spanned by pairwise differences $\xi = f_t^{(i)} - g_l^{(\tau)}$ with zero mean, a Mahalanobis distance metric is derived to reflect the properties of the log-likelihood ratio test, i.e., $d_M^2(\xi) = \xi^T M \xi$. Here the Mahalanobis matrix M is computed by performing eigen-analysis to clip the spectrum of $\hat{M}$, where $\hat{M} = \Sigma_+^{-1} - \Sigma_-^{-1}$, $\Sigma_+ = \sum_{y_{i\tau}=1} \xi \xi^T$ and $\Sigma_- = \sum_{y_{i\tau}=0} \xi \xi^T$.

Having learned M, we perform Cholesky decomposition $M = LL^T$ to calculate the KISSME projection matrix L. Accordingly, we update BNSR by embedding the original feature space into the current KISSME subspace, i.e.,

$$\min_{X,E} \quad \|X\|_1 + \frac{1}{2}\|E\|_F^2$$
$$s.t. \quad L^h DX + E = L^h P, 0 \le X \le 1, \mathbf{1}_1^T X = \mathbf{1}_2^T \tag{5}$$

where $L^h \in \mathbb{R}^{u \times d}$ is the KISSME projection matrix in h^{th} iteration, u is the dimension of embedding space.

As the training goes on, more precise BNSR model can be yielded by a discriminative metric. In turn, more reliable pairwise labels outputted by BNSR lead to a more discriminative metric. Finally, the BNSR is updated dynamically until the maximum number of iterations or the estimated number of positive pairs tends to be stable. Although the alternating iteration mechanism has been widely used, our work innovatively defines a similarity probability based on sparse representation, and improves the iteration strategy with new solution that integrates bi-directional representation and the iterative mechanism.

2.4 Person Sequence Matching

In this section, we briefly describe the testing process. Suppose there are a target set T containing K number of person sequences and a person sequence Q as query. As described in Sect. 2.1, we first partition these person sequences by k-means algorithm and collect all the clustering centroids. Formally, $T = [T^{(1)}, T^{(2)}, \cdots, T^{(K)}]$ and $Q = [q_1, q_2, \cdots, q_k]$, where $T^{(l)} \in \mathbb{R}^{d \times k}$, $q_s \in \mathbb{R}^{d \times 1}$, d

is the dimension of person image feature and k is the number of clusters for each person sequence. Then, we project T and Q into the KISSME embedding space by the projection matrix L learned in Sect. 2.3.

$$T' = LT = [T'^{(1)}, T'^{(2)}, \cdots, T'^{(K)}]$$
$$Q' = LQ = [q'_1, q'_2, \cdots, q'_k] \tag{6}$$

where $T'^{(l)} \in \mathbb{R}^{u \times k}$, $q'_s \in \mathbb{R}^{u \times 1}$. Finally, we solve an Elasticnet sparse representation [20] to perform person identity matching as follows.

$$\min_{X,E} \lambda_1 \|X\|_1 + \lambda_2 \|X\|_F^2 + \frac{1}{2}\|E\|_2^F \tag{7}$$
$$s.t \quad T'X + E = Q'$$

where λ_1 and λ_2 are the trade-off parameters to control the sparsity and smoothness of the coefficient matrix X, T' is treated as the dictionary and E is a residual matrix.

Consequently, according to the sparse coefficient matrix X, the identity of the query person sequence Q' can be determined by calculating the reconstruction residuals. Specifically, for q'_s, its reconstruction residual from $T'^{(l)}$ is $r_s(T'^{(l)}) = \|q'_s - T'^{(l)}x_{sl} - e_s\|_2$, where x_{sl} is the corresponding coefficient sub-vector and e_s is the sth column vector of E. To average the residuals of all the q'_s in Q', we measure the difference between Q' and $T'^{(l)}$ by $R(T'^{(l)}) = \sum_{s=1}^{k} r_s(T'^{(l)})$ and classify the query Q to the same identity with $T'^{(l^*)}$, $l^* = \arg\max_l R(T'^{(l)})$.

3   Experimental Results

In this section, we perform experimental evaluation on three benchmark datasets, PRID 2011 [5], iLIDS-VID [2] and MARS [18]. **PRID 2011** [5] dataset contains images in two disjointed camera views captured on a street. Camera-a and Camera-b consist of 385 and 749 distinct person image sequences respectively with an average of about 100 images per sequence. **iLIDS-VID** [2] dataset is captured from a crowded airport. In each camera view, 300 person image sequences are available and every person sequence has between 23–192 frames. **MARS** [18] dataset is a large scale dataset captured from six cameras in a university campus. It contains 17503 person sequences of 1261 identities. The Cumulative Match Characteristic (CMC) curve [19] is utilized to evaluate the performance and the accuracy of Rank1, Rank5, Rank10 and Rank20 are reported.

3.1   Implementation Details

PRID 2011 and iLIDS-VID datasets are randomly split into two halves, one for training and the other for testing. For these two datasets, we repeat 10 random training/testing splits and report the average performance to ensure statistically stable results. For MARS dataset, a simplified experimental setting is applied in

Table 1. Comparison with the state-of-the-art unsupervised multi-shot person reID methods on PRID 2011, iLIDS-VID and MARS.

Datasets	PRID 2011				iLIDS-VID				MARS			
Rank	1	5	10	20	1	5	10	20	1	5	10	20
Salience [17]	25.8	43.6	52.6	62.0	10.2	24.8	35.5	52.9	–	–	–	–
DVDL [6]	40.6	69.7	77.8	85.6	25.9	48.2	57.3	68.9	–	–	–	–
MDTS [12]	41.7	67.1	79.4	90.1	31.5	62.1	72.8	82.4	–	–	–	–
GRDL [8]	41.6	76.4	84.6	89.9	25.7	49.9	63.2	77.6	19.3	33.2	41.6	46.5
UnKISS [7]	58.1	81.9	89.6	96.0	35.9	63.3	74.9	83.4	22.3	37.4	47.2	53.6
SMP [11]	80.9	95.6	98.8	99.4	41.7	66.3	74.1	80.7	23.6	35.8	–	44.9
DGM [16]	83.3	96.7	**98.9**	99.6	42.6	67.7	76.6	85.8	36.8	54.0	**61.6**	**68.5**
DGM+ [16]	–	–	–	–	–	–	–	–	26.8	40.9	48.9	56.5
TAUDL [9]	49.4	78.7	–	98.9	26.7	51.3	–	82.0	–	–	–	–
RACE [15]	50.6	79.4	88.6	91.8	19.3	39.3	53.3	68.7	–	–	–	–
UTAL [10]	54.7	83.1	–	96.2	35.1	50.9	–	83.8	–	–	–	–
DAL [4]	85.3	97.0	98.8	99.6	56.9	80.6	87.3	91.9	–	–	–	–
UGA [14]	80.9	94.4	–	**100**	57.3	72.0	–	87.3	–	–	–	–
DBNSR	**89.9**	**97.0**	98.8	99.3	**62.7**	**89.1**	**92.7**	**95.6**	**39.4**	**54.7**	60.9	65.6

this paper. For training, we randomly select 625 different sequences for different identities from camera-1 and the same number of sequences from the rest set (i.e. camera 2–6) are randomly selected. Both of them are then used to formulate a DBNSR model for label eaimation. For testing, 634 different sequences for different identities from camera-1 are selected to server as query and the same number of sequences from the rest set are randomly selected to server as gallery. Unless specified, the number of clusters k is set to 4, the maximum number of dynamic iteration is set to 10, the $\lambda_1 = \lambda_2 = 0.01$ in Eq. (7). The handcraft discriptor GOG [13] is selected on all three datasets. The original 7567-dimensional GOG feature for each person image are reduced to 600-dimensional by the PCA method for efficiency considerations on all datasets. Our source code is made publicly available[1].

3.2 Comparison with the State-of-the-Art Methods

On PRID 2011 and iLIDS-VID datasets, we first compare the proposed method with seven non-deep methods. It is noted in Table 1 that our proposed method achieves superior performance on both datasets. The Rank1 accuracy of our DBNSR method outperforms the second-best DGM [16] 6.6% and 20.1% on the two datasets respectively. Then we compare our method with the deep based unsupervised multi-shot person reID methods TAUDL [9], RACE [15], UTAL [10], UGA [14] and DAL [4]. It can be observed that our method can still achieve 4.6% improvement in Rank1 accuracy over the DAL on PRID 2011 and 5.4%

---

[1] https://github.com/xiaobaoli15/DBNSR-reid.

improvement over the UGA on iLIDS-VID. In addition, we also have comparable results for other Ranks.Understandably, due to limited training data on PRID 2011 and iLID-SVID, deep feature do not perform well, which is generally reported in previous works such as DGM [16].

On MARS dataset, we compare the proposed DBNSR with four unsupervised multi-shot methods. All of them are the non-deep methods like ours. It is shown in Table 1 that the proposed method significantly outperforms other unsupervised re-ID methods in Rank1 accuracy. Concretely, the proposed DBNSR method obtains 39.4% Rank1 accuracy, which surpasses the DGM method by 2.6%. Meanwhile, for fair comprison, we reproduce the second-best method DGM [16] on MARS with the source code supplied by authors, which is denoted as DGM+. We configure DGM+ with GOG discriptor and the same person sequence clustering as our DBNSR method. Obviously, our method still achieves the better results under the same experimental settings and a significant performance boosting is obtained by 12.8% in Rank1 accuracy.

The improvements can be attributed to three folds: (1) NSR model can effectively explore the complementary information in the same person sequence by a global perspective to assist label estimation. (2) The forward and backward NSR compute the probabilities between two cameras respectively, the mutual correlation of person sequences under different cameras is used to further filter some unreliable pairwise labels. (3) The iterative mechanism helps to construct a robust BNSR model and learn a discriminative KISSME metric. For more detailed analysis, see the subsequent experiments. In particular, to give a time complexity analysis, we take iLIDS-VID database (150 person sequences for gallery and another 150 for probe) as an example and test the average testing time for each sequence. The average time is 0.0147 s, which is acceptable.

3.3   Ablation Study

Comparison NSR with Euclidean Distance. To verify the advantage of the proposed NSR model for label estimation, we compare it with the 'Euclidean' method with the same parameter settings. NSR and 'Euclidean' indicate that the similarity between person images are calculated by applying NSR model proposed in Eq. (1) and Euclidean distance respectively. It is noted that we similarly configure 'Euclidean' method with the person sequence clustering and bi-directional strategy, as well as alternating iteration mechanism. The results are illustrated in Table 2. It is noted that NSR method accomplishes the consistently improvements on three datasets. Specifically, we have 0.9%, 2.86% and 2.84% improvements in Rank1 accuracy on three datasets respectively. The main reason behind of the improvements is that our proposed NSR can focus on the global information and effectively leverage the complementary information contained in each person image sequence.

Evaluation of Bi-directional Strategy. We remove the bidirectional strategy form DBNSR leading to the 'DBNSR w/o B' method, which indicates that only the forward or backward NSR model is applied for label estimation. As can be

Table 2. Ablation studies on PRID 2011, iLIDS-VID and MARS. 'Purely unsupervised' indicates person matching in original feature space directly without the label estimation and metric learning. 'Euclidean' indicates that Euclidean distance is applied for the label estimation. 'DBNSR w/o B' indicates that the bi-directional strategy is removed. 'DBNSR w/o D' indicates that dynamic iteration procedure is removed. 'Fully supervised' indicates supervised learning, i.e., the setting with ground truth label.

Datasets	PRID 2011			iLIDS-VID			MARS		
Rank	1	5	10	1	5	10	1	5	10
Purely unsupervised	54.61	78.65	85.51	22.07	44.87	56.2	24.92	41.64	48.42
Euclidean	88.99	97.75	99.10	59.87	78.07	83.13	36.59	55.52	59.31
DBNSR w/o B	88.09	96.29	97.30	59.73	78.72	84.20	38.17	55.36	61.04
DBNSR w/o D	88.65	97.42	98.76	57.87	75.73	80.47	35.49	53.31	59.31
DBNSR	89.89	96.97	98.20	62.73	79.73	84.80	39.43	54.73	60.88
Fully supervised	92.47	97.98	98.76	72.40	89.13	92.67	42.59	59.62	65.46

noted from the Table 2, compared with the DBNSR method, the Rank1 accuracy decreased by 1.8%, 3% and 1.3% on three datasets respectively. This is mainly because that DBNSR mines the mutual correlation of person image sequences under different cameras, which can further filter the unreliable pairwise labels output by NSR, thus helps to learn a more discriminative metric.

Evaluation of Dynamic Iteration Procedure. To demonstrate the effectiveness of the dynamic iteration procedure, we compare our DBNSR method with the 'DBNSR w/o D' method. The results of DBNSR are clearly better than the 'DBNSR w/o D' with 1.24%, 4.86% and 3.94% improvement in Rank1 accuracy on three datasets. The main reason is that the dynamic iteration procedure progressively updates the BNSR and KISSME metric by using the intermediate estimated labels. It improves the correctness of the pairwise labels output by BNSR and ensures learning a more discriminative metric.

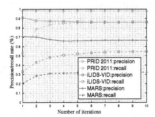

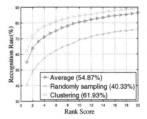

Fig. 2. The varying trends of precision and recall with regard to the estimated positive pairs as the iteration proceeds on three datasets.

Fig. 3. Evaluation of the clustering on iLIDS-VID.

3.4   Analysis

Evaluation of the Label Estimation. To evaluate the effectiveness of label estimation, two measurements precision and recall are calculated. Figure 2 illustrates the varying trends of precision and recall as the iteration proceeds. We observe a consistent varying trend, that is, the precision instantly declining while the recall progressively growing on three datasets, and finally both of them tend to be stable. We first analyze the reason for the decline in precision. Although increasingly positive pairs are estimated as the iteration goes on, it is inevitable that some false positive pairs will be outputted due to drastic cross-view appearance variation. In reverse, it is noted that the recall is progressively growth as the iteration proceeds, that is to say, the more truly positive pairs can be inferred. This suggests that the robustness of the learned metric model is gradually strengthening.

Evaluation of Clustering. To verify the validity of clustering, we compare it with 'Randomly sampling' and 'Average', i.e., randomly sampling some person images from each person sequence and taking the average feature as the representation of each person sequence respectively. In experiments, we fix the number of clusters and the sampling images as 6. From the Fig. 3, we observe consistent improvements on iLIDS-VID dataset with our clustering method. This suggests that modeling each person sequence with clustering method can retain more discriminating information.

Evaluation of the Number of Dynamic Iterations. To evaluate the impact of the number of dynamic iterations, we report the Rank1 accuracy and the number of estimated positive pairs at each iteration on three datasets. We perform 10 iterations and the results are shown in Fig. 4. At the beginning of the iteration, only a small number of cross-camera person sequences are infered as positive pairs. As the iteration proceeds, the Rank1 accuracy is gradually improved as more positive pairs are output. Finally, the DBNSR model tends to converge when the number of dynamic iterations reaches 5 or 6. We also note that the Rank1 accuracy has a slightly decline during the iterative process. It is inevitably that a few false pairwise labels are outputted, which degrades the discriminability of KISSME. Nevertheless, we can still bring 1.24%, 4.86% and 3.94% improvements in Rank1 on the three datasets by this iterative strategy.

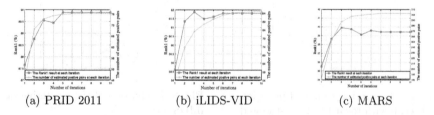

(a) PRID 2011   (b) iLIDS-VID   (c) MARS

Fig. 4. Rank1 results of person reID and the number of estimated positive pairs at each iteration on the three datasets.

4   Conclusion

In this paper, we presented a Dynamic Bi-directional Normalized Sparse Representation (DBNSR) method for unsupervised multi-shot person reID by constraining each element in sparse representation coefficient vector with a probability property. It is capable of effectively measure the similarity among samples by a global perspective. Meanwhile, only both person image sequences that represented mutually with maximum probability were considered a positive pair of the cross camera. An iterative procedure was introduced to progressively update BNSR and KISSME metric with intermediate estimated labels, leading to a more discriminative KISSME. Finally, we verified the effectiveness of the DBNSR for the unsupervised multi-shot person reID on three datasets.

Acknowledgement. This work is partially supported by Natural Science Foundation of China under Grant 62006017 and Beijing Natural Science Foundation under Grant L191016.

References

1. Bak, S., Carr, P.: Person re-identification using deformable patch metric learning. In: IEEE Winter Conference on Applications of Computer Vision, pp. 1–9. IEEE (2016)
2. Bialkowski, A., Denman, S., Sridharan, S., Fookes, C., Lucey, P.: A database for person re-identification in multi-camera surveillance networks. In: International Conference on Digital Image Computing Techniques and Applications, pp. 1–8. IEEE (2012)
3. Boyd, S., Parikh, N., Chu, E., Peleato, B., Eckstein, J.: Distributed optimization and statistical learning via the alternating direction method of multipliers. Found. Trends Mach. Learn. **3**(1), 1–122 (2010)
4. Chen, Y., Zhu, X., Gong, S.: Deep association learning for unsupervised video person re-identification. In: British Machine Vision Conference, p. 48 (2018)
5. Hirzer, M., Beleznai, C., Roth, P.M., Bischof, H.: Person re-identification by descriptive and discriminative classification. In: Heyden, A., Kahl, F. (eds.) SCIA 2011. LNCS, vol. 6688, pp. 91–102. Springer, Heidelberg (2011). https://doi.org/10.1007/978-3-642-21227-7_9
6. Karanam, S., Li, Y., Radke, R.J.: Person re-identification with discriminatively trained viewpoint invariant dictionaries. In: Proceedings of the IEEE International Conference on Computer Vision, pp. 4516–4524 (2015)
7. Khan, F.M., Bremond, F.: Unsupervised data association for metric learning in the context of multi-shot person re-identification. In: IEEE International Conference on Advanced Video and Signal Based Surveillance, pp. 256–262. IEEE (2016)
8. Kodirov, E., Xiang, T., Fu, Z., Gong, S.: Person re-identification by unsupervised ℓ_1 graph learning. In: Leibe, B., Matas, J., Sebe, N., Welling, M. (eds.) ECCV 2016, Part I. LNCS, vol. 9905, pp. 178–195. Springer, Cham (2016). https://doi.org/10.1007/978-3-319-46448-0_11
9. Li, M., Zhu, X., Gong, S.: Unsupervised person re-identification by deep learning tracklet association. In: Ferrari, V., Hebert, M., Sminchisescu, C., Weiss, Y. (eds.) ECCV 2018, Part IV. LNCS, vol. 11208, pp. 772–788. Springer, Cham (2018). https://doi.org/10.1007/978-3-030-01225-0_45

10. Li, M., Zhu, X., Gong, S.: Unsupervised tracklet person re-identification. IEEE Trans. Pattern Anal. Mach. Intell. **42**(7), 1770–1782 (2020). https://doi.org/10.1109/TPAMI.2019.2903058

11. Liu, Z., Wang, D., Lu, H.: Stepwise metric promotion for unsupervised video person re-identification. In: Proceedings of the IEEE International Conference on Computer Vision, pp. 2429–2438 (2017)

12. Ma, X., et al.: Person re-identification by unsupervised video matching. Pattern Recognit. **65**, 197–210 (2017)

13. Matsukawa, T., Okabe, T., Suzuki, E., Sato, Y.: Hierarchical gaussian descriptor for person re-identification. In: Proceedings of the IEEE Conference on Computer Vision and Pattern Recognition, pp. 1363–1372 (2016)

14. Wu, J., Yang, Y., Liu, H., Liao, S., Lei, Z., Li, S.Z.: Unsupervised graph association for person re-identification. In: Proceedings of the IEEE Conference on International Conference on Computer Vision, pp. 8321–8330 (2019)

15. Ye, M., Lan, X., Yuen, P.C.: Robust anchor embedding for unsupervised video person re-identification in the wild. In: Ferrari, V., Hebert, M., Sminchisescu, C., Weiss, Y. (eds.) ECCV 2018, Part VII. LNCS, vol. 11211, pp. 176–193. Springer, Cham (2018). https://doi.org/10.1007/978-3-030-01234-2_11

16. Ye, M., Ma, A.J., Zheng, L., Li, J., Yuen, P.C.: Dynamic label graph matching for unsupervised video re-identification. In: Proceedings of the IEEE International Conference on Computer Vision, pp. 5142–5150 (2017)

17. Zhao, R., Ouyang, W., Wang, X.: Unsupervised salience learning for person re-identification. In: Proceedings of the IEEE Conference on Computer Vision and Pattern Recognition, pp. 3586–3593 (2013)

18. Zheng, L., et al.: MARS: a video benchmark for large-scale person re-identification. In: Leibe, B., Matas, J., Sebe, N., Welling, M. (eds.) ECCV 2016, Part VI. LNCS, vol. 9910, pp. 868–884. Springer, Cham (2016). https://doi.org/10.1007/978-3-319-46466-4_52

19. Zheng, L., Yang, Y., Hauptmann, A.G.: Person re-identification: Past, present and future. arXiv preprint arXiv:1610.02984 (2016)

20. Zou, H., Hastie, T.: Regularization and variable selection via the elastic net. J. Roy. Stat. Soc. Ser. B Stat. Methodol. **67**(2), 301–320 (2005)

Classifier Belief Optimization for Visual Categorization

Gang Yang[1,2] and Xirong Li[1,2(✉)]

[1] Key Lab of Data Engineering and Knowledge Engineering, Beijing, China
[2] School of Information, Renmin University of China, Beijing, China
{yanggang,xirong}@ruc.edu.cn

Abstract. Classifier belief represents the confidence of a classifier making judgment about a special instance. Based on classifier belief, we propose an approach to realize classifier belief optimization. Through enriching prior knowledge and thus reducing the scope of candidate classes, our approach improves classification accuracy. A feature perturbation strategy containing an objective optimization is developed to automatically generate labeled instances. Moreover, we propose a classifier consensus strategy (CCS) for classifier optimization. CCS enables a given classifier to take full advantage of the test data to enrich prior knowledge. Experiments on three benchmark datasets and three classical classifiers justify the validity of the proposed approach. We improve the classification accuracy of a linear SVM by 6%.

Keywords: Image perturbation · Classifier belief · Belief optimization · Image classification

1 Introduction

Classification, aiming to classify a novel instance into a set of predefined classes, is a long-standing challenge in artificial intelligence [2]. Recent advances are mainly attributed to the advent of deep (convolutional) neural networks that have unified feature representation and classifier training into a joint end-to-end learning framework [9]. This paper looks into a different direction, proposing a generic approach to improve classification by manipulating features and enhancing classifier confidence, based on the imitation of human behavior.

A large number of algorithms originating from the simulations of the law of nature [3], have great advantages in practical applications. These algorithms normally mimic the action of insect, bird or human [3]. But there are few jobs imitating human cognitive behavior to increase algorithm ability due to its complexity. Here we make an exploration to optimize classifier by mimicking the cognition processes of human on aspects of prior knowledge and human consensus. When recognizing an ambiguous object, people often refer to others'

This work was supported by the Fundamental Research Funds for the Central Universities, and the Research Funds of Renmin University of China (20XNA031).

J. Lokoč et al. (Eds.): MMM 2021, LNCS 12572, pp. 567–579, 2021.
https://doi.org/10.1007/978-3-030-67832-6_46

advice and tend to trust the person who is highly confident with her advice. High confidence plays a crucial factor when people make a decision. Generally, the more prior knowledge a person learned, the higher confidence he has, where the prior knowledge means the cognition on classified objects. Therefore, accumulating training instances is a crucial factor to improve machine learning and build a more effective classifier. There are many classical methods to accumulate training dataset in data augmentation [19], but most of them only produce new images by manipulating the labeled images. That limits their generalizations. There are less work to generate instances at the feature level, and there are few jobs to improve classifier by optimizing classifier belief. Moreover, prior knowledge about invariant of a classification problem ought to be incorporated into the training procedure, which is helpful to obtain the best possible performance [15]. Therefore, we believe test instances with classifier beliefs are helpful to improve classification, and they are also useful to optimize classifier. Observations on human cognition behavior reveal if allowing people to modify the recognized image as few as possible to increase their recognition belief and further recognize the objects in image, they normally draw the most similar objects with less modification and higher belief [20]. The characteristic brings us inspiration that through enhancing belief and modifying features of instances to form consensus will be an effective way to optimize classifiers.

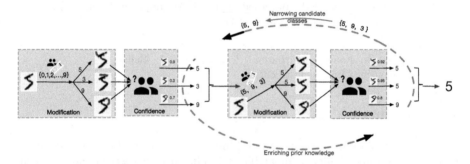

Fig. 1. A schematic process of identifying handwriting digits, in which feature modification is permitted to increase recognition confidence. The digits containing red pixels represent the features of the generated instances by image modification, integers denote the recognized results, decimals denote the recognition confidences, and braces {...} represent the limitation of candidate classes.

Based on above consideration and inspiration, we propose a novel approach that is by mimicking the cognition processes of human to optimize classifier. The basic idea of our approach is that the new evolutional instances generated by a rule of less feature perturbation and higher belief difference from the labeled instances are used to augment data at the feature level, and these from the test instances are provided to classifiers to get consensus of classification through gradually reducing the scope of candidate classes. Unlike other methods of data augmentation, our approach directly generates the feature of instance by a feature perturbation strategy which mimics the image modification. In our approach, as particle swarm optimization (PSO) [3] originates as a method to simulate human social behavior, it is introduced to mimic the human behavior of identifying objects in group with a constraint of the belief difference that denoting people confidence. A classifier consensus strategy (CCS) is proposed to take full advantage of the test instances by imitating the people consensus to enrich prior knowledge. Experiments on image datasets demonstrate our approach improves classifier effectively. Moreover, it is a valuable exploration that classification is improved based on classifier belief and utilizing test instances.

The main contributions of this paper are: (1) At the feature level, our approach efficiently simulates the process of people identifying objects that is through modifying image features and enhancing recognition confidence to improve classification accuracy. (2) The classifier consensus strategy (CCS) enables our approach to generate new labeled instances from test instances and reduce the scope of candidate classes to decrease the difficulty of classification. (3) CCS makes an exploration of taking full advantage of test instances to optimize classifiers. Our experiments reveal the exploration of CCS is effective and valuable.

2   Related Work

Previously, classifier optimization mainly focuses on performance improvement by tuning classifier structure and extending training instances [19]. Especially, extending training instances through wide assortment-distortion (e.g. rotations, scaling) and random noises [21] can increase classification accuracy, and further improve algorithm robustness to some extent. New instances generated by affine transformations and elastic distortions on original instances can form soft margin separating hyperplane to classify non-separable instances [14]. Moreover, researches in recent years, especially some work of pattern recognitions using deep learning, validate that generating adequate training instances is an effective way to optimize classifiers [12]. It further reveals the importance of labeled instances. However, tagging images is a high cost work. Therefore, enriching prior knowledge by generating labeled instances automatically is valuable for classifier.

On the other hand, belief and belief function have combined with classifiers to provide input feature uncertainty and to modify the decision rules that allowing for ambiguous pattern selection [15]. Dempster-Shafer theory of belief functions [4] is adopted to combine classifier results from different classifiers and arrives at the final solution that takes into account all the available results [17]. However, belief function embedded in those classifiers focuses on assigning different belief principles and assumptions on the classifiers and the prediction categories. Few jobs are devoted to generating training instances based on the belief of classifier. Moreover, in previous research, the way of generating labeled instances mainly focuses on utilizing training and validation dataset to augment data. Few researchers pay attention to optimize classification through utilizing test data. Although transductive support vector machines [6, 22] temporarily treat test instances as prior knowledge to optimize classification, these unlabeled test instances normally have detrimental effects especially when they rely on clustering to generate instances [22].

Notably, in this paper we focus on the belief optimization method for classifiers to improve their effectiveness. Although in recent years deep learning has gained remarkable performance on classification [11, 23], we here do not consider them as the optimized classifiers as considering their efficiency. The classifiers based on deep learning can also be optimized by our method, which will be our future research work.

3   Classifier Belief Optimization

A specific process of people recognizing a handwriting digit schematically that our approach mimic is shown in Fig. 1. For a handwritten digit five shown in Fig. 1, a person may incorrectly recognize it as digit three or nine due to its ambiguous appearance. Moreover, confidence about the decision varies over persons. Now these people are asked to modify the image with minimal strokes so that they would expect others to make the right decision with higher confidences. The minimal-strokes constraint allows one to draw (and thus allows others to observe) many incrementally changed instances. The iterative process continues until a consensus is reached on correctly recognizing the digit. Based on mimicking the above process, we propose a classifier belief optimization approach, where we substitute classifiers, belief and feature perturbation for people, confidence, and instance modification respectively. The approach is denoted in Algorithm 1.

Algorithm 1 : *Classifier belief optimization approach*

1: Initiate coefficients, parameters and features of the training dataset X.
2: Generate new instances $\hat{X}$ by the feature perturbation strategy with PSO solving on X.
3: Build $\hat{X}'$ from $\hat{X}$ by the instance selection strategy.
4: Construct a new training dataset with $X \cup \hat{X}'$.
5: Build classifiers C with each C_k training on subset X_k separately. Here, $X_k \subset \{X \cup \hat{X}'\}$, $C_k \in C$, and $k \in \{1, ..., K\}$.
6: Classify a test instance x by C with the classifier consensus strategy and the feature perturbation strategy in PSO solving, thus to generate new instances with classified results.
7: Narrow candidate classes according to the classifier consensus strategy.
8: **if** classification results on x and the generated instances are the same, or the process reaches a pre-specified epoch ϵ, **then**
9:    get final result of x by the majority strategy.
10: **else**
11:    **goto** step 4 with the new generated instances, the new candidate classes and x.
12: **end if**

In Algorithm 1, the classifier belief optimization approach has two stages. Steps 1 to 4 forms stage 1, denoted as BOP_1, to optimize classifier by mimicking the cognition behavior of human on already known objects (training instances). Steps 4 to 12 constructs stage 2, denoted as BOP_2, which mimicking the human identification process on unknown ambiguous objects (test instances). In BOP_1, new labeled instances are generated according to a feature perturbation strategy and a instance selection strategy to build a new training set. These instances form new cognition on their classes to classifiers. In BOP_1, classifiers learn on the new training dataset to improve their performance. In BOP_2, the training dataset is split to several subsets for classifier training respectively. Then classifiers, representing people, identify a test instance in the scope of candidate classes. Due to effect of the feature perturbation strategy, many instances related to the test instance are generated in step 6. These new instances represent the modified images by people, and PSO solving imitates the rule of instance modification that the modification should be less but with higher confidence. According to the classifier consensus strategy, if the classifiers (people) get consensus, then output this result. These instances with their results are put into the training set, and they are regarded as the prior knowledge for further classification. If no consensus, then BOP_2 narrows its candidate classes and drives classifiers (people) to classify it again within the narrowed scope of classes. BOP_2 is an iterative process. When BOP_2 reaches a pre-specified epoch ϵ, classification on that instance terminates. The ultimate result is achieved by a simple majority.

3.1   Definitions and Strategies

Considering a multi-class classification, where a specific instance x in a dataset X is to be classified into one of k classes. A classifier C_j has a confidence value of b_i that x belongs to the i-th class, where $b_i \in [0,1]$ and $\sum_{i=1}^{k} b_i = 1$. We use b_m and b_{sm} to denote the first and second largest confidence values, respectively.

Classifier belief with respect to a specific instance is represented by the largest confidence value of the classifier, i.e., b_m.

Belief difference is defined as $b_m - b_{sm}$. A larger belief difference means the classifier gets an obvious classification result on the instance, and thus the classifier is more confident about the result.

Belief optimization drives classifier to obtain larger belief difference when targeting a specific classification task. Classifiers with belief optimization are more robust than before, as belief optimization improves their separating hyperplane. Moreover, by supervising the changes of belief difference, belief optimization guides classifier to generate more labeled instances to enrich their prior knowledge.

Feature perturbation strategy is concerned about how to modify feature of instance to enlarge the belief difference of classifier. Feature perturbation strategy will cause feature modification of the classified instance and guide change of the classifier belief. This is a rule of human cognition [20]. In our approach, it is designed to make the classifier gain larger belief difference with less feature modification on the original instances. According to label propagation technique [15], the feature perturbation strategy is formulated as follows:

$$\min_{W,\hat{X}} \frac{\|\hat{X} - W\overline{X}\|_F^2 + \lambda tr(W\overline{X}L\overline{X}^T W^T) + \gamma\|\hat{X} - X\|_1}{2(b_m - b_{sm})} \qquad (1)$$

where X is a feature matrix with each row representing an original instance, $\hat{X} \in R^{M \times N}$ denotes the ideal perturbed feature matrix with each row being a new generated instance, $\overline{X} \in R^{M \times N}$ denotes the average feature matrix that each row is set as the mean features of a batch of instances of a class, $W \in R^{M \times M}$ denotes a correlation matrix between $\hat{X}$ and $\overline{X}$ representing feature perturbation, λ and γ are two positive regularization parameters, and $tr()$ is the trace of a matrix. To calculate L, an undirected graph $G = \{V, A\}$ is constructed. Its vertex set V is the set of original instances, and its linear kernel matrix $A \in R^{N \times N}$ is the affine matrix over the original supervised instances. In Eq. 1, L, the normalized Laplacian matrix of G, is expressed by $L = I - D^{-1/2}AD^{-1/2}$, where I is an identity matrix and D is a diagonal matrix with its i-th diagonal entry being the sum of the i-th row of A. Then, the feature perturbation strategy is transformed to be an objective optimization problem, shown in Eq. 2, to generate amounts of perturbed features of instances $\hat{X}^*$ and modification W^*.

$$W^*, \hat{X}^* = arg\min_{W,\hat{X}} \frac{\|\hat{X} - W\overline{X}\|_F^2 + \lambda tr(W\overline{X}L\overline{X}^T W^T) + \gamma\|\hat{X} - X\|_1}{2(b_m - b_{sm})}. \qquad (2)$$

In Eq. 2, the first term denotes the Frobenius norm fitting constraint [1,7], which means that $W\overline{X}$ should not change too much from $\overline{X}$ and should be similar with $\hat{X}$. The second term denotes the smoothness constraint, also known as Laplacian regularization [8], which means the $W\overline{X}$ should not change too much among these similar instances. The third term denotes the L_1-norm fitting constraint, which can impose direct noise reduction on the original X due to the nice property of L_1-norm optimization [13]. With the effect of Eq. 2 optimization, a large number of instances $\hat{X}^*$ are generated with labels. $\hat{X}^*$ are reasonable as they are generated according to the statistical mean of a class.

Instance selection strategy is presented to select the crucial instances from the new instances generated by the feature perturbation strategy, because not all of the generated instances are helpful to optimize classifier. The instance selection strategy is presented as follows.

$$\hat{x}_i^j \in \hat{X}'_{train} \begin{cases} if \ \hat{x}_{i \cdot p}^j < \theta \ \& \ \hat{x}_{i \cdot b}^j > \eta \ \& \ \hat{y}_i^j \neq y_i \\ if \ \hat{x}_{i \cdot p}^j < \theta \ \& \ \hat{x}_{i \cdot b}^j < \eta \ \& \ \hat{y}_i^j = y_i \\ if \ \hat{x}_{i \cdot p}^j > \theta \ \& \ \hat{x}_{i \cdot b}^j > \eta \ \& \ \hat{y}_i^j = y_i \end{cases} \qquad (3)$$

where $\hat{x}_i^j$ is a perturbed instance related with x_i, $\hat{y}$ is the classified results, y_i is the labeled class of x_i, $\hat{x}_{i \cdot p}^j = \|w\hat{x}_i^j - x_i\|$, $\hat{x}_{i \cdot b}^j = b_m - b_{sm}$, and two thresholds θ and η about the feature perturbation and the belief difference control the instance selection. The instance selection strategy includes three scenarios: if a generated instance cannot be predicted correctly, its perturbation is little, and its classifier belief is high, then it is selected; if a generated instance can be predicted correctly, its perturbation is little, and its classifier belief is low, then it is selected; if a training instance can be predicted correctly, its perturbation is large, and its classifier belief is high, then it is selected also. The selected instances are put into the training set to form a new training set. Trained on the new training set, the classifiers are optimized effectively.

Classifier consensus strategy (CCS): Assume $x_i (i \in N)$ is a test instance i denoted by features, $\hat{x}_i^j (j \in N')$ is an instance j generated from x_i based on the feature perturbation strategy, N' is the number of the generated instances, and C_k is a classifier ($k \in K$, K is the number of classifiers). When $K \times (N'+1)$ classification results are the same, the test instances x_i and all $\hat{x}_i^j$ labeled with their classification results are put into training set to retrain new classifiers. When their classification results are different, the classification results can form new candidate classes for the instance x_i, and further classification for x_i just needs to do within the new candidate classes CCS enables classifiers to produce many new labeled instances from the test instances to enrich their prior knowledge. Moreover, CCS decreases the classification complexity by gradually reducing the scope of candidate classes. Based on the thought of CCS, it's easy to form more effective classification algorithms through introducing classification probability and statistical rules.

PSO solving: Our approach uses the particle swarm optimization (PSO) algorithm to directly imitate the behavior of people modifying the image to identify object. PSO is originally proposed, based on the inspiration from the swarming behavior of animals and human social behavior [3]. In our approach, aiming to minimize the objective optimization (Eq. 2) with less feature perturbation and larger belief difference, PSO is naturally adopted to gradually modify images to increase their recognition accuracy. Here, a particle swarm is the population of particles, in which each particle is a new generated instance that flies through the search space and is attracted to previously visited locations with low fitness. The particles are initialized by the features of the original instances, and the fitness function is set as Eq. 2. Each particle consists of a position vector $\overrightarrow{x}$, which is encoded as the perturbed feature of an instance and represents a candidate solution to the optimization problem, a fitness of $\overrightarrow{x}$ solution, a velocity vector $\overrightarrow{v}$ and a memory vector $\overrightarrow{p}$ of the best candidate solution encountered by the particle with its recorded fitness. The position of a particle is updated by $\overrightarrow{x}(t+1) = \overrightarrow{x}(t) + \overrightarrow{v}(t+1)$ and its velocity is changed according to $\overrightarrow{v}(t+1) = \alpha \overrightarrow{v}(t) + \varphi_1(\overrightarrow{p} - \overrightarrow{x}(t)) + \varphi_2(\overrightarrow{p}_g - \overrightarrow{x}(t))$, where φ_1 and φ_2 are uniformly distributed random number within $[0,1]$ that determines the weights between the attraction to position $\overrightarrow{p}$, which is the best position found by the particle so far, and the overall best position $\overrightarrow{p}_g$ found by all particles. When PSO gets convergence, the particles with the low fitness are regarded as the generated instances with the perturbed features. These generated instances are related to their original instances, and they are classified in step 2, 6 of Algorithm 1.

3.2   Key Procedure of Our Approach

With the guidance of classifier belief, BOP_1 generates more effective labeled instances at the feature level for classifiers to increase their classification accuracy. In detail, although many algorithms can produce new instances for classifier, they lack the guidance of classifier belief and barely take into account the difference degree of the new instance. In our approach, the generated instances should be recognized with higher classifier beliefs so that the classifier builds a more effective model with high robustness. So, the feature perturbation strategy transforms the instance generation to be an objective optimization (Eq. 2). As the particle swarm optimization (PSO) algorithm originally has bionic characteristic to simulate human social behavior, it is especially fit for the optimization problem to generate large numbers of new instances with high classifier beliefs. In the PSO solving of BOP_1, the optimization objective of PSO is minimizing Eq. 2, the particles are initialized as the features of the instances in the same class. The saturated particles are the generated instances with the larger belief difference and low feature perturbation. PSO solving of BOP_1 ensures the generated instances are effective and diverse. The instance selection strategy filters out the noise instances. Then a new training dataset including the original training set and the selected instances is formed. BOP_2 realizes the classifier belief optimization on test data, and it attempts to take advantage of the test instance to increase the prior knowledge. After BOP_1, several classifiers imitating people are trained on the subsets of the new training dataset. Every subset contains only the training instances of the candidate classes. In BOP_2, these classifiers predict each test instance separately also with the feature perturbation strategy and PSO solving. Different with BOP_1, the class of the test instance is unknown, $\overline{X}$ of feature perturbation strategy is replaced by a matrix whose row is noisy features of the test instance (x_i). Then with PSO solving, many new instances are generated from x_i no matter whether their classification results are right or not. Then CCS mimics the consensus of human to decide x_i class. If all prediction results on x_i and its new instances are the same, which means consensus, CCS puts x_i and its related new instances into the training set. They are labeled with their consensus results. If there are different prediction results, then the right one normally exists in them. CCS utilizes these prediction results to narrow the candidate classes of x_i. The new candidate classes of x_i are equal to the predicted results of the generated instances, i.e., $\bigcup\{\hat{y}_i^j\}, j \in \{1, 2, ..., N'\}$. To further identify x_i, classifiers are retrained on the training dataset with the new scope of candidate classes. BOP_2 runs iteratively until either CCS gives final consensus classification or its running reaches a pre-specified epoch. Notably, our approach manipulates feature of object directly, so it is a general way to optimize classifiers in many research fields.

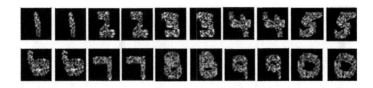

Fig. 2. The instances generated by BOP_1 on the Mnist dataset.

4 Experiments

4.1 Datasets and Settings

To evaluate the effectiveness of our approach, three benchmark datasets and three classical classification algorithms are tested under various classification conditions and settings. The three datasets are the Mnist, the Oxford 102 Flower and the Caltech-UCSD Birds-200-2011 datasets, and the three classification algorithms are linear SVM [5], KNN [10] and Softmax [9]. The Mnist dataset consists of 60,000 training digit images and 10,000 testing digit images, which is widely used in classification research. The Flower dataset is provided by the University of Oxford, consisting of 8189 images divided into 102 flower classes [16]. The Caltech-UCSD Birds-200-2011 (CUB) dataset is an extended version of the CUB-200 dataset, consisting of 11,788 images divided into 200 bird classes. The linear SVM [5] is used as a basic classifier on the Mnist. We apply deep learning features with 4096 dimensions extracted from fc7 layer of CaffeNet on the Flower and the CUB dataset. In our experiments, coefficients λ and γ are both set 1, threshold θ is set to 0.8 according to the value of $||X - \overline{X}||$, $\eta = 0.5$, and the threshold ϵ is set to 10 epochs. After data shuffling, the training dataset is split to 10 subsets averagely.

4.2 Results and Analysis

We demonstrate the effectiveness of our approach on the three classifiers and datasets. Firstly, we apply BOP_1 to optimize linear SVM on the Mnist dataset, and to validate how much belief improvement after optimization. After BOP_1, a new training dataset is generated, which is about 3 times larger than the original training dataset. A new classifier is trained on the new generated training dataset, and gets 95.13% classification accuracy on the test dataset, which increases 2% over the original linear SVM.

On the Mnist dataset, the mean classifier belief of the correctly classified instances is 0.9488 after belief optimization of BOP_1, but the original mean value is 0.8594. After BOP_1 on the Mnist, some generated instances are shown in Fig. 2. The generated instances just modify a few pixels of digits due to the effect of the feature perturbation strategy. However, there is a significant improvement on the classifier beliefs, averaging about 0.2. Classifiers trained on the generated instances are more robust than before, as the generated instances optimize the decision boundary of the classifiers.

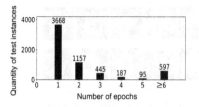 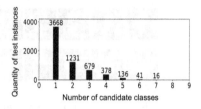

Fig. 3. The relationship among candidate classes, test instances and epochs, illustrating CCS effect on the Flower dataset. The left figure reveals how many epochs a test instance needs to get final classification, and the right one shows the distribution relationship between test instances and their candidate classes after one epoch. Generally, to a classification problem, the less candidate classes, the easier classification. In the Flower dataset, initially all test instances are classified within 102 classes. After the effect of CCS, 1231 instances just belonging to 2 classes are revealed. So finally our approach just needs to decide which class the instances belongs to among the two classes. The problem becomes easier. After one epoch, top@k ($k \leq 9$) classification accuracy is 92.3%, which represents the problem is simplified to classify only in no more than 9 classes in the following processing if 92.3% is taken as a benchmark.

BOP_2 is especially fit for the classification task containing many categories. In the iterative process of BOP_2, a complex classification problem is gradually transformed to be an easy problem with a small number of categories. Figure 3 shows the iterative results on test dataset of the Flower dataset within 7 epochs. In Fig. 3, we can find that 59.6% test instances are directly convergent to the unique classes in one epoch. After two epochs, about 78.4% test instances have gotten convergent to the unique classes. Generally, after 7 epochs of belief optimization, our approach can totally reach a saturated state to yield a deterministic solution. In this test, CCS affects this process clearly, and it not only reduces the problem complexity but also decreases the difficulty of searching.

Table 1. The mean accuracy (in %) comparison on three datasets.

Classifier	Mnist	Flower	CUB
Original linear SVM	92.96	79.72	50.35
Transductive SVM	96.21	82.16	-
CNNaug-SVM	-	86.8	**56.8**
Linear SVM with BOP_1	95.13	81.85	50.93
Linear SVM with BOP_1 & BOP_2	**98.24**	**87.38**	53.32

On the Mnist, Flower and CUB datasets, we compare the optimization effect of BOP_1 and BOP_2 on the linear SVM, and compare our algorithm with transductive SVM [22] and CNNaug-SVM [18]. As the transductive SVM mainly supports binary classification, we construct a hierarchical transductive SVM

Table 2. The mean accuracy (in %) of the linear SVM, KNN, Softmax classifiers and their optimized classifiers by our approach.

Classifier	Mnist	Flower	CUB
SVM	93.0	79.7	50.4
SVM with BOP_1 & BOP_2	**98.2**	**87.4**	**53.3**
KNN	96.6	38.8	34.4
KNN with BOP_1 & BOP_2	**98.3**	**84.7**	**47.9**
Softmax	92.5	79.8	51.2
Softmax with BOP_1 & BOP_2	**97.1**	**86.7**	**54.2**

to realize multi-class classification. The comparison is shown in Table 1. From Table 1, we can see BOP_1 and BOP_2 can improve the classification accuracies of the linear SVM. Although transductive SVM can also optimize SVM classifier to some extent, it shows poor performance on the Flower dataset possibly because the size of category is too large. On the Flower dataset, our approach only uses the flower cut, and does not use any other additional optimization ways, such as flower mask. However, we get 87.38% classification accuracy on the Flower dataset. The result is superior to the best accuracy 86.8% revealed in [18], who mixed multiple optimization methods including the way of augmenting training set by introducing cropped and rotated instances and masking segmentation to extract the specific flowers. On the CUB dataset, which is mainly used for fine-grained classification, we achieve a comparable result. Possibly, as the categories of the CUB dataset have tiny feature difference, the feature perturbation strategy cannot generate effective instances with right labels. Furthermore, Table 2 shows clearly that our approach can optimize three classifiers (Linear SVM, KNN and Softmax). On the three datasets, the accuracies of three classifiers are all enhanced by our approach. It demonstrates that our approach adapts classifiers widely and it is a general way for classifiers. The performance gain is obtained at the cost of extra computational overhead. For example, on the Flower dataset, it takes the baseline Linear SVM 11 s to train and predict. For SVM with BOP_1, it takes 128 s, and around one hour for SVM with BOP_2. Numbers are measured on a Ubuntu computer with 32G RAM and a dual 2.4 GHz CPU. The bottleneck lies in the prediction stage, as the models need to classify many generated instances. As PSO has the superiority of parallel computing, parallel computing can be introduced to improve our approach efficiency.

5   Conclusion

In this paper, an approach of classifier belief optimization, embedded with a feature perturbation strategy and a classifier consensus strategy (CCS), is proposed. Our approach effectively mimics human cognizing processes that is through modifying less content of the recognized object to increase recognition belief so as to make confident judgment. The feature perturbation strategy transforms the instance generation to an objective optimization problem, thereby generating effective labeled instances. CCS is first proposed to provide an enlightening method for classifier optimization, which is utilizing test instances to generate more labeled instances and enrich the prior knowledge of classifier. Experimental results demonstrate our approach optimizes classifiers effectively and widely, and our exploration is valuable. In the near future, we will use our method to make data augmentation, and then research a way of training deep neural networks with these augmented data to optimize the deep learning methods.

References

1. Bay, H., Tuytelaars, T., Van Gool, L.: SURF: speeded up robust features. In: Leonardis, A., Bischof, H., Pinz, A. (eds.) ECCV 2006, Part I. LNCS, vol. 3951, pp. 404–417. Springer, Heidelberg (2006). https://doi.org/10.1007/11744023_32
2. Bishop, C.M.: Pattern Recognition and Machine Learning. Springer, New York (2007)
3. Bonyadi, M.R., Michalewicz, Z.: Analysis of stability, local convergence, and transformation sensitivity of a variant of the particle swarm optimization algorithm. IEEE Trans. Evol. Comput. **20**(3), 370–385 (2016)
4. Bundy, A., Wallen, L.: Dempster-Shafer Theory. Springer, Heidelberg (1984)
5. Chang, C.C., Lin, C.J.: LIBSVM: a library for support vector machines. ACM Trans. Intell. Syst. Technol. **2**(3), 27 (2011)
6. Chapelle, O., Schölkopf, B., Zien, A.: Semi-supervised learning. In: PAKDD, pp. 588–595 (2006)
7. Custódio, A.L., Rocha, H., Vicente, L.N.: Incorporating minimum Frobenius norm models in direct search. Comput. Optim. Appl. **46**(2), 265–278 (2010). https://doi.org/10.1007/s10589-009-9283-0
8. Fu, Z., Lu, Z., Ip, H.H.S., Peng, Y., Lu, H.: Symmetric graph regularized constraint propagation. In: AAAI, pp. 350–355 (2011)
9. Goodfellow, I., Bengio, Y., Courville, A.: Deep Learning. MIT Press, Cambridge (2016)
10. Hall, P., Park, B.U., Samworth, R.J.: Choice of neighbor order in nearest-neighbor classification. Ann. Stat. **36**(5), 2135–2152 (2008)
11. He, K., Zhang, X., Ren, S., Sun, J.: Deep residual learning for image recognition. In: 2016 IEEE Conference on Computer Vision and Pattern Recognition (CVPR), pp. 770–778 (2016)
12. Hinton, G.E., Salakhutdinov, R.R.: A better way to pretrain deep boltzmann machines. In: NIPS, pp. 2447–2455 (2012)
13. Kostina, E.A., Prischepova, S.V.: A new algorithm for minimax and l1-norm optimization. Optimization **44**(3), 263–289 (1998)
14. Lauer, F., Suen, C.Y., Bloch, G.: A trainable feature extractor for handwritten digit recognition. Pattern Recogn. **40**(6), 1816–1824 (2007)
15. Lu, Z., Wang, L., Wen, J.R.: Direct semantic analysis for social image classification. In: AAAI, pp. 1258–1264 (2014)
16. Nilsback, M.E., Zisserman, A.: Automated flower classification over a large number of classes. In: Proceedings of ICVGIP. Citeseer (2008)
17. Quost, B., Denœux, T., Masson, M.H.: Pairwise classifier combination using belief functions. Pattern Recogn. Lett. **28**(5), 644–653 (2007)

18. Sharif Razavian, A., Azizpour, H., Sullivan, J., Carlsson, S.: CNN features off-the-shelf: an astounding baseline for recognition. In: CVPR Workshops, pp. 806–813 (2014)
19. Shen, B., Liu, B.D., Wang, Q., Fang, Y., Allebach, J.P.: SP-SVM: large margin classifier for data on multiple manifolds. In: AAAI, pp. 2965–2971 (2015)
20. Skinner, B.: The Technology of Teaching. Appleton Century Crofts, New York (1968)
21. Vincent, P., Larochelle, H., Bengio, Y., Manzagol, P.A.: Extracting and composing robust features with denoising autoencoders. In: ICML, pp. 1096–1103 (2008)
22. Wang, J., Shen, X., Pan, W.: On transductive support vector machines. Contemp. Math. **443**, 7–20 (2007)
23. Zhang, H., et al.: ResNeSt: split-attention networks. arXiv preprint arXiv:2004.08955 (2020)

Fine-Grained Generation for Zero-Shot Learning

Weimin Sun[2], Jieping Xu[1,2], and Gang Yang[1,2](✉)

[1] Key Lab of Data Engineering and Knowledge Engineering, Beijing, China
[2] School of Information, Renmin University of China, Beijing, China
yanggang@ruc.edu.cn

Abstract. Although zero-shot learning (ZSL) has achieved success in recognizing unseen classes images, most previous studies focus on feature projection from one domain to another, neglecting the domain shift problem caused by differences in classes. In this paper, we propose two novel methods in terms of attributes and features for ZSL problem. The first is Sample-Level Attribute Generation via GAN (SLA-GAN) that generates sample-level attributes. Considering the influence of lighting, environment, weather and other factors, the description based on class-level attributes will be biased. SLA-GAN generates sample-level attributes to describe each sample. Specially, we train a conditional Wasserstein GAN in which the generator synthesizes sample-level attributes from features and the discriminator distinguishes the sample-level from class-level attributes. Apart from that, we propose a novel method Fine-Grained Sample Generation via GAN (FGS-GAN) which can generate the unseen samples from the most similar samples of seen classes. Finally, we replace the class-level attributes with sample-level attributes in FGS-GAN and analyze the effects of sample-level attributes on synthesized features. Experiments on five benchmark data set show that our models outperform state-of-the-art methods in ZSL.

Keywords: Zero-shot learning · Domain shift · GAN · Sample-level attributes

1 Introduction

With continuous development of deep learning models, images classification has achieved great success and been applied in many fields. In these models, images can be easily recognized, as long as this class of samples are provided during training. However, in reality world, human needs to identify some classes samples which they know nothing about except some semantic descriptions. In order to deal with such problem, zero-shot learning methods (ZSL) are proposed. Different from the conventional classification models, in the training set and test

---

This work is supported by the Fundamental Research Funds for the Central Universities, and the Research Funds of Renmin University of China (20XNA031).

J. Lokoč et al. (Eds.): MMM 2021, LNCS 12572, pp. 580–591, 2021.
https://doi.org/10.1007/978-3-030-67832-6_47

Class-level	Attributes					
	Tail	Spot	Orange	Fur	Four Feet	...
	0.267	0.009	0.072	0.186	0.276	...
Sample-level	Fine-grained Attributes					
	0.017	0.122	0.247	0.310	0.256	...
	0.131	0.004	0.033	0.219	0.094	...
	0.275	0.228	0.104	0.189	0.116	...
	0.286	0.139	0.118	0.134	0.056	...

Fig. 1. Showcase of class-level attributes and various sample-level attributes. In zero-shot learning, the class-level attributes are judged by scholars and describe the general attributes of all samples in a class. Sample-level attributes are the real values that we generate to describe each sample instead of class. Due to the differences in descriptions between samples of one class, we utilize sample-level attributes as guidance to generate high-quality samples.

set of ZSL, not only the samples are disjoint, but also the classes are disjoint, so semantic descriptions are used to connect seen and unseen classes. For example, zebra and horse are two classes and disjoint, but we can recognize zebra images by the combination of images of horse and the descriptions of black-and-white stripes.

Recently, one of the methods to solve the domain shift problem in ZSL is to use GAN to generate unseen classes samples, which transforms unsupervised learning into supervised learning. Semantic descriptions as the only guidance for generating samples play an important role. Class-level attributes are the description of the whole class, but in reality world, due to the influence of lighting, environment, weather and other factors, the description based on class-level attributes will be biased.

As we can see from Fig. 1, the attribute values of "tail" in four images are different. In the bottom two images, the sample-level attributes of tails are more obvious, so their attribute values are closer to the class-level attribute value but the top two images are the opposite. If the above two images are described by class-level attributes, there will be a large error in the subsequent results. In addition, it is difficult to guarantee the quality of generating samples only using semantic descriptions as guidance. For example, attribute "black and white stripes" can represent many animals, such as zebra, panda and Bengal tiger, but if adding an image of horse as guidance, the generating samples are clearly close to zebras. Thus, zero-shot learning based on GAN must handle two issues: inconsistency between class-level attributes and samples, and insufficient guidance for generating samples. In this paper, we take these two issues into consideration and propose two novel methods that respectively resolve them.

First of all, we propose Sample-Level Attribute Generation via GAN (SLA-GAN) method to generate sample-level attributes. Specially, we train a conditional Wasserstein GANs in which the generator synthesizes sample-level attributes from features and the discriminator distinguishes the sample-level from class-level attributes. Here, class-level attributes are used as a guidance to keep the synthesized attributes close to the real. It should be noted that, we add the noise in GAN network to ensure the synthesized sample-level attributes are not exactly the class-level attributes. Furthermore, to ensure the high-quality of synthesized samples and provide sufficient information for generating, we propose Fine-Grained Sample Generation via GAN (FGS-GAN) method where samples of unseen classes are synthesized from samples of seen classes in feature space, under a guidance of semantic descriptions. Thus, finding the right "seen-unseen" pairs is of great vital. As the semantic descriptions are the only connection between seen and unseen classes, we use the similarity of attributes as a measure. The smaller the Euclidean distance between the two sets of attributes, the more similar the two classes are. Finally, we combine the two methods and use the sample-level attributes to guide the generation of unseen samples. Through above two methods, we can guarantee that each sample-level attribute is highly related to sample and the generated fine-grained samples of unseen classes have higher quality.

In sum, our contributions are as follows.

- We propose a novel method FGS-GAN to improve the quality of synthesized samples which generates unseen samples from seen samples in feature space, guided by semantic description. This method provides more side information for generating samples than before.
- To bridge the gap between class-level attributes and samples, we introduce sample-level attributes which is defined as the description of sample. Sample-level attributes are generated from visual features. We regularize sample-level attributes should be close to their class-level attributes so that attributes of different classes are clearly distinguished in semantic space.
- We conduct experiments on five benchmark data sets and analyze the effects of sample-level attributes. The results show that our model performs state-of-the-art in zero-shot learning setting and sample-level attributes improve the quality of synthesized features.

2   Related Work

ZSL is first introduced by Lampert et al. [1] who tackles the problem by introducing attribute-based classification. They propose a Direct Attribute Prediction (DAP) model which maps features into attribute embedding through several classifiers and then gets the corresponding class by semantic dictionary which is defined specifically by human. Although this method can well define the relationship between features and semantics, it does not perform well for classification. Akata et al. [2] proposes to embed each class in the space of attribute vectors and measure the compatibility between an image and a label embedding.

However, ZSL typically suffers from the project domain shift problem, so Elyor et al. [3] introduces the encoder-decoder paradigm where an encoder aims to project a visual feature vector into the semantic space and the decoder is able to reconstruct the original visual feature from semantic space. Through adding this restriction, it is ensured that the mapping function keeps all the information of the original input layer as much as possible.

Nowadays, the research on ZSL has become more in-depth. In [5], authors propose to use Variational Autoencoder (VAE) to get a shared latent space of image features and class embeddings which can save visual features and side-information better. Because of the information loss caused by the mapping of visual features to semantic space, [6] proposes a new latent visual embedding. In this new latent visual embedding, each image is divided into several small regions and each region is represented by a set of low dimensional vectors. So the latent visual embedding is represented by the sum of these low dimensional vectors.

In ZSL, there are two main problems, namely the hubness problem and the domain shift problem. Hubness problem means that in high dimensional space, some points will become the nearest neighbors of most points and domain shift problem means that visual features may vary greatly in different categories, although they share the same attribute. Most of the researches are based on one of them, and few of them are conducted at the same time. In [7], authors propose a novel method called Semantically Aligned Bias Reducing (SABR) which solves these two problems. It uses a latent space to learn the relationship between the semantic space and the labels which preserves the information of the class to tackle the hubness problem and then use cross-validation process and a novel weak transfer constraint to deal with domain shift problem. In [8], authors decompose this task into three sub-tasks. The first task is to train a model to classify the seen class and the second is to train a model to classify the unseen class. The third task is to train a gating binary classifier to judge whether it belongs to seen classes or unseen classes.

3   Our Proposed Approach

In this section, we first give the notations and definitions of problems, show the overall procedure of our model, and then introduce our two novel methods in detail.

3.1   Definitions and Notations

Suppose $\{S = (x, y, a) | x \subseteq X^s, y \subseteq Y^s, a \subseteq A\}$ represents the sets of seen class samples, where x is the visual features nowadays normally deep learning features, y is corresponding class label of x and a denotes a set of attributes of class y. In zero-shot learning setting, we have unseen class samples represented by $\{U = (x^u, y^u, a^u) | x^u \subseteq X^u, y^u \subseteq Y^u, a^u \subseteq A\}$. Different from traditional image classification, seen and unseen classes are disjoint which means $Y^s \cap Y^u = \varnothing$.

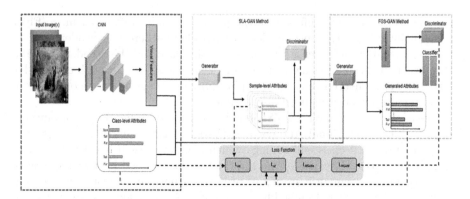

Fig. 2. An illustration of the proposed SLA-GAN method and FGS-GAN method. Firstly, visual features are extracted from input images by convolutional neural network and used as sample information with class-level attributes. Secondly, SLA-GAN method takes the visual features as input and generates sample-level attributes. Thirdly, FGS-GAN method uses the visual features and generated sample-level attributes of seen samples to generate unseen samples. Finally, at recognition stage, a classifier is trained with the generated unseen samples and then predicts the final result of real unseen samples. The specific loss functions of each procedure are in the gray box.

The goal of zero-shot learning is to predict the label of sample x^u in Y^u. In generalized zero-shot learning setting, seen and unseen class samples are provided for testing. So the goal of generalized zero-shot learning is to predict the label of sample in seen and unseen classes.

3.2   Overall Procedure

Our methods are proposed mainly based on two assumptions: the class-level attributes are unsatisfied to represent each image effectively, and the images of unseen class could be generated efficiently according to sample-level attributes. From the consideration of the two assumptions, a general procedure containing our SLA-GAN and FGS-GAN methods is constructed to generate sample-level attributes and fine-grained samples of unseen classes, as shown in Fig. 2. Firstly, images are fed into a convolutional neural network to learn the visual features, and then both visual features and class-level attributes are taken as inputs for our methods. The procedure in yellow box, named as SLA-GAN method, could generate sample-level attributes, using class-level attributes and visual features. The second procedure, named as FGS-GAN method, is to generate fine-grained samples. Specially, samples of unseen classes are synthesized from the most similar samples of seen classes in feature space, under a guidance of attributes. Besides, in order to improve the quality of generated samples, we replace class-level attributes with sample-level attributes. Finally, we train a classifier with these samples of unseen classes generated from FGS-GAN method, and then use the classifier to test the real unseen class samples. The specific loss functions are in the gray box.

3.3   Sample-Level Attribute Generation via GAN (SLA-GAN)

The key of using GAN to address zero-shot learning problem is generating high-quality samples, by the guidance of semantic description. So here semantic descriptions which are class-level attributes determine the quality of generated samples. However, class-level attributes only capture the weakly information of sample and are not discriminative enough to represent samples. What's more, visual features generated from class-level are also limited by the gap. In order to make the sets of attributes and samples more consistent in embedding space, we introduce a new method Sample-Level Attribute Generation via GAN (SLA-GAN) that generates sample-level attributes.

As shown in Fig. 2, the sample-level attributes are extracted according to visual features. To learn an effective set of attributes for compact affective representation of visual features, we take the structure of GAN model. To be more details, Given the seen samples $\{X, Y, A\}$ and random noises $z \sim \mathcal{N}(0, 1)$, the GAN generator G_s of SLA-GAN uses the x and z to generate fine-grained attributes. At the same time, the GAN discriminator D_s of SLA-GAN takes the class-level attributes of images a and $G_s(x, z)$ as inputs to discriminate whether input attributes are sample-level attributes or class-level and classifies the inputs. To learn the generator parameters, the output of the generator $G_s(x, z)$ and class-level attributes a should be close enough by optimizing Mean Squared Error (MSE) loss:

$$\mathcal{L}_{A_s} = ||G_s(x, z) - a||_2^2 \tag{1}$$

Noises z guarantees that the synthesized sample-level attributes were similar to class-level attributes, but were not exactly. Formally, the loss of G_s can be formulated as follows:

$$\mathcal{L}_{G_s} = -\mathbb{E}[D_s(G_s(x, z))] \tag{2}$$

where the term is the Wasserstein loss. Similarly, the loss of the discriminator D_s can be formulated as follows:

$$\mathcal{L}_{D_s} = \mathbb{E}[D_s(G_s(x, z))] - \mathbb{E}[D_s(a)] - \lambda\mathbb{E}[logP(y|G_s(x, z))] + \mathbb{E}[logP(y|a)] \tag{3}$$

The third and forth term are respectively supervised classification loss on sample-level attributes and class-level attributes. Finally, the loss of $\mathcal{L}_{WGAN_s}$ is formulated as:

$$\mathcal{L}_{WGAN_s} = min_{G_s, D_s}(L_{D_s} + L_{G_s}) \tag{4}$$

3.4   Fine-Grained Sample Generation via GAN (FGS-GAN)

Although attributes play an important role in guiding generating unseen samples, the information it provides is limited. Considering the visual features of different image are interlinked, we propose a new method FGS-GAN method that generates unseen samples from samples of seen classes which are conditioned by attributes. To be more details, We pair each unseen class with the most similar seen class as a guidance to solve domain shift problem.

We call the most similar sample as raw sample and synthesized sample as target sample. Given the raw samples $\{X, A\}$ and the target sample $\{X^t, Y^t, A^t\}$, the GAN generator G_f of FGS-GAN uses the input x, a and a^t to synthesize target features $(G_f(x, a, a^t))^v$ and attributes $(G_f(x, a, a^t))^a$. At the same time, the GAN discriminator D_f of FGS-GAN takes the raw features of image x and $(G_f(x, a, a^t))^v$ as inputs to discriminate whether an input feature is target or raw. Just like SLA-GAN method, the attributes constraint should be optimized as follows:

$$\mathcal{L}_{A_f} = \left|\left|(G_f(x, a, a^t))^v - a^t\right|\right|_2^2 \tag{5}$$

The loss of the discriminator G_f can be formulated as follows:

$$\mathcal{L}_{G_f} = -\mathbb{E}[D_f((G_f(x, a, a^t))^v)] + \left|\left|(G_f(x, a, a^t))^v - x^t\right|\right|_2^2 \tag{6}$$

where the second term is the loss between synthesized features and target sample features. And the loss of D_f are as follows:

$$\mathcal{L}_{D_f} = \mathbb{E}[D_f((G_f(x, a, a^t))^v)] - \mathbb{E}[D_f(x^t)] - \lambda\mathbb{E}[logP(y|(G_f(x, a, a^t))^v)] + \mathbb{E}[logP(y|x^t)] \tag{7}$$

Finally, the loss of $\mathcal{L}_{WGAN_f}$ which is like $\mathcal{L}_{D_s}$ is formulated as:

$$\mathcal{L}_{WGAN_f} = min_{G_f, D_f}(L_{D_f} + L_{G_f}) \tag{8}$$

Apart from that, to bridge the gap between seen and unseen classes, choosing suitable samples of proper class is of great importance. Based on the idea of [15], in semantic space, each node represents a class which consists of a set of attributes and similar classes are distributed closely, so we take the distances of different classes in the semantic space to measure the similarity. The weights that calculate similarities of different classes as follows:

$$s_{ij} = \frac{exp(-d_{ij})}{\sum_{i,j=1}^{T}(-d_{ij})} \tag{9}$$

Where d_{ij} represents the Mahalanobis distance between classes i and j. Through the weights, we can pair the most similar seen class for each unseen class.

4   Experiments

In order to verify the validity of model, we carried out experiments on five standard datasets in conventional and generalized ZSL settings. In this section, we will represent and discuss the results of the experiment.

4.1   Experiment Settings

Datasets. To evaluate model, we conduct experiments on five standard datasets: Caltech-UCSD Birds-200-2011 (CUB), Animals with Attributes 1 (AWA1), Animals with Attributes 2 (AWA2), Attribute Pascal and Yahoo (APY) and Scene UNderstanding (SUN). The specific split of dataset is shown in Table 1.

Table 1. Summary of five attribute datasets for ZSL

Dataset	Attributes	Samples	Seen classes (val)	Unseen classes	Samples (train)	Samples (test unseen/seen)
SUN	102	131067	645 (65)	72	10320	1440/2580
APY	64	15399	20 (5)	12	5932	7924/1483
AWA1	85	30475	40 (13)	10	5932	5685/4958
AWA2	85	37322	40 (13)	10	23527	7913/5882
CUB	312	11788	150 (50)	50	7057	2679/1764

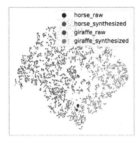 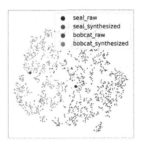

Fig. 3. The t-SNE visualization of horse and giraffe's set of sample-level attributes. In the graph, each node represents a set of attributes and the same color represents from one class. The blue and red points represent class-level attributes, and the yellow and green dots represent synthesized sample-level attributes. (Color figure online)

4.2 Implementation Details

In our mode, the GAN utilizes multiple fully connected layers activated by Rectified Linear Unit (ReLU). Specially, the Generator of FGS-GAN is a symmetric network which gradually regresses the input to the dimension of 1024, 512, 256, and finally the dimension of semantic attributes and then raises it to the dimension of features. The Discriminator of FGS-GAN and SLA-GAN contains two branches, one of which is used to discriminate whether the samples are true or false and the other classifies the inputs. To demonstrate the high-quality of synthesized samples, we compare our models with other generative methods.

4.3 Effects of the New Sample-Level Attributes

As semantic attributes bridge the gap between seen and unseen classes and guide the Generator to synthesize new samples, we explore their effects by visualizing class-level and the new sets of sample-level attributes. For the convenience of the comparison of the spatial differences between different classes, we put two different classes into each figure. In Fig. 3 left, we choose horse and giraffe in AWA2 as a comparison. The blue and red dots represent the class-level attributes, and the yellow and green dots represent the new sets of sample-level attributes

Table 2. The effects of set of sample-level attributes on five datasets in ZSL.

Datasets	SLA-GAN	SLA+FGS-GAN	Improvement
SUN	56.9	57.7	0.8
APY	40.8	42.6	1.8
AWA1	66.4	69.4	3
AWA2	66.2	69.5	3.3
CUB	52.4	52.7	0.3

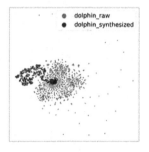 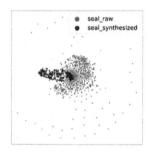

Fig. 4. The t-SNE visualization of dolphin and seal features. The red points represent the newly generated features, and the green points represent the raw features. (Color figure online)

generated by SLA-GAN. In Fig. 3 right, we choose bobcat and seal in AWA2 as a comparison.

From the Fig. 3, we observe that new generated sets of sample-level attributes are all distributed around the class-level points, and the points between different classes are clearly bounded by distinct boundaries. For example, in Fig. 3 left, the two raw points are very close to each other, which is not conducive to distinguish the two classes, but the new points are well distributed in the figure, and there is a obvious dividing line between different classes. In addition, we replace class-level attributes with sample-level attributes in FGS-GAN. From Table 2, we observe that FGS-GAN with sample-level attributes achieves 3.3%, 3.0%, 1.8%,0.8% and 0.3% improvements on AWA2, AWA1, APY, SUN and CUB. These achievements show the effects of new sets of sample-level attributes.

4.4   Effects of the New Fine-Grained Samples

We further analyze the high-quality samples generated by FGS-GAN through visualizing them. The visualization of features is shown in Fig. 4. From the Fig. 4, we observe that the spatial distribution of the unseen class features is centered on a point, gathering a large number of feature points, with the periphery as a circular scattered dry point, and the generated features are distributed in this central area. Therefore, from the spatial distribution of the whole graph, we can

Table 3. The results is evaluated by average top-1 accuracy on five datasets SUN, APY, AWA1, AWA2 and CUB in ZSL.

Approaches	SUN	APY	AWA1	AWA2	CUB
SJE [2]	53.7	32.09	65.6	61.9	53.9
CONSE [14]	44.2	26.9	45.6	44.5	34.3
SYNC [15]	56.3	23.9	54.0	46.6	**55.6**
DEVISE [17]	56.5	39.8	54.2	59.7	52.0
ESZSL [19]	54.5	38.3	58.2	58.6	53.9
SSE [18]	51.5	34.0	60.1	61.0	43.9
LATEM [4]	55.3	35.2	55.1	55.8	49.3
SAE [3]	40.3	8.3	53.0	54.1	33.3
FGS-GAN	56.9	40.8	66.4	66.2	52.4
SLA+FGS-GAN	**57.7**	**42.6**	**69.4**	**69.5**	52.7

Table 4. The results in generalized zero-shot learning are evaluated by average top-1 accuracy on five datasets SUN, APY, AWA1, AWA2 and CUB. The bottom two sets of data are the results of our model.

Method	APY			AWA1			AWA2			CUB			SUN		
	tu	ts	H	tu	ts	H	tu	ts	H	tu	ts	H	tu	ts	H
SJE [2]	3.7	55.7	6.9	11.3	74.6	19.6	8.0	73.9	14.4	23.5	59.2	33.6	14.1	30.5	19.8
CONSE [14]	0.0	**91.2**	0.0	0.4	**88.6**	0.8	0.5	**90.6**	1.0	1.6	**72.2**	3.1	6.8	39.9	11.6
SYNC [15]	7.4	66.3	13.3	8.9	87.3	16.2	10.0	90.5	18.0	11.5	70.9	19.8	7.9	43.3	13.4
GAZSL [11]	14.2	78.6	24.0	29.6	84.2	43.8	35.4	86.9	50.3	31.7	61.3	41.8	22.1	39.3	28.3
DCN [16]	14.2	75.0	23.9	25.5	84.2	39.1	–	–	–	28.4	60.7	38.7	25.5	37.0	30.2
TCN [13]	24.1	64.0	35.1	49.4	76.5	60.0	**61.2**	65.8	**63.4**	**52.6**	52.0	**52.3**	31.2	37.3	34.0
PREN [12]	–	–	–	–	–	–	32.4	88.6	47.4	35.2	55.8	43.1	35.4	27.2	30.8
LisGAN [10]	–	–	–	**52.6**	76.3	**62.3**	–	–	–	46.5	57.9	51.6	**42.9**	37.8	40.2
GDAN [9]	**30.4**	75.0	**43.4**	–	–	–	32.1	67.5	43.5	39.3	66.7	49.5	38.1	**89.9**	**53.4**
SAE [3]	0.4	80.9	0.9	1.8	77.1	3.5	1.1	82.2	2.2	7.8	54.0	13.6	8.8	18.0	11.8
SLA-GAN	15.7	76.5	26.0	21.2	83.5	33.8	21.4	86.2	34.3	21.6	54.8	30.9	17.4	36.7	23.6
SLA+FGS-GAN	14.4	75.9	24.2	21.5	84.1	34.3	27.7	86.4	42.0	23.5	55.9	33.1	18.0	34.2	23.6

get that the newly generated features are consistent with the original features of the unseen class.

4.5 Results Analysis

In order to demonstrate the effectiveness of our methods, we compare our methods with other generative models in ZSL. The results are shown in Table 3. As we can see that APY, AWA1 and AWA2 help much in increasing the prediction accuracy on unseen classes. As our model uses the principle of transferring the features of the most similar class to the target class to generate new samples, the newly generated samples themselves are an unsupervised way which can't be controlled, so the classification effect of the generated samples will be poor in the data sets with more classes. We can also see from the table that the accuracy in AWA1, AWA2 and APY improves 3.0%, 1.6% and 0.5% respectively in SLA+FGS-GAN, which is mainly due to the refinement of the set of sample-level attributes.

In GZSL, the test set contains both seen and unseen classes, so it is more practical for real recognition. In GZSL, we use ts to represent the accuracy of the seen classes, tu to represent the accuracy of the unseen classes, and H to represent their harmonic mean. Since some studies were only carried out in ZSL, we chose some other recent research results in GZSL for comparison in Table 4. It can be seen from the table that SLA+FGS-GAN has a great deviation for the prediction of the unseen classes compared to other methods. As FGS-GAN uses the most similar seen classes to generate unseen classes, the new sample features bias towards seen classes. Therefore, it is not a good choice to use seen classes as guiding features in GZSL. Just like some previous methods, e.g., CONSE, SYNV and SAE, perform well on the accuracy of the seen classes, their performances degrade dramatically on the unseen classes, especially to a larger number of unseen classes. In order to solve this problem, our follow-up work will focus on how to eliminate the bias effect of guided features on the generated features.

5   Conclusion

In this paper, we propose a novel method FGS-GAN that generates unseen samples to deal with zero-shot learning problem. In this method, unseen samples are generated from the seen samples which are the most similar class in semantic space. To guarantee that semantic descriptions are close to each sample, we introduce sample-level attributes instead of class-level attributes to help generate samples. Experiments on five standard data sets show that our models outperform state-of-the-art methods in ZSL and sample-level attributes capture the variance between samples. However, in GZSL, due to the bias effect of seen classes, it is not a good choice to use the most similar seen classes as guiding features. In our future work, we will continue to explore other meaningful information to help GAN generate high-quality samples of unseen classes.

References

1. Lampert, C.H., Nickisch, H., Harmeling, S.: Learning to detect unseen object classes by between-class attribute transfer. In: IEEE Conference on Computer Vision and Pattern Recognition (2009)
2. Akata, Z., Perronnin, F., Harchaoui, Z., Schmid, C.: Label-embedding for attribute-based classification. In: IEEE Conference on Computer Vision and Pattern Recognition (2013)
3. Kodirov, E., Xiang, T., Gong, S.: Semantic autoencoder for zero-shot learning. In: IEEE Conference on Computer Vision and Pattern Recognition (2017)
4. Xian, Y., Akata, Z., Sharma, G., et al.: Latent embeddings for zero-shot classification. In: IEEE Conference on Computer Vision and Pattern Recognition (2016)

5. Zhu, P., Wang, H., Saligrama, V.: Generalized zero-shot recognition based on visually semantic embedding. In: IEEE Conference on Computer Vision and Pattern Recognition (2019)
6. Schonfeld, E., Ebrahimi, S., Sinha, S., et al.: Generalized zero-and few-shot learning via aligned variational autoencoders. In: IEEE Conference on Computer Vision and Pattern Recognition (2019)
7. Paul, A., Krishnan, N.C., Munjal, P.: Semantically aligned bias reducing zero shot learning. In: IEEE Conference on Computer Vision and Pattern Recognition (2019)
8. Atzmon, Y., Chechik, G.: Adaptive confidence smoothing for generalized zero-shot learning. In: IEEE Conference on Computer Vision and Pattern Recognition (2018)
9. Huang, H., Wang, C., Yu, P.S., Wang, C.-D.: Generative dual adversarial network for generalized zero-shot learning. In: IEEE Conference on Computer Vision and Pattern Recognition (2019)
10. Li, J., Jin, M., Lu, K., Ding, Z., Zhu, L., Huang, Z.: Leveraging the invariant side of generative zero-shot learning. In: IEEE Conference on Computer Vision and Pattern Recognition (2019)
11. Zhu, Y., Elhoseiny, M., Liu, B., et al.: A generative adversarial approach for zero-shot learning from noisy texts. In: IEEE Conference on Computer Vision and Pattern Recognition (2018)
12. Ye, M., Guo, Y.: Progressive ensemble networks for zero-shot recognition. In: IEEE Conference on Computer Vision and Pattern Recognition (2019)
13. Jiang, H., Wang, R., Shan, S., et al.: Transferable contrastive network for generalized zero-shot learning. In: IEEE International Conference on Computer Vision (2019)
14. Norouzi, M., Mikolov, T., Bengio, S., et al.: Zero-shot learning by convex combination of semantic embeddings. In: IEEE International Conference on International Conference on Learning Representations (2014)
15. Changpinyo, S., Chao, W.L., Gong, B., et al.: Synthesized classifiers for zero-shot learning. In: IEEE Conference on Computer Vision and Pattern Recognition (2016)
16. Liu, S., Long, M., Wang, J., et al.: Generalized zero-shot learning with deep calibration network. In: IEEE Conference on Neural Information Processing Systems (2018)
17. Frome, A., Corrado, G.S., Shlens, J., et al.: Devise: a deep visual-semantic embedding model. In: IEEE Conference on Neural Information Processing Systems (2013)
18. Zhang, Z., Saligrama, V.: Zero-shot learning via semantic similarity embedding. In: IEEE International Conference on Computer Vision (2015)
19. Romera-Paredes, B., Torr, P.H.S.: An embarrassingly simple approach to zero-shot learning. In: International Conference on Machine Learning (2015)

Fine-Grained Image-Text Retrieval via Complementary Feature Learning

Min Zheng[1(✉)], Yantao Jia[2], and Huajie Jiang[2]

[1] Beijing Key Lab of Transportation Data Analysis and Mining,
Beijing Jiaotong University, Beijing 100044, China
`zhengmin@bjtu.edu.cn`
[2] Huawei Technologies Co., Ltd, Beijing 100085, China

Abstract. Fine-grained image-text retrieval task aims to search the sample of same fine-grained subcategory from one modal (e.g., image) to another (e.g., text). The key is to learn an effective feature representation and accomplish the alignment between images and texts. This paper proposes a novel Complementary Feature Learning (CFL) method for fine-grained image-text retrieval. Firstly CFL encodes images and texts by Convolutional Neural Network and Bidirectional Encoder Representations from Transformers. Further, with the help of Frequent Pattern Mining technique (for images) and special classification token of Bidirectional Encoder Representations from Transformers (for texts), a stronger fine-grained feature is learned. Secondly the image information and text information are aligned in a common latent space by pairwise dictionary learning. Finally, a score function can be learned to measure the relevance between image-text pairs. Further, we verify our method on two specific fine-grained image-text retrieval tasks. Extensive experiments demonstrate the effectiveness of our CFL.

Keywords: Complementary Feature Learning · Fine-grained image-text retrieval · Pairwise dictionary alignment

1 Introduction

In recent years, different modalities of media data such as image, text, and video, are growing rapidly on the Internet. It is prevalent to enable computers to understand, match, and transform such cross-modal data. Image-text cross-modal retrieval is thus one of the most fundamental topics. It takes one type (e.g., image) of data as the query to retrieve relevant data of another type (e.g., text) [20]. The challenge here is how to match the image-text data by learning an effective feature and accomplishing the alignment between images and texts.

Over the past decades, various image-text retrieval approaches have been proposed [15,16] and they generally aim at coarse-grained samples. In a coarse-grained text-to-image retrieval system, when a user submits a description of *"Western Meadowlark"* as a query, it just returns some coarse-grained results

© Springer Nature Switzerland AG 2021
J. Lokoč et al. (Eds.): MMM 2021, LNCS 12572, pp. 592–604, 2021.
https://doi.org/10.1007/978-3-030-67832-6_48

Text Query:
bird with a yellow and black chest and neck, and a dull white and gray wings and tail.

Image Retrieval Results:

| Western Meadowlark | Spotted Catbird | Summer Tanager | | Western Meadowlark | Western Meadowlark | Western Meadowlark |
| (a) Coarse-grained Text-to-Image Retrieval | | | | (b) Fine-grained Text-to-Image Retrieval | | |

Fig. 1. The difference between coarse-grained and fine-grained text-to-image retrieval system.

that related to the category of *"Bird"*, such as *"Western Meadowlark"*, *"Summer Tanager"*, or *"Spotted Catbird"*, as is shown in Fig. 1(a). However, in many real-world scenarios, e.g., automatic biodiversity monitoring, climate change evaluation, intelligent retail, intelligent transportation, etc., the retrieval results are required to be further fine-grained. To tackle such problem, our work focuses on a more competitive task, fine-grained image-text retrieval, which aims to return the exactly same subcategory results. That is, as is shown in Fig. 1(b), when the query is a description of *"Western Meadowlark"*, the retrieval results must be *"Western Meadowlark"*, even though *"Spotted Catbird"* is similar to *"Western Meadowlark"*. Currently, there is only one method that concentrates on fine-grained image-text retrieval task. He *et al.* [22] constructed a new fine-grained cross-model retrieval dataset and presented a FGCross-Net, which considers three constraints.

In this paper, we propose a novel method, Complementary Feature Learning (CFL), for fine-grained image-text retrieval. Here, "complementary feature" refers to local features which possess inner correlation and can be mutually complementary to each other. Concretely, CFL contains three steps. Firstly, CFL encodes images and texts by Convolutional Neural Network (CNN) and Bidirectional Encoder Representations from Transformers (BERT), then learns the complementary features of images and texts by Frequent Pattern Mining (FPM) technique and [CLS] of BERT, respectively. Secondly, CFL utilizes pairwise dictionary alignment technique to construct a latent space so that the image-text can be aligned. Finally, CFL designs a score function in the latent space to measure the relevance between image-text pairs.

The main contributions of our work are summarized as follows:

- We propose a Complementary Feature Mining (CFM) module to mine inner correlation of local features. Previous work [22] only focuses on local features, but ignores the inner correlation.
- We design a Pairwise Dictionary Alignment (PDA) module, which directly learns a latent space and enforces features of images and texts to be the same to accomplish the alignment. Previous works e.g. [6, 19] learn latent features for images and texts independently and learn a transformation from one to another. Further, We use an alternating optimization, it will be converged less than 30 iterations.

- Compared with baselines (e.g. FGCrossNet [22]) which solve the subcategory-specific task alone, we incrementally propose a novel task, namely, instance-specific fine-grained image-text retrieval.

2   Related Works

In this section, we briefly review the related works about fine-grained representation and FPM technique.

Fine-grained Representation. Existing fine-grained image representation methods can be broadly divided into two groups: 1) feature extracting by localization [23, 25]. They capture salient regions and extract features from the corresponding regions. 2) end-to-end feature encoding [2, 21]. They directly learn a discriminative fine-grained representation by deep neural networks. Similarly, there are also many fine-grained text representation methods [8, 11].

Above-mentioned methods all learn global/local features, but neglect inner correlation of features. Our work aims at mining inner correlation of features to make the fine-grained representation stronger.

Frequent Pattern Mining. FPM is a prevalent technique in the field of data mining, and has been widely used in many areas like marketing, advertising, scientific and social network analysis [10, 14]. FPM was first introduced by Agrawal *et al.* [1]. Later, more and more methods have been proposed [5, 17].

FPM can mine interesting correlation or association among attributes/items in large datasets. Inspired by, we employ classical FP-Growth algorithm [5] to mine inner correlation of features, that is, the proposed complementary features.

3   Method

Figure 2 illustrates the overview of the proposed CFL method. In this section, we firstly formulate CFL. Then we elaborate the details of CFM module and PDA module. Finally, score function is presented.

3.1   Problem Formulation

Formally, let $V = \{v_i\}_{i=1}^n$ be a set of image features, where v_i denotes the feature of the i-th image. Similarly, let $T = \{t_i\}_{i=1}^n$ be a set of text features, where t_i denotes the feature of the i-th text. The goal of our CFL is to construct a new latent feature space $Z = \{z_i\}_{i=1}^n$, then we can perform the fine-grained image-text retrieval task in Z by matching the similarity between image-text pairs, where z_i denotes the new latent feature of the i-th sample.

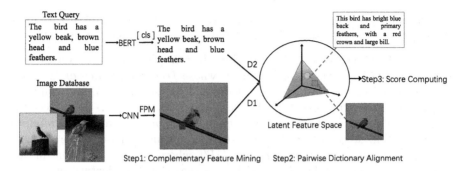

Fig. 2. The architecture of CFL. (Color figure online)

3.2 Complementary Features for Image

To learn the stronger fine-grained image representation, we propose to learn complementary features by FPM. In the following, the motivation and algorithm will be detailed.

a. Why Learn Complementary Features? Fine-grained image representation learning is challenging since that the distinctions in different subcategories are subtle. Thus, the main requisite is to localize the discriminative distinctions to distinguish similar subcategories. Besides, discriminative distinctions correspond to different semantics, and different semantics can be complementary and jointly compose the correlation of a subcategory. For example, {*yellow beak, white throat, black tail*} → {*California Gull*} indicates that the bird belongs to *"California Gull"* subcategory when it has the local features of *"yellow beak"*, *"white throat"*, *"black tail"* at the same time. On the other hand, in data mining, FPM is widely used to discover the interesting correlation or co-activation in large datasets. Inspired by the above observation, we propose to learn complementary features by FPM [5].

b. How to Learn Complementary Features? The following notations are used in our paper. Let $B = \{B_i\}_{i=1}^{c}$ be a set of feature maps, where B_i denotes the i-th feature map. For each B_i, there are a set of local positions $P = \{p_i\}_{i=1}^{h \times w}$. Here, ***local position*** could be regarded as ***item*** in data mining, ***feature map*** could be regarded as ***transaction*** in data mining, which is the input of FPM. The output of FPM are called ***frequent pattern***, that is, ***complementary local positions*** in our task.

There are three procedures to learn the complementary features, mask generation, frequent pattern tree construction, and frequent pattern mining.

Mask Generation. In this procedure, we aim to generate the input of FPM [5]. Feeding an image into CNN, it will be embedded in a tensor of size $h \times w \times c$, where h, w, c represents the height, width, and the number of feature maps. We calculate the mean value δ of the tensor as the threshold. Then we scan B, for $P = \{p_i\}_{i=1}^{h \times w}$, if the value of p_i is higher than δ, the value of p_i is set to 1. If not, the value is set to 0. In this manner, we generate the mask of feature map, $B' = \{B'_i\}^c_{i=1}$. B' is the same size as B and we use it as the input of FPM.

Frequent Pattern Tree Construction. In this procedure, we aim to filter out the local positions $P = \{p_i\}^{h \times w}_{i=1}$ in B' whose *frequency* (times of "$p_i = 1$") is higher than *support* (*support* is a threshold, we set it as 8), and compress them into a prefix-tree structure. We scan the $P = \{p_i\}^{h \times w}_{i=1}$ of B', collect the *frequency* of p_i, retain the p_i whose *frequency* $\geq$ *support*, and sort the retained p_i of each B'_i in descending order, $P' = \{p'_i\}^n_{i=1}$. Then we create the prefix-tree. For B'_1, let the descending order P' be $[p'_1|P']$, where p'_1 is the first element and P' is the remaining list. For $B' = \{B'_i\}^c_{i=2}$, if they share an identical prefix, the shared parts can be merged using one prefix structure as long as the *frequency* is registered properly.

Frequent Pattern Mining. In this procedure, we aim to mine complementary features from the prefix-tree. With the help of pattern fragment growth algorithm [5], we obtain the complementary local positions. These complementary local positions are frequent and co-activated, and can be mutually enhanced and cooperatively compose the correlation of a subcategory. Finally, in order to unify the feature dimension of each image and yield the stronger fine-grained representation, we encode the features of complementary local positions by pooling operation.

3.3 Complementary Features for Text

Similarly, we also propose to learn complementary features for texts. The motivation and algorithm will be detailed in the following.

a. Why Learn Complementary Features? Texts contain contextual relation. E.g., *"Least Auklet has orange beak, white throat, grey crown"*, $\{orange\ beak, white\ throat, grey\ crown\}$ is a set of contextual and relevant phrases, which can be mutually complementary and jointly compose the correlation of a subcategory *"Least Auklet"*.

The BERT [3] model applies a transformer encoder to attend to bi-directional contexts during pre-training. Thus, BERT could encode the text input into the contextual feature. In addition, BERT has two special tokens to obtain a single contiguous sequence for each input sequence. The first is a special classification token [CLS], and the second is a sentence pairs separated token [SEP].

b. How to Learn Complementary Features? Inspired by BERT's success in NLP tasks, we present to employ [CLS] of BERT to learn complementary features for texts. Specially, giving an input sequence of tokens $X = \{[CLS], x_i, [SEP]\}^n_{i=1}$ to BERT, we obtain a sequence of textual features $T = \{t_{CLS}, t_i, t_{SEP}\}^n_{i=1}$, where x_i is the ith token in the sentence and t_i is the feature of x_i. Since that BERT is designed to pre-train deep bi-directional representations by jointly conditioning on both left and right context in all layers, the sequence of features $\{t_i\}^n_{i=1}$ have the contextual correlation. In additional,

t_{CLS} is designed to encode the whole contextual feature of $T = \{t_i,\}_{i=1}^n$. Consequently, we retain the t_{CLS} of token [CLS] to represent the complementary features.

3.4 Pairwise Dictionary Alignment

The key issue of achieving image-text retrieval is to measure the similarity of image-text pair. Thus we need to construct a common latent feature space, where the features of different modalities can be aligned. In our work, we present to utilize dictionary learning technique to construct the latent feature space, where dictionary bases are learned in the image space and text space respectively to reconstruct the features of images and texts via matrices called reconstruction coefficients. Then the reconstruction coefficients can be viewed as new latent features.

Mathematically, the objective function can be formulated as:

$$
\mathcal{L} = \arg\min_{D_1,D_2,Z}(\|V - D_1 Z\|_F^2 + \alpha\,\|T - D_2 Z\|_F^2),
$$
$$
s.t.\quad \|\boldsymbol{d}_1^i\|_2^2 \le 1,\quad \|\boldsymbol{d}_2^i\|_2^2 \le 1, \forall i, \tag{1}
$$

where $V \in \mathbb{R}^{j\times l}$ and $T \in \mathbb{R}^{p\times l}$ are respectively the set of image features and text features, j, p are the dimensions of image feature and text feature and l is the number of samples. $D_1 \in \mathbb{R}^{j\times k}$ and $D_2 \in \mathbb{R}^{p\times k}$ are two dictionary bases in image space and text space, where k is the dimension of the latent space. $Z \in \mathbb{R}^{k\times l}$ is the new features of V and T. By forcing the latent features of corresponding V and T to be same Z, the two spaces are aligned, thus the similarities between image-text pairs can be computed. α is a parameter controlling the relative importance of the image space and text space. d_i^1 denotes the i-th column of D_1 and d_i^2 is the i-th column of D_2. In our experiments, we set α as 0.1.

3.5 Optimization

Equation 1 is not convex for D_1, D_2 and Z simultaneously, but it is convex for each of them separately. Thus, we utilize an alternating optimization method.

Joint Optimization. After all variables in our framework are initialized separately, we jointly optimize them as follows:

(1) Fix D_1, D_2 and update Z by Eq.1. Forcing the derivative of Eq. 1 to be 0 and the closed-form solution for Z is

$$
Z = (\tilde{D}^T \tilde{D})^{-1} \tilde{D}^T \tilde{X}, \tag{2}
$$

where

$$
\tilde{X} = \begin{bmatrix} V \\ \alpha T \end{bmatrix}, \tilde{D} = \begin{bmatrix} D_1 \\ \alpha D_2 \end{bmatrix}.
$$

(2) Fix Z and update D_1. The subproblem can be formulated as:

$$
\arg\min_{D_1} \|V - D_1 Z\|_F^2 \quad s.t.\quad \|\boldsymbol{d}_1^i\|_2^2 \le 1, \forall i. \tag{3}
$$

This problem can be optimized by the Lagrange dual. Thus the analytical solution for Eq. 3 is

$$D_1 = (VZ^T)(ZZ^T + \Lambda)^{-1}, \tag{4}$$

where Λ is a diagonal matrix construct by all the Lagrange dual variables.

(3) Fix Z and update D_2. The subproblem can be formulated as:

$$\arg \min_{D_2} \|T - D_2 Z\|_F^2 \quad s.t. \quad \|d_2^i\|_2^2 \leq 1, \forall i. \tag{5}$$

Similarly, this problem can be also optimized by the Lagrange dual. Thus the analytical solution for Eq. 5 is

$$D_2 = (TZ^T)(ZZ^T + \Lambda)^{-1}. \tag{6}$$

The speed for the optimization is very fast and it will be converged less than 30 iterations.

Table 1. The statistics of fine-grained image-text retrieval datasets.

Dataset	Category	Training	Testing
CUB_img [18]	200	5994	5794
PKU FG-XMedia [22]	200	4000	4000
CUB_txt [13]	200	5994	5794

3.6   Score Function

In the test process, we project images into the latent space by

$$\arg \min_{Z_1} \|V - D_1 Z_1\|_F^2 + \gamma \|Z_1\|_F^2, \tag{7}$$

where V represents the test images and Z_1 is the corresponding features in the latent space. Similarly, we project texts into the latent space by

$$\arg \min_{Z_2} \|T - D_2 Z_2\|_F^2 + \gamma \|Z_2\|_F^2, \tag{8}$$

where T represents the test texts and Z_2 is the corresponding features in the latent space. Then, we apply cosine distance as the score function to measure the similarities between Z_1 and Z_2. Finally, we return the candidates (images or texts) based on the similarities.

4 Experiments

4.1 Datasets and Evaluation Metrics

Datasets. We evaluate our model on the widely used fine-grained image dataset (*CUB_img* [18]), where two kinds of text information are utilized: subcategory-specific (*PKU FG-XMedia* [22]) and instance-specific (*CUB_txt* [13]). The details with category numbers and data splits are summarized in Table 1.

Evaluation Metrics. We report the performance of bi-directional fine-grained image-text retrieval tasks: (1) image query versus text gallery (image-to-text); (2) text query versus image gallery (text-to-image). We use the commonly used metric, mean average precision (mAP) score, to evaluate the performance of fine-grained image-text retrieval.

4.2 Implementation Details

All the experiments are run on a computer with Intel Xeon E5-2695 v4, 251.8G main memory, and an eight Nvidia TITAN Xp GPU.

Image Feature. We apply the pre-trained VggNet-16 as the image encoder. Note that VggNet-16 can be replaced with any CNN model. Specifically, we send an image of size 224×224 to VggNet-16, in $pool_5$, we get a tensor of size $7 \times 7 \times 512$. In order to learn complementary features, we employ FPM to mine complementary local positions. Finally, in order to unify the feature dimension of each image, we concatenate the max-pooling (512-*dimension*) and average-pooling (512-*dimension*) features of complementary local positions, avg+maxPool (1024-*dimension*), as the feature.

Table 2. The mAP scores of bi-directional results on subcategory-specific task, where *CUB_img* [18] (for images) and *PKU FG-XMedia* [22] (for texts) are used.

Method	Image-to-text	Text-to-image	Average
MHTN [6]	0.116	0.124	0.120
ACMR [19]	0.162	0.075	0.119
JRL [24]	0.160	0.190	0.175
GSPH [9]	0.140	0.179	0.160
CMDN [12]	0.099	0.123	0.111
SCA [7]	0.050	0.050	0.050
GXN [4]	0.023	0.035	0.029
FGCrossNet [22]	0.210	0.255	0.233
Our CFL	**0.245**	**0.281**	**0.263**

Text Feature. Similarly, we employ the pre-trained BERT as the text encoder. BERT has 12 self-attention layers, 12 heads, 768 hidden units for each token and

110M parameters in total. In our experiments, we feed the BERT a sequence of tokens, and obtain a sequence of contextual features, each feature is 768-*dimension*. In order to unify the texts of different length, we only retain the embedding t_{CLS} of token [CLS] as the text feature, which is 768-*dimension*.

4.3   Comparisons with State-of-the-Art Methods

To verify the proposed CFL on the subcategory-specific task, we compare CFL with several state-of-the-art methods in Table 2, including seven coarse-grained methods [4, 6, 7, 9, 12, 19, 24] and one fine-grained method [22].

Generally, coarse-grained methods focus on utilizing the global representations to express the whole image and text. They work well on coarse-grained scenario that contains object of different categories, but the performance is limited on fine-grained task since that fine-grained task is required to distinguish different subcategories instead of categories, whose distinctions are subtler.

Among the compared methods, FGCrossNet [22] achieves the best performance. This is because that FGCrossNet [22] pays attention to explore the most salient details and distinctions in both images and texts. Meanwhile, FGCross-Net [22] jointly considers three constraints: classification constraint, center constraint, and ranking constraint. Such three constraints ensure the learning of discriminative features for fine-grained subcategories, the compactness characteristic of the features of the same subcategory, and the sparsity characteristic of the features of different subcategories, respectively. However, such joint constraint manner is limited towards the fine-grained image-text retrieval. This is because that the text information are less than image information (8000 VS. 11788), which is prone to overfit.

Our CFL achieves new state-of-the-art on bi-directional subcategory-specific task. This benefits from two aspects. Firstly, in the procedure of feature extraction, we learn complementary features. For image features, we learn complementary local positions by FPM. For text features, we retain the feature of [CLS] in BERT to represent the contextual correlation of the whole text. Both image features and text features can provide complementary correlation of a subcategory. Second, in the procedure of alignment, it is contributed by the good reconstruction property of the dictionary learning technique. Since that images and texts are associated through a common latent feature space, the corresponding sample variation is not very large. Thus the dictionary learned on the image samples can have a good reconstruction to the same subcategory of text samples. With

Table 3. Comparisons of CFL on subcategory-specific (*CUB_img* [18] + *PKU FG-XMedia* [22]) and instance-specific (*CUB_img* [18] + *CUB_txt* [13]) tasks.

Dataset	Image-to-text	Text-to-image	Average
Subcategory-specific	0.245	0.281	0.263
Instance-specific	0.285	0.288	0.287

Table 4. The mAP scores of bi-directional results on instance-specific task, where *CUB_img* [18] (for images) and *CUB_txt* [13] (for texts) are used.

Method	Image-to-text	Text-to-image	Average
MHTN [6]	0.153	0.174	0.164
ACMR [19]	0.175	0.095	0.135
JRL [24]	0.162	0.178	0.170
GSPH [9]	0.136	0.159	0.148
CMDN [12]	0.123	0.110	0.117
SCA [7]	0.113	0.085	0.099
GXN [4]	0.075	0.056	0.066
FGCrossNet [22]	0.218	0.259	0.239
Our CAA	**0.285**	**0.288**	**0.287**

the help of discriminative property of latent features, the retrieval performance in the latent space can be improved further.

4.4   Instance-Specific Fine-Grained Image-Text Retrieval

Considering that one-one retrieval is needed in real world, we propose a novel task, instance-specific fine-grained image-text retrieval. To the best of our knowledge, we are the first to propose the task for fine-grained image-text retrieval.

Table 3 shows the comparisons of CFL on two fine-grained tasks. We can observe that the performance on instance-specific task outperforms it on subcategory-specific task($0.245 \rightarrow 0.285$, $0.281 \rightarrow 0.288$). This is because that instance-specific *CUB_txt* [13] provide direct descriptions towards to each image, so that we can mine the inner correlation of a subcategory. For instance, in terms of text-to-image direction, when we submit the query *"White Pelican has white wings and has a yellow belly."*, CFL could mine {*white wing, yellow belly*} as a set of complementary features, they can be mutually reinforced, and enhance the representation of subcategory *"White Pelican"*. But subcategory-specific *PKU FG-XMedia* [22] rarely provide direct descriptions towards to each image, they tend to the description about habits customs, even background and noise, e.g., *"White Pelican often occurs in flocks. The vertical plate near the tip of the bill indicates breeding individuals."*, it is hard for us to learn the correlation towards to the instance *"White Pelican"*. So the performance is lower than instance-specific task. Furthermore, to demonstrate the effectiveness of our CFL on the proposed instance-specific task, we compare CFL with several state-of-the-art methods in Table 4.

4.5   Ablation Study

We conduct ablation studies to better understand the impact of each component, as is shown in Table 5. We use VggNet-16 and $BERT_{base}$ as our backbone.

Table 5. Ablation studies of CFL on subcategory-specific and instance-specific task. CFL consists of CFI (Complementary Features for Image), CFT (Complementary Features for Text), and PDA (Pairwise Dictionary Alignment). We measure mAP accuracy.

Method	Subcategory-specific			Instance-specific		
	Image-to-text	Text-to-image	Average	Image-to-text	Text-to-image	Average
VggNet-16/$BERT_{base}$	0.202	0.268	0.235	0.235	0.238	0.237
VggNet-16+CFI/$BERT_{base}$	0.237	0.271	0.254	0.272	0.238	0.255
VggNet-16/$BERT_{base}$+CFT	0.212	0.275	0.244	0.239	0.279	0.259
VggNet-16/$BERT_{base}$/PDA	0.239	0.275	0.257	0.256	0.278	0.267
CFL(Ours)	**0.245**	**0.281**	**0.263**	**0.285**	**0.288**	**0.287**

4.6   Analysis of Loss Function

The best value for α is chosen by five-fold cross-validation, and the scope of α is set in $[0.001, 0.01, 0.1, 1, 10]$. In our experiments, we set α as 0.1, as is shown in Fig. 3.

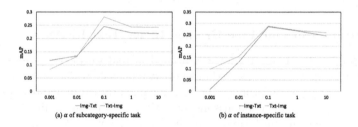

Fig. 3. Analysis of parameter α.

4.7   Qualitative Results

In Fig. 4(a), we visualize the image features to better understand the proposed complementary features. From top to below: original image, heat map of FGCrossNet [22], heat map of CFL. FGCrossNet [22] only focuses on the most discriminative detail, while CFL could accurately capture complementary details, e.g., belly, tail, and feet of the bird. Besides, complementary features have good interpretability, i.e., co-activated details usually have a stronger semantic information. In Fig. 4(b)(c), we visualize some examples on subcategory-specific and instance-specific fine-grained text-to-image retrieval tasks.

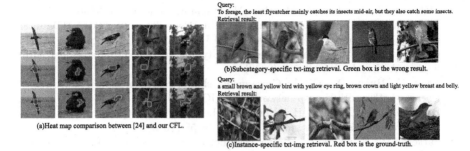

Fig. 4. Qualitative results.

5 Conclusion

In this paper, we propose a novel Complementary Feature Learning for fine-grained image-text retrieval. We discover that complementary features could describe the inner correlation of a subcategory and further enhance the fine-grained representation, so we learn complementary features by FPM (for images) and special classification token [CLS] in BERT (for texts). Then in order to unify different semantic of two modalities, we utilize dictionary learning technique to construct a new latent feature space, and thus the score function can be computed. Furthermore, we verify our method on two specific fine-grained image-text retrieval task: subcategory-specific and instance-specific retrieval. Extensive experiments demonstrate the effectiveness of our method.

References

1. Agrawal, R., Imielinski, T., Swami, A.N.: Mining association rules between sets of items in large databases. In: SIGMOD 1993 (1993)
2. Chen, Y., Bai, Y., Zhang, W., Mei, T.: Destruction and construction learning for fine-grained image recognition. In: CVPR, pp. 5152–5161 (2019)
3. Devlin, J., Chang, M.W., Lee, K., Toutanova, K.: Bert: pre-training of deep bidirectional transformers for language understanding. ArXiv abs/1810.04805 (2019)
4. Gu, J., Cai, J., Joty, S.R., Niu, L., Wang, G.: Look, imagine and match: Improving textual-visual cross-modal retrieval with generative models. In: CVPR, pp. 7181–7189 (2018)
5. Han, J., Pei, J., Yin, Y.: Mining frequent patterns without candidate generation. In: SIGMOD 2000 (2000)
6. Huang, X., Peng, Y., Yuan, M.: MHTN: modal-adversarial hybrid transfer network for cross-modal retrieval. IEEE Trans. Cybern. **50**, 1047–1059 (2017)
7. Lee, K.H., Chen, X.D., Hua, G., Hu, H., He, X.: Stacked cross attention for image-text matching. ArXiv abs/1803.08024 (2018)
8. Lin, Y., Zhong Ji, H.: An attentive fine-grained entity typing model with latent type representation. In: EMNLP/IJCNLP (2019)
9. Mandal, D., Chaudhury, K.N., Biswas, S.: Generalized semantic preserving hashing for n-label cross-modal retrieval. In: CVPR, pp. 2633–2641 (2017)

10. Mehrotra, A., Hendley, R., Musolesi, M.: Prefminer: mining user's preferences for intelligent mobile notification management. In: Proceedings of the 2016 ACM International Joint Conference on Pervasive and Ubiquitous Computing (2016)
11. Onoe, Y., Durrett, G.: Fine-grained entity typing for domain independent entity linking. ArXiv abs/1909.05780 (2020)
12. Peng, Y., Huang, X., Qi, J.: Cross-media shared representation by hierarchical learning with multiple deep networks. In: IJCAI (2016)
13. Reed, S., Akata, Z., Lee, H., Schiele, B.: Learning deep representations of fine-grained visual descriptions. In: CVPR, pp. 49–58 (2016)
14. Sarker, I.H., Salim, F.D.: Mining user behavioral rules from smartphone data through association analysis. ArXiv abs/1804.01379 (2018)
15. Song, Y., Soleymani, M.: Polysemous visual-semantic embedding for cross-modal retrieval. In: CVPR, June 2019
16. Su, S., Zhong, Z., Zhang, C.: Deep joint-semantics reconstructing hashing for large-scale unsupervised cross-modal retrieval. In: ICCV, October 2019
17. Tlili, R., Slimani, Y.: Executing association rule mining algorithms under a grid computing environment. In: PADTAD 2011 (2011)
18. Wah, C., Branson, S., Welinder, P., Perona, P., Belongie, S.: The Caltech-UCSD Birds-200-2011 Dataset. Technical report (2011)
19. Wang, B., Yang, Y., Xu, X., Hanjalic, A., Shen, H.T.: Adversarial cross-modal retrieval. ACM MM (2017)
20. Wang, K., Yin, Q., Wang, W., Wu, S., Wang, L.: A comprehensive survey on cross-modal retrieval. ArXiv abs/1607.06215 (2016)
21. Wei, X., Zhang, Y., Gong, Y., Zhang, J., Zheng, N.: Grassmann pooling as compact homogeneous bilinear pooling for fine-grained visual classification. In: ECCV (2018)
22. He, X., Peng, Y., Xie, L.: A new benchmark and approach for fine-grained cross-media retrieval. In: ACM MM (2019)
23. Yu, C., Zhao, X., Zheng, Q., Zhang, P., You, X.: Hierarchical bilinear pooling for fine-grained visual recognition. In: ECCV (2018)
24. Zhai, X., Peng, Y., Xiao, J.: Learning cross-media joint representation with sparse and semisupervised regularization. TCSVT **24**, 965–978 (2014)
25. Zheng, H., Fu, J., Zha, Z.J., Luo, J.: Looking for the devil in the details: learning trilinear attention sampling network for fine-grained image recognition. In: CVPR, pp. 5007–5016 (2019)

Considering Human Perception and Memory in Interactive Multimedia Retrieval Evaluations

Luca Rossetto[1]([⊠])(iD), Werner Bailer[2](iD), and Abraham Bernstein[1](iD)

[1] University of Zurich, Zurich, Switzerland
{rossetto,bernstein}@ifi.uzh.ch
[2] Joanneum Research, Graz, Austria
werner.bailer@joanneum.at

Abstract. Experimental evaluations dealing with visual known-item search tasks, where real users look for previously observed and memorized scenes in a given video collection, represent a challenging methodological problem. Playing a searched "known" scene to users prior to the task start may not be sufficient in terms of scene memorization for re-identification (i.e., the search need may not necessarily be successfully "implanted"). On the other hand, enabling users to observe a known scene played in a loop may lead to unrealistic situations where users can exploit very specific details that would not remain in their memory in a common case. To address these issues, we present a proof-of-concept implementation of a new visual known-item search task presentation methodology that relies on a recently introduced deep saliency estimation method to limit the amount of revealed visual video contents. A filtering process predicts and subsequently removes information which in an unconstrained setting would likely not leave a lasting impression in the memory of a human observer. The proposed presentation setting is compliant with a realistic assumption that users perceive and memorize only a limited amount of information, and at the same time allows to play the known scene in the loop for verification purposes. The new setting also serves as a search clue equalizer, limiting the rich set of present exploitable content features in video and thus unifies the perceived information by different users. The performed evaluation demonstrates the feasibility of such a task presentation by showing that retrieval is still possible based on query videos processed by the proposed method. We postulate that such information incomplete tasks constitute the necessary next step to challenge and assess interactive multimedia retrieval systems participating at visual known-item search evaluation campaigns.

Keywords: Retrieval evaluation · Query generation · Interactive retrieval · Human perception and memory

1 Introduction

When evaluating retrieval approaches, the different campaigns aim to simulate a realistic search scenario in a controlled environment. In the case of interactive

© Springer Nature Switzerland AG 2021
J. Lokoč et al. (Eds.): MMM 2021, LNCS 12572, pp. 605–616, 2021.
https://doi.org/10.1007/978-3-030-67832-6_49

video retrieval, one of these scenarios is that a user of a search system has seen a specific part of a video in the past, of which they know that it is contained within a given dataset, and wants to retrieve this exact video segment as effectively as possible. This scenario can be simulated by showing such a video segment to users in a controlled environment and have them simultaneously search for it using different systems, implementing different approaches. Such a setup does however not accurately represent the conditions of the original scenario, since the users participating in the evaluation are not only aware that they will need to retrieve the video at the time they see it, but they also know the properties of the retrieval systems they are to use for that task. The evaluation participants therefore have the opportunity to pay special attention to certain aspects of the video which can be most effectively used for a query in a particular system, even though they might not have paid any attention to these aspects when looking at the same video outside of an evaluation setting. An example of how this can be exploited is shown in Fig. 1, which shows the queries of two visual known-item search tasks used in the 2019 Video Browser Showdown (VBS) [34]. The red highlights emphasize legible text which was successfully used to efficiently retrieve the relevant segment during the evaluation. This text is however of minor semantic importance to the events shown in the video and would therefore probably not be remembered – or even perceived – by somebody who saw the video in an unrelated context in the past and now wants to retrieve these sequences. The task during the evaluation setting is therefore arguably not able to accurately simulate the real-world setting which is to be evaluated. To overcome this, we argue that it is insufficient to present a multimedia document directly as a query for known-item search tasks. Rather, when presenting queries to evaluation participants, one needs to consider the effects of human attention as it would likely operate in an actual unconstrained setting without specific priming which would lead to an inaccurate mental representation of the relevant document, as well as human memory effects which would, over time, alter these mental representations even further. As a proof-of-concept and first step into this direction, we propose a saliency-based filtering approach for the generation of evaluation queries, which limits the information in the video to the aspects to which a user would likely have paid attention in a regular setting. It does this by removing specific details to avoid their exploitation in a query. The method thereby implicitly predicts and subsequently removes information a human would *not* pay attention to and would therefore not remember afterwards.

After discussing some relevant related work in Sect. 2, we introduce the proposed proof-of-concept method and its implementation in Sects. 3 and 4 respectively. Section 5 outlines the evaluation procedure and Sect. 6 shows its results. Finally, Sect. 7 concludes and offers some outlook.

2   Related Work

Video is often used as a metaphor for human memory on anything from a personal to a societal level. The relation between video and memory is a manifold

Fig. 1. Example key-frames from two visual known-item search tasks of the 2019 video browser showdown, referencing V3C [35] videos 03482 (top) and 02380 (bottom). The red boxes highlight text which was successfully used to retrieve the relevant sequence during the VBS, even though it would probably not be remembered in a real-world setting. (Color figure online)

one, instigating research in the natural and social sciences [5] as well as the humanities [22], most of which is outside the scope for this work. In practice, however, human memory is often far less precise than video, being not only affected by forgetfulness after the fact but already impeded by selective perception and inattentional blindness [39], which can lead an observer to not even *see* certain aspects of a scene in case their attention is otherwise occupied. For query presentation, we aim to mimic the situation that the searcher remembers a scene view in video or real life some time ago. We are thus interested in long term memory of visual information, discarding cues in the query video that are not memorable. Mandler and Ritchey [28] found that humans can remember information well if can be organised in visual schema, i.e., represented in terms of their properties and arrangement. Thus anything that is coincidentally in the video, but not related to the main person/object/action of interest should thus be suppressed.

In film, an individual's memory is commonly but not exclusively depicted in *Flashbacks* [17] which are sequences outside of the temporal order of the main narrative, usually delineated with some visual transition. During a flashback or other memory sequence, various visual cues are used to help the audience identify the memory sequence. These queues usually degrade the visual fidelity of the presentation with film noise or sepia effects, vignetting or the reduction of color to monochrome [30]. Sometimes, localized effects are used to highlight particular parts of the memory, such as the selective saturation or desaturation of objects or people [16].

While human memory has a large capacity to capture multi-modal impressions in great detail [8], not all of them are equally *memorable*. Research on the *memorability* of images has shown that the likelihood of an image being remembered by a human observer is largely independent of the observers themselves [18] and can be estimated with a high degree of reliability. [21] presented such a memorability estimation method with a near human level rank correlation, concluding that *"predicting human cognitive abilities is within reach for the field of computer vision"*. The method shows that spatially concentrated saliency, providing a 'point of focus' increases the memorability of an image and that image memorability is positively correlated with (human) body parts and faces while being negatively correlated with natural scenes. [6] meanwhile shows that while human faces are generally a memorable part of an image, some faces are more memorable than others and that this difference is consistent across different observers. A study of the effect on overall image memorability based on different objects being visible is presented in [14]. It again confirms the positive correlation between localized saliency and memorability and shows that objects which appear towards the center of an image are more memorable, which validates the vignetting effect as an illustration for memory discussed above. The study also finds that certain 'object categories' such as people, animals or vehicles are inherently more memorable than buildings or furniture.

Less research has yet been conducted in the area of the memorability of video [11,38], which is also considerably more difficult due to its temporal aspects and multi-modal nature. Most recent research activities in this area have clustered around a recently introduced MediaEval[1] task on short- and long-term video memorability prediction [10]. Several participating teams [9,37,40,41] found that image memorability estimation do not directly translate to video memorability and that the results are worse for the long-term estimates than for the short-term ones, indicating that the temporal and multi-modal aspects of video have non-negligible effects on memory formation. All of the proposed methods also do consider the video scene as a whole and do not aim to identify or isolate the aspects which are especially memorable. This would however be a requirement for isolating especially memorable components of a video. In contrast, the concept of *saliency* can be applied locally and describes how much any particular region, in this case of an image, stands out with respect to its neighbors. Based on the observation that most existing work on memorability treats entire media items, Akgunduz et al. [3] performed an experiment in which participants were asked to identify the regions they thought helped them remembering an image. The authors found that the regions were more consistent across participants for correctly remembered images than those for false positives. They found however low overlap of these regions with an image saliency method they used for comparison. The authors thus used the data from their experiments to train a CNN for predicting regions impacting memorability.

Saliency estimation is a common task in image processing with various applications in computer vision as well as image and video coding [13]. Various methods have been proposed for the estimation of saliency in images and later videos, using both engineered and learned features. For this work, we use a recently proposed deep-learning based method [19] which is temporally consistent and has a high accuracy when compared to a human eye-gaze ground truth.

---

[1] http://www.multimediaeval.org/.

In contrast to the visual domain, comparatively little work has been done in acoustic saliency or memorability detection. While there are methods for estimating both the saliency [33] and the memorability [32] of an auditory signal, they detect the salient segments of a signal (i.e., operate in the time domain) as a whole and do not isolate the salient aspects of a signal (i.e., in the frequency domain) analogously to a saliency heat map which can be produced from an image. Some novel multi-modal audio separation methods [15,42] which jointly consider aural and visual information could however form a basis for future extensions in such a direction.

3   Methodology

The proposed method aims at providing a first-order approximation of the effects of human visual attention and, by extension, memory by removing non-salient information from the video. The reasoning behind this approach is that, if an observer does not deliberately focus on specific details they know to be useful for a particular task, they will by default (meaning in the absence of such a task) focus only on the most inherently salient aspects of the video, which in turn will be the only aspects they would be able to remember at a later date. Despite saliency only being one predictive component of memorability, (as discussed in Sect. 2), we use it over a direct attempt at memorability estimation, since saliency can be locally estimated with a high temporal consistency, which is not currently feasible for memorability but required for filtering. We also argue that many factors influence if a salient region caused an impression sufficient to form a lasting memory, some of which might be different from individual to individual and therefore not feasibly predictable by any one model. A non-salient region however does more reliably predict a part of the video to which, little attention would be payed in an unconstrained setting. We therefore use a low saliency estimate for a region as a prediction, that this particular region would ultimately *not* be remembered, which justifies the removal of its contents.

To estimate the visual saliency, the method proposed in [19] is used, which uses a deep convolutional neural network architecture to predict a heat map of eye-gaze information, based on a sequence of consecutive video frames. Since the human visual system favors attention to the center of their visual field, the estimation of eye-gaze serves as an ideal basis for our approach.

The full processing pipeline is illustrated in Fig. 2. The block labelled *Saliency Estimation* in the top row predicts an eye-gaze heat map to be used as an input of a mixer, which overlays the unmodified salient foreground over a desaturated and blurred version of the input video, used as a background. This visual degradation process is inspired by visual effects used in film to indicate flashbacks or other memory scenes and is designed in such a way as to give some visual context to the unmodified parts of the image, without providing any semantic information. We choose this degradation process over stylization methods such as [12] in order to generate a smoother transition between the filtered and the unfiltered parts of the video and also to remove additional color- and shape information, since such information could still be used for query formulation.

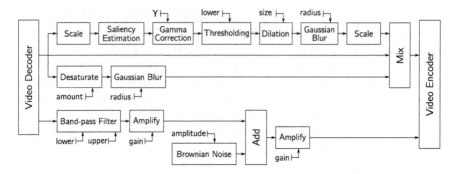

Fig. 2. Illustration of the video filtering pipeline, the upper part describing the filtering of visual information and the lower part describing the filtering of the audio signal. The used input parameters are: $\gamma = 0.8$, lower threshold = 0.5, dilation size = 4 pixel, blur radius = 5 pixel, saturation = 10%, background blur radius = 3%, lower frequency cut-off = 100 Hz, upper frequency cut-off = 2 kHz, noise amplitude = 0.005, amplifier gain = 20%. Parameters were determined empirically.

Before the eye-gaze prediction can be used as an input mask, it is passed through a gamma correction and threshold step to extenuate regions with a high probability and remove regions with a low probability of being looked at directly. The resulting mask is dilated and blurred to ensure a smoother transition between foreground and background during mixing before being scaled to the full size of the input video.

Since isolating the salient aspects of an audio signal appears to be infeasible, we instead apply a content independent filter to the audio signal. The filter primarily consists of a band-pass filter which heavily attenuates all frequencies outside of a narrow range similar to the one used by analog telephones. The remaining pipeline is concerned with the introduction of some Brownian noise in order to hide some additional details as well as steps for amplitude adjustment. In addition, the encoder uses MP3 as output audio format and is set to the lowest supported bit-rate in order to further reduce the audio content based on the encoders internal heuristics.

Figure 3 shows examples of the filter in action. It can be seen, that areas which capture the visual attention are largely preserved while many details, like the person in the background of the first image, the signs and posters in the second image or the captions in the third image become unrecognizable.

4 Implementation

We implemented the filtering pipeline as a standalone application in Java, using TensorFlow [1] for the evaluation of the saliency estimation neural network, BoofCV [2] for image processing and FFmpeg[2] for video decoding and encoding.

---

[2] https://ffmpeg.org/.

Fig. 3. Examples of the proposed method: original frames from V3C videos (left to right) 00801, 06777 and 07453 above and filtered versions of the same frames below.

A pre-trained instance of the neural network[3] was provided by the authors of [19]. The parameters of the filter pipeline indicated in Fig. 2 can be freely adjusted using an external configuration file. We provide the implementation as open source software via GitHub.[4]

5   Evaluation

We evaluated the proposed method at the 9th Video Browser Showdown (VBS) co-located with the 2020 International Conference on Multimedia Modeling during a dedicated, private session using 10 different interactive video retrieval systems [4,20,23–27,29,31,36] in one dedicated evaluation session. This session was split into two tracks with 10 participants in each, leaving one participant per system. In both of the two tracks, participants were given 6 visual known-item search queries taken from the first shard [7] of the V3C dataset [35]. For both tracks, 3 of the queries were processed with the proposed method while the others were kept unmodified. The modifications were alternated between the two tracks, and the queries were presented in the same order in both sessions. The tasks during this session were equivalent to the regular visual known-item search tasks of VBS during which participants are given 5 min to find the presented video sequence of 20 s in a video dataset of roughly 1,000 h.

The 6 used query videos were randomly selected from the dataset and only checked for visual diversity and uniqueness. The videos did not contain any easily identifiable or reproducible components, such as distinctive visible text or spoken dialogue.

---

[3] https://github.com/remega/OMCNN_2CLSTM.
[4] https://github.com/lucaro/VideoSaliencyFilter.

6   Results

During the evaluation session, the 20 participants made a total of 66 submissions for the 2 × 6 evaluated tasks, 33 of which were correct. This number of submissions is substantially lower than what we expected, based on the data of previous VBS evaluations, independently of the application of the filtering method. This might be caused by the fact that during this special evaluation session, each participating search system was only operated by one person at a time, rather than the usual two in regular VBS settings. Of the 33 correct submissions, 15 were made for queries with unmodified videos while 18 submissions were made correctly for the queries processed by the proposed filtering approach. Figure 4 shows a breakdown of the number of correct and incorrect submissions with respect to task and filtering. There is no clearly discernible pattern relating the number of correct or incorrect submissions per task with the application of the proposed filter.

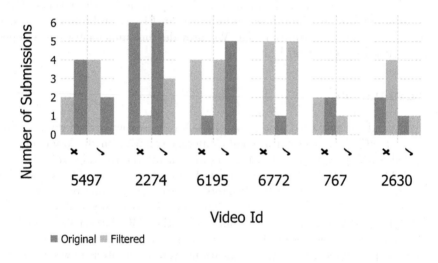

Fig. 4. Number of correct (✓) and incorrect (✗) submissions per video

Focusing only on the correct submissions, Fig. 5 shows the individual submission times per task. While there are differences in submission times within the different tasks, there appears to be no substantial overall difference with respect to the filter. The aggregated distributions of submission times of correct submissions with respect to the application of the filter are illustrated in Fig. 5b. There again appears not to be any substantial difference depending on the filter.

Based on the results presented above, we cannot see any substantial difference in retrieval performance between the tasks using the unfiltered videos and those using the filtered ones, which leads us to conclude that successful retrieval of the target sequence is still possible using the filtered videos and that the filtering hence does not negatively impact the solubility of the retrieval task.

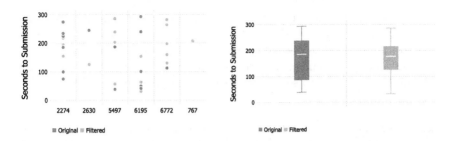

(a) Times of correct submission per (b) Time distributions of correct submis-
video   sions

Fig. 5. Times of correct and incorrect submissions per type

The fact that none of the 6 video segments happened to contain any easily
exploitable components, such as recognizable text or distinctive dialogue supports the assumption that the filter leaves sufficient information intact, seeing
that such aspects would have been removed by the proposed method, as illustrated in Fig. 3. It is therefore reasonable to assume that the filtering could
be used in an interactive video retrieval evaluation setting without negatively
impacting the task as it is intended. Due to the small number of results only
limited conclusions can be drawn. A larger-scale evaluation would be needed
to make any strong quantitative statements about the different effects of the
method on different types of query videos.

7   Conclusion and Outlook

In this paper, we presented a saliency based method for the generation of query
videos containing only partial information for use in the evaluation of interactive video retrieval systems. This filtering method serves as a proof-of-concept
for the feasibility of considering human perception and memory effects in the
context of the evaluation of interactive multimedia retrieval approaches. The
performed experiments indicate that the proposed method, while predicting and
subsequently removing many distinctive details from the video, to which presum-
ably *little to no* attention would have been paid outside of an explicit retrieval
scenario, does not negatively impact retrieval performance when compared to
unfiltered videos. The results, therefore, indicate that such a method could be
used in interactive video retrieval evaluation campaigns to more accurately simulate the desired real-world use case.

While the presented method serves as a first feasibility demonstration, the
problem of task generation for such retrieval evaluations is however far from
solved. For an accurate simulation of the scenario of a human user trying to
use a retrieval system in order to find a multimedia document they encountered before and only partially remember, additional aspects such as longer-
term human memory effects would need to be taken into account, which are not

considered by this method. Further research in the area of multi-modal memorability estimation and, especially, localization, as well as the necessary multimedia decomposition methods is needed in order to more accurately isolate the relevant aspects of a query document in order to consistently 'implant' the information need which is supposed to serve as a basis for the relevant evaluation task into a user.

Acknowledgements. The authors would like to thank all the participants of the 2020 Video Browser Showdown who contributed to the dedicated evaluation of the queries produced using the approach presented in this paper.

References

1. Abadi, M., et al.: Tensorflow: a system for large-scale machine learning. In: 12th USENIX Symposium on Operating Systems Design and Implementation (OSDI 16), pp. 265–283 (2016). https://www.usenix.org/system/files/conference/osdi16/osdi16-abadi.pdf
2. Abeles, P.: BoofCV v0.25 (2016). http://boofcv.org/
3. Akagunduz, E., Bors, A., Evans, K.: Defining image memorability using the visual memory schema. IEEE Trans. Pattern Anal. Mach. Intell. **42**(9), 2165–2178 (2019)
4. Andreadis, S., et al.: VERGE in VBS 2020. In: Ro, Y.M., et al. (eds.) MMM 2020. LNCS, vol. 11962, pp. 778–783. Springer, Cham (2020). https://doi.org/10.1007/978-3-030-37734-2_69
5. Bainbridge, W.A., Hall, E.H., Baker, C.I.: Drawings of real-world scenes during free recall reveal detailed object and spatial information in memory. Nat. Commun. **10**(1), 1–13 (2019)
6. Bainbridge, W.A., Isola, P., Oliva, A.: The intrinsic memorability of face photographs. J. Exp. Psychol. Gen. **142**(4), 1323 (2013)
7. Berns, F., Rossetto, L., Schoeffmann, K., Beecks, C., Awad, G.: V3C1 Dataset: an evaluation of content characteristics. In: Proceedings of the 2019 on International Conference on Multimedia Retrieval, pp. 334–338 (2019)
8. Brady, T.F., Konkle, T., Alvarez, G.A., Oliva, A.: Visual long-term memory has a massive storage capacity for object details. Proc. Nat. Acad. Sci. **105**(38), 14325–14329 (2008)
9. Chaudhry, R., Kilaru, M., Shekhar, S.: Show and recall@ MediaEval 2018 ViMem-Net: predicting video memorability (2018)
10. Cohendet, R., Demarty, C.H., Duong, N., Sjöberg, M., Ionescu, B., Do, T.T.: MediaEval 2018: predicting media memorability task. arXiv preprint arXiv:1807.01052 (2018)
11. Cohendet, R., Yadati, K., Duong, N.Q., Demarty, C.H.: Annotating, understanding, and predicting long-term video memorability. In: Proceedings of the 2018 ACM on International Conference on Multimedia Retrieval, pp. 178–186. ACM (2018)
12. DeCarlo, D., Santella, A.: Stylization and abstraction of photographs. ACM Trans. Graph. **21**(3), 769–776 (2002). https://doi.org/10.1145/566654.566650
13. Deng, X., Xu, M., Jiang, L., Sun, X., Wang, Z.: Subjective-driven complexity control approach for HEVC. IEEE Trans. Circ. Syst. Video Technol. **26**(1), 91–106 (2015)

14. Dubey, R., Peterson, J., Khosla, A., Yang, M.H., Ghanem, B.: What makes an object memorable? In: Proceedings of the IEEE International Conference on Computer Vision, pp. 1089–1097 (2015)
15. Ephrat, A., et al.: Looking to listen at the cocktail party: a speaker-independent audio-visual model for speech separation. ACM Trans. Graph. **37**(4), 112:1–112:11 (2018). https://doi.org/10.1145/3197517.3201357
16. Fletcher, D.: Rocketman. Paramount Pictures, May 2019
17. Hayward, S.: Cinema Studies: The Key Concepts (Routledge Key Guides). Flashback, Routledge (2000)
18. Isola, P., Xiao, J., Parikh, D., Torralba, A., Oliva, A.: What makes a photograph memorable? IEEE Trans. Pattern Anal. Mach. Intell. **36**(7), 1469–1482 (2013)
19. Jiang, L., Xu, M., Liu, T., Qiao, M., Wang, Z.: DeepVS: a deep learning based video saliency prediction approach. In: Ferrari, V., Hebert, M., Sminchisescu, C., Weiss, Y. (eds.) Computer Vision – ECCV 2018. LNCS, vol. 11218, pp. 625–642. Springer, Cham (2018). https://doi.org/10.1007/978-3-030-01264-9_37
20. Jónsson, B., Khan, O.S., Koelma, D.C., Rudinac, S., Worring, M., Zahálka, J.: Exquisitor at the video browser showdown 2020. In: Ro, Y.M., et al. (eds.) MMM 2020. LNCS, vol. 11962, pp. 796–802. Springer, Cham (2020). https://doi.org/10.1007/978-3-030-37734-2_72
21. Khosla, A., Raju, A.S., Torralba, A., Oliva, A.: Understanding and predicting image memorability at a large scale. In: Proceedings of the IEEE International Conference on Computer Vision. pp. 2390–2398 (2015)
22. Kilbourn, R.: Memory and the Flashback in Cinema (2013). https://doi.org/10.1093/obo/9780199791286-0182
23. Kim, B., Shim, J.Y., Park, M., Ro, Y.M.: Deep learning-based video retrieval using object relationships and associated audio classes. In: Ro, Y.M., et al. (eds.) MMM 2020. LNCS, vol. 11962, pp. 803–808. Springer, Cham (2020). https://doi.org/10.1007/978-3-030-37734-2_73
24. Kratochvíl, M., Veselý, P., Mejzlík, F., Lokoč, J.: SOM-Hunter: video browsing with relevance-to-SOM feedback loop. In: Ro, Y.M., et al. (eds.) MMM 2020. LNCS, vol. 11962, pp. 790–795. Springer, Cham (2020). https://doi.org/10.1007/978-3-030-37734-2_71
25. Le, N.-K., Nguyen, D.-H., Tran, M.-T.: An interactive video search platform for multi-modal retrieval with advanced concepts. In: Ro, Y.M., et al. (eds.) MMM 2020. LNCS, vol. 11962, pp. 766–771. Springer, Cham (2020). https://doi.org/10.1007/978-3-030-37734-2_67
26. Leibetseder, A., Münzer, B., Primus, J., Kletz, S., Schoeffmann, K.: diveXplore 4.0: the ITEC deep interactive video exploration system at VBS2020. In: Ro, Y.M., et al. (eds.) MMM 2020. LNCS, vol. 11962, pp. 753–759. Springer, Cham (2020). https://doi.org/10.1007/978-3-030-37734-2_65
27. Lokoč, J., Kovalčík, G., Souček, T.: VIRET at video browser showdown 2020. In: Ro, Y.M., et al. (eds.) MMM 2020. LNCS, vol. 11962, pp. 784–789. Springer, Cham (2020). https://doi.org/10.1007/978-3-030-37734-2_70
28. Mandler, J.M., Ritchey, G.H.: Long-term memory for pictures. J. Exp. Psychol. Hum. Learn. Mem. **3**(4), 386 (1977)
29. Nguyen, P.A., Wu, J., Ngo, C.-W., Francis, D., Huet, B.: VIREO @ video browser showdown 2020. In: Ro, Y.M., et al. (eds.) MMM 2020. LNCS, vol. 11962, pp. 772–777. Springer, Cham (2020). https://doi.org/10.1007/978-3-030-37734-2_68
30. Nolan, C.: Memento. In: Newmarket Films, September 2000

31. Park, S., Song, J., Park, M., Ro, Y.M.: IVIST: interactive video search tool in VBS 2020. In: Ro, Y.M., et al. (eds.) MMM 2020. LNCS, vol. 11962, pp. 809–814. Springer, Cham (2020). https://doi.org/10.1007/978-3-030-37734-2_74

32. Ramsay, D., Ananthabhotla, I., Paradiso, J.: The intrinsic memorability of everyday sounds. In: Audio Engineering Society Conference: 2019 AES International Conference on Immersive and Interactive Audio. Audio Engineering Society (2019)

33. Rodriguez-Hidalgo, A., Peláez-Moreno, C., Gallardo-Antolín, A.: Echoic logsurprise: a multi-scale scheme for acoustic saliency detection. Expert Syst. Appl. **114**, 255–266 (2018)

34. Rossetto, L., et al.: Interactive video retrieval in the age of deep learning-detailed evaluation of VBS 2019. IEEE Trans. Multimedia **23**, 243–256 (2020)

35. Rossetto, L., Schuldt, H., Awad, G., Butt, A.A.: V3C – a research video collection. In: Kompatsiaris, I., Huet, B., Mezaris, V., Gurrin, C., Cheng, W.-H., Vrochidis, S. (eds.) MMM 2019. LNCS, vol. 11295, pp. 349–360. Springer, Cham (2019). https://doi.org/10.1007/978-3-030-05710-7_29

36. Sauter, L., Amiri Parian, M., Gasser, R., Heller, S., Rossetto, L., Schuldt, H.: Combining boolean and multimedia retrieval in vitrivr for large-scale video search. In: Ro, Y.M., et al. (eds.) MMM 2020. LNCS, vol. 11962, pp. 760–765. Springer, Cham (2020). https://doi.org/10.1007/978-3-030-37734-2_66

37. Savii, R.M., dos Santos, S.F., Almeida, J.: Gibis at MediaEval 2018: predicting media memorability task. In: Working Notes Proceedings of the MediaEval 2018 Workshop. CEUR-WS (2018)

38. Shekhar, S., Singal, D., Singh, H., Kedia, M., Shetty, A.: Show and recall: learning what makes videos memorable. In: Proceedings of the IEEE International Conference on Computer Vision Workshops, pp. 2730–2739 (2017)

39. Simons, D.J., Chabris, C.F.: Gorillas in our midst: sustained inattentional blindness for dynamic events. Perception **28**(9), 1059–1074 (1999)

40. Smeaton, A.F., et al.: Dublin's participation in the predicting media memorability task at MediaEval, vol. 2018 (2018)

41. Wang, S., Wang, W., Chen, S., Jin, Q.: RUC at MediaEval 2018: visual and textual features exploration for predicting media memorability. In: Working Notes Proceedings of the MediaEval 2018 Workshop. CEUR-WS (2018)

42. Zhao, H., Gan, C., Rouditchenko, A., Vondrick, C., McDermott, J., Torralba, A.: The sound of pixels. In: Ferrari, V., Hebert, M., Sminchisescu, C., Weiss, Y. (eds.) ECCV 2018. LNCS, vol. 11205, pp. 587–604. Springer, Cham (2018). https://doi.org/10.1007/978-3-030-01246-5_35

Learning Multi-level Interaction Relations and Feature Representations for Group Activity Recognition

Lihua Lu[1,2,3](✉), Yao Lu[3], and Shunzhou Wang[3]

[1] Inspur Electronic Information Industry Co., Ltd., Jinan, China
[2] State Key Laboratory of High-End Server and Storage Technology, Jinan, China
[3] School of Computer Science, Beijing Institute of Technology, Beijing, China
`lulihua@bit.edu.cn`

Abstract. Group activity recognition is an challenging task with a major issue that reasons about complex interaction relations in the context of multi-person scenes. Most existing approaches concentrate on capturing interaction relations and learning features of the group activity at individual or group levels. These approaches lose sight of multi-level structures and interaction relations of the group activity. To overcome this challenge, we propose a Multi-level Interaction Relation model (MIR) to flexibly and efficiently learn multi-level structures of the group activity and capture multi-level interaction relations in the group activity. MIR employs graph pooling and unpooling networks to build multi-grained group relation graphs, and thus divide the group activity into multiple levels. Specifically, the Key Actor based Group Pooling layer (KeyPool) selects key persons in the activity to build the coarser-grained graph while the Key Actor based Group Unpooling layer (KeyUnPool) reconstructs the finer-grained graph according the corresponding KeyPool. Multiple KeyPool and KeyUnPool progressively build multi-grained graphs and learn multi-level structures of the group activity. Thanks to graph convolutions performed on multi-grained relation graphs, multi-level interactions are finally captured. In addition, graph readout (GR) layers are added to obtain multi-level spatio-temporal features of The group activity. Experimental results on two publicly available datasets demonstrate the effectiveness of KeyPool and KeyUnPool, and show our model can further improve the performance of group activity recognition.

Keywords: Group activity recognition · Multi-level structures · Multi-grained relation graphs · Multi-level interactions and features · Graph convolutional networks · Graph pooling networks

1 Introduction

Group activity recognition aims to recognize the group activity in the context of multi-person scenes, which plays important role in many practical applications,

J. Lokoč et al. (Eds.): MMM 2021, LNCS 12572, pp. 617–628, 2021.
https://doi.org/10.1007/978-3-030-67832-6_50

such as sports video analysis, video surveillance and social scene understanding. It is an challenging task since it needs to model jointly the behaviours of multiple actors and reason about interaction relations between actors. Most existing methods [1,6,15] follows a two-stage recognition pipeline, which firstly obtains person-level features using deep neural networks, and then globally aggregates these person-level features into the group-level features. These methods take group activity recognition into account from individual and group perspectives with two major issues. First, learning multi-level structures of the group activity, i.e., individuals, multi-grained subgroups, and the global group. Second, capturing multi-level interaction relations in the activity, i.e., interactions among different individuals or different subgroups, interactions between the individual or subgroup and the global group, and so on.

Recent works [13,21,24] apply graph convolutional networks (GCNs) to group activity recognition, which can automatically build a relation graph from the video, and adaptively capture interactions between actors by performing graph convolution operations on the graph. Wu et al. [24] propose to build a relation graph to simultaneously capture the appearance and position interaction relations between actors. However, above methods ignore hierarchical structures of the group activity and are unable to learn multi-level interactions and features of the activity. Some researches [5,8,23,26] study group activity recognition from multiple levels. However, these methods need to manually define fixed subgroups in advance, which is inflexible to generalize.

In this work, we propose a Multi-level Interaction Relation model (MIR) that employs graph convolution and graph pooling networks to flexibly infer multi-level structures and interaction relations of the group activity, and further learn multi-level feature representations for the group activity recognition. We propose to flexibly learn multi-level structures of the group activity by designing key-actor based group pooling and unpooling layers. Multiple KeyPool and KeyUnpool layers progressively divide the group activity into multiple levels, and build multi-grained group relation graphs. Multi-level interactions can be automatically learned by performing graph convolutions on multi-grained graphs. Finally, the graph readout layers are added to obtain multi-level spatio-temporal features of the group activity.

The major contributions of this paper are threefold:

- We propose the MIR that breaks the typical two-stage recognition pipeline for group activity recognition. The proposed model empolys graph pooling and unpooling networks, which can adaptively divide the group activity into multiple levels, and learn multi-level structures of the group activity.
- KeyPool and KeyUnPool layers play important roles in our model. The KeyPool selects key persons in the activity to build the coarser-grained graph while the KeyUnPool reconstructs the finer-grained graph according the corresponding KeyPool. Multiple KeyPool and KeyUnPool layers progressively build multi-grained graphs, and thus reason about multi-level structures of the group activity. We explore different graph pooling and convolutional networks in our paper.

– Multi-level interactions are automatically captured by graph convolutions performed on multi-grained graphs. Multi-level feature representations of the group activity are learned by using multiple GR layers. These features are more discriminative and efficient for group activity recognition.

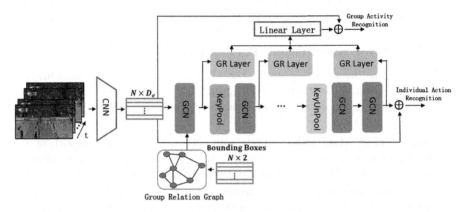

Fig. 1. The proposed Multi-level Interaction Relation (MIR) model for group activity recognition.

2   Approach

2.1   The Overview of Our Model

The overall network framework is illustrated in Fig. 1. Firstly, given a video sequence and a set of person detections encoded as bounding boxes $B_t = \{b_t^i | i = 1, ..., N\} \in \mathbb{R}^{N \times 4}$ for each frame $I_t \in \mathbb{R}^{H_0 \times W_0 \times 3}$, we take Inception-v3 [19] as the backbone to extract the fixed-size representations $f_t^i \in \mathbb{R}^{K \times K \times D}, i \in \{1, ..., N\}$ for each person detection b_t^i, where N is the number of bounding boxes, $K \times K$ is the size of the fixed representation in pixels, D is the number of features, and $H_0 \times W_0$ is the size of the video frame. We then use a $N \times D_e$ matrix X to represent feature vectors of individuals in the collective activity.

Secondly, we build the original group relation graph according to individuals' bounding boxes B_t, where each node denotes a person and each edge denotes the relation between two persons forced in the neighborhood. Concretely, the edge connects persons whose Euclidean distance is below the predefined threshold μ. The distance threshold μ is a hyper-parameter in our network, which is empirically initialized as $\frac{1}{5}$ of the image width. Afterwards, we apply a GCN to capture original interactions between individuals. We stack several KeyPool layers, each of which is followed by a GCN layer, to build a coarser-grained graph layer by layer. And then we stack several KeyUnPool layers, each of which is followed by a GCN layer, to restore a finer-grained graph layer by layer.

Finally, one more GCN layer is added to compute $N \times D_e$ features, which are fused with original individuals' features to generate the final representations for individuals' actions. Furthermore, we add several GR layers, each of which globally aggregates all nodes' features into the graph-level features. Then a linear layer is added to aggregate multi-level graph-level features into a more compact multi-level feature representations of the group activity. Two classifiers respectively for recognizing individual actions and group activity will be applied.

2.2   Key-Actor Based Group Pooling Layer

In the KeyPool layer (as shown in Fig. 2), the person scoring mechanism is employed to select the key actors in the group activity, and then build a coarser-grained relation graph composed of these key actors.

Person Scoring Mechanism. Only some key actors play an important role in identifying the group activity [16,20,21,25]. The person scoring mechanism calculates the score of each person, and selects key actors with high scores to construct a coarser-grained relation graph of the group activity. In order to make full use of the topology structure and deep features of the relation graph, the person scoring mechanism uses self-attention pooling [9] to calculate individual scores.

Self-attention Pooling. Self-attention pooling computes scores for each person by performing graph convolution on the relation graph. Rank these scores and select K person nodes with K-largest scores to build a smaller and coarser relation graph. The GCN used can be implemented in many forms, such as GraphConv [14], GCN [7], GAT [22] and so on. Taking GCN as an example, the individual scoring mechanism is calculated as follows:

$$Z = \sigma\left(A^{(l)}X^{(l)}W^{(l)}\right) \qquad (1)$$

where $A = \tilde{D}^{-\frac{1}{2}}\tilde{A}\tilde{D}^{-\frac{1}{2}}$, $\tilde{A} \in \mathbb{R}^{N \times N}$ is the adjacency matrix of the relation graph, $\tilde{D} \in \mathbb{R}^{N \times N}$ is the degree matrix of the adjacency matrix $\tilde{A}$, $W \in \mathbb{R}^{F \times 1}$ is the learnable parameter matrix in GCN, $Z \in \mathbb{R}^{N \times 1}$ is the obtained persons' scores, l denotes l-th group graph pooling layer and σ is the nonlinear activation function tanh.

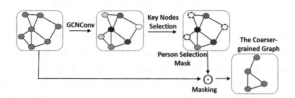

Fig. 2. Key-actor based group pooling layer (KeyPool).

Build a Coarser-Grained Relation Graph. Compute the person selection mask by selecting K nodes with K-largest scores.

$$k = \lceil \lambda N \rceil \tag{2}$$

$$idx = rank\,(Z, k) \tag{3}$$

$$Z_{mask} = Z_{idx} \tag{4}$$

where $\lambda \in (0, 1]$ is the pooling ratio, function $rank$ returns indices of the K-largest in Z, $\cdot_{idx}$ is an indexing operation and Z_{mask} is the final person selection mask.

Build a coarser-grained relation graph and compute node features according to the person selection mask.

$$\tilde{X}^{(l)} = X_{idx,:}^{(l)} \tag{5}$$

$$A^{(l+1)} = A_{idx,idx}^{(l)} \tag{6}$$

$$X^{(l+1)} = \tilde{X}^{(l)} \odot Z_{mask} \tag{7}$$

where $X_{idx,:}$ is the row-wise indexed feature matrix, $A_{idx,idx}$ is the row-wise and column-wise indexed adjacency matrix, $\odot$ denotes the broadcasted element-wise product, $A^{(l+1)}$ and $X^{(l+1)}$ respectively represent the adjacency matrix and feature matrix of the new relation graph consisting of the selected key nodes.

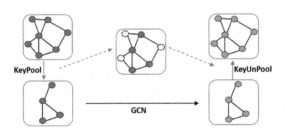

Fig. 3. Key-actor based group unpooling layer (KeyUnPool).

2.3   Key-Actor Based Group Unpooling Layer

KeyUnPool is the inverse operation of KeyPool and aims to reconstruct a finer-grained relation graph. As shown in Fig. 3, the KeyUnPool layer puts back key nodes to their original positions in the finer relation graph according to indices recorded by the KeyPool layer, and thus a fine-grained relation graph is restored. The following GCN layer captures interactions between nodes. To better reconstruct the fine-grained relation graph, we add the skip-connection connecting the corresponding KeyPool and KeyUnPool layers, which can transfer the topology structure and deep features of the relation graph from KeyPool layer to KeyUnPool layer. The formulation is as follows:

$$X^{(l+1)} = distribute\left(0_{N \times D_e}, X^{(l)}, idx\right) \tag{8}$$

where $idx \in \mathbb{Z}^{*k}$ are indices of k key nodes, $X^{(l)}$ is the l-th feature matrix, $0_{N \times D_e}$ denotes the initial feature matrix of the reconstructed by the KeyUn-Pool layer, with the value of 0. Function $distribute$ distributes row vectors in $X^{(l)}$ into $0_{N \times D_e}$ according to their corresponding indices recorded in idx, and $X^{(l+1)}$ represents the reconstructed finer-grained relation graph, whose row vectors with indices in idx are updated by row vectors in $X^{(l)}$ while other row vectors remain 0.

2.4 Multi-level Features of the Group Activity

Based on graph pooling and convolutional networks, individual action recognition is a task of node classification while group activity recognition is a task of graph classification. The key to graph classification is to effectively aggregate features of the nodes on the graph into graph-level representations. Here, we add a graph readout (GR) layer similar to [9] after each GCN layer to obtain the graph-level representation of the group activity (as shown in Fig. 1). Formally, the readout layer is as follows:

$$f = \frac{1}{N} \sum_{i=1}^{N} x_i \, || \, max_{i=1}^{N} x_i \tag{9}$$

where $||$ denotes the operation of concatenation.

Afterwards, we fuse together the outputs of multiple graph readout layers, and feed the resulting vector into a linear layer to compute a compact feature representation. At the same time, we maxpool all the original nodes' features to be the original feature of the group activity, which is fused with the output of the linear layer to be the final multi-level feature representations of the group activity.

3 Experiments

3.1 Datasets and Implementation Details

Datasets. In this section, we deploy experiments on two publicly available datasets, namely the Collective Activity dataset and the Volleyball dataset for the task of collective activity recognition.

The Collective Activity Dataset (CAD). [2] consists of 44 video clips in total (about 2500 frames shot by low-resolution cameras), five group activities: crossing, waiting, queuing, walking and talking, and six individual actions: N/A, crossing, waiting, queuing, walking and talking. We follow the experimental setting of [24] and select $\frac{1}{3}$ of the video sequences for testing and the rest for training.

The Volleyball Dataset (VD). [6] contains labels for people locations, as well as their collective and individual actions. The dataset consists of 55 volleyball games with 4830 labeled frames, where each player is annotated by the bounding box with one of the 9 individual action labels, and the collective scene is assigned with one of the 8 collective activity labels that define which part of the game is happening. In our experiments, we use a temporal window of length $T = 10$ which corresponds to 5 frames before the annotated frame, and 4 frames after. We used frames from $\frac{2}{3}$rd of the videos for training, and the remaining $\frac{1}{3}$rd for testing.

Implement Details. Given ground-truth bounding boxes, we adopt Inception-v3 as the backbone to extract features for each person. We also experiment with VGG [18] network for fair comparison with previous methods. Similar to ARG [24], we randomly sample three ordered frames from the video to build the original relation graph and train our model. We adopt stochastic gradient descent with ADAM to learn the network parameters with fixed hyper-parameters to $\beta_1 = 0.9, \beta_2 = 0.999, \epsilon = 10^{-8}$. Besides, the pooling ratio $\lambda = \{0.9, 0.8, 0.6\}$. For the Volleyball dataset, we train the network in 200 epochs using minibatch size of 32 and a learning rate ranging from 0.0002 to 0.00001. For the Collective Activity dataset, we use minibatch size of 16 with a learning rate of 0.0001, and train the network in 80 epochs.

3.2 Ablation Studies

Analysis of Different Graph Convolutional and Pooling Networks. Our model relies on graph pooling and convolutional networks. We deploy experiments to compare three implementation forms of graph convolutional networks: GCN [7], GAT [22] and GraphConv [14], and two implementation forms of graph pooling networks: mapping pooling (TopK) [3] and self-attention Pooling (SAGPool) [9]. Since SAGPool uses graph convolution to compute attention weights, it has three variants represented as SAGPool-GCN, SAGPool-GAT, and SAGPool-GraphConv. The experimental results are shown in Table 1. It can be seen that using SAGPool-GCN and GAT to respectively implement the group graph pooling layer and the graph convolution layer can achieve the best recognition performance.

Table 1. Results of different implementation of graph pooling and graph convolutional networks on the Volleyball dataset.

Method	TopK	SAGPool-GraphConv	SAGPool-GCN	SAGPool-GAT
GCN	91.1	91.0	91.9	91.2
GAT	91.9	91.6	92.6	92.1

Analysis of Multiple Key-Actor Based Group Pooling and Unpooling Layers. We deploy a set of experiments to compare the effect of different numbers of key actor group pooling and unpooling layers. Results are shown in Table 2. It can be concluded that multiple corresponding group pooling and unpooling layers can improve the performance of group activity recognition. Specifically, two sets of corresponding group pooling and unpooling layers can achieve the highest recognition accuracy of 92.6%. Therefore, we use two sets of group pooling and unpooling modules in the following experiments. In addition, it can be seen that three pooling and unpooling layers degrade the performance since too many layers lead to a large number of parameters making the model easy to overfit.

Table 2. Results of different number of group pooling and unpooling layers on the Volleyball dataset.

Number	0	1	2	3
G-MCA	91.6	92.2	92.6	92.4

3.3   Comparison with the State-of-the-Art

For fair comparison and good performance, we use GAT [22] and SAPool [9] to respectively complement graph convolution and pooling operations in the following experiments.

Results on the Volleyball Dataset. Table 3 provides the comparison results of our proposed method and the state-of-the-art methods on the Volleyball dataset. G-MCA, G-MPCA and P-MCA respectively denote the accuracy of group activity recognition, the mean accuracy of group activity recognition and the accuracy of individual action recognition. Our model outperforms state-of-the-art methods and improve the recognition performance to 92.6%. 1) Our model achieves better results than existing methods [1,13,15,20,21,24,25] following a two-stage pipeline. Recent works such as ARG [24] and GIAM [13] employ graph convolutional networks to automatically capture interactions between actors, and improve the performance by a large margin. Differently, our model uses KeyPool and KeyUnPool layers to build multi-grained relation graphs and learn multi-level interactions, which improves the accuracy of group activity recognition. 2) Our model outperforms these works [5,8] aiming to learn multi-level structures and interactions of the group activity. For example, HRN [5] regards group activity as three levels of individuals, subgroups, and groups. However, these methods divide the group activity into multiple fixed levels in advance, which are not flexible and not easy to expand. Our method uses graph pooling to construct multi-grained relation graph, which adaptively divides the group activity into multiple levels. Figure 4 shows visual results of our model.

Table 3. Comparison with state-of-the-arts on the Volleyball dataset.

Method	Backbone	G-MCA	G-MPCA	P-MCA
HDTM [6]	AlexNet	81.9	82.9	–
SSU [1]	Inception-v3	90.6	–	81.8
PC-TDM [25]	AlexNet	87.7	88.1	–
stagNet [15]	VGG16	89.3	84.4	82.3
HAC [8]	GoogLeNet	–	85.1	–
HRN [5]	VGG19	89.5	–	–
CCG-LSTM [20]	AlexNet	–	89.3	–
SPTS [21]	VGG16	91.2	91.4	–
HAIM [11]	Inception-v3	91.4	91.9	82.2
ST-SAM [12]	Inception-v3	91.7	92.2	82.5
ARG [24]	Inception-v3	92.5	–	**83.0**
PRL [4]	VGG16	91.4	91.8	–
GAIM [13]	Inception-v3	92.1	92.6	82.6
Ours	VGG16	92.1	92.2	82.6
Ours	Inception-v3	**92.6**	**92.8**	82.8

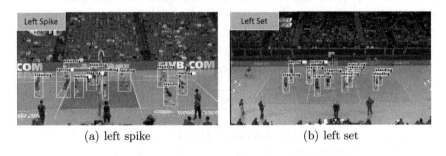

(a) left spike (b) left set

Fig. 4. Visualization results on the Volleyball dataset.

Figure 5(b) and Fig. 5(a) respectively shows the confusion matrix of our model and the baseline on the Volleyball dataset. It can be concluded that our method works well in every category, and improves the recognition accuracy higher than 92.5% except for the category "r-set". However, our method has confusions between "pass" and "set" categories as these two kinds of activities have similar interaction relations.

Results on Collective Activity Dataset. Table 4 provides the comparison results of our proposed method and the state-of-the-art methods on the Collective Activity dataset. Our method also works well on the Collective Activity dataset, and shows its effectiveness and generality. Our model outperforms most two-stage models [6, 10, 13, 15], which recognize the group activity follows a two-

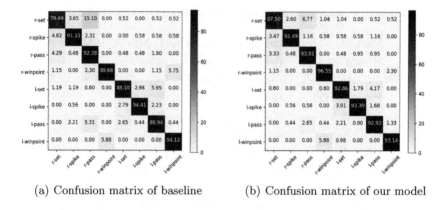

(a) Confusion matrix of baseline   (b) Confusion matrix of our model

Fig. 5. Confusion matrix on the Volleyball dataset.

stage pipeline, concentrating on learning interactions between actors. However, these methods neglects multi-level structures of the group activity. Differently, our method proposes KeyPool and KeyUnPool layers to adaptively learn multi-level structures of the group activity and capture multi-level interactions between actors. However, ARG achieves a better result than our model since multiple pooling and unpooling modules increase the size of the network parameters, and are unfriendly to the smaller Collective Activity dataset.

Table 4. Comparison with state-of-the-arts on the Collective Activity dataset.

Method	Backbone	G-MCA	G-MPCA
HDTM [6]	AlexNet	81.5	80.9
SBGAR [10]	Inception-v3	86.1	86.2
CERN [17]	VGG16	87.2	88.3
stagNet [15]	VGG16	89.1	83.0
HAIM [11]	Inception-v3	89.5	89.1
ST-SAM [12]	Inception-v3	89.9	89.4
GAIM [13]	Inception-v3	90.6	**90.3**
ARG [24]	Inception-v3	**91.0**	–
Ours	Inception-v3	90.2	90.0
Ours	VGG16	89.7	89.3

4   Conclusion

We propose a multi-level interactions and feature representation learning method for group activity recognition, which is based on graph pooling and convolutional networks. Multiple key-actor based group pooling layers selects key persons in the group activity layer by layer to build relation graphs ranging from fine to coarse grain, and thus adaptively learn multi-level structure of the group activity. Multiple key-actor based group unpooling layers layer by layer restore relation graphs from coarse to fine grain, which rely on key actors retained in corresponding pooling modules. Thus, multiple pooling and unpooling layers build multi-grained relation graphs, on which the graph convolution is performed to learn multi-level interactions. Finally, the graph readout layer is used to obtain multi-level spatio-temporal features of the group activity. Experimental results on two publicly available datasets show our model can further improve the performance of group activity recognition. The quantitative and visual results of ablation studies on the Volleyball dataset prove the effectiveness of the key-actor based group pooling and unpooling layers.

References

1. Bagautdinov, T., Alahi, A., Fleuret, F., Fua, P., Savarese, S.: Social scene understanding: end-to-end multi-person action localization and collective activity recognition. In: Proceedings of the IEEE Conference on Computer Vision and Pattern Recognition (CVPR), pp. 4315–4324 (2017)
2. Choi, W., Shahid, K., Savarese, S.: What are they doing?: collective activity classification using spatio-temporal relationship among people. In: Proceedings of the IEEE Conference on International Conference on Computer Vision Workshops (ICCV Workshops), pp. 1282–1289. IEEE (2009)
3. Gao, H., Ji, S.: Graph U-Nets. In: Proceedings of the International Conference on Machine Learning (ICML), pp. 2083–2092 (2019)
4. Hu, G., Cui, B., He, Y., Yu, S.: Progressive relation learning for group activity recognition. In: Proceedings of the IEEE Conference on Computer Vision and Pattern Recognition (CVPR), pp. 980–989 (2020)
5. Ibrahim, M.S., Mori, G.: Hierarchical relational networks for group activity recognition and retrieval. In: Ferrari, V., Hebert, M., Sminchisescu, C., Weiss, Y. (eds.) ECCV 2018. LNCS, vol. 11207, pp. 742–758. Springer, Cham (2018). https://doi.org/10.1007/978-3-030-01219-9_44
6. Ibrahim, M.S., Muralidharan, S., Deng, Z., Vahdat, A., Mori, G.: A hierarchical deep temporal model for group activity recognition. In: Proceedings of the IEEE Conference on Computer Vision and Pattern Recognition (CVPR), pp. 1971–1980 (2016)
7. Kipf, T.N., Welling, M.: Semi-supervised classification with graph convolutional networks. arXiv preprint arXiv:1609.02907 (2016)
8. Kong, L., Qin, J., Huang, D., Wang, Y., Van Gool, L.: Hierarchical attention and context modeling for group activity recognition. In: IEEE International Conference on Acoustics, Speech and Signal Processing (ICASSP), pp. 1328–1332. IEEE (2018)
9. Lee, J., Lee, I., Kang, J.: Self-attention graph pooling. In: Proceedings of the International Conference on Machine Learning (ICML), pp. 3734–3743 (2019)
10. Li, X., Choo Chuah, M.: SBGAR: semantics based group activity recognition. In: Proceedings of the IEEE Conference on International Conference on Computer Vision (ICCV), pp. 2876–2885 (2017)

11. Lu, L., Di, H., Lu, Y., Zhang, L., Wang, S.: A two-level attention-based interaction model for multi-person activity recognition. Neurocomputing **322**, 195–205 (2018)

12. Lu, L., Di, H., Lu, Y., Zhang, L., Wang, S.: Spatio-temporal attention mechanisms based model for collective activity recognition. Sig. Process. Image Commun. **74**, 162–174 (2019)

13. Lu, L., Lu, Y., Yu, R., Di, H., Zhang, L., Wang, S.: GAIM: graph attention interaction model for collective activity recognition. IEEE Trans. Multimedia **22**(2), 524–539 (2019)

14. Morris, C., et al.: Weisfeiler and leman go neural: higher-order graph neural networks. In: Proceedings of the AAAI Conference on Artificial Intelligence (AAAI), vol. 33, pp. 4602–4609 (2019)

15. Qi, M., Wang, Y., Qin, J., Li, A., Luo, J., Van Gool, L.: stagNet: an attentive semantic RNN for group activity and individual action recognition. IEEE Trans. Circuits Syst. Video Technol. (TCSVT) **30**(2), 549–565 (2020)

16. Ramanathan, V., Huang, J., Abu-El-Haija, S., Gorban, A., Murphy, K., Fei-Fei, L.: Detecting events and key actors in multi-person videos. In: Proceedings of the IEEE Conference on Computer Vision and Pattern Recognition (CVPR), pp. 3043–3053 (2016)

17. Shu, T., Todorovic, S., Zhu, S.C.: CERN: confidence-energy recurrent network for group activity recognition. In: Proceedings of the IEEE Conference on Computer Vision and Pattern Recognition (CVPR), pp. 5523–5531 (2017)

18. Simonyan, K., Zisserman, A.: Very deep convolutional networks for large-scale image recognition. arXiv preprint arXiv:1409.1556 (2014)

19. Szegedy, C., Vanhoucke, V., Ioffe, S., Shlens, J., Wojna, Z.: Rethinking the inception architecture for computer vision. In: Proceedings of the IEEE Conference on Computer Vision and Pattern Recognition (CVPR), pp. 2818–2826 (2016)

20. Tang, J., Shu, X., Yan, R., Zhang, L.: Coherence constrained graph LSTM for group activity recognition. IEEE Trans. Pattern Anal. Mach. Intell. (TPAMI), 1 (2019)

21. Tang, Y., Lu, J., Wang, Z., Yang, M., Zhou, J.: Learning semantics-preserving attention and contextual interaction for group activity recognition. IEEE Trans. Image Process. (TIP) **28**(10), 4997–5012 (2019)

22. Veličković, P., Cucurull, G., Casanova, A., Romero, A., Lio, P., Bengio, Y.: Graph attention networks. arXiv preprint arXiv:1710.10903 (2017)

23. Wang, M., Ni, B., Yang, X.: Recurrent modeling of interaction context for collective activity recognition. In: Proceedings of the IEEE Conference on Computer Vision and Pattern Recognition (CVPR), pp. 3048–3056 (2017)

24. Wu, J., Wang, L., Wang, L., Guo, J., Wu, G.: Learning actor relation graphs for group activity recognition. In: Proceedings of the IEEE Conference on Computer Vision and Pattern Recognition (CVPR), pp. 9964–9974 (2019)

25. Yan, R., Tang, J., Shu, X., Li, Z., Tian, Q.: Participation-contributed temporal dynamic model for group activity recognition. In: ACM International Conference on Multimedia (ACMMM), pp. 1292–1300 (2018)

26. Yang, L., Peng, H., Zhang, D., Fu, J., Han, J.: Revisiting anchor mechanisms for temporal action localization. IEEE Trans. Image Process. **29**, 8535–8548 (2020)

A Structured Feature Learning Model for Clothing Keypoints Localization

Ruhan He[ID], Yuyi Su[ID], Tao Peng[(✉)][ID], Jia Chen[ID], Zili Zhang[ID],
and Xinrong Hu[ID]

Engineering Research Center of Hubei Province for Clothing Information,
Wuhan Textile University, Wuhan 430200, China
pt@wtu.edu.cn

Abstract. Visual fashion analysis has attracted many attentions in the recent years. Especially, as a fundamental technology, clothing keypoints localization has great application potential. However, most of researchers seldomly consider the inherent structural information of clothing and process clothing images as ordinary images. In this paper, a Structured Feature Learning Model (SFLM) is proposed to exploit the structure information of clothing, which models the relationships among clothing keypoints on the feature layer and passes the information among the neighboring keypoints. The model introduces the bi-directional tree and the geometrical transform kernels to construct the information flow and capture the relationships respectively. Therefore, the clothing keypoints features and their relationships can be well jointly learned. The proposed model improves feature learning substantially. We demonstrate that our proposed model has an excellent ability to learn advanced deep feature representations for clothing keypoints localization. Experimental results show that the proposed model outperforms the state-of-the-arts on the DeepFashion and FLD dataset. The code will be available at https:// github.com/suyuyiS/SFLM.

Keywords: Clothing keypoints localization · Structured feature learning · Bi-directional tree · Geometrical transform kernels

1 Introduction

With the rapid development of e-commerce and online shopping, clothing visual analysis has received great attention in computer vision. Especially in recent years, thanks to large-scale clothing datasets [6,16,18,34], the modeles based on deep learning have achieved great success in this field, such as clothing retrieval [6,11,29], analysis [14,28], attribute prediction [15,16,25] and so on.

This work attempts to solve a basic but challenging problem in visual fashion analysis, namely the keypoints localization in clothing. The success of previous deep learning based fashion models [5,6,16,18,30] have proven the potential of applying neural network in this area. However, few of them attacked how to

© Springer Nature Switzerland AG 2021
J. Lokoč et al. (Eds.): MMM 2021, LNCS 12572, pp. 629–640, 2021.
https://doi.org/10.1007/978-3-030-67832-6_51

L.Collar   L.Sleeve   L.Waistline   L.Hem

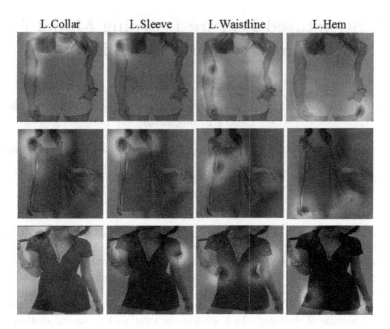

Fig. 1. The response of different images on the same feature channel

inject clothing structure information (such as the geometric relationship between keypoints) into a fashion model. We discover that independent prediction of a keypoint location from heatmap can be refined by modeling the spatial relationship among correlated keypoints. Figure 1 shows the responses of feature maps of keypoints for different input images. We can observe that some other keypoints features also respond when predict a certain keypoint feature in the feature map, which shows that there is a strong dependence between these keypoints. For example, when predict the keypoint of the left collar, the features of the left sleeve and waist keypoint both respond. Similarly, when predict the keypoint on the left, the keypoint feature on the right also responds, which shows that there is a symmetrical relationship between the keypoints features. Hence, in this paper, we propose a new model namely structured feature learning model (SFLM) to exploit the structure information of clothing keypoints at the feature level. Our proposed model shows that the spatial and co-occurrence relationship among feature maps can be modeled by a set of geometrical transform kernels. These kernels can be implemented with convolution and the relationships can be learned in end-to-end learning system.

Meanwhile, it is important to design proper information flow among clothing keypoints, so that features at a keypoint can be optimized by receiving messages from highly correlated keypoints and will not be disturbed by less correlated keypoints in distance. The proposed SFLM model connects correlated keypoints and passes messages along a bi-directional tree structure. Therefore, every keypoint can receive information from all the neighboring keypoints. Thus, the clothing keypoints features and their relationships can be well jointly learned in our model.

The contributions of this work are summarized as three-fold. First, it proposes an end-to-end structured feature learning model named SFLM to capture rich structural information among clothing keypoints at the feature level for clothing keypoints localization. Second, it shows that the relationships among feature maps of neighboring clothing keypoints can be learned by the introduced geometrical transform kernels and can be easily implemented with convolutional layers. Third, a bi-directional tree structure is designed, so that each keypoint can receive information from all the correlated keypoints and optimize its features. To demonstrate the strength of our proposed model, we conduct experiments by using two datasets, Deepfashion [16] and FLD [18]. Experimental results show that our model outperforms the state-of-the-art methods.

2   Related Works

2.1   Clothing Keypoint Localization

Extensive research works have been devoted to clothing keypoints localization and achieved excellent performance [2,8,16–19,27,30,33]. Liu et al. [16] firstly introduced neural network into clothing keypoints localization. They identified the localization as a regression task and designed the FastionNet directly to regress keypoints coordinates. Liu et al. [18] suggested pseudo label to enhance the invariance of clothing keypoints. Yan et al. [30] combined selective dilated convolution and recurrent spatial transformer for localizing cloth keypoints in unconstrained scenes. The success of those deep learning based fashion models demonstrated the strong representation power of neural network. However, they seldomly explored the rich structure information of clothing. In comparison, we propose a structured feature learning model that incorporates both powerful learning capabilities of neural networks and high-level semantic relations in visual fashion.

2.2   Structural Features Learning

Recently some research efforts have modeled structural information for mining correlations among labels or objects in images, which have been proved effective in many tasks [1,3,4,13,20,24,26,31]. Yang et al. [31] proposed the flexible mixture-of-parts model to combine part detection results with a tree-structured model, which provided simple and exact inference. Li et al. [13] built a subgraph-based model for scene graph generation using bottom-up relationship inference of objects in images. Chu et al. [3] modeled structural information to enhance the correlations among body joints at the feature level in human pose estimation. Wang et al. [25] captured kinematic and symmetry grammar of clothing keypoints for mining geometric relationships among keypoints. They modeled grammar message passing processing as a bidirectional convolutional recurrent neural network for training in an end-to-end manner. Similar to these fields, the garments also have rich inherent structural information. In this paper, we propose fashion structural model that account for dependent and symmetric relations in clothing.

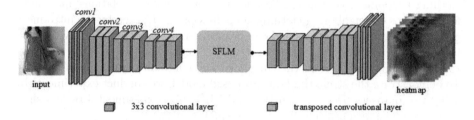

Fig. 2. Illustration of our proposed network. Our network consists of basic convolutional network VGG for feature extraction, the structured feature learning model for modeling rich structure features of clothing, and the upsampling network for predicting the keypoints heatmaps.

3 Our Approach

In this section, we first present our localization framework for clothing keypoints, then introduce our SFLM model in detail.

3.1 Keypoints Localization Framework

Problem Formulation. Clothing keypoints localization aims to predict the positions of N functional keypoints defined on the garment item, such as the corners of neckline, hemline, and cuff. Given an image I, the goal is to predict cloth keypoint positions P:

$$P = \{P_n : n = 1, 2..., N\}, P_n \in \mathbb{R}^2 \tag{1}$$

where P_n can be any pixel locations (x, y) in an image.

Many researchers directly used CNN [9,10,12,22,23] which had a good effect on image classification and recognition, and regarded it as a regression problem of keypoints. However, it has two drawbacks. First, the clothing image itself has rich structural information. If the network model of ordinary images is used to process the clothing image directly, the rich structural information of the clothing will be ignored, fail to better prediction of keypoints. Second, the way of directly regressing the coordinates of keypoints will greatly damage the ability of spatial generalization and is difficult to learn directly.

To address the above problems, we introduce higher-level semantic information to model the clothing structure features. Instead of regressing keypoint positions P directly, we learn to predict a confidence map of positional distribution (heatmap) for each keypoint, given the input image. The overall architecture of the proposed model is illustrated in Fig. 2

For more accurate keypoints localization, we produce high-resolution keypoints heatmaps which have the same size to the input image. To increase the spatial size of the feature map, we use several transposed convolutions. At the end of the upsampling network, we utilize a 1×1 convolution to produce a heatmap for each keypoint.

3.2   SFLM Model

Bi-Directional Tree Structure. In this paper, we utilize $N = 8$ clothing keypoints, defined as left/right collar, left/right sleeve, left/right waistline, and left/right hem, following previous settings [16,18]. The rich inherent natural structure of clothing involves this task, which prompts us to infer the location of keypoints in a global way.

To enhance the features obtained at a keypoint, one expects to receive information from all the other keypoints with a fully connected graph. However, in order to directly model the relationship among features of keypoints in distance, large transform kernels have to be introduced and they are difficult to learn. A better way is to propagate information between them through intermediate keypoints on a designed graph. The adjacent keypoints on the graph are relatively close and the relationship is relatively stable. In this work, we design a message passing scheme so that each keypoint receives messages from all the other in an efficient way by saving intermediate messages, a tree structure shown in Fig. 3 A and B is chosen.

In Fig. 3, we use VGG network [22] for feature extraction. After the conv4_3 layer of VGG, each garment keypoint has an independent set of 128 feature maps. Denote h_{conv4} as the feature map obtained in the conv4 layer and it is a 4,096 dimensional feature channels. The 128 dimensional feature vector for garment keypoint n in the conv5 layer is computed as:

$$h^n_{conv5} = \sigma \left(h_{conv4} \otimes w^n_{conv5} + b_{conv4} \right) \tag{2}$$

where $\otimes$ denotes convolution, σ is a nonlinear function, w^n_{conv5} is the filter bank for keypoint n including 128 filters, b_{conv4} is the bias, and h^n_{conv5} is the feature tensor contains 128 feature maps for garment keypoint n.

In Fig. 3 A, information flows from root keypoints to leaf keypoints. Let $\{A_n\}$ be the original feature maps directly obtained from the conv4 layer. Here, $\{A_n\}$ is the concrete case of h^n_{conv5} in Eq. (2), n is the index of keypoints. The refined feature maps after message passing are denoted by $\left\{ A'_n \right\}$.

$$A_n = \sigma \left(h_{conv4} \otimes w^{a_n} \right) \tag{3}$$

where h_{conv4} are the conv4 feature maps, w^{a_n} is the filter bank for keypoint n, and σ is the rectified linear unit. The process of refining features is explained below.

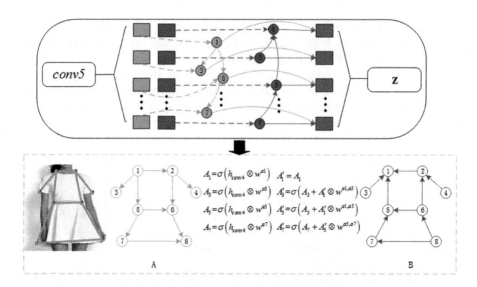

Fig. 3. Illustration of the proposed SFLM. A and B show the details of the bi-directional tree which have information flows in opposite directions. The process of updating feature maps are also illustrated. Dashed line is copy operation and solid line is convolution.

Since A_1 is at the root keypoints in the downward direction tree, it does not receive information from other keypoints, so the refined feature maps is the same as the original ones, i.e.

$$A_1^{'} = A_1 \tag{4}$$

A_3 is updated by receiving information from $A_1^{'}$,

$$A_3^{'} = \sigma\left(A_3 + A_1^{'} \otimes w^{a_1,a_3}\right) \tag{5}$$

where w^{a_1,a_3} is a collection of transform kernels between keypoint A_1 and keypoint A_3. A_6 is updated by receiving information from both $A_2^{'}$ and $A_5^{'}$,

$$A_6^{'} = \sigma\left(A_6 + A_2^{'} \otimes w^{a_2,a_6} + A_5^{'} \otimes w^{a_5,a_6}\right) \tag{6}$$

Feature maps of other keypoints are updated in a similar way.

To obtain complementary features, we design another branch with the same tree structure but opposite information flow in Fig. 3 B. The feature maps $\{B_n\}$ are obtained in the same way as $\{A_n\}$, but the refined feature maps $\left\{B_n^{'}\right\}$ are updated in the opposite order as indicated by the arrows' direction in Fig. 3 B. Complementary features are first obtained from different flow directions separately and then combined by concatenation.

$$z_n = \left[A_n^{'}, B_n^{'}\right] \otimes w^n \tag{7}$$

The final feature maps z_n of keypoint n is predicted from the combined feature maps through 1×1 convolution across feature maps in Eq. (7).

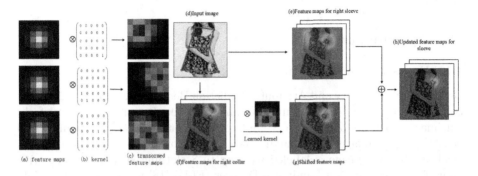

Fig. 4. (a)–(c) show that feature maps can be shifted through convolution with kernels. (d)–(h) show an example of updating feature maps by passing information between keypoints.

Information Passing. In previous works, messages could be passed by distance transfer [7,21] and CRF [4,32]. RNN also passes information at the feature level [25]. It is different from ours mainly in the way of sharing weights. RNN shares feature channels at different time steps and it requires the transfer matrix between features of successive time steps to be shared among all the time steps. Chu et al. [3] showed that under a convolutional neural network, messages can be passed between feature maps through the introduced geometrical transform kernels. We also adopt this messages passing method to enhance the features learned at each keypoint. In our model, clothing keypoints have their own feature channels and the geometrical transform kernels are not shared. This is because feature channels for each keypoint have different semantic meanings and the relationships between feature maps of neighbor keypoint are part specific.

Figure 4 (a)–(c) shows that convolution with asymmetric kernels could geometrically shift the feature responses. (a) is a feature map assuming Gaussian distribution. (b) are different kernels for illustration. (c) are the transformed feature maps after convolution. The feature map has been shifted towards different directions and sum up to different values.

In order to illustrate the process of information passing, an example is shown in Fig. 4 (d)–(h). Given an input image in (d), its feature maps for sleeve and collar are shown in (e) and (f). One of the collar feature maps has high response. One expects to use high response collar feature maps to reduce false alarms and enhance the responses on the right sleeve. It is not suitable to directly add both feature maps, since there is a spatial mismatch between the two keypoints. Instead, we first shift right collar feature maps towards the right sleeve through the geometrical transform kernels and then add the transformed feature maps to right sleeve. The refined feature maps in (h) have much better prediction. Since each feature map captures detailed structure information of the keypoint, the relative spatial distribution between the two maps is stable and the kernel can be easily learned.

4 Experiments

4.1 Datasets and Evaluation

DeepFashion: Category and Attribute Prediction Benchmark (DeepFashion) [16] is a large-scale visual fashion understanding dataset. It contains 289,222 fashion images with annotations of 8 kinds of keypoints, 46 categories and 1,000 attributes. Each image has a bounding box for the clothing. For fashion keypoints localization, each image is labeled with up to 8 clothing keypoints along with their visibilities. Fashion Landmark Dataset (FLD) [18] is a clothing keypoints dataset with more diverse variations, which contains 123,016 images annotated at most 8 keypoints and bounding boxes per image. Normalized Error (NE) metric [18] is adopted for evaluation. NE refers to the $\ell 2$ distance between predicted keypoints and groundtruth in the normalized coordinate space (i.e., normalized with respect to the width/height of the image).

Table 1. Quantitative results for clothing keypoints localization on the DeepFashion-C dataset [16] with Normalized Error (NE). Lower values are better. The best scores are marked in **bold**.

DeepFashion									
Method	L.Collar	R.Collar	L.Sleeve	R.Sleeve	L.Waistline	R.Waistline	L.Hem	R.Hem	Avg.
FashionNet [16]	0.0854	0.0902	0.0973	0.0935	0.0854	0.0845	0.0812	0.0823	0.0872
DFA [18]	0.0628	0.0638	0.0658	0.0621	0.0726	0.0702	0.0658	0.0663	0.0660
DLAN [30]	0.0570	0.0611	0.0672	0.0647	0.0703	0.0694	0.0624	0.0627	0.0643
BCRNNs [25]	0.0415	0.0404	0.0496	0.0449	0.0502	0.0523	0.0537	0.0551	0.0484
Ours	**0.0316**	**0.0330**	**0.0428**	**0.0442**	**0.0378**	**0.0369**	**0.0454**	**0.0466**	**0.0398**

Table 2. Quantitative results for clothing keypoints localization on the FLD dataset [18] with Normalized Error (NE). Lower values are better. The best scores are marked in **bold**.

FLD									
Method	L.Collar	R.Collar	L.Sleeve	R.Sleeve	L.Waistline	R.Waistline	L.Hem	R.Hem	Avg.
FashionNet [16]	0.0781	0.0803	0.0975	0.0923	0.0874	0.0821	0.0802	0.0893	0.0859
DFA [18]	0.0480	0.0480	0.0910	0.0890	-	-	0.0710	0.0720	0.0680
DLAN [30]	0.0531	0.0547	0.0705	0.0735	0.0752	0.0748	0.0693	0.0675	0.0672
BCRNNs [25]	0.0463	0.0471	**0.0627**	0.0614	0.0635	0.0692	0.0635	0.0527	0.0583
Ours	**0.0420**	**0.0386**	0.0675	**0.0609**	**0.0535**	**0.0446**	**0.0571**	**0.0491**	**0.0517**

4.2 Experimental Details and Results

Experimental Details. We follow the dataset split in DeepFashion [16,25] for training and testing. More specifically, 209,222 fashion images are used for training, 40,000 images are used for validation and remaining 40,000 images are for testing. Follow the protocol in FLD [18], 83,033 images and 19,992 fashion images are used for training and validating, 19,991 images are used for testing. We crop each image using ground truth bounding box and resize the cropped image to 224 × 224. All the training data are augmented by scaling, rotation, and flipping. We use the batch size of 50 images on 4 GTX 2080Ti GPUs. And we use Adam to optimize the loss function, the initial learning rate is set to 1e−3. On FLD, we linearly drop the learning rate by a factor of 10 every 20 epochs. On DeepFashion, we linearly decrease the learning rate by a factor of 10 every 10 epochs. We set the Mean Squared Error (MSE) equation as an objective function between the final predicted heatmaps and ground-truth.

Experimental Results. We conduct experiments on two large datasets and compare results of the proposed network with the state-of-the-art methods [16,18,25,30]. Our proposed network outperforms all the competitors at 0.0398 on DeepFashion and consistently outperforms other competitors on all of the clothing keypoints, as shown in Table 1. Meanwhile, we report the comparison results on the FLD dataset in Table 2. Our model again achieves state-of-the-art at 0.0517. It is hard to discriminate between waistlines and hems keypoints which have the largest error rate in other methods. Our proposed model achieves performance improvements in localization waistlines and hems keypoints. From these results, it is proved that our network learns more advanced feature representations for clothing keypoints localization with the aid of the proposed SFLM.

Fig. 5. Visual results for clothing keypoints localization, red and blue circles indicate ground-truth and predicted keypoints, respectively.

We also visualize clothing keypoints localization results in Fig. 5. We can see that the proposed model discriminates right and left-side keypoints even in the back-view and side-view. For complex background, diverse clothing styles and pose, multiple scales and views, our model succeed to predict correct clothing keypoints. Benefiting from modeling spatial and symmetrical relations of keypoints by a tree structure, SFLM can mine semantic coherency of structure and enhance the semantic correlations and constrains among keypoints.

5   Conclusion

In this paper, we propose a clothing keypoints localization network with a structured feature learning model named SFLM. The bi-directional tree structure is designed to capture more spatial details and structure features, which contributes to making more accurate and precise keypoints localization. The method of information transmission can be realized through a geometric transformation kernel. Experimental results on two public datasets show that this model significantly improves feature learning. Compared with recent methods, our model has achieved state-of-the-art performances on Deepfashion and FLD fashion datasets. In future work, we hope to design better information transmission methods and introduce an attention mechanism to better learn the information among keypoints on the feature layer.

Acknowledgment. This work is supported by National Natural Science Foundation of China (No. 61170093).

References

1. Andriluka, M., Pishchulin, L., Gehler, P., Schiele, B.: 2D human pose estimation: new benchmark and state of the art analysis. In: 2014 IEEE Conference on Computer Vision and Pattern Recognition, pp. 3686–3693 (2014)
2. Chen, Y., Wang, Z., Peng, Y., Zhang, Z., Yu, G., Sun, J.: Cascaded pyramid network for multi-person pose estimation (2018)
3. Chu, X., Ouyang, W., Li, H., Wang, X.: Structured feature learning for pose estimation. In: 2016 IEEE Conference on Computer Vision and Pattern Recognition (CVPR), pp. 4715–4723 (2016)
4. Chu, X., Ouyang, W., Li, H., Wang, X.: CRF-CNN: modeling structured information in human pose estimation. In: Proceedings of the 30th International Conference on Neural Information Processing Systems, NIPS 2016, Red Hook, NY, USA, pp. 316–324. Curran Associates Inc. (2016)
5. Corbière, C., Ben-Younes, H., Ramé, A., Ollion, C.: Leveraging weakly annotated data for fashion image retrieval and label prediction. In: 2017 IEEE International Conference on Computer Vision Workshops (ICCVW), pp. 2268–2274 (2017)
6. Ge, Y., Zhang, R., Wang, X., Tang, X., Luo, P.: Deepfashion2: a versatile benchmark for detection, pose estimation, segmentation and re-identification of clothing images. In: 2019 IEEE/CVF Conference on Computer Vision and Pattern Recognition (CVPR), pp. 5332–5340 (2019)

7. Girshick, R.B., Iandola, F.N., Darrell, T., Malik, J.: Deformable part models are convolutional neural networks. In: 2015 IEEE Conference on Computer Vision and Pattern Recognition (CVPR), pp. 437–446 (2015)
8. Gong, K., Liang, X., Zhang, D., Shen, X., Lin, L.: Look into person: self-supervised structure-sensitive learning and a new benchmark for human parsing. In: The IEEE Conference on Computer Vision and Pattern Recognition (CVPR), July 2017
9. He, K., Zhang, X., Ren, S., Sun, J.: Deep residual learning for image recognition. In: 2016 IEEE Conference on Computer Vision and Pattern Recognition (CVPR), pp. 770–778 (2016)
10. Huang, G., Liu, Z., van der Maaten, L., Weinberger, K.Q.: Densely connected convolutional networks. In: Proceedings of the IEEE Conference on Computer Vision and Pattern Recognition (2017)
11. Huang, J., Feris, R., Chen, Q., Yan, S.: Cross-domain image retrieval with a dual attribute-aware ranking network. In: 2015 IEEE International Conference on Computer Vision (ICCV), pp. 1062–1070 (2015)
12. Krizhevsky, A., Sutskever, I., Hinton, G.E.: ImageNet classification with deep convolutional neural networks. Commun. ACM **60**(6), 84–90 (2017). https://doi.org/10.1145/3065386
13. Li, Y., Ouyang, W., Zhou, B., Cui, Y., Shi, J., Wang, X.: Factorizable net: an efficient subgraph-based framework for scene graph generation. ArXiv abs/1806.11538 (2018)
14. Liang, X., Lin, L., Yang, W., Luo, P., Huang, J., Yan, S.: Clothes co-parsing via joint image segmentation and labeling with application to clothing retrieval. IEEE Trans. Multimed. **18**(6), 1175–1186 (2016)
15. Liu, J., Lu, H.: Deep fashion analysis with feature map upsampling and landmark-driven attention. In: Leal-Taixé, L., Roth, S. (eds.) ECCV 2018. LNCS, vol. 11131, pp. 30–36. Springer, Cham (2019). https://doi.org/10.1007/978-3-030-11015-4_4
16. Liu, Z., Luo, P., Qiu, S., Wang, X., Tang, X.: DeepFashion: powering robust clothes recognition and retrieval with rich annotations. In: 2016 IEEE Conference on Computer Vision and Pattern Recognition (CVPR), pp. 1096–1104 (2016)
17. Liu, Z., Luo, P., Wang, X., Tang, X.: Deep learning face attributes in the wild. In: 2015 IEEE International Conference on Computer Vision (ICCV), pp. 3730–3738 (2015)
18. Liu, Z., Yan, S., Luo, P., Wang, X., Tang, X.: Fashion landmark detection in the wild. ArXiv abs/1608.03049 (2016)
19. Newell, A., Yang, K., Deng, J.: Stacked hourglass networks for human pose estimation. In: Leibe, B., Matas, J., Sebe, N., Welling, M. (eds.) ECCV 2016. LNCS, vol. 9912, pp. 483–499. Springer, Cham (2016). https://doi.org/10.1007/978-3-319-46484-8_29
20. Ouyang, W., Chu, X., Wang, X.: Multi-source deep learning for human pose estimation. In: 2014 IEEE Conference on Computer Vision and Pattern Recognition, pp. 2337–2344 (2014)
21. Ouyang, W., et al.: DeepID-Net: deformable deep convolutional neural networks for object detection. IEEE Trans. Pattern Anal. Mach. Intell. **39**(7), 1320–1334 (2017). https://doi.org/10.1109/tpami.2016.2587642. https://doi.org/10.1109/TPAMI.2016.2587642
22. Simonyan, K., Zisserman, A.: Very deep convolutional networks for large-scale image recognition. CoRR abs/1409.1556 (2015)
23. Szegedy, C., et al.: Going deeper with convolutions. In: 2015 IEEE Conference on Computer Vision and Pattern Recognition (CVPR), pp. 1–9 (2015)

24. Wang, F., Li, Y.: Beyond physical connections: tree models in human pose estimation. In: 2013 IEEE Conference on Computer Vision and Pattern Recognition, pp. 596–603 (2013)
25. Wang, W., Xu, Y., Shen, J., Zhu, S.C.: Attentive fashion grammar network for fashion landmark detection and clothing category classification. In: 2018 IEEE/CVF Conference on Computer Vision and Pattern Recognition, pp. 4271–4280 (2018)
26. Wang, Y., Tran, D., Liao, Z.: Learning hierarchical poselets for human parsing. In: CVPR 2011, pp. 1705–1712 (2011)
27. Wei, S.E., Ramakrishna, V., Kanade, T., Sheikh, Y.: Convolutional pose machines. In: CVPR (2016)
28. Yamaguchi, K., Kiapour, M.H., Ortiz, L.E., Berg, T.L.: Parsing clothing in fashion photographs. In: 2012 IEEE Conference on Computer Vision and Pattern Recognition, pp. 3570–3577 (2012)
29. Yamaguchi, K., Kiapour, M.H., Ortiz, L.E., Berg, T.L.: Retrieving similar styles to parse clothing. IEEE Trans. Pattern Anal. Mach. Intell. **37**(5), 1028–1040 (2015)
30. Yan, S., Liu, Z., Luo, P., Qiu, S., Wang, X., Tang, X.: Unconstrained fashion landmark detection via hierarchical recurrent transformer networks. In: Proceedings of the 25th ACM International Conference on Multimedia, MM 2017, New York, NY, USA, pp. 172–180. Association for Computing Machinery (2017). https://doi.org/10.1145/3123266.3123276
31. Yang, Y., Ramanan, D.: Articulated human detection with flexible mixtures of parts. IEEE Trans. Pattern Anal. Mach. Intell. **35**(12), 2878–2890 (2013)
32. Zheng, S., et al.: Conditional random fields as recurrent neural networks. In: 2015 IEEE International Conference on Computer Vision (ICCV), pp. 1529–1537 (2015)
33. Zhu, X., Ramanan, D.: Face detection, pose estimation, and landmark localization in the wild. In: 2012 IEEE Conference on Computer Vision and Pattern Recognition, pp. 2879–2886 (2012)
34. Zou, X., Kong, X., Wong, W., Wang, C., Liu, Y., Cao, Y.: FashionAI: a hierarchical dataset for fashion understanding. In: 2019 IEEE/CVF Conference on Computer Vision and Pattern Recognition Workshops (CVPRW), pp. 296–304 (2019)

Automatic Pose Quality Assessment for Adaptive Human Pose Refinement

Gang Chu, Chi Xie, and Shuang Liang[✉]

School of Software Engineering, Tongji University, Shanghai, China
{chugang,chixie,shuangliang}@tongji.edu.cn

Abstract. Multi-person pose estimation from a 2D image is an essential technique for many computer vision tasks. Although the development of deep convolutional neural networks has brought large improvement to human pose estimation, some complex cases are still challenging to even state-of-the-art approaches. The forms of people in the images are diverse. The quality of estimated poses is difficult to guarantee. Estimated poses usually cannot be directly used in practical application scenarios. In this paper, we propose a pose quality assessment model and an adaptive human pose refinement method. The pose quality assessment model can measure per-joint pose quality with a quality score and select qualified estimated poses. The adaptive pose refinement method can handle each estimated pose respectively, until reaching a certain standard. Our experiments show the effectiveness of the pose quality assessment model and confirm that adaptive pose refinement method performs better than generally refining all poses once. Our adaptive pose refinement method reaches state-of-the-art performance.

Keywords: Human pose estimation · Pose quality assessment · Adaptive pose refinement

1 Introduction

Multi-person pose estimation is the fundamental for many computer vision tasks such as human action recognition, human-computer interaction and video surveillance analyses. It aims to detect precise locations of each person's body joints like shoulder, hip and ankle in a single RGB image. Recent years, the continued development of deep convolutional neural network methods [13,17,20,21] achieves noticeable progress on human pose estimation performance. However, there still remain a lot of challenges like person-person overlapping, person-object occlusion, human scale difference and background cluttering.

After analyzing results of some state-of-the-art approaches, we find that the quality of output poses varies greatly when human scale, human action type or image background complexity is different. Take the approach of Xiao et al. [21] with ResNet-50 [7] backbone as an example, some estimated human poses of MSCOCO validation dataset [10] are shown in Fig. 1. When there are crowds

© Springer Nature Switzerland AG 2021
J. Lokoč et al. (Eds.): MMM 2021, LNCS 12572, pp. 641–652, 2021.
https://doi.org/10.1007/978-3-030-67832-6_52

Fig. 1. Some multi-person pose estimation results of [21] on MSCOCO validation dataset. Poses IoU above 0.9 are colored with green and poses IoU below 0.6 are colored with red. (Color figure online)

in the image or the background is messy, even the pose quality of similar scale people in the same image may vary a lot. 277 images contain estimation results with both poses IoU (Intersection of Union) above 0.9 and poses IoU below 0.6, accounting for more than 10% of MSCOCO validation dataset.

Furthermore, we calculate the IoU distribution of all estimated poses. Although about 61.4% estimated poses' IoU reaches 0.9, there are still more than 7% poses with IoU below 0.6, as shown in Fig. 2. Low quality poses may contain incorrect predictions like joint position jitter and joints missing. However, for many practical application scenes such as intelligent video surveillance, the captured human poses should have enough confidence to distinguish whether a person violates certain rules. Current deep learning approaches usually cannot guarantee their estimated poses' quality, and the usage of human pose estimation technique in realistic scenarios is very limited.

Meanwhile, existing human pose estimation or pose refinement approaches usually handle all input data with the same network and a general workflow. These approaches may be not suitable for all samples, especially the complex ones. We need a more flexible workflow to adapt the diversity of input images.

In real life situations, we can apply review mechanism to solve the problem of standardizing output. In this work, we introduce a network reviewer to supervise output results. Our contributions can be summarized as follows:

- We propose a pose quality assessment model to automatically get per-joint quality of input poses. This starts the exploration of standardizing output pose quality. Human pose estimation technique can play its role in more practical application scenarios.

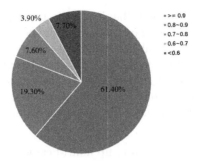

Fig. 2. IoU distribution of poses estimated by [21] on MSCOCO validation dataset.

- We propose an adaptive pose refinement method to iteratively refine each estimated pose respectively. Estimated poses with various errors can be refined to their best conditions with flexible time and computation cost.
- The proposed pose quality assessment model can effectively distinguish predicted joint quality and select output poses which reach our standard. The proposed adaptive pose refinement method performs better than generally refining all poses once and reaches state-of-the-art performance.

2   Related Works

2.1   General Human Pose Estimation Methods

Recent years, with the development of deep convolutional neural networks, great progress has been made in multi-person pose estimation. In general, these methods can be divided into two groups: top-down methods and bottom-up methods. Top-down methods usually have better accuracy. However, they rely heavily on body box detecting result accuracy and the inference time will increase significantly when the number of people in the image increases. Bottom-up methods' inference time is usually not affected by the number of people, but these methods need an extra step to assign detected joints to each human body. Meanwhile, the quality of bottom-up methods' output poses usually has greater difference.

Top-Down Methods. Top-down methods' person boxes are pre-generated. The main effort is to estimate human pose from cropped single person image part. Previous single person pose estimation methods [13,20] contribute mainly on the improvement of backbone architecture. Recent years, Chu et al. [5] enhance the stacked hourglass network [13] by introducing a multi-context attention mechanism. Sun et al. [18] propose a method to combine heatmap-based method and regression method. Sun et al. [19] introduce human structure by adding bone loss which improves the performance of regression methods.

For typical top-down multi-person pose estimation methods, Chen et al. [4] propose cascaded pyramid network which contains Globalnet that is responsible for the detection of easier human keypoints and Refinenet that solves the detection of more difficult or invisible keypoints through higher-level semantic information. Xiao et al. [21] propose a very simple network architecture with a ResNet [7] backbone and several deconvolution layers to generate the keypoint heatmap. This method acquires excellent results. Continuously, Sun et al. [17] propose HRNet to maintain high-resolution feature representation. HRNet performs multi-scale feature fusion through repeated cross parallel convolutions, which further improves the results of human pose estimation.

Bottom-Up Methods. For bottom-up multi-person pose estimation methods [2,9,15], the progress mainly comes from two aspects: human body joint detection network and detected joint assignment algorithm. Cao et al. [2] propose part affinity fields (PAF), a 2D vector to record limb position and direction, to connect joints by greedy algorithm. Papandreou et al. [15] use a full convolutional network to first find all keypoints of each person in the image then predict the relative position relationships of all keypoint pairs. Kreiss et al. [9] propose Pif-Paf which added PIF to [2]. The PIF information is used to determine whether the position on the picture is the position of a human joint.

Besides, Kocabas et al. [8] propose RPN(Pose Residual Network) to combine bottom-up and top-down methods. This method still needs to detect person boxes so the efficiency isn't improved. Nie et al. [14] propose a single-stage method for bottom-up multi-person pose estimation which achieves end-to-end training. Absolute position of each joint is transformed to a vector form a root joint. The root joint of each human body can be directly find from the heatmap and other joints' positions can be calculated by learned joint-joint vectors.

2.2   Human Pose Refinement Methods

There are many methods [3,4,13,20] trying to refine the estimated poses during learning. Newell et al. [13], Wei et al. [20], and Chen et al. [4] adopt a multi-stage network architecture to refine the pose estimation results of the previous stage at each stage via end-to-end learning. Carreria et al. [3] learn the error in each iteration and transform the error into the input pose of next iteration. The estimation and refinement module of these methods are all combined into a single model. The refinement modules of these methods cannot be separated from the whole model or directly applied to any existing poses.

Recently, while there are still difficult cases for current state-of-the-art methods, some independent pose refinement methods [6,12] are proposed for estimated pose from any existing approaches. Fieraru et al. [6] propose a simple post-processing network which learns new heatmap and offset from old heatmap and input image to refine the estimated poses of any other methods. Furthermore, Moon et al. [12] propose a coarse-to-fine network to refine estimated human poses. These methods just generally do pose refining once for all estimated poses and still cannot guarantee the quality of refined poses.

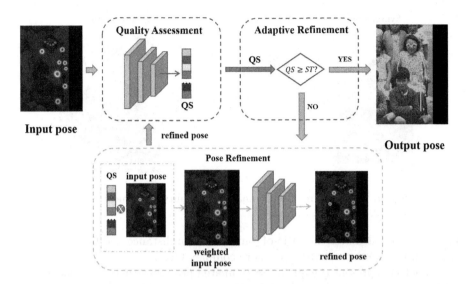

Fig. 3. Adaptive human pose refinement algorithm workflow. Given an estimated body pose and the original RGB image, firstly we get the quality score of each joint through the pose assessment network. While the quality score doesn't reach our threshold, new input data will be generated with the input pose, quality score and the original image. Then the new input data will be sent to our pose refinement network and the refined pose will get a new quality score.

3   Method

3.1   Human Pose Quality Assessment Model

To solve the problem of standardizing estimated pose quality, we propose a human pose quality assessment model as an automatic-reviewer. The model takes synthesized error pose heatmap and corresponding image area as input. Directly regression method is chosen to infer the quality score QS for each joint of the input pose. The model architecture is shown in Fig. 4.

Input Data. The input data of our pose quality assessment network is the original person image I concatenated with the input pose pseudo-heatmap H. To generate the synthesized pseudo-heatmap, we use Gaussian heatmap representation as follows:

$$H_j(x,y) = e^{-\frac{(x-x_j)^2+(y-y_j)^2}{2\sigma_j^2}} \tag{1}$$

where $H_j(x,y)$ is the value of position (x,y) on j'th joint's pseudo-heatmap, (x_j, y_j) is the position of j'th joint and σ_j is the scale of j'th body part.

Quality Score. The key to our pose quality assessment model is a proper metric to define per-joint pose quality. MPII dataset [1] uses PCKh as the evaluation

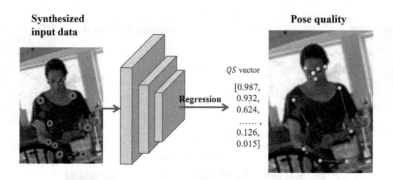

Fig. 4. Architecture of our human pose quality assessment model.

metric which calculates the ratio of joint deviation distance and body head size, while MSCOCO dataset [10] uses more complex OKS.

To better represent the quality of estimated poses, we choose to generate our quality score using the form like OKS. Our target quality score QS of each input body joint j is calculated as follows:

$$QS_j = e^{-\frac{d_j^2}{cs\sigma_j^2}} \tag{2}$$

where d is the Euclidean distance between j'th joint's ground truth position and predicted position, σ is the scale of j'th body part, s is the area of corresponding person box and c is a constant to control QS change rate which set to 2 here.

The QS value ranges from 0 to 1 and predicted joint with smaller error has higher QS. Compared with PCKh, QS changes slower when the deviation is very small or very large. For a medium deviation, QS changes faster and such distance is usually for judging the predicted joint position's correctness. This means that QS value range of obviously correct or incorrect predictions is small. There is larger value range of predicted joints not easy to distinguish.

Loss Function. According to our statics, there are much more high quality estimated joints. To solve the imbalance, we use a weighted L1 loss. The weight of j'th joint is defined as follows:

$$w_j = \begin{cases} \frac{\sum (QS^{gt}>T)}{N}, & \text{if } QS_j^{gt} \le T \\ \frac{\sum (QS^{gt}\le T)}{N}, & \text{if } QS_j^{gt} > T \end{cases} \tag{3}$$

where N is the number of human body joints and T is a threshold of QS and set to 0.75 here.

3.2   Base Human Pose Refinement Model

Our base human pose refinement model also takes a lightweight backbone. We use direct regression method to get the refined joint position coordinates and $L1$

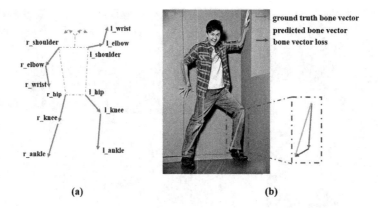

Fig. 5. (a) Bone vectors. The bone vectors are shoulder-elbow, elbow-wrist, hip-knee and knee-ankle. (b) Bone vector loss. The bone vector loss is also a vector pointing from the ground truth bone vector to the predicted bone vector.

loss as base loss function L_J as follows:

$$L_J = \sum_j ||J_j^{pred} - J_j^{gt}||_1 * v_j \tag{4}$$

where J_j is the j'th joint's position coordinate and v_j is j'th joint's visibility.

To better refine error poses, we add bone vector loss for limb joints including ankles, knees, elbows and wrists to make use of human structure. The bone vectors and bone vector loss are shown in Fig. 5. Let $J = \{J_k | k = 1, 2, ..., n\}$ for $n = 8$ limb joints' positions, $p(k)$ for k'th joint's father joint index, the bone vector B_k is defined as follows:

$$B_k = J_k - J_{p(k)} = (x_k - x_{p(k)}, y_k - y_{p(k)}) \tag{5}$$

The bone vector loss is defined using $L1$ form as follows:

$$L_B = \sum_k ||B_k^{pred} - B_k^{gt}||_1 * v_k v_{p(k)} \tag{6}$$

3.3 Adaptive Human Pose Refinement

Based on our human pose quality assessment model and base pose refinement model, we propose an adaptive human pose refinement algorithm. The workflow of our adaptive refinement algorithm is shown in Fig. 3.

Firstly, we set a quality score output standard ST and a maximum refining time MR. Each input pose will get a quality score QS. If the QS reaches ST, the input pose will output directly. Otherwise, new input pose will be synthesized by original input pose and obtained quality score. Then the new input data will be sent to the refinement model. New refined pose will be reviewed again and

Fig. 6. Per-joint quality score visualization of our pose quality assessment model. Body joints are colored with green if $QS > 0.75$, red if $QS < 0.5$ or yellow otherwise. (Color figure online)

get a new QS. This refinement and assessment step loops until new QS reaches ST or total refine time RT reaches MR.

To make full use of our per-joint pose quality assessment result and get information more from high quality input joints, we take an adaptive input pseudo-heatmap synthesizing method. Each joint's QS will generate a weight for this joint's heatmap. The adaptive pseudo-heatmap H' is calculated as follows:

$$H'_j(x,y) = e^{-\frac{(x-x_j)^2+(y-y_j)^2}{2\sigma_j^2}} * e^{-\beta QS_j} \tag{7}$$

where β is a constant to control the range of QS weight and set to 5 here.

4   Experiments

In this section, we evaluate our proposed approaches and perform visualization results of our methods. We use ShufffleNetV2 [11] as the backbone for both our pose quality assessment model and base pose refinement model on PyTorch [16]. While training, for both networks, Adam optimizer is used. The base learning rate is $5e^{-4}$ and drops to $1e^{-4}$ at 60 epochs, $2e^{-5}$ at 100 epochs and $4e^{-6}$ at 150 epochs. There are 200 epochs in total for both two models. We conduct all the experiments on two Tesla K80 GPUs.

4.1   Data Preprocessing

The proposed human pose assessment network and base pose refinement network are both trained and evaluated on MSCOCO keypoint detection dataset [10]. To be independent of different first-stage human pose estimation approaches, we use

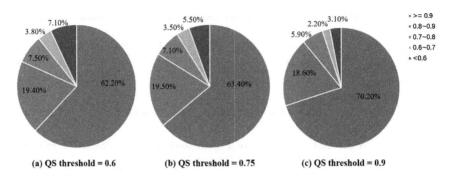

Fig. 7. Selected poses IoU distributions with different thresholds. Our pose quality assessment model can effectively select high quality poses.

Table 1. Average precisions of our human pose quality assessment model on synthesized poses of MSCOCO validation dataset. A predicted joint position is considered to be correct if it's QS reaches the threshold.

Threshold	Shoulders	Elbows	Wrists	Hips	Knees	Ankles	Mean
0.5	96.4	95.0	93.3	94.8	94.0	95.5	95.7
0.69	98.0	98.3	97.2	98.6	97.4	97.7	98.2
0.75	98.3	98.7	97.5	99.1	98.0	98.2	98.5

synthesized error poses to train our networks instead of real estimated poses. The poses are synthesized by the same method as Moon et al. [12]. We select three groups of hyper parameters randomly to increase pose quality diversity.

4.2 Human Pose Quality Assessment

We evaluate our pose quality assessment model on synthesized error poses of MSCOCO validation dataset. The evaluation result is shown in Table 1. We take a QS threshold T to judge whether the synthesized joint position is acceptable. When $QS > T$, the joint position is considered qualified. From Table 1 we can see that pose quality assessment accuracy reaches 95.7% with $T = 0.5$. When T increases, the accuracy will further increase. Some visualization results of error pose per-joint quality assessment are shown in Fig. 6.

Besides, to verify that the pose quality assessment model can control output pose quality of existing first-stage human pose estimation approaches, we evaluate our pose quality assessment model on estimated poses by Xiao et al. [21] with backbone ResNet-50. We set a group of output standards using mean QS threshold to select qualified poses. The selected poses' IoU distributions are shown in Fig. 7. With QS selection, the ratio of high quality output poses increases obviously. When the QS threshold is 0.9, ratio of poses $IoU > 0.9$ increases 8.8% and ratio of poses $IoU < 0.6$ decreases to 3.1%. Meanwhile, the number of images containing both poses $IoU > 0.9$ and poses $IoU < 0.6$ drops from 227 to 113.

Table 2. Pose refinement results on synthesized data of MSCOCO validation dataset.

Type	AP	$AP_{:50}$	$AP_{:75}$	AP_M	AP_L	AR	$AR_{:50}$	$AR_{:75}$	AR_M	AR_L
Synthesized pose	43.8	90.7	34.6	48.9	39.8	55.0	94.9	55.7	54.4	55.8
+ Base refine(L_J)	60.5	92.1	67.9	64.1	57.6	71.6	95.8	80.7	70.7	73.0
+ Base refine($L_J + L_B$)	61.7	93.4	69.4	65.2	58.9	72.6	96.2	81.7	71.8	74.0
+ Adaptive refine	**62.9**	**93.8**	**70.7**	**66.3**	**60.2**	**73.6**	**96.7**	**82.4**	**73.0**	**74.6**

Table 3. Pose refinement results on real estimated poses of MSCOCO validation dataset by Xiao et al. [21] with backbone ResNet-50.

Method	AP	$AP_{:50}$	$AP_{:75}$	AP_M	AP_L	AR	$AR_{:50}$	$AR_{:75}$	AR_M	AR_L
Simple (ResNet-50) [21]	68.6	89.1	75.5	66.9	71.8	**79.3**	94.0	**85.3**	75.9	84.5
+ PoseFix [12]	**72.5**	90.5	**79.6**	**68.9**	79.0	78.0	**94.1**	84.4	73.4	84.1
+ Ours (Base)	70.3	89.6	77.3	67.9	75.7	79.2	94.0	84.5	75.8	84.4
+ Ours (Adaptive)	72.1	**90.6**	78.6	68.4	77.9	**79.3**	**94.1**	84.9	**75.9**	**84.8**

4.3   Human Pose Refinement

We evaluate our base pose refinement model and adaptive pose refinement algorithm on both synthesized error poses and real estimated poses by Xiao et al. [21] on MSCOCO validation dataset. The refinement results are shown in Table 2 and Table 3. After experiments on ST ranging from 0.6 to 0.9 and MR ranging from 2 to 5, we set ST to be 0.85 and MR to be 3 for the final experiments. Some adaptively refined pose visualization results are shown in Fig. 8.

From Table 2 we can see that our base pose refinement model can obviously improve the quality of synthesized error poses. The results are better if adding our bone vector loss. Furthermore, with our adaptive refinement algorithm, the final results' AP can increase another 1.2%.

Fig. 8. Adaptive pose refinement results visualization of MSCOCO validation dataset.

For the refinement results of real estimated poses by Xiao et al. [21] with backbone ResNet-50, as shown in Table 3, though our lightweight base pose refinement model cannot improve the poses as much as Moon et al. [12] because of different backbones (ShufffleNetV2 VS ResNet-50), our adaptive algorithm can make up for this and reaches the state-of-the-art performance. The final refinement time of our adaptive pose refinement algorithm is 1.62 times persample. Our adaptive pose refinement algorithm can effectively improve base refinement model performance with flexible time and computation cost.

5   Conclusion and Discussion

In this paper, we propose a human pose quality assessment model to automatically get estimated poses' per-joint quality and an adaptive pose refinement method to refine each estimated pose respectively. With them, standardizing the quality of output poses becomes possible and human pose estimation technique can be used in more practical application scenarios, while estimated error poses can be refined to their best conditions with minimized time and computation cost. The performance can be further improved by exploring more suitable backbone networks and detailed algorithms.

Acknowledgments. This work is supported by Natural Science Foundation of Shanghai (No.19ZR1461200, No.20ZR1473500) and National Natural Science Foundation of China (No.62076183, No.61976159). The authors would also like to thank the anonymous reviewers for their valuable comments and suggestions.

References

1. Andriluka, M., Pishchulin, L., Gehler, P., Schiele, B.: 2D human pose estimation: New benchmark and state of the art analysis. In: Proceedings of the IEEE Conference on Computer Vision and Pattern Recognition, pp. 3686–3693 (2014)
2. Cao, Z., Simon, T., Wei, S.E., Sheikh, Y.: Realtime multi-person 2D pose estimation using part affinity fields. In: Proceedings of the IEEE Conference on Computer Vision and Pattern Recognition, pp. 7291–7299 (2017)
3. Carreira, J., Agrawal, P., Fragkiadaki, K., Malik, J.: Human pose estimation with iterative error feedback. In: Proceedings of the IEEE Conference on Computer Vision and Pattern Recognition, pp. 4733–4742 (2016)
4. Chen, Y., Wang, Z., Peng, Y., Zhang, Z., Yu, G., Sun, J.: Cascaded pyramid network for multi-person pose estimation. In: Proceedings of the IEEE Conference on Computer Vision and Pattern Recognition, pp. 7103–7112 (2018)
5. Chu, X., Yang, W., Ouyang, W., Ma, C., Yuille, A.L., Wang, X.: Multi-context attention for human pose estimation. In: Proceedings of the IEEE Conference on Computer Vision and Pattern Recognition, pp. 1831–1840 (2017)
6. Fieraru, M., Khoreva, A., Pishchulin, L., Schiele, B.: Learning to refine human pose estimation. In: Proceedings of the IEEE Conference on Computer Vision and Pattern Recognition Workshops, pp. 205–214 (2018)

7. He, K., Zhang, X., Ren, S., Sun, J.: Deep residual learning for image recognition. In: Proceedings of the IEEE Conference on Computer Vision and Pattern Recognition, pp. 770–778 (2016)
8. Kocabas, M., Karagoz, S., Akbas, E.: Multiposenet: fast multi-person pose estimation using pose residual network. In: Proceedings of the European Conference on Computer Vision, pp. 417–433 (2018)
9. Kreiss, S., Bertoni, L., Alahi, A.: Pifpaf: composite fields for human pose estimation. In: Proceedings of the IEEE Conference on Computer Vision and Pattern Recognition, pp. 11977–11986 (2019)
10. Lin, T.Y., et al.: Microsoft COCO: common objects in context. In: Fleet, D., Pajdla, T., Schiele, B., Tuytelaars, T. (eds.) ECCV 2014. LNCS, vol. 8693, pp. 740–755. Springer, Cham (2014). https://doi.org/10.1007/978-3-319-10602-1_48
11. Ma, N., Zhang, X., Zheng, H.T., Sun, J.: Shufflenet v2: practical guidelines for efficient cnn architecture design. In: Proceedings of the European Conference on Computer Vision, pp. 116–131 (2018)
12. Moon, G., Chang, J.Y., Lee, K.M.: Posefix: model-agnostic general human pose refinement network. In: Proceedings of the IEEE Conference on Computer Vision and Pattern Recognition, pp. 7773–7781 (2019)
13. Newell, A., Yang, K., Deng, J.: Stacked hourglass networks for human pose estimation. In: Leibe, B., Matas, J., Sebe, N., Welling, M. (eds.) ECCV 2016. LNCS, vol. 9912, pp. 483–499. Springer, Cham (2016). https://doi.org/10.1007/978-3-319-46484-8_29
14. Nie, X., Feng, J., Zhang, J., Yan, S.: Single-stage multi-person pose machines. In: Proceedings of the IEEE International Conference on Computer Vision, pp. 6951–6960 (2019)
15. Papandreou, G., Zhu, T., Chen, L.C., Gidaris, S., Tompson, J., Murphy, K.: Personlab: person pose estimation and instance segmentation with a bottom-up, part-based, geometric embedding model. In: Proceedings of the European Conference on Computer Vision, pp. 269–286 (2018)
16. Paszke, A., et al.: Pytorch: an imperative style, high-performance deep learning library. In: Advances in Neural Information Processing Systems, pp. 8026–8037 (2019)
17. Sun, K., Xiao, B., Liu, D., Wang, J.: Deep high-resolution representation learning for human pose estimation. In: Proceedings of the IEEE Conference on Computer Vision and Pattern Recognition, pp. 5693–5703 (2019)
18. Sun, X., Shang, J., Liang, S., Wei, Y.: Compositional human pose regression. In: Proceedings of the IEEE International Conference on Computer Vision, pp. 2602–2611 (2017)
19. Sun, X., Xiao, B., Wei, F., Liang, S., Wei, Y.: Integral human pose regression. In: Proceedings of the European Conference on Computer Vision, pp. 529–545 (2018)
20. Wei, S.E., Ramakrishna, V., Kanade, T., Sheikh, Y.: Convolutional pose machines. In: Proceedings of the IEEE Conference on Computer Vision and Pattern Recognition, pp. 4724–4732 (2016)
21. Xiao, B., Wu, H., Wei, Y.: Simple baselines for human pose estimation and tracking. In: Proceedings of the European Conference on Computer Vision, pp. 466–481 (2018)

Deep Attributed Network Embedding with Community Information

Li Xue[1,2], Wenbin Yao[1,2(✉)], Yamei Xia[1], and Xiaoyong Li[3]

¹ School of Computer Science, Beijing University of Posts
and Telecommunications, Beijing 100876, China
ymxia@bupt.edu.cn
² Beijing Key Laboratory of Intelligent Telecommunications Software
and Multimedia, Beijing University of Posts
and Telecommunications, Beijing 100876, China
³ School of Cyberspace Security, Beijing University of Posts and
Telecommunications, Beijing 100876, China

Abstract. Attributed Network Embedding (ANE) aims to learn low-dimensional representation for each node while preserving topological information and node attributes. ANE has attracted increasing attention due to its great value in network analysis such as node classification, link prediction, and node clustering. However, most existing ANE methods only focus on preserving attribute information and local structure, while ignoring the community information. Community information reveals an implicit relationship between vertices from a global view, which can be a supplement to local information and help improve the quality of embedding. So, those methods just produce sub-optimal results for failing to preserve community information. To address this issue, we propose a novel method named DNEC to exploit local structural information, node attributes, and community information simultaneously. A novel deep neural network is designed to preserve both local structure and node attributes. At the same time, we propose a community random walk method and incorporate triplet-loss to preserve the community information. We conduct extensive experiments on multiple real-world networks. The experimental results show the effectiveness of our proposed method.

Keywords: Graph structured data · Network embedding · Deep learning · Node classification

1 Introduction

Networks are important and ubiquitous structures in the real world, including social networks, citation networks, and communication networks. Network Embedding (NE) aims to map vertex into low-dimensional space and is valuable

National Nature Science Foundation of China (61672111) and the Joint Fund of NSFC-General Technology Fundamental Research (U1836215,U1536111).

J. Lokoč et al. (Eds.): MMM 2021, LNCS 12572, pp. 653–665, 2021.
https://doi.org/10.1007/978-3-030-67832-6_53

for many data-mining applications such as node classification, link prediction [1], visualization [2], and anomaly detection [3].

Inspired by the success of Word2vec [4], early works based on skip-gram [5] mainly focus on exploring network structure. Node2Vec [6] explores network structure by biased random walks. Line [7] designs two loss functions to preserve network structure. Those methods only concentrate on preserving the local structure, ignoring community information. CARE [8] adopts a community-aware random walk to preserve community information. COME [9] designs a novel community embedding framework. M-NMF [10] designs a loss function based on modularity to preserve community structure. However, those NE methods just concentrate on network structure and pay less attention to node attributes, which play an important role in many applications. So, those NE methods just consider plain network and are not suitable for attributed networks.

Thus, another line of works is proposed for attributed network embedding, such as TADW [11] and DANE [12]. TADW incorporates node attributes into the matrix factorization framework. DANE designs two autoencoders to preserve node attributes and network structure together. However, those ANE methods don't take community information into account. When the network is sparse and the attribute is noisy, utilizing community structure can greatly improve the quality of node representations.

In order to obtain node representation of high quality, we try to incorporate network structure, node attributes, and community structure into the ANE framework. We propose a novel framework, called DNEC, which preserves community structure. DNEC employs two embedding layers to compress network structure and attribute separately and generate structure representation and attribute representation. Structure representation and attribute representation are connected as the input of the shared encoder. The shared encoder will compress two different representations into the unified representations spaces. Dual decoder employs two traditional fully connected neural networks to reconstruct node attributes and structure of the network. To preserve community structure, we propose a biased random walk to construct community triplets to calculate triplet-loss. In summary, our main contributions can be summarized as follows:

(1) We design a novel ANE framework, which seamlessly integrates network structure, node attributes, and community structure into low-dimensional representation space.
(2) A biased random walk is proposed to construct community triplets and then calculate community triplet-loss.
(3) We evaluate and validate our method through three tasks: node classification, node clustering, and visualization. Experimental result demonstrate the effectiveness of our method.

2   Related Work

Some earlier works can be traced back to the graph embedding problem, such as Laplacian Eigenmaps and LPP [13], which utilizes manifold learning to capture structure proximity. Inspired by word2vec [4], Deepwalk [14] generates node sequences by truncating random walks and train skip-gram model to preserve structural proximity. Node2vec [8] introduces a biased random walk to explore network structure flexibly. Line [7] proposes an explicit objective function to preserve first-order proximity and second-order proximity. Deepwalk [14], Node2vec [6], and Line [7] are all based on shallow neural network that cannot preserve the non-linear structure of the network. SDNE [15] employs autoencoder to preserve first-order proximity, second-order proximity, and non-linear structure of the network simultaneously. DNGR [16] introduces a random-surfing model and directly construct positive pointwise mutual information matrix (PPMI) and employs stacked denoising autoencoder to extract feature. GraRep [17] calculates similarity matrices of the different order, factorize these matrices to retain representations of the different order. The above-mentioned works ignore community structure. CARE designs a community-aware random walk to generate node sequence and feed into skip-gram to preserve the local structure and community information. The M-NMF [10] adopts modular non-negative matrix factorization to retain the node's representation which preserves both the community structure and node's local structure simultaneously.

The above NE methods just explore the structure of networks. Thus, they are not suitable for attributed network containing rich semantic information that should be preserved to improve the quality of representations. State-of-the-art ANE models considering both node attributes and network structure have a better performance. TADW proves that deepwalk is equivalent to matrix factorization and incorporates text information into the matrix factorization framework to preserve node attributes. DANE utilizes two autoencoders to extract node attributes and network structure respectively. Attribute representation and structure representation are connected as the final representation. Tri-Dnr [18] incorporates network structure, node content, and node label into a unified framework to learn the representation of the node.

3   Problem Definition

We consider an attributed information network $G = (V, X, A)$, where $V = \{v_1, , , v_n\}$, $X = \{x_1, , , x_n\}$ and $A = \{a_1, , , a_n\}$ represent the node set, set of attribute vectors and set of adjacent vectors respectively. In detail, attribute vector x_i and adjacent vector a_i is associated with the node v_i. In case of unweighted networks, if v_i is connected to v_j, $a_{ij} = 1$, otherwise, $a_{ij} = 0$. In case of weighted networks, if v_i is connected to v_j, a_{ij} reflects how strongly two individual nodes are connected to each other, otherwise, $a_{ij} = 0$. x_i that holds l different attributes and each element x_{ij} represents whether node v_i contains the j-th attribute. We define a function $com(v_i)$. When $com(v_i) = c$, the vertex v_i belongs to community c. Attributed network consist of network structure and node attributes of vital significance. The aim of ANE is to learn the low-dimensional representation of each node, while preserving node attributes and network structure.

4   The Model

In Sect. 4.1, we firstly perform community detection on the whole graph. After community detection, each node in network is assigned to corresponding community. Then, we perform community random walk to construct community triplets. In Sect. 4.2, Deep Attribute Network Embedding (DNE) framework is designed to integrate network structure and attributes and map two information into the unified representations spaces. In Sect. 4.3, we use community triplets to calculate community triplet-loss and form the final model DNEC.

4.1   Construct Community Triplets

Firstly, we adopts infomap [19] to obtain community information. According to community information, we perform community random walk on the whole graph.

Community Detection: Adjacent matric only reflects the local relationship between nodes. Community structure can reveal the hidden relationship between nodes. To obtain Community structure, we use Infomap [19] to get every node's community. Infomap encodes the shortest vertex sequence based on information theory, and detects communities through a deterministic greedy search strategy. In order to obtain the vertex sequence, a random walk strategy is used to collect high-order information. The greedy search strategy integrates information on a global view and integrates communities. Because random walk and greedy search are common strategies for obtaining community information, Infomap is employed as community detection module.

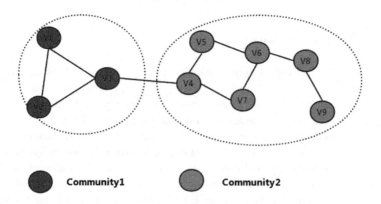

Fig. 1. Simple network with two communities

Community Triplets Construction: On the basis of community detection, we know the community distribution of each node. We perform biased random walk to construct community triplets. For each node a, which belong to community $com(a)$, we randomly select node p belonging to the community $com(a)$. Then, we chose another community which is not equal to the community $com(a)$ and randomly select a node f from this community. we get triplet $< a, p, f >$, where $com(a) = com(p)$ and $com(a) \neq com(f)$. Repeat the above process to construct t triplets for each node in network. For v_1 in Fig. 1, we randomly select a node v_3 from the first community and randomly select a node v_7 from the second community. Then, we obtain a community triple $< v_1, v_3, v_7 >$. Then, we construct t triplets for v_1. We construct community triplets set $ComSet$ for the whole graph. There are $n \times t$ triplets in $ComSet$.

4.2   Framework of DNE

The framework of DNE is as shown in the Fig. 2. DNE is consist of embedding layer, shared encoder and dual decoder. Embedding layer is designed to extract two different representations. Shared encoder is designed to map two representations into unified representations spaces. Finally, dual decoder is designed to reconstruct adjacent and node attributes respectively.

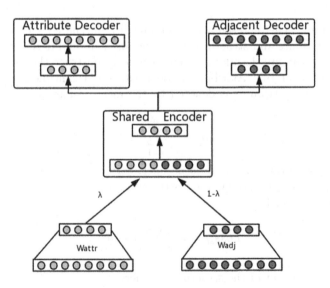

Fig. 2. The framework of the deep model of DNE

Embedding Layer: We design two fully connected layers to extract two different representations and use weight λ and $1-\lambda$ to connect two representations. As shown in Fig. 2, Attribute embedding layer and structure embedding layer compress structural vector and attribute vector into two representations respectively. The structure vector of v_i is a_i and the attribute vector of v_i is a_i. The weights of two layer are W_{attr} and W_{stru} separately. The final output of embedding layer of node v_i is denoted as follows:

$$h_i^{(0)} = [\lambda\sigma(W_{attr} \cdot x_i), (1 - \lambda)\sigma(W_{stru} \cdot a_i)] \tag{1}$$

where W_{attr} and W_{struc} are the weight parameters to be learned. σ is the activation function.

Shared Encoder: To compress attribute and structure into common representation space, we then use a fully connected neural network of multiple layers to map each node into a non-linear latent representation space. The input data of shared encoder is the output of embedding layer $h_i^{(0)}$ and the representation of hidden layers can be denoted as follows:

$$h_i^{(t)} = f(W^t(h_i^{(t-1)}) + b^t) \tag{2}$$

where W^t is the t−th hidden layer weight matrix, b^t is the biases and $f(.)$ is the activation function. The final representation of node v_i is represented as $emb(v_i)$.

Dual Decoder: The representations obtained by the shared encoder layer contains both attribute and structure and is the input of dual decoder. Attributed decoder and structure decoder are designed to reconstruct the node attribute and structure separately. Attribute decoder consists of multiple layers. The loss of reconstructing attributes is denoted by the mean square error (MSE) given by

$$Loss_{attr} = \frac{1}{n}\sum_{i=1}^{n}(x_i - \hat{x}_i)^2 \tag{3}$$

where $\hat{x}_i$ is the output of attribute decoder. Structure decoder consist of multiple layers and directly reconstructs structure vector of node v_i. The structure reconstruct loss is as follows:

$$Loss_{stru} = \frac{1}{n}\sum_{i=1}^{n}(a_i - \hat{a}_i)^2 \tag{4}$$

where $\hat{a}_i$ is the output of the structure decoder.

4.3   DNEC

The homogeneity theory indicates that nodes with same community should be closer to each other in low-dimensional space, while nodes belong to different communities should stay away from each other in the representation space. Therefore, we calculate the community triplet-loss on the basis of DNE and form

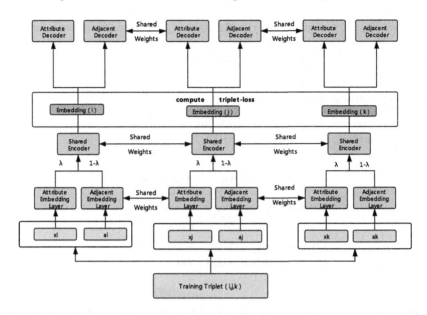

Fig. 3. DNEC: The framework of the deep model of DNE with Triplet-loss

the final model DNEC. Overall, we define the following community triplet-loss function as follows:

$$Loss_{com} = \sum_{<a,p,f> \in ComSet} max(dis(a,p) - dis(a,f) + margin, 0) \qquad (5)$$

where $dis(a,p) = (emb(a) - emb(p))^2$, $com(a) = com(p)$, $com(a) \neq com(f)$. In Fig. 3, all triplets in $ComSet$ are used as training sets to train the model. Given a triplet $< a, p, f >$, we get the node's representation $< emb(a), emb(p), emb(f) >$ through embedding layer and shared encoder. Then, we calculate the $Loss_{com}$ of all triplets in $ComSet$. Minimize L_{com}, $dis(a,p)$ becomes smaller and $dis(a,f)$ becomes bigger. Nodes in the same community will be closer to each other and nodes in the different communities will be away from each other in the representation space.

In order to retain node attributes, local structure, and community structure, we designed the DNEC model. Overall, we minimize the following loss function:

$$L_{total} = Loss_{attr} + Loss_{stru} + Loss_{com} \qquad (6)$$

5   Experiment

In this part, we conduct experiments on three public datasets such: cora, citeseer, and pubmed. We compare our method with the state-of-art methods. The experimental results prove that our method has significant improvements over baselines. Firstly, we introduce the datasets we used in the experiments, and then simply list the comparison methods, finally, we present the experimental results and discuss the advantages of our method.

5.1 Experimental Settings

Datasets : An overview of the network datasets we consider in our experiments is given in Table 1.

Table 1. Statistics of the datasets

Datasets	Nodes	Edges	Features	Classes
Cora	2708	5429	1433	7
Citeseer	3327	4732	3707	6
PubMed	19717	44338	500	3

The datasets are paper citation networks. The nodes in Table 1 represent papers. The edge of each network is the citation relationship between two papers. The attribute of each node is the bag-of-words representation of the corresponding paper.

Baselines: We use the following five state-of-the-art NE methods as our baselines. All baselines are published recently and all have good performance on NE. The descriptions of the baselines are as follows:

Deepwalk [14]: uses random walk to generate node sequences and feed node sequences into skip-gram to learn node representation vector of the nodes using only structure.

Line [7]: exploits the network structure's first-order proximity and second-order proximity.

Node2vec [6]: uses two parameters to simulate BFS and DFS search strategies to generate node sequences and then preserve global and local proximity by a flexible random-walk way.

TADW [11]: incorporates text into Matrix Factorization and preserve node content and network struct simultaneously.

DANE [12]: adopts two deep neural networks to extract node structure and node attribute separately and connect two different representations as the final representation.

Parameter Settings. For a fair comparison, we set the embedding dimension to 100 for all methods. For Deepwalk and Node2vec, we set the window size t to 10 and walk length l to 80. For Node2vec, we set the BFS parameter q to 2.0 and DFS to 0.5. For LINE, the starting value of learning rate is 0.025. The number of negative samples is set as 5 and the number of training samples are set as 10,000. For TADW, we set the parameters λ to 0.5. For DANE, we set the parameters as shown in the paper. For our method, we set λ to 0.5, margin to 0.5 and t to 5. We summarize the parameter settings of the three datasets in Table 2. For PubMed, the network structure contains more useful information than node attribute. So, we set the dimension of Attribute Embedding layer to 200 and set the dimension of Structure Embedding layer to 800.

Table 2. Parameter settings of the three datasets

Datasets	Attr-Emb	Stru-Emd	Shar-Encoder	Attr-Decoder	Stru-Decoder
Cora	512	512	1024-512-100	100-512-1433	100-512-2708
Citeseer	512	512	1024-512-100	100-512-3707	100-512-3327
PubMed	200	800	1000-500-100	100-200-500	100-800-19717

5.2 Results and Analysis

Node Classification. We conduct node classification on learned node's representation to demonstrate the great performance of on semi-supervised classification task. We applied the Lib-SVM(SVM) software packages as the classifier for all baselines. For a comprehensive assessment, we randomly select $\{10\%, 30\%, 50\%\}$ nodes from the dataset as the training set, and the remaining nodes as the testing set. We adopt the method of five-fold cross-validation to train the SVM classifier with training set and use Micro-F1 (Mi-F1) and Macro-F1 (Ma-F1) as Metrics on the testing set to measure the classification result. The average accuracy of node classification of all methods are

Table 3. Average of Micro-F1 and Macro-F1 scores in Cora dataset

Training percent	10%		30%		50%	
Method	Mi-F1	Ma-F1	Mi-F1	Ma-F1	Mi-F1	Ma-F1
Deepwalk	0.7568	0.7498	0.8064	0.7943	0.8287	0.8177
Node2vec	0.7477	0.7256	0.8201	0.8121	0.8235	0.8162
Line	0.7338	0.7191	0.8122	0.8105	0.8353	0.8254
TADW	0.7510	0.7234	0.8006	0.7801	0.8354	0.8187
DANE	0.7867	0.7748	0.8281	0.8127	0.8502	0.8377
DNEC	**0.7979**	**0.7832**	**0.8384**	**0.8213**	**0.8697**	**0.8456**

shown in Tables 3, 4, and 5, where the best results are bold. We find that our method performs better than baselines. Deepwalk, Node2Vec and Line just consider structure. So, the performance of those methods are worsen than TADW.

Because TADW considers attributed information on three datasets. DANE perform better than TADW. Because DANE employs deep neural network to persevere structure information and attributed information. It can be seen from Tables 3, 4, and 5, our method uses a more reasonable method to map structure and node attributes into the unified representation spaces. In the network, nodes with same community tent to have same category. Community triplet-loss will pull nodes with same category cluster in representation spaces. So, DNEC performs better than all baselines.

Table 4. Average of Micro-F1 and Macro-F1 scores in Citeseer dataset

Training percent	10%	30%	50%
Method	Mi-F1 Ma-F1	Mi-F1 Ma-F1	Mi-F1 Ma-F1
Deepwalk	0.5052 0.4645	0.5783 0.5329	0.5900 0.5486
Node2vec	0.5233 0.4832	0.6110 0.5651	0.6335 0.5972
Line	0.5139 0.4726	0.5761 0.5384	0.6075 0.5700
TADW	0.6048 0.5344	0.6481 0.5769	0.6578 0.5897
DANE	0.6444 0.6043	0.7137 0.6718	0.7393 0.6965
DNEC	**0.6534 0.6219**	**0.7248 0.6956**	**0.7524 0.7126**

Table 5. Average of Micro-F1 and Macro-F1 scores in PubMed dataset

Training percent	10%	30%	50%
Method	Mi-F1 Ma-F1	Mi-F1 Ma-F1	Mi-F1 Ma-F1
Deepwalk	0.8047 0.7873	0.8168 0.8034	0.8176 0.8034
Node2vec	0.8027 0.7849	0.8110 0.7965	0.8103 0.7981
Line	0.8037 0.7892	0.8129 0.8007	0.8110 0.7994
TADW	0.8258 0.8143	0.8286 0.8214	0.8343 0.8294
DANE	0.8298 0.8179	0.8311 0.8205	0.8475 0.8349
DNEC	**0.8395 0.8279**	**0.8473 0.8341**	**0.8582 0.8421**

Node Clustering. To prove the performance of our method on node clustering task, we apply K-means on cora dataset. We use the label information as the true community information and use the clustering accuracy to measure the clustering result. The result is shown in Table 6, the clustering accuracy of our method is higher than all baselines. The accuracy of DANE is higher than Deepwalk, Node2vec. Because DANE preserves non-linear structure and attributed

Table 6. Clustering Accuracy

Method	Cora	Citeseer	Pubmed
Deepwalk	0.6813	0.4145	0.6660
Node2vec	0.6473	0.4504	0.6754
Line	0.4789	0.3913	0.6614
TADW	0.5993	0.6642	0.6257
DANE	0.7027	0.4797	0.6942
DNEC	**0.7213**	**0.6942**	**0.7181**

information. DNEC has the best performance for the reason that DNEC incorporates local structure, node attributes and community information. Equipped with triplet-loss, nodes with same community will cluster in low-dimensional space.

Visualization. To further show the embedding result obtained by our method, we apply t-sne to visualize the node's representation in lwo-dimensional space.we conduct t-sne task on citeseer dataset. The result is shown in Fig. 4. The boundary of TADW is not explicit. Because DANE consider node attribute and network structure together and uses non-linear neural network, the boundary of different class is more explicit than TADW. We can see from Fig. 4 that the visualization of our method have clear boundaries and compact cluster. Because triplet-loss makes nodes in same community cluster in representation spaces and make nodes in different communities away from each other.

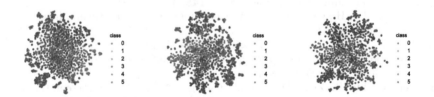

Fig. 4. t-SNE visualization the dataset Citeseer by using TADW, DANE, and our proposed method. The left is the visualization using TADW, and the right is the visualization using the method we proposed, and the median is the visualization using DANE.

6 Conclusion

In this paper, we propose ANE framework, using a more reasonable way to preserve both the network topology and the node attribute. We also take community information into account to improve the quality of representations. The experimental results prove that our method has a great performance on node classification, node clustering, and visualization tasks. Compared to the previous works, we incorporate community information into ANE and obtain a better performance. In future, we will consider the scalability of our method in heterogeneous networks.

References

1. Dong, Y., Zhang, J., Tang, J., Chawla, N.V., Wang, B.: CoupledLP: link prediction in coupled networks. In: 21th International Conference on Knowledge Discovery and Data Mining(SIGKDD 2015), pp. 199–208 (2015)
2. Tang, J., Liu, J., Zhang, M., Mei, Q.: Visualizing large-scale and high-dimensional data. In: 25th International Conference on World Wide Web(WWW 2016), pp. 287–297 (2016)
3. Bhuyan, M.H., Bhattacharyya, D.K., Kalita, J.K.: Network anomaly detection: methods, systems and tools. Commun. Surv. Tutorials **2014**, 303–336 (2014)
4. Mikolov, T., Chen, K., Corrado, G., Dean, J.: Efficient estimation of word representations in vector space. In:1st International Conference on Learning Representations (ICLR 2013), pp. 1–12 (2013)
5. Tomas, M., Ilya, S., Kai, C., Greg, S., Je, D.: Distributed representations of words and phrases and their compositionality. In Advances in neural information processing systems, pp. 3111–3119 (2013)
6. Grover, A., Leskovec, J.: node2vec: scalable feature learning for networks. In:22nd International Conference on Knowledge Discovery and Data Mining (KDD 2016), pp. 855–864. ACM (2016)
7. Tang, J., Qu, M., Wang, M., Zhang, M., Yan, J., Mei, Q.: LINE: large-scale information network embedding. In: 24th International Conference on World Wide Web (WWW 2015), pp. 1067–1077 (2015)
8. Keikha, M.M., Rahgozar, M., Asadpour, M.: Community aware random walk for network embedding. Knowl. Based Syst. **148**, 47–54 (2018)
9. Yang, C., Lu, H., Chen, K.: CONE: Community Oriented Network. http://arxiv.org/abs/1709.01554
10. Yang, L., Cao, X., Wang, C., Zhang, W.: Modularity based community detection with deep learning. In: 25th International Joint Conference on Artificial Intelligence (AAAI 2016), pp. 2252–2258 (2016)
11. Yang, C., Liu, Z., Zhao, D., Sun, M., Chang, E.Y.: Network representation learning with rich text information. In: 24th International Conference on Artifificial Intelligence (IJCAI 2015), pp. 2111–2117 (2015)
12. Hongchang, G., Heng, H.: Deep Attributed network embedding. In: 27th International Joint Conference on Artificial Intelligence (IJCAI 2018), pp. 3364–3370 (2018)
13. Belkin, M., Niyogi, P.: Laplacian Eigenmaps and spectral techniques for embedding and clustering. In: Advances Neural Information Processing Systems, pp. 585–591 (2001)
14. Perozzi, B., Al-Rfou, R., Skiena, S.: DeepWalk: online learning of social representations. In: 20th International Conference on Knowledge Discovery and Data Mining (KDD 2014), pp. 701–710. ACM (2014)
15. Wang, D., Cui, P., Zhu, W.: Structural deep network embedding. In: 22nd SIGKDD International Conference on Knowledge Discovery and Data Mining (SIGKDD 2016), pp. 1225–1234. ACM (2016)

16. Cao, S., Lu, W., Xu, Q.: Deep neural networks for learning graph representations. In: 30th AAAI Conference on Artificial Intelligence (AAAI 2016), pp. 1145–1152 (2016)

17. Cao S., Lu W., Xu Q.: GraRep: learning graph representations with global structural. In 24th International Conference on Information and Knowledge Management (CIKM 2015), pp. 891–900. ACM (2015)

18. Pan, S., Wu, J., Zhu, X., Zhang, C., Wang, Y.: Tri-party deep network representation. In: 25th International Joint Conference on Artificial Intelligence (IJCAI 2016), pp. 1895–1901 (2016)

19. Rosvall, M., Bergstrom, C.: Maps of random walks on complex networks reveal community structure. In: Proceedings of the National Academy of Sciences of the United States of America, vol. 105(4), pp. 1118–1123 (2018)

An Acceleration Framework for Super-Resolution Network via Region Difficulty Self-adaption

Zhenfang Guo[1], Yuyao Ye[1], Yang Zhao[2], and Ronggang Wang[1(✉)]

[1] School of Electronic and Computer Engineering,
Peking University Shenzhen Graduate School,
Peking University Campus, Shenzhen, Guangdong 518055, China
{guodaxia,yeyuyao}@pku.edu.cn, rgwang@pkusz.edu.cn
[2] School of Computers and Information, Hefei University of Technology,
Hefei, China
yzhao@hfut.edu.cn

Abstract. With the development of deep neural network (DNN), many DNN-based super-resolution (SR) models have achieved state-of-the-art (SOTA) performance. But the applications of these SOTA models are limited by the high computational and memory costs. We observed that different image regions have different difficulties in the process of SR reconstruction. However, current DNN-based SR models process different types of regions equally, and thus involve much redundant computation in the regions with low SR difficulty. To address this limitation, this paper proposes a general acceleration framework for SR networks, which first distinguishes the SR difficulty of image regions, and then applies large model and light model for difficult regions and easy regions respectively. Experimental results demonstrated that the proposed acceleration framework can accelerate SOTA SR networks with 2–4 times without reducing of quality performance.

Keywords: Super resolution · Accelerate · Image region classification

1 Introduction

Super resolution aims to recover high-resolution (HR) images from their low-resolution (LR) counterparts. With the development of deep learning, a number of SR methods have been proposed [1]. Due to the powerful feature representation and model fitting capabilities of deep neural network, convolutional neural network (CNN)-based SR methods have achieved significant performance improvements against traditional ones. In order to improve SR performance, more and more complex SR methods [2–4] have been proposed. Unfortunately, although these networks achieve impressive performance, high computational and memory costs limit the applications of these SOTA models. Therefore, it's necessary to research the acceleration of image SR process.

© Springer Nature Switzerland AG 2021
J. Lokoč et al. (Eds.): MMM 2021, LNCS 12572, pp. 666–677, 2021.
https://doi.org/10.1007/978-3-030-67832-6_54

In this years, a series of methods have been proposed to investigate compact deep neural networks (DNN) such as network-pruning [5,6], weight-quantification [7,8], knowledge distillation [9], etc. Network-pruning prunes the unimportant weights or filters to accelerate the model [5,10]. Weight-quantification quantifies the weights and activations to several bits data to achieve large compression and speed-up ratios. Knowledge distillation methods transferred knowledge from a larger model to a smaller model [11]. In addition, efficient neural architecture design [12–14] and neural architecture search [15–17] can establish highly efficient deep networks with fewer parameters and calculations. However these methods often focus on classification, segmentation and other high-level semantic information tasks. High level semantic information is based on a large receptive field. Thus even if operations like pruning, quantization and distillation are carried out, the final feature extraction and ensemble will not be greatly affected, and the model can still converge to satisfactory performance. However, when these methods are applied to SR task, they often fail to achieve satisfactory performance. One reason is that the SR task is based on the low-level semantic information, but pruning, quantization and distillation operations reduce the ability to extract low-level pixel-wise information. Some works have also been devoted to the light-weight of SR networks, such as VDSR [18] and CARN [19]. Nevertheless, these networks still involve redundant computation.

Human visual system (HVS) is much more sensitive to edges than flat area. Similarly, in the process of SR, we have observed that the loss of details in LR image compared with HR image mainly exist in regions of edges and textures. Consequently, for the flat regions, the content loss is of very small magnitude. In other words, although flat regions usually account for the majority of image content, they do not need a large SR network to reconstruct them. Some traditional methods mainly focus on edges and simply upsampled flat area to accelerate the total SR process [29]. However, current SR networks often treat all regions of the image equally, which results in much redundant computation within flat regions.

Based on these observations, we propose an accelerated SR network architecture based on region difficulty self-adaption. We first designed a patch classification network to estimate the difficulty of upsampling this patch by analyzing its texture composition. Then, we can divide all the patches of input image into two parts: easy data and hard data. For the hard data, we use a more complex SR network to recover better details. For the easy data, we utilize lighter network to reduce computational cost. Finally, all the reconstructed patches are put together to obtain the whole SR image. The experimental results show that our framework achieves a good acceleration effect under the premise of ensuring the quality of SR.

2   Related Work

We first review the development of several CNN-based image and video SR methods and then discuss several CNN acceleration techniques related to our work.

2.1 Single Image SR and Video SR

The application of shallow CNN to SR tasks was first proposed by Dong et al. [1]. After that, FASTER SRCNN [20] is proposed by using channels shrinking and smaller convolutional kernels. Kim et al. then trained much deeper VDSR [18] network by introducing residual learning strategy. Lim et al. proposed a very deep and wide network named EDSR by cascading modified residual blocks. In [21] SRGAN is proposed by using Generative Adversarial Networks (GAN) [22] to further improve the subjective quality of restored image [23,24].

In recent three years, more and more SOTA SR networks have been proposed, driven by some influential competitions such as NTIRE series [30,31].

Although these networks achieve state-of-the-art performance, their high computational cost and memory footprint limit their applications.

Traditional multi-frame SR often meet the difficulty to accurately align different frames at pixel level, hence single image SR receives much more attention in past decades. However, with the development of DNN-based flow-estimation, intra-frame alignment, and deformable convolution, many SOTA multi-frame SR methods have been proposed recently [32,33]. Compared with single image SR, video SR makes use of more information in adjacent frames, and thus can achieve better visual performance. For instance, Wang X.T et al. [25] proposed SOTA EDVR method based on multi-level deformable convolution and temporal-spatial attention. Unfortunately, with the improvement of performance, the complexity introduced by these video SR models also increases dramatically.

2.2 Network Acceleration

At present, neural network acceleration can be divided into two parts: model compression and compact model design.

Model Compression. For a given neural network, model compression aims to reduce the computation, energy and storage cost, such as network-pruning, weight-quantification, knowledge distillation. Network-pruning can be divided into structured pruning and unstructured pruning, unstructured pruning cuts out the unimportant connections between neurons. Structured pruning further targets on removing useless channels or layers for acceleration. The quantitative operation first analyses the distribution characteristics of the parameters in the network, and then represents weights or activations in neural networks with discrete values for compression and calculation acceleration. Specifically, binarization methods [26] with only 1-bit values can extremely accelerate the model by efficient binary operations. Quantization needs hardware support. Distillation design a smaller model compared with original model as student model, and take original model as teacher model. Distillation uses the transfer learning method to make the student model learn the knowledge of the teacher model as much as possible.

Compact Model Design. A series of compact models have been proposed in recent years such as SqueezeNet [27], mobileNet, efficientNet [28] etc. SqueezeNet desighed a module named FireModule, in which 1×1 convolution is used to down-up dimensions of the featuremap. MobileNet introduces DepthWise Separable Convolution and Group Convolution, which saves large amount of convolution computation. EfficientNet explores the relationship between network's performance and network's depth, convolution kernel size and feature map resolution to find the best balance. These models have achieved excellent acceleration effect.

3   Motivation

The spatial information distributions of different regions are quite different. For example, some regions are flat and monotonous, while other regions are rich in texture details. We have noticed that the difficulty for magnifying these regions is also different. Existing CNN-based SR networks ignore these differences and treat all regions equally, which results in a great waste of computing resources. To demonstrate this, we carry out a simple experiment as follows.

As shown in the Fig. 1, we used EDVR and bilinear interpolation to reconstruct the input image separately, and then subtract the reconstructed images with ground truth to find the differences. (a) donates the region with different texture in images, (b) is the difference got by EDVR, (c) present the difference got by bilinear interpolation. Comparing the differences from two methods, we can find that different from the rich texture areas, in the flat areas, even using bilinear interpolation can achieve comparable performance with that of EDVR. Hence, reconstructing these flat areas with EDVR means a lot of redundant computation. At the same time, it does not bring much performance improvement. As a result, we tend to propose a certain method to distinguish the degree of difficulty for SR and then use SR networks with different computational complexities accordingly. As a result, we can achieve considerable acceleration effect under the premise of SR quality.

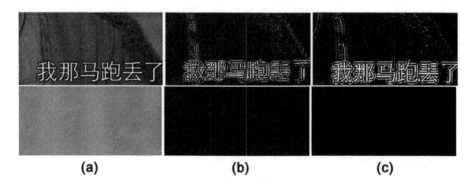

(a)   (b)   (c)

Fig. 1. Differences between upsampled image and GT, (a) GT images, (b) differences between EDVR results and GT, (c) differences between interpolated results and GT

Based on the above observations, we design a general acceleration framework for SOTA SR networks. In the proposed framework, we first divide the input image into a group of patches and put each patch into a lightweight classification network to determine its difficulty for SR. Then the patches with lower difficulty are upsampled with lighter SR network, and these difficult patches are reconstructed with complex SOTA network. Finally, these two types of magnified patches are pieced together as the final output.

4   Our Architecture

Our framework consists of two parts: the lightweight classification network and the two-branch SR framework.

4.1   Lightweight Classification Network

In general, we think that the flat regions of image with less difficulty for SR, and the region with complex texture with more difficulty for SR. However, according to our experiments, there are some exceptions. For some regions with irregular texture and very complex texture, it's easier for SR. Therefore, we don't simply divide the image according to the traditional methods, such as gradient or local differences [29]. For the same reason, it is also not reasonable to train the classification network with manual labeling.

To solve this problem, we propose to embed the classification network into the whole SR framework, and then train it end-to-end by using unsupervised learning. The goal of classification network is to obtain an optimal balance between the SR performance and computation by dividing appropriate groups. The architecture of the patch classification network is shown in Fig. 2. First, the feature of the input image is extracted through several stacked convolution layers and max-pooling operations. Finally, the feature map is reshaped and then inputted into a full connection layer. After the full connection layer, the weight-vector is obtained via a softmax layer.

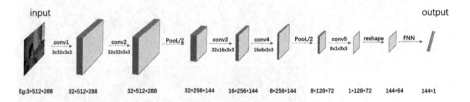

Fig. 2. Architecture of patch classification network

4.2   Two-Branch SR Network

We aim to propose a general acceleration framework that can be applied to different SR networks. Hence, the proposed method merely designs the acceleration mechanism without modifying the architecture of SR networks. In this paper, we directly use the EDVR [25], which has achieved SOTA performance on video SR tasks but also suffers from high computational cost, as the basic SR model.

For the branch that reconstructs these difficult patches, we apply normal EDVR that contains 128 feature channels, 8 deformable convolution groups, 5 residual blocks to extract feature map before multi-frame alignment, and 40 residual blocks to reconstruct the features. For these patches with lower difficulty in another branch, a much lighter EDVR is used with corresponding hyperparameters as 32,1,5,5, respectively.

4.3   Training Phase

Through the classification network, we get a vector of $N \times 1$, denoted as W_1, where each value is between 0 and 1 representing the difficulty for SR. On the other hand, we reshape the image into $N \times C \times BH \times BW$ data blocks. Where N is the number of blocks, C denotes the number of image channels, BH, BW represent the size of each patch. Then we put these blocks into EDVR to get the SR results as $R1$, which shape is $N \times C \times sBH \times sBW$. At the same time, we reshape the ground truth into $N \times C \times sBH \times sBW$ (s denotes the multiples of SR) data blocks, denoted as $R2$. After that, the distance between $R1$ and $R2$ is calculated by an optional criterion such as L_2, denoted as $diff$. The value of each element represents the quality of SR for each patch. We think that under the same network the area with good SR performance has a relatively lower difficulty of SR, and vice versa. Hence, we multiply $diff$ by W_1 to get loss1:

$$loss1 = W_1 \times \frac{1}{N} \sum_{c,x,y} \sqrt{(R1[c,x,y] - R2[c,x,y])^2} \tag{1}$$

where x, y are vertical and horizontal indices, and c is channel indices. In addition, we subtract W_1 from 1 and then sum all the elements to get loss2:

$$loss2 = \sum_N (1 - W_1) \tag{2}$$

The function of loss1 is to select as many blocks as possible from all the data blocks and divide them into low SR difficulty, so as to ensure the acceleration effect. Loss2 restricts loss1 from dividing the data blocks with high SR difficulty into low ones, so as to ensure the overall SR quality of the whole image. The final loss is:

$$loss = loss1 + \lambda loss2 \tag{3}$$

We can get different acceleration effects by changing the value of λ. The whole training process is shown in Fig. 3.

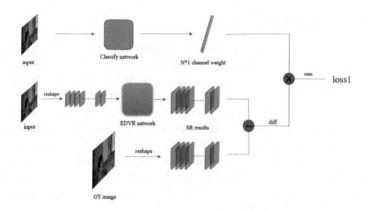

Fig. 3. Training process

4.4 Inference Phase

The inference phase is shown in Fig. 4. In the inference phase, in order to get the exact classification results (0 or 1) from W_1, we first merge W_1 and $1 - W_1$ to form a $N \times 2$ matrix and then use argmax to get a $N \times 1$ result. Each element in the result denotes whether this block belongs to easy data or hard data. The size of each data block is $1/s$ of the original image, s is usually 4 or 8. Through the classification network, the input image patches are classified into two categories: low SR difficulty and high SR difficulty. We then process these two types of patches with lightweight SR model and complex SR model separately. At last, the SR results of all patches are combined to form the final SR result.

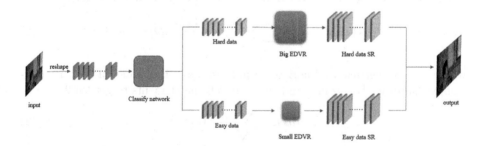

Fig. 4. Inference process

5   Experiment

We use the video resources provided by Youku company as the dataset [34] to train our classification network, and use the REDS dataset [35] to train out

EDVR model under 4× SR task. We train our classification network with ADAM optimizer by setting $\beta_1 = 0.9$, $\beta_2 = 0.999$, and $\varepsilon = 10^{-8}$. We set minibatch size as 16. The learning rate is initialized as 10^{-4} and halved at every 2×10^3 minibatch updates. When calculating *diff*, we use SSIM as optional criterion. We set s as 4 and λ as 1.5 in our experiment. The Youku dataset includes 950 video clips with low-resolution of 512×288 or 480×270 and corresponding high-resolution of 2048×1152 or 1920×1080. The scene styles of each segment are different. We choose 900 of them as training sets and 50 as test sets to train our classification network. The effect of classification network is shown in Fig. 5.

Fig. 5. Patch classification results, (a) with gradient-based method, (b) with the proposed classification network

As shown in Fig. 5, the marked area in blue or red are that with low SR difficulty, or to say these regions can be upsampled with lighter SR models. Figure 5(b) is the result achieved by our classification network and Fig. 5(a) is the result got by gradient-based method. In Fig. 5(b) we can see that although this patch classification network is trained via unsupervised learning, the network can effectively distinguish important foreground regions such as facial and texture areas from the fuzzy background area while gradient-based method can't distinguish these foreground regions as Fig. 5(a) shown. Therefore, the impact of acceleration using our classification network on the subjective feeling is minimized as much as possible. Previous network acceleration methods like to choose FLOPs(floating point of operations) as the evaluation standard to evaluate the acceleration effect. But according to our experiments, FLOPs is often directly proportional to the inference time on CPU, but when inference using GPU, due to GPU's parallel computing methods and other acceleration principles, FLOPs can not represent the real acceleration effect on GPUs. Therefore, we directly use the model inference time as the standard to evaluate the architecture's acceleration effect.

We calculated the time cost of each part in our acceleration framework. Taking 540p to 2K magnification as an example, the average computing time of EDVR reconstruction, patch classification, reshape operation, and other operations account for 98.40%, 0.15%, 1.39% and 0.06%, respectively.

To explore the impact of different hardware platforms on our framework, we do our tests on TITAN V and Tesla V100 respectively. The experiment is done under the input image resolution of 512×288. The results are shown in Table 1 1. Obviously, different platforms have no effect on our acceleration framework.

Table 1. Requested SR time of an image (512×288) on different platforms

	TITAN V	Tesla V100
Our architecture	**0.3440**	**0.2867**
EDVR	1.0890	0.9308

We selected ten groups of representative scene pictures from all the pictures in the test set with resolution of $512 \times 288 - 2048 \times 1152$ to complete objective and subjective evaluation. In addition, we downloaded some 4K videos from Youtube [36] and then made them as test set to evaluate our framework under resolution of $960 \times 540 - 3840 \times 2160$. For objective evaluation, we list their SR results before and after acceleration in Table 2 and Table 3. We can find that under different styles and resolution of images, our acceleration framework can achieve about three times acceleration effect with minimal SR performance loss. For subjective evaluation we invited ten observers and gave them ten pairs of anonymous images. Observers is required to choose one image with better visual quality in each pair. But if they can not distinguish the differences, they can also select the result as "no differences". As last, the selections of "no differences", EDVR results, and our results account for 91%, 5%, and 4%, respectively. Some SR results for 2K images are illustrated in Fig. 6. By comparing the results in Fig. 6(a) and (b), there is almost no visual quality difference between the results of normal EDVR and the proposed acceleration framework.

Table 2. Acceleration effect on images ($512 \times 288 - 2048 \times 1152$) with different style

	Our acceleration framework			EDVR			Acceleration times
	Time	PSNR	SSIM	Time	PSNR	SSIM	
img1-1	0.2759	38.0194	0.9793	0.9300	**38.0236**	0.9794	3.37
img1-2	0.3058	**37.8173**	0.9768	0.9277	37.8155	**0.9769**	3.03
img1-3	0.2730	**39.4054**	0.9836	0.9281	39.4017	**0.9837**	3.40
img1-4	0.2899	39.1261	0.9804	0.9261	**39.1920**	**0.9811**	3.19
img1-5	0.2773	43.9609	0.9811	0.9290	**43.9974**	**0.9816**	3.35
img1-6	0.2861	**44.3085**	0.9827	0.9356	44.2790	**0.9830**	3.27
img1-7	0.2801	45.5510	0.9851	0.9261	**45.6111**	**0.9856**	3.31
img1-8	0.2807	45.0941	0.9838	0.9281	**45.2534**	**0.9845**	3.31
img1-9	0.2808	40.6550	0.9838	0.9256	**40.6629**	**0.9844**	3.30
img1-10	0.2844	40.6068	0.9835	0.9302	**40.6223**	**0.9840**	3.27
Avg	0.2834	41.4545	0.9820	0.9287	**41.4859**	**0.9824**	3.28

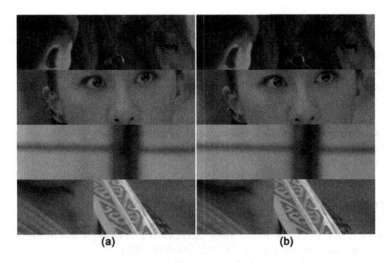

Fig. 6. SR results comparison, (a) normal EDVR, (b) the proposed acceleration framework

Table 3. Acceleration effect on images ($960 \times 540 - 3840 \times 2160$) with different style

	Our acceleration framework			EDVR			Acceleration times
	Time	PSNR	SSIM	Time	PSNR	SSIM	
img2-1	0.8220	39.7403	0.9798	2.4823	**39.7522**	**0.9800**	3.02
img2-2	0.82988	39.8121	0.9799	2.4727	**39.8247**	**0.9801**	2.98
img2-3	0.8139	31.2097	0.9293	2.4743	**31.2132**	**0.9293**	3.04
img2-4	0.7683	31.4931	0.9341	2.4816	**31.4977**	**0.9341**	3.23
img2-5	0.8835	31.7583	0.9383	2.4738	**31.7778**	**0.9385**	2.80
img2-6	0.7943	46.0140	0.9939	2.4703	**46.0254**	**0.9939**	3.11
img2-7	0.8213	45.9885	0.9941	2.4720	**46.0021**	**0.9941**	3.01
img2-8	0.8204	46.0912	0.9940	2.4857	**46.1092**	**0.9940**	3.03
img2-9	0.8330	39.1671	0.9765	2.4741	**39.1707**	**0.9765**	2.97
img2-10	0.8588	39.1648	0.9767	2.4734	**39.1680**	**0.9767**	2.88
Avg	0.8226	39.0439	0.9697	2.4760	**39.0541**	**0.9697**	3.01

Through the experiment, we found that our SR architecture can achieve about three times acceleration effect with minimal SR performance loss on different kinds of GPUs and different input size and there is almost no difference between original SR result and accelerated SR result.

6   Conclusion

This paper proposed an acceleration framework for recent SOTA but complex SR models. The proposed method first classifies different difficulties of image patches, and then applies large and light SR models for difficult and easy patches respectively. Note that the proposed acceleration framework is plug and play for various SR networks, and by modifying the parameters of loss function, it can achieve different acceleration effects. Our method can solve the problem of high computational cost in application of large SR networks, and thus has great application value in the industrial field.

Acknowledgements. Thanks to National Natural Science Foundation of China 61672063,61972129, Shenzhen Research Projects of JCYJ20180503182128089 and 201806080921419290.

References

1. Dong, C., Loy, C.C., He, K.M., Tang, X.O.: Learning a deep convolutional network for image super-resolution. In: ECCV, 184–199 (2014)
2. Lim, B., Son, S., Kim, H., Nah, S., Lee, K.M.: Enhanced deep residual networks for single image super-resolution. In: CVPR (2017)
3. Zhang, Y.L., Tian, Y.P., Kong, Y., Zhong, B., Fu, Y.: Residual dense network for image super-resolution. In: CVPR, pp. 2472–2481 (2018)
4. Zhang, Y.L., Li, K.P., Li, K., Wang, L.C., Zhong, B.N., Fu, Y.: Image super-resolution using very deep residual channel attention networks. In: ECCV, pp. 1646–1654 (2018)
5. Han, S., Mao, H.Z., Dally, W.J.: Compressing deep neural networks with pruning, trained quantization and Huffman coding. In: ICLR (2016)
6. Luo, J.H., Wu, J.X., Lin, W.Y.: ThiNet: a filter level pruning method for deep neural network compression. In: ICCV, pp. 5058–5066 (2017)
7. Jacob, B., et al.: Quantization and training of neural networks for efficient integer-arithmetic-only inference. In: CVPR, pp. 2704–2713 (2018)
8. Rastegari, M., Ordonez, V., Redmon, J., Farhadi, A.: XNOR-Net: ImageNet classification using binary convolutional neural networks. In: Leibe, B., Matas, J., Sebe, N., Welling, M. (eds.) ECCV 2016. LNCS, vol. 9908, pp. 525–542. Springer, Cham (2016). https://doi.org/10.1007/978-3-319-46493-0_32
9. Hinton, G., Vinyals, O., Dean, J.: Distilling the knowledge in a neural network. In: arXiv preprint arXiv:1503.02531 (2015)
10. Li, H., Kadav, A., Durdanovic, I., Samet, H., Graf, H.P.: Pruning filters for efficient convnets. In: ICLR (2017)
11. Hinton, G., Oriol, V., Dean, J.: Distilling the knowledge in a neural network. In: arXiv preprint arXiv:1503.02531 (2015)
12. Howard, A.G., et al.: MobileNets: efficient convolutional neural networks for mobile vision applications. In: arXiv preprint arXiv:1704.04861 (2017)
13. Howard, A., et al.: Searching for mobilenetv3. In: ICCV (2019)
14. Zhang, X.Y., Zhou, X.Y., Lin, M.X., Sun, J.: ShuffleNet: an extremely efficient convolutional neural network for mobile devices. In: CVPR (2018)
15. Baker, B., Gupta, O., Naik, N., Raskar, R.: Designing neural network architectures using reinforement learning. In: ICLR (2017)
16. Liu, C., et al.: Progressive neural architecture search. In: ECCV (2018)
17. Pham, H., Guan, M.Y., Zoph, B., Le, Q.V., Dean, J.: Efficient neural architecture search via parameter sharing. In: ICML (2018)

18. Kim, J., Lee, J.K., Lee, K.M.: Accurate image super-resolution using very deep convolutional networks. In: IEEE Conference on Computer Vision and Pattern Recognition, pp. 1646–1654 (2016)
19. Ahn, N., Kang, B., Sohn, K.A.: Fast, accurate, and lightweight super-resolution with cascading residual network. In: ECCV, pp. 252–268 (2018)
20. Dong, C., Loy, C.C., Tang, X.: Accelerating the super-resolution convolutional neural network. In: ECCV, pp. 391–407 (2016)
21. Ledig, C., et al.: Photo-realistic single image super-resolution using a generative adversarial network. In: arXiv preprint arXiv:1609.04802 (2016)
22. Goodfellow, I., et al.: Generative adversarial nets. In: NIPS (2014)
23. Dosovitskiy, A., Brox, T.: Generating images with perceptural similarity metrics based on deep networks. In: arXiv preprint arXiv:1602.02644 (2016)
24. Justin, J., Alexandre, A., Li, F.F.: Perceptual losses for real-time style transfer and super-resolution. In: ECCV, pp. 694–711 (2016)
25. Wang, X.T., Chan, K.C., Yu, K., Dong, C., Loy, C.C.: EDVR: video restoration with enhanced deformable convolutional networks. In: CVPR Workshops (2019)
26. Liu, Z.C., Wu, B.Y., Luo, W.H., Yang, X., Liu, W., Cheng, K.T.: Bi-Real Net: enhancing the performance of 1-bit CNNs with improved representational capability and advanced training algorithm. In: ECCV (2018)
27. Iandola, F.N., Moskewicz, M.W., Ashraf, K., Han, S., Dally, W.J., Keutzer, K.: SqueezeNet: Alexnet-level accuracy with 50x fewer parameters and 1 Mb model size. In: arXiv preprint arXiv:1602.07360 (2016)
28. Tan, M., Le, Q.V.: EfficientNet: rethinking model scaling for convolutional neural networks. In: ICML (2019)
29. Jia, W., Zhao, Y., Wang, R.G., Li, S.J., Min, H., Liu, X.P.: Are recent SISR techniques suitable for industrial applications at low magnification? IEEE Trans. Ind. Electron. **66**(12), 9828–9836 (2018)
30. Timofte, R., Gu, S.H., Wu, J.Q., Gool, L.V., Zhang, L., Yang, M.H., et al.: NTIRE 2018 challenge on single image super-resolution: methods and results. In: CVPR Workshop (2018)
31. Abdelhamed, A., Timofte, R., Brown, M.S., Yu, S., Park, B.J., et al.: NTIRE 2019 challenge on real image denoising: methods and results. In: CVPR workshop (2019)
32. Wang, W., Ren, C., He, X.H., Chen, H.G., Qing, L.B.: Video super-resolution via residual learning. IEEE Access **6**, 23767–23777 (2018)
33. Wang, Z.Y., Yi, P., Jiang, K., Jiang, J., Han, Z., Lu, T., Ma, J.Y.: Multi-memory convolutional neural network for video super-resolution. IEEE Trans. Image Process. **28**(5), 2530–2544 (2019)
34. Tianchi Homepage: https://tianchi.aliyun.com/dataset/dataDetail?dataId=39568. Accessed 4 May 2020
35. Seungjun Nah Homepage: https://seungjunnah.github.io/Datasets/reds.html. Accessed 6 July 2020
36. Youtube Homepage: https://www.youtube.com/watch?v=LXb3EKWsInQ. Accessed 15 Aug 2020

Spatial Gradient Guided Learning and Semantic Relation Transfer for Facial Landmark Detection

Jian Wang[1], Yaoyi Li[1], and Hongtao Lu[1,2(✉)]

[1] Key Lab of Shanghai Education Commission for Intelligent Interaction and
Cognitive Engineering, Department of Computer Science and Engineering,
Shanghai Jiao Tong University, Shanghai, China
htlu@sjtu.edu.cn
[2] MoE Key Lab of Artificial Intelligence, AI Institute, Shanghai Jiao Tong
University, Shanghai, China

Abstract. Pixel-wise losses are widely used in heatmap regression networks to detect facial landmarks, however, those losses are not consistent with the evaluation criteria in testing, which is evaluating the error between the highest pixel position in the predicted heatmap and the ground-truth heatmap. In this paper, we proposed a novel spatial-gradient consistency loss function (called Grad loss), which maintains a similar spatial structure in the heatmap with ground-truth. To reduce the quantization error caused by downsampling in the network, we also propose a new post-processing strategy based on the Gaussian prior. To further improve face alignment accuracy, we introduce Spatial-Gradient Enhance attention and Relation-based Reweighing Module to transfer semantic information and spatial information between high-resolution and low-resolution representations. Extensive experiments on several benchmarks (e.g., 300W, AFLW, COFW, WFLW) show that our method outperforms the state-of-the-art by impressive margins.

Keywords: Facial landmark detection · Face alignment · Heatmap regression

1 Introduction

Facial landmark detection, also known as face alignment, is a fundamental step before several face-related tasks, such as face recognition and face editing. Methods towards accurate facial landmark localization were widely studied in these years. While classic CNN architectures were used to directly regress coordinates of landmarks, recent developed fully-convolutional networks like HourGlass [9] have proved their stability and accuracy in facial landmark regression.

In this type of networks, the coordinate regression task is re-formulated by regressing a Gaussian heatmap around each landmark coordinate on each channel. In the training phase, pixel-wise loss functions such as MSE (Mean Square

© Springer Nature Switzerland AG 2021
J. Lokoč et al. (Eds.): MMM 2021, LNCS 12572, pp. 678–690, 2021.
https://doi.org/10.1007/978-3-030-67832-6_55

Error) loss or Smooth L1 loss are used to supervise the network to shrink into the Gaussian region and suppress the background regions into zeros. The coordinates are obtained by locating the position of the highest pixel. To avoid large memory consumption of the network, the final output feature is usually downsampled into 1/4 of the original resolution. It is worthy noting that quantization error is introduced during the above resolution reduction. To reduce this error, a hand-crafted shifting from the highest activation to the second highest activation is usually performed such as [11]. Although the above pipeline has performed well, it still faces the following disadvantages. A generated heatmap with lower MSE loss does not necessarily mean lower localization error. The reason is that MSE loss focus on the absolute pixel-error at each position, but our goal is actually to generate a heatmap with the same highest position with ground-truth. Besides, the quantization error cannot be estimated accurately by hand-craft operation.

To improve from the above aspects, we first propose a Grad loss to focus on the relative error between each pixel and its neighbors. The proposed loss will tolerate the absolute pixel error and punish those errors which affect the localization of the highest pixel. In the experiments, we observe that the network with our loss function could generate a heatmap with similar structure, which is shown in Fig. 1.

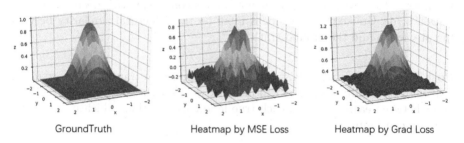

GroundTruth   Heatmap by MSE Loss   Heatmap by Grad Loss

Fig. 1. Compared to our baseline, our approach generates a heatmap with better Gaussian structure.

To reduce the quantization error, we take full advantage of the prior that the heatmap is actually generated by a Gaussian function and then introduce a Maximum Likelihood Estimation method to find a more precise location of the highest pixel. Different from the existing hand-crafted operations, our method adaptively estimates the quantization error according to the predicted heatmap.

Meanwhile, although multi-scale features are fused in the SOTA network, low-resolution features always contribute few to the localization result because of lacking accurate spatial information and the semantic relation in them is not fully utilized. Therefore, we propose a Spatial-Gradient Enhance module to emphasize the edge signal in low-resolution features by combining the original features with extra gradient information. Furthermore, a Relation-based Reweighing Module is introduced to transfer semantic relation from low-resolution features to high-resolution.

Experimental results show our approach outperforms existing methods on multiple datasets, and further improves the performance in other tasks such as human pose estimation.

2   Related Work

Heatmap Regression Network. With the development of FCN (Fully Convolutional Network), heatmap regression models are becoming the mainstream of several detection areas. Marek et al. [5] first proposed to aggregate landmark heatmap into the training process for facial landmark detection. In recent work, multi-scale architectures like stacked HourGlass [9] improved the location accuracy to a new level. Sun et al. proposed a new parallel multi-scale backbone, HR-Net (High Resolution Network) [11], and achieved state-of-the-art with parallel multi-resolution sub-networks and repeated multi-scale fusion.

Loss Functions Design. Compared to network architectures, loss functions were rarely studied in heatmap regression. MSE Loss, L1 Loss or Smooth L1 Loss are commonly used. All the above losses tend to optimize the mean absolute pixel error. However, this target is not always consistent with decreasing localization error. Unlike them, we focus more on the structural similarity between the prediction and the ground-truth.

Post Process Strategy. Post-processing is applied to transform the predicted heatmaps to coordinates. [10] introduced extra offset channels, which predict an offset between each pixel and each true landmark position, which increases the memory consumption a lot.

Multi-scale Fusion. Multi-scale features fusion an important role in facial landmark detection. Most works just concatenate multi-scale features, which ignored the different emphases in different scales. [8] applies a static kernel to fuse local contexts and further aggregates them by dilated convolution. Differently, we integrate more edge information into low-resolution features and aggregate semantic context into high-resolution features.

3   Method

In facial landmark detection, a group of heatmaps are predicted and each heatmap represents the coordinates of a landmark by giving a highest response in the landmark position. We first introduce our Gard loss which guides the network to focus on the localization error between prediction and the groundtruth. Then we utilize the Gaussian prior of the heatmap to estimate a corresponding quantization error and extend our predicted coordinates from integer into accurate floating point representation. To facilitate the multi-scale features fusion, we describe two effective modules to exchange information between features from different branches.

3.1 Grad Loss

The ground-truth heatmap is generated by plotting a Gaussian distribution around the landmark coordinate $(x_g t, y_g t)$:

$$Gaussian(x, y) = \exp\left(-\left(\frac{(x - x_{gt})^2}{2\sigma^2} + \frac{(y - y_{gt})^2}{2\sigma^2}\right)\right) \tag{1}$$

As shown in Fig. 2, here "Loc Error" means Localization Error, although the 2nd heatmap has lower MSE loss, its highest pixel position is wrong. In contrast, the 3rd heatmap has a larger MSE loss, but its final localization result is correct.

Ground Truth

MSE =1
Loc Error = 1
Grad Error = 8

MSE = 5
Loc Error = 0
Grad Error = 4

Fig. 2. MSE loss and grad loss.

From the above observation, we expect our loss function to ignore errors when the same error occurs in each position, because these errors will not affect the localization of the peak position. In fact, we only require that each pixel has the same error with its neighbors. Therefore, we relax our loss function into a local form. For a predicted heatmap H and ground truth H^* with size $m \times n$, we notate $\left(H_{i,j} - H^*_{i,j}\right)$ as $d_{i,j}$, hence our loss definition is adapted into:

$$\mathcal{L}(H, H^*) = \frac{1}{mn} \sum_{i=1,j=1}^{m,n} \left(\frac{[(d_{i,j}) - (d_{i-1,j})]^2}{2} + \frac{[(d_{i,j}) - (d_{i,j-1})]^2}{2}\right) \tag{2}$$

Eq. (2) shows that if the predicted heatmap has a lower error, each pixel must have a similar error with its two neighbors. Another view of our loss function is to re-arrange it as:

$$\mathcal{L}(H, H^*) = \frac{1}{mn} \sum_{i=1,j=1}^{m,n} \left(\frac{[(H_{i,j} - H_{i-1,j}) - (H^*_{i,j} - H^*_{i-1,j})]^2}{2} + \frac{[(H_{i,j} - H_{i,j-1}) - (H^*_{i,j} - H^*_{i,j-1})]^2}{2}\right) \tag{3}$$

In this form, our loss can be explained as minimizing the difference between the spatial gradient map G^* of the predicted heatmap and the ground-truth gradient map G, in which the gradient is defined as the difference between a pixel and its left neighbor and above neighbor. The basic formula of our Grad loss will be:

$$\mathcal{L} = \sum_{i=1, j=1}^{m,n} (G_{i,j}^* - G_{i,j})^2 \tag{4}$$

which can be optimized similarly as MSE Loss.

3.2   MLE for Offset Location

Quantization Error. In the original resolution of the input image, a landmark coordinate is (x_o, y_o). To reduce the memory consumption, we downsample the ground-truth heatmap into $1/4$, as a result, the coordinate we use in the training phase would be $(\lfloor x_o/4 \rfloor, \lfloor y_o/4 \rfloor)$ where $\lfloor \rfloor$ means floor operator, then the upper-bound of the quantization error will be 3 pixels in the final prediction.

Benefiting from above Grad loss, our predicted heatmap have a well Gaussian structure around the peak position $(\hat{x}, \hat{y})$. Notice that $(\hat{x}, \hat{y})$ are integer coordinates. By utilizing the prior that the pixels in the heatmap follow a Gaussian distribution, we can fit the actual Gaussian center (x_{gt}, y_{gt}) which are float point numbers.

All neighbors of $(\hat{x}, \hat{y})$ satisfy the Eq. (1). Take a log-likelihood of all neighbors, we can get:

$$l(\theta) = -\frac{1}{2\sigma^2} \sum_{i=0}^{m} [(x_i - x_{gt})^2 + (y_i - y_{gt})^2] \tag{5}$$

where m is the total number of the neighbors, we can apply Newton-Raphson method to solve (x_{gt}, y_{gt}) iteratively and the initial values of (x_{gt}, y_{gt}) is $(\hat{x}, \hat{y})$. Due to the space limitation, we will not describe this algorithm in details.

3.3   Multi-scale Feature Fusion

Spatial-Gradient Enhance Module. In the final stage of the HRNet, low-resolution features are upsampled and concatenated with other branches. However, the upsampled features are smooth and lacking of clear edge information, which is essential for localization tasks. To tackle this, we propose to transfer spatial gradient information from high-resolution features to low-resolution.

Given an high-resolution feature map $\mathbf{F}^h \in \mathbb{R}^{C \times H \times W}$ and an low-resolution feature map $\mathbf{F}^l \in \mathbb{R}^{C \times H' \times W'}$, we obtain the spatial edge information of each heatmap by Laplacian operator which is defined as:

$$F = \begin{pmatrix} -1 & -1 & -1 \\ -1 & 8 & -1 \\ -1 & -1 & -1 \end{pmatrix} \tag{6}$$

Then we apply a Batch Normalization to scale the gradient map adaptively and a 1×1 convolution to change the channel dimension to be consistent with other scales. The learned gradient maps will be added by low-resolution feature maps to enhance their edges. An illustration of SGE module is presented in Fig. 3 We apply above SGE module between each pair of different scales.

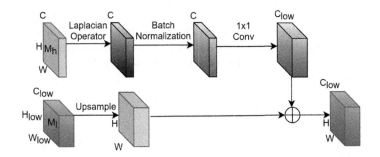

Fig. 3. Illustration of spatial gradient enhance module.

Relation-Based Reweighing Module. Our RRM (Relation-based Reweighing Module) can be abstracted into a concise formulation which is also the paradigm of channel-wise attention:

$$F(x) = x \cdot \delta(f(g(x))) \tag{7}$$

where g is feature extractor, f works as intra-channel learning, δ is activation function. In our design, $g(x)$ is a second-order relation extractor, $f(\cdot)$ is SVD(singular value decomposition) reduction. The most different design is that we transfer the final channel attention to other scale branches rather than the original.

Similarly a 1×1 convolution is utilized to change the channel dimension. Then we use normalized Gram matrix as the relation between different channels. Given a flatten feature map $X \in \mathbb{R}^{C \times HW}$, the Gram Matrix is $G \in \mathbb{R}^{C \times C}$:

$$G_{ij} = \sum_{k=1}^{HW} X_{ik} \cdot X_{jk} \tag{8}$$

Here i, j mean different channel indexes, k is the pixel index in the flatten $H \times W$ vector. The feature maps are normalized before being flatten to make sure the relation is mapped into $[-1, 1]$.

Next we encode the relation matrix into a channel weight vector. To achieve this, we apply SVD to the relation matrix G:

$$G^{C \times C} = U \Sigma_V^T \tag{9}$$

where $\Sigma_{C\times C}$ is a diagonal matrix which consists of all singular values. We select the singular vector $\Sigma'_{C\times 1}$ corresponding to the largest singular value σ to reduce the relation matrix. Sigmoid activation function is used to map W into $(0, 1)$.

$$W_{C\times 1} = Sigmoid(U\Sigma') \tag{10}$$

The channel weight vector represents the semantic importance of different channels. We utilize semantic information in low-resolution features to reweigh high-resolution features. The illustration can be seen in Fig. 4.

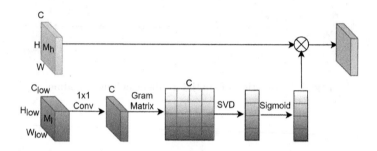

Fig. 4. Illustration of relation-based reweighing module.

3.4 Regression Head Design

We combine the above two effective modules in the final regression head of the network. The design of the final regression head is shown in Fig. 5, and we use HRNet [11] as our backbone network before the regression head.

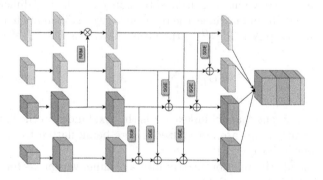

Fig. 5. The architecture of the regression part of the network.

4 Experiments

4.1 Datasets

We evaluate our method on several commonly used facial landmark benchmarks. **AFLW** [15] is a 19 points annotation facial landmark dataset with large head pose and Euler angle variation. **COFW** [1] contains samples with different degrees of occlusion. **300W** [16] is the most commonly used benchmark for facial landmark localization with 68 points. We follow the official experiment setting, training on the 3148 images training set and testing in 4 modes: full test, common subset, challenging subset, and private set. **WFLW** [13] is recently proposed to improve the facial landmark detection robustness for variations in expression, pose, and occlusion.

4.2 Evaluation Metrics

Normalized Mean Error (NME) is wildly used to evaluate the effectiveness of facial landmark detection. We use inter-ocular distance (the distance of outer eye corners) as the normalization factor. **Failure Rate (FR)** is also used to evaluate localization quality. It measures the number of samples with a larger error than a threshold. For all test dataset, we use 8% and 10% as threshold respectively.

Table 1. Comparison results on AFLW dataset.

Method	Full(%)	$FR_{0.1}$(%)	Frontal(%)	Profile(%)
DCFE (ECCV18) [12]	2.17	–	–	–
LAB (CVPR18) [13]	1.85	–	1.62	1.95
Wing (CVPR18) [3]	1.65	–	–	–
ODN(CVPR2019) [17]	1.63	–	**1.38**	1.74
SA+GHCU (CVPR19) [7]	1.60	–	–	
HRNet (baseline) [11]	1.57	0.05	1.46	1.62
Ours	**1.50**	**0**	**1.38**	**1.55**

4.3 Implementation Details

We evaluate the effectiveness of our approach based HRNet [11]. All the faces are cropped according to the annotation and resized to 256×256. The standard derivation for generating Gaussian heatmap is 2.0. Several data augmentation technique is applied including $[-30°, +30°]$ rotation, random horizontal flipping and random rescaling between $[0.75, 1.25]$. The epoch setting and the learning rate strategy are the same with HRNet. The downsample scale factor is 4, which means the final size of the output heatmap is 64×64.

4.4   Evaluation on Benchmarks

Experiment results on the AFLW dataset can be seen in Table 1. The extreme pose variant is a tricky problem for facial landmark detection. Compared our baseline, our approach makes a further improvement both on the frontal faces and profiles. Because our Grad loss guides the network to generate well-organized Gaussian structure in the output heatmaps, our failure rate on 10% NME is 0, which means all the images in the testset are predicted without a large error.

The most challenging problem in COFW is the occlusion. In quantitative results shown in Table 2, we outperform the result of the state of the arts and achieves 3.32 NME. Moreover, we again reduce the failure rate at 10% NME to 0, which indicates the strong capability of occlusion robustness.

We achieve the best results in 300W with a large margin compared to the precious state of the art, see Table 3. What stands out is that the failure rate is reduced to 0 again. In 300W private testset, we still outperform all the other previous work except for the DCFE [13] which exploit extra 3D information.

WFLW is the hardest benchmark among all open datasets. Again we show a positive comparison results in Table 4. We achieve state of the art in all subset in WFLW, proving our approach effective in all extreme conditions such as expressions, makeup or blurry faces.

Table 2. Evaluation on the COFW dataset

Method	NME(%)	$FR_{0.08}$	$FR_{0.1}$
Human	5.60	0	0
TCDCN (ECCV14) [14]	8.05	–	–
DAC-CSR (CVPR17) [4]	6.03	–	4.73
PCD-CNN (CVPR18) [6]	5.77	–	3.73
DCFE (ECCV18) [12]	5.27	7.29	–
LAB (w/B) [13]	3.92	–	0.39
HRNet [11]	3.45	**0.39**	0.19
Ours	**3.32**	**0.39**	0

4.5   Quality Results

Here we show several visualization results of our proposed methods. It's obvious that our method could handle extreme poses better.

5   Ablation Study

To verify the effectiveness of our each independent contribution, We first make a comparison of our three contributions on the 300W and COFW dataset to study

Table 3. Evaluation on 300W.

Method	300W				300W Private testset		
	Common	Challenging	Full	$FR_{0.1}$	NME	AUC	$FR_{0.1}$
PCD-CNN[6]	3.67	7.62	4.44	–	–	–	–
SAN [2]	3.34	6.60	3.98	–	–	–	–
DAN [5]	3.19	5.24	3.59	–	4.30	47.00	2.67
Wing [3]	3.01	6.01	3.60	–	–	–	–
HRNet [11]	2.87	5.15	3.34	0.15	3.85	61.55	–
Ours	2.78	**4.83**	**3.18**	0	**3.74**	**62.92**	**0.17**
Method with extra info.							
LAB(w/B) [13]	2.98	5.19	3.49	–	–	58.85	0.83
DCFE(w/3D)	**2.76**	5.22	3.24	–	–	–	–

Table 4. Evaluation on WFLW.

Method	Full test	Large pose	Expression	Illustration	Makeup	Occlusion	Blur
SDM	10.29	24.10	11.45	9.32	9.38	13.03	11.28
LAB	5.27	10.24	5.51	5.23	5.15	6.79	6.32
Wing	5.11	8.75	5.36	4.93	5.41	6.37	5.81
HRNet	4.60	7.94	4.85	4.55	4.29	5.44	5.42
Ours	**4.44**	**7.61**	**4.68**	**4.35**	**4.22**	**5.21**	**5.16**

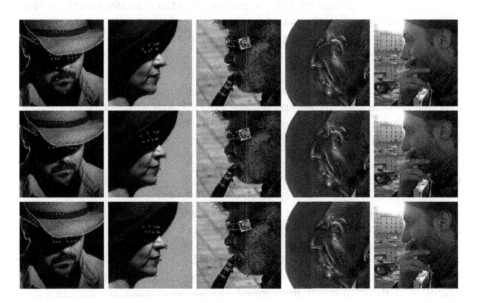

Fig. 6. Visualization samples of our methods. The first row is groundtruth, the second row shows the results from HRNet and the last row is ours.

Table 5. Improvement by different components

Method	300W			COFW	
	Full	$FR_{0.08}$	$FR_{0.1}$	NME	$FR_{0.1}$
MSE (baseline)	3.34	1.74	0.58	3.45	0.20
Grad	3.28	0.73	0	3.42	0
MSE+MLE	3.28	1.16	0.44	3.40	0.20
Grad+MLE	3.23	0.87	0	3.37	0
Grad+MLE+SGE+RRM	3.18	0.58	0	3.32	0

whether they are effective. As seen in Table 5, each component in our approach will improve the accuracy for an obvious margin.

Here we compare results with MLE+MSE and to show that Our Grad loss works collaboratively with our MLE post-processing, rather than a stand-alone component.

Table 6. Grad loss in MPii pose estimation.

Metrics	Methods	Head	Shoulder	Elbow	Wrist	Hip	Knee	Ankle	Mean
PCK@0.1	HRNet	**44.543**	37.313	37.498	36.869	15.146	25.873	27.184	33.149
	Ours	43.008	**39.232**	**38.419**	**38.585**	**16.185**	**27.626**	**28.223**	**34.338**
PCK@0.2	HRNet	80.014	74.032	69.439	65.978	44.937	57.889	58.360	65.587
	Ours	**81.412**	**75.510**	**70.309**	**66.645**	**47.100**	**59.198**	**59.471**	**66.792**
PCK@0.5	HRNet	97.101	**95.941**	90.336	86.449	89.095	**87.084**	**83.278**	**90.330**
	Ours	**97.169**	**95.941**	**90.387**	**86.466**	**89.181**	86.621	82.853	90.242

We also verify our Grad loss in pose estimation task. We follow the same experiment setting as HRNet and replace the MSE loss with our Grad loss. The result is shown in Table 6. We outperform HRNet significantly in PCK@0.1 and PCK@0.2, and perform better in several body parts under PCK@0.5 (Fig. 6).

6   Conclusion

In this paper, we have revisited the optimization goal in facial landmark detection. We propose Grad loss to guide the network to optimize the localization error rather than the pixel error. Meanwhile, we introduce a new post-processing strategy based on Gaussian prior to exploit the distribution structure of the heatmap. We also present two effective components, Spatial Gradient Enhance module and Relation-based Reweighing Module to enhance the low-resolution and high-resolution representation separately. Experiments show our approach outperforms the state-of-the-art on several datasets by significant margins.

Acknowledgement. This paper is supported by NSFC (No. 61772330, 61533012, 61876109), China Next Generation Internet IPv6 project (Grant No. NGII20170609) and Shanghai authentication Key Lab. (2017XCWZK01).

References

1. Burgos-Artizzu, X.P., Perona, P., Dollár, P.: Robust face landmark estimation under occlusion. In: IEEE International Conference on Computer Vision, ICCV 2013, Sydney, Australia, 1–8 December 2013, pp. 1513–1520 (2013)
2. Dong, X., Yan, Y., Ouyang, W., Yang, Y.: Style aggregated network for facial landmark detection. In: 2018 IEEE Conference on Computer Vision and Pattern Recognition, CVPR 2018, Salt Lake City, UT, USA, 18–22 June 2018, pp. 379–388 (2018)
3. Feng, Z., Kittler, J., Awais, M., Huber, P., Wu, X.-J.: Wing loss for robust facial landmark localisation with convolutional neural networks. In: 2018 IEEE Conference on Computer Vision and Pattern Recognition, CVPR 2018, Salt Lake City, UT, USA, 18–22 June 2018, pp. 2235–2245 (2018)
4. Feng, Z.-H., Kittler, J., Christmas, W.J., Huber, P., Wu, X.: Dynamic attention-controlled cascaded shape regression exploiting training data augmentation and fuzzy-set sample weighting. In: 2017 IEEE Conference on Computer Vision and Pattern Recognition, CVPR 2017, Honolulu, HI, USA, 21–26 July 2017, pp. 3681–3690 (2017)
5. Kowalski, M., Naruniec, J., Trzcinski, T.: Deep alignment network: a convolutional neural network for robust face alignment. In: 2017 IEEE Conference on Computer Vision and Pattern Recognition Workshops, CVPR Workshops 2017, Honolulu, HI, USA, 21–26 July 2017, pp. 2034–2043 (2017)
6. Kumar, A., Chellappa, R.: Disentangling 3D pose in a dendritic CNN for unconstrained 2D face alignment. In: 2018 IEEE Conference on Computer Vision and Pattern Recognition, CVPR 2018, Salt Lake City, UT, USA, 18–22 June 2018, pp. 430–439 (2018)
7. Liu, Z., et al.: Semantic alignment: finding semantically consistent ground-truth for facial landmark detection. In: IEEE Conference on Computer Vision and Pattern Recognition, CVPR 2019, Long Beach, CA, USA, 16–20 June 2019, pp. 3467–3476 (2019)
8. Merget, D., Rock, M., Rigoll, G.: Robust facial landmark detection via a fully-convolutional local-global context network. In: 2018 IEEE Conference on Computer Vision and Pattern Recognition, CVPR 2018, Salt Lake City, UT, USA, 18–22 June 2018, pp. 781–790 (2018)
9. Newell, A., Yang, K., Deng, J.: Stacked hourglass networks for human pose estimation. In: Leibe, B., Matas, J., Sebe, N., Welling, M. (eds.) ECCV 2016. LNCS, vol. 9912, pp. 483–499. Springer, Cham (2016). https://doi.org/10.1007/978-3-319-46484-8_29
10. Papandreou, G., et al.: Towards accurate multi-person pose estimation in the wild. In: 2017 IEEE Conference on Computer Vision and Pattern Recognition, Honolulu, HI, USA, 21–26 July 2017, pp. 3711–3719 (2017)
11. Sun, K., et al.: High-resolution representations for labeling pixels and regions. CoRR, abs/1904.04514 (2019)

12. Valle, R., Buenaposada, J.M., Valdés, A., Baumela, L.: A deeply-initialized coarse-to-fine ensemble of regression trees for face alignment. In: Ferrari, V., Hebert, M., Sminchisescu, C., Weiss, Y. (eds.) Computer Vision – ECCV 2018. LNCS, vol. 11218, pp. 609–624. Springer, Cham (2018). https://doi.org/10.1007/978-3-030-01264-9_36

13. Wu, W., Qian, C., Yang, S., Wang, Q., Cai, Y., Zhou, Q.: Look at boundary: a boundary-aware face alignment algorithm. In: 2018 IEEE Conference on Computer Vision and Pattern Recognition, CVPR 2018, Salt Lake City, UT, USA, 18–22 June 2018, pp. 2129–2138 (2018)

14. Zhang, Z., Luo, P., Loy, C.C., Tang, X.: Facial landmark detection by deep multi-task learning. In: Fleet, D., Pajdla, T., Schiele, B., Tuytelaars, T. (eds.) ECCV 2014. LNCS, vol. 8694, pp. 94–108. Springer, Cham (2014). https://doi.org/10.1007/978-3-319-10599-4_7

15. Koestinger, M., Wohlhart, P., Roth, P.M., Bischof, H.: Annotated facial landmarks in the wild: a large-scale, real-world database for facial landmark localization. In: Proceedings of the First IEEE International Workshop on Benchmarking Facial Image Analysis Technologies

16. Sagonas, C., Tzimiropoulos, G., Zafeiriou, S., Pantic, M.: 300 faces in-the-wild challenge: the first facial landmark localization challenge. In: 2013 IEEE International Conference on Computer Vision Workshops, Sydney, Australia, 1–8 December 2013, pp. 397–403 (2013)

17. Zhu, M., Shi, D., Zheng, M., Sadiq, M.: Robust facial landmark detection via occlusion-adaptive deep networks. In: IEEE Conference on Computer Vision and Pattern Recognition, CVPR 2019, Long Beach, CA, USA, 16–20 June 2019, pp. 3486–3496 (2019)

18. Xiong, X., De la Torre, F.: Supervised descent method and its applications to face alignment. In: 2013 IEEE Conference on Computer Vision and Pattern Recognition, Portland, OR, USA, 23–28 June 2013, pp. 532–539 (2013)

DVRCNN: Dark Video Post-processing Method for VVC

Donghui Feng[1], Yiwei Zhang[2], Chen Zhu[2], Han Zhang[2], and Li Song[1,2(✉)]

[1] Cooperative Medianet Innovation Center, Shanghai, China
`faymek@sjtu.edu.cn`
[2] Institute of Image Communication and Network Engineering, Shanghai Jiao Tong University, Shanghai, China
`{6000myiwei,zhuchenzc,zetallica,song_li}@sjtu.edu.cn`

Abstract. Low-light videos are usually accompanied with acquisition noise, motion blur and some other specific distortions, which makes it hard to compress by the video coding technologies and generates less satisfying compressed videos. In order to enhance both the subjective and objective quality of compressed dark videos, we propose a novel learning based post-processing scheme for the most recent VVC. Specifically, we adopt a multi-scale residue learning structure, named Dark Video Restoration Convolutional Neural Network (DVRCNN), as an additional out-loop post-processing method. To avoid the over-smooth effect by MSE metric, SSIM and texture loss are also added to the final loss function. Luma and chroma components are decomposed then fed to two corresponding models separately. Compared with VVC baseline on the six sequences given in ICME 2020 Grand Challenge, our approach significantly reduces the BD-rate by 36.08% and achieves a fair promotion on both objective and subjective quality, especially for the low bit-rate compressed sequence with severe distortion. Validation results show that the proposed model generates well to continuous scenes and variable bitrates.

Keywords: Dark video · Post-processing · Versatile video coding · Convolutional Neural Network

1 Introduction

Videos captured in low light conditions are often encountered in cinema as a result of artistic perspective or the nature of a scene. As a subcategory of natural video content, they often appear in concerts, shows, surveillance camera footage and shots of wildlife at night. In such dark videos, due to the limitation of hardware, acquisition noise and motion blur are simultaneously produced, bringing special characteristics to video compression, which makes it hard to generate subjective satisfactory compressed video.

This work was supported by the Shanghai Key Laboratory of Digital Media Processing and Transmissions, 111 Project (B07022 and Sheitc No.150633) and MoE-China Mobile Research Fund Project(MCM20180702).

ⓒ Springer Nature Switzerland AG 2021
J. Lokoč et al. (Eds.): MMM 2021, LNCS 12572, pp. 691–703, 2021.
https://doi.org/10.1007/978-3-030-67832-6_56

In practice, most of the lossy video coding technologies follow the block-based hybrid coding framework, which includes block-based prediction, transformation, quantization and entropy coding. Thus, the lossy video coding technologies by nature contain distortion and artifact. In High Efficiency Video Coding (HEVC) standard [14], deblocking filter and sample adaptive offset (SAO) was proposed as the in-loop filtering methods to resolve these problems.

The most recent video coding standard named Versatile Video Coding (VVC) [1] still following the block-based processing procedure but incorporated with many advanced technologies. In the VVC standard, up to 4 algorithms are committed to reducing distortion and artifacts at the in-loop filtering step, such as luma mapping with chroma scaling (LMCS), deblocking filter, sample adaptive offset (SAO) and adaptive loop filter (ALF) [3]. These new tools enable around 30% of coding gain beyond HEVC [13]. However, all these in-loop filtering technologies contained in the video coding standard are manually designed based on the characteristics of normal video content. Due to the different characteristics of dark video, traditional in-loop filtering may not be able to handle the distortion and artifacts contained in the compressed dark video.

Recently, there have been many research efforts in employing Convolutional Neural Network (CNN) to solve the traditional filtering problem in the video coding task. Significant gains have been achieved through traditional methods. Most existing CNN-based approaches can roughly be divided into two aspects. Approaches designed to replace or incorporate with in-loop filters at encoder end [7,10,11,16,17] and out-loop restoration approaches to improve reconstruction quality at decoder end [4,9,15]. Nevertheless, all these learning based filtering approaches just take into account the luma component to improve the compress performance of normal video content. In terms of low light video, most of the work focuses on denoising and enhancement, but fewer approaches are reported to improve dark video encoding. Details of related works are shown in Sect. 2.

To improve the perceptual quality of compressed low-light videos beyond the current state of the art VVC, we propose a multi-scale residue learning dark video restoration CNN (DVRCNN) post-processing method. To avoid the over-smooth effect by MSE metric, we also add SSIM and texture loss to the total loss function. In dark videos, the luma component is more severely impaired. Therefore, our method trains two corresponding post processing models for different components respectively. The structure of DVRCNN will be detailed in Sect. 3.

In our experiments, an average of 36.08% reduction of BD-rate is achieved when computing PSNR-YUV in the six sequences. When using PSNR-Y, the reduction drops to 33.07%. It turns out that the chroma tends to perform better than the luma. All sequences have achieved significant gain on both PSNR and VMAF scores. The complete validation demonstrates that the proposed model generates well to c continuous scene and variable bitrates. All the results show that our model can apply to video post-processing problems comprehensively.

2   Related Works

In the domain of artifact reduction of video coding, there are two aspects of methods as mentioned previously. One is the normative in-loop filtering coding tools, which perform at the encoder to generate better references for the following to-be-coded frames. In addition to the in-loop filter, post-processing is usually adopted at the decoder side to improve the quality of reconstructed videos without overhead. It should be noted that these post-processing methods can also be integrated into the coding loop to generate better references as the in-loop approach. There have been many research efforts employing CNN to solve the in-loop filtering and post-processing problems and significant gains have been obtained over traditional methods. Some recent proposals are summarized as follows.

2.1   In-Loop Filters

In terms of in-loop filters, the CNN models are designed to replace or incorporate the traditional in-loop filters. W. Park *et al.* proposed an In-loop Filter CNN (IFCNN) for replacing SAO [11]. Compared to HEVC baseline, the BD-rate results of reducing 4.8% in all-intra configuration and 2.8% on average. Y. Dai *et al.* proposed a Variable filter size Residue learning CNN (VRCNN) as the replacement of both DB and SAO in HEVC intra coding [16]. In their experiments, VRCNN is reported to achieve a promising result of an average 4.6% BD-rate reduction.

VRCNN and IFCNN are both shallow networks with less than 5 layers. Through using a deeper network of 30 layers, J. Kang *et al.* proposed a multi-modal/multi-scale CNN (MMS-net) to replace exiting DB and SAO in HEVC [7]. Their method consists of two sub-networks of different scales, which reduces the average BD-rate by 4.55% and 8.5% in AI configuration, respectively.

In addition to replacing the traditional in-loop filters, the CNN-based methods can also be incorporated with the existing filters. One typical work is the Residual Highway CNN (RHCNN) [17], which is used as the last in-loop filter. The average BD-rate reduction is 5.70%, 5.68%, and 4.35% in AI, Low-Delay (LDP) and Random-Access (RA) configurations of HEVC, respectively. The CNN model can also be incorporated between several traditional filters. For example, a Multi-channel Long-Short-Term Dependency Residual Network (MLSDRN) [10] is inserted between Deblocking and SAO in HEVC, obtaining 6.0%, 8.1%, and 7.4% BD-rate savings in different configurations.

2.2   Post-processing Filters

The post-processing methods, usually out-of-loop filters, improve the quality of reconstructed video in a convenient manner at the decoder side. For applications limited by bandwidth and time delay, it's an available scheme to compensate for the performance.

To some extent, post-processing is similar to the restoration task of single images or videos. Inspired by the superior performance of learning based restoration, C. Li *et al.* proposed a post-processing CNN with 20 convolution layers in [4]. The network structure is similar to [8] but adopted additional information contained in bitstream. Compared to HEVC baseline, their approach achieves an average BD-rate reduction of 1.6% on the six test sequences in the ICIP 2017 Grand Challenge.

More recently, T. Wang *et al.* proposed a Deep CNN-based Auto-Decoder (DCAD) post-processing method [15]. Their approach can further improve the coding efficiency and achieve average BD-rate reduction of 5.0%, 6.4%, 5.3% and 5.5% for AI, LDP, LDB, and RA configurations, respectively. L. Ma *et al.* proposed a Residual-based Video Restoration Network (Residual VRN) [9]. Compared to HEVC baseline, their method performs better than DCAD with an average BD-rate reduction of 7.4%, 9.4%, 7.4% and 7.6% for AI, LDP, LDB, and RA configurations, respectively.

3 Proposed Approach

3.1 Overall Framework of Our Proposed Method

In order to deal with the unique characteristics Of low light video, our proposed approach simultaneously processes both luma and chroma components, which are very different from previous post-processing methods that were designed only for luma components.

The overall framework of our method is shown in Fig. 1. We trained two individual DVRCNN models for luma and chroma pictures, respectively. When dealing with a decoded picture in case of 4:2:0 color format, the decoded picture is first separated into one luma picture and two chroma pictures. Then the luma picture and the chroma pictures are respectively subjected to the corresponding DVRCNN post-processing model to obtain output restored pictures. Finally, the output pictures, including one luma picture and two chroma pictures, are reconstituted to the output enhanced picture, which is the same size as the decoded picture.

3.2 Proposed Network Structure

The input of the loop filter is the reconstructed frame, and the output is the filtered frame, which should be as close to the original frame as possible. Obviously, it has become a key issue to design a proper CNN structure to model the nonlinear map between them. By observing the results of previous work, it's always a dilemma to decide the complexity of network structure. Obviously, complex models can more closely approximate the real distribution of distortion to obtain high gains, but computational efficiency is still a major concern in coding.

To balance between model complexity and filter gain, here we adopt a moderately deep network structure, dark video restoration CNN, referred as DVRCNN.

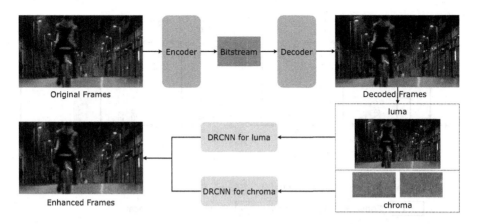

Fig. 1. Overall framework of our proposed DVRCNN post-processing scheme.

Nine convolution blocks, four Max Pooling layers, and four Up Sampling layers are linked to map the reconstructed frame to the residual frame non-linearly. The network is constructed on top of a residual learning structure [5] to accelerate training. The enhanced frame is finally generated by adding the residual frame to an identity skip connection. The structure of DVRCNN is illustrated in Fig. 2.

In general, The structure of the model is divided into two parts (Table 1). The first half is a pooling layer after every two convolutions. After each pooling layer, higher-dimensional features of the input image will be extracted. The feature maps are also directly concatenated with the output of the deconvolution layer in the same size. Such a skip-connection can cope with distortions of different scales in the input image. Severely distorted images are compensated by extracting higher-dimensional feature maps from multiple convolutional layers and pooling layers.

The second half of the model is to achieve upsampling by deconvolution after every two convolutions, thereby restoring the feature map to the same size as the input. After convolution and activation of the last layer in the network, the feature map is added to the input image to get the output enhanced image.

We introduce the nonlinear function PReLU as the activation function to enlarge the network's capacity. In the last convolution, we choose *tanh* activation function to eliminate nonlinear distortion after adding to the original image. Meanwhile, we choose the BatchNorm layer as the normalization item in our model. As mentioned in [12], the BatchNorm layer effectively solve the problem of data distribution shifting during training and improve the speed of training.

3.3   Loss Function

The input of the model is the frame $Y_n, n \in (1, ..., N)$, from the compressed video Y. The output is the enhanced frame $\hat{Y}_n = F(Yn|\theta), n \in (1, ..., N)$, where θ is the whole parameters set of DVRCNN.

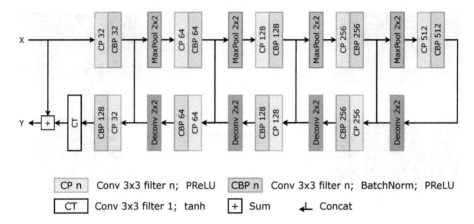

CP n │ Conv 3x3 filter n; PReLU   CBP n │ Conv 3x3 filter n; BatchNorm; PReLU

CT │ Conv 3x3 filter 1; tanh   + │ Sum   ⌐ Concat

Fig. 2. The structure of DVRCNN: there are eighteen layers in DVRCNN, including nine combination layers (each combination layer consists of a convolution layer, a PReLU layer, or a convolution layer, a BatchNorm layer and and a PReLU layer).

We use the frame $X_n, n \in (1, ..., N)$ from the origin video X as the ground truth. The low-light images are more interfered by degradations than bright-light ones. For seeking a proper restoration function, the objective turns to minimize the loss function as follows:

$$\text{Loss} = \text{MSE}(X_n, \hat{Y}_n) + \lambda_1 \text{SSIM}(X_n, \hat{Y}_n) + \lambda_2 ||\nabla X_n - \nabla \hat{Y}_n||_2^2 \qquad (1)$$

Mean-Squared-Error metric is the ideal loss function to increase PSNR performance. But the resulting images are caused to be too smooth due to the implicit Gaussian prior. Considering that the structural and texture information in the dark video is relatively weak, we choose SSIM and texture metric as additional items of the loss function. The SSIM metric reflects the structural similarity between images. And the texture information can be obtained through the Scharr filter, which computes the gradient of an image. Thus, the total loss function can guarantee both objective quality and perceptual quality will be improved together.

4 Experiments and Discussion

4.1 Training Models

The training and test data comes from the six dark sequences in ICME2020 Grand Challenge: Encoding in the Dark [6]. To meet the bitrate requirements of the challenge, each sequence is compressed by VTM-7.0 under random access (RA) configurations and we use *QP* and *QPIncrementFrame* options to arrive at the target bitrate within 3%. We extract the luma and chroma pictures separately from each frame and crop them into patches of size 64×64. The corresponding sub-pictures of the original YUV sequences are taken as the ground truth. One pair of related image patches are taken as one sample. 90% of the samples are used for training, and the remaining 10% are used as test data. For the luma model, we get 3029400 samples for training, 336600 samples for testing, and for the chroma model, we get 801900 samples for training and 89100 samples for testing.

Table 1. The structure of DVRCNN and specification for each layer.

Layers	Input	Operation	Kernle	Stride	Filters
conv1–1	Y or UV	Conv& PReLU	3×3	1	32
conv1–2	conv1–1	Conv& BatchNorm& PReLU	3×3	1	32
pool1	conv1–2	Max Pooling	2×2	2	32
conv2–1	pool1	Conv& PReLU	3×3	1	64
conv2–2	conv2–1	Conv& BatchNorm& PReLU	3×3	1	64
pool2	conv2–2	Max Pooling	2×2	2	64
conv3–1	pool2	Conv& PReLU	3×3	1	128
conv3–2	conv3–1	Conv& BatchNorm& PReLU	3×3	1	128
pool3	conv3–2	Max Pooling	2×2	2	128
conv4–1	pool3	Conv& PReLU	3×3	1	256
conv4–2	conv4–1	Conv& BatchNorm& PReLU	3×3	1	256
pool4	conv4–2	Max Pooling	2×2	2	256
conv5–1	pool4	Conv& PReLU	3×3	1	512
conv5–2	conv5–1	Conv& BatchNorm& PReLU	3×3	1	512
up1	conv5–2	Deconv	2×2	2	256
conv6–1	up1,pool4	Conv& PReLU	3×3	1	256
conv6–2	conv6–1	Conv& BatchNorm& PReLU	3×3	1	256
up2	conv6–2	Deconv	2×2	2	128
conv7–1	up2,pool3	Conv& PReLU	3×3	1	128
conv7–2	conv7–1	Conv& BatchNorm& PReLU	3×3	1	128
up3	conv7-2	Deconv	2×2	2	64
conv8–1	up3,pool2	Conv& PReLU	3×3	1	64
conv8–2	conv8–1	Conv& BatchNorm& PReLU	3×3	1	64
up4	conv8–2	Deconv	2×2	2	32
conv9–1	up4,pool1	Conv& PReLU	3×3	1	32
conv9–2	conv9–1	Conv& BatchNorm& PReLU	3×3	1	128
conv10	conv9–2	ConvTanh	3×3	1	1

In our experiments, we use PyTorch to realize the model. The mini-batch size is 128 and λ_1, λ_2 are set to –0.075, 1.5. The optimizer is Adam with momentum parameters β_1, β_2 set to 0.9 and 0.99. We also adopt The strategy of step learning rate, and gradually adjust the learning rate from 3×10^{-4} to 10^{-6} according to the change of the loss value.

Considering that there are quite a lot image blocks in a frame of dark video with low brightness, this means that these image blocks carry less information, and the compression distortion of these blocks is relatively small, but they occupy most of a mini-batch. Therefore, in the last few epochs of training, we extract the first 2/3 maximum value from the loss vector of a mini-batch and use the average value as the loss of this mini-batch to update the gradient. By doing this, the samples suffering heavy distortion can be extracted from the mini-batch.

Table 2. The BD-rate and BD-PSNR results compared to VTM-7.0 baseline

Sequences	PSNR-Y		PSNR-YUV	
	BD-PSNR(dB)	BD-rate(%)	BD-PSNR(dB)	BD-rate(%)
Campfire	1.14	−27.73	1.22	−30.57
DinnerScene	0.46	−25.26	0.49	−30.37
ELFuente-Cars	1.07	−25.79	1.13	−28.83
ELFuente-Cyclist	2.42	−68.55	2.58	−72.48
ELFuente-Palacio	1.85	−45.46	1.94	−48.55
SmokeClear	0.12	−5.63	0.12	−5.68
Overall	1.18	−33.07	1.25	−36.08

4.2 Comparison with VVC

The overall performance of our proposed method is summarised in Table 2, where VTM-7.0 is used as anchor. Compared with VVC, our approach achieves an average BD-rate reduction of 33.7% and a BD-PNSR increase of 1.18(dB) for luma component. The biggest BD-rate reduction can be 68.55%. As for all three components, the average BD-rate reduction is 36.08% and average BD-PSNR increase is 1.25(dB), which verifies our proposed post-processing method outperforms original VVC when dealing with low-light video compression tasks.

In addition to the objective quality, we further compare the subjective quality of our proposed method with VVC. We use the VMAF as the subjective metric [2]. The quality of each sequence is summarized in Table 3. It can be noticed both the PSNR-YUV and the VMAF scores of our approach are superior than VTM-7.0 baseline at each bitrate point.

To intuitively demonstrate the performance of our proposed post-processing method. The rate-distortion curves of ELFuente-Cyclist is shown in Fig. 3. Our proposed method achieves better performance at all bitrate points for both objective and subjective quality metrics.

4.3 Validation

To perform complete validation on the limited sequences, we adopt a new division method to get training and validation datasets and use them to train new models. For convenience, we specify the 6 dark video sequences with 4 bitrates as S1-S6 and R1-R4, and we make data specs to perform validation. Detailed specifications are in Table 4. Training data drops S6 ,R2 and the last 10 % frames from all the YUV files. Thus, the validation set can be made by the dropped data.

Table 3. Per-sequence performance.

Sequence	Bitrate	PSNR-YUV		VMAF	
		Base	Our	Our	Our
Campfire	637.53	32.06	**33.53**	52.40	**61.89**
	1300.70	34.16	**35.49**	69.11	**75.06**
	2511.70	36.46	**37.57**	83.53	**86.71**
	4378.53	38.63	**39.43**	92.99	**94.55**
DinnerScene	49.85	41.90	**43.05**	71.07	**81.45**
	71.01	42.91	**43.63**	79.63	**85.67**
	101.39	43.60	**44.01**	85.20	**88.66**
	200.47	44.28	**44.38**	90.43	**91.74**
ELFuente-Cars	83.62	37.30	**39.62**	47.81	**64.06**
	148.32	39.52	**41.04**	63.19	**73.64**
	275.41	41.63	**42.37**	76.60	**81.53**
	540.54	43.75	**44.02**	87.16	**89.26**
ELFuente-Cyclist	70.18	36.43	**40.65**	57.85	**83.62**
	122.02	38.58	**41.82**	72.27	**89.90**
	216.02	40.37	**42.38**	83.14	**92.35**
	400.18	41.81	**42.89**	90.27	**94.41**
ELFuente-Palacio	101.55	34.64	**37.49**	51.53	**70.07**
	166.94	36.78	**39.34**	67.19	**80.88**
	294.19	38.94	**40.44**	80.53	**86.31**
	509.50	40.63	**41.36**	88.58	**90.62**
SmokeClear	214.59	40.39	**40.65**	33.46	**34.89**
	410.52	42.45	**42.59**	42.96	**44.49**
	692.62	43.57	**43.66**	51.34	**53.04**
	1414.97	44.53	**44.58**	62.61	**64.38**

For validation result in Table 5, we can see that our method performs well on the sequences the model has seen during the training process. Both the unseen rate and unseen frame have been improved in PSNR and VMAF by our method.

Generally speaking, for texture the model has seen in the training process, it can restore the similar texture in the image block of different rate or different frame. Therefore, our method can have a good performance on the unseen frame and unseen rate. While for the unseen sequence SmokeClear, its objective quality is slightly reduced, which is an intuitive conclusion. When conducting experiments on such few video scenarios, the statistical model can hardly generalize to unfamiliar textures.

For sequences with low bitrate and severe distortion, our method yields higher quality improvement. Among the results of all sequences, results of sequence ELFuente-Cyclist are especially good because this sequence has the most complex texture information than other sequences. Besides, from Fig. 4a we can see that our method can effectively restore the blurred texture in the decoded image. Its subjective quality also improved a lot.

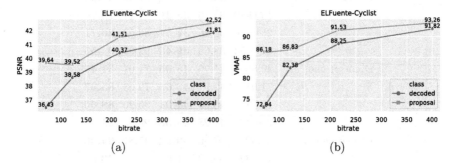

(a)   (b)

Fig. 3. Rate distortion curve of ELFuente-Cyclist sequence. (a), (b) show the PSNR, and VMAF of our approach and baseline (VTM-7.0), respectively.

Table 4. Training and validation data specification.

Mark	[S]equence	[R]ate	Frame
all	1,2,3,4,5,6	1,2,3,4	100%
train	1,2,3,4,5	1,3,4	First 90%
val sequence	6	1,3,4	First 90%
val rate	1,2,3,4,5	2	First 90%
val frame	1,2,3,4,5	1,3,4	Last 10%
var srf	6	2	Last 10%

For other sequences, our method also achieves an improvement on PSNR and VMAF, except for the sequence SmokeClear. But as Fig. 4b shows, it is hard to find the difference between the images even in a close look. This is due to the fact that the design of our model's loss function makes the model pay more attention to subjective quality during the training process. Although its objective quality drops, its subjective quality remains unchanged.

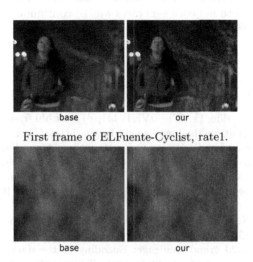

base   our

First frame of ELFuente-Cyclist, rate1.

base   our

First frame of SmokeClear, rate4.

Fig. 4. Some typical frames generated by our proposed method and baseline.

Table 5. Training and validation performance.

Mark	PSNR-Y			PSNR-UV			PSNR-YUV			VMAF		
	Base	Our	Gain	Base	Our	Gain	Base	Our	Gain	Base	Our	Gain
train	37.55	38.71	1.16	41.98	43.22	1.24	38.59	39.76	1.17	87.35	90.59	3.25
val seq	40.70	40.01	−0.70	70.03	62.92	−7.11	42.46	41.76	−0.70	88.96	88.53	−0.43
val rate	37.03	37.41	0.37	41.50	42.11	0.61	38.08	38.49	0.41	85.37	87.61	2.24
val frame	37.30	37.75	0.45	41.81	42.37	0.56	38.35	38.82	0.47	86.53	88.38	1.85
val srf	40.78	39.96	−0.82	69.42	62.82	−6.59	42.54	41.71	−0.83	89.77	89.50	−0.28
all	37.83	38.53	0.69	42.71	43.70	0.99	38.94	39.67	0.73	87.16	89.44	2.28

5   Conclusion

In this paper, we propose a convolutional neural network based post-processing method to improve the quality of compressed low light video content. Our proposed method adopts a multi-scale residue learning structure named DVRCNN at the decoder side. The proposed DVRCNN takes both luma and chroma components simultaneously and contains separate models for different components. The loss function combined with MSE, SSIM and texture has greatly promoted the objective and subjective quality metrics for all bitrate points beyond VVC, especially for the low bit-rate compressed sequence with severe distortion. The component separation strategy has also been proven to be effective, since the chroma component performs much higher than the luma. Validation results show that the proposed network generates well to continuous scenes and variable bitrates. It's powerful enough to apply to dark video post-processing problems comprehensively.

References

1. Versatile Video Coding (VVC)—JVET. https://jvet.hhi.fraunhofer.de/
2. VMAF - video multi-method assessment fusion. https://github.com/Netflix/vmaf
3. Bross, B., Chen, J., Liu, S., Wang, Y.-K.: Versatile video coding (draft 10). http://phenix.it-sudparis.eu/jvet/doc_end_user/current_document.php?id=10399
4. Li, C., Song, L., Xie, R., Zhang, W.: CNN based post-processing to improve HEVC. In: 2017 IEEE International Conference on Image Processing (ICIP), pp. 4577–4580 (2017)
5. He, K., Zhang, X., Ren, S., Sun, J.: Deep Residual Learning for Image Recognition. arXiv:1512.03385 (2015)
6. ICME: ICME 2020 grand challenge: Encoding in the dark—visual information laboratory. Accessed 20 Mar 2020, https://vilab.blogs.bristol.ac.uk/?p=2311
7. Kang, J., Kim, S., Lee, K.M.: Multi-modal/multi-scale convolutional neural network based in-loop filter design for next generation video codec. In: Processing, I.I.C.o.I. (ed.) 2017 IEEE International Conference on Image Processing. IEEE (2017). https://doi.org/10.1109/icip.2017.8296236
8. Kim, J., Lee, J.K., Lee, K.M.: Accurate image super-resolution using very deep convolutional networks. In: 2016 IEEE Conference on Computer Vision and Pattern Recognition (CVPR). IEEE (2016). https://doi.org/10.1109/cvpr.2016.182
9. Ma, L., Tian, Y., Huang, T.: Residual-based video restoration for HEVC intra coding. In: Data, I.I.C.o.M.B. (ed.) 2018 IEEE Fourth International Conference on Multimedia Big Data (BigMM). IEEE (2018). https://doi.org/10.1109/bigmm.2018.8499072
10. Meng, X., Chen, C., Zhu, S., Zeng, B.: A new HEVC in-loop filter based on multi-channel long-short-term dependency residual networks. In: 2018 Data Compression Conference. IEEE (2018). https://doi.org/10.1109/dcc.2018.00027
11. Park, W.S., Kim, M.: CNN-based in-loop filtering for coding efficiency improvement. In: 2016 IEEE 12th Image, Video, and Multidimensional Signal Processing Workshop (IVMSP). IEEE (2016). https://doi.org/10.1109/ivmspw.2016.7528223
12. Ioffe, S., Szegedy, C.: Batch normalization: accelerating deep network training by reducing internal covariate shift. In: Proceedings of the 32nd International Conference on Machine Learning, pp. 448–456 (2015)
13. Sidaty, N., Hamidouche, W., Deforges, O., Philippe, P.: Compression efficiency of the emerging video coding tools. In: 2017 IEEE International Conference on Image Processing (ICIP), pp. 2996–3000 (2017)
14. Sullivan, G.J., Ohm, J.R., Han, W.J., Wiegand, T.: Overview of the high efficiency video coding (HEVC) standard. IEEE Trans. Circ. Syst. Video Technol. **22**(12), 1649–1668 (2012)

15. Wang, T., Chen, M., Chao, H.: A novel deep learning-based method of improving coding efficiency from the decoder-end for HEVC. In: 2017 Data Compression Conference (DCC), pp. 410–419 (2017)
16. Dai, Y., Liu, D., Wu, F.: A convolutional neural network approach for post-processing in HEVC intra coding. In: Amsaleg, L., Guðmundsson, G.Þ., Gurrin, C., Jónsson, B.Þ., Satoh, S. (eds.) MMM 2017. LNCS, vol. 10132, pp. 28–39. Springer, Cham (2017). https://doi.org/10.1007/978-3-319-51811-4_3
17. Zhang, Y., Shen, T., Ji, X., Zhang, Y., Xiong, R., Dai, Q.: Residual highway convolutional neural networks for in-loop filtering in HEVC. IEEE Trans. Image Process. Publ. IEEE Signal Process. Soc. 27(8), 3827–3841 (2018). https://doi.org/10.1109/tip.2018.2815841

An Efficient Image Transmission Pipeline for Multimedia Services

Zeyu Wang$^{(\boxtimes)}$

Shandong University, Qingdao, China
`zywangx@gmail.com`

Abstract. The transmitting costs of image data strongly impact the user experience in multimedia services such as Instagram and Twitter. In this paper, we design a novel image transmission pipeline for both efficiently reducing data usage and preserving image quality in those services. Through analyzing the varying features in resized image, we found that high-frequency details achieve a major loss. Based on this impact, we build a series of mechanisms to construct our pipeline: 1) an image resampling mechanism, 2) a high-frequency feature extraction technique, and 3) an image reconstruction method based on the resampled image and its local features. Besides, we also introduce an adaptive binning approach for improving the performance of feature extraction. Finally, we conduct several experiments which show that the proposed pipeline significantly outperforms other baselines in preserving image quality and transmitting time, and is comparable in reducing data usage.

Keywords: Image transmission · Data usage · Multimedia services · Image quality

1 Introduction

Multimedia services have already improved the quality of our daily life in a wide variety of aspects significantly. While bringing a lot of benefits, users are faced with more and more problems with managing online data usage [6]. Most mobile internet users are highly cost-sensitive to data usage in multimedia services and they would like to take any possible strategies to reduce data usage [14].

As we all know, image plays a significant role in multimedia services. The development of portable phones and cameras made it possible to share and access high-resolution images everywhere. However, transmitting images would cost a large data stream every time, such as several megabytes for mobile cameras and tens of megabytes (or even larger) for professional cameras. Hence it's crucial if we can both reduce the data cost and maintain image quality in the image transmission of multimedia services.

How to find a balance between data cost and the performance of multimedia services? This question has been studied for decades [15]. But so far, all of the previous approaches were proposed from a data management perspective and

© Springer Nature Switzerland AG 2021
J. Lokoč et al. (Eds.): MMM 2021, LNCS 12572, pp. 704–715, 2021.
https://doi.org/10.1007/978-3-030-67832-6_57

paid little attention to the user-side, which dramatically reduces the scope of their applicability. E.g., sometimes users are forced to upload a low-resolution image to share their emotions such as Twitter or WeChat. There's still no effective way to find a balance between reducing data usage and preserving image quality in multimedia services. We aim to tackle this problem and fill the gaps between data usage and users' concerns about image transmission.

For achieving this goal, we propose a novel pipeline in the image transmission process of online multimedia services. Our key idea is to decompose a high-resolution image as a combination of its low-resolution version and notable key features. We first propose a gradient-aware image resampling method for representing the major contents of input images as a low-resolution one. Then we design a high-frequency feature extraction method using Wavelet Transform and introduce an adaptive binning method for better recognizing key features. Finally, we present an image reconstructing approach by combining its major contents and key features. An illustrated instance of our image transmission pipeline is presented in Fig. 1.

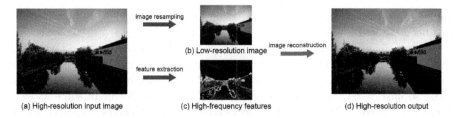

Fig. 1. An illustration of our image transmission pipeline. Our pipeline mainly contains three steps, image resampling, high-frequency feature extraction, and image reconstruction. The blue arrow means these steps are employed from the sender's end, while the red arrow means this step is conducted on the receiver's end. (Color figure online)

We also conduct several studies to demonstrate that our pipeline can preserve the overall quality and significantly reduce data usage.

Organization. The remainder of this paper is structured as follows. Section 2 introduces the previous achievements related to our mechanism. By then, Sect. 3 analyzes the changes of local features in image resamplings. Section 4 introduces the image transmission pipeline we proposed. Hereafter, the default settings and overall results of our experiments are presented in Sect. 5. Finally, we conclude our work and discuss future work in Sect. 6.

2   Related Work

In this section, we briefly discuss related categories of previous works, the impact of data usage for users, image compression methods, and image resampling methods.

2.1 Users' Concerns about Data Usage

Users are highly cost-sensitive to mobile data usage regardless of their income level [6]. Mobile users are more aware of their online services will cost data than PC users, but they still cannot find an appropriate way to manage their data cost for everyday services [14].

Users have designed many strategies to reduce data cost, such as disconnecting to the web [12]. And they are very concerned about how to improve their data usage [12,14]. In other words, users experience still has a strong negative correlation with their data cost.

To overcome the data usage constraint, researchers also presented some efficient ways. Under the resource-constrained settings, previous works have studied many aspects of managing data plans and quota-based data plans [12].

However, no matter how well we can manage our data plan, the essential data usage, e.g., viewing high-resolution images, cannot be reduced.

2.2 Image Compression Methods

Image compression is a probable approach for reducing data cost of images which has been studied for decades [15].

Lossy image compression methods can provide larger compression ratios with less visible artifacts. The Discrete Cosine Transform (i.e., JPEG) is the most famous and widely used transformation for Lossy compression. There are also more sophisticated transformations that could perform better in some aspects, such as the Wavelet Transform (i.e., JPEG2000). These formats have been widely applied, but it still remains several megabytes or even more for general images [5].

More recently, methods inspired by video codecs also achieved good performance such as inter-frame prediction. Two typical formats, WebP, and BPG (Better Portable Graphics) can improve the compression ratio and coding efficiency, but these formats are still not commonly applied, and they may not achieve any major improvement and lack several features [18].

As is well-known, larger compression ratios will cause serious quality descend in many aspects [18]. Hence, there occur numerous complaints from users about the current compression methods applied in famous services such as Facebook[1] and Instagram[2].

2.3 Image Resampling Methods

Little attention of image transmissions studies has been paid to reduce data usage, hence we discuss another related literature: *Image Resampling*. "Image resampling or downsampling reduces the resolution of the image without increasing the physical size of the image, by *throwing away* pixels and determining the

---

[1] https://www.howtogeek.com/343729/why-your-facebook-photos-look-so-bad-and-what-you-can-do-about-it.

[2] https://forum.fujifeed.com/t/uploading-to-instagram-without-compression/233.

color of the remaining pixels based on the combined color of the pixels that were discarded."[3]

The most basic idea is average resampling and bicubic resampling by employing mean and bicubic filters. However, these ideas are too naive to preserve good image quality, hence, many new methods have been proposed.

A content-adaptive method was proposed by Kopf et al. [8] via using adaptive shapes of convolutional kernels in resampling. Hereafter, Öztireli et al. [13] presented a perceptual-based method based on optimizing the visual perception via deriving the structural similarity index (SSIM) [?] of images. More recently, Liu et al. [9] introduced a novel method by optimizing two L_0-regularized priors. However, these methods are always time-consuming and may decrease the quality of original high-resolution images (see Sect. 5).

To overcome the problems of those related works, we attempt to find a different way to represent images. Our pipeline contains an efficient image resampling method and can significantly reduce data usage. And the proposed pipeline can be applied to enhance any kinds of image compression methods.

3   Features in Image Resamplings

In this section, we aim to find which kind of local features of an image changed the most after resampling.

Let's consider a situation about downsampling a small patch in an image first (e.g., resample an image from 3840×2160 to 1920×1080).

Assuming there are a given input image I, a small patch P_o from I, and its corresponding patch P_d in the downscaled image I_D.

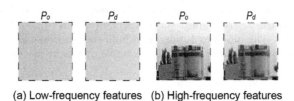

(a) Low-frequency features   (b) High-frequency features

Fig. 2. Comparison of local-frequency (a) and high-frequency (b) features in image resamplings. P_o is from the original image, and P_d is from the 4× resampled version.

A small patch will only contain simple structures. if P_o mainly contains low-frequency features, P_d can preserve the major continuous variation of color and luminance channels. As shown in Fig. 2(a), the major contents of P_o and P_d are similar. It is clear that their contexts both reveal a slight color variation.

However, for a high-frequency patch P_o (with sharp features), P_d may totally obscure the rapid changes and result in visible artifacts by mixing pixels with a

---

[3] http://www.enfocus.com/manuals/Extra/PreflightChecks/17/en-us/common/pr/concept/c_aa1035373.html.

large difference. As shown in Fig. 2(b), the edges of major contents of P_o are not obvious in P_d. The sharp edge at the boundary of the main shape has almost been obscured in P_d which are particularly clear in P_o.

Furthermore, for the cases about resampling an area which contains a wide variety of different patterns and structures, we consider resampling the whole image I.

It is hard and costly to separate the overall image into higher and lower-frequency parts, so we compute the gradient orientation of each image to better accommodate human detection [3].

By comparing the local gradient features of different areas, we found that the conclusion of small patches is also suitable for the overall image I.

As shown in Fig. 3, the gradient map reveals that the major structure of low and medium frequency information in I (e.g., the continuous dark densities as shown in the red box) can be well preserved in I_D. However, the high-frequency details (e.g., the edge of characters as shown in the blue box) show a massive reduction. The blue box highlights a low-frequency comparison, while the red box indicates a high-frequency comparison.

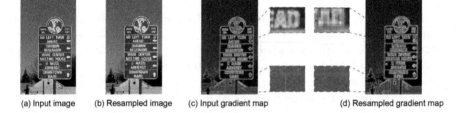

(a) Input image   (b) Resampled image   (c) Input gradient map   (d) Resampled gradient map

Fig. 3. An overall comparison of the features in a target image. (a) shows the original image, and (b) is the 2× resampled version, while (c) and (d) are their corresponding gradient maps. The blue box (upper one) indicates an example of high-frequency details, and the red box (lower one) is an example of low-frequency features. (Color figure online)

In summary, local patches with a larger gradient or more high-frequency features are more likely to be obscured after resampling. And our conclusion is also consistent with previous analysis [7]. Hence, it is necessary for us to find an appropriate way to preserve high-frequency features.

4   Image Transmission Pipeline

In this section, we introduce the technical details of our pipeline.

4.1   Gradient-Aware Image Resampling

We aim to generate a proper low-resolution image that can preserve major contents and some details.

In detail, for a given high-resolution image I, we would like to create an output image I_D with the same aspect ratio and smaller pixels.

Before introducing our technique, we first briefly review the general Gaussian kernel for image resampling. A local Gaussian kernel function in a given 2D domain Ω can be expressed as:

$$G(i) = \sum_{j \in \Omega} \frac{1}{2\pi\sqrt{|\boldsymbol{H}|}} exp(-\frac{1}{2}\boldsymbol{j}^t \boldsymbol{H}^{-1} \boldsymbol{j}), \tag{1}$$

where i is the target point, j is the neighbor pixel of i in the processed domain Ω, $\boldsymbol{j}$ is a column vector of the position of j, and $\boldsymbol{H}$ is the bandwidth vector which can rotate and scale a patch. Here, we denote $\boldsymbol{H}$ as a row vector hence we need to inverse it to compute its product.

For a point i, we first compute the major orientation $\{v_i^1, v_i^2\}$ of the local color variation for the neighbor pixels of its corresponding kernel area. Since this principal directions maximize color variance (i.e., gradient), we use them to adjust the shape of the Gaussian kernel:

$$\boldsymbol{H}_i = \boldsymbol{H} * [v_i^1, v_i^2], \tag{2}$$

which means we rotate the original bandwidth vector $\boldsymbol{H}$ to compute an anisotropic bandwidth $\boldsymbol{H}_i$ at point i based on its local color variation.

Then we generate a gradient-aware proxy image I_D^0 by enhancing the gradient orientations. This proxy image I_D^0 is applied to refine the final output and computed by:

$$I_D^0(i) = \frac{1}{n} \sum_{j \in \Omega_i} I(j) \boldsymbol{H}_i * G(i), \tag{3}$$

where Ω_i is the kernel area of pixel i, $I(j)$ is the neighbor pixels of i in the original image I, and n is the sum of the kernel values and employed as a normalization factor, its equation is:

$$n = \sum_{q \in \Omega_i} ||i - j||_2. \tag{4}$$

However, simplified enhance the gradient orientation of the original image may cause visual artifacts which may expand the color on this orientation as shown in Fig. 4(b). Hence, we adjust the proxy image by addressing the effect of the corresponding position of original image and output I_D as follows,

$$I_D(i) = \frac{1}{n} \sum_{j \in \Omega_i} I(j) exp(-\frac{||i - j||_2}{2\sigma_s^2} - \frac{||I_D^0(i) - I_D^0(j)||_2}{2\sigma_r^2}), \tag{5}$$

in which σ_s and σ_r is employed to control the effect of original image and the proxy image. That is to say, a larger σ_s will decrease the impact of the original image, and a larger σ_r will reduce the gradient enhancement in the proxy image. We empirically define $\sigma_s = \sigma_r = 1$ for simplifying computation.

To explain why we adjust the proxy image, Fig. 4 shows a simple example combined by two concentric circles in which (a) shows the original image, (b)

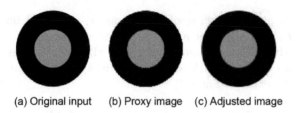

(a) Original input   (b) Proxy image   (c) Adjusted image

Fig. 4. An example of the over-enhancement in the proxy image.

is the proxy image, (c) is the final output of our approach. It's obvious that strong distortions are created on the edge of the circle because the gradient information is over-enhanced, and such distortions can easily be refined by the adjusted image such as Fig. 4(c).

4.2   High-Frequency Features Extraction

Using low-resolution image itself is not enough to reconstruct a high quality high-resolution image. Hence, based on our previous analysis (see Sect. 3) we employ the Wavelet Transform to extract the local high-frequency features [2] for improving the quality of reconstruction.

Our feature extraction method follows three steps. For a given image I, a general wavelet function can be defined as:

$$W(x_i, y_i) = \int_{\Omega_{x_i}} \int_{\Omega_{y_i}} I(x_j, y_j) * G(x_i, y_i) dx_j dy_j. \tag{6}$$

Here, for fitting the description of DWT, we denote (x_i, y_i) as the position of pixel i on the image. In other words, $I(x_j, y_j)$ is equal to $I(j)$, and $G(x_i, y_i)$ refers to $G(i)$ described in Sect. 4.1.

Since many wavelet transforms are complex and hard to explain, we employ the simple but efficient DWT (discrete wavelet transform) method. DWT is always employed to conduct a multi-resolution analysis (i.e., identify and extract signal details at several resolutions) of a signal [17]. For example, 2D DWT can hierarchically decompose a digital image into a series of successively lower resolution images and their associated detail images [11]. Hence, DWT can well preserve high-frequency features.

However, high-frequency features may not spread the whole image. Hence we separate the original image into different bins and run DWT respectively. For a single bin, if the high-frequency features are not obvious enough, this bin will not be preserved. Figure 5 shows an illustration of our bin-based feature extraction. As shown in (c), we will only output the feature of the bottom bin because the top bin does not contain attractive high-frequency information. Besides, because the output features only contains a part of the images with a rest empty region, so we store these features using efficient sparse representation [10].

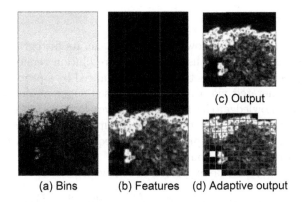

(a) Bins   (b) Features   (c) Output / (d) Adaptive output

Fig. 5. An example of bin-based feature extraction. (a) is two bins of an input image, (b) shows the overall features of bins, (c) illustrates the high-frequency output and (d) shows the adaptive output.

The default setting of bin size is 5% of the whole image, and the lower bound of high-frequency is 10% of the bin with the most obvious features. These two values are selected experimentally for computation efficiency.

4.3 Quadtree-Based Adaptive Binning

Furthermore, to better explore the two hyperparameters of binning (bin size and lower bound of high-frequency), we proposed a quadtree-based approach. This approach can output different scale of bins based on its corresponding local features.

A quadtree is a tree-like data structure whose each internal node has four children. This structure has two positive properties for our task: i) it can decompose a 2D space into adaptable cells and ii) cells can split iteratively.

The image is separated into four equal cells at first, i.e., the first level of nodes in the quadtree. These nodes are regarded as positive nodes at the beginning. Then we summarize the features in each node, and if there are no high-frequency features in a node, this node will be denoted as a negative node. We employ interquartile range (IQR) as the threshold T of the high-frequency features: T = $F_{75} - F_{25}$ in which F_i refers to the ith percentage of the sorted frequency of the whole image. Here we select IQR as a measurement because it has been widely accepted as a robust statistic metric in detecting low, median and high components in the value range [4]. On the third step, positive nodes are separated again, and these steps will iteratively be computed until there are no positive nodes. Besides, as recommended by previous study [19], we define the max depth of quadtree as 8 which is close to 0.3% of the original image.

Figure 5(d) illustrates a sample output of the quadtree-based adaptive binning approach, which can better separate the high-frequency features in the original bin.

4.4 Image Reconstruction

When the server received the low-resolution image, its histogram and its high-frequency features, we can reconstruct its high-resolution version.

Our image reconstruction method is also enhanced by a proxy image I_P. The proxy image is generated via a naive Bayes-based super-resolution model [16]. To the best our knowledge, the local naive Bayes formulation model currently achieves the fastest computation time in image super-resolution. After generating the proxy image, we map the previous high-frequency features into the proxy image to reconstruct our final output image O.

Mathematically, O can be expressed as follows,

$$O(i) = \frac{1}{n} \sum_{j \in \Omega_i} I_P(j) exp(-\frac{||i-j||_2}{2\sigma_s^2} - \frac{||F_{bin}(i) - F_{bin}(j)||_2}{2\sigma_r^2}). \tag{7}$$

where $O(i)$ refers to the value of pixel i in output image, the $F_{bin}(i)$ refers to the corresponding feature bin of i, and σ_s and σ_r are equal with Eq. 5.

5 Evaluation

We introduced the initial settings of our studies in Sect. 5.1. Studied the quality of the images in Sect. 5.2 and analyzed the data usage in Sect. 5.3.

5.1 Default Settings

To better capture the features of user's real photos, we employ the sample set from a recent published FAID dataset [1] which consists of 120 real-world photos and 500 more high-resolution images randomly sampled from paints to scenes captured by mobile phones from wallhaven[4]. The file sizes range from 1 to 7 MB and the minimal resolution is 1080×1440 which can represent real-world usage scenarios.

Afterwards, we employ two most basic resampling approach, average resampling technique *Avg.* and bicubic resampling technique *Bic.*, and three prior methods (see Sect. 2.3) on image resampling: *C13* (content-adaptive method [8]), *P15* (perceptual-based approach [13]), and *L18* (L_0-regularized technique [9]). The methods are tested on a machine with Qualcomm® Snapdragon™865 CPU and Adreno™650 GPU.

5.2 Image Quality Study

For measuring the quality of images, we utilized the two most successful image quality metrics: SSIM (structural similarity index measure) and PSNR (peak signal-to-noise ratio). SSIM ranges from 0 to 0 which assesses the similarity of two images by comparing the perception-based structures. PSNR evaluates the

---

[4] https://alpha.wallhaven.cc/.

signal-to-noise ratio which always ranges from 20 dB to 40 dB. Higher is better for both indexes.

At first, we define a *resampling ratio* as the resampled image size, for example, $2\times$ means the resolution of the resampled image is $\frac{H}{2} \times \frac{W}{2}$ if the original image is $H \times W$. And it is obvious that a smaller resampling ratio will result in higher image quality but will also cause higher computational cost and larger data usage. Experimentally, we evaluate the image quality reconstructed using three fixed resampling ratio: $2\times$, $3\times$, and $4\times$. The average results for comparison are shown in Table 1 (SSIM) and Table 2 (PSNR).

Table 1. The overall results of output image quality using SSIM. M. refers to methods and R. refers to resampling factor. Best results are in bold.

	C13	P15	L18	Avg	Bic	Ours1	Ours2
$2\times$	0.82	0.83	0.76	0.70	0.73	0.83	**0.85**
$3\times$	0.74	0.75	0.70	0.66	0.68	**0.78**	**0.78**
$4\times$	0.70	0.69	0.68	0.64	0.64	0.73	**0.73**

Table 2. The overall results of output image quality using PSNR (dB). Best results are in bold.

	C13	P15	L18	Avg	Bic	Ours1	Ours2
$2\times$	30.39	30.35	29.11	27.54	28.12	30.87	**31.12**
$3\times$	27.20	28.12	27.08	25.61	26.23	**28.64**	28.33
$4\times$	26.00	26.08	25.35	24.62	24.14	26.45	**26.70**

Ours1 refers to our pipeline with basic binning, and *Ours2* is the adaptive version.

It is obvious that both of our methods outperform the baselines in preserving image quality.

Our two methods achieved Top 2 performance, while the adaptive version performs better for most cases. Besides, $2\times$ achieves the highest quality of images, and the quality difference is not severe between $3\times$ and $4\times$. Hence, we recommended employing $2\times$ as the resampling ratio for faithfully preserving image quality and $4\times$ for the demand for computational efficiency.

And since the two most basic methods (*Avg.* and *Bic.*) always perform the worst, we exclude them in the following analysis.

5.3   Data Usage Analysis

We evaluate the performance of reducing data usage with $2\times$, and $4\times$ resampling ratio. Figure 6 indicates the results.

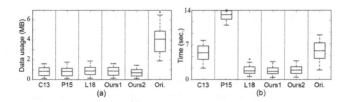

Fig. 6. Comparison of the over all data usage and transmission time in 2× resampling ratio among the original image, our methods and the baseline methods. The shadow (e.g., the *P15* column of (b)) means there are some data points whose transmission time are out of the range (14 s.).

Figure 6(a) shows the data usage of the original image and all the methods while (b) shows the corresponding uploading time.

It's clear that our method can significantly reduce data usage compared to the high-resolution image and is comparable with other baselines. Besides, both versions of our pipeline can achieve more effective computation time than the other methods.

In detail, our methods are comparable with *L18* [9] in transmitting time, but can better preserve image quality (See Sect. 5.2). And we can achieve around 3 and 9 times faster than *C13* [8] and *P15* [13] respectively.

The adaptive binning version is slightly slower than the original version and performs better in reducing data usage.

Because the results of 4× are similar to 2× shown in Fig. 6, we do not present the results in the paper for the page limit.

Finally, we recommend using the proposed pipeline with adaptive binning which performs the best in preserving image quality, is faster than most baselines and can reduce more data usage than the original version.

6   Conclusion

Dedicated to both reducing image data usage and preserving image quality, we designed a novel image transmission pipeline. Our pipeline utilizes a series of image representation and reconstruction mechanisms.

We first propose a gradient-aware resampling method to generate a low-resolution image via analyzing local features. Then we proposed an adaptive binning technique for better inferring the high-frequency features. By combining the previous representation, we can reconstruct a high-resolution image. Finally, we conducted experiments to address the effectiveness of our pipeline for satisfying image quality and data usage. For future work, we would try to improve the performance of feature extraction via various transforms such as Dual-tree complex wavelet transform and Shearlet transform.

References

1. Aksoy, Y., et al.: A dataset of flash and ambient illumination pairs from the crowd. In: ECCV (2018)
2. Antonini, M., Barlaud, M., Mathieu, P., Daubechies, I.: Image coding using wavelet transform. IEEE Trans. Image Process. **1**(2), 205–220 (1992)
3. Dalal, N., Triggs, B.: Histograms of oriented gradients for human detection. In: IEEE Computer Society Conference on Computer Vision and Pattern Recognition, CVPR 2005, vol. 1, pp. 886–893. IEEE (2005)
4. Dwork, C., Lei, J.: Differential privacy and robust statistics. In: Proceedings of the Forty-first Annual ACM Symposium on Theory of Computing, STOC 2009, pp. 371–380. ACM, New York (2009). https://doi.org/10.1145/1536414.1536466
5. Ginesu, G., Pintus, M., Giusto, D.D.: Objective assessment of the webP image coding algorithm. Signal Process. Image Commun. **27**(8), 867–874 (2012)
6. Heuveldop, N., et al.: Ericsson Mobility Report. Ericsson, Stockholm (2017)
7. Kang, C., Xiang, S., Liao, S., Xu, C., Pan, C.: Learning consistent feature representation for cross-modal multimedia retrieval. IEEE Trans. Multimedia **17**(3), 370–381 (2015)
8. Kopf, J., Shamir, A., Peers, P.: Content-adaptive image downscaling. ACM Trans. Graph. **32**(6), 173:1–173:8 (2013). https://doi.org/10.1145/2508363.2508370
9. Liu, J., He, S., Lau, R.W.H.: l_0 -regularized image downscaling. IEEE Trans. Image Process. **27**(3), 1076–1085 (2018). https://doi.org/10.1109/TIP.2017.2772838
10. Mairal, J., Elad, M., Sapiro, G.: Sparse representation for color image restoration. IEEE Trans. Image Process. **17**(1), 53–69 (2008)
11. Mallat, S.: A Wavelet Tour of Signal Processing. Elsevier, Amsterdam (1999)
12. Mathur, A., Schlotfeldt, B., Chetty, M.: A mixed-methods study of mobile users' data usage practices in south africa. In: Proceedings of the 2015 ACM International Joint Conference on Pervasive and Ubiquitous Computing, pp. 1209–1220. ACM (2015)
13. Öztireli, A.C., Gross, M.: Perceptually based downscaling of images. ACM Trans. Graph. **34**(4), 77:1–77:10 (2015). https://doi.org/10.1145/2766891
14. Phokeer, A., Densmore, M., Johnson, D., Feamster, N.: A first look at mobile internet use in township communities in South Africa. In: Proceedings of the 7th Annual Symposium on Computing for Development, p. 15. ACM (2016)
15. Rabbani, M., Jones, P.W.: Digital Image Compression Techniques, vol. 7. SPIE Press, Bellingham (1991)
16. Salvador, J., Perez-Pellitero, E.: Naive bayes super-resolution forest. In: Proceedings of the IEEE International Conference on Computer Vision, pp. 325–333 (2015)
17. Shensa, M.J.: The discrete wavelet transform: wedding the a trous and Mallat algorithms. IEEE Trans. Signal Process. **40**(10), 2464–2482 (1992)
18. Taubman, D., Marcellin, M.: JPEG2000 Image Compression Fundamentals, Standards and Practice. Springer, Heidelberg (2013). https://doi.org/10.1007/978-1-4615-0799-4
19. Veenadevi, V.: Fractal image compression using quadtree decomposition and huffman coding. Signal Image Process. Int. J. **3**, 207–212 (2012). https://doi.org/10.5121/sipij.2012.3215

Gaussian Mixture Model Based Semi-supervised Sparse Representation for Face Recognition

Xinxin Shan and Ying Wen[✉]

Department of Communication and Electronic Engineering,
East China Normal University, Shanghai, China
ywen@cs.ecnu.edu.cn

Abstract. Sparse representation generally relies on supervised learning, however, the samples in real life are often unlabeled and sparse representation cannot make use of the information of the unlabeled samples. In this paper, we propose a Gaussian Mixture Model based Semi-supervised Sparse Representation (GSSR) for face recognition, and it takes full advantage of unlabeled samples to improve the performance of sparse representation. Firstly, we present a semi-supervised sparse representation, which is a linear additive model with rectification and makes all rectified samples conform to Gaussian distribution. Then, we reconstruct a new dictionary that derived from predicting the labels of unlabeled samples through Expectation-Maximization algorithm. Finally, we use the new dictionary embedded into sparse representation to recognize faces. Experiments on AR, LFW and PIE databases show that our method effectively improves the classification accuracy and has superiority even with a few unlabeled samples.

Keywords: Face recognition · Semi-supervised learning · Sparse representation · Gaussian Mixture Model

1 Introduction

Face recognition has gained its popularity with the development of computer technology. Sparse Representation Classification (SRC) proposed by Wright *et al.* [16] attracted many researches' interests due to its good performance of face recognition. To improve the accuracy of SRC, Alajmi *et al.* [1] exploited nonlocal sparsity by adaptively estimating the sparse code changes and regularization parameters for face recognition. Furthermore, with deep learning getting more and more popular in recent years, He et al. [7] combined it with SRC to achieve effective results.

As a fact, many algorithms based on the original SRC require a large number of aligned samples to form the sparse matrix for training, especially in deep neural network, abundant training samples are badly needed [5,7]. One issue that influences the real-world application in face recognition is the shortage of labeled

© Springer Nature Switzerland AG 2021
J. Lokoč et al. (Eds.): MMM 2021, LNCS 12572, pp. 716–727, 2021.
https://doi.org/10.1007/978-3-030-67832-6_58

samples to train the model. Even worse, these labeled samples are usually covered with occlusion or noise. In order to deal with the problem of inadequate training samples, two techniques are listed as follows. (i) Constructing the auxiliary dictionary. The auxiliary dictionary can make full use of the intrinsic information of the training samples to expand the information of samples and make up for the shortage of the training samples. Deng et al. [3,4] utilized an auxiliary dictionary by Extended Sparse Representation-Based Classifier (ESRC) and Superposed SRC (SSRC). Wei and Wang [14] learned an auxiliary dictionary from external data for undersampled face recognition. In these methods, the prototype dictionary is built from mean values of labeled samples per class and the variation dictionary is obtained by subtracting from the original samples, therefore the auxiliary dictionary do not describe samples accurately enough. (ii) Semi-supervised learning. Semi-supervised learning can carry out machine learning with labels for unlabeled samples, which brings unlabeled samples into the scope of supervised learning and expands the sample set to make up for the shortage of training samples. Yan and Wang [15] constructed a l_1 graph by sparse representation. Gao et al. [6] used a probalistic framework named Semi-Supervised Sparse Representation based Classification (S^3RC) to pursue a better prototype dictionary. Wan and Wang [12] presented a cost-sensitive framework for semi-supervised face recognition incorporating label propagation and classifier learning. However, the above semi-supervised learning algorithms for face recognition mostly pay more attention to constructing the graph by sparse techniques, which do not make full use of the auxiliary dictionary.

In this paper, we propose a Gaussian Mixture Model based Semi-supervised Sparse Representation (GSSR) for face recognition. The proposed method includes four parts, i.e., sample rectification, Expectation-Maximization (EM) based Gaussian Mixture Model (GMM) [6] construction, new dictionary construction and classification. Generally, each face can be viewed as the combination of a prototype and a variation [2,4]. The variation of a face contains linear (e.g. occlusion and illumination) and non-linear (e.g. expression and pose) parts. When the linear variation is removed from the original samples, the rectified samples will follow GMM. Then, we can predict the labels of unlabeled samples and re-estimate prototypes and variations of the whole samples by EM algorithm based on GMM. Thus the dictionary can be reconstructed with all labeled and unlabeled samples. In this case, the unlabeled samples contribute to training our model thus compensating the shortage of labeled samples. Lastly, the reconstructed dictionary will be utilized for face recognition based on sparse representation. Compared with deep learning methods, our machine learning method only needs a small number of training samples, which requires less computing power but achieves better results on small sample size.

There are two main contributions of our method.

- Our semi-supervised sparse representation method makes full use of the unlabeled samples. After rectification, all samples conform to GMM. In this case, we can predict the labels of unlabeled samples and jointly update the prototypes and variations by EM algorithm.

– We propose a new sparse representation based on dictionary construction.
  The new prototype dictionary can better express gallery samples and the new
  variation dictionary can exactly describe the non-linear variations of samples,
  which can effectively improve the accuracy of classification.

2   GMM Based Semi-supervised Sparse Representation

2.1   Proposed Semi-supervised Sparse Representation

The appearance of a face is affected by prototype μ, variation ϵ and small dense
noise u, thus a face sample y can be represented by a linear additive model:
$y = \mu + \epsilon + u$. Assume that there is a N-samples dataset $\mathbf{Y} = [y_1; y_2; ...; y_N] \in
\mathbb{R}^{N \times D}$ including L labeled samples of K classes from a total of N face samples,
where D is the dimension of sample. We use the dataset to construct a prototype
dictionary $\mathbf{P} \in \mathbb{R}^{K \times D}$ plus a variation dictionary $\mathbf{V} \in \mathbb{R}^{L \times D}$ model. Then, a face
sample y can be described by the linear additive model: $y = \mathbf{P}\alpha + \mathbf{V}\beta + u$, where
α and β are sparse coefficients associated elements in the prototype dictionary
and the variation dictionary, respectively.

In this case, we can get the rectified unlabeled sample $\hat{y}$ of a testing sample
y as : $\hat{y} = y - \mathbf{V}\hat{\beta} = \mathbf{P}\hat{\alpha} + u$.

The two coefficients α and β can be recovered by solving the following l_1-
minimization problem after normalizing each sample in $\mathbf{P}$ and $\mathbf{V}$:

$$\begin{bmatrix} \hat{\alpha} \\ \hat{\beta} \end{bmatrix} = \arg \min_{\alpha, \beta} \left\| [\mathbf{P} \ \ \mathbf{V}] \begin{bmatrix} \alpha \\ \beta \end{bmatrix} - y \right\|_2^2 + \lambda \left\| \begin{bmatrix} \alpha \\ \beta \end{bmatrix} \right\|_1, \tag{1}$$

where the regularization parameter λ is a preset value to restrain and balance
the two terms.

Given a dataset $\mathbf{Y} = [\mathbf{Y}_1; \mathbf{Y}_2; ...; \mathbf{Y}_K] \in \mathbb{R}^{L \times D}$, in which $\mathbf{Y}_k = [y_1;
y_2; ...; y_{l_k}] \in \mathbb{R}^{l_k \times D}$ is the collection of k-th class labeled samples, where l_k is
the number of samples in k-th class and $L = \sum_{k=1}^{K} l_k$.

We use the prototype μ_k of k-th class to represent the prototype dictionary.
Generally, since it is difficult to acquire each centroid of per class, the mean
value $\bar{\mu}_k$ is used to form $\mathbf{P}$ and the variation dictionary $\mathbf{V}$ can be obtained by:

$$\mathbf{P} = [\bar{\mu}_1; \bar{\mu}_2; ...; \bar{\mu}_K], \quad \mathbf{V} = [\mathbf{Y}_1 - \mathbf{e}_1\bar{\mu}_1; \mathbf{Y}_2 - \mathbf{e}_2\bar{\mu}_2; ...; \mathbf{Y}_K - \mathbf{e}_K\bar{\mu}_K], \tag{2}$$

where $\mathbf{e}_k = [1; 1; ...; 1] \in \mathbb{R}^{l_k \times 1}$.

On account of the finite labeled samples and a large number of available
unlabeled samples in real life, we expect to make use of all samples to optimize
the composition of dictionary and enhance the expressiveness of dictionary. Thus,
we propose a new semi-supervised learning to improve the representation of
dictionary to obtain better recognition effect.

We consider L labeled and $N - L$ unlabeled samples simultaneously, then
the rectified sample $\hat{y}_k$ can be obtained by:

$$\hat{y}_i = \begin{cases} \bar{\mu}_{c_i} & \text{if } i \in \{1, 2, ..., L\} , \\ y_i - \mathbf{V}\hat{\beta} & \text{if } i \in \{L+1, L+2, ..., N\} , \end{cases} \tag{3}$$

where $c_i \in \{1, 2, ..., K\}$ indicates the label of the k-th labeled sample, $\bar{\mu}_{c_i}$ is the mean value of labeled samples in c_i-th class, and $\hat{\beta}$ is estimated by Eq. (1). Thus, we obtain the rectified dataset $\hat{\mathbf{Y}} = [\hat{y}_1; \hat{y}_2; ...; \hat{y}_N]$.

However, the prototype and variation dictionary as aforesaid are gained roughly, so that they can not accurately represent the prototype and variation of samples. Different from the previous methods for $\mathbf{P}$ and $\mathbf{P}$ obtained, after removing the linear variation of all the samples, our method re-estimates $\mathbf{P}^*$ and $\mathbf{V}^*$ jointly by iteratively updating in EM algorithm. The new $\mathbf{P}^*$ and $\mathbf{V}^*$ can better describe the properties and variations of face sample.

Therefore, we substitute $\mathbf{P}^*$ and $\mathbf{V}^*$ for $\mathbf{P}$ and $\mathbf{V}$ of Eq. (1), the residual can be estimated by:

$$r_k(\hat{y}) = \left\| [\mathbf{P}^* \quad \mathbf{V}^*] \begin{bmatrix} \hat{\alpha} \\ \hat{beta} \end{bmatrix} - \hat{y} \right\|_F^2, \quad k \in \{1, 2, ..., K\}. \tag{4}$$

Finally, the label of a testing sample y is:

$$label(y) = \arg \min_{c_k} r_k(\hat{y}). \tag{5}$$

Next, we focus on predicting labels of unlabeled samples by EM algorithm based on GMM and constructing $\mathbf{P}^*$ and $\mathbf{V}^*$ for classification in GSSR.

2.2 Construction of Dictionary in GSSR

Gaussian Mixture Model for Face Data. $\hat{y}$ is also made up of two independent Gaussian latent variables: $\hat{y} = \hat{\mu} + \hat{\epsilon}$, where $\hat{\mu}$ is the prototype and $\hat{\epsilon}$ is the face variation of $\hat{y}$. They respectively follow two Gaussian distributions $\mathcal{N}(0, S_{\hat{\mu}})$ and $\mathcal{N}(0, S_{\hat{\epsilon}})$, where $S_{\hat{\mu}}$ and $S_{\hat{\epsilon}}$ are the covariances of $\hat{\mu}$ and $\hat{\epsilon}$:

$$S_{\hat{\mu}} = cov(\hat{\mu}), \; S_{\hat{\epsilon}} = cov(\hat{\epsilon}). \tag{6}$$

Then, we derive $\hat{\mu}$ and $\hat{\epsilon}$ of the rectified face samples $\hat{\mathbf{Y}}_k$. We already acquire $\hat{\mathbf{Y}}_k = [\hat{y}_1; \hat{y}_2; ...; \hat{y}_n]$ of the k-th class that gathers n rectified samples and some of them are unlabeled with predicted labels.

$\hat{\mathbf{Y}}_k$ can be decomposed into $\mathbf{Q}$ and $\mathbf{h}$, among which $\mathbf{h} = [\hat{\mu}_k; \hat{\epsilon}_1; \hat{\epsilon}_2; ...; \hat{\epsilon}_n] \in \mathcal{N}(0, \sigma_{\mathbf{h}})$ is relative latent variable, and $\sigma_{\mathbf{h}} = diag(S_{\hat{\mu}_k}, S_{\hat{\epsilon}_1}, S_{\hat{\epsilon}_2}, ..., S_{\hat{\epsilon}_n})$. Thus, the relationship between $\hat{\mathbf{Y}}_k$ and $\mathbf{h}$ is: $\hat{\mathbf{Y}}_k = \mathbf{Q}\mathbf{h}$, $\mathbf{Q} = [\mathbf{I}, diag(\mathbf{I})]$, where $\mathbf{I} \in \mathbb{R}^{D \times D}$ is an identity matrix and $\mathbf{0} \in \mathbb{R}^{D \times D}$ is a zero matrix.

Assuming that $\sigma_{\hat{\mathbf{Y}}_k}$ is reversible and $\hat{\mathbf{Y}}_k \in \mathcal{N}(0, \sigma_{\hat{y}})$, $\sigma_{\hat{y}} = \mathbf{Q}\sigma_{\mathbf{h}}\mathbf{Q}^T$ then:

$$\sigma_{\hat{y}} = \begin{bmatrix} S_{\hat{\mu}_k} + S_{\hat{\epsilon}_1} & S_{\hat{\mu}_k} & \cdots & S_{\hat{\mu}_k} \\ S_{\hat{\mu}_k} & S_{\hat{\mu}_k} + S_{\hat{\epsilon}_2} & \cdots & S_{\hat{\mu}_k} \\ \vdots & \vdots & \ddots & \vdots \\ S_{\hat{\mu}_k} & S_{\hat{\mu}_k} & \cdots & S_{\hat{\mu}_k} + S_{\hat{\epsilon}_n} \end{bmatrix} = \begin{bmatrix} F_k + G_1 & F_k & \cdots & F_k \\ F_k & F_k + G_2 & \cdots & F_k \\ \vdots & \vdots & \ddots & \vdots \\ F_k & F_k & \cdots & F_k + G_n \end{bmatrix}^{-1} \tag{7}$$

If considering $\mathbf{h}$ and $\hat{\mathbf{Y}}_k$ together as a random vector that conforms to a multivariate Gaussian distribution, according to the deduction in [8], we can get the expectation of the hidden variable $\mathbf{h}$:

$$E(\mathbf{h}|\hat{\mathbf{Y}}_k) = cov(\mathbf{h}, \hat{\mathbf{Y}}_k) \cdot cov(\hat{\mathbf{Y}}_k, \hat{\mathbf{Y}}_k)^{-1} \cdot \hat{\mathbf{Y}}_k = cov(\mathbf{h}, \mathbf{Qh}) \cdot cov(\mathbf{Qh}, \mathbf{Qh})^{-1} \cdot \hat{\mathbf{Y}}_k$$

$$= cov(\mathbf{h}, \mathbf{h})\mathbf{Q}^T \cdot (\mathbf{Q}cov(\mathbf{h}, \mathbf{h})\mathbf{Q}^T)^{-1} \cdot \hat{\mathbf{Y}}_k = \mathbf{Q}^{-1} \cdot \hat{\mathbf{Y}}_k. \tag{8}$$

In addition, $\mathbf{Q}$ is row full rank and we can solve its Moore-Penrose generalized inverse matrix, so that the hidden variable $\mathbf{h}$ can be represented as: $\mathbf{h} = \mathbf{Q}^{-1}\hat{\mathbf{Y}}_k$. For further simple calculation, we rewritten it as follows:

$$\mathbf{h} = \mathbf{Q}^{-1}(\sigma_{\hat{y}}\sigma_{\hat{y}}^{-1})\hat{\mathbf{Y}}_k = \mathbf{Q}^{-1}(\mathbf{Q}\sigma_{\mathbf{h}}\mathbf{Q}^T)\sigma_{\hat{y}}^{-1}\hat{\mathbf{Y}}_k = \sigma_{\mathbf{h}}\mathbf{Q}^T\sigma_{\hat{y}}^{-1}\hat{\mathbf{Y}}_k. \tag{9}$$

We denote $\hat{y}_{i,k}$ as the i-th sample of the k-th class when $\hat{y}_i \in \hat{\mathbf{Y}}_k$, where $i \in \{1, 2, ..., n\}$ and $k \in \{1, 2, ..., K\}$. When combined with Eq. (7) and the value of related variables, the prototype $\hat{\mu}_k$ and the i-th variation $\hat{\epsilon}_{i,k}$ of each rectified sample in the k-th class can be solved out as:

$$\hat{\mu}_k = \sum_{j=1}^n S_{\hat{\mu}_k}(nF_k + G_j)\hat{y}_{j,k}, \tag{10}$$

$$\hat{\epsilon}_{i,k} = \sum_{j=1}^n S_{\hat{\epsilon}_{i,k}}F_k\hat{y}_{j,k} + \hat{y}_{i,k}. \tag{11}$$

Considering the whole rectified dataset $\hat{\mathbf{Y}}$ containing K classes can be viewed as K Gaussian distributions [6], we can construct GMM with the prior probability π_k, the mean value $\hat{\mu}_k$ and the standard deviation σ_k of k-th class. Then, the rectified sample $\hat{y}_k \in \mathcal{N}(\hat{\mu}_k, \sigma_k)$ and $\theta = \{\hat{\mu}_k, \sigma_k, \pi_k, \text{ for } k = (1, 2, ..., K)\}$ can be optimized as:

$$\hat{\theta} = \arg\max_\theta log\, p(\hat{\mathbf{Y}}|\theta), \quad s.t. \sum_{k=1}^K \pi_k = 1, \tag{12}$$

where the log likelihood $log\, p(\hat{\mathbf{Y}}|\theta)$ is calculated as follows:

$$log\, p(\hat{\mathbf{Y}}|\theta) = log \prod_{i=1}^N p(\hat{y}_i|\theta)^{z_{i,k}} = log \left(\prod_{i=1}^L p(\hat{y}_i|\theta)^{z_{i,k}} \prod_{i=L+1}^N p(\hat{y}_i|\theta)^{z_{i,k}} \right)$$

$$= \sum_{i=1}^L log\, \pi_{c_i}\mathcal{N}(\hat{y}_i|\hat{\mu}_{c_i}, \sigma_{c_i}) + \sum_{i=L+1}^N \sum_{k=1}^K z_{i,k}log\, \pi_k\mathcal{N}(\hat{y}_i|\hat{\mu}_i, \sigma_i), \tag{13}$$

where $z_{i,k}$ is an indicator that will be interpreted in the following subsection, which shows whether the sample $\hat{y}_i$ belongs to the k-th class or not.

Expectation-Maximization Algorithm for Semi-supervised Learning. Due to the existence of linear variations, initial prototype and variation variables obtained from the original samples can not represent the property of samples well, but it will be improved after rectification in linear additive model. In the next steps, our semi-supervised method uses EM algorithm to predict the labels of unlabeled samples, estimate the prototype and variation based on GMM, and use them to reconstruct the prototype and variation dictionaries.

Initialization: For the i-th rectified sample of the k-th class, the relevant variables should be initialized first:

$$\hat{\mu}'_k = \frac{1}{l_k} \sum_{j=1}^{l_k} \hat{y}_{j,k}, \ \hat{\epsilon}'_{i,k} = \hat{y}_{i,k} - \hat{\mu}'_k, \tag{14}$$

$$\sigma_k = \mathbf{I}, \ \pi_k = l_k/L. \tag{15}$$

E-step: Predict the labels of unlabeled samples. If $\hat{y}_i$ is a labeled sample in the dataset, $i \in \{1, 2, ..., L\}$, when $\hat{y}_i \in \hat{\mathbf{Y}}_k$, $z_{i,k} = 1$, otherwise, $z_{i,k} = 0$.

For a rectified unlabeled sample $\hat{y}_i$, the probability that it comes from the k-th class in GMM can be viewed as the indicator $z_{i,k}$, which is estimated by the variables in the previous iteration:

$$z_{i,k}^{(t)} = \frac{\pi_k^{(t-1)} \frac{1}{|\sigma_k^{(t-1)}|^{\frac{1}{2}}} exp(-\frac{1}{2} \left\| \hat{y}_i - \hat{\mu}_k^{(t-1)} \right\|_{\sigma_k^{(t-1)}}^2)}{\sum_{j=1}^{K} \pi_j^{(t-1)} \frac{1}{|\sigma_j^{(t-1)}|^{\frac{1}{2}}} exp(-\frac{1}{2} \left\| \hat{y}_i - \hat{\mu}_j^{(t-1)} \right\|_{\sigma_j^{(t-1)}}^2)}. \tag{16}$$

Therefore, labels of the whole rectified $\hat{\mathbf{Y}}$ are obtained according to the indicators.

M-step: Update the values of prototypes and variations. After acquiring the indicators, for all samples, we can get unlabeled samples $\hat{\mu}'_k$ by Eq. (14) and labeled samples $\hat{\mu}_k$ by Eq. (10). To exploit the information from combination of both labeled and unlabeled samples, so as to get a more accurate prototype, we define a weight matrix $\mathbf{w} = [w_1, \ w_2]^T$ that can balance $\hat{\mu}'_k$ and $\hat{\mu}_k$ to update the whole prototypes $\hat{\mu}_k^{(t)}$ by:

$$\hat{\mu}_k^{(t)} = [\hat{\mu}'_k, \ \hat{\mu}_k] \mathbf{w}. \tag{17}$$

Next, on the basis of Maximum Likelihood Estimate, we can update other parameters of GMM as follows:

$$N_k^{(t)} = \sum_{i=1}^{N} z_{i,k}^{(t)}, \ \pi_k^{(t)} = \frac{N_k^{(t)}}{N}, \ \sigma_k^{(t)} = \frac{1}{N_k^{(t)}} \sum_{i=1}^{N} z_{i,k}^{(t)}(\hat{y}_i - \hat{\mu}_k^{(t)})(\hat{y}_i - \hat{\mu}_k^{(t)})^T. \tag{18}$$

The parameters above are used to renew $z_{i,k}^{(t+1)}$ from Eq. (16) in *E*-step. After obtaining the updated $\hat{\epsilon}_{i,k}^{(t)}$ by Eq. (11), $S_{\hat{\mu}}$ and $S_{\hat{\epsilon}}$ can be respectively updated by Eq. (6).

The conditions to stop the *E*-step and *M*-step are when the log likelihood $log \, p(\hat{\mathbf{Y}}|\theta)$ in Eq. (13) converges or $S_{\hat{\mu}}$ and $S_{\hat{\epsilon}}$ in Eq. (6) concurrently converge.

Finally, we obtain the updated variables $\hat{\mu}_k$ and $\hat{\epsilon}_{i,k}$ by EM algorithm, which will be used to reconstruct the auxiliary dictionary for classification.

Dictionary Reconstruction and Classification. After EM algorithm, we use $\hat{\mu}_k$ and $\hat{\epsilon}_{i,k}$ to reconstruct the prototype and variation dictionaries by:

$$\mathbf{P}^* = [\hat{\mu}_1; \hat{\mu}_2; ...; \hat{\mu}_K], \ \mathbf{V}^* = [\hat{\epsilon}_{1,1}; \hat{\epsilon}_{1,2}; ...; \hat{\epsilon}_{i,k}; ...; \hat{\epsilon}_{l_K,K}]. \tag{19}$$

We use the new $\mathbf{P}^*$ and $\mathbf{V}^*$ to express Eq. (1) for re-estimating $al\hat{p}ha$ and $b\hat{e}ta$. Therefore, the residual and label of rectified sample $\hat{y}$ of the testing sample y can be obtained by Eq. (4) and Eq. (5).

The proposed algorithm is summarized in Algorithm 1.

Algorithm 1: Gaussian Mixture Model Based Semi-supervised Sparse Representation for Face Recognition

---

Input : The matrix of labeled and unlabeled samples $\mathbf{Y}$, the testing sample y that belongs to unlabeled samples, and the weight w_1 and w_2 of matrix $\mathbf{w}$ and the parameter λ. We use LBP to extract face feature and apply the dimensional reduction such as PCA on face samples $\mathbf{Y}$ and y.

1 Construct the initial prototype dictionary $\mathbf{P}$ and the initial variation dictionary $\mathbf{V}$ by Eq.(2).
2 Solve the l_1-minimization problem to obtain the sparse coefficient vectors $\hat{alpha}$ and $\hat{beta}$ by Eq.(1).
3 Get rectified labeled and unlabeled samples $\hat{\mathbf{Y}}$ by Eq.(3) utilizing $\hat{beta}$.
4 Initialize some parameters by Eq.(15).
5 **repeat**
6   **E-step**: Obtain the indicator $z_{i,k}$ by Eq.(16).
7   **M-step**: Calculate $\hat{\mu}'_k$ according to the indicator $z_{i,k}$ of the unlabeled sample by Eq.(14) and get $\hat{\mu}_k$ by Eq.(10). Then, update the parameters $\theta = \{\hat{\mu}_k, \sigma_k, \pi_k, \text{ for } k = (1, 2, ..., K)\}$ of GMM by Eq.(17) and Eq.(18). Compute $\hat{\epsilon}_{i,k}$, by Eq.(11).
8 **until** Eq.(13) converges or Eq.(6) converges;
9 Reconstruct $\mathbf{P}^*$ and $\mathbf{V}^*$ by Eq.(19) with the updated $\hat{\mu}_k$ and $\hat{\epsilon}_{i,k}$ in EM algorithm.
10 Calculate the residual $r_k(\hat{y})$ of the testing sample y by the new residual calculation formula Eq.(4).
Output: The label that indicates the class of y by Eq.(5).

---

3   Experimental Results

3.1   Databases and Settings

Databases. The face databases in the experiments include the AR [9], LFW [10] and PIE [11] databases. Samples and detailed information are respectively shown in Fig. 1 and Table 1.

(a)

(b)

(c)

Fig. 1. Samples from (a) AR database; (b) LFW database; (c) PIE database

Table 1. All databases used in our experiments.

Name	Class	Sum
AR [9]	100	26 × 100
LFW [10]	94	8 × 94
PIE [11]	38	24 × 38

Detailed Settings. We use LBP to extract face feature in our algorithm. Due to original samples have higher dimensions, we apply PCA to reduce the dimension of face samples. The parameter $\lambda = 0.001$ [6] in Eq. (1). $\mathbf{w} = [w_1, w_2] = [0.5, 0.5]$ is selected as trade-off in order to get balanced and better experimental results on all face databases. We carry out the comparative experiments with currently popular SRC based methods, such as SRC [16], SSRC [3], S^3RC [6] and SMSRC [13] to show the strength of our algorithm. All experimental results are the average of 20 runs.

3.2 Experiments on AR Database

AR database is with facial expression, illumination and occlusions. The experiments on this database are divided into two parts: unlabeled samples without/with auxiliary. Specifically, the general experiments contain two datasets respectively consist of training and testing samples, while unlabeled samples with auxiliary include the third unlabeled training dataset. Through these two kinds of experiments, we can fully validate the contribution of unlabeled samples in our semi-supervised algorithm.

Unlabeled Samples Without Auxiliary. In this experiment, the datasets include two parts: training and testing datasets. That is, all unlabeled samples that contribute to improving our method are made up of testing samples. We first randomly choose a session, and from it randomly select 2–13 per class as the training datasets. The dimension of samples is reduced to 100. Then, we randomly use 1–13 samples in another session to form the testing datasets. The results of 2, 4 and 6 labeled images per class are shown in Fig. 2.

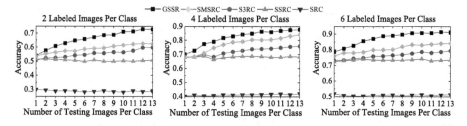

Fig. 2. Accuracy vs. the number of unlabeled testing samples with different numbers of labeled training sets on AR database. Dimension of samples is 100.

It is obvious that the accuracy of GSSR and S^3RC improves as the number of unlabeled sample increases, while the other methods are not affected by unlabeled samples. Our method performs better on samples with higher dimensions. Moreover, the accuracy of all supervised methods is lower than that of semi-supervised methods, which shows the advantages of semi-supervised learning. Comparing with the semi-supervised method S^3RC, the accuracy of our method increases about 10% on average. In a word, the accuracy of GSSR is the highest.

Unlabeled Samples with Auxiliary. For further showing the semi-supervised superiority, we bring in auxiliary unlabeled samples to implement the experiments. In the experiments, the datasets are divided into three groups: training, auxiliary and testing. The auxiliary unlabeled samples are only used to train our model and the unlabeled testing samples are used to calculate the accuracy. We do two groups of experiments: one is fixing the number of training samples and changing the number of testing samples; another is the opposite.

Firstly, we randomly select 2 labeled samples per class from one session to form the training datasets, and 1–11 in remains as the auxiliary unlabeled dataset. From another session, we randomly select 1–13 unlabeled samples as the testing dataset. Experimental results of 1, 5 and 13 unlabeled testing datasets per class are randomly selected to show in Fig. 3 and the results of other number of unlabeled testing datasets are similar.

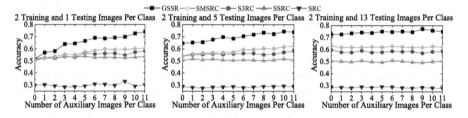

Fig. 3. Accuracy vs. the number of auxiliary unlabeled samples under fixed 2 training and 1, 5, 13 testing samples on AR database. Dimension of samples is 100.

In the following experiments, we select 1 unlabeled testing sample per class from one session with different amount of labeled training samples from 2 to 12 per class in another session. Figure 4 shows the results of 3, 5 and 7 labeled training samples and the results of different amount of them are also similar.

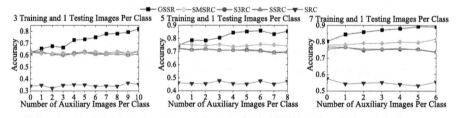

Fig. 4. Accuracy vs. the number of auxiliary unlabeled samples under fixed 3, 5, 7 training and 1 testing samples on AR database. Dimension of samples is 100.

From Fig. 3, we can find that the accuracy of classification is obviously improved with the increase of the number of auxiliary unlabeled samples, when using the fixed number of training or testing samples. The introduction of the auxiliary samples boosts our method performance but has no effect on other methods even S^3RC due to under-utilization of unlabeled samples. In especial, the results of the first figure in Fig. 4

show that when the maximum number of auxiliary samples are adopted, the accuracy even increases about 22.5% compared to that without using them. Thus, the unlabeled samples play a crucial role in our semi-supervised learning method.

3.3 Experiments on LFW Database

LFW is a public benchmark for face verification, to further study the performance of the proposed method, we test these methods on it. The number of samples in labeled training datasets are randomly selected from 3 to 5 for each class, and from 1 to all the remaining samples per class are used as unlabeled testing datasets. GSSR-CNN means that we use CNN as feature extractor and GSSR as classifier such as [6,7]. The average results are shown in Fig. 5.

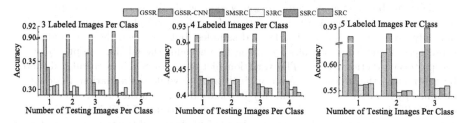

Fig. 5. Accuracy vs. the number of unlabeled testing samples with different numbers of labeled training sets on LFW database. Dimension of samples is 100.

Although the accuracy is not high, our method still outperforms other compared methods. It can be seen that using unlabeled samples to reconstruct the dictionary are helpful to improve classification precision.

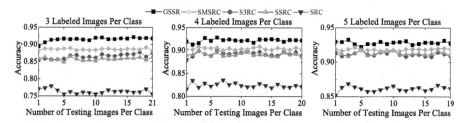

Fig. 6. Accuracy vs. the number of unlabeled testing samples with different numbers of labeled training samples on PIE database. Dimension of samples is 100.

3.4 Experiments on PIE Database

The CMU Pose, Illumination and Expression (PIE) database is also used to test the performance of the method. In this database, we randomly select 3, 4 and 5 labeled samples per class as the training datasets and the number of unlabeled testing samples for each class in the testing datasets is selected from 1 to the maximum of all the remains. The average experimental results are shown in Fig. 6.

It is notable that our semi-supervised algorithm is effective on this database.

4   Discussion and Conclusions

Experimental results indicate that the semi-supervised sparse representation based on GMM for face recognition can achieve satisfactory performance. Semi-supervised learning has more obvious advantages than supervised learning methods. Our proposed method is superior to the other semi-supervised method S^3RC. We take the following three aspects to illustrate. (i) The results of the experiments with auxiliary of AR database obviously show that S^3RC does not make full use of the information of auxiliary unlabeled samples to improve precision, while the performance improvement of our method is obvious with the addition of auxiliary samples. Because our method not only predicts the labels of unlabeled samples, but also uses them to update the prototypes of the whole samples by taking into account the labeled samples to renew the prototype dictionary. (ii) The variation dictionary of S^3RC is calculated merely by subtracting the prototypes from original samples while our variation dictionary is obtained by iterative re-estimation. (iii) To some extent, from the standpoint algorithm of S^3RC [6], its experimental results depend on the outputs of SSRC that are initially used to get prototypes and variations. Instead of doing subtraction, we re-estimate the variations, which are used to reconstruct a new dictionary to describe the samples well. In this paper, experimental results of the proposed GSSR demonstrate that the dictionary reconstruction and semi-supervised learning of our method is capable of improving the classification accuracy effectively.

Acknowledgement. This work was supported in part by 2030 National Key AI Program of China (2018AAA0100500), the National Nature Science Foundation of China (no.6177-3166), and Projects of International Cooperation of Shanghai Municipal Science and Technology Committee (14DZ2260800).

References

1. Alajmi, M., Awedat, K., Essa, A., Alassery, F., Faragallah, O.S.: Efficient face recognition using regularized adaptive non-local sparse coding. IEEE Access **7**, 10653–10662 (2019)
2. Chen, D., Cao, X., Wang, L., Wen, F., Sun, J.: Bayesian face revisited: a joint formulation. Eur. Conf. Comput. Vis. **7574**, 566–579 (2012)
3. Deng, W., Hu, J., Guo, J.: Extended SRC: undersampled face recognition via intraclass variant dictionary. IEEE Trans. Pattern Anal. Mach. Intell. **34**(9), 1864–1870 (2012)
4. Deng, W., Hu, J., Guo, J.: In defense of sparsity based face recognition. In: Proceedings of the IEEE Computer Society Conference on Computer Vision and Pattern Recognition, pp. 399–406 (2013)
5. Duan, Y., Lu, J., Zhou, J.: UniformFace: learning deep equidistributed representation for face recognition. In: IEEE Conference on Computer Vision and Pattern Recognition, pp. 3415–3424 (2019)

6. Gao, Y., Ma, J., Yuille, A.L.: Semi-supervised sparse representation based classification for face recognition with insufficient labeled samples. IEEE Trans. Image Process. **26**(5), 2545–2560 (2017)
7. He, L., Li, H., Zhang, Q., Sun, Z.: Dynamic feature learning for partial face recognition. IEEE Trans. Image Process. **28**(2), 791–802 (2019)
8. Kaare Brandt, M.S.P.: The Matrix Cookbook, pp. 1–72 (2012)
9. Liya, D., Martinez, A.M.: Features versus context: an approach for precise and detailed detection and delineation of faces and facial features. IEEE Trans. Pattern Anal. Mach. Intell. **32**(11), 2022–2038 (2010)
10. Sanderson, C., Lovell, B.C.: Multi-region probabilistic histograms for robust and scalable identity inference. In: Tistarelli, M., Nixon, M.S. (eds.) ICB 2009. LNCS, vol. 5558, pp. 199–208. Springer, Heidelberg (2009). https://doi.org/10.1007/978-3-642-01793-3_21
11. Sim, T., Baker, S., Bsat, M.: The CMU Pose, Illumination, and Expression (PIE) Database of Human Faces. Technical Report, CMU-RI-TR-01-02, Carnegie Mellon University, Pittsburgh, PA (2001)
12. Wan, J., Wang, Y.: Cost-sensitive label propagation for semi-supervised face recognition. IEEE Trans. Inf. Forensics Secur. **14**, 1–15 (2018)
13. Wang, Y., Zheng, K.: Semi-supervised mixed sparse representation based classification for face recognition. In: ACM International Conference Proceeding Series, vol. 3663, pp. 149–153 (2020)
14. Wei, C.P., Wang, Y.C.F.: Undersampled face recognition with one-pass dictionary learning. In: Proceedings - IEEE International Conference on Multimedia and Expo 2015, vol. Augus, no. 6, pp. 1722–1734 (2015)
15. Yan, S., Wang, H.: Semi-supervised Learning by Sparse Representation, pp. 792–801 (2013)
16. Zhang, H., Zhang, Y., Huang, T.S.: Pose-robust face recognition via sparse representation. Pattern Recogn. **46**(5), 1511–1521 (2013)

Correction to: Crossed-Time Delay Neural Network for Speaker Recognition

Liang Chen, Yanchun Liang, Xiaohu Shi, You Zhou, and Chunguo Wu

Correction to:
Chapter "Crossed-Time Delay Neural Network for Speaker Recognition" in: J. Lokoč et al. (Eds.): *MultiMedia Modeling*, LNCS 12572, https://doi.org/10.1007/978-3-030-67832-6_1

The book was inadvertently published with a typo in the third author's name "Xiaoshu Shi", i.e., an extra "s" was added whereas it should have read "Xiaohu Shi". This has been now corrected with the erratum.

The updated version of this chapter can be found at
https://doi.org/10.1007/978-3-030-67832-6_1

© Springer Nature Switzerland AG 2021
J. Lokoč et al. (Eds.): MMM 2021, LNCS 12572, p. C1, 2021.
https://doi.org/10.1007/978-3-030-67832-6_59

Author Index

Printed in the United States
by Baker & Taylor Publisher Services